GENERAL MOTORS

FULL-SIZE VANS
1987-97 REPAIR MANUAL

CHILTON'S™

President	Dean F. Morgantini, S.A.E.
Vice President–Finance	Barry L. Beck
Vice President–Sales	Glenn D. Potere
Executive Editor	Kevin M. G. Maher
Production Manager	Ben Greisler, S.A.E.
Project Managers	Michael Abraham, George B. Heinrich III, S.A.E., Will Kessler, A.S.E., S.A.E., Richard Schwartz
Schematics Editor	Christopher G. Ritchie
Editor	Thomas A. Mellon, S.A.E.

CHILTON™ Automotive Books
PUBLISHED BY W. G. NICHOLS, INC.

Manufactured in USA
© 1998 W. G. Nichols
1020 Andrew Drive
West Chester, PA 19380
ISBN 0-8019-8819-5
Library of Congress Catalog Card No. 97-77878
1234567890 7654321098

™Chilton is a registered trademark of the Chilton Company and is licensed to W. G. Nichols, Inc.

Contents

Contents

7 DRIVE TRAIN

8 SUSPENSION AND STEERING

9 BRAKES

10 BODY AND TRIM

GLOSSARY

MASTER INDEX

SAFETY NOTICE

Proper service and repair procedures are vital to the safe, reliable operation of all motor vehicles, as well as the personal safety of those performing repairs. This manual outlines procedures for servicing and repairing vehicles using safe, effective methods. The procedures contain many NOTES, CAUTIONS and WARNINGS which should be followed along with standard procedures to eliminate the possibility of personal injury or improper service which could damage the vehicle or compromise its safety.

It is important to note that the repair procedures and techniques, tools and parts for servicing motor vehicles, as well as the skill and experience of the individual performing the work vary widely. It is not possible to anticipate all of the conceivable ways or conditions under which vehicles may be serviced, or to provide cautions as to all of the possible hazards that may result. Standard and accepted safety precautions and equipment should be used when handling toxic or flammable fluids, and safety goggles or other protection should be used during cutting, grinding, chiseling, prying, or any other process that can sauce material removal or projectiles.

Some procedures require the use of tools specially designed for a specific purpose. Before substituting another tool or procedure,you must be completely satisfied that neither your personal safety, not the performance of the vehicle will be endangered.

Although information in this manual is based on industry sources and is complete as possible at the time of publication, the possibility exists that some vehicle manufacturers made later changes which could not be included here. While striving for total accuracy, W. G. Nichols, Inc. cannot assume responsibility for any errors, changes or omissions that may occur in the compilation of this data.

PART NUMBERS

Part numbers listed in this reference are not recommendations by Chilton for any product by brand name. They are references that can be used with interchange and aftermarket supplier catalogs to locate each brand supplier's discrete part number.

SPECIAL TOOLS

Special tools are recommended by the vehicle manufacturer to perform their specific job. use has been kept to a minimum, but where absolutely necessary, they are referred to in the text by the part number of the tool manufacturer. These tools can be purchased, under the appropriate part number, from your local dealer or regional distributor, or an equivalent tool can be purchased locally from a tool supplier or parts outlet. Before substituting any tool for the one recommended, read the SAFETY NOTICE at the top of this page.

ACKNOWLEDGMENTS

Portions of the materials contained herein have been reprinted with the permission of General Motors Corporation, Service Technology Group.

No part of this publication may be reproduced, transmitted or stored in any form or by any means, electronic or mechanical, including photocopy, recording, or by information storage or retrieval system without prior written permission from the publisher.

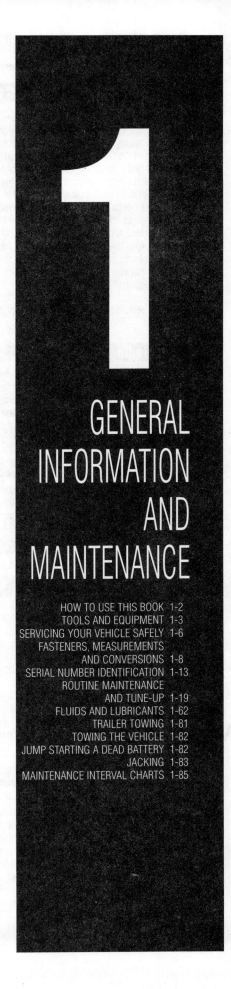

1

GENERAL INFORMATION AND MAINTENANCE

HOW TO USE THIS BOOK

Chilton's Total Car Care manual for the Chevrolet/GMC full size vans is intended to help you learn more about the inner workings of your vehicle while saving you money on its upkeep and operation.

The beginning of the book will likely be referred to the most, since that is where you will find information for maintenance and tune-up. The other sections deal with the more complex systems of your vehicle. Operating systems from engine through brakes are covered to the extent that the average do-it-yourselfer becomes mechanically involved. This book will not explain such things as rebuilding a differential for the simple reason that the expertise required and the investment in special tools make this task uneconomical. It will, however, give you detailed instructions to help you change your own brake pads and shoes, replace spark plugs, and perform many more jobs that can save you money, give you personal satisfaction and help you avoid expensive problems.

A secondary purpose of this book is a reference for owners who want to understand their vehicle and/or their mechanics better. In this case, no tools at all are required.

Where to Begin

Before removing any bolts, read through the entire procedure. This will give you the overall view of what tools and supplies will be required. There is nothing more frustrating than having to walk to the bus stop on Monday morning because you were short one bolt on Sunday afternoon. So read ahead and plan ahead. Each operation should be approached logically and all procedures thoroughly understood before attempting any work.

All sections contain adjustments, maintenance, removal and installation procedures, and in some cases, repair or overhaul procedures. When repair is not considered practical, we tell you how to remove the part and then how to install the new or rebuilt replacement. In this way, you at least save the labor costs. Backyard repair of some components is just not practical.

Avoiding Trouble

Many procedures in this book require you to "label and disconnect . . . " a group of lines, hoses or wires. Don't be lulled into thinking you can remember where everything goes—you won't. If you hook up vacuum or fuel lines incorrectly, the vehicle will run poorly, if at all. If you hook up electrical wiring incorrectly, you may instantly learn a very expensive lesson.

You don't need to know the official or engineering name for each hose or line. A piece of masking tape on the hose and a piece on its fitting will allow you to assign your own label such as the letter A or a short name. As long as you remember your own code, the lines can be reconnected by matching similar letters or names. Do remember that tape will dissolve in gasoline or other fluids; if a component is to be washed or cleaned, use another method of identification. A permanent felt-tipped marker can be very handy for marking metal parts. Remove any tape or paper labels after assembly.

Maintenance or Repair?

It's necessary to mention the difference between maintenance and repair. Maintenance includes routine inspections, adjustments, and replacement of parts which show signs of normal wear. Maintenance compensates for wear or deterioration. Repair implies that something has broken or is not working. A need for repair is often caused by lack of maintenance. Example: draining and refilling the automatic transmission fluid is maintenance recommended by the manufacturer at specific mileage intervals. Failure to do this can ruin the transmission, requiring very expensive repairs. While no maintenance program can prevent items from breaking or wearing out, a general rule can be stated: MAINTENANCE IS CHEAPER THAN REPAIR.

Two basic mechanic's rules should be mentioned here. First, whenever the left side of the vehicle or engine is referred to, it is meant to specify the driver's side. Conversely, the right side of the vehicle means the passenger's side. Second, most screws and bolts are removed by turning counterclockwise, and tightened by turning clockwise.

Safety is always the most important rule. Constantly be aware of the dangers involved in working on an automobile and take the proper precautions. See the information in this section regarding SERVICING YOUR VEHICLE SAFELY and the SAFETY NOTICE on the acknowledgment page.

Avoiding the Most Common Mistakes

Pay attention to the instructions provided. There are 3 common mistakes in mechanical work:

1. Incorrect order of assembly, disassembly or adjustment. When taking something apart or putting it together, performing steps in the wrong order usually just costs you extra time; however, it CAN break something. Read the entire procedure before beginning disassembly. Perform everything in the order in which the instructions say you should, even if you can't immediately see a reason for it. When you're taking apart something that is very intricate, you might want to draw a picture of how it looks when assembled at one point in order to make sure you get everything back in its proper position. We will supply exploded views whenever possible. When making adjustments, perform them in the proper order; often, one adjustment affects another, and you cannot expect even satisfactory results unless each adjustment is made only when it cannot be changed by any other.

2. Overtorquing (or undertorquing). While it is more common for overtorquing to cause damage, undertorquing may allow a fastener to vibrate loose causing serious damage. Especially when dealing with aluminum parts, pay attention to torque specifications and utilize a torque wrench in assembly. If a torque figure is not available, remember that if you are using the right tool to perform the job, you will probably not have to strain yourself to get a fastener tight enough. The pitch of most threads is so slight that the tension you put on the wrench will be multiplied many times in actual force on what you are tightening. A good example of how critical torque is can be seen in the case of spark plug installation, especially where you are putting the plug into an aluminum cylinder head. Too little torque can fail to crush the gasket, causing leakage of combustion gases and consequent overheating of the plug and engine parts. Too much torque can damage the threads or distort the plug, changing the spark gap.

There are many commercial products available for ensuring that fasteners won't come loose, even if they are not torqued just right (a very common brand is Loctite®). If you're worried about getting something together tight enough to hold, but loose enough to avoid mechanical damage during assembly, one of these products might offer substantial insurance. Before choosing a threadlocking compound, read the label on the package and make sure the product is compatible with the materials, fluids, etc. involved.

3. Crossthreading. This occurs when a part such as a bolt is screwed into a nut or casting at the wrong angle and forced. Crossthreading is more likely to occur if access is difficult. It helps to clean and lubricate fasteners, then to start threading with the part to be installed positioned straight in. Then, start the bolt, spark plug, etc. with your fingers. If you encounter resistance, unscrew the part and start over again at a different angle until it can be inserted and turned several times without much effort. Keep in mind that many parts, especially spark plugs, have tapered threads, so that gentle turning will automatically bring the part you're threading to the proper angle, but only if you don't force it or resist a change in angle. Don't put a wrench on the part until it's been tightened a couple of turns by hand. If you suddenly encounter resistance, and the part has not seated fully, don't force it. Pull it back out to make sure it's clean and threading properly.

Always take your time and be patient; once you have some experience, working on your vehicle may well become an enjoyable hobby.

TOOLS AND EQUIPMENT

▶ **See Figures 1 thru 15 (p. 3–5)**

Naturally, without the proper tools and equipment it is impossible to properly service your vehicle. It would also be virtually impossible to catalog every tool that you would need to perform all of the operations in this book. Of course, It would be unwise for the amateur to rush out and buy an expensive set of tools on the theory that he/she may need one or more of them at some time.

The best approach is to proceed slowly, gathering a good quality set of those tools that are used most frequently. Don't be misled by the low cost of bargain tools. It is far better to spend a little more for better quality. Forged wrenches, 6 or 12-point sockets and fine tooth ratchets are by far preferable to their less expensive counterparts. As any good mechanic can tell you, there are few worse experiences than trying to work on a vehicle with bad tools. Your monetary savings will be far outweighed by frustration and mangled knuckles.

Begin accumulating those tools that are used most frequently: those associated with routine maintenance and tune-up. In addition to the normal assortment of screwdrivers and pliers, you should have the following tools:

• Wrenches/sockets and combination open end/box end wrenches in sizes from ⅛–¾ in. or 3mm–19mm (depending on whether your vehicle uses standard or metric fasteners) and a ¹³⁄₁₆ in. or ⅝ in. spark plug socket (depending on plug type).

➡**If possible, buy various length socket drive extensions. Universal-joint and wobble extensions can be extremely useful, but be careful when using them, as they can change the amount of torque applied to the socket.**

• Jackstands for support.
• Oil filter wrench.
• Spout or funnel for pouring fluids.
• Grease gun for chassis lubrication (unless your vehicle is not equipped with any grease fittings—for details, please refer to information on Fluids and Lubricants found later in this section).
• Hydrometer for checking the battery (unless equipped with a sealed, maintenance-free battery).
• A container for draining oil and other fluids.
• Rags for wiping up the inevitable mess.

In addition to the above items there are several others that are not absolutely necessary, but handy to have around. These include Oil Dry® (or an equivalent oil absorbent gravel—such as cat litter) and the usual supply of lubricants, antifreeze and fluids, although these can be purchased as needed. This is a basic list for routine maintenance, but only your personal needs and desire can accurately determine your list of tools.

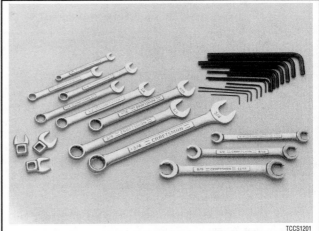
TCCS1201
Fig. 2 In addition to ratchets, a good set of wrenches and hex keys will be necessary

TCCS1202
Fig. 3 A hydraulic floor jack and a set of jackstands are essential for lifting and supporting the vehicle

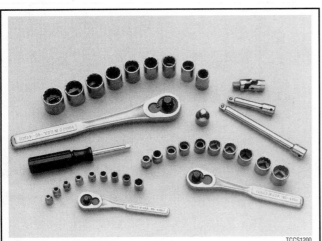
TCCS1200
Fig. 1 All but the most basic procedures will require an assortment of ratchets and sockets

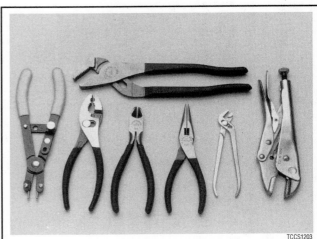
TCCS1203
Fig. 4 An assortment of pliers, grippers and cutters will be handy for old rusted parts and stripped bolt heads

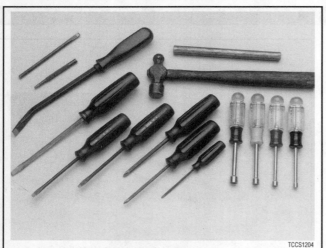

Fig. 5 Various drivers, chisels and prybars are great tools to have in your toolbox

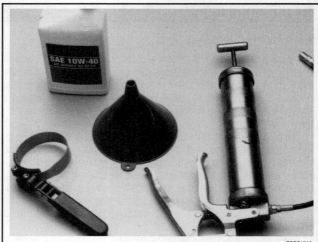

Fig. 8 A few inexpensive lubrication tools will make maintenance easier

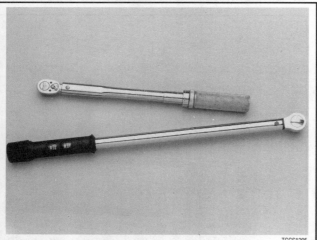

Fig. 6 Many repairs will require the use of a torque wrench to assure the components are properly fastened

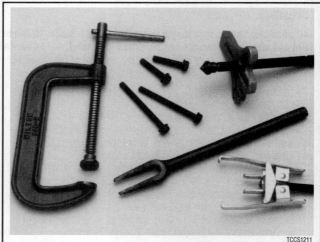

Fig. 9 Various pullers, clamps and separator tools are needed for many larger, more complicated repairs

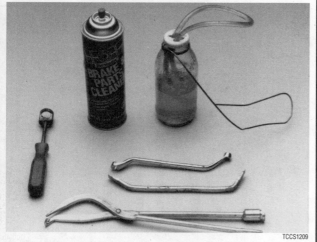

Fig. 7 Although not always necessary, using specialized brake tools will save time

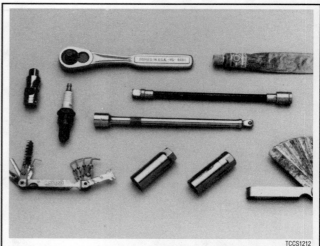

Fig. 10 A variety of tools and gauges should be used for spark plug gapping and installation

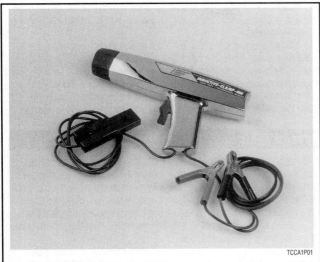

Fig. 11 Inductive type timing light

TCCA1P01

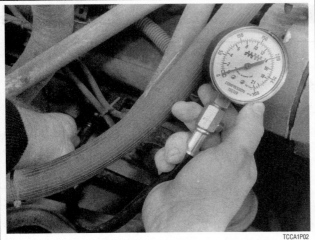

Fig. 12 A screw-in type compression gauge is recommended for compression testing

TCCA1P02

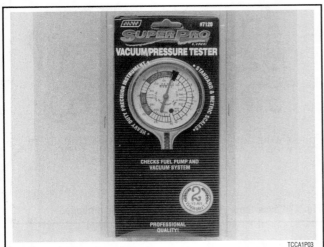

Fig. 13 A vacuum/pressure tester is necessary for many testing procedures

TCCA1P03

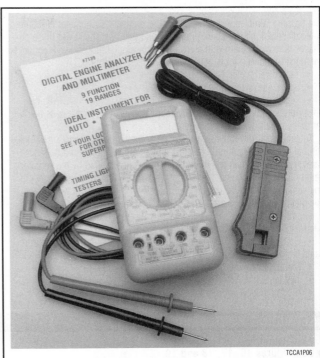

Fig. 14 Most modern automotive multimeters incorporate many helpful features

TCCA1P06

After performing a few projects on the vehicle, you'll be amazed at the other tools and non-tools on your workbench. Some useful household items are: a large turkey baster or siphon, empty coffee cans and ice trays (to store parts), ball of twine, electrical tape for wiring, small rolls of colored tape for tagging lines or hoses, markers and pens, a note pad, golf tees (for plugging vacuum lines), metal coat hangers or a roll of mechanics's wire (to hold things out of the way), dental pick or similar long, pointed probe, a strong magnet, and a small mirror (to see into recesses and under manifolds).

A more advanced set of tools, suitable for tune-up work, can be drawn up easily. While the tools are slightly more sophisticated, they need not be outrageously expensive. There are several inexpensive tach/dwell meters on the market that are every bit as good for the average mechanic as a professional model. Just be sure that it goes to a least 1200–1500 rpm on the

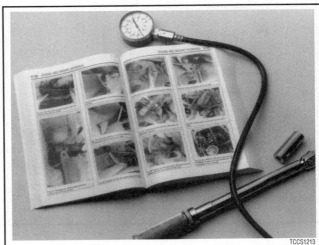

Fig. 15 Proper information is vital, so always have a Chilton Total Car Care manual handy

TCCS1213

tach scale and that it works on 4, 6 and 8-cylinder engines. (If you have one or more vehicles with a diesel engine, a special tachometer is required since diesels don't use spark plug ignition systems). The key to these purchases is to make them with an eye towards adaptability and wide range. A basic list of tune-up tools could include:

- Tach/dwell meter.
- Spark plug wrench and gapping tool.
- Feeler gauges for valve or point adjustment. (Even if your vehicle does not use points or require valve adjustments, a feeler gauge is helpful for many repair/overhaul procedures).

A tachometer/dwell meter will ensure accurate tune-up work on vehicles without electronic ignition. The choice of a timing light should be made carefully. A light which works on the DC current supplied by the vehicle's battery is the best choice; it should have a xenon tube for brightness. On any vehicle with an electronic ignition system, a timing light with an inductive pickup that clamps around the No. 1 spark plug cable is preferred.

In addition to these basic tools, there are several other tools and gauges you may find useful. These include:

- Compression gauge. The screw-in type is slower to use, but eliminates the possibility of a faulty reading due to escaping pressure.
- Manifold vacuum gauge.
- 12V test light.
- A combination volt/ohmmeter

- Induction Ammeter. This is used for determining whether or not there is current in a wire. These are handy for use if a wire is broken somewhere in a wiring harness.

As a final note, you will probably find a torque wrench necessary for all but the most basic work. The beam type models are perfectly adequate, although the newer click types (breakaway) are easier to use. The click type torque wrenches tend to be more expensive. Also keep in mind that all types of torque wrenches should be periodically checked and/or recalibrated. You will have to decide for yourself which better fits your purpose.

Special Tools

Normally, the use of special factory tools is avoided for repair procedures, since these are not readily available for the do-it-yourself mechanic. When it is possible to perform the job with more commonly available tools, it will be pointed out, but occasionally, a special tool was designed to perform a specific function and should be used. Before substituting another tool, you should be convinced that neither your safety nor the performance of the vehicle will be compromised.

Special tools can usually be purchased from an automotive parts store or from your dealer. In some cases special tools may be available directly from the tool manufacturer.

SERVICING YOUR VEHICLE SAFELY

◆ See Figures 16, 17, 18 and 19

It is virtually impossible to anticipate all of the hazards involved with automotive maintenance and service, but care and common sense will prevent most accidents.

The rules of safety for mechanics range from "don't smoke around gasoline," to "use the proper tool(s) for the job." The trick to avoiding injuries is to develop safe work habits and to take every possible precaution.

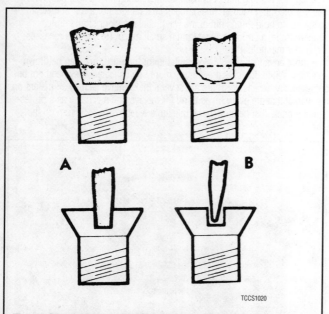

TCCS1020

Fig. 16 Screwdrivers should be kept in good condition to prevent injury or damage which could result if the blade slips from the screw

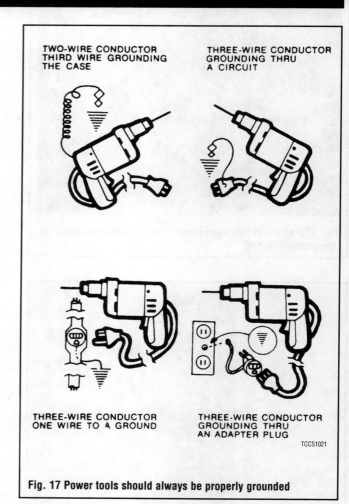

TWO-WIRE CONDUCTOR THIRD WIRE GROUNDING THE CASE

THREE-WIRE CONDUCTOR GROUNDING THRU A CIRCUIT

THREE-WIRE CONDUCTOR ONE WIRE TO A GROUND

THREE-WIRE CONDUCTOR GROUNDING THRU AN ADAPTER PLUG

TCCS1021

Fig. 17 Power tools should always be properly grounded

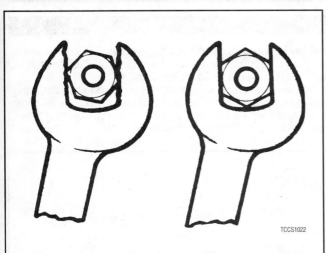

Fig. 18 Using the correct size wrench will help prevent the possibility of rounding off a nut

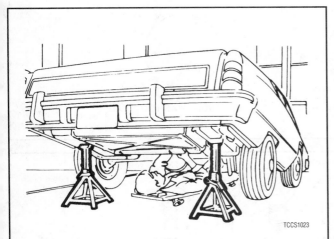

Fig. 19 NEVER work under a vehicle unless it is supported using safety stands (jackstands)

Do's

- Do keep a fire extinguisher and first aid kit handy.
- Do wear safety glasses or goggles when cutting, drilling, grinding or prying, even if you have 20–20 vision. If you wear glasses for the sake of vision, wear safety goggles over your regular glasses.
- Do shield your eyes whenever you work around the battery. Batteries contain sulfuric acid. In case of contact with the eyes or skin, flush the area with water or a mixture of water and baking soda, then seek immediate medical attention.
- Do use safety stands (jackstands) for any undervehicle service. Jacks are for raising vehicles; jackstands are for making sure the vehicle stays raised until you want it to come down. Whenever the vehicle is raised, block the wheels remaining on the ground and set the parking brake.
- Do use adequate ventilation when working with any chemicals or hazardous materials. Like carbon monoxide, the asbestos dust resulting from some brake lining wear can be hazardous in sufficient quantities.

- Do disconnect the negative battery cable when working on the electrical system. The secondary ignition system contains EXTREMELY HIGH VOLTAGE. In some cases it can even exceed 50,000 volts.
- Do follow manufacturer's directions whenever working with potentially hazardous materials. Most chemicals and fluids are poisonous if taken internally.
- Do properly maintain your tools. Loose hammerheads, mushroomed punches and chisels, frayed or poorly grounded electrical cords, excessively worn screwdrivers, spread wrenches (open end), cracked sockets, slipping ratchets, or faulty droplight sockets can cause accidents.
- Likewise, keep your tools clean; a greasy wrench can slip off a bolt head, ruining the bolt and often harming your knuckles in the process.
- Do use the proper size and type of tool for the job at hand. Do select a wrench or socket that fits the nut or bolt. The wrench or socket should sit straight, not cocked.
- Do, when possible, pull on a wrench handle rather than push on it, and adjust your stance to prevent a fall.
- Do be sure that adjustable wrenches are tightly closed on the nut or bolt and pulled so that the force is on the side of the fixed jaw.
- Do strike squarely with a hammer; avoid glancing blows.
- Do set the parking brake and block the drive wheels if the work requires a running engine.

Don'ts

- Don't run the engine in a garage or anywhere else without proper ventilation—EVER! Carbon monoxide is poisonous; it takes a long time to leave the human body and you can build up a deadly supply of it in your system by simply breathing in a little every day. You may not realize you are slowly poisoning yourself. Always use power vents, windows, fans and/or open the garage door.
- Don't work around moving parts while wearing loose clothing. Short sleeves are much safer than long, loose sleeves. Hard-toed shoes with neoprene soles protect your toes and give a better grip on slippery surfaces. Jewelry such as watches, fancy belt buckles, beads or body adornment of any kind is not safe working around a vehicle. Long hair should be tied back under a hat or cap.
- Don't use pockets for toolboxes. A fall or bump can drive a screwdriver deep into your body. Even a rag hanging from your back pocket can wrap around a spinning shaft or fan.
- Don't smoke when working around gasoline, cleaning solvent or other flammable material.
- Don't smoke when working around the battery. When the battery is being charged, it gives off explosive hydrogen gas.
- Don't use gasoline to wash your hands; there are excellent soaps available. Gasoline contains dangerous additives which can enter the body through a cut or through your pores. Gasoline also removes all the natural oils from the skin so that bone dry hands will suck up oil and grease.
- Don't service the air conditioning system unless you are equipped with the necessary tools and training. When liquid or compressed gas refrigerant is released to atmospheric pressure it will absorb heat from whatever it contacts. This will chill or freeze anything it touches. Although refrigerant is normally non-toxic, R-12 becomes a deadly poisonous gas in the presence of an open flame. One good whiff of the vapors from burning refrigerant can be fatal.
- Don't use screwdrivers for anything other than driving screws! A screwdriver used as an prying tool can snap when you least expect it, causing injuries. At the very least, you'll ruin a good screwdriver.
- Don't use a bumper or emergency jack (that little ratchet, scissors, or pantograph jack supplied with the vehicle) for anything other than changing a flat! These jacks are only intended for emergency use out on the road; they are NOT designed as a maintenance tool. If you are serious about maintaining your vehicle yourself, invest in a hydraulic floor jack of at least a 1½ ton capacity, and at least two sturdy jackstands.

FASTENERS, MEASUREMENTS AND CONVERSIONS

Bolts, Nuts and Other Threaded Retainers

♦ See Figures 20, 21, 22 and 23

Although there are a great variety of fasteners found in the modern car or truck, the most commonly used retainer is the threaded fastener (nuts, bolts, screws, studs, etc). Most threaded retainers may be reused, provided that they are not damaged in use or during the repair. Some retainers (such as stretch bolts or torque prevailing nuts) are designed to deform when tightened or in use and should not be reinstalled.

Whenever possible, we will note any special retainers which should be replaced during a procedure. But you should always inspect the condition of a retainer when it is removed and replace any that show signs of damage. Check all threads for rust or corrosion which can increase the torque

POZIDRIVE   PHILLIPS RECESS   TORX®   CLUTCH RECESS

 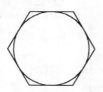 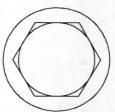

INDENTED HEXAGON   HEXAGON TRIMMED   HEXAGON WASHER HEAD

TCCS1037

Fig. 20 Here are a few of the most common screw/bolt driver styles

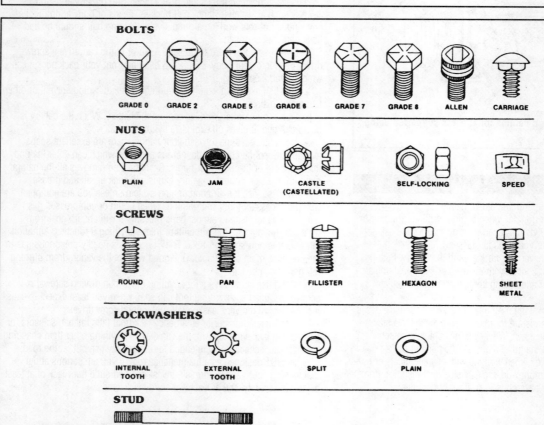

TCCS1036

Fig. 21 There are many different types of threaded retainers found on vehicles

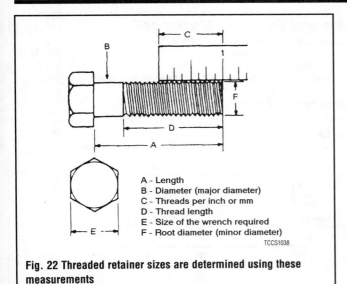

Fig. 22 Threaded retainer sizes are determined using these measurements

A - Length
B - Diameter (major diameter)
C - Threads per inch or mm
D - Thread length
E - Size of the wrench required
F - Root diameter (minor diameter)

TCCS1038

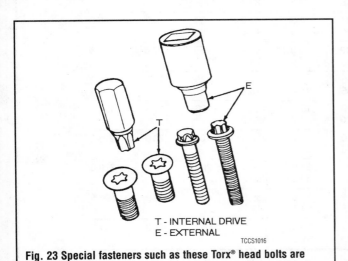

T - INTERNAL DRIVE
E - EXTERNAL

TCCS1016

Fig. 23 Special fasteners such as these Torx® head bolts are used by manufacturers to discourage people from working on vehicles without the proper tools

necessary to achieve the desired clamp load for which that fastener was originally selected. Additionally, be sure that the driver surface of the fastener has not been compromised by rounding or other damage. In some cases a driver surface may become only partially rounded, allowing the driver to catch in only one direction. In many of these occurrences, a fastener may be installed and tightened, but the driver would not be able to grip and loosen the fastener again. (This could lead to frustration down the line should that component ever need to be disassembled again).

If you must replace a fastener, whether due to design or damage, you must ALWAYS be sure to use the proper replacement. In all cases, a retainer of the same design, material and strength should be used. Markings on the heads of most bolts will help determine the proper strength of the fastener. The same material, thread and pitch must be selected to assure proper installation and safe operation of the vehicle afterwards.

Thread gauges are available to help measure a bolt or stud's thread. Most automotive and hardware stores keep gauges available to help you select the proper size. In a pinch, you can use another nut or bolt for a thread gauge. If the bolt you are replacing is not too badly damaged, you can select a match by finding another bolt which will thread in its place. If you find a nut which threads properly onto the damaged bolt, then use that nut to help select the replacement bolt. If however, the bolt you are replacing is so badly damaged (broken or drilled out) that its threads cannot be

used as a gauge, you might start by looking for another bolt (from the same assembly or a similar location on your vehicle) which will thread into the damaged bolt's mounting. If so, the other bolt can be used to select a nut; the nut can then be used to select the replacement bolt.

In all cases, be absolutely sure you have selected the proper replacement. Don't be shy, you can always ask the store clerk for help.

✳✳ WARNING

Be aware that when you find a bolt with damaged threads, you may also find the nut or drilled hole it was threaded into has also been damaged. If this is the case, you may have to drill and tap the hole, replace the nut or otherwise repair the threads. NEVER try to force a replacement bolt to fit into the damaged threads.

Torque

Torque is defined as the measurement of resistance to turning or rotating. It tends to twist a body about an axis of rotation. A common example of this would be tightening a threaded retainer such as a nut, bolt or screw. Measuring torque is one of the most common ways to help assure that a threaded retainer has been properly fastened.

When tightening a threaded fastener, torque is applied in three distinct areas, the head, the bearing surface and the clamp load. About 50 percent of the measured torque is used in overcoming bearing friction. This is the friction between the bearing surface of the bolt head, screw head or nut face and the base material or washer (the surface on which the fastener is rotating). Approximately 40 percent of the applied torque is used in overcoming thread friction. This leaves only about 10 percent of the applied torque to develop a useful clamp load (the force which holds a joint together). This means that friction can account for as much as 90 percent of the applied torque on a fastener.

TORQUE WRENCHES

♦ See Figures 24 and 25

In most applications, a torque wrench can be used to assure proper installation of a fastener. Torque wrenches come in various designs and most automotive supply stores will carry a variety to suit your needs. A torque wrench should be used any time we supply a specific torque value for a fastener. A torque wrench can also be used if you are following the general guidelines in the accompanying charts. Keep in mind that because there is no worldwide standardization of fasteners, the charts are a general guideline and should be used with caution. Again, the general rule of "if you are using the right tool for the job, you should not have to strain to tighten a fastener" applies here.

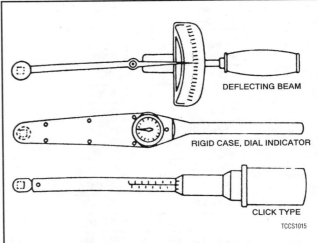

DEFLECTING BEAM

RIGID CASE, DIAL INDICATOR

CLICK TYPE

TCCS1015

Fig. 24 Various styles of torque wrenches are usually available at your local automotive supply store

Standard Torque Specifications and Fastener Markings

In the absence of specific torques, the following chart can be used as a guide to the maximum safe torque of a particular size/grade of fastener.

- There is no torque difference for fine or coarse threads.
- Torque values are based on clean, dry threads. Reduce the value by 10% if threads are oiled prior to assembly.
- The torque required for aluminum components or fasteners is considerably less.

U.S. Bolts

SAE Grade Number	1 or 2			5			6 or 7		
Number of lines always 2 less than the grade number.									
Bolt Size (Inches)—(Thread)	**Maximum Torque**			**Maximum Torque**			**Maximum Torque**		
	Ft./Lbs.	Kgm	Nm	Ft./Lbs.	Kgm	Nm	Ft./Lbs.	Kgm	Nm
¼ — 20	5	0.7	6.8	8	1.1	10.8	10	1.4	13.5
— 28	6	0.8	8.1	10	1.4	13.6			
5/16 — 18	11	1.5	14.9	17	2.3	23.0	19	2.6	25.8
— 24	13	1.8	17.6	19	2.6	25.7			
⅜ — 16	18	2.5	24.4	31	4.3	42.0	34	4.7	46.0
— 24	20	2.75	27.1	35	4.8	47.5			
7/16 — 14	28	3.8	37.0	49	6.8	66.4	55	7.6	74.5
— 20	30	4.2	40.7	55	7.6	74.5			
½ — 13	39	5.4	52.8	75	10.4	101.7	85	11.75	115.2
— 20	41	5.7	55.6	85	11.7	115.2			
9/16 — 12	51	7.0	69.2	110	15.2	149.1	120	16.6	162.7
— 18	55	7.6	74.5	120	16.6	162.7			
⅝ — 11	83	11.5	112.5	150	20.7	203.3	167	23.0	226.5
— 18	95	13.1	128.8	170	23.5	230.5			
¾ — 10	105	14.5	142.3	270	37.3	366.0	280	38.7	379.6
— 16	115	15.9	155.9	295	40.8	400.0			
⅞ — 9	160	22.1	216.9	395	54.6	535.5	440	60.9	596.5
— 14	175	24.2	237.2	435	60.1	589.7			
1 — 8	236	32.5	318.6	590	81.6	799.9	660	91.3	894.8
— 14	250	34.6	338.9	660	91.3	849.8			

Metric Bolts

Relative Strength Marking	4.6, 4.8			8.8		
Bolt Markings						
Bolt Size Thread Size x Pitch (mm)	**Maximum Torque**			**Maximum Torque**		
	Ft./Lbs.	Kgm	Nm	Ft./Lbs.	Kgm	Nm
6 x 1.0	2–3	.2–.4	3–4	3–6	4–.8	5–8
8 x 1.25	6–8	.8–1	8–12	9–14	1.2–1.9	13–19
10 x 1.25	12–17	1.5–2.3	16–23	20–29	2.7–4.0	27–39
12 x 1.25	21–32	2.9–4.4	29–43	35–53	4.8–7.3	47–72
14 x 1.5	35–52	4.8–7.1	48–70	57–85	7.8–11.7	77–110
16 x 1.5	51–77	7.0–10.6	67–100	90–120	12.4–16.5	130–160
18 x 1.5	74–110	10.2–15.1	100–150	130–170	17.9–23.4	180–230
20 x 1.5	110–140	15.1–19.3	150–190	190–240	26.2–46.9	160–320
22 x 1.5	150–190	22.0–26.2	200–260	250–320	34.5–44.1	340–430
24 x 1.5	190–240	26.2–46.9	260–320	310–410	42.7–56.5	420–550

Fig. 25 Standard and metric bolt torque specifications based on bolt strengths—WARNING: use only as a guide

TCCS1098

Beam Type

▶ See Figure 26

The beam type torque wrench is one of the most popular types. It consists of a pointer attached to the head that runs the length of the flexible beam (shaft) to a scale located near the handle. As the wrench is pulled, the beam bends and the pointer indicates the torque using the scale.

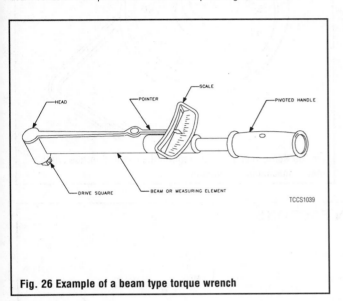

Fig. 26 Example of a beam type torque wrench

Click (Breakaway) Type

▶ See Figure 27

Another popular design of torque wrench is the click type. To use the click type wrench you pre-adjust it to a torque setting. Once the torque is reached, the wrench has a reflex signaling feature that causes a momentary breakaway of the torque wrench body, sending an impulse to the operator's hand.

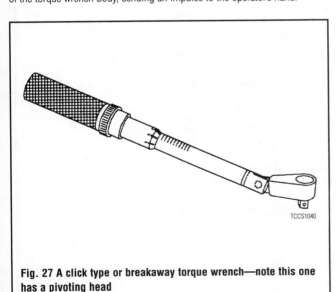

Fig. 27 A click type or breakaway torque wrench—note this one has a pivoting head

Pivot Head Type

▶ See Figure 28

Some torque wrenches (usually of the click type) may be equipped with a pivot head which can allow it to be used in areas of limited access. BUT, it must be used properly. To hold a pivot head wrench, grasp the handle

lightly, and as you pull on the handle, it should be floated on the pivot point. If the handle comes in contact with the yoke extension during the process of pulling, there is a very good chance the torque readings will be inaccurate because this could alter the wrench loading point. The design of the handle is usually such as to make it inconvenient to deliberately misuse the wrench.

➡ **It should be mentioned that the use of any U-joint, wobble or extension will have an effect on the torque readings, no matter what type of wrench you are using. For the most accurate readings, install the socket directly on the wrench driver. If necessary, straight extensions (which hold a socket directly under the wrench driver) will have the least effect on the torque reading. Avoid any extension that alters the length of the wrench from the handle to the head/driving point (such as a crow's foot). U-joint or Wobble extensions can greatly affect the readings; avoid their use at all times.**

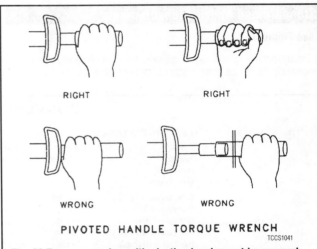

Fig. 28 Torque wrenches with pivoting heads must be grasped and used properly to prevent an incorrect reading

Rigid Case (Direct Reading)

▶ See Figure 29

A rigid case or direct reading torque wrench is equipped with a dial indicator to show torque values. One advantage of these wrenches is that they can be held at any position on the wrench without affecting accuracy. These wrenches are often preferred because they tend to be compact, easy to read and have a great degree of accuracy.

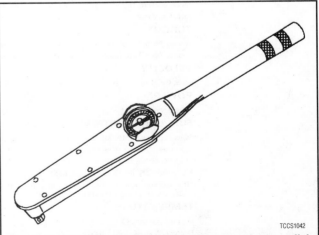

Fig. 29 The rigid case (direct reading) torque wrench uses a dial indicator to show torque

TORQUE ANGLE METERS

▶ **See Figure 30**

Because the frictional characteristics of each fastener or threaded hole will vary, clamp loads which are based strictly on torque will vary as well. In most applications, this variance is not significant enough to cause worry. But, in certain applications, a manufacturer's engineers may determine that more precise clamp loads are necessary (such is the case with many aluminum cylinder heads). In these cases, a torque angle method of installation would be specified. When installing fasteners which are torque angle tightened, a predetermined seating torque and standard torque wrench are usually used first to remove any compliance from the joint. The fastener is then tightened the specified additional portion of a turn measured in degrees. A torque angle gauge (mechanical protractor) is used for these applications.

Standard and Metric Measurements

▶ **See Figure 31**

Throughout this manual, specifications are given to help you determine the condition of various components on your vehicle, or to assist you in

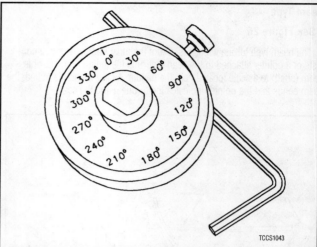

TCCS1043

Fig. 30 Some specifications require the use of a torque angle meter (mechanical protractor)

CONVERSION FACTORS

LENGTH-DISTANCE

Inches (in.)	x 25.4	= Millimeters (mm)	x .0394	= Inches
Feet (ft.)	x .305	= Meters (m)	x 3.281	= Feet
Miles	x 1.609	= Kilometers (km)	x .0621	= Miles

VOLUME

Cubic Inches (in3)	x 16.387	= Cubic Centimeters	x .061	= in3
IMP Pints (IMP pt.)	x .568	= Liters (L)	x 1.76	= IMP pt.
IMP Quarts (IMP qt.)	x 1.137	= Liters (L)	x .88	= IMP qt.
IMP Gallons (IMP gal.)	x 4.546	= Liters (L)	x .22	= IMP gal.
IMP Quarts (IMP qt.)	x 1.201	= US Quarts (US qt.)	x .833	= IMP qt.
IMP Gallons (IMP gal.)	x 1.201	= US Gallons (US gal.)	x .833	= IMP gal.
Fl. Ounces	x 29.573	= Milliliters	x .034	= Ounces
US Pints (US pt.)	x .473	= Liters (L)	x 2.113	= Pints
US Quarts (US qt.)	x .946	= Liters (L)	x 1.057	= Quarts
US Gallons (US gal.)	x 3.785	= Liters (L)	x .264	= Gallons

MASS-WEIGHT

Ounces (oz.)	x 28.35	= Grams (g)	x .035	= Ounces
Pounds (lb.)	x .454	= Kilograms (kg)	x 2.205	= Pounds

PRESSURE

Pounds Per Sq. In. (psi)	x 6.895	= Kilopascals (kPa)	x .145	= psi
Inches of Mercury (Hg)	x .4912	= psi	x 2.036	= Hg
Inches of Mercury (Hg)	x 3.377	= Kilopascals (kPa)	x .2961	= Hg
Inches of Water (H$_2$O)	x .07355	= Inches of Mercury	x 13.783	= H$_2$O
Inches of Water (H$_2$O)	x .03613	= psi	x 27.684	= H$_2$O
Inches of Water (H$_2$O)	x .248	= Kilopascals (kPa)	x 4.026	= H$_2$O

TORQUE

Pounds-Force Inches (in-lb)	x .113	= Newton Meters (N·m)	x 8.85	= in-lb
Pounds-Force Feet (ft-lb)	x 1.356	= Newton Meters (N·m)	x .738	= ft-lb

VELOCITY

Miles Per Hour (MPH)	x 1.609	= Kilometers Per Hour (KPH)	x .621	= MPH

POWER

Horsepower (Hp)	x .745	= Kilowatts	x 1.34	= Horsepower

FUEL CONSUMPTION*

Miles Per Gallon IMP (MPG)	x .354	= Kilometers Per Liter (Km/L)	
Kilometers Per Liter (Km/L)	x 2.352	= IMP MPG	
Miles Per Gallon US (MPG)	x .425	= Kilometers Per Liter (Km/L)	
Kilometers Per Liter (Km/L)	x 2.352	= US MPG	

*It is common to covert from miles per gallon (mpg) to liters/100 kilometers (1/100 km), where mpg (IMP) x 1/100 km = 282 and mpg (US) x 1/100 km = 235.

TEMPERATURE

Degree Fahrenheit (°F)	= (°C x 1.8) + 32
Degree Celsius (°C)	= (°F – 32) x .56

TCCS1044

Fig. 31 Standard and metric conversion factors chart

their installation. Some of the most common measurements include length (in. or cm/mm), torque (ft. lbs., inch lbs. or Nm) and pressure (psi, in. Hg, kPa or mm Hg). In most cases, we strive to provide the proper measurement as determined by the manufacturer's engineers.

Though, in some cases, that value may not be conveniently measured with what is available in your toolbox. Luckily, many of the measuring devices which are available today will have two scales so the Standard or Metric measurements may easily be taken. If any of the various measuring tools which are available to you do not contain the same scale as listed in the specifications, use the accompanying conversion factors to determine the proper value.

The conversion factor chart is used by taking the given specification and multiplying it by the necessary conversion factor. For instance, looking at the first line, if you have a measurement in inches such as "free-play should be 2 in." but your ruler reads only in millimeters, multiply 2 in. by the conversion factor of 25.4 to get the metric equivalent of 50.8mm. Likewise, if the specification was given only in a Metric measurement, for example in Newton Meters (Nm), then look at the center column first. If the measurement is 100 Nm, multiply it by the conversion factor of 0.738 to get 73.8 ft. lbs.

SERIAL NUMBER IDENTIFICATION

Vehicle

The Vehicle Identification Number (VIN) plate is mounted on the driver's side of the instrument panel, and is visible through the windshield.

A 17-character code is used:

The first character is the country of origin:

- 1 = United States
- 2 = Canada
- 3 = Mexico

The second character indicates the manufacturer: G = General Motors

The third character indicates the make: Chevrolet (C) or GMC (T).

The fourth character is the Gross Vehicle Weight range in pounds, as follows:

- B = 3,001–4,000
- C = 4,001–5,000
- D = 5,001–6,000
- E = 6,001–7,000
- F = 7,001–8,000
- G = 8,001–9,000
- H = 9,001–10,000
- J = 10,001–14,000
- K = 14,001–16,000

The fifth character is vehicle line and chassis type: G = full-sized van.

88191P01

The Vehicle Identification Number (VIN) is visible through the windshield

The sixth character is the weight code rating, as follows:

- 1 = ½ ton
- 2 = ¾ ton
- 3 = 1 ton

The seventh character is the body type, as follows:

- 0 = chassis only
- 1 = cutaway van
- 2 = forward control
- 3 = 4-door cab
- 4 = 2-door cab
- 5 = van
- 6 = Suburban
- 7 = motor home chassis
- 8 = Blazer/Jimmy
- 9 = extended cab

The eighth character is the engine code, as follows:

- C = 8–379 (6.2L) diesel
- H = 8–305 (5.0L)
- J = 8–379 (6.2L) diesel
- K = 8–350 (5.7L) with TBI
- M = 8–350 (5.7L) with 4-bbl. carburetor
- N = 8–454 (7.4L) with TBI
- T = 6–292 (4.8L)
- W = 8–454 (7.4L) with 4-bbl. carburetor
- Z = 6–262 (4.3L)

The ninth character is a check digit.

The tenth character is the year code:

- H = 1987
- J = 1988
- K = 1989
- L = 1990

The eleventh character denotes the assembly plant, as folows:

- B = Baltimore, MD
- E = Pontiac East, MI
- F = Flint, MI
- J = Janesville, WI
- S = St. Louis, MO
- V = Pontiac, MI
- Z = Fort Wayne, IN
- 0 = Pontiac, MI
- 1 = Oshawa, ON
- 2 = Moraine, OH
- 3 = Detroit, MI
- 4 = Scarborough, ON
- 7 = Lordstown, OH
- 8 = Shreveport, LA

The last six numbers make up the consecutive serial number.

VEHICLE IDENTIFICATION CHART

Engine Code						Model Year	
Code	Liters	Cu. In. (cc)	Cyl.	Fuel Sys.	Eng. Mfg.	Code	Year
C	6.2	379 (6210)	8	DSL	CPC	H	1987
F	6.5	395 (6473)	8	DSL	CPC	J	1988
H	5.0	305 (4999)	8	TFI	CPC	K	1989
J	6.2	379 (6210)	8	DSL	CPC	L	1990
K	5.7	350 (5735)	8	TFI	CPC	M	1991
M	5.0	305 (4999)	8	MFI	CPC	N	1992
N	7.4	454 (7440)	8	TFI	CPC	P	1993
P	6.5	395 (6473)	8	DSL	CPC	R	1994
R	2.8	173 (2835)	6	TFI	CPC	S	1995
R	5.7	350 (5735)	8	MFI	CPC	T	1996
S	6.5	395 (6473)	8	DSL	CPC	V	1997
W	4.3	263 (4293)	6	MFI	CPC		
Y	6.5	395 (6473)	8	DSL	CPC		
Z	4.3	263 (4293)	6	TFI	CPC		
Z	4.3	263 (4293)	6	MFI	CPC		

TFI - Throttle body Fuel Injection

MFI - Multi-Port Fuel Injection

DSL - Diesel

CPC - Chevrolet/Pontiac/Canada

88191C01

Engine

♦ **See Figures 32, 33, 34, 35 and 36**

On the 1987–92 4.3L V6 engine, the engine identification number is found on a machined pad on the block, at the front just below the right side cylinder head.

On the 1993–97 4.3L V6 engine, the engine identification number is found on a machined pad on the rear of the cylinder block, below and behind the left cylinder head where the engine mates with the bell housing.

On V8 gasoline engines, the engine identification number is usually found on a machined pad on the block, at the front just below the right side cylinder head. The engine identification number is sometimes also found on a machined pad on the left, rear upper side of the block, where the engine mates with the bell housing.

On V8 diesel engines, the engine identification number is found on a machined pad on the front of the block, between the left cylinder head and the thermostat housing, and/or on a machined pad on the left rear of the block, just behind the left cylinder head. The engine number is broken down as follows:

Example—F1210TFA

- F—Manufacturing Plant: F=Flint and T=Tonawanda
- 12—Month of Manufacture (December)
- 10—Day of Manufacturer (Tenth)
- T—Van engine
- FA—Transmission and Engine Combination

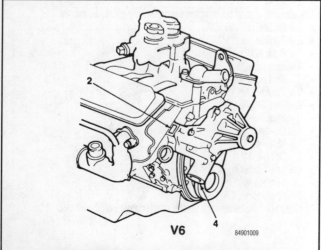

Fig. 32 Engine identification number location—1987–92 4.3L engine

V6

84901009

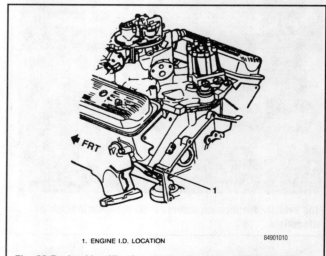

1. ENGINE I.D. LOCATION

84901010

Fig. 33 Engine identification number location—1993–97 4.3L engine

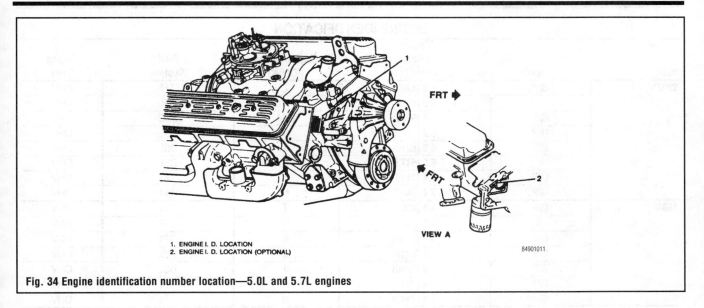

1. ENGINE I. D. LOCATION
2. ENGINE I. D. LOCATION (OPTIONAL)

84901011

Fig. 34 Engine identification number location—5.0L and 5.7L engines

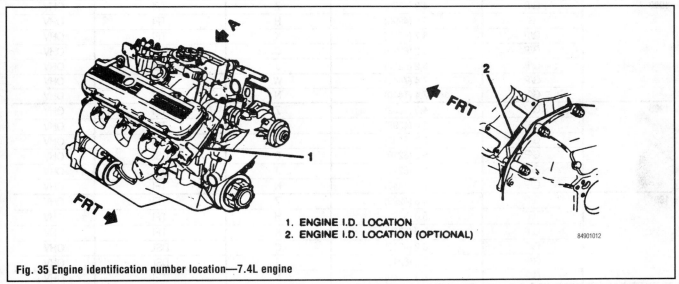

1. ENGINE I.D. LOCATION
2. ENGINE I.D. LOCATION (OPTIONAL)

84901012

Fig. 35 Engine identification number location—7.4L engine

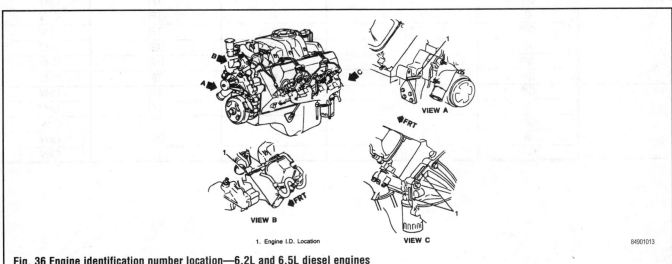

VIEW A

VIEW B

VIEW C

1. Engine I.D. Location

84901013

Fig. 36 Engine identification number location—6.2L and 6.5L diesel engines

ENGINE IDENTIFICATION

Year	Model	Engine Displacement Liters (cc)	Engine Series (ID/VIN)	Fuel System	Engine Type
1987	G/P	4.3 (4293)	Z	TFI	OHV
	G	5.0 (4999)	H	DSL	OHV
	G/P	5.7 (5735)	K/M	4BC	OHV
	G/P	6.2 (6210)	C	DSL	OHV
	G/P	6.2 (6210)	J	DSL	OHV
	P	6.5 (6473)	F	DSL	OHV
	G/P	7.4 (7440)	W	TFI	OHV
	G/P	7.4 (7440)	N	TFI	OHV
1988	G/P	4.3 (4293)	Z	TFI	OHV
	G	5.0 (4999)	H	TFI	OHV
	G/P	5.7 (5735)	K	TFI	OHV
	G/P	6.2 (6210)	C	DSL	OHV
	G/P	6.2 (6210)	J	DSL	OHV
	G/P	7.4 (7440)	W	TFI	OHV
	G/P	7.4 (7440)	N	TFI	OHV
1989	G/P	4.3 (4293)	Z	TFI	OHV
	G	5.0 (4999)	H	TFI	OHV
	G/P	5.7 (5735)	K	TFI	OHV
	G/P	6.2 (6210)	C	DSL	OHV
	G/P	6.2 (6210)	J	DSL	OHV
	G/P	7.4 (7440)	W	TFI	OHV
	G/P	7.4 (7440)	N	TFI	OHV
1990	G/P	4.3 (4293)	Z	TFI	OHV
	G	5.0 (4999)	H	TFI	OHV
	G/P	5.7 (5735)	K	TFI	OHV
	G/P	6.2 (6210)	C	DSL	OHV
	G/P	6.2 (6210)	J	DSL	OHV
	G/P	7.4 (7440)	N	TFI	OHV
1991	G/P	4.3 (4293)	Z	TFI	OHV
	G	5.0 (4999)	H	TFI	OHV
	G/P	5.7 (5735)	K	TFI	OHV
	G/P	6.2 (6210)	C	DSL	OHV
	G/P	6.2 (6210)	J	DSL	OHV
	G/P	7.4 (7440)	N	TFI	OHV
1992	G/P	4.3 (4293)	Z	TFI	OHV
	G	5.0 (4999)	H	TFI	OHV
	G/P	5.7 (5735)	K	TFI	OHV
	G	6.2 (6210)	C	DSL	OHV
	G/P	6.2 (6210)	J	DSL	OHV
	G/P	7.4 (7440)	N	TFI	OHV
1993	G/P	4.3 (4293)	Z	TFI	OHV
	G	5.0 (4999)	H	TFI	OHV
	G/P	5.7 (5735)	K	TFI	OHV
	G	6.2 (6210)	C/J	DSL	OHV
	G/P	7.4 (7440)	N	TFI	OHV

88191C02

ENGINE IDENTIFICATION

Year	Model	Engine Displacement Liters (cc)	Engine Series (ID/VIN)	Fuel System	Engine Type
1994	G/P	4.3 (4293)	Z	TFI	OHV
	G/P	5.0 (4999)	H	TFI	OHV
	G	5.7 (5735)	K	TFI	OHV
	G/P	6.5 (6505)	F/P/Y	DSL	OHV
	G/P	7.4 (7440)	N	TFI	OHV
1995	G/P	4.3 (4293)	Z	TFI	OHV
	G	5.0 (4999)	H	TFI	OHV
	G/P	5.7 (5735)	K	TFI	OHV
	G/P	6.5 (6505)	F/P/Y	DSL	OHV
	G/P	7.4 (7440)	N	TFI	OHV
1996	G/P	4.3 (4293)	W	MFI	OHV
	G	5.0 (4999)	M	MFI	OHV
	G/P	5.7 (5735)	R	MFI	OHV
	G/P	6.5 (6374)	F/Y	DSL	OHV
	G/P	7.4 (7440)	J	MFI	OHV
1997	G/P	4.3 (4293)	W	MFI	OHV
	G	5.0 (4999)	M	MFI	OHV
	G/P	5.7 (5735)	R	MFI	OHV
	G/P	6.5 (6374)	F/Y	DSL	OHV
	G/P	7.4 (7440)	N/J	MFI	OHV

4BC-Four Barrel Carburetor
TFI-Throttle body Fuel Injection
DSL-Diesel

MFI - Multi-Port Fuel Injection
OHV - Overhead Valve

88191C03

Transmission

▶ **See Figures 37 and 38**

The Muncie 3-speed manual transmission serial number is located on the lower left side of the case, adjacent to the rear of the cover.

The New Process 4-speed transmission is numbered on the rear of the case, above the output shaft.

The Muncie 117mm 4-speed transmission is numbered on the rear of the case, above the output shaft.

The NVG 4500 5-speed transmissions are numbered on the top, left side of the case, near the bell housing.

The Turbo Hydra-Matic is identified by a plate attached to the right side, which is stamped with the serial number.

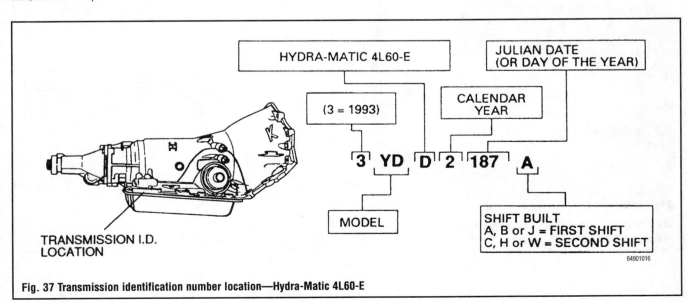

Fig. 37 Transmission identification number location—Hydra-Matic 4L60-E

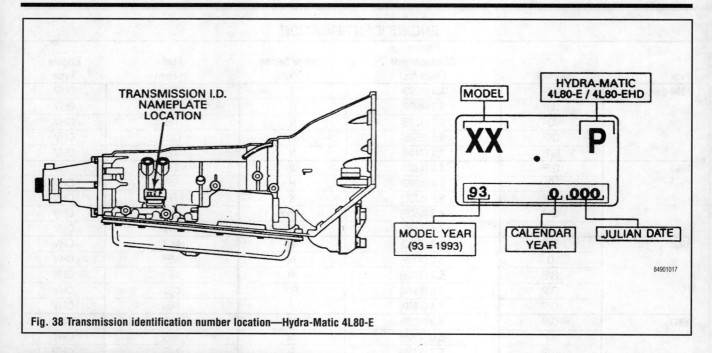

Fig. 38 Transmission identification number location—Hydra-Matic 4L80-E

Drive Axle

The drive axle serial number is stamped on the axle shaft housing, where it connects to the differential housing.

Front axles on four wheel drive models are marked on the front of the left axle tube.

Service Parts Identification Label

▶ See Figure 39

The service parts identification label, commonly known as the option list, is usually located on the inside of the glove compartment door. On some vans, you may have to look for it on an inner fender panel. The label lists the vehicle serial number, wheelbase, all Regular Production Options (RPOs) and all special equipment. Probably the most valuable piece of information on this label is the paint code, a useful item when you need to match the vehicle's original paint.

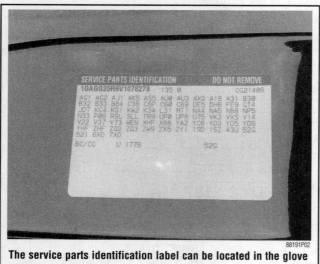

The service parts identification label can be located in the glove box or on a door jam

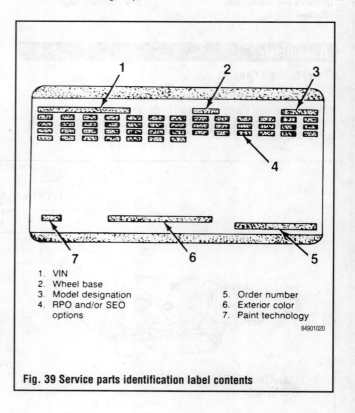

1. VIN
2. Wheel base
3. Model designation
4. RPO and/or SEO options
5. Order number
6. Exterior color
7. Paint technology

Fig. 39 Service parts identification label contents

ROUTINE MAINTENANCE AND TUNE-UP

UNDERHOOD MAINTENANCE COMPONENT LOCATIONS

1. Air filter housing
2. Power steering pump reservoir
3. Brake master cylinder
4. Windshield washer fluid reservoir
5. Radiator hose
6. Engine oil dipstick
7. Engine oil filler cap
8. Automatic transmission dipstick and filler tube
9. Engine coolant reservoir
10. Radiator cap
11. Battery
12. Belt and vacuum hose routing label
13. Air bag warning label

Proper maintenance and tune-ups are the key to long and trouble-free vehicle life, and the work can yield its own rewards. Studies have shown that a properly tuned and maintained vehicle can achieve better gas mileage than an out-of-tune vehicle. As a conscientious owner and driver, set aside a Saturday morning, say once a month, to check or replace items which could cause major problems later. Keep your own personal log to jot down which services you performed, how much the parts cost you, the date, and the exact odometer reading at the time. Keep all receipts for such items as engine oil and filters, so that they may be referred to in case of related problems or to determine operating expenses. As a do-it-yourselfer, these receipts are the only proof you have that the required maintenance was performed. In the event of a warranty problem, these receipts will be invaluable.

The literature provided with your vehicle when it was originally delivered includes the factory recommended maintenance schedule. If you no longer have this literature, replacement copies are usually available from the dealer. A maintenance schedule is provided later in this section, in case you do not have the factory literature.

Air Cleaner

The element should be replaced at the recommended intervals shown in the Maintenance Intervals chart later in this section. If your van is operated under severely dusty conditions or severe operating conditions, more frequent changes will certainly be necessary. Inspect the element at least twice a year. Early spring and early fall are good times for inspection. Remove the element and check for any perforations or tears in the filter. Check the cleaner housing for signs of dirt or dust that may have leaked through the filter element or in through the snorkel tube. Position a droplight on one side of the element and look through the filter at the light. If no glow of light can be seen through the element material, replace the filter. If holes in the filter element are apparent or signs of dirt seepage through the filter are evident, replace the filter.

REMOVAL & INSTALLATION

▶ **See Figure 40, 41, 42, 43 and 44**

1. On early model vehicles, remove the wingnut(s) and lift off the housing cover. On late model and 6.5L diesel vehicles, lift the wire tabs to release the retaining clips and separate the two case halves.

2. On the 6.5L diesel, position the cover with the air cleaner flexible hose off to the side.

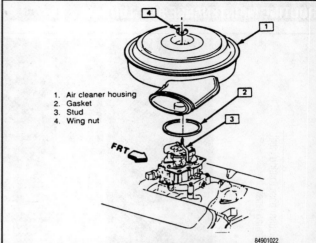

1. Air cleaner housing
2. Gasket
3. Stud
4. Wing nut

Fig. 41 Exploded view of the air cleaner housing—1987–92 7.4L engine

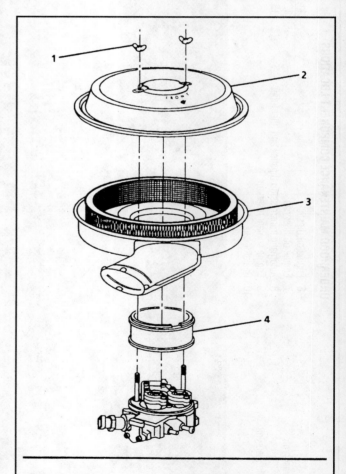

1	WING NUT	4	AIR CLEANER EXTENSION
2	2 HOLE COVER	5	TBI ASSEMBLY
3	AIR CLEANER ASSEMBLY		

Fig. 42 Exploded view of the air cleaner housing—1993–95 gasoline engines

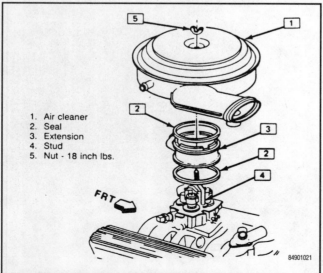

1. Air cleaner
2. Seal
3. Extension
4. Stud
5. Nut - 18 inch lbs.

Fig. 40 Exploded view of the air cleaner housing—1987–92 gasoline engines except the 7.4L

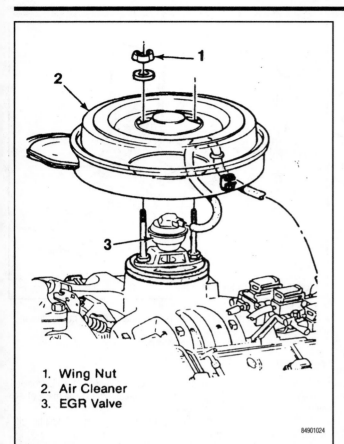

1. Wing Nut
2. Air Cleaner
3. EGR Valve

84901024

Fig. 43 Exploded view of the air cleaner housing—6.2L diesel engine

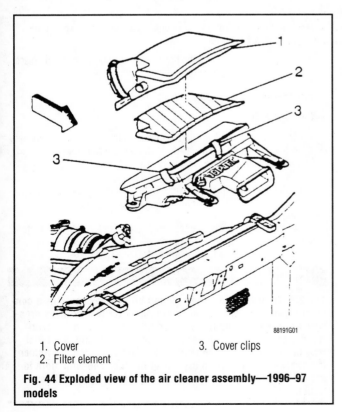

1. Cover
2. Filter element
3. Cover clips

88191G01

Fig. 44 Exploded view of the air cleaner assembly—1996–97 models

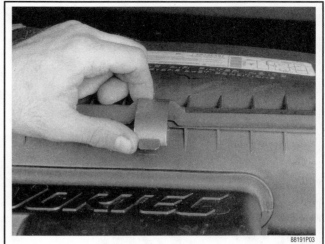

88191P03

Unsnap the air cleaner housing clips and separate the two halves . . .

88191P04

. . . then remove the filter element from the housing

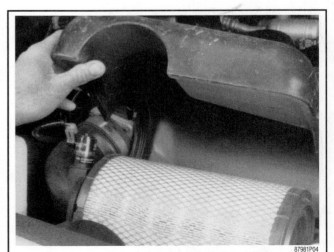

87981P04

On newer vehicles, lift up the air cleaner cover—1996 van shown

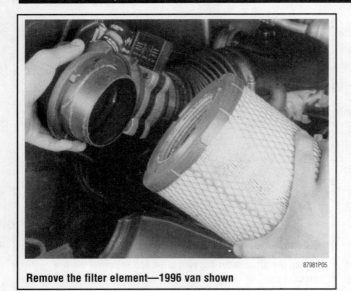

Remove the filter element—1996 van shown

87981P05

3. Withdraw the element from the housing and discard it.

4. With a clean rag, remove any dirt or dust from the front cover and also from the element seating surface.

To install:

5. Position and install the new filter element so that it seats properly in the housing.

6. On the 6.5L diesel, position the cover with the attached hose over the element and snap the retaining clips into place. On all other engines, install the housing lid and tighten the wingnut(s) to about 18 inch lbs. (2 Nm) and fasten the retaining clips.

✳✳ WARNING

Do not drive the vehicle with the air cleaner removed. Doing so will allow dirt and a variety of other foreign particles to enter the engine, causing damage and wear. Also, backfiring could cause a fire in the engine compartment.

Fuel Filter

REMOVAL & INSTALLATION

Carbureted Gasoline Engines

FILTER IN CARBURETOR
▶ See Figure 45

The fuel filter should be serviced at the interval given on the Maintenance Interval chart. Two types of fuel filters are used, a bronze type and a paper element type. Filter replacement should be attempted only when the engine is cold. Additionally, it is a good idea to place some absorbent rags under the fuel fittings to catch the gasoline which will spill out when the lines are loosened.

1. Disengage the fuel line connection at the intake fuel filter nut. Plug the opening to prevent loss of fuel.

2. Remove the intake fuel filter nut from the carburetor with a 1 in. open end wrench (or adjustable wrench).

3. Remove the filter element and spring.

4. Check the element for restrictions by blowing on the cone end. Air should pass freely.

5. Clean or replace the element, as necessary.

To install:

6. Install the element spring, then the filter element in the carburetor. Bronze filters should have the small section of the cone facing out.

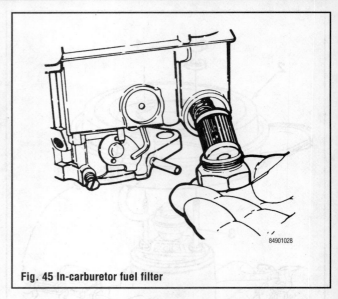

Fig. 45 In-carburetor fuel filter

84901028

7. Install a new gasket on the intake fuel nut. Install the nut in the carburetor body and tighten securely.

8. Install the fuel line and tighten the connector.

INLINE FILTER

Some vans may have an inline filter. This is a can-shaped device located in the fuel line between the pump and the carburetor. It may be made of either plastic or metal. To replace the filter:

1. Place some absorbent rags under the filter. Remember, it will be full of gasoline when removed.

2. Use a pair of pliers to expand the clamp on one end of the filter, then slide the clamp down past the point to which the filter pipe extends into the rubber hose. Do the same with the other clamp.

3. Gently twist and pull the hoses free of the filter pipes. Remove and discard the old filter.

➡**Most replacement filters come with new hoses that should be installed with a new filter.**

4. Install the new filter into the hoses, slide the clamps back into place, and check for leaks with the engine idling.

Fuel Injected Gasoline Engines

▶ See Figure 46

The inline filter on the fuel injected models is found along the frame rail.

1. You must first relieve the fuel system pressure as follows:

   a. Disconnect the negative battery cable.

   b. Loosen the filler cap.

   c. Connect a fuel pressure gauge to the fuel pressure tap. Wrap a shop towel around the fitting while connecting the gauge to avoid spilling fuel.

   d. Connect a bleed hose to the gauge and insert the other end into a suitable container for storing fuel.

   e. Open the valve and bleed the system pressure.

✳✳ CAUTION

The 220 TBI unit used on the V6 and V8 engines contains a constant bleed feature in the pressure regulator that relieves pressure any time the engine is turned off. Therefore, no special relief procedure is required; however, a small amount of fuel may be released when the fuel line is disconnected. To reduce the chance of personal injury, cover the fuel line with cloth to collect the fuel and then place the cloth in an approved container.

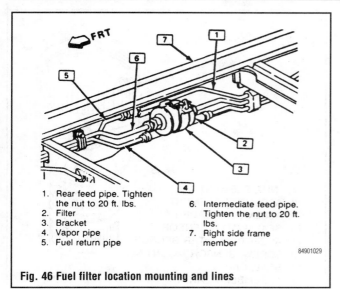

1. Rear feed pipe. Tighten the nut to 20 ft. lbs.
2. Filter
3. Bracket
4. Vapor pipe
5. Fuel return pipe
6. Intermediate feed pipe. Tighten the nut to 20 ft. lbs.
7. Right side frame member

84901029

Fig. 46 Fuel filter location mounting and lines

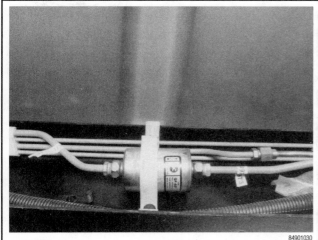

84901030

On gasoline fuel injected vehicles, the fuel filter is found along the frame rail

88191P05

The fuel filter may be adjacent to the fuel tank

2. Disconnect the fuel lines.
3. Remove the fuel filter from the retainer or mounting bolt.

To install:

4. Install the filter and tighten the bolt to 12 ft. lbs. (16 Nm). Connect the fuel lines and tighten the nuts to 20 ft. lbs. (26 Nm).
5. Road test the van and check for any leaks.

➡ **The filter has an arrow (fuel flow direction) on the side of the case, be sure to install it correctly in the system, with the arrow facing away from the fuel tank.**

Diesel Engines

6.2L ENGINE

▶ **See Figures 47 and 48**

The fuel/water separator is usually located on the header assembly.

1. Drain the fuel from the fuel filter by opening both the air bleed and the water drain valve, allowing the fuel to drain out into an appropriate container.
2. Remove the fuel tank cap to release any pressure or vacuum in the tank.
3. Unstrap both bail wires with a screwdriver and remove the filter.

To install:

4. Before installing the new filter, insure that both filter mounting plate fittings are clear of dirt.
5. Install the new filter and snap into place with the bail wires.
6. Close the water drain valve and open the air bleed valve. Connect a ⅛ in. (3mm) I.D. hose to the air bleed port and place the other end into a suitable container.
7. Disconnect the fuel injection pump shut-off solenoid wire.
8. Crank the engine for 10–15 seconds, then wait one minute for the starter motor to cool. Repeat until clear fuel is observed coming from the air bleed.

➡ **If the engine is to be cranked, or starting attempted with the air cleaner removed, care must be taken to prevent dirt from being pulled into the air inlet manifold, which could result in engine damage.**

9. Close the air bleed valve, reconnect the injection pump solenoid wire and replace the fuel tank cap.
10. Start the engine, allow it to idle for 5 minutes and check the fuel filter for leaks.

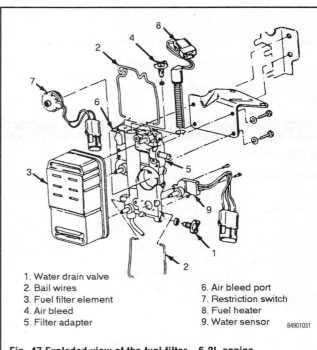

1. Water drain valve
2. Bail wires
3. Fuel filter element
4. Air bleed
5. Filter adapter
6. Air bleed port
7. Restriction switch
8. Fuel heater
9. Water sensor

84901031

Fig. 47 Exploded view of the fuel filter—6.2L engine

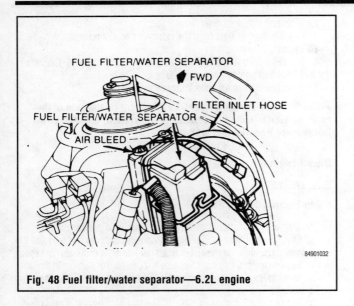

Fig. 48 Fuel filter/water separator—6.2L engine

6.5L ENGINE

◆ **See Figure 49**

1. Remove the fuel tank cap to release any pressure or vacuum in the tank.
2. Spin off the element nut at the top of the filter—it looks like a large knurled knob.
3. Lift the filter element out of the header assembly.

To install:

4. Clean the mating surfaces on the header assembly and the filter. Align the widest key slot in the element cap with that in the header assembly, push the element down until the two surfaces make contact, then tighten the nut by hand.
5. Open the air bleed valve on top of the filter assembly. Connect a hose to the bleeder valve and insert the other end into a suitable glass container.
6. Disconnect the fuel injection pump shut-down solenoid wire, then crank the engine in 10–15 second intervals until clear, clean fuel is coming out of the hose.

➡**Wait about one minute between cranking intervals!**

7. Remove the hose and close the bleeder valve.
8. Connect the shut-down solenoid wire and install the fuel cap. Start the engine and allow it to idle for a few minutes. Check for leaks.

PCV Valve

◆ **See Figures 50 and 51**

➡**Diesel engines do not utilize a PCV system.**

The PCV valve, which is the heart of the positive crankcase ventilation system, should be changed as noted in the Maintenance Intervals chart at the end of this section. The main thing to keep in mind is that the valve should be free of dirt and residue and should be in working order. As long as the valve is not showing signs of becoming damaged or gummed up, it should perform its function properly. When the valve becomes sticky and will not operate freely, it should be replaced.

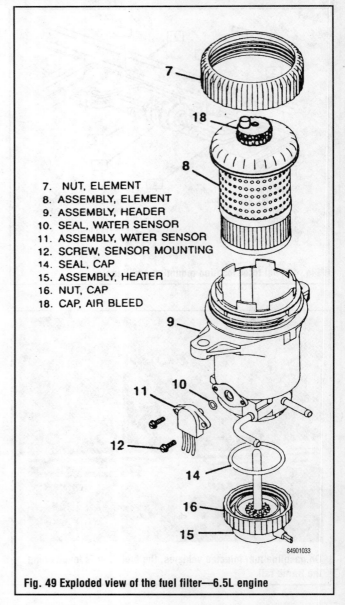

7. NUT, ELEMENT
8. ASSEMBLY, ELEMENT
9. ASSEMBLY, HEADER
10. SEAL, WATER SENSOR
11. ASSEMBLY, WATER SENSOR
12. SCREW, SENSOR MOUNTING
14. SEAL, CAP
15. ASSEMBLY, HEATER
16. NUT, CAP
18. CAP, AIR BLEED

Fig. 49 Exploded view of the fuel filter—6.5L engine

The PCV valve is used to control the rate at which crankcase vapors are returned to the intake manifold. The action of the valve plunger is controlled by intake manifold vacuum and the spring. During deceleration and idle, when manifold vacuum is high, it overcomes the tension of the valve spring and the plunger bottoms in the manifold end of the valve housing. Because of the valve construction, it reduces, but does not stop, the passage of vapors to the intake manifold. When the engine is lightly accelerated or operated at constant speed, spring tension matches intake manifold vacuum pull and the plunger takes a mid-position in the valve body, allowing more vapors to flow into the manifold.

The valve is either mounted on the valve cover or in the line which runs from the intake manifold to the crankcase. Do not attempt to adjust or repair the valve. If the valve is faulty, replace it.

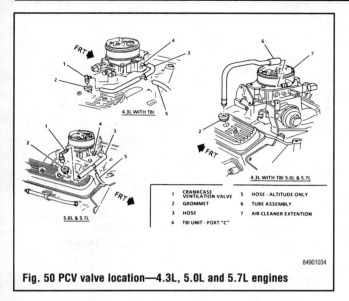

Fig. 50 PCV valve location—4.3L, 5.0L and 5.7L engines

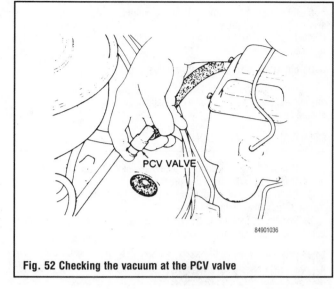

Fig. 52 Checking the vacuum at the PCV valve

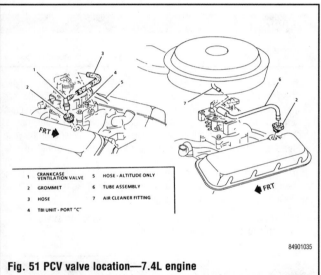

Fig. 51 PCV valve location—7.4L engine

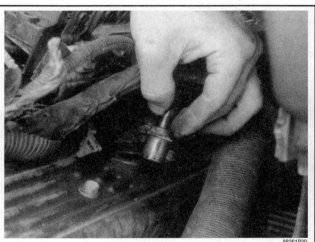

The PCV valve is normally fitted to a rubber grommet in the valve cover

TESTING

♦ See Figure 52

An inoperative PCV system will cause rough idling, sludge and oil dilution. In the event of erratic idle, never attempt to compensate by disconnecting the PCV system. Disconnecting the PCV system will adversely affect engine ventilation. It could also shorten engine life through the buildup of sludge.

1. Remove the engine cover located between the driver and passenger seats. Refer to Section 10 for this procedure.
2. With the engine idling, remove the PCV valve from the rocker cover or line. If the valve is not plugged, a hissing sound will be heard. A strong vacuum should be felt when you place your finger over the valve.
3. Reinstall the PCV valve and allow about a minute for pressure to drop.
4. Remove the crankcase intake air cleaner. Cover the opening in the rocker cover with a piece of stiff paper. The paper should be sucked against the opening with noticeable force.
5. With the engine stopped, remove the PCV valve and shake it. A rattle or clicking should be heard to indicate that the valve is free.

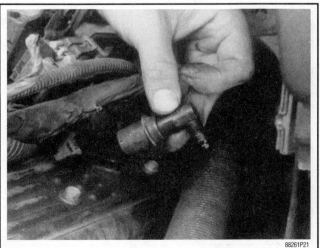

Once it is removed from the grommet, carefully pull the PCV valve free of the vacuum hose

6. If the system performs as indicated in Steps 2, 3, 4 and 5, no further service is required, unless replacement is specified in the Maintenance Intervals Chart. If the system does not pass these tests, the valve should be replaced with a new one.

➡**Do not attempt to clean a PCV valve.**

7. After checking and/or servicing the Crankcase Ventilation System, any components that do not allow passage of air to the intake manifold should be replaced.

REMOVAL & INSTALLATION

1. Remove the engine cover located between the driver and passenger seats. Refer to Section 10 for this procedure.
2. Remove the PCV valve from the cylinder head cover or from the manifold-to-crankcase hose.
3. Visually inspect all hose connections and hoses for cracks, clogs or deterioration and replace as necessary.

Crankcase Depression Regulator and Flow Control Valve

SERVICING

◗ **See Figures 53 and 54**

➡**This system is found only on diesel engines.**

The Crankcase Depression Regulator (CDR) is designed to scavenge crankcase vapors in basically the same manner as the PCV valve on gasoline engines. The valve is located by the right cylinder head cover. On this system, the valve and filter are replaced as an assembly.

The ventilation pipes and tubes should also be cleaned and replaced as wear and tear dictates.

➡**Do not attempt to test the crankcase controls on these diesels. Instead, clean the valve cover filter assembly and vent pipes and check the vent pipes. Replace the breather cap assembly every 30,000 miles (48,000 km). Replace all rubber fittings as required every 15,000 miles (24,000 km).**

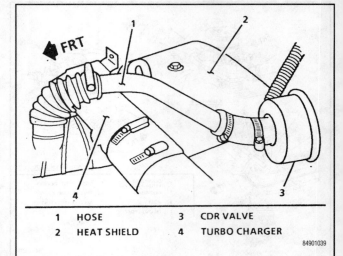

| 1 | HOSE | 3 | CDR VALVE |
| 2 | HEAT SHIELD | 4 | TURBO CHARGER |

Fig. 54 CDR valve—6.5L engine

Evaporative Canister

SERVICING

The only regular maintenance that need be performed on the evaporative emission canister is to regularly change the filter (on those 1987–90 models which utilize one; 1991–97 vans do not have a canister filter) and check the condition of the hoses. If any hoses need replacement, use only hoses which are marked EVAP. No other type should be used. Whenever the vapor vent hose is replaced, the restrictor adjacent to the canister should also be replaced.

The evaporative emission canister is either located on the left side of the engine compartment or is secured to the underbody of the vehicle, with a filter located in its bottom (if applicable).

➡**For further information on the evaporative emission system, please refer to Section 4 of this manual.**

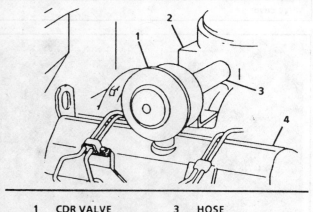

| 1 | CDR VALVE | 3 | HOSE |
| 2 | INTAKE MANIFOLD | 4 | RIGHT VALVE COVER |

Fig. 53 CDR valve—6.2L engine

The EVAP canister on 1996–97 models (arrow) is secured to the frame rail, beneath the van

To service the canister filter:

1. Note the installed positions of the hoses, tagging them as necessary, in case any have to be removed.
2. Loosen the clamps and remove the canister.
3. Pull the filter out and throw it away.
4. Install a new canister filter.
5. Install the canister and tighten the clamps.
6. Check the hoses.

Battery

PRECAUTIONS

Always use caution when working on or near the battery. Never allow a tool to bridge the gap between the negative and positive battery terminals. Also, be careful not to allow a tool to provide a ground between the positive cable/terminal and any metal component on the vehicle. Either of these conditions will cause a short circuit, leading to sparks and possible personal injury.

Do not smoke, have an open flame or create sparks near a battery; the gases contained in the battery are very explosive and, if ignited, could cause severe injury or death.

Remove the battery from the vehicle

Loosen the battery hold-down device retainer . . .

Use a wire brush to clean any rust from the battery tray

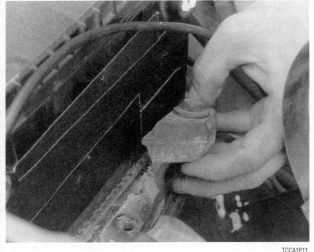

. . . then remove the battery hold-down device

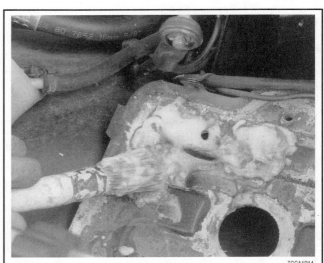

Brush on a solution of baking soda and water to clean the tray

TCCA1P15

After cleaning the tray thoroughly, wash it off with some water

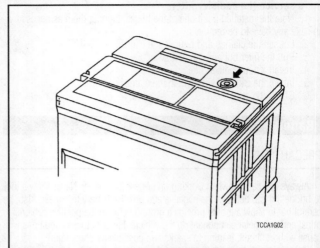

TCCA1G02

Fig. 55 A typical location for the built-in hydrometer on mainte-nance-free batteries

All batteries, regardless of type, should be carefully secured by a battery hold-down device. If this is not done, the battery terminals or casing may crack from stress applied to the battery during vehicle operation. A battery which is not secured may allow acid to leak out, making it discharge faster; such leaking corrosive acid can also eat away at components under the hood.

Always visually inspect the battery case for cracks, leakage and corrosion. A white corrosive substance on the battery case or on nearby components would indicate a leaking or cracked battery. If the battery is cracked, it should be replaced immediately.

REMOVAL & INSTALLATION

1. Disconnect the negative and then the positive battery cables.
2. Loosen the hold-down clamp or strap retainers.
3. Remove the battery hold-down device.
4. Remove the battery from the vehicle.

While the battery is removed, it is a good idea and opportunity to check the condition of the battery tray. Clear it of any debris, and check it for soundness (the battery tray can be cleaned with a baking soda and water solution). Rust should be wire brushed away, and the metal given a couple coats of anti-rust paint.

To install:

5. Install the battery and tighten the hold-down clamp or strap securely. Do not overtighten, as this can crack the battery case.
6. Connect the positive and then the negative battery cables.

GENERAL MAINTENANCE

▶ **See Figure 55**

A battery that is not sealed must be checked periodically for electrolyte level. You cannot add water to a sealed maintenance-free battery (though not all maintenance-free batteries are sealed); however, a sealed battery must also be checked for proper electrolyte level, as indicated by the color of the built-in hydrometer "eye."

Always keep the battery cables and terminals free of corrosion. Check these components about once a year. Refer to the removal, installation and cleaning procedures outlined in this section.

Keep the top of the battery clean, as a film of dirt can help completely discharge a battery that is not used for long periods. A solution of baking soda and water may be used for cleaning, but be careful to flush this off with clear water. DO NOT let any of the solution into the filler holes. Baking soda neutralizes battery acid and will de-activate a battery cell.

Batteries in vehicles which are not operated on a regular basis can fall victim to parasitic loads (small current drains which are constantly drawing current from the battery). Normal parasitic loads may drain a battery on a vehicle that is in storage and not used for 6–8 weeks. Vehicles that have additional accessories such as a cellular phone, an alarm system or other devices that increase parasitic load may discharge a battery sooner. If the vehicle is to be stored for 6–8 weeks in a secure area and the alarm system, if present, is not necessary, the negative battery cable should be disconnected at the onset of storage to protect the battery charge.

Remember that constantly discharging and recharging will shorten battery life. Take care not to allow a battery to be needlessly discharged.

BATTERY FLUID

Check the battery electrolyte level at least once a month, or more often in hot weather or during periods of extended vehicle operation. On non-sealed batteries, the level can be checked either through the case on translucent batteries or by removing the cell caps on opaque-cased types. The electrolyte level in each cell should be kept filled to the split ring inside each cell, or the line marked on the outside of the case.

If the level is low, add only distilled water through the opening until the level is correct. Each cell is separate from the others, so each must be checked and filled individually. Distilled water should be used, because the chemicals and minerals found in most drinking water are harmful to the battery and could significantly shorten its life.

If water is added in freezing weather, the vehicle should be driven several miles to allow the water to mix with the electrolyte. Otherwise, the battery could freeze.

Although some maintenance-free batteries have removable cell caps for access to the electrolyte, the electrolyte condition and level on all sealed maintenance-free batteries must be checked using the built-in hydrometer "eye." The exact type of eye varies between battery manufacturers, but most apply a sticker to the battery itself explaining the possible readings. When in doubt, refer to the battery manufacturer's instructions to interpret battery condition using the built-in hydrometer.

➡**Although the readings from built-in hydrometers found in sealed batteries may vary, a green eye usually indicates a properly charged battery with sufficient fluid level. A dark eye is normally an indicator of a battery with sufficient fluid, but one which may be low in charge. And a light or yellow eye is usually an indication that electrolyte supply has dropped below the necessary level for battery (and hydrometer) operation. In this last case, sealed batteries with an insufficient electrolyte level must usually be discarded.**

Checking the Specific Gravity

▶ See Figure 56

A hydrometer is required to check the specific gravity on all batteries that are not maintenance-free. On batteries that are maintenance-free, the specific gravity is checked by observing the built-in hydrometer "eye" on the top of the battery case. Check with your battery's manufacturer for proper interpretation of its built-in hydrometer readings.

✳✳ CAUTION

Battery electrolyte contains sulfuric acid. If you should splash any on your skin or in your eyes, flush the affected area with plenty of clear water. If it lands in your eyes, get medical help immediately.

The fluid (sulfuric acid solution) contained in the battery cells will tell you many things about the condition of the battery. Because the cell plates must be kept submerged below the fluid level in order to operate, maintaining the fluid level is extremely important. And, because the specific gravity of the acid is an indication of electrical charge, testing the fluid can be an aid in determining if the battery must be replaced. A battery in a vehicle

If the fluid level is low, add only distilled water through the opening until the level is correct

On non-maintenance-free batteries, the fluid level can be checked through the case on translucent models; the cell caps must be removed on other models

Check the specific gravity of the battery's electrolyte with a hydrometer

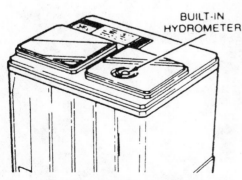

Location of indicator on sealed battery

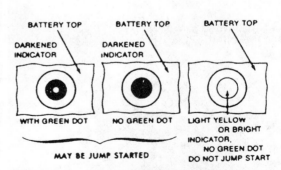

Check the appearance of the charge indicator on top of the battery before attempting a jump start; if it's not green or dark, do not jump start the car

Fig. 56 A typical sealed (maintenance-free) battery with a built-in hydrometer—NOTE that the hydrometer eye may vary between battery manufacturers; always refer to the battery's label

with a properly operating charging system should require little maintenance, but careful, periodic inspection should reveal problems before they leave you stranded.

As stated earlier, the specific gravity of a battery's electrolyte level can be used as an indication of battery charge. At least once a year, check the specific gravity of the battery. It should be between 1.20 and 1.26 on the gravity scale. Most auto supply stores carry a variety of inexpensive battery testing hydrometers. These can be used on any non-sealed battery to test the specific gravity in each cell.

The battery testing hydrometer has a squeeze bulb at one end and a nozzle at the other. Battery electrolyte is sucked into the hydrometer until the float is lifted from its seat. The specific gravity is then read by noting the position of the float. If gravity is low in one or more cells, the battery should be slowly charged and checked again to see if the gravity has come up. Generally, if after charging, the specific gravity between any two cells varies more than 50 points (0.50), the battery should be replaced, as it can no longer produce sufficient voltage to guarantee proper operation.

CABLES

▶ **See Figures 57, 58, 59, 60 and 61 (p. 31–32)**

Once a year (or as necessary), the battery terminals and the cable clamps should be cleaned. Loosen the clamps and remove the cables, negative cable first. On batteries with posts on top, the use of a puller specially made for this purpose is recommended. These are inexpensive and available in most auto parts stores. Side terminal battery cables are secured with a small bolt.

Clean the cable clamps and the battery terminal with a wire brush, until all corrosion, grease, etc., is removed and the metal is shiny. It is especially important to clean the inside of the clamp thoroughly (an old knife is useful here), since a small deposit of foreign material or oxidation there will prevent a sound electrical connection and inhibit either starting or charging. Special tools are available for cleaning these parts, one type for conventional top post batteries and another type for side terminal batteries. It is also a good idea to apply some dielectric grease to the terminal, as this will aid in the prevention of corrosion.

After the clamps and terminals are clean, reinstall the cables, negative cable last; DO NOT hammer the clamps onto battery posts. Tighten the clamps securely, but do not distort them. Give the clamps and terminals a thin external coating of grease after installation, to retard corrosion.

Check the cables at the same time that the terminals are cleaned. If the cable insulation is cracked or broken, or if the ends are frayed, the cable should be replaced with a new cable of the same length and gauge.

. . . then disconnect the cable from the battery

A wire brush may be used to clean any corrosion or foreign material from the cable

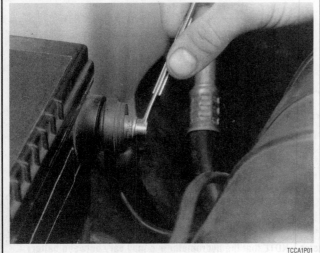

Loosen the battery cable retaining nut . . .

The wire brush can also be used to remove any corrosion or dirt from the battery terminal

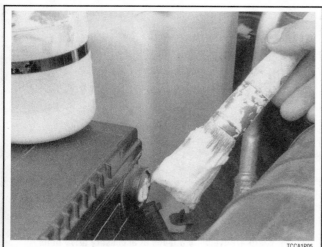

The battery terminal can also be cleaned using a solution of baking soda and water

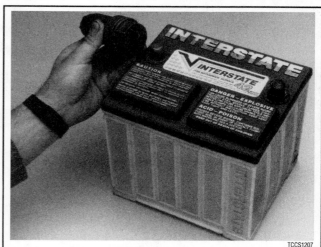

Fig. 58 The underside of this special battery tool has a wire brush to clean post terminals

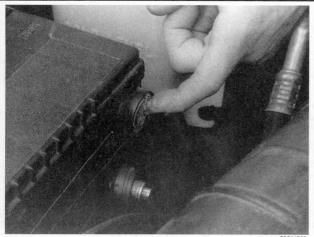

Before connecting the cables, it's a good idea to coat the terminals with a small amount of dielectric grease

Fig. 59 Place the tool over the battery posts and twist to clean until the metal is shiny

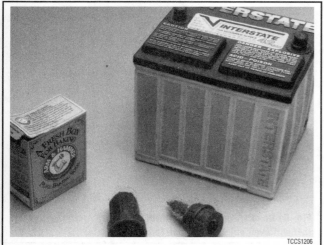

Fig. 57 Maintenance on top post batteries is performed with household items, as well as special tools like this post cleaner

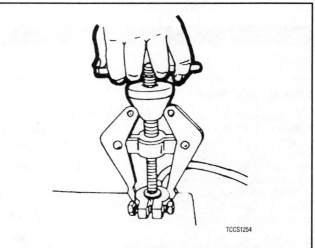

Fig. 60 A special tool is available to pull the clamp from the post

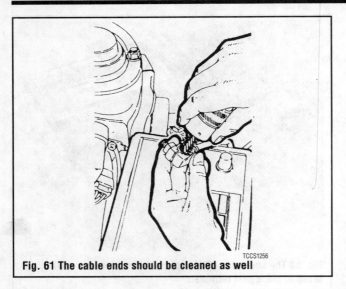

Fig. 61 The cable ends should be cleaned as well

CHARGING

※ CAUTION

The chemical reaction which takes place in all batteries generates explosive hydrogen gas. A spark can cause the battery to explode and splash acid. To avoid serious personal injury, be sure there is proper ventilation and take appropriate fire safety precautions when connecting, disconnecting, or charging a battery and when using jumper cables.

A battery should be charged at a slow rate to keep the plates inside from getting too hot. However, if some maintenance-free batteries are allowed to discharge until they are almost "dead," they may have to be charged at a high rate to bring them back to "life." Always follow the charger manufacturer's instructions on charging the battery.

REPLACEMENT

When it becomes necessary to replace the battery, select one with an amperage rating equal to or greater than the battery originally installed. Deterioration and just plain aging of the battery cables, starter motor, and associated wires makes the battery's job harder in successive years. The slow increase in electrical resistance over time makes it prudent to install a new battery with a greater capacity than the old.

Belts

INSPECTION

▶ **See Figures 62 thru 68**

Inspect the belts for signs of glazing or cracking. A glazed belt will be perfectly smooth from slippage, while a good belt will have a slight texture of fabric visible. Cracks will usually start at the inner edge of the belt and run outward. All worn or damaged drive belts should be replaced immediately. It is best to replace all drive belts at one time, as a preventive maintenance measure, during this service operation.

Newer models have certain components driven by a serpentine belt. Serpentine belts are automatically tensioned by a system of idler and tensioner pulleys, and thus, require no adjustment.

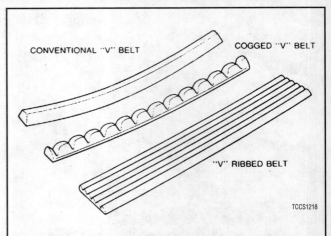

Fig. 62 There are typically 3 types of accessory drive belts found on vehicles today

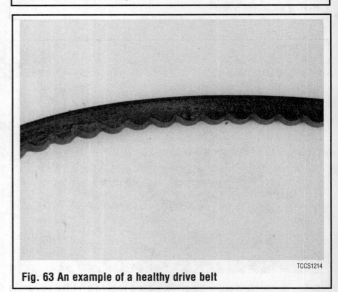

Fig. 63 An example of a healthy drive belt

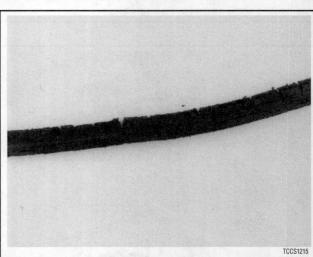

Fig. 64 Deep cracks in this belt will cause flex, building up heat that will eventually lead to belt failure

Fig. 65 The cover of this belt is worn, exposing the critical rein-forcing cords to excessive wear

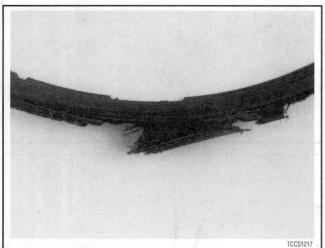

Fig. 66 Installing too wide a belt can result in serious belt wear and/or breakage

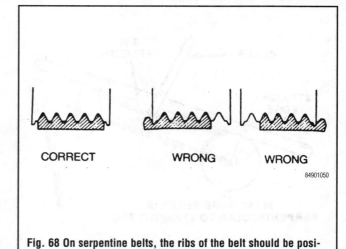

Fig. 68 On serpentine belts, the ribs of the belt should be positioned in the pulley grooves as shown

V-Belts

♦ See Figures 69 and 70

Belt tension should be checked with a gauge made for the purpose. If a tension gauge is not available, tension can be checked with moderate thumb pressure applied to the belt at its longest span midway between pulleys. If the belt has a free span less than 12 in. (305mm), it should deflect approximately 1/8–1/4 in. (3–6mm). If the span is longer than 12 in. (305mm), deflection can range between 1/8 in. (3mm) and 3/8 in. (9.5mm).

If a tension gauge is available use the following procedure:

1. Place a belt tension gauge at the center of the greatest span of a warm (not hot) drive belt and measure the tension.

2. If the belt is not within the specification, loosen the component mounting bracket and adjust to specification.

3. Run the engine at idle for 15 minutes to allow the belt to reseat itself in the pulleys.

4. Allow the drive belt to cool and re-measure the tension. Adjust as necessary to meet the following specifications:

• V6 and V8 gasoline engines: used belt—90 ft. lbs. (122 Nm); new belt—135 ft. lbs. (183 Nm).

• 6.2L and 6.5L diesel engines: used belt—67 ft. lbs. (90 Nm); new belt—146 ft. lbs. (197 Nm).

➡**A belt is considered "used" after 15 minutes of operation.**

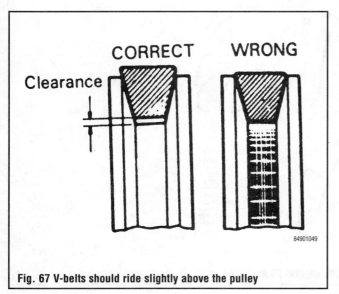

Fig. 67 V-belts should ride slightly above the pulley

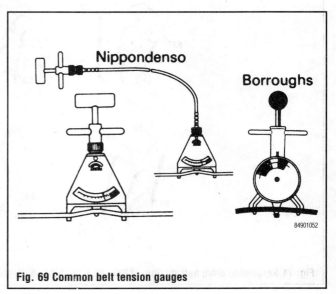

Fig. 69 Common belt tension gauges

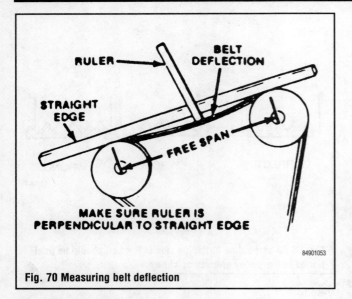

Fig. 70 Measuring belt deflection

Serpentine Drive Belts

The serpentine belt tension can be checked by simply observing the belt's acceptable wear range indicator, located on the tensioner spindle. If the belt does not meet the specification, it must be replaced.

DRIVE BELT ROUTING

▶ See Figures 71 thru 95 (p. 34–39)

A label is normally provided in the engine compartment which details the proper belt routing for the original engine installed in the vehicle. Check the routing label (or vehicle emission control label) for an illustration which resembles your engine first. If no label is present or if the label does not match your engine, refer to the routing diagrams found in this section. In cases where engine swaps were made, determine the year or the engine using your codes, or visually match the accessories to the diagrams provided.

The drive belt routing schematic is usually found on a label in the engine compartment

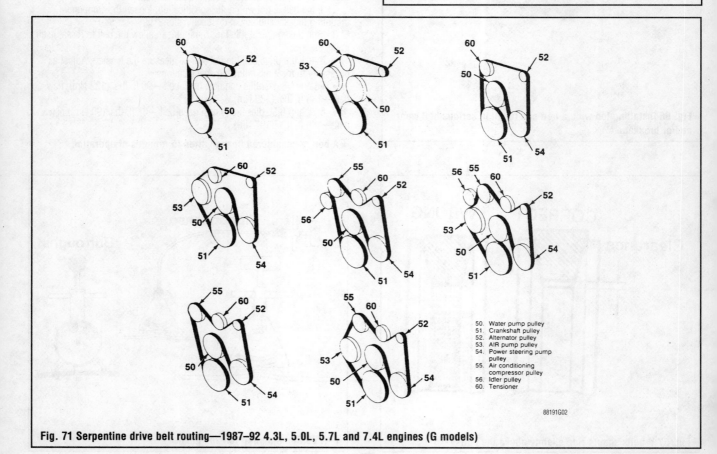

50. Water pump pulley
51. Crankshaft pulley
52. Alternator pulley
53. AIR pump pulley
54. Power steering pump pulley
55. Air conditioning compressor pulley
56. Idler pulley
60. Tensioner

Fig. 71 Serpentine drive belt routing—1987–92 4.3L, 5.0L, 5.7L and 7.4L engines (G models)

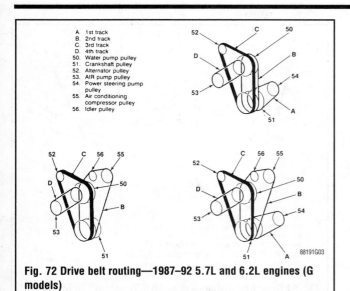

A. 1st track
B. 2nd track
C. 3rd track
D. 4th track
50. Water pump pulley
51. Crankshaft pulley
52. Alternator pulley
53. AIR pump pulley
54. Power steering pump pulley
55. Air conditioning compressor pulley
56. Idler pulley

Fig. 72 Drive belt routing—1987–92 5.7L and 6.2L engines (G models)

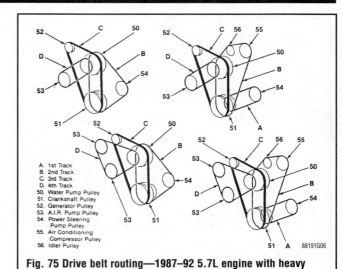

A. 1st Track
B. 2nd Track
C. 3rd Track
D. 4th Track
50. Water Pump Pulley
51. Crankshaft Pulley
52. Generator Pulley
53. A.I.R. Pump Pulley
54. Power Steering Pump Pulley
55. Air Conditioning Compressor Pulley
56. Idler Pulley

Fig. 75 Drive belt routing—1987–92 5.7L engine with heavy duty emissions (P models)

Fig. 73 Drive belt routing—1987–92 5.7L engine with heavy duty emissions (G models)

A. 1st track
B. 2nd track
C. 3rd track
D. 4th track
50. Water pump pulley
51. Crankshaft pulley
52. Alternator pulley
53. AIR pump pulley
54. Power steering pump pulley
55. Air conditioning compressor pulley
56. Idler pulley

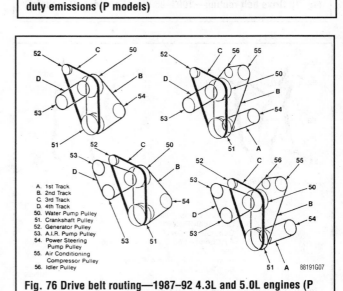

A. 1st Track
B. 2nd Track
C. 3rd Track
D. 4th Track
50. Water Pump Pulley
51. Crankshaft Pulley
52. Generator Pulley
53. A.I.R. Pump Pulley
54. Power Steering Pump Pulley
55. Air Conditioning Compressor Pulley
56. Idler Pulley

Fig. 76 Drive belt routing—1987–92 4.3L and 5.0L engines (P models)

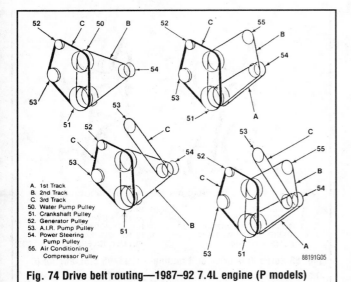

A. 1st Track
B. 2nd Track
C. 3rd Track
50. Water Pump Pulley
51. Crankshaft Pulley
52. Generator Pulley
53. A.I.R. Pump Pulley
54. Power Steering Pump Pulley
55. Air Conditioning Compressor Pulley

Fig. 74 Drive belt routing—1987–92 7.4L engine (P models)

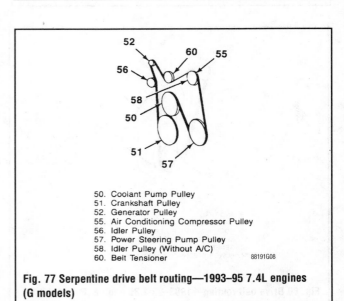

50. Coolant Pump Pulley
51. Crankshaft Pulley
52. Generator Pulley
55. Air Conditioning Compressor Pulley
56. Idler Pulley
57. Power Steering Pump Pulley
58. Idler Pulley (Without A/C)
60. Belt Tensioner

Fig. 77 Serpentine drive belt routing—1993–95 7.4L engines (G models)

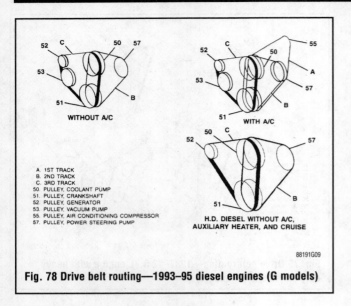

A. 1ST TRACK
B. 2ND TRACK
C. 3RD TRACK
50. PULLEY, COOLANT PUMP
51. PULLEY, CRANKSHAFT
52. PULLEY, GENERATOR
53. PULLEY, VACUUM PUMP
55. PULLEY, AIR CONDITIONING COMPRESSOR
57. PULLEY, POWER STEERING PUMP

88191G09

Fig. 78 Drive belt routing—1993–95 diesel engines (G models)

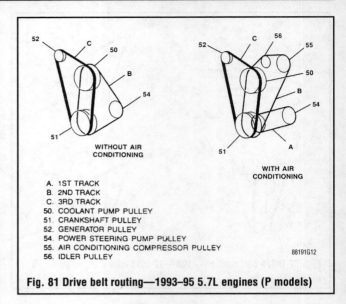

A. 1ST TRACK
B. 2ND TRACK
C. 3RD TRACK
50. COOLANT PUMP PULLEY
51. CRANKSHAFT PULLEY
52. GENERATOR PULLEY
54. POWER STEERING PUMP PULLEY
55. AIR CONDITIONING COMPRESSOR PULLEY
56. IDLER PULLEY

88191G12

Fig. 81 Drive belt routing—1993–95 5.7L engines (P models)

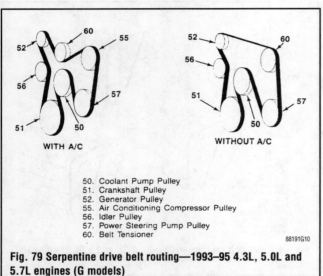

50. Coolant Pump Pulley
51. Crankshaft Pulley
52. Generator Pulley
55. Air Conditioning Compressor Pulley
56. Idler Pulley
57. Power Steering Pump Pulley
60. Belt Tensioner

88191G10

Fig. 79 Serpentine drive belt routing—1993–95 4.3L, 5.0L and 5.7L engines (G models)

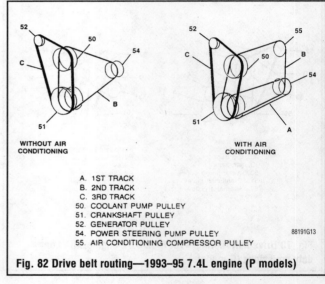

A. 1ST TRACK
B. 2ND TRACK
C. 3RD TRACK
50. COOLANT PUMP PULLEY
51. CRANKSHAFT PULLEY
52. GENERATOR PULLEY
54. POWER STEERING PUMP PULLEY
55. AIR CONDITIONING COMPRESSOR PULLEY

88191G13

Fig. 82 Drive belt routing—1993–95 7.4L engine (P models)

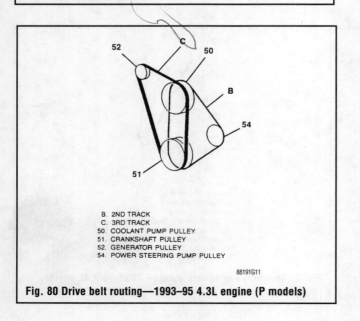

B. 2ND TRACK
C. 3RD TRACK
50. COOLANT PUMP PULLEY
51. CRANKSHAFT PULLEY
52. GENERATOR PULLEY
54. POWER STEERING PUMP PULLEY

88191G11

Fig. 80 Drive belt routing—1993–95 4.3L engine (P models)

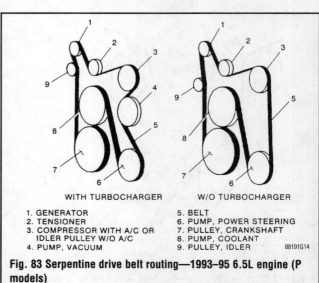

1. GENERATOR
2. TENSIONER
3. COMPRESSOR WITH A/C OR IDLER PULLEY W/O A/C
4. PUMP, VACUUM
5. BELT
6. PUMP, POWER STEERING
7. PULLEY, CRANKSHAFT
8. PUMP, COOLANT
9. PULLEY, IDLER

88191G14

Fig. 83 Serpentine drive belt routing—1993–95 6.5L engine (P models)

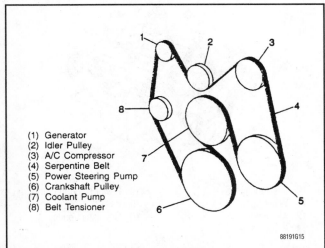

(1) Generator
(2) Idler Pulley
(3) A/C Compressor
(4) Serpentine Belt
(5) Power Steering Pump
(6) Crankshaft Pulley
(7) Coolant Pump
(8) Belt Tensioner

88191G15

Fig. 84 Serpentine drive belt routing—1996–97 4.3L, 5.0L and 5.7L engines with A/C (G models)

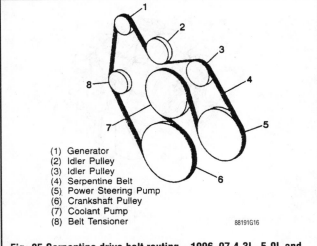

(1) Generator
(2) Idler Pulley
(3) Idler Pulley
(4) Serpentine Belt
(5) Power Steering Pump
(6) Crankshaft Pulley
(7) Coolant Pump
(8) Belt Tensioner

88191G16

Fig. 85 Serpentine drive belt routing—1996–97 4.3L, 5.0L and 5.7L engines without A/C (G models)

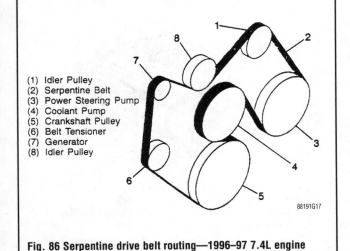

(1) Idler Pulley
(2) Serpentine Belt
(3) Power Steering Pump
(4) Coolant Pump
(5) Crankshaft Pulley
(6) Belt Tensioner
(7) Generator
(8) Idler Pulley

88191G17

Fig. 86 Serpentine drive belt routing—1996–97 7.4L engine without A/C (G models)

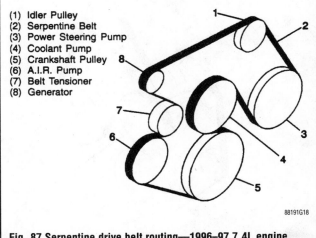

(1) Idler Pulley
(2) Serpentine Belt
(3) Power Steering Pump
(4) Coolant Pump
(5) Crankshaft Pulley
(6) A.I.R. Pump
(7) Belt Tensioner
(8) Generator

88191G18

Fig. 87 Serpentine drive belt routing—1996–97 7.4L engine with air pump, but no A/C (G models)

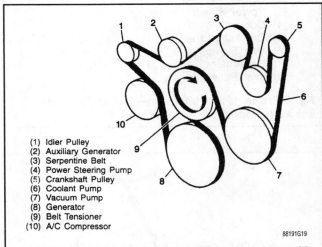

(1) Idler Pulley
(2) Auxiliary Generator
(3) Serpentine Belt
(4) Power Steering Pump
(5) Crankshaft Pulley
(6) Coolant Pump
(7) Vacuum Pump
(8) Generator
(9) Belt Tensioner
(10) A/C Compressor

88191G19

Fig. 88 Serpentine drive belt routing—1996–97 ambulance with 6.5L engine (G models)

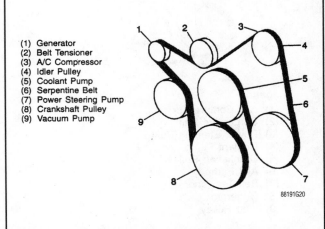

(1) Generator
(2) Belt Tensioner
(3) A/C Compressor
(4) Idler Pulley
(5) Coolant Pump
(6) Serpentine Belt
(7) Power Steering Pump
(8) Crankshaft Pulley
(9) Vacuum Pump

88191G20

Fig. 89 Serpentine drive belt routing—1996–97 6.5L diesel engine (G models)

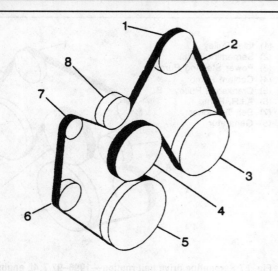

Legend

(1) A/C Compressor
(2) Serpentine Belt
(3) Power Steering Pump
(4) Coolant Pump
(5) Crankshaft Pulley
(6) Belt Tensioner
(7) Generator
(8) Idler Pulley

88191G21

Fig. 90 Serpentine drive belt routing—1996–97 7.4L engine with A/C (G models)

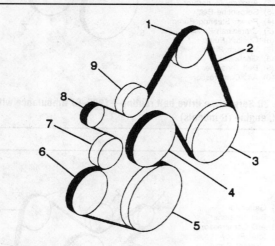

Legend

(1) A/C Compressor
(2) Serpentine Belt
(3) Power Steering Pump
(4) Coolant Pump
(5) Crankshaft Pulley
(6) AIR Pump
(7) Belt Tensioner
(8) Generator
(9) Idler Pulley

88191G22

Fig. 91 Serpentine drive belt routing—1996–97 7.4L engine with air pump and A/C (G models)

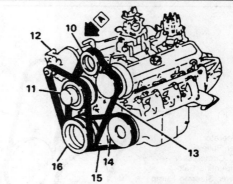

10. Idler pulley
11. Water pump
12. Alternator
13. Belt
14. Power steering pump
15. Belt
16. Crankshaft pulley

88191G23

Fig. 92 Drive belt routing—1996–97 5.7L engine (P models)

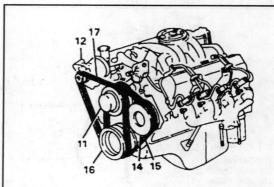

11. Water pump
12. Alternator
14. Power steering pump
15. Belt
16. Crankshaft pulley
17. Belt

88191G24

Fig. 93 Drive belt routing—1996–97 diesel engines (P models)

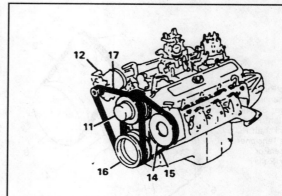

11. Water pump
12. Alternator
14. Power steering pump
15. Belt
16. Crankshaft pulley
17. Belt

88191G25

Fig. 94 Drive belt routing—1996–97 4.3L engine (P models)

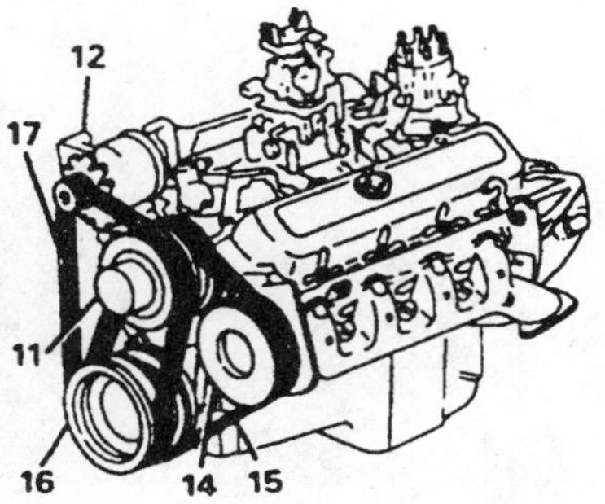

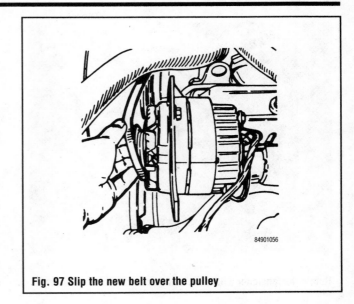

11. Water pump
12. Alternator
14. Power steering pump
15. Belt
16. Crankshaft pulley
17. Belt

88191G26

Fig. 95 Drive belt routing—1996–97 7.4L engine (P models)

REMOVAL & INSTALLATION

V-Belts

♦ See Figures 96, 97 and 98

1. Loosen the driven accessory's pivot and mounting bolts. Remove the belt.
2. Install the belt. Move the accessory toward or away from the engine until the tension is correct. You can use a wooden hammer handle, or broomstick, as a lever, but do not use anything metallic, such as a prybar. Certain models may utilize an adjusting bolt to do this work for you. Simply loosen the mounting bolt and turn the adjuster!
3. Tighten the bolts and recheck the tension. If new belts have been installed, run the engine for a few minutes, then recheck and readjust as necessary.

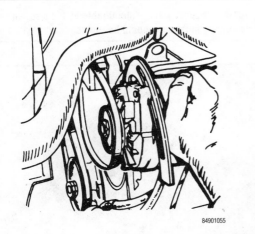

84901055

Fig. 96 Push the component toward the engine and slip off the belt

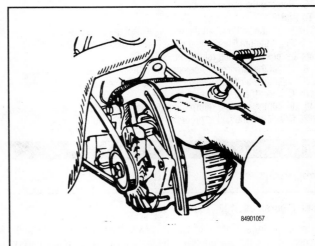

84901056

Fig. 97 Slip the new belt over the pulley

84901057

Fig. 98 Pull outward on the component and tighten the adjusting and mounting bolts

It is better to have belts too loose than too tight, because over-tightened belts will lead to bearing failure, particularly in the water pump and alternator. However, loose belts place an extremely high impact load on the driven component due to the whipping action of the belt.

Serpentine Drive Belts

1. For safety purposes, disconnect the negative battery cable.

➡**It may be necessary to remove the air filter housing to gain access to the belt tensioner.**

2. If necessary, remove the air filter housing cover and filter as outlined in this section.
3. Tag and disconnect the hoses and loosen the housing retainers. Remove the housing from the engine compartment.
4. Using a ½ in. breaker bar with a socket placed on the tensioner pulley bolt, rotate the tensioner to relieve belt tension.

Rotate the tensioner with a breaker bar to relieve belt tension

87981P09

Fig. 100 A hose clamp that is too tight can cause older hoses to separate and tear on either side of the clamp

TCCS1220

5. Remove the serpentine belt.

To install:

6. Route the belt over all the pulleys except the tensioner.

7. Place the breaker bar and socket on the tensioner pulley bolt and rotate the tensioner to the released position.

8. Install the air cleaner housing and tighten the retainers.

9. Install the air filter element and housing cover.

10. Connect the negative battery cable.

11. Install the belt and return the pulley to its original position.

12. Check that the belt is properly seated in each pulley.

Hoses

INSPECTION

♦ **See Figures 99, 100, 101 and 102**

Upper and lower radiator hoses, along with the heater hoses, should be checked for deterioration, leaks and loose hose clamps at least every 15,000 miles (24,000 km). It is also wise to check the hoses periodically in early spring and at the beginning of the fall or winter when you are performing other maintenance. A quick visual inspection could discover

Fig. 101 A soft spongy hose (identifiable by the swollen section) will eventually burst and should be replaced

TCCS1221

Fig. 99 The cracks developing along this hose are a result of age-related hardening

TCCS1219

Fig. 102 Hoses are likely to deteriorate from the inside if the cooling system is not periodically flushed

TCCS1222

a weakened hose which might leave you stranded if it remains unrepaired.

Whenever you are checking the hoses, make sure the engine and cooling system are cold. Visually inspect for cracking, rotting or collapsed hoses, and replace as necessary. Run your hand along the length of the hose. If a weak or swollen spot is noted when squeezing the hose wall, the hose should be replaced.

REMOVAL & INSTALLATION

1. Remove the radiator pressure cap.

✳✳ CAUTION

Never remove the pressure cap while the engine is running, or personal injury from scalding hot coolant or steam may result. If possible, wait until the engine has cooled to remove the pressure cap. If this is not possible, wrap a thick cloth around the pressure cap and turn it slowly to the stop. Step back while the pressure is released from the cooling system. When you are sure all the pressure has been released, use the cloth to turn and remove the cap.

2. Position a clean container under the radiator and/or engine draincock or plug, then open the drain and allow the cooling system to drain to an appropriate level. For some upper hoses, only a little coolant must be drained. To remove hoses positioned lower on the engine, such as a lower radiator hose, the entire cooling system must be emptied.

✳✳ CAUTION

When draining coolant, keep in mind that cats and dogs are attracted by ethylene glycol antifreeze, and are quite likely to drink any that is left in an uncovered container or in puddles on the ground. This will prove fatal in sufficient quantity. Always drain coolant into a sealable container. Coolant may be reused unless it is contaminated or several years old.

3. Loosen the hose clamps at each end of the hose requiring replacement. Clamps are usually either of the spring tension type (which require pliers to squeeze the tabs and loosen) or of the screw tension type (which require screw or hex drivers to loosen). Pull the clamps back on the hose away from the connection.

4. Twist, pull and slide the hose off the fitting, taking care not to damage the neck of the component from which the hose is being removed.

➡**If the hose is stuck at the connection, do not try to insert a screwdriver or other sharp tool under the hose end in an effort to free it, as the connection and/or hose may become damaged. Heater connections especially may be easily damaged by such a procedure. If the hose is to be replaced, use a single-edged razor blade to make a slice along the portion of the hose which is stuck on the connection, perpendicular to the end of the hose. Do not cut deep, so as to prevent damaging the connection. The hose can then be peeled from the connection and discarded.**

5. Clean both hose mounting connections. Inspect the condition of the hose clamps and replace them, if necessary.

To install:

6. Dip the ends of the new hose into clean engine coolant to ease installation.

7. Slide the clamps over the replacement hose, then slide the hose ends over the connections into position.

8. Position and secure the clamps at least ¼ in. (6.35mm) from the ends of the hose. Make sure they are located beyond the raised bead of the connector.

9. Close the radiator or engine drains and properly refill the cooling system with the clean drained engine coolant or a suitable mixture of ethylene glycol coolant and water.

10. If available, install a pressure tester and check for leaks. If a pressure tester is not available, run the engine until normal operating temperature is reached (allowing the system to naturally pressurize), then check for leaks.

✳✳ CAUTION

If you are checking for leaks with the system at normal operating temperature, BE EXTREMELY CAREFUL not to touch any moving or hot engine parts. Once temperature has been reached, shut the engine OFF, and check for leaks around the hose fittings and connections which were removed earlier.

Spark Plugs

▶ **See Figure 103**

A typical spark plug consists of a metal shell surrounding a ceramic insulator. A metal electrode extends downward through the center of the insulator and protrudes a small distance. Located at the end of the plug and attached to the side of the outer metal shell is the side electrode. The side electrode bends in at a 90(angle so that its tip is just past and parallel to the tip of the center electrode. The distance between these two electrodes (measured in thousandths of an inch or hundredths of a millimeter) is called the spark plug gap.

The spark plug does not produce a spark, but instead provides a gap across which the current can arc. The coil produces anywhere from 20,000 to 50,000 volts (depending on the type and application) which travels through the wires to the spark plugs. The current passes along the center electrode and jumps the gap to the side electrode, and in so doing, ignites the air/fuel mixture in the combustion chamber.

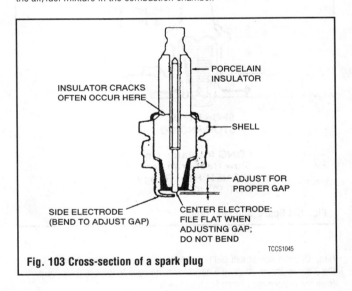

Fig. 103 Cross-section of a spark plug

SPARK PLUG HEAT RANGE

▶ **See Figure 104**

Spark plug heat range is the ability of the plug to dissipate heat. The longer the insulator (or the farther it extends into the engine), the hotter the plug will operate; the shorter the insulator (the closer the electrode is to the block's cooling passages) the cooler it will operate. A plug that absorbs little heat and remains too cool will quickly accumulate deposits of oil and carbon since it is not hot enough to burn them off. This leads to plug fouling and consequently to misfiring. A plug that absorbs too much heat will have no deposits but, due to the excessive heat, the electrodes will burn away quickly and might possibly lead to preignition or other ignition problems. Preignition takes place when plug tips get so hot that they glow sufficiently to ignite the air/fuel mixture before the actual spark occurs. This early ignition will usually cause a pinging during low speeds and heavy loads.

The general rule of thumb for choosing the correct heat range when picking a spark plug is: if most of your driving is long distance, high speed travel, use a colder plug; if most of your driving is stop and go, use a hotter

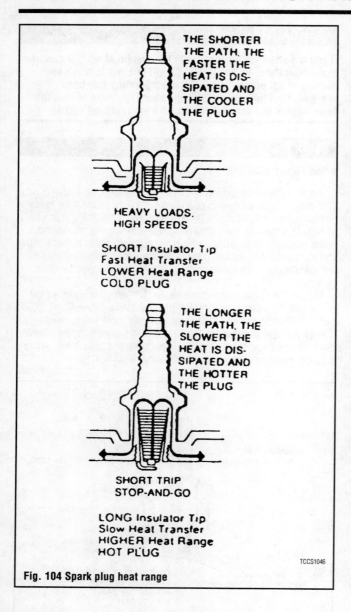

THE SHORTER THE PATH, THE FASTER THE HEAT IS DISSIPATED AND THE COOLER THE PLUG

HEAVY LOADS,
HIGH SPEEDS

SHORT Insulator Tip
Fast Heat Transfer
LOWER Heat Range
COLD PLUG

THE LONGER THE PATH, THE SLOWER THE HEAT IS DISSIPATED AND THE HOTTER THE PLUG

SHORT TRIP
STOP-AND-GO

LONG Insulator Tip
Slow Heat Transfer
HIGHER Heat Range
HOT PLUG

TCCS1046

Fig. 104 Spark plug heat range

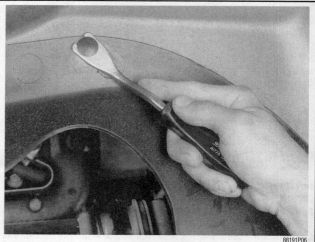

After the van has been raised and the wheel removed, unsnap the access panel retaining clips and remove the panel

88191P06

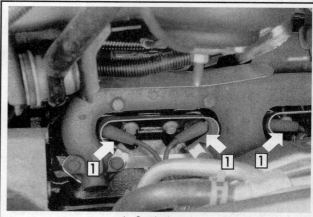

1. Spark plug wires

88191P07

After the panel has been removed, it will allow access to the spark plugs and wires

plug. Original equipment plugs are generally a good compromise between the 2 styles and most people never have the need to change their plugs from the factory-recommended heat range.

REMOVAL & INSTALLATION

A set of spark plugs usually requires replacement after about 20,000–30,000 miles (32,000–48,000 km), depending on your style of driving. In normal operation, plug gap increases about 0.001 in. (0.025mm) for every 2500 miles (4000 km). As the gap increases, the plug's voltage requirement also increases. It requires a greater voltage to jump the wider gap and about two to three times as much voltage to fire the plug at high speeds than at idle. The improved air/fuel ratio control of modern fuel injection, combined with the higher voltage output of modern ignition systems, will often allow an engine to run significantly longer on a set of standard spark plugs, but keep in mind that efficiency will drop as the gap widens (along with fuel economy and power).

When you're removing spark plugs, work on one at a time. Don't start by removing the plug wires all at once because, unless you number them, they may become mixed up. Take a minute before you begin and number the wires with tape.

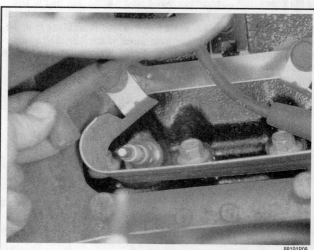

88191P08

Disconnect the spark plug wire by pulling on the boot, NOT THE WIRE

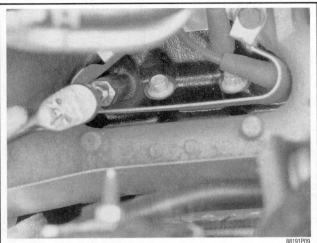

Use a ratchet, extension and spark plug socket to remove the spark plugs from the bores

1. Disconnect the negative battery cable, and if the vehicle has been run recently, allow the engine to thoroughly cool.

2. Raise the front of the vehicle and support it with jackstands.

3. Check for access to the plugs on your vehicle. The wheelwells of most vans covered in this manual are designed to allow access to the sides of the engine. A rubber cover may be draped over the opening, and it may require the removal of one or more plastic body snap-fasteners (which may be pried loose with a special C-shaped tool) before you can move it aside for clearance. If this is your best access point, raise the front of the vehicle and support it with jackstands, then remove the tire and wheel assemblies.

➡**On some models, the engine cover may be removed to provide additional access to the spark plugs. This will be necessary if you also plan to check or replace the spark plug wires.**

4. Carefully twist the spark plug wire boot to loosen it, then pull upward and remove the boot from the plug. Be sure to pull on the boot and not on the wire, otherwise the connector located inside the boot may become separated.

5. Using compressed air (and safety glasses), blow any water or debris from the spark plug well to assure that no harmful contaminants are allowed to enter the combustion chamber when the spark plug is removed. If compressed air is not available, use a rag or a brush to clean the area.

➡**Remove the spark plugs when the engine is cold, if possible, to prevent damage to the threads. If removal of the plugs is difficult, apply a few drops of penetrating oil or silicone spray to the area around the base of the plug, and allow it a few minutes to work.**

6. Using a spark plug socket that is equipped with a rubber insert to properly hold the plug, turn the spark plug counterclockwise to loosen and remove the spark plug from the bore.

✳✳ WARNING

Be sure not to use a flexible extension on the socket. Use of a flexible extension may allow a shear force to be applied to the plug. A shear force could break the plug off in the cylinder head, leading to costly and frustrating repairs.

To install:

7. Inspect the spark plug boot for tears or damage. If a damaged boot is found, the spark plug wire must be replaced.

8. Using a wire feeler gauge, check and adjust the spark plug gap. When using a gauge, the proper size should pass between the electrodes with a slight drag. The next larger size should not be able to pass, while the next smaller size should pass freely.

9. Carefully thread the plug into the bore by hand. If resistance is felt before the plug is almost completely threaded, back the plug out and begin threading again. In small, hard to reach areas, an old spark plug wire and boot could be used as a threading tool. The boot will hold the plug while you twist the end of the wire, and the wire is supple enough to twist before it would allow the plug to crossthread.

✳✳ WARNING

Do not use the spark plug socket to thread the plugs. Always carefully thread the plug by hand or using an old plug wire to prevent the possibility of crossthreading and damaging the cylinder head bore.

10. Carefully tighten the spark plug. If the plug you are installing is equipped with a crush washer, seat the plug, then tighten about ¼ turn to crush the washer. If you are installing a tapered seat plug, tighten the plug to specifications provided by the vehicle or plug manufacturer.

11. Apply a small amount of silicone dielectric compound to the end of the spark plug lead or inside the spark plug boot to prevent sticking, then install the boot to the spark plug and push until it clicks into place. The click may be felt or heard, then gently pull back on the boot to assure proper contact.

12. Install the engine cover.

13. Install the tire and wheel assemblies, raise the vehicle with the jack and remove the jackstands.

14. Lower the vehicle, start the engine and drive the van to check for proper operation.

INSPECTION & GAPPING

◆ **See Figures 105 thru 114 (p. 44–46)**

Check the plugs for deposits and wear. If they are not going to be replaced, clean the plugs thoroughly. Remember that any kind of deposit will decrease the efficiency of the plug. Plugs can be cleaned on a spark plug cleaning machine, which can sometimes be found in service stations, or you can do an acceptable job of cleaning with a stiff brush. If the plugs are cleaned, the electrodes must be filed flat. Use an ignition points file, not an emery board or the like, which will leave deposits. The electrodes must be filed perfectly flat with sharp edges; rounded edges reduce the spark plug voltage by as much as 50%.

Check spark plug gap before installation. The ground electrode (the L-shaped one connected to the body of the plug) must be parallel to the center electrode and the specified size wire gauge (please refer to the Tune-Up Specifications chart for details) must pass between the electrodes with a slight drag.

➡**NEVER adjust the gap on a used platinum type spark plug.**

Always check the gap on new plugs, as they are not always set correctly at the factory. Do not use a flat feeler gauge when measuring the gap on a used plug, because the reading may be inaccurate. A round-wire type gapping tool is the best way to check the gap. The correct gauge should pass through the electrode gap with a slight drag. If you're in doubt, try one size smaller and one larger. The smaller gauge should go through easily, while the larger one shouldn't go through at all. Wire gapping tools usually have a bending tool attached. Use that to adjust the side electrode until the proper distance is obtained. Absolutely never attempt to bend the center electrode! Also, be careful

Fig. 105 A normally worn spark plug should have light tan or gray deposits on the firing tip

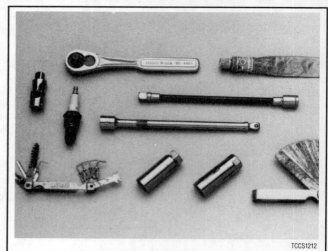

Fig. 107 A variety of tools and gauges are needed for spark plug service

Fig. 106 A carbon fouled plug, identified by soft, sooty, black deposits, may indicate an improperly tuned vehicle. Check the air cleaner, ignition components and engine control system

Fig. 108 A physically damaged spark plug may be evidence of severe detonation in that cylinder. Watch that cylinder carefully between servicing, as continued detonation will not only damage the plug, but could also damage the engine

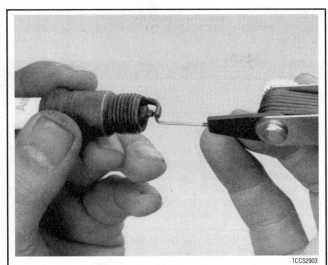

Fig. 109 Checking the spark plug gap with a feeler gauge

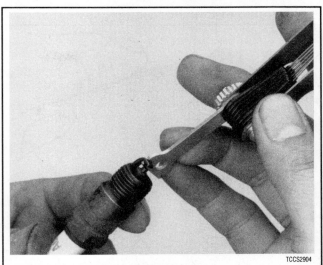

Fig. 111 Adjusting the spark plug gap

Fig. 110 An oil fouled spark plug indicates an engine with worn piston rings and/or bad valve seals, allowing excessive oil to enter the chamber

Fig. 112 This spark plug has been left in the engine too long, as evidenced by the extreme gap. Plugs with such an extreme gap can cause misfiring and stumbling, accompanied by a noticeable lack of power

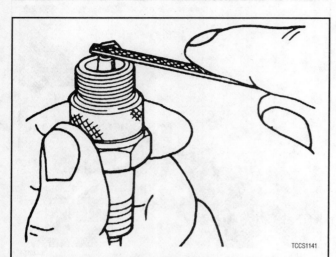

Fig. 113 If the standard plug is in good condition, the electrode may be filed flat—WARNING: do not file platinum plugs

not to bend the side electrode too far or too often as it may weaken and break off within the engine, requiring removal of the cylinder head to retrieve it.

Spark Plug Wires

TESTING

▶ **See Figures 117 and 118**

At every tune-up/inspection, visually check the spark plug cables for burns cuts, or breaks in the insulation. Check the boots and the nipples on the distributor cap and/or coil. Replace any damaged wiring.

Every 50,000 miles (80,000 km) or 60 months, the resistance of the wires should be checked with an ohmmeter. Wires with excessive resistance will cause misfiring, and may make the engine difficult to start in damp weather.

To check resistance:
1. Remove the engine cover to gain access to the distributor.
2. Remove the distributor cap, leaving the wires in place.

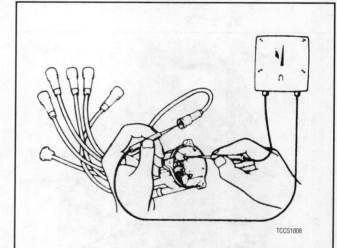

Fig. 117 Checking plug wire resistance through the distributor cap with an ohmmeter

Fig. 114 A bridged or almost bridged spark plug, identified by a build-up between the electrodes and caused by excessive carbon or oil build-up on the plug

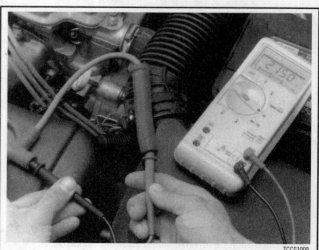

Fig. 118 Checking individual plug wire resistance with a digital ohmmeter

3. Connect one lead of an ohmmeter to an electrode within the cap.

4. Connect the other lead to the corresponding spark plug terminal (remove it from the spark plug for this test).

5. Replace any wire which shows a resistance over 30,000 ohms. Generally speaking, however, resistance should not be over 25,000 ohms, and 30,000 ohms must be considered the outer limit of acceptability.

It should be remembered that resistance is also a function of length. The longer the wire, the greater the resistance. Thus, if the wires on your van are longer than the factory originals, the resistance will be higher, possibly outside these limits.

6. Install the engine cover.

REMOVAL & INSTALLATION

When installing new wires, replace them one at a time to avoid mix-ups. Start by replacing the longest one first.

1. Remove the engine cover to gain access to the distributor.

2. Remove the spark plug wire by gripping the boot firmly and disengaging the wire from the spark plug and the distributor.

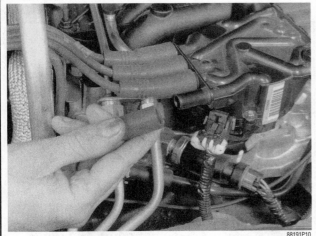

Remove the engine cover to gain access to the distributor, then disengage the wires from the distributor

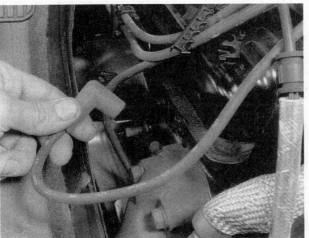

Disengage the spark plug wires from the plugs. They can be accessed either through the panel at the wheelwell or at the engine cover (as shown)

3. Install the boot of the new wire firmly over the spark plug. Route the wire over the same path as the original.

4. Install the engine cover.

Distributor Cap and Rotor

REMOVAL & INSTALLATION

Carbureted Engines

1. Remove the engine cover to gain access to the distributor.

2. Remove the feed and module wire terminal connectors from the distributor cap.

3. Remove the retainer and spark plug wires from the cap.

4. Depress and release the 4 distributor cap-to-housing retainers and lift off the cap assembly.

5. Remove the 4 coil cover screws and cover.

6. Using a finger or a blunt drift, push the spade terminals up out of the distributor cap.

7. Remove all 4 coil screws and lift the coil, coil spring and rubber seal washer out of the cap coil cavity.

Disengage the feed wires . . .

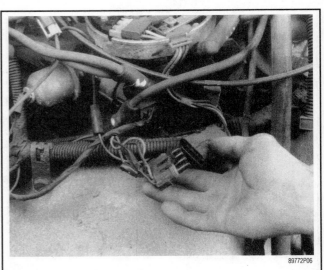

. . . and the module harness

After unfastening the spark plug wires and retaining screws, remove the distributor cap

Unfasten the rotor retaining screws . . .

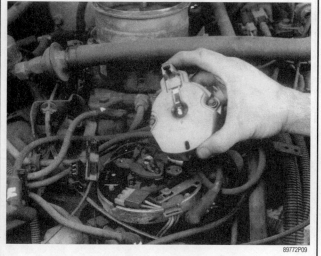

. . . then remove the rotor from the distributor housing

8. Remove the two rotor attaching screws (if equipped) and rotor.

9. Using a new distributor cap and rotor, reverse the above procedures to assemble, being sure to clean and lubricate the rubber seal washer with dielectric lubricant.

Fuel Injected Engines

1. Remove the engine cover to gain access to the distributor.
2. Tag and remove the spark plug wires.
3. Loosen the cap retaining fasteners and remove the cap.
4. Remove the rotor from the distributor shaft.
5. Installation is the reverse of removal.
6. Install the engine cover.

INSPECTION

1. Remove the engine cover to gain access to the distributor.
2. Remove the distributor cap and rotor as described in this section.
3. Check the cap for wear, electrode cracks or damage. Replace if defective.
4. Check the rotor for cracks and wear. Replace if defective.
5. Install the engine cover.

Tag all the spark plug wires and matching cap terminals before removal

Release the distributor cap hold-down screws

88261P33

Remove the cap for inspection, replacement or access to the rotor

88261P34

Carefully pull the rotor from the distributor shaft. Note that this type of rotor does not have retaining screws

Ignition Timing

GENERAL INFORMATION

➡**This procedure does not apply to diesel engines.**

Ignition timing is the measurement, in degrees of crankshaft rotation, of the point at which the spark plugs fire in each of the cylinders. It is measured in degrees before or after Top Dead Center (TDC) of the compression stroke. Ignition timing is controlled by turning the distributor in the engine.

Ideally, the air/fuel mixture in the cylinder will be ignited by the spark plug just as the piston passes TDC of the compression stroke. If this happens, this piston will be beginning the power stroke just as the compressed and ignited air/fuel mixture starts to expand. The expansion of the air/fuel mixture then forces the piston down on the power stroke and turns the crankshaft.

Because it takes a fraction of a second for the spark plug to ignite the gases in the cylinder, the spark plug must fire a little before the piston reaches TDC. Otherwise, the mixture will not be completely ignited as the piston passes TDC and the full benefit of the explosion will not be used by the engine. The timing measurement is given in degrees of crankshaft rotation before the piston reaches TDC (BTDC). If the setting for the ignition

timing is 5 degrees BTDC, the spark plug must fire 5 degrees before that piston reaches TDC. This only holds true, however, when the engine is at idle speed.

As the engine speed increases, the pistons go faster. The spark plugs have to ignite the fuel even sooner if it is to be completely ignited when the piston reaches TDC. To do this, the distributor has a means to advance the timing of the spark as the engine speed increases.

If the ignition is set too far advanced (BTDC), the ignition and expansion of the fuel in the cylinder will occur too soon and tend to force the piston down while it is still traveling up. This causes engine ping. If the engine is too far retarded after TDC (ATDC), the piston will have already passed TDC and started on its way down when the fuel is ignited. This will cause the piston to be forced down for only a portion of its travel. This will result in poor engine performance and lack of power.

Timing should be checked at each tune-up and any time the points are adjusted or replaced. It isn't likely to change much with HEI. The timing marks consist of a notch on the rim of the crankshaft pulley or vibration damper and a graduated scale attached to the engine front (timing) cover. A stroboscopic flash (dynamic) timing light must be used, as a static light is too inaccurate for emission controlled engines.

There are three basic types of timing lights available. The first is a simple neon bulb with two wire connections. One wire connects to the spark plug terminal and the other plugs into the end of the spark plug wire for the No. 1 cylinder, thus connecting the light in series with the spark plug. This type of light is pretty dim and must be held very closely to the timing marks to be seen. Sometimes a dark corner has to be sought out to see the flash at all. This type of light is very inexpensive. The second type operates from the vehicle battery—two alligator clips connect to the battery terminals, while an adapter enables a third clip to be connected between the No. 1 spark plug and wire. This type is a bit more expensive, but it provides a nice bright flash that you can see even in bright sunlight. It is the type most often seen in professional shops. The third type replaces the battery power source with 115 volt current.

Some timing lights have other features built into them, such as dwell meters, or tachometers. These are convenient, in that they reduce the tangle of wires under the hood when you're working, but may duplicate the functions of tools you already have. One worthwhile feature, which is becoming more of a necessity with higher voltage ignition systems, is an inductive pickup. The inductive pickup clamps around the No. 1 spark plug wire, sensing the surges of high voltage electricity as they are sent to the plug. The advantage is that no mechanical connection is inserted between the wire and the plug, which eliminates false signals to the timing light. A timing light with an inductive pickup should be used on HEI systems.

INSPECTION AND ADJUSTMENT

HEI Systems

◆ **See Figures 119 and 120**

1. Start the engine and allow it to reach operating temperature. Stop the engine and connect the timing light to the No. 1 (left front) spark plug wire, at the plug or at the distributor cap. You can also use the No. 6 wire, if it is more convenient. Numbering is illustrated in this section.

➡**Do not pierce the plug wire insulation with HEI; it will cause a miss. The best method is to use an inductive pickup timing light.**

2. Clean off the timing marks and mark the pulley or damper notch and timing scale with white chalk.

3. Disconnect and plug the vacuum line at the distributor on models with a carburetor. This is done to prevent any distributor vacuum advance. On fuel injected models, disengage the timing connector which comes out of the harness conduit next to the distributor; this will put the system in the bypass mode. Check the underhood emission sticker for any other hoses or wires which may need to be disconnected.

4. Start the engine and adjust the idle speed to that specified on the Underhood Emissions label. With an automatic transmission, set the speci-

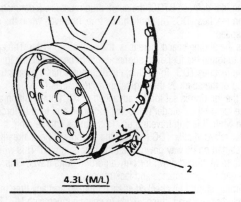

4.3L (M/L)

1   BALANCER TIMING GROOVE

2   TIMING TAB

88261G49

Fig. 119 Timing marks are found on the crankshaft damper (balancer) and the engine front cover—late model 4.3L engine shown (others similar)

88261G51

Fig. 120 View of the typical timing mark scale

88261P35

Aim the timing light at the crankshaft damper timing mark, but WATCH OUT for moving engine parts

fied idle speed in Park. It will be too high, since it is normally (in most cases) adjusted in Drive. You can disconnect the idle solenoid, if any, to get the speed down. Otherwise, adjust the idle speed screw.

The tachometer connects to the **TACH** terminal on the distributor and to a ground on models with a carburetor. On models with fuel injection, the tachometer connects to the **TACH** terminal on the ignition coil. Some tachometers must connect to the **TACH** terminal and to the positive battery terminal. Some tachometers won't work with HEI.

✷✷ WARNING

Never ground the HEI TACH terminal; serious system damage will result.

5. Aim the timing light at the pointer marks. Be careful not to touch the fan, because it may appear to be standing still. If the pulley or damper notch isn't aligned with the proper timing mark (see the Underhood Emissions label), the timing will have to be adjusted.

➡**Top Dead Center or TDC corresponds to 0°. Before Top Dead Center, BTDC or B may be shown as BEFORE. After Top Dead Center, ATDC, or A may be shown as AFTER.**

6. Loosen the distributor base clamp locknut. You can buy specialty wrenches which make this task a lot easier.

7. Turn the distributor slowly to adjust the timing, holding it by the body and not the cap. Turn the distributor in the direction of rotor rotation to retard, and against the direction of rotation to advance.

8. Tighten the locknut. Check the timing again, in case the distributor moved slightly as you tightened it.

9. Reinstall the distributor vacuum line or the timing connector. Correct the idle speed.

10. Stop the engine and disconnect the timing light.

Distributor Ignition (DI) Systems

1995 MODELS

➡**Refer to the underhood label for the proper timing setting.**

1. Engage the parking brake, block the wheels and set the transmission in P.

2. Disconnect the Ignition Control (IC) system by disengaging the "set timing connector". This is a single wire sealed connector that has a tan with black stripe lead. This wire comes out of the wiring harness below the heater case.

3. With the ignition switch **OFF**, connect the timing light pickup lead to the No. 1 spark plug wire.

4. Start the engine and point the timing light at the timing mark on the balancer or pulley and check the timing.

5. If the timing is not within specifications, refer to the underhood emission sticker and loosen the distributor hold-down bolt. Slowly rotate the distributor until the proper timing setting is achieved.

6. Tighten the hold-down bolt and recheck the timing.

7. Turn the ignition **OFF**, remove the timing light and engage the "set timing" connector.

1996–97 MODELS

The ignition timing is preset and cannot be adjusted. If the distributor position is moved, crossfiring may be induced. To check distributor position, do the following:

➡**An OBD II compliant scan tool is required for this procedure.**

1. With the ignition **OFF**, attach the scan tool to the Data Link Connector (DLC).

2. Start the engine and bring the vehicle to operating temperature.

3. Monitor cam retard on the scan tool.

4. If cam retard is between -2° and +2°, the distributor is properly adjusted.

5. If cam retard is not between -2° and +2° the distributor must be adjusted.

6. With the engine **OFF**, loosen the distributor hold-down bolt.

7. Start the engine and check the cam retard reading. Rotate the distributor counterclockwise to compensate for a negative reading and clockwise to compensate for a positive reading.

8. Momentarily raise the engine speed to over 1000 RPM and check the cam retard reading.

9. If the proper reading is not achieved, repeat Steps 7 and 8.

10. When the proper reading has been achieved, tighten the distributor hold-down bolt and disconnect the scan tool.

Valve Lash

Valve lash adjustment determines how far the valves enter the cylinder and how long they stay open and/or closed.

➡**While all the valve adjustments must be made as accurately as possible, it is better to have the valve adjustment slightly loose than slightly tight, as a burned valve may result from overly tight adjustments.**

All of the engines covered in this manual utilize hydraulic lifters. The purpose of the hydraulic lifters is to automatically maintain zero valve lash, therefore no periodic adjustments are required on engines equipped with them. However, many of the vehicles utilize rocker arms that are retained by adjusting nuts. If the rocker arms and nuts are loosened or removed, they must be properly adjusted upon installation in order for the lifters to work.

ADJUSTMENT

4.3L Engine

VIN Z

▶ **See Figures 121 and 122**

➡**This engine utilizes hydraulic valve lifters which means that a valve adjustment is NOT a regular maintenance item. The valves must only be adjusted if the rocker arms have been disturbed for any reason such as cylinder head, camshaft, pushrod or lifter removal.**

Some models utilize a screw in type rocker arm studs with positive stop shoulders, no adjustment is necessary or possible.

Other models utilize pressed-in rocker arm studs, use the following procedure to tighten the rocker arms nuts and properly center the pushrod on the hydraulic lifter:

1. Disconnect the negative battery cable.
2. Remove the engine cover.
3. Remove the rocker arm covers.

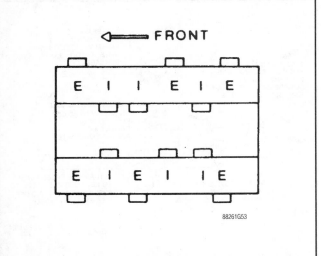

Fig. 121 Valve arrangement—4.3L engine (E=exhaust; I=intake)

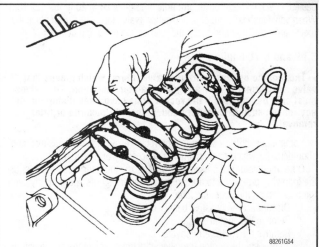

Fig. 122 Adjust the rockers, by rotating the pushrods between your thumb and forefinger to feel for play

4. To prepare the engine for valve adjustment, rotate the crankshaft until the mark on the damper pulley aligns with the 0 degree mark on the timing plate and the No. 1 piston is on its compression stroke. You will know the No. 1 piston is on its compression stroke because both the intake and exhaust valves will remain closed as the crankshaft damper mark approaches the timing scale.

➡**Another method to tell when the piston is coming up on the compression stroke is by removing the spark plug and placing your thumb over the hole; you will feel the air being forced out of the spark plug hole. Stop turning the crankshaft when the TDC timing mark on the crankshaft pulley is directly aligned with the timing mark pointer or the zero mark on the scale.**

5. With the engine on the compression stroke, adjust the exhaust valves of cylinders No. 1, 5 and 6 and the intake valves of cylinders No. 1, 2 and 3 by performing the following procedures:

   a. Back out the adjusting nut until lash can be felt at the pushrod.

   b. While rotating the pushrod, turn the adjusting nut inward until all the lash is removed.

   c. When the play has disappeared, turn the adjusting nut inward 1 additional turn for 1987–93 engines and 1¾ turns for 1994 engines.

6. Rotate the crankshaft 1 complete revolution and align the mark on the damper pulley with the 0 degree mark on the timing plate; the engine is now positioned on the No. 4 firing position. This time the No. 4 cylinder valves remain closed as the timing mark approaches the scale. Adjust the exhaust valves of cylinders No. 2, 3 and 4 and the intake valves of cylinders No. 4, 5 and 6 by performing the following procedures:

   a. Back out the adjusting nut until lash can be felt at the pushrod.

   b. While rotating the pushrod, turn the adjusting nut inward until all the lash is removed.

   c. When the play has disappeared, turn the adjusting nut inward 1 additional turn for 1987–93 engines and 1¾ turns for 1994 engines.

7. Install the rocker arm covers.

8. Connect the negative battery cable, and verify that there are no leaks.

9. Turn the engine **OFF**, then install the engine cover. You may wish to allow the engine to cool first, as you will be working near hot components.

VIN W

The 4.3L (VIN W) and some 4.3L (VIN Z) engines are equipped with screw-in type rocker arm studs with positive stop shoulders. Because the shoulders allow the rocker arms to be tightened into proper position, no adjustments are necessary or possible. If a valve train problem is suspected, check that the rocker arm nuts are tightened to 20 ft. lbs. (27 Nm). When valve lash falls out of specification (valve tap is heard), replace the rocker arm, pushrod and hydraulic lifter on the offending cylinder.

5.0L and 5.7L Engines

➡**This engine utilizes hydraulic valve lifters, which means that valve adjustment is NOT a regular maintenance item. The valves must only be adjusted if the rocker arms have been disturbed for any reason such as cylinder head, camshaft, pushrod or lifter removal.**

Some models utilize screw-in type rocker arm studs with positive stop shoulders, for which no adjustment is necessary or possible.

Other models utilize pressed-in rocker arm studs; for these models, use the following procedure to tighten the rocker arms nuts and properly center the pushrod on the hydraulic lifter:

1. Disconnect the negative battery cable.
2. Remove the engine cover.
3. Remove the rocker arm covers.
4. To prepare the engine for valve adjustment, rotate the crankshaft until the mark on the damper pulley aligns with the 0 degree mark on the timing plate and the No. 1 piston is on its compression stroke. You will know the No. 1 piston is on its compression stroke because both the intake and exhaust valves will remain closed as the crankshaft damper mark approaches the timing scale.

➡**Another method to tell when the piston is coming up on the compression stroke is by removing the spark plug and placing your thumb over the hole; you will feel the air being forced out of the spark plug hole. Stop turning the crankshaft when the TDC timing mark on the crankshaft pulley is directly aligned with the timing mark pointer or the zero mark on the scale.**

5. With the engine on the compression stroke, adjust the exhaust valves of cylinders No. 1, 3, 4 and 8 and the intake valves of cylinders No. 1, 2, 5 and 7 by performing the following procedures:
   a. Back out the adjusting nut until lash can be felt at the pushrod.
   b. While rotating the pushrod, turn the adjusting nut inward until all the lash is removed.
   c. When the play has disappeared, turn the adjusting nut inward 1 additional turn.
6. Rotate the crankshaft 1 complete revolution and align the mark on the damper pulley with the 0 degree mark on the timing plate; the engine is now positioned on the No. 6 firing position. This time the No. 6 cylinder valves remain closed as the timing mark approaches the scale. Adjust the exhaust valves of cylinder No. 2, 5, 6 and 7 and the intake valves of cylinders No. 3, 4, 6 and 8 by performing the following procedures:
   a. Back out the adjusting nut until lash can be felt at the pushrod.
   b. While rotating the pushrod, turn the adjusting nut inward until all the lash is removed.
   c. When the play has disappeared, turn the adjusting nut inward 1 additional turn.
7. Install the rocker arm covers.
8. Connect the negative battery cable, and verify that there are no leaks.
9. Turn the engine **OFF**, then install the engine cover. You may wish to allow the engine to cool first, as you will be working near hot components.

Idle Speed and Mixture Adjustments

CARBURETED ENGINES

Mixture screws are concealed under staked-in plugs. Idle mixture is adjustable only during carburetor overhaul, and requires the addition of propane as an artificial mixture enricher. For these reasons, mixture adjustments are not considered part of routine maintenance. Refer to Section 5 for these procedures.

5.7L Engines

▶ **See Figures 123 and 124**

1. All adjustments should be made with the engine at normal operating temperature, air cleaner on, choke open, and air conditioning off, unless otherwise noted. Set the parking brake and block the rear wheels. Automatic transmissions should be set in Drive, manuals in Neutral, unless otherwise noted in the procedures or on the emission control label.
2. Refer to the underhood emission sticker and prepare the vehicle for adjustment as specified on the sticker. On models without a solenoid, turn the idle speed screw to obtain the idle speed listed in the underhood emission control label. On models with a solenoid, turn the solenoid screw to obtain the idle speed listed in the underhood emission control label. Disconnect the wire at the air conditioning compressor and turn the air conditioning on. Rev the engine momentarily to fully extend the solenoid plunger. Turn the solenoid screw to obtain the solenoid idle speed listed on the underhood emission sticker. Reconnect the air conditioning wire at the compressor.

GASOLINE FUEL INJECTED ENGINES

The fuel injected vehicles are controlled by a computer which supplies the correct amount of fuel during all engine operating condi-

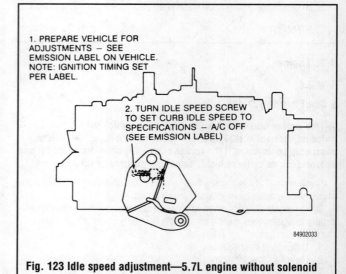

Fig. 123 Idle speed adjustment—5.7L engine without solenoid

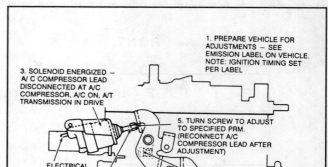

Fig. 124 Idle speed adjustment—5.7L engine with solenoid

tions and controls idle speed; no adjustment is necessary or possible.

DIESEL ENGINES

Idle Speed Adjustment

◆ See Figure 125

➡A special tachometer suitable for diesel engines must be used, since a gasoline engine type tachometer will not work with diesel engines.

1. Set the parking brake and block the drive wheels.
2. Run the engine to normal operating temperature. The air cleaner must be mounted and all accessories turned off.
3. Install the diesel tachometer as per the manufacturer's instructions.
4. Adjust the low idle speed screw on the fuel injection pump to the specification listed on the underhood label in Neutral or P for both manual and automatic transmissions.

➡All idle speeds are to be set within 25 rpm of the specified values.

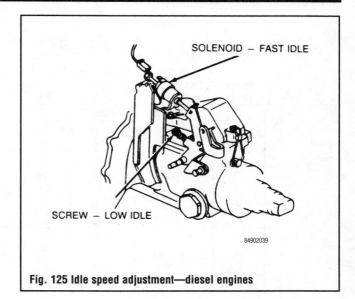

Fig. 125 Idle speed adjustment—diesel engines

GASOLINE ENGINE TUNE-UP SPECIFICATIONS

Year	Engine ID/VIN	Engine Displacement Liters (cc)	Spark Plugs Gap (in.)	Ignition Timing (deg.) MT	Ignition Timing (deg.) AT	Fuel Pump (psi)	Idle Speed (rpm) MT	Idle Speed (rpm) AT	Valve Clearance In.	Valve Clearance Ex.
1987	Z	4.3 (4293)	0.040	4B	①	9–13	700	700	HYD	HYD
	H	5.0 (4999)	0.045	4B	4B	4.0–6.5	700	700	HYD	HYD
	K	5.7 (5735)	0.045	①	4B	4.0–6.5	700	700	HYD	HYD
	N	7.4 (7440)	0.045	4B	4B	9–13	700	700	HYD	HYD
	W	7.4 (7440)	0.045	4B	4B	4.0–6.5	700	700	HYD	HYD
1988	Z	4.3 (4293)	0.040	4B	①	9–13	700	700	HYD	HYD
	H	5.0 (4999)	0.045	4B	4B	4.0–6.5	700	700	HYD	HYD
	K	5.7 (5735)	0.045	①	4B	4.0–6.5	700	700	HYD	HYD
	N	7.4 (7440)	0.045	①	4B	9–13	700	700	HYD	HYD
	W	7.4 (7440)	0.045	①	4B	4.0–6.5	700	700	HYD	HYD
1989	Z	4.3 (4293)	0.040	①	①	9–13	700	700	HYD	HYD
	H	5.0 (4999)	0.045	①	①	4.0–6.5	700	700	HYD	HYD
	K	5.7 (5735)	0.045	①	①	4.0–6.5	700	700	HYD	HYD
	N	7.4 (7440)	0.045	①	①	9–13	700	700	HYD	HYD
	W	7.4 (7440)	0.045	①	①	4.0–6.5	①	①	HYD	HYD
1990	Z	4.3 (4293)	0.040	①	①	9–13	①	①	HYD	HYD
	H	5.0 (4999)	0.045	①	①	9–13	①	①	HYD	HYD
	K	5.7 (5735)	0.045	①	①	9–13	①	①	HYD	HYD
	N	7.4 (7440)	0.045	①	①	9–13	①	①	HYD	HYD
	W	7.4 (7440)	0.045	①	①	9–13	①	①	HYD	HYD
1991	Z	4.3 (4293)	0.040	①	①	9–13	①	①	HYD	HYD
	H	5.0 (4999)	0.045	①	①	9–13	①	①	HYD	HYD
	K	5.7 (5735)	0.045	①	①	9–13	①	①	HYD	HYD
	N	7.4 (7440)	0.045	①	①	26–32	①	①	HYD	HYD
1992	Z	4.3 (4293)	0.035	①	①	9–13	①	①	HYD	HYD
	H	5.0 (4999)	0.045	①	①	9–13	①	①	HYD	HYD
	K	5.7 (5735)	0.045	①	①	9–13	①	①	HYD	HYD
	N	7.4 (7440)	0.045	①	①	26–32	①	①	HYD	HYD
1993	Z	4.3 (4293)	0.035	①	①	9–13	①	①	HYD	HYD
	H	5.0 (4999)	0.045	①	①	9–13	①	①	HYD	HYD
	K	5.7 (5735)	0.045	①	①	9-13	①	①	HYD	HYD
	N	7.4 (7440)	0.045	①	①	9–13	①	①	HYD	HYD
1994	Z	4.3 (4293)	0.035	①	①	9–13	①	①	HYD	HYD
	H	5.0 (4999)	0.045	①	①	9–13	①	①	HYD	HYD
	K	5.7 (5735)	0.045	①	①	9–13	①	①	HYD	HYD
	N	7.4 (7440)	0.045	①	①	9–13	①	①	HYD	HYD

GASOLINE ENGINE TUNE-UP SPECIFICATIONS

Year	Engine ID/VIN	Engine Displacement Liters (cc)	Spark Plugs Gap (in.)	Ignition Timing (deg.) MT	AT	Fuel Pump (psi)	Idle Speed (rpm) MT	AT	Valve Clearance In.	Ex.
1995	Z	4.3 (4293)	0.035	④	④	9-13	①	725	HYD	HYD
	H	5.0 (4999)	0.035	①	①	9-13	①	①	HYD	HYD
	K	5.7 (5735)	0.035	①	①	9-13	①	①	HYD	HYD
	N	7.4 (7440)	0.035	①	①	26-32	①	①	HYD	HYD
1996	W	4.3 (4293)	0.060	③	③	58-64 ②	①	625	HYD	HYD
	M	5.0 (4999)	0.060	③	③	60-66 ②	①	550	HYD	HYD
	R	5.7 (5735)	0.060	③	③	60-66 ②	①	525	HYD	HYD
	J	7.4 (7440)	0.060	③	③	60-66 ②	①	675 ⑤	HYD	HYD
1997	W	4.3 (4293)	0.060	③	③	58-64 ②	①	625	HYD	HYD
	M	5.0 (4999)	0.060	③	③	60-66 ②	①	550	HYD	HYD
	R	5.7 (5735)	0.060	③	③	60-66 ②	①	525	HYD	HYD
	J	7.4 (7440)	0.060	③	③	60-66 ②	①	675 ⑤	HYD	HYD

NOTE: The Vehicle Emission Control Information label often reflects specification changes made during production. The label figures must be used if they differ from those in this chart.

HYD - Hydraulic

① Refer to underhood label for exact setting
② With key on and engine off
③ Ignition timing is preset and cannot be adjusted

④ Over 8500: GVW:
Manual: 565-615
Automatic: 525-575
⑤ Over 8500 GVW

88191C05

DIESEL ENGINE TUNE-UP SPECIFICATIONS

Year	Engine ID/VIN	Engine Displacement cu. in. (cc)	Valve Clearance Intake (in.)	Exhaust (in.)	Injection Pump Setting (deg.)	Injection Nozzle Pressure (psi) New	Used	Idle Speed (rpm)	Cranking Compression Pressure (psi)
1987	C	6.2 (6210)	HYD	HYD	①	1600	1500	①	NA
	J	6.2 (6210)	HYD	HYD	①	1600	1500	①	NA
1988	C	6.2 (6210)	HYD	HYD	①	1600	1500	①	NA
	J	6.2 (6210)	HYD	HYD	①	1600	1500	①	NA
1989	C	6.2 (6210)	HYD	HYD	①	1600	1500	①	NA
	J	6.2 (6210)	HYD	HYD	①	1600	1500	①	NA
1990	C	6.2 (6210)	HYD	HYD	①	1600	1500	①	NA
	J	6.2 (6210)	HYD	HYD	①	1600	1500	①	NA
1991	C	6.2 (6210)	HYD	HYD	①	1600	1500	①	NA
	J	6.2 (6210)	HYD	HYD	①	1600	1500	①	NA
1992	C	6.2 (6210)	HYD	HYD	①	1600	1500	①	NA
	J	6.5 (6473)	HYD	HYD	①	1600	1500	①	NA
	F	6.2 (6210)	HYD	HYD	①	1600	1500	①	NA
1993	C	6.2 (6210)	HYD	HYD	②	1600	1500	①	NA
	J	6.2 (6210)	HYD	HYD	②	1600	1500	①	NA
	F	6.5 (6473)	HYD	HYD	①	1600	1500	①	NA
1994	F	6.5 (6473)	HYD	HYD	①	1600	1500	①	NA
	P	6.5 (6473)	HYD	HYD	①	1600	1700	①	NA
	Y	6.5 (6473)	HYD	HYD	①	1600	1500	①	NA
1995	F	6.5 (6473)	HYD	HYD	①	1600	1500	①	NA
	P	6.5 (6473)	HYD	HYD	①	1800	1700	①	NA
	Y	6.5 (6473)	HYD	HYD	①	1600	1500	①	NA
1996	F	6.5 (6473)	HYD	HYD	①	1800	1700	①	NA
	Y	6.5 (6473)	HYD	HYD	①	1800	1700	①	NA
1997	F	6.5 (6473)	HYD	HYD	①	1800	1700	①	NA
	Y	6.5 (6473)	HYD	HYD	①	1800	1700	①	NA

NOTE: The Vehicle Emission Control Information label often reflects specification changes made during production. The label figures must be used if they differ from those in this chart

HYD - Hydraulic
NA - Not Available

① Refer to Vehicle Emission Control Information label
② Set by aligning marks on top of engine front cover and injection pump flange

88191C06

5. Adjust the fast idle speed as follows:

   a. Remove the connector from the fast idle solenoid. Use an insulated jumper wire from the battery positive terminal to the solenoid terminal to energize the solenoid.

   b. Open the throttle momentarily to ensure that the fast idle solenoid plunger is energized and fully extended.

   c. Adjust the extended plunger by turning the hex-head screw to an engine speed of 800 rpm (check the underhood label) while in Neutral.

   d. Remove the jumper wire and reinstall the connector to the fast idle solenoid.

6. Disconnect and remove the tachometer.

Air Conditioning System

SYSTEM SERVICE & REPAIR

➤It is recommended that the A/C system be serviced by an EPA Section 609 certified automotive technician utilizing a refrigerant recovery/recycling machine.

The do-it-yourselfer should not service his/her own vehicle's A/C system for many reasons, including legal concerns, personal injury, environmental damage and cost. The following are some of the reasons why you may decide not to service your own vehicle's A/C system.

According to the U.S. Clean Air Act, it is a federal crime to service or repair (involving the refrigerant) a Motor Vehicle Air Conditioning (MVAC) system for money without being EPA certified. It is also illegal to vent R-12 and R-134a refrigerants into the atmosphere. Selling or distributing A/C system refrigerant (in a container which contains less than 20 pounds of refrigerant) to any person who is not EPA 609 certified is also not allowed by law.

State and/or local laws may be more strict than the federal regulations, so be sure to check with your state and/or local authorities for further information. For further federal information on the legality of servicing your A/C system, call the EPA Stratospheric Ozone Hotline.

➤Federal law dictates that a fine of up to $25,000 may be levelled on people convicted of venting refrigerant into the atmosphere. Additionally, the EPA may pay up to $10,000 for information or services leading to a criminal conviction of the violation of these laws.

When servicing an A/C system, you run the risk of handling or coming in contact with refrigerant, which may result in skin or eye irritation or frostbite. Although low in toxicity (due to chemical stability), inhalation of concentrated refrigerant fumes is dangerous and can result in death; cases of fatal cardiac arrhythmia have been reported in people accidentally subjected to high levels of refrigerant. Some early symptoms include loss of concentration and drowsiness.

➤Generally, the limit for exposure is lower for R-134a than it is for R-12. Exceptional care must be practiced when handling R-134a.

Also, refrigerants can decompose at high temperatures (near gas heaters or open flame), which may result in hydrofluoric acid, hydrochloric acid and phosgene (a fatal nerve gas).

R-12 refrigerant can damage the environment because it is a Chlorofluorocarbon (CFC), which has been proven to add to ozone layer depletion, leading to increasing levels of UV radiation. UV radiation has been linked with an increase in skin cancer, suppression of the human immune system, an increase in cataracts, damage to crops, damage to aquatic organisms, an increase in ground-level ozone, and increased global warming.

R-134a refrigerant is a greenhouse gas which, if allowed to vent into the atmosphere, will contribute to global warming (the Greenhouse Effect).

It is usually more economically feasible to have a certified MVAC automotive technician perform A/C system service on your vehicle. Some possible reasons for this are as follows:

• While it is illegal to service an A/C system without the proper equipment, the home mechanic would have to purchase an expensive refrigerant recovery/recycling machine to service his/her own vehicle.

• Since only a certified individual may purchase refrigerant—according to the Clean Air Act, there are specific restrictions on selling or distributing A/C system refrigerant—it is legally impossible (unless certified) for the home mechanic to service his/her own vehicle. Procuring refrigerant in an illegal fashion exposes one to the risk of paying a $25,000 fine to the EPA.

R-12 Refrigerant Conversion

If your vehicle still uses R-12 refrigerant, one way to save A/C system costs down the road is to investigate the possibility of having your system converted to R-134a. The older R-12 systems can be easily converted to R-134a refrigerant by a certified automotive technician by installing a few new components and changing the system oil.

The cost of R-12 is steadily rising and will continue to increase, because it is no longer imported or manufactured in the United States. Therefore, it is often possible to have an R-12 system converted to R-134a and recharged for less than it would cost to just charge the system with R-12.

If you are interested in having your system converted, contact local automotive service stations for more details and information.

PREVENTIVE MAINTENANCE

▶ **See Figure 126**

Although the A/C system should not be serviced by the do-it-yourselfer, preventive maintenance can be practiced and A/C system inspections can be performed to help maintain the efficiency of the vehicle's A/C system. For preventive maintenance, perform the following:

• The easiest and most important preventive maintenance for your A/C system is to be sure that it is used on a regular basis. Running the system for five minutes each month (no matter what the season) will help ensure that the seals and all internal components remain lubricated.

➤Some newer vehicles automatically operate the A/C system compressor whenever the windshield defroster is activated. When running, the compressor lubricates the A/C system components; therefore, the A/C system would not need to be operated each month.

• In order to prevent heater core freeze-up during A/C operation, it is necessary to maintain proper antifreeze protection. Use a hand-held coolant tester (hydrometer) to periodically check the condition of the antifreeze in your engine's cooling system.

➤Antifreeze should not be used longer than the manufacturer specifies.

• For efficient operation of an air conditioned vehicle's cooling system, the radiator cap should have a holding pressure which meets manufacturer's specifications. A cap which fails to hold these pressures should be replaced.

TCCS1233

A coolant tester can be used to determine the freezing and boiling levels of the coolant in your vehicle

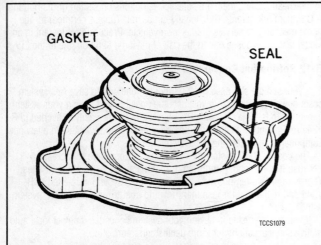

Fig. 126 To ensure efficient cooling system operation, inspect the radiator cap gasket and seal

• Any obstruction of, or damage to, the condenser configuration will restrict air flow which is essential to its efficient operation. It is, therefore, a good rule to keep this unit clean and in proper physical shape.

➡**Bug screens which are mounted in front of the condenser (unless they are original equipment) are regarded as obstructions.**

• The condensation drain tube expels any water which accumulates on the bottom of the evaporator housing into the engine compartment. If this tube is obstructed, the air conditioning performance can be restricted and condensation buildup can spill over onto the vehicle's floor.

SYSTEM INSPECTION

▶ **See Figure 127**

Although the A/C system should not be serviced by the do-it-yourselfer, preventive maintenance can be practiced and A/C system inspections can be performed to help maintain the efficiency of the vehicle's A/C system. For A/C system inspection, perform the following:

The easiest and often most important check for the air conditioning system consists of a visual inspection of the system components. Visually inspect the air conditioning system for refrigerant leaks, damaged compressor clutch, abnormal compressor drive belt tension and/or condition,

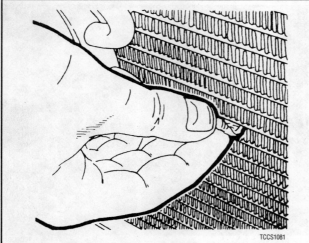

Fig. 127 Periodically remove any debris from the condenser and radiator fins

plugged evaporator drain tube, blocked condenser fins, disconnected or broken wires, blown fuses, corroded connections and poor insulation.

A refrigerant leak will usually appear as an oily residue at the leakage point in the system. The oily residue soon picks up dust or dirt particles from the surrounding air and appears greasy. Through time, this will build up and appear to be a heavy, dirt impregnated grease.

For a thorough visual and operational inspection, check the following:

• Check the surface of the radiator and condenser for dirt, leaves or other material which might block air flow.

• Check for kinks in hoses and lines. Check the system for leaks.

• Make sure the drive belt is properly tensioned. When the air conditioning is operating, make sure the drive belt is free of noise or slippage.

• Make sure the blower motor operates at all appropriate positions, then check for distribution of the air from all outlets with the blower on **HIGH** or **MAX**.

➡**Keep in mind that under conditions of high humidity, air discharged from the A/C vents may not feel as cold as expected, even if the system is working properly. This is because vaporized moisture in humid air retains heat more effectively than dry air, thereby making humid air more difficult to cool.**

• Make sure the air passage selection lever is operating correctly. Start the engine and warm it to normal operating temperature, then make sure the temperature selection lever is operating correctly.

Windshield Wipers

ELEMENT (REFILL) CARE AND REPLACEMENT

For maximum effectiveness and longest element life, the windshield and wiper blades should be kept clean. Dirt, tree sap, road tar and so on will cause streaking, smearing and blade deterioration if left on the glass. It is advisable to wash the windshield carefully with a commercial glass cleaner at least once a month. Wipe off the rubber blades with the wet rag afterwards. Do not attempt to move wipers across the windshield by hand; damage to the motor and drive mechanism will result.

To inspect and/or replace the wiper blade elements, place the wiper switch in the **LOW** speed position and the ignition switch in the **ACC** position. When the wiper blades are approximately vertical on the windshield, turn the ignition switch to **OFF**.

Examine the wiper blade elements. If they are found to be cracked, broken or torn, they should be replaced immediately. Replacement intervals will vary with usage, although ozone deterioration usually limits element life to about one year. If the wiper pattern is smeared or streaked, or if the blade chatters across the glass, the elements should be replaced. It is easiest and most sensible to replace the elements in pairs.

If your vehicle is equipped with aftermarket blades, there are several different types of refills and your vehicle might have any kind. Aftermarket blades and arms rarely use the exact same type blade or refill as the original equipment. Here are some typical aftermarket blades; not all may be available for your vehicle:

The Anco® type uses a release button that is pushed down to allow the refill to slide out of the yoke jaws. The new refill slides back into the frame and locks in place.

Some Trico® refills are removed by locating where the metal backing strip or the refill is wider. Insert a small screwdriver blade between the frame and metal backing strip. Press down to release the refill from the retaining tab.

Other types of Trico® refills have two metal tabs which are unlocked by squeezing them together. The rubber filler can then be withdrawn from the frame jaws. A new refill is installed by inserting the refill into the front frame jaws and sliding it rearward to engage the remaining frame jaws. There are usually four jaws; be certain when installing that the refill is engaged in all of them. At the end of its travel, the tabs will lock into place on the front jaws of the wiper blade frame.

Another type of refill is made from polycarbonate. The refill has a simple locking device at one end which flexes downward out of the groove into which the jaws of the holder fit, allowing easy release. By sliding the new

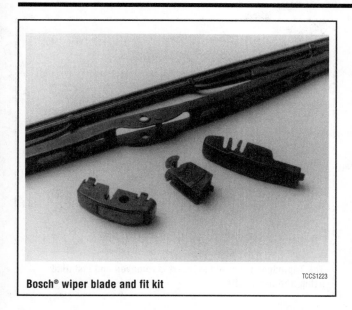

Bosch® wiper blade and fit kit

TCCS1223

Trico® wiper blade and fit kit

TCCS1226

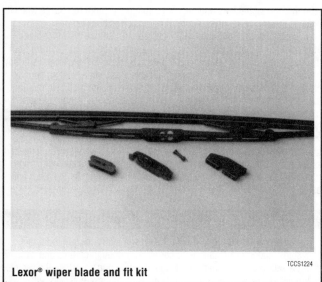

Lexor® wiper blade and fit kit

TCCS1224

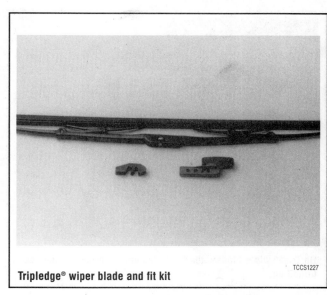

Tripledge® wiper blade and fit kit

TCCS1227

Pylon® wiper blade and adaptor

TCCS1225

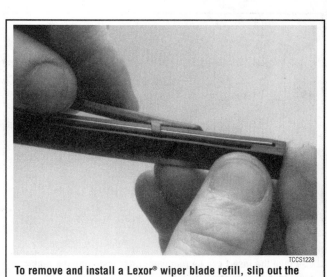

TCCS1228

To remove and install a Lexor® wiper blade refill, slip out the old insert and slide in a new one

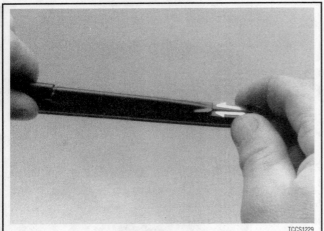

On Pylon® inserts, the clip at the end has to be removed prior to sliding the insert off. Don't forget to attach the clip after the new insert is installed

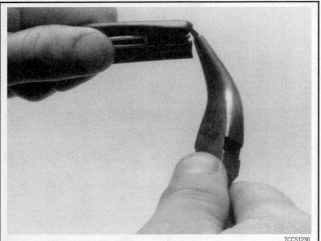

On Trico® wiper blades, the tab at the end of the blade must be turned up . . .

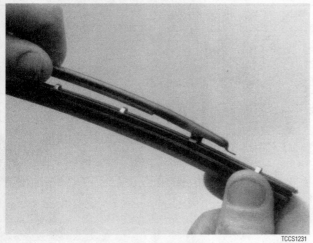

. . . then the insert can be removed. After installing the replacement insert, bend the tab back

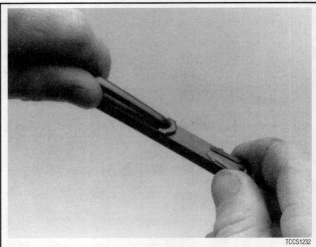

The Tripledge® wiper blade insert is removed and installed using a retaining clip

refill through all the jaws and pushing through the slight resistance when it reaches the end of its travel, the refill will lock into position.

To replace the Tridon® refill, it is necessary to remove the wiper blade. This refill has a plastic backing strip with a notch about 1 in. (25mm) from the end. Hold the blade (frame) on a hard surface so that the frame is tightly bowed. Grip the tip of the backing strip and pull up while twisting counterclockwise. The backing strip will snap out of the retaining tab. Do this for the remaining tabs until the refill is free of the blade. The length of these refills is molded into the end and they should be replaced with identical types.

Regardless of the type of refill used, be sure to follow the part manufacturer's instructions closely. Make sure that all of the frame jaws are engaged as the refill is pushed into place and locked. If the metal blade holder and frame are allowed to touch the glass during wiper operation, the glass will be scratched.

Tires and Wheels

Common sense and good driving habits will afford maximum tire life. Fast starts, sudden stops and hard cornering are tough on tires and will shorten their useful life span. Make sure that you don't overload the vehicle or run with incorrect pressure in the tires. Both of these practices will increase tread wear.

➡For optimum tire life, keep the tires properly inflated, rotate them often and have the wheel alignment checked periodically.

Inspect your tires frequently. Be especially careful to watch for bubbles in the tread or sidewall, deep cuts or underinflation. Replace any tires with bubbles in the sidewall. If cuts are so deep that they penetrate to the cords, discard the tire. Any cut in the sidewall of a radial tire renders it unsafe. Also look for uneven tread wear patterns that may indicate the front end is out of alignment or that the tires are out of balance.

TIRE ROTATION

◗ See Figures 128, 129 and 130

Tires must be rotated periodically to equalize wear patterns that vary with a tire's position on the vehicle. Tires will also wear in an uneven way as the front steering/suspension system wears to the point where the alignment should be reset.

Rotating the tires will ensure maximum life for the tires as a set, so you will not have to discard a tire early due to wear on only part of the tread. Regular rotation is required to equalize wear.

When rotating "unidirectional tires," make sure that they always roll in

RECOMMENDED ROTATION PATTERNS WITH SINGLE REAR WHEELS

FOUR TIRE ROTATION	FIVE TIRE ROTATION
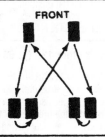	

RECOMMENDED ROTATION PATTERNS WITH DUAL REAR WHEELS

SIX TIRE ROTATION

FOR TRUCKS WITH THE SAME TIRE SIZES AND LOAD RANGES ON THE FRONT AND REAR.	FOR TRUCK WITH DIFFERENT TIRE SIZES AND/OR LOAD RANGES ON THE FRONT AND REAR

88191G27

Fig. 128 Common tire rotation patterns

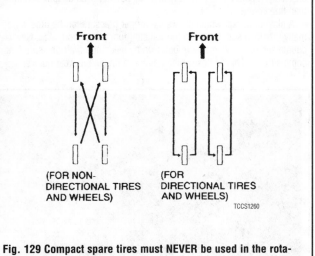

Fig. 129 Compact spare tires must NEVER be used in the rotation pattern

TCCS1234

Fig. 130 Unidirectional tires are identifiable by sidewall arrows and/or the word "rotation"

the same direction. This means that a tire used on the left side of the vehicle must not be switched to the right side and vice-versa. Such tires should only be rotated front-to-rear or rear-to-front, while always remaining on the same side of the vehicle. These tires are marked on the sidewall as to the direction of rotation; observe the marks when reinstalling the tire(s).

Some styled or "mag" wheels may have different offsets front to rear. In these cases, the rear wheels must not be used up front and vice-versa. Furthermore, if these wheels are equipped with unidirectional tires, they cannot be rotated unless the tire is remounted for the proper direction of rotation.

➡ **The compact or space-saver spare is strictly for emergency use. It must never be included in the tire rotation or placed on the vehicle for everyday use.**

TIRE DESIGN

▶ **See Figure 131**

For maximum satisfaction, tires should be used in sets of four. Mixing of different types (radial, bias-belted, fiberglass belted) must be avoided. In most cases, the vehicle manufacturer has designated a type of tire on which the vehicle will perform best. Your first choice when replacing tires should be to use the same type of tire that the manufacturer recommends.

When radial tires are used, tire sizes and wheel diameters should be selected to maintain ground clearance and tire load capacity equivalent to the original specified tire. Radial tires should always be used in sets of four.

※※ CAUTION

Radial tires should never be used on only the front axle.

When selecting tires, pay attention to the original size as marked on the tire. Most tires are described using an industry size code sometimes referred to as P-Metric. This allows the exact identification of the tire specifications, regardless of the manufacturer. If selecting a different tire size or brand, remember to check the installed tire for any sign of interference with the body or suspension while the vehicle is stopping, turning sharply or heavily loaded.

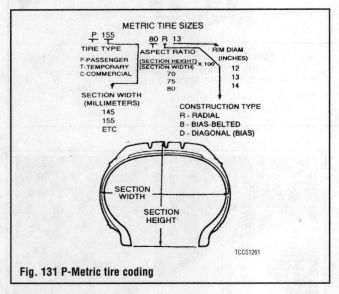

Fig. 131 P-Metric tire coding

Snow Tires

Good radial tires can produce a big advantage in slippery weather, but in snow, a street radial tire does not have sufficient tread to provide traction and control. The small grooves of a street tire quickly pack with snow and the tire behaves like a billiard ball on a marble floor. The more open, chunky tread of a snow tire will self-clean as the tire turns, providing much better grip on snowy surfaces.

To satisfy municipalities requiring snow tires during weather emergencies, most snow tires carry either an M + S designation after the tire size stamped on the sidewall, or the designation "all-season." In general, no change in tire size is necessary when buying snow tires.

Most manufacturers strongly recommend the use of 4 snow tires on their vehicles for reasons of stability. If snow tires are fitted only to the drive wheels, the opposite end of the vehicle may become very unstable when braking or turning on slippery surfaces. This instability can lead to unpleasant endings if the driver can't counteract the slide in time.

Note that snow tires, whether 2 or 4, will affect vehicle handling in all non-snow situations. The stiffer, heavier snow tires will noticeably change the turning and braking characteristics of the vehicle. Once the snow tires are installed, you must re-learn the behavior of the vehicle and drive accordingly.

➡**Consider buying extra wheels on which to mount the snow tires. Once done, the "snow wheels" can be installed and removed as needed. This eliminates the potential damage to tires or wheels from seasonal removal and installation. Even if your vehicle has styled wheels, see if inexpensive steel wheels are available. Although the look of the vehicle will change, the expensive wheels will be protected from salt, curb hits and pothole damage.**

TIRE STORAGE

If they are mounted on wheels, store the tires at proper inflation pressure. All tires should be kept in a cool, dry place. If they are stored in the garage or basement, do not let them stand on a concrete floor; set them on strips of wood, a mat or a large stack of newspaper. Keeping them away from direct moisture is of paramount importance. Tires should not be stored upright, but in a flat position.

INFLATION & INSPECTION

▶ **See Figures 132 thru 139 (p. 60–62)**

The importance of proper tire inflation cannot be overemphasized. A tire employs air as part of its structure. It is designed around the supporting strength of the air at a specified pressure. For this reason, improper inflation drastically reduces the tire's ability to perform as intended. A tire will lose some air in day-to-day use; having to add a few pounds of air periodically is not necessarily a sign of a leaking tire.

Two items should be a permanent fixture in every glove compartment: an accurate tire pressure gauge and a tread depth gauge. Check the tire pressure (including the spare) regularly with a pocket type gauge. Too often, the gauge on the end of the air hose at your corner garage is not accurate because it suffers too much abuse. Always check tire pressure when the tires are cold, as pressure increases with temperature. If you must move the vehicle to check the tire inflation, do not drive more than a mile before checking. A cold tire is generally one that has not been driven for more than three hours.

A plate or sticker which shows the proper pressure for the tires is normally provided somewhere in the vehicle (door post, hood, etc.). Never counteract excessive pressure build-up by bleeding off air pressure (letting some air out). This will cause the tire to run hotter and wear quicker.

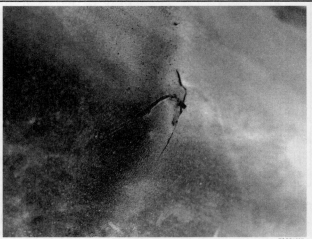

Fig. 132 Tires should be checked frequently for any sign of puncture or damage

TCCS1095

Fig. 133 Tires with deep cuts, or cuts which show bulging, should be replaced immediately

> ### ✳✳ CAUTION
>
> **Never exceed the maximum tire pressure embossed on the tire! This is the pressure to be used when the tire is at maximum loading, but it is rarely the correct pressure for everyday driving. Consult the owner's manual or the tire pressure sticker for the correct tire pressure.**

Once you've maintained the correct tire pressures for several weeks, you'll be familiar with the vehicle's braking and handling characteristics. Slight adjustments in tire pressures can fine-tune these attributes, but never change the cold pressure specification by more than 2 psi. A slightly lower tire pressure will give a softer ride, but also yield lower fuel mileage. A slightly harder tire will give crisper dry road handling, but can cause skidding on wet surfaces. Unless you're fully attuned to the vehicle, stick to the recommended inflation pressures.

All tires made since 1968 have built-in tread wear indicator bars that show up as ½ in. (13mm) wide smooth bands across the tire when ¹⁄₁₆ in. (1.5mm) of tread remains. The appearance of tread wear indicators means that the tires should be replaced. In fact, many states have laws prohibiting the use of tires with less than this amount of tread.

You can check your own tread depth with an inexpensive gauge or by

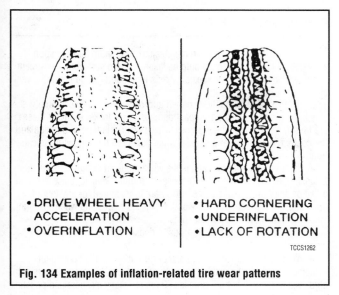

- **DRIVE WHEEL HEAVY ACCELERATION**
- **OVERINFLATION**

- **HARD CORNERING**
- **UNDERINFLATION**
- **LACK OF ROTATION**

TCCS1262

Fig. 134 Examples of inflation-related tire wear patterns

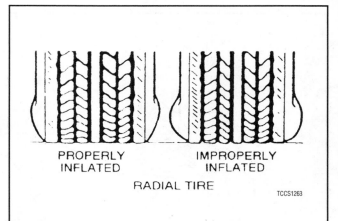

PROPERLY INFLATED

IMPROPERLY INFLATED

RADIAL TIRE

TCCS1263

Fig. 135 Radial tires have a characteristic sidewall bulge; don't try to measure pressure by looking at the tire. Use a quality air pressure gauge

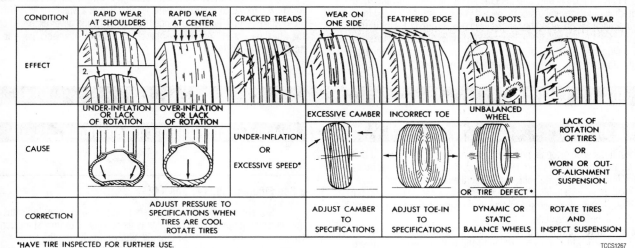

CONDITION	RAPID WEAR AT SHOULDERS	RAPID WEAR AT CENTER	CRACKED TREADS	WEAR ON ONE SIDE	FEATHERED EDGE	BALD SPOTS	SCALLOPED WEAR
EFFECT							
CAUSE	UNDER-INFLATION OR LACK OF ROTATION	OVER-INFLATION OR LACK OF ROTATION	UNDER-INFLATION OR EXCESSIVE SPEED*	EXCESSIVE CAMBER	INCORRECT TOE	UNBALANCED WHEEL OR TIRE DEFECT *	LACK OF ROTATION OF TIRES OR WORN OR OUT-OF-ALIGNMENT SUSPENSION.
CORRECTION	ADJUST PRESSURE TO SPECIFICATIONS WHEN TIRES ARE COOL ROTATE TIRES			ADJUST CAMBER TO SPECIFICATIONS	ADJUST TOE-IN TO SPECIFICATIONS	DYNAMIC OR STATIC BALANCE WHEELS	ROTATE TIRES AND INSPECT SUSPENSION

*HAVE TIRE INSPECTED FOR FURTHER USE.

TCCS1267

Fig. 136 Common tire wear patterns and causes

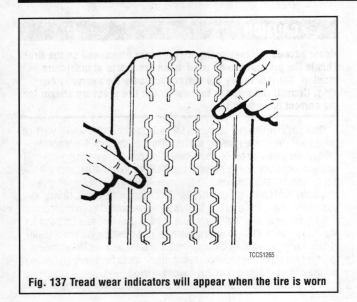

Fig. 137 Tread wear indicators will appear when the tire is worn

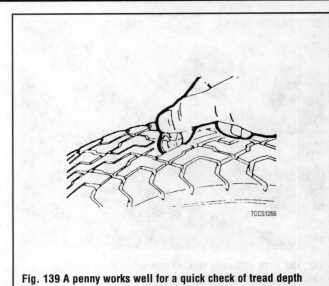

Fig. 139 A penny works well for a quick check of tread depth

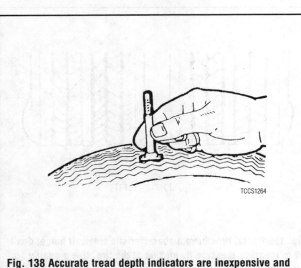

Fig. 138 Accurate tread depth indicators are inexpensive and handy

using a Lincoln head penny. Slip the Lincoln penny (with Lincoln's head upside-down) into several tread grooves. If you can see the top of Lincoln's head in 2 adjacent grooves, the tire has less than 1/16 in. (1.5mm) of tread left and should be replaced. You can measure snow tires in the same manner by using the "tails" side of the Lincoln penny. If you can see the top of the Lincoln memorial, it's time to replace the snow tire(s).

CARE OF SPECIAL WHEELS

If you have invested money in magnesium, aluminum alloy or sport wheels, special precautions should be taken to make sure your investment is not wasted and that your special wheels look good for the life of the vehicle.

Special wheels are easily damaged and/or scratched. Occasionally check the rims for cracking, impact damage or air leaks. If any of these are found, replace the wheel. In order to prevent this type of damage and the costly replacement of a special wheel, observe the following precautions:

• Use extra care not to damage the wheels during removal, installation, balancing, etc. After removal of the wheels from the vehicle, place them on a mat or other protective surface. If they are to be stored for any length of time, support them on strips of wood. Never store tires and wheels upright, since the tread may develop flat spots.

• When driving, watch for hazards; it doesn't take much to crack a wheel.

• When washing, use a mild soap or non-abrasive dish detergent (keeping in mind that detergent tends to remove wax). Avoid cleansers with abrasives or the use of hard brushes. There are many cleaners and polishes for special wheels.

• If possible, remove the wheels during the winter. Salt and sand used for snow removal can severely damage the finish of a wheel.

• Make certain the recommended lug nut torque is never exceeded or the wheel may crack. Never use snow chains on special wheels; severe scratching will occur.

FLUIDS AND LUBRICANTS

Fluid Disposal

Used fluids such as engine oil, transmission fluid, antifreeze and brake fluid are hazardous wastes and must be disposed of properly. Before draining any fluids, consult with your local authorities; in many areas, waste oil and other automotive fluids are being accepted as a part of recycling programs. A number of service stations and auto parts stores are also accepting waste fluids for recycling.

Be sure of the recycling center's policies before draining any fluids, as many will not accept different fluids that have been mixed together.

Fuel and Engine Oil Recommendations

OIL

▶ See Figures 140, 141 and 142

The Society of Automotive Engineers (SAE) grade number indicates the viscosity of the engine oil, which is its resistance to flow at a given temperature. The lower the SAE grade number, the lighter the oil. For example, the mono-grade oils begin with SAE 5 weight, which is a thin, light oil, and continue in viscosity up to SAE 80 or 90 weight, which are heavy gear lubricants. These oils are also known as "straight weight", meaning they are of a single viscosity, and do not vary with engine temperature.

Multi-viscosity oils offer the important advantage of being adaptable to temperature extremes. These oils have designations such as 10W-40, 20W-50, etc. The 10W-40 means that in winter (the "W" in the designation) the oil acts like a thin 10 weight oil, allowing the engine to spin easily when cold, and offering rapid lubrication. Once the engine has warmed up, however, the oil acts like a straight 40 weight, maintaining good lubrication and protection for the engine's internal components. A 20W-50 oil would therefore be slightly heavier than, and not as ideal in cold weather as, the 10W-40, but would offer better protection at higher rpm and temperatures because, when warm, it acts like a 50 weight oil. Whichever oil viscosity you choose when changing the oil, make sure you are anticipating the temperatures your engine will be operating in until the oil is changed again. Refer to the oil viscosity chart for oil recommendations according to temperature.

The American Petroleum Institute (API) designation indicates the classification of engine oil used under certain given operating conditions. Only oils designated for use "Service SG" or greater should be used. Oils of the SG type perform a variety of functions inside the engine in addition to the

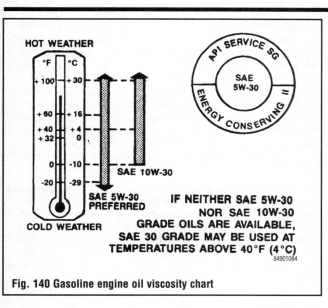

Fig. 140 Gasoline engine oil viscosity chart

Fig. 141 Look for the API oil identification label when choosing your engine oil

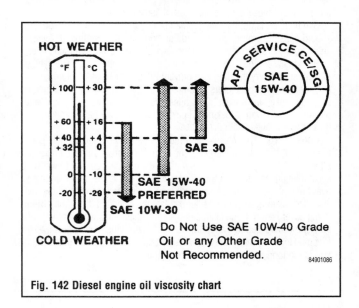

Fig. 142 Diesel engine oil viscosity chart

RECOMMENDED LUBRICANTS

Component	Lubricant
Engine Oil	API SG/CE
Coolant	Ethylene Glycol Anti-Freeze
Manual Transmission	
Muncie 117mm	API GL5, SAE 80W-90
Getrag 85mm	Synchromesh Transmission Fluid
NVG 4500	Castrol Syntorq GL-4
NVG 5LM60	Synchromesh Transmission Fluid
Automatic Transmission	AFT Dexron® II
Transfer Case	
Differential	API GL-5, SAE 80W-90
Master Cylinder	DOT 3 Brake Fluid
Power Steering	GM Power Steering Fluid
Manual Steering Gear	GM Lubricant
Multi-Purpose Grease	NLGI #2

84901151

basic function as a lubricant. Through a balanced system of metallic detergents and polymeric dispersants, engine oil prevents the formation of high and low temperature deposits and also keeps sludge and particles of dirt in suspension. Acids, particularly sulfuric acid, as well as other by-products of combustion, are neutralized. Both the SAE grade number and the APE designation can be found on top of the oil can.

Diesel engines also require SG or higher rated engine oil. In addition, the oil must qualify for a CC or greater rating. The API has a number of different diesel engine ratings, including CB, CC, and CD. Any of these other ratings are fine, as long as the designation CC appears on the can along with them. Do not use oil labeled only SG or only CC. Both designations must always appear together.

For recommended oil viscosities, refer to the chart. Note that 10W-30 and 10W-40 grade oils are not recommended for sustained high speed driving when the temperature rises above the indicated limit.

Synthetic Oil

There are many excellent synthetic and fuel-efficient oils currently available that can provide better gas mileage, longer service life and, in some cases, better engine protection. These benefits do not come without a few hitches, however; the main one being the price of synthetic oils, which is three or four times the price per quart of conventional oil.

Synthetic oil is not for every van and every type of driving, so you should consider your engine's condition and your type of driving. Also, check your van's warranty conditions regarding the use of synthetic oils.

Brand new engines are a wrong candidate for synthetic oil. The synthetic oils are so slippery that they can prevent the proper break-in of new engines; most manufacturers recommend that you wait until the engine is properly broken in, at least 3000 miles (4800 km), before using synthetic oil. Also, if your van is leaking oil past old seals, you'll have a much greater leak problem with synthetics.

Consider your type of driving. If most of your accumulated mileage is high speed, highway type driving, the more expensive synthetic oils may be a benefit. Extended highway driving gives the engine a chance to warm up, accumulating less acids in the oil and putting less stress on the engine over the long run. Under these conditions, the oil change interval can be extended (as long as your oil filter can last the extended life of the oil) up to the advertised mileage claims of the synthetics. Vans with synthetic oils may show increased fuel economy in highway driving, due to less internal friction. However, many automotive experts agree that 50,000 miles (80,000 km) is too long to keep any oil in your engine.

FUEL

Gasoline Engines

It is important to use fuel of the proper octane rating in your van. Octane rating is based on the quantity of anti-knock compounds added to the fuel and it determines the speed at which the gasoline will burn. The lower the octane rating, the faster it burns. The higher the octane, the slower the fuel will burn and the greater the percentage of compounds in the fuel which prevent spark ping (knock), detonation and preignition (dieseling).

As the temperature of the engine increases, the air/fuel mixture exhibits a tendency to ignite before the spark plug is fired. If fuel with an octane rating too low for the engine is used, this will allow combustion to occur before the piston has completed its compression stroke, thereby creating a very high pressure very rapidly.

Fuel of the proper octane rating, for the compression ratio and ignition timing of your van, will slow the combustion process sufficiently to allow the spark plug enough time to ignite the mixture completely and smoothly. Many non-catalyst models are designed to run on regular fuel. The use of some super-premium fuel is no substitution for a properly tuned and maintained engine. Chances are that if your engine exhibits any signs of spark ping, detonation or pre-ignition when using regular fuel, the ignition timing should be checked against specifications or the cylinder head should be removed for decarbonizing.

Vehicles equipped with catalytic converters must use UNLEADED GASOLINE ONLY. Use of leaded fuel (if available) shortens the life of spark plugs,

exhaust systems and EGR valves and can damage the catalytic converter. Most converter equipped models are designed to operate using unleaded gasoline with a minimum rating of 87 octane. Use of unleaded gasoline with octane ratings lower than 87 can cause persistent spark knock which could lead to engine damage.

Light spark knock may be noticed when accelerating or driving up hills. The slight knocking may be considered normal (with 87 octane) because maximum fuel economy is obtained under conditions of occasional light spark knock. Gasoline with an octane rating higher than 87 may be used, but is not necessary (in most cases) for proper operation.

If spark knock is constant, when using 87 octane, at cruising speeds on level ground, an ignition timing adjustment may be required.

➡**Your engine's fuel requirement can change with time, mainly due to carbon buildup, which changes the compression ratio. If your engine pings, knocks or runs on, switch to a higher grade of fuel. Sometimes just changing brands will cure the problem. If it becomes necessary to retard the timing from specifications, don't change it more than a few degrees. Retarded timing will reduce power output and fuel mileage and will increase the engine temperature.**

Diesel Engines

Diesel engines require the use of diesel fuel. At no time should gasoline be substituted. Two grades of diesel fuel are manufactured, #1 and #2, although #2 grade is generally more available. Better fuel economy results from the use of #2 grade fuel. In some northern parts of the U.S. and in most parts of Canada, #1 grade fuel is available in the winter or a winterized blend of #2 grade is supplied in winter months. When the temperature falls below 20°F (−7°C), #1 grade or winterized #2 grade fuel are the only fuels that can be used. Cold temperatures cause unwinterized #2 to thicken (it actually gels), blocking the fuel lines and preventing the engine from running.

- Do not use home heating oil in your van.
- Do not use ether or starting assist fluids in your van.
- Do not use any fuel additives recommended for use in gasoline engines.

It is normal that the engine noise level is louder during the warm-up period in winter. It is also normal that whitish/blue smoke may be emitted from the exhaust after starting and during warm-up. The amount of smoke depends upon the outside temperature.

OPERATION IN FOREIGN COUNTRIES

If you plan to drive your van outside the United States or Canada, there is a possibility that fuels will be too low in anti-knock quality and could produce engine damage. It is wise to consult with local authorities upon arrival in a foreign country to determine the best fuels available.

Engine

❊❊ CAUTION

Prolonged and repeated skin contact with used engine oil, with no effort to remove the oil, may be harmful. Always follow these simple precautions when handling used motor oil:

- Avoid prolonged skin contact with used motor oil.
- Remove oil from skin by washing thoroughly with soap and water or waterless hand cleaner. Do not use gasoline, thinners or other solvents.
- Avoid prolonged skin contact with oil-soaked clothing.

OIL LEVEL CHECK

Every time you stop for fuel, check the engine oil as follows:
1. Park the van on level ground.
2. When checking the oil level it is best for the engine to be at operating temperature, although checking the oil immediately after stopping will

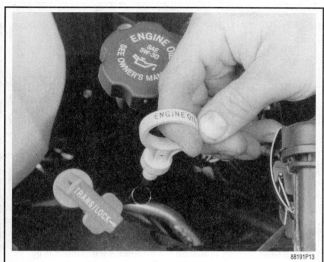

Pull the dipstick from the tube, wipe it clean and reinsert it

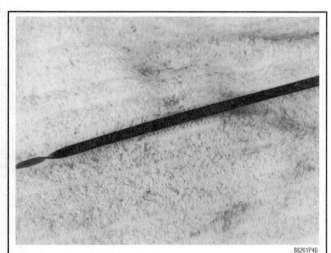

Remove the dipstick again, hold it horizontally and read the level using the stick's markings

If additional oil needs to be added, remove the cap from the filler tube

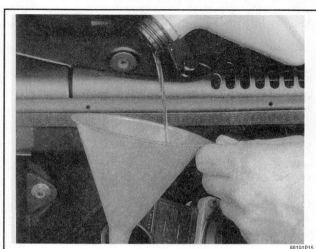

Use a funnel (which will prevent spillage) and add the correct amount and grade of engine oil

lead to a false reading. Wait a few minutes after turning off the engine to allow the oil to drain back into the crankcase.

3. Open the hood and locate the dipstick, which is on the left side of the engine. Pull the dipstick from its tube, wipe it clean and reinsert it.

4. Pull the dipstick out again and, holding it horizontally, read the oil level. The oil should be between the **FULL** or **OPERATING RANGE** and **ADD** or **ADD OIL** marks on the dipstick.

5. If the oil is below the **ADD** mark, add oil of the proper viscosity through the capped opening on top of the cylinder head cover. See the "Oil and Fuel Recommendations chart" in this section for the proper viscosity and rating of oil to use.

6. Reinsert the dipstick and check the oil level again after adding any oil. Be careful not to overfill the crankcase. Approximately one quart of oil will raise the level from the **ADD** to the **FULL** mark. Excess oil will generally be consumed at an accelerated rate.

OIL & FILTER CHANGE

▶ **See Figure 143**

The oil should be changed every 7500 miles (12,000 km). General Motors recommends changing the oil filter with every other oil change; we suggest that the filter be changed with every oil change. There is approximately 1 quart of dirty oil left remaining in the old oil filter if it is not changed! A few dollars more every year seems a small price to pay for extended engine life—so change the filter every time you change the oil!

The oil drain plug is located on the bottom, rear of the oil pan (bottom of the engine, underneath the van).

The mileage figures given are the recommended intervals assuming normal driving and conditions. If your van is being used under dusty, polluted or off-road conditions, change the oil and filter more frequently than specified. The same goes for vans driven in stop-and-go traffic or only for short distances. Always drain the oil after the engine has been running long enough to bring it to normal operating temperature. Hot oil will flow easier and more contaminants will be removed along with the oil than if it were drained cold. To change the oil and filter:

➡**If the engine is equipped with an oil cooler, this will also have to be drained, using the drain plug. Be sure to add enough oil to fill the cooler in addition to the engine.**

1. Warm the oil by running the engine for a short period of time or at least until the needle on the temperature gauge rises above the **C** mark. This will make the oil flow more freely from the oil pan.

2. Park on a level surface, apply the parking brake and block the wheels.

Raise the van and support it with jackstands positioned below the frame rail

Use a filter wrench to loosen the oil filter, then remove it by hand

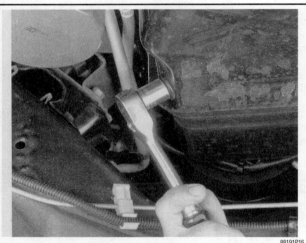

Loosen the drain plug using a ratchet and socket (shown) or a box end wrench

Fig. 143 Before installing a new oil filter, lightly coat the rubber gasket with clean oil

3. Raise the front of the van and support it with jackstands.

4. Stop the engine. Raise the hood and remove the oil filler cap from the top of the valve cover. This allows air to enter the engine as the oil drains, promoting quicker drainage. Remove the dipstick, wipe it off and set it aside.

5. Position a suitable oil drain pan beneath the drain plug.

➡All diesel and gasoline engines covered by this manual hold approximately 5–8 quarts of oil, so choose a drain pan that exceeds this amount to allow for movement of the oil when the pan is pulled from under the vehicle. This will prevent time lost to the cleaning up of messy oil spills.

6. With the proper size socket or wrench (DO NOT use regular or locking pliers), loosen the drain plug. Unscrew the drain plug while maintaining a slight upward force on it to keep the oil from running out around it (and your hand). Allow the oil to drain into the drain pan.

✳✳ CAUTION

The engine oil will be hot. Keep your arms, face and hands away from the oil as it is draining.

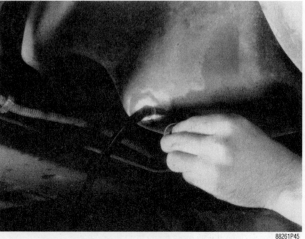

Unthread the plug, then withdraw it (and your hand) quickly to keep from getting burned by the hot oil

7. Remove the drain pan and wipe any excess oil from the area around the hole using a clean rag.

8. Clean the threads of the drain plug and the drain plug gasket to remove any sludge deposits that may have accumulated.

9. Place the drain pan under the oil filter location to prevent spilling any oil from the filter on the ground.

10. Using a filter wrench, loosen the oil filter by turning it counterclockwise, then unscrew the filter the rest of the way by hand. Keep the filter end up so that the oil does not spill out. Tilt the filter into the drain pan to drain the oil.

11. Remove the drain pan from under the vehicle and position it off to the side.

12. With a clean rag, wipe off the filter seating surface to ensure a proper seal. Make sure that the old gasket is not stuck to the seating surface. If it is, remove it and thoroughly clean the seating surface of the old gasket material.

13. Open a container of new oil and smear some of this oil onto the rubber gasket of the new oil filter. Get a feel for where the filter post is and start the filter by hand until the gasket contacts the seat. Tighten the filter an additional ¾ turn with your hand.

14. Install the drain plug and metal gasket. Be sure that the plug is tight enough that the oil does not leak out, but not tight enough to strip the threads. Over time you will develop a sense of what the proper tightness of the drain plug is. If a torque wrench is available, tighten the plug to 20 ft. lbs. (27 Nm) on gasoline engines or 30 ft. lbs. (40 Nm) on diesel engines.

➡**Replace the drain plug gasket at every third or fourth oil change.**

15. Through a suitable plastic or metal funnel, add clean new oil of the proper grade and viscosity through the oil filler on top of the valve cover. Be sure that the oil level registers near the full mark on the dipstick.

16. Install and tighten the oil filler cap.

17. Start the engine and allow it to run for several minutes. Check for leaks at the filter and drain plug. Sometimes leaks will not be revealed until the engine reaches normal operating temperature.

18. Stop the engine and recheck the oil level. Add oil as necessary.

When you have finished this job, you will notice that you now possess several quarts of dirty oil. The best thing to do with it is to pour it into plastic jugs, such as milk or anti-freeze containers. Then, find a gas station or service garage which accepts waste oil for recycling and dispose of it there.

Manual Transmission

FLUID RECOMMENDATIONS

- Muncie 117mm: API GL-5, SAE 80W-90
- Muncie 76mm 3-speed: SAE 80W-90 GL-5. For vehicles normally operated in cold climates, use SAE 80W GL-5 gear lubricant.
- New Process 89mm 4-speed: Dexron® II ATF.
- The NVG 4500 5-speed: Castrol Syntorq GL-4

LEVEL CHECK

▶ **See Figure 144**

Check the lubricant level at least twice a year, even more frequently if driven in deep water.

1. With the van parked on a level surface, remove the filler plug from the side of the transmission case. Be careful not to take out the drain plug at the bottom.

2. If lubricant begins to trickle out of the hole, there is enough. If not, carefully insert a finger (watch out for sharp threads) and check that the level is up to the edge of the hole.

3. If not, add sufficient lubricant with a funnel and tube, or a squeeze bulb to bring it to the proper level. You can also use a common kitchen baster.

4. Install the plug and tighten to 17 ft. lbs. (23 Nm). Road test the van and check for any leaks.

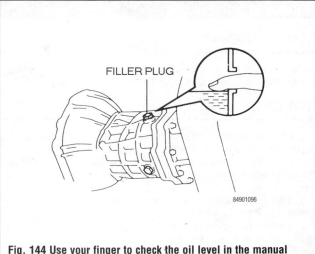

Fig. 144 Use your finger to check the oil level in the manual transmission

DRAIN & REFILL

▶ **See Figure 145**

No intervals are specified for changing the transmission lubricant, but it is a good idea on a used vehicle, one that has been worked hard, or one driven in deep water. The vehicle should be on a level surface and the lubricant should be at operating temperature.

1. Position the van on a level surface.

2. Place a pan of sufficient capacity under the transmission drain plug.

3. Remove the upper (fill) plug to provide a vent opening.

4. Remove the lower (drain) plug and let the lubricant drain out.

✳✳ CAUTION

The oil will be hot! Be careful when you remove the plug or you'll be taking a bath in hot gear oil.

5. Install the drain plug and tighten to 17 ft. lbs. (23 Nm).

6. Add lubricant with a suction gun or squeeze bulb.

7. Reinstall the filler plug. Run the engine and check for leaks.

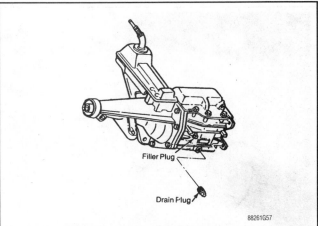

Fig. 145 The filler plug is normally found about mid-way up the side of the transmission, while drain plugs are found towards the bottom of the housing

Automatic Transmission

FLUID RECOMMENDATIONS

Use Dexron II® (or the latest superseding) automatic transmission fluid type for 1987–95 models and Dexron III® for 1996–97 models.

LEVEL CHECK

Check the level of the fluid at least once a month. The fluid level should be checked with the engine at normal operating temperature and running. If the van has been running at high speed for a long period, in city traffic on a hot day, or pulling a trailer, let it cool down for about thirty minutes before checking the level.

1. Park the van on a level surface with the engine idling. Shift the transmission into **P** and set the parking brake.

2. Remove the dipstick (on newer models, you may have to flip up the handle first), wipe it clean and reinsert if firmly. Be sure that it has been pushed all the way in.

3. Remove the dipstick and check the fluid level while holding it horizontally. All models have a HOT and a COLD side to the dipstick.

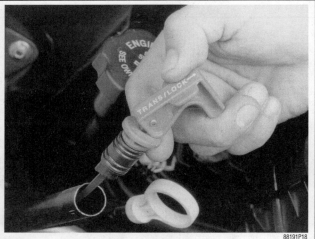

Unlock the dipstick handle (if applicable), withdraw the dipstick from the tube, wipe it clean and reinsert it again

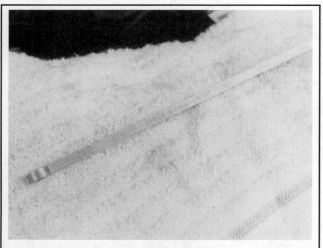

Withdraw the dipstick again, hold it horizontally and make sure the fluid level is within the given range(s)

If needed, add transmission fluid through the dipstick tube using a funnel to avoid spillage

- **COLD:** the fluid level should fall in this range when the engine has been running for only a short time.
- **HOT:** the fluid level should fall in this range when the engine has reached normal operating temperatures.

4. Early models have two dimples below the ADD mark; the level should be between these when the engine is cold.

5. If the fluid level is not within the proper area on either side of the dipstick, pour ATF into the dipstick tube. This is easily done with the aid of a funnel. Check the level often as you are filling the transmission. Be extremely careful not to overfill it. Overfilling will cause slippage, seal damage and overheating. Approximately one pint of ATF will raise the level from one notch to the other.

❊❊ WARNING

The fluid on the dipstick should always be a bright red color. It if is discolored (brown or black), or smells burnt, serious transmission troubles, probably due to overheating, should be suspected. The transmission should be inspected by a qualified service technician to locate the cause of the burnt fluid.

DRAIN & REFILL

▶ **See Figure 147 (p. 70)**

1. The fluid should be drained with the transmission warm. It is easier to change the fluid if the van is raised somewhat from the ground, but this is not always easy without a lift. The transmission must be level for it to drain properly.

2. Raise the van and support it with jackstands.

3. Place a shallow pan underneath to catch the transmission fluid (about 5 pints). Loosen all the pan bolts, then pull one corner down to drain most of the fluid. If it sticks, VERY CAREFULLY pry the pan loose. You can buy aftermarket drain plug kits that makes this operation a bit less messy, once installed.

➥**If the fluid removed smells burnt, serious transmission troubles, probably due to overheating, should be suspected.**

4. On newer model vehicles, loosen the drain pan plug and drain the fluid into a suitable container.

5. After all the fluid has been drained, install the drain plug.

6. On vans without a drain plug, remove the pan bolts and empty out the pan. On some models, there may not be much room to access the bolts at the front of the pan.

7. Clean the pan with solvent and allow it to air dry.

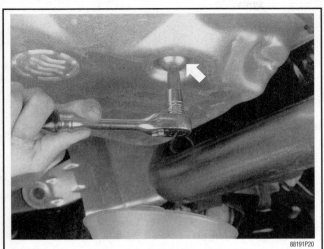

On 1996–97 models, the pan is equipped with a drain plug which makes it easier to drain the fluid . . .

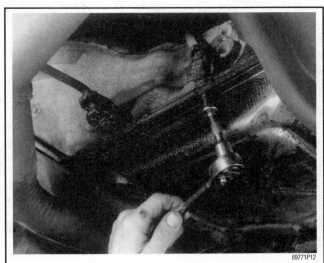

On pre-1996 models, remove the transmission pan retainers

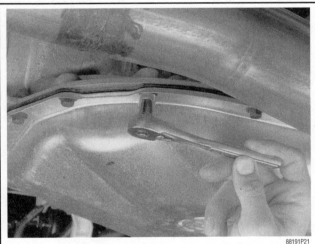

. . . then loosen the pan retainers and remove the pan to gain access to the filter

Allow the fluid to drain, then lower the pan

Raise the van and support it with jackstands positioned beneath the frame rail

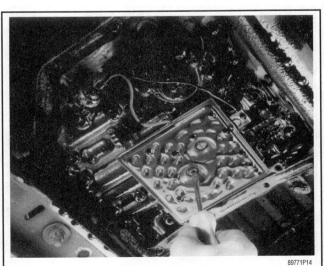

Unfasten the transmission filter retaining screws . . .

. . . then remove the filter from the transmission valve body

Remove the filter from the transmission

Be sure the old filter gasket is removed with the filter and is not stuck to the valve body

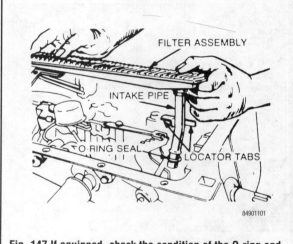

Fig. 147 If equipped, check the condition of the O-ring and replace it as necessary

Remove the old gasket; always replace it with a new one

➡If you use a rag to wipe out the pan, you risk leaving bits of lint and threads in the transmission.

8. Remove the filter or strainer retaining bolts. On the Turbo Hydra-Matic 400, there are two screws securing the filter or screen to the valve body. A reusable strainer may be found on some models. The strainer may be cleaned in solvent and air dried thoroughly. The filter and gasket must be replaced.

To install:

9. Install a new gasket and filter.

10. Install a new gasket on the pan, and tighten the bolts evenly to 12 ft. lbs. (16 Nm) in a crisscross pattern.

11. Using a funnel, add DEXRON® II (or the latest superseding) automatic transmission fluid type for 1987–95 models and Dexron II® for 1996–97 models through the dipstick tube. The correct amount is stated in the Capacities Chart at the end of this section. Do not overfill.

12. With the gearshift lever in **PARK**, start the engine and let it idle. Do not race the engine.

13. Move the gearshift lever through each position, while depressing the brake pedal. Return the lever to **PARK**, and check the fluid level with the engine idling. The level should be between the two dimples on the dipstick, about ¼ in. (6mm) below the ADD mark. Add fluid, if necessary.

14. Check the fluid level after the van has been driven enough to thoroughly warm up the transmission. If the transmission is overfilled, the excess must be drained off. Overfilling causes aerated fluid, resulting in transmission slippage and probable damage.

Rear Axle

FLUID RECOMMENDATIONS

Rear axles use SAE 80W-90 GL-5 gear oil. Positraction® axles must use special lubricant available from dealers. If the special fluid is not used, noise, uneven operation, and damage will result. There is also a Positraction® additive used to cure noise and slippage. Positraction® axles have an identifying tag, as well as a warning sticker near the jack or on the rear wheelwell.

LEVEL CHECK

▶ **See Figure 148**

Lubricant levels in the rear axle should be checked as specified in the Maintenance Interval Charts, later in this section. To check the lubricant level:

1. Park on level ground.
2. Remove the filler plug from the differential housing cover.
3. If lubricant trickles out, there is enough. If not, carefully insert a finger and check that the level is up to the bottom of the hole. Front axles should be full up to the level of the hole when warm, and ½ in. (12.7mm) below when cool.
4. Lubricant may be added with a funnel or a squeeze bulb. Rear axles use SAE 80W-90 GL-5 gear lubricant.

Positraction® limited slip axles must use a special lubricant available from dealers. If the special fluid is not used, noise, uneven operation, and damage will result. There is also a Positraction® additive to cure noise and slippage. Positraction® axles have an identifying tag, as well as a warning sticker near the jack or on the rear wheelwell.

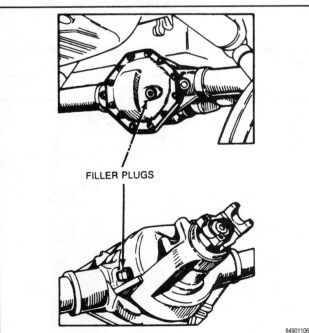

Fig. 148 The rear axle differential filler plug may be in either of these locations

FILLER PLUGS

Use a ratchet and extension to remove the filler plug and check the axle fluid

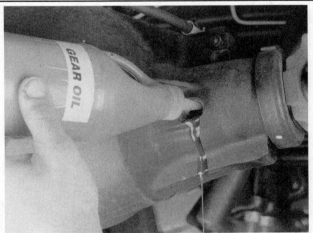

Gear oil can be added using a pump or a squeeze bottle until it begins to trickle out, then reinstall the filler plug

DRAIN & REFILL

No intervals are specified for changing axle lubricant, but it is a good idea, especially if you have driven in water above the axle vents.

1. Park the vehicle on the level with the axles at normal operating temperature.
2. Place a pan of at least 6 pints capacity under the differential housing.
3. Remove the filler plug.
4. If you have a drain plug, remove it. If not, unbolt and remove the differential cover.
5. Install the drain plug or differential cover. Use a new gasket if the differential cover has been removed.
6. Install the drain plug and tighten it so it will not leak. Do not overtighten.

➡**It is usually a good idea to replace the gasket at this time.**

7. Refill the differential with the proper lubricant—do not overfill!
8. Install and tighten the filler plug to the following specifications:
   - 8⅝ in.—26 ft. lbs. (35 Nm)
   - 9½ in.—26 ft. lbs. (35 Nm)
   - 9¾ in.—26 ft. lbs. (35 Nm)
   - 10½ in.—26 ft. lbs. (35 Nm)
9. Road test the van and check for any leaks.

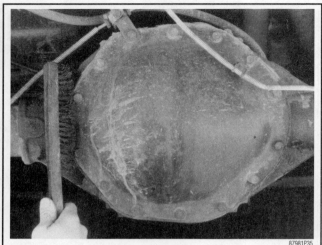

Using a wire brush, clean the bolts and edges of the differential cover

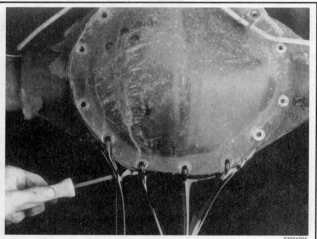

After removing the bolts, carefully pry the bottom of the cover off and drain the fluid

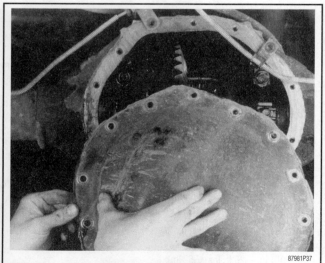

After the oil has drained, remove the differential cover

Cooling System

▶ **See Figures 149, 150, 151, 152 and 153**

For most of the vans covered in this manual (except 1996–97 models), you should inspect, flush and refill the cooling system with fresh coolant (antifreeze) at least once every two years or 30,000 miles (48,000 km). If the coolant is left in the system too long, it loses its ability to prevent rust or corrosion. If the coolant has too much water, it won't protect against freezing and can boil over in the summer.

The cooling systems for all 1996–97 models were originally filled at the factory with silicate-free DEX-COOL® coolant meeting GM specification 6277M. The fluid is easily identified because of its orange color (instead of the green that is normally associated with ethylene glycol antifreeze). If your cooling system is filled with DEX-COOL®, then no periodic service is required, other than fluid level checks, for 150,000 miles (240,000 km) or 5 years, whichever comes first. BUT if you add a silicate coolant to the system (even in small amounts), premature engine, heater core or radiator corrosion may occur. In addition, the coolant will have to be changed sooner (every 30,000 miles/48,000 km or 2 years, just like in vehicles not using DEX-COOL®).

Fig. 149 The cooling system should be pressure tested once a year

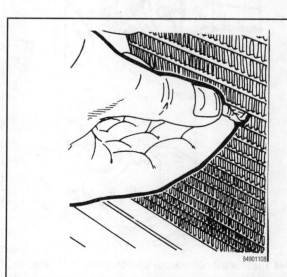

Fig. 150 Remove any debris from the radiator's cooling fins

Fig. 151 Coolant condition can be checked with an inexpensive tester

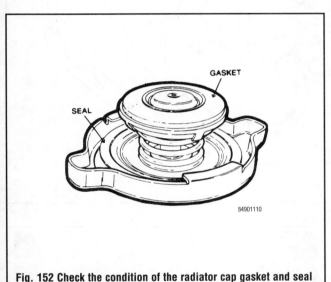

Fig. 152 Check the condition of the radiator cap gasket and seal

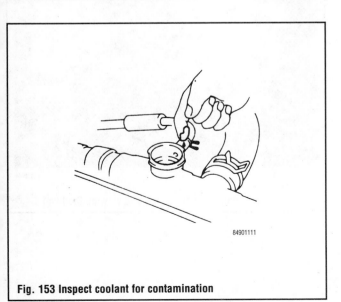

Fig. 153 Inspect coolant for contamination

FLUID RECOMMENDATIONS

The recommended coolant mixture for 1987–95 Chevy/GMC vans is 50/50 ethylene glycol and water for year round use. Use a good quality antifreeze with water pump lubricants, rust inhibitors and other corrosion inhibitors, along with acid neutralizers. 1996–97 models were factory equipped with GM DEX-COOL® silicate-free coolant, which is easily identified by its orange color. GM does not recommend any other type of coolant for these vehicles.

LEVEL CHECK

▶ **See Figure 154**

1. Check the level on the see-through expansion tank.

☀ CAUTION

The radiator coolant is under pressure when hot. To avoid the danger of physical harm, coolant level should be checked or replenished only when the engine is cold. To remove the radiator cap when the engine is hot, first cover the cap with a thick rag, or wear a heavy glove for protection. Press down on the cap slightly and slowly turn it counterclockwise until it reaches the first stop. Allow all the pressure to vent (indicated when the hissing sound stops). When the pressure is released, press down on the cap and continue to rotate it counterclockwise. Some radiator caps have a lever for venting the pressure, but you should still exercise extreme caution when removing the cap.

2. Check the level and, if necessary, add coolant through the expansion tank to the proper level. Use a 50/50 mix of ethylene glycol antifreeze and water on 1987–95 models and GM DEX-COOL® on 1996–97 models. Alcohol or methanol base coolants are not recommended. Antifreeze solutions should be used, even in summer, to prevent rust and to take advantage of the solution's higher boiling point compared to plain water. This is imperative on air conditioned vans; the heater core can freeze if it isn't protected. Coolant should be added through the coolant recovery tank, not the radiator filler neck.

☀ WARNING

Never add large quantities of cold coolant to a hot engine! A cracked engine block may result!

Each year the cooling system should be serviced as follows:
- Wash the radiator cap and filler neck with clean water.
- Check the coolant for proper level and freeze protection.
- Have the system pressure tested at 15 psi (103 kPa). If a replacement cap is installed, be sure that it conforms to the original specifications.
- Tighten the hose clamps and inspect all hoses. Replace hoses that are swollen, cracked or otherwise deteriorated.
- Clean the frontal area of the radiator core and the air conditioning condenser, if so equipped.

DRAIN, FLUSH & REFILL

The cooling system in your van accumulates some internal rust and corrosion during normal operation. A simple method of keeping the system clean is known as flushing the system. It is performed by circulating a can of radiator flush through the system, then draining and refilling the system with the recommended coolant and water mixture. Radiator flush is marketed by several different manufacturers, and is available in containers at many automotive departments, parts stores, and hardware stores. This operation should be performed every 30,000 miles (48,000 km) or once every 2 years for vehicles with silicate based coolant; every 150,000 miles (240,000 km) or once every 5 years for vehicles using GM DEX-COOL® coolant.

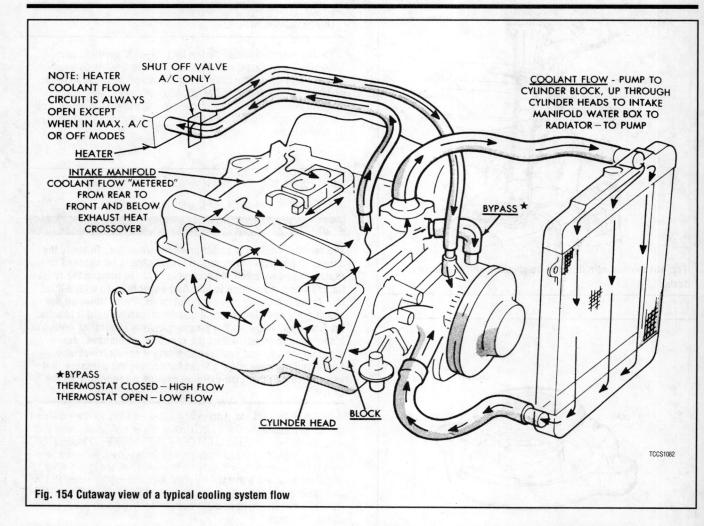

NOTE: HEATER COOLANT FLOW CIRCUIT IS ALWAYS OPEN EXCEPT WHEN IN MAX. A/C OR OFF MODES

SHUT OFF VALVE A/C ONLY

<u>HEATER</u>

<u>INTAKE MANIFOLD</u>
COOLANT FLOW "METERED" FROM REAR TO FRONT AND BELOW EXHAUST HEAT CROSSOVER

COOLANT FLOW - PUMP TO CYLINDER BLOCK, UP THROUGH CYLINDER HEADS TO INTAKE MANIFOLD WATER BOX TO RADIATOR – TO PUMP

BYPASS ★

★BYPASS
THERMOSTAT CLOSED – HIGH FLOW
THERMOSTAT OPEN – LOW FLOW

CYLINDER HEAD

BLOCK

TCCS1082

Fig. 154 Cutaway view of a typical cooling system flow

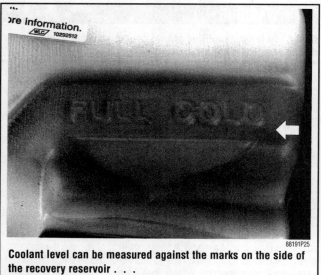

Coolant level can be measured against the marks on the side of the recovery reservoir . . .

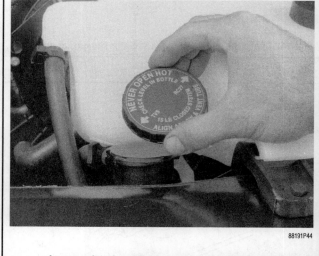

. . . or by removing the radiator cap and viewing the level

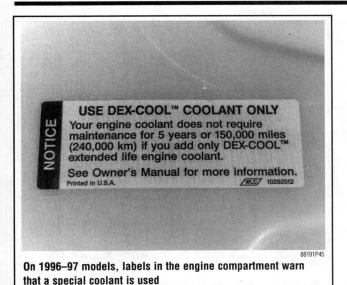

On 1996–97 models, labels in the engine compartment warn that a special coolant is used

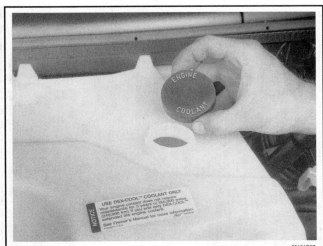

To replenish the cooling system, remove the recovery reservoir cap . . .

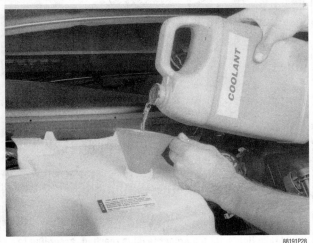

. . . then, using a funnel, add coolant until it reaches the full mark on the side of the reservoir . . .

. . . or, the radiator cap can be removed and the coolant added there

✳✳ CAUTION

When draining the coolant, keep in mind that cats and dogs are attracted by ethylene glycol antifreeze, and are quite likely to drink any that is left in an uncovered container or in puddles on the ground. This will prove fatal in sufficient quantity. Always drain the coolant into a sealable container. Coolant should be reused unless it is contaminated or several years old.

1. Drain the existing antifreeze and coolant. Open the radiator and engine drain petcocks (located near the bottom of the radiator and engine block, respectively), or disconnect the bottom radiator hose at the radiator outlet.

2. Close the petcock or reconnect the lower hose and fill the system with water—hot water if the engine is at operating temperature.

3. Add a can of quality radiator flush to the radiator or recovery tank, following the instructions on the can.

4. Idle the engine as long as specified on the can of flush, or until the upper radiator hose gets hot.

5. Drain the system again. There should be quite a bit of scale and rust in the drained water.

6. Refill the system with water and repeat the process (do not add additional radiator flush) until the drained water is mostly clear.

7. Close all petcocks and connect all hoses.

8. Flush the coolant recovery reservoir with water and leave empty.

9. Determine the capacity of your van's cooling system (see the Capacities specifications in this guide). Add the correct mixture AND TYPE of coolant—refer to the fluid recommendations in this section if you are unsure. Fill the radiator to about ½ in. (13mm) from the bottom of the filler neck.

10. Start the vehicle and allow it to reach normal operating temperature. When the thermostat opens, air which was trapped in the engine will be expelled, causing the coolant level to drop. Add the correct type and mixture of coolant and water until the level reaches the bottom of the filler neck, then replace the radiator cap.

11. Turn the vehicle off and add the same mixture and type of coolant to the recovery tank, but do not exceed the ADD or COLD marks on the side of the tank.

12. Run the engine to operating temperature, then stop the engine and check for leaks. Check the coolant level and top up if necessary.

13. Check the protection level of the coolant with an antifreeze tester (a small, inexpensive syringe type device available at auto parts stores). The tester has five or six small colored balls inside, each of which signify a certain temperature rating. Insert the tester in the recovery tank and suck just

enough coolant into the syringe to float as many individual balls as you can (without sucking in too much coolant and floating all the balls at once). A chart provided with the tester will equate the number of floating balls with a certain temperature level of protection. For example, three floating balls might mean the coolant will protect your engine down to 5°F (-15°C).

Brake Master Cylinder

FLUID RECOMMENDATIONS

Use only Heavy Duty Brake fluid meeting or exceeding DOT 3 standards.

LEVEL CHECK

▶ **See Figure 155**

Chevrolet and GMC vans are equipped with a dual braking system, which allows a vehicle to be brought to a safe stop in the event of failure in either the front or rear brakes. The dual master cylinder has 2 entirely separate reservoirs, one connected to the front brakes and the other connected to the rear brakes. In the event of failure in either portion, the remaining part is not affected. Fluid level in the master cylinder should be checked on a regular basis.

The master cylinder is mounted to the left side of the firewall.
1. Clean away all of the dirt around the cover of the master cylinder.
2. Be sure that the vehicle is resting on a level surface.
3. Carefully pry the clip from the top of the master cylinder to release the cover. On some later models, just pull up on the tabs.
4. The fluid level should be approximately ¼ in. (6mm) from the top of the master cylinder, or at least above the **MIN** mark. If not, add fluid until the level is correct. Replacement fluid should be Delco Supreme No. 11, DOT 3, or its equivalent.

➡**It is normal for the fluid level to fall as the disc brake pads wear.**

✳✳ WARNING

Brake fluid dissolves paint! It also absorbs moisture from the air. Never leave a container or the master cylinder uncovered any longer than necessary!

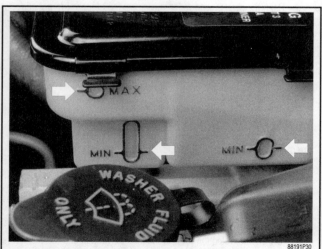

The master cylinder brake fluid level can be referenced against the marks on the side of the reservoir

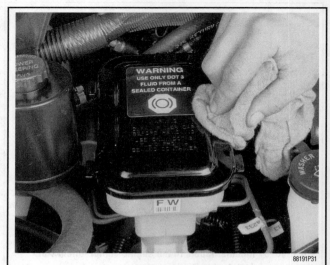

Use a cloth to clean the dirt and debris from the cover . . .

. . . then remove the cover from the master cylinder

Add brake fluid until the proper level is reached, according to the marks on the side of the reservoir

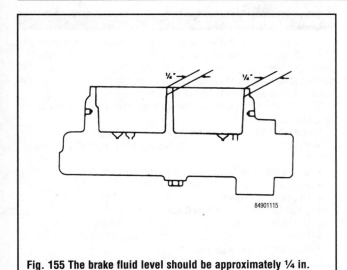

Fig. 155 The brake fluid level should be approximately ¼ in. below the top of the master cylinder

5. Install the cover of the master cylinder. On most models there is a rubber gasket under the cover, which fits into 2 slots on the cover. Be sure that this is seated properly.
6. Push the clip back into place and be sure that it seats in the groove on top of the cover.

Clutch Master Cylinder

FLUID RECOMMENDATIONS

Use only Heavy Duty Brake fluid meeting DOT 3 standards.

LEVEL CHECK

The clutch master cylinder is located on the firewall in the engine compartment.
1. Clean away all of the dirt around the cover of the master cylinder.
2. Be sure that the vehicle is resting on a level surface.
3. Carefully remove the cover from the master cylinder.
4. The fluid level should be approximately ¼ in. (6mm) from the top of the master cylinder, or at least above the **MIN** mark. If not, add fluid until the level is correct. Replacement fluid should be Delco Supreme No. 11, DOT 3, or its equivalent.
5. Install the cover of the master cylinder.

Power Steering Pump

FLUID RECOMMENDATIONS

Use GM Power Steering fluid, or its equivalent.

LEVEL CHECK

Check the dipstick in the pump reservoir when the fluid is at operating temperature. The fluid should be between the **HOT** and **COLD** marks. If the fluid is at room temperature, the fluid should be between the **ADD** and **COLD** marks. The fluid does not require periodic changing.

On systems with a remote reservoir, the level should be maintained approximately ½–1 in. (13–25mm) from the top with the wheels in the full left turn position.

Unscrew the power steering pump cap/dipstick

Use a funnel when adding the fluid to avoid spillage

Steering Gear

FLUID RECOMMENDATIONS

Use GM Lubricant (part No. 1051052) or equivalent.

LEVEL CHECK

No lubrication is needed for the life of the gear, except in the event of seal replacement or overhaul, when the gear should be refilled with a 13 oz. container of Steering Gear Lubricant (Part No. 1051052) or its equivalent, which meets GM Specification GM 4673M.

Chassis Greasing

Refer to the diagrams for chassis points to be lubricated. Not all vehicles have all the fittings illustrated. Water resistant EP chassis lubricant (grease) conforming to GM specification 6031-M should be used for all chassis grease points.

Once every year or 7500 miles (12,067 km), the front suspension ball joints, both upper and lower on each side of the van, must be greased. Most vans covered in this guide should be equipped with grease nipples on the ball joints, although some may have plugs which must be removed and nipples fitted.

✳✳ WARNING

Do not pump so much grease into the ball joint that excess grease squeezes out of the rubber boot, since this would destroy the watertight seal.

1. Raise up the front end of the van and safely support it with jackstands. Block the rear wheels and firmly apply the parking brake.

2. If the van has been parked in temperatures below 20°F (-7°C) for any length of time, park it in a heated garage for an hour or so until the ball joints loosen up enough to accept the grease.

3. Depending on which front wheel you work on first, turn the wheel and tire outward, either full-lock right or full-lock left. You now have the ends of the upper and lower suspension control arms in front of you; the grease nipples are visible pointing up (top ball joint) and down (lower ball joint) through the end of each control arm.

➡ **If the nipples are not accessible enough, remove the wheel and tire.**

4. Wipe all dirt and crud from the nipples or from around the plugs (if installed). If plugs are on the van, remove them and install grease nipples in the holes (nipples are available in various thread sizes at most auto parts stores).

5. Using a hand operated, low pressure grease gun loaded with a quality chassis grease, grease the ball joint only until the rubber joint boot begins to swell out.

The steering linkage should be greased at the same interval as the ball joints. Grease nipples are installed on the steering tie rod ends on most models.

6. Wipe all dirt and crud from around the nipples at each tie rod end.

7. Using a hand operated, low pressure grease gun loaded with a suitable chassis grease, grease the linkage until the old grease begins to squeeze out around the tie rod ends.

8. Wipe off the nipples and any excess grease. Also grease the nipples on the steering idler arms.

Use chassis grease on the parking brake cable where it contacts the cable guides, levers and linkage.

Apply a small amount of clean engine oil to the kickdown and shift linkage points at 7500 mile (12,000 km) intervals.

Body Lubrication and Maintenance

LOCK CYLINDERS

Apply graphite lubricant sparingly through the key slot. Insert the key and operate the lock several times to be sure that the lubricant is worked into the lock cylinder.

HOOD LATCH & HINGES

Clean the latch surfaces and apply clean engine oil to the latch pilot bolts and the spring anchor. Also lubricate the hood hinges with engine oil. Use a chassis grease to lubricate all the pivot points in the latch release mechanism.

DOOR HINGES

The gas tank filler door and van doors should be wiped clean and lubricated with clean engine oil once a year. The door lock cylinders and latch mechanisms should be lubricated periodically with a few drops of graphite lock lubricant or a few shots of silicone spray.

BODY DRAIN HOLES

Be sure that the drain holes in the doors and rocker panels are cleared of obstruction. A small punch, screwdriver or unbent wire coat hanger can be used to clear them of any debris.

Front Wheel Bearings

Only the front wheel bearings require periodic maintenance. A premium high melting point grease meeting GM specification 6031-M must be used. Long fiber type greases must not be used. This service is recommended at the intervals in the Maintenance Intervals Chart or whenever the van has been driven in water up to the hubs.

Before handling the bearings, there are a few things that you should remember to do and not to do.

Remember to do the following:
• Remove all outside dirt from the housing before exposing the bearing.
• Treat a used bearing as gently as you would a new one.
• Work with clean tools in clean surroundings.
• Use clean, dry canvas gloves, or at least clean, dry hands.
• Clean solvents and flushing fluids are a must.
• Use clean paper when laying out the bearings to dry.
• Protect disassembled bearings from rust and dirt. Cover them up.
• Use clean rags to wipe bearings.
• Keep the bearings in oil-proof paper when they are to be stored or are not in use.
• Clean the inside of the housing before replacing the bearing.

Do not do the following:
• Don't work in dirty surroundings.
• Don't use dirty, chipped or damaged tools.
• Try not to work on wooden work benches or use wooden mallets.
• Don't handle bearings with dirty or moist hands.
• Do not use gasoline for cleaning; use a safe solvent.
• Do not spin dry bearings with compressed air. They will be damaged.
• Do not spin dirty bearings.
• Avoid using cotton waste or dirty cloths to wipe bearings.
• Try not to scratch or nick bearing surfaces.
• Do not allow the bearing to come in contact with dirt or rust at any time.

REMOVAL, PACKING & INSTALLATION

➡ **Sodium based grease is not compatible with lithium based grease. Read the package labels and be careful not to mix the two types. If there is any doubt as to the type of grease used, completely clean the old grease from the bearing and hub before replacing.**

2-Wheel Drive Models

◗ **See Figures 156 thru 169 (p. 79–81)**

1. Raise and support the front end on jackstands.
2. Remove the wheel.
3. Dismount the caliper and wire it out of the way.
4. Pry out the grease cap, remove the cotter pin, spindle nut and washer, then remove the hub. Do not drop the wheel bearings.
5. Remove the outer roller bearing assembly from the hub. The inner bearing assembly will remain in the hub and may be removed after prying out the inner seal. Discard the seal.
6. Clean all parts in a non-flammable solvent and let them air dry. Never spin dry a bearing with compressed air! Check for excessive wear and damage.

To install:

7. Using a hammer and drift, remove the bearing races from the hub. They are driven out from the inside. When installing new races, make sure that they are not cocked and that they are fully seated against the hub shoulder.

8. Pack both wheel bearings using high melting point wheel bearing grease for disc brakes. Ordinary grease will melt and ooze out, ruining the pads. Bearings should be packed using a cone-type wheel bearing greaser tool. If one is not available, they may be packed by hand.

9. Place a healthy glob of grease in the palm of one hand and force

Fig. 156 Pry the dust cap from the hub, taking care not to distort or damage its flange

Fig. 159 Loosen and remove the castellated nut from the spindle

Fig. 157 Once the bent ends are cut, grasp the cotter pin and pull or pry it free of the spindle

Fig. 160 Remove the washer from the spindle

Fig. 158 If difficulty is encountered, gently tap on the pliers with a hammer to help free the cotter pin

Fig. 161 With the nut and washer out of the way, the outer bearing may be removed from the hub

Fig. 162 Pull the hub and inner bearing assembly from the spindle

Fig. 165 Thoroughly pack the bearing with fresh, high temperature wheel bearing grease before installation

Fig. 163 Use a small prytool to remove the old inner bearing seal

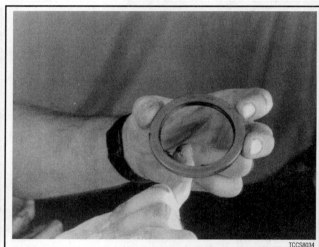

Fig. 166 Apply a thin coat of fresh grease to the new inner bearing seal lip

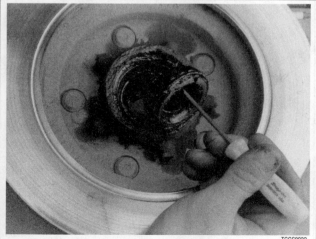

Fig. 164 With the seal removed, the inner bearing may be withdrawn from the hub

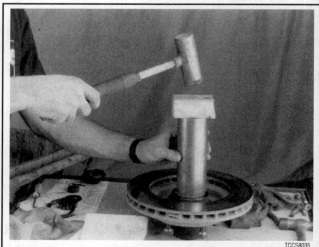

Fig. 167 Use a suitably sized driver to install the inner bearing seal to the hub

Fig. 168 Tighten the nut to specifications while gently spinning the wheel, then adjust the bearing

Fig. 169 After the bearings are adjusted, install the dust cap by gently tapping on the flange

the edge of the bearing into it so that the grease fills the bearing. Do this until the whole bearing is packed.

10. Place the inner bearing in the hub and install a new inner seal, making sure that the seal flange faces the bearing race.

11. Carefully install the wheel hub over the spindle.

12. Using your hands, firmly press the outer bearing into the hub. Install the spindle washer and nut.

13. Spin the wheel hub by hand and tighten the nut until it is just snug; 12 ft. lbs. (16 Nm).

14. Back off the nut until it is loose, then finger-tighten it. Loosen the nut until either hole in the spindle lines up with a slot in the nut and insert a new cotter pin.

15. There should be 0.001–0.005 in. (0.025–0.127mm) end-play on 1987–90 models. On 1991–97 models, end-play should be 0.005–0.008 in. This can be measured with a dial indicator, if you wish.

16. Replace the dust cap, wheel and tire.

TRAILER TOWING

General Recommendations

Your vehicle was primarily designed to carry passengers and cargo. It is important to remember that towing a trailer will place additional loads on your vehicle's engine, drive train, steering, braking and other systems. However, if you decide to tow a trailer, using the proper equipment is a must.

Local laws may require specific equipment such as trailer brakes or fender mounted mirrors. Check your local laws.

Trailer Weight

The weight of the trailer is the most important factor. A good weight-to-horsepower ratio is about 35:1; that is, 35 lbs. of Gross Combined Weight (GCW) for every horsepower your engine develops. Multiply the engine's rated horsepower by 35 and subtract the combined weight of the vehicle, passengers and luggage. The number remaining is the approximate maximum weight you should tow, although a numerically higher axle ratio may help compensate for heavier weight.

Hitch (Tongue) Weight

▶ See Figure 170

Calculate the hitch weight in order to select a proper hitch. The weight of the hitch is usually 9–11% of the trailer gross weight and should be measured with the trailer loaded. Hitches fall into various categories: those that mount on the frame and rear bumper, the bolt-on type, or the weld-on distribution type used for larger trailers. Axle mounted or clamp-on bumper hitches should never be used.

Check the gross weight rating of your trailer. Tongue weight is usually figured as 10% of gross trailer weight. Therefore, a trailer with a maximum gross weight of 2000 lbs. will have a maximum

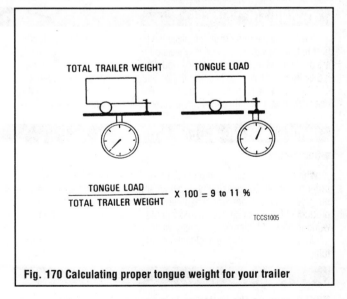

Fig. 170 Calculating proper tongue weight for your trailer

tongue weight of 200 lbs. Class I trailers fall into this category. Class II trailers are those with a gross weight rating of 2000–3000 lbs., while Class III trailers fall into the 3500–6000 lbs. category. Class IV trailers are those over 6000 lbs. and are for use with fifth wheel trucks, only.

When you've determined the hitch that you'll need, follow the manufacturer's installation instructions, exactly, especially when it comes to fastener torques. The hitch will be subjected to a lot of stress and good hitches come with hardened bolts. NEVER substitute an inferior bolt for a hardened bolt.

Cooling

ENGINE

Overflow Tank

One of the most common, if not THE most common, problem associated with trailer towing is engine overheating. If you have a cooling system without an expansion tank, you'll definitely need to get an aftermarket expansion tank kit, preferably one with at least a 2 quart capacity. These kits are easily installed on the radiator's overflow hose, and come with a pressure cap designed for expansion tanks.

Flex Fan

Another helpful accessory for vehicles using a belt-driven radiator fan is a flex fan. These fans are large diameter units designed to provide more airflow at low speeds, by using fan blades that have deeply cupped surfaces. The blades then flex, or flatten out, at high speed, when less cooling air is needed. These fans are far lighter in weight than stock fans, requiring less horsepower to drive them. Also, they are far quieter than stock fans. If you do decide to replace your stock fan with a flex fan, note that if your vehicle has a fan clutch, a spacer will be needed between the flex fan and water pump hub.

Oil Cooler

Aftermarket engine oil coolers are helpful for prolonging engine oil life and reducing overall engine temperatures. Both of these factors increase engine life. While not absolutely necessary in towing Class I and some Class II trailers, they are recommended for heavier Class II and all Class III towing. Engine oil cooler systems usually consist of an adapter, screwed on in place of the oil filter, a remote filter mounting and a multi-tube, finned heat exchanger, which is mounted in front of the radiator or air conditioning condenser.

TOWING THE VEHICLE

Release the parking brake and place the transmission in Neutral. It is best to tow the van with its drive wheels off the ground. If the drive wheels are on the ground, the transmission and differential must operate properly. If they do not, place a dolly under the wheels or disconnect the driveshaft.

If the van is being towed on its front wheels, the steering wheel should be clamped in a straight ahead position by a steering wheel clamping

JUMP STARTING A DEAD BATTERY

▶ See Figure 171

Whenever a vehicle is jump started, precautions must be followed in order to prevent the possibility of personal injury. Remember that batteries contain a small amount of explosive hydrogen gas which is a by-product of battery charging. Sparks should always be avoided when working around batteries, especially when attaching jumper cables. To minimize the possibility of accidental sparks, follow the procedure carefully.

✳✳ WARNING

NEVER hook up the batteries in a series circuit or the entire electrical system will go up in smoke, including the starter!

Vehicles equipped with a diesel engine may utilize two 12 volt batteries. If so, the batteries are connected in a parallel circuit (positive terminal to positive terminal, negative terminal to negative terminal). Hooking the batteries up in parallel circuit increases battery cranking power without increasing total battery voltage output. Output remains at

TRANSMISSION

An automatic transmission is usually recommended for trailer towing. Modern automatics have proven reliable and, of course, easy to operate, in trailer towing. The increased load of a trailer, however, causes an increase in the temperature of the automatic transmission fluid. Heat is the worst enemy of an automatic transmission. As the temperature of the fluid increases, the life of the fluid decreases.

It is essential, therefore, that you install an automatic transmission cooler. The cooler, which consists of a multi-tube, finned heat exchanger, is usually installed in front of the radiator or air conditioning compressor, and hooked in-line with the transmission cooler tank inlet line. Follow the cooler manufacturer's installation instructions.

Select a cooler of at least adequate capacity, based upon the combined gross weights of the vehicle and trailer.

Cooler manufacturers recommend that you use an aftermarket cooler in addition to, and not instead of, the present cooling tank in your radiator. If you do want to use it in place of the radiator cooling tank, get a cooler at least two sizes larger than normally necessary.

➡A transmission cooler can, sometimes, cause slow or harsh shifting in the transmission during cold weather, until the fluid has a chance to come up to normal operating temperature. Some coolers can be purchased with or retrofitted with a temperature bypass valve, which will allow fluid flow through the cooler only when the fluid has reached a certain operating temperature.

Handling A Trailer

Towing a trailer with ease and safety requires a certain amount of experience. It's a good idea to learn the feel of a trailer by practicing turning, stopping and backing in an open area such as an empty parking lot.

device, such as that provided by a towing service or towing system manufacturer. It is not advisable to use the steering column lock to hold the wheels in the straight ahead position.

Whenever possible, follow the vehicle manufacturer's recommendations for maximum towing speed (35 mph) and distance (50 miles).

12 volts. On the other hand, hooking two 12 volt batteries up in a series circuit (positive terminal to negative terminal, positive terminal to negative terminal) increases total battery output to 24 volts (12 volts plus 12 volts).

Jump Starting Precautions

• Be sure that both batteries are of the same voltage. Vehicles covered by this manual and most vehicles on the road today utilize a 12 volt charging system.

• Be sure that both batteries are of the same polarity (have the same terminal, in most cases NEGATIVE grounded).

• Be sure that the vehicles are not touching or a short could occur.

• On serviceable batteries, be sure the vent cap holes are not obstructed.

• Do not smoke or allow sparks anywhere near the batteries.

• In cold weather, make sure the battery electrolyte is not frozen. This can occur more readily in a battery that has been in a state of discharge.

• Do not allow electrolyte to contact your skin or clothing.

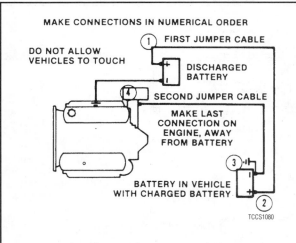

Fig. 171 Connect the jumper cables to the batteries and engine in the order shown

Jump Starting Procedure

1. Make sure that the voltages of the 2 batteries are the same. Most batteries and charging systems are of the 12 volt variety.

2. Pull the jumping vehicle (with the good battery) into a position so the jumper cables can reach the dead battery and that vehicle's engine. Make sure that the vehicles do NOT touch.

3. Place the transmissions of both vehicles in **Neutral** (MT) or **P** (AT), as applicable, then firmly set their parking brakes.

➡️**If necessary for safety reasons, the hazard lights on both vehicles may be operated throughout the entire procedure without significantly increasing the difficulty of jumping the dead battery.**

4. Turn all lights and accessories OFF on both vehicles. Make sure the ignition switches on both vehicles are turned to the **OFF** position.

5. Cover the battery cell caps with a rag, but do not cover the terminals.

6. Make sure the terminals on both batteries are clean and free of corrosion or proper electrical connection will be impeded. If necessary, clean the battery terminals before proceeding.

7. Identify the positive (+) and negative (-) terminals on both batteries.

8. Connect the first jumper cable to the positive (+) terminal of the dead battery, then connect the other end of that cable to the positive (+) terminal of the booster (good) battery.

9. Connect one end of the other jumper cable to the negative (-) terminal on the booster battery and the final cable clamp to an engine bolt head, alternator bracket or other solid, metallic point on the engine with the dead battery. Try to pick a ground on the engine that is positioned away from the battery in order to minimize the possibility of the 2 clamps touching should one loosen during the procedure. DO NOT connect this clamp to the negative (-) terminal of the bad battery.

❄❄ CAUTION

Be very careful to keep the jumper cables away from moving parts (cooling fan, belts, etc.) on both engines.

10. Check to make sure that the cables are routed away from any moving parts, then start the donor vehicle's engine. Run the engine at moderate speed for several minutes to allow the dead battery a chance to receive some initial charge.

11. With the donor vehicle's engine still running slightly above idle, try to start the vehicle with the dead battery. Crank the engine for no more than 10 seconds at a time and let the starter cool for at least 20 seconds between tries. If the vehicle does not start in 3 tries, it is likely that something else is also wrong or that the battery needs additional time to charge.

12. Once the vehicle is started, allow it to run at idle for a few seconds to make sure that it is operating properly.

13. Turn ON the headlights, heater blower and, if equipped, the rear defroster of both vehicles in order to reduce the severity of voltage spikes and subsequent risk of damage to the vehicles' electrical systems when the cables are disconnected. This step is especially important to any vehicle equipped with computer control modules.

14. Carefully disconnect the cables in the reverse order of connection. Start with the negative cable that is attached to the engine ground, then the negative cable on the donor battery. Disconnect the positive cable from the donor battery and finally, disconnect the positive cable from the formerly dead battery. Be careful when disconnecting the cables from the positive terminals not to allow the alligator clips to touch any metal on either vehicle or a short and sparks will occur.

JACKING

▸ **See Figure 172**

Your vehicle was supplied with a jack for emergency road repairs. This jack is fine for changing a flat tire or other short term procedures not requiring you to go beneath the vehicle. If it is used in an emergency situation, carefully follow the instructions provided either with the jack or in your owner's manual. Do not attempt to use the jack on any portions of the vehicle other than specified by the vehicle manufacturer. Always block the diagonally opposite wheel when using a jack.

A more convenient way of jacking is the use of a garage or floor jack. You may use the floor jack to raise your Chevrolet and GM vans.

Never place the jack under the radiator, engine or transmission components. Severe and expensive damage will result when the jack is raised. Additionally, never jack under the floorpan or bodywork; the metal will deform.

Whenever you plan to work under the vehicle, you must support it on jackstands or ramps. Never use cinder blocks or stacks of wood to support the vehicle, even if you're only going to be under it for a few minutes. Never crawl under the vehicle when it is supported only by the tire-changing jack or other floor jack.

➡️**Always position a block of wood or small rubber pad on top of the jack or jackstand to protect the lifting point's finish when lifting or supporting the vehicle.**

Small hydraulic, screw, or scissors jacks are satisfactory for raising the vehicle. Drive-on trestles or ramps are also a handy and safe way to both raise and support the vehicle. Be careful though, some ramps may be too steep to drive your vehicle onto without scraping the front bottom panels. Never support the vehicle on any suspension member (unless specifically instructed to do so by a repair manual) or by an underbody panel.

Jacking Precautions

The following safety points cannot be overemphasized:
- Always block the opposite wheel or wheels to keep the vehicle from rolling off the jack.
- When raising the front of the vehicle, firmly apply the parking brake.
- When the drive wheels are to remain on the ground, leave the vehicle in gear to help prevent it from rolling.
- Always use jackstands to support the vehicle when you are working underneath. Place the stands beneath the vehicle's jacking brackets. Before climbing underneath, rock the vehicle a bit to make sure it is firmly supported.

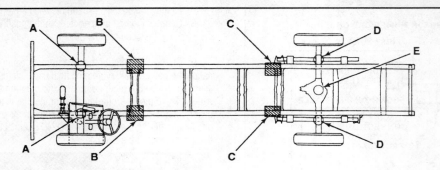

A. Front axle; at the spring mount.
B. Frame; at the crossmember, just behind the spring mount.
C. Frame; at the crossmember.
D. Rear Axle; at the spring mount.
E. Rear Axle; at the differential.

○ Floor Jack

▨ Hoist

88191G28

Fig. 172 Typical vehicle lifting points

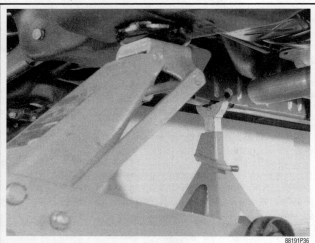

88191P36

When raising the front of the van, always support the vehicle with jackstands

88191P38

Raise the rear of the van with a hydraulic jack beneath any one of the lifting points . . .

88191P37

Be sure to position the jackstands beneath the frame rail

88191P39

. . . then position jackstands at the appropriate points of the frame rail

MAINTENANCE INTERVAL CHARTS

◆ **See Figures 173, 174 and 175 (p. 85–87)**

When performing a maintenace service, the following charts should be used as a general guideline only. Always consult your owner's manual first, since it will reflect any changes in the manufacturer's service procedures.

➡ If the maintenance charts in your owner's manual differ from the charts illustrated, use the schedule in the owner's manual.

Item No.	Service		If your driving conditions meet those specified in "Scheduled Maintenance Services" in this Section (or see Index), use Maintenance Schedule I (+)							
		Miles (000)	7.5	15	22.5	30	37.5	45	52.5	60
		Kilometers (000)	12.5	25	37.5	50	62.5	75	87.5	100
1	Engine Oil Change*—Every 12 Months, or		●	●	●	●	●	●	●	●
	Oil Filter Change*—Every 12 Months, or		●	●	●	●	●	●	●	●
2	Chassis Lubrication—Every 12 Months, or		●	●	●	●	●	●	●	●
3	Clutch Fork Ball Stud Lubrication					●				●
5	Cooling System Service*—Every 24 Months or					●				●
6	Air Cleaner Filter Replacement*					●				●
7	Front Wheel Bearing Repack					●				●
8	Transmission Service **									
10	Fuel Filter Replacement*$									●
11	Spark Plugs Replacement*					●				●
12	Spark Plug Wire Inspection*									●
15	Engine Timing Check*$									●
16	Fuel Tank, Cap and Lines Inspection*$									●
18	Engine Accessory Drive (Serpentine) Belt Inspection*									●
24	Tire and Wheel Rotation**		●		●		●		●	
25	Drive Axle Service**		●	●	●	●	●	●	●	●
26	Brake Systems Inspection**									

* An Emission Control Service
** See "Explanation of Scheduled Maintenance Services" in the Index
$ The California Air Resources Board has determined that the failure to perform this maintenance item will not nullify the emission warranty or limit recall liability prior to the completion of vehicle useful life. General Motors, however, urges that all recommended maintenance services be performed at the indicated intervals and the maintenance be recorded.

THE SERVICES SHOWN ON THIS CHART UP TO 60,000 MILES (100 000 km) ARE TO BE DONE AFTER 60,000 MILES AT THE SAME INTERVALS.

T0403/T0903

88191C07

Fig. 173 Maintenance interval chart for gasoline engines with light duty emissions

If your driving conditions meet those specified in "Scheduled Maintenance Services" in this Section (or see Index), use Maintenance Schedule 1 (+)

88191C08

Item No.	Service	3 / 5	6 / 10	9 / 15	12 / 20	15 / 25	18 / 30	21 / 35	24 / 40	27 / 45	30 / 50	33 / 55	36 / 60	39 / 65	42 / 70	45 / 75	48 / 80	51 / 85	54 / 90	57 / 95	60 / 100
	Miles (000) / Kilometers (000) →																				
1	Engine Oil Change* – Every 12 Months, or	•	•	•	•	•	•	•	•	•	•	•	•	•	•	•	•	•	•	•	•
	Oil Filter Change* – Every 12 Months, or		•		•		•		•		•		•		•		•		•		•
2	Chassis Lubrication – Every 12 Months, or		•		•		•		•		•		•		•		•		•		•
3	Clutch Fork Ball Stud Lubrication				•								•								•
5	Cooling System Service* – Every 24 Months or								•								•				
6	Air Cleaner Filter Replacement								•								•				•
7	Front Wheel Bearing Repack								•								•				•
8	Transmission Service**																				•
10	Fuel Filter Replacement*								•						•						
11	Spark Plugs Replacement*										•		•								•
12	Spark Plug Wire Inspection*										•		•								•
13	EGR System Inspection*								•								•				•
14	Electronic Vacuum Regulator Valve (EVRV) Inspection*																				•
15	Engine Timing Check ▲*								•		•		•				•				•
16	Fuel Tank, Cap and Lines Inspection*										•										
17	Thermostatically Controlled Air Cleaner Inspection ▲*								•				•				•				•
18	Engine Accessory Drive (Serpentine) Belt Inspection*				•								•				•				•
19	Evaporative Control System Inspection*												•				•				•
20	Shields and Underhood Insulation Inspection ▲■				•				•								•				•
21	Air Intake System Inspection ▲■								•				•				•				
22	Thermostatically Controlled Engine Cooling Fan Check ▲■ – Every 12 Months or				•				•				•				•				•
24	Tire and Wheel Rotation**		•						•						•		•		•		•
25	Drive Axle Service**		•		•		•		•				•		•		•		•		•
26	Brake Systems Inspection**																				

THE SERVICES SHOWN ON THIS CHART UP TO 60,000 MILES (100,000 km) ARE TO BE DONE AFTER 60,000 MILES AT THE SAME INTERVALS.
TD407

* An Emission Control Service
** See "Explanation of Scheduled Maintenance Services" in this section.
▲ Also a Noise Emission Control Service
■ Applicable only to vehicles sold in the United States

Fig. 174 Maintenance interval chart for gasoline engines with heavy duty emissions

If your driving conditions meet those specified in "Scheduled Maintenance Services" in this section, use Maintenance Schedule I (+).

Item No.	Service — Miles (000)	2.5	5	7.5	10	12.5	15	17.5	20	22.5	25	27.5	30	32.5	35	37.5	40	42.5	45	47.5	50	52.5	55	57.5	60
	Kilometers (000)	4	8	12	16	20	24	28	32	36	40	44	48	52	56	60	64	68	72	76	80	84	88	92	100
1	Engine Oil Change* —Every 12 Months, or		•		•		•		•		•		•		•		•		•		•		•		•
	Oil Filter Change* —Every 12 Months, or		•				•				•				•				•				•		•
2	Chassis Lubrication—Every 12 Months, or		•		•		•		•		•		•		•		•		•		•		•		•
3	Clutch Fork Ball Stud Lubrication												•												•
4	Engine Idle Speed Adjustment*		•										•												•
5	Cooling System Service* —Every 24 Months or												•												•
6	Air Cleaner Filter Replacement* ★												•												•
7	Front Wheel Bearing Repack												•												•
8	Transmission Service**												•												•
9	CDRV System Inspection*												•												•
10	Fuel Filter Replacement*												•												•
13	EGR System Inspection*												•												•
18	Engine Accessory Drive (Serpentine) Belt Inspection*												•												•
20	Shields and Underhood Insulation Inspection ▲■								•				•				•				•				•
21	Air Intake System Inspection ▲■								•				•				•				•				•
22	Thermostatically Controlled Engine Cooling Fan Check ▲■ —Every 12 Months or				•								•												•
23	Exhaust Pressure Regulator Valve Inspection*												•												•
24	Tire and Wheel Rotation**		•				•				•				•				•				•		
25	Drive Axle Service**		•				•				•				•				•				•		•
26	Brake Systems Inspection**						•						•						•						•

* An Emission Control Service
** See "Explanation of Scheduled Maintenance Services" in this section.
▲ Also a Noise Emission Control Service (applicable to vehicles with engine VIN code Y).
■ Applicable only to trucks sold in the United States

THE SERVICES SHOWN ON THIS CHART UP TO 60,000 MILES (100 000 km) ARE TO BE DONE AFTER 60,000 MILES AT THE SAME INTERVALS.

88191C09

Fig. 175 Maintenance interval chart for diesel engines with light duty emissions

CAPACITIES

Year	Model	Engine ID/VIN	Engine Displacement Liters (cc)	Engine Filter (qts.)	Transmission			Drive Axle Rear	Fuel Tank (gal.)	Cooling System (qts.)	
					4-Spd	5-Spd	Auto.			w/AC	w/oAC
1987	G/P	Z	4.3 (4293)	5.0	①	①	②	③	22.0	11.0	11.0
	G	H	5.0 (4999)	5.0	①	①	②	③	22.0	17.0	17.0
	G/P	K/M	5.7 (5735)	5.0	-	①	②	③	22.0	17.0	17.0
	G/P	C	6.2 (6210)	7.0	-	①	②	③	22.0	25.5	25.5
	G/P	J	6.2 (6210)	7.0	-	①	②	③	22.0	25.5	25.5
	P	F	6.5 (6473)	7.0	-	①	②	③	22.0	24.0	⑤
	G/P	W	7.4 (7440)	6.0	-	①	②	③	22.0	23.0	23.0
	G/P	N	7.4 (7440)	6.0	-	①	②	③	22.0	23.0	23.0
1988	G/P	Z	4.3 (4293)	5.0	①	①	②	③	22.0	11.0	11.0
	G	H	5.0 (4999)	5.0	①	①	②	③	22.0	17.0	17.0
	G/P	K	5.7 (5735)	5.0	①	①	②	③	22.0	17.0	17.0
	G/P	C	6.2 (6210)	7.0	-	①	②	③	22.0	25.5	25.5
	G/P	J	6.2 (6210)	7.0	-	①	②	③	22.0	25.5	25.5
	G/P	W	7.4 (7440)	6.0	-	①	②	③	22.0	23.0	23.0
	G/P	N	7.4 (7440)	6.0	-	①	②	③	22.0	23.0	23.0
1989	G/P	Z	4.3 (4293)	5.0	①	①	②	③	22.0	11.0	11.0
	G	H	5.0 (4999)	5.0	①	①	②	③	22.0	17.0	17.0
	G/P	K	5.7 (5735)	5.0	①	①	②	③	22.0	17.0	17.0
	G/P	C	6.2 (6210)	7.0	-	①	②	③	22.0	25.5	25.5
	G/P	J	6.2 (6210)	7.0	-	①	②	③	22.0	25.5	25.5
	G/P	W	7.4 (7440)	6.0	-	①	②	③	22.0	23.0	23.0
	G/P	N	7.4 (7440)	6.0	-	①	②	③	22.0	23.0	23.0
1990	G/P	Z	4.3 (4293)	5.0	①	①	②	③	22.0	11.0	11.0
	G	H	5.0 (4999)	5.0	①	①	②	③	22.0	17.0	17.0
	G/P	K	5.7 (5735)	5.0	①	①	②	③	22.0	17.0	17.0
	G/P	C	6.2 (6210)	7.0	-	①	②	③	22.0	25.5	25.5
	G/P	J	6.2 (6210)	7.0	-	①	②	③	22.0	25.5	25.5
	G/P	N	7.4 (7440)	7.0	-	①	②	③	22.0	23.0	23.0
1991	G/P	Z	4.3 (4293)	5.0	①	①	②	③	22.0	23.0	23.0
	G	H	5.0 (4999)	5.0	①	①	②	③	22.0	11.0	11.0
	G/P	K	5.7 (5735)	5.0	①	①	②	③	22.0	17.0	17.0
	G/P	C	6.2 (6210)	7.0	-	①	②	③	22.0	17.0	17.0
	G/P	J	6.2 (6210)	7.0	-	①	②	③	22.0	25.5	25.5
	G/P	N	7.4 (7440)	7.0	-	①	②	③	22.0	25.5	25.5
1992	G/P	Z	4.3 (4293)	5.0	-	①	②	③	22.0	23.0	23.0
	G	H	5.0 (4999)	5.0	-	①	②	③	22.0	23.0	23.0
	G/P	K	5.7 (5735)	5.0	-	①	②	③	22.0	11.0	11.0
	G	C	6.2 (6210)	7.0	-	①	②	③	22.0	17.0	17.0
	G/P	J	6.2 (6210)	7.0	-	①	②	③	22.0	17.0	17.0
	G/P	N	7.4 (7440)	7.0	-	①	②	③	22.0	25.5	25.5
1993	G/P	Z	4.3 (4293)	5.0	-	①	②	③	22.0 ④	25.5	25.5
	G	H	5.0 (4999)	5.0	-	①	②	③	22.0 ④	23.0	23.0
	G/P	K	5.7 (5735)	5.0	-	①	②	③	⑥	23.0	23.0
	G	C/J	6.2 (6210)	7.0	-	①	②	③	22.0 ④	24.0	⑤
	G/P	N	7.4 (7440)	6.0	-	①	②	⑦	⑧	24.5	⑤

88191C10

CAPACITIES

Year	Model	Engine ID/VIN	Engine Displacement Liters (cc)	Engine Filter (qts.)	Transmission 4-Spd	Transmission 5-Spd	Transmission Auto.	Drive Axle Rear	Fuel Tank (gal.)	Cooling System (qts.) w/AC	Cooling System (qts.) w/oAC
1994	G/P	Z	4.3 (4293)	5.0	-	①	②	③	22.0 ④	11.0	⑤
	G/P	H	5.0 (4999)	5.0	-	①	②	③	22.0 ④	17.0	⑤
	G	K	5.7 (5735)	5.0	-	①	②	③	22.0 ⑥	18.0	⑤
	G/P	F/P/Y	6.5 (6505)	7.0	-	①	②	③	22.0 ④	24.0	⑤
	G/P	N	7.4 (7440)	6.0	-	①	②	③	⑧	24.5	⑤
1995	G/P	Z	4.3 (4293)	5.0	-	①	②	③	22.0 ④	11.0	⑤
	G	H	5.0 (4999)	5.0	-	①	②	③	22.0 ④	17.0	⑤
	G/P	K	5.7 (5735)	5.0	-	①	②	③	⑩	18.0	⑤
	G/P	F/P/Y	6.5 (6505)	7.0	-	①	②	③	22.0 ④	24.0	⑤
	G/P	N	7.4 (7440)	6.0	-	①	②	③	⑧	24.5	⑤
1996	G/P	W	4.3 (4293)	5.0	-	①	②	③	22.0 ⑨	11.0	⑤
	G	M	5.0 (4999)	5.0	-	①	②	③	22.0 ⑨	17.0	⑤
	G/P	R	5.7 (5735)	5.0	-	①	②	③	⑨	18.0	⑤
	G/P	F/Y	6.5 (6374)	7.0	-	①	②	③	22.0 ⑨	24.0	⑤
	G/P	J	7.4 (7440)	6.0	-	①	②	③	⑧		⑤
1997	G/P	W	4.3 (4293)	5.0	-	①	②	③	22.0 ⑨	11.0	⑤
	G	M	5.0 (4999)	5.0	-	①	②	③	22.0 ⑨	17.0	⑤
	G/P	R	5.7 (5735)	5.0	-	①	②	③	⑨	18.0	⑤
	G/P	F/Y	6.5 (6374)	7.0	-	①	②	③	22.0 ⑨	24.0	⑤
	G/P	N/J	7.4 (7440)	6.0	-	①	②	③	⑧	24.5	⑤

① 117mm: 8.4 pts.
  85mm: 3.6 pts.
  New Venture gear 4500: 8.0 pts.
  New Venture gear 5LM60: 4.4 pts.

② 350C trans.: 6.3 pts.
  THM400 and 4L80 trans.: 9.0 pts.
  THM700 R4 and 4L60 trans.: 10.0 pts.
  THM700 R4 and 4L80-E trans.: 14.3 pts.

③ 8.5" ring gear: 4.2 pts.
  9.5" ring gear: 6.5 pts.
  9.75" ring gear: 6.0 pts.
  10.5" ring gear: 6.5 pts.

④ Available with 32 and 41 gallon tanks
⑤ Add three qts. with rear heater
⑥ Short bed: 20 gals
  Long bed: 34 gals.

⑦ 8.5" ring gear: 4.2 pts.
  9.5" ring gear: 6.5 pts.
  Chrevolet 10.5" ring gear: 6.5 pts.
  Dana 9.5" ring gear: 6.0 pts.
  Rockwell 12" ring gear: 12.5 pts.

⑧ Available with a variety of fuel tanks
⑨ Available with 31 and 40 gallon tanks
⑩ Short bed: 26 gals
  Long bed: 34 gals.

88191C11

ENGLISH TO METRIC CONVERSION: MASS (WEIGHT)

Current **mass** measurement is expressed in pounds and ounces (lbs. & ozs.). The metric unit of mass (or weight) is the kilogram (kg). Even although this table does not show conversion of masses (weights) larger than 15 lbs, it is easy to calculate larger units by following the data immediately below.

To convert ounces (oz.) to grams (g): multiply th number of ozs. by 28
To convert grams (g) to ounces (oz.): multiply the number of grams by .035

To convert pounds (lbs.) to kilograms (kg): multiply the number of lbs. by .45
To convert kilograms (kg) to pounds (lbs.): multiply the number of kilograms by 2.2

lbs	kg	lbs	kg	oz	kg	oz	kg
0.1	0.04	0.9	0.41	0.1	0.003	0.9	0.024
0.2	0.09	1	0.4	0.2	0.005	1	0.03
0.3	0.14	2	0.9	0.3	0.008	2	0.06
0.4	0.18	3	1.4	0.4	0.011	3	0.08
0.5	0.23	4	1.8	0.5	0.014	4	0.11
0.6	0.27	5	2.3	0.6	0.017	5	0.14
0.7	0.32	10	4.5	0.7	0.020	10	0.28
0.8	0.36	15	6.8	0.8	0.023	15	0.42

ENGLISH TO METRIC CONVERSION: TEMPERATURE

To convert Fahrenheit (°F) to Celsius (°C): take number of °F and subtract 32; multiply result by 5; divide result by 9

To convert Celsius (°C) to Fahrenheit (°F): take number of °C and multiply by 9; divide result by 5; add 32 to total

Fahrenheit (F)		Celsius (C)		Fahrenheit (F)		Celsius (C)		Fahrenheit (F)		Celsius (C)	
°F	°C	°C	°F	°F	°C	°C	°F	°F	°C	°C	°F
−40	−40	−38	−36.4	80	26.7	18	64.4	215	101.7	80	176
−35	−37.2	−36	−32.8	85	29.4	20	68	220	104.4	85	185
−30	−34.4	−34	−29.2	90	32.2	22	71.6	225	107.2	90	194
−25	−31.7	−32	−25.6	95	35.0	24	75.2	230	110.0	95	202
−20	−28.9	−30	−22	100	37.8	26	78.8	235	112.8	100	212
−15	−26.1	−28	−18.4	105	40.6	28	82.4	240	115.6	105	221
−10	−23.3	−26	−14.8	110	43.3	30	86	245	118.3	110	230
−5	−20.6	−24	−11.2	115	46.1	32	89.6	250	121.1	115	239
0	−17.8	−22	−7.6	120	48.9	34	93.2	255	123.9	120	248
1	−17.2	−20	−4	125	51.7	36	96.8	260	126.6	125	257
2	−16.7	−18	−0.4	130	54.4	38	100.4	265	129.4	130	266
3	−16.1	−16	3.2	135	57.2	40	104	270	132.2	135	275
4	−15.6	−14	6.8	140	60.0	42	107.6	275	135.0	140	284
5	−15.0	−12	10.4	145	62.8	44	112.2	280	137.8	145	293
10	−12.2	−10	14	150	65.6	46	114.8	285	140.6	150	302
15	−9.4	−8	17.6	155	68.3	48	118.4	290	143.3	155	311
20	−6.7	−6	21.2	160	71.1	50	122	295	146.1	160	320
25	−3.9	−4	24.8	165	73.9	52	125.6	300	148.9	165	329
30	−1.1	−2	28.4	170	76.7	54	129.2	305	151.7	170	338
35	1.7	0	32	175	79.4	56	132.8	310	154.4	175	347
40	4.4	2	35.6	180	82.2	58	136.4	315	157.2	180	356
45	7.2	4	39.2	185	85.0	60	140	320	160.0	185	365
50	10.0	6	42.8	190	87.8	62	143.6	325	162.8	190	374
55	12.8	8	46.4	195	90.6	64	147.2	330	165.6	195	383
60	15.6	10	50	200	93.3	66	150.8	335	168.3	200	392
65	18.3	12	53.6	205	96.1	68	154.4	340	171.1	205	401
70	21.1	14	57.2	210	98.9	70	158	345	173.9	210	410
75	23.9	16	60.8	212	100.0	75	167	350	176.7	215	414

TCCS1C01

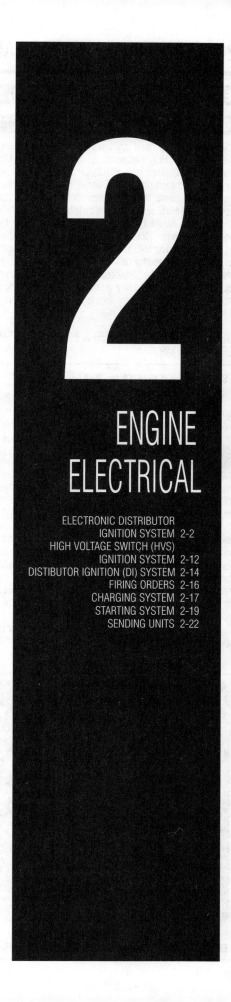

2

ENGINE
ELECTRICAL

ELECTRONIC DISTRIBUTOR IGNITION SYSTEM

General Information

There are four general ignition systems used on these vehicles: High Energy Ignition (HEI), Electronic Spark Timing (EST), High Voltage Switch (HVS) and Distributor Ignition (DI) systems. The HEI and EST systems are very similar to each other and differ more in nomenclature than anything else. These systems use distributors that contain pickups and electronic modules. The HVS system uses a distributor that contains nothing but a rotor and cap. All the HVS does is distribute the spark to the appropriate cylinder; the Engine Control Module (ECM) takes care of the rest of the timing parameters. The HVS distributor does contain a camshaft position sensor, but it is not used for timing determination. The Distributor Ignition (DI) system consists of the distributor, Hall effect switch (camshaft position sensor), ignition coil, secondary wires, spark plugs, knock sensor and crankshaft position sensor. The system is regulated by the Vehicle Control Module (VCM).

HIGH ENERGY IGNITION (HEI) & ELECTRONIC SPARK TIMING (EST) SYSTEMS

◆ See Figures 1 thru 12 (p. 2–8)

The HEI/EST system operates in basically the same manner as the conventional points type ignition system, with the exception of the type of switching device used. A toothed iron timer core is mounted on the distributor shaft, which rotates inside of an electronic pole piece. The pole piece has internal teeth (corresponding to those on the timer core) and contains a permanent magnet and pick-up coil (not to be confused with the ignition coil). The pole piece senses the magnetic field of the timer core teeth and sends a signal to the ignition module, which electronically controls the primary coil voltage. The ignition coil operates in basically the same manner as a conventional ignition coil (though the ignition coils DO NOT interchange).

Some distributors use a Hall effect device to act as the switching device. This type of distributor uses a slotted vane that passes between a magnet and the Hall effect device to signal when to initiate a spark. The Hall effect device is a solid state sensor that acts as a magnetic activated switch. The slots in the vane effectively change the magnetic field set up by the magnet, causing the Hall effect device to switch on and off. This signal is sent to the ignition module and processed in the same way that the above mentioned pick-up coil type distributor does.

The 4.3L engines through 1995 use a knock sensor to retard the timing when knock is sensed. The knock sensor is located on the block and it sends a signal to the Electronic Spark Control (ESC) module located on a bracket at the back of the engine. The ESC module in turn sends a signal to the ECM to retard the timing.

➡**The HEI/EST systems contain a capacitor within the distributor, which is primarily used for radio interference suppression purposes.**

None of the electrical components used in the HEI systems are adjustable. If a component is found to be defective, it must be replaced.

IGNITION COIL

Carbureted Engines

1. Connect an ohmmeter between the **TACH** and **BAT** terminals in the distributor cap. The primary coil resistance should be less than one ohm (zero or nearly zero).
2. To check the coil secondary resistance, connect an ohmmeter between the rotor button and the **BAT** terminal. Then connect the ohmmeter between the ground terminal and the rotor button. The resistance in both cases should be between 6000 and 30,000 ohms.
3. Replace the coil only if the readings in Step 1 and 2 are infinite.

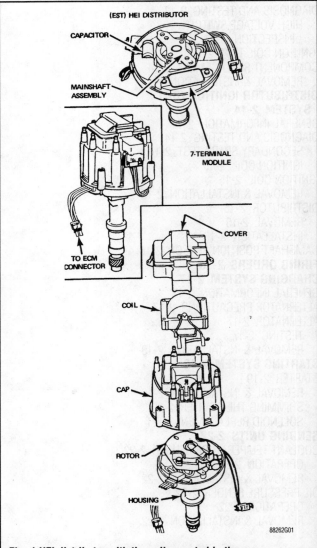

Fig. 1 HEI distributor with the coil mounted in the cap

EST distributor at home nestled at the back of the 4.3L engine

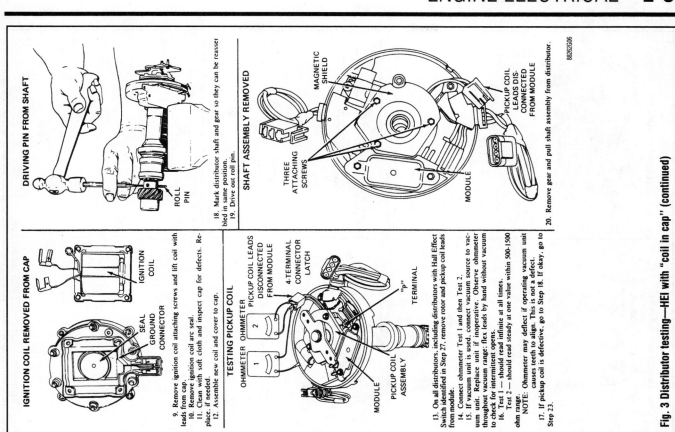

88262G06

DRIVING PIN FROM SHAFT

ROLL PIN

18. Mark distributor shaft and gear so they can be reassembled in same position.
19. Drive out roll pin.

SHAFT ASSEMBLY REMOVED

MAGNETIC SHIELD

PICKUP COIL LEADS DISCONNECTED FROM MODULE

THREE ATTACHING SCREWS

MODULE

20. Remove gear and pull shaft assembly from distributor.

IGNITION COIL REMOVED FROM CAP

IGNITION COIL

SEAL
GROUND
CONNECTOR

9. Remove ignition coil attaching screws and lift coil with leads from cap.
10. Remove ignition coil arc seal.
11. Clean with soft cloth and inspect cap for defects. Replace, if needed.
12. Assemble new coil and cover to cap.

TESTING PICKUP COIL

OHMMETER OHMMETER

PICKUP COIL LEADS DISCONNECTED FROM MODULE

4-TERMINAL CONNECTOR LATCH

"P" TERMINAL

MODULE

PICKUP COIL ASSEMBLY

13. On all distributors, including distributors with Hall Effect Switch identified in Step 27, remove rotor and pickup coil leads from module.
14. Connect ohmmeter Test 1 and then Test 2.
15. If vacuum unit is used, connect vacuum source to vacuum unit. Replace unit if inoperative. Observe ohmmeter throughout vacuum range: flex leads by hand without vacuum to check for intermittent opens.
16. Test 1 — should read infinite at all times.
    Test 2 — should read steady at one value within 500-1500 ohm range.
    NOTE: Ohmmeter may deflect if operating vacuum unit causes teeth to align. This is not a defect.
17. If pickup coil is defective, go to Step 18. If okay, go to Step 23.

Fig. 3 Distributor testing—HEI with "coil in cap" (continued)

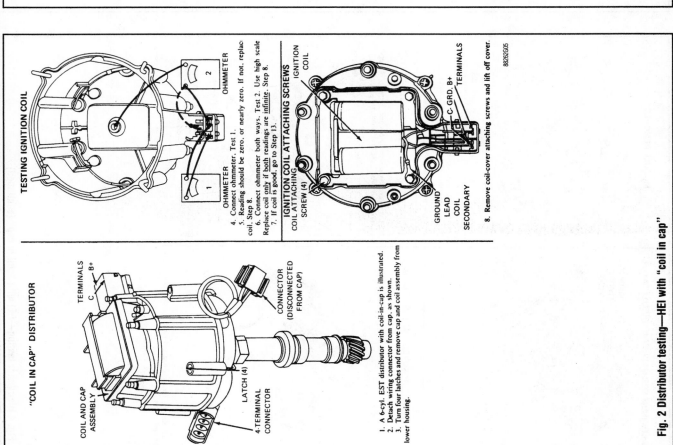

88262G05

TESTING IGNITION COIL

OHMMETER 2

OHMMETER 1

4. Connect ohmmeter. Test 1.
5. Reading should be zero, or nearly zero. If not, replace coil. Step 8.
6. Connect ohmmeter both ways. Test 2. Use high scale. Replace coil only if both readings are infinite. Step 8.
7. If coil is good, go to Step 13.

IGNITION COIL ATTACHING SCREWS

IGNITION COIL

COIL ATTACHING SCREW (4)

TERMINALS
C. GRD. B+

GROUND LEAD COIL SECONDARY

8. Remove coil-cover attaching screws and lift off cover.

"COIL IN CAP" DISTRIBUTOR

TERMINALS
C   B+

COIL AND CAP ASSEMBLY

CONNECTOR (DISCONNECTED FROM CAP)

LATCH (4)

4-TERMINAL CONNECTOR

1. A 6-cyl. EST distributor with coil-in-cap is illustrated.
2. Detach wiring connector from cap, as shown.
3. Turn four latches and remove cap and coil assembly from lower housing.

Fig. 2 Distributor testing—HEI with "coil in cap"

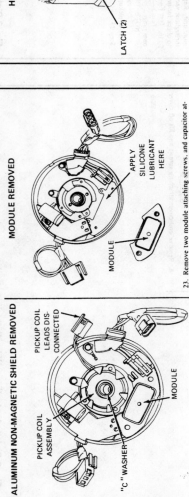

MODULE REMOVED

MODULE

APPLY SILICONE LUBRICANT HERE

23. Remove two module attaching screws, and capacitor attaching screw. Lift module, capacitor and harness assembly from base.
24. Disconnect wiring harness from module.
25. Check module with an approved module tester.
26. Install module, wiring harness, and capacitor assembly. Use silicone lubricant on housing under module.

DISTRIBUTOR WITH HALL EFFECT SWITCH

27. The procedures previously covered, Steps 1 - 26, apply also to distributors with Hall Effect Switches.

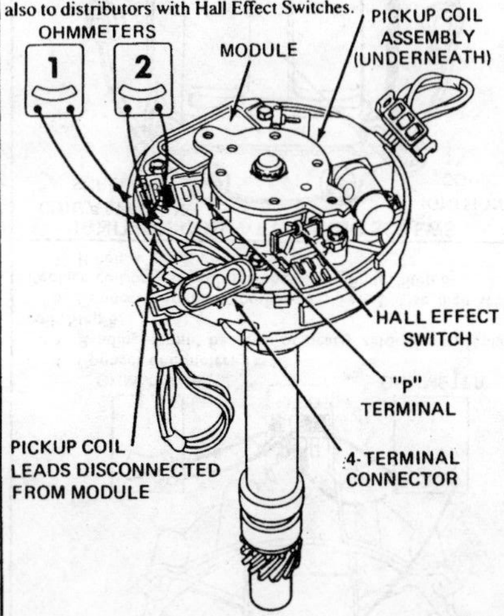

HALL EFFECT SWITCH

"P" TERMINAL

4-TERMINAL CONNECTOR

PICKUP COIL ASSEMBLY (UNDERNEATH)

MODULE

1 OHMMETERS 2

PICKUP COIL LEADS DISCONNECTED FROM MODULE

ALUMINUM NON-MAGNETIC SHIELD REMOVED

PICKUP COIL LEADS DISCONNECTED

PICKUP COIL ASSEMBLY

MODULE

"C" WASHER

21. Remove three attaching screws and remove magnetic shield.

PICKUP COIL REMOVED AND DISASSEMBLED

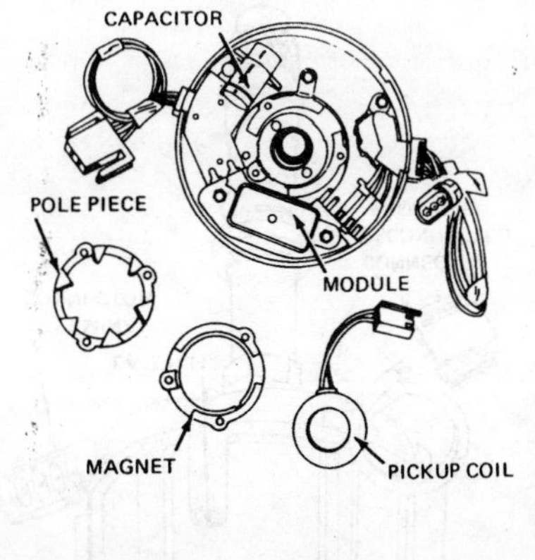

MODULE

PICKUP COIL

CAPACITOR

POLE PIECE

MAGNET

22. Remove retaining ring and remove pickup coil, magnet and pole piece.

88262G07

Fig. 4 Distributor testing—HEI with "coil in cap" (continued)

TESTING PICKUP COIL

PICKUP COIL ASSEMBLY

PICKUP COIL LEADS DISCONNECTED FROM MODULE

MODULE

1 OHMMETER

2 OHMMETER

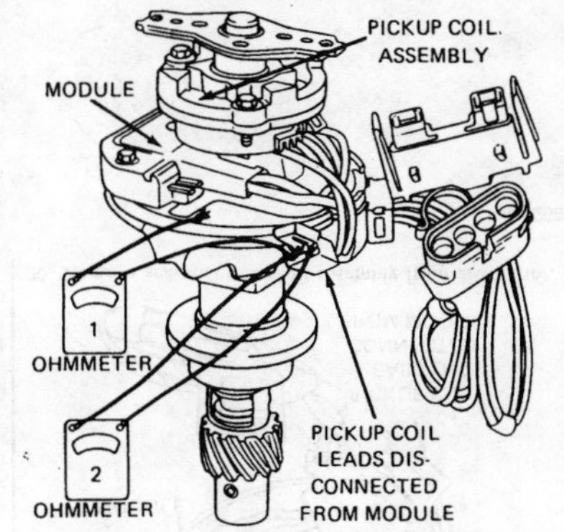

3. Remove rotor and pickup coil leads from module.
4. Connect ohmmeter Part 1 and Part 2.
5. If vacuum unit is used, connect vacuum source to vacuum unit. Replace vacuum unit if inoperative.
6. Observe ohmmeter throughout vacuum range: if no vacuum unit is used, flex leads by hand to check for intermittent opens.

Step 1 — Should read infinite at all times. If not, pickup coil is defective.

Step 2 — Should read one steady value between 500-1500 ohms as vacuum is operated, or as leads are flexed by hand. If not, pickup coil is defective.

7. Ohmmeter may deflect if operating vacuum unit causes teeth to align. This is not a defect.

DRIVING PIN FROM SHAFT

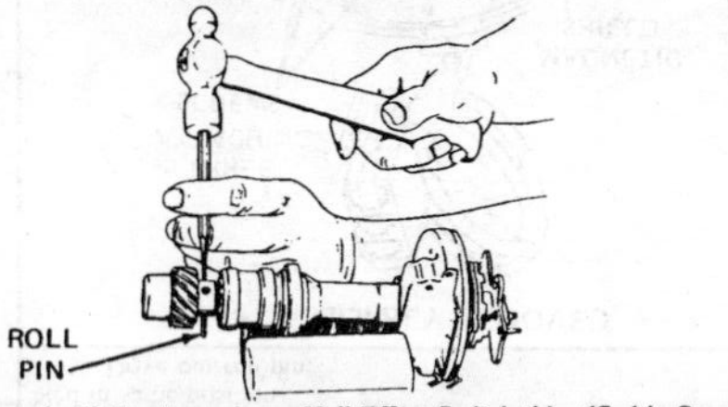

ROLL PIN

8. If distributor has a Hall Effect Switch (identified in Step 12), remove this switch by detaching screws. Then drive roll pin from gear and remove shaft assembly. Mark gear and shaft for correct reassembly.

HEI/EST DISTRIBUTOR

IGNITION COIL CONNECTOR TERMINALS LATCH B+

C-

4-TERMINAL CONNECTOR

LATCH (2)

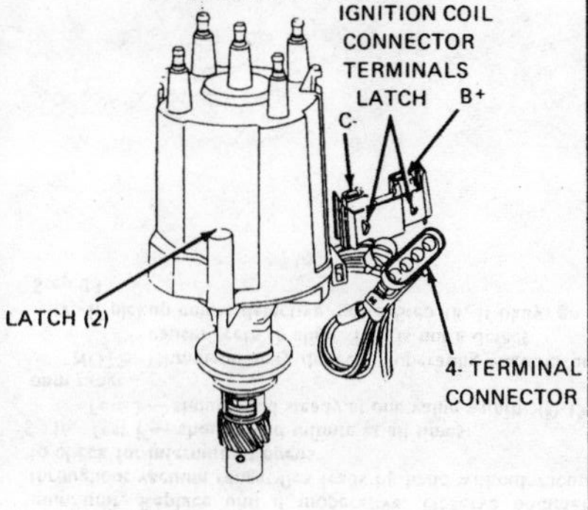

1. A typical distributor used with a separately mounted coil is shown.

TESTING IGNITION COIL

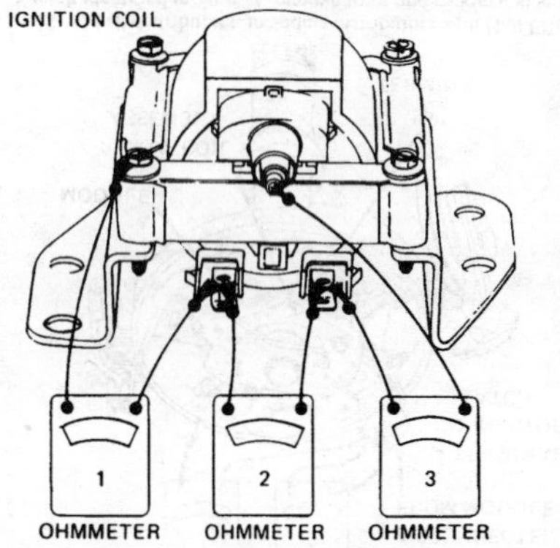

IGNITION COIL

1 OHMMETER

2 OHMMETER

3 OHMMETER

2. Check ignition coil with ohmmeter for opens and grounds:

Step 1. — Use high scale. Should read very high (infinite). If not, replace coil.

Step 2. — Use low scale. Should read very low or zero. If not, replace coil.

Step 3. — Use high scale. Should not read infinite. If it does, replace coil.

88262G08

Fig. 5 Distributor testing—HEI with remote coil

IGNITION SYSTEM CHECK

(REMOTE COIL / SEALED MODULE CONNECTOR DISTRIBUTOR) ALL ENGINES EXCEPT 2.5L TRUCK

Test Description: Numbers below refer to circled numbers on the diagnostic chart.

1. Two wires are checked, to ensure that an open is not present in a spark plug wire.

1A. If spark occurs with EST connector disconnected, pick-up coil output is too low for EST operation.

2. A spark indicates the problem must be the distributor cap or rotor.

3. Normally, there should be battery voltage at the "C" and "+" terminals. Low voltage would indicate an open or a high resistance circuit from the distributor to the coil or ignition switch. If "C" terminal voltage was low, but "+" terminal voltage is 10 volts or more, circuit from "C" terminal to ignition coil or ignition coil primary winding is open.

4. Checks for a shorted module or grounded circuit from the ignition coil to the module. The distributor module should be turned "OFF," so normal voltage should be about 12 volts. If the module is turned "ON," the voltage would be low, but above 1 volt. This could cause the ignition coil to fail from excessive heat. With an open ignition coil primary winding, a small amount of voltage will leak through the module from the "Bat." to the "tach" terminal.

5. Applying a voltage (1.5 to 8 volts) to module terminal "P" should turn the module "ON" and the "tach" terminal voltage should drop to about 7-9 volts. This test will determine whether the module or coil is faulty or if the pick-up coil is not generating the proper signal to turn the module "ON." This test can be performed by using a DC battery with a rating of 1.5 to 8 volts. The use of the test light is mainly to allow the "P" terminal to be probed more easily. Some digital multi-meters can also be used to trigger the module by selecting ohms, usually the diode position. In this position the meter may have a voltage across it's terminals which can be used to trigger the module. The voltage in the ohm's position can be checked by using a second meter or by checking the manufacturer's specification of the tool being used.

6. This should turn "OFF" the module and cause a spark. If no spark occurs, the fault is most likely in the ignition coil because most module problems would have been found before this point in the procedure. A module tester could determine which is at fault.

Fig. 7 Ignition system check—4.3L engine except with HVS

DISTRIBUTOR WITH HALL EFFECT SWITCH

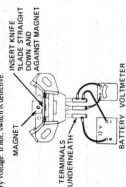

12. If distributor has a Hall Effect Switch, this switch was removed in Step 8.
13. The procedures previously covered, Steps 1-11, apply also to distributors with Hall Effect Switches.

TESTING HALL EFFECT SWITCH

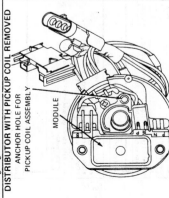

INSERT KNIFE BLADE STRAIGHT DOWN AND AGAINST MAGNET

14. Connect 12-volt battery and voltmeter to switch, carefully note polarity markings.

With knife blade, voltmeter should read less than 0.5 volts. If not, switch is defective. With knife blade, voltmeter should read within 0.5 volts of battery voltage. If not, switch is defective.

REASSEMBLY

17. Wipe distributor base and module clean, apply silicone lubricant between module and base for heat dissipation.
18. Attach module to base. Attach wiring connectors to module.
19. Assemble pickup and thin "C" washer.
20. Assemble shaft, gear parts and roll pin.
21. If fused, assemble Hall Effect Switch.
22. Spin shaft to insure that teeth do not touch.
23. Loosen, then re-tighten pickup coil teeth and Hall Effect Switch teeth, if used, to eliminate contact.
24. Install rotor and cap.

REMOVE PICKUP COIL

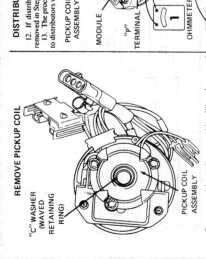

9. To remove pickup coil, remove thin "C" washer (waved retaining ring).

DISTRIBUTOR WITH PICKUP COIL REMOVED

10. Lift pickup coil assembly straight up to remove from distributor.

REMOVING MODULE

11. Disconnect wiring connectors from module. Remove two screws to remove module. Test module with an approved module tester.

Fig. 6 Distributor testing—HEI with remote coil (continued)

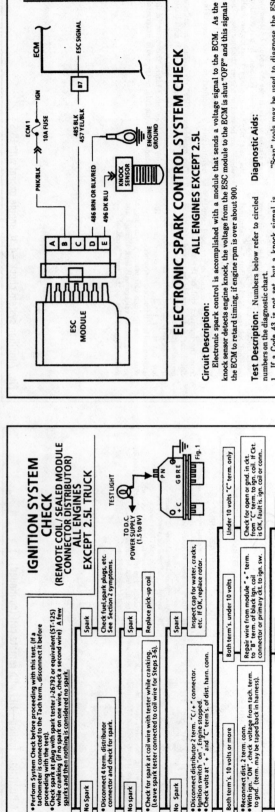

ELECTRONIC SPARK CONTROL SYSTEM CHECK
ALL ENGINES EXCEPT 2.5L

Circuit Description:

Electronic spark control is accomplished with a module that sends a voltage signal to the ECM. As the knock sensor detects engine knock, the voltage from the ESC module to the ECM is shut "OFF" and this signals the ECM to retard timing, if engine rpm is over about 900.

Test Description: Numbers below refer to circled numbers on the diagnostic chart.

1. If a Code 43 is not set, but a knock signal is indicated while running at 1500 rpm, listen for an internal engine noise. Under a no load condition there should not be any detonation, and if knock is indicated, an internal engine problem may exist.

2. Usually a knock signal can be generated by tapping on the right exhaust manifold. This test can also be performed at idle. Test number 1 was run at 1500 rpm to determine if a constant knock signal was present, which would affect engine performance.

3. This tests whether the knock signal is due to the sensor, a basic engine problem, or the ESC module.

4. If the module ground circuit is faulty, the ESC module will not function correctly. The test light should light indicating the ground circuit is OK.

5. Contacting CKT 496, with a test light to 12 volts, should generate a knock signal to determine whether the knock sensor is faulty, or the ESC module can't recognize a knock signal.

Diagnostic Aids:

"Scan" tools may be used to diagnose the ESC system. The knock signal can be monitored to see if the knock sensor is detecting a knock condition and if the ESC module is functioning, knock signal should display "YES", whenever detonation is present. For 2.5L engines, the knock retard position on the "Scan" displays the amount of spark retard the ECM is commanding. The ECM can retard the timing up to 20 degrees.

This check should be used after other causes of spark knock have been checked such as engine timing, EGR systems, engine temperature or excessive engine noise.

88262C41

Fig. 9 Ignition system check—4.3L engine except with HVS (continued)

Fig. 8 Ignition system check—4.3L engine except with HVS (continued)

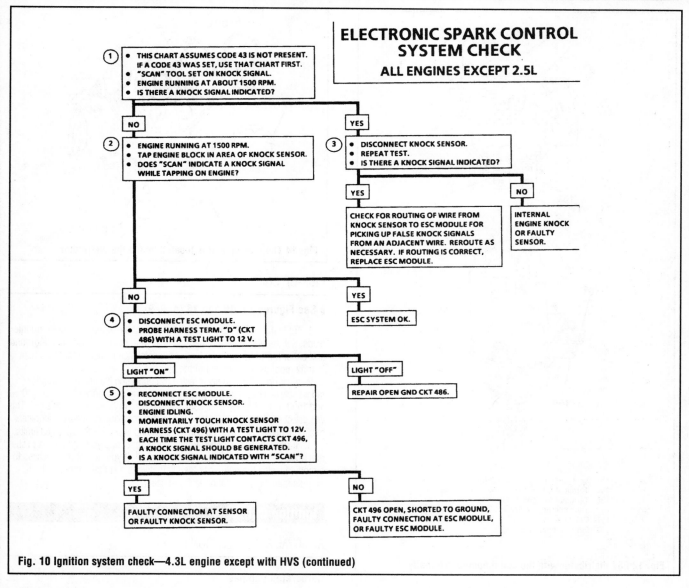

ELECTRONIC SPARK CONTROL SYSTEM CHECK
ALL ENGINES EXCEPT 2.5L

① • THIS CHART ASSUMES CODE 43 IS NOT PRESENT. IF A CODE 43 WAS SET, USE THAT CHART FIRST.
• "SCAN" TOOL SET ON KNOCK SIGNAL.
• ENGINE RUNNING AT ABOUT 1500 RPM.
• IS THERE A KNOCK SIGNAL INDICATED?

NO

② • ENGINE RUNNING AT 1500 RPM.
• TAP ENGINE BLOCK IN AREA OF KNOCK SENSOR.
• DOES "SCAN" INDICATE A KNOCK SIGNAL WHILE TAPPING ON ENGINE?

YES

③ • DISCONNECT KNOCK SENSOR.
• REPEAT TEST.
• IS THERE A KNOCK SIGNAL INDICATED?

YES

CHECK FOR ROUTING OF WIRE FROM KNOCK SENSOR TO ESC MODULE FOR PICKING UP FALSE KNOCK SIGNALS FROM AN ADJACENT WIRE. REROUTE AS NECESSARY. IF ROUTING IS CORRECT, REPLACE ESC MODULE.

NO

INTERNAL ENGINE KNOCK OR FAULTY SENSOR.

NO

④ • DISCONNECT ESC MODULE.
• PROBE HARNESS TERM. "D" (CKT 486) WITH A TEST LIGHT TO 12 V.

YES

ESC SYSTEM OK.

LIGHT "ON"

⑤ • RECONNECT ESC MODULE.
• DISCONNECT KNOCK SENSOR.
• ENGINE IDLING.
• MOMENTARILY TOUCH KNOCK SENSOR HARNESS (CKT 496) WITH A TEST LIGHT TO 12V.
• EACH TIME THE TEST LIGHT CONTACTS CKT 496, A KNOCK SIGNAL SHOULD BE GENERATED.
• IS A KNOCK SIGNAL INDICATED WITH "SCAN"?

LIGHT "OFF"

REPAIR OPEN GND CKT 486.

YES

FAULTY CONNECTION AT SENSOR OR FAULTY KNOCK SENSOR.

NO

CKT 496 OPEN, SHORTED TO GROUND, FAULTY CONNECTION AT ESC MODULE, OR FAULTY ESC MODULE.

Fig. 10 Ignition system check—4.3L engine except with HVS (continued)

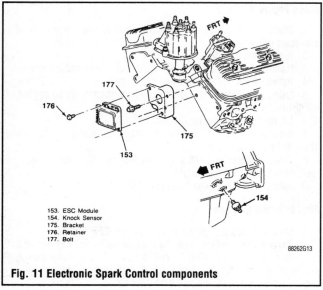

176
177
175
153
154

153. ESC Module
154. Knock Sensor
175. Bracket
176. Retainer
177. Bolt

88262G13

Fig. 11 Electronic Spark Control components

➡ **These resistance checks will not disclose shorted coil windings. This condition can be detected only with scope analysis or a suitably designed coil tester. If these instruments are unavailable, replace the coil with a known good coil as a final coil test.**

Fuel Injected Engines

♦ See Figure 13 (p. 8)

1. Tag and disconnect the distributor lead and wiring from the coil.
2. Connect an ohmmeter as shown in Step 1 of the accompanying illustration. Place the ohmmeter on the high scale. The reading should be infinite.
3. Connect an ohmmeter as shown in Step 2 of the same illustration. Place the ohmmeter on the low scale. The reading should be very low or zero. If not, replace the coil.
4. Connect an ohmmeter as shown in Step 3 of the same illustration. Place the ohmmeter on the high scale. The meter should not read infinite. If it does, replace the coil.
5. Connect the distributor lead and wiring.

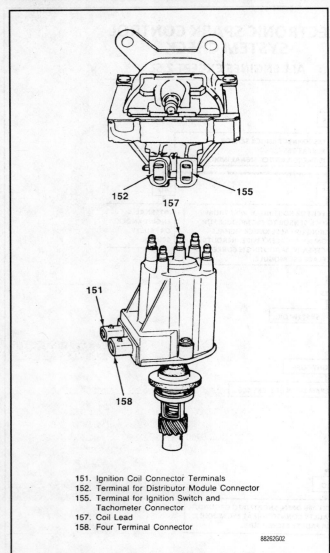

151. Ignition Coil Connector Terminals
152. Terminal for Distributor Module Connector
155. Terminal for Ignition Switch and
     Tachometer Connector
157. Coil Lead
158. Four Terminal Connector

88262G02

Fig. 12 EST distributor with the coil mounted externally

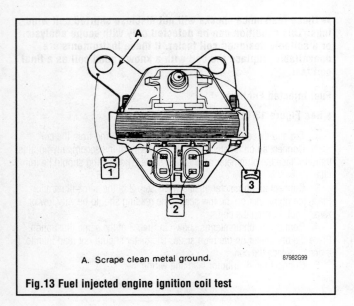

A. Scrape clean metal ground.

87982G99

Fig.13 Fuel injected engine ignition coil test

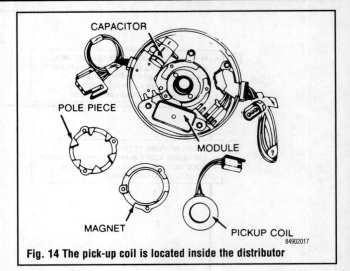

84902017

Fig. 14 The pick-up coil is located inside the distributor

PICK-UP COIL

▶ **See Figures 14, 15 and 16 (p. 8–9)**

1. To test the pick-up coil, first disconnect the white and green module leads. Set the ohmmeter on the high scale and connect it between a ground and either the white or green lead. Any resistance measurement less than infinity requires replacement of the pick-up coil.

2. Pick-up coil continuity is tested by connecting the ohmmeter (on low range) between the white and green leads. Normal resistance is between 500 and 1500 ohms. Move the vacuum advance arm while performing this test. This will detect any break in coil continuity. Such a condition can cause intermittent misfiring. Replace the pick-up coil if the reading is outside the specified limits.

3. If no defects have been found at this time, and you still have a problem, then the module will have to be checked. If you do not have access to a module tester, the only possible alternative is a substitution test. If the module fails the substitution test, replace it.

Ignition Coil

REMOVAL & INSTALLATION

Carbureted Engines

▶ **See Figure 17 (p. 9)**

1. Disconnect the feed and module wire terminal connectors from the distributor cap.
2. Remove the ignition set retainer.
3. Remove the 4 coil cover-to-distributor cap screws and coil cover.
4. Remove the 4 coil-to-distributor cap screws.
5. Using a blunt drift, press the coil wire spade terminals up and out of the distributor cap.
6. Lift the coil up out of the distributor cap.
7. Remove and clean the coil spring, rubber seal washer and coil cavity of the distributor cap.
8. Coat the rubber seal with a dielectric lubricant furnished in the replacement ignition coil package.
9. Reverse the above procedures to install.

Fuel Injected Engines

1. Make sure that the ignition switch is in the **OFF** position.
2. Tag and disconnect the coil wire and the connector on the side of the coil.
3. Remove the nuts holding the coil and bracket assembly to the engine and lift out the coil. The coil is riveted to the bracket; to remove it will require drilling the rivets and punching them out.

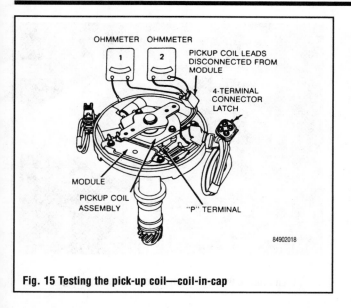

Fig. 15 Testing the pick-up coil—coil-in-cap

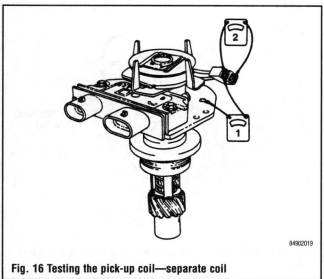

Fig. 16 Testing the pick-up coil—separate coil

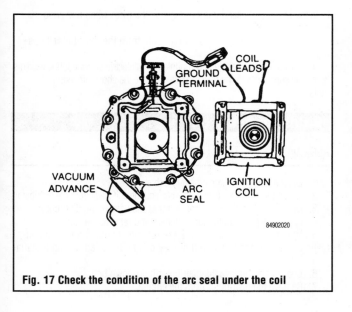

Fig. 17 Check the condition of the arc seal under the coil

Be careful not to break the locktabs when unplugging the connectors

4. Position the coil on the engine and tighten the nuts.
5. Attach the coil wire and electrical connectors.

Vacuum Advance Unit

REMOVAL & INSTALLATION

1. Remove the distributor cap and rotor as previously described.
2. Disconnect the vacuum hose from the vacuum advance unit.
3. Remove the two vacuum advance retaining screws, pull the advance unit outward, rotate and disengage the operating rod from its tang.
4. Reverse the above procedure to install.

Ignition Module

REMOVAL & INSTALLATION

▶ **See Figure 18**

1. Remove the distributor cap and rotor as previously described.
2. Disconnect the harness connector and pickup coil spade connectors

Disengage the distributor feed wires . . .

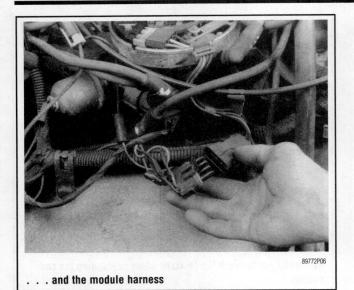

89772P06

. . . and the module harness

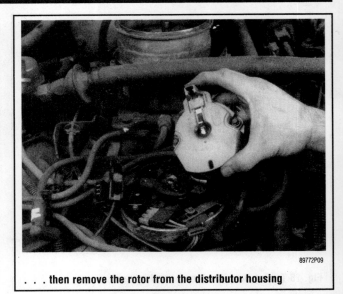

89772P09

. . . then remove the rotor from the distributor housing

89772P07

After unfastening the spark plug wires and retaining screws, remove the distributor cap

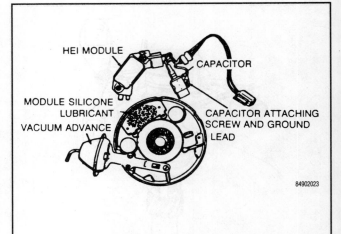

84902023

Fig. 18 Be sure to coat the mating surfaces with silicone lubricant

89772P08

Unfasten the rotor retaining screws . . .

from the module. Be careful not to damage the wires when removing the connector.

3. Remove the two screws and module from the distributor housing.

4. Coat the bottom of the new module with dielectric silicone lubricant. This is usually supplied with the new module. Reverse the above procedure to install.

Distributor

REMOVAL

1. Disconnect the negative battery cable.
2. Tag and remove the spark plug wires and the coil leads from the distributor.
3. Disengage the electrical connector at the base of the distributor.
4. Loosen the distributor cap fasteners and remove the cap.
5. Using a marker, matchmark the rotor-to-housing and housing-to-engine block positions so that they can be matched during installation.
6. Loosen and remove the distributor hold-down bolt.
7. Remove the distributor from the engine.

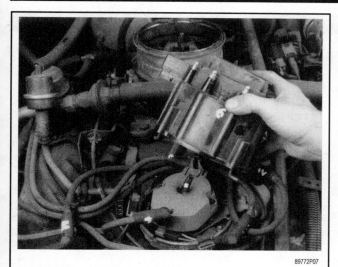

Unfasten and remove the distributor cap

Using a distributor wrench, unfasten the hold-down bolt and clamp

If necessary, unfasten the retaining screws and remove the rotor

Remove the distributor from the engine

INSTALLATION

Engine Not Disturbed

1. Install the distributor in the engine making sure that the matchmarks are properly aligned.
2. Install and tighten the hold-down bolt.
3. Install the distributor cap and engage the electrical connector at the base of the distributor.
4. Install the spark plug wires and coil leads.
5. Connect the negative battery cable.

Engine Disturbed

1. Remove the No. 1 cylinder spark plug. Turn the engine using a socket wrench on the large bolt on the front of the crankshaft pulley. Place a finger near the No. 1 spark plug hole and turn the crankshaft until the piston reaches Top Dead Center (TDC). As the engine approaches TDC, you will feel air being expelled by the No. 1 cylinder. The timing mark on the crankshaft pulley should now be aligned with the **0** mark on the timing scale. If the position is not being met, turn the engine another full turn (360 degrees). Once the engine's position is correct, install the spark plug.
2. Turn the rotor so that it will point to the No. 1 terminal of the distributor cap.
3. Install the distributor in the engine. It may be necessary to turn the rotor a little in either direction, in order to engage the gears.
4. Tap the starter a few times to ensure that the oil pump shaft is mated to the distributor shaft.
5. Bring the engine to TDC again and check that the rotor is pointed toward the No. 1 terminal of the cap. If the marks are all aligned, install and tighten the hold-down bolt.
6. Install the cap and fasten the mounting screws.
7. Engage the electrical connections and the spark plug wires.

HIGH VOLTAGE SWITCH (HVS) IGNITION SYSTEM

General Information

▶ **See Figures 19, 20, 21, 22 and 23**

The High Voltage Switch (HVS) ignition system is used only on the 1995 4.3L (VIN W) engine. The ignition system is controlled by the Vehicle Control Module (VCM-A). The VCM-A obtains information from various engine sensors, then uses it to compute the desired spark timing, as well as control the dwell and firing of the ignition coil by way of an ignition control line to the coil driver. The High Voltage Switch (HVS) assembly resembles a distributor, containing both a cap and rotor. But, unlike a distributor ignition system, ignition timing is preset and cannot be adjusted because the HVS is mounted in a fixed position (it cannot be rotated). The HVS provides spark at exactly the right time to ignite the air/fuel mixture, producing peak performance and fuel economy. The HVS system is comprised of the following parts:

- Vehicle Control Module (VCM-A)
- Crankshaft position sensor
- Ignition coil driver module
- Ignition coil
- High voltage switch

The Vehicle Control Module (VCM-A, often referred to in the past as an ECM) is located on the right-hand side fenderwell of the vehicle. It is the control center for fuel emissions, automatic transmission control functions and the anti-lock brake system. The VCM-A constantly monitors information from sensors in the engine and controls the component systems. It is designed to process the various input information, then send the necessary electrical responses. The ignition module that is used on the Distributor Ignition (DI) system is not used. All Ignition Control (IC) and bypass functions are controlled by the VCM-A.

The Crankshaft Position Sensor (CKP) is a digital sensor that provides reference information to the VCM-A for spark and fuel delivery. It is located in the front timing chain cover and is perpendicular to the crankshaft target wheel. There is an air gap between the sensor and the target wheel which is not adjustable. The target wheel has three slots 60ʃ apart and is keyed to the crankshaft. As the target wheel rotates, the slots passing by the sensor create a change in the magnetic field of the sensor which results in an induced voltage pulse. One revolution of the crankshaft results in three

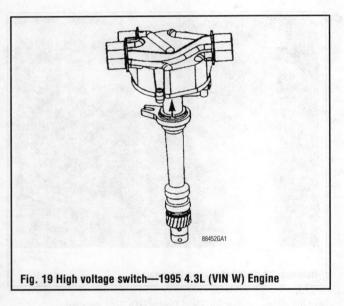

Fig. 19 High voltage switch—1995 4.3L (VIN W) Engine

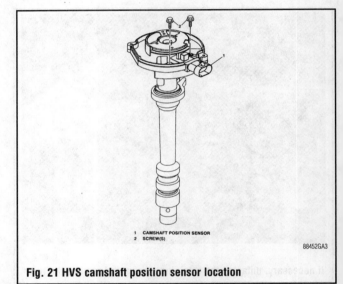

1 CAMSHAFT POSITION SENSOR
2 SCREW(S)

88452GA3

Fig. 21 HVS camshaft position sensor location

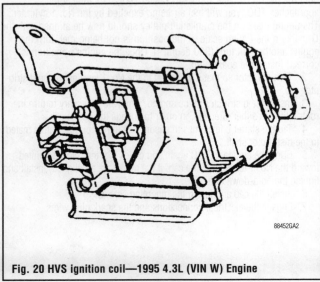

88452GA2

Fig. 20 HVS ignition coil—1995 4.3L (VIN W) Engine

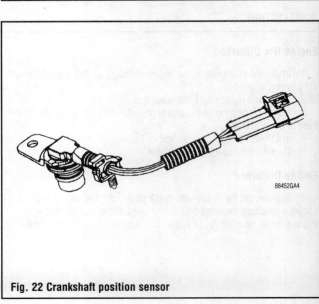

88452GA4

Fig. 22 Crankshaft position sensor

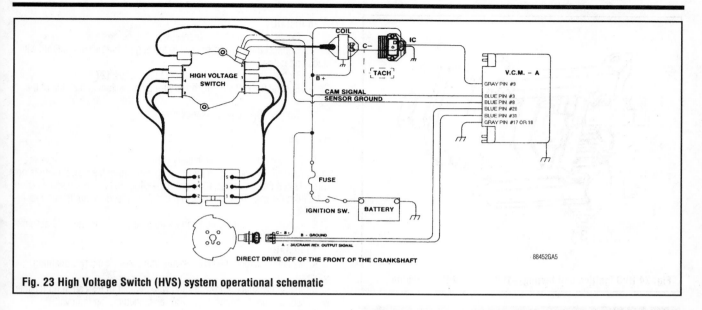

Fig. 23 High Voltage Switch (HVS) system operational schematic

pulses (3x signal). From these pulses, the VCM-A is able to determine crankshaft position and engine speed. The VCM-A then activates the fuel injector and provides spark to the High Voltage Switch. There is a very important relationship between the crankshaft position sensor and the target wheel in that the sensor must be perpendicular to the target wheel and have the precise air gap.

The Ignition Coil Driver (ICD) module is mounted on a bracket next to the ignition coil. The ICD controls the communication between the ignition coil and the VCM-A. The VCM-A sends a signal to the ICD commanding it to turn current on and off to the ignition coil at the proper times.

The High Voltage Switch is an assembly that looks similar to a distributor. It contains the Camshaft Position (CMP) sensor, cap, rotor and shaft. The High Voltage Switch shaft is driven by the camshaft and rotates like a distributor, providing spark to the correct cylinder via the cap and rotor.

The Camshaft Position (CMP) sensor is located within the HVS. Its operation is very similar to the Crankshaft Position (CKP) sensor, but it provides one pulse per camshaft revolution (1x signal). The VCM-A uses this signal, along with the crankshaft position, to determine which cylinder(s) are misfiring. It connects to the VCM-A through the primary engine harness and provides cylinder identification. The VCM-A controls the dwell and firing of the ignition coil through an ignition control line to the coil driver.

➡**The Camshaft Position sensor does not have any effect on driveability. Its only purpose is to provide the VCM-A with cylinder identification and other needed information for misfire diagnostic trouble codes.**

HVS SERVICE PRECAUTIONS

- When making compression checks, disconnect the HVS electrical connector to disable the ignition and fuel injection system. Refer to Section 3 for compression check procedures.
- No periodic lubrication of the high voltage switch is required. Engine oil lubricates the lower bushing and the upper bushing is prelubricated and sealed.
- There is no manual dwell adjustment.
- The spark plug wires are made of a material which is very pliable and soft. It is very important to route the spark plug wires correctly to prevent chafing or cutting.

Diagnosis and Testing

HIGH VOLTAGE SWITCH INSPECTION

1. Visually inspect the HVS cap for cracks or tiny holes. Replace the cap if it is damaged or worn.
2. Check the metal terminals in the cap for corrosion. If any corrosion is found, scrape the terminals clean with a suitable scraping tool or replace the cap.
3. Inspect the HVS rotor for wear or burning at the outer terminal. A build-up of carbon on the terminal means the rotor has worn and needs to be replaced.
4. Check the HVS shaft for shaft-to-bushing looseness. Place the shaft in the housing. If the shaft wobbles, replace the housing and/or shaft.
5. Visually inspect the HVS housing for cracks or damage.

IGNITION COIL TEST

▶ **See Figure 24**

If the trouble has been narrowed down to one of the components in the ignition system, the following test can help pinpoint the problem. An ohmmeter with both high and low ranges should be used. This test is made with the negative battery cable disconnected.

1. Disconnect the high voltage switch lead and the wiring from the ignition coil.
2. Set the ohmmeter to the HIGH scale, then connect it to the coil, as shown in Step 1 of the illustration. The reading should be infinite. If not, verify a proper test connection to be assured of a true test result and, if still not infinite, replace the coil.
3. Set the ohmmeter to the LOW scale, then connect it as shown in Step 2 of the illustration. The reading should be very low or zero. If not, verify a proper test connection and replace the coil.
4. Set the ohmmeter on the HIGH scale, then connect it to the coil as shown in Step 3 of the illustration. The ohmmeter should NOT read infinite. If it does, verify the connection and replace the coil.
5. Reconnect the high voltage switch lead and wiring to the coil.

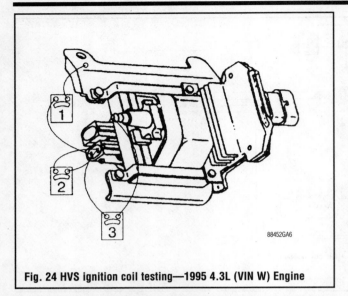

Fig. 24 HVS ignition coil testing—1995 4.3L (VIN W) Engine

Component Replacement

REMOVAL & INSTALLATION

Ignition Coil

1. Disconnect the negative battery cable.
2. Disengage the wiring connectors from the side of the coil.
3. Disconnect the coil wire.
4. Unfasten the nuts holding the coil bracket and coil to the engine bracket or manifold.
5. Drill and punch out the two rivets holding the coil to the bracket, then remove the bracket and the coil.

➡**A replacement coil kit comes with two screws to attach the coil to the bracket.**

To install:

6. Connect the coil to the bracket with two screws.
7. Connect the coil and bracket to the engine bracket or manifold with studs and nuts.
8. Tighten the coil hold-down nuts to 20 ft. lbs. (27 Nm).
9. Engage the coil wire, then the wiring connectors at the side of the coil.
10. Connect the negative battery cable.

HVS Cap

1. Disconnect the negative battery cable.
2. Remove the retainer and spark plug wires from the cap. If there is no wire retainer, be sure to tag all of the spark plug wires before disconnecting them from the cap. This will ease cap installation and ensure the correct firing order.
3. Loosen the two retaining screws holding the cap to the HVS assembly and remove the cap.

To install:

4. Install the cap to the HVS assembly and secure the two retaining screws.
5. Install the spark plug wires and wire retainer to the cap. If no retainer was used, be sure to connect the wires as tagged during removal.
6. Connect the negative battery cable.

Rotor

1. Disconnect the negative battery cable.
2. Remove the cap from the HVS housing assembly.
3. Remove the rotor attaching screws and note the position of the rotor (also note from which holes the screws were removed), then remove the rotor.

To install:

4. Install the rotor in the position noted earlier, then secure the rotor using the attaching screws.
5. Install the cap to the HVS housing assembly.
6. Connect the negative battery cable.

DISTRIBUTOR IGNITION (DI) SYSTEM

General Information

The Distributor Ignition (DI) system consists of the distributor, Hall effect switch (camshaft position sensor), ignition coil, secondary wires, spark plugs, knock sensor and crankshaft position sensor. The system is controlled by the Vehicle Control Module (VCM). The VCM, using information from various engine sensors, controls the spark timing, dwell, and firing of the ignition coil. It is used on 1993–96 models.

Diagnosis and Testing

The symptoms of a defective component within the DI system are exactly the same as those you would encounter in a conventional or HEI system. Some of these symptoms are:

- Hard or no starting
- Rough Idle
- Poor fuel economy
- Engine misses under load or while accelerating

If you suspect a problem in the ignition system, there are certain preliminary checks which you should carry out before you begin to check the electronic portions of the system. First, it is extremely important to make sure the vehicle's battery is in a good state of charge. A defective or poorly charged battery will cause the various components of the ignition system to read incorrectly when they are being tested. Second, make sure all wiring connections are clean and tight, not only at the battery, but also at the distributor cap, ignition coil and electronic control module.

1. Check the cap for tiny holes and carbon tracks as follows:
   a. Remove the cap and place an ohmmeter lead on the cap terminal.
   b. Use the other lead to probe all the other terminals and the center carbon button.
2. If the readings are not infinite, the cap must be replaced.

SECONDARY SPARK TEST

It is imperative to check the secondary ignition circuit first. If the secondary circuit checks out properly, then the engine condition is probably not the fault of the ignition system. To check the secondary ignition system, perform a simple spark test.

1. Remove one of the plug wires and insert some sort of extension in the plug socket. An old spark plug with the ground electrode removed makes a good extension.
2. Hold the wire and extension about ¼ in. (0.25mm) away from the block and crank the engine.
3. If a normal spark occurs, then the problem is most likely not in the ignition system. Check for fuel system problems, or fouled spark plugs.
4. If, however, there is no spark or a weak spark, test the ignition coil as well as the camshaft and crankshaft position sensors. For testing the camshaft and crankshaft position sensors, refer to Section 4.

IGNITION COIL

▶ **See Figure 25**

➡**Make sure the ignition switch is OFF.**

1. Tag and disconnect the wires from the ignition coil.
2. Using a digital ohmmeter set on the high scale, probe the ignition coil as shown in Step 1 of the accompanying illustration.
3. The reading should be infinite. If not, replace the coil.
4. Using the low scale of the ohmmeter, probe the ignition coil as shown in Step 2 of the accompanying illustration. The reading should be 0.1 ohms; if not, replace the coil.
5. Using the high scale of the ohmmeter, probe the ignition coil as shown in Step 3 of the accompanying illustration. The reading should be 5k–25k ohms; if not, replace the coil.
6. Reconnect the wires to the ignition coil.

Remove the engine cover to gain access to the distributor on DI equipped models

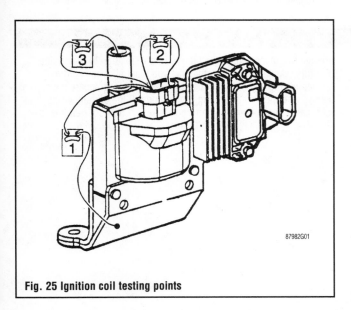

Fig. 25 Ignition coil testing points

Ignition Coil

REMOVAL & INSTALLATION

▶ **See Figures 26, 27 and 28**

1. Tag and disengage the wiring connectors from the coil and the coil wire.
2. Unfasten the retainers securing the coil bracket and coil to the manifold.
3. Remove the coil and bracket and drill out the two rivets securing the coil to the bracket.
4. Remove the coil from the bracket.
To install:

➡**The replacement coil kit may come with the two screws to attach the coil to the bracket. If not, you must supply your own screws.**

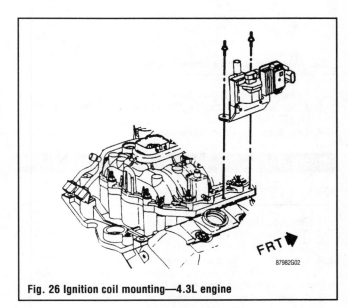

Fig. 26 Ignition coil mounting—4.3L engine

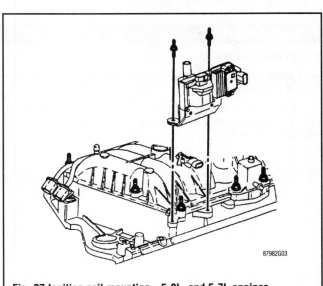

Fig. 27 Ignition coil mounting—5.0L and 5.7L engines

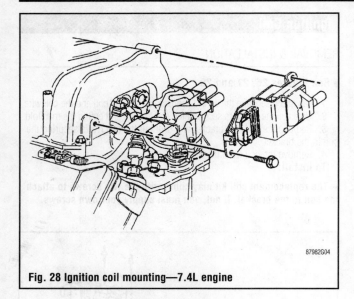

Fig. 28 Ignition coil mounting—7.4L engine

87982G04

5. Fasten the coil to the bracket using two screws.
6. Fasten the coil and bracket to the manifold. Tighten the retainers to 20 ft. lbs. (27 Nm).
7. Engage the coil wire and the wiring connectors to the coil.

Distributor

REMOVAL

1. Disconnect the negative battery cable.
2. Tag and remove the spark plug wires and the coil leads from the distributor.
3. Disengage the electrical connector at the base of the distributor.
4. Loosen the distributor cap fasteners and remove the cap.
5. Using a marker, matchmark the rotor-to-housing and housing-to-engine block positions so that they can be matched during installation.
6. Loosen and remove the distributor hold-down bolt.
7. Remove the distributor from the engine.

FIRING ORDERS

▶ **See Figures 29 and 30**

➡**To avoid confusion, remove and tag the spark plug wires one at a time, for replacement.**

If a distributor is not keyed for installation with only one orientation, it could have been removed previously and rewired. The resultant wiring would hold the correct firing order, but could change

INSTALLATION

Engine Not Disturbed

1. Install the distributor in the engine, making sure that the matchmarks are properly aligned.
2. Install the hold-down bolt and tighten it to 20 ft. lbs. (27 Nm).
3. Install the distributor cap and engage the electrical connector at the base of the distributor.
4. Install the spark plug wires and coil leads.
5. Connect the negative battery cable.

Engine Disturbed

1. Remove the No. 1 cylinder spark plug. Turn the engine using a socket wrench on the large bolt on the front of the crankshaft pulley. Place a finger near the No. 1 spark plug hole and turn the crankshaft until the piston reaches Top Dead Center (TDC). As the engine approaches TDC, you will feel air being expelled by the No. 1 cylinder. If the position is not being met, turn the engine another full turn (360 degree). Once the engine's position is correct, install the spark plug.
2. Align the pre-drilled indent hole in the distributor driven gear with the white painted alignment line on the lower portion of the shaft housing.
3. Using a long screwdriver, align the oil pump drive shaft in the engine with the mating drive tab in the distributor.
4. Install the distributor in the engine.
5. When the distributor is fully seated, the rotor segment should be aligned with the pointer cast in the distributor base. The pointer will have a "6" or "8" cast into it indicating a 6 or 8-cylinder engine. If the rotor segment is not within a few degrees of the pointer, the distributor gear may be off a tooth or more. If this is the case, repeat the process until the rotor aligns with the pointer.
6. Install the cap and fasten the mounting screws.
7. Tighten the distributor mounting bolt to 20 ft. lbs. (27 Nm).
8. Engage the electrical connections and the spark plug wires.

Camshaft Position Sensor

For information on the camshaft position sensor, please refer to Section 4.

the relative placement of the plug towers in relation to the engine. For this reason, it is imperative that you label all wires before disconnecting any of them. Also, before removal, compare the current wiring with the accompanying illustrations. If the current wiring does not match, make notes in your book to reflect how your engine is wired.

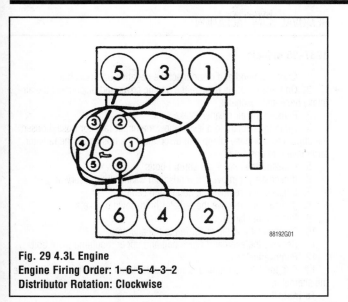

Fig. 29 4.3L Engine
Engine Firing Order: 1–6–5–4–3–2
Distributor Rotation: Clockwise

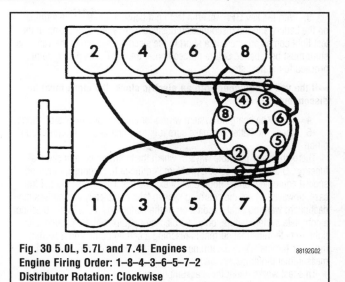

Fig. 30 5.0L, 5.7L and 7.4L Engines
Engine Firing Order: 1–8–4–3–6–5–7–2
Distributor Rotation: Clockwise

CHARGING SYSTEM

General Information

The automotive charging system provides electrical power for operation of the vehicle's ignition and starting systems and all the electrical accessories. The battery serves as an electrical surge or storage tank, storing (in chemical form) the energy originally produced by the engine driven alternator. The system also provides a means of regulating alternator output to protect the battery from being overcharged and to avoid excessive voltage to the accessories.

Alternator Precautions

To prevent damage to the alternator and regulator, the following precautionary measures must be taken when working with the electrical system.

• Never reverse the battery connections. Always check the battery polarity visually. This is to be done before any connections are made to ensure that all of the connections correspond to the battery ground polarity of the vehicle.

• Booster batteries must be connected properly. Make sure the positive cable of the booster battery is connected to the positive terminal of the battery which is getting the boost.

• Disconnect the battery cables before using a fast charger; the charger has a tendency to force current through the diodes in the opposite direction for which they were designed.

• Never use a fast charger as a booster for starting the vehicle.

• Never disconnect the voltage regulator while the engine is running, unless as noted for testing purposes.

• Do not ground the alternator output terminal.

• Do not operate the alternator on an open circuit with the field energized.

• Do not attempt to polarize the alternator.

• Disconnect the battery cables and remove the alternator before using an electric arc welder on the vehicle.

• Protect the alternator from excessive moisture. If the engine is to be steam cleaned, cover or remove the alternator.

Alternator

TESTING

◆ **See Figure 31**

If you suspect a defect in your charging system, first perform these general checks before going on to more specific tests.

1. Check the condition of the alternator belt and tighten it if necessary.
2. Clean the battery cable connections at the battery. Make sure the connections between the battery cables and battery clamps are good. Reconnect the negative terminal only and proceed to the next step.

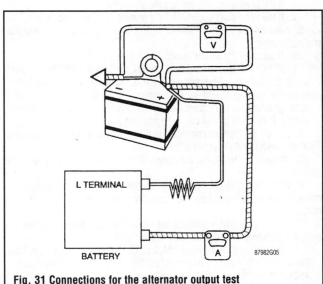

Fig. 31 Connections for the alternator output test

3. With the key **OFF**, insert a test light between the positive terminal on the battery and the disconnected positive battery terminal clamp. If the test light comes on, there is a short in the electrical system of the van. The short must be repaired before proceeding. If the light does not come on, proceed to the next step.

➡️**If the van is equipped with an electric clock, the clock must be disconnected.**

4. Check the charging system wiring for any obvious breaks or shorts.
5. Check the battery to make sure it is fully charged and in good condition.

There are many possible ways in which the charging system can malfunction. Often the source of a problem is difficult to diagnose, requiring special equipment and a good deal of experience. This is usually not the case, however, where the charging system fails completely and causes the dashboard warning light to come on or the battery to "die". To troubleshoot a complete system failure, only two pieces of equipment are needed: a test light, to determine that current is reaching a certain point; and a current indicator (ammeter), to determine the direction of the current flow and its measurement in amps.

This test works under three assumptions:
- The battery is known to be good and fully charged.
- The alternator belt is in good condition and adjusted to the proper tension.
- All connections in the system are clean and tight.

➡️**In order for the current indicator to give a valid reading, the van must be equipped with battery cables which are of the same gauge size and quality as original equipment battery cables.**

6. With the ignition switch **ON** and the engine not running, the charge indicator light should be on. If not, disengage the wiring harness at the alternator and use a fused jumper wire with a 5-amp fuse to ground the "L" terminal in the wiring harness.
   a. If the lamp lights, replace the alternator.
   b. If the lamp does not light, check for an open circuit between the grounding lead and the ignition switch.
7. With the ignition switch **ON** and the engine running, the lamp should be off. If not, stop the engine, turn the ignition switch **ON**, and disconnect the wiring harness.
   a. If the lamp goes out, replace the alternator.
   b. If the lamp stays on, check for a grounded "L" terminal wire.
8. If the vehicle voltmeter shows high or low voltage readings with the engine running:
   a. Disengage the wiring harness from the alternator.
   b. With the engine off and ignition **ON**, connect a digital multimeter set on the DC scale, from ground to the "L" terminal in the wiring harness. The reading should equal the battery's voltage; if not, there is an open, grounded or high resistance circuit between the terminal and the battery. Repair this circuit before performing any more tests.
9. Engage the harness connector to the alternator and run the engine at 2500 rpm with the accessories off.
10. Measure the voltage at the battery. If it is above 16 volts, replace the alternator.
11. With the engine off, connect an ammeter at the alternator output terminal. The ammeter must have the capability to measure 115 amps of current.
12. Connect a digital multimeter set on the DC scale across the alternator and a carbon pile across the battery.
   a. Run the engine at 2500 RPM, turn on all the accessories and load the battery with a carbon pile to obtain maximum amperage. Maintain voltage at 13 volts or more.
   b. If the output is within 15 amps of the rated output, the alternator is OK: Refer to the alternator specifications in this section.
   c. If the output is not within 15 amps, the alternator must be replaced.

REMOVAL & INSTALLATION

1987–95 Models

1. Open the hood and disconnect the negative battery cable.
2. On G-van models remove the engine cover and disconnect the air intake hose and resonator.
3. Remove the air cleaner intake duct.
4. Drain the coolant to a level below the upper radiator hose. Loosen the upper radiator hose clamp and disconnect the hose from the radiator and move it to one side.
5. Loosen the radiator fan shroud bolts.
6. If necessary, remove the windshield washer fluid reservoir.
7. If necessary, remove the hood latch cable.
8. If necessary, remove the radiator hold-down brackets.
9. Remove the fan shroud.
10. Disconnect and tag all wiring to the alternator.
11. Remove the alternator brace bolt and upper mounting pivot bolt.
12. Remove the drive belt.
13. Support the alternator and remove the lower mounting bolt. Remove the alternator.

To install:

14. Install the unit and tighten the lower mounting bolt to the following figures:
- All gasoline engines:18 ft. lbs. (25 Nm)
- All diesel engines: 32 ft. lbs. (43 Nm)
15. Install the upper mounting/pivot bolt and the drive belt.
16. Reconnect the wires at the alternator.
17. Adjust the belt to have ½ in. (13mm) depression under thumb pressure on its longest run.
18. Tighten the upper mounting bolt to the following figures:
- 4.3L engine: 37 ft. lbs. (50 Nm)
- 5.0L engine: 37 ft. lbs. (50 Nm)
- 5.7L engine: 37 ft. lbs. (50 Nm)
- 7.4L engine:18 ft. lbs. (25 Nm)
- Diesel engines: 20 ft. lbs. (27 Nm)
19. Place the fan shroud back in its original position.
20. If removed, install the radiator hold-down brackets and the hood latch cable.
21. If removed install the windshield washer fluid reservoir.
22. Install the upper radiator hose, tighten the hose clamp and replenish the cooling system

88262P90

Before removing the positive lead from the alternator, disconnect the negative battery cable

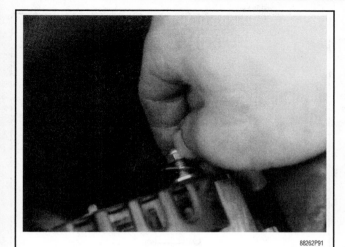

Be careful when removing the locknut, as the terminal stud sometimes will rotate with the nut

Remove the drive belt, loosen the mounting bolts and remove the alternator

23. Tighten the fan shroud bolts.
24. Install the air cleaner intake duct.
25. On G-van models install the air intake hose, resonator and engine cover.
26. Reconnect the negative battery cable.
27. Close the hood, start the vehicle and check for normal operation.

1996–97 Models

1. Open the hood and disconnect the negative battery cable.
2. Remove the plastic coolant reservoir from the engine compartment.
3. Remove the air cleaner assembly from the engine compartment.
4. Remove the upper fan shroud.
5. Loosen the serpentine belt tensioner and slip the belt off the alternator.
6. Disconnect the heater hose pipe from the alternator (gasoline engines only).
7. Disconnect the oil fill bracket from the generator bracket (gasoline engines only).
8. Disconnect and tag all wiring to the alternator.
9. Remove the alternator front mounting bolt.

10. Support the alternator and remove the rear mounting bolt. Remove the alternator.
To install:
11. Install the unit and tighten the rear mounting bolt to 18 ft. lbs. (25 Nm)
12. Install the front mounting bolt and tighten it to 37 ft. lbs. (50 Nm).
13. Reconnect the wires at the alternator.
14. Loosen the serpentine belt tensioner and reinstall the belt on the alternator pulley. Release the belt tensioner.
15. Connect the oil fill bracket to the alternator bracket (gasoline engines only).
16. Connect the heater hose pipe to the alternator (gasoline engines only).
17. Install the upper fan shroud.
18. Install the air cleaner assembly.
19. Install the plastic coolant reservoir.
20. Reconnect the negative battery cable.
21. Close the hood, start the vehicle and check for normal operation.

STARTING SYSTEM

Starter

The starting motor is a specially designed, direct current electric motor capable of producing a great amount of power for its size. One thing that allows the motor to produce a great deal of power is its tremendous rotating speed. It drives the engine through a tiny pinion gear (attached to the starter's armature), which drives the very large flywheel ring gear at a greatly reduced speed. Another factor allowing it to produce so much power is that only intermittent operation is required of it. Thus, little allowance for air circulation is required, and the windings can be built into a very small space.

REMOVAL & INSTALLATION

▶ **See Figures 32 and 33**

The following is a general procedure for all vans covered in this manual, and may vary slightly depending on model and series.
1. Disconnect the negative battery cable at the battery.
2. Raise and support the vehicle.
3. Disconnect and tag all wires at the solenoid terminal.

➡**Reinstall all nuts as soon as they are removed, since the thread sizes are different.**

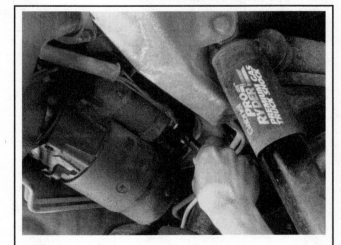

Disconnect the negative battery cable before removing the starter cables

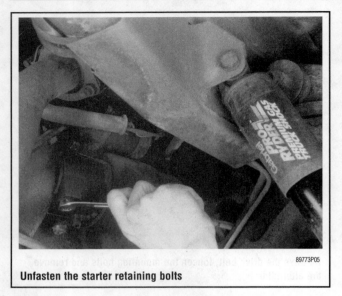
Unfasten the starter retaining bolts

89773P05

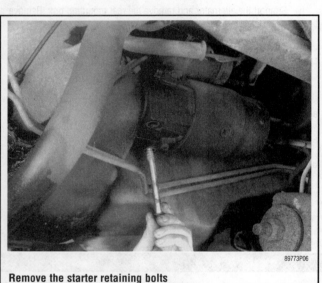
Remove the starter retaining bolts

89773P06

Remove the starter from the van

89773P07

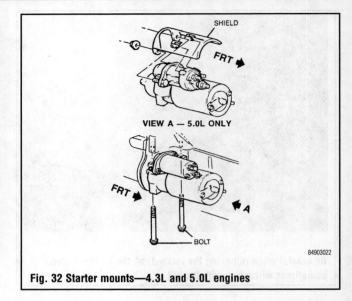
Fig. 32 Starter mounts—4.3L and 5.0L engines

84903022

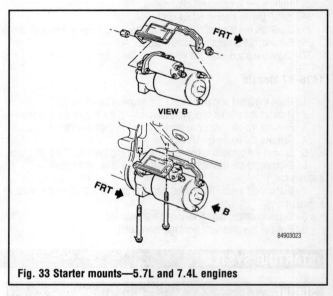
Fig. 33 Starter mounts—5.7L and 7.4L engines

84903023

4. Remove the front bracket from the starter and the mounting bolts. On engines with a solenoid heat shield, remove the front bracket upper bolt and detach the bracket from the starter.

5. Remove the front bracket bolt or nut. Lower the starter, front end first, then remove the unit from the van.

To install:

6. Position the starter and tighten all bolts to 35 ft. lbs. (45 Nm)

7. Reconnect all wires.

SHIMMING THE STARTER

▶ See Figures 34, 35 and 36

Starter noise during cranking and after the engine fires is often a result of too much or too little distance between the starter pinion gear and the flywheel. A high pitched whine during cranking (before the engine fires) can be caused by the pinion and flywheel being too far apart. Likewise, a whine after the engine starts (as the key is released) is often a result of the pinion-flywheel relationship being too close. In both cases flywheel damage can occur. Shims are available in 0.015 in. (0.3mm) sizes to properly adjust the starter on its mount. You will also need a flywheel turning tool, available at most auto parts stores or from most auto tool store or salesperson.

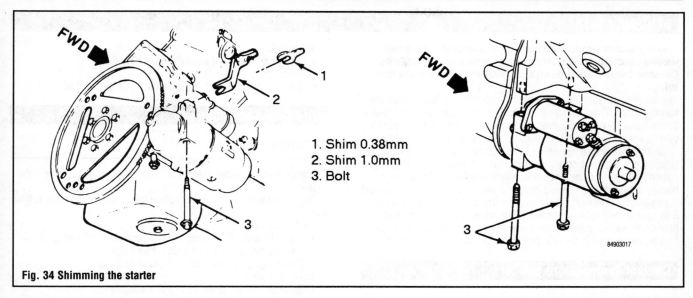

1. Shim 0.38mm
2. Shim 1.0mm
3. Bolt

Fig. 34 Shimming the starter

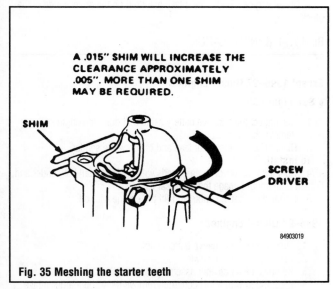

A .015" SHIM WILL INCREASE THE CLEARANCE APPROXIMATELY .005". MORE THAN ONE SHIM MAY BE REQUIRED.

SHIM

SCREW DRIVER

Fig. 35 Meshing the starter teeth

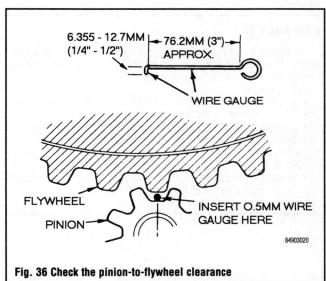

6.355 - 12.7MM (1/4" - 1/2")   76.2MM (3") APPROX.

WIRE GAUGE

FLYWHEEL

PINION

INSERT 0.5MM WIRE GAUGE HERE

Fig. 36 Check the pinion-to-flywheel clearance

If your van's starter emits the above noises, follow the shimming procedure:
1. Disconnect the negative battery cable.
2. Remove the flywheel inspection cover on the bottom of the bellhousing.
3. Using the flywheel turning tool, turn the flywheel and examine the flywheel teeth. If damage is evident, the flywheel should be replaced.
4. Insert a screwdriver into the small hole in the bottom of the starter and move the starter pinion and clutch assembly so the pinion and flywheel teeth mesh. If necessary, rotate the flywheel so that a pinion tooth is directly in the center of the two flywheel teeth and on the centerline of the two gears, as shown in the accompanying illustration.
5. Check the pinion-to-flywheel clearance by using a 0.020 in. (0.5mm) wire gauge (a spark plug wire gauge may work here, or you can make your own). Make sure you center the pinion tooth between the flywheel teeth and the gauge—NOT in the corners, as you may get a false reading. If the clearance is under this minimum, shim the starter away from the flywheel by adding shim(s) one at a time to the starter mount. Check clearance after adding each shim.
6. If the clearance is a good deal over 0.020 in. (0.5mm)—in the

vicinity of 0.050 in. (1.3mm) plus, shim the starter towards the flywheel. Broken or severely mangled flywheel teeth are also a good indicator that the clearance here is too great. Shimming the starter towards the flywheel is done by adding shims to the outboard starter mounting pad only. Check the clearance after each shim is added. A shim of 0.015 in. (0.3mm) at this location will decrease the clearance about 0.010 in. (0.2mm).

SOLENOID REPLACEMENT

1. Disconnect the negative battery cable.
2. Remove the screw and washer from the field strap terminal.
3. Remove the two solenoid-to-housing retaining screws and the motor terminal bolt.
4. Remove the solenoid by twisting the unit 90 degrees.
5. To replace the solenoid, reverse the above procedure. Make sure the return spring is on the plunger, and rotate the solenoid unit into place on the starter.

SENDING UNITS

➡This section describes the operating principles of sending units, warning lights and gauges. Sensors which provide information to the Electronic Control Module (ECM) are covered in Section 4 of this manual.

Instrument panels contain a number of indicating devices (gauges and warning lights). These devices are composed of two separate components. One is the sending unit, mounted on the engine or other remote part of the vehicle, and the other is the actual gauge or light in the instrument panel.

Several types of sending units exist, however most can be characterized as being either a pressure type or a resistance type. Pressure type sending units convert liquid pressure into an electrical signal which is sent to the gauge. Resistance type sending units are most often used to measure temperature and use variable resistance to control the current flow back to the indicating device. Both types of sending units are connected in series by a wire to the battery (through the ignition switch). When the ignition is turned **ON**, current flows from the battery through the indicating device and on to the sending unit.

Coolant Temperature Sender

OPERATION

▶ **See Figure 37**

The coolant temperature sender changes resistance as the coolant temperature increases and decreases. The coolant temperature sender can be found at these different locations as follows:
1987–93 models:
- 4.3L engines: in the left cylinder head between spark plugs # 3 and 5
- 5.0/5.7L engines: in the left cylinder head above the # 1 spark plug
- 7.4L engines: in the left cylinder head above the # 3 spark plug
- Diesel engines: near the front of the left cylinder head before the exhaust manifold
1994–97 models:
- Gasoline engines: in the middle of the cylinder head on the driver's side
- Diesel engines: in the left front of the cylinder head

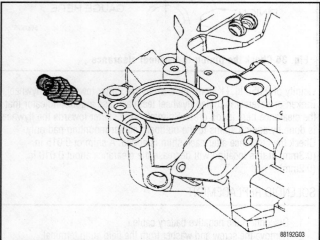

Fig. 37 Location of the engine coolant temperature sender— 1994–97 5.0L and 5.7L engines

REMOVAL & INSTALLATION

1. Disconnect the negative battery cable and drain the engine coolant.
2. If necessary to gain access to the sender, the engine cover may have to be removed.
3. Disconnect the electrical lead and unscrew the sender.

To install:
4. Install the sender and connect the electrical lead.
5. Install the engine cover.
6. Connect the battery cable and fill the engine with coolant.

Oil Pressure Sender

OPERATION

The oil pressure sender relays to the dash gauge the oil pressure in the engine.

The oil pressure sender can be found at these different locations as follows:
1987–93 models:
- 4.3L, 5.0L and 5.7L engines: at the left front side of the distributor
- 7.4L engines: at the front left side of the block
- Diesel engines: left side above the flywheel housing
1994–97 models:
- Gasoline engines: at the top rear of the engine block
- Diesel engines: under the intake manifold on the driver's side of the block

REMOVAL & INSTALLATION

Except 1996–97 Diesel Engines

▶ **See Figure 38**

1. Disconnect the negative battery cable and drain the engine oil.
2. Remove the engine cover.
3. Disconnect the electrical lead and unscrew the sender.
To install:
4. Coat the first two or three threads with sealer. Install the sender and tighten until snug. Engage the electrical lead.
5. Connect the battery cable and fill the engine with oil.

1996–97 Diesel Engines

1. Disconnect the negative battery cable.
2. Remove the engine cover.
3. Remove the air cleaner assembly.
4. If equipped with a turbocharger, remove the turbocharger intake

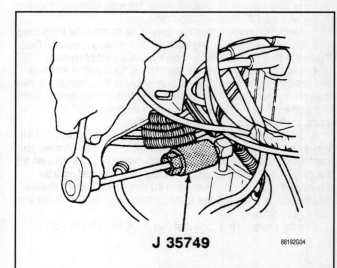

J 35749

Fig. 38 Removing the oil pressure sender—1994–97 models

cover and cover the intake opening to prevent dirt entering the tur-bocharger.

5. Disengage the sender electrical connection and remove the sender from the engine block.

➡**A 1¹/₁₆ in. crow's foot wrench is required to remove the sender from the block.**

To install:

6. Install the sender in the block and engage the electrical connection.
7. If equipped with a turbocharger, remove the cover placed over the intake opening.
8. Install the turbocharger intake cover.
9. Install the air cleaner assembly.
10. Install the engine cover and connect the negative battery cable.

Troubleshooting Basic Starting System Problems

Problem	Cause	Solution
Starter motor rotates engine slowly	• Battery charge low or battery defective	• Charge or replace battery
	• Defective circuit between battery and starter motor	• Clean and tighten, or replace cables
	• Low load current	• Bench-test starter motor. Inspect for worn brushes and weak brush springs.
	• High load current	• Bench-test starter motor. Check engine for friction, drag or coolant in cylinders. Check ring gear-to-pinion gear clearance.
Starter motor will not rotate engine	• Battery charge low or battery defective	• Charge or replace battery
	• Faulty solenoid	• Check solenoid ground. Repair or replace as necessary.
	• Damaged drive pinion gear or ring gear	• Replace damaged gear(s)
	• Starter motor engagement weak	• Bench-test starter motor
	• Starter motor rotates slowly with high load current	• Inspect drive yoke pull-down and point gap, check for worn end bushings, check ring gear clearance
	• Engine seized	• Repair engine
Starter motor drive will not engage (solenoid known to be good)	• Defective contact point assembly	• Repair or replace contact point assembly
	• Inadequate contact point assembly ground	• Repair connection at ground screw
	• Defective hold-in coil	• Replace field winding assembly
Starter motor drive will not disengage	• Starter motor loose on flywheel housing	• Tighten mounting bolts
	• Worn drive end busing	• Replace bushing
	• Damaged ring gear teeth	• Replace ring gear or driveplate
	• Drive yoke return spring broken or missing	• Replace spring
Starter motor drive disengages prematurely	• Weak drive assembly thrust spring	• Replace drive mechanism
	• Hold-in coil defective	• Replace field winding assembly
Low load current	• Worn brushes	• Replace brushes
	• Weak brush springs	• Replace springs

TCCS2C01

Troubleshooting Basic Charging System Problems

Problem	Cause	Solution
Noisy alternator	• Loose mountings • Loose drive pulley • Worn bearings • Brush noise • Internal circuits shorted (High pitched whine)	• Tighten mounting bolts • Tighten pulley • Replace alternator • Replace alternator • Replace alternator
Squeal when starting engine or accelerating	• Glazed or loose belt	• Replace or adjust belt
Indicator light remains on or ammeter indicates discharge (engine running)	• Broken belt • Broken or disconnected wires • Internal alternator problems • Defective voltage regulator	• Install belt • Repair or connect wiring • Replace alternator • Replace voltage regulator/alternator
Car light bulbs continually burn out— battery needs water continually	• Alternator/regulator overcharging	• Replace voltage regulator/alternator
Car lights flare on acceleration	• Battery low • Internal alternator/regulator problems	• Charge or replace battery • Replace alternator/regulator
Low voltage output (alternator light flickers continually or ammeter needle wanders)	• Loose or worn belt • Dirty or corroded connections • Internal alternator/regulator problems	• Replace or adjust belt • Clean or replace connections • Replace alternator/regulator

TCCS2C02

3

ENGINE AND ENGINE OVERHAUL

ENGINE MECHANICAL 3-20
EXHAUST SYSTEM 3-77
ENGINE RECONDITIONING 3-80

GENERAL ENGINE SPECIFICATIONS

Year	Engine ID/VIN	Engine Displacement Liters (cc)	Fuel System Type	Net Horsepower @ rpm	Net Torque @ rpm (ft. lbs.)	Bore x Stroke (in.)	Compression Ratio	Oil Pressure @ rpm
1987	Z	4.3 (4293)	TFI	①	②	4.00x3.48	9.3:1	18@2000
	H	5.0 (4999)	TFI	165@4400	240@2000	3.74x3.48	9.0:1	18@2000
	K/M	5.7 (5735)	4BC	③	④	4.00x3.48	8.5:1	18@2000
	C	6.2 (6210)	DSL	130@3600	240@2000	3.98x3.80	21.3:1	35@2000
	J	6.2 (6210)	DSL	135@3600	240@2000	3.98x3.80	21.3:1	35@2000
	F	6.5 (6473)	DSL	⑤	⑥	4.05x3.80	21.0:1	40-45@2000
	W	7.4 (7440)	TFI	230@3600	385@1600	4.25x4.00	8.0:1	40@2000
	N	7.4 (7440)	TFI	230@3600	385@1600	4.25x4.00	8.0:1	40@2000
1988	Z	4.3 (4293)	TFI	①	②	4.00x3.48	9.3:1	18@2000
	H	5.0 (4999)	TFI	165@4400	240@2000	3.74x3.48	9.0:1	18@2000
	K	5.7 (5735)	TFI	③	④	4.00x3.48	8.5:1	18@2000
	C	6.2 (6210)	DSL	130@3600	240@2000	3.98x3.80	21.3:1	35@2000
	J	6.2 (6210)	DSL	135@3600	240@2000	3.98x3.80	21.3:1	35@2000
	F	6.5 (6473)	DSL	⑤	⑥	4.05x3.80	21.0:1	40-45@2000
	W	7.4 (7440)	TFI	230@3600	385@1600	4.25x4.00	8.0:1	40@2000
	N	7.4 (7440)	TFI	230@3600	385@1600	4.25x4.00	8.0:1	40@2000
1989	Z	4.3 (4293)	TFI	①	②	4.00x3.48	9.3:1	18@2000
	H	5.0 (4999)	TFI	165@4400	240@2000	3.74x3.48	9.0:1	18@2000
	K	5.7 (5735)	TFI	③	④	4.00x3.48	8.5:1	18@2000
	C	6.2 (6210)	DSL	130@3600	240@2000	3.98x3.80	21.3:1	35@2000
	J	6.2 (6210)	DSL	135@3600	240@2000	3.98x3.80	21.3:1	35@2000
	F	6.5 (6473)	DSL	⑤	⑥	4.05x3.80	21.0:1	40-45@2000
	W	7.4 (7440)	TFI	230@3600	385@1600	4.25x4.00	8.0:1	40@2000
	N	7.4 (7440)	TFI	230@3600	385@1600	4.25x4.00	8.0:1	40@2000
1990	Z	4.3 (4293)	TFI	①	②	4.00x3.48	9.3:1	18@2000
	H	5.0 (4999)	TFI	165@4400	240@2000	3.74x3.48	9.0:1	18@2000
	K	5.7 (5735)	TFI	③	④	4.00x3.48	8.5:1	18@2000
	C	6.2 (6210)	DSL	130@3600	240@2000	3.98x3.80	21.3:1	35@2000
	J	6.2 (6210)	DSL	135@3600	240@2000	3.98x3.80	21.3:1	35@2000
	F	6.5 (6473)	DSL	⑤	⑥	4.05x3.80	21.0:1	40-45@2000
	N	7.4 (7440)	TFI	230@3600	385@1600	4.25x4.00	8.0:1	40@2000
1991	Z	4.3 (4293)	TFI	①	②	4.00x3.48	9.3:1	18@2000
	H	5.0 (4999)	TFI	165@4400	240@2000	3.74x3.48	9.0:1	18@2000
	K	5.7 (5735)	TFI	③	④	4.00x3.48	8.5:1	18@2000
	C	6.2 (6210)	DSL	130@3600	240@2000	3.98x3.80	21.3:1	35@2000
	J	6.2 (6210)	DSL	135@3600	240@2000	3.98x3.80	21.3:1	35@2000
	F	6.5 (6473)	DSL	⑤	⑥	4.05x3.80	21.0:1	40-45@2000
	N	7.4 (7440)	TFI	230@3600	385@1600	4.25x4.00	8.0:1	40@2000
1992	Z	4.3 (4293)	TFI	①	②	4.00x3.48	9.3:1	18@2000
	H	5.0 (4999)	TFI	165@4400	240@2000	3.74x3.48	9.0:1	18@2000
	K	5.7 (5735)	TFI	③	④	4.00x3.48	8.5:1	18@2000
	C	6.2 (6210)	DSL	130@3600	240@2000	3.98x3.80	21.3:1	35@2000
	J	6.2 (6210)	DSL	135@3600	240@2000	3.98x3.80	21.3:1	35@2000
	F	6.5 (6473)	DSL	⑤	⑥	4.05x3.80	21.0:1	40-45@2000
	N	7.4 (7440)	TFI	230@3600	385@1600	4.25x4.00	8.0:1	40@2000

88193C01

GENERAL ENGINE SPECIFICATIONS

Year	Engine ID/VIN	Engine Displacement Liters (cc)	Fuel System Type	Net Horsepower @ rpm	Net Torque @ rpm (ft. lbs.)	Bore x Stroke (in.)	Compression Ratio	Oil Pressure @ rpm
1993	Z	4.3 (4293)	TFI	①	②	4.00x3.48	9.3:1	18@2000
	H	5.0 (4999)	TFI	165@4400	240@2000	3.74x3.48	9.0:1	18@2000
	K	5.7 (5735)	TFI	③	④	4.00x3.48	8.5:1	18@2000
	C	6.2 (6210)	DSL	130@3600	240@2000	3.98x3.80	21.3:1	35@2000
	J	6.2 (6210)	DSL	135@3600	240@2000	3.98x3.80	21.3:1	35@2000
	F	6.5 (6473)	DSL	⑤	⑥	4.05x3.80	21.0:1	40-45@2000
	N	7.4 (7440)	TFI	230@3600	385@1600	4.25x4.00	8.0:1	40@2000
1994	Z	4.3 (4293)	MFI	①	②	4.00x3.48	9.1:1	18@2000
	Z	4.3 (4293)	TFI	①	②	4.00x3.48	9.1:1	18@2000
	H	5.0 (4999)	TFI	175@4200	265@2800	3.74x3.48	9.0:1	18@2000
	K	5.7 (5735)	MFI	③	④	4.00x3.48	9.1:1	18@2000
	K	5.7 (5735)	TFI	③	④	4.00x3.48	9.1:1	18@2000
	F	6.5 (6473)	DSL	⑤	⑥	4.05x3.80	21.5:1	40-45@2000
	Y	6.5 (6473)	DSL	⑦	⑧	4.06x3.82	21.5:1	40-45@2000
	N	7.4 (7440)	TFI	230@3600	385@1600	4.25x4.00	8.0:1	40@2000
1995	Z	4.3 (4293)	MFI	①	②	4.00x3.48	9.1:1	18@2000
	Z	4.3 (4293)	TFI	①	②	4.00x3.48	9.1:1	18@2000
	H	5.0 (4999)	TFI	175@4200	265@2800	3.74x3.48	9.1:1	18@2000
	K	5.7 (5735)	MFI	③	④	4.00x3.48	9.1:1	18@2000
	K	5.7 (5735)	TFI	③	④	4.00x3.48	9.1:1	18@2000
	F	6.5 (6473)	DSL	190@3400	⑥	4.06x3.82	21.5:1	40-45@2000
	Y	6.5 (6473)	DSL	⑦	⑧	4.06x3.82	21.5:1	40-45@2000
	N	7.4 (7440)	TFI	230@3600	385@1600	4.25x4.00	7.9:1	25@2000
1996	W	4.3 (4293)	MFI		⑨	4.00x3.48	9.2:1	18@2000
	X	4.3 (4293)	MFI		⑩	4.00x3.48	9.2:1	18@2000
	M	5.0 (4999)	MFI	220@4600	285@2800	3.74x3.48	9.4:1	18@2000
	R	5.7 (5735)	MFI	250@4600	335@2800	4.00x3.48	9.4:1	18@2000
	F/Y	6.5 (6473)	DSL	⑤	⑥	4.05x3.80	21.5:1	40-45@2000
	N/J	7.4 (7440)	MFI	290@4200	410@3200	4.25x4.00	9.0:1	40@2000
1997	W	4.3 (4293)	MFI		⑨	4.00x3.48	9.2:1	18@2000
	X	4.3 (4293)	MFI		⑩	4.00x3.48	9.2:1	18@2000
	M	5.0 (4999)	MFI	220@4600	285@2800	3.74x3.48	9.4:1	18@2000
	R	5.7 (5735)	MFI	250@4600	335@2800	4.00x3.48	9.4:1	18@2000
	F/Y	6.5 (6473)	DSL	⑤	⑥	4.05x3.80	21.5:1	40-45@2000
	N/J	7.4 (7440)	MFI	290@4200	410@3200	4.25x4.00	9.0:1	40@2000

TFI - Throttle body fuel injection
MFI - Multi-port fuel injection
DSL - Diesel

① G/P- Van: 165@4000
② G/P-Van: 230@2400
③ Below 8500 GVWR: 210@4000
  Above 8500 GVWR: 190@4000

④ Below 8500 GVWR: 300@2800
  Above 8500 GVWR: 300@2400
⑤ Below 15,000 GVWR: 180@3400
  Above 15,000 GVWR: 190@3400
⑥ Below 15,000 GVWR: 385@1700
  Above 15,000 GVWR: 380@1700

⑦ Below 8500 GVWR: 155@3600
  Above 8500 GVWR: 160@3600
⑧ Below 8500 GVWR: 275@1700
  Above 8500 GVWR: 290@1700
⑨ 2WD: 245@2800
⑩ 2WD: 235@2800

88193C02

VALVE SPECIFICATIONS

Year	Engine ID/VIN	Engine Displacement Liters (cc)	Seat Angle (deg.)	Face Angle (deg.)	Spring Test Pressure (lbs. @ in.)	Spring Installed Height (in.)	Stem-to-Guide Clearance (in.)		Stem Diameter (in.)	
							Intake	Exhaust	Intake	Exhaust
1987	Z	4.3 (4293)	46	45	194-206 @ 1.25	1.72	0.0010-0.0027	0.0010-0.0027	0.3410-0.3417	0.3410-0.3417
	H	5.0 (4999)	46	45	76-84 @ 1.70	1.72	0.0010-0.0027	0.0010-0.0027	0.3410-0.3417	0.3410-0.3417
	K	5.7 (5735)	46	45	76-84 @ 1.70	1.72	0.0010-0.0027	0.0010-0.0027	0.3410-0.3417	0.3410-0.3417
	M	5.7 (5735)	46	45	76-84 @ 1.70	1.72	0.0010-0.0027	0.0010-0.0027	0.3410-0.3417	0.3410-0.3417
	C/J	6.2 (6210)	46	45	80 @ 1.81	1.81	0.0010-0.0027	0.0010-0.0027	0.3414	0.3414
	N	7.4 (7440)	46	45	74-86 @ 1.80	1.80	0.0010-0.0027	0.0012-0.0029	0.3410-0.3417	0.3410-0.3417
	W	7.4 (7440)	46	45	74-86 @ 1.80	1.80	0.0010-0.0027	0.0012-0.0029	0.3410-0.3417	0.3410-0.3417
1988	Z	4.3 (4293)	46	45	194-206 @ 1.25	1.72	0.0010-0.0027	0.0010-0.0027	0.3410-0.3417	0.3410-0.3417
	H	5.0 (4999)	46	45	76-84 @ 1.70	1.72	0.0010-0.0027	0.0010-0.0027	0.3410-0.3417	0.3410-0.3417
	K	5.7 (5735)	46	45	76-84 @ 1.70	1.72	0.0010-0.0027	0.0010-0.0027	0.3410-0.3417	0.3410-0.3417
	M	5.7 (5735)	46	45	76-84 @ 1.70	1.72	0.0010-0.0027	0.0010-0.0027	0.3410-0.3417	0.3410-0.3417
	C/J	6.2 (6210)	46	45	80 @ 1.81	1.81	0.0010-0.0027	0.0010-0.0027	0.3414	0.3414
	N	7.4 (7440)	46	45	74-86 @ 1.80	1.80	0.0010-0.0027	0.0012-0.0029	0.3410-0.3417	0.3410-0.3417
	W	7.4 (7440)	46	45	74-86 @ 1.80	1.80	0.0010-0.0027	0.0012-0.0029	0.3410-0.3417	0.3410-0.3417
1989	Z	4.3 (4293)	46	45	194-206 @ 1.25	1.72	0.0010-0.0027	0.0010-0.0027	0.3410-0.3417	0.3410-0.3417
	H	5.0 (4999)	46	45	76-84 @ 1.70	1.72	0.0010-0.0027	0.0010-0.0027	0.3410-0.3417	0.3410-0.3417
	K	5.7 (5735)	46	45	76-84 @ 1.70	1.72	0.0010-0.0027	0.0010-0.0027	0.3410-0.3417	0.3410-0.3417
	C/J	6.2 (6210)	46	45	80 @ 1.81	1.81	0.0010-0.0027	0.0010-0.0027	0.3414	0.3414
	N	7.4 (7440)	46	45	76-84 @ 1.70	1.80	0.0010-0.0027	0.0012-0.0029	0.3410-0.3417	0.3410-0.3417
	W	7.4 (7440)	46	45	76-84 @ 1.70	1.80	0.0010-0.0027	0.0012-0.0029	0.3410-0.3417	0.3410-0.3417
1990	Z	4.3 (4293)	46	45	194-206 @ 1.25	1.72	0.0010-0.0027	0.0010-0.0027	0.3410-0.3417	0.3410-0.3417
	H	5.0 (4999)	46	45	76-84 @ 1.70	1.72	0.0010-0.0027	0.0010-0.0027	0.3410-0.3417	0.3410-0.3417
	K	5.7 (5735)	46	45	70-84 @ 1.70	1.72	0.0010-0.0027	0.0010-0.0027	0.3410-0.3417	0.3410-0.3417
	C/J	6.2 (6210)	46	45	80 @ 1.81	1.81	0.0010-0.0027	0.0010-0.0027	0.3414	0.3414

88193C03

VALVE SPECIFICATIONS

Year	Engine ID/VIN	Engine Displacement Liters (cc)	Seat Angle (deg.)	Face Angle (deg.)	Spring Test Pressure (lbs. @ in.)	Spring Installed Height (in.)	Stem-to-Guide Clearance (in.)		Stem Diameter (in.)	
							Intake	Exhaust	Intake	Exhaust
1990	N	7.4 (7440)	46	45	74-86@1.80	1.80	0.0010-0.0027	0.0012-0.0029	0.3410-0.3417	0.3410-0.3417
	W	7.4 (7440)	46	45	74-86@1.80	1.80	0.0010-0.0027	0.0012-0.0029	0.3410-0.3417	0.3410-0.3417
1991	Z	4.3 (4293)	46	45	194-206@1.25	1.72	0.0010-0.0027	0.0010-0.0027	0.3410-0.3417	0.3410-0.3417
	H	5.0 (4999)	46	45	76-84@1.70	1.72	0.0010-0.0027	0.0010-0.0027	0.3410-0.3417	0.3410-0.3417
	K	5.7 (5735)	46	45	76-84@1.70	1.72	0.0010-0.0027	0.0010-0.0027	0.3410-0.3417	0.3410-0.3417
	C/J	6.2 (6210)	46	45	80@1.81	1.81	0.0010-0.0027	0.0010-0.0027	0.3414	0.3414
	N	7.4 (7440)	46	45	74-86@1.80	1.80	0.0010-0.0027	0.0012-0.0029	0.3410-0.3417	0.3410-0.3417
1992	Z	4.3 (4293)	46	45	194-206@1.25	1.72	0.0010-0.0027	0.0010-0.0027	NA	NA
	H	5.0 (4999)	46	45	76-84@1.70	1.72	0.0010-0.0027	0.0010-0.0027	NA	NA
	K	5.7 (5735)	46	45	76-84@1.70	1.72	0.0010-0.0027	0.0010-0.0027	NA	NA
	C/J	6.2 (6210)	46	45	230@1.39	1.81	0.0010-0.0027	0.0010-0.0027	NA	NA
	F	6.5 (6473)	46	45	230@1.39	1.81	0.0010-0.0027	0.0010-0.0027	NA	NA
	N	7.4 (7440)	46	45	74-86@1.80	1.80	0.0010-0.0027	0.0012-0.0029	NA	NA
1993	Z	4.3 (4293)	46	45	194-206@1.25	1.72	0.0010-0.0027	0.0010-0.0027	NA	NA
	H	5.0 (4999)	46	45	76-84@1.70	1.72	0.0010-0.0027	0.0010-0.0027	NA	NA
	K	5.7 (5735)	46	45	76-84@1.70	1.72	0.0010-0.0027	0.0010-0.0027	NA	NA
	C	6.2 (6210)	46	45	230@1.39	1.81	0.0010-0.0027	0.0010-0.0027	NA	NA
	J	6.2 (6210)	46	45	230@1.39	1.81	0.0010-0.0027	0.0010-0.0027	NA	NA
	N	7.4 (7440)	46	45	74-86@1.80	1.80	0.0010-0.0027	0.0012-0.0029	NA	NA
1994	Z	4.3 (4293)	46	45	194-206@1.25	1.72	0.0010-0.0027	0.0010-0.0027	NA	NA
	H	5.0 (4999)	46	45	76-84@1.70	1.72	0.0010-0.0027	0.0010-0.0027	NA	NA
	K	5.7 (5735)	46	45	76-84@1.70	1.72	0.0010-0.0027	0.0010-0.0027	NA	NA
	F	6.5 (6473)	46	45	230@1.39	1.81	0.0010-0.0027	0.0010-0.0027	NA	NA
	P	6.5 (6473)	46	45	230@1.39	1.81	0.0010-0.0027	0.0010-0.0027	NA	NA

88193C04

VALVE SPECIFICATIONS

Year	Engine ID/VIN	Engine Displacement Liters (cc)	Seat Angle (deg.)	Face Angle (deg.)	Spring Test Pressure (lbs. @ in.)	Spring Installed Height (in.)	Stem-to-Guide Clearance (in.)		Stem Diameter (in.)	
							Intake	Exhaust	Intake	Exhaust
1994	Y	6.5 (6473)	46	45	230@1.39	1.81	0.0010-0.0027	0.0010-0.0027	NA	NA
	N	7.4 (7440)	46	45	74-86@1.80	1.80	0.0010-0.0027	0.0012-0.0029	NA	NA
1995	Z	4.3 (4293)	46	45	194-206@1.25	1.69-1.71	0.0010-0.0027	0.0010-0.0027	NA	NA
	H	5.0 (4999)	46	45	76-84@1.70	1.72	0.0010-0.0027	0.0010-0.0027	NA	NA
	K	5.7 (5735)	46	45	76-84@1.70	1.72	0.0010-0.0027	0.0010-0.0027	NA	NA
	F	6.5 (6473)	46	45	230@1.39	1.81	0.0010-0.0027	0.0010-0.0027	NA	NA
	P	6.5 (6473)	46	45	230@1.39	1.81	0.0010-0.0027	0.0010-0.0027	NA	NA
	Y	6.5 (6473)	46	45	230@1.39	1.81	0.0010-0.0027	0.0010-0.0027	NA	NA
	N	7.4 (7440)	46	45	205-225@1.40	1.80	0.0010-0.0027	0.0012-0.0029	NA	NA
1996-97	W	4.3 (4293)	46	45	187-203@1.27	1.69-1.71	0.0010	0.0020	NA	NA
	M	5.0 (4999)	46	45	187-203@1.27	1.69-1.71	0.0010-0.0027	0.0010-0.0027	NA	NA
	R	5.7 (5735)	46	45	187-203@1.27	1.69-1.71	0.0010-0.0027	0.0010-0.0027	NA	NA
	F/Y	6.5 (6473)	46	45	230@1.40	1.80	0.0010-0.0027	0.0010-0.0027	NA	NA
	J/N	7.4 (7440)	46	45	238-262@1.34	1.83	0.0010- ① 0.0029	0.0012- ① 0.0031	NA	NA

NA - Not Available
① Service limit:
   Intake: 0.0037 MAX
   Exhaust: 0.0049 MAX

88193C05

CAMSHAFT SPECIFICATIONS

All measurements given in inches.

Year	Engine ID/VIN	Displacement Liters (cc)	Journal Diameter					Elevation		Bearing Clearance	Camshaft End-Play
			1	2	3	4	5	Intake	Exhaust		
1987	Z	4.3 (4293)	1.8682-1.8692	1.8682-1.8692	1.8682-1.8692	1.8682-1.8692	N/A	0.3570	0.3900	0.0010-0.0030	0.0040-0.0120
	H	5.0 (4999)	1.8682-1.8692	1.8682-1.8692	1.8682-1.8692	1.8682-1.8692	1.8682-1.8692	0.2484	0.2667	N/A	0.0040-0.0120
	K	5.7 (5735)	1.8682-1.8692	1.8682-1.8692	1.8682-1.8692	1.8682-1.8692	1.8682-1.8692	0.2600	0.2733	N/A	0.0040-0.0120
	C	6.2 (6210)	2.1633-2.1642	2.1633-2.1642	2.1633-2.1642	2.1633-2.1642	2.0067-2.0089	0.2808	0.2808		N/A
	J	6.2 (6210)	2.1633-2.1642	2.1633-2.1642	2.1633-2.1642	2.1633-2.1642	2.0067-2.0089	0.2808	0.2808		N/A
	N	7.4 (7440)	1.9482-1.9492	1.9482-1.9492	1.9482-1.9492	1.9482-1.9492	1.9482-1.9492	0.2341-0.2345	0.2529-0.2531	N/A	N/A
	W	7.4 (7440)	1.9482-1.9492	1.9482-1.9492	1.9482-1.9492	1.9482-1.9492	1.9482-1.9492	0.2341-0.2345	0.2529-0.2531	N/A	N/A
1988	Z	4.3 (4293)	1.8682-1.8692	1.8682-1.8692	1.8682-1.8692	1.8682-1.8692	N/A	0.3570	0.3900	0.0010-0.0030	0.0040-0.0120
	H	5.0 (4999)	1.8682-1.8692	1.8682-1.8692	1.8682-1.8692	1.8682-1.8692	1.8682-1.8692	0.2484	0.2667	N/A	0.0040-0.0120
	K	5.7 (5735)	1.8682-1.8692	1.8682-1.8692	1.8682-1.8692	1.8682-1.8692	1.8682-1.8692	0.2600	0.2733	N/A	0.0040-0.0120
	C	6.2 (6210)	2.1633-2.1642	2.1633-2.1642	2.1633-2.1642	2.1633-2.1642	2.0067-2.0089	0.2808	0.2808		N/A
	J	6.2 (6210)	2.1633-2.1642	2.1633-2.1642	2.1633-2.1642	2.1633-2.1642	2.0067-2.0089	0.2808	0.2808		N/A
	N	7.4 (7440)	1.9482-1.9492	1.9482-1.9492	1.9482-1.9492	1.9482-1.9492	1.9482-1.9492	0.2341-0.2345	0.2529-0.2531	N/A	N/A
	W	7.4 (7440)	1.9482-1.9492	1.9482-1.9492	1.9482-1.9492	1.9482-1.9492	1.9482-1.9492	0.2341-0.2345	0.2529-0.2531	N/A	N/A
1989	Z	4.3 (4293)	1.8682-1.8692	1.8682-1.8692	1.8682-1.8692	1.8682-1.8692	N/A	0.3570	0.3900	0.0010-0.0030	0.0040-0.0120
	H	5.0 (4999)	1.8682-1.8692	1.8682-1.8692	1.8682-1.8692	1.8682-1.8692	1.8682-1.8692	0.2484	0.2667	N/A	0.0040-0.0120
	K	5.7 (5735)	1.8682-1.8692	1.8682-1.8692	1.8682-1.8692	1.8682-1.8692	1.8682-1.8692	0.2600	0.2733	N/A	0.0040-0.0120
	C	6.2 (6210)	2.1633-2.1642	2.1633-2.1642	2.1633-2.1642	2.1633-2.1642	2.0067-2.0089	0.2808	0.2808		N/A
	J	6.2 (6210)	2.1633-2.1642	2.1633-2.1642	2.1633-2.1642	2.1633-2.1642	2.0067-2.0089	0.2808	0.2808		N/A
	N	7.4 (7440)	1.9482-1.9492	1.9482-1.9492	1.9482-1.9492	1.9482-1.9492	1.9482-1.9492	0.2341-0.2345	0.2529-0.2531	N/A	N/A
	W	7.4 (7440)	1.9482-1.9492	1.9482-1.9492	1.9482-1.9492	1.9482-1.9492	1.9482-1.9492	0.2341-0.2345	0.2529-0.2531	N/A	N/A
1990	Z	4.3 (4293)	1.8682-1.8692	1.8682-1.8692	1.8682-1.8692	1.8682-1.8692	N/A	0.3570	0.3900	0.0010-0.0030	0.0040-0.0120
	H	5.0 (4999)	1.8682-1.8692	1.8682-1.8692	1.8682-1.8692	1.8682-1.8692	1.8682-1.8692	0.2484	0.2667	N/A	0.0040-0.0120

88193C06

CAMSHAFT SPECIFICATIONS

All measurements given in inches.

Year	Engine ID/VIN	Displacement Liters (cc)	Journal Diameter					Elevation		Bearing Clearance	Camshaft End-Play
			1	2	3	4	5	Intake	Exhaust		
1990	K	5.7 (5735)	1.8682-1.8692	1.8682-1.8692	1.8682-1.8692	1.8682-1.8692	1.8682-1.8692	0.2600	0.2733	N/A	0.0040-0.0120
	C	6.2 (6210)	2.1633-2.1642	2.1633-2.1642	2.1633-2.1642	2.1633-2.1642	2.0067-2.0089	0.2808	0.2808		N/A
	J	6.2 (6210)	2.1633-2.1642	2.1633-2.1642	2.1633-2.1642	2.1633-2.1642	2.0067-2.0089	0.2808	0.2808		N/A
	N	7.4 (7440)	1.9482-1.9492	1.9482-1.9492	1.9482-1.9492	1.9482-1.9492	1.9482-1.9492	0.2341-0.2345	0.2529-0.2531	N/A	N/A
1991	Z	4.3 (4293)	1.8682-1.8692	1.8682-1.8692	1.8682-1.8692	1.8682-1.8692	N/A	0.3570	0.3900	0.0010-0.0030	0.0040-0.0120
	H	5.0 (4999)	1.8682-1.8692	1.8682-1.8692	1.8682-1.8692	1.8682-1.8692	1.8682-1.8692	0.2484	0.2667	N/A	0.0040-0.0120
	K	5.7 (5735)	1.8682-1.8692	1.8682-1.8692	1.8682-1.8692	1.8682-1.8692	1.8682-1.8692	0.2600	0.2733	N/A	0.0040-0.0120
	C	6.2 (6210)	2.1633-2.1642	2.1633-2.1642	2.1633-2.1642	2.1633-2.1642	2.0067-2.0089	0.2808	0.2808		N/A
	J	6.2 (6210)	2.1633-2.1642	2.1633-2.1642	2.1633-2.1642	2.1633-2.1642	2.0067-2.0089	0.2808	0.2808		N/A
	N	7.4 (7440)	1.9482-1.9492	1.9482-1.9492	1.9482-1.9492	1.9482-1.9492	1.9482-1.9492	0.2341-0.2345	0.2529-0.2531	N/A	N/A
1992	Z	4.3 (4293)	1.8682-1.8692	1.8682-1.8692	1.8682-1.8692	1.8682-1.8692	N/A	0.2340	0.2570..	0.0010-0.0030	0.0040-0.0120
	H	5.0 (4999)	1.8682-1.8692	1.8682-1.8692	1.8682-1.8692	1.8682-1.8692	1.8682-1.8692	0.2336	0.2565	N/A	0.0040-0.0120
	K	5.7 (5735)	1.8682-1.8692	1.8682-1.8692	1.8682-1.8692	1.8682-1.8692	1.8682-1.8692	0.2565	0.2690	N/A	0.0040-0.0120
	C	6.2 (6210)	2.1633-2.1642	2.1633-2.1642	2.1633-2.1642	2.1633-2.1642	2.0067-2.0089	0.2808	0.2808	0.0010-0.0040	0.0020-0.0120
	J	6.2 (6210)	2.1633-2.1642	2.1633-2.1642	2.1633-2.1642	2.1633-2.1642	2.0067-2.0089	0.2808	0.2808	0.0010-0.0040	0.0020-0.0120
	F	6.5 (6473)	2.1642-2.1663	2.1642-2.1663	2.1642-2.1663	2.1642-2.1663	2.0067-2.0089	0.2808	0.2808	N/A	0.0020-0.0120
	N	7.4 (7440)	1.9482-1.9492	1.9482-1.9492	1.9482-1.9492	1.9482-1.9492	1.9482-1.9492	0.2341-0.2345	0.2529-0.2531	N/A	N/A
1993	Z	4.3 (4293)	1.8682-1.8692	1.8682-1.8692	1.8682-1.8692	1.8682-1.8692	N/A	0.2340	0.2570..	0.0010-0.0030	0.0040-0.0120
	H	5.0 (4999)	1.8682-1.8692	1.8682-1.8692	1.8682-1.8692	1.8682-1.8692	1.8682-1.8692	0.2336	0.2565	N/A	0.0040-0.0120
	K	5.7 (5735)	1.8682-1.8692	1.8682-1.8692	1.8682-1.8692	1.8682-1.8692	1.8682-1.8692	0.2565	0.2690	N/A	0.0040-0.0120
	C	6.2 (6210)	2.1633-2.1642	2.1633-2.1642	2.1633-2.1642	2.1633-2.1642	2.0067-2.0089	0.2808	0.2808	0.0010-0.0040	0.0020-0.0120
	J	6.2 (6210)	2.1633-2.1642	2.1633-2.1642	2.1633-2.1642	2.1633-2.1642	2.0067-2.0089	0.2808	0.2808	0.0010-0.0040	0.0020-0.0120
	F	6.5 (6473)	2.1642-2.1663	2.1642-2.1663	2.1642-2.1663	2.1642-2.1663	2.0067-2.0089	0.2808	0.2808	N/A	0.0020-0.0120
	N	7.4 (7440)	1.9482-1.9492	1.9482-1.9492	1.9482-1.9492	1.9482-1.9492	1.9482-1.9492	0.2341-0.2345	0.2529-0.2531	N/A	N/A

88193C07

CAMSHAFT SPECIFICATIONS
All measurements given in inches.

Year	Engine ID/VIN	Displacement Liters (cc)	Journal Diameter 1	2	3	4	5	Elevation Intake	Exhaust	Bearing Clearance	Camshaft End-Play
1994	Z	4.3 (4293)	1.8682-1.8692	1.8682-1.8692	1.8682-1.8692	1.8682-1.8692	N/A	0.2340	0.2570..	0.0010-0.0030	0.0040-0.0120
	H	5.0 (4999)	1.8682-1.8692	1.8682-1.8692	1.8682-1.8692	1.8682-1.8692	1.8682-1.8692	0.2336	0.2565	N/A	0.0040-0.0120
	K	5.7 (5735)	1.8682-1.8692	1.8682-1.8692	1.8682-1.8692	1.8682-1.8692	1.8682-1.8692	0.2565	0.2690	N/A	0.0040- 0 0.0120
	Y	6.5 (6473)	2.1642-2.1663	2.1642-2.1663	2.1642-2.1663	2.1642-2.1663	2.0067-2.0089	0.2808	0.2808	N/A	0.0020-0.0120
	P	6.5 (6473)	2.1642-2.1663	2.1642-2.1663	2.1642-2.1663	2.1642-2.1663	2.0067-2.0089	0.2808	0.2808	N/A	0.0020-0.0120
	N	7.4 (7440)	1.9482-1.9492	1.9482-1.9492	1.9482-1.9492	1.9482-1.9492	1.9482-1.9492	0.2341-0.2345	0.2529-0.2531	N/A	N/A
1995	Z	4.3 (4293)	1.8682-1.8692	1.8682-1.8692	1.8682-1.8692	1.8682-1.8692	N/A	0.2340	0.2570..	0.0010-0.0030	0.0040-0.0120
	H	5.0 (4999)	1.8682-1.8692	1.8682-1.8692	1.8682-1.8692	1.8682-1.8692	1.8682-1.8692	0.2336	0.2565	N/A	0.0040-0.0120
	K	5.7 (5735)	1.8682-1.8692	1.8682-1.8692	1.8682-1.8692	1.8682-1.8692	1.8682-1.8692	0.2565	0.2690	N/A	0.0040-0.0120
	Y	6.5 (6473)	2.1642-2.1663	2.1642-2.1663	2.1642-2.1663	2.1642-2.1663	2.0067-2.0089	0.2808	0.2808	N/A	0.0020-0.0120
	F	6.5 (6473)	2.1642-2.1663	2.1642-2.1663	2.1642-2.1663	2.1642-2.1663	2.0067-2.0089	0.2808	0.2808	N/A	0.0020-0.0120
	N	7.4 (7440)	1.9477-1.9497	1.9477-1.9497	1.9477-1.9497	1.9477-1.9497	1.9477-1.9497	0.2485-0.2489	0.2535-0.2539	N/A	N/A
1996	W	4.3 (4293)	1.8677-1.8697	1.8677-1.8697	1.8677-1.8697	1.8677-1.8697	N/A	0.2761-0.2765	0.2853-0.2857	N/A	0.001-0.0090
	M	5.0 (4999)	1.8677-1.8697	1.8677-1.8697	1.8677-1.8697	1.8677-1.8697	1.8677-1.8697	0.274-0.2780	0.283-0.2870	N/A	N/A
	R	5.7 (5735)	1.8677-1.8697	1.8677-1.8697	1.8677-1.8697	1.8677-1.8697	1.8677-1.8697	0.274-0.2780	0.283-0.2870	N/A	N/A
	F	6.5 (6473)	2.1658-2.1680	2.1658-2.1680	2.1658-2.1680	2.1658-2.1680	2.0082-2.0104	0.2810	0.2810	N/A	0.0020-0.0120
	P	6.5 (6473)	2.1658-2.1680	2.1658-2.1680	2.1658-2.1680	2.1658-2.1680	2.0082-2.0104	0.2810	0.2810	N/A	0.0020-0.0120
	J	7.4 (7440)	1.9477-1.9497	1.9477-1.9497	1.9477-1.9497	1.9477-1.9497	1.9477-1.9497	0.2821	0.2843	N/A	N/A
1997	W	4.3 (4293)	1.8677-1.8697	1.8677-1.8697	1.8677-1.8697	1.8677-1.8697	N/A	0.2761-0.2765	0.2853-0.2857	N/A	0.001-0.0090
	M	5.0 (4999)	1.8677-1.8697	1.8677-1.8697	1.8677-1.8697	1.8677-1.8697	1.8677-1.8697	0.274-0.2780	0.283-0.2870	N/A	N/A
	R	5.7 (5735)	1.8677-1.8697	1.8677-1.8697	1.8677-1.8697	1.8677-1.8697	1.8677-1.8697	0.274-0.2780	0.283-0.2870	N/A	N/A
	Y	6.5 (6473)	2.1658-2.1680	2.1658-2.1680	2.1658-2.1680	2.1658-2.1680	2.0082-2.0104	0.2810	0.2810	N/A	0.0020-0.0120
	F	6.5 (6473)	2.1658-2.1680	2.1658-2.1680	2.1658-2.1680	2.1658-2.1680	2.0082-2.0104	0.2810	0.2810	N/A	0.0020-0.0120
	J	7.4 (7440)	1.9477-1.9497	1.9477-1.9497	1.9477-1.9497	1.9477-1.9497	1.9477-1.9497	0.2821	0.2843	N/A	N/A

N/A - Not Available

88193C08

CRANKSHAFT AND CONNECTING ROD SPECIFICATIONS

All measurements are given in inches.

Year	Engine ID/VIN	Engine Displacement Liters (cc)	Crankshaft Main Brg. Journal Dia.	Main Brg Oil Clearance	Shaft End-play	Thrust on No.	Connecting Rod Journal	Oil Clearance	Side Clearance
1987	Z	4.3 (4293)	②	③	0.0020-0.0060	3	2.2487-2.2497	0.0013-0.0035	0.0060-0.0140
	H	5.0 (4999)	③	③	0.0020-0.0060	5	2.0990-2.1000	0.0013-0.0035	0.0060-0.0140
	K	5.7 (5735)	②	③	0.0020-0.0060	5	2.0988-2.0998	0.0013-0.0035	0.0060-0.0140
	C	6.2 (6210)	⑤	⑥	0.0020-0.0070	3	2.3980-2.3990	0.0017-0.0039	0.0070-0.0240
	J	6.2 (6210)	⑤	⑥	0.0020-0.0070	3	2.3980-2.3990	0.0017-0.0039	0.0070-0.0240
	N	7.4 (7440)	⑦	⑧	0.0060-0.0100	5	2.1990-2.2000	0.00009-0.0025	0.0130-0.0230
	W	7.4 (7440)	⑦	⑧	0.0060-0.0100	5	2.1990-2.2000	0.00009-0.0025	0.0130-0.0230
1988	Z	4.3 (4293)	②	③	0.0020-0.0060	3	2.2487-2.2497	0.0013-0.0035	0.0060-0.0140
	H	5.0 (4999)	②	③	0.0020-0.0060	5	2.0990-2.1000	0.0013-0.0035	0.0060-0.0140
	K	5.7 (5735)	②	③	0.0020-0.0060	5	2.0988-2.0998	0.0013-0.0035	0.0060-0.0140
	C	6.2 (6210)	⑤	⑥	0.0020-0.0070	3	2.3980-2.3990	0.0017-0.0039	0.0070-0.0240
	J	6.2 (6210)	⑤	⑥	0.0020-0.0070	3	2.3980-2.3990	0.0017-0.0039	0.0070-0.0240
	N	7.4 (7440)	⑦	⑧	0.0060-0.0100	5	2.1990-2.2000	0.00009-0.0025	0.0130-0.0230
	W	7.4 (7440)	⑦	⑧	0.0060-0.0100	5	2.1990-2.2000	0.00009-0.0025	0.0130-0.0230
1989	Z	4.3 (4293)	②	③	0.0020-0.0060	3	2.2487-2.2497	0.0013-0.0035	0.0060-0.0140
	H	5.0 (4999)	②	③	0.0020-0.0060	5	2.0988-2.0998	0.0013-0.0035	0.0060-0.0140
	K	5.7 (5735)	②	③	0.0020-0.0060	5	2.0988-2.0998	0.0013-0.0035	0.0060-0.0140
	C	6.2 (6210)	⑤	⑥	0.0020-0.0070	3	2.3980-2.3990	0.0017-0.0039	0.0070-0.0240
	J	6.2 (6210)	⑤	⑥	0.0020-0.0070	3	2.3980-2.3990	0.0017-0.0039	0.0070-0.0240
	N	7.4 (7440)	⑦	⑧	0.0060-0.0100	5	2.1990-2.2000	0.00009-0.0025	0.0130-0.0230
	W	7.4 (7440)	⑦	⑧	0.0060-0.0100	5	2.1990-2.2000	0.00009-0.0025	0.0130-0.0230

88193C09

CRANKSHAFT AND CONNECTING ROD SPECIFICATIONS

All measurements are given in inches.

| Year | Engine ID/VIN | Engine Displacement Liters (cc) | Crankshaft | | | | Connecting Rod | | |
			Main Brg. Journal Dia.	Main Brg Oil Clearance	Shaft End-play	Thrust on No.	Journal	Oil Clearance	Side Clearance
1990	Z	4.3 (4293)	②	③	0.0020-0.0060	3	2.2487-2.2497	0.0013-0.0035	0.0060-0.0140
	H	5.0 (4999)	②	③	0.0020-0.0060	5	2.0988-2.0998	0.0013-0.0035	0.0060-0.0140
	K	5.7 (5735)	②	③	0.0020-0.0060	5	2.0988-2.0998	0.0013-0.0035	0.0060-0.0140
	C	6.2 (6210)	⑤	⑥	0.0020-0.0070	3	2.3980-2.3990	0.0017-0.0039	0.0070-0.0240
	J	6.2 (6210)	⑤	⑥	0.0020-0.0070	3	2.3980-2.3990	0.0017-0.0039	0.0070-0.0240
	N	7.4 (7440)	⑦	⑧	0.0060-0.0100	5	2.1990-2.2000	0.00009-0.0025	0.0130-0.0230
1991	Z	4.3 (4293)	②	③	0.0020-0.0060	3	2.2487-2.2497	0.0013-0.0035	0.0060-0.0140
	H	5.0 (4999)	②	③	0.0020-0.0060	5	2.0988-2.0998	0.0013-0.0035	0.0060-0.0140
	K	5.7 (5735)	②	③	0.0020-0.0060	5	2.0988-2.0998	0.0013-0.0035	0.0060-0.0140
	C	6.2 (6210)	④	⑤	0.0020-0.0070	3	2.3980-2.3990	0.0017-0.0039	0.0070-0.0240
	J	6.2 (6210)	④	⑤	0.0020-0.0070	3	2.3980-2.3990	0.0017-0.0039	0.0070-0.0240
	N	7.4 (7440)	⑥	⑦	0.0060-0.0100	5	2.1990-2.2000	0.00009-0.0025	0.0130-0.0230
1992	Z	4.3 (4293)	②	③	0.0020-0.0060	3	2.2487-2.2497	0.0013-0.0035	0.0060-0.0140
	H	5.0 (4999)	②	③	0.0020-0.0060	5	2.0990-2.1000	0.0013-0.0035	0.0060-0.0140
	K	5.7 (5735)	②	③	0.0020-0.0060	5	2.0988-2.0998	0.0013-0.0035	0.0060-0.0140
	C	6.2 (6210)	④	⑤	0.0020-0.0070	3	2.3980-2.3990	0.0017-0.0039	0.0070-0.0240
	J	6.2 (6210)	④	⑤	0.0020-0.0070	3	2.3980-2.3990	0.0017-0.0039	0.0070-0.0240
	F	6.5 (6473)	④	⑤	0.0020-0.0070	3	2.3980-2.3990	0.0017-0.0039	0.0070-0.0240
	N	7.4 (7440)	⑥	⑦	0.0060-0.0100	5	2.1990-2.2000	0.00009-0.0025	0.0130-0.0230
1993	Z	4.3 (4293)	②	③	0.0020-0.0060	3	2.2487-2.2497	0.0013-0.0035	0.0060-0.0140
	H	5.0 (4999)	②	③	0.0020-0.0060	3	2.0988-2.0998	0.0013-0.0035	0.0060-0.0140
	K	5.7 (5735)	②	③	0.002-0.0060	3	2.0988-2.0998	0.0013-0.0035	0.0060-0.0140

88193C10

CRANKSHAFT AND CONNECTING ROD SPECIFICATIONS
All measurements are given in inches.

| Year | Engine ID/VIN | Engine Displacement Liters (cc) | Crankshaft | | | | Connecting Rod | | |
			Main Brg. Journal Dia.	Main Brg Oil Clearance	Shaft End-play	Thrust on No.	Journal	Oil Clearance	Side Clearance
1993	C	6.2 (6210)	④	⑤	0.0020-0.0070	3	2.3980-2.3990	0.0017-0.0039	0.0070-0.0240
	J	6.2 (6210)	④	⑤	0.0020-0.0070	3	2.3980-2.3990	0.0017-0.0039	0.0070-0.0240
	F	6.5 (6473)	④	⑤	0.0020-0.0070	3	2.3980-2.3990	0.0017-0.0039	0.0070-0.0240
	N	7.4 (7440)	⑥	⑦	0.0060-0.0100	5	2.1990-2.2000	0.00009-0.0025	0.0130-0.0230
1994	Z	4.3 (4293)	②	③	0.0020-0.0060	3	2.2487-2.2497	0.0013-0.0035	0.0060-0.0140
	H	5.0 (4999)	②	③	0.0020-0.0060	5	2.0988-2.0998	0.0013-0.0035	0.0060-0.0140
	K	5.7 (5735)	②	③	0.0020-0.0060	5	2.0988-2.0998	0.0013-0.0035	0.0060-0.0140
	Y	6.5 (6473)	④	⑤	0.0040-0.0098	3	2.3980-2.3990	0.0017-0.0039	0.0070-0.0240
	P	6.5 (6473)	④	⑤	0.0040-0.0098	3	2.3980-2.3990	0.0017-0.0039	0.0070-0.0240
	N	7.4 (7440)	⑥	⑦	0.0060-0.0100	5	2.1990-2.2000	0.00009-0.0025	0.0130-0.0230
1995	Z	4.3 (4293)	②	③	0.0020-0.0060	3	2.2487-2.2497	0.0013-0.0035	0.015-0.0460
	H	5.0 (4999)	②	③	0.002-0.0060	5	2.0988-2.0998	0.0013-0.0035	0.0060-0.0140
	K	5.7 (5735)	②	③	0.0020-0.0060	5	2.0988-2.0998	0.0013-0.0035	0.0060-0.0140
	Y	6.5 (6473)	④	⑤	0.0040-0.0098	3	2.3980-2.3990	0.0017-0.0039	0.0070-0.0240
	F	6.5 (6473)	④	⑤	0.0040-0.0098	3	2.3980-2.3990	0.0017-0.0039	0.0070-0.0240
	N	7.4 (7440)	⑥	⑦	0.0060-0.0100	5	2.1990-2.2000	0.00009-0.0025	0.0130-0.0230
1996	W	4.3 (4293)	⑨	NA	0.002-0.0080	4	2.2487-2.2497	0.0010-0.003	0.006-0.0170
	M	5.0 (4999)	⑪	NA	0.0020-0.0080	5	2.0978-2.0998	0.0013-0.0035	0.006-0.0140
	R	5.7 (5735)	⑪	NA	0.0020-0.0080	5	2.0978-2.0998	0.0013-0.0035	0.006-0.0140
	Y	6.5 (6473)	⑩	NA	0.0039-0.0010	3	⑫	0.0018-0.0039	0.0067-0.0248
	P	6.5 (6473)	⑩	NA	0.0039-0.0010	3	⑫	0.0018-0.0039	0.0067-0.0248
	J	7.4 (7440)	⑬	NA	0.0050-0.0110	5	2.1990-2.1996	0.0011-0.0029	0.0130-0.0230

88193C11

CRANKSHAFT AND CONNECTING ROD SPECIFICATIONS
All measurements are given in inches.

| Year | Engine ID/VIN | Engine Displacement Liters (cc) | Crankshaft | | | | Connecting Rod | | |
			Main Brg. Journal Dia.	Main Brg Oil Clearance	Shaft End-play	Thrust on No.	Journal	Oil Clearance	Side Clearance
1997	W	4.3 (4293)	⑨	NA	0.0020-0.0080	4	2.2487-2.2497	0.0010-0.003	0.006-0.0170
	M	5.0 (4999)	⑪	NA	0.0020-0.0080	5	2.0978-2.0998	0.0013-0.0035	0.006-0.0140
	R	5.7 (5735)	⑪	NA	0.0020-0.0080	5	2.0978-2.0998	0.0013-0.0035	0.006-0.0140
	Y	6.5 (6473)	⑩	NA	0.0039-0.0010	3	⑫	0.0018-0.0039	0.0067-0.0248
	F	6.5 (6473)	⑩	NA	0.0039-0.0010	3	⑫	0.0018-0.0039	0.0067-0.0248
	J	7.4 (7440)	⑬	NA	0.0050-0.0110	5	2.1990-2.1996	0.0011-0.0029	0.0130-0.0230

① No. 1 2.4484-2.4493
  Nos. 2-3 : 2.4485-2.4494
  No. 4 : 2.4479-2.4488
② No. 1 : 2.4484-2.4493
  Nos. 2-3: 2.4481-2.4490
  No. 4 :2.4479-2.4488
③ Nos. 1 : 0.0008-0.0020
  Nos. 2-3 : 0.0011-0.0023
  Nos. 4 0.0017-0.0032
④ Nos. 1-6. 0.0010-0.0024
  No. 7 : 0.0016-0.0035

⑤ 1-4: 2.9495-2.9504
  No. 5 : 2.9493-2.9502
⑥ 1-4: 0.0083
  No. 5 : 0.0055-0.0093
⑦ 1-4: 2.7481-2.7490
  No. 5 : 2.7476-2.7486
⑧ Nos. 1-4 : 0.0013-0.0025
  No 5 : 0.0024-0.0040
⑨ Two dots : 1.9983-1.9989
  One dot : 1.9989-1.9994

⑩ No. 1 2.4488-2.4495
  Nos. 2-3 : 2.4485-2.4494
  No. 4 : 2.4480-2.4489
⑩ Blue
  Nos. 1-4 : 2.9517-2.9520
  No. 5 : 2.9515-2.9518
Orange or Red
  Nos. 1-4 : 2.9518-2.9522
White
  Nos. 1-4 : 2.9524-2.9527
  No. 5 : 2.9522-2.9525

⑪ No. 1 0.0007-0.0021
  Nos. 2-4 : 0.0009-0.0024
  No. 5 : 0.0010-0.0027
⑫ Green
  2.399-2.400
Yellow
  2.400-2.401
⑬ All : 2.7482-2.7489

88193C12

PISTON AND RING SPECIFICATIONS

All measurements are given in inches.

Year	Engine ID/VIN	Engine Displacement Liters (cc)	Piston Clearance	Ring Gap		Ring Side Clearance		
				Top Compression	Oil Control	Top Compression	Bottom Compression	Oil Control
1987	Z	4.3 (4293)	0.0007-0.0017	0.010-0.020	0.015-0.055	0.0012-0.0032	0.0012-0.0032	0.0020-0.0070
	H	5.0 (4999)	0.0007-0.0017	0.010-0.020	0.015-0.055	0.0012-0.0032	0.0012-0.0032	0.0020-0.0070
	K	5.7 (5735)	0.0007-0.0017	0.010-0.020	0.015-0.055	0.0012-0.0032	0.0012-0.0032	0.0020-0.0070
	C	6.2 (6210)	①	0.010-0.020	0.0090-0.0.02	0.0200-0.0070	0.0200-0.0300	0.0010-0.0030
	J	6.2 (6210)	①	0.010-0.020	0.0090-0.0.02	0.0200-0.0070	0.0200-0.0300	0.0010-0.0030
	N	7.4 (7440)	0.0030-0.0042	0.010-0.018	0.010-0.030	0.0012-0.0029	0.0012-0.0029	0.0050-0.0065
	W	7.4 (7440)	0.0030-0.0042	0.010-0.018	0.010-0.030	0.0012-0.0029	0.0012-0.0029	0.0050-0.0065
1988	Z	4.3 (4293)	0.0007-0.0017	0.010-0.020	0.015-0.055	0.0012-0.0032	0.0012-0.0032	0.0020-0.0070
	H	5.0 (4999)	0.0007-0.0017	0.010-0.020	0.015-0.055	0.0012-0.0032	0.0012-0.0032	0.0020-0.0070
	K	5.7 (5735)	0.0007-0.0017	0.010-0.020	0.015-0.055	0.0012-0.0032	0.0012-0.0032	0.0020-0.0070
	C	6.2 (6210)	①	0.010-0.020	0.0090-0.0.02	0.0200-0.0070	0.0200-0.0300	0.0010-0.0030
	J	6.2 (6210)	①	0.010-0.020	0.0090-0.0.02	0.0200-0.0070	0.0200-0.0300	0.0010-0.0030
	N	7.4 (7440)	0.0030-0.0042	0.010-0.018	0.010-0.030	0.0012-0.0029	0.0012-0.0029	0.0050-0.0065
	W	7.4 (7440)	0.0042	0.010-0.018	0.010-0.030	0.0012-0.0029	0.0012-0.0029	0.0050-0.0065
1989	Z	4.3 (4293)	0.0007-0.0017	0.010-0.020	0.015-0.055	0.0012-0.0032	0.0012-0.0032	0.0020-0.0070
	H	5.0 (4999)	0.0007-0.0017	0.010-0.020	0.015-0.055	0.0012-0.0032	0.0012-0.0032	0.0020-0.0070
	K	5.7 (5735)	0.0007-0.0017	0.010-0.020	0.015-0.055	0.0012-0.0032	0.0012-0.0032	0.0020-0.0070
	C	6.2 (6210)	①	0.010-0.020	0.0090-0.0.02	0.0200-0.0070	0.0200-0.0300	0.0010-0.0030
	J	6.2 (6210)	①	0.010-0.020	0.0090-0.0.02	0.0200-0.0070	0.0200-0.0300	0.0010-0.0030
	N	7.4 (7440)	0.0030-0.0042	0.010-0.018	0.010-0.030	0.0012-0.0029	0.0012-0.0029	0.0050-0.0065
	W	7.4 (7440)	0.0030-0.0042	0.010-0.018	0.010-0.030	0.0012-0.0029	0.0012-0.0029	0.0050-0.0065

88193C13

PISTON AND RING SPECIFICATIONS

All measurements are given in inches.

Year	Engine ID/VIN	Engine Displacement Liters (cc)	Piston Clearance	Ring Gap Top Compression	Ring Gap Oil Control	Ring Side Clearance Top Compression	Ring Side Clearance Bottom Compression	Ring Side Clearance Oil Control
1990	Z	4.3 (4293)	0.0007-0.0017	0.010-0.020	0.015-0.055	0.0012-0.0032	0.0012-0.0032	0.0020-0.0070
	H	5.0 (4999)	0.0007-0.0017	0.010-0.020	0.015-0.055	0.0012-0.0032	0.0012-0.0032	0.0020-0.0070
	K	5.7 (5735)	0.0007-0.0017	0.010-0.020	0.015-0.055	0.0012-0.0032	0.0012-0.0032	0.0020-0.0070
	C	6.2 (6210)	①	0.010-0.002	0.0090-0.0.02	0.0200-0.0070	0.0200-0.0300	0.0010-0.0030
	J	6.2 (6210)	①	0.010-0.020	0.0090-0.0.02	0.0200-0.0070	0.0200-0.0300	0.0010-0.0030
	N	7.4 (7440)	0.0030-0.0042	0.010-0.018	0.010-0.030	0.0012-0.0029	0.0012-0.0029	0.0050-0.0065
1991	Z	4.3 (4293)	0.0007-0.0017	0.010-0.020	0.015-0.055	0.0012-0.0032	0.0012-0.0032	0.0020-0.0070
	H	5.0 (4999)	0.0007-0.0017	0.010-0.020	0.015-0.055	0.0012-0.0032	0.0012-0.0032	0.0020-0.0070
	K	5.7 (5735)	0.0007-0.0017	0.010-0.020	0.015-0.055	0.0012-0.0032	0.0012-0.0032	0.0020-0.0070
	C	6.2 (6210)	①	0.01-0.0.02	0.0090-0.0.02	0.0200-0.0070	0.0200-0.0300	0.0010-0.0030
	J	6.2 (6210)	①	0.010-0.020	0.0090-0.0.02	0.0200-0.0070	0.0200-0.0300	0.0010-0.0030
	N	7.4 (7440)	0.0030-0.0040	0.010-0.018	0.010-0.030	0.0012-0.0029	0.0012-0.0029	0.0050-0.0065
1992	Z	4.3 (4293)	0.0007-0.0017	0.010-0.020	0.015-0.055	0.0012-0.0032	0.0012-0.0032	0.0020-0.0070
	H	5.0 (4999)	0.0007-0.0017	0.010-0.020	0.015-0.055	0.0012-0.0032	0.0012-0.0032	0.0020-0.0070
	K	5.7 (5735)	0.0007-0.0017	0.010-0.020	0.015-0.055	0.0012-0.0032	0.0012-0.0032	0.0020-0.0070
	C	6.2 (6210)	①	0.030-0.055	0.76-0.178	0.075-1.0000	0.040-0.0960	0.040-0.0960
	J	6.2 (6210)	①	0.030-0.055	0.76-0.178	0.075-1.0000	0.040-0.0960	0.040-0.0960
	F	6.5 (6473)	②	0.26-0.5100	0.25-0.51	④	0.030-0.0790	0.040-0.090
	N	7.4 (7440)	0.0030-0.0042	0.010-0.018	0.010-0.030	0.0012-0.0029	0.0012-0.0029	0.0050-0.0065
1993	Z	4.3 (4293)	0.0007-0.0017	0.010-0.020	0.015-0.055	0.0012-0.0032	0.0012-0.0032	0.0020-0.0070
	H	5.0 (4999)	0.0007-0.0021	0.010-0.020	0.010-0.030	0.0012-0.0032	0.0012-0.0032	0.0020-0.0070
	K	5.7 (5735)	0.0007-0.0021	0.010-0.020	0.010-0.030	0.0012-0.0032	0.0012-0.0032	0.0020-0.0070

88193C14

PISTON AND RING SPECIFICATIONS
All measurements are given in inches.

Year	Engine ID/VIN	Engine Displacement Liters (cc)	Piston Clearance	Ring Gap Top Compression	Ring Gap Oil Control	Ring Side Clearance Top Compression	Ring Side Clearance Bottom Compression	Ring Side Clearance Oil Control
1993	C	6.2 (6210)	①	0.030-0.055	0.76-0.178	0.075-1.0000	0.040-0.0960	0.040-0.0960
	J	6.2 (6210)	①	0.030-0.055	0.76-0.178	0.075-1.0000	0.040-0.0960	0.040-0.0960
	F	6.5 (6473)	②	0.010-0.020	0.010-0.020	③	0.0015-0.0030	0.0015-0.0035
	N	7.4 (7440)	0.0003-0.0042	0.010-0.018	0.010-0.030	0.0012-0.0029	0.0012-0.0029	0.0050-0.0065
1994	Z	4.3 (4293)	0.0007-0.0017	0.010-0.020	0.015-0.055	0.0012-0.0032	0.0012-0.0032	0.0020-0.0070
	H	5.0 (4999)	0.0007-0.0021	0.010-0.020	0.010-0.030	0.0012-0.0032	0.0012-0.0032	0.0020-0.0070
	K	5.7 (5735)	0.0007-0.0021	0.010-0.020	0.010-0.030	0.0012-0.0032	0.0012-0.0032	0.0020-0.0070
	Y	6.5 (6473)	②	0.010-0.020	0.010-0.020	③	0.0015-0.0030	0.0015-0.0035
	P	6.5 (6473)	②	0.010-0.020	0.010-0.020	③	0.0015-0.0030	0.0015-0.0035
	N	7.4 (7440)	0.0018-0.0030	0.010-0.018	0.010-0.030	0.0012-0.0029	0.0012-0.0029	0.0050-0.0065
1995	Z	4.3 (4293)	0.0007-0.0024	0.010-0.020	0.015-0.055	0.0012-0.0032	0.0012-0.0032	0.0020-0.0070
	H	5.0 (4999)	0.0007-0.0021	0.010-0.020	0.010-0.030	0.0012-0.0032	0.0012-0.0032	0.0020-0.0070
	K	5.7 (5735)	0.0007-0.0021	0.010-0.020	0.010-0.030	0.0012-0.0032	0.0012-0.0032	0.0020-0.0070
	Y	6.5 (6473)	②	0.010-0.020	0.010-0.020	③	0.0015-0.0030	0.0015-0.0035
	F	6.5 (6473)	②	0.010-0.020	0.010-0.020	③	0.0015-0.0030	0.0015-0.0035
	N	7.4 (7440)	0.0018-0.0030	0.010-0.018	0.010-0.030	0.0012-0.0029	0.0012-0.0029	0.0050-0.0065
1996	W	4.3 (4293)	0.0007-0.0017	0.010-0.030	0.015-0.065	0.0012-0.0042	0.0012-0.0042	0.0020-0.0080
	M	5.0 (4999)	0.0007-0.0021	0.010-0.020	0.010-0.030	0.0012-0.0032	0.0012-0.0032	0.0020-0.0070
	R	5.7 (5735)	0.0007-0.0021	0.010-0.020	0.010-0.030	0.0012-0.0032	0.0012-0.0032	0.0020-0.0070
	Y	6.5 (6473)	②	0.010-0.020	0.010-0.020	③	0.0015-0.0030	0.0015-0.0035
	P	6.5 (6473)	②	0.010-0.0200	0.010-0.0200	③ 0.0031	0.0031	0.0015-0.0035
	J	7.4 (7440)	0.0018-0.0030	0.010-0.018	0.010-0.030	0.0012-0.0029	0.0012-0.0029	0.0050-0.0065

88193C15

PISTON AND RING SPECIFICATIONS

All measurements are given in inches.

Year	Engine ID/VIN	Engine Displacement Liters (cc)	Piston Clearance	Ring Gap		Ring Side Clearance		
				Top Compression	Oil Control	Top Compression	Bottom Compression	Oil Control
1997	W	4.3 (4293)	0.0007- 0.0017	0.010- 0.030	0.015- 0.065	0.0012- 0.0042	0.0012- 0.0042	0.0020- 0.0080
	M	5.0 (4999)	0.0007- 0.0021	0.010- 0.020	0.010- 0.030	0.0012- 0.0032	0.0012- 0.0032	0.0020- 0.0070
	R	5.7 (5735)	0.0007- 0.0021	0.010- 0.020	0.010- 0.030	0.0012- 0.0032	0.0012- 0.0032	0.0020- 0.0070
	Y	6.5 (6473)	②	0.010- 0.020	0.010- 0.020	③	0.0015- 0.0030	0.0015- 0.0035
	F	6.5 (6473)	②	0.010- 0.0200	0.010- 0.0200	③ 0.0031	0.0015- 0.0031	0.0015- 0.0035
	J	7.4 (7440)	0.0018- 0.0030	0.010- 0.018	0.010- 0.030	0.0012- 0.0029	0.0012- 0.0029	0.0050- 0.0065

① Bohn pistons Nos. 1-6: 0.0035-0.0.004
Bohn pistons Nos. 7-8: 0.004-0.005
Zoliner Pistons Nos: 1-6: 0.004-0.005
Zoliner piston Nos. 7-8: 0.004-0.005

② 1-6-0.037-0.047
7-8-0.0042-. 0.0052+C28
③ Bohn pistons Nos. 1-6: 0.002-0.003
Bohn pistons Nos. 7-8: 0.002-0.004

④ Keystone type ring

88193C16

TORQUE SPECIFICATIONS
All readings in ft. lbs.

Year	Engine ID/VIN	Engine Displacement Liters (cc)	Cylinder Head Bolts	Main Bearing Bolts	Rod Bearing Bolts	Crankshaft Damper Bolts	Flywheel Bolts	Manifold		Spark Plugs	Lug Nut
								Intake	Exhaust		
1987	Z	4.3 (4293)	65	80	45	70	75	36	⑨	22	90
	H	5.0 (4999)	65	④	45	70	60	35	⑨	17-27	⑪
	K/M	5.7 (5735)	65	④	45	70	60	35	⑨	17-27	⑪
	C	6.2 (6210)	①	③	48	200	60	31	25	-	⑪
	J	6.2 (6210)	①	③	48	200	65	31	26	-	⑪
	F	6.5 (6473)	①	③	48	200	66	31	26	-	⑪
	W	7.4 (7440)	80	110	50	85	65	30	25	17-27	⑪
	N	7.4 (7440)	80	110	50	85	65	30	25	22	⑪
1988	Z	4.3 (4293)	65	80	45	70	75	36	⑨	22	90
	H	5.0 (4999)	65	④	45	70	60	35	⑨	17-27	⑪
	K	5.7 (5735)	65	④	45	70	60	35	⑨	17-27	⑪
	C	6.2 (6210)	①	③	48	200	60	31	25	-	⑪
	J	6.2 (6210)	①	③	48	200	65	31	26	-	⑪
	W	7.4 (7440)	80	110	50	85	65	30	25	17-27	⑪
	N	7.4 (7440)	80	110	50	85	65	30	25	22	⑪
1989	Z	4.3 (4293)	65	80	45	70	75	36	⑨	22	90
	H	5.0 (4999)	65	④	45	70	60	35	⑨	17-27	⑪
	K	5.7 (5735)	65	④	45	70	60	35	⑨	17-27	⑪
	C	6.2 (6210)	①	③	48	200	60	31	25	-	⑪
	J	6.2 (6210)	①	③	48	200	65	31	26	-	⑪
	W	7.4 (7440)	80	110	50	85	65	30	25	17-27	⑪
	N	7.4 (7440)	80	110	50	85	65	36	25	22	⑪
1990	Z	4.3 (4293)	65	80	45	70	75	35	⑨	22	90
	H	5.0 (4999)	65	④	45	70	60	35	⑨	17-27	⑪
	K	5.7 (5735)	65	④	45	70	60	31	⑨	17-27	⑪
	C	6.2 (6210)	①	③	48	200	60	31	25	-	⑪
	J	6.2 (6210)	①	③	48	200	60	30	26	-	⑪
	N	7.4 (7440)	80	110	48	85	65	30	20	17-27	⑪
1991	Z	4.3 (4293)	65	75	20 ⑥	70	75	36	⑨	22	90
	H	5.0 (4999)	65	④	45	70	75	35	⑨	15	⑪
	K	5.7 (5735)	65	④	45	70	60	35	⑨	15	⑪
	C	6.2 (6210)	①	③	48	200	66	31	-	-	⑪
	J	6.2 (6210)	①	③	48	200	66	31	-	-	⑪
	N	7.4 (7440)	80	100	48	85	65	40	25	22	90
1992	Z	4.3 (4293)	65	75	20 ⑥	70	75	36	⑨	22	⑪
	H	5.0 (4999)	65	④	45	70	75	35	⑨	15	⑪
	K	5.7 (5735)	65	④	45	70	60	35	⑨	15	⑪
	C	6.2 (6210)	①	③	48	200	66	31	26	-	⑪
	J	6.2 (6210)	①	③	48	200	66	31	26	-	⑪
	N	7.4 (7440)	80	100	48	85	65	40	40	22	⑪
1993	Z	4.3 (4293)	65	75	20 ⑥	70	75	35	⑨	22	90
	H	5.0 (4999)	65	④	45	70	75	35	⑨	15	⑪
	K	5.7 (5735)	65	④	45	70	75	35	⑨	15	⑪
	C	6.2 (6210)	①	③	48	200	66	31	26	-	⑪

88193C17

TORQUE SPECIFICATIONS
All readings in ft. lbs.

Year	Engine ID/VIN	Engine Displacement Liters (cc)	Cylinder Head Bolts	Main Bearing Bolts	Rod Bearing Bolts	Crankshaft Damper Bolts	Flywheel Bolts	Manifold Intake	Manifold Exhaust	Spark Plugs	Lug Nut
1993	J	6.2 (6210)	①	③	48	200	66	31	26	-	⑪
	F	6.5 (6473)	①	③	48	200	66	31	26	-	⑪
	N	7.4 (7440)	80	100	48	85	65	40	40	22	⑪
1994	Z	4.3 (4293)	65	75	20 ⑥	70	75	35	⑨	11	90
	H	5.0 (4999)	65	④	45	70	75	35	⑨	15	⑪
	K	5.7 (5735)	65	④	45	70	75	35	⑨	15	⑪
	F	6.5 (6473)	①	③	48	200	66	31	26	-	⑪
	P	6.5 (6473)	①	③	48	200	66	31	26	-	⑪
	Y	6.5 (6473)	①	③	48	200	66	31	26	-	⑪
	N	7.4 (7440)	80	100	48	85	65	35	40	22	⑪
1995	Z	4.3 (4293)	65	81	20 ⑥	70	74	35	⑨	11	90
	H	5.0 (4999)	65	④	45	70	75	35	⑨	15	⑪
	K	5.7 (5735)	65	④	45	70	75	35	⑨	15	⑪
	F	6.5 (6473)	①	③	48	200	66	31	26	-	⑪
	P	6.5 (6473)	①	③	48	200	66	31	26	-	⑪
	Y	6.5 (6473)	①	③	48	200	66	31	26	-	⑪
	N	7.4 (7440)	80	100	48	85	65	35	40	22	⑪
1996	W	4.3 (4293)	②	77	20 ⑥	74	74	⑧	⑩	11	90
	M	5.0 (4999)	②	⑤	⑦	74	74	⑧	⑩	15	⑪
	R	5.7 (5735)	②	⑤	⑦	74	74	⑧	⑩	15	⑪
	F	6.5 (6473)	①	③	48	200	65	31	26	-	⑪
	S	6.5 (6473)	①	③	48	200	65	31	26	-	⑪
	J	7.4 (7440)	85	100	45	110	67	30	22	15	⑪
1997	W	4.3 (4293)	②	77	20 ⑥	74	74	⑧	⑩	11	90
	M	5.0 (4999)	②	⑤	⑦	74	74	⑧	⑩	15	⑪
	R	5.7 (5735)	②	⑤	⑦	74	74	⑧	⑩	15	⑪
	F	6.5 (6473)	①	③	48	200	65	31	26	-	⑪
	S	6.5 (6473)	①	③	48	200	65	31	26	-	⑪
	J	7.4 (7440)	85	100	45	110	67	30	22	15	⑪

* NOTE: Applies to Lower Manifold only.

① Apply sealer
Step 1: 20 ft. lbs.
Step 2: 50 ft. lbs.
Step32: 1/4 turn.

② 1st pass: 22 ft. lbs.
2nd pass:
Short bolt: Plus 55 degrees
Medium bolt: Plus 65 degrees
Long bolt: Plus 75 degrees

③ Outer bolts: 100 ft. lbs.
Inner bolts: 111 ft. lbs.

④ Outer bolts on caps 2-4: 70 ft. lbs
All others: 80 ft. lbs.

⑤ Outer bolts on caps 2-4: 67 ft. lbs.
All others: 74 ft. lbs.

⑥ plus an additional 60 degree turn
tubular steel 26 ft. lbs.

⑦ Coat threads with sealant
Tighten all bolts to 20 ft. lbs.
Retorque to 50 ft. lbs.

⑧ Lower intake manifold:
1st pass: 27 in. lbs.
2nd pass: 106 in. lbs.
Final pass: 11 ft. lbs.
Upper manifold bolts:
1st pass: 44 in. lbs.
2nd pass: 88 in. lbs.

⑨ Two center bolts: 26 ft. lbs.
All others: 20 ft. lbs.

⑩ Tighten bolts to 12 ft. lbs.
Retorque to 22 ft. lbs.

⑪ All 5 & 6 stud single rear wheels: 110 ft. lbs
All 8 stud single rear wheels: 120 ft. lbs.
All 8 stud dual rear wheels: 140 ft. lbs.
All 10 stud dual wheels: 175 ft. lbs.

88193C18

ENGINE MECHANICAL

Engine

REMOVAL & INSTALLATION

▸ **See Figure 1**

In the process of removing the engine, you will come across a number of steps which call for the removal of a separate component or system, such as "disconnect the exhaust system" or "remove the radiator." In most instances, a detailed removal procedure can be found elsewhere in this manual.

It is virtually impossible to list each individual wire and hose which must be disconnected, simply because so many different model and engine combinations have been manufactured. Careful observation and common sense are the best possible approaches to any repair procedure.

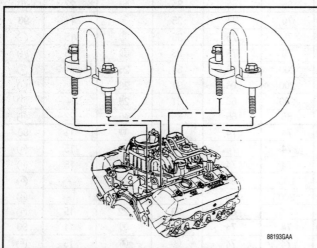

Fig. 1 Universal lift brackets should be installed in place of the proper intake manifold bolts

Removal and installation of the engine can be made easier if you follow these basic points:
- If you have to drain any of the fluids, use a suitable container.
- Always tag any wires or hoses and, if possible, the components they came from before disconnecting them.
- Because there are so many bolts and fasteners involved, store and label the retainers from components separately in muffin pans, jars or coffee cans. This will prevent confusion during installation.
- After unbolting the transmission, always make sure it is properly supported.
- If it is necessary to disconnect the air conditioning system, have this service performed by a qualified technician using a recovery/recycling station. If the system does not have to be disconnected, unbolt the compressor and set it aside.
- When unbolting the engine mounts, always make sure the engine is properly supported. When removing the engine, make sure that any lifting devices are properly attached to the engine. It is recommended that if your engine is supplied with lifting hooks, your lifting apparatus be attached to them.
- Lift the engine from its compartment slowly, checking that no hoses, wires or other components are still connected.
- After the engine is clear of the compartment, place it on an engine stand or workbench.
- After the engine has been removed, you can perform a partial or full teardown of the engine using the procedures outlined in this manual.

1. Disconnect the negative battery cable, then the positive battery cable, at the battery.
2. Remove the engine cover.
3. Drain the cooling system.

✴✴ **CAUTION**

When draining the coolant, keep in mind that cats and dogs are attracted by ethylene glycol antifreeze, and are quite likely to drink any that is left in an uncovered container or in puddles on the ground. This will prove fatal in sufficient quantity. Always drain the coolant into a sealable container. Coolant should be reused unless it is contaminated or several years old.

4. Remove the air cleaner.
5. Remove the radiator coolant reservoir bottle.
6. Remove the upper radiator support.
7. Remove the grille and the lower grille valance.
8. If necessary, remove the front bumper.

✴✴ **CAUTION**

Please refer to Section 1 before discharging the compressor or disconnecting air conditioning lines. Damage to the air conditioning system or personal injury could result. Consult your local laws concerning refrigerant discharge and recycling. In many areas it may be illegal for anyone but a certified technician to service the A/C system. Always use an approved recovery station when discharging the air conditioning.

9. Discharge the air conditioning system and remove the air conditioning vacuum reservoir.
10. Remove the air conditioning condenser from in front of the radiator.
11. If the van is equipped with an automatic transmission, remove the fluid cooler lines from the radiator.
12. Disconnect the radiator hoses at the radiator.
13. Loosen the radiator support bracket and remove the radiator and the shroud.
14. Disconnect the accelerator and cruise control linkages.
15. Disconnect all hoses and wires at the fuel unit.
16. Remove the fuel supply unit and cap the lines.
17. On 1996–97 models, remove the intake manifold.
18. On turbocharged engines, remove the turbocharger assembly.
19. On diesel engines, remove the lower intake manifold if equipped.
20. On diesel engines, remove the exhaust manifolds if necessary.
21. Disconnect the engine wiring harness from the firewall connection.
22. Tag and disconnect all vacuum lines.
23. Remove the power steering pump. It's not necessary to disconnect the hoses; just lay the pump aside.
24. Disconnect the heater hoses at the engine.
25. On some models it may be necessary to remove the thermostat housing.
26. Remove the oil filler and automatic transmission tubes.
27. Raise and support the van on jackstands.
28. Remove the cruise control servo, servo bracket and transducer.
29. Drain the engine oil.
30. Disconnect the exhaust pipes at the manifolds.
31. Remove the driveshaft and plug the end of the transmission.
32. Disconnect the transmission shift linkage and the speedometer cable.
33. Remove the fuel line from the fuel tank and at the fuel pump.
34. Remove the transmission mounting bolts.
35. Lower the van, support the transmission and engine.
36. On 1996–97 models, install lifting hooks J-41427 as follows:
   a. Disconnect the spark plug wires and remove the distributor cap.
   b. Remove the two right rear lower intake manifold retainers and install lifting hook J-41427 (the one marked "right"). Tighten the bolts to 11 ft. lbs. (15 Nm).
   c. Remove the air conditioning compressor and the accessory drive bracket.

d. Disconnect the EGR tube and the two left lower bolts from the intake manifold.

e. Install the lifting hook J-41427 (the one marked "left") and tighten the bolts to 11 ft. lbs. (15 Nm).

37. Remove the engine mount bracket-to-frame bolts.

38. Remove the engine mount through-bolts.

39. Raise the engine slightly and remove the engine mounts. Support the engine with wood between the oil pan and the crossmember.

40. Remove the manual transmission and clutch as follows:

a. Remove the clutch housing rear bolts.

b. Remove the bolts attaching the clutch housing to the engine and remove the transmission and clutch as a unit.

➡**Support the transmission as the last bolt is being removed to prevent damaging the clutch.**

c. Remove the starter and clutch housing rear cover.

d. Loosen the clutch mounting bolts a little at a time to prevent distorting the disc until spring pressure is released. Remove all of the bolts, the clutch disc and the pressure plate.

41. Remove the automatic transmission as follows:

a. Lower the engine and support it on blocks.

b. Remove the starter and converter housing underpan.

c. Remove the flywheel-to-converter attaching bolts.

d. Support the transmission on blocks.

e. Disconnect the detent cable on the Turbo Hydra-Matic.

f. Remove the transmission-to-engine mounting bolts.

42. Attach an engine crane to the engine.

a. Remove the blocks from the engine only and glide the engine away from the transmission.

To install:

43. Raise the engine slightly and install the engine mounts. Tighten the bolts to specification.

44. Install the manual transmission and clutch as follows:

a. Install the clutch disc and the pressure plate. Tighten the clutch mounting bolts a little at a time to prevent distorting the disc.

b. Install the starter and clutch housing rear cover.

c. Install the bolts attaching the clutch housing to the engine and install the transmission and clutch as a unit. Tighten the bolts to specification.

d. Install the clutch housing rear bolts.

45. Install the automatic transmission as follows:

a. Position the transmission.

b. Install the transmission-to-engine mounting bolts.

c. Connect the throttle linkage and detent cable.

d. Install the flywheel-to-converter attaching bolts. Tighten the bolts to specification.

e. Install the starter and converter housing underpan.

46. Install the engine mount through-bolts. Tighten the bolts to specification.

47. Install the engine mount bracket-to-frame bolts. Tighten the bolts to specification.

48. Install the clutch cross-shaft.

49. Install the transmission mounting bolts. Tighten the bolts to specification.

50. Connect the transmission shift linkage and the speedometer cable.

51. Install the driveshaft.

52. Remove the lifting hooks and install the compressor, EGR valve tube and intake manifold retaining bolts.

53. Install the condenser.

54. Install the hood latch support.

55. Install the lower fan shroud and filler panel.

56. Install the transmission dipstick tube and the accelerator cable at the tube.

57. Install the coolant hose at the intake manifold and the PCV valve.

58. Install the distributor cap.

59. Install the cruise control servo, servo bracket and transducer.

60. Install the oil filler pipe and automatic transmission filler pipe.

61. Install the engine dipstick tube.

62. If removed, install the thermostat housing.

63. Connect the heater hoses at the engine.

64. Connect the engine wiring harness to the firewall connection.

65. Install the radiator and the shroud.

66. Install the radiator support bracket.

67. On diesel engines, install the exhaust manifolds if removed.

68. On diesel engines, install the lower intake manifold if removed.

69. On 1996–97 models, install the intake manifold.

70. Install the fuel supply unit.

71. Connect the lines to the fuel supply unit.

72. Connect the accelerator and cruise control linkages.

73. Install the windshield wiper jar and bracket.

74. Install the air conditioning condenser.

75. Install the air conditioning vacuum reservoir.

76. Have the air conditioning system charged by a qualified technician using a recovery/recycling station.

❄❄ CAUTION

Please refer to Section 1 before discharging the compressor or disconnecting air conditioning lines. Damage to the air conditioning system or personal injury could result. Consult your local laws concerning refrigerant discharge and recycling. In many areas it may be illegal for anyone but a certified technician to service the A/C system. Always use an approved recovery station when discharging the air conditioning.

77. If the van is equipped with an automatic transmission, install the fluid cooler lines at the radiator.

78. Install the radiator coolant reservoir bottle.

79. Connect the radiator hoses at the radiator.

80. Install the upper radiator support the grille and the lower grille valance.

81. Install the air cleaner.

82. Install the air stove pipe.

83. Install the engine cover.

84. Fill the cooling system.

85. Connect the battery cables.

Valve/Cylinder Head Cover

REMOVAL & INSTALLATION

Gasoline Engines

▶ **See Figures 2, 3 and 4 (p. 22–23)**

1. Disconnect the negative battery cable. Remove the air cleaner assembly.

2. If applicable, remove the coolant recovery reservoir.

3. Remove the engine cover.

4. Tag, disconnect and reposition as necessary any vacuum or PCV hoses that obstruct the cylinder head covers.

5. If applicable, remove the EGR tube.

6. Disconnect electrical wire(s) (spark plug, etc.) from the cylinder head cover clips. You may also have to remove or move the alternator brace and PCV pipe.

7. Unbolt and remove the cover(s).

➡**Do not pry the covers off if they seem stuck. Instead, gently tap around each cover with a rubber mallet until the old gasket or sealer breaks loose.**

To install:

8. Install a new gasket or apply RTV (or any equivalent) sealer to the cover prior to installation. If using sealer, follow directions on the tube.

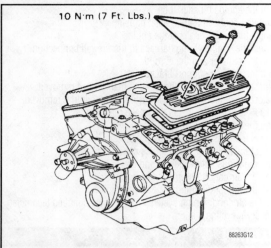

10 N·m (7 Ft. Lbs.)

88263G12

Fig. 2 Exploded view of a typical 4.3L rocker arm cover mounting

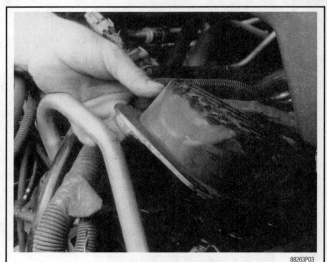

88263P03

Lift and remove the valve cover from the cylinder head

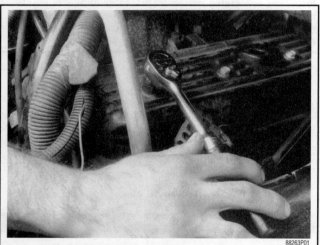

88263P01

Loosen the valve cover retaining bolts using a wrench or ratchet and suitable driver . . .

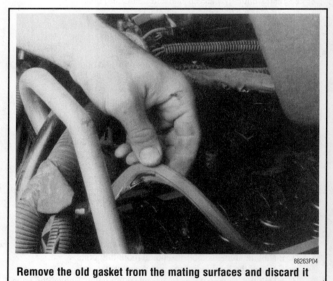

88263P04

Remove the old gasket from the mating surfaces and discard it

88263P02

. . . then remove the bolts from the cover

9. Install the cover and mounting bolts. Tighten the bolts as follows:
- 1987–95 4.3L engines: 90 inch lbs. (10 Nm)
- 1987–95 5.0L, 5.7L engines: 95 inch lbs. (11 Nm)
- 1996–97 4.3L, 5.0L and 5.7L engines: 106 inch lbs. (12 Nm)
- 1987–91 7.4L engines: 115 inch lbs. (13 Nm)
- 1992–97 7.4L engines: 60 inch lbs. (7 Nm)
10. If equipped, install the EGR tube.
11. Connect and reposition all vacuum and PCV hoses, and reconnect electrical and/or spark plug wires at the cover clips. Install the air cleaner.
12. If applicable, install the coolant recovery reservoir.
13. Install the engine cover.
14. Reconnect the battery cable.

Diesel Engines

RIGHT SIDE

1. Remove the engine cover.
2. Remove the intake manifold.
3. Remove the fuel injection lines for all except the No. 5 and No. 7 injectors.
4. Disconnect the glow plug wires.
5. Remove the wiring harness from the clip.

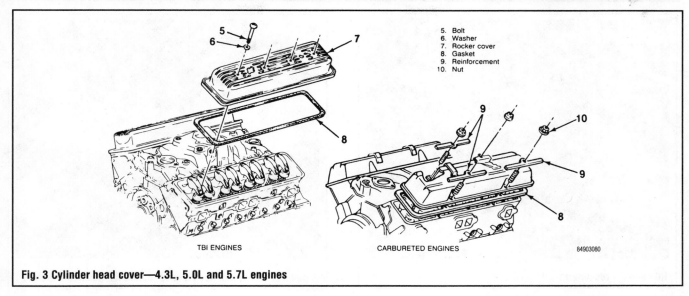

5. Bolt
6. Washer
7. Rocker cover
8. Gasket
9. Reinforcement
10. Nut

TBI ENGINES   CARBURETED ENGINES   84903080

Fig. 3 Cylinder head cover—4.3L, 5.0L and 5.7L engines

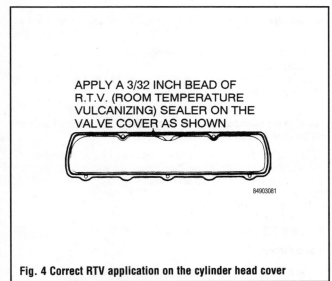

APPLY A 3/32 INCH BEAD OF
R.T.V. (ROOM TEMPERATURE
VULCANIZING) SEALER ON THE
VALVE COVER AS SHOWN

84903081

Fig. 4 Correct RTV application on the cylinder head cover

6. Remove the CDR valve.
7. Remove the cover bolts.
8. Remove the cover. If the cover sticks, jar it loose with a plastic or rubber mallet. NEVER pry it loose!
9. Installation is the reverse of removal. Clean all old RTV gasket material from the mating surfaces. Apply a ⁵⁄₁₆ in. (8mm) bead of sealer to the head mating surfaces. Tighten the cover bolts to 16 ft. lbs. (22 Nm).
10. Install the engine cover.

LEFT SIDE

1. Remove the engine cover.
2. Remove the intake manifold.
3. Remove the fuel injection lines.
4. On vans with air conditioning, remove the upper fan shroud.
5. On vans with air conditioning, remove the compressor drive belt.
6. On vans with air conditioning, remove the left exhaust manifold.
7. Remove the dipstick tube
8. On vans with air conditioning, dismount the compressor and move it out of the way. It may be possible to avoid disconnecting the refrigerant lines. If not, Discharge the system and disconnect the lines. Cap all openings at once. See Section 1 for discharging procedures.
9. Remove the dipstick tube front bracket from the stud.

10. Remove the wiring harness brackets.
11. Remove the rocker arm cover bolts and fuel return bracket.
12. Remove the cover. If the cover sticks, jar it loose with a plastic or rubber mallet. NEVER pry it loose!
13. Installation is the reverse of removal. Clean all old RTV gasket material from the mating surfaces. Apply a ⁵⁄₁₆ in. (8mm) bead of sealer to the head mating surfaces. Tighten the cover bolts to 16 ft. lbs. (22 Nm).
14. Install the engine cover.

Rocker Arms

REMOVAL & INSTALLATION

4.3L, 5.0L and 5.7L Engines

1. Remove the engine cover.
2. Remove the cylinder head cover.
3. Remove the rocker arm nut. If you are only replacing the pushrod, back the nut off until you can swing the rocker out of the way.
4. Remove the rocker arms and balls as a unit.

➡**Always remove each set of rocker arms (one set per cylinder) as a unit.**

5. Lift out the pushrods and pushrod guides.
   To install:
6. Install the pushrods and their guides. Make sure that they seat properly in each lifter.
7. Position a set of rocker arms (for one cylinder) in the proper location.

➡**Install the rocker arms for each cylinder only when the lifters are off the cam lobe and both valves are closed.**

8. Coat the replacement rocker arm with Molykote® or its equivalent, and the rocker arm and pivot with SAE 90 gear oil, and install the pivots.
9. Install the nuts and tighten alternately as detailed in the valve lash adjustment procedure later in this section.
10. Install the engine cover.

7.4L Engines

1. Remove the engine cover.
2. Remove the cylinder head cover.
3. Remove the rocker arm bolt. If you are only replacing the pushrod, back the nut off until you can swing the rocker out of the way.
4. Remove the rocker arms and balls as a unit.

Remove the rocker arm nut

87983P31

Remove the rocker arms

87983P32

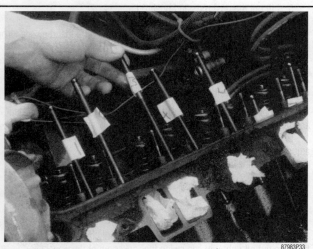

Tag the pushrods before removal as they must be installed in the same order

87983P33

A piece of cardboard may be used to hold the pushrods in order

87983P34

➡**Always remove each set of rocker arms (one set per cylinder) as a unit.**

　5. Lift out the pushrods and pushrod guides.
　To install:
　6. Install the pushrods and their guides. Make sure that they seat properly in each lifter.
　7. Position a set of rocker arms (for one cylinder) in the proper location.

➡**Install the rocker arms for each cylinder only when the lifters are off the cam lobe and both valves are closed.**

　8. Coat the replacement rocker arm with Molykote® or its equivalent, and the rocker arm and pivot with SAE 90 gear oil, and install the pivots.
　9. Install the bolts and tighten them to 40 ft. lbs. (54 Nm) on 1987–95 models and 45 ft. lbs. (61 Nm) and 1996–97 models.
　10. Install the engine cover.

6.2L and 6.5L Diesel Engines

▶ **See Figures 5 and 6**

　1. Remove the engine cover.

➡**Rotate the engine until the mark on the crankshaft balancer is at 2 o'clock. Rotate the crankshaft counterclockwise 3½ in. (88mm) aligning the crankshaft balancer mark with the first lower water pump bolt, about 12:30. This will ensure that no valves are close to a piston crown**

　2. Remove the cylinder head cover.
　3. The rocker assemblies are mounted on two short rocker shafts per cylinder head, with each shaft operating four rockers. Remove the two bolts which secure each rocker shaft assembly, and remove the shaft. Mark the shafts so they can be installed in their original locations.
　4. Remove the pushrods. The pushrods MUST be installed in the original direction! A paint stripe usually identifies the upper end of each rod, but if you can't see it, make sure to mark each rod yourself.
　5. Insert a small prybar into the end of the rocker shaft bore and break off the end of the nylon retainers. Pull off the retainers with pliers and then slide off the rockers.
　To install:
　6. Make sure first that the rocker arms and springs go back on the shafts in the exact order in which they were removed. Its a good idea to coat them with engine oil.
　7. Center the rockers on the corresponding holes in the shaft and install new plastic retainers using a ½ in. (13mm) drift.
　8. Install the pushrods with their marked ends up.

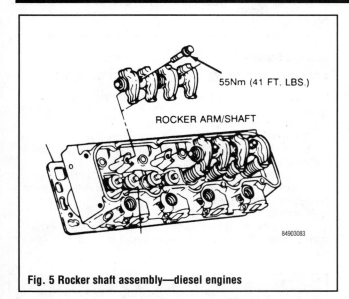

55Nm (41 FT. LBS.)

ROCKER ARM/SHAFT

84903083

Fig. 5 Rocker shaft assembly—diesel engines

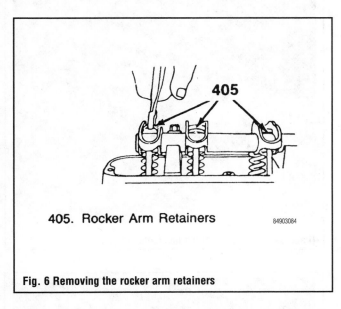

405

405. Rocker Arm Retainers 84903084

Fig. 6 Removing the rocker arm retainers

9. Install the rocker shaft assemblies and make sure that the ball ends of the pushrods seat themselves in the rockers.

10. Rotate the engine clockwise until the mark on the torsional damper aligns with the **0** on the timing tab. Rotate the engine counterclockwise 3½ in. (88mm) measured at the damper. You can estimate this by checking that the mark on the damper is now aligned with the FIRST lower water pump bolt. BE CAREFUL! This ensures that the piston is away from the valves.

11. Install the rocker shaft bolts and tighten them to 40 ft. lbs. (55 Nm).

12. Install the cylinder head cover.

13. Install the engine cover.

INSPECTION

- Inspect the rocker arm bolts for signs of cracking at the bolt shoulder.
- Inspect the rocker arms and balls at their mating surfaces. They should be smooth, with no signs of scoring or other damage.
- Check the surfaces where the rocker contacts the valve stem or pushrod. They should be smooth, with no signs of scoring or other damage.
- Roll the pushrod on a flat surface to see if its bent—replace it if it is.
- Check the ends of the pushrods for signs of scoring or any roughness.

Rocker Stud

REPLACEMENT

➡The following tools will be necessary for this procedure: Rocker stud replacement tool J-5802-01, Reamer J-5715 or Reamer J-6036 and Installer J-6880, or their equivalents.

4.3L, 5.0L and 5.7L Engines

▸ **See Figures 7, 8 and 9**

1. Remove the valve cover.
2. Remove the engine cover.
3. Remove the rocker arm cover.
4. Remove the rocker arm.
5. Place the tool over the stud. Install the nut and flat washer.
6. Tighten the nut to remove the stud.

To install:

7. Using one of the reamers, ream the stud hole as necessary.
8. Coat the lower end of the new stud with SAE 80W-90 gear oil.
9. Using the installing tool, install the new stud. The stud is properly installed when the tool bottoms on the cylinder head.
10. Install the rocker arm(s) and adjust the valves.

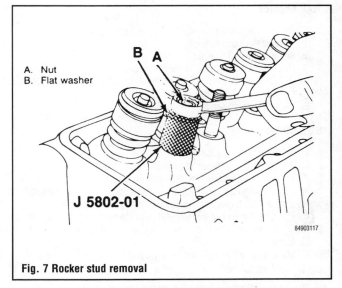

A. Nut
B. Flat washer

B A

J 5802-01

84903117

Fig. 7 Rocker stud removal

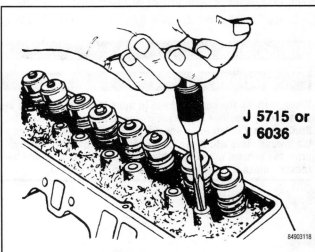

J 5715 or
J 6036

84903118

Fig. 8 Reaming the rocker stud bore

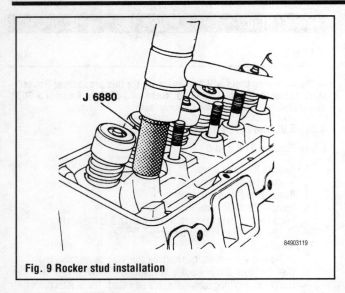

Fig. 9 Rocker stud installation

11. Install the cover.
12. Install the engine cover.

7.4L Engines

1. Remove the engine cover.
2. Remove the valve cover.
3. Remove the rocker arm.
4. Using a deep socket, unscrew the stud.
5. To install, simply reverse the removal procedures. Tighten the stud to 50 ft. lbs. (68 Nm). Adjust the valves.
6. Install the engine cover.

6.2L Diesel Engine

1. Remove the engine cover.
2. Remove the valve cover as previously explained.
3. The rocker assemblies are mounted on two short rocker shafts per cylinder head, with each shaft operating four rockers. Remove the two bolts which secure each rocker shaft assembly, and remove the shaft.
4. The rocker arms can be removed from the shaft by removing the cotter pin on the end of each shaft. The rocker arms and springs slide off.
   To install:
5. Make sure first that the rocker arms and springs go back on the shafts in the exact order in which they were removed.

➡**Always install new cotter pins on the rocker shaft ends.**

6. Install the rocker shaft assemblies, tighten the bolts to 41 ft. lbs. (55 Nm).

Thermostat

❋❋ CAUTION

When draining the coolant, keep in mind that cats and dogs are attracted by ethylene glycol antifreeze, and are quite likely to drink any that is left in an uncovered container or in puddles on the ground. This will prove fatal in sufficient quantity. Always drain the coolant into a sealable container. Coolant should be reused unless it is contaminated or several years old.

REMOVAL & INSTALLATION

Gasoline Engines

▶ **See Figures 10, 11, 12, 13 and 14 (p. 27–28)**

1. Disconnect the negative battery cable and remove the engine cover.
2. Remove the air cleaner and intake duct.
3. If applicable, remove the coolant recovery reservoir.
4. Drain the radiator until the coolant is below the thermostat level (below the level of the intake manifold).
5. Remove the upper radiator hose from the outlet elbow.
6. Remove the water outlet elbow assembly from the engine. Remove the thermostat from the engine.
   To install:
7. Clean the gasket surfaces on the water outlet elbow and the intake manifold. Use a new gasket when installing the elbow to the manifold.

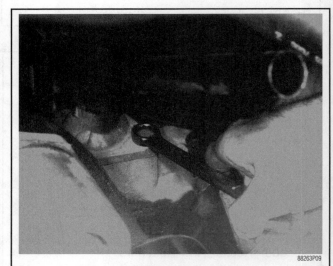

If access is difficult with the hose attached . . .

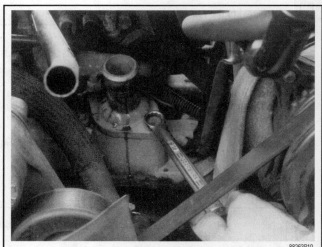

. . . remove the hose, then loosen and remove the housing retainers

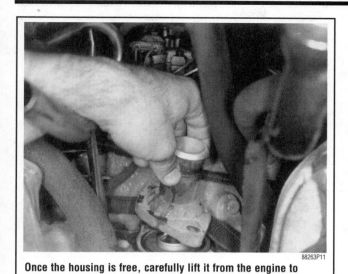

Once the housing is free, carefully lift it from the engine to expose the thermostat

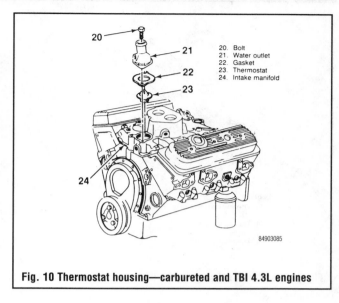

Fig. 10 Thermostat housing—carbureted and TBI 4.3L engines

20. Bolt
21. Water outlet
22. Gasket
23. Thermostat
24. Intake manifold

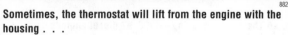

Sometimes, the thermostat will lift from the engine with the housing . . .

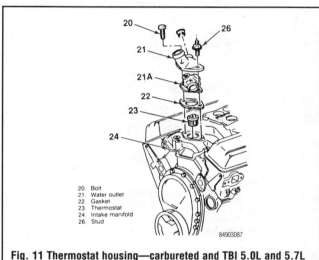

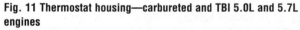

Fig. 11 Thermostat housing—carbureted and TBI 5.0L and 5.7L engines

20. Bolt
21. Water outlet
22. Gasket
23. Thermostat
24. Intake manifold
26. Stud

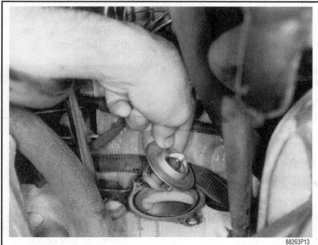

. . . otherwise, note the direction it is installed, then lift the thermostat from the engine

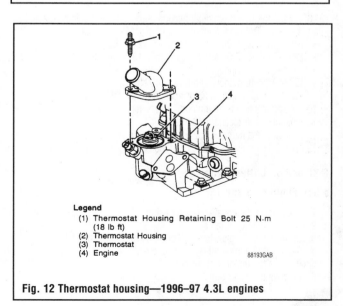

Legend
(1) Thermostat Housing Retaining Bolt 25 N·m (18 lb ft)
(2) Thermostat Housing
(3) Thermostat
(4) Engine

Fig. 12 Thermostat housing—1996–97 4.3L engines

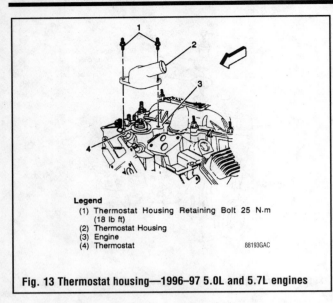

Legend
(1) Thermostat Housing Retaining Bolt 25 N·m (18 lb ft)
(2) Thermostat Housing
(3) Engine
(4) Thermostat

88193GAC

Fig. 13 Thermostat housing—1996–97 5.0L and 5.7L engines

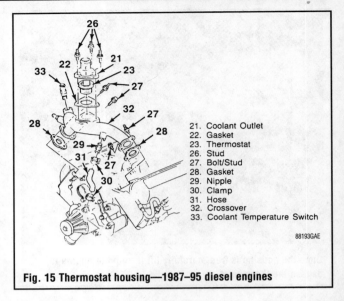

21. Coolant Outlet
22. Gasket
23. Thermostat
26. Stud
27. Bolt/Stud
28. Gasket
29. Nipple
30. Clamp
31. Hose
32. Crossover
33. Coolant Temperature Switch

88193GAE

Fig. 15 Thermostat housing—1987–95 diesel engines

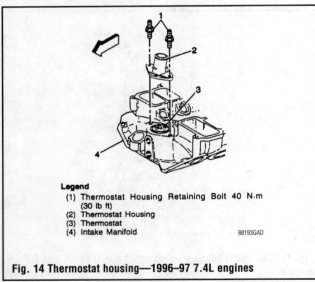

Legend
(1) Thermostat Housing Retaining Bolt 40 N·m (30 lb ft)
(2) Thermostat Housing
(3) Thermostat
(4) Intake Manifold

88193GAD

Fig. 14 Thermostat housing—1996–97 7.4L engines

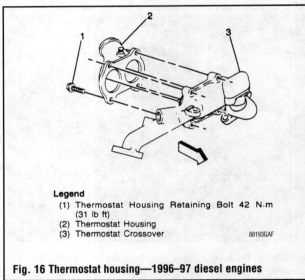

Legend
(1) Thermostat Housing Retaining Bolt 42 N·m (31 lb ft)
(2) Thermostat Housing
(3) Thermostat Crossover

88193GAF

Fig. 16 Thermostat housing—1996–97 diesel engines

8. Install the new thermostat making sure the spring side is inserted into the engine. Tighten the thermostat housing bolts as follows:
- 1987–95 4.3L, 5.0L and 5.7L models: 21 ft. lbs. (28 Nm)
- 1996–97 4.3L, 5.0L and 5.7L models: 18 ft. lbs. (25 Nm)
- 1987–95 7.4L models: 27 ft. lbs. (37 Nm)
- 1996–97 7.4L models: 30 ft. lbs. (40 Nm)

9. Connect the upper radiator hose to the outlet elbow.
10. If applicable, install the coolant recovery reservoir.
11. Install the air cleaner and intake duct.
12. Connect the negative battery cable and install the engine cover.
13. Refill the cooling system. Start the engine and check for leaks.

6.2L and 6.5L Diesel Engines

▶ **See Figures 15 and 16**

1. Disconnect the negative battery cable.
2. Remove the upper fan shroud.
3. Drain the cooling system to a point below the thermostat.
4. Remove the engine oil dipstick tube brace and the oil fill brace.
5. Remove the upper radiator hose.
6. Remove the water outlet.

7. Remove the thermostat and gasket.
8. Installation is the reverse of removal.
9. Use a new gasket coated with sealer, Make sure that the spring end of the thermostat is in the engine. Tighten the bolts to 35 ft. lbs. (47 Nm) on 1987–91 models and 31 ft. lbs. (42 Nm) on 1992–97 models.

Upper Intake Manifold

REMOVAL & INSTALLATION

4.3L Engines

1996–97 MODELS

▶ **See Figure 17**

The intake manifold assembly is a two-piece design. The upper portion is made from a composite material and the lower portion is cast-aluminum. The throttle body attaches to the upper manifold. The lower manifold has an Exhaust Gas Recirculation (EGR) port cast into the manifold for mixture of exhaust gases with the fuel and air mixture. The EGR valve bolts into the lower intake manifold.

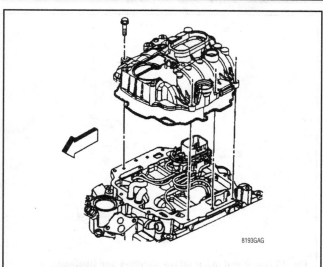

Fig. 17 Upper intake manifold mounting—1996–97 models

The Central Sequential Multi-port Fuel Injection (CSFI) system uses multiple injectors to meter and distribute fuel to each engine cylinder. The CSFI unit is retained by a bracket bolted to the lower intake manifold. The fuel meter body also houses the pressure regulator. Metal inlet and outlet fuel lines and nylon delivery tubes connect to the CSFI unit. The delivery tubes independently distribute fuel to each cylinder through nozzles located at the port entrance of each manifold runner where the fuel is atomized.

> ❄ **CAUTION**
>
> **Fuel injection systems remain under pressure, even after the engine has been turned off. The fuel system pressure must be relieved before disconnecting any fuel lines. Failure to do so may result in fire and/or personal injury.**

1. Disconnect the negative battery cable.
2. Remove the engine cover.
3. Remove the coolant reservoir.
4. Drain the cooling system.

> ❄ **CAUTION**
>
> **When draining engine coolant, keep in mind that cats and dogs are attracted to ethylene glycol antifreeze and could drink any that is left in an uncovered container or in puddles on the ground. This will prove fatal in sufficient quantity. Always drain coolant into a sealable container. Coolant should be reused unless it is contaminated or is several years old.**

5. Remove the air cleaner intake duct.
6. Remove the wiring harness connectors and brackets and move them aside.
7. Disconnect the throttle linkage and bracket from the upper intake manifold.
8. Remove the cruise control cable (if equipped).
9. Disconnect the fuel lines and bracket from the rear of the manifold.
10. Remove the brake booster vacuum hose and PCV hose at the upper intake manifold.
11. Remove the ignition coil and bracket.
12. Remove the purge solenoid and bracket.

➡**Note the location of the manifold bolts and studs before removal for reassembly in their original positions.**

13. Remove the intake manifold bolts and studs.

➡**Do not disassemble the CSFI unit.**

14. Remove the upper intake manifold.
15. Clean the old gasket from both mating surfaces.

To install:

16. Install the upper intake manifold gasket.
17. Install the upper intake manifold.

➡**When installing the upper intake manifold be careful not to pinch the injector wires between the upper and lower intake manifolds.**

18. Install the upper intake manifold mounting bolts and studs in the same locations as prior to removal.
19. Tighten the bolts and studs in a crisscross pattern, first to 44 inch lbs. (5 Nm) and then to 88 inch lbs. (10 Nm).
20. Install the purge solenoid and bracket.
21. Install the ignition coil and bracket.
22. Install the PCV hose and the brake booster vacuum hose.
23. Connect the fuel lines and bracket to the rear of the manifold.
24. Install the throttle linkage and bracket to the upper intake manifold.
25. Install the throttle linkage cable.
26. Install the cruise control cable (if equipped).
27. Install the wiring harness connectors and brackets.
28. Install the air cleaner intake duct.
29. Install the coolant recovery reservoir.
30. Install the engine cover and replenish the cooling system.
31. Connect the negative battery cable.
32. Start the vehicle and verify no leaks.

5.0 and 5.7L Engines

▶ **See Figure 18**

The 5.0L and 5.7L engines use a two-piece intake manifold design. The upper portion is made from a composite material and lower portion is cast-aluminum. The throttle body attaches to the upper manifold. The lower manifold has an Exhaust Gas Recirculation (EGR) port cast into the manifold for mixture of exhaust gases with the fuel and air mixture. The EGR valve bolts to the lower intake manifold.

The Central Sequential Multi-port Fuel Injection (CSFI) system uses multiple injectors to meter and distribute fuel to each engine cylinder. The CSFI unit is retained by a bracket bolted to the lower intake manifold. The fuel meter body also houses the pressure regulator. Metal inlet and outlet fuel lines and nylon delivery tubes connect to the CSFI unit. The delivery tubes independently distribute fuel to each cylinder through nozzles located at the port entrance of each manifold runner where the fuel is atomized.

Note that the lower intake manifold gaskets are NOT reusable on the 5.0L and 5.7L engines.

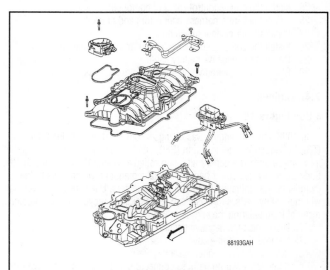

Fig. 18 Upper intake manifold assembly—1996–97 models

✖✖ CAUTION

Fuel injection systems remain under pressure, even after the engine has been turned off. The fuel system pressure must be relieved before disconnecting any fuel lines. Failure to do so may result in fire and/or personal injury.

1. Disconnect the negative battery cable.
2. Remove the engine cover.
3. Remove the air cleaner intake duct.
4. Remove the coolant recovery reservoir.
5. Remove the wiring harness connectors and brackets and move them aside.
6. Disconnect the throttle linkage and bracket from the upper intake manifold.
7. Remove the cruise control cable (if equipped).
8. Remove the fuel lines and the bracket from the rear of the intake manifold.
9. Remove the PCV valve and hose.
10. Remove the ignition coil and bracket.
11. Remove the purge solenoid and bracket.

➡**Note the location of the manifold bolts and studs before removal for reassembly in their original positions.**

12. Remove the intake manifold bolts and studs.

➡**Do not disassemble the CSFI unit.**

13. Remove the upper intake manifold.
14. Clean the old gasket residue from both mating surfaces.

To install:
15. Install the upper intake manifold gasket.
16. Install the upper intake manifold.

➡**When installing the upper intake manifold be careful not to pinch the injector wires between the upper and lower intake manifolds.**

17. Install the upper intake manifold mounting bolts and studs in the same locations as prior to removal.
18. Tighten the bolts and studs in a crisscross pattern in 2 steps, first to 44 inch lbs. (5 Nm) and then to 83 inch lbs. (10 Nm).
19. Install the purge solenoid and bracket.
20. Install the PCV hose.
21. Install the fuel lines and the bracket at the rear of the intake manifold.
22. Install the ignition coil and bracket.
23. Install the throttle linkage and bracket to the upper intake manifold.
24. Install the throttle linkage cable.
25. Install the cruise control cable (if equipped).
26. Install the wiring harness connectors and brackets.
27. Install the air cleaner intake duct.
28. Install the coolant recovery reservoir and the engine cover.
29. Connect the negative battery cable.
30. Start the vehicle and verify that there are no leaks.

7.4L Engines

◗ **See Figure 19**

In 1996, the 7.4L engine was changed from Throttle Body Fuel Injection (TBI) to Sequential Fuel Injection (SFI). The intake manifold was changed to a two-piece unit. The upper half, often called a "plenum" mounts the throttle body assembly. The lower half of the intake manifold, which bolts to the cylinder heads, contains the fuel rail and injectors. Use care when working with light alloy parts. Work as clean as possible to prevent dirt and foreign material from entering the engine.

1. Disconnect the negative battery cable.
2. Remove the engine cover.
3. Remove the air cleaner assembly.
4. Remove the wiring harness connectors and brackets and move them aside.

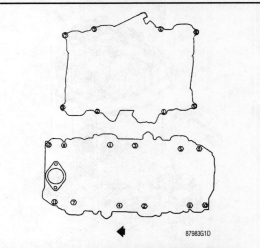

Fig. 19 Upper and lower intake manifold bolt tightening sequence—1996–97 7.4L engines

5. Remove the throttle and cruise control linkage (if equipped).
6. Remove the throttle body electrical connectors.
7. Remove the PCV valve and hose.
8. Remove the EGR inlet tube.
9. Remove the purge solenoid and connectors.
10. Remove the ignition coil and bracket.
11. Remove the #8 spark plug wire from the distributor.
12. Remove the upper intake manifold bolts and remove the upper intake manifold.

To install:
13. Clean all parts well. Clean all traces of gasket from the sealing surfaces.
14. Install a new upper intake manifold gasket.
15. Carefully place the upper intake manifold into position.
16. Before installing the upper intake manifold bolts coat at least 8 threads with a threadlocking sealant such as GM P/N 12345493 or its equivalent.
17. Install the bolts and tighten them in two steps, first to 72 inch lbs. (8Nm) then to 10 ft. lbs. (14 Nm). Install the two corner bolts first to help align the two halves.
18. Connect the #8 spark plug wire.
19. Install the ignition coil and bracket.
20. Install the purge canister and connectors.
21. Install the EGR inlet tube.
22. Install the PCV valve and hose.
23. Install the throttle body electrical connectors.
24. Install the throttle and cruise control linkage and bracket.
25. Install the wiring harness connectors and brackets.
26. Install the air cleaner assembly and the engine cover.
27. Connect the negative battery cable, start the vehicle and check for leaks.

Lower Intake Manifold

REMOVAL & INSTALLATION

4.3L Engines

1987–95 MODELS

◗ **See Figures 20, 21 and 22 (p. 32–33)**

1. Disconnect the negative battery cable. Drain the cooling system.
2. Remove the engine cover.
3. Remove the air cleaner assembly.

➥Mark the relationship of the distributor and rotor for proper reassembly

    4. Remove the distributor.
    5. Disconnect the accelerator and cruise control cables with their brackets.
    6. Remove the cruise control transducer (if equipped).
    7. Remove the air conditioner compressor without disconnecting the lines and set it aside.
    8. Remove the alternator bracket and the idler pulley bracket at the manifold.
    9. Disconnect all electrical connections and vacuum lines from the manifold. Remove the EGR valve if necessary.
    10. Disconnect the fuel line at the intake manifold.
    11. Remove the heater pipe.
    12. Disconnect the upper radiator hose and pull it off.
    13. Tag and disconnect the power brake vacuum pipe and the EGR vacuum line.
    14. Tag and disconnect the coil wires and if necessary remove the coil.
    15. Remove the sensors and bracket on the right side. Disconnect the wiring harness on the right side and position it out of the way.
    16. If equipped, disconnect the transmission dipstick tube.

➥Mark the location of the intake manifold studs for proper reassembly

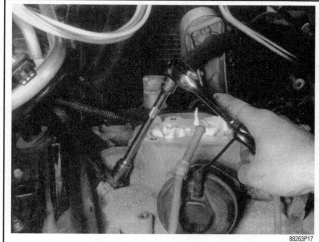

A ratchet with various extensions will be very helpful for manifold bolt removal

Disconnect all lines, hoses . . .

Loosen and remove the intake manifold retaining bolts . . .

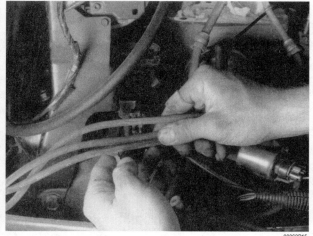

. . . and wiring from the intake manifold or from manifold mounted support brackets

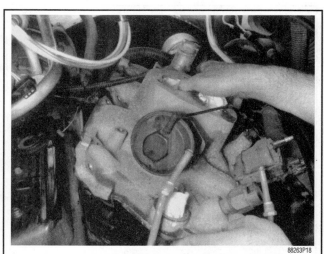

. . . then remove the manifold—the carburetor (or TBI unit) need not be removed

17. Remove the intake manifold bolts. Remove the manifold and the gaskets. Remember to reinstall the O-ring between the intake manifold and timing chain cover during assembly, if so equipped.

To install:

➡**Before installing the intake manifold, be sure that the gasket surfaces are thoroughly clean.**

18. Use plastic gasket retainers to prevent the manifold gasket from slipping out of place, if so equipped. Coat the front and rear sealing surfaces with a 0.19 in. (5mm) bead of RTV sealant. Extend the bead approximately ½ in. (13mm) down each head to help retain the gaskets.

19. Install the manifold and the gaskets. Remember to reinstall the O-ring between the intake manifold and timing chain cover, if so equipped.

20. Install the intake manifold bolts and tighten them to 35 ft. lbs. (48 Nm) in the sequence shown. On the final tightening sequence tighten bolt #9 to 41 ft. lbs. (56 Nm).

21. Connect the transmission dipstick tube, if removed.

22. Connect the coil wires. Install the sensors and bracket on the right side. Connect the wiring harness.

23. Connect the power brake vacuum pipe and the EGR vacuum line.

24. Connect the upper radiator hose.

25. Install the heater pipe.

26. Connect the fuel line(s).

27. Connect all electrical connections and vacuum lines at the manifold. Install the EGR valve.

28. Install the rear air conditioner compressor.

29. Install the alternator bracket and the idler pulley bracket at the manifold.

30. If equipped, install the cruise control transducer.

31. Connect the accelerator and cruise control cables with their brackets.

32. Install the distributor.

33. Install the air cleaner assembly.

34. Install the engine cover.

35. Fill the cooling system.

1996–97 MODELS

◆ **See Figure 23**

1. Remove the upper intake manifold using the recommended procedure outlined in this section.

2. Remove the distributor.

3. Disconnect the upper radiator hose from the thermostat housing.

4. Disconnect the heater hose from the lower intake manifold.

5. Remove the coolant bypass hose.

6. Remove the EGR valve.

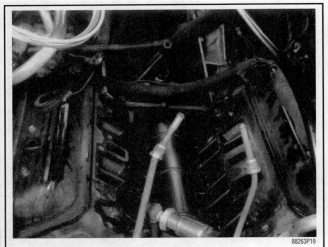

Once the manifold has been removed, you have free access to the lifter valley

88263P19

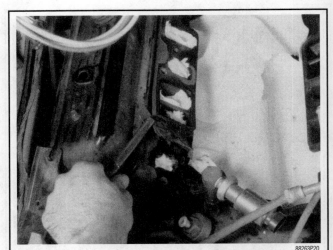

To keep debris out of the engine, cover all openings before cleaning the gasket surfaces

88263P20

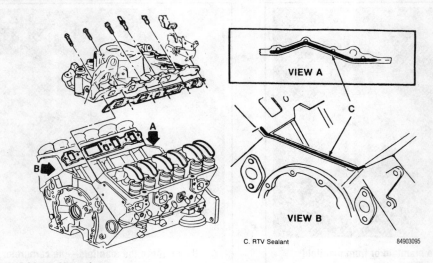

C. RTV Sealant   84903095

Fig. 20 Intake manifold—4.3L engines

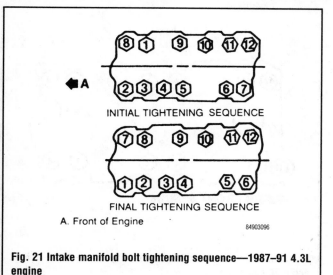

Fig. 21 Intake manifold bolt tightening sequence—1987–91 4.3L engine

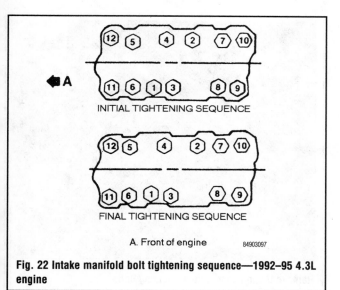

Fig. 22 Intake manifold bolt tightening sequence—1992–95 4.3L engine

20. Apply gasket sealer to the front and rear sealing surfaces of the engine block. Extend the sealer approximately ½-inch (13mm) onto the heads.

21. Install the lower intake manifold.

22. Apply sealer to the lower intake manifold bolts prior to installation.

23. Install the bolts and tighten in sequence and in 3 steps as follows:
    a. First step to 26 inch lbs. (3 Nm).
    b. Second step to 106 inch lbs. (12 Nm).
    c. Final step to 11 ft. lbs. (15 Nm).

24. Install the PCV valve and hose.

25. Install the EGR tube, clamp and bolt.

26. Install the ignition coil and bracket.

27. Install the transmission oil level indicator and tube, if equipped.

28. Connect the wiring harnesses and brackets to the lower manifold.

29. Connect the fuel pressure and return lines to the lower intake manifold.

30. Install the EGR valve.

31. Install the coolant bypass hose.

32. Connect the heater hose to the lower intake manifold.

33. Connect the upper radiator hose to the thermostat housing.

34. Disconnect the accelerator and cruise control cables with their brackets.

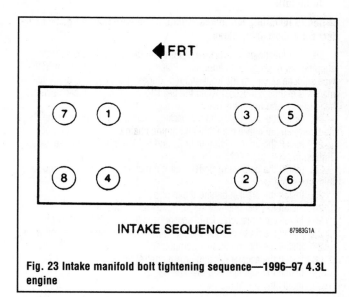

Fig. 23 Intake manifold bolt tightening sequence—1996–97 4.3L engine

35. Install the EGR tube.

36. Install the A/C compressor and bracket.

37. Install the distributor.

38. Connect the negative battery cable.

39. Start the vehicle and check the ignition timing (not adjustable).

40. Verify no oil, coolant, vacuum or fuel leaks.

5.0L and 5.7L Engines

1987–95 MODELS

◆ See Figures 24 and 25

1. Disconnect the negative battery cable. Drain the cooling system.

2. Remove the engine cover.

3. Remove the air cleaner assembly.

4. If necessary, remove the coolant recovery reservoir.

5. Remove the upper radiator hose from the thermostat housing.

6. Disconnect the heater pipe at the rear of the manifold.

7. Disconnect the rear alternator brace at the manifold.

8. Disengage all electrical connections and vacuum lines from the manifold. Remove the EGR valve if necessary.

7. Disconnect the fuel pressure and return lines from the lower intake manifold.

8. Disconnect the wiring harnesses and brackets from the lower manifold.

9. Disconnect the accelerator and cruise control cables with their brackets.

10. Remove the transmission oil level indicator and tube, if equipped.

11. Remove the ignition coil and bracket.

12. Remove the EGR tube, clamp and bolt.

13. Remove the PCV valve and hose.

14. Remove the A/C compressor and bracket, but do NOT disconnect the lines. Move the compressor out of the way. Take care not to kink the A/C lines.

15. Loosen the compressor mounting bracket and slide it forward, but do NOT remove it.

16. Remove the lower intake manifold bolts.

17. Remove the lower intake manifold.

To install:

18. Clean all gasket surfaces completely.

19. Install the intake manifold gaskets with the port blocking plates facing the rear. Factory gaskets should have the words "This Side Up" visible.

➡**Mark the relationship of the distributor and rotor for proper reassembly**

9. Remove the distributor.
10. Disconnect the fuel line at the intake manifold.
11. Remove the accelerator and cruise control linkage.
12. Remove the air conditioner compressor rear bracket.
13. Remove the brake booster vacuum pipe and then disconnect the coil wires.
14. Remove the emission control sensors and their bracket from the right side.
15. Remove the fuel line bracket at the rear of the manifold and position the fuel lines out of the way.
16. Remove the bracket behind the idler pulley.
17. Remove the carburetor or TBI unit if necessary. Refer to Section 5 for this procedure.

➡**Mark the location of the intake manifold studs for proper reassembly**

18. Remove the intake manifold bolts. Remove the manifold and the gaskets. Remember to reinstall the O-ring between the intake manifold and timing chain cover during assembly, if so equipped.

To install:

➡**Before installing the intake manifold, be sure that the gasket surfaces are thoroughly clean.**

19. Use plastic gasket retainers to prevent the manifold gasket from slipping out of place, if so equipped. Place a ³⁄₁₆ in. (5mm) bead of RTV type silicone sealer on the front and rear ridges of the cylinder block-to-manifold mating surfaces. Extend the bead ½ in. (13mm) up each cylinder head to seal and retain the manifold side gaskets.
20. Install the manifold and the gaskets. Remember to reinstall the O-ring between the intake manifold and timing chain cover, if so equipped.
21. Install the intake manifold bolts and tighten in the proper sequence. Tighten to 35 ft. lbs. (48Nm).
22. Install the carburetor or TBI unit if removed. Refer to Section 5 for this procedure.
23. Install the bracket behind the idler pulley.
24. Install the fuel line bracket at the rear of the manifold.
25. Install the emission control sensors and their bracket on the right side.
26. Install the brake booster vacuum pipe and then connect the coil wires.
27. Install the air conditioner compressor rear bracket.
28. Install the accelerator and cruise control linkage.
29. Install the fuel line and bracket.
30. Install the distributor.

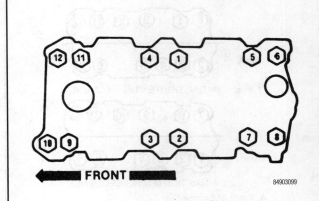

Fig. 25 Intake manifold bolt tightening sequence—1987–95 5.0L and 5.7L engines

Remove the intake manifold retaining bolts

Fig. 24 Intake manifold—5.0L and 5.7L engines

Remove the intake manifold

87983P39

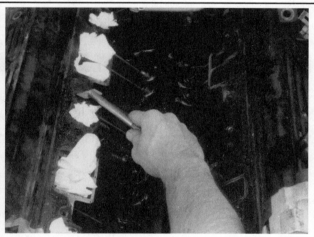

Using a scraper, clean the intake manifold gasket mating surfaces

87983P40

31. Engage all electrical connections and vacuum lines at the manifold. Install the EGR valve.

32. Connect the rear alternator brace at the manifold.

33. Connect the heater pipe to the rear of the manifold.

34. Install the upper radiator hose.

35. If removed, install the coolant recovery reservoir.

36. Install the air cleaner assembly.

37. Connect the negative battery cable. Fill the cooling system.

1996–97 MODELS

▶ See Figure 26

1. Remove the upper intake manifold using the recommended procedure outlined in this section.

2. Remove the distributor.

3. Disconnect the upper radiator hose from the thermostat housing.

4. Disconnect the heater hose from the lower intake manifold.

5. Remove the coolant bypass hose.

6. Remove the EGR valve.

7. Disconnect the fuel pressure and return lines from the lower intake manifold.

8. Disconnect the wiring harnesses and brackets from the lower manifold.

9. Remove the left side valve cover.

10. Remove the transmission oil level indicator and tube, if equipped.

11. Remove the EGR tube, clamp and bolt.

12. Remove the PCV valve and hose.

13. Remove the A/C compressor and bracket, but do NOT disconnect the lines. Move the compressor out of the way. Take care not to kink the A/C lines.

14. Loosen the compressor mounting bracket and slide it forward, but do NOT remove it.

15. Remove the power brake vacuum tube.

16. Remove the lower intake manifold bolts.

17. Remove the lower intake manifold.

To install:

18. Clean all gasket surfaces completely.

19. Install the intake manifold gaskets with the port blocking plates facing the rear. Factory gaskets should have the words "This Side Up" visible.

20. Apply gasket sealer to the front and rear sealing surfaces of the engine block. Extend the sealer approximately ½-inch (13mm) onto the heads.

21. Install the lower intake manifold.

22. Apply sealer to the lower intake manifold bolts prior to installation.

23. Install the bolts and tighten in sequence and in 3 steps as follows:

   a. First step to 71 inch lbs. (8 Nm).

   b. Second step to 106 inch lbs. (12 Nm).

   c. Final step to 11 ft. lbs. (15 Nm).

24. Install the power brake vacuum tube.

25. Install the PCV valve and hose.

26. Install the EGR tube, clamp and bolt.

27. Install the transmission oil level indicator and tube, if equipped.

28. Install the left side valve cover.

29. Connect the wiring harnesses and brackets to the lower manifold.

30. Connect the fuel pressure and return lines to the lower intake manifold.

31. Install the EGR valve.

32. Install the coolant bypass hose.

33. Connect the heater hose to the lower intake manifold.

34. Connect the upper radiator hose to the thermostat housing.

35. Install the A/C compressor and bracket.

36. Install the distributor.

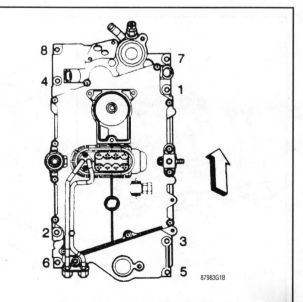

87983G1B

Fig. 26 Intake manifold bolt tightening sequence—1996–97 5.0L and 5.7L engines

37. Connect the negative battery cable.
38. Start the vehicle and check the ignition timing (not adjustable).
39. Verify no oil, coolant, vacuum or fuel leaks.

6.2L Diesel Engine

▶ **See Figure 27**

1. Disconnect both batteries.
2. Remove the engine cover.
3. Remove the air cleaner assembly and, if applicable, the air intake duct.
4. Remove the crankcase ventilator tubes, and disconnect the secondary fuel filter lines. Remove the secondary filter and adapter.
5. Remove the thermostat bolts and the upper radiator hose.
6. Loosen the vacuum pump hold-down clamp and rotate the pump to gain access to the nearest manifold bolt.
7. Remove the EPR/EGR boost solenoids and bracket, if equipped. Tag and disconnect the EGR and crankcase vent hoses.
8. Remove the heater hose bracket, tag and disconnect any vacuum lines and electrical connections as necessary.
9. If equipped with a turbocharger remove the long pencil brace.
10. Remove the fuel line brackets and ground straps.
11. Remove the rear air conditioning bracket, if equipped.
12. Remove the intake manifold bolts. The injection line clips are retained by these bolts.
13. Remove the intake manifold.

➡ **If the engine is to be further serviced with the manifold removed, install protective covers over the intake ports.**

To install:

14. Clean the manifold gasket surfaces on the cylinder heads and install new gaskets before installing the manifold.

➡ **The gaskets have an opening for the EGR valve on light duty installations. An insert covers this opening on heavy duty installations.**

15. Install the manifold. Tighten the bolts in the sequence illustrated to 32 ft. lbs. (42 Nm).
16. The secondary filter must be filled with clean diesel fuel before it is reinstalled.
17. Install the rear air conditioning bracket, if equipped.

18. Install the ground straps and fuel line brackets.
19. Install the turbocharger pencil brace, if equipped.
20. Engage any electrical connections and vacuum hoses that were removed.
21. Install the EPR/EGR valve bracket. Reconnect the hoses.
22. Tighten the vacuum pump hold-down clamp.
23. Install the upper radiator hose and the thermostat bolts.
24. Install the secondary filter and adapter.
25. Connect the secondary fuel filter lines.
26. Install the crankcase ventilator tubes.
27. Install the air cleaner assembly.
28. Connect both batteries.

6.5L Diesel Engine

▶ **See Figures 27 and 28**

1. Have the A/C system discharged by a qualified technician using approved equipment.
2. Disconnect both batteries.
3. Remove the engine cover.
4. Remove the air cleaner assembly and if applicable the air intake duct.
5. Remove the Crankcase Depression Regulator (CDR) vent hose.
6. Disconnect the fuel lines and brackets.
7. Remove the wiring harness and all connections and brackets.
8. Remove the oil and transmission dipstick tubes.
9. Remove the rear A/C line.

✳✳ WARNING

Do not attempt to remove center intake manifold with the with the left and right intake manifolds as an assembly as this may damage the gaskets, turbocharger and center intake manifold during reassembly.

10. Remove the center intake manifold.
11. Remove the upper intake manifold.
12. Remove the glow plug relay.
13. Tag the fuel line clips, lower intake manifold studs and brackets before removal to aid during installation.
14. Loosen the manifold studs and fuel line clips, then remove the lower manifold and gaskets.

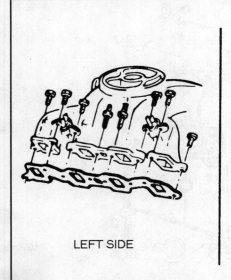 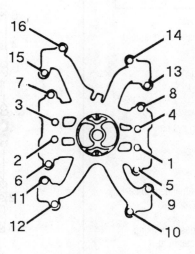 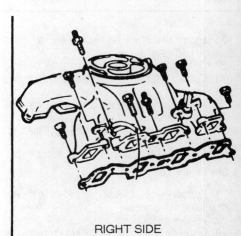

LEFT SIDE

16
15
7
3
14
13
8
4
2
6
11
12
1
5
9
10

RIGHT SIDE

84903100

Fig. 27 Intake manifold bolt tightening sequence—6.2L diesel engine (1987–95 6.5L engine similar)

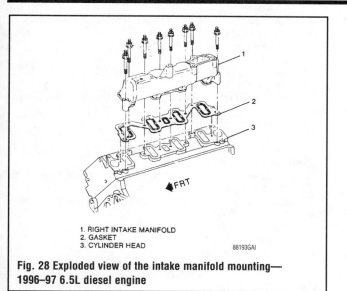

Fig. 28 Exploded view of the intake manifold mounting— 1996–97 6.5L diesel engine

1. RIGHT INTAKE MANIFOLD
2. GASKET
3. CYLINDER HEAD

88193GAI

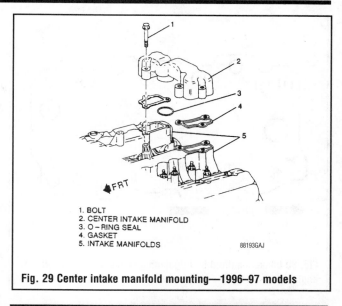

Fig. 29 Center intake manifold mounting—1996–97 models

1. BOLT
2. CENTER INTAKE MANIFOLD
3. O–RING SEAL
4. GASKET
5. INTAKE MANIFOLDS

88193GAJ

➡If the engine is to be further serviced with the manifold removed, install protective covers over the intake ports.

To install:

15. Clean the manifold gasket surfaces on the cylinder heads and install new gaskets before installing the manifold.
16. Install the lower manifold. Apply Teflon sealer to the bolts and tighten them in the sequence illustrated to 31 ft. lbs. (42 Nm).
17. Install the center intake manifold.
18. Install the ground straps and fuel line brackets.
19. Engage any electrical connections and vacuum hoses that were removed.
20. Install the engine oil and transmission dipstick tubes.
21. Install the CDR vent hose.

➡Always install a new O-ring between the upper manifold and turbocharger. Coat the O-ring with clean engine oil before installation.

22. Install the upper manifold and tighten the bolts to 17 ft. lbs. (23 Nm).
23. Connect the A/C lines and have the system recharged by a qualified technician using approved equipment.
24. Install the glow plug relay.
25. Install the air cleaner assembly.
26. Install the engine cover.
27. Connect both batteries.

CENTER INTAKE MANIFOLD

▶ See Figure 29

1. Disconnect the negative battery cable and remove the engine cover.
2. Loosen the center intake manifold bolts and remove the manifold.

To install:

➡Install a new O-ring lubricated with clean engine oil between the manifold and the turbocharger

3. Install the manifold and tighten the bolts to 17 ft. lbs. (23 Nm).
4. Install the engine cover and connect the negative battery cable.

7.4L Engines

1987–95 MODELS

▶ See Figures 30, 31 and 32

1. Disconnect the battery.
2. Remove the engine cover.

✳✳ CAUTION

When draining engine coolant, keep in mind that cats and dogs are attracted to ethylene glycol antifreeze and could drink any that is left in an uncovered container or in puddles on the ground. This will prove fatal in sufficient quantity. Always drain coolant into a sealable container. Coolant should be reused unless it is contaminated or is several years old.

3. Drain the cooling system.
4. Remove the air cleaner assembly.
5. Remove the upper radiator hose, thermostat housing and the bypass hose, if necessary.
6. Disconnect the heater hose and pipe.
7. Tag and disconnect all electrical connections and vacuum lines from the manifold and move them to the side.
8. Disconnect the accelerator linkage.
9. Disconnect the cruise control cable, if equipped.
10. Disconnect the TVS cable.
11. Remove the fuel line at the manifold.
12. Remove the TBI unit, if necessary. Refer to Section 5 for this procedure.

➡Mark the relationship of the distributor and rotor for proper reassembly

13. Remove the distributor, if necessary.
14. Remove the cruise control transducer, if equipped.
15. Disconnect the ignition coil wires and remove the coil if necessary.
16. Remove the EGR solenoid and bracket.
17. Remove the MAP sensor and bracket.
18. Remove the air conditioning compressor.
19. Remove the front alternator/AIR pump bracket, if necessary.
20. Remove the intake manifold bolts.
21. Remove the manifold and the gaskets and seals.

➡Remember to reinstall the O-ring between the intake manifold and timing chain cover during assembly, if so equipped.

To install:

➡Before installing the intake manifold, be sure that the gasket surfaces are thoroughly clean.

22. Install the manifold and the gaskets and seals.
23. Install the intake manifold bolts. Tighten the bolts to 30 ft. lbs. (40 Nm) in the proper sequence.
24. Install the front alternator/AIR pump bracket, if removed.

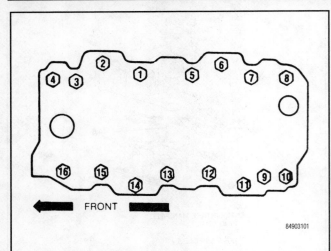

Fig. 30 Intake manifold bolt tightening sequence—1987–90 7.4L engines

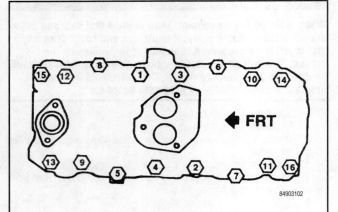

Fig. 31 Intake manifold bolt tightening sequence—1991–94 7.4L engine

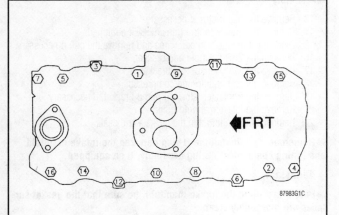

Fig. 32 Intake manifold bolt tightening sequence—1995 7.4L engine

25. Install the air conditioning compressor rear bracket, if removed.
26. Install the MAP sensor and bracket.
27. Install the EGR solenoid and bracket.
28. Connect the ignition coil wires.
29. Install the cruise control transducer, if equipped.
30. Install the distributor.
31. Install the TBI unit, if removed. Refer to Section 5 for this procedure.
32. Install the fuel line at the manifold.
33. Connect the TVS cable.
34. Connect the cruise control cable, if equipped.
35. Connect the accelerator linkage.
36. Connect all electrical connections and vacuum lines at the manifold.
37. Connect the heater hose and pipe.
38. Install the upper radiator hose, thermostat housing and the bypass hose.
39. Install the air cleaner assembly.
40. Fill the cooling system.
41. Install the engine cover.
42. Connect the battery.

1996–97 MODELS

1. Have the A/C system discharged. Recover the refrigerant using the appropriate recycling equipment.
2. Remove the upper intake manifold using the recommended procedure outlined in this section.
3. Remove the A/C lines at the compressor.
4. Remove the distributor using the recommended procedure. Mark the relationship of the distributor housing and rotor for proper reassembly.
5. Drain the engine coolant. Remove the upper radiator hose at the thermostat housing.
6. Disconnect the heater hose from the manifold.
7. Disconnect the fuel line brackets and rail.
8. Disconnect the water pump bypass hose.
9. Remove the lower intake manifold bolts and remove the lower intake manifold and gaskets.

To install:
10. Clean all parts well:
    a. Clean all traces of gasket from the sealing surfaces.
    b. Inspect for cracks, broken flanges and gasket surface damage.
    c. Clean excessive carbon buildup in the exhaust passages.
    d. Clean scale and deposits from the coolant passages.
    e. Clean the EGR passage of carbon deposits.
11. Install the gaskets to the cylinder head in their proper position. Factory-type gaskets should be stamped "This Side Up".
12. Install the front and rear intake manifold seals to the block.
13. Apply a ³⁄₁₆-inch (5mm) bead of RTV GM #1052289, or equivalent, to the four seal corners of the block. Extend the bead approximately ½-inch (13mm) up the cylinder head to seal and retain the gaskets.
14. Carefully place the lower intake manifold into position on the engine.
15. Apply sealer, GM #1052080, or equivalent, to the lower intake manifold bolts. Install the lower manifold bolts and tighten them in sequence to 30 ft. lbs. (40 Nm).
16. Install the water pump bypass hose.
17. Install the wiring harness connectors and brackets.
18. Install the fuel line brackets and fuel rail.
19. Install the heater hose.
20. Install the upper radiator hose.
21. Install the A/C lines to the compressor.
22. Install the distributor. Note the relationship of the distributor housing and rotor made at disassembly.
23. Install the upper intake manifold using the procedure in this section.
24. Fill the cooling system.

➡The 1996–97 models should have come with DEX-COOL™. This orange-color coolant is low in silicates and is designed to protect the aluminum components in the cooling system.

25. Connect the negative battery cable.
26. Start the engine. Check for coolant, oil and vacuum leaks and for proper engine operation.
27. Install the engine cover.
28. Have the A/C system recharged.

Exhaust Manifold

REMOVAL & INSTALLATION

4.3L Engines

▶ See Figure 33

On some engines, tab locks are used on the front and rear pairs of bolts on each exhaust manifold. When removing the bolts, straighten the tabs from beneath the van using a suitable tool. When installing the tab locks, bend the tabs against the sides of the bolt, not over the top of the bolt.

1987–95 MODELS

1. Disconnect the negative battery cable. Remove the air cleaner assembly.
2. Remove the engine cover.
3. Raise the vehicle and support it with jackstands.
4. Remove the hot air shroud, (if so equipped). Disconnect the exhaust pipe at the manifold.
5. Lower the van.
6. Disconnect the O_2 sensor wire on the left side manifold. Do not remove the sensor unless you intend to replace it.
7. Disconnect the rear power steering pump bracket at the left manifold.
8. Remove the heat stove pipe on the right side manifold.
9. Remove the AIR hose at the check valve, if equipped.
10. Remove the manifold bolts and remove the manifold(s). Some models have lock tabs on the front and rear manifold bolts which must be removed before removing the bolts. These tabs can be bent with a drift pin.
To install:
11. Clean both the manifold and cylinder block mating surfaces and install the manifold. Install the flat washers and then the tab washers and

insert the bolts. Tighten the two center bolts to 26 ft. lbs. (36 Nm); the outside bolts to 20 ft. lbs. (28 Nm) and then bend the tab washers against the bolt heads.
12. Install the AIR hose at the check valve, if equipped.
13. Install the heat stove pipe on the right side manifold.
14. Connect the rear power steering pump bracket at the left manifold.
15. Connect the O_2 sensor wire on the left side manifold.
16. Raise the van and support it with jackstands.
17. Connect the exhaust pipe at the manifold. Install the hot air shroud.
18. Lower the van.
19. Install the air cleaner. Connect the negative battery cable.
20. Install the engine cover.

1996–97 MODELS

▶ See Figures 34 and 35

1. Disconnect the negative battery cable. Remove the air cleaner assembly.
2. Remove the engine cover.
3. If applicable, remove the coolant recovery reservoir.
4. Raise the vehicle and support it with jackstands.
5. Remove the hot air shroud, (if so equipped). Disconnect the exhaust pipe at the manifold.
6. Lower the van.
7. If necessary, remove the EGR inlet pipe from the left manifold.
8. Unfasten the manifold retainers and remove the manifold.
To install:
9. Clean the manifold-to-cylinder head mating surfaces.
10. Install the manifold and tighten the retainers in the following sequence:
• Bolts on the center exhaust tube: 11 ft. lbs. (15 Nm)
• Bolts on the front and rear exhaust tubes: 22 ft. lbs. (30 Nm)
11. Bend the tab washers over the bolts.
12. If removed, install the EGR inlet pipe.
13. Raise the vehicle and support it with jackstands.
14. Install the exhaust pipe at the manifold.
15. Install the hot air shroud, If equipped.
16. Lower the vehicle.
17. Install the engine cover.

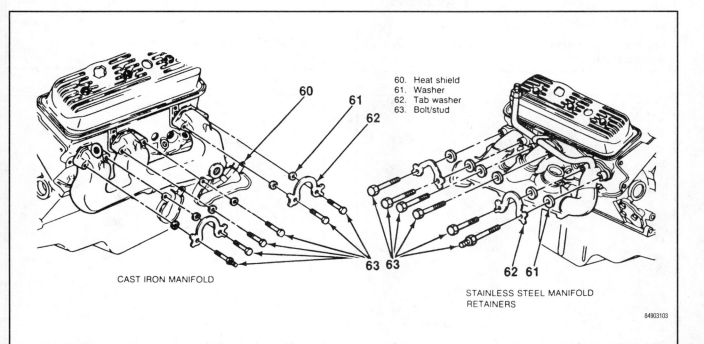

60. Heat shield
61. Washer
62. Tab washer
63. Bolt/stud

CAST IRON MANIFOLD

STAINLESS STEEL MANIFOLD RETAINERS

84903103

Fig. 33 Exhaust manifold—4.3L engine

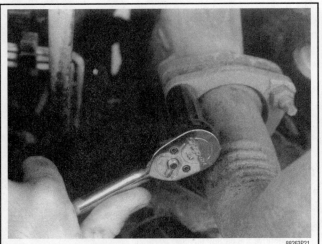

Loosen the retainers and disconnect the exhaust pipe from the manifold

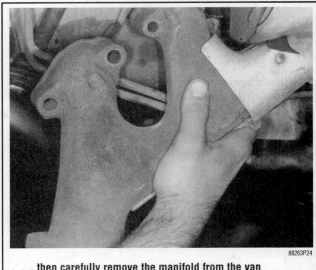

. . . then carefully remove the manifold from the van

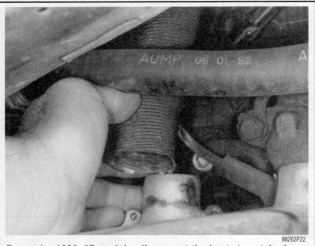

Except for 1996–97 models, disconnect the heat stove tube from the exhaust manifold

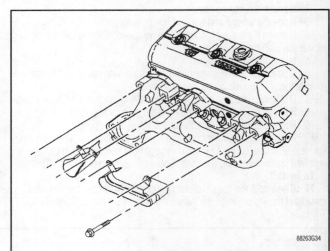

Fig. 34 Exploded view of the heat shields—1996–97 4.3L engine

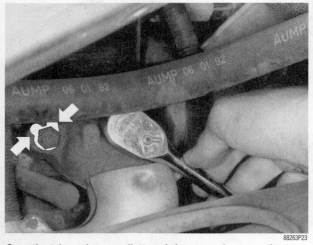

Once the tab washers are flattened, loosen and remove the manifold retaining bolts . . .

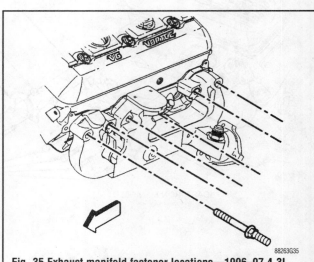

Fig. 35 Exhaust manifold fastener locations—1996–97 4.3L engine

18. If removed, install the coolant recovery reservoir.
19. Install the air cleaner and intake duct.
20. Connect the negative battery cable.

5.0L and 5.7L Engines

▶ **See Figure 36**

On some engines, tab locks are used on the front and rear pairs of bolts on each exhaust manifold. When removing the bolts, straighten the tabs from beneath the van using a suitable tool. When installing the tab locks, bend the tabs against the sides of the bolt, not over the top of the bolt.

1. Disconnect the negative battery cable. Remove the air cleaner.
2. Disconnect the negative battery cable and remove the engine cover.
3. If necessary, remove the air cleaner assembly and coolant recovery reservoir.
4. On 1996–97 models, disconnect the EGR inlet tube and the oil dipstick tube.
5. If necessary, tag and disconnect the ignition wires from the spark plugs.
6. Raise the van and support it with jackstands.
7. Remove the hot air shroud, (if so equipped). Disconnect the exhaust pipe at the manifold.
8. Lower the van.

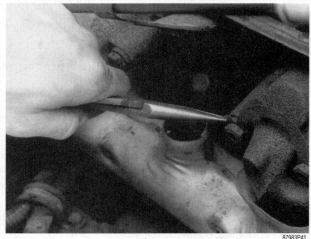
Use a pair of needlenose pliers to bend back the locktabs on the exhaust manifold

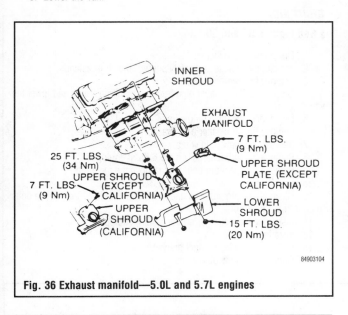
Fig. 36 Exhaust manifold—5.0L and 5.7L engines

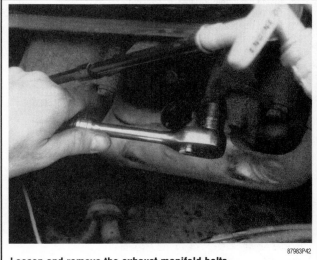
Loosen and remove the exhaust manifold bolts

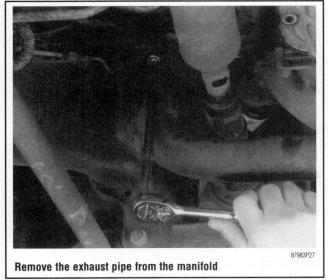
Remove the exhaust pipe from the manifold

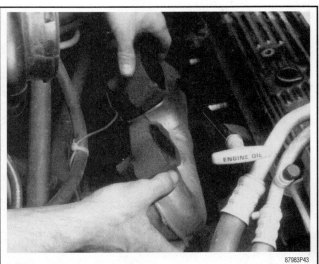
Remove the exhaust manifold

9. Disconnect the O(SUB)2(/SUB) sensor wire on the left side manifold. Do not remove the sensor unless you intend to replace it.

10. On some models it may be necessary to remove the left side floor panel to gain access to the exhaust manifold.

11. Remove the heat stove pipe on the right side manifold.

12. Disconnect the rear power steering pump bracket at the left manifold.

13. Remove the dipstick tube bracket on the right manifold.

14. Remove the manifold bolts and remove the manifold(s). Some models have locktabs on the front and rear manifold bolts which must be removed before removing the bolts. These tabs can be bent with a drift pin or needlenose pliers.

To install:

15. Clean both the manifold and cylinder block mating surfaces and install the manifold. Install the flat washers and then the tab washers and insert the bolts. On 1987–95 models, tighten the two center bolts to 26 ft. lbs. (36 Nm); the outside bolts to 20 ft. lbs. (28 Nm) and then bend the tab washers against the bolt heads. On 1996–97 models, tighten the bolts in two passes in the sequence illustrated. On the first pass, tighten the bolts to 11 ft. lbs. (15 Nm) and on the second pass to 22 ft. lbs. (30 Nm).

16. Install the dipstick tube bracket on the right manifold.

17. If removed install the EGR inlet tube.

18. If removed, connect the ignition wires to the spark plugs.

19. Install the left floor panel, if removed.

20. Connect the rear power steering pump bracket at the left manifold.

21. Install the heat stove pipe on the right side manifold.

22. Connect the O(SUB)2(/SUB) sensor wire on the left side manifold.

23. Raise the van and support it with jackstands.

24. Connect the exhaust pipe at the manifold. Install the hot air shroud.

25. Lower the van.

26. Install the air cleaner assembly and coolant recovery reservoir.

27. Connect the negative battery cable.

28. Install the engine cover.

7.4L Engines

RIGHT SIDE

▶ **See Figure 37**

1. Disconnect the negative battery cable.

2. Remove the engine cover.

3. Remove the heat stove pipe, if applicable.

4. Remove the dipstick tube.

5. Disconnect the AIR hose at the check valve, if equipped.

6. Remove the spark plugs.

7. Disconnect the exhaust pipe at the manifold.

8. Remove the manifold bolts and spark plug heat shields.

9. Remove the manifold.

To install:

10. Clean the mating surfaces.

11. Clean the stud threads.

12. Install the manifold and bolts. Tighten the bolts to 40 ft. lbs. (54 Nm) and if equipped with nuts (late model vehicles) tighten those to 22 ft. lbs. (30 Nm) starting from the center bolts and working towards the outside.

13. Connect the exhaust pipe at the manifold.

14. Install the spark plugs.

15. Connect the AIR hose at the check valve, if equipped.

16. Install the dipstick tube.

17. Install the heat stove pipe, if applicable.

18. Connect the battery.

19. Install the engine cover.

6.2L and 6.5L Diesel Engines

RIGHT SIDE

▶ **See Figures 38 and 39**

1. Disconnect the batteries.

2. Jack up the vehicle and safely support it with jackstands.

3. Remove the engine cover.

4. Disconnect the exhaust pipe from the manifold flange and lower the van.

5. Disconnect the glow plug wires.

6. Remove the air cleaner duct bracket.

7. Remove the glow plug wires.

8. Remove the turbocharger on the 6.5L, if equipped.

9. Remove the manifold bolts and remove the manifold.

To install:

10. Clean all mating surfaces and install the manifold. Tighten the bolts to 26 ft. lbs. (35 Nm).

11. Install the turbocharger on the 6.5L, if equipped.

12. Install the glow plugs.

13. Install the air cleaner duct bracket.

14. Connect the glow plug wires.

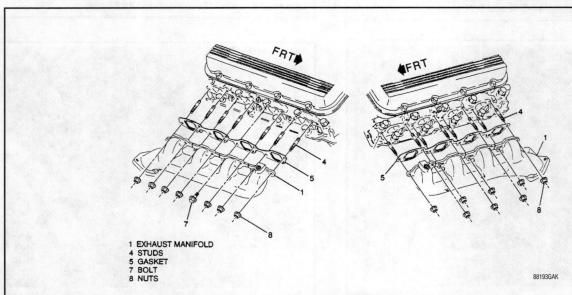

1 EXHAUST MANIFOLD
4 STUDS
5 GASKET
7 BOLT
8 NUTS

88193GAK

Fig. 37 Exploded view of the exhaust manifold mounting—1996–97 model shown (others similar)

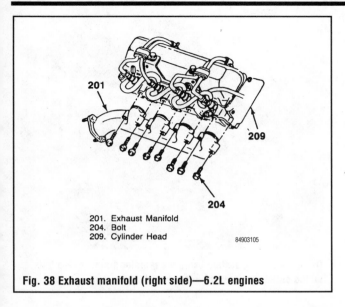

201. Exhaust Manifold
204. Bolt
209. Cylinder Head

84903105

Fig. 38 Exhaust manifold (right side)—6.2L engines

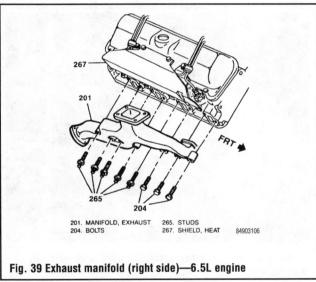

201. MANIFOLD, EXHAUST   265. STUDS
204. BOLTS   267. SHIELD, HEAT

84903106

Fig. 39 Exhaust manifold (right side)—6.5L engine

15. Raise the vehicle and support it with jackstands.
16. Connect the exhaust pipe to the manifold flange and lower the van.
17. Connect the batteries.
18. Install the engine cover.

LEFT SIDE

▶ **See Figure 40**

1. Disconnect the batteries, negative cable first.
2. Remove the engine cover.
3. Remove the dipstick tube nut, and remove the dipstick tube.
4. Disconnect the glow plug wires.
5. Raise the vehicle and safely support it with jackstands.
6. Disconnect the exhaust pipe at the manifold flange.
7. Remove the manifold bolts. Remove the manifold from underneath the van.

To install:

8. Install the manifold and tighten the bolts to 26 ft. lbs. (35 Nm).
9. Connect the exhaust pipe to the manifold flange.
10. Lower the vehicle and connect the glow plug wires.
11. Install the dipstick tube and tighten the nut.
12. Connect the batteries, positive cable first.
13. Install the engine cover.

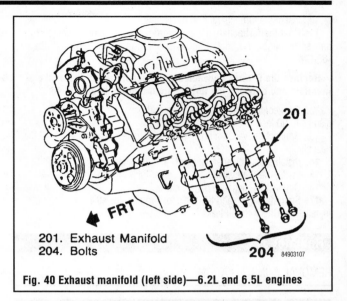

201. **Exhaust Manifold**
204. **Bolts**

84903107

Fig. 40 Exhaust manifold (left side)—6.2L and 6.5L engines

Turbocharger

REMOVAL & INSTALLATION

▶ **See Figure 41**

1. Disconnect the negative battery and remove the engine cover.
2. Remove the CDR valve.
3. Remove the air cleaner assembly and air duct.
4. Remove the heat shield from the turbocharger.
5. Remove the center intake manifold.
6. Tag and remove the vacuum hose from the wastegate actuator.
7. Disconnect the exhaust pipe, exhaust clamps and retaining bolts from the turbocharger.
8. Remove the turbocharger from the engine.

To install:

9. Before installing the turbocharger, perform the following checks.
   a. Check the intake and exhaust systems leading to and from the turbocharger for dirt and debris. Even small pieces of dirt can cause severe damage.
   b. Ensure the exhaust manifold-to-turbocharger mating surfaces and clean.
   c. Make sure the oil feed and return passages in the block and turbocharger are free of clean and open.

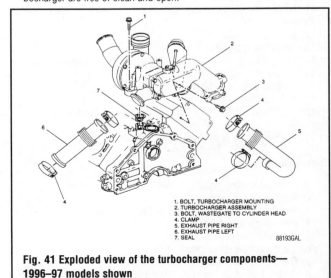

1. BOLT, TURBOCHARGER MOUNTING
2. TURBOCHARGER ASSEMBLY
3. BOLT, WASTEGATE TO CYLINDER HEAD
4. CLAMP
5. EXHAUST PIPE RIGHT
6. EXHAUST PIPE LEFT
7. SEAL

88193GAL

Fig. 41 Exploded view of the turbocharger components—1996–97 models shown

10. Install the turbocharger on the engine.

11. Coat the turbocharger retaining bolts with a high temperature anti-seize compound, install the bolts and tighten them to 48 ft. lbs. (65 Nm).

➡ **Replace the O-rings between the turbocharger and the intake manifold and between the turbocharger and the engine block.**

12. Connect the exhaust pipes to the turbocharger and tighten the clamps to 90 inch lbs. (10 Nm).

13. Connect the vacuum hose to the wastegate actuator and install the heat shield.

14. Install the air cleaner assembly and air intake duct.

15. Install the CDR valve and the center intake manifold.

16. Connect the negative battery cable.

17. Start the engine and let it idle for two minutes after finishing the installation. Check for oil leaks.

Radiator

REMOVAL & INSTALLATION

✳✳ CAUTION

When draining the coolant, keep in mind that cats and dogs are attracted by ethylene glycol antifreeze, and are quite likely to drink any that is left in an uncovered container or in puddles on the ground. This will prove fatal in sufficient quantity. Always drain the coolant into a sealable container. Coolant should be reused unless it is contaminated or several years old.

Gasoline Engines

1. Drain the cooling system.
2. Remove the coolant recovery reservoir, if applicable.
3. If necessary, remove the air cleaner assembly.
4. If necessary, remove the hood latch.
5. If there is a fan shroud, remove the shroud or shroud halves (upper and lower) attaching retainers.
6. Disconnect the radiator upper and lower hoses and, if applicable, the transmission coolant lines.
7. If applicable, remove the oil cooler lines from the radiator.
8. Remove the radiator upper panel if so equipped.
9. Disengage any electrical connections from the radiator.
10. On 1996–97 models, remove the fan and clutch assembly.
11. Remove the radiator attaching bolts and remove the radiator.

To install:
12. Install the radiator.
13. Install the upper panel, if removed.
14. Connect the engine oil cooler and transmission oil cooler lines.
15. Engage the electrical connections to the radiator.
16. Connect the upper and lower radiator hoses.
17. Install and the shroud.
18. If removed., install the air cleaner assembly and coolant recovery reservoir.
19. Fill the cooling system and check for leaks.

Diesel Engines

1. Drain the cooling system.
2. Remove the air intake snorkel.
3. Remove the windshield washer bottle.
4. Remove the hood release cable.
5. Remove the upper fan shroud.
6. Disconnect the upper radiator hose.
7. Disconnect the transmission cooler lines.
8. On the 6.2L diesel engine, unplug the low coolant sensor wire.

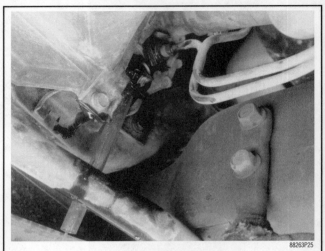

Drain the cooling system using the radiator draincock—a tube on the outlet may prevent a mess

On some models, you must remove the hood latch—start by matchmarking it . . .

. . . then loosen the retaining bolts . . .

. . . and remove the latch assembly from the radiator support

With the retainers removed, carefully lift the upper fan shroud from the engine compartment

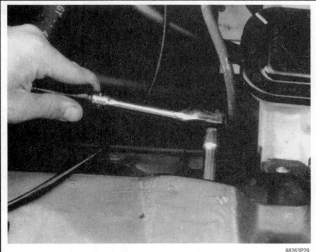

Loosen the retainers for the upper fan shroud . . .

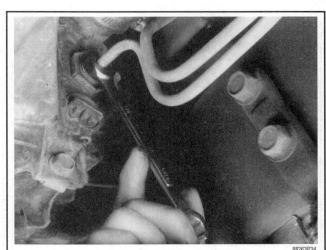

Loosen and disconnect any threaded transmission or oil cooler lines

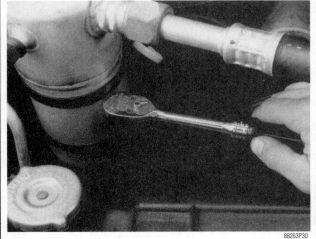

. . . being careful not to miss any (a long extension is handy for the upper-to-lower shroud bolts)

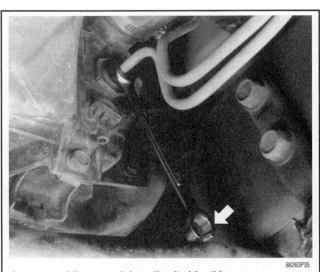

An open-end line wrench is well suited for this purpose

Disengage the overflow hose from the radiator

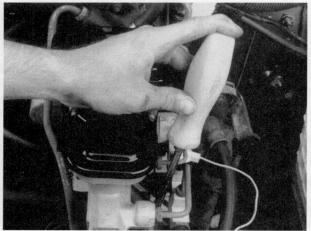

Loosen the clamps and disconnect the remaining radiator hoses . . .

. . . then carefully lift the radiator from the engine compartment

9. Disconnect the overflow hose.
10. Disconnect the engine oil cooler lines.
11. Disconnect the lower radiator hose.
12. On the 6.2L diesel engine, remove the brake master cylinder. See Section 9.
13. Remove the fasteners securing the radiator, then remove the radiator from the vehicle.
To install:
14. Position the radiator at its mounting points and install its retainers. Tighten to 71 inch lbs. (9 Nm).
15. If removed, install the brake master cylinder.
16. Connect the lower radiator hose.
17. Connect the engine oil cooler lines.
18. Connect the overflow hose.
19. If removed, engage the low coolant sensor wire.
20. Connect the transmission cooler lines.
21. Connect the upper radiator hose.
22. Install the upper fan shroud.
23. Install the hood release cable.
24. Install the windshield washer bottle.
25. Install the air intake snorkel.
26. Fill the cooling system.

Engine Fan

REMOVAL & INSTALLATION

▶ **See Figures 42 and 43**

1. Disconnect the negative battery cable.
2. If necessary remove the air cleaner assembly and coolant recovery reservoir.
3. Remove the radiator shroud.
4. Remove the drive belt, if necessary.
5. Remove the fan clutch-to-water pump pulley nuts and lift out the fan/clutch assembly.
6. Remove the fan clutch bolts and separate the fan from the clutch.
To install:
7. Install the fan on the fan clutch, then position the fan/clutch assembly on the water pump pulley. Tighten the retainers as follows:
- 1987–95 gasoline engines: 26 ft. lbs. (35 Nm)
- 1996–97 4.3L, 5.0L and 5.7L gasoline engines: 42 ft. lbs. (57 Nm)
- 7.4L and diesel engines: 18 ft. lbs. (24 Nm)
8. Install the fan shroud.

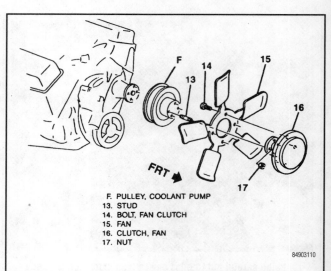

F. PULLEY, COOLANT PUMP
13. STUD
14. BOLT, FAN CLUTCH
15. FAN
16. CLUTCH, FAN
17. NUT

Fig. 42 Engine fan and clutch assembly—gasoline engines

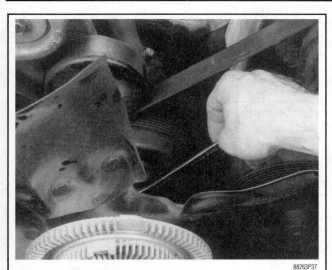

Loosen the fan-to-pulley retainers . . .

. . . then remove the fan from the water pump pulley and engine compartment

9. If removed, install the drive belt.
10. If removed, install the coolant recovery reservoir and air cleaner assembly.
11. Connect the battery cable.

Auxiliary Cooling Fan

REMOVAL & INSTALLATION

1. Remove the grille.
2. Unplug the fan harness connector.
3. Remove the fan-to-brace bolts and lift out the fan.
4. Installation is the reverse of removal. Tighten the bolts to 53 ft. lbs. (72 Nm).

TESTING

♦ See Figures 44 and 45

For testing the auxiliary cooling fan, refer to the cooling fan circuit illustration and the diagnosis chart.

Water Pump

REMOVAL & INSTALLATION

❋❋ CAUTION

When draining the coolant, keep in mind that cats and dogs are attracted by ethylene glycol antifreeze, and are quite likely to drink any that is left in an uncovered container or in puddles on the ground. This will prove fatal in sufficient quantity. Always drain the coolant into a sealable container. Coolant should be reused unless it is contaminated or several years old.

4.3L, 5.0L, 5.7L and 7.4L Engines

♦ See Figures 46, 47 and 48 (p. 49)

1. Disconnect the negative battery cable.
2. Drain the radiator. Remove the fan shroud.
3. Remove the drive belt(s).
4. Remove the alternator and other accessories, if necessary.

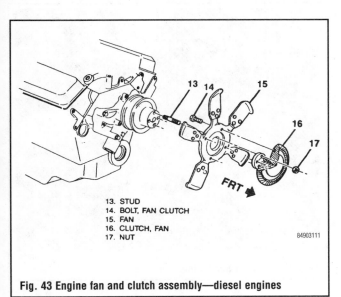

13. STUD
14. BOLT, FAN CLUTCH
15. FAN
16. CLUTCH, FAN
17. NUT

Fig. 43 Engine fan and clutch assembly—diesel engines

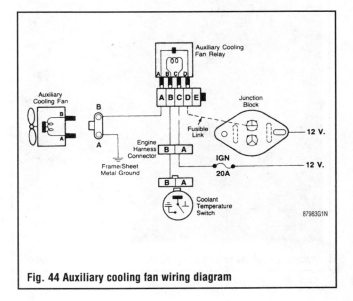

Fig. 44 Auxiliary cooling fan wiring diagram

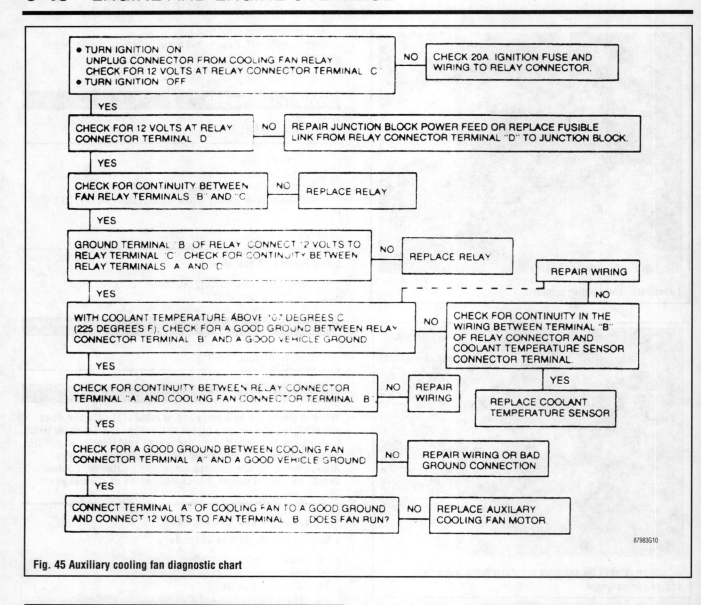

- TURN IGNITION "ON"
  UNPLUG CONNECTOR FROM COOLING FAN RELAY
  CHECK FOR 12 VOLTS AT RELAY CONNECTOR TERMINAL "C"
- TURN IGNITION "OFF"

→ NO → CHECK 20A IGNITION FUSE AND WIRING TO RELAY CONNECTOR.

YES

CHECK FOR 12 VOLTS AT RELAY CONNECTOR TERMINAL "D"

→ NO → REPAIR JUNCTION BLOCK POWER FEED OR REPLACE FUSIBLE LINK FROM RELAY CONNECTOR TERMINAL "D" TO JUNCTION BLOCK.

YES

CHECK FOR CONTINUITY BETWEEN FAN RELAY TERMINALS "B" AND "C"

→ NO → REPLACE RELAY

YES

GROUND TERMINAL "B" OF RELAY CONNECT 12 VOLTS TO RELAY TERMINAL "C" CHECK FOR CONTINUITY BETWEEN RELAY TERMINALS "A" AND "D"

→ NO → REPLACE RELAY

REPAIR WIRING

NO

YES

WITH COOLANT TEMPERATURE ABOVE "07" DEGREES C (225 DEGREES F), CHECK FOR A GOOD GROUND BETWEEN RELAY CONNECTOR TERMINAL "B" AND A GOOD VEHICLE GROUND

→ NO → CHECK FOR CONTINUITY IN THE WIRING BETWEEN TERMINAL "B" OF RELAY CONNECTOR AND COOLANT TEMPERATURE SENSOR CONNECTOR TERMINAL.

YES

CHECK FOR CONTINUITY BETWEEN RELAY CONNECTOR TERMINAL "A" AND COOLING FAN CONNECTOR TERMINAL "B"

→ NO → REPAIR WIRING

REPLACE COOLANT TEMPERATURE SENSOR

YES

CHECK FOR A GOOD GROUND BETWEEN COOLING FAN CONNECTOR TERMINAL "A" AND A GOOD VEHICLE GROUND

→ NO → REPAIR WIRING OR BAD GROUND CONNECTION.

YES

CONNECT TERMINAL "A" OF COOLING FAN TO A GOOD GROUND AND CONNECT 12 VOLTS TO FAN TERMINAL "B" DOES FAN RUN?

→ NO → REPLACE AUXILARY COOLING FAN MOTOR.

87983G10

Fig. 45 Auxiliary cooling fan diagnostic chart

87983P49

Disconnect the lower radiator hose from the water pump inlet

87983P50

Remove the water pump attaching bolts

Remove the water pump from the vehicle

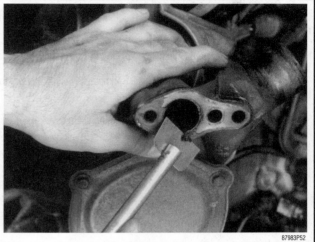

Using a scraper, clean the old gasket from both mating surfaces of the water pump

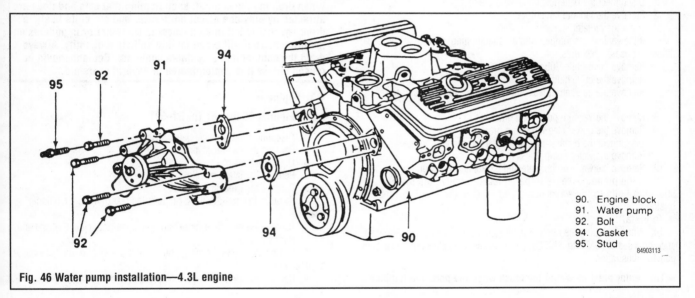

90. Engine block
91. Water pump
92. Bolt
94. Gasket
95. Stud

Fig. 46 Water pump installation—4.3L engine

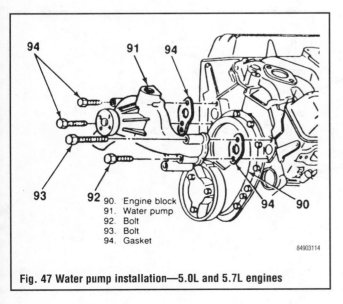

90. Engine block
91. Water pump
92. Bolt
93. Bolt
94. Gasket

Fig. 47 Water pump installation—5.0L and 5.7L engines

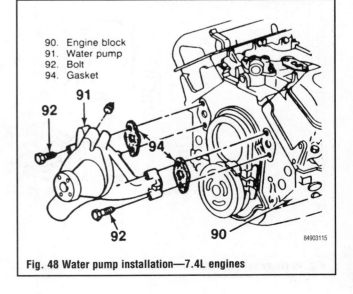

90. Engine block
91. Water pump
92. Bolt
94. Gasket

Fig. 48 Water pump installation—7.4L engines

5. Remove the fan, fan clutch and pulley.

6. Remove any accessory brackets that might interfere with water pump removal.

7. Disconnect the lower radiator hose from the water pump inlet and the heater hose from the nipple on the pump. On the 7.4L engine, remove the bypass hose.

8. Remove the bolts, then pull the water pump assembly away from the timing cover.

To install:

9. Clean all old gasket material from the timing chain cover.

10. Install the pump assembly with a new gasket. Tighten the bolts to 30 ft. lbs. (41 Nm).

11. Connect the hose between the water pump inlet and the nipple on the pump. Connect the heater hose and the bypass hose (7.4L only).

12. Install the fan, fan clutch and pulley.

13. Install and adjust the alternator and other accessories, if necessary.

14. Install the drive belt (s). Install the upper radiator shroud

15. Fill the cooling system. Connect the battery.

6.2L and 6.5L Diesel Engines

▶ **See Figure 49**

1. Disconnect the batteries, negative cable first.

2. Remove the fan and fan shroud.

3. Drain the radiator.

4. If the vehicle is equipped with air conditioning, remove the air conditioning hose bracket nuts.

5. Remove the oil filler tube.

6. Remove the drive belt(s).

7. Remove the generator pivot bolt and remove the generator lower bracket.

8. Remove the vacuum pump and bracket.

9. Remove the power steering pump bracket.

10. Disconnect the bypass hose and the lower radiator hose.

11. Remove the water pump bolts.

12. Remove the water pump plate and gasket and water pump.

13. If the pump gasket is to be replaced, remove the plate attaching bolts to the water pump and remove (and replace) the gasket.

To install:

14. When installing the pump, the flanges must be free of oil. Apply an anaerobic sealer (GM part #1052357 or equivalent) as shown in the accompanying illustration.

➡ **The sealer must be wet to the touch when the bolts are tightened.**

15. Attach the water pump and plate assembly. Tighten the bolts to 17 ft. lbs. (23 Nm), except the three lower right side bolts. Tighten these three to 31 ft. lbs. (42 Nm).

16. Connect the bypass hose and the lower radiator hose.

17. Install the power steering pump mounting bracket.

18. Install the alternator lower bracket.

19. Install the alternator pivot bolt.

20. Install the drive belt (s).

21. Install the oil filler tube.

22. If the vehicle is equipped with air conditioning, install the air conditioning hose bracket nuts.

23. Fill the radiator.

24. Install the fan and fan shroud.

25. Connect the batteries.

Cylinder Head

REMOVAL & INSTALLATION

✴✴ CAUTION

When draining the coolant, keep in mind that cats and dogs are attracted by ethylene glycol antifreeze, and are quite likely to drink any that is left in an uncovered container or in puddles on the ground. This will prove fatal in sufficient quantity. Always drain the coolant into a sealable container. Coolant should be reused unless it is contaminated or several years old.

4.3L Engine

▶ **See Figures 50 thru 57 (p. 51–52)**

1. Disconnect the negative battery cable.

2. Remove the engine cover.

3. Drain the coolant.

4. Remove the intake manifold.

5. Remove the exhaust manifold.

6. If applicable, remove the air pipe at the rear of the right cylinder head.

7. Remove the alternator mounting bolt at the right cylinder head and, if necessary, the alternator.

8. Remove the power steering pump and brackets from the left cylinder head, and lay them aside.

9. Remove the air conditioner compressor, and lay it aside. Remove the

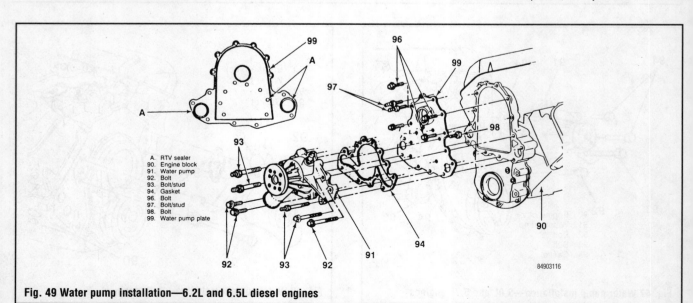

A. RTV sealer
90. Engine block
91. Water pump
92. Bolt
93. Bolt/stud
94. Gasket
96. Bolt
97. Bolt/stud
98. Bolt
99. Water pump plate

Fig. 49 Water pump installation—6.2L and 6.5L diesel engines

84903116

Fig. 50 Prepare the cylinder head by removing the rocker arm cover, intake manifold and exhaust manifold

Fig. 53 Once all the bolts are removed, break the gasket seal and lift the cylinder head from the block

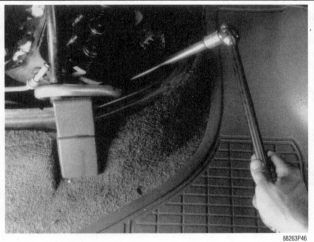

Fig. 51 Loosen the cylinder head bolts using the reverse order of the tightening sequence

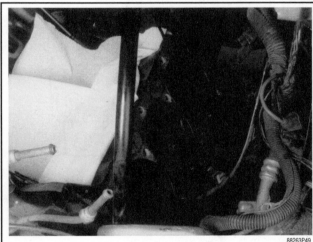

Fig. 54 Protect the lifter valley and piston bores using rags or a plastic cover . . .

Fig. 52 A breaker bar, socket and various length extensions are necessary to remove the bolts

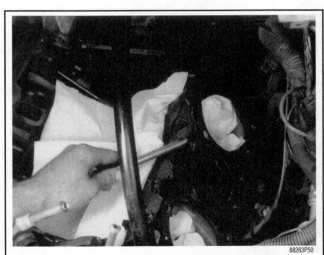

Fig. 55 . . . then carefully clean all the old gasket and debris from the gasket mating surfaces

Fig. 56 Upon installation, tighten the cylinder head bolts in the proper sequence

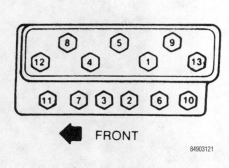

Fig. 57 Cylinder head bolt tightening sequence—1987–97 4.3L engines

spark plug wires at their brackets, the ground strap from the right side and the coolant sensor wire from the left head.

10. Remove the cylinder cover.
11. Remove the spark plugs.
12. Remove the pushrods.
13. Remove the cylinder head bolts in the reverse order of the tightening sequence.
14. Remove the cylinder head and gasket.

To install:

15. Clean all gasket mating surfaces, install a new gasket and reinstall the cylinder head. Install the cylinder heads using new gaskets. Make sure the gasket has the word **HEAD** up.

➡️**Coat a steel gasket on both sides with sealer. If a composition gasket is used, do not use sealer.**

16. Clean the cylinder head bolts, apply sealer to the threads, and install them hand-tight.
17. Tighten the head bolts a little at a time in the sequence shown. Tighten the bolts in three stages:
1987–95 models:
- First pass: 25 ft. lbs. (34 Nm)
- Second pass: 45 ft. lbs. (61 Nm)
- Final pass: 65 ft. lbs. (90 Nm)

On 1996–97 models install the bolts in sequence to 22 ft. lbs. (30 Nm). The bolts must then be tightened again in sequence in the following order:
- Short length bolt: (11, 7, 3, 2, 6, 10) 55 degrees
- Medium length bolt: (12, 13) 65 degrees
- Long length bolts: (1, 4, 8, 5, 9) 75 degrees
18. Install the pushrods.
19. If necessary, adjust the rocker arms.
20. Install the spark plugs.
21. Install the rocker arm cover.
22. Install the air conditioner compressor.
23. Install the power steering pump and brackets.
24. Install the alternator or the alternator mounting bolt at the cylinder head.
25. If removed, install the air pipe at the rear of the head.
26. Install the exhaust manifold.
27. Install the intake manifold.
28. Fill the engine with coolant.
29. Connect the negative battery cable.
30. Install the engine cover.

5.0L and 5.7L Engines

♦ **See Figures 58 thru 63**

1. Disconnect the negative battery cable and drain the coolant.
2. Remove the engine cover.
3. If applicable, remove the coolant recovery reservoir.
4. Remove the intake manifold.
5. Remove the exhaust manifolds and position them out of the way.
6. Remove the ground strap at the rear of the right AIR pipe, If equipped.
7. If the van is equipped with air conditioning, remove the air conditioning compressor and the forward mounting bracket and lay the compressor aside. Do not disconnect any of the refrigerant lines.
8. Remove the EGR inlet tube.
9. On the right side cylinder head, disconnect the fuel pipe and move it out of the way. Remove the spark plug wires and disconnect the wiring harness bracket.
10. Remove the nut and stud attaching the main accessory bracket to the cylinder head. You may have to loosen the remaining bolts and studs in order to remove the head.
11. Tag and disconnect the coolant sensor wire. Remove the spark plug wire bracket.
12. Remove the cylinder head covers. Remove the spark plugs.
13. Back off the rocker arm nuts and pivot the rocker arms out of the

Fig. 58 Using a breaker bar, remove the cylinder head bolts in the reverse order of the tightening sequence

Fig. 59 After removing all the cylinder head bolts, remove the cylinder head

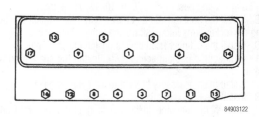

Fig. 62 Cylinder head bolt tightening sequence—1987–96 5.0L and 5.7L engines

Fig. 60 Remove and discard the old cylinder head gasket

Fig. 63 Using a torque wrench, tighten the cylinder head bolts in sequence

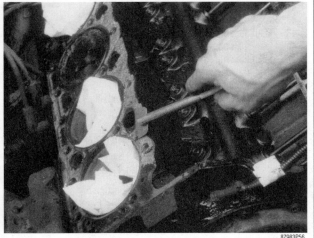

Fig. 61 Using a scraper, remove the old gasket residue from both mating surfaces

way so that the pushrods can be removed. Identify the pushrods so that they can be installed in their original positions.

14. Remove the cylinder head bolts in the reverse order of the tightening sequence and then remove the heads.

To install:

15. Inspect the cylinder head and block mating surfaces. Clean all old gasket material.

16. Install the cylinder heads using new gaskets. Install the gaskets with the word **HEAD** up.

➡Coat a steel gasket on both sides with sealer. If a composition gasket is used, do not use sealer.

17. Clean the bolts, apply sealer to the threads, and install them hand-tight.

18. Tighten the cylinder head bolts a little at a time, in the sequence shown. Tighten the bolts in three stages:

1987–95 models.
- First pass: 25 ft. lbs. (34 Nm)
- Second pass: 45 ft. lbs. (61 Nm)
- Final pass: 65 ft. lbs. (90 Nm)

On 1996– models install the bolts in sequence to 22 ft. lbs. (30 Nm). The bolts must then be tightened again in sequence in the following order:

- Short length bolt: (3, 4, 7, 8, 11, 12, 15, 16) 55 degrees
- Medium length bolt: (14, 17) 65 degrees
- Long length bolts: (1, 2, 5, 6, 9, 10, 13) 75 degrees

19. Install the pushrods so that they are in their original positions. Swing the rocker arms into position and tighten the bolts.
20. Install the cylinder head covers. Install the spark plugs.
21. Connect the coolant sensor wire. Install the spark plug wire bracket.
22. Install main accessory bracket to the cylinder head.
23. Install the EGR vent tube.
24. Connect the fuel pipe. Install the spark plug wires and Connect the wiring harness bracket.
25. Install the air conditioning compressor and the forward mounting bracket.
26. Connect the ground strap to the rear of the right AIR pipe.
27. Install the exhaust manifolds.
28. Install the intake manifold.
29. If removed, install the coolant recovery reservoir.
30. Connect the negative battery cable and fill the engine with coolant.
31. Install the engine cover.

6.2L and 6.5L Diesel Engines

▶ See Figure 64

RIGHT SIDE

1. Disconnect the negative battery cable. Drain the cooling system.
2. Remove the engine cover.
3. Remove the intake manifold.
4. Remove the fuel injection lines. Refer to Section 5 for this procedure.
5. Remove the cruise control transducer (if so equipped).
6. Remove the upper fan shroud.
7. Remove the air conditioning compressor belt.
8. Remove the exhaust manifold.
9. Disconnect and label the glow plug wiring. Use a proper removal tool. DO NOT pull on the harness wire!
10. Remove the oil dipstick tube.
11. Remove the oil fill tube upper bracket.
12. Remove the rocker arm cover(s), after removing any accessory brackets which interfere with cover removal.

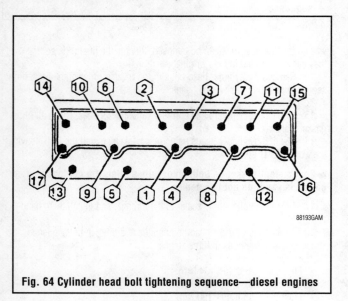

Fig. 64 Cylinder head bolt tightening sequence—diesel engines

88193GAM

✳✳ CAUTION

The EPA warns that prolonged contact with used engine oil may cause a number of skin disorders, including cancer! You should make every effort to minimize you exposure to used engine oil. Protective gloves should be worn when changing the oil. Wash your hands and any other exposed skin areas as soon as possible after exposure to used engine oil. Soap and water, or waterless hand cleaner should be used.

13. Remove the rocker arm assemblies. It is a good practice to number or mark the parts to avoid interchanging them.
14. Remove the pushrods. Keep them in order.
15. Remove the air cleaner resonator and bracket.
16. Remove the automatic transmission dipstick and tube.
17. Drain the cooling system.
18. Disconnect the heater hoses at the head.
19. Disconnect the upper radiator hose.
20. Disconnect the bypass hose.
21. Remove the alternator upper bracket.
22. Remove the coolant crossover pipe and thermostat.
23. Remove the head bolts.
24. Remove the cylinder head.

To install:

25. Clean the mating surfaces of the head and block thoroughly.
26. Install a new head gasket on the engine block. Do NOT coat the gaskets with any sealer on either engine. The gaskets have a special coating that eliminates the need for sealer. The use of sealer will interfere with this coating and cause leaks. Install the cylinder head onto the block.
27. Clean the head bolts thoroughly. The left rear head bolt must be installed into the head prior to head installation. Coat the threads and heads of the head bolts with sealing compound (GM part #1052080 or equivalent) before installation. Tighten the head bolts in three stages: 20 ft. lbs. (25 Nm); 50 ft. lbs. (68 Nm) and finally, ¼ turn more.
28. Install the coolant crossover pipe and thermostat.
29. Install the alternator upper bracket.
30. Connect the bypass hose.
31. Connect the upper radiator hose.
32. Connect the heater hoses at the head.
33. Install the automatic transmission dipstick and tube.
34. Install the air cleaner resonator and bracket.
35. Install the pushrods.
36. Install the rocker arm assemblies.
37. Adjust the valves.
38. Install the rocker arm cover(s).
39. Install the oil fill tube upper bracket.
40. Install the oil dipstick tube.
41. Connect the glow plug wiring.
42. Install the exhaust manifold.
43. Install the air conditioning compressor belt.
44. Install the upper fan shroud.
45. Install the cruise control transducer.
46. Install the fuel injection lines. See Section 5.
47. Install the intake manifold.
48. Fill the cooling system and connect the battery cable.

LEFT SIDE

1. Disconnect the negative battery cable and drain the cooling system.
2. Remove the engine cover.
3. If necessary, remove the coolant recovery reservoir.
4. Remove the intake manifold.
5. Remove the fuel injection lines. See Section 5.
6. Remove the cruise control transducer.
7. Remove the upper fan shroud.
8. Remove the air conditioning compressor belt.
9. Remove the exhaust manifold.

10. Remove the power steering pump lower adjusting bolts.
11. Disconnect and label the glow plug wiring.
12. Remove the air conditioning compressor and position it out of the way. DO NOT DISCONNECT ANY REFRIGERANT LINES!
13. Remove the power steering pump and position it out of the way. DO NOT DISCONNECT THE FLUID LINES!
14. Remove the oil dipstick tube.
15. Disconnect the transmission detent cable.
16. Remove the glow plug controller and bracket.
17. Remove the rocker arm cover(s), after removing any accessory brackets which interfere with cover removal.
18. Remove the rocker arm assemblies. It is a good practice to number or mark the parts to avoid interchanging them.
19. Remove the pushrods. Keep them in order.
20. Remove the air cleaner resonator and bracket.
21. Remove the automatic transmission dipstick and tube.
22. Remove the alternator upper bracket.
23. Remove the coolant crossover pipe and thermostat.
24. Remove the head bolts.
25. Remove the cylinder head.

To install:

26. Clean the mating surfaces of the head and block thoroughly.
27. Install a new head gasket on the engine block. Do NOT coat the gaskets with any sealer on either engine. The gaskets have a special coating that eliminates the need for sealer. The use of sealer will interfere with this coating and cause leaks. Install the cylinder head onto the block.
28. Clean the head bolts thoroughly. The left rear head bolt must be installed into the head prior to head installation. Coat the threads and heads of the head bolts with sealing compound (GM part #1052080 or equivalent) before installation. Tighten the head bolts in three stages: 20 ft. lbs. (25 Nm); 50 ft. lbs. (68 Nm) and finally, ¼ turn more.
29. Install the coolant crossover pipe and thermostat.
30. Install the alternator upper bracket.
31. Install the automatic transmission dipstick and tube.
32. Install the air cleaner resonator and bracket.
33. Install the pushrods.
34. Install the rocker arm assemblies.
35. Adjust the valves.
36. Install the rocker arm cover(s).
37. Install the oil fill tube upper bracket.
38. Install the oil dipstick tube.
39. Connect the glow plug wiring.
40. Install the compressor.
41. Install the power steering pump.
42. Install the glow plug controller.
43. Install the exhaust manifold.
44. Connect the detent cable.
45. Install the air conditioning compressor belt.
46. Install the upper fan shroud.
47. Install the cruise control transducer.
48. Install the fuel injection lines. See Section 5.
49. Install the intake manifold.
50. Install the coolant recovery reservoir, if removed.
51. Connect the battery cable and fill the cooling system.
52. Install the engine cover.

7.4L Engines

▶ **See Figure 65**

1. Disconnect the negative battery cable and drain the cooling system.
2. Remove the engine cover.
3. Remove the intake manifold.
4. Remove the exhaust manifolds.
5. Remove the alternator and bracket.
6. Remove the AIR pump, if equipped.

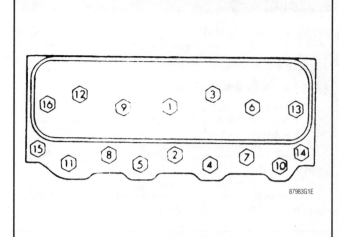

Fig. 65 Cylinder head bolt tightening sequence—1987–96 7.4L engines

7. If the vehicle is equipped with air conditioning, remove the air conditioning compressor and the forward mounting bracket and lay the compressor aside. Do not disconnect any of the refrigerant lines.
8. Remove the rocker arm cover.
9. Remove the spark plugs.
10. Remove the AIR pipes at the rear of the head, if equipped.
11. Disconnect the ground strap at the rear of the head.
12. Disconnect the temperature sensor wire.
13. Back off the rocker arm nuts and pivot the rocker arms out of the way so that the pushrods can be removed. Identify the pushrods so that they can be installed in their original positions.
14. Remove the cylinder head bolts and remove the heads.

To install:

➡ **The cylinder head should be cleaned and inspected for warpage or damage before installation. Refer to the cleaning and inspection procedures in the engine reconditioning portion of this section.**

15. Thoroughly clean the mating surfaces of the head and block. Clean the bolt holes thoroughly.
16. Install the cylinder heads using new gaskets. Install the gaskets with the word **HEAD** up.

➡ **Coat a steel gasket on both sides with sealer. If a composition gasket is used, do not use sealer.**

17. Clean the bolts, apply sealer to the threads, and install them hand-tight.
18. Tighten the head bolts a little at a time in the sequence shown. On 1987–95 models, tighten the bolts in three stages: 30 ft. lbs. (40 Nm), 60 ft. lbs. (80 Nm) and finally to 81 ft. lbs. (110 Nm). On 1996–97 models tighten the bolts in three stages: 30 ft. lbs. (40 Nm), 60 ft. lbs. (80 Nm) and finally to 85 ft. lbs. (115 Nm).
19. Install the intake and exhaust manifolds.
20. Install the pushrods.
21. Install the rocker arms and adjust them as described in this section.
22. Connect the temperature sensor wire.
23. Connect the ground strap at the rear of the head.
24. Install the AIR pipes at the rear of the head.
25. Install the spark plugs.
26. Install the rocker arm cover.
27. Install the air conditioning compressor and the forward mounting bracket.
28. Install the AIR pump.
29. Install the alternator.
30. Connect the battery cable and refill the cooling system.
31. Install the engine cover.

Oil Pan

REMOVAL & INSTALLATION

4.3L Engines

▶ See Figures 66 thru 71

A one-piece oil pan gasket is used.

1. Disconnect the negative battery cable. Raise the vehicle, support it safely, and drain the engine oil.
2. Remove the exhaust crossover pipe, if necessary.
3. Remove the oil cooler lines from the oil pan and from the adapter, if equipped.
4. Remove the oil filter and oil filter adapter, if equipped.
5. Remove the transmission oil cooler line bracket from the oil pan, if equipped (on models with automatic transmission only).

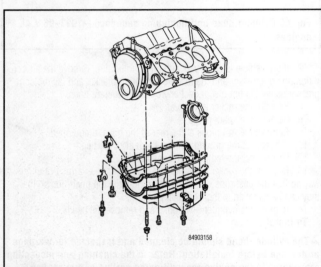

Fig. 66 Exploded view of the oil pan—4.3L engines

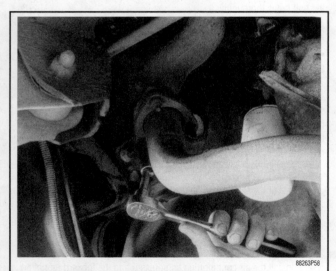

Fig. 67 Loosen the exhaust pipe bolts for clearance

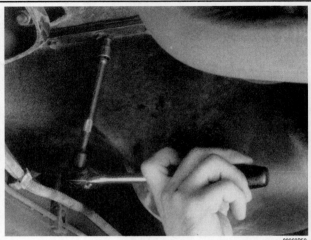

Fig. 68 Loosen and remove the oil pan retaining bolts (a variety of sockets and extensions will be helpful)

6. Remove the torque converter cover (on models with automatic transmission).
7. Remove the strut rods at the flywheel cover.
8. Remove the strut rod brackets at the front engine mountings, if necessary.
9. Remove the starter and starter opening shield, If equipped.
10. Remove the oil pan bolts, nuts and reinforcements.
11. Remove the oil pan and gaskets.

✳✳ CAUTION

The EPA warns that prolonged contact with used engine oil may cause a number of skin disorders, including cancer! You should make every effort to minimize you exposure to used engine oil. Protective gloves should be worn when changing the oil. Wash your hands and any other exposed skin areas as soon as possible after exposure to used engine oil. Soap and water, or waterless hand cleaner should be used.

To install:
12. Thoroughly clean all gasket surfaces and install a new gasket, using only a small amount of sealer at the front and rear corners of the oil pan.
13. Install the oil pan and new gaskets.
14. Install the oil pan bolts, nuts and reinforcements. On 1987–95 models, tighten the pan bolts to 100 inch lbs. (11 Nm) and tighten the nuts at the corners to 17 ft. lbs. (23 Nm). On 1996–97 models, tighten the bolts to 18 ft. lbs. (25 Nm) and then tighten the nuts to 18 ft. lbs. (25 Nm).
15. Install the transmission oil cooler line bracket (on models with automatic transmission).
16. Install oil filter adapter, oil cooler and the oil filter.
17. Install the starter and opening shield.
18. Install the strut rod brackets at the front engine mountings, if removed.
19. Install the strut rods at the flywheel cover, if removed.
20. Install the torque converter cover (on models with automatic transmission), if removed.
21. Install the exhaust crossover pipe, if removed.
22. Connect the negative battery cable.
23. Fill the crankcase with the correct grade and amount of engine oil.

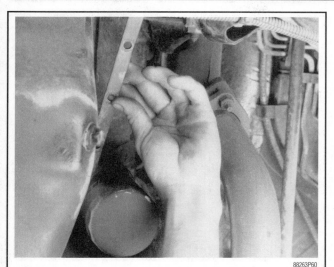

Fig. 69 If equipped, remove the oil pan reinforcements . . .

Fig. 70 . . . then lower the pan from the vehicle

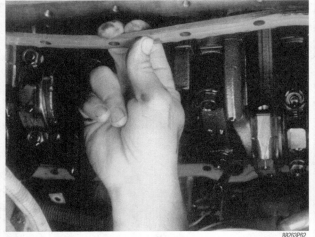

Fig. 71 Remove the old gasket material and use a scraper to clean the mating surfaces

5.0L and 5.7L Engines

♦ See Figures 72 thru 80 (p. 57–59)

1. Disconnect the negative battery cable. Drain the cooling system. Drain the engine oil.
2. If necessary, remove the engine oil dipstick.
3. Remove the oil cooler lines from the adapter.
4. If equipped, remove the exhaust crossover pipe.
5. If equipped with automatic transmission, remove the converter housing cover and the transmission oil cooler line retainer from the bracket.
6. Remove the starter brace and bolt and swing the starter aside.
7. Remove the oil pan and discard the gaskets.
8. Installation is the reverse of removal. Clean all gasket surfaces and use new gaskets to assemble. Use gasket sealer to retain side gaskets to the cylinder block. Install a new oil pan rear seal in the rear main bearing cap slot with the ends butting the side gaskets. Install a new front seal in the crankcase front cover with the ends butting the side gaskets. On 1987–95 models, tighten the pan bolts to 100 inch lbs. (11 Nm) and tighten the nuts at the corners to 17 ft. lbs. (23 Nm). On 1996–97 models tighten the bolts to 18 ft. lbs. (25 Nm). Fill the engine with oil and check for leaks.

Fig. 72 Remove the bolts from the oil filter adapter

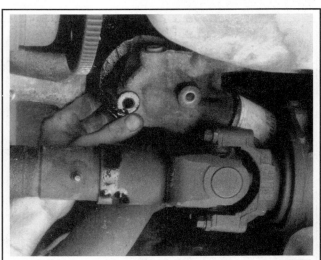

Fig. 73 Remove the oil filter adapter

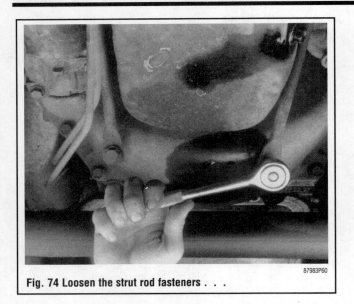

Fig. 74 Loosen the strut rod fasteners . . .

Fig. 75 . . . then remove the strut rods

Fig. 76 Remove the torque converter cover

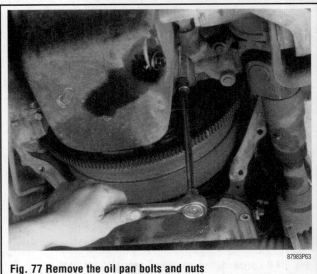

Fig. 77 Remove the oil pan bolts and nuts

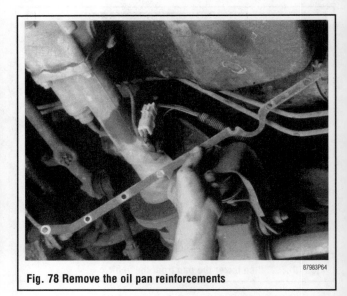

Fig. 78 Remove the oil pan reinforcements

Fig. 79 Remove the oil pan from the vehicle

Fig. 80 Remove the old gasket from both mating surfaces

7.4L Engines

1987–94 MODELS

▶ **See Figure 81**

1. Disconnect the battery.
2. If equipped, remove the oil pressure gauge tube.
3. Remove the distributor cap.
4. Raise and support the front end on jackstands.
5. Drain the engine oil.
6. Remove the flywheel strut rods and cover.
7. Remove the oil cooler lines from the filter housing.
8. Remove the starter assembly.
9. Support the engine with a floor jack.

> ※ **WARNING**
>
> **Do not place the jack under the pan, sheet metal or pulley!**

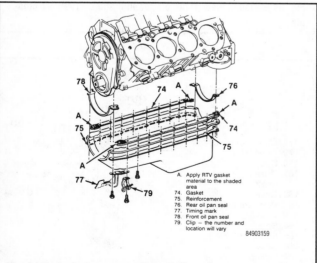

A. Apply RTV gasket material to the shaded area
74. Gasket
75. Reinforcement
76. Rear oil pan seal
77. Timing mark
78. Front oil pan seal
79. Clip — the number and location will vary

Fig. 81 Typical oil pan mounting—7.4L engines

10. Remove the engine mount through-bolts.
11. Raise the engine just enough to remove the pan.
12. Remove the oil pan and discard the gaskets.

To install:

13. Clean all mating surfaces thoroughly.
14. Apply RTV gasket material to the front and rear corners of the gaskets.
15. Coat the gaskets with adhesive sealer and position them on the block.
16. Install the oil pan.
17. Install the pan bolts, clips and reinforcements. Tighten the pan-to-cover bolts to 70 inch lbs. (8 Nm); the pan-to-block bolts to 13 ft. lbs. (18 Nm).
18. Lower the engine onto the mounts.
19. Install the engine mount through-bolts.
20. Connect the oil cooler lines.
21. Install the starter assembly.
22. Install the flywheel cover and strut rods.
23. Install the oil pressure gauge tube.
24. Connect the battery.
25. Fill the crankcase with the correct grade and amount of engine oil.

1995–97 MODELS

1. Disconnect the negative battery cable and remove the oil level indicator and tube.
2. Raise the vehicle, support it safely with jackstands and drain the oil.
3. If necessary, remove the oil dipstick tube.
4. Remove the flywheel/torque converter cover.
5. Remove the exhaust crossover pipe.
6. Remove the oil filter and adapter, if equipped.
7. Remove the oil cooler line retainer from the bracket, if equipped.
8. Remove the transmission oil cooler line retainer from the bracket, if equipped.
9. Remove the starter assembly, if necessary.
10. Remove the oil pan bolts, nuts and strut rods, if equipped.
11. Remove the oil pan and gasket.

To install:

12. Thoroughly clean all gasket surfaces and install a new gasket, using only a small amount of sealer at the front and rear corners of the oil pan.
13. Install the oil pan and new gaskets.
14. Install the oil pan bolts, nuts and strut rods. On 1995 model tighten the bolts to 100 inch lbs. (11 Nm) and the nuts to 16 ft. lbs. (22 Nm). On 1996–97 models, tighten the pan bolts and nuts to 18 ft. lbs. (25 Nm).
15. Install the transmission oil cooler line bracket (on models with automatic transmission).
16. Install oil filter adapter, oil cooler and the oil filter.
17. If removed, install the starter assembly.
18. Install the strut rod brackets at the front engine mountings, if removed.
19. Install the strut rods at the flywheel cover, if removed.
20. Install the torque converter cover (on models with automatic transmission), if removed.
21. Install the exhaust crossover pipe, if removed.
22. Install the oil dipstick tube.
23. Connect the negative battery cable.
24. Fill the crankcase with the correct grade and amount of engine oil.

6.2L and 6.5L Diesel Engines

▶ **See Figure 82**

1. Remove the engine cover.
2. Disconnect the batteries and remove the engine oil dipstick.
3. Remove the dipstick tube.
4. Raise and support the van. Drain the oil.
5. Remove the flywheel cover.
6. Remove the oil cooler lines at the filter base and the transmission cooler lines

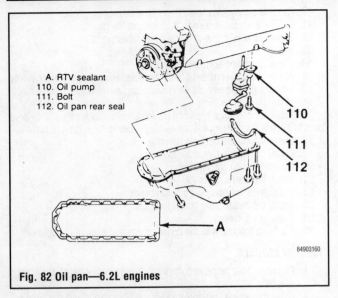

A. RTV sealant
110. Oil pump
111. Bolt
112. Oil pan rear seal

Fig. 82 Oil pan—6.2L engines

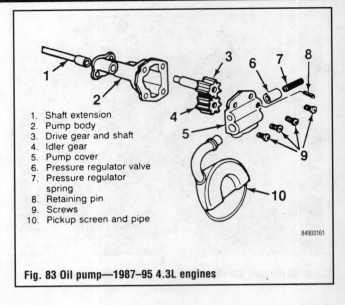

1. Shaft extension
2. Pump body
3. Drive gear and shaft
4. Idler gear
5. Pump cover
6. Pressure regulator valve
7. Pressure regulator spring
8. Retaining pin
9. Screws
10. Pickup screen and pipe

Fig. 83 Oil pump—1987–95 4.3L engines

7. If equipped, remove the cable clamps and cable from the oil pan.

8. On 1987–94 6.2L models, remove the transmission and flywheel.

9. Remove the oil pan.

To install:

10. Using new gaskets coated with sealer, position the oil pan on the block and install the bolts. Tighten the bolts to 89 inch lbs. (10 Nm), except for the two rear bolts. Tighten them to 17 ft. lbs. (23 Nm).

11. On 1987–94 6.2L models, install the transmission and flywheel.

12. Install the oil cooler lines at the filter base and connect the transmission cooler lines.

13. Install the flywheel cover.

14. Lower the vehicle.

15. Connect the batteries.

16. Install the engine oil dipstick tube and dipstick.

17. Change the oil and filter.

Oil Pump

REMOVAL & INSTALLATION

4.3L, 5.0L, 5.7L and 7.4L Engines

▶ **See Figures 83, 84, 85 and 86**

1. Remove the oil pan.

2. Remove the bolt attaching the pump to the rear main bearing cap. Remove the pump and the extension shaft, which will come out behind it.

To install:

3. If the pump has been disassembled, is being replaced, or for any reason oil has been removed from it, it must be primed. It can either be filled with oil before installing the cover plate (and oil kept within the pump during handling), or the entire pump cavity can be filled with petroleum jelly.

➡**If the pump is not primed, the engine could be damaged before it receives adequate lubrication when you start it.**

4. Engage the extension shaft with the oil pump shaft. Align the slot on the top of the extension shaft with the drive tang on the lower end of the distributor driveshaft, and then position the pump at the rear main bearing cap so the mounting bolt can be installed. The installed position of the oil pump screen is with the bottom edge parallel to the oil pan rails. Install the bolt, tightening to 65 ft. lbs. (90 Nm).

5. Install the oil pan.

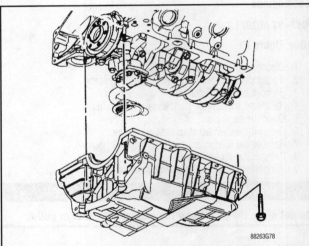

Fig. 84 Exploded view of the oil pan mounting—1996–97 models

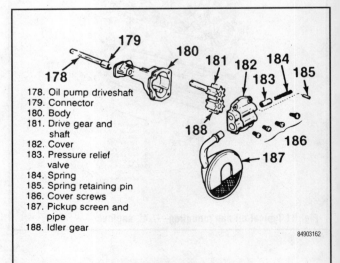

178. Oil pump driveshaft
179. Connector
180. Body
181. Drive gear and shaft
182. Cover
183. Pressure relief valve
184. Spring
185. Spring retaining pin
186. Cover screws
187. Pickup screen and pipe
188. Idler gear

Fig. 85 Oil pump—5.0L and 5.7L engines

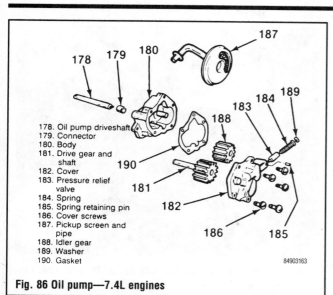

178. Oil pump driveshaft
179. Connector
180. Body
181. Drive gear and shaft
182. Cover
183. Pressure relief valve
184. Spring
185. Spring retaining pin
186. Cover screws
187. Pickup screen and pipe
188. Idler gear
189. Washer
190. Gasket

84903163

Fig. 86 Oil pump—7.4L engines

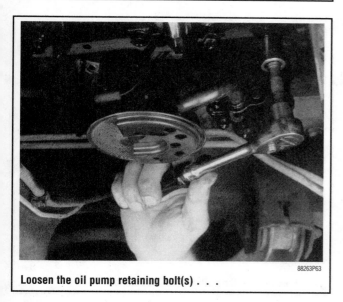

Loosen the oil pump retaining bolt(s) . . .

88263P63

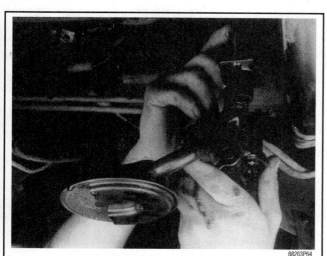

. . . then remove the oil pump and extension shaft from the engine

88263P64

6.2L and 6.5L Diesel Engines

1987–95 MODELS

♦ **See Figure 87**

1. Drain the oil.
2. Lower the oil pan enough to gain access to the pump.
3. Rotate the crankshaft so that the forward crankshaft throw and No. 1 and No. 2 connecting rod journals are up.
4. Remove the bolt retaining the pump to the main bearing cap. Let the pump and extension shaft fall into the pan.
5. Remove the pan from the vehicle.

To install:

6. Maneuver the pan, pump and extension shaft into position.
7. Position the pump on the bearing cap.
8. Align the extension shaft hex with the drive hex on the oil pump drive or vacuum pump. The pump should push easily into place. Install the pump and tighten the bolt to 65 ft. lbs. (90 Nm).
9. Install the pan and fill the engine with oil.

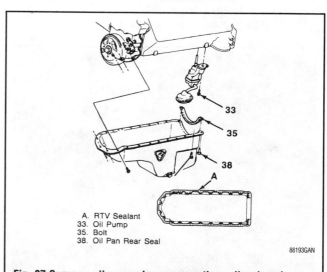

A. RTV Sealant
33. Oil Pump
35. Bolt
38. Oil Pan Rear Seal

86193GAN

Fig. 87 Common oil pan and pump mounting—diesel engines

1996–97 MODELS

1. Remove the oil pump.
2. Remove the bolt attaching the pump to the rear main bearing cap. Remove the pump and the hex drift.

To install:

3. If the pump has been disassembled, is being replaced, or for any reason oil has been removed from it, it must be primed. It can either be filled with oil before installing the cover plate (and oil kept within the pump during handling), or the entire pump cavity can be filled with petroleum jelly.

➡**If the pump is not primed, the engine could be damaged before it receives adequate lubrication when you start it.**

4. Install the oil pump and extension shaft.
5. Align the extension shaft hex with the drive hex and push the pump into place.
6. Install the bolt, tightening to 65 ft. lbs. (90 Nm).
7. Install the oil pan.

INSPECTION

1. Inspect the pump body for wear, cracks or other damage.
2. Inspect the inside of the pump cover for cracks or wear that might allow oil to leak past the gear ends.

3. Inspect the gears for wear.

4. Inspect the drive gear and shaft for improper fit in the pump body.

5. Inspect the pick-up screen and pipe for damage and/or loose fit.

6. Check that the pressure regulator valve slides freely in its bore without sticking or binding.

7. Oil pump gears, cover and body are serviced as a unit. If any single part is damaged, replace the entire assembly.

Crankshaft Damper

REMOVAL & INSTALLATION

➡**A torsional damper puller tool is required to perform this procedure.**

1. Disconnect the negative battery cable.
2. Remove the fan shroud assembly.
3. Remove the cooling fan belts, fan and pulley.
4. If necessary, remove the radiator.
5. Remove the accessory drive pulley (crankshaft pulley on diesel engines).
6. Remove the torsional damper bolt.
7. Remove the torsional damper using a suitable puller.

Loosen and remove the retaining bolts around the perimeter of the pulley face . . .

On some models you will have to remove the damper hub-to-crankshaft bolt before the pulley

. . . then remove the pulley from the damper

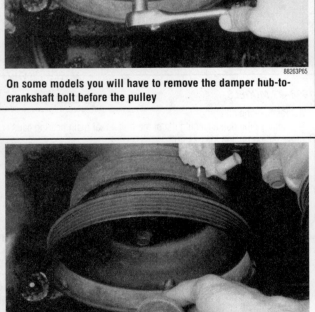

The hub bolt on this engine has a large flat washer which spreads the clamp load on the pulley

Use a suitable (non-jawed) puller to loosen the damper on the crankshaft

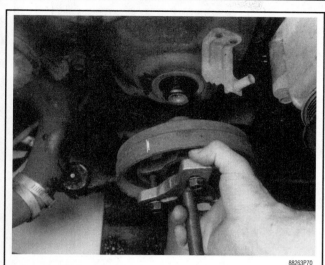

Once loosened, the damper is easily removed

88263P70

If necessary, drive a new oil seal into place before reinstalling the damper

88263P71

➡Make sure you do not lose the crankshaft key, if it has been removed.

To install:

    8. Coat the crankshaft stub with engine oil.

    9. Position the crankshaft key if one was used. If you pulled the crank seal, replace it with the open end facing in.

➡The inertial weight section of the damper is attached to the hub with a rubber-like material. The correct installation procedures, with the proper tools, MUST be followed or the resultant movement of the inertial weight will destroy the tuning of the damper!

    10. Thread the stud on the tool into the end of the crankshaft.

    11. Position the damper on the shaft and tap it into place with a plastic mallet (lightly!). Make sure the key is in place by securing it with a little RTV sealant.

    12. Install the bearing, washer and nut and then turn the nut until the damper is pulled into position. Remove the tool.

    13. Make sure the damper is all the way on, then install the bolt. Tighten the bolt as follows:

- 1987–95 models: 4.3L, 5.0L & 5.7L engines: 70 ft. lbs. (95 Nm)
- 1996–97 models: 4.3L, 5.0L & 5.7L engines: 74 ft. lbs. (100 Nm)
- 6.2L & 6.5L engine: 200 ft. lbs. (270 Nm)

- 1987–95 models: 7.4L engine: 85 ft. lbs. (115 Nm)
- 1996–97 models: 7.4L engine: 110 ft. lbs. (149 Nm)
14. Install the remaining components and road test the van.

Timing Chain Cover and Seal

REMOVAL & INSTALLATION

4.3L, 5.0L and 5.7L Engines

▶ See Figures 88, 89, 90, 91 and 92 (p. 64–65)

    1. Drain the cooling system.

    2. Drain the oil and remove the oil pan.

    3. Remove the crankshaft pulley and damper.

    4. Remove the water pump.

    5. If equipped, remove the crankshaft position sensor.

    6. Remove the bolts holding the timing case cover to the block and remove the cover and gaskets.

    7. Use a suitable tool to pry the old seal out of the front face of the cover.

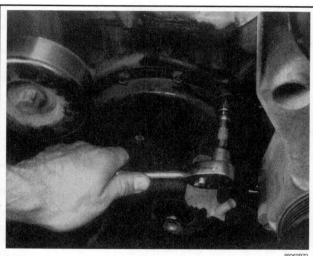

Loosen and remove the timing cover retaining bolts . . .

88263P72

. . . then carefully break the gasket seal . . .

88263P73

. . . remove the cover from the engine compartment

88263P74

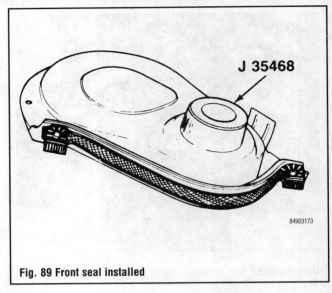

J 35468

84903170

Fig. 89 Front seal installed

Using a seal puller, remove the old seal from the front cover

87983P73

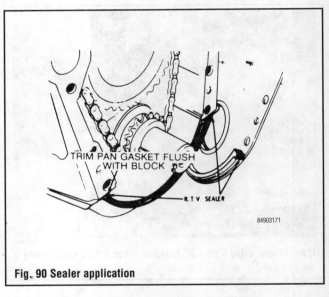

TRIM PAN GASKET FLUSH WITH BLOCK

R.T.V. SEALER

84903171

Fig. 90 Sealer application

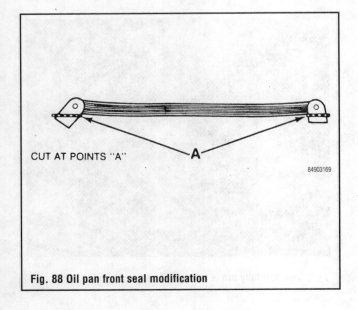

CUT AT POINTS "A"

A

84903169

Fig. 88 Oil pan front seal modification

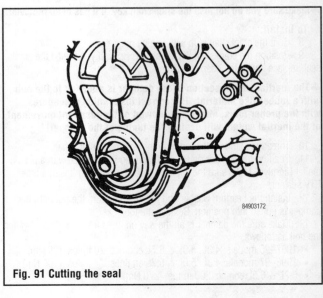

84903172

Fig. 91 Cutting the seal

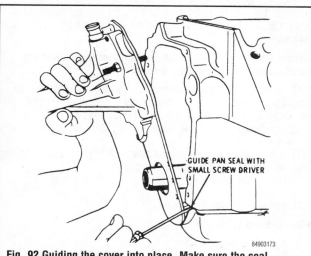

Fig. 92 Guiding the cover into place. Make sure the seal remains undisturbed

To install:

8. Install the new seal so that the open end is toward the inside of the cover.

➡**Coat the lip of the new seal with oil prior to installation.**

9. Check that the timing chain oil slinger is in place against the crankshaft sprocket.

10. Apply sealer to the front cover as shown in the accompanying illustration. Install the cover carefully onto the locating dowels.

11. On 1987–95 models, tighten the attaching screws to 124 inch lbs. (14 Nm) on the 4.3L and 100 inch lbs. (11 Nm) on the 5.0L and 5.7L.

12. On 1996–97 models, tighten the attaching screws to 106 inch lbs. (12 Nm) on the 4.3L, 5.0L and 5.7L models.

13. Install the remaining components and fill the engine with oil and coolant. Road test the van.

7.4L Engines

➡**Special tool J-22102, or its equivalent seal driver, will be necessary for this job.**

1. Disconnect the negative battery cable.
2. Drain the cooling system.
3. Remove the water pump.
4. Remove the crankshaft pulley and damper.
5. If equipped, remove the crankshaft position sensor.
6. Remove the oil pan.
7. Remove the front cover bolts.
8. Pull off the cover and gaskets.
9. Use a suitable tool to pry the old seal out of the front face of the cover.

To install:

10. Using seal driver J-22102, or equivalent, install the new seal so that the open end is toward the inside of the cover.

➡**Coat the lip of the new seal with oil prior to installation.**

11. Install a new front pan seal, cutting the tabs off.

12. Coat a new cover gasket with adhesive sealer and position it on the block.

13. Apply a 1/8 in. (bead of RTV gasket material to the front cover. Install the cover carefully onto the locating dowel.

14. On 1987–95 models, tighten the retaining bolts to 100 inch lbs. (11 Nm).

15. On 1996–97 models, tighten the retaining bolts to 89 inch lbs. (10 Nm).

16. Install the oil pan.
17. If removed, install the crankshaft position sensor.
18. Install the damper.
19. Install the water pump.
20. Fill the crankcase with the proper amount and grade of engine oil.
21. Connect the battery cables and fill the cooling system.

6.2L and 6.5L Diesel Engines

➡ **See Figure 93**

1. Drain the cooling system.
2. Remove the water pump.
3. Rotate the crankshaft to align the marks on the injection pump driven gear and the camshaft gear as shown in the illustration.
4. Scribe a mark aligning the injection pump flange and the front cover.
5. Remove the crankshaft pulley and torsional damper.
6. If equipped, remove the crankshaft position sensor.
7. Remove the front cover-to-oil pan bolts (4).
8. Remove the two fuel return line clips.
9. Remove the injection pump retaining nuts from the front cover.
10. Remove the baffle. Remove the remaining cover bolts, and remove the front cover.
11. If the front cover oil seal is to be replaced, it can now be pried out of the cover with a suitable prying tool. Press the new seal into the cover evenly.

➡**The oil seal can also be replaced with the front cover installed. Remove the torsional damper first, then pry the old seal out of the cover using a suitable prying tool. Use care not to damage the surface of the crankshaft. Install the new seal evenly into the cover and install the damper.**

To install:

12. To install the front cover, first clean both sealing surfaces until all traces of old sealer are gone. Apply a 3/32 in. (2mm) bead of sealant (GM sealant #1052357 or equivalent) to the sealing surface as shown in the illustration. Apply a bead of RTV type sealer to the bottom portion of the front cover which attached to the oil pan. Install the front cover.

13. Install the baffle.

14. Install the injection pump, making sure the scribe marks on the pump and front cover are aligned.

15. Install the injection pump driven gear, making sure the marks on the cam gear and pump are aligned. Be sure the dowel pin and the three holes on the pump flange are also aligned.

16. Install the fuel line clips, the front cover-to-oil bolts, and the tor-

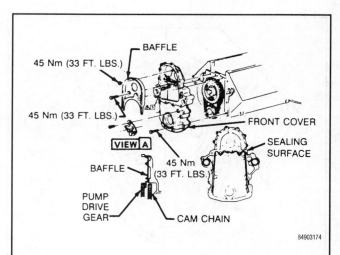

Fig. 93 Front cover installation showing sealer application—diesel engines

sional damper and crankshaft pulley. Tighten the cover-to-block bolts to 33 ft. lbs. (45 Nm) on 1987–95 models and 30 ft. lbs. (40 Nm).

17. If equipped, tighten the baffle bolts and nut to 33 ft. lbs. (45 Nm), the injection pump nuts to 31 ft. lbs. (42 Nm) and the injection pump bolts to 17 ft. lbs. (23 Nm).

Timing Chain

REMOVAL & INSTALLATION

4.3L, 5.0L, 5.7L and 7.4L Engines

▶ **See Figure 94**

1. On some models it may be necessary to remove the grille assembly. Refer to Section 10 for this procedure.

2. If necessary, remove the air cleaner assembly and the coolant recovery reservoir.

3. Remove the radiator, water pump, the torsional damper and the crankcase front cover. This will allow access to the timing chain.

4. Crank the engine until the timing marks on both sprockets are nearest each other and in line between the shaft centers.

5. On 1996–97 vehicles remove the crankshaft position sensor reluctor ring. On 7.4L engines tool J-41371 or its equivalent puller must be used to remove the reluctor ring.

6. Take out the bolts that hold the camshaft gear to the camshaft. This gear is a light press fit on the camshaft and will come off easily. It is located by a dowel. The chain comes off with the camshaft gear.

➡ **A gear puller will be required to remove the crankshaft gear.**

To install:

7. Without disturbing the position of the engine, mount the new crankshaft gear on the shaft, and mount the chain over the camshaft gear. Arrange the camshaft gear in such a way that the timing marks will line up between the shaft centers and the camshaft locating dowel will enter the dowel hole in the cam sprocket.

8. Place the cam sprocket, with its chain mounted over it, in position on the front of the van and pull up with the three bolts that hold it to the camshaft.

9. After the gears are in place, turn the engine two full revolutions to make certain that the timing marks are in correct alignment between the shaft centers.

10. On 1987–95 models 4.3L 5.0L and 5.7L models, tighten the camshaft sprocket bolts (and nut on the 4.3L), to 21 ft. lbs. (28 Nm). On the 7.4L, tighten them to 20 ft. lbs. (26 Nm).

11. On 1996–97 models, tighten the camshaft sprocket bolts (and nut on the 4.3L) to 18 ft. lbs. (25 Nm). On the 7.4L, tighten them to 25 ft. lbs. (34 Nm).

➡ **When installing the crankshaft position sensor you must use install a new oil ring seal onto the sensor.**

12. Install the crankshaft position sensor reluctor ring onto the crankshaft until it is firmly seated against the crankshaft sprocket. On 1996–97 7.4L vehicles replace the reluctor ring with a new component.

13. If removed, install the air cleaner assembly and the coolant recovery reservoir.

14. Install the front cover, torsional damper, water pump and the radiator.

15. If removed, install the grille assembly.

End-play of the camshaft is zero.

6.2L and 6.5L Diesel Engines

▶ **See Figures 95 and 96**

1. Remove the front cover.

2. Remove the bolt and washer attaching the camshaft gear and the injection pump gear. Crank the engine until the timing marks on both sprockets are nearest each other and in line between the shaft centers.

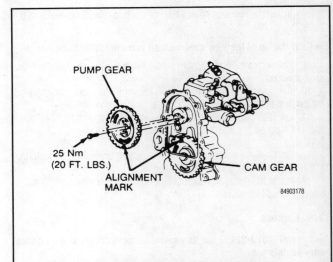

Fig. 95 Timing mark alignment—6.2L and 6.5L engines

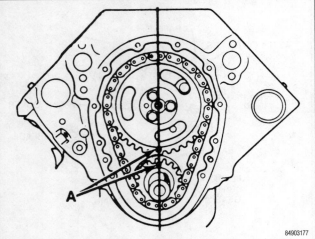

Fig. 94 Timing mark alignment—4.3L, 5.0L, 5.7L and 7.4L engines

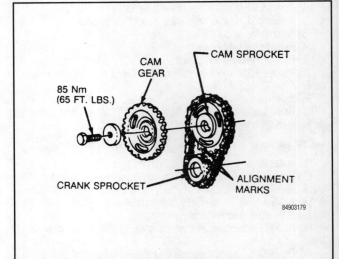

Fig. 96 Timing chain installation—6.2L and 6.5L engines

3. Remove the camshaft sprocket, timing chain and crankshaft sprocket as a unit.

To install:

4. Install the camshaft sprocket, timing chain and crankshaft sprocket as a unit, aligning the timing marks on the sprockets as shown in the illustration. On 1987–95 models, tighten the camshaft gear bolt to 75 ft. lbs. (100 Nm). On 1996–97 models, tighten the camshaft gear bolt to 125 ft. lbs. (171 Nm).

5. Rotate the crankshaft 360° so that the camshaft gear and the injection pump gear are aligned as shown in the illustration (accompanying the diesel Front Cover Removal Procedure). On 1987–95 models, tighten the bolt to 17 ft. lbs. (23 Nm). On 1996–97 models, tighten the camshaft gear bolt to 20 ft. lbs. (25 Nm).

6. Install the front cover as previously detailed. The injection pump must be re-timed since the timing chain assembly was removed. See Section 5 for this procedure.

Camshaft, Bearing and Lifters

REMOVAL & INSTALLATION

4.3L, 5.0L and 5.7L Engines

▶ See Figures 97, 98, 99, 100 and 101

✳✳ CAUTION

Please refer to Section 1 before discharging the compressor or disconnecting air conditioning lines. Damage to the air conditioning system or personal injury could result. Consult your local laws concerning refrigerant discharge and recycling. In many areas it may be illegal for anyone but a certified technician to service the A/C system. Always use an approved recovery station when discharging the air conditioning.

1. Disconnect the negative battery cable.
2. On some models it may be necessary to remove the grille and hood assemblies.
3. Remove the air cleaner assembly and if equipped, remove the coolant recovery reservoir.

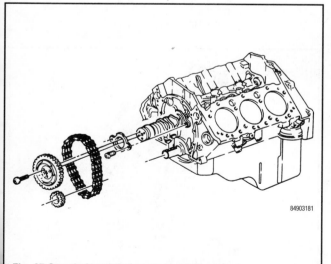

Fig. 97 Camshaft and timing chain—4.3L engine

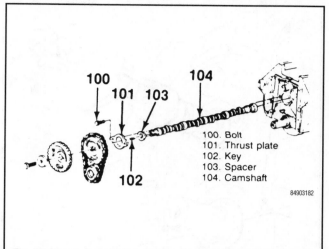

100. Bolt
101. Thrust plate
102. Key
103. Spacer
104. Camshaft

Fig. 98 Camshaft and related parts—5.0L, 5.7L, 6.2L, 6.5L and 7.4L engines

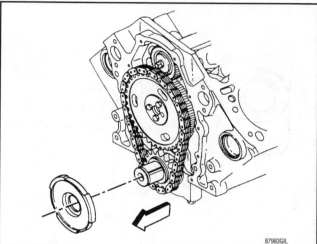

Fig. 99 Crankshaft position sensor reluctor ring location—4.3L, 5.0L and 5.7L engines

✳✳ CAUTION

Please refer to Section 1 before discharging the compressor or disconnecting air conditioning lines. Damage to the air conditioning system or personal injury could result. Consult your local laws concerning refrigerant discharge and recycling. In many areas it may be illegal for anyone but a certified technician to service the A/C system. Always use an approved recovery station when discharging the air conditioning.

4. Have the system discharged by a qualified technician using approved equipment.
5. Drain the cooling system then remove the radiator.
6. Remove the air conditioning condenser.
7. Tag and disengage any vacuum lines and electrical connections which will hinder the removal of the camshaft.
8. Mark the distributor as to location in the block. Remove the distributor and spark plugs.

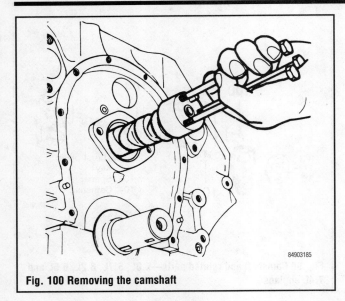

Fig. 100 Removing the camshaft

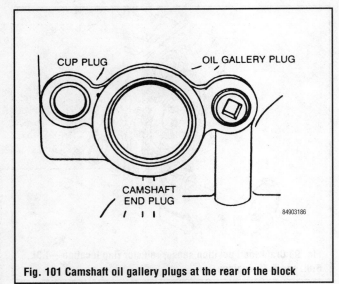

Fig. 101 Camshaft oil gallery plugs at the rear of the block

9. Remove the valve covers.
10. Remove the drive belt(s).
11. If necessary remove the alternator and its retaining brackets.
12. Remove the water pump.
13. Remove the engine oil dipstick tube.
14. Remove the valve lifters and pushrods.
15. Remove the crankshaft pulley and damper.
16. Remove the front cover, timing chain and sprockets.
17. Install two 5⁄16 in.–18 bolts in the holes in the front of the camshaft and carefully pull the camshaft from the block.

To install:

18. Liberally coat camshaft and bearing with heavy engine oil or engine assembly lubricant and insert the cam into the engine.
19. Install the timing chain.
20. Install the reluctor ring, lifters and pushrods.
21. Install the intake manifold.
22. Install the distributor using the locating marks made during removal. (If any problems are encountered, refer to distributor removal and installation)
23. Install the damper and water pump.
24. Install the valve covers and the cooling fan.
25. Engage all vacuum and electrical connections.

26. Install the radiator and condenser.
27. Fill the cooling system with the right amount and grade of oil.
28. Install coolant recovery reservoir and the air cleaner assembly.
29. Install the engine cover and connect the battery cable.

7.4L Engines

▶ **See Figure 102**

1. Disconnect the negative battery cable.
2. Remove the air cleaner.
3. Remove the grille.
4. Remove the air conditioning compressor from its brackets and move the compressor out of the way without disconnecting the lines.
5. Drain the cooling system.
6. Remove the fan shroud and radiator.
7. Remove the drive belt(s), loosen the alternator bolts and move the alternator to one side.
8. Remove the cylinder head covers.
9. Disconnect the hoses from the water pump.
10. Remove the water pump.
11. Remove the torsional damper and pulley.
12. Remove the front cover.
13. Mark the distributor as to location in the block. Remove the distributor.
14. Remove the intake manifold.
15. Mark the lifters, pushrods, and rocker arms as to location so that they may be installed in the same position. Remove these parts.
16. Rotate the camshaft so that the timing marks align.
17. Remove the camshaft sprocket bolts.
18. Pull the camshaft sprocket and timing chain off. The sprocket is a tight fit, so you'll have to tap it loose with a plastic mallet.
19. Install two 5⁄16 in.–18 bolts in the holes in the front of the camshaft and carefully pull the camshaft from the block.

To install:

20. Liberally coat camshaft and bearing with heavy engine oil or engine assembly lubricant and insert the cam into the engine.
21. Install the distributor using the locating marks made during removal. (If any problems are encountered, refer to distributor removal and installation)
22. Install the camshaft sprocket bolts and tighten them to 20 ft. lbs. (27 Nm) on 1987–95 models or 10 ft. lbs. (14 Nm) on 1996–97 models.
23. Install the lifters, pushrods, and rocker arms.
24. Install the intake manifold.
25. Install the front cover.
26. Install the torsional damper and pulley.

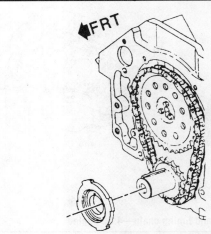

Fig. 102 Crankshaft position sensor reluctor ring location—7.4L engines

27. Install the water pump.
28. Connect the hoses at the water pump.
29. Install the cylinder head covers.
30. Install the alternator and drive belt(s).
31. Install the fan shroud and radiator.
32. Fill the cooling system.
33. Install the air conditioning compressor.
34. Install the grille.
35. Install the air cleaner.
36. Connect the battery.

Diesel Engines

1. Disconnect the negative battery cable.
2. Drain the cooling system.
3. Remove the air inlet duct and hood latch.
4. If equipped, remove the cruise control motor and windshield washer reservoir.
5. Remove the fan shroud.
6. Remove the radiator and fan.
7. Remove the headlight bezels, grille, bumper and lower valance panel.
8. Remove the coolant recovery reservoir.
9. If necessary, remove the upper tie bar.

✳✳ CAUTION

Please refer to Section 1 before discharging the compressor or disconnecting air conditioning lines. Damage to the air conditioning system or personal injury could result. Consult your local laws concerning refrigerant discharge and recycling. In many areas it may be illegal for anyone but a certified technician to service the A/C system. Always use an approved recovery station when discharging the air conditioning.

10. Remove the condenser.
11. If applicable, remove the vacuum pump and the oil pump drive.
12. If necessary, remove the power steering pump and the generator and lay them aside.
13. If the van is equipped with air conditioning, remove the compressor (with the lines attached) and position it out of the way.
14. Remove the cylinder head covers.
15. On early model vehicles, remove the rocker shaft assemblies and pushrods. Place the pushrods in order in a rack (easily by punching holes in a piece of heavy cardboard and numbering the holes) so that they can be installed in correct order.
16. On late model engines, remove the cylinder heads as previously detailed.
17. Remove the front cover.
18. Remove the timing chain assembly.
19. Remove the fuel pump. Remove the front engine mount through-bolts.
20. Remove the camshaft retainer plate.
21. Remove the camshaft by carefully sliding it out of the block.

➡**Whenever a new camshaft installed, GM recommends replacing all the valve lifters, as well as the oil filter. The engine oil must be changed. These measures will help ensure proper wear characteristics of the new camshaft.**

To install:

22. Coat the camshaft lobes with Molykote® or an equivalent lube. Liberally tube the camshaft journals with clean engine oil and install the camshaft carefully.
23. Install the camshaft retainer plate and tighten the bolts to 17 ft. lbs. (23 Nm).
24. Install the front engine mount bolts and tighten them to 70 ft. lbs. (95 Nm). Tighten the nut to 50 ft. lbs. (70 Nm).

25. Install the fuel pump.
26. Install the timing chain assembly.
27. Install the front cover.
28. Install the valve lifters, guide plates and clamps, and rotate the crankshaft so that the lifters are free to travel.
29. Install the cylinder heads.
30. Install the pushrods in their original order. Install the rocker shaft assemblies, then install the cylinder head covers.
31. Install the oil pump drive.
32. Install the compressor.
33. Install the power steering pump.
34. Install the alternator.
35. Install the water pump.
36. Install the vacuum pump.
37. Install the radiator and fan.
38. Install the air conditioning condenser. Have the A/C system charged by a qualified, certified technician. Refer to Section 1 for additional information.
39. Install the fan shroud.
40. Install the grille, valance and headlight bezel assemblies.
41. Fill the cooling system and connect the battery.
42. Install the engine cover.

INSPECTION

Run-Out

▶ See Figure 103

Camshaft runout should be checked when the camshaft has been removed from the engine. An accurate dial indicator is needed for this procedure; engine specialists and most machine shops have this equipment. If you have access to a dial indicator, or can take your camshaft to someone who does, measure the camshaft bearing journal run-out. If the run-out exceeds the limit replace the camshaft.

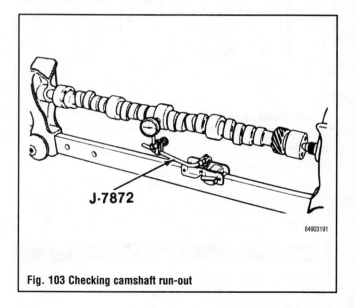

J-7872

84903191

Fig. 103 Checking camshaft run-out

Lobe Height

▶ See Figures 104 and 105

Use a micrometer to check camshaft (lobe) height, making sure the anvil and the spindle of the micrometer are positioned directly on the heel and tip of the camshaft lobe as shown in the accompanying illustration.

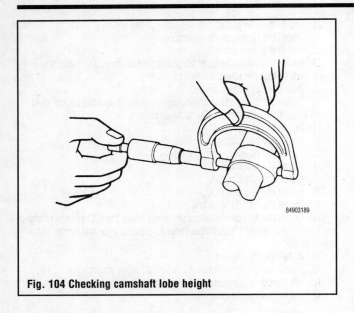

Fig. 104 Checking camshaft lobe height

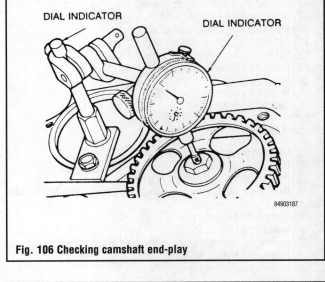

Fig. 106 Checking camshaft end-play

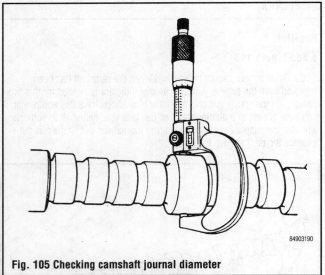

Fig. 105 Checking camshaft journal diameter

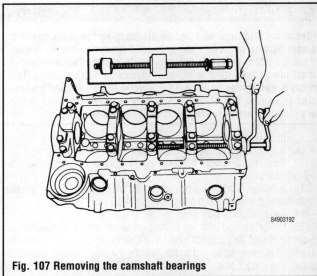

Fig. 107 Removing the camshaft bearings

End-Play

▶ See Figure 106

After the camshaft has been installed, end-play should be checked. The camshaft sprocket should then be installed. Use a dial gauge to check the end-play, by moving the camshaft forward and backward. End-play specifications should be as noted in the Camshaft Specifications chart.

Bearings

REMOVAL & INSTALLATION

▶ See Figures 107, 108, 109, 110 and 111

If excessive camshaft wear is found, or if the engine is completely rebuilt, the camshaft bearings should be replaced.

➡**The front and rear bearings should be removed last, and installed first. Those bearings act as guides for the other bearings and pilot.**

1. Drive the camshaft rear plug from the block.
2. Assemble the removal puller with its shoulder on the bearing to be removed. Gradually tighten the puller nut until the bearing is removed.
3. Remove the remaining bearings, leaving the front and rear for last. To

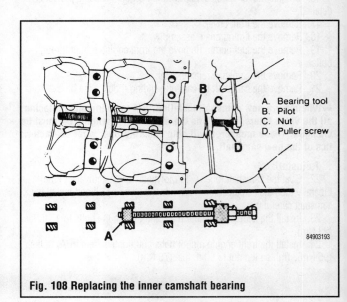

Fig. 108 Replacing the inner camshaft bearing

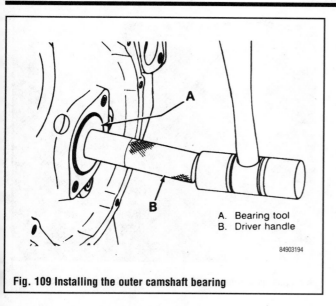

A. Bearing tool
B. Driver handle

84903194

Fig. 109 Installing the outer camshaft bearing

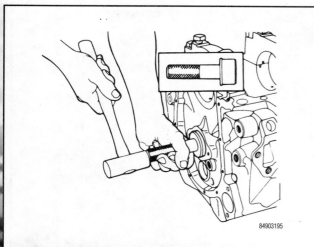

84903195

Fig. 110 Installing the front camshaft bearing on the diesel. The bearing tool is shown in the inset

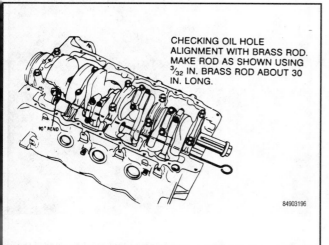

CHECKING OIL HOLE ALIGNMENT WITH BRASS ROD. MAKE ROD AS SHOWN USING $\frac{3}{32}$ IN. BRASS ROD ABOUT 30 IN. LONG.

90° BEND

84903196

Fig. 111 Make this simple tool to check camshaft bearing oil hole alignment

remove these, reverse the position of the puller, so as to pull the bearings towards the center of the block. Leave the tool in this position, pilot the new front and rear bearings on the installer, and pull them into position.

4. Return the puller to its original position and pull the remaining bearings into position.

➡You must make sure that the oil holes of the bearings and block align when installing the bearings. If they don't align, the camshaft will not get proper lubrication and may seize or at least be seriously damaged. To check for correct oil hole alignment, use a piece of brass rod with a 90° bend in the end as shown in the illustration. Check all oil hole openings. The wire must enter each hole, or the hole is not properly aligned.

5. Replace the camshaft rear plug, and stake it into position. On the diesel, coat the outer diameter of the new plug with GM sealant #1052080 or equivalent, and install it flush to $\frac{1}{32}$ in. (0.794mm) deep.

Lifters

REMOVAL & INSTALLATION

4.3L, 5.0L, 5.7L and 7.4L Engines

1. Remove the cylinder head cover.
2. Remove the intake manifold.
3. Back off the rocker arm adjusting nuts and remove the pushrods. Keep them in order for installation.
4. Remove the lifter retainer bolts, retainer and restrictor.
5. Remove the lifters. If your are going to re-use the lifters, remove them one at a time and mark each one for installation. They **must** be re-installed in the same locations. If a lifter is stuck, it can be removed with a grasping-type lifter tool, available from most auto parts stores.
6. Inspect each lifter thoroughly. If any of them shows any signs of wear, heat bluing or damage, replace the whole set.
7. Coat each lifter with engine oil supplement prior to installation. Tighten the retainer bolts to 12 ft. lbs. (16 Nm). Adjust the valves as described in the valve lash procedure.

6.2L and 6.5L Diesel Engines

◆ See Figure 112 (p. 73)

1. Remove the cylinder head cover.
2. Remove the rocker arm shaft, rocker arms and pushrods. Keep all parts in order and properly identified for installation.
3. Remove the clamps and lifter guide plates.

88263P54

Remove the bolts from the lifter retainers (if equipped) . . .

88263P55

. . . then remove the lifter retainer from the lifter valley

TCCS3812

A magnet is helpful to pull a well oiled lifter from the bore . . .

88263P56

Remove the restrictor for the lifter(s) you are servicing . . .

88263P57

. . . then grasp and remove the lifter from the bore

TCCS3813

. . . but a slide hammer type removal tool must be used if the lifter is stuck

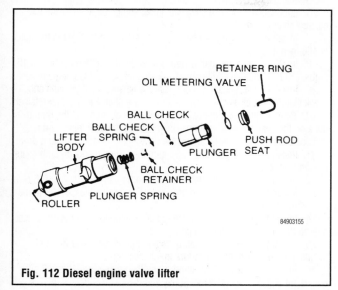

Fig. 112 Diesel engine valve lifter

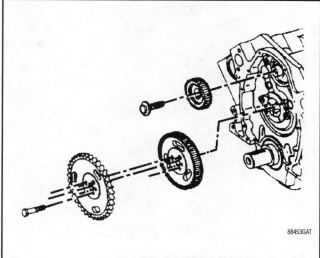

Fig. 113 View of the balance shaft drive and driven gears

4. Remove the lifters by reaching through the access holes in the cylinder head with a magnetic lifter tool. If you are going to re-use the lifters, remove them one at a time and mark each one for installation. They **must** be re-installed in the same locations. If a lifter is stuck, it can be removed with a grasping-type lifter tool, available form most auto parts stores.

To install:

5. Inspect each lifter thoroughly. If any of them shows any signs of wear, heat bluing or damage, replace the whole set.

➡**Some engines will have both standard and 0.010 in. (.0039mm) oversize lifters. The oversized lifters will have "10" etched into the side. The block will be stamped "OS" on the cast pad next to the lifter bore. and on the top rail of the crankcase above the lifter bore.**

✳✳ WARNING

New lifters must be primed before installation. Damage to the lifters and engine will result if new lifters are installed dry!

6. Prime new lifters by immersing them in clean kerosene or diesel fuel and working the lifter plunger while the unit is submerged.

7. Prior to installation, coat the lifter roller with engine oil supplement. Re-used lifters must be installed in their original positions!

8. Install the lifters.

9. Install the guide plates and clamps. Tighten the clamp bolts to 18 ft. lbs. (26 Nm).

10. After all the clamps are installed, turn the crankshaft by hand, 2 full turns (720°) to ensure free movement of the lifters in the guide plates. If the crankshaft won't turn, one or more lifters may be jamming in the guide plates.

11. The remainder of assembly the reverse of disassembly.

Balance Shaft

REMOVAL & INSTALLATION

▶ **See Figures 113, 114, 115 and 116**

✳✳ CAUTION

When draining engine coolant, keep in mind that cats and dogs are attracted to ethylene glycol antifreeze and could drink any that is left in an uncovered container or in puddles on the ground. This will prove fatal in sufficient quantity. Always drain coolant into a sealable container. Coolant should be reused unless it is contaminated or is several years old.

Fig. 114 View of the balance shaft location—1994 4.3L engine

Fig. 115 Unfasten the balance shaft gear bolt . . .

Fig. 116 . . . then remove the gear

88453P58

1. Disconnect the negative battery cable and remove the engine cover.
2. Remove the air cleaner and coolant recovery reservoir.
3. Have the air conditioning system discharged by a qualified technician using a proper refrigerant recovery/recycling station.
4. Remove the air conditioning compressor, bracket and accessory drive bracket.
5. Properly relieve the fuel system pressure.
6. Drain the engine cooling system.
7. Remove the upper radiator shroud, then disengage the oil and transmission cooler lines at the radiator.
8. Tag and disengage all hoses from the radiator.
9. Remove the radiator and air conditioning condenser from the vehicle.
10. Remove the fan assembly.
11. Carefully release the belt tension, then remove the serpentine drive belt.
12. If equipped, unfasten the pencil brace at the water pump, then remove the water pump.
13. Remove the crankshaft pulley and damper. For details, please refer to the procedure in this section.
14. If necessary, remove the flywheel inspection cover.
15. Remove the front cover. For details, please refer to the procedure in this section.
16. Remove the timing chain and sprockets. For details, please refer to the procedure in this section.
17. Unfasten the balance shaft gear bolt, then remove the gear.
18. Remove the balance shaft retainer.
19. Remove the intake manifold assembly. For details, please refer to the procedure in this section.
20. Remove the lifter retainer.
21. Remove the balance shaft and front bearing by gently driving them out using a soft faced mallet.
22. Using tool J-38834 or its equivalent, remove the balance shaft rear bearing.

➥The balance shaft and drive and driven gears are serviced only as a set, including the gear bolt. The balance shaft and front bearing are serviced as a package.

❊❊ WARNING

The front bearing must not be removed from the balance shaft.

To install:
23. Inspect the balance shaft gears for damage, such as nicks and burrs.
24. Using a putty knife, clean the gasket mounting surfaces. Using solvent, clean the oil and grease from the gasket mounting surfaces.
25. Lubricate the balance shaft rear bearing with clean engine oil, then install the bearing using tool J-38834 or its equivalent.

26. Lubricate the balance shaft with clean engine oil, then install the balance shaft into the block.
27. Install the balance shaft bearing retainer and bolts. Tighten the bolts to 106 inch lbs. (12 Nm).
28. Install the balance shaft driven gear and bolt. Tighten the bolt to 15 ft. lbs. (20 Nm) plus an additional 35 degrees using a torque/angle meter.
29. Install the lifter retainer, then rotate the balance shaft by hand and check that there is clearance between the balance shaft and the lifter retainer.
30. Temporarily install the balance shaft drive gear so that the timing mark on the gear points straight up, then remove the drive gear, turn the balance shaft so the timing mark on the driven gear is facing straight down.
31. Install the drive gear and make sure the timing marks on both gears line up (dot-to-dot).
32. Install the drive gear retaining bolt and tighten to 12 ft. lbs. (16 Nm).
33. Install the intake manifold assembly. For details, please refer to the procedure in this section.
34. Install the timing chain and sprocket assemblies. For details, please refer to the procedure in this section.
35. Install the front cover, seal, bolts and the oil pan assembly. For details, please refer to the procedure in this section.
36. Install the flywheel inspection cover, then using tool J-39046 or its equivalent engage the crankshaft pulley and damper. For details, please refer to the procedure in this section.
37. Install the water pump, then engage the pencil brace to the pump.
38. Install the serpentine drive belt.
39. Install the fan assembly.
40. Install the air conditioning compressor bracket and bracket.
41. Install the air conditioning condenser and the radiator assemblies. Engage all hoses removed from the radiator.
42. Engage the oil and transmission cooler lines at the radiator, then install the radiator shroud.
43. Install the coolant recovery reservoir.
44. Install the air cleaner assembly and connect the negative battery cable.
45. Fill the crankcase with the correct grade and amount of oil.
46. Fill the cooling system with coolant.
47. Start the vehicle and check for leaks.
48. Have the air conditioning system charged by a qualified technician using a proper refrigerant recovery/recycling station.
49. Install the engine cover.

Rear Main Oil Seal

REMOVAL & INSTALLATION

1987–90 7.4L Engines

▶ See Figures 117, 118, 119, 120 and 121

1. Remove the oil pan, oil pump and rear main bearing cap.
2. Remove the oil seal from the bearing cap by prying it out with a suitable tool.
3. Remove the upper half of the seal with a small punch. Drive it around far enough to be gripped with pliers.
   To install:
4. Clean the crankshaft and bearing cap.
5. Coat the lips and bead of the seal with light engine oil, keeping oil from the ends of the seal.
6. Position the fabricated tool between the crankshaft and seal seat.
7. Position the seal between the crankshaft and tip of the tool so that the seal bead contacts the tip of the tool. The oil seal lip should face forward.
8. Roll the seal around the crankshaft using the tool to protect the seal bead from the sharp corners of the crankcase.
9. The installation tool should be left installed until the seal is properly positioned with both ends flush with the block.
10. Remove the tool.
11. Install the other half of the seal in the bearing cap using the tool in the same manner as before. Light thumb pressure should install the seal.

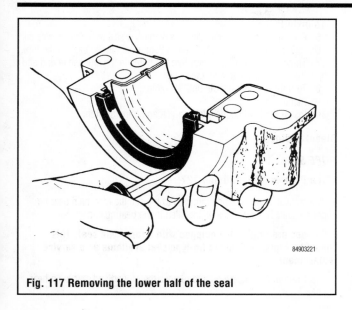

Fig. 117 Removing the lower half of the seal

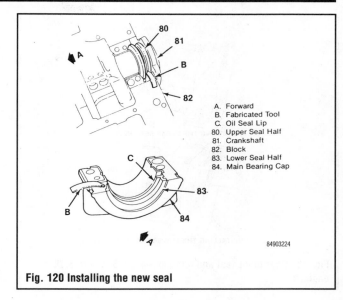

A. Forward
B. Fabricated Tool
C. Oil Seal Lip
80. Upper Seal Half
81. Crankshaft
82. Block
83. Lower Seal Half
84. Main Bearing Cap

Fig. 120 Installing the new seal

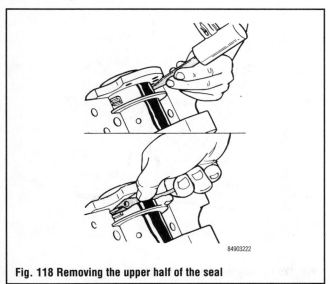

Fig. 118 Removing the upper half of the seal

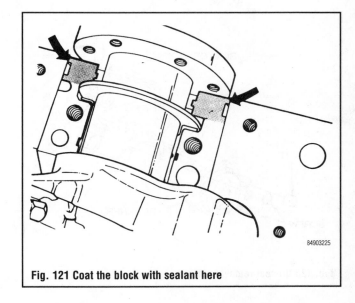

Fig. 121 Coat the block with sealant here

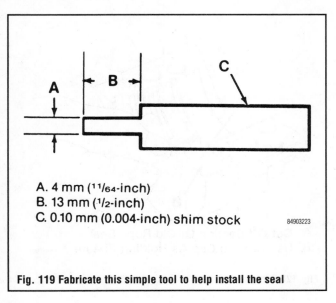

A. 4 mm (¹¹/₆₄-inch)
B. 13 mm (¹/₂-inch)
C. 0.10 mm (0.004-inch) shim stock

Fig. 119 Fabricate this simple tool to help install the seal

12. Install the bearing cap with sealant applied to the mating areas of the cap and block. Keep sealant from the ends of the seal.

13. Tighten the main bearing cap retaining bolts to 10 ft. lbs. (14 Nm). Tap the end of the crankshaft first rearward, then forward with a lead hammer. This will line up the rear main bearing and the crankshaft thrust surfaces. Tighten the main bearing cap 110 ft. lbs. (150 Nm).

14. Install the oil pump.

15. Install the oil pan.

4.3L, 5.0L, 5.7L and 1991–97 7.4L Engines

▶ See Figures 122, 123 and 124

➡Special tool J-35621 (or J-38841), or its equivalent seal installer, will be necessary for this job.

1. Remove the transmission.

2. With manual transmission, remove the clutch.

3. Remove the flywheel or flexplate.

4. Insert a small prying tool in the notches provided in the seal retainer and pry out the old seal. Be VERY CAREFUL to avoid nicking or scratching the sealing surfaces of the crankshaft.

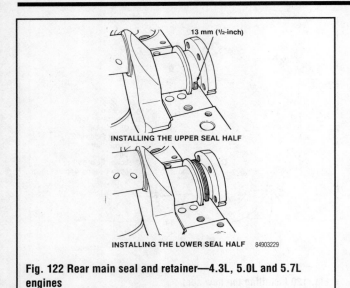

Fig. 122 Rear main seal and retainer—4.3L, 5.0L and 5.7L engines

To install:

5. Coat the inner and outer diameters of the new seal with clean engine oil.
6. Using seal tool J-35621, or equivalent, position the seal on the tool.
7. Thread the attaching screws into the holes in the crankshaft end and tighten them securely with a screwdriver.
8. Turn the installer handle until it bottoms.
9. Remove the tool.
10. Install the flywheel/flexplate, clutch and transmission.

Diesel Engines

ROPE SEAL

▶ See Figures 125, 126 and 127

The crankshaft need not be removed to replace the rear main bearing upper oil seal. The lower seal is installed in the bearing cap.

➡Engines are originally equipped with a rope-type seal. This should be replaced with the lip-type seal available as a service replacement.

1. Drain the crankcase oil and remove the oil pan and rear main bearing cap.

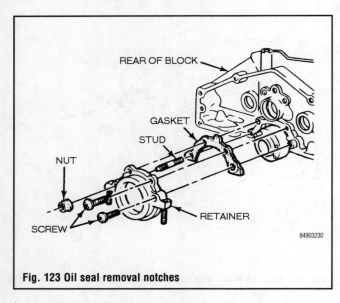

Fig. 123 Oil seal removal notches

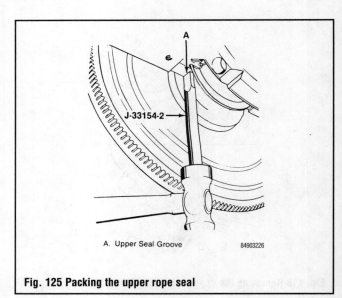

A. Upper Seal Groove

Fig. 125 Packing the upper rope seal

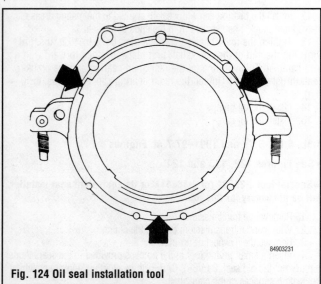

Fig. 124 Oil seal installation tool

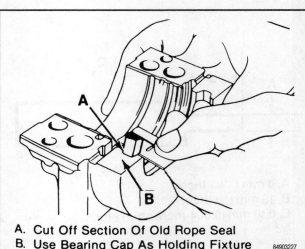

A. Cut Off Section Of Old Rope Seal
B. Use Bearing Cap As Holding Fixture

Fig. 126 Trim the rope seal

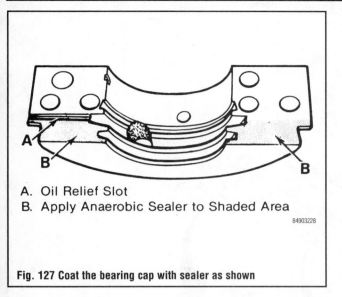

A. Oil Relief Slot
B. Apply Anaerobic Sealer to Shaded Area

84903228

Fig. 127 Coat the bearing cap with sealer as shown

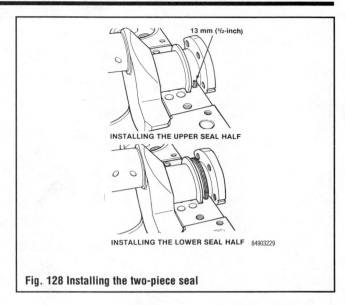

INSTALLING THE UPPER SEAL HALF

INSTALLING THE LOWER SEAL HALF   84903229

Fig. 128 Installing the two-piece seal

2. Using a special main seal tool or a tool that can be made from a dowel (see illustration), drive the upper seal into its groove on each side until it is tightly packed. This is usually ¼–¾ in. (6–19mm).

3. Measure the amount the seal was driven up on one side. Add ¹⁄₁₆ in. (2mm) and cut another length from the old seal. Use the main bearing cap as a holding fixture when cutting the seal as illustrated. Carefully trim protruding seal.

4. Work these two pieces of seal up into the cylinder block on each side with two nailsets or small screwdrivers. Using the packing tool again, pack these pieces into the block, then trim the flush with a razor blade or hobby knife as shown. Do not scratch the bearing surface with the razor.

➡It may help to use a bit of oil on the short pieces of the rope seal when packing it into the block.

5. Apply Loctite® # 496 sealer or equivalent to the rear main bearing cap and install the rope seal. Cut the ends of the seal flush with the cap.

6. Check to see if the rear main cap with the new seal will seat properly on the block. Place a piece of Plastigage® on the rear main journal, install the cap and tighten to 70 ft. lbs. (94 Nm). Remove the cap and check the Plastigage® against specifications. If out of specs, recheck the end of the seal for fraying that may be preventing the cap from seating properly.

7. Make sure all traces of Plastigage® are removed from the crankshaft journal. Apply a thin film of sealer (GM part # 1052357 or equivalent) to the bearing cap. Keep the sealant off of both the seal and the bearing.

8. Just before assembly, apply a light coat of clean engine oil on the crankshaft surface that will contact the seal.

9. Install the bearing cap and tighten to specification.

10. Install the oil pump and oil pan.

TWO-PIECE LIP SEAL

▶ **See Figure 128**

1. Disconnect the negative battery cable. Drain the oil.
2. Remove the oil pan and oil pump.

3. Loosen the bolts and remove the rear main bearing cap. Pull out the old rope seal.

4. Clean the upper and lower seal grooves. Clean the main bearing cap and block mating surfaces and then check the bearing clearance.

5. Coat the inner side of the seal halves where they contact the crankshaft and slide them into position.

6. Roll one seal half into the cylinder block groove until ½ in. (13mm) of the seal's end is protruding from the block.

7. Insert the other half into the opposite side of the groove. The ends of the seals (where they touch) should now be at either the 4 and 10 o'clock or the 8 and 2 o'clock positions. This is the only way you will be able to align the main bearing cap and seal lips properly!

8. Coat the seal groove in the bearing cap lightly with adhesive. Apply a thin film of anaerobic sealant to the cap (stay away from the oil hole!!), coat the bolts with oil and tap them into position. Tighten all bolts to specification, loosen and then re-tighten.

9. Install the oil pan and pump. Fill the engine with oil and connect the battery cable.

Flywheel and Ring Gear

REMOVAL & INSTALLATION

The ring gear is an integral part of the flywheel and is not replaceable.

1. Remove the transmission.

2. Remove the six bolts attaching the flywheel to the crankshaft flange. Remove the flywheel.

3. Inspect the flywheel for cracks, and inspect the ring gear for burrs or worn teeth. Replace the flywheel if any damage is apparent. Remove burrs with a mill file.

4. Install the flywheel. The flywheel will only attach to the crankshaft in one position, as the bolt holes are unevenly spaced. Install the bolts and torque to specification.

EXHUAST SYSTEM

Inspection

▶ **See Figures 129, 130 and 131 (p. 78–79)**

➡Safety glasses should be worn at all times when working on or near the exhaust system. Older exhaust systems will almost always be covered with loose rust particles which will shower you when disturbed. These particles are more than a nuisance and could injure your eye.

✵ CAUTION

Do **NOT** perform exhaust repairs or inspection with the engine or exhaust hot. Allow the system to cool completely before attempting any work. Exhaust systems are noted for sharp edges, flaking metal and rusted bolts. Gloves and eye protection are required. A healthy supply of penetrating oil and rags is highly recommended.

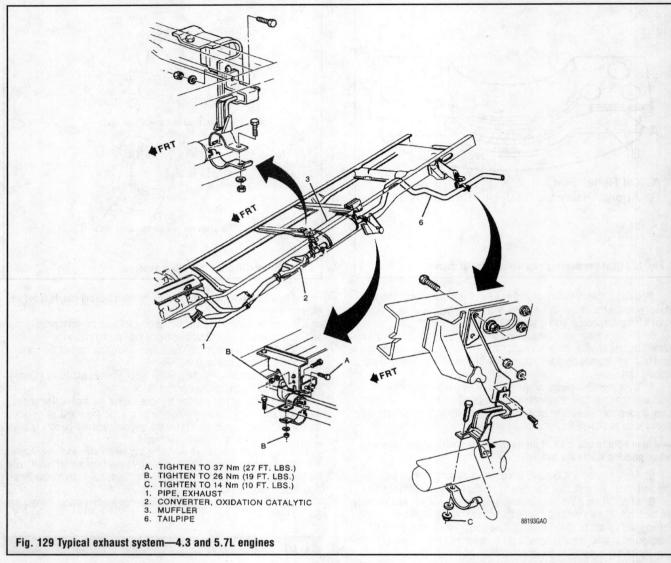

A. TIGHTEN TO 37 N·m (27 FT. LBS.)
B. TIGHTEN TO 26 N·m (19 FT. LBS.)
C. TIGHTEN TO 14 N·m (10 FT. LBS.)
1. PIPE, EXHAUST
2. CONVERTER, OXIDATION CATALYTIC
3. MUFFLER
6. TAILPIPE

88193GA0

Fig. 129 Typical exhaust system—4.3 and 5.7L engines

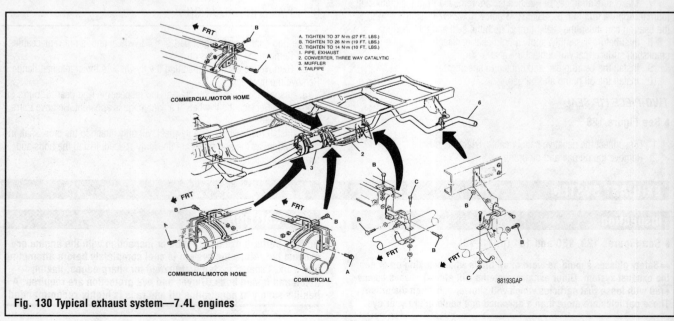

A. TIGHTEN TO 37 N·m (27 FT. LBS.)
B. TIGHTEN TO 26 N·m (19 FT. LBS.)
C. TIGHTEN TO 14 N·m (10 FT. LBS.)
1. PIPE, EXHAUST
2. CONVERTER, THREE WAY CATALYTIC
3. MUFFLER
6. TAILPIPE

COMMERCIAL/MOTOR HOME

COMMERCIAL/MOTOR HOME

COMMERCIAL

88193GAP

Fig. 130 Typical exhaust system—7.4L engines

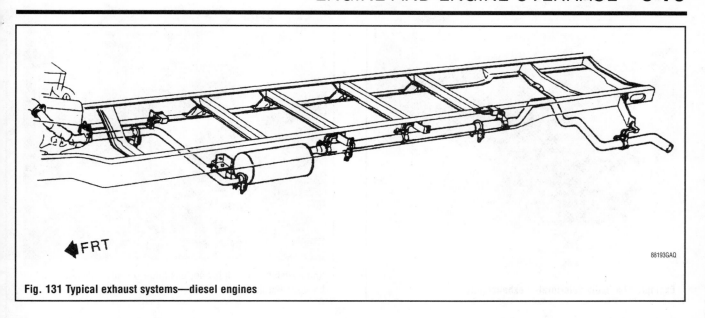

Fig. 131 Typical exhaust systems—diesel engines

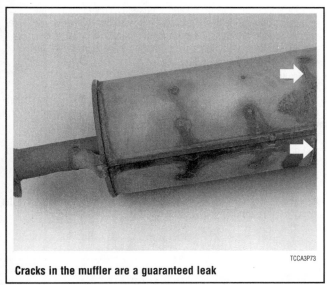

Cracks in the muffler are a guaranteed leak

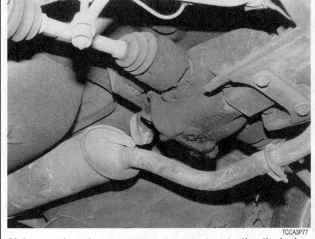

Make sure the exhaust components are not contacting the body or suspension

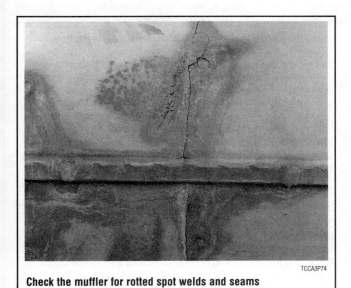

Check the muffler for rotted spot welds and seams

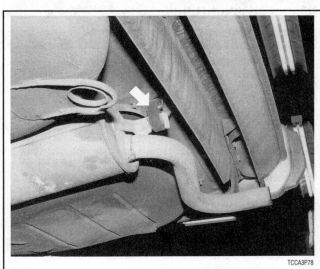

Check for overstretched or torn exhaust hangers

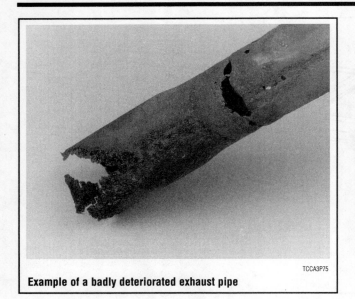

TCCA3P75

Example of a badly deteriorated exhaust pipe

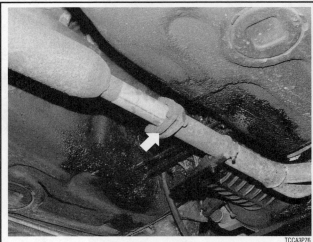

TCCA3P76

Some systems, like this one, use large O-rings ("donuts") in between the flanges

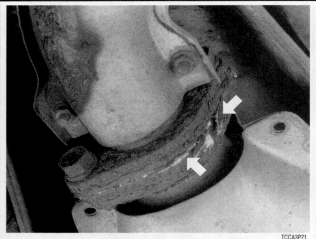

TCCA3P71

Inspect flanges for gaskets that have deteriorated and need replacement

Your vehicle must be raised and supported safely to inspect the exhaust system properly. By placing 4 safety stands under the vehicle for support should provide enough room for you to slide under the vehicle and inspect the system completely. Start the inspection at the exhaust manifold or turbocharger pipe where the header pipe is attached and work your way to the back of the vehicle. On dual exhaust systems, remember to inspect both sides of the vehicle. Check the complete exhaust system for open seams, holes loose connections, or other deterioration which could permit exhaust fumes to seep into the passenger compartment. Inspect all mounting brackets and hangers for deterioration, some models may have rubber O-rings that can be overstretched and non-supportive. These components will need to be replaced if found. It has always been a practice to use a pointed tool to poke up into the exhaust system where the deterioration spots are to see whether or not they crumble. Some models may have heat shield covering certain parts of the exhaust system, it will be necessary to remove these shields to have the exhaust visible for inspection also.

ENGINE RECONDITIONING

Determining Engine Condition

Anything that generates heat and/or friction will eventually burn or wear out (ie. a light bulb generates heat, therefore its life span is limited). With this in mind, a running engine generates tremendous amounts of both; friction is encountered by the moving and rotating parts inside the engine and heat is created by friction and combustion of the fuel. However, the engine has systems designed to help reduce the effects of heat and friction and provide added longevity. The oiling system reduces the amount of friction encountered by the moving parts inside the engine, while the cooling system reduces heat created by friction and combustion. If either system is not maintained, a break-down will be inevitable. Therefore, you can see how regular maintenance can affect the service life of your vehicle. If you do not drain, flush and refill your cooling system at the proper intervals, deposits will begin to accumulate in the radiator, thereby reducing the amount of heat it can extract from the coolant. The same applies to your oil and filter; if it is not changed often enough it becomes laden with contaminates and is unable to properly lubricate the engine. This increases friction and wear.

There are a number of methods for evaluating the condition of your

engine. A compression test can reveal the condition of your pistons, piston rings, cylinder bores, head gasket(s), valves and valve seats. An oil pressure test can warn you of possible engine bearing, or oil pump failures. Excessive oil consumption, evidence of oil in the engine air intake area and/or bluish smoke from the tail pipe may indicate worn piston rings, worn valve guides and/or valve seals. As a general rule, an engine that uses no more than one quart of oil every 1000 miles is in good condition. Engines that use one quart of oil or more in less than 1000 miles should first be checked for oil leaks. If any oil leaks are present, have them fixed before determining how much oil is consumed by the engine, especially if blue smoke is not visible at the tail pipe.

COMPRESSION TEST

A noticeable lack of engine power, excessive oil consumption and/or poor fuel mileage measured over an extended period are all indicators of internal engine wear. Worn piston rings, scored or worn cylinder bores, blown head gaskets, sticking or burnt valves, and worn valve seats are all possible culprits. A check of each cylinder's compression will help locate the problem.

Gasoline Engines

➡A screw-in type compression gauge is more accurate than the type you simply hold against the spark plug hole. Although it takes slightly longer to use, it's worth the effort to obtain a more accurate reading.

1. Make sure that the proper amount and viscosity of engine oil is in the crankcase, then ensure the battery is fully charged.
2. Warm-up the engine to normal operating temperature, then shut the engine **OFF**.
3. Disable the ignition system.
4. Label and disconnect all of the spark plug wires from the plugs.
5. Thoroughly clean the cylinder head area around the spark plug ports, then remove the spark plugs.
6. Set the throttle plate to the fully open (wide-open throttle) position. You can block the accelerator linkage open for this, or you can have an assistant fully depress the accelerator pedal.
7. Install a screw-in type compression gauge into the No. 1 spark plug hole until the fitting is snug.

❊❊ WARNING

Be careful not to crossthread the spark plug hole.

8. According to the tool manufacturer's instructions, connect a remote starting switch to the starting circuit.
9. With the ignition switch in the **OFF** position, use the remote starting switch to crank the engine through at least five compression strokes (approximately 5 seconds of cranking) and record the highest reading on the gauge.
10. Repeat the test on each cylinder, cranking the engine approximately the same number of compression strokes and/or time as the first.
11. Compare the highest readings from each cylinder to that of the others. The indicated compression pressures are considered within specifications if the lowest reading cylinder is within 75 percent of the pressure recorded for the highest reading cylinder. For example, if your highest reading cylinder pressure was 150 psi (1034 kPa), then 75 percent of that would be 113 psi (779 kPa). So the lowest reading cylinder should be no less than 113 psi (779 kPa).
12. If a cylinder exhibits an unusually low compression reading, pour a tablespoon of clean engine oil into the cylinder through the spark plug hole and repeat the compression test. If the compression rises after adding oil, it means that the cylinder's piston rings and/or cylinder bore are damaged or

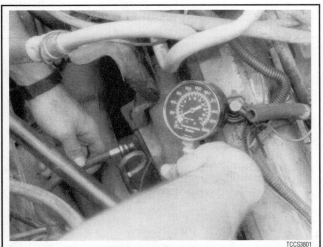

TCCS3801

A screw-in type compression gauge is more accurate and easier to use without an assistant

worn. If the pressure remains low, the valves may not be seating properly (a valve job is needed), or the head gasket may be blown near that cylinder. If compression in any two adjacent cylinders is low, and if the addition of oil doesn't help raise compression, there is leakage past the head gasket. Oil and coolant in the combustion chamber, combined with blue or constant white smoke from the tail pipe, are symptoms of this problem. However, don't be alarmed by the normal white smoke emitted from the tail pipe during engine warm-up or from cold weather driving. There may be evidence of water droplets on the engine dipstick and/or oil droplets in the cooling system if a head gasket is blown.

Diesel Engines

Checking cylinder compression on diesel engines is basically the same procedure as on gasoline engines except for the following:

1. A special compression gauge adaptor suitable for diesel engines (because these engines have much greater compression pressures) must be used.
2. Remove the injector tubes and remove the injectors from each cylinder.

❊❊ WARNING

Do not forget to remove the washer underneath each injector. Otherwise, it may get lost when the engine is cranked.

3. When fitting the compression gauge adaptor to the cylinder head, make sure the bleeder of the gauge (if equipped) is closed.
4. When reinstalling the injector assemblies, install new washers underneath each injector.

OIL PRESSURE TEST

Check for proper oil pressure at the sending unit passage with an externally mounted mechanical oil pressure gauge (as opposed to relying on a factory installed dash-mounted gauge). A tachometer may also be needed, as some specifications may require running the engine at a specific rpm.

1. With the engine cold, locate and remove the oil pressure sending unit.
2. Following the manufacturer's instructions, connect a mechanical oil pressure gauge and, if necessary, a tachometer to the engine.
3. Start the engine and allow it to idle.
4. Check the oil pressure reading when cold and record the number. You may need to run the engine at a specified rpm, so check the specifications chart located earlier in this section.
5. Run the engine until normal operating temperature is reached (upper radiator hose will feel warm).
6. Check the oil pressure reading again with the engine hot and record the number. Turn the engine **OFF**.
7. Compare your hot oil pressure reading to that given in the chart. If the reading is low, check the cold pressure reading against the chart. If the cold pressure is well above the specification, and the hot reading was lower than the specification, you may have the wrong viscosity oil in the engine. Change the oil, making sure to use the proper grade and quantity, then repeat the test.

Low oil pressure readings could be attributed to internal component wear, pump related problems, a low oil level, or oil viscosity that is too low. High oil pressure readings could be caused by an overfilled crankcase, too high of an oil viscosity or a faulty pressure relief valve.

Buy or Rebuild?

Now that you have determined that your engine is worn out, you must make some decisions. The question of whether or not an engine is worth rebuilding is largely a subjective matter and one of personal worth. Is the engine a popular one, or is it an obsolete model? Are parts available? Will it get acceptable gas mileage once it is rebuilt? Is the car it's being put into worth keeping? Would it be less expensive to buy a new engine, have your engine rebuilt by a pro, rebuild it yourself or buy a used engine from a salvage yard? Or would it be simpler and less expensive to buy another car? If you have considered all these matters and more, and have still decided to rebuild the engine, then it is time to decide how you will rebuild it.

➡**The editors at Chilton feel that most engine machining should be performed by a professional machine shop. Don't think of it as wasting money, rather, as an assurance that the job has been done right the first time. There are many expensive and specialized tools required to perform such tasks as boring and honing an engine block or having a valve job done on a cylinder head. Even inspecting the parts requires expensive micrometers and gauges to properly measure wear and clearances. Also, a machine shop can deliver to you clean, and ready to assemble parts, saving you time and aggravation. Your maximum savings will come from performing the removal, disassembly, assembly and installation of the engine and purchasing or renting only the tools required to perform the above tasks. Depending on the particular circumstances, you may save 40 to 60 percent of the cost doing these yourself.**

A complete rebuild or overhaul of an engine involves replacing all of the moving parts (pistons, rods, crankshaft, camshaft, etc.) with new ones and machining the non-moving wearing surfaces of the block and heads. Unfortunately, this may not be cost effective. For instance, your crankshaft may have been damaged or worn, but it can be machined undersize for a minimal fee.

So, as you can see, you can replace everything inside the engine, but, it is wiser to replace only those parts which are really needed, and, if possible, repair the more expensive ones. Later in this section, we will break the engine down into its two main components: the cylinder head and the engine block. We will discuss each component, and the recommended parts to replace during a rebuild on each.

Engine Overhaul Tips

Most engine overhaul procedures are fairly standard. In addition to specific parts replacement procedures and specifications for your individual engine, this section is also a guide to acceptable rebuilding procedures. Examples of standard rebuilding practice are given and should be used along with specific details concerning your particular engine.

Competent and accurate machine shop services will ensure maximum performance, reliability and engine life. In most instances it is more profitable for the do-it-yourself mechanic to remove, clean and inspect the component, buy the necessary parts and deliver these to a shop for actual machine work.

Much of the assembly work (crankshaft, bearings, piston rods, and other components) is well within the scope of the do-it-yourself mechanic's tools and abilities. You will have to decide for yourself the depth of involvement you desire in an engine repair or rebuild.

TOOLS

The tools required for an engine overhaul or parts replacement will depend on the depth of your involvement. With a few exceptions, they will be the tools found in a mechanic's tool kit (see Section 1 of this manual). More in-depth work will require some or all of the following:
• A dial indicator (reading in thousandths) mounted on a universal base
• Micrometers and telescope gauges
• Jaw and screw-type pullers
• Scraper
• Valve spring compressor
• Ring groove cleaner
• Piston ring expander and compressor
• Ridge reamer
• Cylinder hone or glaze breaker
• Plastigage®
• Engine stand

The use of most of these tools is illustrated in this section. Many can be rented for a one-time use from a local parts jobber or tool supply house specializing in automotive work.

Occasionally, the use of special tools is called for. See the information on Special Tools and the Safety Notice in the front of this book before substituting another tool.

OVERHAUL TIPS

Aluminum has become extremely popular for use in engines, due to its low weight. Observe the following precautions when handling aluminum parts:
• Never hot tank aluminum parts (the caustic hot tank solution will eat the aluminum.
• Remove all aluminum parts (identification tag, etc.) from engine parts prior to the tanking.
• Always coat threads lightly with engine oil or anti-seize compounds before installation, to prevent seizure.
• Never overtighten bolts or spark plugs especially in aluminum threads.

When assembling the engine, any parts that will be exposed to frictional contact must be prelubed to provide lubrication at initial start-up. Any product specifically formulated for this purpose can be used, but engine oil is not recommended as a prelube in most cases.

When semi-permanent (locked, but removable) installation of bolts or nuts is desired, threads should be cleaned and coated with Loctite® or another similar, commercial non-hardening sealant.

CLEANING

Before the engine and its components are inspected, they must be thoroughly cleaned. You will need to remove any engine varnish, oil sludge and/or carbon deposits from all of the components to insure an accurate inspection. A crack in the engine block or cylinder head can easily become overlooked if hidden by a layer of sludge or carbon.

Most of the cleaning process can be carried out with common hand tools and readily available solvents or solutions. Carbon deposits can be chipped away using a hammer and a hard wooden chisel. Old gasket material and varnish or sludge can usually be removed using a scraper and/or cleaning solvent. Extremely stubborn deposits may require the use of a power drill with a wire brush. If using a wire brush, use extreme care around any critical machined surfaces (such as the gasket surfaces, bearing saddles, cylinder bores, etc.). USE OF A WIRE BRUSH IS NOT RECOMMENDED ON ANY ALUMINUM COMPONENTS. Always follow any safety recommendations given by the manufacturer of the tool and/or solvent. You should always wear eye protection during any cleaning process involving scraping, chipping or spraying of solvents.

An alternative to the mess and hassle of cleaning the parts yourself is to drop them off at a local garage or machine shop. They will, more than

TCCS3132

Use a gasket scraper to remove the old gasket material from the mating surfaces

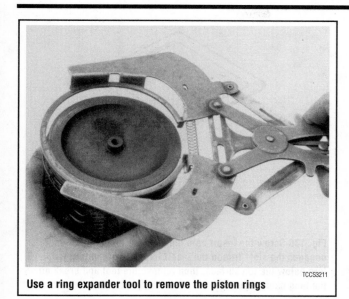

Use a ring expander tool to remove the piston rings

likely, have the necessary equipment to properly clean all of the parts for a nominal fee.

✳✲ CAUTION

Always wear eye protection during any cleaning process involving scraping, chipping or spraying of solvents.

Remove any oil galley plugs, freeze plugs and/or pressed-in bearings and carefully wash and degrease all of the engine components including the fasteners and bolts. Small parts such as the valves, springs, etc., should be placed in a metal basket and allowed to soak. Use pipe cleaner type brushes, and clean all passageways in the components. Use a ring expander and remove the rings from the pistons. Clean the piston ring grooves with a special tool or a piece of broken ring. Scrape the carbon off of the top of the piston. You should never use a wire brush on the pistons. After preparing all of the piston assemblies in this manner, wash and degrease them again.

✳✲ WARNING

Use extreme care when cleaning around the cylinder head valve seats. A mistake or slip may cost you a new seat.

When cleaning the cylinder head, remove carbon from the combustion chamber with the valves installed. This will avoid damaging the valve seats.

REPAIRING DAMAGED THREADS

▶ **See Figures 132, 133, 134, 135 and 136**

Several methods of repairing damaged threads are available. Heli-Coil® (shown here), Keenserts® and Microdot® are among the most widely used. All involve basically the same principle—drilling out stripped threads, tapping the hole and installing a prewound insert—making welding, plugging and oversize fasteners unnecessary.

Two types of thread repair inserts are usually supplied: a standard type for most inch coarse, inch fine, metric course and metric fine thread sizes and a spark lug type to fit most spark plug port sizes. Consult the individual tool manufacturer's catalog to determine exact applications. Typical thread repair kits will contain a selection of prewound threaded inserts, a tap (corresponding to the outside diameter threads of the insert) and an installation tool. Spark plug inserts usually differ because they require a tap equipped with pilot threads and a combined reamer/tap section. Most manufacturers also supply blister-packed thread repair inserts separately in addition to a master kit containing a variety of taps and inserts plus installation tools.

Before attempting to repair a threaded hole, remove any snapped, broken

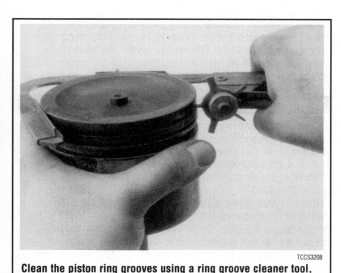

Clean the piston ring grooves using a ring groove cleaner tool, or . . .

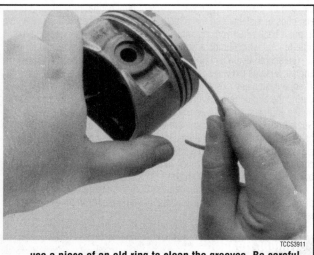

. . . use a piece of an old ring to clean the grooves. Be careful, the ring can be quite sharp

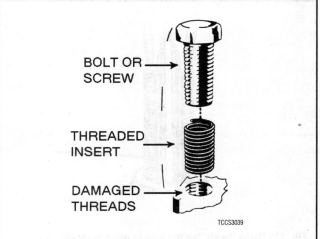

Fig. 132 Damaged bolt hole threads can be replaced with thread repair inserts

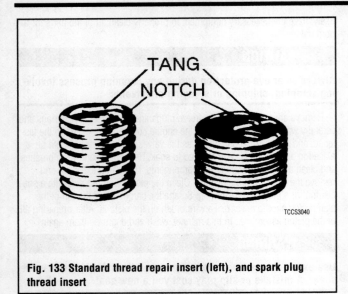

Fig. 133 Standard thread repair insert (left), and spark plug thread insert

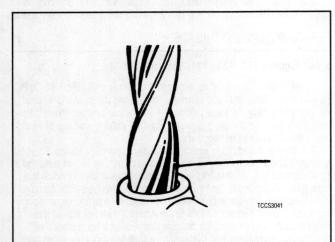

Fig. 134 Drill out the damaged threads with the specified size bit. Be sure to drill completely through the hole or to the bottom of a blind hole

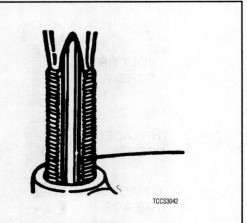

Fig. 135 Using the kit, tap the hole in order to receive the thread insert. Keep the tap well oiled and back it out frequently to avoid clogging the threads

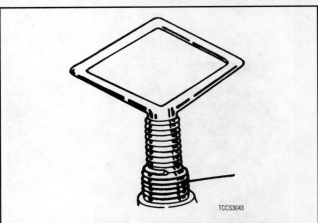

Fig. 136 Screw the insert onto the installer tool until the tang engages the slot. Thread the insert into the hole until it is ¼–½ turn below the top surface, then remove the tool and break off the tang using a punch

or damaged bolts or studs. Penetrating oil can be used to free frozen threads. The offending item can usually be removed with locking pliers or using a screw/stud extractor. After the hole is clear, the thread can be repaired, as shown in the series of accompanying illustrations and in the kit manufacturer's instructions.

Engine Preparation

To properly rebuild an engine, you must first remove it from the vehicle, then disassemble and diagnose it. Ideally you should place your engine on an engine stand. This affords you the best access to the engine components. Follow the manufacturer's directions for using the stand with your particular engine. Remove the flywheel or flexplate before installing the engine to the stand.

Now that you have the engine on a stand, and assuming that you have drained the oil and coolant from the engine, it's time to strip it of all but the necessary components. Before you start disassembling the engine, you may want to take a moment to draw some pictures, or fabricate some labels or containers to mark the locations of various components and the bolts and/or studs which fasten them. Modern day engines use a lot of little brackets and clips which hold wiring harnesses and such, and these holders are often mounted on studs and/or bolts that can be easily mixed up. The manufacturer spent a lot of time and money designing your vehicle, and they wouldn't have wasted any of it by haphazardly placing brackets, clips or fasteners on the vehicle. If it's present when you disassemble it, put it back when you assemble, you will regret not remembering that little bracket which holds a wire harness out of the path of a rotating part.

You should begin by unbolting any accessories still attached to the engine, such as the water pump, power steering pump, alternator, etc. Then, unfasten any manifolds (intake or exhaust) which were not removed during the engine removal procedure. Finally, remove any covers remaining on the engine such as the rocker arm, front or timing cover and oil pan. Some front covers may require the vibration damper and/or crank pulley to be removed beforehand. The idea is to reduce the engine to the bare necessities (cylinder head(s), valve train, engine block, crankshaft, pistons and connecting rods), plus any other 'in block' components such as oil pumps, balance shafts and auxiliary shafts.

Finally, remove the cylinder head(s) from the engine block and carefully place on a bench. Disassembly instructions for each component follow later in this section.

Cylinder Head

There are two basic types of cylinder heads used on today's automobiles: the Overhead Valve (OHV) and the Overhead Camshaft (OHC). The latter can also be broken down into two subgroups: the Single Overhead Camshaft (SOHC) and the Dual Overhead Camshaft (DOHC). Generally, if there is only a single camshaft on a head, it is just referred to as an OHC head. Also, an engine with a OHV cylinder head is also known as a pushrod engine.

Most cylinder heads these days are made of an aluminum alloy due to its light weight, durability and heat transfer qualities. However, cast iron was the material of choice in the past, and is still used on many vehicles today. Whether made from aluminum or iron, all cylinder heads have valves and seats. Some use two valves per cylinder, while the more hi-tech engines will utilize a multi-valve configuration using 3, 4 and even 5 valves per cylinder. When the valve contacts the seat, it does so on precision machined surfaces, which seals the combustion chamber. All cylinder heads have a valve guide for each valve. The guide centers the valve to the seat and allows it to move up and down within it. The clearance between the valve and guide can be critical. Too much clearance and the engine may consume oil, lose vacuum and/or damage the seat. Too little, and the valve can stick in the guide causing the engine to run poorly if at all, and possibly causing severe damage. The last component all cylinder heads have are valve springs. The spring holds the valve against its seat. It also returns the valve to this position when the valve has been opened by the valve train or camshaft. The spring is fastened to the valve by a retainer and valve locks (sometimes called keepers). Aluminum heads will also have a valve spring shim to keep the spring from wearing away the aluminum.

An ideal method of rebuilding the cylinder head would involve replacing all of the valves, guides, seats, springs, etc. with new ones. However, depending on how the engine was maintained, often this is not necessary. A major cause of valve, guide and seat wear is an improperly tuned engine. An engine that is running too rich, will often wash the lubricating oil out of the guide with gasoline, causing it to wear rapidly. Conversely, an engine which is running too lean will place higher combustion temperatures on the valves and seats allowing them to wear or even burn. Springs fall victim to the driving habits of the individual. A driver who often runs the engine rpm to the redline will wear out or break the springs faster then one that stays well below it. Unfortunately, mileage takes it toll on all of the parts. Generally, the valves, guides, springs and seats in a cylinder head can be machined and re-used, saving you money. However, if a valve is burnt, it may be wise to replace all of the valves, since they were all operating in the same environment. The same goes for any other component on the cylinder head. Think of it as an insurance policy against future problems related to that component.

Unfortunately, the only way to find out which components need replacing, is to disassemble and carefully check each piece. After the cylinder head(s) are disassembled, thoroughly clean all of the components.

DISASSEMBLY

Before disassembling the cylinder head, you may want to fabricate some containers to hold the various parts, as some of them can be quite small (such as keepers) and easily lost. Also keeping yourself and the components organized will aid in assembly and reduce confusion. Where possible, try to maintain a components original location; this is especially important if there is not going to be any machine work performed on the components.

1. If you haven't already removed the rocker arms and/or shafts, do so now.
2. Position the head so that the springs are easily accessed.
3. Use a valve spring compressor tool, and relieve spring tension from the retainer.

➡**Due to engine varnish, the retainer may stick to the valve locks. A gentle tap with a hammer may help to break it loose.**

4. Remove the valve locks from the valve tip and/or retainer. A small magnet may help in removing the locks.
5. Lift the valve spring, tool and all, off of the valve stem.
6. If equipped, remove the valve seal. If the seal is difficult to remove with the valve in place, try removing the valve first, then the seal. Follow the steps below for valve removal.
7. Position the head to allow access for withdrawing the valve.

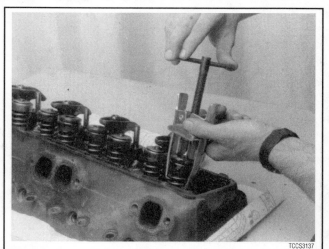

TCCS3137

When removing an OHV valve spring, use a compressor tool to relieve the tension from the retainer

TCCS3138

A small magnet will help in removal of the valve locks

TCCS3139

Be careful not to lose the small valve locks (keepers)

Remove the valve seal from the valve stem—O-ring type seal shown

Removing an umbrella/positive type seal

Invert the cylinder head and withdraw the valve from the valve guide bore

➡**Cylinder heads that have seen a lot of miles and/or abuse may have mushroomed the valve lock grove and/or tip, causing difficulty in removal of the valve. If this has happened, use a metal file to carefully remove the high spots around the lock grooves and/or tip. Only file it enough to allow removal.**

8. Remove the valve from the cylinder head.

9. If equipped, remove the valve spring shim. A small magnetic tool or screwdriver will aid in removal.

10. Repeat Steps 3 though 9 until all of the valves have been removed.

INSPECTION

Now that all of the cylinder head components are clean, it's time to inspect them for wear and/or damage. To accurately inspect them, you will need some specialized tools:

- 0–1 inch micrometer for the valves
- Dial indicator or inside diameter gauge for the valve guides
- Spring pressure test gauge

If you do not have access to the proper tools, you may want to bring the components to a shop that does.

Valves

The first thing to inspect are the valve heads. Look closely at the head, margin and face for any cracks, excessive wear or burning. The margin is the best place to look for burning. It should have a squared edge with an even width all around the diameter. When a valve burns, the margin will look melted and the edges rounded. Also inspect the valve head for any signs of tulipping. This will show as a lifting of the edges or dishing in the center of the head and will usually not occur to all of the valves. All of the heads should look the same, any that seem dished more than others are probably bad. Next, inspect the valve lock grooves and valve tips. Check for any burrs around the lock grooves, especially if you had to file them to remove the valve. Valve tips should appear flat, although slight rounding with high mileage engines is normal. Slightly worn valve tips will need to be machined flat. Last, measure the valve stem diameter with the micrometer. Measure the area that rides within the guide, especially towards the tip where most of the wear occurs. Take several measurements along its length and compare them to each other. Wear should be even along the length with little to no taper. If no minimum diameter is given in the specifications, then the stem should not read more than 0.001 in. (0.025mm) below the specification. Any valves that fail these inspections should be replaced.

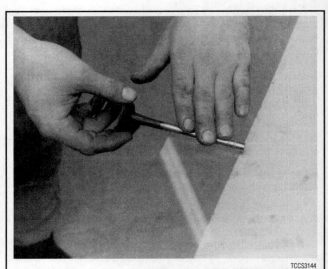

Valve stems may be rolled on a flat surface to check for bends

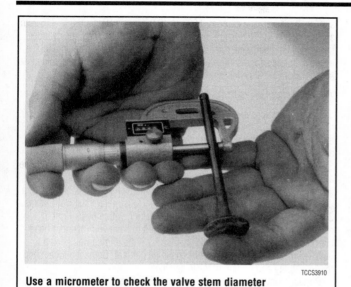

Use a micrometer to check the valve stem diameter

Springs, Retainers and Valve Locks

The first thing to check is the most obvious, broken springs. Next check the free length and squareness of each spring. If applicable, insure to distinguish between intake and exhaust springs. Use a ruler and/or carpenters square to measure the length. A carpenters square should be used to check the springs for squareness. If a spring pressure test gauge is available, check each springs rating and compare to the specifications chart. Check the readings against the specifications given. Any springs that fail these inspections should be replaced.

The spring retainers rarely need replacing, however they should still be checked as a precaution. Inspect the spring mating surface and the valve lock retention area for any signs of excessive wear. Also check for any signs of cracking. Replace any retainers that are questionable.

Valve locks should be inspected for excessive wear on the outside contact area as well as on the inner notched surface. Any locks which appear worn or broken and its respective valve should be replaced.

Use a caliper to check the valve spring free-length

Check the valve spring for squareness on a flat surface; a carpenter's square can be used

Cylinder Head

There are several things to check on the cylinder head: valve guides, seats, cylinder head surface flatness, cracks and physical damage.

VALVE GUIDES

Now that you know the valves are good, you can use them to check the guides, although a new valve, if available, is preferred. Before you measure anything, look at the guides carefully and inspect them for any cracks, chips or breakage. Also if the guide is a removable style (as in most aluminum heads), check them for any looseness or evidence of movement. All of the guides should appear to be at the same height from the spring seat. If any seem lower (or higher) from another, the guide has moved. Mount a dial indicator onto the spring side of the cylinder head. Lightly oil the valve stem and insert it into the cylinder head. Position the dial indicator against the valve stem near the tip and zero the gauge. Grasp the valve stem and wiggle towards and away from the dial indicator and observe the readings. Mount the dial indicator 90 degrees from the initial point and zero the gauge and again take a reading.

A dial gauge may be used to check valve stem-to-guide clearance; read the gauge while moving the valve stem

Compare the two readings for a out of round condition. Check the readings against the specifications given. An Inside Diameter (I.D.) gauge designed for valve guides will give you an accurate valve guide bore measurement. If the I.D. gauge is used, compare the readings with the specifications given. Any guides that fail these inspections should be replaced or machined.

VALVE SEATS

A visual inspection of the valve seats should show a slightly worn and pitted surface where the valve face contacts the seat. Inspect the seat carefully for severe pitting or cracks. Also, a seat that is badly worn will be recessed into the cylinder head. A severely worn or recessed seat may need to be replaced. All cracked seats must be replaced. A seat concentricity gauge, if available, should be used to check the seat run-out. If run-out exceeds specifications the seat must be machined (if no specification is given use 0.002 in. or 0.051mm).

CYLINDER HEAD SURFACE FLATNESS

After you have cleaned the gasket surface of the cylinder head of any old gasket material, check the head for flatness.

Place a straightedge across the gasket surface. Using feeler gauges, determine the clearance at the center of the straightedge and across the cylinder head at several points. Check along the centerline and diagonally on the head

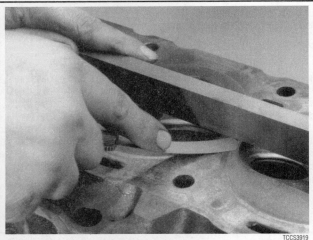

TCCS3919

Check the head for flatness across the center of the head surface using a straightedge and feeler gauge

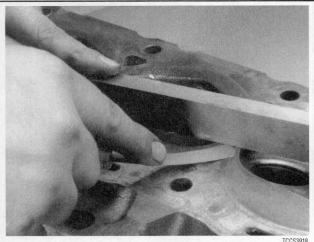

TCCS3918

Checks should also be made along both diagonals of the head surface

surface. If the warpage exceeds 0.003 in. (0.076mm) within a 6.0 in. (15.2cm) span, or 0.006 in. (0.152mm) over the total length of the head, the cylinder head must be resurfaced. After resurfacing the heads of a V-type engine, the intake manifold flange surface should be checked, and if necessary, milled proportionally to allow for the change in its mounting position.

CRACKS AND PHYSICAL DAMAGE

Generally, cracks are limited to the combustion chamber, however, it is not uncommon for the head to crack in a spark plug hole, port, outside of the head or in the valve spring/rocker arm area. The first area to inspect is always the hottest: the exhaust seat/port area.

A visual inspection should be performed, but just because you don't see a crack does not mean it is not there. Some more reliable methods for inspecting for cracks include Magnaflux®, a magnetic process or Zyglo®, a dye penetrant. Magnaflux® is used only on ferrous metal (cast iron) heads. Zyglo® uses a spray on fluorescent mixture along with a black light to reveal the cracks. It is strongly recommended to have your cylinder head checked professionally for cracks, especially if the engine was known to have overheated and/or leaked or consumed coolant. Contact a local shop for availability and pricing of these services.

Physical damage is usually very evident. For example, a broken mounting ear from dropping the head or a bent or broken stud and/or bolt. All of these defects should be fixed or, if unrepairable, the head should be replaced.

REFINISHING & REPAIRING

Many of the procedures given for refinishing and repairing the cylinder head components must be performed by a machine shop. Certain steps, if the inspected part is not worn, can be performed yourself inexpensively. However, you spent a lot of time and effort so far, why risk trying to save a couple bucks if you might have to do it all over again?

Valves

Any valves that were not replaced should be refaced and the tips ground flat. Unless you have access to a valve grinding machine, this should be done by a machine shop. If the valves are in extremely good condition, as well as the valve seats and guides, they may be lapped in without performing machine work.

It is a recommended practice to lap the valves even after machine work has been performed and/or new valves have been purchased. This insures a positive seal between the valve and seat.

LAPPING THE VALVES

➡ **Before lapping the valves to the seats, read the rest of the cylinder head section to insure that any related parts are in acceptable enough condition to continue.**

➡ **Before any valve seat machining and/or lapping can be performed, the guides must be within factory recommended specifications.**

1. Invert the cylinder head.
2. Lightly lubricate the valve stems and insert them into the cylinder head in their numbered order.
3. Raise the valve from the seat and apply a small amount of fine lapping compound to the seat.
4. Moisten the suction head of a hand-lapping tool and attach it to the head of the valve.
5. Rotate the tool between the palms of both hands, changing the position of the valve on the valve seat and lifting the tool often to prevent grooving.
6. Lap the valve until a smooth, polished circle is evident on the valve and seat.
7. Remove the tool and the valve. Wipe away all traces of the grinding compound and store the valve to maintain its lapped location.

❊❊ WARNING

Do not get the valves out of order after they have been lapped. They must be put back with the same valve seat they were lapped with.

Springs, Retainers and Valve Locks

There is no repair or refinishing possible with the springs, retainers and valve locks. If they are found to be worn or defective, they must be replaced with new (or known good) parts.

Cylinder Head

Most refinishing procedures dealing with the cylinder head must be performed by a machine shop. Read the sections below and review your inspection data to determine whether or not machining is necessary.

VALVE GUIDE

➡️**If any machining or replacements are made to the valve guides, the seats must be machined.**

Unless the valve guides need machining or replacing, the only service to perform is to thoroughly clean them of any dirt or oil residue.

There are only two types of valve guides used on automobile engines: the replaceable-type (all aluminum heads) and the cast-in integral-type (most cast iron heads). There are four recommended methods for repairing worn guides.

- Knurling
- Inserts
- Reaming oversize
- Replacing

Knurling is a process in which metal is displaced and raised, thereby reducing clearance, giving a true center, and providing oil control. It is the least expensive way of repairing the valve guides. However, it is not necessarily the best, and in some cases, a knurled valve guide will not stand up for more than a short time. It requires a special knurlizer and precision reaming tools to obtain proper clearances. It would not be cost effective to purchase these tools, unless you plan on rebuilding several of the same cylinder head.

Installing a guide insert involves machining the guide to accept a bronze insert. One style is the coil-type which is installed into a threaded guide. Another is the thin-walled insert where the guide is reamed oversize to accept a split-sleeve insert. After the insert is installed, a special tool is then run through the guide to expand the insert, locking it to the guide. The insert is then reamed to the standard size for proper valve clearance.

Reaming for oversize valves restores normal clearances and provides a true valve seat. Most cast-in type guides can be reamed to accept an valve with an oversize stem. The cost factor for this can become quite high as you will need to purchase the reamer and new, oversize stem valves for all guides which were reamed. Oversizes are generally 0.003 to 0.030 in. (0.076 to 0.762mm), with 0.015 in. (0.381mm) being the most common.

To replace cast-in type valve guides, they must be drilled out, then reamed to accept replacement guides. This must be done on a fixture which will allow centering and leveling off of the original valve seat or guide, otherwise a serious guide-to-seat misalignment may occur making it impossible to properly machine the seat.

Replaceable-type guides are pressed into the cylinder head. A hammer and a stepped drift or punch may be used to install and remove the guides. Before removing the guides, measure the protrusion on the spring side of the head and record it for installation. Use the stepped drift to hammer out the old guide from the combustion chamber side of the head. When installing, determine whether or not the guide also seals a water jacket in the head, and if it does, use the recommended sealing agent. If there is no water jacket, grease the valve guide and its bore. Use the stepped drift, and hammer the new guide into the cylinder head from the spring side of the cylinder head. A stack of washers the same thickness as the measured protrusion may help the installation process.

VALVE SEATS

➡️**Before any valve seat machining can be performed, the guides must be within factory recommended specifications.**

➡️**If any machining or replacements were made to the valve guides, the seats must be machined.**

If the seats are in good condition, the valves can be lapped to the seats, and the cylinder head assembled. See the valves section for instructions on lapping.

If the valve seats are worn, cracked or damaged, they must be serviced by a machine shop. The valve seat must be perfectly centered to the valve guide, which requires very accurate machining.

CYLINDER HEAD SURFACE

If the cylinder head is warped, it must be machined flat. If the warpage is extremely severe, the head may need to be replaced. In some instances, it may be possible to straighten a warped head enough to allow machining. In either case, contact a professional machine shop for service.

CRACKS AND PHYSICAL DAMAGE

Certain cracks can be repaired in both cast iron and aluminum heads. For cast iron, a tapered threaded insert is installed along the length of the crack. Aluminum can also use the tapered inserts, however welding is the preferred method. Some physical damage can be repaired through brazing or welding. Contact a machine shop to get expert advice for your particular dilemma.

ASSEMBLY

The first step for any assembly job is to have a clean area in which to work. Next, thoroughly clean all of the parts and components that are to be assembled. Finally, place all of the components onto a suitable work space and, if necessary, arrange the parts to their respective positions.

1. Lightly lubricate the valve stems and insert all of the valves into the cylinder head. If possible, maintain their original locations.
2. If equipped, install any valve spring shims which were removed.
3. If equipped, install the new valve seals, keeping the following in mind:
- If the valve seal presses over the guide, lightly lubricate the outer guide surfaces.
- If the seal is an O-ring type, it is installed just after compressing the spring but before the valve locks.
4. Place the valve spring and retainer over the stem.
5. Position the spring compressor tool and compress the spring.
6. Assemble the valve locks to the stem.
7. Relieve the spring pressure slowly and insure that neither valve lock becomes dislodged by the retainer.
8. Remove the spring compressor tool.
9. Repeat Steps 2 through 8 until all of the springs have been installed.

Engine Block

GENERAL INFORMATION

A thorough overhaul or rebuild of an engine block would include replacing the pistons, rings, bearings, timing belt/chain assembly and oil pump. For OHV engines also include a new camshaft and lifters. The block would then have the cylinders bored and honed oversize (or if using removable cylinder sleeves, new sleeves installed) and the crankshaft would be cut undersize to provide new wearing surfaces and perfect clearances. However, your particular engine may not have everything worn out. What if only the piston rings have worn out and the clearances on everything else are still within factory specifications? Well, you could just replace the rings and put it back together, but this would be a very rare example. Chances are, if one component in your engine is worn, other components are sure to follow, and soon. At the very least, you should always replace the rings, bearings and oil pump. This is what is commonly called a "freshen up".

Cylinder Ridge Removal

Because the top piston ring does not travel to the very top of the cylinder, a ridge is built up between the end of the travel and the top of the cylinder bore.

Pushing the piston and connecting rod assembly past the ridge can be difficult, and damage to the piston ring lands could occur. If the ridge is not removed before installing a new piston or not removed at all, piston ring breakage and piston damage may occur.

➡It is always recommended that you remove any cylinder ridges before removing the piston and connecting rod assemblies. If you know that new pistons are going to be installed and the engine block will be bored oversize, you may be able to forego this step. However, some ridges may actually prevent the assemblies from being removed, necessitating its removal.

There are several different types of ridge reamers on the market, none of which are inexpensive. Unless a great deal of engine rebuilding is anticipated, borrow or rent a reamer.

1. Turn the crankshaft until the piston is at the bottom of its travel.
2. Cover the head of the piston with a rag.
3. Follow the tool manufacturers instructions and cut away the ridge, exercising extreme care to avoid cutting too deeply.
4. Remove the ridge reamer, the rag and as many of the cuttings as possible. Continue until all of the cylinder ridges have been removed.

DISASSEMBLY

The engine disassembly instructions following assume that you have the engine mounted on an engine stand. If not, it is easiest to disassemble the engine on a bench or the floor with it resting on the bellhousing or transmission mounting surface. You must be able to access the connecting rod fasteners and turn the crankshaft during disassembly. Also, all engine covers (timing, front, side, oil pan, whatever) should have already been removed. Engines which are seized or locked up may not be able to be completely disassembled, and a core (salvage yard) engine should be purchased.

If not done during the cylinder head removal, remove the pushrods and lifters, keeping them in order for assembly. Remove the timing gears and/or timing chain assembly, then remove the oil pump drive assembly and withdraw the camshaft from the engine block. Remove the oil pick-up and pump assembly. If equipped, remove any balance or auxiliary shafts. If necessary, remove the cylinder ridge from the top of the bore. See the cylinder ridge removal procedure earlier in this section.

Rotate the engine over so that the crankshaft is exposed. Use a number punch or scribe and mark each connecting rod with its respective cylinder number. The cylinder closest to the front of the engine is always number 1. However, depending on the engine placement, the front of the engine could either be the flywheel or damper/pulley end. Generally the front of the engine faces the front of the vehicle. Use a number punch or scribe and also mark the main bearing caps from front to rear with the front most cap being number 1 (if there are five caps, mark them 1 through 5, front to rear).

✳ WARNING

Take special care when pushing the connecting rod up from the crankshaft because the sharp threads of the rod bolts/studs will score the crankshaft journal. Insure that special plastic caps are installed over them, or cut two pieces of rubber hose to do the same.

Again, rotate the engine, this time to position the number one cylinder bore (head surface) up. Turn the crankshaft until the number one piston is at the bottom of its travel, this should allow the maximum access to its connecting rod. Remove the number one connecting rods fasteners and cap and place two lengths of rubber hose over the rod bolts/studs to protect the crankshaft from damage. Using a sturdy wooden dowel and a hammer, push the connecting rod up about 1 in. (25mm) from the crankshaft and remove the upper bearing insert. Continue pushing or tapping the connecting rod up until the piston rings are out of the cylinder bore. Remove the piston and rod by hand, put the upper half of the bearing insert back into the rod, install the cap with its bearing insert installed, and hand-tighten the cap fasteners. If the parts are kept in order in this manner, they will not get lost and you will be able to tell which bearings came form what cylinder if any problems are discovered and diagnosis is necessary. Remove all the other piston assemblies in the same manner.

TCCS3803

Place rubber hose over the connecting rod studs to protect the crankshaft and cylinder bores from damage

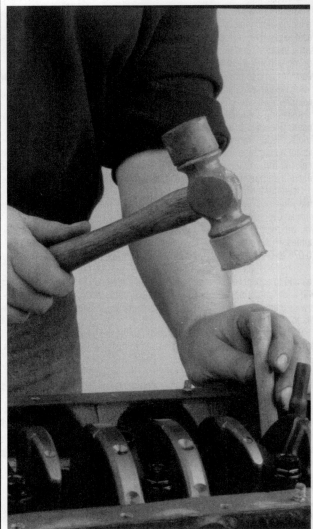

TCCS3804

Carefully tap the piston out of the bore using a wooden dowel

On V-style engines, remove all of the pistons from one bank, then reposition the engine with the other cylinder bank head surface up, and remove that banks piston assemblies.

The only remaining component in the engine block should now be the crankshaft. Loosen the main bearing caps evenly until the fasteners can be turned by hand, then remove them and the caps. Remove the crankshaft from the engine block. Thoroughly clean all of the components.

INSPECTION

Now that the engine block and all of its components are clean, it's time to inspect them for wear and/or damage. To accurately inspect them, you will need some specialized tools:

- Two or three separate micrometers to measure the pistons and crankshaft journals
- A dial indicator
- Telescoping gauges for the cylinder bores
- A rod alignment fixture to check for bent connecting rods

If you do not have access to the proper tools, you may want to bring the components to a shop that does.

Generally, you shouldn't expect cracks in the engine block or its components unless it was known to leak, consume or mix engine fluids, it was severely overheated, or there was evidence of bad bearings and/or crankshaft damage. A visual inspection should be performed on all of the components, but just because you don't see a crack does not mean it is not there. Some more reliable methods for inspecting for cracks include Magnaflux®, a magnetic process or Zyglo®, a dye penetrant. Magnaflux® is used only on ferrous metal (cast iron). Zyglo® uses a spray on fluorescent mixture along with a black light to reveal the cracks. It is strongly recommended to have your engine block checked professionally for cracks, especially if the engine was known to have overheated and/or leaked or consumed coolant. Contact a local shop for availability and pricing of these services.

Engine Block

ENGINE BLOCK BEARING ALIGNMENT

Remove the main bearing caps and, if still installed, the main bearing inserts. Inspect all of the main bearing saddles and caps for damage, burrs or high spots. If damage is found, and it is caused from a spun main bearing, the block will need to be align-bored or, if severe enough, replacement. Any burrs or high spots should be carefully removed with a metal file.

Place a straightedge on the bearing saddles, in the engine block, along the centerline of the crankshaft. If any clearance exists between the straightedge and the saddles, the block must be align-bored.

Align-boring consists of machining the main bearing saddles and caps by means of a flycutter that runs through the bearing saddles.

DECK FLATNESS

The top of the engine block where the cylinder head mounts is called the deck. Insure that the deck surface is clean of dirt, carbon deposits and old gasket material. Place a straightedge across the surface of the deck along its centerline and, using feeler gauges, check the clearance along several points. Repeat the checking procedure with the straightedge placed along both diagonals of the deck surface. If the reading exceeds 0.003 in. (0.076mm) within a 6.0 in. (15.2cm) span, or 0.006 in. (0.152mm) over the total length of the deck, it must be machined.

CYLINDER BORES

The cylinder bores house the pistons and are slightly larger than the pistons themselves. A common piston-to-bore clearance is 0.0015–0.0025 in. (0.0381mm–0.0635mm). Inspect and measure the cylinder bores. The bore should be checked for out-of-roundness, taper and size. The results of this inspection will determine whether the cylinder can be used in its existing size and condition, or a rebore to the next oversize is required (or in the case of removable sleeves, have replacements installed).

The amount of cylinder wall wear is always greater at the top of the cylinder than at the bottom. This wear is known as taper. Any cylinder that has a taper of 0.0012 in. (0.305mm) or more, must be rebored.

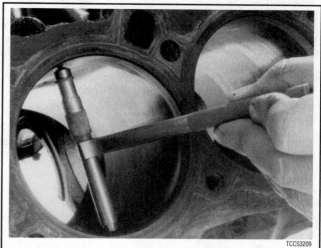

Use a telescoping gauge to measure the cylinder bore diameter—take several readings within the same bore

Measurements are taken at a number of positions in each cylinder: at the top, middle and bottom and at two points at each position; that is, at a point 90 degrees from the crankshaft centerline, as well as a point parallel to the crankshaft centerline. The measurements are made with either a special dial indicator or a telescopic gauge and micrometer. If the necessary precision tools to check the bore are not available, take the block to a machine shop and have them mike it. Also if you don't have the tools to check the cylinder bores, chances are you will not have the necessary devices to check the pistons, connecting rods and crankshaft. Take these components with you and save yourself an extra trip.

For our procedures, we will use a telescopic gauge and a micrometer. You will need one of each, with a measuring range which covers your cylinder bore size.

1. Position the telescopic gauge in the cylinder bore, loosen the gauges lock and allow it to expand.

➡**Your first two readings will be at the top of the cylinder bore, then proceed to the middle and finally the bottom, making a total of six measurements.**

2. Hold the gauge square in the bore, 90 degrees from the crankshaft centerline, and gently tighten the lock. Tilt the gauge back to remove it from the bore.
3. Measure the gauge with the micrometer and record the reading.
4. Again, hold the gauge square in the bore, this time parallel to the crankshaft centerline, and gently tighten the lock. Again, you will tilt the gauge back to remove it from the bore.
5. Measure the gauge with the micrometer and record this reading. The difference between these two readings is the out-of-round measurement of the cylinder.
6. Repeat steps 1 through 5, each time going to the next lower position, until you reach the bottom of the cylinder. Then go to the next cylinder, and continue until all of the cylinders have been measured.

The difference between these measurements will tell you all about the wear in your cylinders. The measurements which were taken 90 degrees from the crankshaft centerline will always reflect the most wear. That is because at this position is where the engine power presses the piston against the cylinder bore the hardest. This is known as thrust wear. Take your top, 90 degree measurement and compare it to your bottom, 90 degree measurement. The difference between them is the taper. When you measure your pistons, you will compare these readings to your piston sizes and determine piston-to-wall clearance.

Crankshaft

Inspect the crankshaft for visible signs of wear or damage. All of the journals should be perfectly round and smooth. Slight scores are normal for a used crankshaft, but you should hardly feel them with your fingernail. When measuring the crankshaft with a micrometer, you will take readings at the front and rear of each journal, then turn the micrometer 90 degrees and take two more readings, front and rear. The difference between the front-to-rear readings is the journal taper and the first-to-90 degree reading is the out-of-round measurement. Generally, there should be no taper or out-of-roundness found, however, up to 0.0005 in. (0.0127mm) for either can be overlooked. Also, the readings should fall within the factory specifications for journal diameters.

If the crankshaft journals fall within specifications, it is recommended that it be polished before being returned to service. Polishing the crankshaft insures that any minor burrs or high spots are smoothed, thereby reducing the chance of scoring the new bearings.

Pistons and Connecting Rods

PISTONS

The piston should be visually inspected for any signs of cracking or burning (caused by hot spots or detonation), and scuffing or excessive wear on the skirts. The wristpin attaches the piston to the connecting rod. The piston should move freely on the wrist pin, both sliding and pivoting. Grasp the connecting rod securely, or mount it in a vise, and try to rock the piston back and forth along the centerline of the wristpin. There should not be any excessive play evident between the piston and the pin. If there are C-clips retaining the pin in the piston then you have wrist pin bushings in the rods. There should not be any excessive play between the wrist pin and the rod bushing. Normal clearance for the wrist pin is approx. 0.001–0.002 in. (0.025mm–0.051mm).

Use a micrometer and measure the diameter of the piston, perpendicular to the wrist pin, on the skirt. Compare the reading to its original cylinder measurement obtained earlier. The difference between the two readings is the piston-to-wall clearance. If the clearance is within specifications, the piston may be used as is. If the piston is out of specification, but the bore is not, you will need a new piston. If both are out of specification, you will need the cylinder rebored and oversize pistons installed. Generally if two or more pistons/bores are out of specification, it is best to rebore the entire block and purchase a complete set of oversize pistons.

TCCS3210

Measure the piston's outer diameter, perpendicular to the wrist pin, with a micrometer

CONNECTING ROD

You should have the connecting rod checked for straightness at a machine shop. If the connecting rod is bent, it will unevenly wear the bearing and piston, as well as place greater stress on these components. Any bent or twisted connecting rods must be replaced. If the rods are straight and the wrist pin clearance is within specifications, then only the bearing end of the rod need be checked. Place the connecting rod into a vice, with the bearing inserts in place, install the cap to the rod and torque the fasteners to specifications. Use a telescoping gauge and carefully measure the inside diameter of the bearings. Compare this reading to the rods original crankshaft journal diameter measurement. The difference is the oil clearance. If the oil clearance is not within specifications, install new bearings in the rod and take another measurement. If the clearance is still out of specifications, and the crankshaft is not, the rod will need to be reconditioned by a machine shop.

➡**You can also use Plastigage® to check the bearing clearances. The assembling section has complete instructions on its use.**

Camshaft

Inspect the camshaft and lifters/followers as described earlier in this section.

Bearings

All of the engine bearings should be visually inspected for wear and/or damage. The bearing should look evenly worn all around with no deep scores or pits. If the bearing is severely worn, scored, pitted or heat blued, then the bearing, and the components that use it, should be brought to a machine shop for inspection. Full-circle bearings (used on most camshafts, auxiliary shafts, balance shafts, etc.) require specialized tools for removal and installation, and should be brought to a machine shop for service.

Oil Pump

➡**The oil pump is responsible for providing constant lubrication to the whole engine and so it is recommended that a new oil pump be installed when rebuilding the engine.**

Completely disassemble the oil pump and thoroughly clean all of the components. Inspect the oil pump gears and housing for wear and/or damage. Insure that the pressure relief valve operates properly and there is no binding or sticking due to varnish or debris. If all of the parts are in proper working condition, lubricate the gears and relief valve, and assemble the pump.

REFINISHING

Almost all engine block refinishing must be performed by a machine shop. If the cylinders are not to be rebored, then the cylinder glaze can be removed with a ball hone. When removing cylinder glaze with a ball hone,

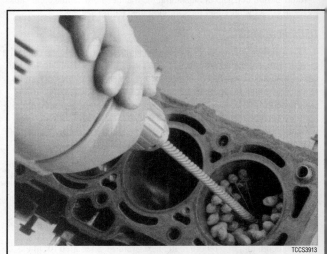

TCCS3913

Use a ball type cylinder hone to remove any glaze and provide a new surface for seating the piston rings

use a light or penetrating type oil to lubricate the hone. Do not allow the hone to run dry as this may cause excessive scoring of the cylinder bores and wear on the hone. If new pistons are required, they will need to be installed to the connecting rods. This should be performed by a machine shop as the pistons must be installed in the correct relationship to the rod or engine damage can occur.

Pistons and Connecting Rods

Only pistons with the wrist pin retained by C-clips are serviceable by the home-mechanic. Press fit pistons require special presses and/or heaters to remove/install the connecting rod and should only be performed by a machine shop.

All pistons will have a mark indicating the direction to the front of the engine and the must be installed into the engine in that manner. Usually it is a notch or arrow on the top of the piston, or it may be the letter F cast or

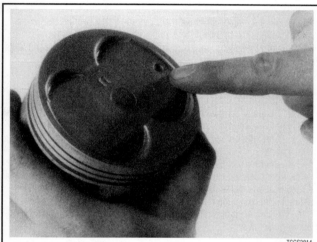

TCCS3814

Most pistons are marked to indicate positioning in the engine (usually a mark means the side facing the front)

stamped into the piston.

C-CLIP TYPE PISTONS

1. Note the location of the forward mark on the piston and mark the connecting rod in relation.
2. Remove the C-clips from the piston and withdraw the wrist pin.

➡**Varnish build-up or C-clip groove burrs may increase the difficulty of removing the wrist pin. If necessary, use a punch or drift to carefully tap the wrist pin out.**

3. Insure that the wrist pin bushing in the connecting rod is usable, and lubricate it with assembly lube.
4. Remove the wrist pin from the new piston and lubricate the pin bores on the piston.
5. Align the forward marks on the piston and the connecting rod and install the wrist pin.
6. The new C-clips will have a flat and a rounded side to them. Install both C-clips with the flat side facing out.
7. Repeat all of the steps for each piston being replaced.

ASSEMBLY

Before you begin assembling the engine, first give yourself a clean, dirt free work area. Next, clean every engine component again. The key to a good assembly is cleanliness.

Mount the engine block into the engine stand and wash it one last time using water and detergent (dishwashing detergent works well). While washing it, scrub the cylinder bores with a soft bristle brush and thoroughly clean all of the oil passages. Completely dry the engine and spray the entire assembly down with an anti-rust solution such as WD-40® or similar product. Take a clean lint-free rag and wipe up any excess anti-rust solution from the bores, bearing saddles, etc. Repeat the final cleaning process on the crankshaft. Replace any freeze or oil galley plugs which were removed during disassembly.

Crankshaft

1. Remove the main bearing inserts from the block and bearing caps.
2. If the crankshaft main bearing journals have been refinished to a definite undersize, install the correct undersize bearing. Be sure that the bearing inserts and bearing bores are clean. Foreign material under inserts will distort bearing and cause failure.
3. Place the upper main bearing inserts in bores with tang in slot.

➡**The oil holes in the bearing inserts must be aligned with the oil holes in the cylinder block.**

4. Install the lower main bearing inserts in bearing caps.
5. Clean the mating surfaces of block and rear main bearing cap.
6. Carefully lower the crankshaft into place. Be careful not to damage bearing surfaces.
7. Check the clearance of each main bearing by using the following procedure:
   a. Place a piece of Plastigage® or its equivalent, on bearing surface across full width of bearing cap and about ¼ in. off center.

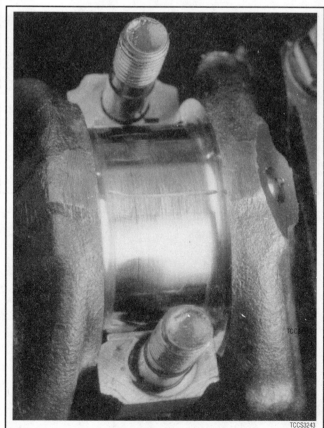

TCCS3243

Apply a strip of gauging material to the bearing journal, then install and torque the cap

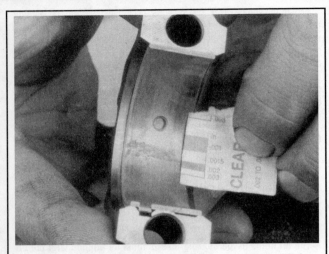

After the cap is removed again, use the scale supplied with the gauging material to check the clearance

TCCS3805

A dial gauge may be used to check crankshaft end-play

TCCS3806

Carefully pry the crankshaft back and forth while reading the dial gauge for end-play

b. Install cap and tighten bolts to specifications. Do not turn crankshaft while Plastigage® is in place.

c. Remove the cap. Using the supplied Plastigage® scale, check width of Plastigage® at widest point to get maximum clearance. Difference between readings is taper of journal.

d. If clearance exceeds specified limits, try a 0.001 in. or 0.002 in. undersize bearing in combination with the standard bearing. Bearing clearance must be within specified limits. If standard and 0.002 in. undersize bearing does not bring clearance within desired limits, refinish crankshaft journal, then install undersize bearings.

8. Install the rear main seal.

9. After the bearings have been fitted, apply a light coat of engine oil to the journals and bearings. Install the rear main bearing cap. Install all bearing caps except the thrust bearing cap. Be sure that main bearing caps are installed in original locations. Tighten the bearing cap bolts to specifications.

10. Install the thrust bearing cap with bolts finger-tight.

11. Pry the crankshaft forward against the thrust surface of upper half of bearing.

12. Hold the crankshaft forward and pry the thrust bearing cap to the rear. This aligns the thrust surfaces of both halves of the bearing.

13. Retain the forward pressure on the crankshaft. Tighten the cap bolts to specifications.

14. Measure the crankshaft end-play as follows:

a. Mount a dial gauge to the engine block and position the tip of the gauge to read from the crankshaft end.

b. Carefully pry the crankshaft toward the rear of the engine and hold it there while you zero the gauge.

c. Carefully pry the crankshaft toward the front of the engine and read the gauge.

d. Confirm that the reading is within specifications. If not, install a new thrust bearing and repeat the procedure. If the reading is still out of specifications with a new bearing, have a machine shop inspect the thrust surfaces of the crankshaft, and if possible, repair it.

15. Rotate the crankshaft so as to position the first rod journal to the bottom of its stroke.

Pistons and Connecting Rods

1. Before installing the piston/connecting rod assembly, oil the pistons, piston rings and the cylinder walls with light engine oil. Install connecting rod bolt protectors or rubber hose onto the connecting rod bolts/studs. Also perform the following:

a. Select the proper ring set for the size cylinder bore.

b. Position the ring in the bore in which it is going to be used.

c. Push the ring down into the bore area where normal ring wear is not encountered.

d. Use the head of the piston to position the ring in the bore so that the ring is square with the cylinder wall. Use caution to avoid damage to the ring or cylinder bore.

e. Measure the gap between the ends of the ring with a feeler gauge. Ring gap in a worn cylinder is normally greater than specification. If the ring gap is greater than the specified limits, try an oversize ring set.

f. Check the ring side clearance of the compression rings with a feeler gauge inserted between the ring and its lower land according to specification. The gauge should slide freely around the entire ring circumference without binding. Any wear that occurs will form a step at the inner portion of the lower land. If the lower lands have high steps, the piston should be replaced.

2. Unless new pistons are installed, be sure to install the pistons in the cylinders from which they were removed. The numbers on the connecting rod and bearing cap must be on the same side when installed in the cylinder bore. If a connecting rod is ever transposed from one engine or cylinder to another, new bearings should be fitted and the connecting rod should be numbered to correspond with the new cylinder number. The notch on the piston head goes toward the front of the engine.

3. Install all of the rod bearing inserts into the rods and caps.

4. Install the rings to the pistons. Install the oil control ring first, then the second compression ring and finally the top compression ring. Use a

Checking the piston ring-to-ring groove side clearance using the ring and a feeler gauge

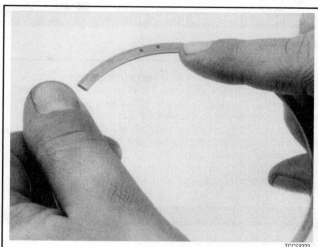

Most rings are marked to show which side of the ring should face up when installed to the piston

The notch on the side of the bearing cap matches the tang on the bearing insert

Install the piston and rod assembly into the block using a ring compressor and the handle of a hammer

piston ring expander tool to aid in installation and to help reduce the chance of breakage.

5. Make sure the ring gaps are properly spaced around the circumference of the piston. Fit a piston ring compressor around the piston and slide the piston and connecting rod assembly down into the cylinder bore, pushing it in with the wooden hammer handle. Push the piston down until it is only slightly below the top of the cylinder bore. Guide the connecting rod onto the crankshaft bearing journal carefully, to avoid damaging the crankshaft.

6. Check the bearing clearance of all the rod bearings, fitting them to the crankshaft bearing journals. Follow the procedure in the crankshaft installation above.

7. After the bearings have been fitted, apply a light coating of assembly oil to the journals and bearings.

8. Turn the crankshaft until the appropriate bearing journal is at the bottom of its stroke, then push the piston assembly all the way down until the connecting rod bearing seats on the crankshaft journal. Be careful not to

allow the bearing cap screws to strike the crankshaft bearing journals and damage them.

9. After the piston and connecting rod assemblies have been installed, check the connecting rod side clearance on each crankshaft journal.

10. Prime and install the oil pump and the oil pump intake tube.

11. Install the balance shaft assembly.

Camshaft, Lifters and Timing assembly

1. Install the camshaft.
2. Install the lifters/followers into their bores.
3. Install the timing gears/chain assembly.

CYLINDER HEAD(S)

1. Install the cylinder head(s) using new gaskets.
2. Assemble the rest of the valve train (pushrods and rocker arms and/or shafts).

Engine Start-up and Break-in

STARTING THE ENGINE

Now that the engine is installed and every wire and hose is properly connected, go back and double check that all coolant and vacuum hoses are connected. Check that you oil drain plug is installed and properly tightened. If not already done, install a new oil filter onto the engine. Fill the crankcase with the proper amount and grade of engine oil. Fill the cooling system with a 50/50 mixture of coolant/water.

1. Connect the vehicle battery.
2. Start the engine. Keep your eye on your oil pressure indicator; if it does not indicate oil pressure within 10 seconds of starting, turn the vehicle off.

❋❋ WARNING

Damage to the engine can result if it is allowed to run with no oil pressure. Check the engine oil level to make sure that it is full. Check for any leaks and if found, repair the leaks before continuing. If there is still no indication of oil pressure, you may need to prime the system.

3. Confirm that there are no fluid leaks (oil or other).
4. Allow the engine to reach normal operating temperature (the upper radiator hose will be hot to the touch).
5. If necessary, set the ignition timing.
6. Install any remaining components such as the air cleaner (if removed for ignition timing) or body panels which were removed.

BREAKING IT IN

Make the first miles on the new engine, easy ones. Vary the speed but do not accelerate hard. Most importantly, do not lug the engine, and avoid sustained high speeds until at least 100 miles. Check the engine oil and coolant levels frequently. Expect the engine to use a little oil until the rings seat. Change the oil and filter at 500 miles, 1500 miles, then every 3000 miles past that.

KEEP IT MAINTAINED

Now that you have just gone through all of that hard work, keep yourself from doing it all over again by thoroughly maintaining it. Not that you may not have maintained it before, heck you could have had one to two hundred thousand miles on it before doing this. However, you may have bought the vehicle used, and the previous owner did not keep up on maintenance. Which is why you just went through all of that hard work. See?

TORQUE SPECIFICATIONS

Component	US	Metric
Thermostat Housing Crossover		
6.2L, 6.5L engines		
1987–97	31 ft. lbs	42 Nm
Turbocharger		
Intake manifold studsManifold studs	31 ft. lbs.	42 Nm
Center intake manifold-to-intake manifold bolts	17 ft. lbs.	23 Nm
Heat shield bolts (top and right)	22 ft. lbs.	30 Nm
Heat shield bolts (left)	17 ft. lbs.	23 Nm
Turbo mounting bolts	48 ft. lbs.	65 Nm
Turbo exhaust clamps	90 in. lbs.	10 Nm
Water pump		
4.3L, 5.0L, 5.7L, 7.4L engines	30 ft. lbs.	41 Nm
6.2L, 6.5L engines		
3 lower right bolts	31 ft. lbs.	42 Nm
All other bolts	17 ft. lbs.	23 Nm
Thermostat		
Gasoline engines		
4.3L, 5.0L and 5.7L models		
1987–95	21 ft. lbs.	28 Nm
4.3L, 5.0L and 5.7L models		
1996–97	18 ft. lbs.	25 Nm
7.4L models		
1987–95	27 ft. lbs	37 Nm
1996–97	30 ft. lbs.	40 Nm
Diesel engines		
1987–91 models	35 ft. lbs.	47 Nm
1992–97 models	31 ft. lbs.	42 Nm

88193C19

USING A VACUUM GAUGE

White needle = steady needle   *Dark needle = drifting needle*

The vacuum gauge is one of the most useful and easy-to-use diagnostic tools. It is inexpensive, easy to hook up, and provides valuable information about the condition of your engine.

Indication: Normal engine in good condition

Gauge reading: Steady, from 17–22 in./Hg.

Indication: Sticking valve or ignition miss

Gauge reading: Needle fluctuates from 15–20 in./Hg. at idle

Indication: Late ignition or valve timing, low compression, stuck throttle valve, leaking carburetor or manifold gasket.

Gauge reading: Low (15–20 in./Hg.) but steady

Indication: Improper carburetor adjustment, or minor intake leak at carburetor or manifold

NOTE: Bad fuel injector O-rings may also cause this reading.

Gauge reading: Drifting needle

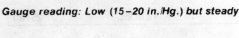

Indication: Weak valve springs, worn valve stem guides, or leaky cylinder head gasket (vibrating excessively at all speeds).

NOTE: A plugged catalytic converter may also cause this reading.

Gauge reading: Needle fluctuates as engine speed increases

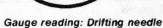

Indication: Burnt valve or improper valve clearance. The needle will drop when the defective valve operates.

Gauge reading: Steady needle, but drops regularly

Indication: Choked muffler or obstruction in system. Speed up the engine. Choked muffler will exhibit a slow drop of vacuum to zero.

Gauge reading: Gradual drop in reading at idle

Indication: Worn valve guides

Gauge reading: Needle vibrates excessively at idle, but steadies as engine speed increases

TCCS3C01

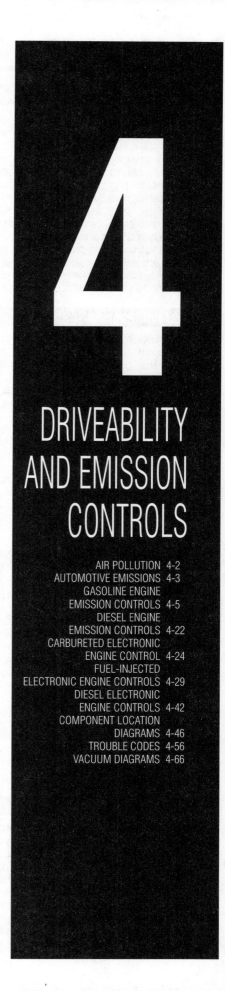

4

DRIVEABILITY AND EMISSION CONTROLS

AIR POLLUTION

The earth's atmosphere, at or near sea level, consists approximately of 78 percent nitrogen, 21 percent oxygen and 1 percent other gases. If it were possible to remain in this state, 100 percent clean air would result. However, many varied sources allow other gases and particulates to mix with the clean air, causing our atmosphere to become unclean or polluted.

Some of these pollutants are visible while others are invisible, with each having the capability of causing distress to the eyes, ears, throat, skin and respiratory system. Should these pollutants become concentrated in a specific area and under certain conditions, death could result due to the displacement or chemical change of the oxygen content in the air. These pollutants can also cause great damage to the environment and to the many man made objects that are exposed to the elements.

To better understand the causes of air pollution, the pollutants can be categorized into 3 separate types, natural, industrial and automotive.

Natural Pollutants

Natural pollution has been present on earth since before man appeared and continues to be a factor when discussing air pollution, although it causes only a small percentage of the overall pollution problem. It is the direct result of decaying organic matter, wind born smoke and particulates from such natural events as plain and forest fires (ignited by heat or lightning), volcanic ash, sand and dust which can spread over a large area of the countryside.

Such a phenomenon of natural pollution has been seen in the form of volcanic eruptions, with the resulting plume of smoke, steam and volcanic ash blotting out the sun's rays as it spreads and rises higher into the atmosphere. As it travels into the atmosphere the upper air currents catch and carry the smoke and ash, while condensing the steam back into water vapor. As the water vapor, smoke and ash travel on their journey, the smoke dissipates into the atmosphere while the ash and moisture settle back to earth in a trail hundreds of miles long. In some cases, lives are lost and millions of dollars of property damage result.

Industrial Pollutants

Industrial pollution is caused primarily by industrial processes, the burning of coal, oil and natural gas, which in turn produce smoke and fumes. Because the burning fuels contain large amounts of sulfur, the principal ingredients of smoke and fumes are sulfur dioxide and particulate matter. This type of pollutant occurs most severely during still, damp and cool weather, such as at night. Even in its less severe form, this pollutant is not confined to just cities. Because of air movements, the pollutants move for miles over the surrounding countryside, leaving in its path a barren and unhealthy environment for all living things.

Working with Federal, State and Local mandated regulations and by carefully monitoring emissions, big business has greatly reduced the amount of pollutant introduced from its industrial sources, striving to obtain an acceptable level. Because of the mandated industrial emission clean up, many land areas and streams in and around the cities that were formerly barren of vegetation and life, have now begun to move back in the direction of nature's intended balance.

Automotive Pollutants

The third major source of air pollution is automotive emissions. The emissions from the internal combustion engines were not an appreciable problem years ago because of the small number of registered vehicles and the nation's small highway system. However, during the early 1950's, the trend of the American people was to move from the cities to the surrounding suburbs. This caused an immediate problem in transportation because the majority of suburbs were not afforded mass transit conveniences. This lack of transportation created an attractive market for the automobile manufacturers, which resulted in a dramatic increase in the number of vehicles produced and sold, along with a marked increase in highway construction

between cities and the suburbs. Multi-vehicle families emerged with a growing emphasis placed on an individual vehicle per family member. As the increase in vehicle ownership and usage occurred, so did pollutant levels in and around the cities, as suburbanites drove daily to their businesses and employment, returning at the end of the day to their homes in the suburbs.

It was noted that a smoke and fog type haze was being formed and at times, remained in suspension over the cities, taking time to dissipate. At first this "smog," derived from the words "smoke" and "fog," was thought to result from industrial pollution but it was determined that automobile emissions shared the blame. It was discovered that when normal automobile emissions were exposed to sunlight for a period of time, complex chemical reactions would take place.

It is now known that smog is a photo chemical layer which develops when certain oxides of nitrogen (NOx) and unburned hydrocarbons (HC) from automobile emissions are exposed to sunlight. Pollution was more severe when smog would become stagnant over an area in which a warm layer of air settled over the top of the cooler air mass, trapping and holding the cooler mass at ground level. The trapped cooler air would keep the emissions from being dispersed and diluted through normal air flows. This type of air stagnation was given the name "Temperature Inversion."

TEMPERATURE INVERSION

In normal weather situations, surface air is warmed by heat radiating from the earth's surface and the sun's rays. This causes it to rise upward, into the atmosphere. Upon rising it will cool through a convection type heat exchange with the cooler upper air. As warm air rises, the surface pollutants are carried upward and dissipated into the atmosphere.

When a temperature inversion occurs, we find the higher air is no longer cooler, but is warmer than the surface air, causing the cooler surface air to become trapped. This warm air blanket can extend from above ground level to a few hundred or even a few thousand feet into the air. As the surface air is trapped, so are the pollutants, causing a severe smog condition. Should this stagnant air mass extend to a few thousand feet high, enough air movement with the inversion takes place to allow the smog layer to rise above ground level but the pollutants still cannot dissipate. This inversion can remain for days over an area, with the smog level only rising or lowering from ground level to a few hundred feet high. Meanwhile, the pollutant levels increase, causing eye irritation, respiratory problems, reduced visibility, plant damage and, in some cases, disease.

This inversion phenomenon was first noted in the Los Angeles, California area. The city lies in terrain resembling a basin and with certain weather conditions, a cold air mass is held in the basin while a warmer air mass covers it like a lid.

Because this type of condition was first documented as prevalent in the Los Angeles area, this type of trapped pollution was named Los Angeles Smog, although it occurs in other areas where a large concentration of automobiles are used and the air remains stagnant for any length of time.

HEAT TRANSFER

Consider the internal combustion engine as a machine in which raw materials must be placed so a finished product comes out. As in any machine operation, a certain amount of wasted material is formed. When we relate this to the internal combustion engine, we find that through the input of air and fuel, we obtain power during the combustion process to drive the vehicle. The by-product or waste of this power is, in part, heat and exhaust gases with which we must dispose.

The heat from the combustion process can rise to over 4000°F (2204°C). The dissipation of this heat is controlled by a ram air effect, the use of cooling fans to cause air flow and a liquid coolant solution surrounding the combustion area to transfer the heat of combustion through the cylinder walls and into the coolant. The coolant is then directed to a thin-finned, multi-tubed radiator, from which the excess heat is transferred to the atmosphere by 1 of the 3 heat transfer methods, conduction, convection or radiation.

The cooling of the combustion area is an important part in the control of exhaust emissions. To understand the behavior of the combustion and transfer of its heat, consider the air/fuel charge. It is ignited and the flame front burns progressively across the combustion chamber until the burning charge reaches the cylinder walls. Some of the fuel in contact with the walls is not hot enough to burn, thereby snuffing out or quenching the combustion process. This leaves unburned fuel in the combustion chamber. This

unburned fuel is then forced out of the cylinder and into the exhaust system, along with the exhaust gases.

Many attempts have been made to minimize the amount of unburned fuel in the combustion chambers due to quenching, by increasing the coolant temperature and lessening the contact area of the coolant around the combustion area. However, design limitations within the combustion chambers prevent the complete burning of the air/fuel charge, so a certain amount of the unburned fuel is still expelled into the exhaust system, regardless of modifications to the engine.

AUTOMOTIVE EMISSIONS

Before emission controls were mandated on internal combustion engines, other sources of engine pollutants were discovered along with the exhaust emissions. It was determined that engine combustion exhaust produced approximately 60 percent of the total emission pollutants, fuel evaporation from the fuel tank and carburetor vents produced 20 percent, with the final 20 percent being produced through the crankcase as a by-product of the combustion process.

Exhaust Gases

The exhaust gases emitted into the atmosphere are a combination of burned and unburned fuel. To understand the exhaust emission and its composition, we must review some basic chemistry.

When the air/fuel mixture is introduced into the engine, we are mixing air, composed of nitrogen (78 percent), oxygen (21 percent) and other gases (1 percent) with the fuel, which is 100 percent hydrocarbons (HC), in a semi-controlled ratio. As the combustion process is accomplished, power is produced to move the vehicle while the heat of combustion is transferred to the cooling system. The exhaust gases are then composed of nitrogen, a diatomic gas (N_2), the same as was introduced in the engine, carbon dioxide (CO_2), the same gas that is used in beverage carbonation, and water vapor (H_2O). The nitrogen (N_2), for the most part, passes through the engine unchanged, while the oxygen (O_2) reacts (burns) with the hydrocarbons (HC) and produces the carbon dioxide (CO_2) and the water vapors (H_2O). If this chemical process would be the only process to take place, the exhaust emissions would be harmless. However, during the combustion process, other compounds are formed which are considered dangerous. These pollutants are hydrocarbons (HC), carbon monoxide (CO), oxides of nitrogen (NOx) oxides of sulfur (SOx) and engine particulates.

HYDROCARBONS

Hydrocarbons (HC) are essentially fuel which was not burned during the combustion process or which has escaped into the atmosphere through fuel evaporation. The main sources of incomplete combustion are rich air/fuel mixtures, low engine temperatures and improper spark timing. The main sources of hydrocarbon emission through fuel evaporation on most vehicles used to be the vehicle's fuel tank and carburetor float bowl.

To reduce combustion hydrocarbon emission, engine modifications were made to minimize dead space and surface area in the combustion chamber. In addition, the air/fuel mixture was made more lean through the improved control which feedback carburetion and fuel injection offers and by the addition of external controls to aid in further combustion of the hydrocarbons outside the engine. Two such methods were the addition of air injection systems, to inject fresh air into the exhaust manifolds and the installation of catalytic converters, units that are able to burn traces of hydrocarbons without affecting the internal combustion process or fuel economy.

To control hydrocarbon emissions through fuel evaporation, modifications were made to the fuel tank to allow storage of the fuel vapors during periods of engine shut-down. Modifications were also made to the air intake system so that at specific times during engine operation, these vapors may be purged and burned by blending them with the air/fuel mixture.

CARBON MONOXIDE

Carbon monoxide is formed when not enough oxygen is present during the combustion process to convert carbon (C) to carbon dioxide (CO_2). An increase in the carbon monoxide (CO) emission is normally accompanied by an increase in the hydrocarbon (HC) emission because of the lack of oxygen to completely burn all of the fuel mixture.

Carbon monoxide (CO) also increases the rate at which the photo chemical smog is formed by speeding up the conversion of nitric oxide (NO) to nitrogen dioxide (NO_2). To accomplish this, carbon monoxide (CO) combines with oxygen (O_2) and nitric oxide (NO) to produce carbon dioxide (CO_2) and nitrogen dioxide (NO_2). ($CO + O_2 + NO = CO_2 + NO_2$).

The dangers of carbon monoxide, which is an odorless and colorless toxic gas are many. When carbon monoxide is inhaled into the lungs and passed into the blood stream, oxygen is replaced by the carbon monoxide in the red blood cells, causing a reduction in the amount of oxygen supplied to the many parts of the body. This lack of oxygen causes headaches, lack of coordination, reduced mental alertness and, should the carbon monoxide concentration be high enough, death could result.

NITROGEN

Normally, nitrogen is an inert gas. When heated to approximately 2500°F (1371°C) through the combustion process, this gas becomes active and causes an increase in the nitric oxide (NO) emission.

Oxides of nitrogen (NOx) are composed of approximately 97–98 percent nitric oxide (NO). Nitric oxide is a colorless gas but when it is passed into the atmosphere, it combines with oxygen and forms nitrogen dioxide (NO_2). The nitrogen dioxide then combines with chemically active hydrocarbons (HC) and when in the presence of sunlight, causes the formation of photo-chemical smog.

Ozone

To further complicate matters, some of the nitrogen dioxide (NO_2) is broken apart by the sunlight to form nitric oxide and oxygen. ($NO_2 +$ sunlight $= NO + O$). This single atom of oxygen then combines with diatomic (meaning 2 atoms) oxygen (O_2) to form ozone (O_3). Ozone is one of the smells associated with smog. It has a pungent and offensive odor, irritates the eyes and lung tissues, affects the growth of plant life and causes rapid deterioration of rubber products. Ozone can be formed by sunlight as well as electrical discharge into the air.

The most common discharge area on the automobile engine is the secondary ignition electrical system, especially when inferior quality spark plug cables are used. As the surge of high voltage is routed through the secondary cable, the circuit builds up an electrical field around the wire, which acts upon the oxygen in the surrounding air to form the ozone. The faint glow along the cable with the engine running that may be visible on a dark night, is called the "corona discharge." It is the result of the electrical field passing from a high along the cable, to a low in the surrounding air, which forms the ozone gas. The combination of corona and ozone has been a major cause of cable deterioration. Recently, different and better quality insulating materials have lengthened the life of the electrical cables.

Although ozone at ground level can be harmful, ozone is beneficial to the earth's inhabitants. By having a concentrated ozone layer called the "ozonosphere," between 10 and 20 miles (16–32 km) up in the atmosphere, much of the ultra violet radiation from the sun's rays are absorbed and screened. If this ozone layer were not present, much of the earth's surface would be burned, dried and unfit for human life.

OXIDES OF SULFUR

Oxides of sulfur (SO_x) were initially ignored in the exhaust system emissions, since the sulfur content of gasoline as a fuel is less than $\frac{1}{10}$ of 1 percent. Because of this small amount, it was felt that it contributed very little to the overall pollution problem. However, because of the difficulty in solving the sulfur emissions in industrial pollutions and the introduction of catalytic converter to the automobile exhaust systems, a change was mandated. The automobile exhaust system, when equipped with a catalytic converter, changes the sulfur dioxide (SO_2) into sulfur trioxide (SO_3).

When this combines with water vapors (H_2O), a sulfuric acid mist (H_2SO_4) is formed and is a very difficult pollutant to handle since it is extremely corrosive. This sulfuric acid mist that is formed, is the same mist that rises from the vents of an automobile battery when an active chemical reaction takes place within the battery cells.

When a large concentration of vehicles equipped with catalytic converters are operating in an area, this acid mist may rise and be distributed over a large ground area causing land, plant, crop, paint and building damage.

PARTICULATE MATTER

A certain amount of particulate matter is present in the burning of any fuel, with carbon constituting the largest percentage of the particulates. In gasoline, the remaining particulates are the burned remains of the various other compounds used in its manufacture. When a gasoline engine is in good internal condition, the particulate emissions are low but as the engine wears internally, the particulate emissions increase. By visually inspecting the tail pipe emissions, a determination can be made as to where an engine defect may exist. An engine with light gray or blue smoke emitting from the tail pipe normally indicates an increase in the oil consumption through burning due to internal engine wear. Black smoke would indicate a defective fuel delivery system, causing the engine to operate in a rich mode. Regardless of the color of the smoke, the internal part of the engine or the fuel delivery system should be repaired to prevent excess particulate emissions.

Diesel and turbine engines emit a darkened plume of smoke from the exhaust system because of the type of fuel used. Emission control regulations are mandated for this type of emission and more stringent measures are being used to prevent excess emission of the particulate matter. Electronic components are being introduced to control the injection of the fuel at precisely the proper time of piston travel, to achieve the optimum in fuel ignition and fuel usage. Other particulate after-burning components are being tested to achieve a cleaner emission.

Good grades of engine lubricating oils should be used, which meet the manufacturers specification. Cut-rate oils can contribute to the particulate emission problem because of their low flash or ignition temperature point. Such oils burn prematurely during the combustion process causing emission of particulate matter.

The cooling system is an important factor in the reduction of particulate matter. The optimum combustion will occur, with the cooling system operating at a temperature specified by the manufacturer. The cooling system must be maintained in the same manner as the engine oiling system, as each system is required to perform properly in order for the engine to operate efficiently for a long time.

Crankcase Emissions

Crankcase emissions are made up of water, acids, unburned fuel, oil fumes and particulates. These emissions are classified as hydrocarbons (HC) and are formed by the small amount of unburned, compressed air/fuel mixture entering the crankcase from the combustion area (between the cylinder walls and piston rings) during the compression and power strokes. The head of the compression and combustion help to form the remaining crankcase emissions.

Since the first engines, crankcase emissions were allowed into the atmosphere through a road draft tube, mounted on the lower side of the engine block. Fresh air came in through an open oil filler cap or breather. The air passed through the crankcase mixing with blow-by gases. The motion of the vehicle and the air blowing past the open end of the road draft tube caused a low pressure area (vacuum) at the end of the tube. Crankcase emissions were simply drawn out of the road draft tube into the air.

To control the crankcase emission, the road draft tube was deleted. A hose and/or tubing was routed from the crankcase to the intake manifold so the blow-by emission could be burned with the air/fuel mixture. However, it was found that intake manifold vacuum, used to draw the crankcase emissions into the manifold, would vary in strength at the wrong time and not allow the proper emission flow. A regulating valve was needed to control the flow of air through the crankcase.

Testing, showed the removal of the blow-by gases from the crankcase as quickly as possible, was most important to the longevity of the engine. Should large accumulations of blow-by gases remain and condense, dilution of the engine oil would occur to form water, soots, resins, acids and lead salts, resulting in the formation of sludge and varnishes. This condensation of the blow-by gases occurs more frequently on vehicles used in numerous starting and stopping conditions, excessive idling and when the engine is not allowed to attain normal operating temperature through short runs.

Evaporative Emissions

Gasoline fuel is a major source of pollution, before and after it is burned in the automobile engine. From the time the fuel is refined, stored, pumped and transported, again stored until it is pumped into the fuel tank of the vehicle, the gasoline gives off unburned hydrocarbons (HC) into the atmosphere. Through the redesign of storage areas and venting systems, the pollution factor was diminished, but not eliminated, from the refinery standpoint. However, the automobile still remained the primary source of vaporized, unburned hydrocarbon (HC) emissions.

Fuel pumped from an underground storage tank is cool but when exposed to a warmer ambient temperature, will expand. Before controls were mandated, an owner might fill the fuel tank with fuel from an underground storage tank and park the vehicle for some time in warm area, such as a parking lot. As the fuel would warm, it would expand and should no provisions or area be provided for the expansion, the fuel would spill out of the filler neck and onto the ground, causing hydrocarbon (HC) pollution and creating a severe fire hazard. To correct this condition, the vehicle manufacturers added overflow plumbing and/or gasoline tanks with built in expansion areas or domes.

However, this did not control the fuel vapor emission from the fuel tank. It was determined that most of the fuel evaporation occurred when the vehicle was stationary and the engine not operating. Most vehicles carry 5–25 gallons (19–95 liters) of gasoline. Should a large concentration of vehicles be parked in one area, such as a large parking lot, excessive fuel vapor emissions would take place, increasing as the temperature increases.

To prevent the vapor emission from escaping into the atmosphere, the fuel systems were designed to trap the vapors while the vehicle is stationary, by sealing the system from the atmosphere. A storage system is used to collect and hold the fuel vapors from the carburetor (if equipped) and the fuel tank when the engine is not operating. When the engine is started, the storage system is then purged of the fuel vapors, which are drawn into the engine and burned with the air/fuel mixture.

GASOLINE ENGINE EMISSION CONTROLS

Crankcase Ventilation System

OPERATION

▶ **See Figures 1 and 2**

The Positive Crankcase Ventilation (PCV) system is used to evacuate the crankcase vapors. Outside vehicle air is routed through the air cleaner to the crankcase where it mixes with the blow-by gases and is passed through the PCV valve. It is then routed into the intake manifold. The PCV valve meters the air flow rate, which varies under engine operation depending on manifold vacuum. In order to maintain idle quality, the PCV valve limits the air flow when intake manifold vacuum is high. If abnormal operating conditions occur, the system will allow excessive blow-by gases to back flow through the crankcase vent tube into the air cleaner. These blow-by gases will then be burned by normal combustion.

A plugged PCV valve or hose may cause rough idle, stalling or slow idle speed, oil leaks, oil in the air cleaner or sludge in the engine. A leaking PCV valve or hose could cause rough idle, stalling or high idle speed.

Other than checking and replacing the PCV valve and associated hoses, there is not service required. Engine operating conditions that would direct suspicion to the PCV system are rough idle, oil present in the air cleaner, oil leaks and excessive oil sludging or dilution. If any of the above conditions exist, remove the PCV valve and shake it. A clicking sound indicates

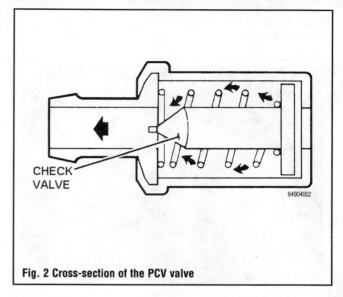

Fig. 2 Cross-section of the PCV valve

that the valve is free. If no clicking sound is heard, replace the valve. Inspect the PCV breather in the air cleaner. Replace the breather if it is so dirty that it will not allow gases to pass through. Check all the PCV hoses for condition and tight connections. Replace any hoses that have deteriorated.

TESTING

▶ **See Figure 3**

With the engine running, remove the PCV from the valve cover and place your thumb over the end of the valve. Check if vacuum is present at the valve. If vacuum is not present, check for plugged hoses, blockage of the manifold port at the throttle body/carburetor unit or a faulty PCV valve. Replace as necessary. With the engine not running, remove the PCV valve from the vehicle. Shake the valve and listen for the rattle of the check valve needle. If no rattle is heard, the valve is defective and must be replaced.

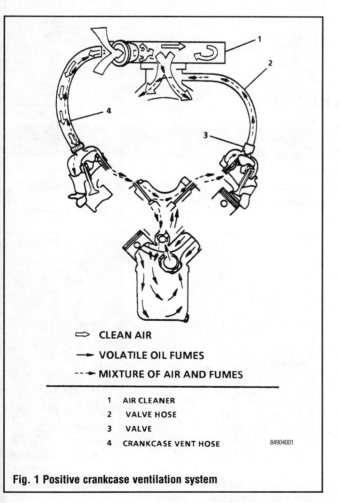

- ⇨ **CLEAN AIR**
- → **VOLATILE OIL FUMES**
- --→ **MIXTURE OF AIR AND FUMES**

1	AIR CLEANER
2	VALVE HOSE
3	VALVE
4	CRANKCASE VENT HOSE

Fig. 1 Positive crankcase ventilation system

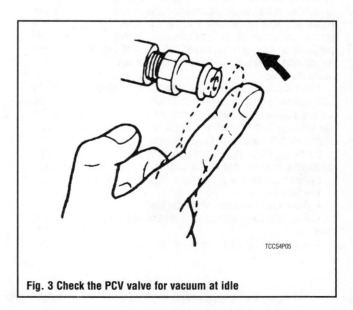

Fig. 3 Check the PCV valve for vacuum at idle

REMOVAL & INSTALLATION

1. To replace the valve, gently pull the hose from the top of the valve, then pull the valve out of the cover grommet.
2. Installation is the reverse of removal.

Grasp the PCV valve to remove it from the grommet in the valve cover

Evaporative Emission Control System

OPERATION

▶ **See Figures 4 thru 12 (p. 7–8)**

The Evaporative Emission Control System (EECS) is designed to prevent fuel tank vapors from being emitted into the atmosphere. Gasoline vapors are absorbed and stored by a fuel vapor charcoal canister. The charcoal canister absorbs the gasoline vapors and stores them until certain engine conditions are met and the vapors can be purged and burned by the engine.

The charcoal canister purge cycle is controlled either by a thermostatic vacuum switch or by a timed vacuum source. The thermostatic switch is installed in the coolant passage and prevents canister purge when engine operating temperature is below 115°F (46°C). The timed vacuum source uses a manifold vacuum-controlled diaphragm to control canister purge. When the engine is running, full manifold vacuum is applied to the top tube of the purge valve which lifts the valve diaphragm and opens the valve.

A vent located in the fuel tank, allows fuel vapors to flow to the charcoal canister. A tank pressure control valve, used on high altitude applications, prevents canister purge when the engine is not running. The fuel tank cap does not normally vent to the atmosphere but is designed to provide both vacuum and pressure relief.

Poor engine idle, stalling and poor driveability can be caused by a damaged canister or split, damaged or improperly connected hoses.

Evidence of fuel loss or fuel vapor odor can be caused by:
- A liquid fuel leak
- A cracked or damaged vapor canister
- A disconnected, misrouted, kinked or damaged vapor pipe or canister hoses
- A damaged air cleaner or improperly seated air cleaner gasket

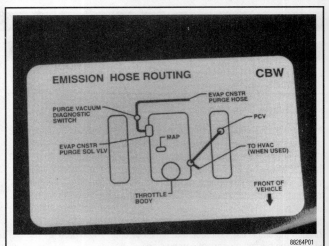

Sample of the emissions related hose routing sticker found on most vehicles

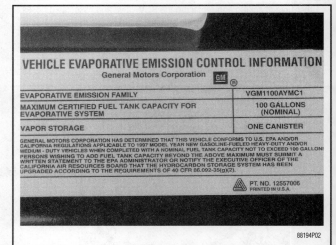

The emissions label under the hood has all of the information pertinent to that vehicle on it

The EVAP canister can be found under the van near the driver's side frame rail—1996–97 models

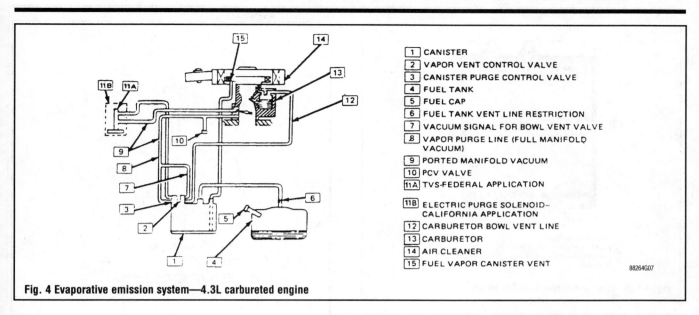

1	CANISTER
2	VAPOR VENT CONTROL VALVE
3	CANISTER PURGE CONTROL VALVE
4	FUEL TANK
5	FUEL CAP
6	FUEL TANK VENT LINE RESTRICTION
7	VACUUM SIGNAL FOR BOWL VENT VALVE
8	VAPOR PURGE LINE (FULL MANIFOLD VACUUM)
9	PORTED MANIFOLD VACUUM
10	PCV VALVE
11A	TVS-FEDERAL APPLICATION
11B	ELECTRIC PURGE SOLENOID– CALIFORNIA APPLICATION
12	CARBURETOR BOWL VENT LINE
13	CARBURETOR
14	AIR CLEANER
15	FUEL VAPOR CANISTER VENT

88264G07

Fig. 4 Evaporative emission system—4.3L carbureted engine

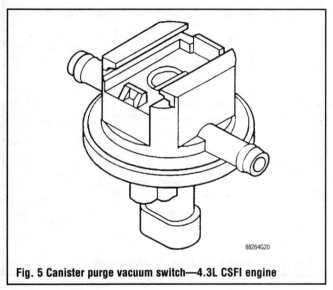

88264G20

Fig. 5 Canister purge vacuum switch—4.3L CSFI engine

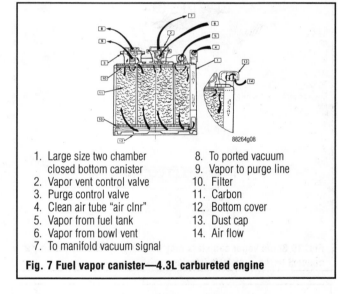

88264g08

1. Large size two chamber closed bottom canister
2. Vapor vent control valve
3. Purge control valve
4. Clean air tube "air clnr"
5. Vapor from fuel tank
6. Vapor from bowl vent
7. To manifold vacuum signal
8. To ported vacuum
9. Vapor to purge line
10. Filter
11. Carbon
12. Bottom cover
13. Dust cap
14. Air flow

Fig. 7 Fuel vapor canister—4.3L carbureted engine

88264P03

Fig. 6 Typical canister mounting—it has two hoses attached with a third nipple blocked off

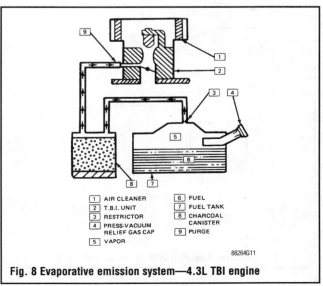

1	AIR CLEANER
2	T.B.I. UNIT
3	RESTRICTOR
4	PRESS-VACUUM RELIEF GAS CAP
5	VAPOR
6	FUEL
7	FUEL TANK
8	CHARCOAL CANISTER
9	PURGE

88264G11

Fig. 8 Evaporative emission system—4.3L TBI engine

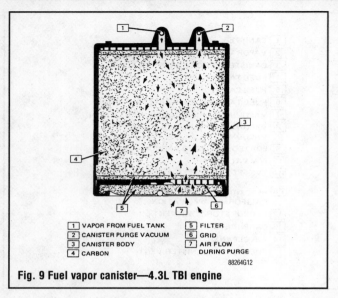

1	VAPOR FROM FUEL TANK	5	FILTER
2	CANISTER PURGE VACUUM	6	GRID
3	CANISTER BODY	7	AIR FLOW
4	CARBON		DURING PURGE

88264G12

Fig. 9 Fuel vapor canister—4.3L TBI engine

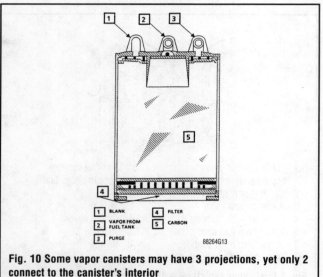

1	BLANK	4	FILTER
2	VAPOR FROM FUEL TANK	5	CARBON
3	PURGE		

88264G13

Fig. 10 Some vapor canisters may have 3 projections, yet only 2 connect to the canister's interior

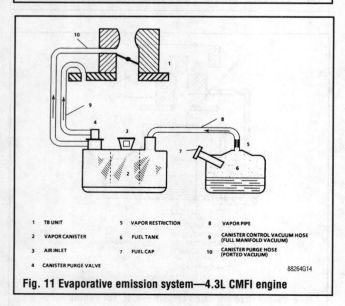

1	TB UNIT	5	VAPOR RESTRICTION	8	VAPOR PIPE
2	VAPOR CANISTER	6	FUEL TANK	9	CANISTER CONTROL VACUUM HOSE (FULL MANIFOLD VACUUM)
3	AIR INLET	7	FUEL CAP	10	CANISTER PURGE HOSE (PORTED VACUUM)
4	CANISTER PURGE VALVE				

88264G14

Fig. 11 Evaporative emission system—4.3L CMFI engine

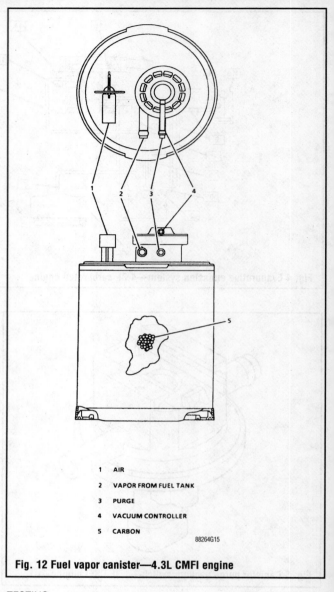

1	AIR
2	VAPOR FROM FUEL TANK
3	PURGE
4	VACUUM CONTROLLER
5	CARBON

88264G15

Fig. 12 Fuel vapor canister—4.3L CMFI engine

TESTING

Vapor Canister

◆ See Figure 13

1. Apply a length of hose to the lower tube of the purge valve assembly and attempt to blow air through it. There should be little or no air passing into the canister.

➡**If the canister is equipped with a constant purge hole, a small amount of air will pass into the canister.**

2. Using a hand-held vacuum pump, apply a vacuum of 15 in. Hg (51 kPa) to the control vacuum (upper) tube. If the vacuum does not hold for at least 20 seconds, the diaphragm is leaking. Replace the canister.

3. If the diaphragm holds vacuum, attempt to blow air through the hose connected to the PCV tube while vacuum is still being applied. An increase of air should be observed. If no increase is noted, the canister must be replaced.

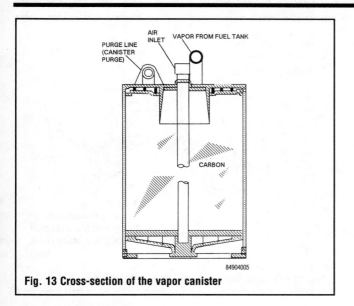

Fig. 13 Cross-section of the vapor canister

Fuel Tank Pressure Control Valve

▶ **See Figure 14**

1. Attach a length of hose to the tank side of the valve assembly and try to blow air through it. Little or no air should pass into the canister.
2. Using a hand-held vacuum pump, apply vacuum equivalent to 15 in. Hg (51 kPa) to the control vacuum tube. If the diaphragm does not hold vacuum, the diaphragm is leaking. Replace the valve.
3. If the diaphragm holds vacuum, attempt to blow air through the hose connected to the valve while vacuum is still being applied. Air should pass. If no air is noted, the valve must be replaced.

Thermostatic Vacuum Switch

1. With engine temperature below 100°F (38°C), apply vacuum to the manifold side of the switch. The switch should hold vacuum.
2. Start and continue to run the engine until the engine temperature increases above 122°F (50°C). The vacuum should drop off.
3. Replace the switch if it fails either test.

REMOVAL & INSTALLATION

Vapor Canister

▶ **See Figures 15 and 16**

1. Tag and disconnect the hoses from the canister.
2. Remove the vapor canister retaining nut.
3. Remove the canister from the vehicle.

To install:

4. Install the canister. If necessary, refer to the vehicle emission control label, located in the engine compartment, for proper routing of the vacuum hoses.

Thermostatic Vacuum Switch

1. Drain the cooling system to below the switch level.
2. Tag and disconnect the vacuum hoses from the switch.
3. Unscrew and remove the thermostatic vacuum switch.

To install:

4. Install the thermostatic vacuum switch. Make sure to apply sealer to the switch threads.

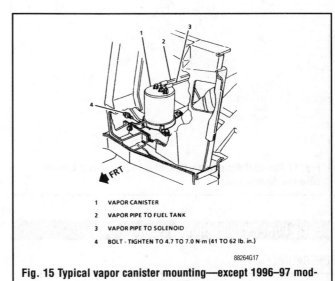

1	VAPOR CANISTER
2	VAPOR PIPE TO FUEL TANK
3	VAPOR PIPE TO SOLENOID
4	BOLT - TIGHTEN TO 4.7 TO 7.0 N·m (41 TO 62 lb. in.)

Fig. 15 Typical vapor canister mounting—except 1996–97 mod-

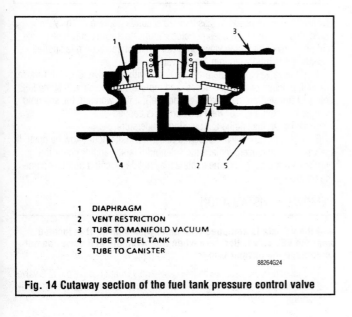

1	DIAPHRAGM
2	VENT RESTRICTION
3	TUBE TO MANIFOLD VACUUM
4	TUBE TO FUEL TANK
5	TUBE TO CANISTER

Fig. 14 Cutaway section of the fuel tank pressure control valve

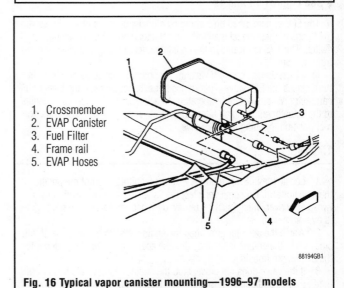

1. Crossmember
2. EVAP Canister
3. Fuel Filter
4. Frame rail
5. EVAP Hoses

Fig. 16 Typical vapor canister mounting—1996–97 models

5. Connect the vacuum hoses.
6. Refill the cooling system.

Canister Purge Solenoid

▶ **See Figure 17**

1. Disconnect the negative battery cable.
2. Disconnect the electrical connectors and hoses from the solenoid.
3. Unfasten the retainers, then pull the solenoid away from the bracket and remove the assembly.

To install:

4. Position the solenoid and fasten its retainers.
5. Engage the electrical connectors and the hoses.
6. Connect the negative battery cable.

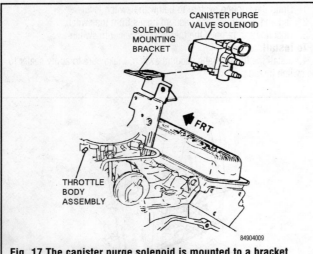

Fig. 17 The canister purge solenoid is mounted to a bracket near the throttle body

---

Early Fuel Evaporation System

OPERATION

▶ **See Figures 18 and 19**

The EFE system, used on carbureted models, consists of an EFE valve at the flange of the exhaust manifold, an actuator, and a thermal vacuum switch. The TVS is located in the coolant outlet housing and directly controls vacuum.

In both systems, manifold vacuum is applied to the actuator which, in turn, closes the EFE valve. This routes hot exhaust gases to the base of the carburetor. When coolant temperatures reach a set limit, vacuum is denied to the actuator, allowing an internal spring to return the actuator to its normal position, opening the EFE valve.

TESTING

1. Locate the EFE valve on the exhaust manifold and not the position of the actuator arm. On some vehicles, the valve and arm are covered by a two-piece cover which must be removed for access. Make sure the engine is overnight cold.
2. Watch the actuator arm when the engine is started. The valve should close when the engine is started cold; the actuator link will be pulled into the diaphragm housing.
3. If the valve does not close, stop the engine. Remove the hose from the EFE valve and apply 10 in. Hg of vacuum by hand pump. The valve should close and stay closed for at least 20 seconds (you will hear it

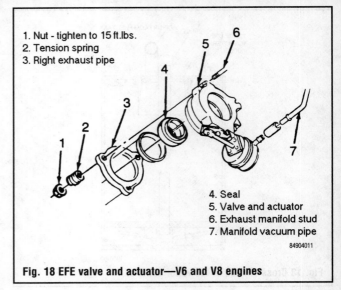

1. Nut - tighten to 15 ft.lbs.
2. Tension spring
3. Right exhaust pipe
4. Seal
5. Valve and actuator
6. Exhaust manifold stud
7. Manifold vacuum pipe

Fig. 18 EFE valve and actuator—V6 and V8 engines

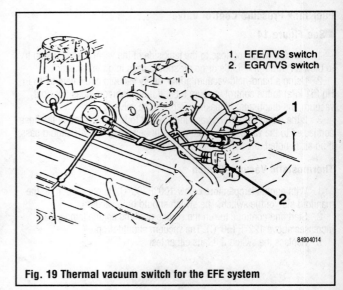

1. EFE/TVS switch
2. EGR/TVS switch

Fig. 19 Thermal vacuum switch for the EFE system

close). If the valve opens in less than 20 seconds, replace it. The valve could also be seized if it does not close; lubricate it with spray type manifold heat valve lube. If the valve does not close when vacuum is applied and when it is lubricated, replace the valve.

4. If the valve closes, the problem is not with the valve. Check for loose, cracked, pinched or plugged hoses, and replace as necessary. Test the EFE solenoid (located on the valve cover bracket); if it is working, the solenoid plunger will emit a noise when the current is applied.
5. Warm up the engine to operating temperature.
6. Watch the EFE valve to see if it has opened. It should now be open. If the valve is still closed, replace the solenoid if faulty, and/or check the engine thermostat; the engine coolant may not be reaching normal operating temperature.

REMOVAL & INSTALLATION

➡**If the vehicle is equipped with an oxygen sensor, it is located near the EFE valve. Use care when removing the EFE valve, as not to damage the oxygen sensor.**

1. Disconnect the negative battery cable and vacuum hose at the EFE valve.
2. Remove the exhaust pipe-to-manifold nuts, and the washers and tension springs, if used.

3. Lower the exhaust crossover pipe. On some models, complete removal of the pipe is not necessary.

4. Remove the EFE valve.

To install:

5. Installation is the reverse of removal. Always install new seals and gaskets. Tighten the exhaust nuts to 22 ft. lbs. (30 Nm). Connect the negative battery cable and vacuum hose to the valve.

Exhaust Gas Recirculation (EGR) System

OPERATION

▶ **See Figures 20 thru 27**

The EGR system's purpose is to control oxides of nitrogen which are formed during the peak combustion temperatures. The end products of combustion are relatively inert gases derived from the exhaust gases, which are directed into the EGR valve to help lower peak combustion temperatures.

The port EGR valve is controlled by a flexible diaphragm which is spring loaded to hold the valve closed. Vacuum applied to the top side of the

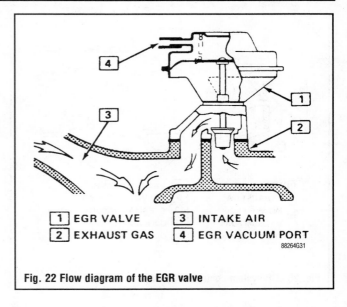

Fig. 22 Flow diagram of the EGR valve

1	EGR VALVE	3	INTAKE AIR
2	EXHAUST GAS	4	EGR VACUUM PORT

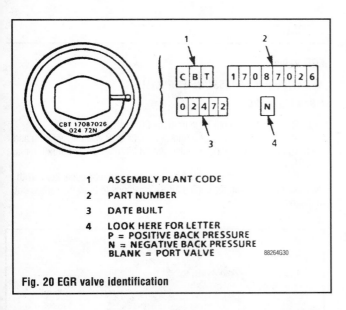

1   ASSEMBLY PLANT CODE

2   PART NUMBER

3   DATE BUILT

4   LOOK HERE FOR LETTER
P = POSITIVE BACK PRESSURE
N = NEGATIVE BACK PRESSURE
BLANK = PORT VALVE

Fig. 20 EGR valve identification

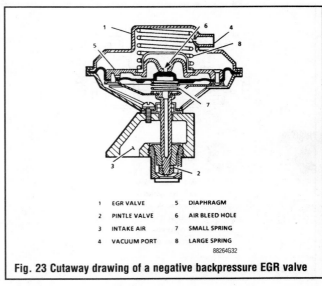

1	EGR VALVE	5	DIAPHRAGM
2	PINTLE VALVE	6	AIR BLEED HOLE
3	INTAKE AIR	7	SMALL SPRING
4	VACUUM PORT	8	LARGE SPRING

Fig. 23 Cutaway drawing of a negative backpressure EGR valve

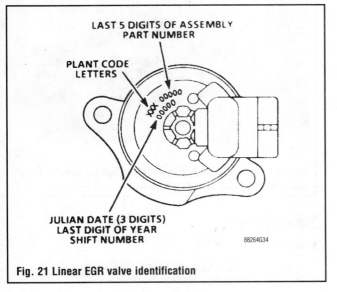

Fig. 21 Linear EGR valve identification

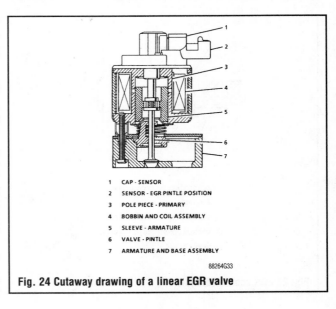

1   CAP - SENSOR

2   SENSOR - EGR PINTLE POSITION

3   POLE PIECE - PRIMARY

4   BOBBIN AND COIL ASSEMBLY

5   SLEEVE - ARMATURE

6   VALVE - PINTLE

7   ARMATURE AND BASE ASSEMBLY

Fig. 24 Cutaway drawing of a linear EGR valve

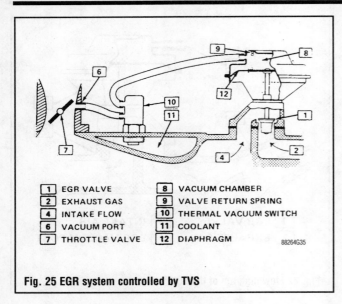

Fig. 25 EGR system controlled by TVS

1	EGR VALVE	8	VACUUM CHAMBER
2	EXHAUST GAS	9	VALVE RETURN SPRING
4	INTAKE FLOW	10	THERMAL VACUUM SWITCH
6	VACUUM PORT	11	COOLANT
7	THROTTLE VALVE	12	DIAPHRAGM

88264G35

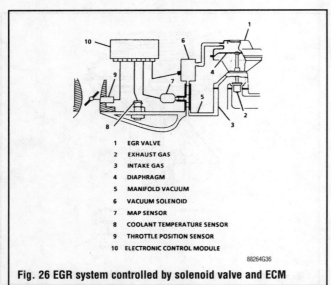

Fig. 26 EGR system controlled by solenoid valve and ECM

1	EGR VALVE
2	EXHAUST GAS
3	INTAKE GAS
4	DIAPHRAGM
5	MANIFOLD VACUUM
6	VACUUM SOLENOID
7	MAP SENSOR
8	COOLANT TEMPERATURE SENSOR
9	THROTTLE POSITION SENSOR
10	ELECTRONIC CONTROL MODULE

88264G36

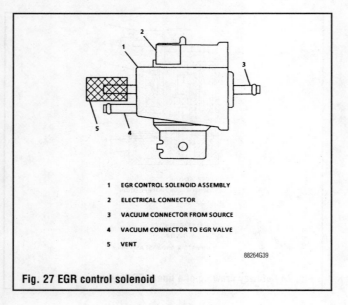

Fig. 27 EGR control solenoid

1	EGR CONTROL SOLENOID ASSEMBLY
2	ELECTRICAL CONNECTOR
3	VACUUM CONNECTOR FROM SOURCE
4	VACUUM CONNECTOR TO EGR VALVE
5	VENT

88264G39

diaphragm overcomes the spring pressure and opens the valve which allows exhaust gas to be pulled into the intake manifold and enter the engine cylinders.

The negative backpressure EGR valve has a bleed valve spring below the diaphragm, and the valve is normally closed. The valve varies the amount of exhaust flow into the manifold, depending on manifold vacuum and variations in exhaust backpressure.

The diaphragm on this valve has an internal air bleed hole which is held closed by a small spring when there is no exhaust backpressure. Engine vacuum opens the EGR valve against the pressure of a large spring. When manifold vacuum combines with negative exhaust backpressure, the vacuum bleed hole opens and the EGR valve closes. This valve will open if vacuum is applied with the engine not running.

The linear EGR valve is operated exclusively by the control module command. The control module monitors various engine parameters by means of the following sensors:

- Throttle Position Sensor (TPS)
- Manifold Absolute Pressure (MAP) sensor
- Engine Coolant Temperature (ECT) sensor
- Pintle position sensor

Output messages are then sent to the EGR system indicating the proper amount of exhaust gas recirculation necessary to lower combustion temperatures.

TESTING

EGR Valve

NEGATIVE BACKPRESSURE EGR VALVE

▶ **See Figure 28**

1. Remove the vacuum hose from the EGR valve.
2. Using a vacuum source, connect it to the EGR valve hose fitting and apply 10 in. Hg (33.8 kPa); the valve should lift off of its seat. If not, replace the EGR valve.
3. Clean the carbon deposits from the valve and intake manifold. With the valve removed, run the engine for 3–5 seconds to blow the carbon out of the intake manifold.

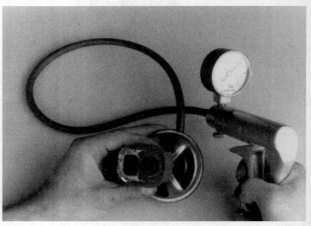

TCCS4P01

Fig. 28 Some EGR valves may be tested using a vacuum pump and watching for diaphragm movement

LINEAR EGR VALVE

▶ **See Figures 29 and 30**

1. Remove the electrical connector from the EGR valve.
2. Measure the resistance between terminals A and E.

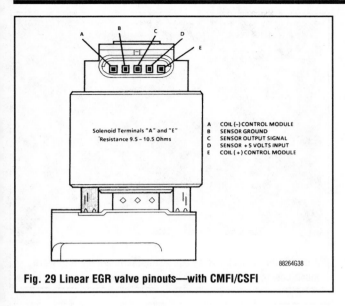

Fig. 29 Linear EGR valve pinouts—with CMFI/CSFI

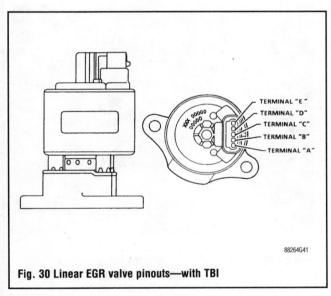

Fig. 30 Linear EGR valve pinouts—with TBI

3. The resistance should be 9.5–10.5 ohms. Replace the valve if the resistance is not in this range.

4. Remove the EGR valve from the engine.

5. Measure the resistance between terminals B and C while moving the pintle in and out. The resistance should change in a smooth fashion without skips or jumps. Replace if necessary.

EGR Control Solenoid

1. Unfasten the electrical connector from the solenoid.

2. Using an ohmmeter, measure the solenoid's resistance, it should be more than 20 ohms. If less than 20 ohms, replace the solenoid and/or possibly the ECM.

Thermostatic Vacuum Switch

If the thermostatic vacuum switch is not working, a Code 32 will store in the ECM memory and a "Service Engine Soon" lamp will light on the instrument panel.

1. Remove the TVS from the engine.

2. Using a vacuum gauge, connect it to one of the hose connections and apply 10 in. Hg (33.8 kPa).

➥A vacuum drop of 2 in. Hg (6.7 kPa) in 2 minutes is allowable.

3. Place the tip of the switch in boiling water. When the switch reaches 195°F (91°C), the valve should open and the vacuum will drop; if not, replace the switch.

REMOVAL & INSTALLATION

EGR Valve

◗ See Figures 31, 32 and 33

1. Disconnect the negative battery cable.

2. Remove the air cleaner assembly or air inlet duct from the engine.

3. Remove the EGR valve vacuum line from the valve (except for linear type EGR valves; if equipped with a linear valve, disconnect the electrical plug.)

4. Remove the EGR bolts and/or nuts and remove the EGR valve and gasket.

To install:

5. Install a new gasket to the EGR valve and attach the EGR valve to the manifold.

6. Install the nuts and/or bolts. Tighten the bolts to 17–18 ft. lbs.

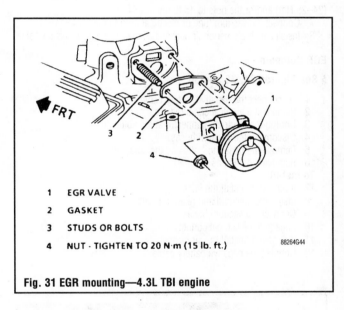

1	EGR VALVE
2	GASKET
3	STUDS OR BOLTS
4	NUT · TIGHTEN TO 20 N·m (15 lb. ft.)

Fig. 31 EGR mounting—4.3L TBI engine

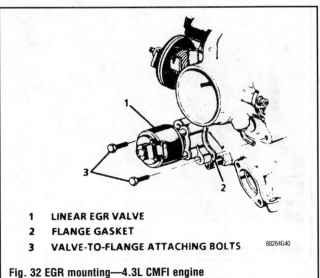

1	LINEAR EGR VALVE
2	FLANGE GASKET
3	VALVE-TO-FLANGE ATTACHING BOLTS

Fig. 32 EGR mounting—4.3L CMFI engine

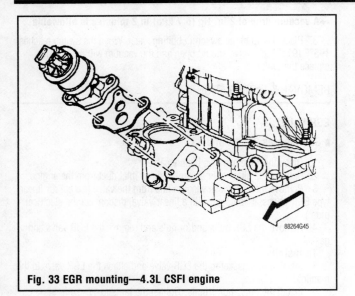

Fig. 33 EGR mounting—4.3L CSFI engine

A distributor wrench makes accessing the mounting hardware much easier

(24–25 Nm) and/or the nuts to 15 ft. lbs. (20 Nm).

7. Connect the vacuum tube or electrical plug to the EGR valve.
8. Install the air cleaner or air duct and connect the negative battery cable.

EGR Solenoid

▶ See Figures 34, 35 and 36

1. Disconnect the negative battery cable.
2. Remove the air cleaner, as required.
3. Unplug the electrical connector at the solenoid.
4. Disconnect the vacuum hoses.
5. Remove the retaining bolts and the solenoid.
6. Remove the filter, as required.

To install:

7. If removed, install the filter.
8. Install the solenoid and retaining bolts.
9. Connect the vacuum hoses.
10. Engage the electrical connector.
11. If removed, install the air cleaner.
12. Connect the negative battery cable.

Pull the EGR valve away, along with the old gasket

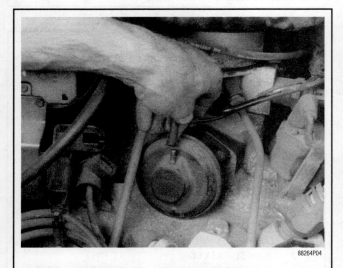

Disconnect the vacuum hose and tag it for identification

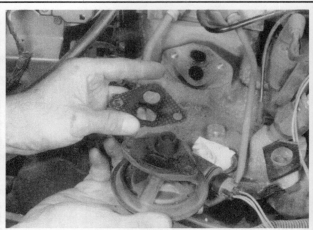

Always use a new gasket when installing. Notice that this one is burned in the center

Location of the linear EGR valve—1996–97 models

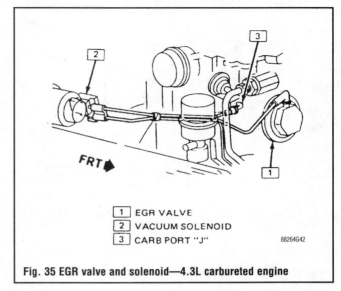

1. EGR VALVE
2. VACUUM SOLENOID
3. CARB PORT "J"

88264G42

Fig. 35 EGR valve and solenoid—4.3L carbureted engine

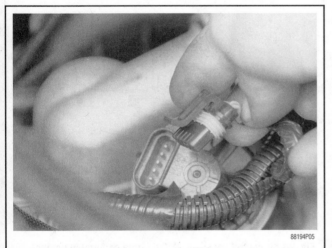

Unplug the electrical connection before loosening the retainers and removing the linear EGR valve

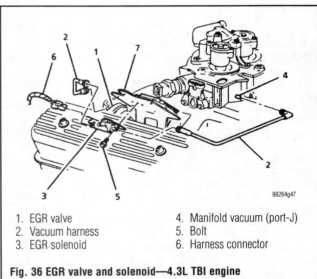

88264g47

1. EGR valve
2. Vacuum harness
3. EGR solenoid
4. Manifold vacuum (port-J)
5. Bolt
6. Harness connector

Fig. 36 EGR valve and solenoid—4.3L TBI engine

Throttle Return Control System

◆ See Figure 37

This system consists of a throttle lever actuator, a solenoid vacuum control valve, and an electronic speed sensor. The throttle lever actuator, mounted on the carburetor, opens the primary throttle plates a preset amount above normal engine idle speed, in response to a signal from the solenoid vacuum control valve. The valve is mounted on the thermostat housing mounting stud. It is held open in response to a signal from the electronic speed sensor. When open, the valve allows a vacuum signal to be sent to the throttle lever actuator. The speed sensor monitors engine speed at the distributor. It supplies an electrical signal to the solenoid valve, as long as a preset engine speed is exceeded. The object of this system is the same as that of the earlier system.

THROTTLE LEVER ACTUATOR

The checking procedure is the same as for earlier years. Follow Steps 1–9 of the Throttle Valve procedure. Adjustment procedures are covered in the carburetor portion of Section 5.

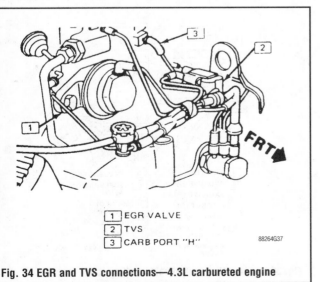

1. EGR VALVE
2. TVS
3. CARB PORT "H"

88264G37

Fig. 34 EGR and TVS connections—4.3L carbureted engine

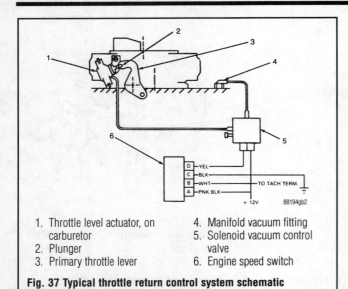

1. Throttle level actuator, on carburetor
2. Plunger
3. Primary throttle lever
4. Manifold vacuum fitting
5. Solenoid vacuum control valve
6. Engine speed switch

Fig. 37 Typical throttle return control system schematic

TRC SYSTEM CHECK

1. Connect a tachometer to the distributor TACH terminal. Start the engine and raise the engine speed to 1890 rpm. The throttle lever actuator on the carburetor should extend.

2. Reduce the engine speed to 1700 rpm. The lever actuator should retract.

3. If the actuator operates outside of the speed limits, the speed switch is faulty and must be replaced. It cannot be adjusted.

4. If the actuator does not operate at all:

a. Check the voltage at the vacuum solenoid and the speed switch with a voltmeter. Connect the negative probe of the voltmeter to the engine ground and the positive probe to the voltage source wire on the component. The positive probe can be inserted on the connector body at the wire side; it is not necessary to unplug the connector. Voltage should be 12 to 14 volts in both cases.

b. If the correct voltage is present at one component but not the other, the engine wiring harness is faulty.

c. If the voltage is not present at all, check the engine harness connections at the distributor and the bulkhead connector, and repair as necessary.

d. If the correct voltage is present at both components, check the solenoid operation: ground the solenoid-to-speed switch connecting wire terminal at the solenoid connector with a jumper wire. This should cause the throttle lever actuator to extend, with the engine running.

e. If the lever actuator does not extend, remove the hose from the solenoid side port which connects the actuator hose. Check the port for obstructions or blockage. If the port is not plugged, replace the solenoid.

f. If the actuator extends in Step 4d, ground the solenoid-to-speed switch wire terminal at the switch. If the actuator does not extend, the wire between the speed switch and the solenoid is open and must be repaired. If the actuator does extend, check the speed switch ground wire for a ground; it should read zero volts with the engine running. Check the speed switch-to-distributor wire for a proper connection. If the ground and distributor wires are properly connected and the actuator still does not extend when the engine speed is above 1,890 rpm, replace the speed switch.

5. If the actuator is extended at all speeds:

a. Remove the connector from the vacuum solenoid.

b. If the actuator remains extended, check the solenoid side port orifice for blockage. If plugged, clear and reconnect the system and recheck. If the actuator is still extended, remove the solenoid connector; if the actuator does not retreat, replace the vacuum solenoid.

c. If the actuator retracts with the solenoid connector off, reconnect it

and remove the speed switch connector. If the actuator retracts, the problem is in the speed switch, which should be replaced. If the actuator does not retract, the solenoid-to-speed switch wire is shorted to ground in the wiring harness. Repair the short.

Air Injector Reactor (AIR) System

▶ **See Figures 38, 39, 40, 41 and 42**

The AIR system injects compressed air into the exhaust system, close enough to the exhaust valves to continue burning the normally unburned segment of the exhaust gases. To do this, the AIR system employs an air injection pump and a system of hoses, valves, tubes, etc., necessary to carry the compressed air from the pump to the exhaust manifolds.

A diverter valve is used to prevent backfiring. The valve senses sudden increases in manifold vacuum and ceases the injection of air during rich periods. During coasting, this valve diverts the entire air flow through a muffler and during high engine speeds, expels it through a relief valve. Check valves in the system prevent exhaust gases from entering the pump.

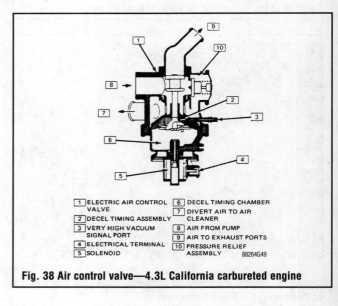

1. ELECTRIC AIR CONTROL VALVE
2. DECEL TIMING ASSEMBLY
3. VERY HIGH VACUUM SIGNAL PORT
4. ELECTRICAL TERMINAL
5. SOLENOID
6. DECEL TIMING CHAMBER
7. DIVERT AIR TO AIR CLEANER
8. AIR FROM PUMP
9. AIR TO EXHAUST PORTS
10. PRESSURE RELIEF ASSEMBLY

Fig. 38 Air control valve—4.3L California carbureted engine

1. AIR FLOW
2. EXHAUST GAS
3. EXHAUST VALVE
4. INTAKE FLOW
5. INTAKE VALVE
6. COMBUSTION CHAMBER
7. VACUUM BLEED VALVE
8. AIR CLEANER
9. DECELERATION VALVE
10. MANIFOLD VACUUM
11. DIAPHRAGM
12. VALVE

Fig. 39 Deceleration control valve airflow

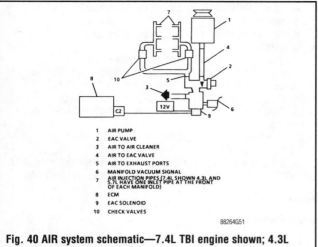

Fig. 40 AIR system schematic—7.4L TBI engine shown; 4.3L and 5.7L engines similar

1 AIR PUMP
2 EAC VALVE
3 AIR TO AIR CLEANER
4 AIR TO EAC VALVE
5 AIR TO EXHAUST PORTS
6 MANIFOLD VACUUM SIGNAL
7 AIR INJECTION PIPES (7.4L SHOWN 4.3L AND 5.7L HAVE ONE INLET PIPE AT THE FRONT OF EACH MANIFOLD)
8 ECM
9 EAC SOLENOID
10 CHECK VALVES

88264G51

TESTING

➡ **The AIR system is not completely silent under normal conditions. Noises will rise in pitch as engine speed increases. If the noise is excessive, temporarily eliminate the air pump by disconnecting its drive belt. If the noise disappears, the air pump is at fault.**

Check Valve

To test the check valve, disconnect the hose at the diverter valve. Place your hand over the check valve and feel for exhaust pulses. If exhaust pulses are present, the check valve must be replaced.

Diverter Valve

▶ **See Figure 43**

Pull off the vacuum line to the top of the valve with the engine running. There should be vacuum in the line; if not, replace the line. No air should be escaping with the engine running at a steady idle. Open and quickly close the throttle. A blast of air should come out of the valve muffler for at least one second.

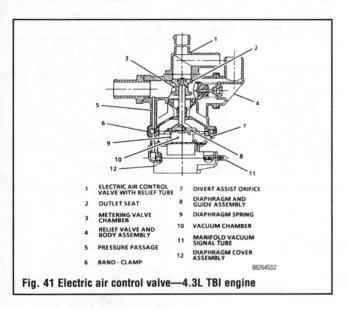

Fig. 41 Electric air control valve—4.3L TBI engine

1 ELECTRIC AIR CONTROL VALVE WITH RELIEF TUBE
2 OUTLET SEAT
3 METERING VALVE CHAMBER
4 RELIEF VALVE AND BODY ASSEMBLY
5 PRESSURE PASSAGE
6 BAND - CLAMP
7 DIVERT ASSIST ORIFICE
8 DIAPHRAGM AND GUIDE ASSEMBLY
9 DIAPHRAGM SPRING
10 VACUUM CHAMBER
11 MANIFOLD VACUUM SIGNAL TUBE
12 DIAPHRAGM COVER ASSEMBLY

88264G52

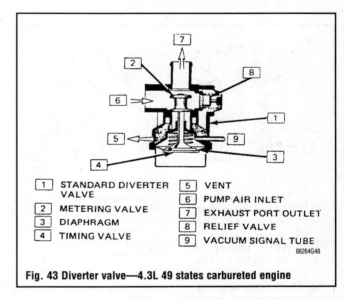

Fig. 43 Diverter valve—4.3L 49 states carbureted engine

1	STANDARD DIVERTER VALVE	5	VENT
2	METERING VALVE	6	PUMP AIR INLET
3	DIAPHRAGM	7	EXHAUST PORT OUTLET
4	TIMING VALVE	8	RELIEF VALVE
		9	VACUUM SIGNAL TUBE

88264G48

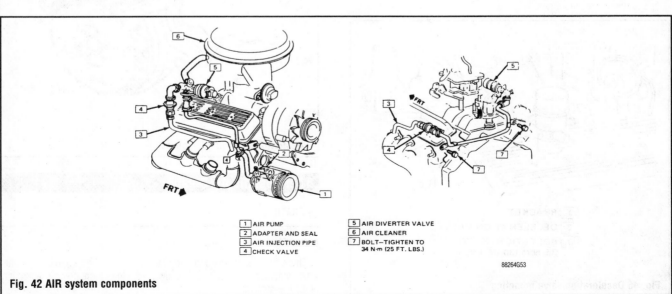

Fig. 42 AIR system components

1 AIR PUMP
2 ADAPTER AND SEAL
3 AIR INJECTION PIPE
4 CHECK VALVE
5 AIR DIVERTER VALVE
6 AIR CLEANER
7 BOLT—TIGHTEN TO 34 N·m (25 FT. LBS.)

88264G53

Air Pump

Disconnect the hose from the diverter valve. Start the engine and accelerate it to about 1500 rpm. The air flow should increase as the engine is accelerated. If no air flow is noted or it remains constant, check the following:

- Drive belt tension.
- Leaking pressure relief valve. If defective, replace the entire relief/diverter valve.
- Foreign matter in pump filter openings. If the pump is defective or excessively noisy, it must be replaced.

REMOVAL & INSTALLATION

▶ **See Figures 44 and 45**

All hoses and fittings should be inspected for condition and tightness of connections. Check the drive belt for wear and tension periodically.

AIR Pump

1. Disconnect the output hose.
2. Hold the pump from turning by pressing the drive belt.
3. Loosen, but do not remove, the pulley bolts.

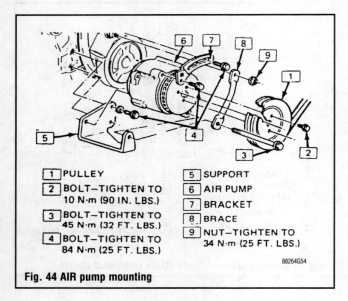

1	PULLEY	5	SUPPORT
2	BOLT—TIGHTEN TO 10 N·m (90 IN. LBS.)	6	AIR PUMP
3	BOLT—TIGHTEN TO 45 N·m (32 FT. LBS.)	7	BRACKET
4	BOLT—TIGHTEN TO 84 N·m (25 FT. LBS.)	8	BRACE
		9	NUT—TIGHTEN TO 34 N·m (25 FT. LBS.)

Fig. 44 AIR pump mounting

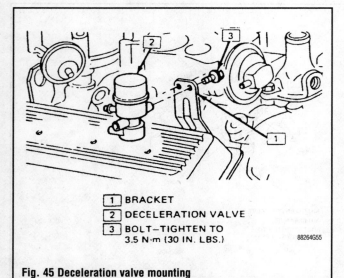

1	BRACKET
2	DECELERATION VALVE
3	BOLT—TIGHTEN TO 3.5 N·m (30 IN. LBS.)

Fig. 45 Deceleration valve mounting

4. Loosen the alternator so the belt can be removed.
5. Remove the pulley.
6. Remove the pump mounting bolts and the pump.

To install:
7. Install the pump with the mounting bolts loose.
8. Install the pulley and tighten the bolts finger-tight.
9. Install the drive belt.
10. Press the drive belt to prevent the pump from turning.
11. Tighten the pulley bolts to 25 ft. lbs. (33 Nm). Tighten the pump mountings.
12. Check and adjust the belt tension.
13. Connect the hose.
14. If any hose leaks are suspected, pour soapy water over the suspected area with the engine running. Bubbles will form wherever air is escaping.

Filter

▶ **See Figure 46**

1. Remove the AIR pump and diverter valve as an assembly.

✳✳ WARNING

Do not clamp the pump in a vise or use a hammer or prybar on the pump housing! Damage to the housing may result.

2. To change the filter, break the plastic fan from the hub. It is seldom possible to remove the fan without breaking it. Wear safety glasses.
3. Remove the remaining portion of the fan filter from the pump hub. Be careful that filter fragments do not enter the air intake hole.

To install:
4. Position a new centrifugal fan filter on the pump hub. Place the pump pulley against the fan filter and install the securing screws. Tighten the screws alternately to 95 inch lbs. (10 Nm). The fan filter will be pressed onto the pump hub.
5. Install the pump on the engine and adjust the drive belt.

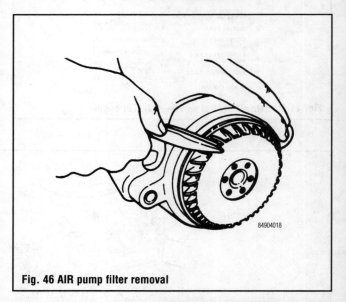

Fig. 46 AIR pump filter removal

Thermostatic Air Cleaner

OPERATION

▶ **See Figure 47**

This system is designed to warm the air entering the carburetor/TBI unit when underhood temperatures are low. This allows more precise calibration of the fuel system.

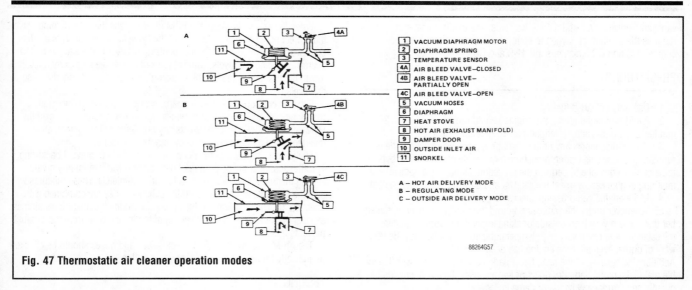

Fig. 47 Thermostatic air cleaner operation modes

The thermostatically controlled air cleaner is composed of the air cleaner body, a filter, sensor unit, vacuum diaphragm, damper door and associated hoses and connections. Heat radiating from the exhaust manifold is trapped by a heat stove and is ducted to the air cleaner to supply heated air to the fuel system. A movable door in the air cleaner snorkel allows air to be drawn in from the heat stove (cold operation) or from the underhood air (warm operation). Periods of extended idling, climbing a grade or high speed operation are followed by a considerable increase in engine compartment temperature. Excessive fuel vapors enter the intake manifold causing an over-rich mixture, resulting in a rough idle. To overcome this, some engines may be equipped with a hot idle compensator.

TESTING

1. Remove the air cleaner assembly and cool to below 40°F (4°C). The damper door should be closed to outside air.
2. Check for the presence and condition of the air cleaner gasket.
3. Reinstall the air cleaner assembly and check to make sure the heat stove tube is connected at the air cleaner snorkel and exhaust manifold.
4. Start the engine and watch the damper in the air cleaner snorkel. As the air cleaner warms up, the damper door should open slowly to the outside air.
5. If the damper fails to operate, check for vacuum at the port on the carburetor/TBI unit. If vacuum is not present, the port must be unclogged.
6. If vacuum was OK at the port, check for vacuum at the damper. If vacuum is present and the damper fails to operate, the vacuum diaphragm must be replaced. If vacuum is not present, the sensor unit in the air cleaner is probably faulty.

REMOVAL & INSTALLATION

▶ **See Figure 48**

Vacuum Diaphragm

1. Remove the air cleaner.
2. If the van uses a plastic heat tube elbow, use a ⅛ in. bit to drill out the two rivets that secure it to the heat tube and remove the elbow.
3. Using a ⅛ in. drill bit again, drill out the two rivets that secure the vacuum diaphragm assembly.
4. Remove the blow-down spring and the carrier assembly.
5. Examine the spring clip on the hot air damper. Replace if necessary.
To install:
6. Install a new assembly with two pop rivets. Install a new blow-down spring.

7. Install the heat elbow with two rivets, if equipped.
8. Install the air cleaner.

Sensor Unit

1. Remove the air cleaner.
2. Label and disconnect the vacuum hoses leading to the sensor.
3. Remove the two clips securing the sensor to the air cleaner.
To install:
4. Position the sensor on the air cleaner.
5. Install the clips securing the sensor.
6. Connect the vacuum hoses and install the air cleaner.

Catalytic Converter

OPERATION

The catalytic converter is a muffler-like container built into the exhaust system to aid in the reduction of exhaust emissions. The catalyst element is coated with a noble metal such as platinum, palladium, rhodium or a combination of them. When the exhaust gases come into contact with the catalyst, a chemical reaction occurs which reduces the pollutants into harmless substances such as water and carbon dioxide.

Two types of catalytic converters are used on Chevrolet/GMC full-size

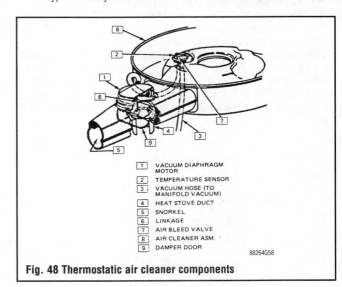

Fig. 48 Thermostatic air cleaner components

vans: an oxidizing type and a three-way type. The oxidizing catalyst requires the addition of oxygen to spur the catalyst into reducing the engine's HC and CO emissions into H_2O and CO_2.

PRECAUTIONS

1. Use only unleaded fuel.
2. Avoid prolonged idling; the engine should run no longer than 20 minutes at curb idle and no longer than 10 minutes at fast idle.
3. Do not disconnect any of the spark plug leads while the engine is running. If any engine testing procedure requires disconnecting or bypassing a control component, perform the procedure as quickly as possible. A misfiring engine can overheat the catalyst and damage the oxygen sensor.
4. Make engine compression checks as quickly as possible.
5. Whenever under the vehicle or around the catalytic converter, remember that it has a very high outside or skin temperature. During operation, the catalyst must reach very high temperatures to work efficiently. Be very wary of burns, even after the engine has been shut off for awhile. Additionally, because of the heat, never park the vehicle on or over flammable materials, particularly dry grass or leaves. Inspect the heat shields frequently and correct any bends or damage.
6. In the unlikely event that the catalyst must be replaced, DO NOT dispose of the old one where anything containing grease, gas or oil can come in contact with it. The catalytic action with these substances will result in heat which may start a fire.

Air Management System

The Air Management System is used to provide additional oxygen to continue the combustion process after the exhaust gases leave the combustion chamber, much the same as the AIR system described earlier in this section. Air is injected into either the exhaust port(s), the exhaust manifold(s) or the catalytic converter by an engine driven air pump. The system is in operation at all times and will bypass air only momentarily during deceleration and at high speeds. The bypass function is performed by the Air Management Valve, a check valve which protects the air pump by preventing any backflow of exhaust gases.

The Air Management System helps to reduce HC and CO content in the exhaust gases by injecting air into the exhaust ports during cold engine operation. This air injection also helps the catalytic converter to reach the proper temperature quicker during warm-up. When the engine is warm (closed loop), the Air Management System injects air into the beds of a 3-way converter to lower the HC and CO content in the exhaust.

The Air Management System utilizes the following components:
1. An engine driven air pump.
2. Air management valves (Air Control and Air Switching)
3. Air flow and control hoses
4. Check valves
5. A dual bed, 3-way catalytic converter

The belt driven, vane type air pump is located at the front of the engine and supplies clean air to the system for purposes already stated. When the engine is cold, the Electronic Control Module (ECM) energizes an air control solenoid. This allows air to flow to the air switching valve. The air switching valve is then energized to direct air into the exhaust ports.

When the engine is warm, the ECM de-energizes the air switching valve, thus directing air between the beds of the catalytic converter. This air then provides additional oxygen for the oxidizing catalyst in the second bed to decrease HC and CO levels, while at the same time keeping oxygen levels low in the first bed, enabling the reducing catalyst to effectively decrease the levels of NOx.

If the air control valve detects a rapid increase in manifold vacuum (deceleration), certain operating modes (wide open throttle, etc.) or if the ECM self-diagnostic system detects any problems in the system, air is diverted to the air cleaner or directly into the atmosphere.

The primary purpose of the ECM's divert mode is to prevent backfiring. Throttle closure at the beginning of deceleration will temporarily create air/fuel mixtures which are too rich to burn completely. These mixtures will become burnable when they reach the exhaust if they are combined with injection air. The next firing of the engine will ignite the mixture causing an exhaust backfire. Momentary diverting of the injection air from the exhaust prevents this.

The Air Management System check valves and hoses should be checked periodically for any leaks, cracks or deterioration.

TESTING

▶ **See Figure 49**

Refer to the accompanying flow chart when testing the Air Management System.

REMOVAL & INSTALLATION

Air Pump

1. Remove the valves and/or adapter at the air pump.
2. Loosen the air pump adjustment bolt and remove the drive belt.
3. Unscrew the three mounting bolts and then remove the pump pulley.
4. Unscrew the pump mounting bolts and then remove the pump.
5. Installation is in the reverse order of removal. Be sure to adjust the drive belt tension after installing it.

Check Valve

1. Release the clamp and disconnect the air hoses from the valve.
2. Unscrew the check valve from the air injection pipe.
3. Installation is in the reverse order of removal.

Air Management Valve

1. Disconnect the negative battery cable.
2. Remove the air cleaner.
3. Tag and disconnect the vacuum hose from the valve.
4. Tag and disconnect the air outlet hoses from the valve.
5. Bend back the lock tabs and then remove the bolts holding the elbow to the valve.
6. Tag and disconnect any electrical connections at the valve, then remove the valve from the elbow.
7. Installation is in the reverse order of removal.

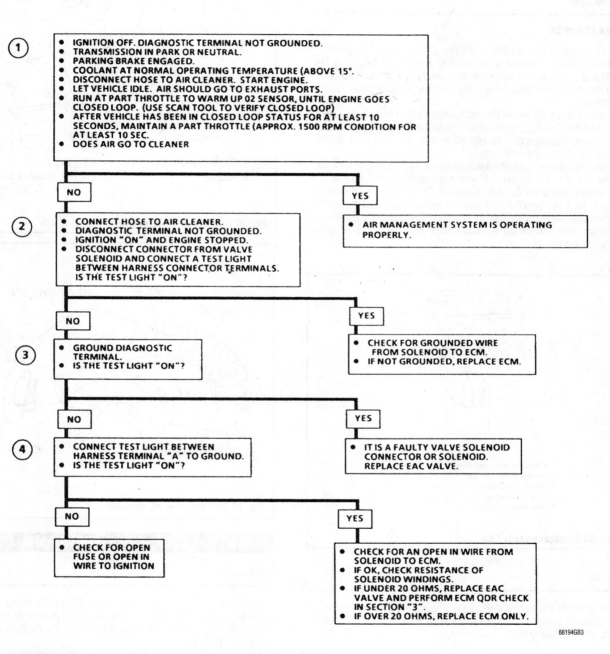

AIR MANAGEMENT CHECK
(ELECTRONIC AIR CONTROL VALVE)

ASSUMES MANIFOLD VACUUM SIGNAL AT VALVE WITH
ENGINE IDLING, AND VOLTAGE ON PIN A WITH IGNITION ON.

①
- IGNITION OFF. DIAGNOSTIC TERMINAL NOT GROUNDED.
- TRANSMISSION IN PARK OR NEUTRAL.
- PARKING BRAKE ENGAGED.
- COOLANT AT NORMAL OPERATING TEMPERATURE (ABOVE 15°.
- DISCONNECT HOSE TO AIR CLEANER.
- LET VEHICLE IDLE. AIR SHOULD GO TO EXHAUST PORTS.
- RUN AT PART THROTTLE TO WARM UP 02 SENSOR, UNTIL ENGINE GOES CLOSED LOOP. (USE SCAN TOOL TO VERIFY CLOSED LOOP)
- AFTER VEHICLE HAS BEEN IN CLOSED LOOP STATUS FOR AT LEAST 10 SECONDS, MAINTAIN A PART THROTTLE (APPROX. 1500 RPM CONDITION FOR AT LEAST 10 SEC.
- DOES AIR GO TO CLEANER

NO

YES

②
- CONNECT HOSE TO AIR CLEANER.
- DIAGNOSTIC TERMINAL NOT GROUNDED.
- IGNITION "ON" AND ENGINE STOPPED.
- DISCONNECT CONNECTOR FROM VALVE SOLENOID AND CONNECT A TEST LIGHT BETWEEN HARNESS CONNECTOR TERMINALS. IS THE TEST LIGHT "ON"?

- AIR MANAGEMENT SYSTEM IS OPERATING PROPERLY.

NO

YES

③
- GROUND DIAGNOSTIC TERMINAL.
- IS THE TEST LIGHT "ON"?

- CHECK FOR GROUNDED WIRE FROM SOLENOID TO ECM.
- IF NOT GROUNDED, REPLACE ECM.

NO

YES

④
- CONNECT TEST LIGHT BETWEEN HARNESS TERMINAL "A" TO GROUND.
- IS THE TEST LIGHT "ON"?

- IT IS A FAULTY VALVE SOLENOID CONNECTOR OR SOLENOID. REPLACE EAC VALVE.

NO

YES

- CHECK FOR OPEN FUSE OR OPEN IN WIRE TO IGNITION

- CHECK FOR AN OPEN IN WIRE FROM SOLENOID TO ECM.
- IF OK, CHECK RESISTANCE OF SOLENOID WINDINGS.
- IF UNDER 20 OHMS, REPLACE EAC VALVE AND PERFORM ECM QDR CHECK IN SECTION "3".
- IF OVER 20 OHMS, REPLACE ECM ONLY.

88194GB3

Fig. 49 Air Management System diagnostic chart

DIESEL ENGINE EMISSION CONTROLS

Crankcase Ventilation System

OPERATION

▶ **See Figure 50**

A Crankcase Depression Regulator Valve (CDRV) is used to regulate (meter) the flow of crankcase gases back into the engine to be burned. The CDRV is designed to limit vacuum in the crankcase as the gases are drawn from the valve covers through the CDRV and into the intake manifold (air crossover).

Fresh air enters the engine through the combination filter, check valve and oil fill cap. The fresh air mixes with blow-by gases and enters both valve covers. The gases pass through a filter installed on the valve covers and are drawn into connecting tubing.

Intake manifold vacuum acts against a spring loaded diaphragm to control the flow of crankcase gases. Higher intake vacuum levels pull the diaphragm closer to the top of the outlet tube. This reduces the amount of gases being drawn from the crankcase and decreases the vacuum level in the crankcase. As the intake vacuum decreases, the spring pushes the diaphragm away from the top of the outlet tube allowing more gases to flow to the intake manifold.

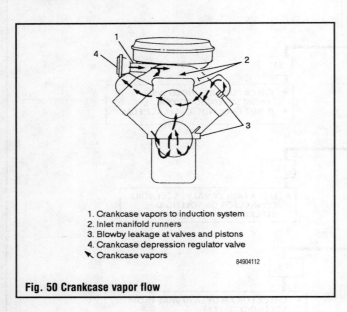

1. Crankcase vapors to induction system
2. Inlet manifold runners
3. Blowby leakage at valves and pistons
4. Crankcase depression regulator valve
↘ Crankcase vapors

84904112

Fig. 50 Crankcase vapor flow

TESTING

Do not attempt to test the valve. If you suspect problems with the system, clean the filter and vent pipes with solvent. Be sure to dry the components before installing them.

REMOVAL & INSTALLATION

▶ **See Figures 51 and 52**

The components of this system can be removed by disconnecting the hoses and pulling the component from its mounting grommet. Be careful not to damage the grommet; replace if necessary.

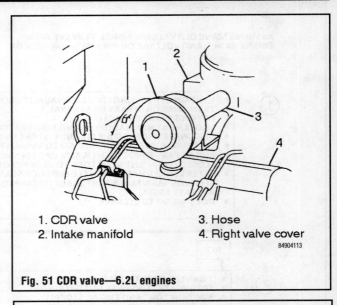

1. CDR valve
2. Intake manifold
3. Hose
4. Right valve cover

84904113

Fig. 51 CDR valve—6.2L engines

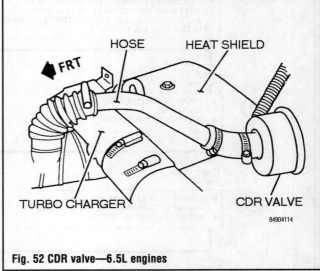

HOSE　　HEAT SHIELD

◀ FRT

TURBO CHARGER

CDR VALVE

84904114

Fig. 52 CDR valve—6.5L engines

Exhaust Gas Recirculation (EGR) System

OPERATION

To lower the formation of nitrogen oxides (NOx) in the exhaust, it is necessary to reduce combustion temperatures. This is done in the diesel, as in the gasoline engine, by introducing exhaust gases into the cylinders through the EGR valve.

The Exhaust Pressure Regulator (EPR) valve and solenoid operate in conjunction with the EGR valve. The EPR valve's job is to increase exhaust backpressure in order to increase EGR flow. The EPR valve is usually open, and the solenoid is normally closed. When energized by the **B+** wire from the Throttle Position Switch (TPS), the solenoid opens, allowing vacuum to the EPR valve, closing it. This occurs at idle. As the throttle is opened, at a calibrated throttle angle, the TPS de-energizes the EPR solenoid, cutting off vacuum to the EPR valve, closing the valve. Two other solenoids are used for EGR valve control. The EGR solenoid allows vacuum to reach the EGR vent solenoid under certain conditions. The vent solenoid then controls the EGR valve to regulate the flow of gasses into the intake manifold.

TESTING

Exhaust Gas Recirculation (EGR) Valve

Apply vacuum to the EGR valve with a hand vacuum pump. The valve should be fully open at 11 in. Hg and closed below 6 in. Hg.

EPR Valve

1. Apply 11 in. Hg vacuum to the EPR valve tube with a hand vacuum pump. Observe the valve actuator lever for movement.
2. If it does not move, spray a penetrating lubricant on the lever and try to free the valve.

❊❊ CAUTION

Make sure the valve is not hot.

3. If the lubricant will not free the valve, it must be replaced.

Vacuum Regulator Valve (VRV)

The Vacuum Regulator Valve is attached to the side of the injection pump and regulates vacuum in proportion to throttle angle. Vacuum from the vacuum pump is supplied to port **A** and vacuum at port **B** is reduced as the throttle is opened. At closed throttle, the vacuum is 15 in.; at half throttle, 6 in.; at wide open throttle there is zero vacuum.

Response Vacuum Reducer (RVR)

Connect a vacuum gauge to the port marked **To EGR** valve to T.C.C. solenoid. Connect a hand operated vacuum pump to the VRV port. Draw a 50.66 kPa (15 in. Hg) vacuum on the pump and the reading on the vacuum gauge should be lower than the vacuum pump reading as follows:
- 0.75 in. Except High Altitude
- 2.5 in. High Altitude

Torque Converter Clutch Operated Solenoid

When the torque converter clutch is engaged, an electrical signal energizes the solenoid allowing ports 1 and 2 to be interconnected. When the solenoid is not energized, port 1 is closed and ports 2 and 3 are interconnected.

Vacuum Pump

Since the air crossover and intake manifold in a diesel engine is unrestricted (unlike a gasoline engine which has throttle plates creating a venturi effect) there is no vacuum source. To provide vacuum, a vacuum pump is mounted in the location occupied by the distributor in a gasoline engine. This pump supplies the air conditioning servos, the cruise control servos, and the transmission vacuum modulator where required.

The pump is a diaphragm type which needs no maintenance. It is driven by a drive gear on its lower end which meshes with gear teeth on the end of the engine's camshaft.

REMOVAL & INSTALLATION

Vacuum Pump

1. Disconnect the batteries.
2. Remove the air cleaner, and cover the intake manifold.
3. Remove the vacuum pump clamp, disconnect the vacuum line and remove the pump.

4. Install a new gasket. Install the pump and reverse the removal procedures for installation.

EGR Valve

◆ See Figure 53

1. Remove the air cleaner assembly and air intake tube.
2. Unplug the vacuum hose from the valve.
3. Remove the studs securing the valve to the intake manifold.
4. Installation is the reverse of removal. Tighten the studs until snug.

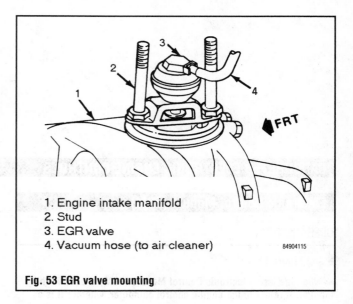

1. Engine intake manifold
2. Stud
3. EGR valve
4. Vacuum hose (to air cleaner)

84904115

Fig. 53 EGR valve mounting

EPR Valve

◆ See Figure 54

1. Raise and safely support the vehicle.
2. Unplug the vacuum hose from the actuator.
3. Disconnect the exhaust pipe from the valve.
4. Remove the studs securing the valve to the exhaust manifold.
5. Installation is the reverse of removal.

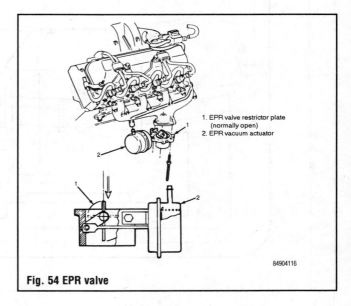

1. EPR valve restrictor plate (normally open)
2. EPR vacuum actuator

84904116

Fig. 54 EPR valve

EGR/EPR Solenoid Assembly

▶ **See Figure 55**

1. Disconnect the negative battery cable.
2. Label and disconnect the vacuum hoses from the assembly.
3. Unplug the solenoid electrical connectors.
4. Remove the retainers securing the assembly to the intake manifold.
5. Installation is the reverse of removal.

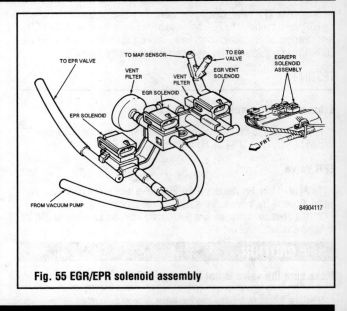

Fig. 55 EGR/EPR solenoid assembly

CARBURETED ELECTRONIC ENGINE CONTROLS

Electronic Control Module (ECM)

OPERATION

▶ **See Figure 56**

➡ When the term Electronic Control Module (ECM) is used in this manual, it refers to the engine control computer, whether it is a

Vehicle Control Module (VCM), Powertrain Control Module (PCM) or Electronic Control Module (ECM).

The ECM is a reliable solid state computer, protected in a metal box. It is used to monitor and control all the functions of the Computer Command Control (CCC) system and is located in one of several places in the passenger compartment (refer to the component location diagrams in this section). The ECM can perform several on-vehicle functions at the same time and has the ability to diagnose itself as well as other CCC system circuits.

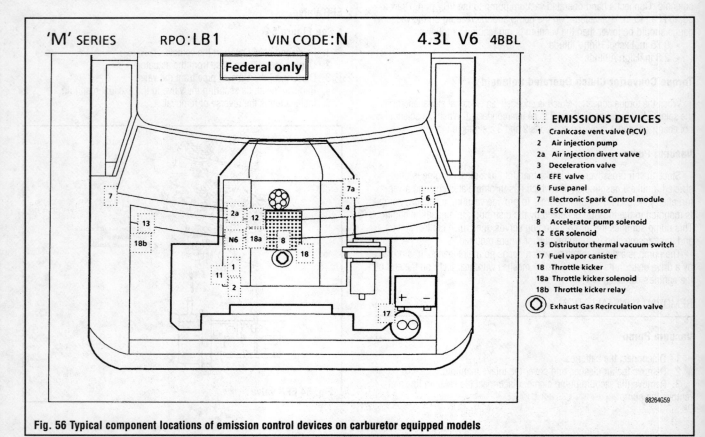

Fig. 56 Typical component locations of emission control devices on carburetor equipped models

REMOVAL & INSTALLATION

1. Disconnect the negative battery cable.
2. Disengage the connectors from the ECM.
3. Remove the ECM mounting hardware.
4. Remove the ECM from the passenger compartment.
5. Installation is the reverse of removal.

Oxygen Sensor

OPERATION

The oxygen sensor is a spark plug shaped device that is screwed into the exhaust manifold on V6 and V8 engines, and into the exhaust pipe on the 4.8L. It monitors the oxygen content of the exhaust gases and sends a voltage signal to the ECM. The ECM monitors this voltage and, depending on the value of the received signal, issues a command to the mixture control solenoid on the carburetor to adjust for rich or lean conditions.

The proper operation of the oxygen sensor depends upon four basic conditions:

1. Good electrical connections. Since the sensor generates low currents, good clean electrical connections at the sensor are a must.
2. Outside air supply. Air must circulate to the internal portion of the sensor. When servicing the sensor, do not restrict the air passages.
3. Proper operating temperatures. The ECM will not recognize the sensor's signals until the sensor reaches approximately 600°F (316°C).
4. Non-leaded fuel. The use of leaded gasoline will damage the sensor very quickly.

TESTING

♦ See Figure 57

1. Start the engine and bring it to normal operating temperature, then run the engine above 1200 rpm for two minutes.
2. Backprobe with a high impedance averaging voltmeter (set to the DC voltage scale) between the oxygen sensor (02S) and battery ground.
3. Verify that the 02S voltage fluctuates rapidly between 0.40–0.60 volts.
4. If the 02S voltage is stabilized at the middle of the specified range (approximately 0.45–0.55 volts) or if the 02S voltage fluctuates very slowly between the specified range (02S signal crosses 0.5 volts less than 5 times in ten seconds), the 02S may be faulty.

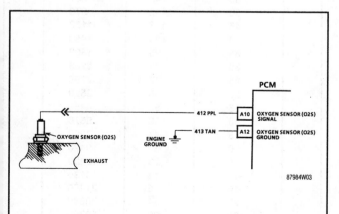

Fig. 57 Oxygen sensor (02S) wiring diagram for PCM equipped models. ECM equipped models terminals are numbered D7 for the sensor signal and D6 for the sensor ground

5. If the 02S voltage stabilizes at either end of the specified range, the ECM is probably not able to compensate for a mechanical problem such as a vacuum leak or a high float level. These types of mechanical problems will cause the 02S to sense a constant lean or constant rich mixture. The mechanical problem will first have to be repaired and then the 02S test repeated.
6. Pull a vacuum hose located after the throttle plate. Voltage should drop to approximately 0.12 volts (while still fluctuating rapidly). This tests the ability of the 02S to detect a lean mixture condition. Reattach the vacuum hose.
7. Richen the mixture using a propane enrichment tool. Voltage should rise to approximately 0.90 volts (while still fluctuating rapidly). This tests the ability of the 02S to detect a rich mixture condition.
8. If the 02S voltage is above or below the specified range, the 02S and/or the 02S wiring may be faulty. Check the wiring for any breaks, repair as necessary and repeat the test.

REMOVAL & INSTALLATION

✳✳ WARNING

The sensor uses a permanently attached pigtail and connector. This pigtail should not be removed from the sensor. Damage or removal of the pigtail or connector could affect the proper operation of the sensor. Keep the electrical connector and louvered end of the sensor clean and free of grease. NEVER use cleaning solvents of any type on the sensor!

➥**The oxygen sensor may be difficult to remove when the temperature of the engine is below 120°F (49°C). Excessive force may damage the threads in the exhaust manifold or exhaust pipe.**

1. Unplug the electrical connector and any attaching hardware.
2. Remove the sensor using an appropriate sized wrench or special socket.

To install:

3. Coat the threads of the sensor with a GM anti-seize compound, part number 5613695, or its equivalent, before installation. New sensors are usually precoated with this compound.

➥**The GM anti-seize compound is NOT a conventional anti-seize paste. The use of a regular paste may electrically insulate the sensor, rendering it useless. The threads MUST be coated with the proper electrically conductive anti-seize compound.**

4. Install the sensor and tighten to 30 ft. lbs. (40 Nm). Use care in making sure the silicone boot is in the correct position to avoid melting it during operation.
5. Engage the electrical connector and attaching hardware if used.

Coolant Temperature Sensor (CTS)

OPERATION

♦ See Figure 58

The coolant temperature sensor is a thermistor (a resistor which changes value based on temperature). Low coolant temperatures produce high resistance (100,000 ohms at -40°F/-40°C) while low temperatures causes low resistance (70 ohms at 266°F/130°C). The sensor is mounted in the coolant stream (usually on the intake manifold) and the ECM supplies a 5 volt signal to the sensor through a resistor in the ECM and measures the voltage. The voltage will be high when the engine is cold, and low when the engine is hot. By measuring the voltage, the ECM knows the engine coolant temperature effects most systems the ECM controls.

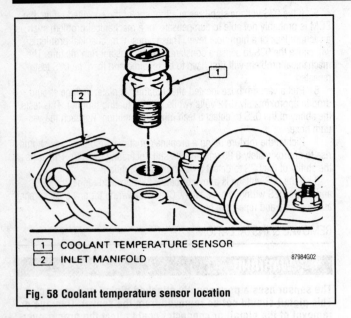

| 1 | COOLANT TEMPERATURE SENSOR |
| 2 | INLET MANIFOLD |

87984G02

Fig. 58 Coolant temperature sensor location

TESTING

▶ **See Figures 59, 60 and 61**

1. Remove the sensor from the vehicle.
2. Immerse the tip of the sensor in container of water.
3. Connect a digital ohmmeter to the two terminals of the sensor.
4. Using a calibrated thermometer, compare the resistance of the sensor to the temperature of the water. Refer to the engine coolant sensor temperature vs. resistance illustration.
5. Repeat the test at two other temperature points, heating or cooling the water as necessary.
6. If the sensor does not meet specification, it must be replaced.

REMOVAL & INSTALLATION

1. Disconnect the negative battery cable.
2. Drain the cooling system below the level of the sensor and disengage the sensor electrical connection.

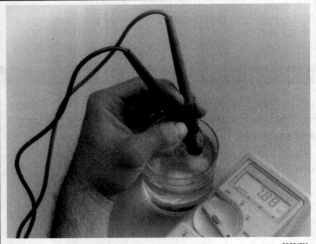

TCCS4P02

Fig. 59 Submerge the end of the coolant temperature sensor in cold or hot water and check the resistance

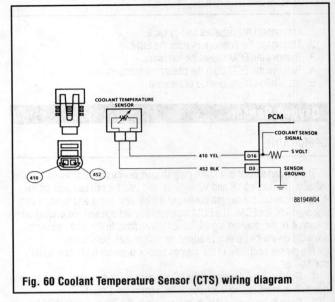

88194W04

Fig. 60 Coolant Temperature Sensor (CTS) wiring diagram

3. Remove the coolant sensor.

To install:

4. Install the sensor and engage the electrical connector.
5. Refill the cooling system and connect the negative battery cable.

ENGINE COOLANT SENSOR		
TEMPERATURE VS. RESISTANCE VALUES (APPROXIMATE)		
°C	°F	OHMS
100	212	177
90	194	241
80	176	332
70	158	467
60	140	667
50	122	973
45	113	1188
40	104	1459
35	95	1802
30	86	2238
25	77	2796
20	68	3520
15	59	4450
10	50	5670
5	41	7280
0	32	9420
-5	23	12300
-10	14	16180
-15	5	21450
-20	-4	28680
-30	-22	52700
-40	-40	100700

87984G38

Fig. 61 Coolant temperature sensor temperature vs. resistance values

Manifold Absolute Pressure (MAP) Sensor

OPERATION

The Manifold Absolute Pressure (MAP) sensor measures the changes in intake manifold pressure, which result from the engine load and speed changes, and converts this to a voltage output.

A closed throttle on engine coastdown will produce a low MAP output, while a wide-open throttle will produce a high output. This high output is produced because the pressure inside the manifold is the same as outside the manifold, so 100 percent of the outside air pressure is measured.

The MAP sensor reading is the opposite of what you would measure on a vacuum gauge. When manifold pressure is high, vacuum is low. The MAP sensor is also used to measure barometric pressure under certain conditions, which allows the ECM to automatically adjust for different altitudes.

The ECM sends a 5 volt reference signal to the MAP sensor. As the manifold pressure changes, the electrical resistance of the sensor also changes. By monitoring the sensor output voltage, the ECM knows the manifold pressure. A higher pressure, low vacuum (high voltage) requires more fuel, while a lower pressure, higher vacuum (low voltage) requires less fuel.

The ECM uses the MAP sensor to control fuel delivery and ignition timing.

TESTING

▶ **See Figure 62**

1. Backprobe with a high impedance voltmeter at MAP sensor terminals A and C.
2. With the key **ON** and engine off, the voltmeter reading should be approximately 5.0 volts.
3. If the voltage is not as specified, either the wiring to the MAP sensor or the ECM may be faulty. Correct any wiring or ECM faults before continuing test.
4. Backprobe with a high impotence voltmeter at MAP sensor terminals B and A.
5. Verify that the sensor voltage is approximately 0.5 volts with the engine not running.
6. Start the vehicle.
7. Verify that the sensor voltage is greater than 1.5 volts at idle.
8. Verify that the sensor voltage increases to approximately 4.5. volts at Wide Open Throttle (WOT).
9. If the sensor voltage is as specified, the sensor is functioning properly.

10. If the sensor voltage is not as specified, check the sensor and the sensor vacuum source for a leak or a restriction. If no leaks or restrictions are found, the sensor may be defective and should be replaced.

REMOVAL & INSTALLATION

1. Disconnect the negative battery cable.
2. Tag and disconnect the vacuum harness assembly.
3. Disengage the electrical connector.
4. Release the locktabs, unfasten the bolts and remove the sensor.
5. Installation is the reverse of removal.

Throttle Position Sensor (TPS)

OPERATION

The Throttle Position Sensor (TPS) is located inside the carburetor. It is a potentiometer with one wire connected to 5 volts from the ECM and the other to ground. A third wire is connected to the ECM to measure the voltage from the TPS.

As the accelerator pedal is moved, the output of the TPS also changes. At a closed throttle position, the output of the TPS is low (approximately 0.5 volts). As the throttle valve opens, the output increases so that, at wide-open throttle, the output voltage should be approximately 4.5 volts.

By monitoring the output voltage from the TPS, the ECM can determine fuel delivery based on throttle valve angle (driver demand).

TESTING

▶ **See Figure 63**

1. Backprobe with a high impedance voltmeter at TPS terminals A and B.
2. With the key **ON** and engine off, the voltmeter reading should be approximately 5.0 volts.
3. If the voltage is not as specified, either the wiring to the TPS or the ECM may be faulty. Correct any wiring or ECM faults before continuing test.
4. Backprobe with a high impedance voltmeter at terminals C and B.
5. With the key **ON** and engine off and the throttle closed, the TPS voltage should be approximately 0.5–1.2 volts.
6. Verify that the TPS voltage increases or decreases smoothly as the

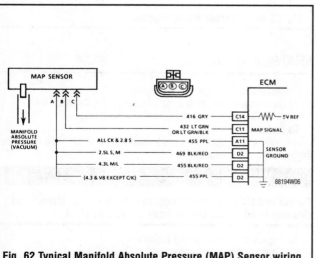

Fig. 62 Typical Manifold Absolute Pressure (MAP) Sensor wiring diagram

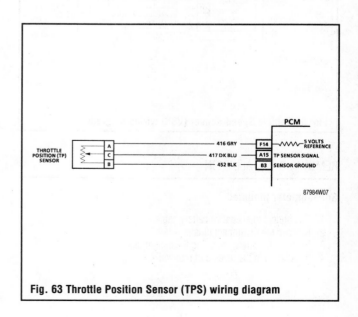

Fig. 63 Throttle Position Sensor (TPS) wiring diagram

throttle is opened or closed. Make sure to open and close the throttle very slowly in order to detect any abnormalities in the TPS voltage reading.

7. If the sensor voltage is not as specified, replace the sensor.

REMOVAL & INSTALLATION

The throttle position sensor is located in the carburetor. Please refer to Section 5 for the carburetor disassembly procedures to remove the TPS.

Vehicle Speed Sensor (VSS)

OPERATION

The vehicle speed sensor is sometimes located behind the speedometer or more commonly on the transmission. It sends a pulsing voltage signal to the ECM, which the ECM converts to vehicle speed. This sensor mainly controls the operation of the Torque Convertor Clutch (TCC) system, shift light and cruise control.

TESTING

▶ See Figure 64

1. Backprobe the VSS terminals with a high impedance voltmeter (set at the AC voltage scale).
2. Safely raise and support the entire vehicle using jackstands. Make absolutely sure the vehicle is secure.
3. Start the vehicle and place it in gear.
4. Verify that the VSS voltage increases as the speed increases.
5. If the VSS voltage is not as specified the VSS may be faulty.

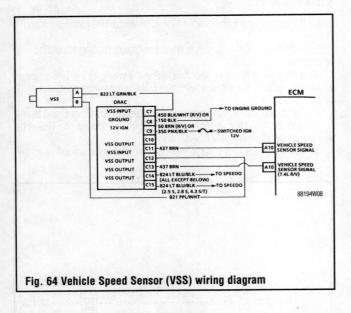

Fig. 64 Vehicle Speed Sensor (VSS) wiring diagram

REMOVAL & INSTALLATION

Speedometer Mounted

1. Disconnect the negative battery cable.
2. Remove the instrument cluster.
3. Remove the screws securing the sensor assembly.
4. Installation is the reverse of removal.

Transmission Mounted

1. Raise and safely support the vehicle.
2. Unplug the electrical connector.
3. Disconnect the speedometer cable from the sensor.
4. Remove the sensor from the transmission.
5. Installation is the reverse of removal.

Knock Sensor

OPERATION

Located in the engine block, the Knock Sensor (KS) retards ignition timing during a spark knock condition to allow the ECM to maintain maximum timing advance under most conditions.

TESTING

▶ See Figure 65

1. Connect a timing light to the vehicle and start the engine.
2. Check that the timing is correct before testing knock sensor operation.
3. If timing is correct, tap on the front of the engine block with a metal object while observing the timing to see if the timing retards.
4. If the timing does not retard, the knock sensor may be defective.

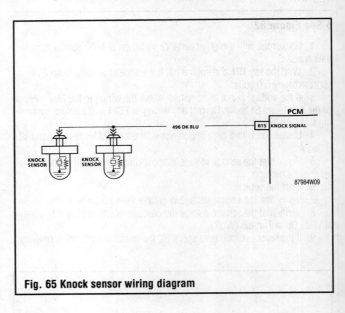

Fig. 65 Knock sensor wiring diagram

REMOVAL & INSTALLATION

1. Disconnect the negative battery cable.
2. Disengage the wiring harness connector from the knock sensor.
3. Remove the knock sensor from the engine block.
To install:
4. Apply a water base caulk to the knock sensor threads and install the sensor in the engine block.

✴✴ WARNING

Do not use silicone tape to coat the knock sensor threads, as this will insulate the sensor from the engine block.

5. Engage the wiring harness connector.
6. Connect the negative battery cable.

FUEL INJECTED ELECTRONIC ENGINE CONTROLS

8819P15

UNDER ENGINE COVER ELECTRONIC ENGINE CONTROL COMPONENTS—1997 MODEL SHOWN (OTHERS SIMILAR)

1. Oil pressure sender
2. Camshaft Position (CMP) sensor
3. Manifold Absolute Pressure (MAP) sensor
4. Idle Air Control (IAC) valve
5. Throttle Position Sensor (TPS)

UNDERHOOD ELECTRONIC ENGINE CONTROL COMPONENTS—1997 MODEL SHOWN (OTHERS SIMILAR)

1. Mass Air Flow (MAF) sensor
2. Intake Air Temperature (IAT) sensor

Electronic Control Module (ECM)

OPERATION

➡**When the term Electronic Control Module (ECM) is used in this manual it will refer to the engine control computer, regardless of whether it is a Vehicle Control Module (VCM), Powertrain Control Module (PCM) or Electronic Control Module (ECM).**

The Electronic Control Module (ECM) is required to maintain the exhaust emissions at acceptable levels. The module is a small, solid state computer which receives signals from many sources and sensors; it uses these data to make judgments about operating conditions and then control output signals to the fuel and emission systems to match the current requirements.

Engines coupled to electronically controlled transmissions employ a Powertrain Control Module (PCM) or Vehicle Control Module (VCM) to oversee both engine and transmission operation. The integrated functions of engine and transmission control allow accurate gear selection and improved fuel economy.

In the event of an ECM failure, the system will default to a pre-programmed set of values. These are compromise values which allow the engine to operate, although at a reduced efficiency. This is variously known as the default, limp-in or back-up mode. Driveability is almost always affected when the ECM enters this mode.

REMOVAL & INSTALLATION

1. Disconnect the negative battery cable.
2. Disengage the connectors from the ECM.
3. Remove the spring retainer off and over the rail of the ECM.
4. Slide the ECM out of the bracket at an angle.
5. Remove the ECM.

To install:

6. Install the ECM into the bracket.
7. Install the spring retainer and engage the electrical connectors.
8. Connect the negative battery cable.

Oxygen Sensor

OPERATION

▶ **See Figure 66**

There are two types of oxygen sensor's used in these vehicles. They are the single wire oxygen sensor (02S) and the heated oxygen sensor (H02S).

The oxygen sensor is a spark plug shaped device that is screwed into the exhaust manifold. It monitors the oxygen content of the exhaust gases and sends a voltage signal to the Electronic Control Module (ECM). The ECM monitors this voltage and, depending on the value of the received signal, issues a command to the mixture control solenoid on the carburetor to adjust for rich or lean conditions.

The heated oxygen sensor has a heating element incorporated into the sensor to aid in the warm up to the proper operating temperature and to maintain that temperature.

The proper operation of the oxygen sensor depends upon four basic conditions:

1. Good electrical connections. Since the sensor generates low currents, good clean electrical connections at the sensor are a must.
2. Outside air supply. Air must circulate to the internal portion of the sensor. When servicing the sensor, do not restrict the air passages.
3. Proper operating temperatures. The ECM will not recognize the sensor's signals until the sensor reaches approximately 600°F (316°C).
4. Non-leaded fuel. The use of leaded gasoline will damage the sensor very quickly.

TESTING

Single Wire Sensor

▶ **See Figure 67**

1. Start the engine and bring it to normal operating temperature, then run the engine above 1200 rpm for two minutes.
2. Backprobe with a high impedance averaging voltmeter (set to the DC voltage scale) between the oxygen sensor (02S) and battery ground.
3. Verify that the 02S voltage fluctuates rapidly between 0.40–0.60 volts.
4. If the 02S voltage is stabilized at the middle of the specified range (approximately 0.45–0.55 volts) or if the 02S voltage fluctuates very slowly between the specified range (02S signal crosses 0.5 volts less than 5 times in ten seconds), the 02S may be faulty.
5. If the 02S voltage stabilizes at either end of the specified range, the ECM is probably not able to compensate for a mechanical problem such as a vacuum leak or a faulty pressure regulator. These types of mechanical problems will cause the 02S to sense a constant lean or constant rich mixture. The mechanical problem will first have to be repaired and then the 02S test repeated.
6. Pull a vacuum hose located after the throttle plate. Voltage should drop to approximately 0.12 volts (while still fluctuating rapidly). This tests the ability of the 02S to detect a lean mixture condition. Reattach the vacuum hose.

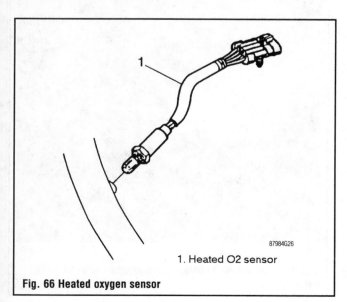

Fig. 66 Heated oxygen sensor

1. Heated O2 sensor

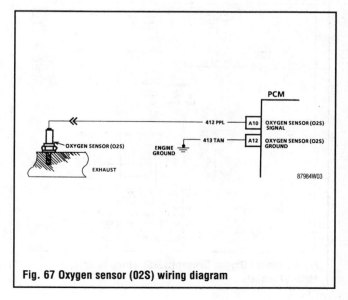

Fig. 67 Oxygen sensor (02S) wiring diagram

7. Richen the mixture using a propane enrichment tool. Voltage should rise to approximately 0.90 volts (while still fluctuating rapidly). This tests the ability of the 02S to detect a rich mixture condition.

8. If the 02S voltage is above or below the specified range, the 02S and/or the 02S wiring may be faulty. Check the wiring for any breaks, repair as necessary and repeat the test.

Heated Oxygen Sensor

▶ See Figures 68 and 69

1. Start the engine and bring it to normal operating temperature, then run the engine above 1200 rpm for two minutes.

2. Turn the ignition **OFF** disengage the H02S harness connector.

3. Connect a test light between harness terminals A and B. With the ignition switch **ON** and the engine off, verify that the test light is lit. If the test light is not lit, either the supply voltage to the H02S heater or the ground circuit of the H02S heater is faulty. Check the H02S wiring and the fuse.

4. Next, connect a high impedance ohmmeter between the H02S terminals B and A and verify that the resistance is 3.5–14.0 ohms.

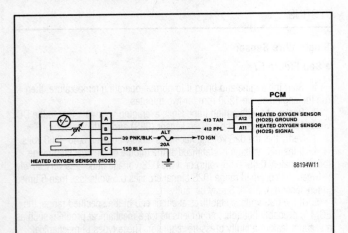

Fig. 68 Heated Oxygen Sensor (H02S) wiring diagram—1995 models shown

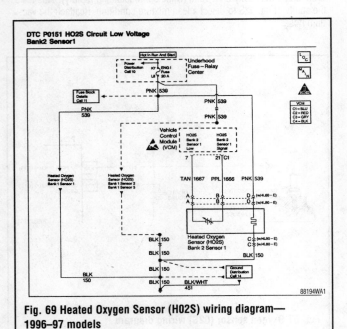

Fig. 69 Heated Oxygen Sensor (H02S) wiring diagram— 1996–97 models

5. If the H02S heater resistance is not as specified, the H02S may be faulty.

6. Start the engine and bring it to normal operating temperature, then run the engine above 1200 rpm for two minutes.

7. Backprobe with a high impedance averaging voltmeter (set to the DC voltage scale) between the oxygen sensor (02S) and battery ground.

8. Verify that the 02S voltage fluctuates rapidly between 0.40–0.60 volts.

9. If the 02S voltage is stabilized at the middle of the specified range (approximately 0.45–0.55 volts) or if the 02S voltage fluctuates very slowly between the specified range (02S signal crosses 0.5 volts less than 5 times in ten seconds), the 02S may be faulty.

10. If the 02S voltage stabilizes at either end of the specified range, the ECM is probably not able to compensate for a mechanical problem such as a vacuum leak or a faulty fuel pressure regulator. These types of mechanical problems will cause the 02S to sense a constant lean or constant rich mixture. The mechanical problem will first have to be repaired and then the 02S test repeated.

11. Pull a vacuum hose located after the throttle plate. Voltage should drop to approximately 0.12 volts (while still fluctuating rapidly). This tests the ability of the 02S to detect a lean mixture condition. Reattach the vacuum hose.

12. Richen the mixture using a propane enrichment tool. Voltage should rise to approximately 0.90 volts (while still fluctuating rapidly). This tests the ability of the 02S to detect a rich mixture condition.

13. If the 02S voltage is above or below the specified range, the 02S and/or the 02S wiring may be faulty. Check the wiring for any breaks, repair as necessary and repeat the test.

REMOVAL & INSTALLATION

✳✳ WARNING

The sensor uses a permanently attached pigtail and connector. This pigtail should not be removed from the sensor. Damage or removal of the pigtail or connector could affect the proper operation of the sensor. Keep the electrical connector and louvered end of the sensor clean and free of grease. NEVER use cleaning solvents of any type on the sensor!

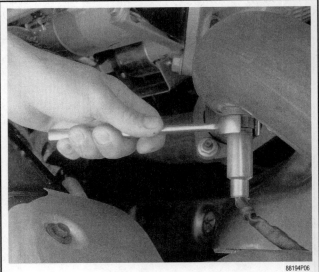

Use a special wrench to unfasten the oxygen sensor from the exhaust pipe

➡The oxygen sensor may be difficult to remove when the temperature of the engine is below 120°F (49°C). Excessive force may damage the threads in the exhaust manifold or exhaust pipe.

1. Disconnect the negative battery cable.
2. Unplug the electrical connector and any attaching hardware.
3. Remove the sensor.

To install:

4. Coat the threads of the sensor with a GM anti-seize compound, part number 5613695, or its equivalent, before installation. New sensors are precoated with this compound.

➡The GM anti-seize compound is NOT a conventional anti-seize paste. The use of a regular paste may electrically insulate the sensor, rendering it useless. The threads MUST be coated with the proper electrically conductive anti-seize compound.

5. Install the sensor and tighten to 30 ft. lbs. (41 Nm). Use care in making sure the silicone boot is in the correct position to avoid melting it during operation.
6. Engage the electrical connector.
7. Connect the negative battery cable.

Crankshaft Position (CKP) Sensor

OPERATION

▶ **See Figure 70**

The Crankshaft Position (CKP) Sensor provides a signal through the ignition module which the ECM uses as a reference to calculate rpm and crankshaft position.

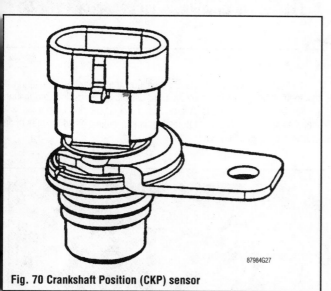

Fig. 70 Crankshaft Position (CKP) sensor

TESTING

▶ **See Figure 71**

1. Disconnect the CKP sensor harness. Connect an LED test light between battery ground and CKP harness terminal A.
2. With the ignition **ON** and the engine off, verify that the test light illuminates.
3. If not as specified, repair or replace the fuse and/or wiring.
4. Carefully connect the test light between CKP harness terminal A and B. Verify that the test light illuminates.
5. If not as specified, repair the CKP harness ground circuit (terminal B).
6. Turn the ignition **OFF** and disconnect the test light.

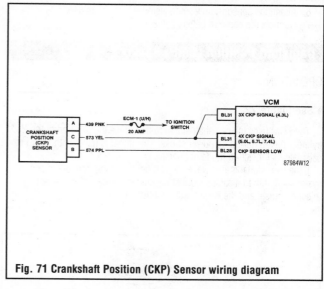

Fig. 71 Crankshaft Position (CKP) Sensor wiring diagram

7. Next, connect suitable jumper wires between the CKP sensor and CKP sensor harness. Connect a duty cycle meter to the jumper wire corresponding to CKP terminal C and battery ground.
8. Crank the engine and verify that the duty cycle signal is between 40–60%.
9. If it is not as specified, the CKP sensor may be faulty.
10. Next, connect a AC volt meter to the jumper wire corresponding to CKP terminal C and battery ground.
11. Crank the engine and verify that the AC voltage signal is at least 10.0 volts.
12. If not as specified the CKP sensor may be faulty.

REMOVAL & INSTALLATION

1. Disconnect the negative battery cable.
2. Detach the sensor harness connector at the sensor.
3. Unfasten the retaining bolt, then remove the sensor from the front cover. Inspect the sensor O-ring for wear, cracks or leakage and replace if necessary.

To install:

4. Lubricate the O-ring with clean engine oil, then place on the sensor. Install the sensor into the front cover.
5. Install the sensor and tighten the retaining bolt.

Location of the Crankshaft Position (CKP) sensor—1997 model shown, others similar

6. Attach the sensor harness connector.
7. Connect the negative battery cable.

Camshaft Position (CMP) Sensor

OPERATION

◆ See Figure 72

The ECM uses the camshaft signal to determine the position of the No. 1 cylinder piston during its power stroke. The signal is used by the ECM to calculate fuel injection mode of operation.

If the cam signal is lost while the engine is running, the fuel injection system will shift to a calculated fuel injected mode based on the last fuel injection pulse, and the engine will continue to run.

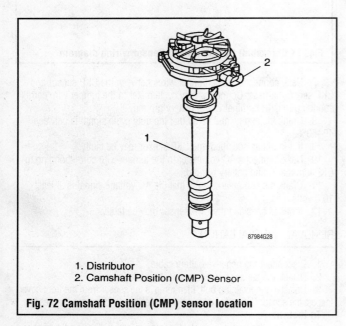

1. Distributor
2. Camshaft Position (CMP) Sensor

Fig. 72 Camshaft Position (CMP) sensor location

TESTING

◆ See Figure 73

1. Disconnect the CMP sensor wiring harness and connect an LED test light between CMP harness terminal C and battery ground.
2. With the ignition **ON** and the engine off, verify that the test light illuminates.
3. If not as specified, repair or replace the fuse and/or wiring.
4. Carefully connect the test light between CMP harness terminal A and C and verify that the test light illuminates.
5. If not as specified, repair the CMP harness ground circuit (terminal A).
6. Turn the ignition **OFF** and disconnect the test light.
7. Next, connect suitable jumper wires between the CMP sensor and CMP sensor harness. Connect a DC volt meter to the jumper wire corresponding to CMP terminal B and battery ground.
8. Start the engine and verify that the voltage signal is 5–7 volts.
9. If it is not as specified, the CMP sensor may be faulty.

REMOVAL & INSTALLATION

1. Disconnect the negative battery cable.
2. Detach the sensor harness connector at the sensor.
3. Unfasten the retaining screw, then remove the sensor.

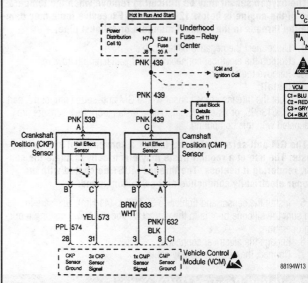

Fig. 73 Camshaft Position (CMP) wiring diagram—1996–97

To install:

4. Install the sensor and tighten the retaining screw, then tighten to 35–53 inch lbs. (4–6 Nm).
5. Attach the sensor harness connector.
6. Connect the negative battery cable.

Mass Air Flow (MAF) Sensor

OPERATION

◆ See Figure 74

The Mass Air Flow (MAF) Sensor measures the amount of air entering the engine during a given time. The ECM uses the mass airflow information for fuel delivery calculations. A large quantity of air entering the engine indicates an acceleration or high load situation, while a small quantity of air indicates deceleration or idle.

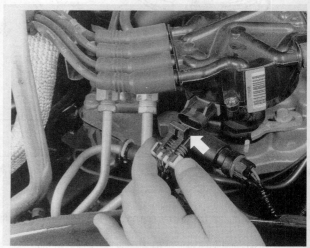

Unplug the Camshaft Position (CMP) sensor electrical connection before loosening the retaining screw

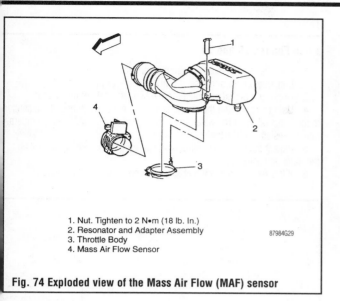

1. Nut. Tighten to 2 N•m (18 lb. In.)
2. Resonator and Adapter Assembly
3. Throttle Body
4. Mass Air Flow Sensor

87984G29

Fig. 74 Exploded view of the Mass Air Flow (MAF) sensor

TESTING

◆ See Figure 75

1. Backprobe with a high impedance voltmeter between MAF sensor terminals C and B.
2. With the ignition **ON** engine off, verify that battery voltage is present.
3. If the voltage is not as specified, either the wiring to the MAF sensor, fuse or the ECM may be faulty. Correct any wiring or ECM faults before continuing test.
4. Disconnect the voltmeter and backprobe with a frequency meter between MAF sensor terminals A and B.
5. Start the engine and wait until it reaches normal idle speed and verify that the MAF sensor output is approximately 2000 Hz.
6. Slowly raise engine speed up to maximum recommended rpm and verify that the MAF sensor output rises smoothly to approximately 8000 Hz.
7. If MAF sensor output is not as specified the sensor may be faulty.

REMOVAL & INSTALLATION

1. Disconnect the negative battery cable.
2. Unplug the electrical connector.

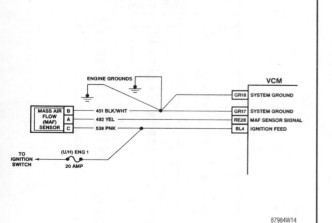

87984W14

Fig. 75 Mass Air Flow (MAF) sensor wiring diagram

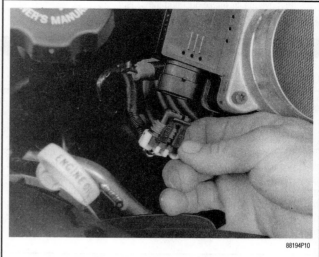

88194P10

Unplug the MAF sensor electrical connection . . .

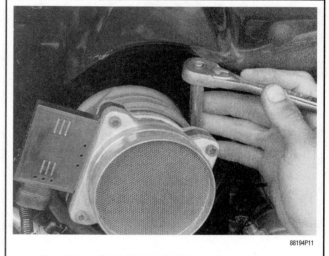

88194P11

. . . then loosen the intake duct retainers

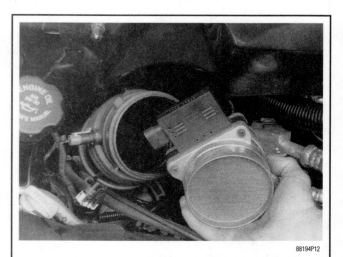

88194P12

Remove the intake duct and MAF sensor from the engine compartment

3. Remove the air intake duct and the sensor.
4. Installation is the reverse of removal.

Engine Coolant Temperature (ECT) Sensor

OPERATION

▶ **See Figures 76 and 77**

The Engine Coolant Temperature (ECT) sensor is mounted in the intake manifold and sends engine temperature information to the ECM. The ECM supplies 5 volts to the coolant temperature sensor circuit. The sensor is a thermistor which changes internal resistance as temperature changes. When the sensor is cold (internal resistance high), the ECM monitors a high signal voltage which it interprets as a cold engine. As the sensor warms (internal resistance low), the ECM monitors a low signal voltage which it interprets as warm engine.

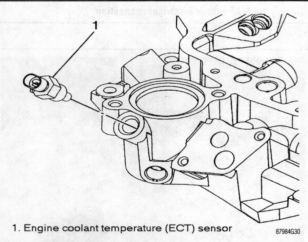

1. Engine coolant temperature (ECT) sensor

Fig. 76 Engine Coolant Temperature (ECT) sensor location— 4.3L, 5.0L and 5.7L engines

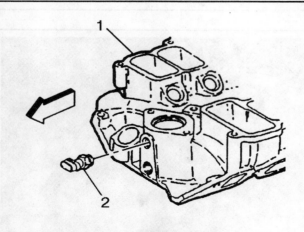

1. Lower intake manifold assembly
2. Engine coolant temperature (ECT) sensor

Fig. 77 Engine Coolant Temperature (ECT) sensor location— 7.4L engines

TESTING

▶ **See Figures 78 and 79**

1. Remove the ECT sensor from the vehicle.
2. Immerse the tip of the sensor in container of water.
3. Connect a digital ohmmeter to the two terminals of the sensor.
4. Using a calibrated thermometer, compare the resistance of the senso to the temperature of the water. Refer to the engine coolant sensor temperature vs. resistance illustration.
5. Repeat the test at two other temperature points, heating or cooling the water as necessary.
6. If the sensor does not met specification, it must be replaced.

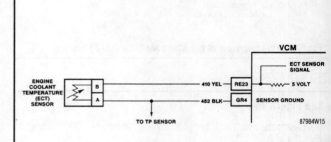

Fig. 78 Engine Coolant Temperature (ECT) sensor wiring diagram

REMOVAL & INSTALLATION

1. Disconnect the negative battery cable.
2. Drain the cooling system below the level of the sensor and disengage the sensor electrical connection.
3. Remove the coolant sensor.

ENGINE COOLANT SENSOR		
TEMPERATURE VS. RESISTANCE VALUES (APPROXIMATE)		
°C	°F	OHMS
100	212	177
90	194	241
80	176	332
70	158	467
60	140	667
50	122	973
45	113	1188
40	104	1459
35	95	1802
30	86	2238
25	77	2796
20	68	3520
15	59	4450
10	50	5670
5	41	7280
0	32	9420
-5	23	12300
-10	14	16180
-15	5	21450
-20	-4	28680
-30	-22	52700
-40	-40	100700

Fig. 79 Engine Coolant Temperature (ECT) sensor temperature vs. resistance values

To install:

4. Install the sensor and engage the electrical connector.
5. Refill the cooling system and connect the negative battery cable.

Intake Air Temperature (IAT) Sensor

OPERATION

▶ See Figure 80

the Intake Air Temperature (IAT) Sensor is a thermistor which changes value based on the temperature of the air entering the engine. Low temperature produces a high resistance, while a high temperature causes a low resistance. The ECM supplies a 5 volt signal to the sensor through a resistor in the ECM and measures the voltage. The voltage will be high when the incoming air is cold, and low when the air is hot. By measuring the voltage, the ECM calculates the incoming air temperature.

the IAT sensor signal is used to adjust spark timing according to incoming air density.

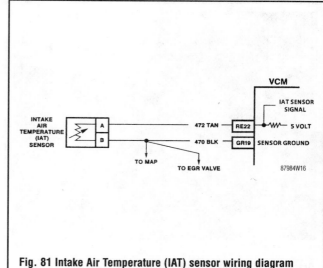

Fig. 81 Intake Air Temperature (IAT) sensor wiring diagram

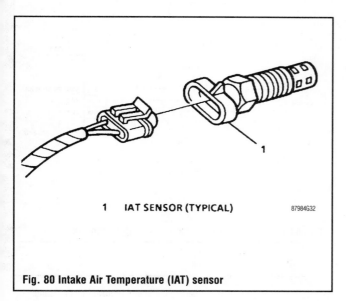

Fig. 80 Intake Air Temperature (IAT) sensor

INTAKE AIR SENSOR		
TEMPERATURE VS. RESISTANCE VALUES (APPROXIMATE)		
°C	°F	OHMS
100	212	177
90	194	241
80	176	332
70	158	467
60	140	667
50	122	973
45	113	1188
40	104	1459
35	95	1802
30	86	2238
25	77	2796
20	68	3520
15	59	4450
10	50	5670
5	41	7280
0	32	9420
-5	23	12300
-10	14	16180
-15	5	21450
-20	-4	28680
-30	-22	52700
-40	-40	100700

87984G39

Fig. 82 Intake Air Temperature (IAT) sensor temperature vs. resistance values

TESTING

▶ See Figures 81 and 82

1. Remove the Intake Air Temperature (IAT) sensor.
2. Connect a digital ohmmeter to the two terminals of the sensor.
3. Using a calibrated thermometer, compare the resistance of the sensor to the temperature of the ambient air. Refer to the temperature vs. resistance illustration.
4. Repeat the test at two other temperature points, heating or cooling the air as necessary with a hair dryer or other suitable tool.
5. If the sensor does not meet specification, it must be replaced.

REMOVAL & INSTALLATION

1. Disconnect the negative battery cable.
2. Disengage the sensor electrical connection.
3. Loosen and remove the IAT sensor.
4. Installation is the reverse of removal.

Unplug the IAT sensor electrical connection

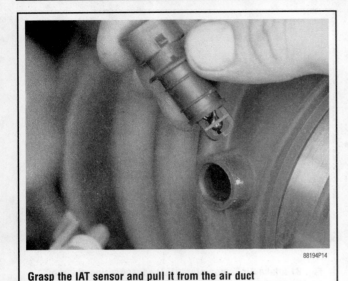

Grasp the IAT sensor and pull it from the air duct

Throttle Position Sensor (TPS)

OPERATION

▶ **See Figure 83**

The Throttle Position Sensor (TPS) is connected to the throttle shaft on the throttle body. It is a potentiometer with one end connected to 5 volts from the ECM and the other to ground.

A third wire is connected to the ECM to measure the voltage from the TPS. As the throttle valve angle is changed (accelerator pedal moved), the output of the TPS also changes. At a closed throttle position, the output of the TPS is low (approximately .5 volts). As the throttle valve opens, the output increases so that, at wide-open throttle, the output voltage should be approximately 4.5 volts.

By monitoring the output voltage from the TPS, the ECM can determine fuel delivery based on throttle valve angle (driver demand).

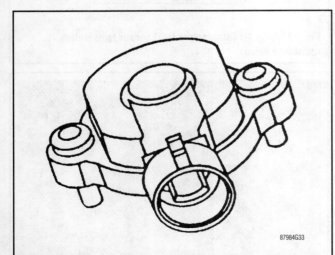

Fig. 83 Common Throttle Position Sensor (TPS) found on GM vans

TESTING

▶ **See Figure 84**

1. Backprobe with a high impedance voltmeter at TPS terminals A and B.
2. With the key **ON** and engine off, the voltmeter reading should be approximately 5.0 volts.
3. If the voltage is not as specified, either the wiring to the TPS or the ECM may be faulty. Correct any wiring or ECM faults before continuing test.
4. Backprobe with a high impedance voltmeter at terminals C and B.
5. With the key **ON** and engine off and the throttle closed, the TPS voltage should be approximately 0.5–1.2 volts.
6. Verify that the TPS voltage increases or decreases smoothly as the throttle is opened or closed. Make sure to open and close the throttle very slowly in order to detect any abnormalities in the TPS voltage reading.
7. If the sensor voltage is not as specified, replace the sensor.

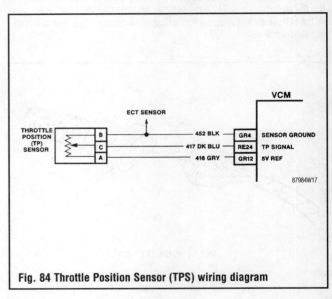

Fig. 84 Throttle Position Sensor (TPS) wiring diagram

REMOVAL & INSTALLATION

1. Disconnect the negative battery cable and remove the air cleaner and gasket.
2. Disengage the electrical connector.
3. Unfasten the two TPS attaching screw assemblies.
4. Remove the TPS from the throttle body assembly.
5. Remove the TPS seal.

To install:
6. Install the TPS seal over the throttle shaft.
7. With the throttle valve closed, install the TPS on the throttle shaft. Rotate it counterclockwise, to align the mounting holes.
8. Install the two TPS attaching screw assemblies.
9. Engage the electrical connector.
10. Install the air cleaner and gasket.
11. Connect the negative battery cable.

Idle Air Control (IAC) Valve

OPERATION

▶ **See Figure 85**

The engine idle speed is controlled by the ECM through the Idle Air Control (IAC) valve mounted on the throttle body. The ECM sends voltage pulses to the IAC motor causing the IAC motor shaft and pintle to move in or out a given distance (number of steps) for each pulse, (called counts).

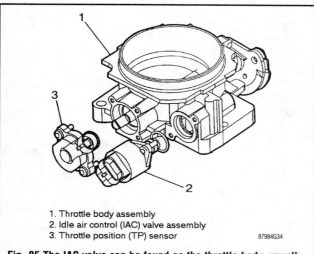

1. Throttle body assembly
2. Idle air control (IAC) valve assembly
3. Throttle position (TP) sensor

87984G34

Fig. 85 The IAC valve can be found on the throttle body, usually next to the throttle position sensor

This movement controls air flow around the throttle plate, which in turn, controls engine idle speed, either cold or hot. IAC valve pintle position counts can be seen using a scan tool. Zero counts corresponds to a fully closed passage, while 140 or more counts (depending on the application) corresponds to full flow.

TESTING

▶ See Figure 86

1. Disengage the IAC electrical connector.
2. Using an ohmmeter, measure the resistance between IAC terminals A and B. Next measure the resistance between terminals C and D.
3. Verify that the resistance between both sets of IAC terminals is 20–80 ohms. If the resistance is not as specified, the IAC may be faulty.
4. Measure the resistance between IAC terminals B and C. Next measure the resistance between terminals A and D.
5. Verify that the resistance between both sets of IAC terminals is infinite. If the resistance is not infinite, the IAC may be faulty.
6. Also, with a small mirror, inspect IAC air inlet passage and pintle for debris. Clean as necessary, as this can cause IAC malfunction.

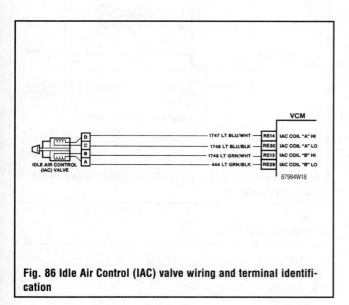

Fig. 86 Idle Air Control (IAC) valve wiring and terminal identification

REMOVAL & INSTALLATION

1. Disconnect the negative battery cable.
2. Disengage the electrical connection.
3. Remove the IAC valve. On thread-mounted units, use 1¼ in. (32mm) wrench and on flange-mounted units, remove the screw assemblies.
4. Remove the IAC valve gasket or O-ring and discard it.
To install:
5. Clean the old gasket material from the surface of the throttle body assembly on the thread mounted valve. On the flange-mounted valve clean the surface to ensure proper O-ring sealing
6. Install the valve with a new gasket or O-ring. Tighten the thread mounted assembly 13 ft. lbs. (18 Nm) and tighten the flange mounted attaching screws to 28 inch. lbs. (3 Nm).
7. Engage the electrical connector to the IAC valve.
8. Connect the negative battery cable.

Manifold Absolute Pressure (MAP) Sensor

OPERATION

▶ See Figure 87

The Manifold Absolute Pressure (MAP) sensor measures the changes in intake manifold pressure, which result from the engine load and speed changes, and converts this to a voltage output.

A closed throttle on engine coastdown will produce a low MAP output, while a wide-open throttle will produce a high output. This high output is produced because the pressure inside the manifold is the same as outside the manifold, so 100 percent of the outside air pressure is measured.

The MAP sensor reading is the opposite of what you would measure on a vacuum gauge. When manifold pressure is high, vacuum is low. The MAP sensor is also used to measure barometric pressure under certain conditions, which allows the ECM to automatically adjust for different altitudes.

The ECM sends a 5 volt reference signal to the MAP sensor. As the manifold pressure changes, the electrical resistance of the sensor also changes. By monitoring the sensor output voltage, the ECM knows the manifold pressure. A higher pressure, low vacuum (high voltage) requires more fuel, while a lower pressure, higher vacuum (low voltage) requires less fuel.

The ECM uses the MAP sensor to control fuel delivery and ignition timing.

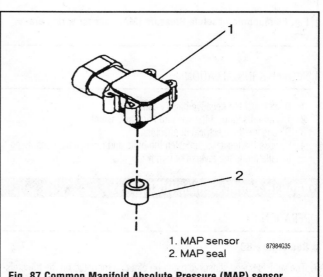

1. MAP sensor
2. MAP seal

87984G35

Fig. 87 Common Manifold Absolute Pressure (MAP) sensor

TESTING

▶ **See Figure 88**

1. Backprobe with a high impedance voltmeter at MAP sensor terminals A and C.
2. With the key **ON** and engine off, the voltmeter reading should be approximately 5.0 volts.
3. If the voltage is not as specified, either the wiring to the MAP sensor or the ECM may be faulty. Correct any wiring or ECM faults before continuing test.
4. Backprobe with the high impotence voltmeter at MAP sensor terminals B and A.
5. Verify that the sensor voltage is approximately 0.5 volts with the engine not running (at sea level).
6. Record MAP sensor voltage with the key **ON** and engine off.
7. Start the vehicle.
8. Verify that the sensor voltage is greater than 1.5 volts (above the recorded reading) at idle.
9. Verify that the sensor voltage increases to approximately 4.5. volts (above the recorded reading) at Wide Open Throttle (WOT).
10. If the sensor voltage is as specified, the sensor is functioning properly.
11. If the sensor voltage is not as specified, check the sensor and the sensor vacuum source for a leak or a restriction. If no leaks or restrictions are found, the sensor may be defective and should be replaced.

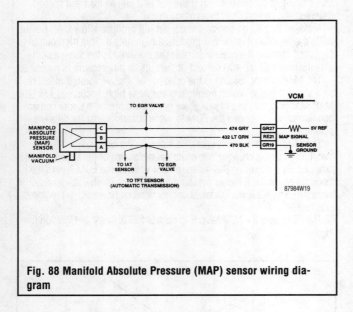

Fig. 88 Manifold Absolute Pressure (MAP) sensor wiring diagram

REMOVAL & INSTALLATION

1. Disconnect the negative battery cable.
2. Tag and disconnect the vacuum harness assembly.
3. Disengage the electrical connector.
4. Release the locktabs, unfasten the bolts and remove the sensor.
5. Installation is the reverse of removal.

Vehicle Speed Sensor (VSS)

OPERATION

▶ **See Figure 89**

The vehicle speed sensor is made up of a coil mounted on the transmission and a tooth rotor mounted to the output shaft of the transmission. As

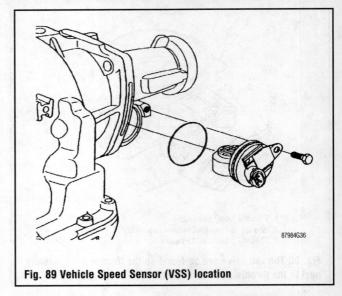

Fig. 89 Vehicle Speed Sensor (VSS) location

each tooth nears the coil, the coil produces an AC voltage pulse. As the vehicle speed increases the number of voltage pulses per second increases.

TESTING

▶ **See Figure 90**

1. To test the VSS, backprobe the VSS terminals with a high impedance voltmeter (set at the AC voltage scale).
2. Safely raise and support the entire vehicle using jackstands. Make absolutely sure the vehicle is stable.
3. Start the vehicle and place it in gear.
4. Verify that the VSS voltage increases as the drive shaft speed increases.
5. If the VSS voltage is not as specified the VSS may be faulty.

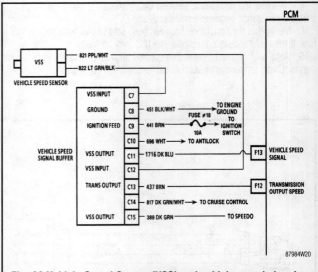

Fig. 90 Vehicle Speed Sensor (VSS) and vehicle speed signal buffer wiring diagram

REMOVAL & INSTALLATION

1. Disconnect the negative battery cable.
2. Disengage the electrical connection.
3. Unfasten the sensor retainers.

4. Remove the sensor and gasket or O-ring.
To install:
5. Install the sensor with a new gasket or O-ring.
6. Fasten the sensor retainers.
7. Engage the electrical connections.
8. Connect the negative battery cable.

Knock Sensor

OPERATION

▶ **See Figure 91**

Located in the engine block, the knock sensor retards ignition timing during a spark knock condition to allow the ECM to maintain maximum timing advance under most conditions.

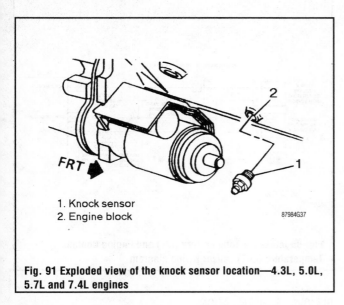

1. Knock sensor
2. Engine block

87984G37

Fig. 91 Exploded view of the knock sensor location—4.3L, 5.0L, 5.7L and 7.4L engines

TESTING

▶ **See Figures 92 and 93**

1. Connect a timing light to the vehicle and start the engine.
2. Check that the timing is correct before testing knock sensor operation.
3. If timing is correct, tap on the front of the engine block with a metal object while observing the timing to see if the timing retards.
4. If the timing does not retard the knock sensor may be defective.

REMOVAL & INSTALLATION

1. Disconnect the negative battery cable.
2. Disengage the wiring harness connector from the knock sensor.
3. Remove the knock sensor from the engine block.

To install:
4. Apply a water base caulk to the knock sensor threads and install the sensor in the engine block.

✳✳ WARNING

Do not use silicon tape to coat the knock sensor threads as this will insulate the sensor from the engine block.

5. Engage the wiring harness connector.
6. Connect the negative battery cable.

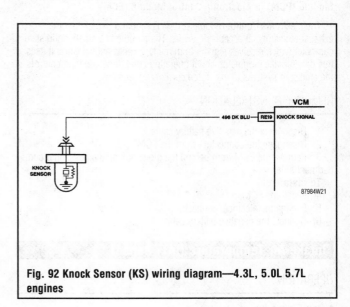

Fig. 92 Knock Sensor (KS) wiring diagram—4.3L, 5.0L 5.7L engines

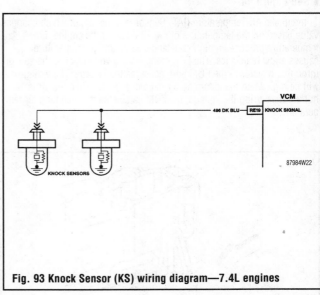

Fig. 93 Knock Sensor (KS) wiring diagram—7.4L engines

DIESEL ELECTRONIC ENGINE CONTROLS

Electronic Control Module (ECM)

OPERATION

➡**When the term Electronic Control Module (ECM) is used in this manual it will refer to the engine control computer regardless that it may be a Vehicle Control Module (VCM), Powertrain Control Module (PCM) or Electronic Control Module (ECM).**

The Electronic Control Module (ECM) is required to maintain the exhaust emissions at acceptable levels. The module is a small, solid state computer which receives signals from many sources and sensors. It uses this data tomake judgments about operating conditions and then controls the emission systems to match the current requirements.

REMOVAL & INSTALLATION

1. Disconnect the negative battery cable.
2. Disengage the connectors from the ECM.
3. Remove the ECM from behind the glove box on the passenger compartment side.
To install:
4. Install the ECM.
5. Engage the electrical connectors.
6. Connect the negative battery cable.

Intake Air Temperature (IAT) Sensor

OPERATION

▶ **See Figure 94**

the Intake Air Temperature (IAT) Sensor is a thermistor which changes value based on the temperature of the air entering the engine. Low temperature produces a high resistance, while a high temperature causes a low resistance. The ECM supplies a 5 volt signal to the sensor through a resistor in the ECM and measures the voltage. The voltage will be high when the incoming air is cold, and low when the air is hot. By measuring the voltage, the ECM calculates the incoming air temperature.

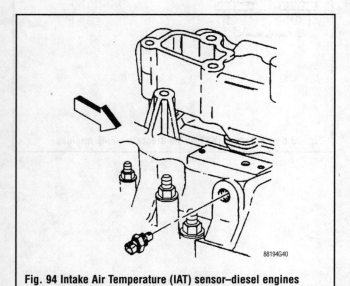

Fig. 94 Intake Air Temperature (IAT) sensor–diesel engines

TESTING

▶ **See Figures 95 and 96**

1. Remove the Intake Air Temperature (IAT) sensor.
2. Connect a digital ohmmeter to the two terminals of the sensor.
3. Using a calibrated thermometer, compare the resistance of the sensor to the temperature of the ambient air. Refer to the temperature vs. resistance illustration.
4. Repeat the test at two other temperature points, heating or cooling the air as necessary with a hair dryer or other suitable tool.
5. If the sensor does not meet specification, it must be replaced.

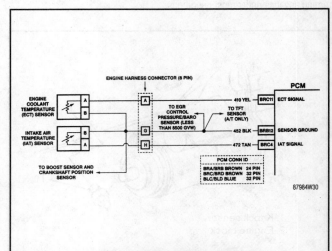

Fig. 95 Intake Air Temperature (IAT) and Engine Coolant Temperature (ECT) sensor wiring diagram

REMOVAL & INSTALLATION

1. Unplug the sensor electrical connection.
2. Loosen and remove the sensor from the vehicle.
3. Installation is the reverse of removal.

INTAKE AIR SENSOR		
TEMPERATURE VS. RESISTANCE VALUES (APPROXIMATE)		
°C	°F	OHMS
100	212	177
90	194	241
80	176	332
70	158	467
60	140	667
50	122	973
45	113	1188
40	104	1459
35	95	1802
30	86	2238
25	77	2796
20	68	3520
15	59	4450
10	50	5670
5	41	7280
0	32	9420
-5	23	12300
-10	14	16180
-15	5	21450
-20	-4	28680
-30	-22	52700
-40	-40	100700

Fig. 96 IAT sensor temperature vs. resistance values

Engine Coolant Temperature (ECT) Sensor

OPERATION

▶ **See Figures 97 and 98**

The Engine Coolant Temperature (ECT) sensor is mounted in the intake manifold and sends engine temperature information to the ECM. The ECM supplies 5 volts to the coolant temperature sensor circuit. The sensor is a thermistor which changes internal resistance as temperature changes. When the sensor is cold (internal resistance high), the ECM monitors a high signal voltage which it interprets as a cold engine. As the sensor warms (internal resistance low), the ECM monitors a low signal voltage which it interprets as warm engine.

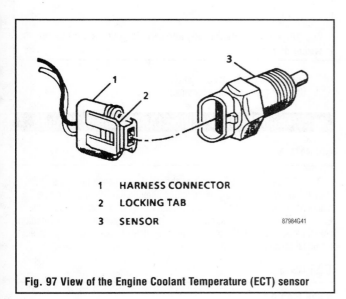

1	**HARNESS CONNECTOR**
2	**LOCKING TAB**
3	**SENSOR**

87984G41

Fig. 97 View of the Engine Coolant Temperature (ECT) sensor

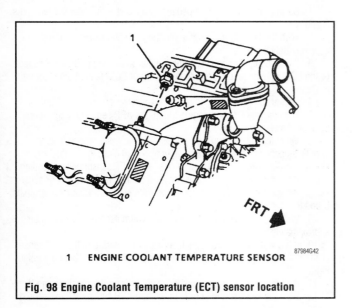

1   **ENGINE COOLANT TEMPERATURE SENSOR**

87984G42

Fig. 98 Engine Coolant Temperature (ECT) sensor location

TESTING

▶ **See Figures 99 and 100**

1. Remove the ECT sensor from the vehicle.
2. Immerse the tip of the sensor in container of water.
3. Connect a digital ohmmeter to the two terminals of the sensor.
4. Using a calibrated thermometer, compare the resistance of the sensor to the temperature of the water. Refer to the engine coolant sensor temperature vs. resistance illustration.
5. Repeat the test at two other temperature points, heating or cooling the water as necessary.
6. If the sensor does not meet specification, it must be replaced.

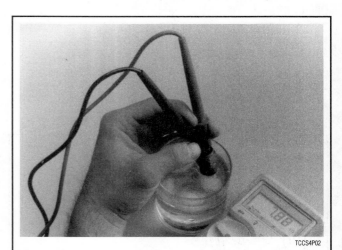

TCCS4P02

Fig. 99 Submerge the end of the temperature sensor in cold or hot water and check resistance

ENGINE COOLANT SENSOR		
TEMPERATURE VS. RESISTANCE VALUES (APPROXIMATE)		
°C	°F	OHMS
100	212	177
90	194	241
80	176	332
70	158	467
60	140	667
50	122	973
45	113	1188
40	104	1459
35	95	1802
30	86	2238
25	77	2796
20	68	3520
15	59	4450
10	50	5670
5	41	7280
0	32	9420
-5	23	12300
-10	14	16180
-15	5	21450
-20	-4	28680
-30	-22	52700
-40	-40	100700

87984G38

Fig. 100 ECT sensor temperature vs. resistance values

REMOVAL & INSTALLATION

1. Disconnect the negative battery cable.
2. Drain the cooling system below the level of the sensor and disengage the sensor electrical connection.
3. Remove the coolant sensor.
To install:
4. Install the sensor and engage the electrical connector.
5. Refill the cooling system and connect the negative battery cable.

Vehicle Speed Sensor (VSS)

OPERATION

▶ See Figure 101

The vehicle speed sensor is made up of a coil mounted on the transmission and a tooth rotor mounted to the output shaft of the transmission. As each tooth nears the coil, the coil produces an AC voltage pulse. As the vehicle speed increases the number of voltage pulses per second increases.

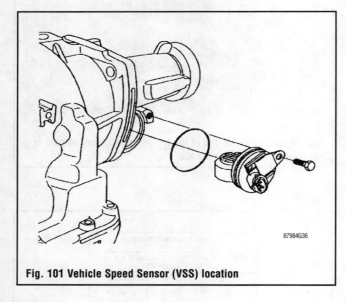

Fig. 101 Vehicle Speed Sensor (VSS) location

TESTING

▶ See Figure 102

1. To test the VSS, backprobe the VSS terminals with a high impedance voltmeter (set at the AC voltage scale).
2. Safely raise and support the entire vehicle using jackstands. Make absolutely sure the vehicle is stable.
3. Start the vehicle and place it in gear.
4. Verify that the VSS voltage increases as the drive shaft speed increases.
5. If the VSS voltage is not as specified the VSS may be faulty.

REMOVAL & INSTALLATION

1. Disconnect the negative battery cable.
2. Disengage the electrical connection.
3. Unfasten the sensor retainers.
4. Remove the sensor and gasket or O-ring.
To install:
5. Install the sensor with a new gasket or O-ring.
6. Fasten the sensor retainers.

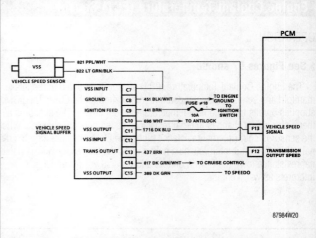

Fig. 102 Speed Sensor (VSS) and vehicle speed signal buffer wiring diagram

7. Engage the electrical connections.
8. Connect the negative battery cable.

Accelerator Pedal Position (APP) Sensor Module

OPERATION

The APP sensor module contains three potentiometers (a device for measuring unknown voltage or potential difference by comparison to a standard voltage). Each of the APP sensors send a varying voltage to the ECM. By monitoring the output voltage from the Accelerator Pedal Position (APP) module, the ECM can determine fuel delivery based on the accelerator pedal position (driver demand).

TESTING

▶ See Figure 103

1. Backprobe with a high impedance voltmeter at APP sensor terminals G and A.
2. With the key **ON** and engine off, the voltmeter reading should be approximately 5.0 volts.
3. If the voltage is not as specified, either the wiring to the APP sensor or the ECM may be faulty. Correct any wiring or ECM faults before continuing test.
4. Backprobe with a high impedance voltmeter at terminals F and A.
5. With the key **ON** and engine idling, the APP sensor voltage should be approximately 0.5 volts.
6. Verify that the APP voltage increases or decreases smoothly as the throttle is opened or closed. Make sure to open and close the throttle very slowly in order to detect any abnormalities in the APP sensor voltage reading.
7. If the APP sensor voltage is not as specified, replace the APP sensor.
8. Backprobe with a high impedance voltmeter at APP sensor terminals D and B.
9. With the key **ON** and engine off, the voltmeter reading should be approximately 5.0 volts.
10. If the voltage is not as specified, either the wiring to the APP sensor or the ECM may be faulty. Correct any wiring or ECM faults before continuing test.
11. Backprobe with a high impedance voltmeter at terminals C and B.
12. With the key **ON** and engine idling, the APP sensor voltage should be approximately 4.5 volts.
13. Verify that the APP voltage decreases smoothly as the throttle is opened. Make sure to open and close the throttle very slowly in order to detect any abnormalities in the APP sensor voltage reading.

approximately 5.0 volts.

17. If the voltage is not as specified, either the wiring to the APP sensor or the ECM may be faulty. Correct any wiring or ECM faults before continuing test.

18. Backprobe with a high impedance voltmeter at terminals K and J.

19. With the key **ON** and engine idling, the APP sensor voltage should be approximately 4.0 volts.

20. Verify that the APP voltage decreases smoothly to about 2.0 volts as the throttle is opened. Make sure to open and close the throttle very slowly in order to detect any abnormalities in the APP sensor voltage reading.

21. If the APP sensor voltage is not as specified, replace the APP sensor module.

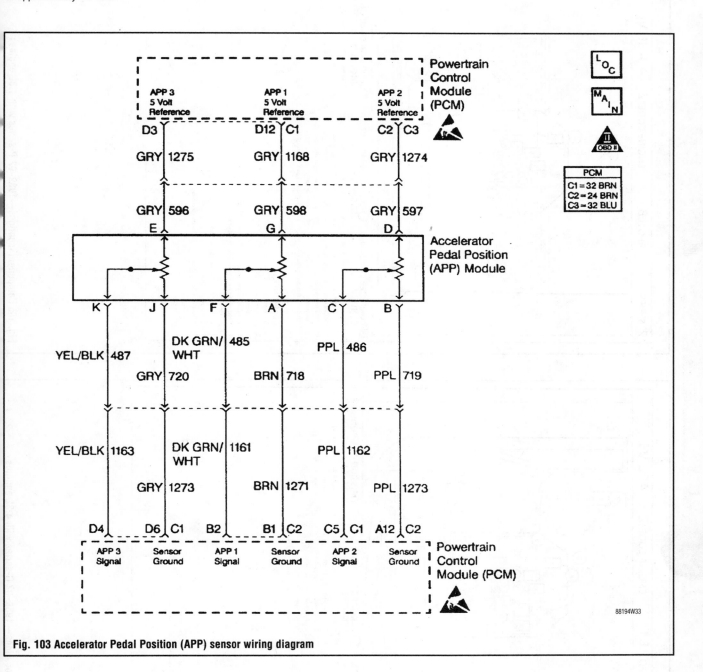

Fig. 103 Accelerator Pedal Position (APP) sensor wiring diagram

COMPONENT LOCATION DIAGRAMS

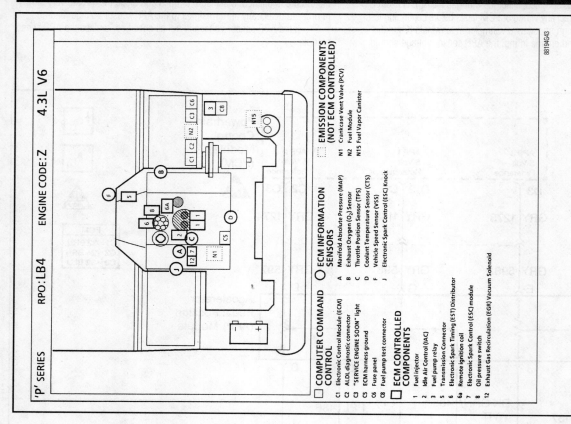

Fig. 105 Component locations—1989–92 P-series with 4.3L engines

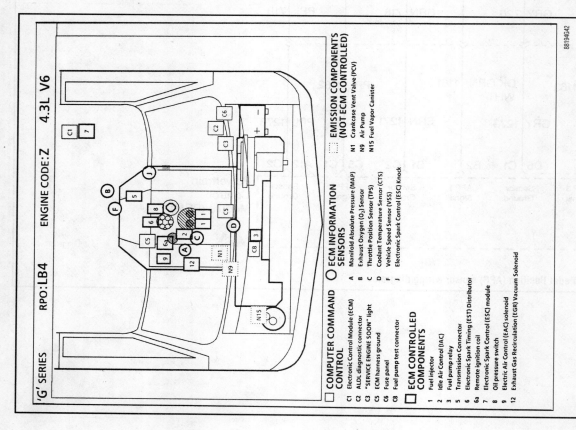

Fig. 104 Component locations—1989–92 G-series with 4.3L engines

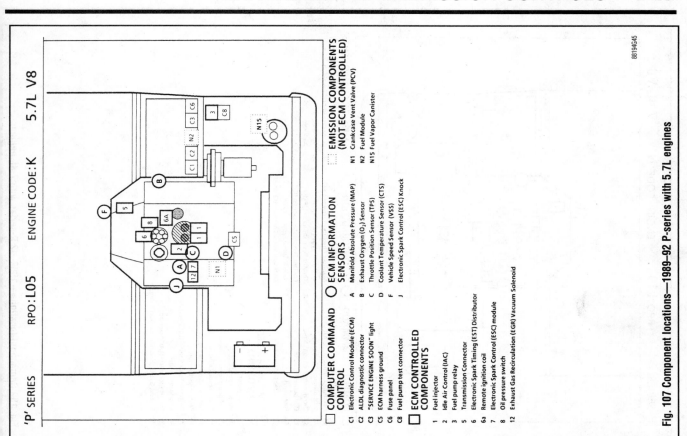

'P' SERIES   RPO: L05   ENGINE CODE: K   5.7L V8

8194G45

□ **COMPUTER COMMAND CONTROL**
C1 Electronic Control Module (ECM)
C2 ALDL diagnostic connector
C3 "SERVICE ENGINE SOON" light
C5 ECM harness ground
C6 Fuse panel
C8 Fuel pump test connector

○ **ECM INFORMATION SENSORS**
A Manifold Absolute Pressure (MAP)
B Exhaust Oxygen (O_2) Sensor
C Throttle Position Sensor (TPS)
D Coolant Temperature Sensor (CTS)
F Vehicle Speed Sensor (VSS)
J Electronic Spark Control (ESC) Knock

□ **ECM CONTROLLED COMPONENTS**
1 Fuel injector
2 Idle Air Control (IAC)
3 Fuel pump relay
5 Transmission Connector
6 Electronic Spark Timing (EST) Distributor
6a Remote ignition coil
7 Electronic Spark Control (ESC) module
8 Oil pressure switch
12 Exhaust Gas Recirculation (EGR) Vacuum Solenoid

⋯ **EMISSION COMPONENTS (NOT ECM CONTROLLED)**
N1 Crankcase Vent Valve (PCV)
N2 Fuel Module
N15 Fuel Vapor Canister

Fig. 107 Component locations—1989–92 P-series with 5.7L engines

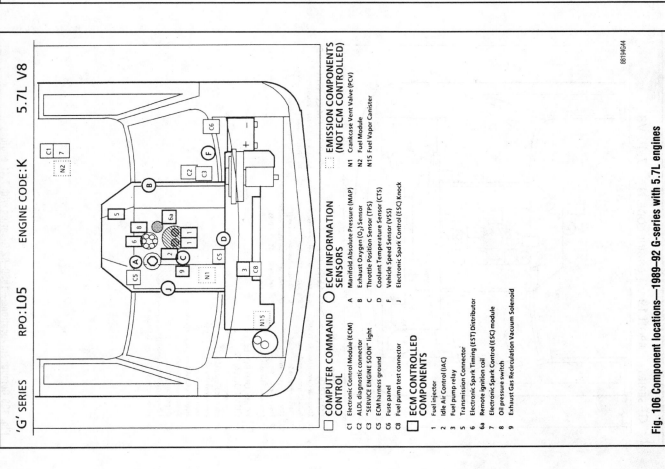

'G' SERIES   RPO: L05   ENGINE CODE: K   5.7L V8

8194G44

□ **COMPUTER COMMAND CONTROL**
C1 Electronic Control Module (ECM)
C2 ALDL diagnostic connector
C3 "SERVICE ENGINE SOON" light
C5 ECM harness ground
C6 Fuse panel
C8 Fuel pump test connector

○ **ECM INFORMATION SENSORS**
A Manifold Absolute Pressure (MAP)
B Exhaust Oxygen (O_2) Sensor
C Throttle Position Sensor (TPS)
D Coolant Temperature Sensor (CTS)
F Vehicle Speed Sensor (VSS)
J Electronic Spark Control (ESC) Knock

□ **ECM CONTROLLED COMPONENTS**
1 Fuel injector
2 Idle Air Control (IAC)
3 Fuel pump relay
5 Transmission Connector
6 Electronic Spark Timing (EST) Distributor
6a Remote ignition coil
7 Electronic Spark Control (ESC) module
8 Oil pressure switch
9 Exhaust Gas Recirculation Vacuum Solenoid

⋯ **EMISSION COMPONENTS (NOT ECM CONTROLLED)**
N1 Crankcase Vent Valve (PCV)
N2 Fuel Module
N15 Fuel Vapor Canister

Fig. 106 Component locations—1989–92 G-series with 5.7L engines

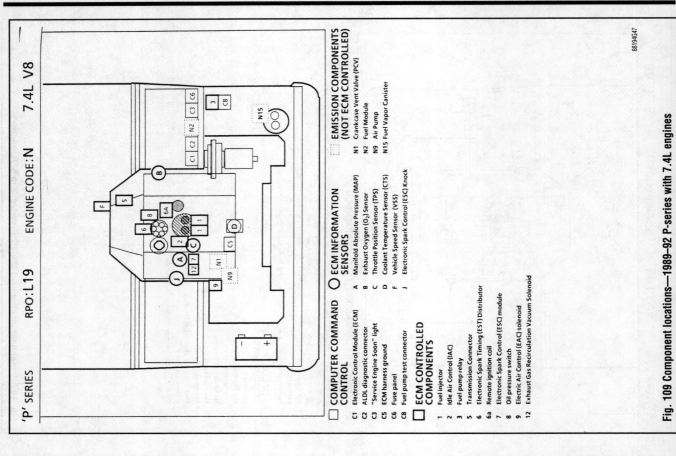

'P' SERIES   RPO: L19   ENGINE CODE: N   7.4L V8

8819_4G47

□ **COMPUTER COMMAND CONTROL**
C1 Electronic Control Module (ECM)
C2 ALDL diagnostic connector
C3 "Service Engine Soon" light
C5 ECM harness ground
C6 Fuse panel
C8 Fuel pump test connector

○ **ECM INFORMATION SENSORS**
A Manifold Absolute Pressure (MAP)
B Exhaust Oxygen (O₂) Sensor
C Throttle Position Sensor (TPS)
D Coolant Temperature Sensor (CTS)
F Vehicle Speed Sensor (VSS)
J Electronic Spark Control (ESC) Knock

▒ **EMISSION COMPONENTS (NOT ECM CONTROLLED)**
N1 Crankcase Vent Valve (PCV)
N2 Fuel Module
N9 Air Pump
N15 Fuel Vapor Canister

□ **ECM CONTROLLED COMPONENTS**
1 Fuel injector
2 Idle Air Control (IAC)
3 Fuel pump relay
5 Transmission Connector
6 Electronic Spark Timing (EST) Distributor
6a Remote ignition coil
7 Electronic Spark Control (ESC) module
8 Oil pressure switch
9 Electric Air Control (EAC) solenoid
12 Exhaust Gas Recirculation Vacuum Solenoid

Fig. 109 Component locations—1989–92 P-series with 7.4L engines

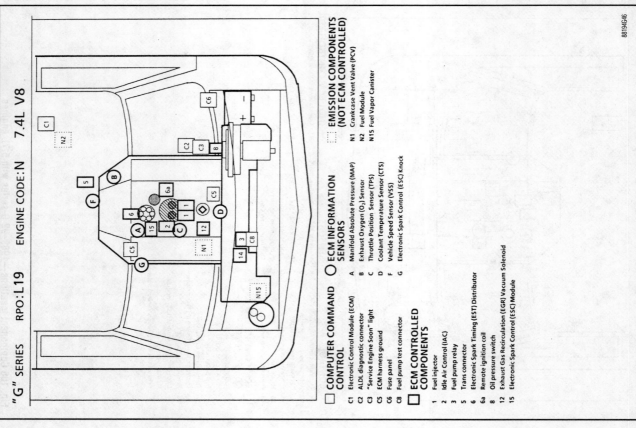

"G" SERIES   RPO: L19   ENGINE CODE: N   7.4L V8

8819_4G46

□ **COMPUTER COMMAND CONTROL**
C1 Electronic Control Module (ECM)
C2 ALDL diagnostic connector
C3 "Service Engine Soon" light
C5 ECM harness ground
C6 Fuse panel
C8 Fuel pump test connector

○ **ECM INFORMATION SENSORS**
A Manifold Absolute Pressure (MAP)
B Exhaust Oxygen (O₂) Sensor
C Throttle Position Sensor (TPS)
D Coolant Temperature Sensor (CTS)
F Vehicle Speed Sensor (VSS)
G Electronic Spark Control (ESC) Knock

▒ **EMISSION COMPONENTS (NOT ECM CONTROLLED)**
N1 Crankcase Vent Valve (PCV)
N2 Fuel Module
N15 Fuel Vapor Canister

□ **ECM CONTROLLED COMPONENTS**
1 Fuel injector
2 Idle Air Control (IAC)
3 Fuel pump relay
5 Trans connector
6 Electronic Spark Timing (EST) Distributor
6a Remote ignition coil
8 Oil pressure switch
12 Exhaust Gas Recirculation (EGR) Vacuum Solenoid
15 Electronic Spark Control (ESC) Module

Fig. 108 Component locations—1989–92 G-series with 7.4L engines

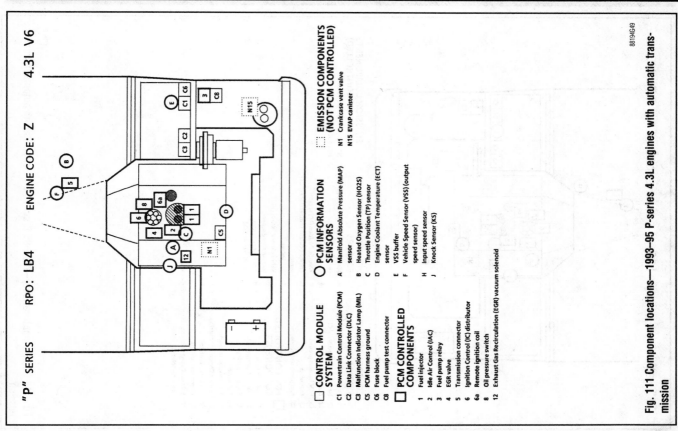

"P" SERIES   RPO: LB4   ENGINE CODE: Z   4.3L V6

CONTROL MODULE SYSTEM
C1 Powertrain Control Module (PCM)
C2 Data Link Connector (DLC)
C3 Malfunction Indicator Lamp (MIL)
C5 PCM harness ground
C6 Fuse block
C8 Fuel pump test connector

PCM CONTROLLED COMPONENTS
1 Fuel injector
2 Idle Air Control (IAC)
3 Fuel pump relay
4 EGR valve
5 Transmission connector
6 Ignition Control (IC) distributor
6a Remote ignition coil
8 Oil pressure switch
12 Exhaust Gas Recirculation (EGR) vacuum solenoid

PCM INFORMATION SENSORS
A Manifold Absolute Pressure (MAP) sensor
B Heated Oxygen Sensor (HO2S)
C Throttle Position (TP) sensor
D Engine Coolant Temperature (ECT) sensor
E VSS buffer
F Vehicle Speed Sensor (VSS) (output speed sensor)
H Input speed sensor
J Knock Sensor (KS)

EMISSION COMPONENTS (NOT PCM CONTROLLED)
N1 Crankcase vent valve
N15 EVAP canister

8819G49

Fig. 111 Component locations—1993–95 P-series 4.3L engines with automatic transmission

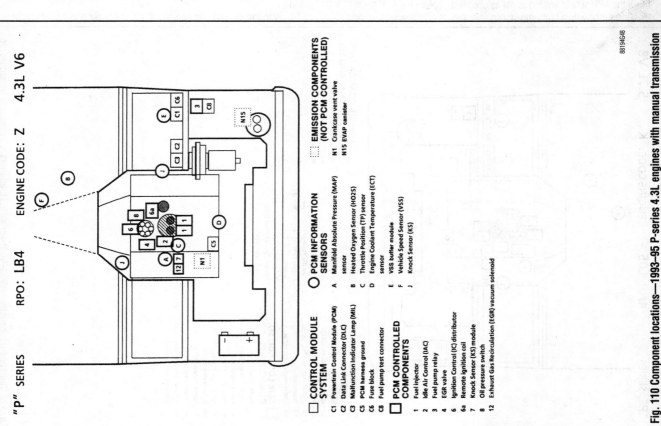

"P" SERIES   RPO: LB4   ENGINE CODE: Z   4.3L V6

CONTROL MODULE SYSTEM
C1 Powertrain Control Module (PCM)
C2 Data Link Connector (DLC)
C3 Malfunction Indicator Lamp (MIL)
C5 PCM harness ground
C6 Fuse block
C8 Fuel pump test connector

PCM CONTROLLED COMPONENTS
1 Fuel injector
2 Idle Air Control (IAC)
3 Fuel pump relay
4 EGR valve
6 Ignition Control (IC) distributor
6a Remote ignition coil
7 Knock Sensor (KS) module
8 Oil pressure switch
12 Exhaust Gas Recirculation (EGR) vacuum solenoid

PCM INFORMATION SENSORS
A Manifold Absolute Pressure (MAP) sensor
B Heated Oxygen Sensor (HO2S)
C Throttle Position (TP) sensor
D Engine Coolant Temperature (ECT) sensor
E VSS buffer module
F Vehicle Speed Sensor (VSS)
J Knock Sensor (KS)

EMISSION COMPONENTS (NOT PCM CONTROLLED)
N1 Crankcase vent valve
N15 EVAP canister

8819G48

Fig. 110 Component locations—1993–95 P-series 4.3L engines with manual transmission

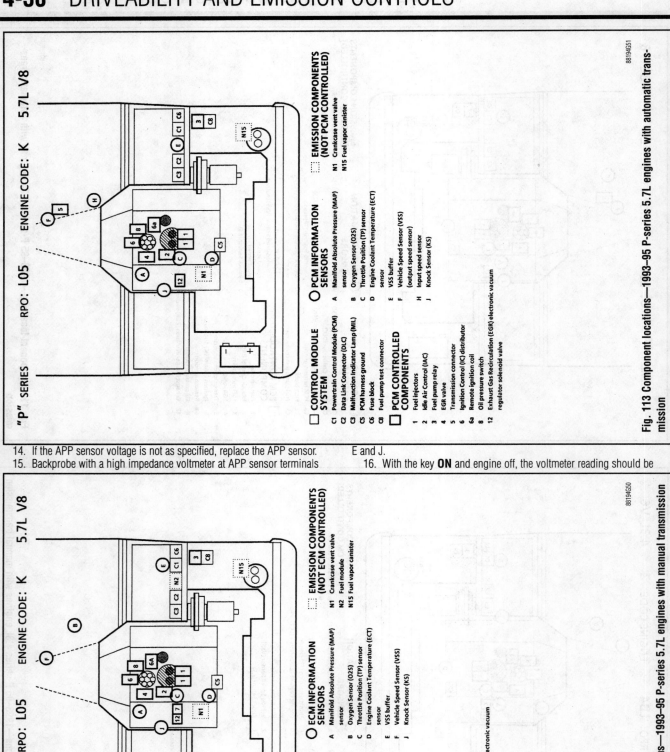

Fig. 113 Component locations—1993–95 P-series 5.7L engines with automatic transmission

88194G51

"P" SERIES RPO: L05 ENGINE CODE: K 5.7L V8

○ **CONTROL MODULE SYSTEM**
C1 Powertrain Control Module (PCM)
C2 Data Link Connector (DLC)
C3 Malfunction Indicator Lamp (MIL)
C5 PCM harness ground
C6 Fuse block
C8 Fuel pump test connector

○ **PCM CONTROLLED COMPONENTS**
1 Fuel injectors
2 Idle Air Control (IAC)
3 Fuel pump relay
4 EGR valve
5 Transmission connector
6 Ignition Control (IC) distributor
6a Remote ignition coil
8 Oil pressure switch
12 Exhaust Gas Recirculation (EGR) electronic vacuum regulator solenoid valve

○ **PCM INFORMATION SENSORS**
A Manifold Absolute Pressure (MAP) sensor
B Oxygen Sensor (O2S)
C Throttle Position (TP) sensor
D Engine Coolant Temperature (ECT) sensor
E VSS buffer
F Vehicle Speed Sensor (VSS) (output speed sensor)
H Input speed sensor
J Knock Sensor (KS)

▦ **EMISSION COMPONENTS (NOT PCM CONTROLLED)**
N1 Crankcase vent valve
N15 Fuel vapor canister

14. If the APP sensor voltage is not as specified, replace the APP sensor.
15. Backprobe with a high impedance voltmeter at APP sensor terminals E and J.
16. With the key **ON** and engine off, the voltmeter reading should be

---

Fig. 112 Component locations—1993–95 P-series 5.7L engines with manual transmission

88194G50

"P" SERIES RPO: L05 ENGINE CODE: K 5.7L V8

○ **CONTROL MODULE SYSTEM**
C1 Engine Control Module (ECM)
C2 Data Link Connector (DLC)
C3 Malfunction Indicator Lamp (MIL)
C5 ECM harness ground
C6 Fuse block
C8 Fuel pump test connector

○ **ECM CONTROLLED COMPONENTS**
1 Fuel injectors
2 Idle Air Control (IAC)
3 Fuel pump relay
4 EGR valve
6 Ignition Control (IC) distributor
6a Remote ignition coil
7 Knock Sensor (KS) module
8 Oil pressure switch
12 Exhaust Gas Recirculation (EGR) electronic vacuum regulator solenoid valve

○ **ECM INFORMATION SENSORS**
A Manifold Absolute Pressure (MAP) sensor
B Oxygen Sensor (O2S)
C Throttle Position (TP) sensor
D Engine Coolant Temperature (ECT) sensor
E VSS buffer
F Vehicle Speed Sensor (VSS)
J Knock Sensor (KS)

▦ **EMISSION COMPONENTS (NOT ECM CONTROLLED)**
N1 Crankcase vent valve
N2 Fuel module
N15 Fuel vapor canister

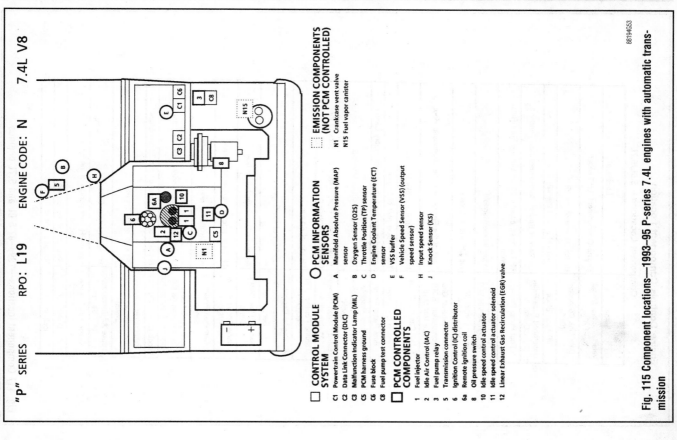

"P" SERIES   **RPO: L19**   **ENGINE CODE: N**   **7.4L V8**

CONTROL MODULE SYSTEM
C1 Powertrain Control Module (PCM)
C2 Data Link Connector (DLC)
C3 Malfunction Indicator Lamp (MIL)
C5 PCM harness ground
C6 Fuse block
C8 Fuel pump test connector

PCM CONTROLLED COMPONENTS
1 Fuel injector
2 Idle Air Control (IAC)
3 Fuel pump relay
5 Transmission connector
6 Ignition Control (IC) distributor
6a Remote ignition coil
8 Oil pressure switch
10 Idle speed control actuator
11 Idle speed control actuator solenoid
12 Linear Exhaust Gas Recirculation (EGR) valve

PCM INFORMATION SENSORS
A Manifold Absolute Pressure (MAP) sensor
B Oxygen Sensor (O2S)
C Throttle Position (TP) sensor
D Engine Coolant Temperature (ECT) sensor
E VSS buffer
F Vehicle Speed Sensor (VSS) (output speed sensor)
H Input speed sensor
J Knock Sensor (KS)

EMISSION COMPONENTS (NOT PCM CONTROLLED)
N1 Crankcase vent valve
N15 Fuel vapor canister

88194G53

Fig. 115 Component locations—1993–95 P-series 7.4L engines with automatic transmission

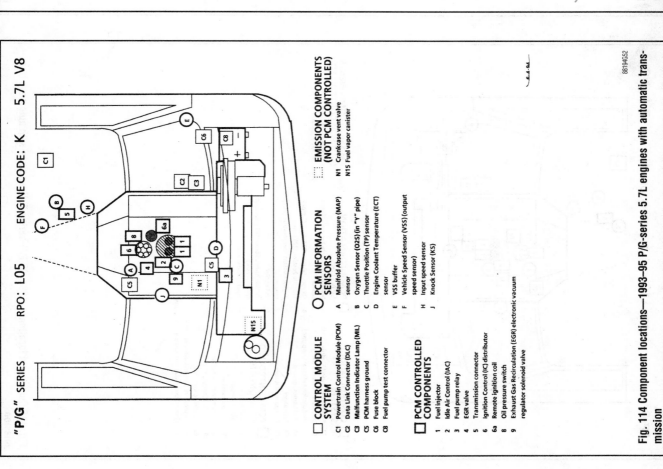

"P/G" SERIES   **RPO: L05**   **ENGINE CODE: K**   **5.7L V8**

CONTROL MODULE SYSTEM
C1 Powertrain Control Module (PCM)
C2 Data Link Connector (DLC)
C3 Malfunction Indicator Lamp (MIL)
C5 PCM harness ground
C6 Fuse block
C8 Fuel pump test connector

PCM CONTROLLED COMPONENTS
1 Fuel injector
2 Idle Air Control (IAC)
3 Fuel pump relay
4 EGR valve
5 Transmission connector
6 Ignition Control (IC) distributor
6a Remote ignition coil
8 Oil pressure switch
9 Exhaust Gas Recirculation (EGR) electronic vacuum regulator solenoid valve

PCM INFORMATION SENSORS
A Manifold Absolute Pressure (MAP) sensor
B Oxygen Sensor (O2S) (in "Y" pipe)
C Throttle Position (TP) sensor
D Engine Coolant Temperature (ECT) sensor
E VSS buffer
F Vehicle Speed Sensor (VSS) (output speed sensor)
H Input speed sensor
J Knock Sensor (KS)

EMISSION COMPONENTS (NOT PCM CONTROLLED)
N1 Crankcase vent valve
N15 Fuel vapor canister

88194G52

Fig. 114 Component locations—1993–95 P/G-series 5.7L engines with automatic transmission

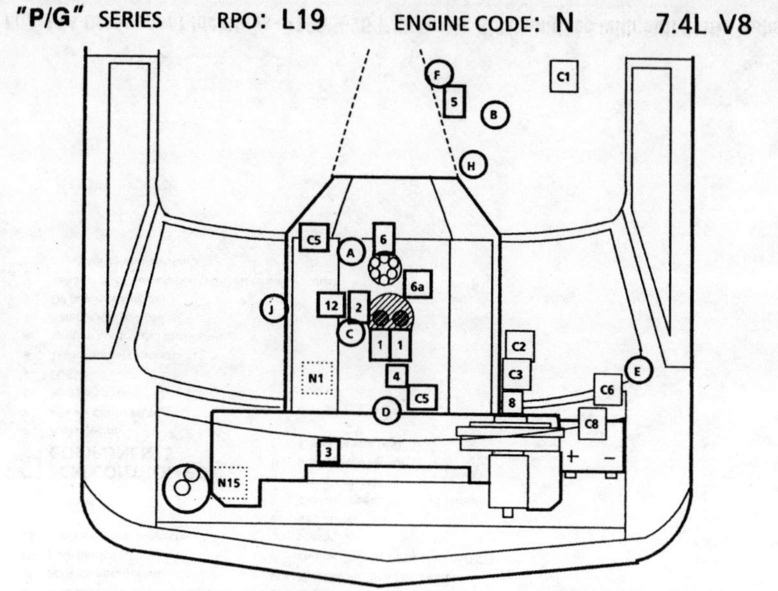

Engine Controls Component Location

Component Locations – 5.0L/5.7L

Name	Location
Vehicle Control Module (VCM)	Engine Compartment, LH Fender
Data Link Connector (DLC)	Under LH side of the I/P
I/P Fuse Block	Lower LH side of the I/P
Underhood Fuse Relay Center	LH Rear of Engine Compartment, on Fender
Fuel Pump Prime Connector	I/P Harness, approx. 20 cm into the Fuse-Relay Center
Fuel Injectors # 1 Through #8 VIN M,R	In the Intake Manifold
Idle Air Control (IAC) Valve Motor	Top LH side of Engine.
Linear Exhaust Gas Recirculation (EGR) Valve VIN M,R	Front of the Engine near the Thermostat Housing
EVAP Canister Purge Solenoid	RH Center on the Intake Manifold
Ignition Coil Driver	Top RH side rear of Engine
Fuel Pump Relay	Located in the Underhood Fuse Relay Center
Manifold Absolute Pressure (MAP) Sensor VIN M,R	Top RH Center of Intake Manifold
Heated Oxygen Sensors #1 through #4	In the Exhaust Pipe, in front and back of the Catalytic Converters
Throttle Position (TP) Sensor	LH top of Engine.
Engine Coolant Temperature (ECT) Sensor	Top front of the Engine.
Mass Air Flow (MAF) Sensor	Air Intake Duct near the air filter
Vehicle Speed Sensor (VSS)	LH Rear side of the Transmission.
Camshaft Position Sensor	In the Distributor, rear top of Engine.
Input Speed Sensor, Transmission (4L80E Automatic Transmission)	LH side of the Transmission, near the front
Knock Sensor VIN (M,R)	RH side of the Engine on the Engine Block
Evaporative Emission Purge Solenoid Vacuum Switch	RH side of the Engine
Intake Air Temperature (IAT) Sensor	In the Air Intake Duct
Crankshaft Position (CKP) Sensor	Lower RH front portion of the Engine block, near the Crankshaft
Distributor	Rear top of the Engine.
Ignition Coil	RH side rear of the Engine

Fig. 117 Component locations—1996-97 5.0L and 5.7L engines

"P/G" SERIES   RPO: L19   ENGINE CODE: N   7.4L V8

CONTROL MODULE SYSTEM
C1 Powertrain Control Module (PCM)
C2 Data Link Connector (DLC)
C3 Malfunction Indicator Lamp (MIL)
C5 PCM harness ground
C6 Fuse panel
C8 Fuel pump test connector

PCM CONTROLLED COMPONENTS
1 Fuel injector
2 Idle air control
3 Fuel pump relay
5 Transmission connector
6 Ignition Control (IC) distributor
6a Remote ignition coil
8 Oil pressure switch (lower front of block)
12 Linear Exhaust Gas Recirculation (EGR) valve

PCM INFORMATION SENSORS
A Manifold Absolute Pressure (MAP) sensor
B Oxygen Sensor (O2S) (in "Y" pipe)
C Throttle Position (TP) sensor
D Engine Coolant Temperature (ECT) sensor
E VSS buffer
F Vehicle Speed Sensor (VSS) (output speed sensor)
H Input speed sensor
J Knock sensor

EMISSION COMPONENTS (NOT PCM CONTROLLED)
N1 Crankcase vent valve
N15 Fuel vapor canister

Fig. 116 Component locations—1994-95 P/G-series 7.4L engines with automatic transmission

Component Locations – 7.4L

Name	Location
Vehicle Control Module (VCM)	Engine Compartment, LH Fender.
Data Link Connector (DLC)	Under the LH side of the I/P
I/P Fuse Block	Lower LH side of the I/P
Underhood Fuse Relay Center	LH Rear of the Engine Compartment, on the Fender
Fuel Pump Prime Connector	I/P Harness, approx. 20 cm into the Fuse- Relay Center
Fuel Injectors # 1 Through #8 VIN J	In the Intake Manifold at each cylinder
Idle Air Control (IAC) Valve Motor	Attatched to the RH rear of the Throttle Body
Linear Exhaust Gas Recirculation (EGR) Valve VIN J	RH side center of the intake manifold
AIR Injection Reaction Pump	Front of the Engine
AIR Injection Reaction Relay	Under Hood Fuse Relay Center
Ignition Coil	Top RH side rear of the Engine
Fuel Pump Relay	Located in the Underhood Fuse Relay Center
Manifold Absolute Pressure (MAP) Sensor VIN J	Top Front Center of the Intake Manifold
Heated Oxygen Sensors #1 through #4	In the Exhaust Pipe, in the front and the back of the Catalytic Converters
Throttle Position (TP) Sensor	On the RH side of the Throttle Body
Engine Coolant Temperature (ECT) Sensor	RH Top of the Engine near the Thermostat Housing
Mass Air Flow (MAF) Sensor	Air Intake Duct near the Air Filter

88194G56

Fig. 119 Component locations—1996–97 7.4L engines

Component Locations – 5.0L/5.7L (cont'd)

Name	Location
Fuel Pump Oil Pressure Switch and Sender	Rear Top Center of the Engine, behind the Distributor
A/C Compressor Low Pressure Cut-off Switch	In the low pressure refrigerant line
A/C High Pressure Cut-off Switch	On the rear portion of A/C Compressor
Brake Pressure Differential Switch	Part of the (EBCM), LH frame rail near center of vehicle.
Wheel Speed Sensor, LH front	At the LH Front Wheel
Wheel Speed Sensor, RH front	At the RH Front Wheel

88194G55

Fig. 118 Component locations—1996–97 5.0L and 5.7L engines (continued)

Engine Controls Component Location

Name	Location
Heated Oxygen Sensor, Bank 2 Sensor 1	In exhaust pipe in front of catalytic converter
Heater and A/C Controller	Center Of IP
IP Fuse Block	At LH lower kick panel
Idle Air Control Valve	Top LH side of engine
Ignition Control Module	Top RH side of engine.
Ignition Coil	Top RH of engine.
Instrument Cluster	LH side of IP
Intake Air Temperature (IAT) Sensor	Part of air intake duct, front of engine compartment
Knock Sensor	Top rear of engine
Manifold Absolute Pressure (MAP) Sensor	Top RH side of engine
Mass Air Flow (MAF) Sensor	Part of air intake duct, front top of engine
Power Steering Control Module	Below center of IP
Radio	Center of I/P
TCC/Stoplamp Switch	Below center of IP, near brake pedal lever
Throttle Position (TP) Sensor	LH top of engine
Underhood Fuse -Relay Center	Engine compartment, left fender
Vehicle Control Module (VCM)	Engine compartment, LH fender
Vehicle Speed Sensor (VSS)	Below LH side of IP, near steering column
C100	LH rear of engine compartment at bulkhead
C103 (M30)	LH on transmission
C103 (MT1)	LH on transmission
C105	Engine harness, RH frame rail near starter
C110	Engine harness, in line to engine sensors
C213	IP harness behind LH side of IP near center of vehicle
C301	Engine harness, in line to fuel pump harness on LH frame rail near EBCM
G100	LH engine compartment, near fender well
G201	IP harness behind LH kick panel near IP fuse block
G103	Engine harness, at generator bracket
P100	LH rear of engine compartment at bulkhead
P101	Under RH side of IP
S101	Engine harness, approx 20 cm from knock sensor breakout toward EBCM
S102	Engine harness, approx 22 cm from EGR sensor breakout toward C100
S103	Engine harness, approx 4 cm from fuel injector breakout toward transmission

Fig. 121 Component locations—1996-97 4.3L engines

Component Locations – 7.4L (cont'd)

Name	Location
Vehicle Speed Sensor (VSS)	LH rear side of the Transmission.
Camshaft Position Sensor	In the Distributor
Input Speed Sensor, Transmission (4L80E Automatic Transmission)	LH side of the Transmission, near the front
Knock Sensor VIN J	LH side Rear of the Engine on the Engine Block. RH side of the Engine Block, below the Exhaust Manifold, Forward of the Starter
Evaporative Emission Purge Solenoid Vacuum Switch	Top RH of the Engine
Intake Air Temperature (IAT) Sensor	In the Air Intake Duct
Crankshaft Position (CKP) Sensor	Lower RH front portion of the Engine block, near the Crankshaft
Distributor	Top of the Engine at the rear.
Fuel Pump Oil Pressure Switch and Sender	Rear Top Center of Engine, behind the Distributor
A/C Compressor Low Pressure Cut-off Switch	In the low pressure refrigerant line
A/C High Pressure Cut-off Switch	On the rear portion of A/C compressor
Brake Pressure Differential Switch	Part of the (EBCM), LH frame rail near center of Vehicle.
Wheel Speed Sensor, LH front	At the LH front wheel
Wheel Speed Sensor, RH front	At the RH front wheel

Fig. 120 Component locations—1996-97 7.4L engines (continued)

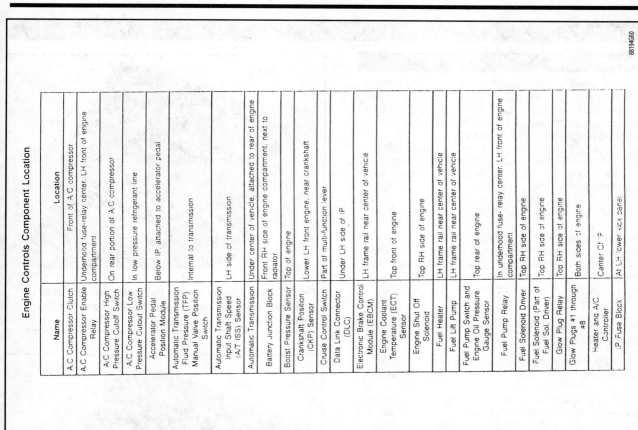

Engine Controls Component Location

Name	Location
A/C Compressor Clutch	Front of A/C compressor
A/C Compressor Enable Relay	Underhood fuse-relay center. LH front of engine compartment
A/C Compressor High Pressure Cutoff Switch	On rear portion of A/C compressor
A/C Compressor Low Pressure Cutout Switch	In low pressure refrigerant line
Accelerator Pedal Position Module	Below IP, attached to accelerator pedal
Automatic Transmission Fluid Pressure (TFP) Manual Valve Position Switch	Internal to transmission
Automatic Transmission Input Shaft Speed (A/T ISS) Sensor	LH side of transmission
Automatic Transmission	Under center of vehicle, attached to rear of engine
Battery Junction Block	Front RH side of engine compartment, next to radiator
Boost Pressure Sensor	Top of engine
Crankshaft Position (CKP) Sensor	Lower LH front engine, near crankshaft
Cruise Control Switch	Part of multi-function lever
Data Link Connector (DLC)	Under LH side of IP
Electronic Brake Control Module (EBCM)	LH frame rail near center of vehicle
Engine Coolant Temperature (ECT) Sensor	Top front of engine
Engine Shut Off Solenoid	Top RH side of engine
Fuel Heater	LH frame rail near center of vehicle
Fuel Lift Pump	LH frame rail near center of vehicle
Fuel Pump Switch and Engine Oil Pressure Gauge Sensor	Top rear of engine
Fuel Pump Relay	In underhood fuse-relay center. LH front of engine compartment
Fuel Solenoid Driver	Top RH side of engine
Fuel Solenoid (Part of Fuel Sol. Driver)	Top RH side of engine
Glow Plug Relay	Top RH side of engine
Glow Plugs #1 through #8	Both sides of engine
Heater and A/C Controller	Center of IP
IP Fuse Block	At LH lower kick panel

88194G60

Fig. 123 Component locations—1996–97 6.5L diesel engines

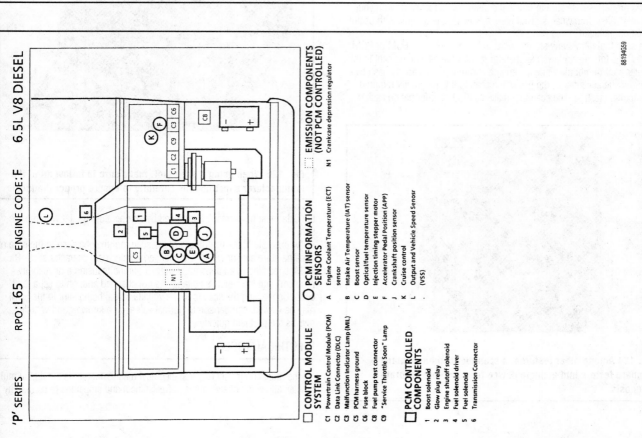

'P' SERIES   RPO:L65   ENGINE CODE:F   6.5L V8 DIESEL

□ **CONTROL MODULE SYSTEM**
C1 Powertrain Control Module (PCM)
C2 Data Link Connector (DLC)
C3 Malfunction Indicator Lamp (MIL)
C5 PCM harness ground
C6 Fuse block
C8 Fuel pump test connector
C9 "Service Throttle Soon" Lamp

□ **PCM CONTROLLED COMPONENTS**
1 Boost solenoid
2 Glow plug relay
3 Engine shutoff solenoid
4 Fuel solenoid driver
5 Fuel solenoid
6 Transmission Connector

○ **PCM INFORMATION SENSORS**
A Engine Coolant Temperature (ECT) sensor
B Intake Air Temperature (IAT) sensor
C Boost sensor
D Optical/fuel temperature sensor
E Injection timing stepper motor
F Accelerator Pedal Position (APP) sensor
J Crankshaft position sensor
K Cruise control
L Output and Vehicle Speed Sensosr (VSS)

▨ **EMISSION COMPONENTS (NOT PCM CONTROLLED)**
N1 Crankcase depression regulator

88194G59

Fig. 122 Typical component locations—diesel engines (except 1996–97 models)

TROUBLE CODES

General Information

Since the control module is programmed to recognize the presence and value of electrical inputs, it will also note the lack of a signal or a radical change in values. It will, for example, react to the loss of signal from the vehicle speed sensor or note that engine coolant temperature has risen beyond acceptable (programmed) limits. Once a fault is recognized, a numeric code is assigned and held in memory. The dashboard warning lamp: CHECK ENGINE or SERVICE ENGINE SOON (SES), will illuminate to advise the operator that the system has detected a fault. This lamp is also known as the Malfunction Indicator Lamp (MIL).

More than one code may be stored. Keep in mind not every engine uses every code. Additionally, the same code may carry different meanings relative to each engine or engine family.

In the event of an computer control module failure, the system will default to a pre-programmed set of values. These are compromise values which allow the engine to operate, although possibly at reduced efficiency. This is variously known as the default, limp-in or back-up mode. Driveability is almost always affected when the ECM enters this mode.

SCAN TOOLS

▶ **See Figures 124, 125, 126, 127 and 128**

On most models, the stored codes may be read with only the use of a small jumper wire, however the use of a hand-held scan tool such as GM's TECH-1® or equivalent is recommended. On 1996 models, an OBD-II compliant scan tool must be used. There are many manufacturers of these tools; a purchaser must be certain that the tool is proper for the intended use. If you own a scan type tool, it probably came with comprehensive instructions on proper use. Be sure to follow the instructions that came with your unit if they differ from what is given here; this is a general guide with useful information included.

The scan tool allows any stored codes to be read from the ECM or PCM memory. The tool also allows the operator to view the data being sent to the computer control module while the engine is running. This ability has obvious diagnostic advantages; the use of the scan tool is frequently required for component testing. The scan tool makes collecting information easier;

Fig. 124 Among other features, a scan tool combines many standard testers into a single device for quick and accurate diagnosis

Fig. 125 Many different types of test equipment, such as this Auto Xray® scan tool, are available through aftermarket tool manufacturers

Fig. 126 When using a scan tool, make sure to follow all of the manufacturer's instructions carefully to ensure proper diagnosis

the data must be correctly interpreted by an operator familiar with the system.

An example of the usefulness of the scan tool may be seen in the case of a temperature sensor which has changed its electrical characteristics. The ECM is reacting to an apparently warmer engine (causing a driveability problem), but the sensor's voltage has not changed enough to set a fault code. Connecting the scan tool, the voltage signal being sent to the ECM may be viewed; comparison to normal values or a known good vehicle reveals the problem quickly.

ELECTRICAL TOOLS

The most commonly required electrical diagnostic tool is the digital multimeter, allowing voltage, ohmage (resistance) and amperage to be read by

TCCS4P12

Fig. 127 Inexpensive scan tools, such as this Auto Xray®, are available to interface with your General Motors vehicle

"SCAN" Position	Units Displayed	Typical Data Value
Engine Speed	Rpm	± 50 RPM from desired rpm in drive (A/T) ± 100 RPM from desired rpm in neutral (M/T)
Desired Idle	Rpm	ECM idle command (varies with temp.)
Coolant Temperature	Degrees Celsius	85° - 105°
IAT/MAT	Degrees Celsius	10° - 90° (varies with underhood temp. and sensor location)
MAP	kPa/Volts	29-48 kPa/1 - 2 volts (varies with manifold and barometric pressures)
Open/Closed Loop	Open/Closed	"Closed Loop" (may enter "Open Loop" with extended idle)
Throt Position	Volts	.30 - 1.33
Throttle Angle	0 - 100%	0
Oxygen Sensor	Millivolts	100 - 999 (varies continuously)
Inj. Pulse Width	Milliseconds	.8 - 3.0
Spark Advance	Degrees	Varies
Engine Speed	Rpm	± 50 RPM from desired rpm in drive (A/T) ± 100 RPM from desired rpm in neutral (M/T)
Fuel Integrator	Counts	110-145
Block Learn	Counts	118-138
Idle Air Control	Counts (steps)	1 - 50
P/N Switch	P-N and R-D-L	Park/Neutral (P/N)
MPH/KPH	0-255	0
TCC	"ON"/"OFF"	"OFF"
Crank Rpm	Rpm	) 796
Ign/Batt Voltage	Volts	13.5 - 14.5
Cooling Fan Relay	"ON"/"OFF"	"OFF" (coolant temperature below 102°C)
A/C Request	"YES"/"NO"	No
A/C Clutch	"ON"/"OFF"	"OFF"
Power Steering	Normal/High Pressure	Normal
Shift Light (M/T)	"ON"/"OFF"	"OFF"

84904059

Fig. 128 Example of scan tool data and typical or baseline values

one instrument. The multimeter must be a high-impedance unit, with 10 megohms of impedance in the voltmeter. This type of meter will not place an additional load on the circuit it is testing; this is extremely important in low voltage circuits. The multimeter must be of high quality in all respects. It should be handled carefully and protected from impact or damage. Replace batteries frequently in the unit.

Other necessary tools include an unpowered test light, a quality tachometer with an inductive (clip-on) pick up, and the proper tools for releasing GM's Metri-Pack, Weather Pack and Micro-Pack terminals as necessary. The Micro-Pack connectors are used at the ECM electrical connector. A vacuum pump/gauge may also be required for checking sensors, solenoids and valves.

Diagnosis and Testing

Diagnosis of a driveability and/or emissions problems requires attention to detail and following the diagnostic procedures in the correct order. Resist the temptation to perform any repairs before performing the preliminary diagnostic steps. In many cases this will shorten diagnostic time and often cure the problem without electronic testing.

The proper troubleshooting procedure for these vehicles is as follows:

VISUAL/PHYSICAL INSPECTION

This is possibly the most critical step of diagnosis and should be performed immediately after retrieving any codes. A detailed examination of connectors, wiring and vacuum hoses can often lead to a repair without further diagnosis. Performance of this step relies on the skill of the technician performing it; a careful inspector will check the undersides of hoses as well as the integrity of hard-to-reach hoses blocked by the air cleaner or other component. Wiring should be checked carefully for any sign of strain, burning, crimping, or terminal pull-out from a connector. Checking connectors at components or in harnesses is required; usually, pushing them together will reveal a loose fit.

INTERMITTENTS

If a fault occurs intermittently, such as a loose connector pin breaking contact as the vehicle hits a bump, the ECM will note the fault as it occurs and energize the dash warning lamp. If the problem self-corrects, as with the terminal pin again making contact, the dash lamp will extinguish after 10 seconds but a code will remain stored in the computer control module's memory.

When an unexpected code appears during diagnostics, it may have been set during an intermittent failure that self-corrected; the codes are still useful in diagnosis and should not be discounted.

CIRCUIT/COMPONENT REPAIR

The fault codes and the scan tool data will lead to diagnosis and checking of a particular circuit. It is important to note that the fault code indicates a fault or loss of signal in an ECM-controlled system, not necessarily in the specific component.

Refer to the appropriate Diagnostic Code chart to determine the codes meaning. The component may then be tested following the appropriate component test procedures found in this section. If the component is OK, check the wiring for shorts or opens. Further diagnoses should be left to an experienced driveability technician.

If a code indicates the ECM to be faulty and the ECM is replaced, but does not correct the problem, one of the following may be the reason:

• There is a problem with the ECM terminal connections: The terminals may have to be removed from the connector in order to check them properly.

• The ECM or PROM is not correct for the application: The incorrect ECM or PROM may cause a malfunction and may or may not set a code.

• The problem is intermittent: This means that the problem is not present at the time the system is being checked. In this case, make a careful physical inspection of all portions of the system involved.

• Shorted solenoid, relay coil or harness: Solenoids and relays are turned on and off by the ECM using internal electronic switches called drivers. Each driver is part of a group of four called Quad-Drivers. A shorted solenoid, relay coil or harness may cause an ECM to fail, and a replacement ECM to fail when it is installed. Use a short tester, J34696, BT 8405, or equivalent, as a fast, accurate means of checking for a short circuit.

• The Programmable Read Only Memory (PROM) may be faulty: Although the PROM rarely fails, it operates as part of the ECM. Therefore, it could be the cause of the problem. Substitute a known good PROM.

• The replacement ECM may be faulty: After the ECM is replaced, the system should be rechecked for proper operation. If the diagnostic code again indicates the ECM is the problem, substitute a known good ECM. Although this is a very rare condition, it could happen.

Reading Codes

1987–95 MODELS

▶ See Figures 129 and 130

Listings of the trouble for the various engine control system covered in this manual are located in this section. Remember that a code only points to the faulty circuit NOT necessarily to a faulty component. Loose, damaged or corroded connections may contribute to a fault code on a circuit when the sensor or component is operating properly. Be sure that the components are faulty before replacing them, especially the expensive ones.

The Assembly Line Diagnostic Link (ALDL) connector or Data Link Connector (DLC) may be located under the dash and sometimes covered with a plastic cover labeled DIAGNOSTIC CONNECTOR.

1. The diagnostic trouble codes can be read by grounding test terminal B. The terminal is most easily grounded by connecting it to terminal A (internal ECM ground). This is the terminal to the right of terminal B on the top row of the ALDL connector.

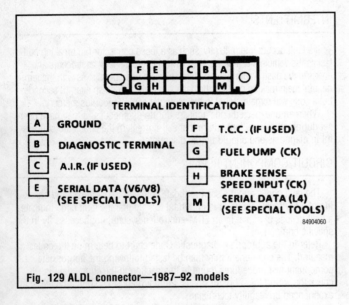

TERMINAL IDENTIFICATION

A	GROUND	**F**	T.C.C. (IF USED)
B	DIAGNOSTIC TERMINAL	**G**	FUEL PUMP (CK)
C	A.I.R. (IF USED)	**H**	BRAKE SENSE SPEED INPUT (CK)
E	SERIAL DATA (V6/V8) (SEE SPECIAL TOOLS)	**M**	SERIAL DATA (L4) (SEE SPECIAL TOOLS)

84904060

Fig. 129 ALDL connector—1987–92 models

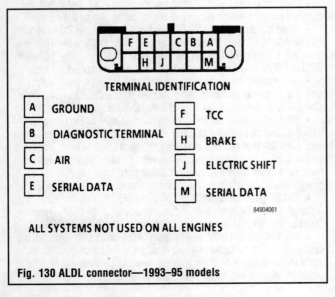

TERMINAL IDENTIFICATION

A	GROUND	**F**	TCC
B	DIAGNOSTIC TERMINAL	**H**	BRAKE
C	AIR	**J**	ELECTRIC SHIFT
E	SERIAL DATA	**M**	SERIAL DATA

84904061

ALL SYSTEMS NOT USED ON ALL ENGINES

Fig. 130 ALDL connector—1993–95 models

2. Once the terminals have been connected, the ignition switch must be moved to the **ON** position with the engine not running.

3. The Service Engine Soon or Check Engine light should be flashing. If it isn't, turn the ignition **OFF** and remove the jumper wire. Turn the ignition **ON** and confirm that light is now on. If it is not, replace the bulb and try again. If the bulb still will not light, or if it does not flash with the test terminal grounded, the system should be diagnosed by an experienced driveability technician. If the light is OK, proceed as follows.

4. The code(s) stored in memory may be read through counting the flashes of the dashboard warning lamp. The dash warning lamp should begin to flash Code 12. The code will display as one flash, a pause and two flashes. Code 12 is not a fault code. It is used as a system acknowledgment or handshake code; its presence indicates that the ECM can communicate as requested. Code 12 is used to begin every diagnostic sequence. Some vehicles also use Code 12 after all diagnostic codes have been sent.

5. After Code 12 has been transmitted 3 times, the fault codes, if any, will each be transmitted 3 times. The codes are stored and transmitted in numeric order from lowest to highest.

➡**The order of codes in the memory does not indicate the order of occurrence.**

6. If there are no codes stored, but a driveability or emissions problem is evident, the system should be diagnosed by an experienced driveability technician.

7. If one or more codes are stored, record them. Refer to the applicable Diagnostic Code chart in this section.

8. Switch the ignition **OFF** when finished with code retrieval or scan tool readings.

➡**After making repairs, clear the trouble codes and operate the vehicle to see if it will reset, indicating further problems.**

1996–97 MODELS

On 1996–97 models, an OBD-II compliant scan tool must be used to retrieve the trouble codes. Follow the scan tool manufacturer's instructions on how to connect the scan tool to the vehicle and how to retrieve the codes.

Clearing Codes

▶ See Figures 131 thru 145 (p. 59–66)

Stored fault codes may be erased from memory at any time by removing power from the ECM for at least 30 seconds. It may be necessary to clear stored codes during diagnosis to check for any recurrence during a test drive, but the stored codes must be written down when retrieved. The codes may still be required for subsequent troubleshooting. Whenever a repair is complete, the stored codes must be erased and the vehicle test driven to confirm correct operation and repair.

❄ WARNING

The ignition switch must be OFF any time power is disconnected or restored to the ECM. Severe damage may result if this precaution is not observed.

Depending on the electrical distribution of the particular vehicle, power to the ECM may be disconnected by removing the ECM fuse in the fusebox, disconnecting the in-line fuse holder near the positive battery terminal or disconnecting the ECM power lead at the battery terminal. Disconnecting the negative battery cable to clear codes is not recommended as this will also clear other memory data in the vehicle such as radio presets.

DIAGNOSTIC CODE IDENTIFICATION

The "Service Engine Soon" light will only be "ON" if the malfunction exists under the conditions listed below. If the malfunction clears, the light will go out and the code will be stored in the ECM/PCM. Any codes stored will be erased if no problem reoccurs within 50 engine starts.

CODE AND CIRCUIT	PROBABLE CAUSE	CODE AND CIRCUIT	PROBABLE CAUSE
Code 13 - Oxygen O₂ Sensor Circuit (Open Circuit)	Indicates that the oxygen sensor circuit or sensor was open for one minute while off idle.	Code 33 - Manifold Absolute Pressure (MAP) Sensor Circuit (Signal Voltage High- Low Vacuum)	MAP sensor output to high for 5 seconds or an open signal circuit.
Code 14 - Coolant Temperature Sensor (CTS) Circuit (High Temperature Indicated)	Sets if the sensor or signal line becomes grounded for 3 seconds.	Code 34 - Manifold Absolute Pressure (MAP) Sensor Circuit (Signal Voltage Low-High Vacuum)	Low or no output from sensor with engine running.
Code 15 - Coolant Temperature Sensor (CTS) Circuit (Low Temperature Indicated)	Sets if the sensor, connections, or wires open for 3 seconds.	Code 35 - Idle Air Control (IAC) System	IAC error
Code 21 - Throttle Position Sensor (TPS) Circuit (Signal Voltage High)	TPS voltage greater than 2.5 volts for 3 seconds with less than 1200 RPM.	Code 42 - Electronic Spark Timing (EST)	ECM/PCM has seen an open or grounded EST or bypass circuit.
Code 22 - Throttle Position Sensor (TPS) Circuit (Signal Voltage Low)	A shorted to ground or open signal circuit will set code in 3 seconds.	Code 43 - Electronic Spark Control (ESC) Circuit	Signal to the ECM/PCM has remained low for too long or the system has failed a functional check.
Code 23 - Intake Air Temperature (IAT) Sensor Circuit (Low Temperature Indicated)	Sets if the sensor, connections, or wires open for 3 seconds.	Code 44 - Oxygen (O₂) Sensor Circuit (Lean Exhaust Indicated)	Sets if oxygen sensor voltage remains below .2 volt for about 20 seconds.
Code 24 - Vehicle Speed Sensor (VSS)	No vehicle speed present during a road load decel.	Code 45 - Oxygen (O₂) Sensor Circuit (Rich Exhaust Indicated)	Sets if oxygen sensor voltage remains above .7 volt for about 1 minute.
Code 25 - Intake Air Temperature (IAT) Sensor Circuit (High Temperature Indicated)	Sets if the sensor or signal line becomes grounded for 3 seconds.	Code 51 - Faulty MEM-CAL or ECM/PCM Problem	Faulty MEM-CAL, PROM, or ECM/PCM.
Code 32 - Exhaust Gas Recirculation (EGR) System	Vacuum switch shorted to ground on start up OR Switch not closed after the ECM/PCM has commanded EGR for a specified period of time. OR EGR solenoid circuit open for a specified period of time.	Code 52 - Fuel CALPAK Missing	Fuel CAL-PAK missing or faulty.
		Code 53 - System Over Voltage	System overvoltage. Indicates a basic generator problem.
		Code 54 - Fuel Pump Circuit (Low Voltage)	Sets when the fuel pump voltage is less than 2 volts when reference pulses are being received.
		Code 55 - Faulty ECM/PCM	Faulty ECM/PCM

8490464

Fig. 132 Fuel injected engine trouble codes through 1995, except with 4L60E and 4L80E transmissions

---

CODE IDENTIFICATION

The "Service Engine Soon" light will only be "ON" if the malfunction exists under the conditions listed below. If the malfunction clears, the light will go out and the code will be stored in the ECM. Any Codes stored will be erased if no problem reoccurs within 50 engine starts.

CODE AND CIRCUIT	PROBABLE CAUSE	CODE AND CIRCUIT	PROBABLE CAUSE
Code 12 - No engine speed reference pulse.	No engine speed sensor reference pulses to the ECM. This code is not stored in memory and will only flash while the fault is present. Normal code with ignition "ON," engine not running.	Code 31 - MAP Sensor Too Low	Absolute Pressure (MAP) circuit signal voltage too low. Engine must run at curb idle for 10 seconds before this code will set.
Code 14 - Coolant Sensor High Temperature Indication	Sets if the sensor or signal line becomes grounded for 10 seconds.	Code 32 - EGR Loop Error	Exhaust Gas Recirculation (EGR) vacuum circuit has seen improper EGR vacuum. Vehicle must be running at road speed approximately 30 mph (48 Km/h) for 10 seconds before this code will set.
Code 15 - Coolant Sensor Low Temperature Indication	Sets if the sensor, connections, or wires open for 10 seconds.	Code 33 - MAP Sensor Too High	Absolute Pressure (MAP) circuit signal voltage too high. Engine must run at curb idle for 10 seconds before this code will set.
Code 21 - TPS Signal Voltage High	Throttle Position Sensor (TPS) circuit voltage high (open circuit or misadjusted TPS). Engine must run 30 seconds, at curb idle speed, before this code will set.	Code 51 - PROM	Faulty or improperly installed PROM. It takes approximately 10 seconds before this code will set.
Code 22 - TPS Signal Voltage Low	Throttle Position Sensor (TPS) circuit voltage low (grounded circuit). Engine must run 2 minutes at 1250 rpm or above before this code will set.	Code 52 - ECM	Fault in ECM circuit. It takes 10 seconds before this code will set.
Code 23 - TPS Not Calibrated	Throttle Position Sensor (TPS) circuit. Voltage not between .25 and 1.3 volts at curb idle speed. Engine must run for 30 seconds, at curb idle, before this code will set.	Code 53 - Five volt Reference Overload	5 volt reference (Vref) circuit overloaded (grounded circuit). It takes 10 seconds before this Code will set.
Code 24 - VSS No Vehicle Speed Indication	Vehicle speed sensor (VSS) circuit (open or grounded circuit). Vehicle must operate at road speed for 10 seconds before this code will set.		

8490119

Fig. 131 Carbureted engine trouble codes

DIAGNOSTIC TROUBLE CODE (DTC) IDENTIFICATION

The MIL (Service Engine Soon) will only be "ON" if the malfunction exists with the conditions listed below. If the malfunction clears, the lamp will go out and the DTC will be stored in the PCM. Any DTCs stored will be erased if no problem reoccurs within 50 engine starts.

DTC AND CIRCUIT	PROBABLE CAUSE	DTC AND CIRCUIT	PROBABLE CAUSE
DTC 51 - Faulty PROM (MEM-CAL) Problem	Faulty PROM (MEM-CAL) or PCM.	*DTC 69 - TCC Stuck "ON"	Slip > -20 and slip 20 TCC is not locked gear = 2, 3 or 4 TPS > 25%, not in P/R/N for 4 seconds.
DTC 53 - System Voltage High	System overvoltage of 19.5 volts for 2 seconds	*DTC 72 - Vehicle Speed Sensor Loss	Not in P/N - Output speed changes greater than 1000 RPM • P/N - Output speed changes greater than 2050 RPM • For 2 seconds
DTC 54 - Fuel Pump Circuit (Low Voltage)	Sets when the fuel pump voltage is less than 2 volts when reference pulses are being received.		
DTC 55 - Faulty PCM	Faulty PCM	*DTC 73 - Pressure Control Solenoid	If return amperage varies more than 0.16 amps. from commanded amperage
*DTC 58 - Transmission Fluid Temperature High	Transmission fluid temperature greater than 154°C (309°F) for one second.	*DTC 75 - System Voltage Low	System voltage < 7.3 at low temperature or < 11.7 at high temperature for 4 seconds.
*DTC 59 - Transmission Fluid Temperature Low	Transmission fluid temperature greater than -33°C (-27°F) for one second.	*DTC 79 - Transmission Fluid Over Temperature	Transmission fluid Temperature > 150°C and < 154°C for 15 minutes.
*DTC 66 - 3-2 Control Solenoid Circuit Fault	At High Duty Cycle the circuit voltage is high OR at Low Duty Cycle the Circuit Voltage is low for four seconds.	*DTC 81 - 2-3 Shift Solenoid Circuit Fault	2-3 shift solenoid is command "ON", and circuit voltage is high for two seconds OR 2-3 shift solenoid is command "OFF", and circuit voltage is low for two seconds.
*DTC 67 Torque Converter Clutch Circuit	TCC is commanded "ON" and circuit voltage remains high for two seconds OR TCC is commanded "OFF" and circuit voltage remains low for two seconds.	*DTC 82 - 1-2 Shift Solenoid Circuit Fault	1-2 shift solenoid is command "ON", and circuit voltage is high for two seconds OR 1-2 shift solenoid is command "OFF" and circuit voltage is low for two seconds.

84904067

Fig. 134 Fuel injected engine trouble codes through 1995 with 4L60E transmissions (continued)

DIAGNOSTIC TROUBLE CODE (DTC) IDENTIFICATION

The MIL (Service Engine Soon) will only be "ON" if the malfunction exists with the conditions listed below. If the malfunction clears, the lamp will go out and the DTC will be stored in the PCM. Any DTCs stored will be erased if no problem reoccurs within 50 engine starts.

DTC AND CIRCUIT	PROBABLE CAUSE	DTC AND CIRCUIT	PROBABLE CAUSE
DTC 13 - Oxygen O2S Sensor Circuit (Open Circuit)	Indicates that the oxygen sensor circuit or sensor was open for one minute while off idle.	DTC 33 - Manifold Absolute Pressure (MAP) Sensor Circuit. (Signal Voltage High - Low Vacuum)	MAP sensor output high for 5 seconds or an open signal circuit.
DTC 14 - Engine Coolant Temperature (ECT) Sensor Circuit (High Temperature Indicated)	Sets if the sensor or signal line becomes grounded or greater than 145°C (294°F) for 0.5 seconds.	DTC 34 - Manifold Absolute Pressure (MAP) Sensor Circuit (Signal Voltage Low - High Vacuum)	Low or no output from MAP sensor with engine operating.
DTC 15 - Engine Coolant Temperature (ECT) Sensor Circuit (Low Temperature Indicated)	Sets if the sensor, connections, or wires open or less than -33°C (-27°F) for 0.5 seconds.	DTC 35 - IAC	IAC error
DTC 16 - Transmission Output Speed Low	Open in CKT 1697/1716 or power loss to VSS buffer	*DTC 37 - Brake Switch Stuck On	With no voltage and vehicle speed is less than 5 mph for 6 seconds, then vehicle speed is 5 - 20 MPH for 6 seconds, then vehicle speed is greater than 20 MPH for 6 seconds, this must occur for 7 times.
DTC 21 - Throttle Position (TP) Sensor Circuit (Signal Voltage High)	TP voltage greater than 4.88 volts 4 seconds with less than 1200 RPM.	*DTC 38 - Brake Switch Stuck Off	With voltage and vehicle speed is greater than 20 MPH for 6 seconds, then vehicle speed is 5 - 20 MPH for 6 seconds. This must occur 7 times.
DTC 22 - Throttle Position (TP) Sensor Circuit (Signal Voltage Low)	A short to ground, open signal circuit, or TP voltage less than 0.16 volts for 4 seconds.	DTC 42 - Ignition Control (IC)	PCM detects an open or grounded IC or bypass circuit.
DTC 24 - Vehicle Speed Sensor (VSS) Signal Low	No vehicle speed sensor signal present during a road load decel.	DTC 43 - Knock Sensor (KS) Circuit	Signal to the PCM has remained low for too long, or the system has failed a functional system check.
DTC 28 - Fluid Pressure Switch Assembly	PCM detects 1 of 2 invalid combinations of the fluid pressure switch range signals	DTC 44 - Oxygen Sensor (O2S) Circuit (Lean Exhaust Indicated)	Sets if oxygen sensor voltage remains less than 0.2 volt for 20 seconds.
DTC 32 - Exhaust Gas Recirculation (EGR) System	Vacuum switch shorted to ground on start up OR Switch not closed after the PCM has commanded EGR for a specified period of time. OR EGR solenoid circuit open for a specified period of time.	DTC 45 - Oxygen Sensor (O2S) Circuit (Rich Exhaust Indicated)	Sets if oxygen sensor voltage remains greater than 0.7 volt for about 1 minute.

84904066

Fig. 133 Fuel injected engine trouble codes through 1995 with 4L60E transmissions

DIAGNOSTIC TROUBLE CODE IDENTIFICATION (Continued)

The MIL (Service Engine Soon) will only be "ON" if the malfunction exists with the conditions listed below. If the malfunction clears, the lamp will go out and the DTC will be stored in the PCM. Any DTCs stored will be erased if no problem reoccurs within 50 engine starts. Note: All DTC(S) with the sign * are transmission related DTC(S) and have descriptions, diagnostic charts
Remember, always start with the lowest numerical DTC first, when diagnosing some engine DTC(S) trigger other transmission DTC(S).

DTC AND CIRCUIT	PROBABLE CAUSE	DTC AND CIRCUIT	PROBABLE CAUSE
DTC 58 - Transmission Fluid Temperature High*	Refer to SECTION 7A-17C.	DTC 82 - 1-2 Shift Solenoid Circuit Fault*	Refer to SECTION 7A-17C.
DTC 59 - Transmission Fluid Temperature Low*	Refer to SECTION 7A-17C.	DTC 83 - TCC Solenoid Circuit Fault*	Refer to SECTION 7A-17C.
DTC 68 - Overdrive Ratio Error*	Refer to SECTION 7A-17C.	DTC 85 - Undefined Ratio*	Refer to SECTION 7A-17C.
DTC 73 - Pressure Control Solenoid*	Refer to SECTION 7A-17C.	DTC 86 - Low Ratio*	Refer to SECTION 7A-17C.
DTC 75 - System Voltage Low*	Refer to SECTION 7A-17C.	DTC 87 - High Ratio*	Refer to SECTION 7A-17C.
DTC 81 - 2-3 Shift Solenoid Circuit Fault*	Refer to SECTION 7A-17C.		

8490469

Fig. 136 Fuel injected engine trouble codes through 1995 with 4L80E transmissions (continued)

DIAGNOSTIC TROUBLE CODE IDENTIFICATION

The MIL (Service Engine Soon) will only be "ON" if the malfunction exists with the conditions listed below. If the malfunction clears, the lamp will go out and the DTC will be stored in the PCM. Any DTCs stored will be erased if no problem reoccurs within 50 engine starts. Note: All DTC(S) with the sign * are transmission related DTC(S) and have descriptions, diagnostic charts
Remember, always start with the lowest numerical DTC first, when diagnosing some engine DTC(S) trigger other transmission DTC(S).

DTC AND CIRCUIT	PROBABLE CAUSE	DTC AND CIRCUIT	PROBABLE CAUSE
DTC 13 - Oxygen Sensor O2S Circuit (Open Circuit)	Indicates that the oxygen sensor circuit or sensor was open for one minute while off idle.	DTC 33 - Manifold Absolute Pressure (MAP) Sensor Circuit (Signal Voltage High - Low Vacuum)	MAP sensor output to high for 5 seconds or an open signal circuit.
DTC 14 - Engine Coolant Temperature (ECT) Sensor Circuit (High Temperature Indicated)	Signal voltage has been greater than 151°C (304°F) for 1 second.	DTC 34 - Manifold Absolute Pressure (MAP) Sensor Circuit (Signal Voltage Low - High Vacuum)	Low or no output from sensor with engine operating.
DTC 15 - Engine Coolant Temperature (ECT) Sensor Circuit (Low Temperature Indicated)	Signal voltage has been less than -37°C (-34°F) for 1 second.	DTC 39 - TCC Stuck "OFF"	Refer to SECTION 7A-17C.
DTC 21 - Throttle Position (TP) Sensor Circuit (Signal Voltage High)	If signal voltage has been greater than 4.9 volts for 1 second.	DTC 42 - Ignition Control (IC)	PCM has an open or grounded IC or bypass circuit.
DTC 22 - Throttle Position (TP) Sensor Circuit (Signal Voltage Low)	DTC 22 will set if TP signal voltage is less than .2 volt for more than 1 second.	DTC 43 - Knock Sensor (KS) Circuit	Signal to the PCM has remained low for too long or the system has failed a functional check.
DTC 24 - Vehicle Speed Sensor (VSS)	With input speed at least 3000 RPM, output speed must read less than 200 RPM for 1.5 seconds.	DTC 44 - Oxygen Sensor O2S Circuit (Lean Exhaust Indicated)	Sets if oxygen sensor voltage remains less than .2 volt for 20 seconds.
DTC 28 - Fluid Pressure Switch Assembly*	Refer to SECTION 7A-17C.	DTC 45 - Oxygen Sensor O2S Circuit (Rich Exhaust Indicated)	Sets if oxygen sensor voltage remains greater than .7 volt for 1 minute.
DTC 32 - Exhaust Gas Recirculation (EGR) System	Vacuum switch shorted to ground on start up OR Switch not closed after the PCM has commanded EGR for a specified period of time OR EGR solenoid circuit open for a specified period of time.	DTC 51 - Faulty PROM (MEM-CAL) Problem	Faulty PROM or PCM.
		DTC 53 - System Over Voltage	Generator voltage is greater than 19.5 volts for 2 seconds.
		DTC 54 - Fuel Pump Circuit (Low Voltage)	Sets when the fuel pump voltage is less than 2 volts when reference pulses are being received.
		DTC 55 - Faulty PCM	Faulty PCM.

8490468

Fig. 135 Fuel injected engine trouble codes through 1995 with 4L80E transmissions

P0500 - Vehicle Speed Sensor (VSS) Circuit
P0506 - Idle System Low - Idle Air Control (IAC) Responding
P0507 - Idle System High - Idle Air Control (IAC) Responding
P1106 - Manifold Absolute Pressure (MAP) Sensor Circuit Intermittent High Voltage
P1107 - Manifold Absolute Pressure (MAP) Sensor Circuit Intermittent Low Voltage
P1111 - Intake Air Temperature (IAT) Sensor Circuit Intermittent High Voltage
P1112 - Intake Air Temperature (IAT) Sensor Circuit Intermittent Low Voltage
P1114 - Engine Coolant Temperature (ECT) Sensor Circuit Intermittent Low Voltage
P1115 - Engine Coolant Temperature (ECT) Sensor Circuit Intermittent High Voltage
P1121 - Throttle Position (TP) Sensor Circuit Intermittent High Voltage
P1122 - Throttle Position (TP) Sensor Circuit Intermittent Low Voltage

P1133 - Heated Oxygen Sensor (HO2S) Insufficient Switching Bank 1, Sensor 1
P1134 - Heated Oxygen Sensor (HO2S) Transition Time Ratio Bank 1, Sensor 1
P1153 - Heated Oxygen Sensor (HO2S) Insufficient Switching Bank 2, Sensor 1
P1154 - Heated Oxygen Sensor (HO2S) Transition Time Ratio Bank 2, Sensor 1
P1345 - Crankshaft Position/Camshaft Position (CKP/CMP) Correlation
P1351 - Ignition Control (IC) Circuit High Voltage
P1361 - Ignition Control (IC) Circuit Low Voltage
P1380 - Electronic Brake Control Module (EBCM) DTC Detected - Rough Road Data Unusable
P1381 - Misfire Detected - No Electronic Brake Control Module (EBCM) VCM Serial Data
P1406 - Exhaust Gas Recirculation (EGR) Valve Pintle Position Circuit
P1415 - AIR System Bank 1
P1416 - AIR System Bank 2
P1441 - Evaporative Emission (EVAP) System Flow During Non-Purge
P1508 - Idle Air Control (IAC) System Low RPM
P1509 - Idle Air Control (IAC) System High RPM

Fig. 138 Trouble code list for 1996–97 gasoline engines (continued)

87984G51

DTC P0101 - Mass Air Flow (MAF) System Performance
DTC P0102 - Mass Air Flow (MAF) Sensor Circuit Low Frequency
DTC P0103 - Mass Air Flow (MAF) Sensor Circuit High Frequency
DTC P0106 - Manifold Absolute Pressure (MAP) System Performance
DTC P0107 - Manifold Absolute Pressure (MAP) Sensor Circuit Low Voltage
DTC P0108 - Manifold Absolute Pressure (MAP) Sensor Circuit High Voltage
P0112 - Intake Air Temperature (IAT) Sensor Circuit Low Voltage
P0113 - Intake Air Temperature (IAT) Sensor Circuit High Voltage
P0117 - Engine Coolant Temperature (ECT) Sensor Circuit Low Voltage
P0118 - Engine Coolant Temperature (ECT) Sensor Circuit High Voltage
P0121 - Throttle Position (TP) System Performance
P0122 - Throttle Position (TP) Sensor Circuit Low Voltage
P0123 - Throttle Position (TP) Sensor Circuit High Voltage
P0125 - Engine Coolant Temperature (ECT) Excessive Time to Closed Loop Fuel Control
P0131 - Heated Oxygen Sensor (HO2S) Circuit Low Voltage Bank 1, Sensor 1
P0132 - Heated Oxygen Sensor (HO2S) Circuit High Voltage Bank 1, Sensor 1
P0133 - Heated Oxygen Sensor (HO2S) Circuit Slow Response Bank 1, Sensor 1
P0134 - Heated Oxygen Sensor (HO2S) Circuit Insufficient Activity Bank 1, Sensor 1
P0135 - Heated Oxygen Sensor (HO2S) Heater Circuit Bank 1, Sensor 1
P0137 - Heated Oxygen Sensor (HO2S) Circuit Low Voltage Bank 1, Sensor 2
P0138 - Heated Oxygen Sensor (HO2S) Circuit High Voltage Bank 1, Sensor 2
P0140 - Heated Oxygen Sensor (HO2S) Circuit Insufficient Activity Bank 1, Sensor 2
P0141 - Heated Oxygen Sensor (HO2S) Heater Circuit Bank 1, Sensor 2
P0143 - Heated Oxygen Sensor (HO2S) Circuit Low Voltage Bank 1, Sensor 3
P0144 - Heated Oxygen Sensor (HO2S) Circuit High Voltage Bank 1, Sensor 3

P0146 - Heated Oxygen Sensor (HO2S) Circuit Insufficient Activity Bank 1, Sensor 3
P0147 - Heated Oxygen Sensor (HO2S) Heater Circuit Bank 1, Sensor 3
P0151 - Heated Oxygen Sensor (HO2S) Circuit Low Voltage Bank 2, Sensor 1
P0152 - Heated Oxygen Sensor (HO2S) Circuit High Voltage Bank 2, Sensor 1
P0153 - Heated Oxygen Sensor (HO2S) Circuit Slow Response Bank 2, Sensor 1
P0154 - Heated Oxygen Sensor (HO2S) Circuit Insufficient Activity Bank 2, Sensor 1
P0155 - Heated Oxygen Sensor (HO2S) Heater Circuit Bank 2, Sensor 1
P0157 - Heated Oxygen Sensor (HO2S) Circuit Low Voltage Bank 2, Sensor 2
P0158 - Heated Oxygen Sensor (HO2S) Circuit High Voltage Bank 2, Sensor 2
P0160 - Heated Oxygen Sensor (HO2S) Circuit Insufficient Activity Bank 2, Sensor 2
P0161 - Heated Oxygen Sensor (HO2S) Heater Circuit Bank 2, Sensor 2
P0171 - Fuel Trim System Lean Bank 1
P0172 - Fuel Trim System Rich Bank 1
P0174 - Fuel Trim System Lean Bank 2
P0175 - Fuel Trim System Rich Bank 2
P0300 - Engine Misfire Detected
P0301 - Cylinder 1 Misfire Detected
P0302 - Cylinder 2 Misfire Detected
P0303 - Cylinder 3 Misfire Detected
P0304 - Cylinder 4 Misfire Detected
P0305 - Cylinder 5 Misfire Detected
P0306 - Cylinder 6 Misfire Detected
P0307 - Cylinder 7 Misfire Detected
P0308 - Cylinder 8 Misfire Detected
P0325 - Knock Sensor (KS) Module Circuit
P0327 - Knock Sensor (KS) Circuit Low Voltage

P0336 - Crankshaft Position (CKP) Sensor Circuit Performance
P0337 - Crankshaft Position (CKP) Sensor Circuit Low Frequency
P0338 - Crankshaft Position (CKP) Sensor Circuit High Frequency
P0339 - Crankshaft Position (CKP) Sensor Circuit Intermittent
P0340 - Camshaft Position (CMP) Sensor Circuit
P0341 - Camshaft Position (CMP) Sensor Circuit Performance
P0401 - Exhaust Gas Recirculation (EGR) System
P0410 - AIR System
P0420 - Three Way Catalytic Converter (TWC) System Low Efficiency Bank 1
P0430 - Three Way Catalytic Converter (TWC) System Low Efficiency Bank 2
P0441 - Evaporative Emission (EVAP) System No Flow During Purge

Fig. 137 Trouble code list for 1996–97 gasoline engines

87984G50

DIAGNOSTIC TROUBLE CODE (DTC) IDENTIFICATION

The MIL (Service Engine Soon) will only be "ON" if the malfunction exists under the conditions listed below. If the malfunction clears, the lamp will go out and the DTC will be stored in the PCM. Any DTCs stored will be erased if no problem reoccurs within 50 engine starts. Note: All DTCs with the sign * are transmission related DTCs.

Remember, always start with the lowest numerical DTC first, when diagnosing some engine DTCs trigger other transmission DTCs.

DTC AND CIRCUIT	PROBABLE CAUSE	DTC AND CIRCUIT	PROBABLE CAUSE
DTC 14 - Engine Coolant Temperature (ECT) Sensor Circuit (High Temperature Indicated)	Sets if the sensor or signal line becomes grounded or greater than 145°C (294°F) for 0.5 seconds.	DTC 32 - Exhaust Gas Recirculation (EGR) System Error	Exhaust Gas Recirculation (EGR) vacuum circuit has seen improper EGR vacuum. Vehicle must be running at road speed approximately 30 mph (48 Km/h) for 10 seconds before this DTC will set.
DTC 15 - Engine Coolant Temperature (ECT) Sensor Circuit (Low Temperature Indicated)	Sets if the sensor, connections, or wires open or less than -33°C (-27°F) for 0.5 seconds.		
DTC 16 - Transmission Output Speed Signal Low	Open in CKT 1716 or power loss to VSS buffer module.	DTC 33 - Manifold Absolute Pressure (MAP) Sensor Circuit (Signal Voltage High - Low Vacuum)	MAP sensor output high for 5 seconds or an open signal circuit.
DTC 21 - Throttle Position (TP) Sensor Circuit (Signal Voltage High)	TP voltage greater than 4.88 volts 4 seconds with less than 1200 RPM.		
DTC 22 - Throttle Position (TP) Sensor Circuit (Signal Voltage Low)	A short to ground, open signal circuit, or TP voltage less than 0.16 volts for 4 seconds.	*DTC 37 - Brake Switch Stuck On	With no voltage and vehicle speed is less than 5 mph for 6 seconds, then vehicle speed is 5 - 20 MPH for 6 seconds, then vehicle speed is greater than 20 MPH for 6 seconds, this must occur for 7 times.
DTC 23 - Throttle Position (TP) Sensor Not Calibrated	Throttle Position TP sensor circuit voltage not between .25 and 1.3 volts at curb idle speed. Engine must run for 30 seconds, at curb idle, before this DTC will set.	*DTC 38 - Brake Switch Stuck Off	With voltage and vehicle speed is greater than 20 MPH for 6 seconds, then vehicle speed is 5 - 20 MPH for 6 seconds. This must occur 7 times.
*DTC 24 - Vehicle Speed Sensor (VSS) Signal Low	No vehicle speed sensor signal present during a road load decel.		
*DTC 28 - Fluid Pressure Switch Assembly	PCM detects 1 of 2 invalid combinations of the fluid pressure switch range signals.		
DTC 31 - MAP Sensor too low	MAP Sensor signal voltage too low. Engine must run at curb idle for 10 seconds before this DTC will set.		

Fig. 140 Trouble code list for 1991–93 diesel engines with 4L60E automatic transmissions

87984656

CODE IDENTIFICATION

The "Service Engine Soon" light will only be "ON" if the malfunction exists under the conditions listed below. If the malfunction clears, the light will go out and the code will be stored in the ECM. Any Codes stored will be erased if no problem reoccurs within 50 engine starts.

CODE AND CIRCUIT	PROBABLE CAUSE	CODE AND CIRCUIT	PROBABLE CAUSE
Code 12 - No engine speed reference pulse.	No engine speed sensor reference pulses to the ECM. This code is not stored in memory and will only flash while the fault is present. Normal code with ignition "ON.", engine not running	Code 31 - MAP Sensor Too Low	Absolute Pressure (MAP) circuit signal voltage too low. Engine must run at curb idle for 10 seconds before this code will set
Code 14 - Coolant Sensor High Temperature Indication	Sets if the sensor or signal line becomes grounded for 5 minutes.	Code 32 - EGR Loop Error	Exhaust Gas Recirculation (EGR) vacuum circuit has seen improper EGR vacuum Vehicle must be running at road speed approximately 30 mph (48 Km/h) for 10 seconds before this code will set.
Code 15 - Coolant Sensor Low Temperature Indication	Sets if the sensor, connections, or wires open for 5 minutes.	Code 33 - MAP Sensor Too High	Absolute Pressure (MAP) circuit signal voltage too high. Engine must run at curb idle for 10 seconds before this code will set.
Code 21 - TPS Signal Voltage High	Throttle Position Sensor (TPS) circuit voltage high (open circuit or misadjusted TPS). Engine must run 30 seconds, at curb idle, before this code will set		
Code 22 - TPS Signal Voltage Low	Throttle Position Sensor (TPS) circuit voltage low (grounded circuit). Engine must run 2 minutes at 1250 rpm or above before this code will set	Code 51 - PROM	Faulty or improperly installed PROM. It takes approximately 10 seconds before this code will set
Code 23 - TPS Not Calibrated	Throttle Position Sensor (TPS) circuit. Voltage not between 25 and 1.3 volts at curb idle speed Engine must run for 30 seconds, at curb idle, before this code will set.	Code 52 - ECM	Fault in ECM circuit. It takes 10 seconds before this code will set.
Code 24 - VSS No Vehicle Speed Indication	Vehicle speed sensor (VSS) circuit (open or grounded circuit). Vehicle must operate at road speed for 10 seconds before this code will set	Code 53 - Five volt Reference Overload	5 volt reference (Vref) circuit overloaded (grounded circuit). It takes 10 seconds before this Code will set.

Fig. 139 Trouble code list for 1987–93 diesel engines with manual transmissions and 1987–90 diesel engines with automatic transmissions

87984655

DIAGNOSTIC TROUBLE CODE (DTC) IDENTIFICATION

The MIL (Service Engine Soon) will only be "ON" if the malfunction exists with the conditions listed below. If the malfunction clears, the lamp will go out and the DTC will be stored in the PCM. Any DTCs stored will be erased if no problem reoccurs within 50 engine starts. Note: All DTCs with the sign * are transmission related DTCs.

Remember, always start with the lowest numerical DTC first, when diagnosing some engine DTCs trigger other transmission DTCs.

DTC AND CIRCUIT	PROBABLE CAUSE	DTC AND CIRCUIT	PROBABLE CAUSE
DTC 51 - Faulty PROM Problem	Faulty PROM or PCM.	*DTC 69 - TCC Stuck "ON"	Slip > -20 and slip 20 TCC is not locked gear = 2, 3 or 4 TPS > 25%, not in P/RN for 4 seconds.
*DTC 52 - Long System Voltage High	Generator Voltage is greater than 16V for 109 minutes.	*DTC 72 - Vehicle Speed Sensor Loss	Not in P/N - Output speed changes greater than 1000 RPM • P/N - Output speed changes greater than 2050 RPM
*DTC 53 - System Voltage High	System overvoltage of 19.5 volts for 2 seconds		
DTC 55 - Faulty PCM	Faulty PCM.		- For 2 seconds
*DTC 58 - Transmission Fluid Temperature High	Transmission fluid temperature greater than 154°C (309°F) for one second.	*DTC 73 - Pressure Control Solenoid	If return amperage varies more than 0.16 amps. from commanded amperage
*DTC 59 - Transmission Fluid Temperature Low	Transmission fluid temperature greater than -33°C (-27°F) for one second.	*DTC 75 - System Voltage Low	System voltage <7.3 at low temperature or <11.7 at high temperature for 4 seconds.
*DTC 66 - 3-2 Control Solenoid Circuit Fault	At High Duty Cycle the circuit voltage is high OR at Low Duty Cycle the Circuit Voltage is low for four seconds.	*DTC 79 - Transmission Fluid Over Temperature	Transmission fluid Temperature >150C and <154C for 15 minutes.
*DTC 67 Torque Converter Clutch Circuit	TCC is commanded "ON", and circuit voltage remains high for two seconds OR TCC is commanded "OFF", and circuit voltage remains low for two seconds.	*DTC 81 - 2-3 Shift Solenoid Circuit Fault	2-3 shift solenoid is command "ON", and circuit voltage is high for two seconds OR 2-3 shift solenoid is command "OFF", and circuit voltage is low for two seconds.
		*DTC 82 - 1-2 Shift Solenoid Circuit Fault.	1-2 shift solenoid is command "ON", and circuit voltage is high for two seconds OR 1-2 shift solenoid is command "OFF" and circuit voltage is low for two seconds.

87984657

Fig. 141 Trouble code list for 1991–93 diesel engines with 4L60E automatic transmissions (continued)

DIAGNOSTIC TROUBLE CODE (DTC) IDENTIFICATION

The MIL (Malfunction Indicator Lamp) will be "ON" if an emission malfunction exists. If the malfunction clears, the lamp will go "OFF" and the DTC will be stored in the PCM. Any DTC(s) stored will be cleared if no problem recurs within 50 engine starts.

❓ **Important**

All DTC(s) with the sign * are transmission related DTC(s).

Remember, always start with the lowest numerical engine DTC first. When diagnosing some engine DTC(s), other transmission symptoms can occur.

DTC NUMBER AND NAME	DTC NUMBER AND NAME
DTC 13 - Engine Shutoff Solenoid Circuit Fault	* DTC 28 - Trans Range Pressure Switch Circuit
DTC 14 - Engine Coolant Temperature (ECT) Sensor Circuit Low (High Temperature Indicated)	DTC 29 - Glow Plug Relay Fault
	DTC 31 - EGR Control Pressure/Baro Sensor Circuit Low (High Vacuum)
DTC 15 - Engine Coolant Temperature (ETC) Sensor Circuit High (Low Temperature Indicated)	DTC 32 - EGR Circuit Error
	DTC 33 - EGR Control Pressure/Baro Sensor Circuit High
DTC 16 - Vehicle Speed Sensor Buffer Fault	DTC 34 - Injection Timing Stepper Motor Fault
DTC 17 - High Resolution Circuit Fault	DTC 35 - Injection Pulse Width Error (Response Time Short)
DTC 18 - Pump Cam Reference Pulse Error	DTC 36 - Injection Pulse Width Error (Response Time Long)
DTC 19 - Crankshaft Position Reference Error	* DTC 37 - TCC Brake Switch Stuck "ON"
DTC 21 - Accelerator Pedal Position 1 Circuit High	* DTC 38 - TCC Brake Switch Stuck Stuck "OFF"
DTC 22 - Accelerator Pedal Position 1 Circuit Low	DTC 41 - Brake Switch Circuit Fault
DTC 23 - Accelerator Pedal Position 1 Circuit Range Fault	DTC 42 - Fuel Temperature Circuit Low (High Temp Indicated)
* DTC 24 - Vehicle Speed Sensor Circuit Low (Output Speed Signal)	DTC 43 - Fuel Temperature Circuit High (Low Temp Indicated)
DTC 25 - Accelerator Pedal Position 2 Circuit High	DTC 44 - EGR Pulse Width Error
DTC 26 - Accelerator Pedal Position 2 Circuit Low	DTC 45 - EGR Vent Error
DTC 27 - Accelerator Pedal Position 2 Circuit Range Fault	DTC 46 - Malfunction Indicator Lamp Circuit Fault

87984658

Fig. 142 Trouble code list for 1994–95 diesel engines

DTC	Description	Illuminate MIL
P0112	IAT Sensor Circuit Low Voltage	Yes
P0113	IAT Sensor Circuit High Voltage	Yes
P0117	ECT Sensor Circuit Low Voltage	Yes
P0118	ECT Sensor Circuit High Voltage	Yes
P0121	APP Sensor 1 Circuit Performance	No
P0122	APP Sensor 1 Circuit Low Voltage	No
P0123	APP Sensor 1 Circuit High Voltage	No
P0182	Fuel Temperature Sensor Circuit Low Voltage	Yes
P0183	Fuel Temperature Sensor Circuit High Voltage	Yes
P0215	Engine Shutoff Control Circuit	No
P0216	Injection Timing Control System	Yes
P0219	Engine Overspeed Condition	No
P0220	APP Sensor 2 Circuit	No
P0221	APP Sensor 2 Circuit Performance	No
P0222	APP Sensor 2 Circuit Low Voltage	No
P0223	APP Sensor 2 Circuit High Voltage	No
P0225	APP Sensor 3 Circuit	No
P0226	APP Sensor 3 Circuit Performance	No
P0227	APP Sensor 3 Circuit Low Voltage	No
P0228	APP Sensor 3 Circuit High Voltage	No
P0231	Lift Pump Secondary Circuit Low Voltage	Yes
P0236	TC Boost System	Yes
P0237	TC Boost Sensor Circuit Low Voltage	Yes
P0238	TC Boost Sensor Circuit High Voltage	Yes
P0251	Injection Pump Cam System	Yes
P0263	Cylinder 8 Balance System	No
P0266	Cylinder 7 Balance System	No
P0269	Cylinder 2 Balance System	No
P0272	Cylinder 6 Balance System	No
P0275	Cylinder 5 Balance System	No
P0278	Cylinder 4 Balance System	No
P0281	Cylinder 3 Balance System	No
P0284	Cylinder 1 Balance System	No
P0335	CKP Sensor Circuit Performance	Yes
P0370	Timing Reference High Resolution	Yes
P0380	Glow plug Circuit Performance	Yes
P0404	EGR System	Yes
P0405	EGR Sensor Circuit Low Voltage	Yes

Fig. 144 Trouble code list for 1996—97 diesel engines

DIAGNOSTIC TROUBLE CODE (DTC) IDENTIFICATION

The MIL (Malfunction Indicator Lamp) will be "ON" if an emission malfunction exists. If the malfunction clears, the lamp will go "OFF" and the DTC will be stored in the PCM. Any DTC(s) stored will be cleared if no problem recurs within 50 engine starts.

Important

All DTC(s) with the sign * are transmission related DTC(s).
Remember, always start with the lowest numerical engine DTC first. When diagnosing some engine DTC(s), other transmission symptoms can occur.

DTC NUMBER AND NAME	DTC NUMBER AND NAME
DTC 47 - Intake Air Temperature Sensor Circuit Low (High Temp Indicated)	* **DTC 72** - Vehicle Speed Sensor Circuit Loss (Output Speed Signal)
DTC 48 - Intake Air Temperature Sensor Circuit High (Low Temp Indicated)	* **DTC 73** - Pressure Control Solenoid Circuit
DTC 49 - Service Throttle Soon Lamp Circuit Fault	* **DTC 75** - System Voltage Low
DTC 51 - PROM Error	**DTC 76** - Resume/Accel Switch Fault
* **DTC 52** - System Voltage High Long	* **DTC 79** - Trans Fluid Overtemp
DTC 53 - System Voltage High	* **DTC 81** - 2-3 Shift Solenoid Circuit
DTC 56 - Injection Pump Calibration Resistor Error	* **DTC 82** - 1-2 Shift Solenoid Circuit
* **DTC 57** - PCM 5 Volt Shorted	**DTC 88** - TDC Offset Error
* **DTC 58** - Trans Fluid Temp Circuit Low	**DTC 91** - Cylinder Balance Fault #1 Cyl
* **DTC 59** - Trans Fluid Temp Circuit High	**DTC 92** - Cylinder Balance Fault #2 Cyl
DTC 63 - Accelerator Pedal Position 3 Circuit High	**DTC 93** - Cylinder Balance Fault #3 Cyl
DTC 64 - Accelerator Pedal Position 3 Circuit Low	**DTC 94** - Cylinder Balance Fault #4 Cyl
DTC 65 - Accelerator Pedal Position 3 Circuit Range Fault	**DTC 95** - Cylinder Balance Fault #5 Cyl
* **DTC 66** - 3-2 Control Solenoid Circuit	**DTC 96** - Cylinder Balance Fault #6 Cyl
* **DTC 67** - TCC Solenoid Circuit	**DTC 97** - Cylinder Balance Fault #7 Cyl
DTC 69 - TCC Stuck "ON"	**DTC 98** - Cylinder Balance Fault #8 Cyl
DTC 71 - Set/Coast Switch Fault	**DTC 99** - Accelerator Pedal Position 2 (5 Bolt Reference Fault)

Fig. 143 Trouble code list for 1994—95 diesel engines

DTC	Description	Illuminate MIL
P0406	EGR Sensor Circuit High Voltage	Yes
P0501	Vehicle Speed Sensor Circuit	No
P0567	Cruise Resume Circuit	No
P0568	Cruise Set Circuit	No
P0571	Cruise Brake Switch Circuit	No
P0601	PCM Memory	No
P0602	PCM Not Programmed	No
P0606	PCM Internal Communication Interrupted	Yes
P1125	APP System	No
P1214	Injection Pump Timing Offset	Yes
P1216	Fuel Solenoid Response Time Too Short	No
P1217	Fuel Solenoid Response Time Too Long	No
P1218	Injection Pump Calibration Circuit	Yes
P1627	A/D Performance	Yes
P1635	5 Volt Reference Low	No
P1641	Malfunction Indicator Lamp (MIL) Control Circuit	No
P1653	EGR Vent Solenoid Control Circuit	Yes
P1654	Service Throttle Soon (STS) Lamp Control Circuit	No
P1655	EGR Solenoid Control Circuit	Yes
P1656	Wastegate Solenoid Control Circuit	Yes

87984G53

Fig. 145 Trouble code list for 1996–97 diesel engines (continued)

VACUUM DIAGRAMS

Following are vacuum diagrams for most of the engine and emissions package combinations covered by this manual. Because vacuum circuits will vary based on various engine and vehicle options, always refer first to the vehicle emission control information label, if present. Should the label be missing, or should vehicle be equipped with a different engine from the vehicle's original equipment, refer to the diagrams below for the same or similar configuration.

If you wish to obtain a replacement emissions label, most manufacturers make the labels available for purchase. The labels can usually be ordered from a local dealer.

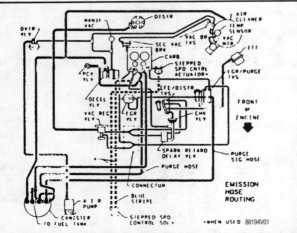

Fig. 146 Vacuum hose routing—1987–88 Federal and high altitude (VIN Z) 4.3L engines with automatic transmissions (G10, 20 and 30 models)

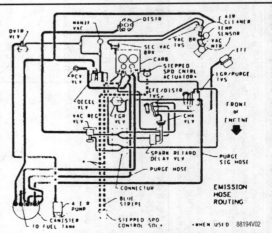

Fig. 147 Vacuum hose routing—1987–88 Federal and high altitude (VIN Z) 4.3L engines with manual transmissions (G10, 20 and 30 models)

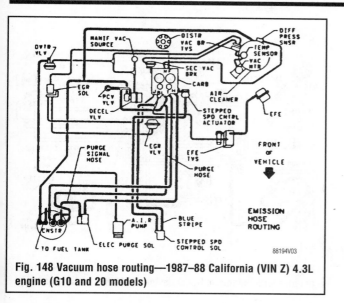

Fig. 148 Vacuum hose routing—1987–88 California (VIN Z) 4.3L engine (G10 and 20 models)

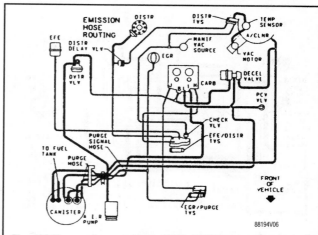

Fig. 151 Vacuum hose routing—1987–88 Federal and high altitude (VIN H) 5.0L engines with manual transmissions (G10 and 20 models)

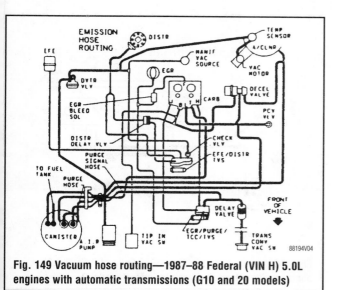

Fig. 149 Vacuum hose routing—1987–88 Federal (VIN H) 5.0L engines with automatic transmissions (G10 and 20 models)

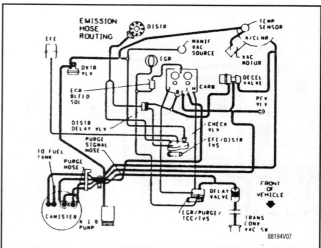

Fig. 152 Vacuum hose routing—1987–88 Federal (VIN K) 5.7L engines with automatic transmissions (G10, 20 and 30 models)

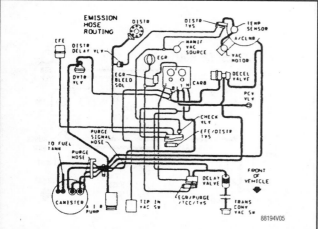

Fig. 150 Vacuum hose routing—1987–88 Federal and high altitude (VIN H) 5.0L and (VIN K) 5.7L engines with automatic transmissions (G10 and 20 models)

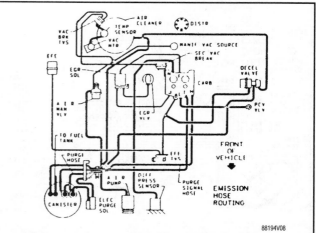

Fig. 153 Vacuum hose routing—1987–88 California (VIN H) 5.0L and (VIN K) 5.7L engines with automatic transmissions (G10, 20 and 30 models)

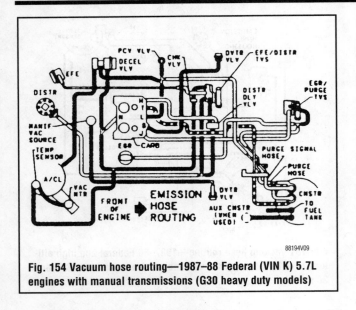

Fig. 154 Vacuum hose routing—1987–88 Federal (VIN K) 5.7L engines with manual transmissions (G30 heavy duty models)

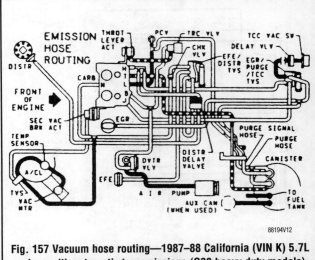

Fig. 157 Vacuum hose routing—1987–88 California (VIN K) 5.7L engines with automatic transmissions (G30 heavy duty models)

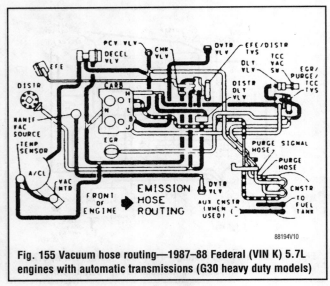

Fig. 155 Vacuum hose routing—1987–88 Federal (VIN K) 5.7L engines with automatic transmissions (G30 heavy duty models)

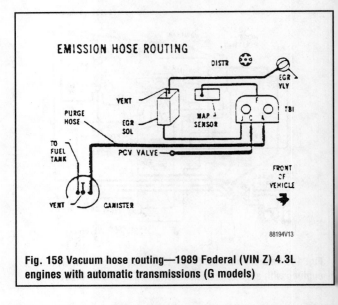

Fig. 158 Vacuum hose routing—1989 Federal (VIN Z) 4.3L engines with automatic transmissions (G models)

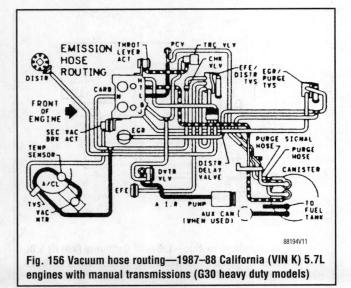

Fig. 156 Vacuum hose routing—1987–88 California (VIN K) 5.7L engines with manual transmissions (G30 heavy duty models)

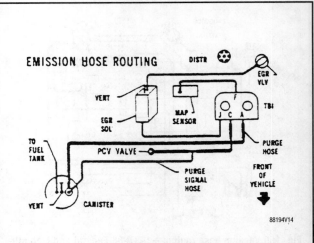

Fig. 159 Vacuum hose routing—1989 high altitude (VIN Z) 4.3L engines with automatic transmissions (G models)

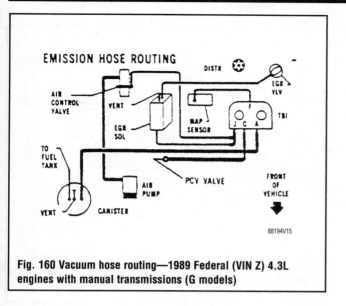

Fig. 160 Vacuum hose routing—1989 Federal (VIN Z) 4.3L engines with manual transmissions (G models)

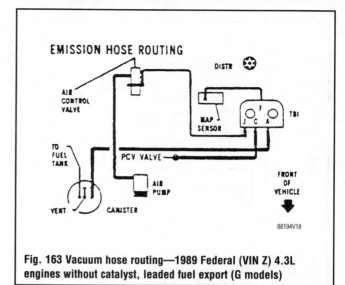

Fig. 163 Vacuum hose routing—1989 Federal (VIN Z) 4.3L engines without catalyst, leaded fuel export (G models)

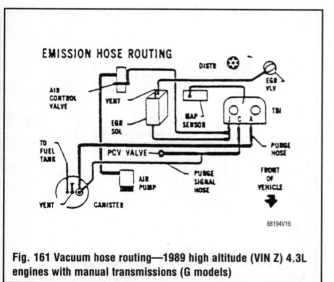

Fig. 161 Vacuum hose routing—1989 high altitude (VIN Z) 4.3L engines with manual transmissions (G models)

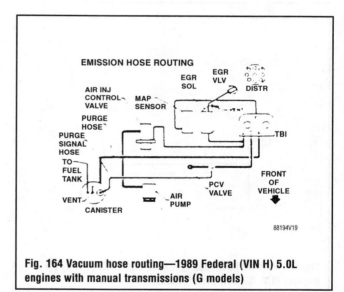

Fig. 164 Vacuum hose routing—1989 Federal (VIN H) 5.0L engines with manual transmissions (G models)

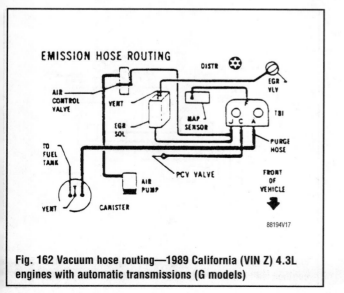

Fig. 162 Vacuum hose routing—1989 California (VIN Z) 4.3L engines with automatic transmissions (G models)

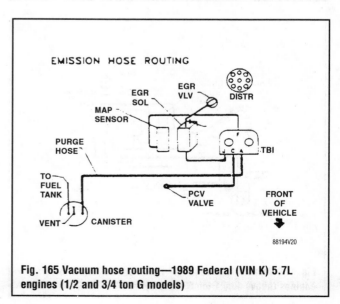

Fig. 165 Vacuum hose routing—1989 Federal (VIN K) 5.7L engines (1/2 and 3/4 ton G models)

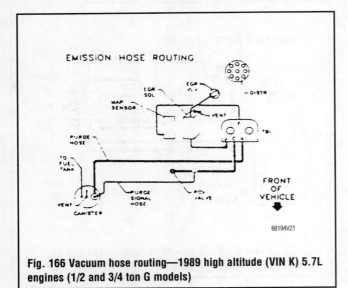

Fig. 166 Vacuum hose routing—1989 high altitude (VIN K) 5.7L engines (1/2 and 3/4 ton G models)

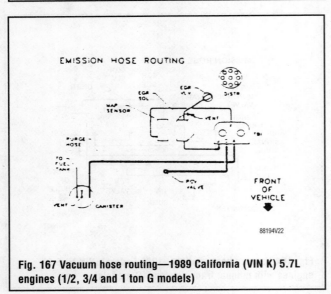

Fig. 167 Vacuum hose routing—1989 California (VIN K) 5.7L engines (1/2, 3/4 and 1 ton G models)

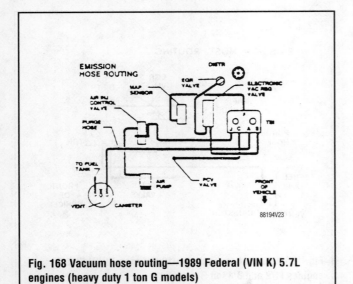

Fig. 168 Vacuum hose routing—1989 Federal (VIN K) 5.7L engines (heavy duty 1 ton G models)

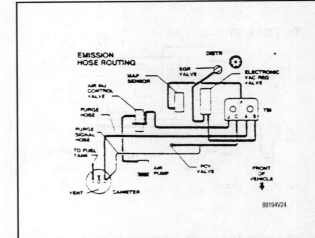

Fig. 169 Vacuum hose routing—1989 high altitude (VIN K) 5.7L engines (1 ton G models)

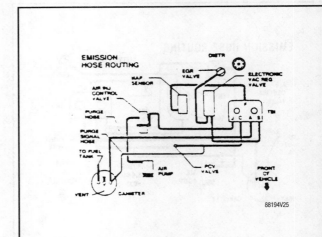

Fig. 170 Vacuum hose routing—1989 Federal (VIN K) 5.7L engines with optional flatbed or van boxes (1 ton G models)

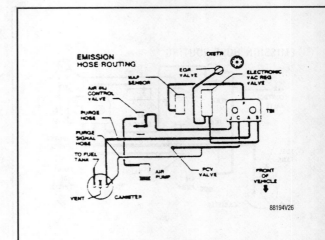

Fig. 171 Vacuum hose routing—1989 high altitude (VIN K) 5.7L engines with optional flatbed or van boxes (1 ton G models)

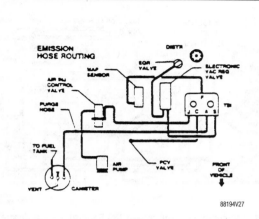

Fig. 172 Vacuum hose routing—1989 Federal (VIN K) 5.7L engines with optional flatbed or van boxes and option NA4 (1 ton G models)

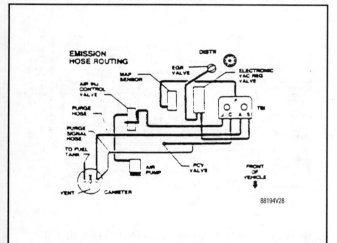

Fig. 173 Vacuum hose routing—1989 high altitude (VIN K) 5.7L engines (1 ton G models)

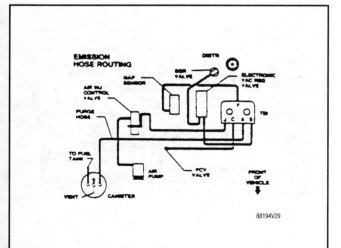

Fig. 174 Vacuum hose routing—1989 California (VIN K) 5.7L engines with optional flatbed or van boxes (1 ton G models)

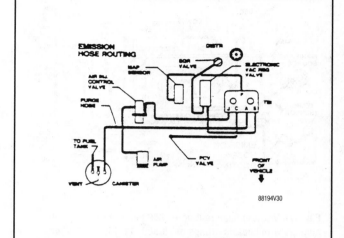

Fig. 175 Vacuum hose routing—1989 California (VIN K) 5.7L engines with base body and option NA4 (1 ton G models)

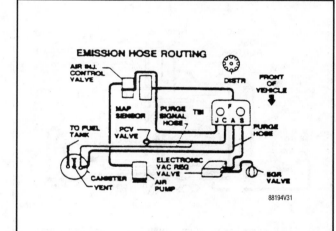

Fig. 176 Vacuum hose routing—1989 high altitude (VIN N) 7.4L engines (G models)

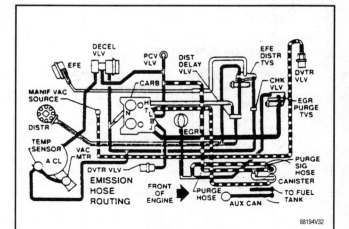

Fig. 177 Vacuum hose routing—1989 Federal and California (VIN W) 7.4L engines with chassis ratings of 14,500 or 16,000 lbs. GVW (P models)

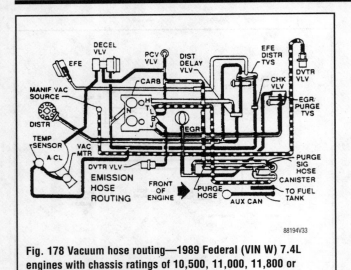

Fig. 178 Vacuum hose routing—1989 Federal (VIN W) 7.4L engines with chassis ratings of 10,500, 11,000, 11,800 or 12,300 lbs. GVW (P models)

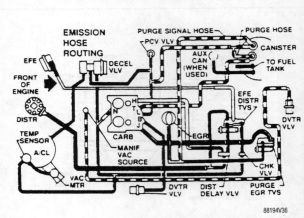

Fig. 181 Vacuum hose routing—1989 Federal and California (VIN W) 7.4L engines with chassis ratings of 12,000 lbs. GVW (P models)

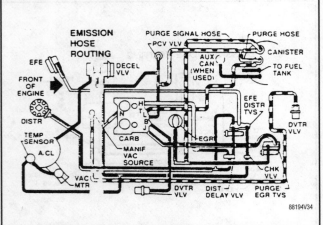

Fig. 179 Vacuum hose routing—1989 Federal and California (VIN W) 7.4L engines with chassis ratings of 14,100 lbs. or above GVW (P models)

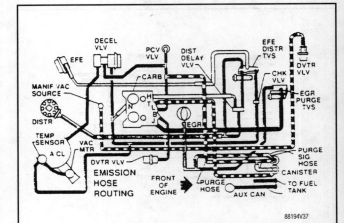

Fig. 182 Vacuum hose routing—1989 Federal (VIN W) 7.4L engines with chassis ratings of 10,500, 11,000, 11,800 or 12,300 lbs. GVW (P models)

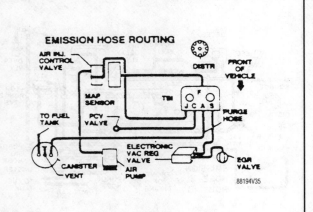

Fig. 180 Vacuum hose routing—1989 California (VIN N) 7.4L engines with base chassis (G models)

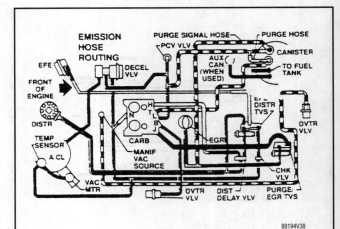

Fig. 183 Vacuum hose routing—1989 Federal (VIN W) 7.4L engines with chassis ratings of 12,000 lbs. GVW (P models)

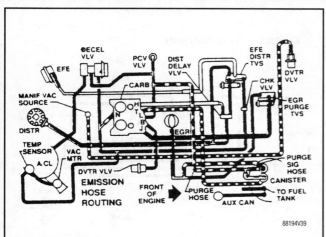

Fig. 184 Vacuum hose routing—1989 California (VIN W) 7.4L engines with chassis ratings of 10,500, 11,000, 11,800 or 12,300 lbs. GVW (P models)

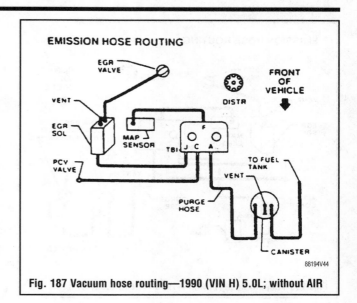

Fig. 187 Vacuum hose routing—1990 (VIN H) 5.0L; without AIR

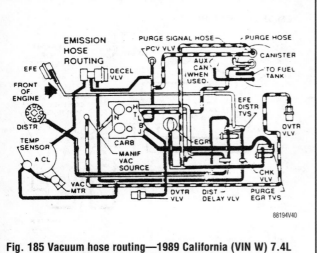
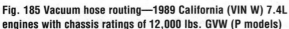

Fig. 185 Vacuum hose routing—1989 California (VIN W) 7.4L engines with chassis ratings of 12,000 lbs. GVW (P models)

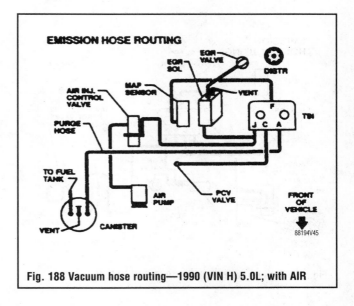

Fig. 188 Vacuum hose routing—1990 (VIN H) 5.0L; with AIR

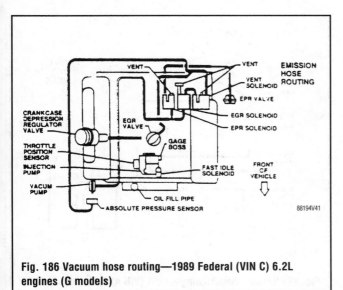

Fig. 186 Vacuum hose routing—1989 Federal (VIN C) 6.2L engines (G models)

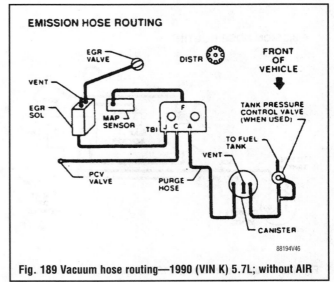

Fig. 189 Vacuum hose routing—1990 (VIN K) 5.7L; without AIR

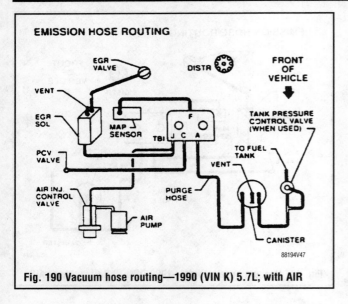

Fig. 190 Vacuum hose routing—1990 (VIN K) 5.7L; with AIR

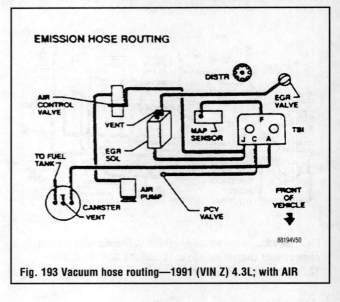

Fig. 193 Vacuum hose routing—1991 (VIN Z) 4.3L; with AIR

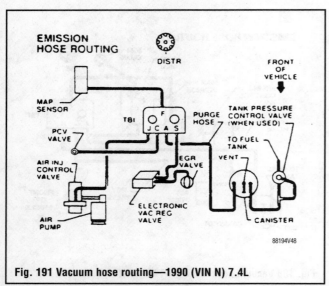

Fig. 191 Vacuum hose routing—1990 (VIN N) 7.4L

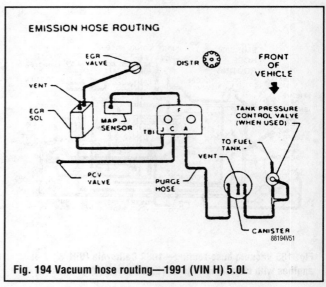

Fig. 194 Vacuum hose routing—1991 (VIN H) 5.0L

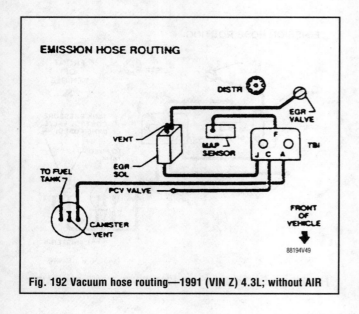

Fig. 192 Vacuum hose routing—1991 (VIN Z) 4.3L; without AIR

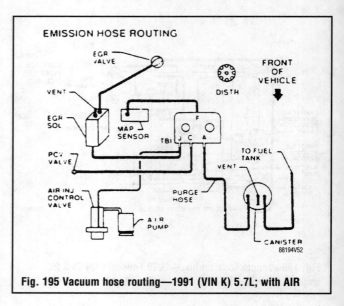

Fig. 195 Vacuum hose routing—1991 (VIN K) 5.7L; with AIR

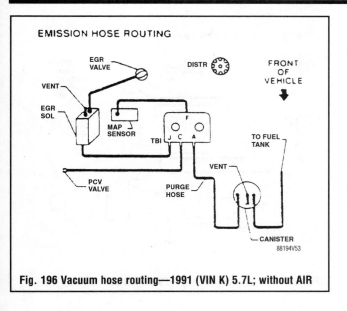

Fig. 196 Vacuum hose routing—1991 (VIN K) 5.7L; without AIR

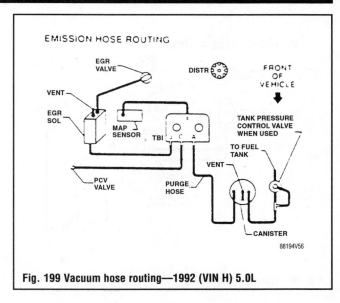

Fig. 199 Vacuum hose routing—1992 (VIN H) 5.0L

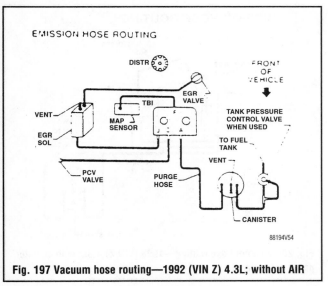

Fig. 197 Vacuum hose routing—1992 (VIN Z) 4.3L; without AIR

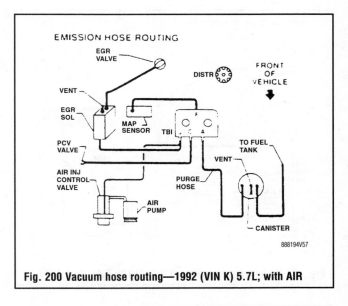

Fig. 200 Vacuum hose routing—1992 (VIN K) 5.7L; with AIR

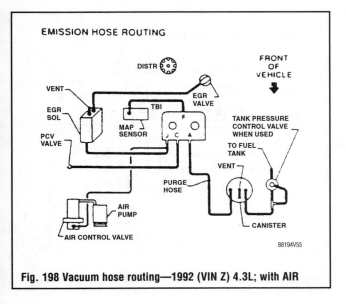

Fig. 198 Vacuum hose routing—1992 (VIN Z) 4.3L; with AIR

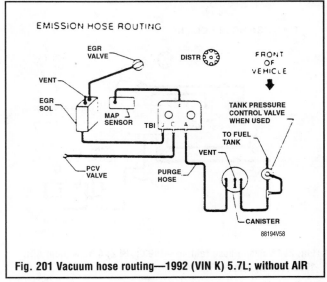

Fig. 201 Vacuum hose routing—1992 (VIN K) 5.7L; without AIR

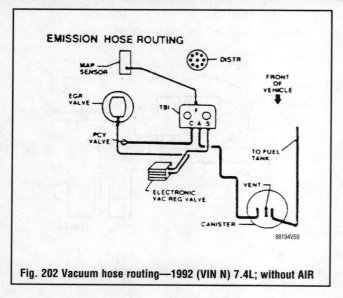

Fig. 202 Vacuum hose routing—1992 (VIN N) 7.4L; without AIR

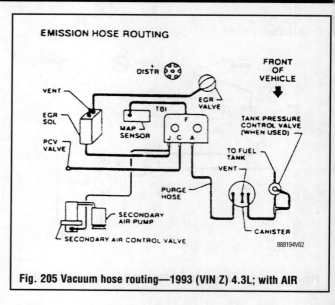

Fig. 205 Vacuum hose routing—1993 (VIN Z) 4.3L; with AIR

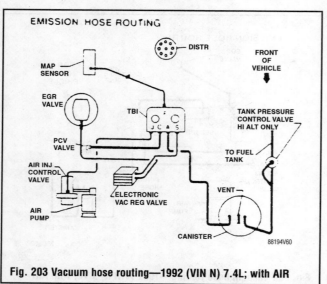

Fig. 203 Vacuum hose routing—1992 (VIN N) 7.4L; with AIR

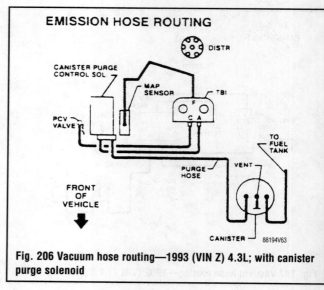

Fig. 206 Vacuum hose routing—1993 (VIN Z) 4.3L; with canister purge solenoid

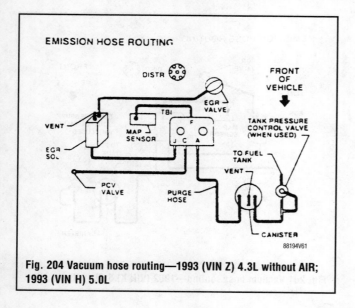

Fig. 204 Vacuum hose routing—1993 (VIN Z) 4.3L without AIR; 1993 (VIN H) 5.0L

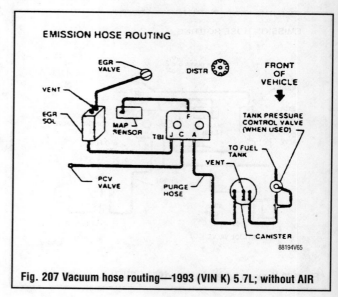

Fig. 207 Vacuum hose routing—1993 (VIN K) 5.7L; without AIR

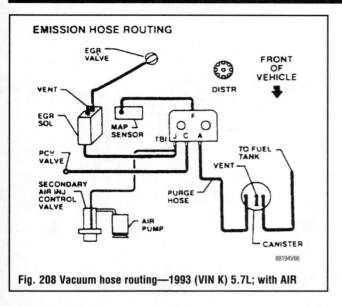

Fig. 208 Vacuum hose routing—1993 (VIN K) 5.7L; with AIR

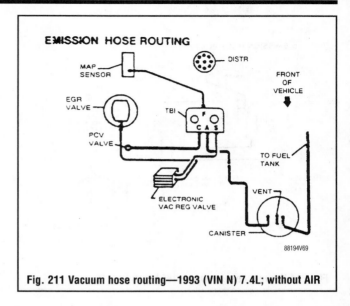

Fig. 211 Vacuum hose routing—1993 (VIN N) 7.4L; without AIR

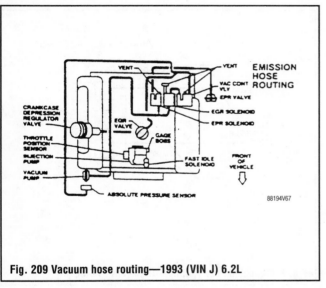

Fig. 209 Vacuum hose routing—1993 (VIN J) 6.2L

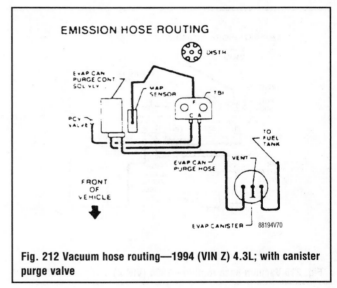

Fig. 212 Vacuum hose routing—1994 (VIN Z) 4.3L; with canister purge valve

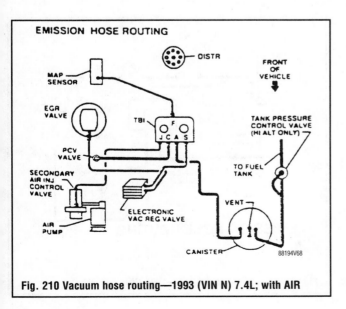

Fig. 210 Vacuum hose routing—1993 (VIN N) 7.4L; with AIR

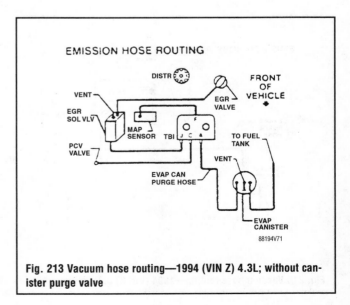

Fig. 213 Vacuum hose routing—1994 (VIN Z) 4.3L; without canister purge valve

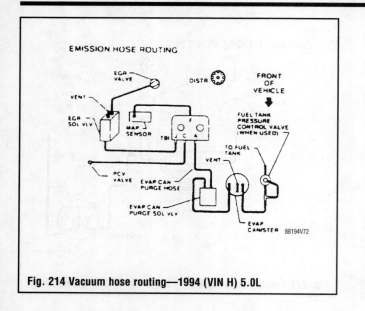

Fig. 214 Vacuum hose routing—1994 (VIN H) 5.0L

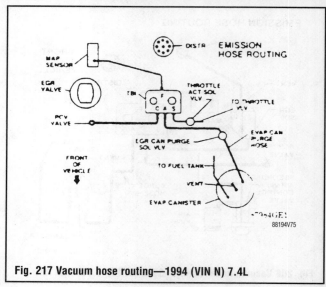

Fig. 217 Vacuum hose routing—1994 (VIN N) 7.4L

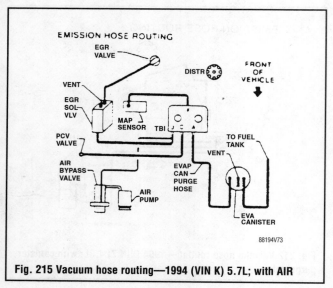

Fig. 215 Vacuum hose routing—1994 (VIN K) 5.7L; with AIR

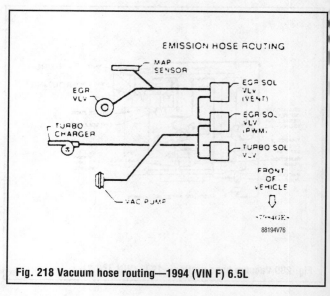

Fig. 218 Vacuum hose routing—1994 (VIN F) 6.5L

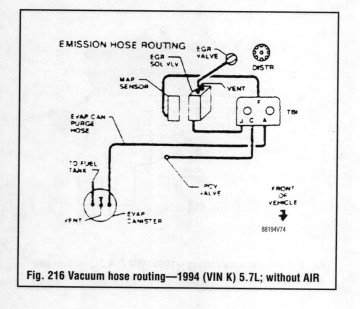

Fig. 216 Vacuum hose routing—1994 (VIN K) 5.7L; without AIR

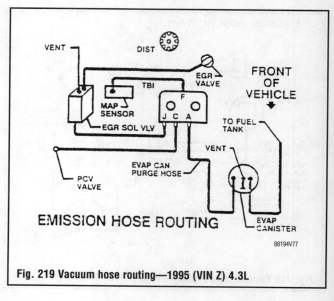

Fig. 219 Vacuum hose routing—1995 (VIN Z) 4.3L

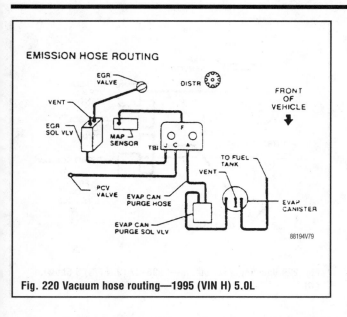

Fig. 220 Vacuum hose routing—1995 (VIN H) 5.0L

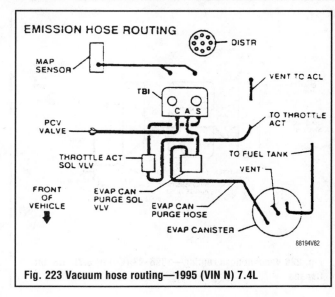

Fig. 223 Vacuum hose routing—1995 (VIN N) 7.4L

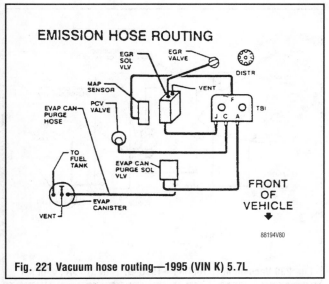

Fig. 221 Vacuum hose routing—1995 (VIN K) 5.7L

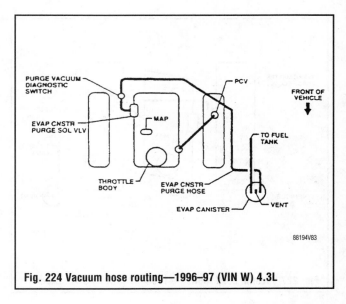

Fig. 224 Vacuum hose routing—1996–97 (VIN W) 4.3L

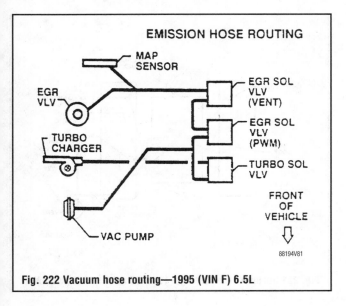

Fig. 222 Vacuum hose routing—1995 (VIN F) 6.5L

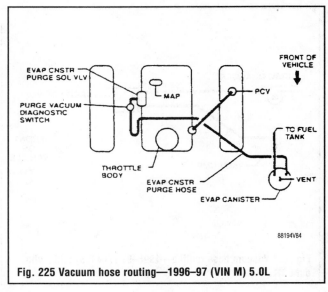

Fig. 225 Vacuum hose routing—1996–97 (VIN M) 5.0L

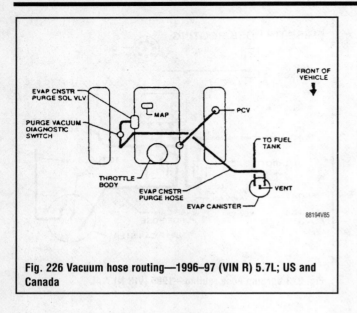

Fig. 226 Vacuum hose routing—1996–97 (VIN R) 5.7L; US and Canada

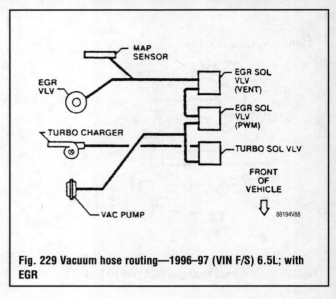

Fig. 229 Vacuum hose routing—1996–97 (VIN F/S) 6.5L; with EGR

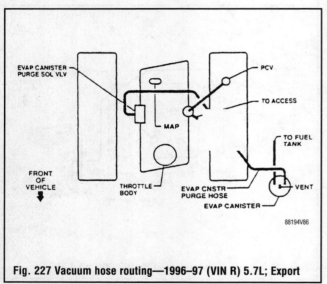

Fig. 227 Vacuum hose routing—1996–97 (VIN R) 5.7L; Export

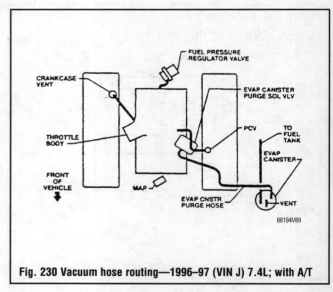

Fig. 230 Vacuum hose routing—1996–97 (VIN J) 7.4L; with A/T

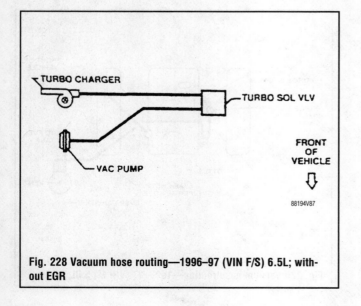

Fig. 228 Vacuum hose routing—1996–97 (VIN F/S) 6.5L; without EGR

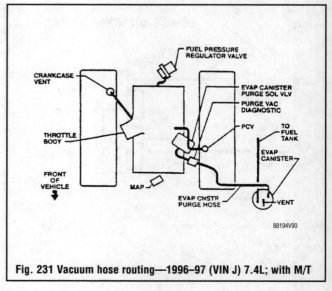

Fig. 231 Vacuum hose routing—1996–97 (VIN J) 7.4L; with M/T

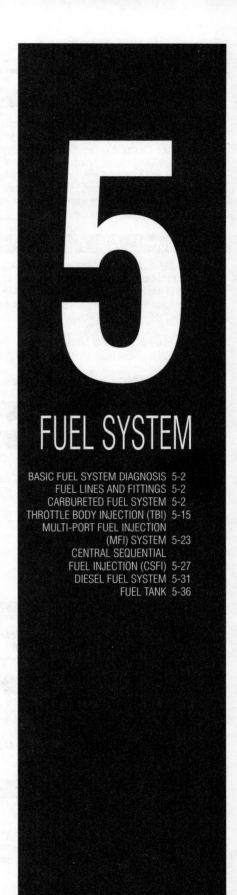

5

FUEL SYSTEM

BASIC FUEL SYSTEM DIAGNOSIS

When there is a problem starting or driving a vehicle, two of the most important checks involve the ignition and the fuel systems. The questions most mechanics attempt to answer first, "is there spark?" and "is there fuel?" will often lead to solving most basic problems. For ignition system diagnosis and testing, please refer to the information on engine electrical components and ignition systems found earlier in this manual. If the ignition system checks out (there is spark), then you must determine if the fuel system is operating properly (is there fuel?).

Precautions

Safety is the most important factor when performing not only fuel system maintenance, but any type of maintenance. Failure to conduct maintenance and repairs in a safe manner may result in serious personal injury or death. Maintenance and testing of the vehicle's fuel system components can be accomplished safely and effectively by adhering to the following rules and guidelines:

• To avoid the possibility of fire and personal injury, always disconnect the negative battery cable unless the repair or test procedure requires that battery voltage be applied.

• Always relieve the fuel system pressure prior to disconnecting any fuel system component (injector, fuel rail, pressure regulator, etc.), fitting or fuel line connection. Exercise extreme caution whenever relieving fuel system pressure to avoid exposing skin, face and eyes to fuel spray. Please be advised that fuel under pressure may penetrate the skin or any part of the body that it contacts.

• Always place a shop towel or cloth around the fitting or connection prior to loosening to absorb any excess fuel due to spillage. Ensure that all fuel spillage (should it occur) is quickly removed from engine surfaces. Ensure that all fuel soaked cloths or towels are deposited into a suitable waste container.

• Always keep a dry chemical (Class B) fire extinguisher near the work area.

• Do not allow fuel spray or fuel vapors to come into contact with a spark or open flame.

• Always use a backup wrench when loosening and tightening fuel line connection fittings. This will prevent unnecessary stress and torsion to fuel line piping. Always follow the proper torque specifications.

• Always replace worn fuel fitting O-rings with new ones. Do not substitute fuel hose or equivalent where fuel pipe is installed.

• Due to the possibility of a fire or explosion, never drain or store gasoline in an open container.

FUEL LINE FITTINGS

Quick-Connect Fittings

REMOVAL & INSTALLATION

▶ See Figure 1

➡ **This procedure requires Tool Set J37088-A or its equivalent fuel line quick-connect separator.**

1. Grasp both sides of the fitting. Twist the female connector ¼ turn in each direction to loosen any dirt within the fittings. Using compressed air, blow out the dirt from the quick-connect fittings at the end of the fittings.

✳✳ CAUTION

Safety glasses MUST be worn when using compressed air to avoid eye injury due to flying dirt particles!

2. For plastic (hand releasable) fittings, squeeze the plastic retainer release tabs, then pull the connection apart.

3. For metal fittings, choose the correct tool from kit J37088-A or its equivalent for the size of the fitting to be disconnected. Insert the proper tool into the female connector, then push inward to release the locking tabs. Pull the connection apart.

4. If it is necessary to remove rust or burrs from the male tube end of a quick-connect fitting, use emery cloth in a radial motion with the tube end to prevent damage to the O-ring sealing surfaces. Using a clean shop towel, wipe off the male tube ends. Inspect all connectors for dirt and burrs. Clean and/or replace if required.

To install:

5. Apply a few drops of clean engine oil to the male tube end of the fitting.

6. Push the connectors together to cause the retaining tabs/fingers to snap into place.

7. Once installed, pull on both ends of each connection to make sure they are secure and check for leaks.

CARBURETED FUEL SYSTEM

Only the 5.7L engine is equipped with a carburetor. Two 4-bbl. carburetors were offered, the M4ME and M4MEF. The difference between the two models is that the M4MEF has a wide open throttle mixture control. The M4ME was used only on some 1987 models. The M4MEF was used for 1988–90 models.

Mechanical Fuel Pump

▶ See Figure 2

The fuel pump is a single action AC diaphragm type.

The pump is operated by an eccentric on the camshaft. A pushrod between the camshaft eccentric and the fuel pump operates the pump rocker arm.

TESTING

Pressure

▶ See Figure 3

Fuel pumps should always be tested on the vehicle. The larger line between the pump and tank is the suction side of the system and the smaller line, between the pump and carburetor, is the pressure side. A leak in the pressure side would be apparent because of dripping fuel. A leak in the suction side is usually only apparent because of a reduced volume of fuel delivered to the pressure side.

1. Tighten any loose line connections and look for any kinks or restrictions.

2. Disconnect the fuel line at the carburetor. Disengage the distributor-to-coil primary wire. Place a container at the end of the fuel line and crank

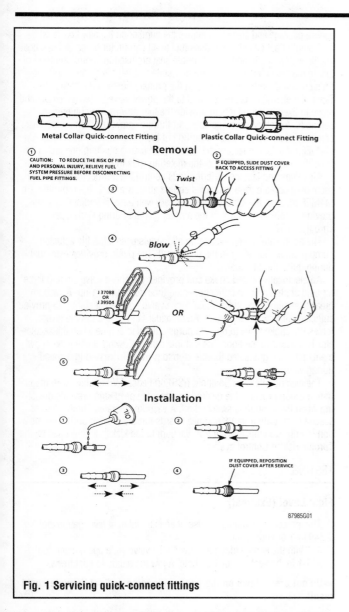

Fig. 1 Servicing quick-connect fittings

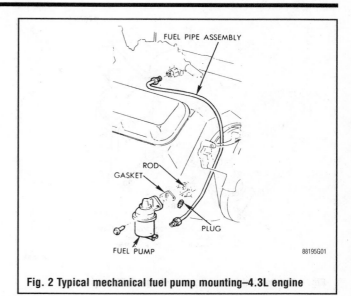

Fig. 2 Typical mechanical fuel pump mounting—4.3L engine

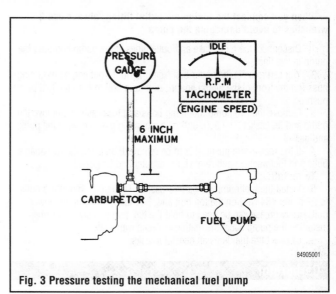

Fig. 3 Pressure testing the mechanical fuel pump

the engine a few revolutions. If little or no fuel flows from the line, either the fuel pump is inoperative or the line is plugged. Blow through the lines with compressed air and try the test again. Reconnect the line.

3. If fuel flows in good volume, check the fuel pump pressure to be sure.

4. Attach a low pressure gauge to the pressure side of the fuel line. On vans equipped with a vapor return system, squeeze off the return hose.

5. Run the engine at idle and note the reading on the gauge. Stop the engine and compare the reading with the specifications listed in the Tune-Up Specifications chart located in Section 1. If the pump is operating properly, the pressure will be as specified and will be constant at idle speed. If pressure varies sporadically or is too high or low, the pump should be replaced.

6. Remove the pressure gauge.

Volume

1. Disconnect the fuel line from the carburetor. Run the fuel line into a suitable measuring container.

2. Run the engine at idle until there is one pint of fuel in the container. One pint should be pumped in 30 seconds or less.

3. If the flow is below minimum, check for a restriction in the line. The only way to check fuel pump pressure is by connecting an accurate pressure gauge to the fuel line at the carburetor level. Never replace a fuel pump without performing this simple test. If the engine seems to be starving out, check the ignition system first. Also check for a plugged fuel filter or a restricted fuel line before replacing the pump.

REMOVAL & INSTALLATION

▶ **See Figure 4**

✻✻ CAUTION

Never smoke when working around gasoline! Avoid all sources of sparks or ignition. Gasoline vapors are EXTREMELY volatile!

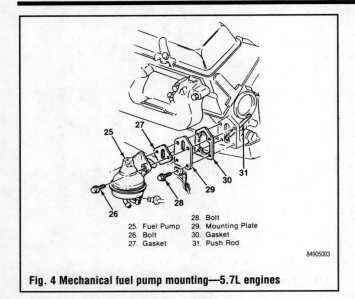

25. Fuel Pump
26. Bolt
27. Gasket
28. Bolt
29. Mounting Plate
30. Gasket
31. Push Rod

84905003

Fig. 4 Mechanical fuel pump mounting—5.7L engines

➡**When you connect the fuel pump outlet fitting, always use 2 wrenches to avoid damaging the pump.**

1. Disconnect the fuel intake and outlet lines at the pump and plug the pump intake line.

2. You can remove the upper bolt from the right front engine mounting boss (on the front of the block) and insert a long bolt to hold the fuel pump pushrod.

3. Remove the two pump mounting bolts and lockwashers; remove the pump and its gasket. The 5.7L utilizes a mounting plate between the pump and gasket.

4. If the rocker arm pushrod is to be removed, unfasten the two adapter bolts and lockwashers and remove the adapter and its gasket.

To install:

5. Install the fuel pump with a new gasket. Tighten the mounting bolts to 27 ft. lbs. (34 Nm) on the top bolt and, 3 ft. lbs. (4 Nm) on the lower bolt. Heavy grease can be used to hold the fuel pump pushrod up when installing the pump. Coat the mating surfaces with sealer.

6. Connect the fuel lines an check for leaks.

Carburetor

DESCRIPTION & OPERATION

These Rochester models are four barrel, two stage carburetors with three major assemblies: the air horn, float bowl, and throttle body. They have six basic operating systems:

1. Float
2. Idle
3. Main Metering
4. Power
5. Pump
6. Choke

The first "M" in the model identification number indicates that the carburetor is of a Modified primary metering "open loop" design. The "4M" is the model designation, indicating it is a four barrel carburetor. The remaining letters designate specific features as follows:

• C—It has an integral Hot Air Choke.
• D—Dual capacity pump valve and a combined mixture control/dual capacity pump solenoid assembly.
• E—Has an electric choke.
• F—Has an adjustable wide open throttle mixture control.

The carburetor identification number is stamped vertically on the float bowl near the secondary throttle lever. Refer to this number before servicing the carburetor. If replacing the float bowl assembly, follow the instructions in the

service package and stamp or engrave the number on the new float bowl.

A single float chamber supplies fuel to all carburetor bores. A float, float needle with pull clip and a float needle seat are used to control the level of fuel in the float chamber. A vacuum-operated power piston and metering rods control the air/fuel metering in the primary bores of the carburetor. Tapered metering rods are attached to the power valve piston assembly and move in fixed metering jets to provide the fuel flow for varying engine demands. A factory-set adjustable part throttle screw, used on all models, precisely positions the tapered portion of the metering rods in the jets. On M4MEF models, the factory-set rich stop adjusting bushing precisely positions the enrichment portion of the metering rods in the jets.

Air valves and tapered metering rods control the air/fuel mixture in the secondary bores during increased engine air flow at wide open throttle. On M4MEF models, the factory-set secondary well air bleed adjusting screw provides additional control of the air/fuel mixture during Wide Open Throttle (WOT).

The accelerator pump system on all models uses a throttle actuated pump plunger, operating in the pump well. The pump provides extra fuel during quick throttle openings.

An electrically heated choke coil provides the choke valve closing force for cold startup and for correct opening time during warm-up. A vacuum break assembly(s) controls initial choke valve opening at startup to provide sufficient air flow to the engine. An unloader tang on the throttle lever forces the choke valve to open to purge a flooded engine when the accelerator is pressed to the floor. The fast idle cam, following choke valve movement, acts as a graduated throttle stop to provide increased idle speed during warm-up.

The electric Idle Stop Solenoid (ISS) on Federal V8 engines with manual transmission provides the desired engine idle speed, and prevents dieseling when the ignition is switched off. A vacuum-operated Throttle Kicker assembly on California V8 engines retards throttle closing during deceleration to improve emission control. Vacuum to the kicker is controlled by the Throttle Return Control system.

TESTING

Float Level (External)

This procedure requires the use of an external float level gauge tool No. J-34935-1 or equivalent.

1. With the engine idling and the choke valve wide open, insert tool J-34935-1 in the vent slot or vent hole. Allow the gauge to float freely.

➡**Do not press down on the gauge. Flooding or float damage could result.**

2. Observe the mark on the gauge that lines up with the top of the casting. The setting should be within $\frac{1}{16}$ in. (1.6mm) of the specified float level setting. Incorrect fuel pressure will adversely affect the fuel level.

3. If not within specification, remove the air horn and adjust the float.

Choke (Engine Off)

1. Remove the air cleaner assembly.
2. Hold the throttle half way down.
3. Open and close the choke several times. Be sure all links are connected and not damaged. Choke valve, linkage, and fast idle cam must operate freely.
4. If the choke valve, linkage or fast idle cam is sticking due to varnish, clean with choke cleaner.
5. Do not lubricate linkage, as lubricant will collect dust and cause sticking.

Electric Choke (On Vehicle)

1. Allow the choke thermostat to stabilize at about 70°F (21°C).
2. Open the throttle to allow the choke valve to close.
3. Start the engine and determine the length of time for the choke valve to reach full open position:

a. If longer than five minutes, check the voltage at the choke stat connector, with the engine running.

b. If voltage is between 12 and 15 volts, check for proper ground between choke cover and choke housing. If correct, replace choke cover assembly.

c. If the voltage is low or zero, check all wires and connections.

Vacuum Break

A hand-operated vacuum pump such as J-23738-A or equivalent will be needed for this procedure.

1. If the vacuum break has an air bleed hole, plug it during this checking procedure.

2. Apply 15 in. Hg (50 kPa) vacuum to the vacuum break with the hand pump.

a. Apply finger pressure to see if the plunger has moved through full travel. If not, replace the vacuum break.

b. Observe the vacuum gauge. Vacuum should hold vacuum for at least twenty seconds. If not, replace the vacuum break.

3. Replace vacuum break hoses that are cracked, cut or hardened.

Idle Stop Solenoid (ISS)

A non-functioning idle stop solenoid (if equipped) could cause stalling or rough idle.

1. Turn the ignition **ON**, but do not start the engine.

2. Open the throttle momentarily to allow the solenoid plunger to extend.

3. Disconnect the wire at the solenoid. The plunger should drop back from the throttle lever.

4. Connect the solenoid wire. The plunger should move out and contact the throttle lever.

5. If the plunger does not move in and out as the wire is disconnected and connected, check the voltage across the feed wire:

a. If 12–15 volts are present in the feed wire, replace the solenoid.

b. If the voltage is low, locate the cause of the open circuit in the solenoid feed wire and repair as necessary.

Throttle Kicker

A hand-operated vacuum pump such as J-23738-A or equivalent will be needed for this procedure.

1. Hold the throttle half way open to allow the plunger to extend fully.

2. Apply 20 in. Hg (67 kPa) vacuum to the throttle kicker with the hand vacuum pump.

a. Apply finger pressure to the plunger to see if it has extended fully. If not, replace the throttle kicker.

b. Observe the vacuum gauge. Vacuum should hold for at least twenty seconds. If not, replace the throttle kicker.

3. Release the vacuum to the throttle kicker.

4. If the plunger does not retract to its starting position, replace kicker.

ADJUSTMENTS

Float

◗ See Figure 5, 6 and 7 (p. 6–8)

A float level T-scale such as J-9789-90 or equivalent and float positioning tool kit J-34817 or equivalent will be needed for this adjustment.

1. Remove the air horn, gasket, power piston and metering rod assembly, and the float bowl insert.

2. Attach float adjustment tool J-34817-1 or equivalent to the float bowl.

3. Place float adjustment tool J-34817-3 or equivalent into float adjustment tool J-34817-1 or equivalent, with the contact pin resting on the outer edge of the float lever.

4. Measure the distance from the top of the casting to the top of the float at a point 3⁄16 in. (2mm) from the large end of the float using the float adjustment tool J-9789-90 or equivalent.

5. If more than 1⁄16 in. (1.6mm) from specification, use the float gauge adjusting tool J-34817-25 or equivalent to bend the lever up or down. Remove the gauge adjusting tool and measure, repeating until within specification.

6. Check the float alignment and reassemble the carburetor.

Pump

◗ See Figure 8 (p. 8)

Float Level T-scale J-9789-90 or equivalent will be needed for this adjustment.

1. The pump link must be in the specified hole to make this adjustment.

2. With the fast idle cam off the cam follower lever, turn the throttle stop screw out so it does not touch the throttle lever.

3. Measure the distance from the top of the choke valve wall to the top of the pump stem.

4. Adjust, if necessary, by supporting the pump lever with a screwdriver and bending it at the notch.

Air Valve Return Spring

◗ See Figure 9 (p. 8)

1. Loosen the setscrew.

2. Turn spring fulcrum pin counterclockwise until the air valves open.

3. Turn the pin clockwise until the air valves close, then the additional turns specified.

4. Tighten the setscrew. Apply lithium grease to the spring contact area.

Choke Stat Lever

Linkage Bending Tool J-9789-111 or equivalent will be needed for this adjustment.

1. Drill out and remove the choke cover attaching rivets. Remove the choke cover and thermostat assembly.

2. Place fast idle cam on high step against the cam follower lever.

3. Push up on the choke stat lever to close the choke valve.

4. Check the stat lever for correct orientation by inserting a 0.120 in. (3mm) plug gauge hole in the choke housing. The gauge should fit in the hole and touch the edge of the lever.

5. Adjust, if necessary, by bending the choke link with J-9789-111 or equivalent.

Choke Link and Fast Idle Cam

◗ See Figures 10 and 11 (p. 8)

Choke Valve Angle Gauge J-26701-A or equivalent will be needed for this adjustment.

1. Attach a rubber band to the vacuum break lever of the intermediate choke shaft.

2. Open the throttle to allow the choke valve to close.

3. Set up J-26701-A or equivalent and set the angle to specification as follows:

a. Rotate the degree scale until zero is opposite the pointer.

b. Center the leveling bubble.

c. Rotate the scale to the specified angle.

4. Place the fast idle cam on the second step against the cam follower lever, with the lever contacting the rise of the high step. If the lever does not contact the cam, turn the fast idle adjusting screw in additional turn(s).

➡**Final fast idle speed adjustment must be performed according to the underhood emission control information label.**

5. Adjust, if bubble is not recentered, by bending the fast idle cam kick lever with pliers.

'M4ME CARBURETOR ADJUSTMENT SPECIFICATIONS

CARBU-RETOR PART NO.	FLOAT LEVEL mm (Inches) + 1/16"	PUMP ROD SETTING mm (Inches)	PUMP ROD LOCA-TION	AIR VALVE SPRING (Turns)	CHOKE COIL LEVER	FAST IDLE CAM (CHOKE ROD) ± 2.5°	VACUUM BREAK FRONT ± 2.5°	VACUUM BREAK REAR ± 3.5°	AIR VALVE ROD mm (Inches)	UN-LOAD-ER ± 4°	PROPANE ENRICH-MENT SPEED
17080212	9.5 (12/32)	7.0 (9/32)	INNER	3/4	.120	46°	24°	30°	.025	40°	
17080213	9.5 (12/32)	7.0 (9/32)	INNER	1	.120	37°	23°	30°	.025	40°	
17080298	9.5 (12/32)	7.0 (9/32)	INNER	1	.120	37°	23°	30°	.025	40°	
17082213	9.5 (12/32)	7.0 (9/32)	INNER	1	.120	37°	23°	30°	.025	40°	
17083298	9.5 (12/32)	7.0 (9/32)	INNER	1	.120	37°	23°	30°	.025	40°	
17084500	9.5 (12/32)	7.0 (9/32)	INNER	1	.120	37°	23°	30°	.025	40°	
17084501	9.5 (12/32)	7.0 (9/32)	INNER	1	.120	37°	23°	30°	.025	40°	
17084502	9.5 (12/32)	7.0 (9/32)	INNER	7/8	.120	46°	24°	30°	.025	40°	
17085000	9.5 (12/32)	7.0 (9/32)	INNER	7/8	.120	46°	24°	30°	0.6 (.025)	40°	
17085001	9.5 (12/32)	7.0 (9/32)	INNER	1	.120	46°	23°	30°	0.6 (.025)	40°	
17085003	10.0 (13/32)	7.0 (9/32)	INNER	7/8	.120	46°	23°	—	0.6 (.025)	35°	
17085004	10.0 (13/32)	7.0 (9/32)	INNER	7/8	.120	46°	23°	—	0.6 (.025)	35°	
17085205	10.0 (13/32)	7.0 (9/32)	INNER	7/8	.120	20°	26°	38°	0.6 (.025)	39°	
17085206	10.0 (13/32)	7.0 (9/32)	INNER	7/8	.120	46°	—	26°	0.6 (.025)	39°	20
17085208	10.0 (13/32)	7.0 (9/32)	INNER	7/8	.120	20°	26°	38°	0.6 (.025)	39°	10
17085209	10.0 (13/32)	9.5 (3/8)	OUTER	7/8	.120	20°	26°	36°	0.6 (.025)	39°	50
17085210	10.0 (13/32)	7.0 (9/32)	INNER	7/8	.120	20°	26°	38°	0.6 (.025)	39°	10
17085211	10.0 (13/32)	9.5 (3/8)	OUTER	7/8	.120	20°	26°	36°	0.6 (0.25)	39°	50
17085212	10.0 (13/32)	7.0 (9/32)	INNER	7/8	.120	46°	23°	—	0.6 (.025)	35°	
17085213	10.0 (13/32)	7.0 (9/32)	INNER	7/8	.120	46°	23°	—	0.6 (.025)	35°	
17085215	10.0 (13/32)	7.0 (9/32)	INNER	7/8	.120	46°	—	26°	0.6 (.025)	32°	
17085216	10.0 (13/32)	7.0 (9/32)	INNER	7/8	.120	20°	26°	38°	0.6 (.025)	39°	
17085217	10.0 (13/32)	7.0 (9/32)	INNER	1/2	.120	20°	26°	36°	0.6 (.025)	39°	
17085219	10.0 (13/32)	7.0 (9/32)	INNER	1/2	.120	20°	26°	36°	0.6 (.025)	39°	
17085220	10.0 (13/32)	9.5 (3/8)	OUTER	7/8	.120	20°	—	26°	0.6 (.025)	32°	75
17085221	10.0 (13/32)	9.5 (3/8)	OUTER	7/8	.120	20°	—	26°	0.6 (.025)	32°	75
17085222	10.0 (13/32)	7.0 (9/32)	INNER	1/2	.120	20°	26°	36°	0.6 (.025)	39°	20

88195G08

Fig. 5 Carburetor adjustment specifications—M4ME models

CARBU-RETOR PART NO.	FLOAT LEVEL mm (Inches) + 1/16"	PUMP ROD SETTING mm (Inches)	PUMP ROD LOCA-TION	AIR VALVE SPRING (Turns)	CHOKE COIL LEVER	FAST IDLE CAM (CHOKE ROD) + 2.5°	VACUUM BREAK FRONT + 2.5°	VACUUM BREAK REAR + 3.5°	AIR VALVE ROD mm (Inches)	UN-LOAD-ER + 4°	PROPANE ENRICH-MENT SPEED
17085223	10.0 (13/32)	9.5 (3/8)	OUTER	1/2	.120	20°	26°	36°	0.6 (.025)	39°	50
17085224	10.0 (13/32)	7.0 (9/32)	INNER	1/2	.120	20°	26°	36°	0.6 (.025)	39°	20
17085225	10.0 (13/32)	9.5 (3/8)	OUTER	1/2	.120	20°	26°	36°	0.6 (.025)	39°	50
17085226	10.0 (13/32)	7.0 (9/32)	INNER	7/8	.120	20°	–	24°	0.6 (.025)	32°	20
17085227	10.0 (13/32)	7.0 (9/32)	INNER	7/8	.120	20°	–	24°	0.6 (.025)	32°	20
17085228	10.0 (13/32)	7.0 (9/32)	INNER	7/8	.120	46°	–	24°	0.6 (.025)	39°	30
17085229	10.0 (13/32)	7.0 (9/32)	INNER	7/8	.120	46°	–	24°	0.6 (.025)	39°	30
17085230	10.0 (13/32)	7.0 (9/32)	INNER	7/8	.120	20°	–	26°	0.6 (.025)	32°	20
17085231	10.0 (13/32)	7.0 (9/32)	INNER	7/8	.120	20°	–	26°	0.6 (.025)	32°	40
17085235	10.0 (13/32)	7.0 (9/32)	INNER	7/8	.120	46°	–	26°	0.6 (.025)	39°	80
17085238	10.0 (13/32)	9.5 (3/8)	OUTER	7/8	.120	20°	–	26°	0.6 (.025)	32°	75
17085239	10.0 (13/32)	9.5 (3/8)	OUTER	7/8	.120	20°	–	26°	0.6 (.025)	32°	75
17085290	10.0 (13/32)	7.0 (9/32)	INNER	7/8	.120	46°	–	24°	0.6 (.025)	39°	30
17085291	10.0 (13/32)	9.5 (3/8)	OUTER	7/8	.120	46°	–	26°	0.6 (.025)	39°	100
17085292	10.0 (13/32)	7.0 (9/32)	INNER	7/8	.120	46°	–	24°	0.6 (.025)	39°	30
17085293	10.0 (13/32)	9.5 (3/8)	OUTER	7/8	.120	46°	–	26°	0.6 (.025)	39°	100
17085294	10.0 (13/32)	7.0 (9/32)	INNER	7/8	.120	46°	–	26°	0.6 (.025)	39°	
17085298	10.0 (13/32)	7.0 (9/32)	INNER	7/8	.120	46°	–	26°	0.6 (.025)	39°	

M4ME CARBURETOR ADJUSTMENT SPECIFICATIONS

88195G09

Fig. 6 Carburetor adjustment specifications—M4ME models (continued)

Primary Side Vacuum Break

▶ See Figure 12

Choke Valve Angle Gauge J-26701-A and Hand Operated Vacuum Pump J-23738-A or equivalents, will be needed for this adjustment.

1. Attach rubber band to the vacuum break lever of the intermediate choke shaft.
2. Open the throttle to allow the choke valve to close.
3. Set up J-26701-A or equivalent and set angle to specifications.
4. Plug the vacuum break bleed holes, if applicable. Apply 15 in. Hg (50 kpa) vacuum to seat the vacuum break plunger.
5. Seat the bucking spring, if so equipped. If necessary, bend the air valve link to permit full plunger travel, then re-apply vacuum to fully retract the plunger.
6. Adjust, if the bubble is not re-centered, by turning the vacuum break adjusting screw.

Secondary Side Vacuum Break

Choke Valve Angle Gauge J-26701-A, Hand Operated Vacuum Pump J-23738-A and Linkage Bending Tool J-9789-111 or equivalents will be needed for this adjustment.

1. Attach a rubber band to the vacuum break lever of the intermediate choke shaft.
2. Open the throttle to allow the choke valve to close.
3. Set up J-26701-A or equivalent and set angle to specification.
4. Plug vacuum break bleed holes, if so equipped. Apply 15 in. Hg (50 kPa) vacuum to seat the vacuum break plunger.
5. Compress the plunger bucking spring, if so equipped. If necessary, bend the air valve link to permit full plunger travel, then re-apply vacuum to fully retract the plunger.
6. Adjust, if bubble is not re-centered, by either supporting the link where shown and bending it with J-9789-111 or equivalent, or by turning the screw with a ⅛ in. hex wrench.

Air Valve Link

▶ See Figure 13 and 14 (p. 9)

Hand Operated Vacuum Pump J-23738-A and Linkage Bending Tool J-9789-111 or equivalents will be needed for this adjustment.

1. Plug vacuum break bleed holes, if applicable. With the air valves closed, apply 15 in. Hg (50 kpa) vacuum to seat the vacuum break plunger.
2. Gauge the clearance between the air valve link and the end of the slot in the air valve lever. Clearance should be 0.025 in. (0.6mm).
3. Adjust, if necessary, by bending the link with J-9789-111 or equivalent.

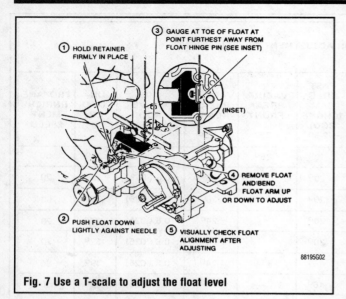

① HOLD RETAINER FIRMLY IN PLACE

③ GAUGE AT TOE OF FLOAT AT POINT FURTHEST AWAY FROM FLOAT HINGE PIN (SEE INSET)

(INSET)

④ REMOVE FLOAT AND BEND FLOAT ARM UP OR DOWN TO ADJUST

② PUSH FLOAT DOWN LIGHTLY AGAINST NEEDLE

⑤ VISUALLY CHECK FLOAT ALIGNMENT AFTER ADJUSTING

88195G02

Fig. 7 Use a T-scale to adjust the float level

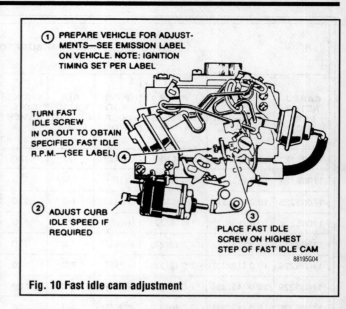

① PREPARE VEHICLE FOR ADJUSTMENTS—SEE EMISSION LABEL ON VEHICLE. NOTE: IGNITION TIMING SET PER LABEL

TURN FAST IDLE SCREW IN OR OUT TO OBTAIN SPECIFIED FAST IDLE R.P.M.—(SEE LABEL)

② ADJUST CURB IDLE SPEED IF REQUIRED

③ PLACE FAST IDLE SCREW ON HIGHEST STEP OF FAST IDLE CAM

88195G04

Fig. 10 Fast idle cam adjustment

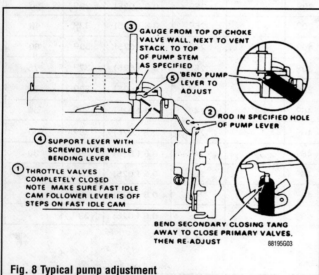

③ GAUGE FROM TOP OF CHOKE VALVE WALL, NEXT TO VENT STACK, TO TOP OF PUMP STEM AS SPECIFIED

⑤ BEND PUMP LEVER TO ADJUST

② ROD IN SPECIFIED HOLE OF PUMP LEVER

④ SUPPORT LEVER WITH SCREWDRIVER WHILE BENDING LEVER

① THROTTLE VALVES COMPLETELY CLOSED NOTE MAKE SURE FAST IDLE CAM FOLLOWER LEVER IS OFF STEPS ON FAST IDLE CAM

BEND SECONDARY CLOSING TANG AWAY TO CLOSE PRIMARY VALVES. THEN RE-ADJUST

88195G03

Fig. 8 Typical pump adjustment

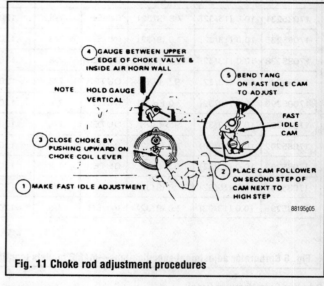

④ GAUGE BETWEEN UPPER EDGE OF CHOKE VALVE & INSIDE AIR HORN WALL

NOTE HOLD GAUGE VERTICAL

⑤ BEND TANG ON FAST IDLE CAM TO ADJUST

FAST IDLE CAM

③ CLOSE CHOKE BY PUSHING UPWARD ON CHOKE COIL LEVER

② PLACE CAM FOLLOWER ON SECOND STEP OF CAM NEXT TO HIGH STEP

① MAKE FAST IDLE ADJUSTMENT

88195g05

Fig. 11 Choke rod adjustment procedures

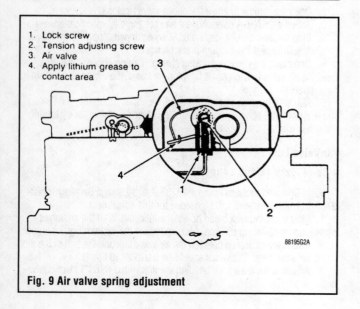

1. Lock screw
2. Tension adjusting screw
3. Air valve
4. Apply lithium grease to contact area

88195G2A

Fig. 9 Air valve spring adjustment

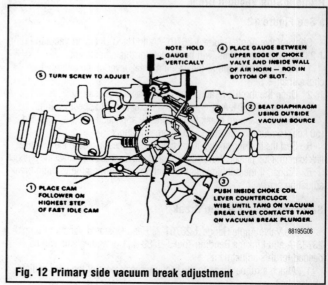

④ PLACE GAUGE BETWEEN UPPER EDGE OF CHOKE VALVE AND INSIDE WALL OF AIR HORN — ROD IN BOTTOM OF SLOT.

NOTE HOLD GAUGE VERTICALLY

⑤ TURN SCREW TO ADJUST

② SEAT DIAPHRAGM USING OUTSIDE VACUUM SOURCE

① PLACE CAM FOLLOWER ON HIGHEST STEP OF FAST IDLE CAM

③ PUSH INSIDE CHOKE COIL LEVER COUNTERCLOCKWISE UNTIL TANG ON VACUUM BREAK LEVER CONTACTS TANG ON VACUUM BREAK PLUNGER.

88195G06

Fig. 12 Primary side vacuum break adjustment

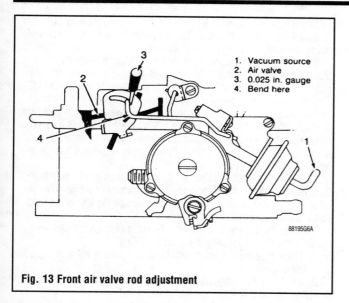

1. Vacuum source
2. Air valve
3. 0.025 in. gauge
4. Bend here

Fig. 13 Front air valve rod adjustment

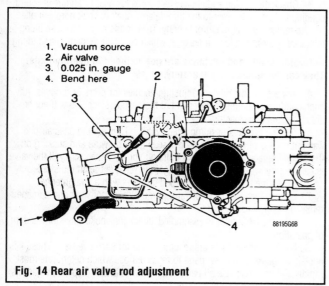

1. Vacuum source
2. Air valve
3. 0.025 in. gauge
4. Bend here

Fig. 14 Rear air valve rod adjustment

Unloader Adjustment

▶ See Figure 15

Choke Valve Angle Gauge J-26701-A and Linkage Bending Tool J-9789-111 or their equivalents will be needed for this adjustment.

1. Attach a rubber band to the vacuum break lever of the intermediate choke shaft.
2. Open the throttle to allow the choke valve to close.
3. Set up J-26701-A or equivalent and set angle to specifications.
4. Hold the secondary lockout lever away from the pin.
5. Hold the throttle lever in wide open position.
6. Adjust, if bubble is not re-centered, by bending fast idle lever with J-9789-111 or their equivalent.

Secondary Throttle Lockout

1. Place the fast idle cam on the high step against the cam follower lever.
2. Hold the throttle lever closed.
3. Gauge the clearance between the lockout lever and pin. It must be 0.010–0.020 in.
4. Adjust, if necessary, by bending the pin.

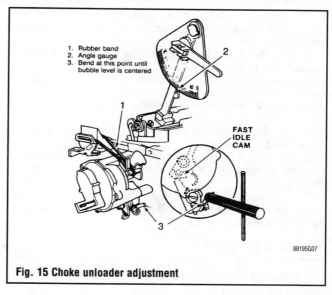

1. Rubber band
2. Angle gauge
3. Bend at this point until bubble level is centered

FAST IDLE CAM

Fig. 15 Choke unloader adjustment

5. Push down on tail of fast idle cam to move lockout lever away from pin.
6. Rotate the throttle lever to bring the lockout pin to the position of minimum clearance with the lockout lever.
7. Gauge the clearance between the lockout lever and pin. The minimum must be 0.015 in.
8. Adjust, if necessary, by filing the end of the pin.

Idle Speed and Mixture

In case of a major carburetor overhaul, throttle body replacement, or high idle CO (when indicated by an emissions inspection), the idle mixture may be adjusted. Adjusting the mixture by other than the following method may violate Federal and/or state laws. Idle mixture needle socket J-29030-B or equivalent is required for this adjustment.

1. Set the parking brake and block the drive wheels.
2. Remove the carburetor from the engine.
3. Drain the fuel from the carburetor into a container. Dispose of the fuel in an approved container.
4. Remove the idle mixture needle plugs as follows:
   a. Invert the carburetor and support it to avoid damaging external components.
   b. Make two parallel hacksaw cuts in the throttle body, between the locator points near one idle mixture needle plug. The distance between the cuts depends on the size of the punch to be used.
   c. Cut down to the plug, but not more than 1/8 in. beyond the locator point.
   d. Place a flat punch at a point near the ends of the saw marks. Hold the punch at a 45° angle and drive it into the throttle body until the casting breaks away, exposing the steel plug.
   e. Use a center punch to break the plug apart, uncover idle mixture needle. Remove all loose pieces of plug.
   f. Repeat the previous steps for the other needle plug.
5. Use idle mixture needle socket J-29030-B or equivalent to lightly seat the idle mixture needles, then back them out three turns.
6. Reinstall the carburetor on the engine.
7. Place the transmission in Park (automatic transmission) or Neutral (manual transmission).
8. Start the engine and bring it to a normal operating temperature, choke valve open, and air conditioning off.
9. Connect a known accurate tachometer to the engine.
10. Check ignition timing, and adjust if necessary, by following the procedure described on the Emission Control Information Label located under the hood on the vehicle.

11. Use idle mixture needle socket J-29030-B or equivalent to turn the mixture needles equally (⅛ turn at a time), in or out, to obtain the highest rpm (best idle).

12. Adjust the idle speed screw (throttle stop) to obtain the base idle speed specified on the underhood emission control information label.

13. Again try to readjust mixture needles to obtain the highest idle rpm. The adjustment is correct when the highest rpm (best idle) is reached with the minimum number of mixture needle turns from the seated position.

14. If necessary, readjust the idle speed screw (throttle stop) to obtain the specified base idle speed.

15. Check (and if necessary adjust) the idle speed solenoid activated speed and fast idle speed. Refer to the underhood emission control information label.

16. Check the throttle kicker and adjust if necessary.

17. Turn off the engine, remove all test equipment and remove the block from the drive wheels.

REMOVAL & INSTALLATION

1. Disconnect the negative battery terminal. Remove the air cleaner assembly and gasket.

2. Disconnect the electrical connectors from the choke and idle stop solenoid.

3. Disconnect and tag the vacuum hoses.

4. Disconnect the accelerator linkage, downshift cable (automatic transmission only) and cruise control linkage (if equipped).

5. Disconnect the fuel line connection at the fuel inlet nut.

6. Remove the carburetor attaching bolts and the carburetor with the flange insulator.

✴✴ CAUTION

Clean the sealing surfaces on the intake manifold and carburetor. Be sure to extinguish all open flames while filling and testing carburetor with gasoline to avoid the risk of fire.

To install:

7. Install the carburetor with a new flange gasket. It is good shop practice to fill the carburetor float bowl before installing the carburetor. This reduces the strain on starting motor and battery and reduces the possibility of backfiring while attempting to start the engine. Operate the throttle several times and check the discharge from pump jets before installing the carburetor.

8. Install the carburetor attaching bolts and torque them to 12 ft. lbs. (16 Nm). Be sure to tighten the bolts in a crisscross pattern.

9. Install the fuel line to the fuel inlet nut, cruise control cable (if equipped), downshift cable (automatic transmission only), accelerator linkage, vacuum hoses, electrical connectors to the choke and idle stop solenoid, air cleaner assembly with gasket and the negative battery terminal.

➡**After servicing the carburetor, tighten the mounting bolts in a clockwise direction to 12 ft. lbs. (16 Nm). When tightening the carburetor at recommended maintenance intervals, check the bolt torque. If less than 5 ft. lbs. (7 Nm), retighten to 8 ft. lbs. (11 Nm); but if greater than 5 ft. lbs. (7 Nm), do not retighten.**

OVERHAUL

◆ **See Figures 16 and 17**

Efficient carburetion depends greatly on careful cleaning and inspection during overhaul, since dirt, gum, water or varnish in or on the carburetor parts are often responsible for poor performance.

Overhaul your carburetor in a clean, dust-free area. Carefully disassemble the carburetor, referring often to the exploded views and directions packaged with the rebuilding kit. Keep all similar and look-alike parts segregated during disassembly and cleaning to avoid accidental interchange during assembly. Make a note of all jet sizes.

When the carburetor is disassembled, wash all parts (except diaphragms, electric choke units, solenoids, pump plunger and any other plastic, leather, fiber or rubber parts) in clean carburetor solvent. DO NOT leave the parts in the solvent any longer than is necessary to sufficiently loosen the deposits. Excessive cleaning may remove the special finish from the float bowl and choke valve bodies, leaving these parts unfit for service. Rinse all parts in clean solvent and blow them dry with compressed air or allow them to air dry. Wipe clean all cork, plastic, leather and fiber parts with a clean, lint-free cloth.

Blow out all passages and jets with compressed air and be sure that there are no restrictions or blockages. Never use wire or similar tools to clean the jets, fuel passages or air bleeds. Clean all jets and valves separately to avoid accidental interchange.

Check all parts for wear or damage. If wear or damage is found, replace the defective parts. Especially check the following:

1. Check the float needle and seat for wear. If wear is found, replace the complete assembly.

2. Check the float hinge pin for wear and the float(s) for dents or distortion. Replace the float if fuel has leaked into it.

3. Check the throttle and choke shaft bores for wear or an out-of-round condition. Damage or wear to the throttle arm, shaft or shaft bore will often require replacement of the throttle body. These parts require a close fitting tolerance; wear may allow air leakage, which could affect starting and idling.

➡**Throttle shafts and bushings are not included in overhaul kits. They can be purchased separately.**

4. Inspect the idle mixture adjusting needles for burrs or grooves. Any such condition requires replacement of the needle, since you will not be able to obtain a satisfactory idle.

5. Test the accelerator pump check valves. They should pass air one way but not the other. Test for proper seating by blowing and sucking on the valve. Replace the valve check ball and spring as necessary. If the valve is satisfactory, wash the valve parts again to remove breath moisture.

6. Check the bowl cover for warped surfaces with a straightedge.

7. Closely inspect the accelerator pump plunger for wear and damage, replacing as necessary.

8. After the carburetor is assembled, check the choke valve for freedom of operation.

Carburetor overhaul kits are recommended for each overhaul. These kits contain all gaskets and new parts to replace those which deteriorate most rapidly. Failure to replace all parts supplied with the kit (especially gaskets) can result in poor performance later.

Some carburetor manufacturers supply overhaul kits of three basic types: minor repair, major repair and gasket kits. Basically, they contain the following:

Minor Repair Kits:
- All gaskets
- Float needle valve
- All diagrams
- Spring for the pump diaphragm

Major Repair Kits:
- All jets and gaskets
- All diaphragms
- Float needle valve
- Pump ball valve
- Float
- Complete intermediate rod
- Intermediate pump lever
- Some cover hold-down screws and washers

Gasket Kits:
- All gaskets

After cleaning and checking all components, reassembly the carburetor, using new parts and referring to the exploded view. When reassembling, make sure that all screws and jets are tight in their seats but DO NOT over-

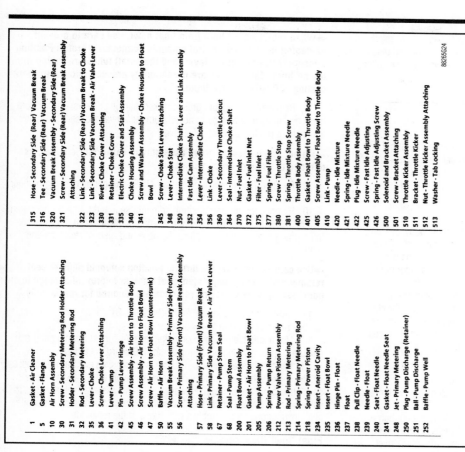

315	Hose - Secondary Side (Rear) Vacuum Break
316	Tee - Secondary Side (Rear) Vacuum Break
320	Vacuum Break Assembly - Secondary Side (Rear)
321	Screw - Secondary Side (Rear) Vacuum Break Assembly Attaching
322	Link - Secondary Side (Rear) Vacuum Break to Choke
323	Link - Secondary Side Vacuum Break - Air Valve Lever
330	Rivet - Choke Cover Attaching
331	Retainer - Choke Cover
335	Electric Choke Cover and Stat Assembly
340	Choke Housing Assembly
341	Screw and Washer Assembly - Choke Housing to Float Bowl
345	Screw - Choke Stat Lever Attaching
348	Lever - Choke Stat
350	Intermediate Choke Shaft, Lever and Link Assembly
352	Fast Idle Cam Assembly
354	Lever - Intermediate Choke
356	Link - Choke
360	Lever - Secondary Throttle Lockout
364	Seal - Intermediate Choke Shaft
370	Nut - Fuel Inlet
372	Gasket - Fuel Inlet Nut
375	Filter - Fuel Filter
377	Spring - Fuel Filter
380	Screw - Throttle Stop
381	Spring - Throttle Stop Screw
400	Throttle Body Assembly
401	Gasket - Float Bowl to Throttle Body
405	Gasket Assembly - Float Bowl to Throttle Body
410	Link - Pump
420	Needle - Idle Mixture
421	Spring - Idle Mixture Needle
422	Plug - Idle Mixture Needle
425	Screw - Fast Idle Adjusting
426	Spring - Fast Idle Adjusting Screw
500	Solenoid and Bracket Assembly
501	Screw - Bracket Attaching
510	Throttle Kicker Assembly
511	Bracket - Throttle Kicker
512	Nut - Throttle Kicker Assembly Attaching
513	Washer - Tab Locking

1	Gasket - Air Cleaner
5	Gasket - Flange
10	Air Horn Assembly
30	Screw - Secondary Metering Rod Holder Attaching
31	Holder - Secondary Metering Rod
32	Rod - Secondary Metering
35	Lever - Choke
36	Screw - Choke Lever Attaching
41	Lever - Pump
42	Pin - Pump Lever Hinge
45	Screw Assembly - Air Horn to Throttle Body
46	Screw Assembly - Air Horn to Float Bowl
47	Screw - Air Horn to Float Bowl (countersunk)
50	Baffle - Air Horn
55	Vacuum Break Assembly - Primary Side (Front)
56	Screw - Primary Side (Front) Vacuum Break Assembly Attaching
57	Hose - Primary Side (Front) Vacuum Break
58	Link - Primary Side Vacuum Break - Air Valve Lever
67	Retainer - Pump Stem Seal
68	Seal - Pump Stem
200	Float Bowl Assembly
201	Gasket - Air Horn to Float Bowl
205	Pump Assembly
206	Spring - Pump Return
212	Power Valve Piston Assembly
213	Rod - Primary Metering
214	Spring - Primary Metering Rod
218	Spring - Power Piston
234	Insert - Aneroid Cavity
235	Insert - Float Bowl
236	Hinge Pin - Float
237	Float
238	Pull Clip - Float Needle
239	Needle - Float
240	Seat - Float Needle
241	Gasket - Float Needle Seat
248	Jet - Primary Metering
250	Plug - Pump Discharge (Retainer)
251	Ball - Pump Discharge
252	Baffle - Pump Well

Fig. 17 Keylist for the M4ME carburetor assembly

88265624

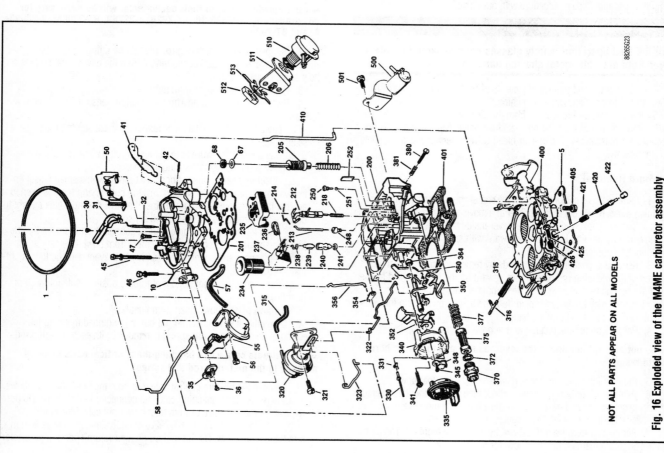

NOT ALL PARTS APPEAR ON ALL MODELS

Fig. 16 Exploded view of the M4ME carburetor assembly

88265623

tighten, for the tips will be distorted. Tighten all screws gradually, in rotation. DO NOT tighten the needle valves into their seats; uneven jetting will result. Always use new gaskets. Be sure to adjust the float level when reassembling.

DISASSEMBLY

Idle Speed Solenoid Removal

Remove the attaching screws, then remove the Idle Speed Solenoid. The Idle Speed Solenoid should not be immersed in any carburetor cleaner, and should always be removed before complete carburetor overhaul, as carburetor cleaner will damage the internal components.

Idle Mixture Needle Plug Removal

1. Use hacksaw to make two parallel cuts in the throttle body, one on each side of the locator points near one idle mixture needle plug. The distance between the cuts will depend on the size of the punch to be used. Cuts should reach down to the steel plug, but should but extend more than ⅛ in. (3mm) beyond the locator points.

2. Place a flat punch at a point near the ends of the saw marks in the throttle body. Hold the punch at a 45° angle, and drive it into the throttle body until the casting breaks away, exposing the hardened steel plug. The plug will break, rather than remaining intact. Remove all the loose pieces.

3. Repeat the procedure for the other idle mixture needle plug.

Idle Air Bleed Valve Removal

1. Cover internal bowl vents and air inlets to the bleed valve with masking tape.

2. Carefully align a ⁷⁄₆₄ in. drill bit on rivet head. Drill only enough to remove head of each rivet holding the idle air bleed valve cover.

3. Use a suitably sized punch to drive out the remainder of the rivet from the castings. Repeat procedure with other rivet.

☼☼ CAUTION

For the next operation, safety glasses must be worn to protect eyes from possible metal shaving damage.

4. Lift off cover and remove any pieces of rivet still inside tower. Use shop air to blow out any remaining chips.

5. Remove idle air bleed valve from the air horn.

6. Remove and discard O-ring seals from valve. New O-ring seals are required for reassembly. The idle air bleed valve is serviced as a complete assembly only.

Air Horn Removal

1. Remove upper choke lever from the end of choke shaft by removing retaining screw. Rotate upper choke lever to remove choke rod from slot in lever.

2. Remove choke rod from lower lever inside the float bowl casting. Remove rod by holding lower lever outward with small screwdriver and twisting rod counterclockwise.

3. Remove secondary metering rods by removing the small screw in the top of the metering rod hanger. Lift upward on the metering rod hanger until the secondary metering rods are completely out of the air horn. Metering rods may be disassembled from the hanger by rotating the ends out of the holes in the end of the hanger.

4. Remove pump link retainer and remove link from pump lever.

➡**Do not attempt to remove the lever, as damage to the air horn could result.**

5. Remove front vacuum break hose from tube on float bowl.

6. Remove 11 air horn-to-bowl screws; then remove the 2 countersunk attaching screws located next to the venturi. If used, remove secondary air baffle deflector from beneath the 2 center air horn screws.

7. Remove air horn from float bowl by lifting it straight up. The air horn gasket should remain on the float bowl for removal later.

➡**When removing air horn from float bowl, use care to prevent damaging the mixture control solenoid connector, Throttle Position Sensor (TPS) adjustment lever, and the small tubes protruding from the air horn. These tubes are permanently pressed into the air horn casting. DO NOT remove them.**

8. Remove front vacuum break bracket attaching screws. The vacuum break assembly may now be removed from the air valve dashpot rod, and the dashpot rod from the air valve lever.

➡**Do not place vacuum break assembly in carburetor cleaner, as damage to vacuum break will occur.**

9. Remove Throttle Position Sensor (TPS) plunger by pushing plunger down through seal in air horn.

10. Remove the throttle position solenoid seal and pump plunger stem seal by inverting air horn and using a small screwdriver to remove staking holding seal retainers in place. Remove and discard retainers and seals.

➡**Use care in removing the throttle position solenoid plunger seal retainer and pump plunger stem seal retainer to prevent damage to air horn casting. New seals and retainers are required for reassembly.**

11. Invert air horn, and use Tool J-28696-4, BT-7967A, or equivalent, to remove rich mixture stop screw and spring.

12. Use a suitable punch to drive the lean mixture screw plug and rich mixture stop screw plug out of the air horn. Discard the plugs.

13. Further disassembly of the air horn is not required for cleaning purposes. The choke valve and choke valve screws, the air valves and air valve shaft should not be removed. However, if it is necessary to replace the air valve closing springs or center plastic eccentric cam, a repair kit is available. Instructions for assembly are included in the repair kit.

Float Bowl Disassembly

➡**The following tools, or their equivalents, will be necessary for this procedure: J-28696-10, BT-7928, J-22769, BT-3006M, J-28696-4, and BT-7928.**

1. Remove solenoid metering rod plunger by lifting straight up.

2. Remove air horn gasket by lifting it from the dowel locating pins on float bowl. Discard gasket.

3. Remove pump plunger from pump well.

4. Remove staking holding Throttle Position Sensor (TPS) in bowl as follows:

    a. Lay a flat tool or metal piece across bowl casting to protect gasket sealing surface.

    b. Use a small screwdriver to depress throttle position solenoid sensor lightly and hold against spring tension.

    c. Observing safety precautions, pry upward with a small chisel or equivalent to remove bowl staking, making sure prying force is exerted against the metal piece and not against the bowl casting. Use care not to damage the throttle position solenoid sensor.

    d. Push up from bottom on electrical connector and remove throttle position solenoid and connector assembly from bowl. Use care in removing sensor and connector assembly to prevent damage to this critical electrical part.

    e. Remove spring from bottom of throttle position solenoid well in float bowl.

5. Remove plastic bowl insert from float bowl.

6. Carefully lift each metering rod out of the guided metering jet, checking to be sure the return spring is removed with each metering rod.

➡**Use extreme care when handling these critical parts to avoid damage to the metering rod and spring.**

7. Remove the mixture control solenoid from the float bowl as follows:

    a. Remove screw attaching solenoid connector to float bowl. Do not remove solenoid connector from float bowl until called for in text.

    b. Use Tool J-28696-10, BT-7928, or equivalent, to remove lean mixture (solenoid) screw. Do not remove plunger return spring or connector and wires from the solenoid body. The mixture control solenoid, with plunger and connector, is only serviced as a complete assembly.

    c. Remove rubber gasket from top of solenoid connector and discard.

    d. Remove solenoid screw tension spring (next to float hanger pin).

  8. Remove float assembly and float needle by pulling up on retaining pin. Remove needle and seat and gasket using set remover Tool J-22769, BT-3006M, or equivalent.

  9. Remove large mixture control solenoid tension spring from boss on bottom of float bowl located between guided metering jets.

  10. If necessary, remove the primary main metering jets using special Tool J-28696-4, BT-7928, or equivalent.

➡**Use care installing tool on jet, to prevent damage to the metering rod guide (upper area), and locating tool over vertical float sections on lower area of jet. Also, no attempt should be made to remove the secondary metering jets (metering orifice plates). These jets are fixed and, if damaged, entire bowl replacement is required.**

  11. Remove the pump discharge check ball retainer and turn the bowl upside down, catching the discharge ball as it falls.

  12. Remove secondary air baffle, if replaced is required.

  13. Remove pump well fill slot baffle only if necessary.

Choke Disassembly

➡**Tools J-9789-118, BT-30-15, or their equivalents, will be necessary for this procedure.**

The tamper-resistant choke cover is used to discourage unnecessary readjustment of the choke thermostatic cover and coil assembly. However, if it is necessary to remove the cover and coil assembly during normal carburetor disassembly for cleaning and normal carburetor disassembly for cleaning and overhaul, the procedures below should be followed.

  1. Support float bowl and throttle body, as an assembly, on a suitable holding fixture such as Tool J-9789-118, BT-30-15, or equivalent.

  2. Carefully align a 5/32 in. drill bit on the rivet head and drill only enough to remove the rivet head. Drill the 2 remaining rivet heads, then use a drift and small hammer to drive the remainder of the rivets out of the choke housing.

➡**Use care in drilling to prevent damage to the choke cover or housing.**

  3. Remove the 2 conventional retainers, retainer with tab, and choke cover assembly from choke housing.

  4. Remove choke housing assembly from float bowl by removing retaining screw and washer inside the choke housing. The complete choke assembly can be removed from the float bowl by sliding outward.

  5. Remove secondary throttle valve lock-out lever from float bowl.

  6. Remove lower choke lever from inside float bowl cavity by inverting bowl.

  7. To disassemble intermediate choke shaft from choke housing, remove coil lever retaining screw at end of shaft inside the choke housing. Remove thermostatic coil lever from flats on intermediate choke shaft.

  8. Remove intermediate choke shaft from the choke housing by sliding it outward. The fast idle cam can now be removed from the intermediate choke shaft. Remove the cup seal from the float bowl for cleaning purposes. DO NOT ATTEMPT TO REMOVE THE INSERT!

  9. Remove fuel inlet nut, gasket, check valve, filter assembly and spring. Discard check valve filter assembly and gasket.

  10. Remove 3 throttle body-to-bowl attaching screws and lockwashers and remove throttle body assembly.

  11. Remove throttle body-to-bowl insulator gasket.

Throttle Body Disassembly

➡**Tools J-29030-B and BT-7610B, or their equivalents, will be necessary for this procedure.**

Place throttle body assembly on carburetor holding fixture to avoid damage to throttle valves.

  1. Remove pump rod from the throttle lever by rotating the rod until the tang on the rod aligns with the slot in the lever.

  2. Use Tool J-29030-B, BT-7610B, or equivalent, to remove idle mixture needles for thorough throttle body cleaning.

  3. Further disassembly of the throttle body is not required for cleaning purposes. The throttle valve screws are permanently staked in place and should not be removed. The throttle body is serviced as a complete assembly.

ASSEMBLY

➡**The following tools, or their equivalents, will be necessary for this procedure: J-29030-B, BT-7610B, J-9789-118, BT-30-15, J-23417, BT-6911, J-28696-4, J-22769, BT-3006M, J-33815-1, BT-8253-A, J-28696-10, and BT-7928.**

  1. Install the lower end of the pump rod in the throttle lever by aligning the tang on the rod with the slot in the lever. The end of the rod should point outward toward the throttle lever.

  2. Install idle mixture needles and springs using Tool J-29030-B, BT-7610B, or equivalent. Lightly seat each needle and then turn counterclockwise 3 turns, the final idle mixture adjustment is made on the vehicle.

  3. If a new float bowl assembly is used, stamp or engrave the model number on the new float bowl. Install new throttle body-to-bowl insulator gasket over 2 locating dowels on bowl.

  4. Install throttle body making certain throttle body is properly located over dowels on float bowl. Install 3 throttle body-to-bowl screws and lockwashers and tighten evenly and securely.

  5. Place carburetor on proper holding fixture such as J-9789-118, BT-30-15 or equivalent.

  6. Install fuel inlet filter spring, a new check valve filter assembly, new gasket and inlet nut. Tighten nut to 18 ft. lbs. (24 Nm).

➡**When installing a service replacement filter, make sure the filter is the type that includes the check valve to meet government safety standard. New service replacement filters with check valve meet this requirement. When properly installed, the hole in the filter faces toward the inlet nut. Ribs on the closed end of the filter element prevent it from being installed incorrectly, unless forced. Tightening beyond the specified torque, 18 ft. lbs. (24 Nm), can damage the nylon gasket.**

  7. Install a new cup seal into the insert on the side of the float bowl for the intermediate choke shaft. The lip on the cup seal faces outward.

  8. Install the secondary throttle valve lock-out lever on the boss of the float bowl, with the recess hole in the lever facing inward.

  9. Install the fast idle cam on the intermediate choke shaft (steps on cam face downward).

  10. Carefully install fast idle cam and intermediate choke shaft assembly in the choke housing. Install the thermostatic coil lever on the flats on the intermediate choke shaft. Inside thermostatic choke coil lever is properly aligned when both inside and outside levers face toward the fuel inlet. Install inside lever retaining screw into the end of the intermediate choke shaft.

  11. Install lower choke rod (inner) lever into cavity in float bowl.

  12. Install choke housing to bowl, sliding intermediate choke shaft into lower (inner) lever. Tool J-23417, BT-6911 or equivalent, can be used to hold the lower choke lever in correct position while installing the choke housing. The intermediate choke shaft lever and fast idle cam are in correct position when the tang on lever is beneath the fast idle cam.

  13. Install choke housing retaining screws and washers. Check linkage for freedom of movement. Do not install choke cover and coil assembly until inside coil lever is adjusted.

  14. If removed, install air baffle in secondary side of float bowl with notches toward the top. Top edge of baffle must be flush with bowl casting.

  15. If removed, install baffle inside of the pump well with slot toward the bottom.

  16. Install pump discharge check ball and retainer screw in the passage next to the pump well.

  17. If removed, carefully install primary main metering jets in bottom of float bowl using or Tool J-28696-4, BT-7928, equivalent.

➡**Use care in installing jets to prevent damage to metering rod guide.**

18. Install large mixture control solenoid tension spring over boss on bottom of float bowl.

19. Install needle seat assembly, with gasket, using seat installer J-22769, BT-3006M, or equivalent.

20. To make adjustment easier, carefully bend float arm before assembly.

21. Install float needle onto float arm by sliding float lever under needle pull clip. Proper installation of the needle pull clip is to hook the clip over the edge of the float on the float arm facing the float pontoon.

22. Install float hinge pin into float arm with end of loop of pin facing pump well. Install float assembly by aligning needle in the seat, and float hinge pin into locating channels in float bowl. DO NOT install float needle pull clip into holes in float arm.

23. Make a float level adjustment as necessary.

24. Install mixture control solenoid screw tension spring between raised bosses next to float hanger pin.

25. Install mixture control solenoid and connector assembly as follows:

a. Install new rubber gasket on top of solenoid connector.

b. Install solenoid carefully in the float chamber, aligning pin on end of solenoid with hole in raised boss at bottom of bowl. Align solenoid connector wires to fit in slot in bowl.

c. Install lean mixture (solenoid) screw through hole in solenoid bracket and tension spring in bowl, engaging first 6 screw threads to assure proper thread engagement.

d. Install mixture control solenoid gauging Tool J-33815-1, BT-8253-A, or equivalent over the throttle side metering jet rod guide, and temporarily install solenoid plunger.

e. Holding the solenoid plunger against the solenoid stop, use Tool J-28696-10, BT-7928, or equivalent, to turn the lean mixture (solenoid) screw slowly clockwise, until the solenoid plunger just contacts the gauging tool. The adjustment is correct when the solenoid plunger is contacting BOTH the solenoid stop and the gauging tool.

f. Remove solenoid plunger and gauging tool.

26. Install connector attaching screw, but DO NOT overtighten, as that could cause damage to the connector.

27. Install throttle position sensor return spring in bottom of well in float bowl.

28. Install throttle position sensor and connector assembly in float bowl by aligning groove in electrical connector with slot in float bowl casting. Push down on connector and sensor assembly so that connector and wires are located below bowl casting surface.

29. Install plastic bowl insert over float valve, pressing downward until properly seated (flush with bowl casting surface).

30. Slide metering rod return spring over metering rod tip until small end of spring stops against shoulder on rod. Carefully install metering rod and spring assembly through holding in plastic bowl insert and gently lower the metering rod into the guided metering jet, until large end of spring seats on the recess on end of jet guide.

✳✳ CAUTION

Do not force metering rod down in jet. Use extreme care when handling these critical parts to avoid damage to rod and spring. If service replacement metering rods, springs and jets are installed, they must be installed in matched sets.

31. Install pump return spring in pump well.

32. Install pump plunger assembly in pump well.

33. Holding down on pump plunger assembly against return spring tension, install air horn gasket by aligning pump plunger stem with hole in gasket, and aligning holes in gasket over throttle position solenoid plunger, solenoid plunger return spring metering rods, solenoid attaching screw and electrical connector. Position gasket over the two dowel locating pins on the float bowl.

34. Holding down on air horn gasket and pump plunger assembly, install the solenoid-metering rod plunger in the solenoid, aligning slot in

end of plunger with solenoid attaching screw. Be sure plunger arms engage top of each metering rod plunger.

35. If a service replacement mixture control solenoid package is installed, the solenoid and plunger MUST be installed as a matched set.

Air Horn Assembly

➡**The following tools, or their equivalents, will be necessary for this procedure: J-28696-10, J-2869-4, BT-7967A, J-34935-1, BT-8420A, BT-7928, J-33815-2, and BT-8353B.**

1. If removed, install the throttle position solenoid adjustment screw in the air horn using Tool J-28696-10, BT-7967A, or equivalent. Final adjustment of the throttle position sensor is made on the vehicle.

2. Inspect the air valve shaft pin for lubrication. Apply a liberal quantity of lithium base grease to the air valve shaft pin, especially in the area contacted by the air valve spring.

3. Install new pump plunger and throttle position solenoid plunger seals and retainers in air horn casting. The lip on the seal faces outward, away from the air horn mounting surface. Lightly stake seal retainer in three places, choosing locations different from the original stakings.

4. Install rich mixture stop screw and rich authority adjusting spring from bottom side of the air horn. Use Tool J-2869-4, BT-7967A, or equivalent, to bottom the stop screw lightly, then back out ¼ turn. Final adjustment procedure will be covered later in this section.

5. Install throttle position solenoid actuator plunger in the seal.

6. Carefully lower the air horn assembly onto the float bowl while positioning the throttle position solenoid adjustment lever over the throttle position solenoid sensor and guiding pump plunger stem through the seal in the air horn casting. To ease installation, insert a thin screwdriver between the air horn gasket and float bowl to raise the throttle position solenoid adjustment lever, positioning it over the throttle position solenoid sensor.

7. Make sure that the bleed tubes and accelerating well tubes are positioned properly through the holes in the air horn gasket. Do not force the air horn assembly onto the bowl, but lower it lightly into place over the 2 dowel locating pins.

8. Install 2 long air horn screws and lockwashers, 9 short screws and lockwashers and 2 countersunk screws located next to the carburetor venturi area. Install secondary air baffle beneath the No. 3 and 4 screws. Tighten all screws evenly and securely.

9. Install air valve rod into slot in the lever on the end of the air valve shaft. Install the other end of the rod in hole in front vacuum break plunger. Install front vacuum break and bracket assembly on the air horn, using 2 attaching screws. Tighten screws securely. Connect pump link to pump lever and install retainer.

➡**Use care installing the roll pin to prevent damage to the pump lever bearing surface and casting bosses.**

10. Install 2 secondary metering rods into the secondary metering rod hanger (upper end of rods point toward each other). Install secondary metering rod holder, with rods, onto air valve cam follower. Install retaining screw and tighten securely. Work air valves up and down several times to make sure they remove freely in both directions.

11. Connect choke rod into lower choke lever inside bowl cavity. Install choke rod in slot in upper choke lever, and position lever on end of choke shaft, making sure flats on end of shaft align with flats in lever. Install attaching screw and tighten securely. When properly installed, the number on the lever will face outward.

12. Adjust the rich mixture stop screw:

a. Insert external float gauging Tool J-34935-1, BT-8420A, or equivalent, in the vertical D-shaped vent hole in the air horn casting (next to the idle air bleed valve) and allow it to float freely.

b. Read (at eye level) the mark on the gauge, in inches, that lines up with the tip of the air horn casting.

c. Lightly press down on gauge, and again read and record the mark on the gauge that lines up with the top of the air horn casting.

d. Subtract gauge UP dimension, found in Step b, from gauge DOWN dimension, found in Step c, and record the difference in fractions of an inch. This difference in dimension is the total solenoid plunger travel.

e. Insert Tool J-28696-10, BT-7928, or equivalent, in the access hole in the air horn, and adjust the rich mixture stop screw to obtain ⅛ in. (3mm) total solenoid plunger travel.

13. With the solenoid plunger travel correctly set, install the plugs supplied in the service kit into the air horn to retain the setting and prevent fuel vapor loss:

a. Install the plug, hollow end down, into the access hole to the lean mixture (solenoid) screw and use a suitably sized punch to drive the plug into the air horn until top of plug is even with the lower edge of the hole chamber.

b. In a similar manner, install the plug over the rich mixture screw access hole and drive the plug into place so that the tip of the plug is 1/16 in. (1.5mm) below the surface of the air horn casting.

14. Install the Idle Air Bleed Valve as follows:

a. Lightly coat 2 new O-ring seals with automatic transmission fluid, to aid in their installation on the idle air bleed valve body. The thick seal goes in the upper groove and the thin seal goes in the lower groove.

b. Install the idle air bleed valve in the air horn, making sure that there is proper thread engagement.

c. Insert idle air bleed valve gauging Tool J-33815-2, BT-8353B, or equivalent, in throttle side D-shaped vent hole of the air horn casting. The upper end of the tool should be positioned over the open cavity next to the idle air bleed valve.

d. Hold the gauging tool down lightly so that the solenoid plunger is against the solenoid stop, then adjust the idle air bleed valve so that the gauging tool will pivot over and just contact the top of the valve.

e. Remove the gauging tool.

f. The final adjustment of the idle air bleed valve is made on the vehicle to obtain idle mixture control.

15. Perform the Air Valve Spring Adjustment and Choke coil Lever Adjustment as previously described.

16. Install the cover and coil assembly in the choke housing, as follows:

a. Place the cam follower on the highest step of the fast idle cam.

b. Install the thermostatic cover and coil assembly in the choke housing, making sure the coil tang engages the inside coil pickup lever. Ground contact for the electric choke is provided by a metal plate located at the rear of the choke cover assembly. DO NOT install a choke cover gasket between the electric choke assembly and the choke housing.

c. A choke cover retainer kit is required to attach the choke cover to the choke housing. Follow the instructions found in the kit and install the proper retainer and rivets using a suitable blind rivet tool.

d. It may be necessary to use an adapter (tube) if the installing tool interferes with the electrical connector tower on the choke cover.

17. Install the hose on the front vacuum brake and on the tube on the float bowl.

18. Position the idle speed solenoid and bracket assembly on the float bowl, retaining it with 2 large countersunk screws.

19. Perform the Choke Rod-Fast Idle Cam Adjustment, Primary (Front) Vacuum Break Adjustment, Air Valve Rod Adjustment—Front, Unloader Adjustment and the Secondary Lockout Adjustment as previously described.

20. Reinstall the carburetor on the vehicle with a new flange gasket.

THROTTLE BODY INJECTION (TBI)

General Information

The electronic fuel injection system is a fuel metering system with the amount of fuel delivered by the Throttle Body Injectors (TBI) determined by an electronic signal supplied by the Electronic Control Module (ECM). The ECM monitors various engine and vehicle conditions to calculate the fuel delivery time (pulse width) of the injectors. The fuel pulse may be modified by the ECM to account for special operating conditions, such as cranking, cold starting, altitude, acceleration and deceleration.

The ECM controls the exhaust emissions by modifying fuel delivery to achieve, as near as possible, an air/fuel ratio of 14.7:1. The injector "on" time is determined by various inputs to the ECM. By increasing the injector pulse, more fuel is delivered, enriching the air/fuel ratio. Decreasing the injector pulse, leans the air/fuel ratio.

The basic TBI unit is made up of two major casting assemblies: (1) a throttle body with a valve to control airflow and (2) a fuel body assembly with an integral pressure regulator and fuel injector to supply the required fuel. An electronically operated device to control the idle speed and a device to provide information regarding throttle valve position are included as part of the TBI unit.

The fuel injector is a solenoid-operated device controlled by the ECM. The incoming fuel is directed to the lower end of the injector assembly which has a fine screen filter surrounding the injector inlet. The ECM actuates the solenoid, which lifts a normally closed ball valve off a seat. The fuel under pressure is injected in a conical spray pattern at the walls of the throttle body bore above the throttle valve. The excess fuel passes through a pressure regulator before being returned to the vehicle fuel tank.

The pressure regulator is a diaphragm-operated relief valve with injector pressure on one side and air cleaner pressure on the other. The function of the regulator is to maintain a constant pressure drop across the injector throughout the operating load and speed range of the engine.

The throttle body portion of the TBI may contain ports located at, above, or below the throttle valve. These ports generate the vacuum signals for the EGR valve, MAP sensor and the canister purge system.

OPERATING MODES

Starting Mode

When the ignition switch is first turned **ON**, the fuel pump relay is energized by the module for 2 seconds in order to build system pressure. In the start mode, the computer module checks the ECT, TP sensor and crank signal in order to determine the best air/fuel ratio for starting. The modules on later model vehicles may also use the IAT or MAT (as equipped) and the MAP sensor. Ratios could range from 1.5:1 at approximately −33°F (−36°C), to 14.7:1 at 201°F (94°C).

Clear Flood Mode

If the engine becomes flooded, it can be cleared by opening the accelerator to the full throttle position. When the throttle is open all the way and engine rpm is less than 600, the computer module will pulse the fuel injector at an air/fuel ratio of 16.5:1 while the engine is turning over in order to clear the engine of excess fuel. If throttle position is reduced below 65 percent, the module will return to the start mode.

Open Loop Mode

When the engine first starts and engine speed rises above 400 rpm, the computer module operates in the Open Loop mode until specific parameters are met. In Open Loop mode, the fuel requirements are calculated based on information from the MAP and ECT sensors. The oxygen sensor signal is ignored during initial engine operation because it needs time to warm up.

Closed Loop Mode
▶ See Figure 18

When the correct parameters are met, the computer module will use O_2 sensor output and adjust the air/fuel mixture accordingly in order to maintain a narrow band of exhaust gas oxygen concentration. When the

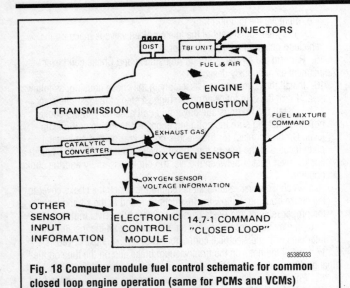

Fig. 18 Computer module fuel control schematic for common closed loop engine operation (same for PCMs and VCMs)

module is correcting and adjusting fuel mixture based on the oxygen sensor signal along with the other sensors, this is known as feedback air/fuel ratio control. The computer module will shift into this Closed Loop mode when:

- Oxygen sensor output voltage is varied, indicating that the sensor has warmed up to operating temperature
- The ECT shows an engine coolant temperature above a specified level.
- The engine has been operating for a programmed amount of time.

Acceleration Mode

If the throttle position and manifold pressure is quickly increased, the module will provide extra fuel for smooth acceleration.

Deceleration Mode

As the throttle closes and the manifold pressure decreases, fuel flow is reduced by the module. If both conditions remain for a specific number of engine revolutions indicating a very fast deceleration, the module may decide fuel flow is not needed and stop the flow by temporarily shutting off the injectors.

Highway Fuel Mode (Semi-Closed Loop)

On some vehicles, the computer control module is programmed to enter a special highway mode to improve fuel economy. If the module senses the correct ECT, ignition control, canister purge activity and a constant engine speed, it will enter highway mode. During this operation, there will be very little adjustment of the long and short term fuel trims, also, the oxygen sensor values will usually read below 100 millivolts.

Decel En-Leanment Mode

On some vehicles, the computer control module is programmed to further reduce emissions by leaning the fuel spray on deceleration. The module does this when a high MAP vacuum (low voltage or pressure) is sensed, BUT it should be noted that the module may do this when the vehicle is not moving. This mode of operation may be misdiagnosed as a lean condition. When diagnosing the control system using a scan tool with the transmission in Park, the oxygen sensor signal low (usually below 100 mV), and both fuel trim numbers around 128 counts, lower the engine speed to 1000 rpm. If the sensor and long term trim numbers respond normally, it is possible that the system was fooled into decel en-leanment operation. If the oxygen sensor and long term numbers do not respond at the lower rpm, there are other problems with the vehicle.

Battery Low Mode

If the computer module detects a low battery, it will increase injector pulse width to compensate for the low voltage and provide proper fuel delivery. It will also increase idle speed to increase alternate output and, in some cases, ignition dwell time to allow for proper engine operation.

Field Service Mode

When the diagnostic terminal of the test connector is grounded with the engine running, the computer control module will enter the Field Service Mode. If the engine is running in Open Loop Mode, the CHECK ENGINE or SERVICE ENGINE SOON Malfunction Indicator Lamp (MIL) will flash quickly, about 2½ times per second. When the engine is in Closed Loop Mode, the MIL will flash only about once per second. If the light stays OFF most of the time in Close Loop, the engine is running lean. If the light is ON most of the time, the engine is running rich.

While the engine continues to operate in Field Service Mode certain conditions will apply:

- The distributor operates with a fixed spark advance (some early model vehicles).
- New trouble codes cannot be stored in computer memory.
- The closed loop timer is bypassed.

➡**For more information concerning the computer control module, self-diagnosis systems and other electronic engine controls, please refer to Section 4 of this manual.**

Fuel Pressure Relief

Prior to servicing any component of the fuel injection system, the fuel pressure must relieved. If fuel pressure is not relieved, serious injury could result.

❋❋ CAUTION

To reduce the chance of personal injury when disconnecting a fuel line, always cover the fuel line with cloth to collect escaping fuel, then place the cloth in an approved container.

1. Disconnect the negative battery cable.
2. Loosen fuel filler cap to relieve fuel tank pressure.
3. The internal constant bleed feature of the Model 220 TBI unit relieves fuel pump system pressure when the engine is turned **OFF**. Therefore, no further action is required.

➡**Allow the engine to set for 5–10 minutes; this will allow the orifice (in the fuel system) to bleed off the pressure.**

4. When fuel service is finished, tighten the fuel filler cap and connect the negative battery cable.

Electric Fuel Pump

REMOVAL & INSTALLATION

◆ **See Figures 19 and 20**

❋❋ CAUTION

The 220 TBI unit has a bleed in the pressure regulator to relieve pressure any time the engine is turned off; however, a small amount of fuel may be released when the fuel line is disconnected. As a precaution, cover the fuel line with a cloth and dispose of properly.

1. With the engine turned **OFF**, relieve the fuel pressure at the pressure regulator. Refer to the fuel relief procedure in this section.
2. Disconnect the negative battery cable.

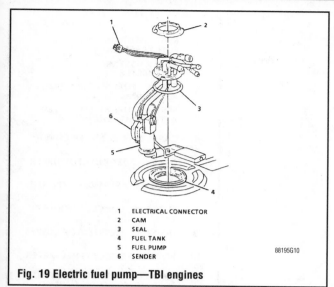

1 ELECTRICAL CONNECTOR
2 CAM
3 SEAL
4 FUEL TANK
5 FUEL PUMP
6 SENDER

88195G10

Fig. 19 Electric fuel pump—TBI engines

TCCS4P04

Fig. 20 Fuel pressure can be checked using an inexpensive pressure/vacuum gauge

3. Raise and support the rear of the vehicle on jackstands.
4. Drain the fuel tank, then remove it.
5. Using a hammer and a drift punch, drive the fuel lever sending device and pump assembly locking ring (located on top of the fuel tank) counterclockwise. Lift the assembly from the tank and remove the pump from the fuel lever sending device.
6. Pull the pump up into the attaching hose while pulling it outward away from the bottom support. Be careful not to damage the rubber insulator and strainer during removal. After the pump assembly is clear of the bottom support, pull it out of the rubber connector.

To install:

7. Connect the fuel pump to the hose.

➡Be careful that you don't fold or twist the strainer when installing the sending unit, or you'll restrict fuel flow.

8. Install a new O-ring on the pump assembly and then position them into the fuel tank.
9. Turn the locking ring clockwise until its tight.
10. Install the fuel tank and connect the battery cable.

TESTING

➡Tools J-29658-82 and J-29658, or their equivalents, will be necessary for this procedure.

1. Disconnect the negative battery cable.
2. Secure two sections of ⅜ in. x 10 in. (9.5mm x 254mm) steel tubing, with a double-flare on one end of each section.
3. Install a flare nut on each section of tubing, then connect each of the sections into the flare nut-to-flare nut adapter, while care included in the gauge adapter tool No. J-29658-82 or equivalent.
4. Attach the pipe and the adapter assembly to the gauge tool No. J-29658 or equivalent.
5. Raise and support the vehicle on jackstands.
6. Remove the air cleaner and plug the THERMAC vacuum port on the TBI.
7. Disconnect the fuel feed hose between the fuel tank and the filter, then secure the other ends of the ⅜ in. (9.5mm) tubing into the fuel hoses with hose clamps.
8. Reconnect the battery cable.
9. Start the engine, check for leaks and observe the fuel pressure, it should be 9–13 psi (62–89 Kpa).
10. Depressurize the fuel system, remove the testing tool, remove the plug from the THERMAC vacuum port, reconnect the fuel line, start the engine and check for fuel leaks.

Throttle Body

◆ See Figure 21

The Model 220 throttle body assembly consists of three major casting assemblies:
• Fuel pressure cover with pressure regulator.
• Fuel metering body with fuel injectors.
• Throttle body with an Idle Air Control (IAC) valve and a Throttle Position (TP) sensor.

The Throttle Position (TP) sensor is a variable resistor used to convert the degree of throttle plate opening to an electrical signal to the computer control module. The module uses this signal as a reference point of throttle valve position. In addition, an Idle Air Control (IAC) assembly, mounted in the throttle body is used to control idle speeds. A cone-shaped valve in the IAC assembly is located in an air passage in the throttle body that leads from the point beneath the air cleaner to below the throttle valve. The module monitors idle speeds and, depending on engine load, moves the IAC cone in the air passage to increase or decrease air bypassing the throttle valve to the intake manifold for control of idle speeds.

The operation of all throttle bodies is basically the same. Each is constantly monitored by the computer control module in order to produce a 14.7:1 air/fuel ratio, which is vital to the catalytic converter operation.

REMOVAL & INSTALLATION

◆ See Figures 22 thru 27 (p. 19)

1. Remove the engine cover.
2. Release the fuel pressure. Refer to the fuel relief procedure in this section.
3. Disconnect the THERMAC hose from the engine fitting and remove the air cleaner.
4. Disengage the electrical connectors at the idle air control, throttle position sensor and the injector. Squeeze the plastic tabs on the injector connections and pull straight up.
5. Disconnect the grommet with wires from the throttle body.
6. Disconnect the throttle linkage, return spring, transmission control cable and cruise control (if equipped).
7. Disconnect the throttle body vacuum hoses, the fuel supply and fuel return lines.
8. Disconnect the bolts securing the throttle body, then remove it.

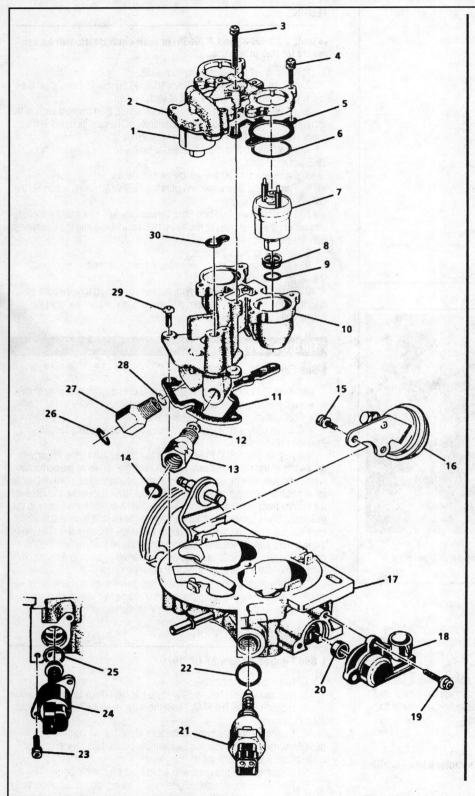

1 REGULATOR ASSEMBLY - FUEL PRESSURE

2 COVER ASSEMBLY - FUEL METER

3 SCREW - FUEL METER COVER ATTACHING - LONG

4 SCREW - FUEL METER COVER ATTACHING - SHORT

5 GASKET - FUEL METER COVER

6 O-RING - FUEL INJECTOR UPPER

7 INJECTOR ASSEMBLY - TBI FUEL

8 FILTER - FUEL INJECTOR INLET

9 O-RING - FUEL INJECTOR LOWER

10 BODY ASSEMBLY - FUEL METER

11 GASKET - THROTTLE BODY TO FUEL METER BODY

12 GASKET - FUEL OUTLET NUT

13 NUT - FUEL OUTLET

14 O-RING - FUEL RETURN LINE

15 SCREW - ISC ACTUATOR ASSEMBLY ATTACHING

16 ACTUATOR ASSEMBLY - IDLE SPEED CONTROL (ISC)

17 BODY ASSEMBLY - THROTTLE

18 SENSOR - THROTTLE POSITION (TP)

19 SCREW - TP SENSOR ATTACHING

20 SEAL - TP SENSOR

21 VALVE ASSEMBLY - IDLE AIR CONTROL (IAC) - THREAD MOUNTED

22 GASKET - IAC VALVE

23 SCREW - IAC VALVE ATTACHING

24 VALVE ASSEMBLY - IDLE AIR CONTROL (IAC) - FLANGE MOUNTED

25 O-RING - IAC VALVE

26 O-RING - FUEL INLET LINE

27 NUT - FUEL INLET

28 GASKET - FUEL INLET NUT

29 SCREW - FUEL METER BODY TO THROTTLE BODY ATTACHING

30 GASKET - FUEL METER OUTLET

85385040

Fig. 21 Exploded view of the model 220 TBI unit

Fig. 22 Tag and disconnect the vacuum lines

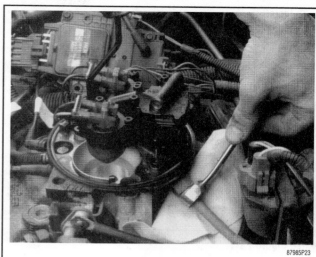

Fig. 25 Use a flare nut wrench to disconnect the fuel lines

Fig. 23 Tag and disengage the electrical connections

Fig. 26 Loosen and remove the bolts securing the throttle body

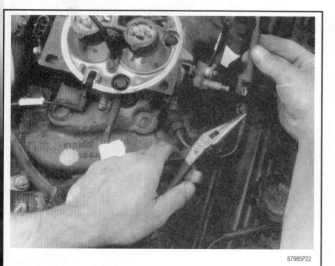

Fig. 24 Disconnect the linkages

Fig. 27 Remove the throttle body from the intake manifold

To install:

9. Replace the manifold gaskets and O-rings.
10. Install the TBI unit and tighten the bolts to 12 ft. lbs. (16 Nm).
11. Install new O-rings into the fuel line nuts and then screw them on by hand. Tighten them to 20 ft. lbs. (26 Nm).
12. Connect the vacuum hoses and bracket.
13. Connect the throttle linkage, transmission control cable, return springs and cruise control cable.
14. Install the grommet (with harness connected) to the TBI.
15. Reconnect all electrical leads. Press the accelerator pedal to the floor and make sure that it releases properly.
16. Turn the ignition switch ON (but don't start the engine!) and check for leaks around the fuel line nuts.
17. Install the air cleaner and start the engine—check for leaks.
18. Install the engine cover.

ADJUSTMENT

▶ **See Figure 28**

Only if parts of the throttle body have been replaced should this procedure be performed; the engine should be at operating temperature.

1. Remove the engine cover.
2. Remove the air cleaner, adapter and gaskets. Discard the gaskets. Plug any vacuum line ports, as necessary.
3. Leave the IAC valve connected and ground the diagnostic terminal (ALDL connector).
4. Turn the ignition switch to the **ON** position, do not start the engine. Wait for at least 30 seconds (this allows the IAC valve pintle to extend and seat in the throttle body).
5. With the ignition switch still in the **ON** position, disconnect the IAC electrical connector.
6. Remove the ground from the diagnostic terminal and start the engine. Let the engine reach normal operating temperature.
7. Apply the parking brake and block the drive wheels. Remove the plug from the idle stop screw by piercing it first with a suitable tool, then applying leverage to the tool to lift the plug out.
8. Adjust the idle stop screw to the proper specifications
9. Turn the ignition **OFF** and reconnect the IAC valve connector. Unplug any plugged vacuum line ports and install the air cleaner, adapter and new gaskets.

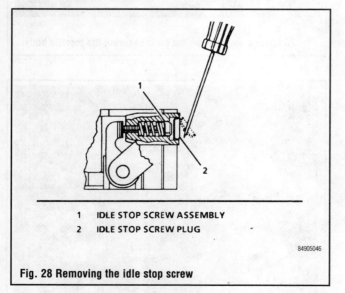

| 1 | IDLE STOP SCREW ASSEMBLY |
| 2 | IDLE STOP SCREW PLUG |

84905046

Fig. 28 Removing the idle stop screw

Fuel Meter Cover

REMOVAL & INSTALLATION

▶ **See Figures 29, 30, 31, 32 and 33**

1. Relieve the fuel system pressure. Refer to the fuel relief procedure in this section.
2. Remove the engine cover and the air cleaner assembly.
3. Disconnect the negative battery cable.
4. Disengage electrical connector at the injector by squeezing the two tabs and pulling straight up.
5. Remove the five screws securing the fuel meter cover to the fuel meter body. Notice the location of the two short screws during removal.

88265P75

Fig. 29 The throttle body can be accessed once the engine cover and air cleaner have been removed

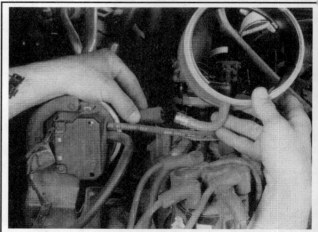

88265P75

Fig. 30 Remove the adapter ring and disconnect from the breather hose

Fig. 31 Unplug the injector electrical connections

Fig. 32 Remove the mounting screws from the meter

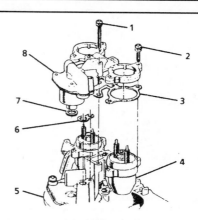

1	FUEL METER COVER ATTACHING SCREW ASSEMBLY - LONG
2	FUEL METER COVER ATTACHING SCREW ASSEMBLY - SHORT
3	FUEL METER COVER GASKET
4	FUEL METER BODY ASSEMBLY
5	THROTTLE BODY ASSEMBLY
6	FUEL METER OUTLET GASKET
7	PRESSURE REGULATOR SEAL
8	FUEL METER COVER ASSEMBLY

Fig. 33 Exploded view of the fuel meter cover mounting

➡The service kits may include a small vial of thread locking compound with directions for use. If the material is not available, use part number 1054.3L4, Loctite® or equivalent. Do not use a higher strength locking compound than recommended, as this may prevent attaching screw removal or breakage of the screw head if removal is again required.

8. Reconnect all the fuel injectors, start the engine and check for leaks.

Fuel Injectors

REMOVAL & INSTALLATION

◆ See Figures 34 thru 41 (p. 22–23)

❄❄❄ WARNING

When removing the injectors, be careful not to damage the electrical connector pins (on top of the injector), the injector fuel filter and the nozzle. The fuel injector is serviced as a complete assembly ONLY. The injector is an electrical component and should not be immersed in any kind of cleaner.

1. Remove the engine cover and air cleaner. Relieve the fuel system pressure. Refer to the fuel relief procedure in this section.
2. At the injector connector(s), squeeze the two tabs together and pull straight up.
3. Remove the fuel meter cover and leave the cover gasket in place.
4. Using a small prybar or tool No. J-26868 or equivalent and a round fulcrum, carefully pry the injector until it is free from the fuel meter body.
5. Remove the small O-ring from the nozzle end of the injector. Carefully rotate the injector's fuel filter back and forth to remove it from the base of the injector.

❄❄❄ CAUTION

Do not remove the four screws securing the pressure regulator to the fuel meter cover! The fuel pressure regulator includes a large spring under heavy tension which, if accidentally released, could cause personal injury! The fuel meter cover is serviced only as a complete assembly and includes the fuel pressure regulator preset and plugged at the factor.

6. Remove the fuel meter cover assembly from the throttle body.

❄❄❄ WARNING

DO NOT immerse the fuel meter cover (with pressure regulator) in any type of cleaner! Immersion of cleaner will damage the internal fuel pressure regulator diaphragms and gaskets.

To install:
7. Be sure to use new gaskets and then install the fuel meter cover. Tighten the attaching screws to 28 inch lbs. (3 Nm).

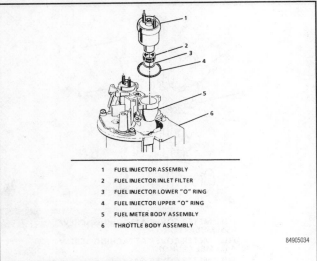

1 FUEL INJECTOR ASSEMBLY
2 FUEL INJECTOR INLET FILTER
3 FUEL INJECTOR LOWER "O" RING
4 FUEL INJECTOR UPPER "O" RING
5 FUEL METER BODY ASSEMBLY
6 THROTTLE BODY ASSEMBLY

84905034

Fig. 34 Fuel injectors and components

88455P26

Fig. 37 . . . then remove the fuel meter cover

88455P24

Fig. 35 Disengage the electrical connection

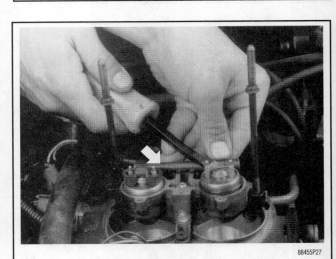

88455P27

Fig. 38 Using a metal dowel as a fulcrum and a prytool to remove the injectors from their bores

88455P25

Fig. 36 Unfasten the fuel meter cover retaining screws . . .

88455P28

Fig. 39 Remove the injectors . . .

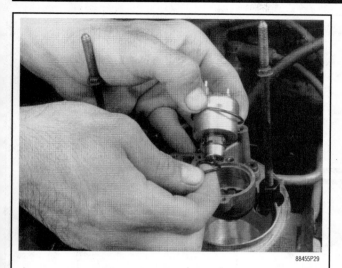

Fig. 40 . . . then remove and discard the O-ring seals

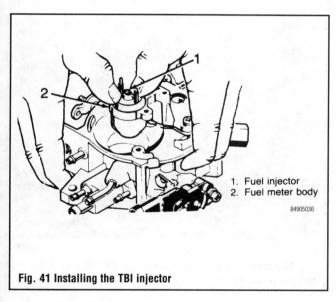

1. Fuel injector
2. Fuel meter body

Fig. 41 Installing the TBI injector

6. Discard the fuel meter cover gasket.
7. Remove the large O-ring and back-up washer (if equipped) from the top of the counterbore of the fuel meter body injector cavity.

MULTI-PORT FUEL INJECTION (MFI)

General Information

In this system, the injectors are controlled individually. Each cylinder receives one charge every two revolutions just before the intake valve opens. This means that the mixture is never static in the intake manifold along with the mixture adjustments that can be made almost simultaneously between the firing of one injector and the next. A camshaft signal sensor or a special distributor reference pulse informs the ECM when the No. 1 cylinder is on the compression stroke. If the sensor fails or the distributor reference pulse is interrupted in any way, the system reverts to pulsing all the injectors simultaneously.

Relieving Fuel System Pressure

➡ Fuel pressure gauge J-34730-1A or its equivalent is required to perform this procedure.

To install:
8. Lubricate the new lower O-rings with automatic transmission fluid and then push on the nozzle end of the injector until it presses against the injector fuel filter.
9. Position the injector back-up washer into the fuel meter bore.
10. Lubricate the new upper O-rings with automatic transmission fluid and then position it over the back-up washer so that it seats properly and is flush with the top of the meter body. Positioning must be correct or the injector will leak after installation.
11. Install the injector so that the raised lug on the injector base is aligned with the notch in the fuel meter body cavity. Press down on the injector until it is fully seated. The electrical terminals should be parallel with the throttle shaft.
12. Install the cover gasket and the meter cover.
13. Reconnect the electrical leads, start the engine and check for leaks.

Fuel Meter Body

REMOVAL & INSTALLATION

1. Relieve the fuel system pressure. Refer to the fuel relief procedure in this section.
2. Raise the hood, install fender covers and remove the air cleaner assembly.
3. Disconnect the negative battery cable.
4. Remove the fuel meter cover assembly.
5. Remove the fuel meter cover gasket, fuel meter outlet gasket and pressure regulator seal.
6. Remove the fuel injectors.
7. Remove the fuel inlet and outlet nuts and gaskets from the fuel meter body.
8. Remove the three screws and lockwashers.
9. Remove the fuel meter body from the throttle assembly.

➡ DO not remove the center screw and staking at each end holding the fuel distribution skirt in the throttle body. The skirt is an integral part of the throttle body and is not serviced separately.

10. Remove the fuel meter body insulator gasket.
To install:
11. Be sure to install new gaskets and O-rings wherever necessary. Apply a threadlocking compound to the fuel meter retaining screws prior to tightening.
12. Install the fuel inlet and fuel outlet nuts and gaskets to the fuel meter body.
13. Install the fuel injectors.
14. Install the fuel meter cover gasket, fuel meter outlet gasket and pressure regulator seal.
15. Install the fuel meter cover assembly.
16. Connect the negative battery cable.
17. Install the air cleaner assembly.

1. Disconnect the negative battery cable.
2. Loosen the fuel filler cap to relieve fuel tank pressure.
3. Connect the fuel pressure gauge to the pressure connection. Wrap a shop towel around the fitting while connecting the gauge to prevent spillage.
4. Install the bleed hose into an approved container and open the valve to bleed the system. The system is now safe for servicing.
5. Drain any fuel remaining in the gauge into an approved container.

Electric Fuel Pump

▸ See Figure 42

All Chevrolet/GMC fuel-injected vehicles are equipped with an electric fuel pump. For a fuel injection system to work properly, the pump must develop pressures well above those of a mechanical fuel pump. This high pressure is maintained within the lines even when the engine is off. Extreme caution must be used to safely release the pressurized fuel before any work is begun.

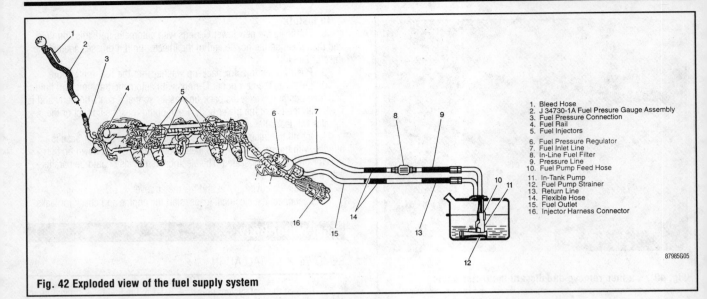

1. Bleed Hose
2. J 34730-1A Fuel Presure Gauge Assembly
3. Fuel Pressure Connection
4. Fuel Rail
5. Fuel Injectors
6. Fuel Pressure Regulator
7. Fuel Inlet Line
8. In-Line Fuel Filter
9. Pressure Line
10. Fuel Pump Feed Hose
11. In-Tank Pump
12. Fuel Pump Strainer
13. Return Line
14. Flexible Hose
15. Fuel Outlet
16. Injector Harness Connector

87985G05

Fig. 42 Exploded view of the fuel supply system

❊❊ CAUTION

Always relieve the fuel pressure within the system before any work is begun on any fuel component. Failure to safely relieve the pressure may result in fire and/or serious injury.

REMOVAL & INSTALLATION

Single Tank

▶ See Figures 43, 44 and 45

1. Disconnect the negative battery cable.
2. Relieve the fuel system pressure. Refer to the fuel system relief procedure in this section.
3. Raise the vehicle and support it safely with jackstands.
4. Drain the fuel system and remove the fuel tank. Refer to the fuel tank removal procedure in this section.
5. Remove the fuel sender assembly turning it counterclockwise using tool J-36608 or its equivalent.
6. Remove the assembly from the tank.

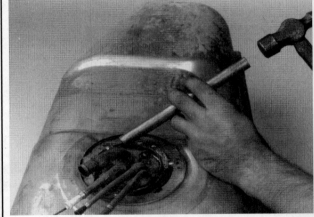

TCCS5P04

Fig. 44 A brass drift and a hammer can be used to loosen the fuel pump locking cam

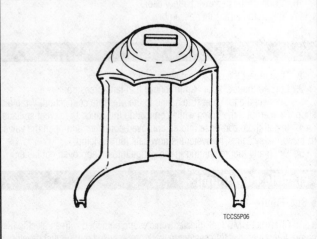

TCCS5P06

Fig. 43 A special tool is usually available to remove or install the fuel pump locking cam

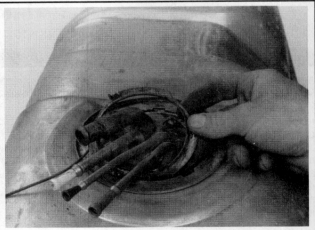

TCCS5P05

Fig. 45 Once the locking cam is released it can be removed to free the fuel pump

7. Pull the pump up into the attaching hose while pulling outward from the bottom support. Do not damage the rubber insulator or the strainer.

8. Inspect the fuel pump attaching hose and the rubber sound insulation for signs of deterioration.

9. Inspect the strainer for blockage and damage.

To install:

10. Install the fuel pump assembly into the attaching hose.

➡**Be careful not to bend or fold over the fuel strainer when installing the fuel sender as this will restrict fuel flow.**

11. Install the fuel sender into the fuel tank. Insert a new O-ring seal.

12. Install the camlock assembly turning it clockwise to lock it.

13. Install the fuel tank. Refer to the fuel tank installation procedure in this section.

14. Connect the negative battery cable.

15. Turn the ignition switch **ON** for 2 seconds then turn the switch **OFF** for 10 seconds. Again, turn the ignition switch **ON** and check for leaks.

Dual Tanks

1. Disconnect the negative battery cable.

2. Loosen the filler cap(s) to relieve fuel tank pressure.

3. Disconnect the fuel pipes from the pump.

4. Slide the pump out of the bracket.

To install:

5. Install new fuel pipe O-rings.

6. Position the pump in the pump bracket.

7. Connect the fuel feed pipe and suction pipe to the fuel pump.

8. Using a backup wrench to stop the fuel pump from turning, tighten the fittings to 22 ft. lbs. (30 Nm).

9. Engage the electrical connector.

10. Connect the negative battery cable.

11. Turn the ignition switch **ON** for 2 seconds then turn the switch **OFF** for 10 seconds. Again, turn the ignition switch **ON** and check for leaks.

Throttle Body

REMOVAL & INSTALLATION

◆ **See Figure 46**

1. Disconnect the negative battery cable.

2. Remove the air inlet duct.

3. Disengage the Idle Air Control (IAC) valve and the Throttle Position Sensor (TPS) electrical connectors.

4. Disconnect the throttle and cruise control cables.

5. Remove the accelerator cable bracket.

6. Unfasten the throttle body retaining nuts and remove the throttle body.

7. Remove and discard the flange gasket.

8. Clean both gasket mating surfaces.

➡**When cleaning the old gasket from the machined aluminum surfaces be careful as sharp tools may damage the sealing surfaces**

To install:

9. Install the new flange gasket and the throttle body assembly.

10. Tighten the throttle body attaching nuts to 18 ft. lbs. (25 Nm).

11. Install the accelerator cable bracket.

12. Connect the throttle and cruise control cables.

13. Engage the IAC valve and the TPS electrical connectors.

14. Install the air inlet duct and connect the negative battery cable.

Fuel Injectors

REMOVAL & INSTALLATION

◆ **See Figure 47**

➡**Use care when removing the injectors to prevent damage to the electrical connector pins on the injector and the nozzle. The fuel injector is serviced as a complete assembly only. Since the injector is an electrical component, it should not be immersed in any type of cleaner.**

1. Disconnect the negative battery cable.

2. Relieve the fuel system pressure. Refer to the fuel system relief procedure in this section.

3. Remove the intake manifold plenum.

4. Remove the fuel rail assembly.

5. Disengage the electrical wiring harness.

6. Disassemble the injector clip and discard it.

7. Remove the injector O-ring seals from both ends of the injector. Save the O-ring backups for use on reassembly.

To install:

8. Install the O-ring backups before installing the O-rings.

9. Lubricate the new injector O-rings with clean engine oil and install them on the injector assembly.

10. Install the fuel injector into the fuel rail injector socket with the electrical connectors facing outward.

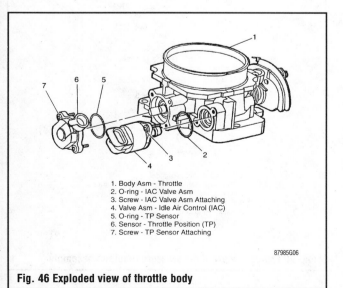

1. Body Asm - Throttle
2. O-ring - IAC Valve Asm
3. Screw - IAC Valve Asm Attaching
4. Valve Asm - Idle Air Control (IAC)
5. O-ring - TP Sensor
6. Sensor - Throttle Position (TP)
7. Screw - TP Sensor Attaching

87985G06

Fig. 46 Exploded view of throttle body

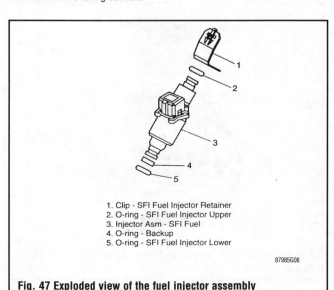

1. Clip - SFI Fuel Injector Retainer
2. O-ring - SFI Fuel Injector Upper
3. Injector Asm - SFI Fuel
4. O-ring - Backup
5. O-ring - SFI Fuel Injector Lower

87985G08

Fig. 47 Exploded view of the fuel injector assembly

11. Install new injector retaining clips on the injector fuel rail assembly by sliding the clip into the injector groove as it snaps onto the fuel rail.

12. Install the fuel rail assembly.

13. Install the manifold plenum.

14. Engage the electrical wiring harness.

15. Connect the negative battery cable.

TESTING

▶ **See Figures 48 and 49**

➡**This test requires the use of fuel injector tester J-34730-3 or its equivalent.**

1. With the engine cool and the ignition turned **OFF**, install the fuel pressure gauge to the fuel pressure connection. Wrap a shop towel around the fitting while connecting the gauge to prevent spillage.

2. Disengage all the fuel injector electrical connectors. Engage the tester to one fuel injector.

3. Turn **ON** the ignition and bleed the air from the pressure gauge.

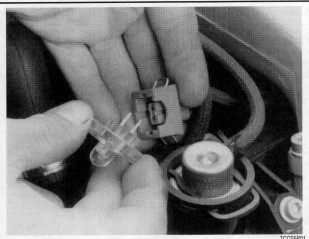

TCCS5P01

Fig. 48 A noid light can be attached to the fuel injector harness in order to test for injector pulse

4. Turn **OFF** the ignition for ten seconds and then turn it **ON** again. This will bring the fuel pressure to its maximum pressure. Record this reading.

5. Press the tester button and record the lowest pressure reading. Subtract this reading from the initial reading obtained and record the result.

6. Connect the tester to each injector and repeat Steps 4 and 5.

7. Pressure should fall between 56–62 psi (430 kPa). Replace any injector that does not meet these specifications.

Fuel Pressure Regulator

REMOVAL & INSTALLATION

▶ **See Figure 50**

1. Disconnect the negative battery cable.

2. Relieve fuel system pressure. Refer to the fuel system relief procedure in this section.

3. Disconnect the ignition coil.

4. Remove the manifold plenum.

5. Disconnect the vacuum line to the regulator.

6. Remove the snapring from the regulator housing.

7. Place a towel under the regulator to absorb any spilled fuel and remove the pressure regulator from the fuel socket.

8. Remove the pressure regulator from the fuel rail.

9. Remove the pressure regulator O-ring filter, O-ring backup and O-ring and discard them.

To install:

10. Before installing the O-rings, lubricate them with clean engine oil and install them on the regulator inlet as a complete assembly.

11. Install the snapring retainer into the slot on the regulator housing.

12. Connect the vacuum line to the regulator.

➡**Ensure that the retainer is properly seated in the slot in the regulator housing. Pull on the regulator to make sure that it is properly seated.**

13. Connect the negative battery cable.

14. Turn the ignition **ON** for 2 seconds and then turn it **OFF** for 10 seconds. Again turn the ignition **ON** and check for leaks.

15. Install the manifold plenum.

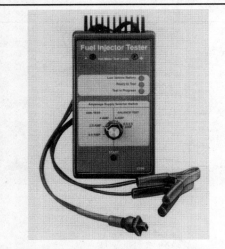

TCCS5P03

Fig. 49 Fuel injector testers can be purchased or sometimes rented

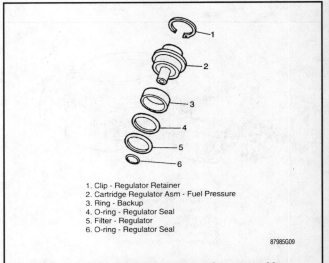

1. Clip - Regulator Retainer
2. Cartridge Regulator Asm - Fuel Pressure
3. Ring - Backup
4. O-ring - Regulator Seal
5. Filter - Regulator
6. O-ring - Regulator Seal

87985G09

Fig. 50 Exploded view of the pressure regulator assembly

Fuel Rail Assembly

REMOVAL & INSTALLATION

▶ **See Figure 51**

➡**Clean the fuel rail assembly before removal. The fittings should be capped to prevent dirt from entering open lines.**

1. Disconnect the negative battery cable.
2. Relieve fuel system pressure. Refer to the fuel system relief procedure in this section.
3. Remove the manifold plenum.
4. Remove the distributor.
5. Disconnect the fuel lines at the rail.
6. Unfasten the fuel pipe bracket bolt.
7. Remove the fuel inlet and return line O-rings and discard them.
8. Disengage the fuel injector electrical connectors and remove from the coil bracket.
9. Unfasten the fuel rail retaining bolts.
10. Disconnect the vacuum line to the fuel pressure regulator.
11. Remove the fuel rail.
12. Remove the O-rings seals and backups from the injectors. Discard the old seals but retain the backups for reuse.

To install:

➡**Ensure that the O-ring backups are on the injectors before installing the O-rings. Lubricate the O-rings with clean engine oil before installation.**

13. Install the fuel rail in the intake manifold. Tilt the fuel rail assembly to install the injectors. Tighten the fuel rail retaining bolts to 89 inch. lbs. (10 Nm).
14. Engage the injector electrical connectors.
15. Install new O-rings on the fuel pipes.
16. Install the fuel return and feed lines.
17. Tighten the fuel pipe nuts to 20 ft. lbs. (27 Nm) using a back-up wrench to prevent the fittings from turning.
18. Connect the negative battery cable.
19. Turn the ignition **ON** for 2 seconds and then turn it **OFF** for 10 seconds. Again turn the ignition **ON** and check for leaks.
20. Install the manifold plenum.

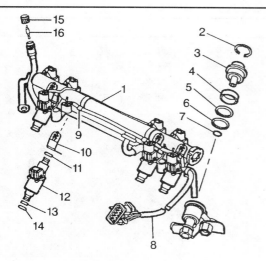

1. Rail Asm - Fuel
2. Clip - Regulator Retainer
3. Cartridge Regulator Asm - Fuel Pressure
4. Ring - Backup
5. O-ring - Regulator Seal
6. Filter - Regulator
7. O-ring - Regulator Seal
8. Wiring Harness - Fuel Injector
9. Retainer Clip - Wiring Harness
10. Clip - SFI Fuel Injector Retainer
11. O-ring - SFI Fuel Injector Upper
12. Injector Asm - SFI Fuel
13. O-ring - Backup
14. O-ring - SFI Fuel Injector Lower
15. Cap - Fuel Pressure Connection
16. Core Asm - Fuel Pressure Connection

87985G10

Fig. 51 Exploded view of the fuel rail assembly

CENTRAL SEQUENTIAL FUEL INJECTION (CSFI)

General Information

The 1996–97 vans are equipped with the Central Sequential Fuel Injection (CSFI) system. Fuel is delivered to the engine by individual fuel injectors and poppet nozzles mounted in the intake manifold near each cylinder. Each is fired sequentially for accuracy and precise metering control.

Relieving Fuel System Pressure

➡**Fuel pressure gauge J 34730-1A or its equivalent is required to perform this procedure.**

1. Disconnect the negative battery cable.
2. Loosen the fuel filler cap to relieve fuel tank pressure.
3. Engage the fuel pressure gauge to the fuel pressure connection. Wrap a shop towel around the fitting while connecting the gauge to prevent spillage.
4. Install the bleed hose into an approved container and open the valve to bleed the system. The system is now safe for servicing.
5. Drain any fuel remaining in the gauge into an approved container.

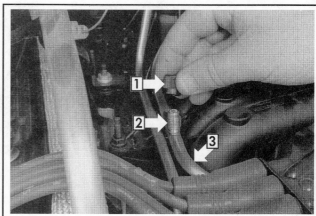

1. Cap
2. Fuel pressure connection
3. Fuel rail

88195P01

Unscrew the fuel pressure connection cap before connecting the fuel pressure gauge—models with CSFI

Electric Fuel Pump

▶ **See Figure 52**

All Chevrolet/GMC Central Sequential Fuel Injection (CSFI) fuel injected vehicles are equipped with an electric fuel pump. For a fuel injection system to work properly, the pump must develop pressures well above those of a mechanical fuel pump. This high pressure is maintained within the lines even when the engine is **OFF**. Extreme caution must be used to safely release the pressurized fuel before any work is begun.

❊❊ CAUTION

Always relieve the fuel pressure within the system before any work is begun on any fuel component. Failure to safely relieve the pressure may result in fire and/or serious injury.

REMOVAL & INSTALLATION

Single Tank

▶ **See Figures 53, 54 and 55**

1. Disconnect the negative battery cable.
2. Relieve the fuel system pressure. Refer to the fuel system relief procedure in this section.
3. Raise the vehicle and support it safely with jackstands.
4. Drain the fuel system and remove the fuel tank. Refer to the fuel tank removal procedure in this section.
5. Remove the fuel sender assembly turning it counterclockwise using tool J-36608 or its equivalent.
6. Remove the fuel pump from the sender assembly. Pull the pump up into the attaching hose while pulling outward from the bottom support. Do not damage the rubber insulator or the strainer.
7. Inspect the fuel pump attaching hose and the rubber sound insulation for signs of deterioration.
8. Inspect the strainer for blockage and damage.

To install:

9. Install the fuel pump assembly into the attaching hose.

➡**Be careful not to bend or fold over the fuel strainer when installing the fuel sender as this will restrict fuel flow.**

10. Install the fuel sender into the fuel tank. Insert a new O-ring seal.
11. Install the camlock assembly turning it clockwise to lock it.

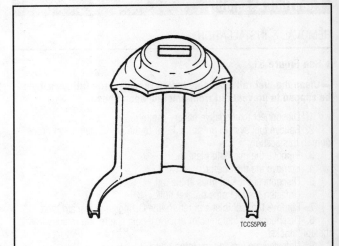

Fig. 53 A special tool is usually available to remove or install the fuel pump locking cam

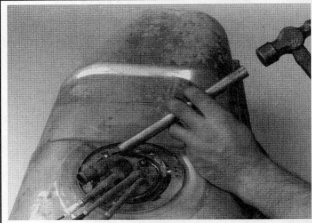

Fig. 54 A brass drift and a hammer can be used to loosen the fuel pump locking cam

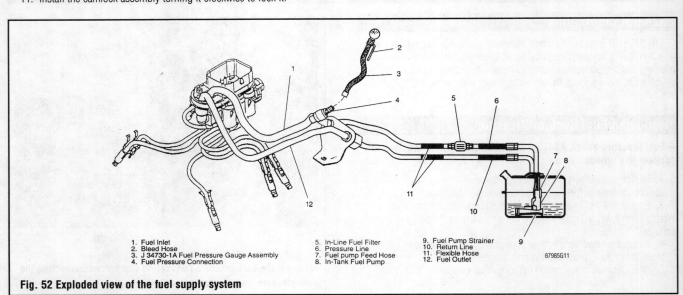

1. Fuel Inlet
2. Bleed Hose
3. J 34730-1A Fuel Pressure Gauge Assembly
4. Fuel Pressure Connection
5. In-Line Fuel Filter
6. Pressure Line
7. Fuel pump Feed Hose
8. In-Tank Fuel Pump
9. Fuel Pump Strainer
10. Return Line
11. Flexible Hose
12. Fuel Outlet

87985G11

Fig. 52 Exploded view of the fuel supply system

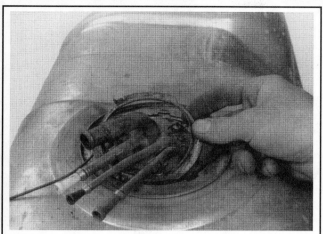

TCCS5P05

Fig. 55 Once the locking cam is released, it can be removed to free the fuel pump

12. Install the fuel tank. Refer to the fuel tank installation procedure in this section.

13. Connect the negative battery cable.

Dual Tanks

1. Disconnect the negative battery cable.
2. Loosen the filler cap(s) to relieve fuel tank pressure.
3. Disconnect the fuel pipes from the pump.
4. Slide the pump out of the bracket.

To install:

5. Install new fuel pipe O-rings.
6. Position the pump in the pump bracket.
7. Connect the fuel feed pipe and suction pipe to the fuel pump.
8. Using a backup wrench to stop the fuel pump from turning, tighten the fittings to 22 ft. lbs. (30 Nm).
9. Engage the electrical connector.
10. Connect the negative battery cable.
11. Turn the ignition switch **ON** for 2 seconds then turn the switch **OFF** for 10 seconds. Again, turn the ignition switch **ON** and check for leaks.

Throttle Body

REMOVAL & INSTALLATION

1. Disconnect the negative battery cable.
2. Remove the air inlet fastener and duct.
3. Disengage the Idle Air Control (IAC) valve and the Throttle Position Sensor (TPS) electrical connectors.
4. Disconnect the throttle and cruise control cables.
5. Disconnect the accelerator cable bracket bolts and nuts.
6. Disengage the wiring harness fastener nut.
7. Unfasten the throttle body retaining nuts and remove the throttle body.
8. Remove and discard the flange gasket.
9. Clean both gasket mating surfaces.

➡**When cleaning the old gasket from the machined aluminum surfaces be careful as sharp tools may damage the sealing surfaces**

To install:

10. Install the new flange gasket and the throttle body assembly.
11. Tighten the throttle body attaching nuts to 18 ft. lbs. (25 Nm).
12. Install the accelerator cable bracket bolts and nuts and tighten to 18 ft. lbs. (25 Nm).
13. Connect the throttle and cruise control cables.

14. Engage the IAC valve and the TPS electrical connectors.
15. Install the air inlet fastener and duct. Connect the negative battery cable.

Fuel Injectors

REMOVAL & INSTALLATION

▶ **See Figures 56 and 57**

1. Disconnect the negative battery cable.
2. Relieve the fuel system pressure. Refer to the fuel system relief procedure in this section.
3. Disengage the fuel meter body electrical connection and the fuel feed and return hoses from the engine fuel pipes.
4. Remove the upper manifold assembly.
5. Tag and remove the poppet nozzle out of the casting socket.
6. Remove the fuel meter body by releasing the locktabs.

➡**Each injector is calibrated. When replacing the fuel injectors, be sure to replace it with the correct injector.**

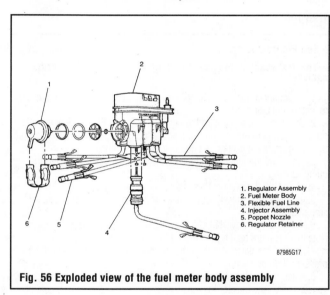

1. Regulator Assembly
2. Fuel Meter Body
3. Flexible Fuel Line
4. Injector Assembly
5. Poppet Nozzle
6. Regulator Retainer

87985G17

Fig. 56 Exploded view of the fuel meter body assembly

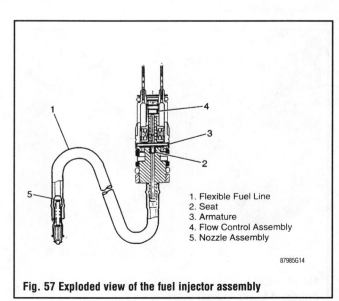

1. Flexible Fuel Line
2. Seat
3. Armature
4. Flow Control Assembly
5. Nozzle Assembly

87985G14

Fig. 57 Exploded view of the fuel injector assembly

7. Disassemble the lower hold-down plate and nuts.

8. While pulling the poppet nozzle tube downward, push with a small screwdriver down between the injector terminals and remove the injectors.

To install:

9. Install the fuel meter body assembly into the intake manifold and tighten the fuel meter bracket retainer bolts to 88 inch. lbs. (10 Nm).

✳✳ CAUTION

To reduce the risk of fire or injury ensure that the poppet nozzles are properly seated and locked in their casting sockets

10. Install the fuel meter body into the bracket and lock all the tabs in place.

11. Install the poppet nozzles into the casting sockets.

12. Engage the electrical connections and install new O-ring seals on the fuel return and feed hoses.

13. Install the fuel feed and return hoses and tighten the fuel pipe nuts to 22 ft. lbs. (30 Nm).

14. Connect the negative battery cable.

15. Turn the ignition **ON** for 2 seconds and then turn it **OFF** for 10 seconds. Again turn the ignition **ON** and check for leaks.

16. Install the manifold plenum.

TESTING

▶ **See Figures 58 and 59**

➡ This test requires the use of fuel injector tester J 39021 or its equivalent.

1. Disconnect the fuel injector harness and attach a noid light in order to test for injector pulse.

2. With the engine cool and the ignition turned **OFF**, install the fuel pressure gauge to the fuel pressure connection. Wrap a shop towel around the fitting while connecting the gauge to prevent spillage.

3. Turn **ON** the ignition and record the fuel gauge pressure with the pump running.

4. Turn **OFF** the ignition. Pressure should drop and hold steady at this point.

5. To perform this test, set the selector switch to the balance test 2.5 amp position.

6. Turn the injector **ON** by depressing the button on the injector tester. Note this pressure reading the instant the gauge needle stops.

7. Repeat the balance test on the remaining injectors and record the pressure drop on each.

8. Start the engine to clear fuel from the intake. Retest the injectors that appear faulty. Any injector that has a plus or minus 1.5 psi (10 kpa) difference from the other injectors is suspect.

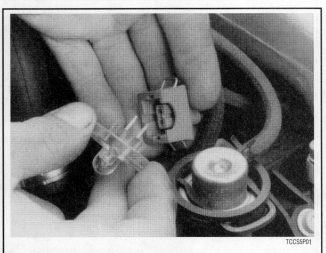

Fig. 58 A noid light can be attached to the fuel injector harness in order to test for injector pulse

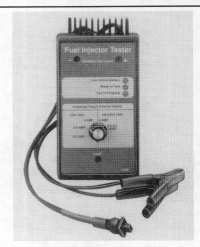

TCCS5P03

Fig. 59 Fuel injector testers can be purchased or sometimes rented

Fuel Pressure Regulator

REMOVAL & INSTALLATION

▶ **See Figure 60**

1. Disconnect the negative battery cable.

2. Relieve the fuel system pressure. Refer to the fuel system relief procedure in this section.

3. Remove the upper manifold assembly.

4. Remove the fuel pressure regulator vacuum tube.

5. Disassemble the fuel pressure regulator snapring retainer.

6. Remove the fuel pressure regulator assembly and the O-rings. Discard the O-rings, filter and back-up O-rings.

To install:

7. Lubricate the O-rings with clean engine oil and install as an assembly.

8. Install the fuel pressure regulator, attach the vacuum tube.

9. Install the snapring retainer.

10. Install the upper manifold assembly.

11. Connect the negative battery cable.

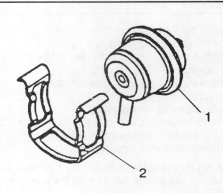

1. Fuel Pressure Regulator
2. Fuel Pressure Regulator Retainer

87985G15

Fig. 60 Exploded view of the fuel pressure regulator

Engine Fuel Pipes

REMOVAL & INSTALLATION

▶ **See Figure 61**

1. Disconnect the negative battery cable.
2. Relieve the fuel system pressure. Refer to the fuel system relief procedure in this section.
3. Remove the fuel lines at the rear of the intake manifold.
4. Remove the nuts and the retainer.
5. Loosen the injector fuel inlet and outlet pipes.
6. Remove the rear fuel line bracket.

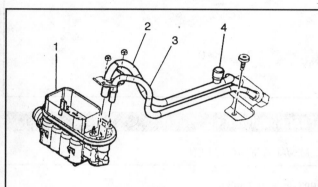

1. Fuel Meter Body
2. Fuel Inlet
3. Fuel Outlet
4. Fuel Pressure Connection

87985G16

Fig. 61 Exploded view of the engine fuel pipes and related components

7. Pull straight up on the fuel pipe to remove the pipes from the injector assembly.
8. Remove the O-rings from both ends of the fuel feed and return pipes.

To install:
9. Install the inlet and outlet of the fuel injector assembly.
10. Apply a few drops of clean engine oil to the male tube ends.
11. Install the fuel pipes to the fuel injector assembly.
12. Install the fuel pipe retainer and attaching nuts. After the pipes are secured, pull up on them gently to ensure that they are properly secured. Tighten the rear fuel line bracket bolt to 53 inch. lbs. (6 Nm) and the fuel pipe retainer nuts to 27 inch lbs. (3 Nm).
13. Tighten the fuel pipe nuts to 22 ft. lbs. (30 Nm) and connect the negative battery cable.
14. Turn the ignition **ON** for 2 seconds then turn it **OFF** for 10 seconds. Again turn the ignition **ON** and check for leaks.

Fuel Pressure Connection

The fuel pressure connection is non-replaceable, but is serviceable.

SERVICE

1. Disconnect the negative battery cable.
2. Relieve the fuel system pressure. Refer to the fuel system relief procedure in this section.
3. Remove the fuel pressure connection cap.
4. Using a valve core removal tool remove the valve core assembly and discard it.

To install:
5. Install a new valve core assembly using a valve core removal tool.
6. Connect the negative battery cable.
7. Turn the ignition **ON** for 2 seconds then turn it **OFF** for 10 seconds. Again turn the ignition **ON** and check for leaks.
8. Install the fuel pressure connection cap.

DIESEL FUEL SYSTEM

Fuel Injection Lines

REMOVAL & INSTALLATION

▶ **See Figure 62**

➡ **When the fuel lines are to be removed, clean all fuel line fittings thoroughly before loosening. Immediately cap the lines, nozzles and pump fittings to maintain cleanliness.**

1. Disconnect both batteries.
2. Disconnect the air cleaner bracket at the valve cover.
3. Remove the crankcase ventilator bracket and move it aside.
4. Disconnect the secondary filter lines.
5. Remove the secondary filter adapter.
6. Loosen the vacuum pump hold-down clamp and rotate the pump in order to gain access to the intake manifold bolt. Remove the intake manifold bolts. The injection line clips are retained by the same bolts.
7. Remove the intake manifold. Install a protective cover (GM part no. J-29664-1 or equivalent) so no foreign material falls into the engine.
8. Remove the injection line clips at the loom brackets.
9. Remove the injection lines at the nozzles and cover the nozzles with protective caps.
10. Remove the injection lines at the pump and tag the lines for later installation.
11. Remove the fuel line from the injection pump.

To install:
12. Install the injection lines at the pump and nozzles. Tighten all fittings to 20 ft. lbs. (25 Nm).
13. Install the injection line clips at the loom bracket.
14. Install the intake manifold.
15. Install the alternator bracket and tighten the manifold bolts.
16. Install the fuel lines at the filter. Tighten the bolts to 9 inch lbs. (1 Nm).
17. Install the filter to the manifold and tighten the bolts to 30 ft. lbs. (40 Nm).
18. Install the air cleaner and the crankcase ventilator bracket.
19. Connect the batteries.

Fuel Injectors

REMOVAL & INSTALLATION

▶ **See Figure 63**

➡ **Special tool J-29873, or its equivalent, an injection nozzle socket, will be necessary for this procedure.**

1. Disconnect the batteries.
2. Disconnect the fuel line clip, and remove the fuel return hose.
3. Remove the fuel injection lines as previously detailed.
4. Using GM special tool J-29873, remove the injector. Always remove the injector by turning the 30mm hex portion of the injector; turning the round portion will damage the injector. Always cap the injector and fuel lines when disconnected, to prevent contamination.

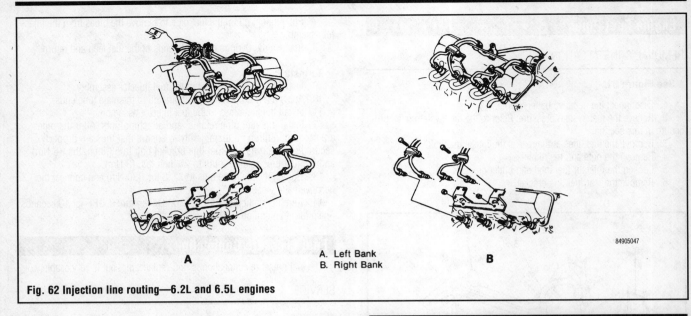

A. Left Bank
B. Right Bank

Fig. 62 Injection line routing—6.2L and 6.5L engines

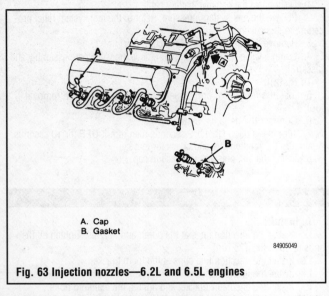

A. Cap
B. Gasket

Fig. 63 Injection nozzles—6.2L and 6.5L engines

5. Install the injector with a new gasket and tighten to 50 ft. lbs. (70 Nm). Connect the injection line and tighten the nut to 20 ft. lbs. (25 Nm). Install the fuel return hose, fuel line clips, and connect the batteries.

TESTING

1. Install a suitable pressure gauge.
2. Open the shut-off valve on the gauge a ¼ turn.

✳✳ CAUTION

When testing nozzle opening pressure, always keep your hands (or any exposed skin!) away from the nozzle. Diesel injectors have sufficient pressure to penetrate your skin!

3. Slowly depress the lever on the gauge. Note when the needle on the gauge stops—the maximum pressure is the opening pressure. Pressure should never fall below 1500 psi (10,342 kPa) on the 6.2L engine or 1700 psi (11,721 kPa) on the 6.5L engine.
4. Replace any injector which does not meets these pressures.

Fuel Supply Pump

REMOVAL & INSTALLATION

1987–90 6.2L Engine

▶ See Figure 64

✳✳ CAUTION

Never smoke when working around diesel fuel! Avoid all sources of sparks or ignition.

1. Disconnect the fuel intake and outlet lines at the pump and plug the pump intake line.
2. You can insert a long bolt to hold the fuel pump pushrod.
3. Remove the two pump mounting bolts and lockwashers; remove the pump and its gasket. The 6.2L utilizes a mounting plate between the pump and gasket.

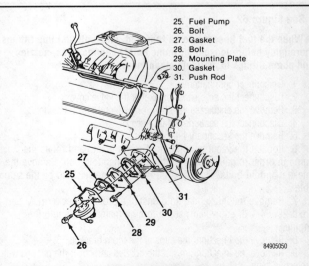

25. Fuel Pump
26. Bolt
27. Gasket
28. Bolt
29. Mounting Plate
30. Gasket
31. Push Rod

Fig. 64 Fuel pump location—1987–90 6.2L engine

4. If the rocker arm pushrod is to be removed, remove the two adapter bolts and lockwashers and remove the adapter and its gasket.

5. Install the fuel pump with a new gasket. Tighten the upper mounting bolts to 24 ft. lbs. (33 Nm) and the lower bolt to 6 ft. lbs. (8 Nm). Heavy grease can be used to hold the fuel pump pushrod up when installing the pump. Coat the mating surfaces with sealant.

6. Connect the fuel lines an check for leaks.

1991–97 Diesel Engines

▶ See Figure 65

1. Disconnect the negative battery cables.
2. Locate the pump on the left frame rail and disconnect the electrical lead from the pump and the harness from the pump support bracket.
3. Use two open end wrenches and disconnect the fuel lines at the pump.
4. Remove the pump support bracket screws and remove it from the brake lines.
5. Remove the pump and bracket.

To install:
6. Attach the pump and bracket to the frame rail.
7. Attach the support bracket to the brake lines.
8. Connect the fuel lines to the pump.
9. Connect the harness to the bracket and then connect the lead to the pump.
10. Connect the batteries.

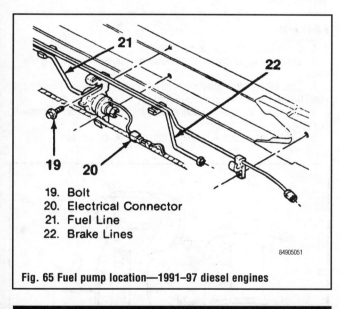

19. Bolt
20. Electrical Connector
21. Fuel Line
22. Brake Lines

Fig. 65 Fuel pump location—1991–97 diesel engines

Fuel Injection Pump

REMOVAL & INSTALLATION

▶ See Figures 66, 67 and 68

1. Disconnect both batteries.
2. Remove the fan and fan shroud.
3. Remove the intake manifold.
4. Remove the fuel lines.
5. Disconnect the accelerator cable at the injection pump, and the detent cable (see illustration) where applicable.
6. Tag and disconnect the necessary wires and hoses at the injection pump.
7. Disconnect the fuel return line at the top of the injection pump.
8. Disconnect the fuel feed line at the injection pump.

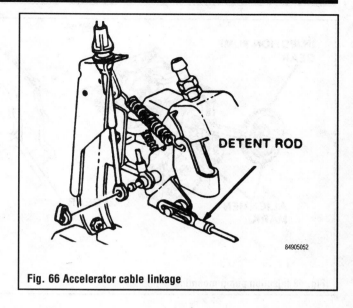

Fig. 66 Accelerator cable linkage

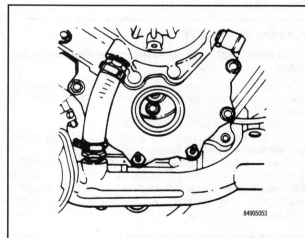

Fig. 67 Rotate the crankshaft so that the injection pump drive gear bolts become visible through the hole

9. Remove the air conditioning hose retainer bracket if equipped with A/C.
10. Remove the oil fill tube, including the crankcase depression valve vent hose assembly.
11. Remove the grommet for the oil filler tube.
12. Scribe or paint a matchmark on the front cover and on the injection pump flange.
13. The crankshaft must be rotated in order to gain access to the injection pump drive gear bolts through the oil filler neck hole.
14. Remove the injection pump-to-front cover attaching nuts. Remove the pump and cap all open lines and nozzles.

To install:
15. Replace the gasket.
16. Align the locating pin on the pump hub with the slot in the injection pump driven gear. At the same time, align the timing marks.
17. Attach the injection pump to the front cover, aligning the timing marks before tightening the nuts to 30 ft. lbs. (40 Nm).
18. Install the drive gear-to-injection pump bolts. Tighten the bolts to 20 ft. lbs. (25 Nm).
19. Install the remaining components as removed. Tighten the fuel feed line at the injection pump to 20 ft. lbs. (25 Nm). Start the engine and check for leaks.

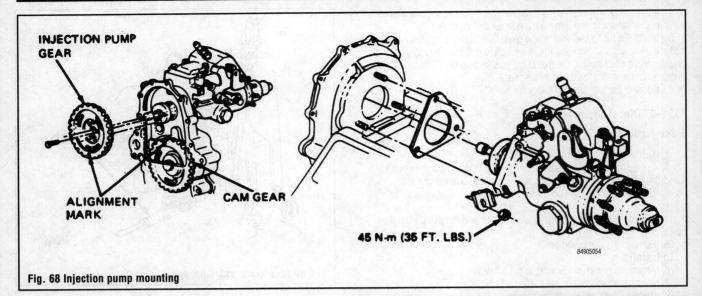

Fig. 68 Injection pump mounting

INJECTION TIMING ADJUSTMENT

♦ **See Figures 69, 70 and 71**

➡**Special tool J-26987, or its equivalent, will be necessary for this procedure.**

For the engine to be properly timed, the lines on the top of the injection pump adapter and the flange of the injection pump must be aligned.

1. The engine must be **OFF** for resetting the timing.
2. Loosen the three pump retaining nuts with tool J-26987, an injection pump intake manifold wrench, or its equivalent.
3. Align the mark on the injection pump with the marks on the adapter and tighten the nuts. Tighten to 30 ft. lbs. (40 Nm). Use a ¾ in. (19.05mm) open-end wrench on the boss at the front of the injection pump to aid in rotating the pump to align the marks.
4. Adjust the throttle rod.

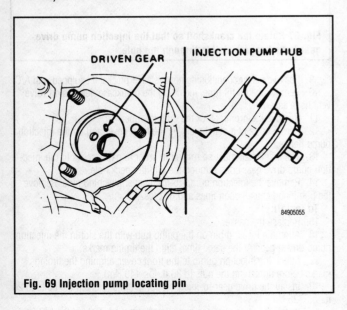

Fig. 69 Injection pump locating pin

Glow Plugs

INSPECTION

♦ **See Figure 72**

1. Check all connections on the controller.
2. Check the upper copper stud nuts on the controller. Do not tighten them.
3. Check the engine harness ground connection and the wiring harness nuts. Tighten them to 44 inch lbs. (5 Nm).
4. Check that the four-wire connector at the controller is seated properly and latched.
5. Tighten the controller mounting nuts to 25 ft. lbs. (35 Nm).

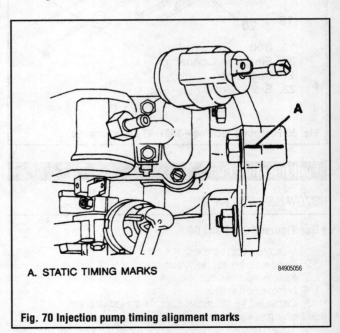

A. STATIC TIMING MARKS

Fig. 70 Injection pump timing alignment marks

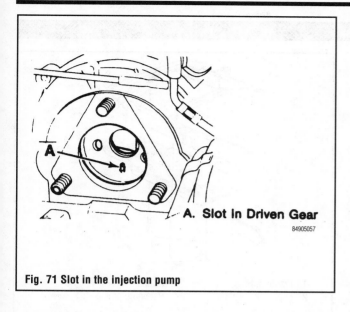

Fig. 71 Slot in the injection pump

A. Slot In Driven Gear

84905057

REMOVAL & INSTALLATION

1. Disconnect the negative battery cables.

2. On the 6.2L engine and the left side only of the 6.5L, disconnect the glow plug lead wires and then remove the plugs. You'll need a ⅜ in. (9.525mm) deep-well socket.

3. On the right side of the 6.5L engine, raise the van and support it with safety stands. Remove the right front tire.

4. Remove the inner splash shield from the fender well.

5. Remove the lead wire from the plug at the No. 2 cylinder. Remove the lead wires from plugs in the Nos. 4 and 6 cylinders at the harness connectors.

6. Remove the heat shroud for the plug in the No. 4 cylinder. Remove the heat shroud for the plug in the No. 6 cylinder. Slide the shrouds back just far enough to allow access so you can unplug the wires.

7. Remove the plugs in cylinders No. 2, 4 and 6.

8. Reach up under the vehicle and disconnect the lead wire at No. 8. Remove the glow plug. You may find that removing the exhaust down pipe make this a bit easier when working on Nos. 6 and 8.

9. Installation is the reverse of removal. Install all glow plugs and carefully tighten them to 13 ft. lbs. (17 Nm) for the right side on the 6.5L; 17 ft. lbs. (23 Nm) on all others.

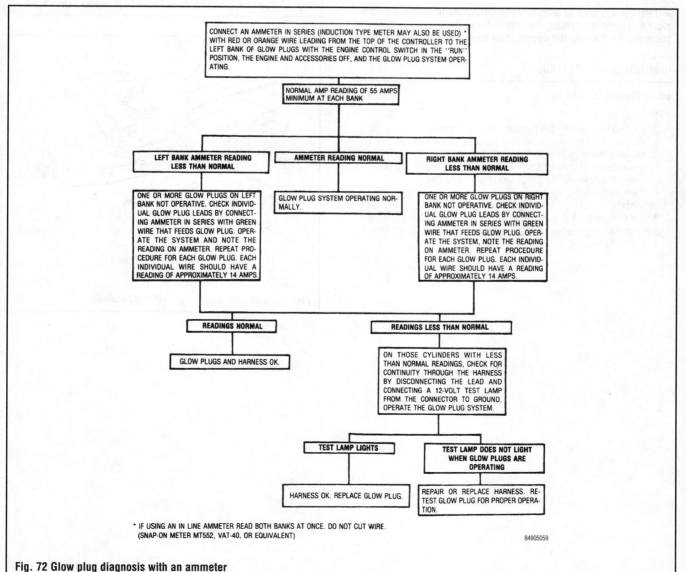

CONNECT AN AMMETER IN SERIES (INDUCTION TYPE METER MAY ALSO BE USED) * WITH RED OR ORANGE WIRE LEADING FROM THE TOP OF THE CONTROLLER TO THE LEFT BANK OF GLOW PLUGS WITH THE ENGINE CONTROL SWITCH IN THE "RUN" POSITION, THE ENGINE AND ACCESSORIES OFF, AND THE GLOW PLUG SYSTEM OPERATING.

NORMAL AMP READING OF 55 AMPS MINIMUM AT EACH BANK

LEFT BANK AMMETER READING LESS THAN NORMAL

AMMETER READING NORMAL

RIGHT BANK AMMETER READING LESS THAN NORMAL

ONE OR MORE GLOW PLUGS ON LEFT BANK NOT OPERATIVE. CHECK INDIVIDUAL GLOW PLUG LEADS BY CONNECTING AMMETER IN SERIES WITH GREEN WIRE THAT FEEDS GLOW PLUG. OPERATE THE SYSTEM AND NOTE THE READING ON AMMETER. REPEAT PROCEDURE FOR EACH GLOW PLUG. EACH INDIVIDUAL WIRE SHOULD HAVE A READING OF APPROXIMATELY 14 AMPS.

GLOW PLUG SYSTEM OPERATING NORMALLY.

ONE OR MORE GLOW PLUGS ON RIGHT BANK NOT OPERATIVE. CHECK INDIVIDUAL GLOW PLUG LEADS BY CONNECTING AMMETER IN SERIES WITH GREEN WIRE THAT FEEDS GLOW PLUG. OPERATE THE SYSTEM, NOTE THE READING ON AMMETER. REPEAT PROCEDURE FOR EACH GLOW PLUG. EACH INDIVIDUAL WIRE SHOULD HAVE A READING OF APPROXIMATELY 14 AMPS.

READINGS NORMAL

GLOW PLUGS AND HARNESS OK.

READINGS LESS THAN NORMAL

ON THOSE CYLINDERS WITH LESS THAN NORMAL READINGS, CHECK FOR CONTINUITY THROUGH THE HARNESS BY DISCONNECTING THE LEAD AND CONNECTING A 12-VOLT TEST LAMP FROM THE CONNECTOR TO GROUND. OPERATE THE GLOW PLUG SYSTEM.

TEST LAMP LIGHTS

HARNESS OK. REPLACE GLOW PLUG.

TEST LAMP DOES NOT LIGHT WHEN GLOW PLUGS ARE OPERATING

REPAIR OR REPLACE HARNESS. RETEST GLOW PLUG FOR PROPER OPERATION.

* IF USING AN IN LINE AMMETER READ BOTH BANKS AT ONCE. DO NOT CUT WIRE. (SNAP-ON METER MT552, VAT-40, OR EQUIVALENT)

84905059

Fig. 72 Glow plug diagnosis with an ammeter

FUEL TANK

Tank Assembly

DRAINING

> ⁂ **CAUTION**
>
> **Disconnect the battery before beginning the draining operation.**

If the vehicle is not equipped with a drain plug, use the following procedure to remove the fuel.

1. Using a 10 ft. (3m) piece of ⅜ in. (9.5mm) hose, cut a flap slit 18 in. (45cm) from one end.
2. Install a pipe nipple, of slightly larger diameter than the hose, into the opposite end of the hose.
3. Install the nipple end of the hose into the fuel tank with the natural curve of the hose pointing downward. Keep feeding the hose in until the nipple hits the bottom of the tank.
4. Place the other end of the hose in a suitable container and insert a air hose pointing it in the downward direction of the slit and inject air into the line.

➡**If the vehicle is to be stored, always drain the fuel from the complete fuel system including the carburetor or throttle body, fuel pump supply, fuel injection pump, fuel lines, and tank.**

REMOVAL & INSTALLATION

▶ **See Figures 73 and 74**

1. Drain the tank.
2. Jack up your vehicle and support it with jackstands.
3. Remove the clamp on the filler neck and the vent tube hose.
4. Remove the gauge hose which is attached to the frame.
5. While supporting the tank securely, remove the support straps.
6. Lower the tank until the gauge wiring can be removed.
7. Remove the tank.

To install:

8. Install the unit in the reverse order of removal. Make certain that the anti-squeak material is replaced and tighten the strap bolts to 33 ft. lbs. (45 Nm).
9. Lower the vehicle.

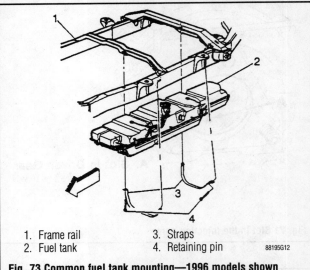

1. Frame rail	3. Straps
2. Fuel tank	4. Retaining pin

88195G12

Fig. 73 Common fuel tank mounting—1996 models shown

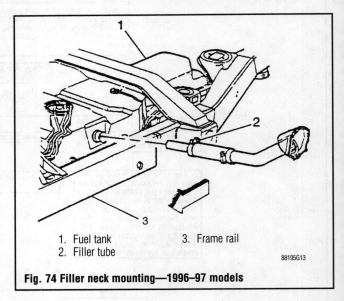

1. Fuel tank	3. Frame rail
2. Filler tube	

88195G13

Fig. 74 Filler neck mounting—1996–97 models

6

CHASSIS
ELECTRICAL

UNDERSTANDING AND TROUBLESHOOTING ELECTRICAL SYSTEMS

Basic Electrical Theory

▶ **See Figure 1**

For any 12 volt, negative ground, electrical system to operate, the electricity must travel in a complete circuit. This simply means that current (power) from the positive terminal (+) of the battery must eventually return to the negative terminal (-) of the battery. Along the way, this current will travel through wires, fuses, switches and components. If, for any reason, the flow of current through the circuit is interrupted, the component fed by that circuit will cease to function properly.

Perhaps the easiest way to visualize a circuit is to think of connecting a light bulb (with two wires attached to it) to the battery—one wire attached to the negative (-) terminal of the battery and the other wire to the positive (+) terminal. With the two wires touching the battery terminals, the circuit would be complete and the light bulb would illuminate. Electricity would follow a path from the battery to the bulb and back to the battery. It's easy to see that with longer wires on our light bulb, it could be mounted anywhere. Further, one wire could be fitted with a switch so that the light could be turned on and off.

The normal automotive circuit differs from this simple example in two ways. First, instead of having a return wire from the bulb to the battery, the current travels through the chassis of the vehicle. Since the negative (-) battery cable is attached to the chassis and the chassis is made of electrically conductive metal, the chassis of the vehicle can serve as a ground wire to complete the circuit. Secondly, most automotive circuits contain multiple components which receive power from a single circuit. This lessens the amount of wire needed to power components on the vehicle.

Fig. 1 This example illustrates a simple circuit. When the switch is closed, power from the positive (+) battery terminal flows through the fuse and the switch, and then to the light bulb. The light illuminates and the circuit is completed through the ground wire back to the negative (-) battery terminal. In reality, the two ground points shown in the illustration are attached to the metal chassis of the vehicle, which completes the circuit back to the battery.

THE WATER ANALOGY

Electricity is the flow of electrons—hypothetical particles thought to constitute the basic "stuff" of electricity. Many people have been taught electrical theory using an analogy with water. In a comparison with water flowing through a pipe, the electrons would be the water.

The flow of electricity can be measured much like the flow of water through a pipe. The unit of measurement used is amperes, frequently abbreviated as amps (a). When connected to a circuit, an ammeter will measure the actual amount of current flowing through the circuit. When relatively few electrons flow through a circuit, the amperage is low. When many electrons flow, the amperage is high.

Just as water pressure is measured in units such as pounds per square inch (psi), electrical pressure is measured in units called volts (v). When a voltmeter is connected to a circuit, it is measuring the electrical pressure. The higher the voltage, the more current will flow through the circuit. The lower the voltage, the less current will flow.

While increasing the voltage in a circuit will increase the flow of current, the actual flow depends not only on voltage, but also on the resistance of the circuit. Resistance is the amount of force necessary to push the current through the circuit. The standard unit for measuring resistance is an ohm (W or omega). Resistance in a circuit varies depending on the amount and type of components used in the circuit. The main factors which determine resistance are:

- **Material**—some materials have more resistance than others. Those with high resistance are said to be insulators. Rubber is one of the best insulators available, as it allows little current to pass. Low resistance materials are said to be conductors. Copper wire is among the best conductors. Most vehicle wiring is made of copper.
- **Size**—the larger the wire size being used, the less resistance the wire will have. This is why components which use large amounts of electricity usually have large wires supplying current to them.
- **Length**—for a given thickness of wire, the longer the wire, the greater the resistance. The shorter the wire, the less the resistance. When determining the proper wire for a circuit, both size and length must be considered to design a circuit that can handle the current needs of the component.
- **Temperature**—with many materials, the higher the temperature, the greater the resistance. This principle is used in many of the sensors on the engine.

OHM'S LAW

The preceding definitions may lead the reader into believing that there is no relationship between current, voltage and resistance. Nothing can be further from the truth. The relationship between current, voltage and resistance can be summed up by a statement known as Ohm's law.

Voltage (E) is equal to amperage (I) times resistance (R): $E = I \times R$
Other forms of the formula are $R = E/I$ and $I = E/R$

In each of these formulas, E is the voltage in volts, I is the current in amps and R is the resistance in ohms. The basic point to remember is that as the resistance of a circuit goes up, the amount of current that flows in the circuit will go down, if voltage remains the same.

Electrical Components

POWER SOURCE

The power source for 12 volt automotive electrical systems is the battery. In most modern vehicles, the battery is a lead/acid electrochemical device consisting of six 2 volt subsections (cells) connected in series, so that the unit is capable of producing approximately 12 volts of electrical pressure. Each subsection consists of a series of positive and negative plates held a short distance apart in a solution of sulfuric acid and water.

The two types of plates are of dissimilar metals. This sets up a chemical reaction, and it is this reaction which produces current flow from the battery when its positive and negative terminals are connected to an electrical load. The power removed from the battery is replaced by the alternator, which forces electrons back through the battery, reversing the normal flow, and restoring the battery to its original chemical state.

GROUND

Two types of grounds are used in automotive electric circuits. Direct ground components are grounded through their mounting points. All other components use some sort of ground wire which is attached to the body or chassis of the vehicle. The electrical current runs through the chassis of the vehicle and returns to the battery through the ground (-) cable; if you look, you'll see that the battery ground cable connects between the battery and the body or chassis of the vehicle.

➥**It should be noted that a good percentage of electrical problems can be traced to bad grounds.**

PROTECTIVE DEVICES

It is possible for large surges of current to pass through the electrical system of your vehicle. If this surge of current were to reach the load in the circuit, it could burn it out or severely damage it. To prevent this, fuses, circuit breakers and/or fusible links are connected into the supply wires of the electrical system. These items are nothing more than a built-in weak spot in the system. When an abnormal amount of current flows through the system, these protective devices work as follows to protect the circuit:

• Fuse—when an excessive electrical current passes through a fuse, the fuse "blows" (the conductor melts) and opens the circuit, preventing the passage of current.

• Circuit Breaker—a circuit breaker is basically a self-repairing fuse. It will open the circuit in the same fashion as a fuse, but when the surge subsides, the circuit breaker can be reset and does not need replacement.

• Fusible Link—a fusible link (fuse link or main link) is a short length of special, Hypalon high temperature insulated wire that acts as a fuse. When an excessive electrical current passes through a fusible link, the thin gauge wire inside the link melts, creating an intentional open to protect the circuit. To repair the circuit, the link must be replaced. Some newer type fusible links are housed in plug-in modules, which are simply replaced like a fuse, while older type fusible links must be cut and spliced if they melt. Since this link is very early in the electrical path, it's the first place to look if nothing on the vehicle works, but the battery seems to be charged and is properly connected.

✳✳ CAUTION

Always replace fuses, circuit breakers and fusible links with identically rated components. Under no circumstances should a component of higher or lower amperage rating be substituted.

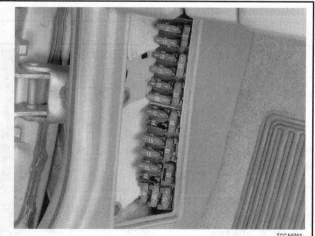

TCCA6P01

Most vehicles use one or more fuse panels. This one is located in the driver's side kick panel

SWITCHES AND RELAYS

▶ **See Figure 2**

Switches are used in electrical circuits to control the passage of current. The most common use is to open and close circuits between the battery and the various electric devices in the system. Switches are rated according to the amount of amperage they can handle. If a sufficient amperage rated switch is not used in a circuit, the switch could overload and cause damage.

Some electrical components which require a large amount of current to operate use a special switch called a relay. Since these circuits carry a large amount of current, the thickness of the wire in the circuit is also greater. If this large wire were connected from the load to the control switch on the dashboard, the switch would have to carry the high amperage load and the dash would be twice as large to accommodate the increased size of the wiring harness. To prevent these problems, a relay is used.

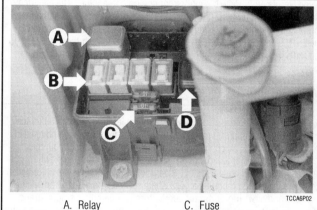

A. Relay	C. Fuse
B. Fusible link	D. Flasher

TCCA6P02

The underhood fuse and relay panel usually contains fuses, relays, flashers and fusible links

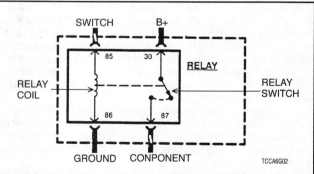

TCCA6G02

Fig. 2 Relays are composed of a coil and a switch. These two components are linked together so that when one operates, the other operates at the same time. The large wires in the circuit are connected from the battery to one side of the relay switch (B+) and from the opposite side of the relay switch to the load (component). Smaller wires are connected from the relay coil to the control switch for the circuit and from the opposite side of the relay coil to ground.

Relays are composed of a coil and a switch. These two components are linked together so that when one operates, the other operates at the same time. The large wires in the circuit are connected from the battery to one side of the relay switch and from the opposite side of the relay switch to the load. Most relays are normally open, preventing current from passing through the circuit. Additional, smaller wires are connected from the relay coil to the control switch for the circuit and from the opposite side of the relay coil to ground. When the control switch is turned on, it grounds the smaller wire to the relay coil, causing the coil to operate. The coil pulls the relay switch closed, sending power to the component without routing it through the inside of the vehicle. Some common circuits which may use relays are the horn, headlights, starter, electric fuel pump and rear window defogger systems.

LOAD

Every complete circuit must include a "load" (something to use the electricity coming from the source). Without this load, the battery would attempt to deliver its entire power supply from one pole to another. The electricity would take a short cut to ground and cause a great amount of damage to other components in the circuit by developing a tremendous amount of heat. This condition could develop sufficient heat to melt the insulation on all the surrounding wires and reduce a multiple wire cable to a lump of plastic and copper.

WIRING & HARNESSES

The average automobile contains about ½ mile of wiring, with hundreds of individual connections. To protect the many wires from damage and to keep them from becoming a confusing tangle, they are organized into bundles, enclosed in plastic or taped together and called wiring harnesses. Different harnesses serve different parts of the vehicle. Individual wires are color coded to help trace them through a harness where sections are hidden from view.

Automotive wiring or circuit conductors can be either single strand wire, multi-strand wire or printed circuitry. Single strand wire has a solid metal core and is usually used inside such components as alternators, motors, relays and other devices. Multi-strand wire has a core made of many small strands of wire twisted together into a single conductor. Most of the wiring in an automotive electrical system is made up of multi-strand wire, either as a single conductor or grouped together in a harness. All wiring is color coded on the insulator, either as a solid color or as a colored wire with an identification stripe. A printed circuit is a thin film of copper or other conductor that is printed on an insulator backing. Occasionally, a printed circuit is sandwiched between two sheets of plastic for more protection and flexibility. A complete printed circuit, consisting of conductors, insulating material and connectors for lamps or other components is called a printed circuit board. Printed circuitry is used in place of individual wires or harnesses in places where space is limited, such as behind instrument panels.

Since automotive electrical systems are very sensitive to changes in resistance, the selection of properly sized wires is critical when systems are repaired. A loose or corroded connection or a replacement wire that is too small for the circuit will add extra resistance and an additional voltage drop to the circuit.

The wire gauge number is an expression of the cross-section area of the conductor. The most common system for expressing wire size is the American Wire Gauge (AWG) system. As gauge number increases, area decreases and the wire becomes smaller. An 18 gauge wire is smaller than a 4 gauge wire. A wire with a higher gauge number will carry less current than a wire with a lower gauge number. Gauge wire size refers to the size of the strands of the conductor, not the size of the complete wire. It is possible, therefore, to have two wires of the same gauge with different diameters because one may have thicker insulation than the other.

12 volt automotive electrical systems generally use 10, 12, 14, 16 and 18 gauge wire. Main power distribution circuits and larger accessories usually use 10 and 12 gauge wire. Battery cables are usually 4 or 6 gauge, although 1 and 2 gauge wires are occasionally used.

It is essential to understand how a circuit works before trying to figure out why it doesn't. An electrical schematic shows the electrical current paths when a circuit is operating properly. Schematics break the entire electrical system down into individual circuits. In a schematic, no attempt is made to represent wiring and components as they physically appear on the vehicle; switches and other components are shown as simply as possible. Face views of harness connectors show the cavity or terminal locations in all multi-pin connectors to help locate test points.

CONNECTORS

Three types of connectors are commonly used in automotive applications: weatherproof, molded and hard shell.

• Weatherproof—these connectors are most commonly used in the engine compartment or where the connector is exposed to the elements. Terminals are protected against moisture and dirt by sealing rings which provide a weathertight seal. All repairs require the use of a special terminal and the tool required to service it. Unlike standard blade type terminals, these weatherproof terminals cannot be straightened once they are bent. Make certain that the connectors are properly seated and all of the sealing rings are in place when connecting leads.

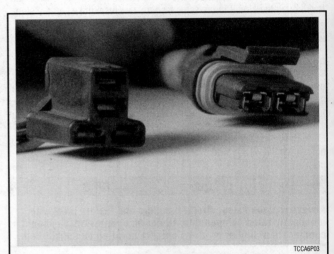

TCCA6P03

Hard shell (left) and weatherproof (right) connectors have replaceable terminals

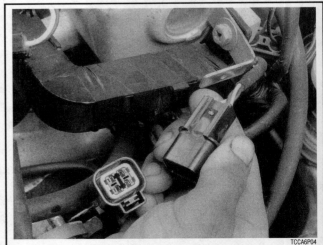

TCCA6P04

Weatherproof connectors are most commonly used in the engine compartment or where the connector is exposed to the elements

• Molded—these connectors require complete replacement of the connector if found to be defective. This means splicing a new connector assembly into the harness. All splices should be soldered to insure proper contact. Use care when probing the connections or replacing terminals in them, as it is possible to create a short circuit between opposite terminals. If this happens to the wrong terminal pair, it is possible to damage certain components. Always use jumper wires between connectors for circuit checking and NEVER probe through weatherproof seals.

• Hard Shell—unlike molded connectors, the terminal contacts in hard-shell connectors can be replaced. Replacement usually involves the use of a special terminal removal tool that depresses the locking tangs (barbs) on the connector terminal and allows the connector to be removed from the rear of the shell. The connector shell should be replaced if it shows any evidence of burning, melting, cracks, or breaks. Replace individual terminals that are burnt, corroded, distorted or loose.

Test Equipment

Pinpointing the exact cause of trouble in an electrical circuit is most times accomplished by the use of special test equipment. The following describes different types of commonly used test equipment and briefly explains how to use them in diagnosis. In addition to the information covered below, the tool manufacturer's instructions booklet (provided with the tester) should be read and clearly understood before attempting any test procedures.

JUMPER WIRES

✳✳ CAUTION

Never use jumper wires made from a thinner gauge wire than the circuit being tested. If the jumper wire is of too small a gauge, it may overheat and possibly melt. Never use jumpers to bypass high resistance loads in a circuit. Bypassing resistances, in effect, creates a short circuit. This may, in turn, cause damage and fire. Jumper wires should only be used to bypass lengths of wire.

Jumper wires are simple, yet extremely valuable, pieces of test equipment. They are basically test wires which are used to bypass sections of a circuit. Although jumper wires can be purchased, they are usually fabricated from lengths of standard automotive wire and whatever type of connector (alligator clip, spade connector or pin connector) that is required for the particular application being tested. In cramped, hard-to-reach areas, it is advisable to have insulated boots over the jumper wire terminals in order to prevent accidental grounding. It is also advisable to include a standard automotive fuse in any jumper wire. This is commonly referred to as a "fused jumper". By inserting an in-line fuse holder between a set of test leads, a fused jumper wire can be used for bypassing open circuits. Use a 5 amp fuse to provide protection against voltage spikes.

Jumper wires are used primarily to locate open electrical circuits, on either the ground (-) side of the circuit or on the power (+) side. If an electrical component fails to operate, connect the jumper wire between the component and a good ground. If the component operates only with the jumper installed, the ground circuit is open. If the ground circuit is good, but the component does not operate, the circuit between the power feed and component may be open. By moving the jumper wire successively back from the component toward the power source, you can isolate the area of the circuit where the open is located. When the component stops functioning, or the power is cut off, the open is in the segment of wire between the jumper and the point previously tested.

You can sometimes connect the jumper wire directly from the battery to the "hot" terminal of the component, but first make sure the component uses 12 volts in operation. Some electrical components, such as fuel injectors, are designed to operate on about 4 volts, and running 12 volts directly to these components will cause damage.

TEST LIGHTS

The test light is used to check circuits and components while electrical current is flowing through them. It is used for voltage and ground tests. To use a 12 volt test light, connect the ground clip to a good ground and probe wherever necessary with the pick. The test light will illuminate when voltage is detected. This does not necessarily mean that 12 volts (or any particular amount of voltage) is present; it only means that some voltage is present. It is advisable before using the test light to touch its ground clip and probe across the battery posts or terminals to make sure the light is operating properly.

✳✳ WARNING

Do not use a test light to probe electronic ignition spark plug or coil wires. Never use a pick-type test light to probe wiring on computer controlled systems unless specifically instructed to do so. Any wire insulation that is pierced by the test light probe should be taped and sealed with silicone after testing.

Like the jumper wire, the 12 volt test light is used to isolate opens in circuits. But, whereas the jumper wire is used to bypass the open to operate the load, the 12 volt test light is used to locate the presence of voltage in a circuit. If the test light illuminates, there is power up to that point in the circuit; if the test light does not illuminate, there is an open circuit (no power). Move the test light in successive steps back toward the power source until the light in the handle illuminates. The open is between the probe and a point which was previously probed.

The self-powered test light is similar in design to the 12 volt test light, but contains a 1.5 volt penlight battery in the handle. It is most often used in place of a multimeter to check for open or short circuits when power is isolated from the circuit (continuity test).

The battery in a self-powered test light does not provide much current. A weak battery may not provide enough power to illuminate the test light even when a complete circuit is made (especially if there is high resistance in the circuit). Always make sure that the test battery is strong. To check the battery, briefly touch the ground clip to the probe; if the light glows brightly, the battery is strong enough for testing.

➡**A self-powered test light should not be used on any computer controlled system or component. The small amount of electricity transmitted by the test light is enough to damage many electronic automotive components.**

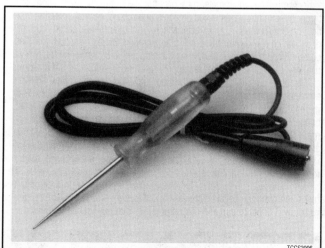

TCCS2006

A 12 volt test light is used to detect the presence of voltage in a circuit

MULTIMETERS

Multimeters are an extremely useful tool for troubleshooting electrical problems. They can be purchased in either analog or digital form and have a price range to suit any budget. A multimeter is a voltmeter, ammeter and ohmmeter (along with other features) combined into one instrument. It is often used when testing solid state circuits because of its high input impedance (usually 10 megaohms or more). A brief description of the multimeter main test functions follows:

• Voltmeter—the voltmeter is used to measure voltage at any point in a circuit, or to measure the voltage drop across any part of a circuit. Voltmeters usually have various scales and a selector switch to allow the reading of different voltage ranges. The voltmeter has a positive and a negative lead. To avoid damage to the meter, always connect the negative lead to the negative (-) side of the circuit (to ground or nearest the ground side of the circuit) and connect the positive lead to the positive (+) side of the circuit (to the power source or the nearest power source). Note that the negative voltmeter lead will always be black and that the positive voltmeter will always be some color other than black (usually red).

• Ohmmeter—the ohmmeter is designed to read resistance (measured in ohms) in a circuit or component. All ohmmeters will have a selector switch which permits the measurement of different ranges of resistance (usually the selector switch allows the multiplication of the meter reading by 10, 100, 1,000 and 10,000). Since the meters are powered by an internal battery, the ohmmeter can be used as a self-powered test light. When the ohmmeter is connected, current from the ohmmeter flows through the circuit or component being tested. Since the ohmmeter's internal resistance and voltage are known values, the amount of current flow through the meter depends on the resistance of the circuit or component being tested. The ohmmeter can also be used to perform a continuity test for suspected open circuits. In using the meter for making continuity checks, do not be concerned with the actual resistance readings. Zero resistance, or any ohm reading, indicates continuity in the circuit. Infinite resistance indicates an opening in the circuit. A high resistance reading where there should be none indicates a problem in the circuit. Checks for short circuits are made in the same manner as checks for open circuits, except that the circuit must be isolated from both power and normal ground. Infinite resistance indicates no continuity to ground, while zero resistance indicates a dead short to ground.

✳✳ WARNING

Never use an ohmmeter to check the resistance of a component or wire while there is voltage applied to the circuit.

• Ammeter—an ammeter measures the amount of current flowing through a circuit in units called amperes or amps. At normal operating voltage, most circuits have a characteristic amount of amperes, called "current draw" which can be measured using an ammeter. By referring to a specified current draw rating, then measuring the amperes and comparing the two values, one can determine what is happening within the circuit to aid in diagnosis. An open circuit, for example, will not allow any current to flow, so the ammeter reading will be zero. A damaged component or circuit will have an increased current draw, so the reading will be high. The ammeter is always connected in series with the circuit being tested. All of the current that normally flows through the circuit must also flow through the ammeter; if there is any other path for the current to follow, the ammeter reading will not be accurate. The ammeter itself has very little resistance to current flow and, therefore, will not affect the circuit, but it will measure current draw only when the circuit is closed and electricity is flowing. Excessive current draw can blow fuses and drain the battery, while a reduced current draw can cause motors to run slowly, lights to dim and other components to not operate properly.

Troubleshooting

When diagnosing a specific problem, organized troubleshooting is a must. The complexity of a modern automotive vehicle demands that you approach any problem in a logical, organized manner. There are certain troubleshooting techniques which are standard:

• Establish when the problem occurs. Does the problem appear only under certain conditions? Were there any noises, odors or other unusual symptoms?

• Isolate the problem area. To do this, make some simple tests and observations, then eliminate the systems that are working properly. Check for obvious problems, such as broken wires and loose or dirty connections. Always check the obvious before assuming something complicated is the cause.

• Test for problems systematically to determine the cause once the problem area is isolated. Are all the components functioning properly? Is there power going to electrical switches and motors. Performing careful, systematic checks will often turn up most causes on the first inspection, without wasting time checking components that have little or no relationship to the problem.

• Test all repairs after the work is done to make sure that the problem is fixed. Some causes can be traced to more than one component, so a careful verification of repair work is important in order to pick up additional malfunctions that may cause a problem to reappear or a different problem to arise. A blown fuse, for example, is a simple problem that may require more than another fuse to repair. If you don't look for a problem that caused a fuse to blow, a shorted wire (for example) may go undetected.

Experience has shown that most problems tend to be the result of a fairly simple and obvious cause, such as loose or corroded connectors, bad grounds or damaged wire insulation which causes a short. This makes careful visual inspection of components during testing essential to quick and accurate troubleshooting.

Testing

OPEN CIRCUITS

1. Isolate the circuit from power and ground.
2. Connect the self-powered test light or ohmmeter ground clip to a good ground and probe sections of the circuit sequentially.
3. If the light is out or there is infinite resistance, the open is between the probe and the circuit ground.
4. If the light is on or the meter shows continuity, the open is between the probe and end of the circuit toward the power source.

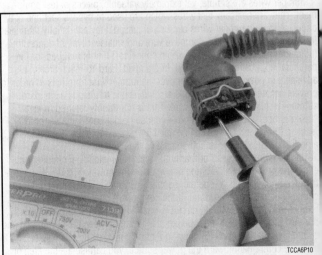

TCCA6P10

The infinite reading on this multimeter (1   .) indicates that the circuit is open

SHORT CIRCUITS

➡**Never use a self-powered test light to perform checks for opens or shorts when power is applied to the electrical system under test. The 12 volt vehicle power will quickly burn out the light bulb in the test light.**

1. Isolate the circuit from power and ground.
2. Connect the self-powered test light or ohmmeter ground clip to a good ground and probe any easy-to-reach test point in the circuit.
3. If the light comes on or there is continuity, there is a short somewhere in the circuit.
4. To isolate the short, probe a test point at either end of the isolated circuit (the light should be on or the meter should indicate continuity).
5. Leave the test light probe engaged and sequentially open connectors or switches, remove parts, etc. until the light goes out or continuity is broken.
6. When the light goes out, the short is between the last two circuit components which were opened.

VOLTAGE

This test determines voltage available from the battery and should be the first step in any electrical troubleshooting procedure. Many electrical problems, especially on computer controlled systems, can be caused by a low state of charge in the battery. Excessive corrosion at the battery cable terminals can cause poor contact that will prevent proper charging and full battery current flow.

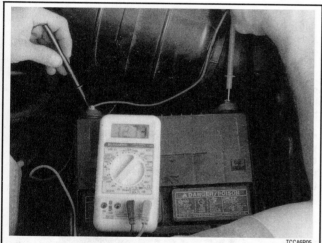

Using a multimeter to check battery voltage. This battery is fully charged

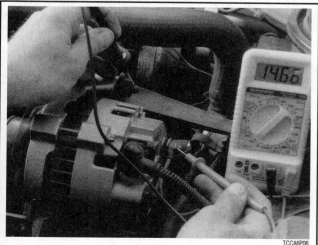

Testing voltage output between the alternator's BAT terminal and ground. This voltage reading is normal

1. Set the voltmeter selector switch to the 20V position.
2. Connect the multimeter negative lead to the battery's negative (-) post or terminal and the positive lead to the battery's positive (+) post or terminal.
3. Turn the ignition switch **ON** to provide a load.
4. A well charged battery should register over 12 volts. If the meter reads below 11.5 volts, the battery power may be insufficient to operate the electrical system properly.

VOLTAGE DROP

When current flows through a load, the voltage beyond the load drops. This voltage drop is due to the resistance created by the load and also by small resistances created by corrosion at the connectors and damaged insulation on the wires. The maximum allowable voltage drop under load is critical, especially if there is more than one load in the circuit, since all voltage drops are cumulative.

This voltage drop test revealed high resistance (low voltage) in the circuit

1. Set the voltmeter selector switch to the 20 volt position.
2. Connect the multimeter negative lead to a good ground.
3. Operate the circuit and check the voltage prior to the first component (load).
4. There should be little or no voltage drop in the circuit prior to the first component. If a voltage drop exists, the wire or connectors in the circuit are suspect.
5. While operating the first component in the circuit, probe the ground side of the component with the positive meter lead and observe the voltage readings. A small voltage drop should be noticed. This voltage drop is caused by the resistance of the component.
6. Repeat the test for each component (load) down the circuit.
7. If a large voltage drop is noticed, the preceding component, wire or connector is suspect.

RESISTANCE

❊❊❊ WARNING

Never use an ohmmeter with power applied to the circuit. The ohmmeter is designed to operate on its own power supply. The normal 12 volt automotive electrical system current could damage the meter!

Checking the resistance of a coolant temperature sensor with an ohmmeter. Reading is 1.04 kilohms

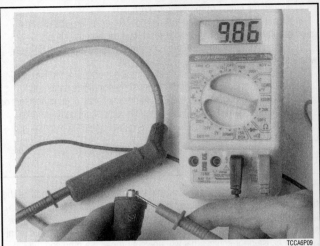

Spark plug wires can be checked for excessive resistance using an ohmmeter

1. Isolate the circuit from the vehicle's power source.
2. Ensure that the ignition key is **OFF** when disconnecting any components or the battery.
3. Where necessary, also isolate at least one side of the circuit to be checked, in order to avoid reading parallel resistances. Parallel circuit resistances will always give a lower reading than the actual resistance of either of the branches.
4. Connect the meter leads to both sides of the circuit (wire or component) and read the actual measured ohms on the meter scale. Make sure the selector switch is set to the proper ohm scale for the circuit being tested, to avoid misreading the ohmmeter test value.

Wire and Connector Repair

Almost anyone can replace damaged wires, as long as the proper tools and parts are available. Automotive wire and terminals are avail-

able to fit almost any need. Even the specialized weatherproof, molded and hard shell connectors are now available from aftermarket suppliers.

Be sure the ends of all the wires are fitted with the proper terminal hardware and connectors. Wrapping a wire around a stud is never a permanent solution and will only cause trouble later. Replace wires one at a time to avoid confusion. Always route wires exactly the same as the factory.

➡️**If connector repair is necessary, only attempt it if you have the proper tools. Weatherproof and hard shell connectors require special tools to release the pins inside the connector. Attempting to repair these connectors with conventional hand tools will damage them.**

BATTERY CABLES

Disconnecting the Cables

When working on any electrical component on the vehicle, it is always a good idea to disconnect the negative (-) battery cable. This will prevent potential damage to many sensitive electrical components such as the Engine Control Module (ECM), radio, alternator, etc.

➡️**Any time you disengage the battery cables, it is recommended that you disconnect the negative (-) battery cable first. This will prevent your accidentally grounding the positive (+) terminal to the body of the vehicle when disconnecting it, thereby preventing damage to the above mentioned components.**

Before you disconnect the cable(s), first turn the ignition to the **OFF** position. This will prevent a draw on the battery which could cause arcing (electricity trying to ground itself to the body of a vehicle, just like a spark plug jumping the gap) and, of course, damaging some components such as the alternator diodes.

When the battery cable(s) are reconnected (negative cable last), be sure to check that your lights, windshield wipers and other electrically operated safety components are all working correctly. If your vehicle contains an Electronically Tuned Radio (ETR), don't forget to also reset your radio stations. Ditto for the clock.

SUPPLEMENTAL INFLATABLE RESTRAINT (SIR) SYSTEM

General Information

The Supplemental Inflatable Restraint (SIR) system offers protection in addition to that provided by the seat belt by deploying an air bag from the center of the steering wheel or dash panel. The air bag deploys when the vehicle is involved in a frontal crash of sufficient force up to 30° off the centerline of the vehicle. To further absorb the crash energy, there is also a knee bolster located beneath the instrument panel in the driver's area and the steering column is collapsible.

The system has an energy reserve, which can store a large enough electrical charge to deploy the air bag(s) for up to ten minutes after the battery has been disconnected or damaged. The system **MUST** be disabled before any service is performed on or around SIR components or SIR wiring.

SERVICE PRECAUTIONS

• When performing service around the SIR system components or wiring, the SIR system **MUST** be disabled. Failure to do so could result in possible air bag deployment, personal injury or unneeded SIR system repairs.

• When carrying a live inflator module, make sure that the bag and trim cover are pointed away from you. Never carry the inflator module by the wires or connector on the underside of the module. In case of accidental deployment, the bag will then deploy with minimal chance of injury.

• When placing a live inflator module on a bench or other surface, always face the bag and trim cover up, away from the surface.

DISABLING THE SYSTEM

▶ See Figures 3, 4 and 5

➡Turn the steering wheel to the straight ahead position, turn the ignition OFF, then remove the key.

1. Disconnect the negative battery cable.
2. Remove the AIR BAG fuse from the fuse block.
3. On all but 1996–97 models, remove the steering column filler panel.
4. On 1996–97 models, remove the driver's and passenger knee bolster panels.
5. On all but 1996–97 models, disengage the Connector Position Assurance (CPA) and the yellow two-way connector located near the base of the steering column.
6. On 1996–97 models, disengage the Connector Position Assurance (CPA) and the yellow two-way connector located near the base of the steer-

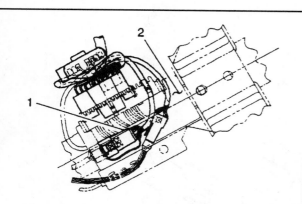

1 SIR STEERING COLUMN CONNECTOR
2 STEERING COLUMN

88196G01

Fig. 3 Location of the yellow two-way connector—except 1996–97 models

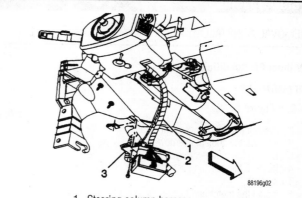

1. Steering column harness
2. Driver yellow 2-way SIR connector
3. Bracket

Fig. 4 Location of the driver's side yellow two-way connector—1996–97 models

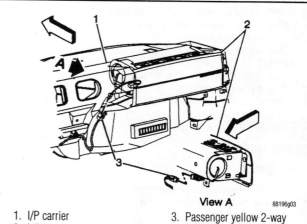

View A 88196g03

1. I/P carrier
2. Inflatable restraint I/P module
3. Passenger yellow 2-way SIR connector

Fig. 5 Location of the passenger's side yellow two-way connector—1996–97 models

ing column and the Connector Position Assurance (CPA) and the yellow two-way connector located behind the passenger bolster panel.
7. Connect the negative battery cable.

ENABLING THE SYSTEM

1. Disconnect the negative battery cable.
2. Turn the ignition switch to **LOCK**, then remove the key.
3. Engage the yellow SIR connector and CPA located near the base of the steering column and also on 1996–97 models the yellow SIR connector and CPA located behind the passenger knee bolster.
4. Install the steering column filler panel or knee bolster (depending on model year).
5. Install the AIR BAG fuse to the fuse block.
6. Connect the negative battery cable.
7. Turn the ignition switch to **RUN** and make sure that the AIR BAG warning lamp flashes seven times and then shuts off. If the warning lamp does not shut off, make sure that the wiring is properly connected. If the light remains on, take the vehicle to a reputable repair facility for service.

HEATING AND AIR CONDITIONING

Blower Motor

REMOVAL & INSTALLATION

Without Air Conditioning

ALL MODELS

▶ See Figure 6

1. Disconnect the battery ground cable.
2. Remove the coolant overflow bottle.
3. Unplug the motor wiring.
4. Remove the attaching screws and lift out the blower motor.

To install:

5. Install the motor and tighten the screws.
6. Engage the motor wiring.
7. Install the coolant overflow bottle.
8. Connect the negative battery cable.

With Air Conditioning

1987–89 MODELS

1. Disconnect the battery ground cable.
2. Remove the power antenna, if so equipped.
3. Remove the coolant overflow bottle.
4. Unplug the motor wiring.
5. Remove the attaching screws and lift out the blower motor.

To install:

6. Install the motor and tighten the screws.
7. Engage the motor wiring.
8. Install the coolant overflow bottle.
9. Install the power antenna, if so equipped.
10. Connect the negative battery cable.

1990–95 MODELS

▶ See Figure 7

1. Disconnect the battery ground cable.
2. Remove the coolant overflow bottle.

3. Unplug the motor wiring.
4. Remove the attaching screws and lift out the blower motor.

To install:

5. Install the motor and tighten the screws.
6. Engage the motor wiring.
7. Install the coolant overflow bottle.
8. Connect the negative battery cable.

1996–97 MODELS

▶ See Figures 8 and 9 (p. 11–12)

1. Remove the coolant recovery tank.
2. Remove the battery from the van.
3. Loosen the evaporator inlet line and the blower motor insulator retainers.
4. Remove the blower motor insulator.
5. Disengage the electrical connection.
6. Remove the attaching screws and lift out the blower motor.

To install:

7. Install the motor and tighten the screws.
8. Engage the motor electrical connection.
9. Install the blower motor cover.
10. Install the insulator cover and evaporator inlet line retainers.
11. Install the battery and coolant recovery tank.

Auxiliary Heater and Air Conditioner

1987 MODELS

▶ See Figure 10 (p. 13)

1. Disconnect the battery ground cable.
2. Disconnect the drain tubes at the rear of the blower-evaporator shroud/duct.
3. Remove the screws securing the shroud to the roof and case.
4. Remove the shroud/duct.
5. Disconnect the blower motor ground straps at the center connector between the motors.
6. Disconnect the blower motor wires.
7. Support the case and remove the lower-to-upper case half screws and lower the case and motor assemblies.

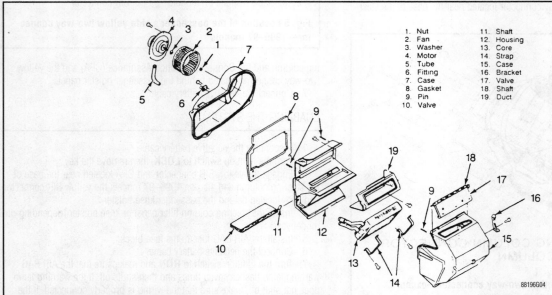

1.	Nut	11.	Shaft
2.	Fan	12.	Housing
3.	Washer	13.	Core
4.	Motor	14.	Strap
5.	Tube	15.	Case
6.	Fitting	16.	Bracket
7.	Case	17.	Valve
8.	Gasket	18.	Shaft
9.	Pin	19.	Duct
10.	Valve		

Fig. 6 Exploded view of the blower motor and heater core assembly

88196G04

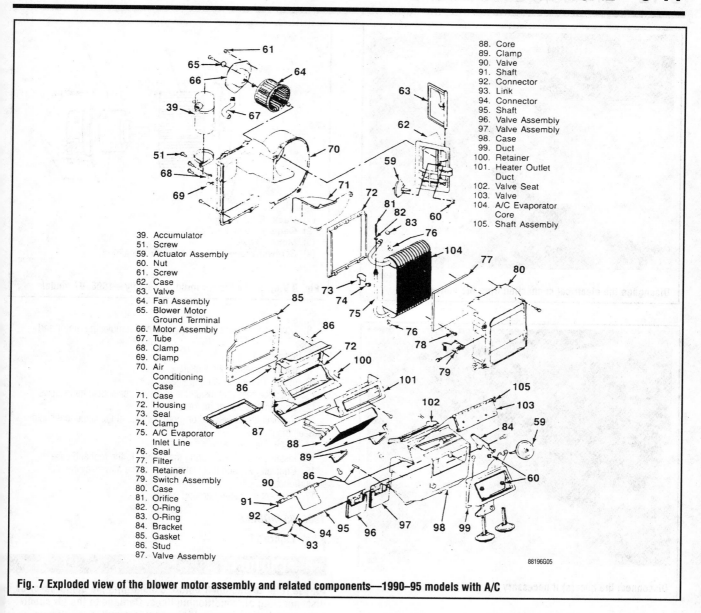

88. Core
89. Clamp
90. Valve
91. Shaft
92. Connector
93. Link
94. Connector
95. Shaft
96. Valve Assembly
97. Valve Assembly
98. Case
99. Duct
100. Retainer
101. Heater Outlet Duct
102. Valve Seat
103. Valve
104. A/C Evaporator Core
105. Shaft Assembly

39. Accumulator
51. Screw
59. Actuator Assembly
60. Nut
61. Screw
62. Case
63. Valve
64. Fan Assembly
65. Blower Motor Ground Terminal
66. Motor Assembly
67. Tube
68. Clamp
69. Clamp
70. Air Conditioning Case
71. Case
72. Housing
73. Seal
74. Clamp
75. A/C Evaporator Inlet Line
76. Seal
77. Filter
78. Retainer
79. Switch Assembly
80. Case
81. Orifice
82. O-Ring
83. O-Ring
84. Bracket
85. Gasket
86. Stud
87. Valve Assembly

88196G05

Fig. 7 Exploded view of the blower motor assembly and related components—1990–95 models with A/C

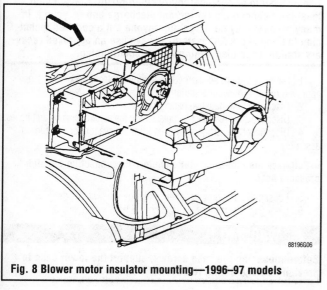

88196G06

Fig. 8 Blower motor insulator mounting—1996–97 models

88196P01

Common blower motor assembly—1997 model shown, others similar

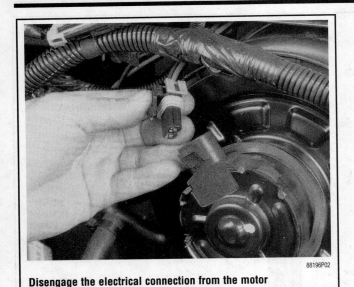

Disengage the electrical connection from the motor

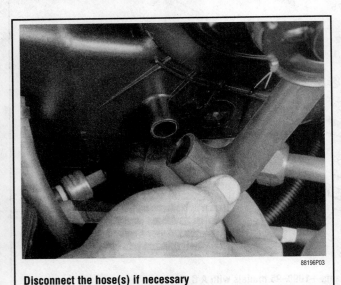

Disconnect the hose(s) if necessary

Loosen the blower motor retainers and remove the motor assembly

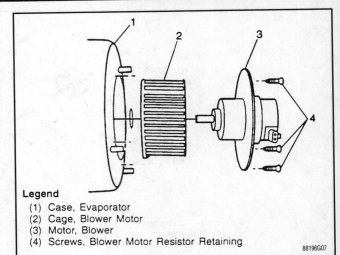

Legend
(1) Case, Evaporator
(2) Cage, Blower Motor
(3) Motor, Blower
(4) Screws, Blower Motor Resistor Retaining

Fig. 9 View of the blower motor assembly—1996–97 models

8. Remove the motor retaining strap and remove the motor and wheels.

To install:

9. Install the motor and wheels.
10. Install the motor retaining strap.
11. Raise the case and Install the lower-to-upper case half screws.
12. Connect the blower motor wires.
13. Connect the blower motor ground straps at the center connector between the motors.
14. Install the shroud/duct.
15. Install the screws securing the shroud to the roof and case.
16. Connect the drain tubes at the rear of the blower-evaporator shroud/duct.
17. Connect the battery ground cable.

1988–95 MODELS

▶ See Figure 11

❊❊ CAUTION

Please refer to Section 1 before discharging the compressor or disconnecting air conditioning lines. Damage to the air conditioning system or personal injury could result. Consult your local laws concerning refrigerant discharge and recycling. In many areas it may be illegal for anyone but a certified technician to service the A/C system. Always use an approved recovery station when discharging the air conditioning.

1. Have the system discharged by a qualified technician using an approved recovery/recycling station.
2. Disconnect the negative battery cable.
3. Disconnect the rear duct by unfastening the screws, clamps and hoses.
4. Disconnect the refrigerant hoses from the evaporator and blower assembly.

➡**Pull back the rubber insulation before disconnecting the high pressure hose**

5. Loosen the ground wire screw and move the wire aside.
6. Disengage the motor electrical connection.

❊❊ WARNING

Before loosening the case screws, support the lower case to prevent damage during removal.

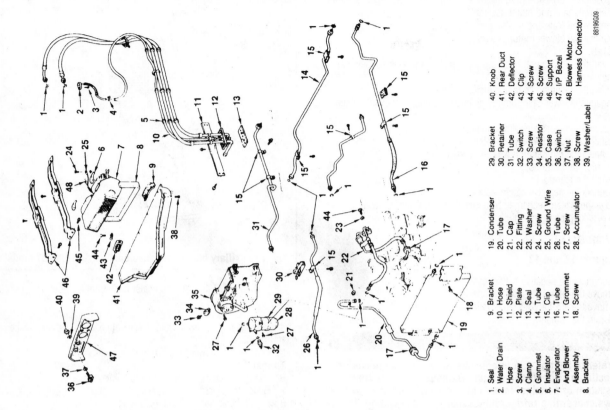

88196G09

1. Seal
2. Water Drain
   Hose
3. Screw
4. Clamp
5. Grommet
6. Insulator
7. Evaporator
   And Blower
   Assembly
8. Bracket

9. Bracket
10. Hose
11. Shield
12. Plate
13. Seal
14. Tube
15. Clip
16. Tube
17. Grommet
18. Screw

19. Condenser
20. Tube
21. Cap
22. Fitting
23. Washer
24. Screw
25. Ground Wire
26. Tube
27. Screw
28. Accumulator

29. Bracket
30. Retainer
31. Tube
32. Switch
33. Screw
34. Resistor
35. Case
36. Switch
37. Nut
38. Screw
39. Washer/Label

40. Knob
41. Rear Duct
42. Deflector
43. Clip
44. Screw
45. Screw
46. Support
47. I/P Bezel
48. Blower Motor
    Harness Connector

Fig. 11 Exploded view of the auxiliary A/C system—1988–95 models

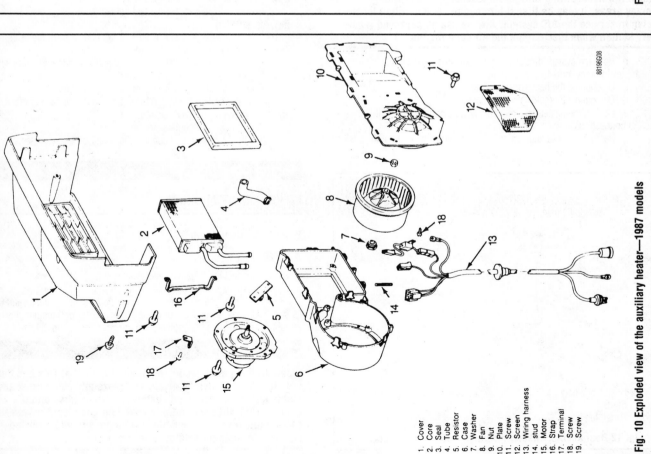

88196G08

1. Cover
2. Core
3. Seal
4. Tube
5. Resistor
6. Case
7. Washer
8. Fan
9. Nut
10. Plate
11. Screw
12. Screen
13. Wiring harness
    stud
14. Motor
15. Motor
16. Strap
17. Terminal
18. Screw
19. Screw

Fig. 10 Exploded view of the auxiliary heater—1987 models

7. Loosen the lower-to-upper evaporator and blower case screws, then remove the lower case and motor assembly.

8. Remove the plate and retaining strap.

9. Remove the blower motor assembly.

To install:

10. Install the blower motor assembly, aligning the wheels so they don't contact the case.

11. Install the retaining strap and plate.

12. Engage the lower case with the motor to the upper case and tighten the screws.

13. Fasten the motor's electrical connection.

14. Install the ground wire and tighten the screw.

15. Connect the refrigerant hoses and install the rubber insulation around the high pressure hose.

16. Install the rear duct.

17. Connect the negative battery cable.

18. Have the system recharged by a qualified technician using an approved recycling/recovery station.

1996–97 MODELS

▶ **See Figures 12 and 13**

1. Disconnect the negative battery cable.
2. Remove the left rear quarter trim panels.
3. Remove the auxiliary heater as follows:
   a. Drain the coolant.

✳✳ CAUTION

Please refer to Section 1 before discharging the compressor or disconnecting air conditioning lines. Damage to the air conditioning system or personal injury could result. Consult your local laws concerning refrigerant discharge and recycling. In many areas, it may be illegal for anyone but a certified technician to service the A/C system. Always use an approved recovery station when discharging the air conditioning.

   b. Have the system discharged by a qualified technician using an approved recovery/recycling station.
   c. Disconnect the heater-to-roof duct.
   d. Disconnect the heater-to-floor duct.
   e. Loosen the heater case retaining screws and disengage the electrical connections.
   f. Remove the A/C and heater cover from the underside of the auxiliary heater.

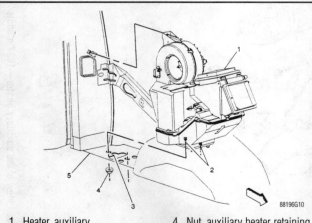

1. Heater, auxiliary
2. Studs
3. Panel, left floor
4. Nut, auxiliary heater retaining
5. Carpet/mat

Fig. 12 Rear auxiliary heater mounting—1996–97 models

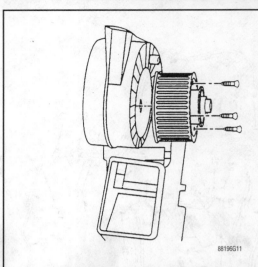

88196G11

Fig. 13 Auxiliary blower motor components—1996–97 models

   g. Disconnect the A/C and heater lines from the underside the auxiliary heater.
   h. Loosen its retaining nuts and remove the auxiliary heater.
4. Disengage the blower motor electrical connections, then loosen the motor retainers.
5. Remove the blower motor from the case.

To install:

6. Engage the motor to the case and tighten the retainers.
7. Fasten the electrical connections to the motor.
8. Install the auxiliary heater as follows:
   a. Install the heater in the van and tighten the retaining nuts to 89 inch lbs. (10 Nm).
   b. Engage the heater and A/C lines to the underside of the heater. Tighten the nut to 18 ft. lbs. (25 Nm).
   c. Install the A/C and heater line cover and fasten the retaining scre▾
   d. Engage the electrical connections.
   e. Connect the heater-to-floor and heater-to-roof ducts.
   f. Have the system recharged by a qualified technician using an approved recycling/recovery station.
   g. Refill the engine coolant system.
9. Install the trim panel and connect the negative battery cables.

Heater Core

REMOVAL & INSTALLATION

Without Air Conditioning

ALL MODELS

1. Disconnect the negative battery cable.
2. Remove the coolant recovery bottle.
3. Place a pan under the van and disconnect the heater intake and out▾let hoses. Quickly remove and plug the hoses and support them in an upright position. Drain the coolant from the heater core into the pan.

✳✳ CAUTION

When draining engine coolant, keep in mind that cats and dogs are attracted to ethylene glycol antifreeze and could drink any that is left in an uncovered container or in puddles on the ground. This will prove fatal in sufficient quantity. Always drain coolant into a sealable container. Coolant should be reused unless it is contaminated or is several years old.

4. Remove the heater distributor duct-to-case attaching screws and the duct-to-engine cover screw. Remove the duct.

5. Remove the engine cover.

6. Remove all the instrument panel attaching screws.

7. Carefully lower the steering column. Raise and support the right side of the instrument panel. Refer to Section 8 for further details.

8. Remove the defroster duct-to-case attaching screws and the two screws attaching the distributor to the heater case.

9. Disconnect the temperature door cable. Carefully fold the cable back and out of the way.

10. Remove the three nuts from the engine compartment side of the distributor case and the screw from the passenger compartment side.

11. Remove the heater case and core assembly.

12. Remove the core retaining straps and remove the core.

To install:

13. Install the core.

14. Install the core retaining straps.

15. Install the heater case and core assembly.

16. Fasten the three nuts on the engine compartment side of the distributor case and the screw on the passenger compartment side.

17. Connect the temperature door cable.

18. Install the defroster duct-to-case attaching screws and the two screws attaching the distributor to the heater case.

19. Install the steering column.

20. Fasten all the instrument panel attaching screws.

21. Install the engine cover.

22. Install the duct. Install the heater distributor duct-to-case attaching screws and the duct-to-engine cover screw.

23. Connect the heater intake and outlet hoses.

24. Fill the cooling system.

25. Install the coolant recovery bottle.

26. Connect the negative battery cable.

With Air Conditioning

1987–89 MODELS

1. Disconnect the battery ground cable.

2. Remove the engine cover.

3. Remove the steering column to instrument panel bolts. Lower the column carefully.

4. Remove the upper and lower instrument panel attaching screws. Remove the radio support bracket screw.

5. Raise and support the right side of the instrument panel.

6. Remove the lower right instrument panel bracket.

7. Remove the vacuum actuator from the kick panel.

8. Disconnect the temperature cable and vacuum hoses at the case. Remove the heater distributor duct from over the engine hump.

9. Remove the two defroster duct-to-firewall attaching screws below the windshield.

10. Under the hood, disconnect and plug the heater hoses at the firewall.

11. Remove the three nuts and one screw (inside) holding the heater case to the firewall.

12. Remove the case from the van. Remove the gasket for access to the screws holding the case together. Remove the temperature cable support bracket. Remove the screws and separate the case. Remove the heater core.

To install:

13. Install the heater core.

14. Assemble the case and fasten the screws.

15. Install the temperature cable support bracket.

16. Position the gasket, then install the case in the van.

17. Fasten the three nuts and one screw (inside) holding the heater case to the firewall.

18. Connect and plug the heater hoses at the firewall.

19. Install the two defroster duct-to-firewall attaching screws below the windshield.

20. Install the heater distributor duct.

21. Connect the temperature cable and vacuum hoses at the case.

22. Install the vacuum actuator at the kick panel.

23. Install the lower right instrument panel bracket.

24. Fasten the radio support bracket screw.

25. Fasten the upper and lower instrument panel attaching screws.

26. Install the steering column to instrument panel bolts.

27. Install the engine cover.

28. Connect the battery ground cable.

29. Refill the cooling system as necessary.

1990–95 MODELS

1. Disconnect the battery ground cable.

2. Remove the engine cover.

3. Remove the steering column-to-instrument panel bolts. Lower the column carefully.

4. Remove the upper and lower instrument panel attaching screws. Remove the radio support bracket screw.

5. Raise and support the right side of the instrument panel.

6. Remove the lower right instrument panel bracket.

7. Remove the vacuum actuator from the kick panel.

8. Disconnect the temperature cable and vacuum hoses at the case. Remove the heater distributor duct from over the engine hump.

9. Remove the two defroster duct-to-firewall attaching screws below the windshield.

10. Under the hood, disconnect and plug the heater hoses at the firewall.

11. Remove the three nuts and one screw (inside) holding the heater case to the firewall.

12. Remove the case from the van. Remove the gasket for access to the screws holding the case together. Remove the temperature cable support bracket. Remove the screws and separate the case. Remove the heater core.

To install:

13. Install the heater core.

14. Assemble the case and fasten the screws.

15. Install the temperature cable support bracket.

16. Position the gasket, then install the case in the van.

17. Fasten the three nuts and one screw (inside) holding the heater case to the firewall.

18. Connect and plug the heater hoses at the firewall.

19. Fasten the two defroster duct-to-firewall attaching screws below the windshield.

20. Install the heater distributor duct.

21. Connect the temperature cable and vacuum hoses at the case.

22. Install the vacuum actuator at the kick panel.

23. Install the lower right instrument panel bracket.

24. Fasten the radio support bracket screw.

25. Fasten the upper and lower instrument panel attaching screws.

26. Fasten the steering column-to-instrument panel bolts.

27. Install the engine cover.

28. Connect the battery ground cable.

29. Refill the cooling system as necessary.

1996–97 MODELS

▶ See Figure 14

1. Drain the coolant.

❄❄ CAUTION

Please refer to Section 1 before discharging the compressor or disconnecting air conditioning lines. Damage to the air conditioning system or personal injury could result. Consult your local laws concerning refrigerant discharge and recycling. In many areas it may be illegal for anyone but a certified technician to service the A/C system. Always use an approved recovery station when discharging the air conditioning.

2. Have the system discharged by a qualified technician using an approved recovery/recycling station.

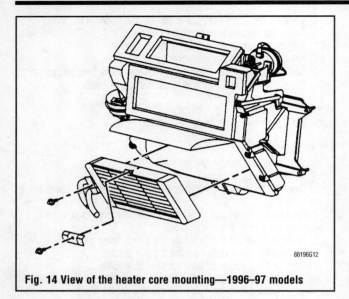

Fig. 14 View of the heater core mounting—1996–97 models

3. Remove the coolant recovery tank and the battery from the van.
4. Remove the A/C accumulator.
5. Disconnect the heater hoses from the core.
6. Remove the right kick panel and knee bolster.
7. Disconnect the outer floor air outlet duct.
8. Loosen the screws front the heater case.
9. Carefully open the heater core access door and loosen the retainers from the core.
10. Remove the heater core.

To install:
11. Install the heater core and fasten the retainers.
12. Carefully close the core access door, then tighten the heater case screws.
13. Connect the outer floor air inlet duct.
14. Unstall the right knee bolster and kick panel.
15. Connect the heater hoses to the core.
16. Install the A/C accumulator.
17. Install the battery and coolant recovery tank.
    a. Have the system recharged by a qualified technician using an approved recycling/recovery station.
    b. Refill the engine coolant system.

Auxiliary Heater and Air Conditioner

1987–95 MODELS

▶ See Figure 15

❉❉ CAUTION

When draining engine coolant, keep in mind that cats and dogs are attracted to ethylene glycol antifreeze and could drink any that is left in an uncovered container or in puddles on the ground. This will prove fatal in sufficient quantity. Always drain coolant into a sealable container. Coolant should be reused unless it is contaminated or is several years old.

1. Drain the cooling system.
2. Disconnect the battery ground cable.
3. Disconnect the heater hoses at the core tubes.
4. Remove the heater case-to-floor studs.
5. Remove the case cover.
6. Disconnect the wiring at the case.
7. Lift the case from the van.
8. Remove the core cover and lift the core and seal from the case.

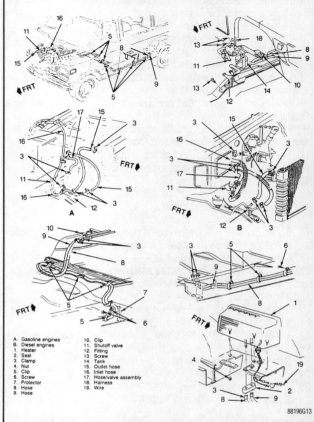

A. Gasoline engines	10. Clip
B. Diesel engines	11. Shutoff valve
1. Heater	12. Fitting
2. Seal	13. Screw
3. Clamp	14. Tank
4. Nut	15. Outlet hose
5. Clip	16. Inlet hose
6. Screw	17. Hose/valve assembly
7. Protector	18. Harness
8. Hose	19. Wire
9. Hose	

Fig. 15 Sectional views of the auxiliary heater plumbing components—1987–95 models

To install:
9. Lower the core and seal into the case.
10. Install the core cover.
11. Install the case in the van.
12. Connect the wiring at the case.
13. Install the case cover.
14. Install the heater case-to-floor studs.
15. Connect the heater hoses at the core tubes.
16. Connect the battery ground cable.
17. Fill the cooling system.

1996–97 MODELS

▶ See Figure 16

1. Disconnect the negative battery cable.
2. Remove the left rear quarter trim panels.
3. Remove the auxiliary heater and A/C as follows:
    a. Drain the coolant.

❉❉ CAUTION

Please refer to Section 1 before discharging the compressor or disconnecting air conditioning lines. Damage to the air conditioning system or personal injury could result. Consult your local laws concerning refrigerant discharge and recycling. In many areas it may be illegal for anyone but a certified technician to service the A/C system. Always use an approved recovery station when discharging the air conditioning.

    b. Have the system discharged by a qualified technician using an approved recovery/recycling station.

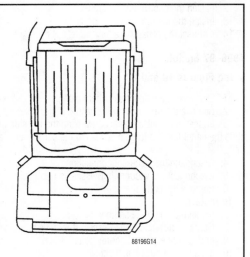

Fig. 16 Heater core assembly—1996–97 models

   c. Disconnect the heater-to-roof duct.

   d. Disconnect the heater-to-floor duct.

   e. Loosen the heater case retaining screws and disengage the electrical connections.

   f. Remove the A/C and heater cover from the underside of the auxiliary heater.

   g. Disconnect the A/C and heater lines from the underside the auxiliary heater.

   h. Loosen the auxiliary heater retaining nuts and remove auxiliary heater.

4. Loosen the retainers from the bottom of the case.

5. Remove the heater core from the case.

To install:

6. Install the heater core in the case and tighten the retainers to the bottom of the case.

7. Install the auxiliary heater as follows:

   a. Install the heater in the van and tighten the retaining nuts to 89 inch lbs. (10 Nm).

   b. Engage the heater and A/C lines to the underside of the heater. Tighten the nut to 18 ft. lbs. (25 Nm).

   c. Install the A/C and heater line cover and fasten the retaining screw.

   d. Engage the electrical connections.

   e. Connect the heater-to-floor and heater-to-roof ducts.

   f. Have the system recharged by a qualified technician using an approved recycling/recovery station.

   g. Refill the engine coolant system.

8. Install the trim panel and connect the negative battery cables.

Air Conditioning Components

REMOVAL & INSTALLATION

Repair or service of air conditioning components is not covered by this manual, because of the risk of personal injury or death, and because of the legal ramifications of servicing these components without the proper EPA certification and experience. Cost, personal injury or death, environmental damage, and legal considerations (such as the fact that it is a federal crime to vent refrigerant into the atmosphere), dictate that the A/C components on your vehicle should be serviced only by a Motor Vehicle Air Conditioning (MVAC) trained, and EPA certified, automotive technician.

If your vehicle's A/C system uses R-12 refrigerant and is in need of recharging, the A/C system can be converted over to R-134a refrigerant (less environmentally harmful and expensive). Refer to Section 1 for additional information on R-12 to R-134a conversions, and for additional considerations dealing with your vehicle's A/C system.

Temperature Control Cable

REMOVAL & INSTALLATION

♦ See Figure 17

The control cable is used on 1987–95 models only. The 1996–97 models utilize vacuum to operate the control doors.

1. Disconnect the negative battery cable.
2. Remove the engine cover and radio.
3. Remove the control assembly.
4. Unfasten the temperature cable retainer from the control assembly and remove the cable eyelet.
5. Disconnect the tab from the slot in the control assembly.
6. Loosen the cable-to-defroster duct screw and retainer.
7. Loosen the cable-to-heater case screw and retainer.
8. Unfasten the adjuster tab retainer from the heater case and remove the adjuster tab.
9. Disconnect the cable-to-heater case tab from the slot in the heater case.
10. Remove the cable.

To install:

11. Attach a wire to the new cable and pull it through from the heater core end of the van.
12. Connect the cable-to-heater case tab to the slot in the case.
13. Connect the adjusting tab to the heater case using the retainer.
14. Fasten the screw and retainer which attach the cable to the heater case.
15. Fasten the screw and retainer which attach the cable to the defroster duct.
16. Connect the tab to the slot in the control assembly.
17. Install the cable outlet to the control assembly using the retainer.
18. Install the control assembly and radio.
19. Install the engine cover and connect the negative battery cable.

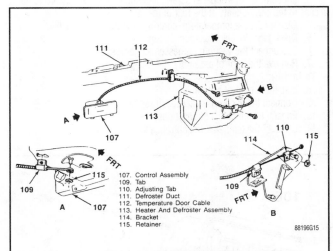

Fig. 17 Temperature control cable routing and mounting—1987–95 models

ADJUSTMENT

1. Remove the instrument panel compartment and door
2. Loosen the cable attaching bolt at the heater case assembly.

→**Ensure that the cable is installed in the bracket on the defroster duct assembly.**

3. Place the temperature lever in the full **COLD** position and hold while tightening the cable attaching screw.
4. Install the instrument panel compartment and door.

Control Panel

REMOVAL & INSTALLATION

1987–90 Models

1. Disconnect the negative battery cable.
2. Remove the headlamp switch control knob.
3. Remove the instrument panel bezel.
4. Remove the control screws.
5. Disconnect the temperature cable eyelet clip and retainer.
6. Remove the control lower right mounting tab through the dash opening.
7. Remove the upper tab and the lower right tab.
8. Disconnect the electrical harness.
9. Disconnect the vacuum harness.
10. Remove the control assembly.

To install:

11. Install the control assembly.
12. Connect the vacuum harness.
13. Connect the electrical harness.
14. Install the upper tab and the lower right tab.
15. Install the control lower right mounting tab through the dash opening.
16. Connect the temperature cable eyelet clip and retainer.
17. Install the control screws.
18. Install the instrument panel bezel.
19. Install the headlamp switch control knob.
20. Connect the negative battery cable.

1991–95 Models

▶ **See Figure 18**

1. Disconnect the negative battery cable.
2. Remove the instrument panel bezel.
3. Loosen the control panel screws and slide the panel forward to gain access to the components at the rear of the unit.
4. Disconnect the temperature control cable from the panel.
5. Disengage the electrical connections.
6. Disconnect the vacuum harnesses as necessary.
7. Remove the control assembly.

To install:

8. Install the control assembly.
9. Connect the vacuum harnesses, if removed.
10. Engage the electrical connections.
11. Connect the temperature control cable.

12. Fasten the control panel screws.
13. Install the instrument panel bezel.
14. Connect the negative battery cable.

1996–97 Models

▶ **See Figures 19 and 20**

1. Disconnect the negative battery cable.
2. Remove the instrument cluster trim plate.
3. Loosen the control panel screw from the left side of the panel and slide the panel forward to gain access to the components at the rear of the unit.
4. Disengage the electrical connections.
5. Disconnect the vacuum harnesses as necessary.
6. Remove the control assembly.

To install:

7. Install the control assembly.
8. Connect the vacuum harnesses, if removed.
9. Engage the electrical connections.
10. Install the control panel screw.
11. Install the instrument cluster trim plate.
12. Connect the negative battery cable.

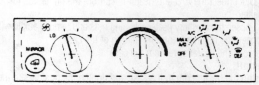

88196G17

Fig. 19 Typical control panel—1996–97 models

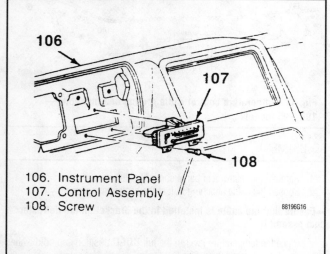

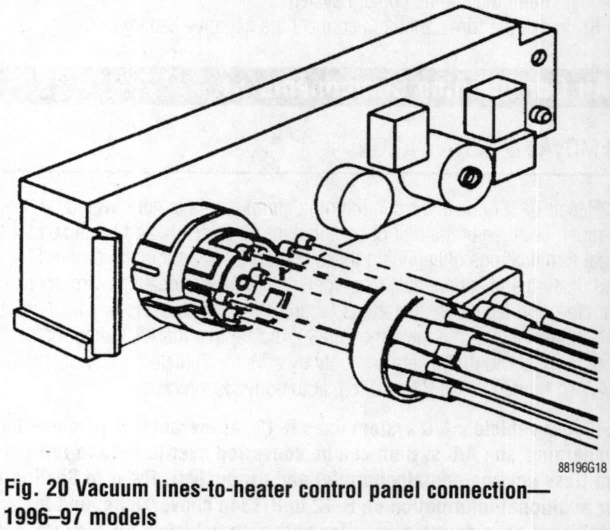

106. Instrument Panel
107. Control Assembly
108. Screw

88196G16

Fig. 18 Control panel mounting—1991–95 models

Fig. 20 Vacuum lines-to-heater control panel connection—1996–97 models

88196G18

Coolant Control Valve

REMOVAL & INSTALLATION

This valve was used on 1987–95 models.

❋❋ CAUTION

When draining engine coolant, keep in mind that cats and dogs are attracted to ethylene glycol antifreeze and could drink any that is left in an uncovered container or in puddles on the ground. This will prove fatal in sufficient quantity. Always drain coolant into a sealable container. Coolant should be reused unless it is contaminated or is several years old.

1. Drain the cooling system.
2. Disconnect the coolant hoses.
3. If necessary, disconnect the vacuum hose.
4. Loosen the screws and remove the valve.

To install:

5. Install the valve and tighten the screws.
6. Connect the vacuum lines, if removed.
7. Connect the coolant hoses and refill the cooling system.

Hot Water Bypass Valve

REMOVAL & INSTALLATION

▶ See Figure 21

This valve was used on 1996–97 models.

❋❋ CAUTION

When draining engine coolant, keep in mind that cats and dogs are attracted to ethylene glycol antifreeze and could drink any that is left in an uncovered container or in puddles on the ground. This will prove fatal in sufficient quantity. Always drain coolant into a sealable container. Coolant should be reused unless it is contaminated or is several years old.

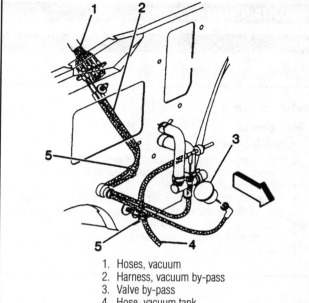

1. Hoses, vacuum
2. Harness, vacuum by-pass
3. Valve by-pass
4. Hose, vacuum tank
5. Clips, retaining

88196G19

Fig. 21 Hot water bypass valve mounting and related components—1996–97 models

1. Drain the cooling system.
2. Remove the heater hose clamps using tool J-39529 or its equivalent
3. Disconnect the heater hoses from the bypass valve(s).
4. Loosen the bolts and remove the valve from the cowl

To install:

5. Install the valve and tighten the bolts to 35 inch lbs. (4 Nm).
6. Connect the heater hoses and install the heater hose clamps using tool J-39529 or its equivalent.
7. Refill the cooling system.

CRUISE CONTROL

General Information

Cruise control maintains a desired vehicle speed under normal driving conditions.

There are two different cruise control systems used on the Chevrolet/GMC full size vans. They are vacuum and electro-motor operated systems.

The vacuum system components are:
- Mode control switches
- Controller (module)
- Servo unit
- Speed sensor
- Vacuum supply
- Electrical and vacuum release switches
- Electrical harness

The Electro-motor system components are:
- Brake release switch
- Multi-function lever
- Module
- VCM or PCM
- Vehicle speed sensor

CRUISE CONTROL TROUBLESHOOTING

Problem	Possible Cause
Will not hold proper speed	Incorrect cable adjustment
	Binding throttle linkage
	Leaking vacuum servo diaphragm
	Leaking vacuum tank
	Faulty vacuum or vent valve
	Faulty stepper motor
	Faulty transducer
	Faulty speed sensor
	Faulty cruise control module
Cruise intermittently cuts out	Clutch or brake switch adjustment too tight
	Short or open in the cruise control circuit
	Faulty transducer
	Faulty cruise control module
Vehicle surges	Kinked speedometer cable or casing
	Binding throttle linkage
	Faulty speed sensor
	Faulty cruise control module
Cruise control inoperative	Blown fuse
	Short or open in the cruise control circuit
	Faulty brake or clutch switch
	Leaking vacuum circuit
	Faulty cruise control switch
	Faulty stepper motor
	Faulty transducer
	Faulty speed sensor
	Faulty cruise control module

Note: Use this chart as a guide. Not all systems will use the components listed.

TCCA6C01

ENTERTAINMENT SYSTEMS

Radio

REMOVAL & INSTALLATION

1987–95 Models

▶ See Figure 22

1. Disconnect the negative battery cable.
2. If necessary, remove the engine cover and air cleaner.
3. If necessary, remove the lower instrument panel extension.
4. Remove the radio bezel.
5. Remove the knobs, washers and nuts from the front of the radio.
6. Remove the rear bracket screw and separate the bracket from the radio.
7. Disengage the electrical connections.
8. Remove the radio.

To install:
9. Install the radio and engage the electrical connections.
10. Engage the radio to the bracket and tighten the screw.
11. Install the washers, nuts and knobs on the front of the radio.
12. Install the radio bezel.
13. If removed, install the lower instrument panel extension.
14. If removed, install the air cleaner and engine cover.
15. Connect the negative battery cable.

1996–97 Models

▶ See Figure 23

1. Disconnect the negative battery cable.
2. Remove the radio bezel.
3. Remove the lower instrument panel extension.
4. Remove bracket screw.
5. Remove the radio nuts.
6. Separate the bracket from the radio.
7. Disengage the electrical connections and antenna.
8. Remove the radio.

To install:
9. Install the radio, then engage the antenna and electrical connections.
10. Engage the radio to the bracket and tighten the screw.
11. Install the radio nuts.
12. If removed, install the lower instrument panel extension.
13. Install the radio bezel.
14. Connect the negative battery cable.

CD Player

REMOVAL & INSTALLATION

1996–97 Models

▶ See Figure 24

1. Disconnect the negative battery cable.
2. Remove the instrument panel trim panel filler and trim panel.
3. Press down on the retaining tabs to disengage the unit from the bracket.
4. Slide the unit forward and disengage the electrical connections.

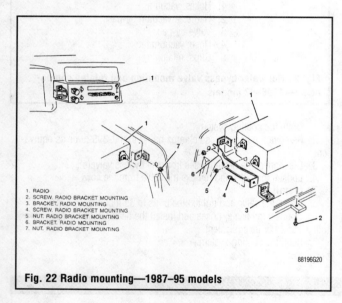

1. RADIO
2. SCREW, RADIO BRACKET MOUNTING
3. BRACKET, RADIO MOUNTING
4. SCREW, RADIO BRACKET MOUNTING
5. NUT, RADIO BRACKET MOUNTING
6. BRACKET, RADIO MOUNTING
7. NUT, RADIO BRACKET MOUNTING

88196G20

Fig. 22 Radio mounting—1987–95 models

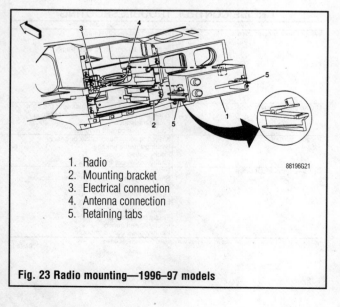

1. Radio
2. Mounting bracket
3. Electrical connection
4. Antenna connection
5. Retaining tabs

88196G21

Fig. 23 Radio mounting—1996–97 models

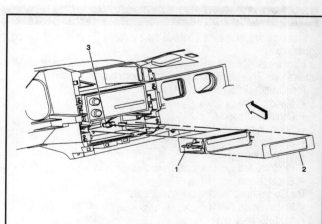

1. CD player
2. Trim panel
3. Electrical connection

88196G22

Fig. 24 Compact disc player mounting—1996–97 models

To install:

5. Engage the electrical connections and install the unit into the bracket.
6. Press the CD player inward to engage the retaining tabs.
7. Install the instrument panel trim panel and trim panel filler.
8. Connect the negative battery cable.

Speakers

REMOVAL & INSTALLATION

1987–95 Models

FRONT LEFT

▶ **See Figure 25**

The front speakers on 1987–95 models are located in the instrument panel.
1. Disconnect the negative battery cable.
2. If necessary, remove the instrument panel bezel.
3. Remove the instrument cluster.
4. Loosen the speaker screws and disengage the electrical connections.
5. Remove the speaker.

To install:

6. Install the speaker and engage the electrical connections.
7. Install the screws and tighten them to 9 inch lbs. (1 Nm).
8. Install the instrument cluster.
9. Install the instrument panel bezel, if removed.
10. Connect the negative battery cable.

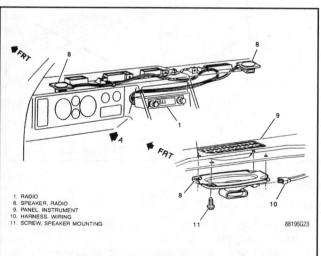

1. RADIO
8. SPEAKER, RADIO
9. PANEL, INSTRUMENT
10. HARNESS, WIRING
11. SCREW, SPEAKER MOUNTING

88196G23

Fig. 25 Front speaker mounting and related components—1987–95 models

FRONT RIGHT

1. Disconnect the negative battery cable and remove the engine cover.
2. Remove the right door lock pillar garnish molding and hinge pillar molding.
3. Remove the radio bezel and radio support bracket screw.
4. Unfasten the instrument panel retainers and pull the panel forward just enough to access the speaker.
5. Disengage the electrical connections, loosen the retaining screws and remove the speaker.

To install:

6. Install the speaker, tighten the screws to 9 inch lbs. (1 Nm) and engage the electrical connections.
7. Push the instrument panel into position and tighten its retainers.
8. Tighten the radio bracket screw and install the radio bezel.
9. Install the right door hinge pillar molding and garnish molding.
10. Install the engine cover and connect the negative battery cable.

REAR CORNER

▶ **See Figure 26**

1. Remove the rear garnish molding.
2. Loosen the speaker housing screws, disengage the electrical connections and remove the housing.
3. Loosen the speaker retaining screws and remove the speaker.

To install:

4. Install the speaker and tighten the screws to 9 inch lbs. (1 Nm).
5. Engage the electrical connections.
6. Install the speaker housing and tighten the screws to 17 inch lbs. (2 Nm).
7. Install the rear garnish.

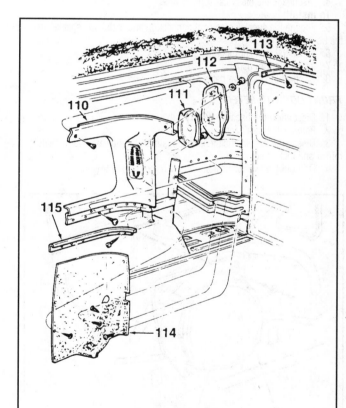

110. Upper Corner Trim Panel
111. Speaker
112. Speaker Insulation
113. Rear Door Upper Molding
114. Lower Corner Trim Panel
115. Trim Strip

88196G24

Fig. 26 Remove the trim panel to gain access to the rear speaker—1987–95 models

REAR SIDE

1. Disconnect the negative battery cable.
2. Remove the rear trim panel screws and pull the panel out just enough to access the speaker.
3. Disengage the electrical connection.

To install:

4. Install the speaker and tighten the retaining nuts.
5. Engage the electrical connection.
6. Install the rear trim panel screws and connect the negative battery cable.

1996–97 Models

FRONT

◆ **See Figure 27**

The front speakers on 1996–97 models are mounted in the door panels.
1. Disconnect the negative battery cable.
2. Remove the door trim panel.
3. Loosen the speaker retaining screws and slide the speaker out of the housing.
4. Disengage the electrical connections.

To install:

5. Engage the speaker electrical connection and install the speaker in the housing.
6. Install the speaker retaining screws.
7. Install the trim panel.
8. Connect the negative battery cable.

FRONT DOOR TWEETER

1. Disconnect the negative battery cable.
2. Remove the trim panel.
3. Disengage the electrical connections from the power window switch, mirror and lock, if equipped.
4. Drill out the tweeter heat stakes, then remove the tweeter.

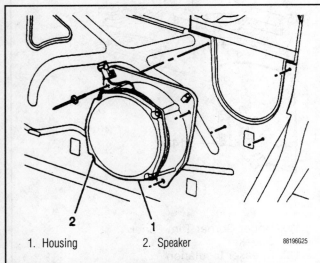

1. Housing   2. Speaker   88196G25

Fig. 27 Front door speaker mounting—1996–97 models

To install:

5. Install the tweeter.
6. Engage the electrical connections.
7. Install the trim panel and connect the negative battery cable.

REAR DOOR

◆ **See Figure 28**

1. Disconnect the negative battery cable.
2. Remove the door trim panel.
3. Loosen the speaker retaining screws and slide the speaker out of the housing.
4. Disengage the electrical connections.

To install:

5. Engage the speaker electrical connection and install the speaker in the housing.
6. Install the speaker retaining screws.
7. Install the trim panel.
8. Connect the negative battery cable.

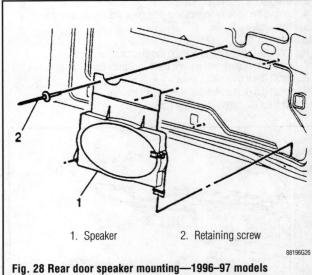

1. Speaker   2. Retaining screw

88196G26

Fig. 28 Rear door speaker mounting—1996–97 models

REAR HEADER

◆ **See Figures 29 and 30**

1. If equipped, carefully pry the speaker grille from the housing.
2. If equipped, remove the header trim panel.
3. Loosen the speaker retaining screws and slide the speaker out of the housing.
4. Disengage the electrical connections.

To install:

5. Engage the speaker electrical connection and install the speaker in the housing.
6. Install the speaker retaining screws.
7. If equipped, press the speaker grille into the housing.
8. If equipped, install the trim panel.

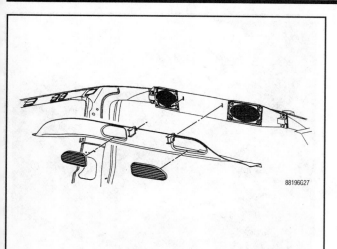

Fig. 29 If equipped, remove the two rear speaker grilles and the header trim panel—1996–97 models

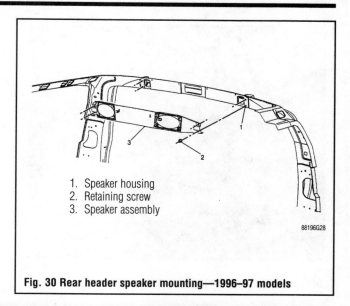

1. Speaker housing
2. Retaining screw
3. Speaker assembly

Fig. 30 Rear header speaker mounting—1996–97 models

WINDSHIELD WIPERS

Blade and Arm

REMOVAL & INSTALLATION

1987–95 Models

▶ **See Figures 31 and 32**

1. To remove the arm, pull the wiper arms away from the glass and release the clip underneath. The wiper arms are splined to the shafts and can be pulled off.

➡**Be sure to matchmark or note the position of the blade or arm before removal.**

2. Disconnect the washer hose.
3. To remove the blade, use a narrow prytool to release the retainer spring then remove the blade.
4. To install the blade, simply snap it back into place.
5. To install the arm, connect the washer hose, position the arm over the shaft and press down. Make sure you install the arms in the same position before removal.

1996–97 Models

▶ **See Figure 33 (p. 25)**

1. Turn the ignition switch to the **ACCY** position and set the wiper switch to the **PULSE** position.
2. Turn the ignition **OFF** when the wipers are in the innerwipe position and not moving (refer to the accompanying illustration).
3. Disconnect the washer hose.
4. Remove the cover from the nut and loosen the nut.
5. Remove the wiper arm.
6. Remove the wiper blade after pushing in the button on the wiper blade clip.

To install:

7. To install the blade, simply snap it back into place.
8. Install the wiper arm and tighten the nut to 19 ft. lbs. (26 Nm). Install the nut cover.

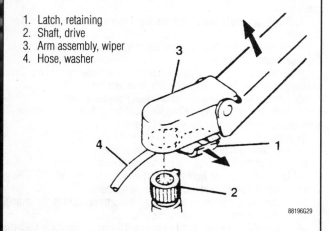

1. Latch, retaining
2. Shaft, drive
3. Arm assembly, wiper
4. Hose, washer

Fig. 31 Release the retaining clip to remove the wiper arm— 1987–95 models

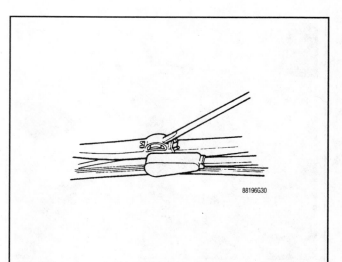

Fig. 32 Insert a prytool into the slot to disengage the blade retaining pin, then remove the blade assembly—1987–95 models

Disconnect the washer hose from the nozzle

Remove the cover from the nut . . .

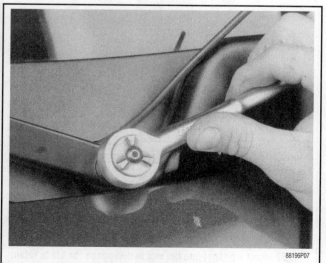

. . . then loosen the wiper arm retaining nut

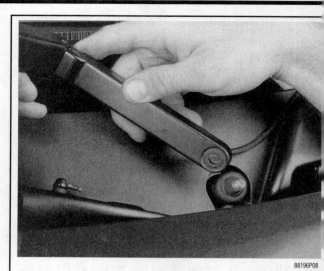

Remove the wiper arms from the van

➥The wiper arms are stamped LH (left hand) and RH (right hand) and should not be interchanged

9. Connect the washer hose and check the wipers for proper operation.

Wiper Motor

REMOVAL & INSTALLATION

1987–95 Models
▶ See Figure 34

1. Be sure that the wiper motor arm is in the **PARK** position. The wiper arms should be in their normal **OFF** position.
2. Open the hood and disconnect the battery ground cable.
3. Raise the hood and remove the exposed cowl cover screws.
4. Remove the wiper arms. This can be done by pulling the wiper arms away from the glass to release the clip underneath. The wiper arms are splined to the shafts and can be pulled off.
5. Unfasten the remaining screws securing the cowl panel and remove it.
6. Loosen the nuts holding the transmission linkage to the wiper motor crank arm.
7. Disengage the power feed to the wiper arm at the connector next to the radio.
8. Remove the flex hose from the left defroster outlet to gain access to the wiper motor screws.
9. Remove the one screw holding the left hand heater duct to the engine shroud and move the heater duct down and out.
10. Remove the windshield washer hoses from the pump.
11. Remove the 3 screws holding the wiper motor to the cowl and lift the wiper motor out from under the dashboard.
To install:
12. Position the wiper motor in the PARK position.
13. Position the wiper motor under the dashboard.
14. Install the 3 screws holding the wiper motor to the cowl.
15. Install the windshield washer hoses at the pump.
16. Install the one screw holding the left-hand heater duct to the engine.
17. Install the flex hose at the left defroster outlet.
18. Engage the power feed to the wiper arm at the connector next to the radio.
19. Tighten the nuts holding the transmission linkage to the wiper motor crank arm.
20. Install the cowl panel.

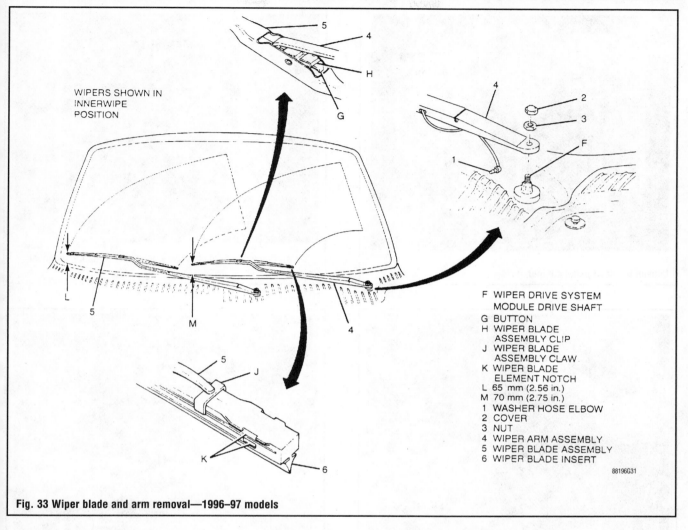

F WIPER DRIVE SYSTEM
  MODULE DRIVE SHAFT
G BUTTON
H WIPER BLADE
  ASSEMBLY CLIP
J WIPER BLADE
  ASSEMBLY CLAW
K WIPER BLADE
  ELEMENT NOTCH
L 65 mm (2.56 in.)
M 70 mm (2.75 in.)
1 WASHER HOSE ELBOW
2 COVER
3 NUT
4 WIPER ARM ASSEMBLY
5 WIPER BLADE ASSEMBLY
6 WIPER BLADE INSERT

88196G31

Fig. 33 Wiper blade and arm removal—1996–97 models

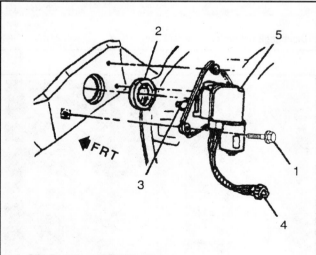

1. BOLT, 4 N·m (35 LBS. IN.)
2. SEAL
3. CRANK ARM
4. HARNESS, WIPER MOTOR
5. ASSEMBLY, WIPER MOTOR

88196G32

Fig. 34 Wiper motor mounting and related components—1987–95 models

21. Install the wiper arms.
22. Install the cowl cover screws.
23. Connect the battery ground cable.
24. Be sure that the wiper motor arm is in the **PARK** position. The wiper arms should be in their normal **OFF** position.

1996–97 Models

▶ **See Figures 35, 36 and 37 (p. 27)**

1. Disconnect the negative battery cable.
2. Disconnect the wiper drive system module (wiper linkage assembly) as follows:
   a. Remove the wiper arms and air inlet screen (cowl panel).
   b. Disengage the electrical connection from the wiper motor.
   c. Loosen the retaining bolts and remove the module.
3. Using tool J-39232 or its equivalent, disconnect the drive link from the wiper motor crank arm.
4. Loosen the wiper motor bolts and remove the wiper motor.
To install:
5. Install the wiper motor and tighten the bolts to 71 inch lbs. (8 Nm).
6. Using tool J-39529 or its equivalent, connect the drive link to the wiper motor crank arm.
7. Install the wiper drive system module as follows:
   a. Install the module and tighten the bolts to 71 inch lbs. (8 Nm).
   b. Engage the electrical connection to the wiper motor.
   c. Install the air inlet screen and wiper arms.
8. Connect the negative battery cable and check for proper operation.

Loosen the cowl panel's upper . . .

88196P09

. . . so that you can access the washer hoses and disconnect them

88196P12

. . . and lower retaining screws

88196P10

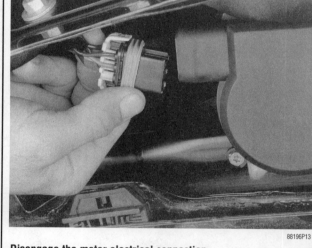

Disengage the motor electrical connection

88196P13

Separate the two halves of the cowl panel and raise them just enough . . .

88196P11

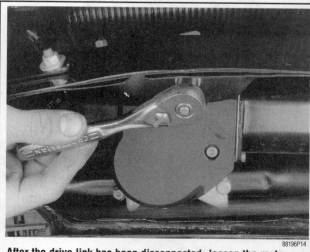

After the drive link has been disconnected, loosen the motor retainers

88196P14

Remove the wiper motor from the engine compartment

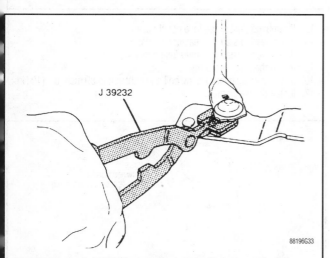

Fig. 35 Use tool J-39232 or equivalent to disconnect the drive link from the wiper motor crank arm—1996–97 models

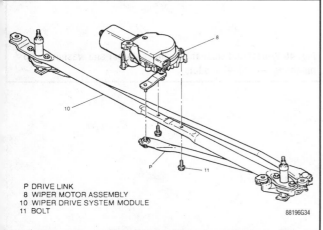

P DRIVE LINK
8 WIPER MOTOR ASSEMBLY
10 WIPER DRIVE SYSTEM MODULE
11 BOLT

Fig. 36 Once the module and wiring have been disconnected, loosen the retainers and remove the wiper motor—1996–97 models

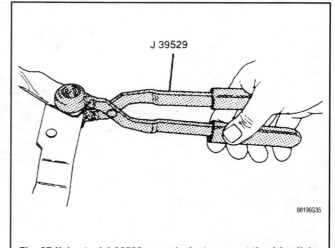

Fig. 37 Using tool J-39529 or equivalent, connect the drive link to the wiper motor crank arm

Windshield Washer Motor

REMOVAL & INSTALLATION

1987–91 Models

▶ **See Figure 38**

1. Disconnect the negative battery cable.
2. Disengage the electrical connection and fluid tubes from the motor.
3. Remove the motor from the bracket.

To install:

4. Install the motor in the bracket, then engage the electrical connections and fluid tubes.
5. Connect the negative battery cable.

1992–95 Models

▶ **See Figure 39**

1. Disconnect the negative battery cable and the hose from the washer pump.
2. Remove the solvent container by sliding it off the bracket.

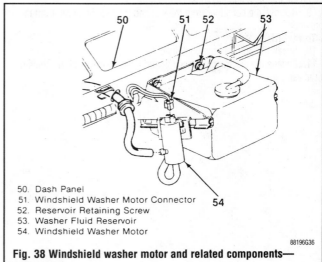

50. Dash Panel
51. Windshield Washer Motor Connector
52. Reservoir Retaining Screw
53. Washer Fluid Reservoir
54. Windshield Washer Motor

Fig. 38 Windshield washer motor and related components—1987–91 models

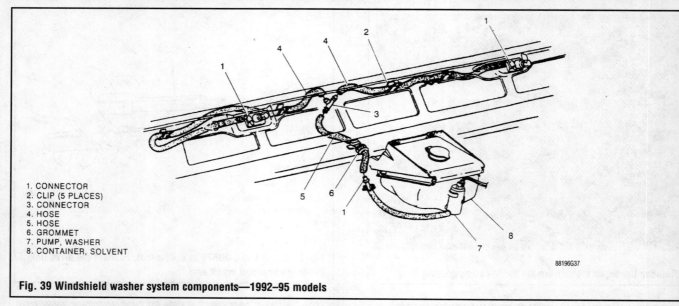

1. CONNECTOR
2. CLIP (5 PLACES)
3. CONNECTOR
4. HOSE
5. HOSE
6. GROMMET
7. PUMP, WASHER
8. CONTAINER, SOLVENT

88196G37

Fig. 39 Windshield washer system components—1992–95 models

3. Disengage the electrical connection from the pump.
4. Remove the washer pump by sliding the stem up and off the seal.

To install:

5. Install the washer pump by pushing the stem down until it is fully seated in the seal.
6. Engage the pump electrical connection and install the solvent container by sliding it into the bracket.
7. Connect the negative battery cable and check for proper operation.

1996–97 Models

▶ **See Figure 40**

1. Disconnect the negative battery cable.
2. Remove the watershield from the front fender.
3. Loosen the solvent container-to-body bolt.
4. Remove the horn assembly.
5. If necessary, remove the main fuse panel.
6. If necessary, detach the master cylinder without disconnecting the lines.
7. If necessary, remove the fuse panel base.
8. Lift the solvent container up enough to access the underneath and disengage the hose and electrical connection.
9. Remove the container from the van and remove the pump from the container.

To install:

10. Install the pump in the container.
11. Engage the electrical connection and hose, then install the container in the van.

12. If removed, install the fuse panel base.
13. If removed, install the master cylinder.
14. If removed, install the main fuse panel.
15. Install the horn assembly.
16. Install the container-to-body bolt and tighten it to 89 inch lbs. (10 Nm).
17. Install the watershield.

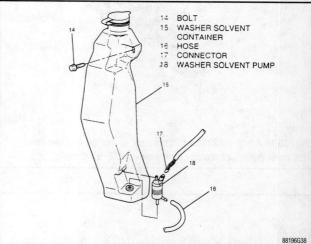

14 BOLT
15 WASHER SOLVENT CONTAINER
16 HOSE
17 CONNECTOR
18 WASHER SOLVENT PUMP

88196G38

Fig. 40 Windshield washer solvent container and washer pump mounting—1996–97 models

INSTRUMENTS AND SWITCHES

❋❋ WARNING

Many solid state electrical components utilized in these vehicles can be damaged by Electrostatic Discharge (ESD). Some of these vehicles will display a label informing you that they will be damaged by ESD and some will not have labels, but they may be damaged also. To avoid possible damage to any of these components, follow the steps outlined below in Handling Electrostatic Discharge (ESD) Sensitive Parts.

Handling Electrostatic Discharge (ESD) Sensitive Parts

♦ See Figure 41

1. Body movement produces an electrostatic charge. To discharge personal static electricity, touch a ground point (metal) on the vehicle. This should be performed any time you:
   - slide across the vehicle seat
   - sit down or get up
   - do any walking
2. Do not touch any exposed terminals on components or connectors with your fingers or any tools.
3. Never use jumper wires, ground a terminal on a component, use test equipment on any component or terminal unless instructed to in a diagnostic or testing procedure. When using test equipment, always connect the ground lead first.

NOTICE

CONTENTS SENSITIVE
TO
STATIC ELECTRICITY

88196G39

Fig. 41 Typical Electrostatic Discharge (ESD) label

Instrument Cluster

REMOVAL & INSTALLATION

1987–90 Models

♦ See Figure 42

1. Disconnect the battery ground cable.
2. Reach up behind the cluster, depress the speedometer cable retaining tang and pull out the cable.
3. On G-series models, remove the clock set stem knob.
4. Remove the cluster bezel retaining screws.

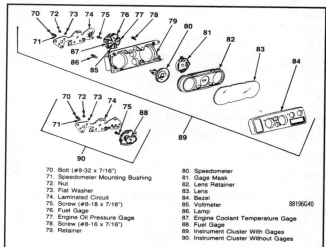

70. Bolt (#8-32 x 7/16")
71. Speedometer Mounting Bushing
72. Nut
73. Flat Washer
74. Laminated Circuit
75. Screw (#8-18 x 7/16")
76. Fuel Gage
77. Engine Oil Pressure Gage
78. Screw (#8-16 x 7/16")
79. Retainer
80. Speedometer
81. Gage Mask
82. Lens Retainer
83. Lens
84. Bezel
85. Voltmeter
86. Lamp
87. Engine Coolant Temperature Gage
88. Fuel Gage
89. Instrument Cluster With Gages
90. Instrument Cluster Without Gages

88196G40

Fig. 42 Exploded view of the instrument cluster and gauge mounting components—1987–90 models

5. Remove the cluster bezel.
6. Remove the cluster retaining screws.
7. Pull the top of the cluster away from the panel and lift out the bottom of the cluster. Pull the cluster out just far enough to unplug the wiring and remove the cluster.

To install:

8. Engage the wiring harness and install the cluster in the panel.
9. Install the cluster retaining screws.
10. Install the bezel and tighten the retaining screws.
11. On G-series models, install the clock set stem knob.
12. Connect the speedometer cable.
13. Connect the negative battery cable and check for proper operation.

1991–95 Models

♦ See Figure 43

1. Set the parking brake, block the wheels and place the transmission in **LOW** gear.
2. Disconnect the negative battery cable.
3. If equipped, tilt the steering wheel to the fully down position.

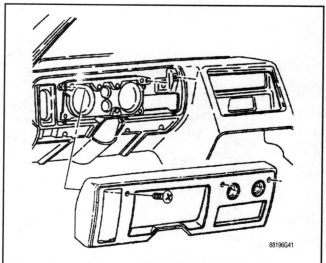

88196G41

Fig. 43 Instrument cluster mounting—1991–95 models

4. If equipped, remove the rear heater and fan control knobs.
5. Loosen the bezel screws and remove the bezel.
6. Lloosen the cluster screws, slide the cluster forward and disengage the electrical connections.
7. Remove the cluster.

To install:

8. Engage the electrical connections and install the cluster. Tighten the screws to 22 inch lbs. (2.5 Nm).
9. Install the bezel and tighten the screws.
10. If removed, install the heater and fan control knobs.
11. Connect the negative battery cable.
12. Set the transmission in **PARK**.
13. Check for proper operation.

1996–97 Models

▶ **See Figure 44**

1. Set the parking brake, block the wheels and place the transmission in **LOW** gear.
2. Disconnect the negative battery cable.
3. Remove the instrument cluster lower trim filler trim panel and trim panel.
4. If equipped, tilt the steering wheel to the fully down position.
5. Loosen the cluster screws, slide the cluster forward and disengage the electrical connections.
6. Remove the cluster.

To install:

7. Engage the electrical connections and install the cluster. Tighten the screws to 18 inch lbs. (2 Nm).
8. Install the cluster trim panel and filler trim panel.
9. Connect the negative battery cable.
10. Set the transmission in **PARK**.
11. Check for proper operation.

Gauges

REMOVAL & INSTALLATION

1987–90 Models

The gauges on these models can be replaced individually as follows:
1. Remove the instrument cluster.
2. If equipped, remove the lens.

3. Disconnect the lamp socket assemblies.
4. Remove the laminated circuit, then remove the cluster case from the bezel.
5. Loosen the gauge bolts and remove the gauge.
6. Installation is the reverse of removal.

1996–97 Models

The gauges are an integral part of the cluster assembly. If any of the gauges is found to be defective, the whole assembly must be replaced.

Headlight Switch

REMOVAL & INSTALLATION

1987–95 Models

▶ **See Figure 45**

1. Disconnect the negative battery cable.
2. Remove the knob assembly as follows:
   a. Pull the knob to the low beam position.
   b. Press the retaining pin out of the switch and remove the knob.
3. Loosen the lower trim panel screws and remove the panel.
4. Loosen the switch nut and remove the switch.

To install:

5. Install the switch and tighten the nut.
6. Install the trim panel and tighten the screws.
7. Install the knob assembly into the switch assembly.
8. Connect the negative battery cable.

1996–97 Models

▶ **See Figure 46**

1. Disconnect the negative battery cable.
2. Remove the instrument cluster lower trim filler panel and trim panel.
3. Disengage the electrical connection from the switch.
4. Remove the switch by releasing the trim panel retainers from the switch.

To install:

5. Install the switch into the trim panel and engage the electrical connection.
6. Install the instrument cluster trim panel and lower trim panel filler.
7. Connect the negative battery cable and check for proper operation.

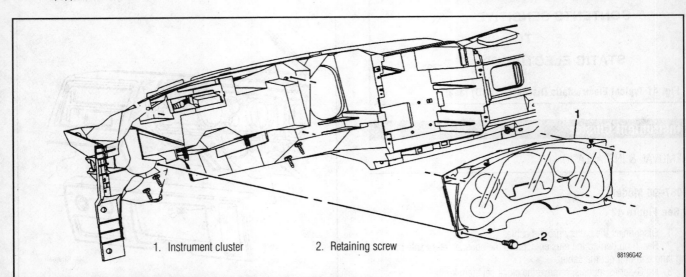

1. Instrument cluster   2. Retaining screw

88196G42

Fig. 44 Exploded view of the instrument cluster mounting—1996–97 models

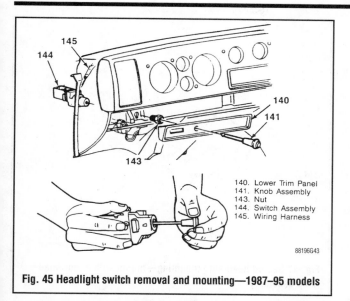

Fig. 45 Headlight switch removal and mounting—1987–95 models

140. Lower Trim Panel
141. Knob Assembly
143. Nut
144. Switch Assembly
145. Wiring Harness

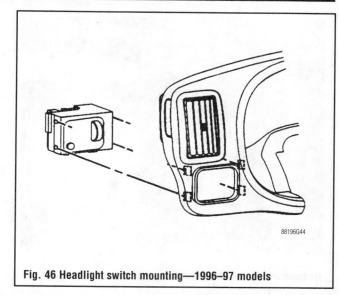

Fig. 46 Headlight switch mounting—1996–97 models

LIGHTING

Headlights

REMOVAL & INSTALLATION

Sealed Beam

▶ See Figures 47 and 48

1. Remove the headlight bezel by unfastening the attaching screws.
2. Remove the spring (if any) from the retaining ring and disengage it from the headlamp adjusting screws.

3. Disconnect the wiring harness connector.

➡ **Do not disturb the adjusting screws.**

4. Remove the retaining ring and the headlamp.
To install:
5. Install the headlamp in the retaining ring.

➡ **The number which is molded into the lens must be at the top.**

6. Install the headlamp assembly, twisting the ring slightly to engage the adjusting screws.
7. Install the retaining ring spring and check the operation of the unit. Install the bezel.

Remove the headlight bezel assembly screws

Remove the bezel assembly

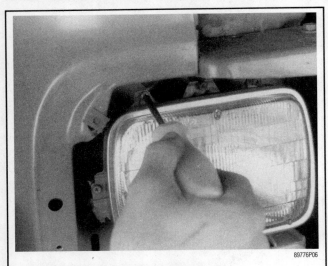

Remove the headlight retaining ring screws

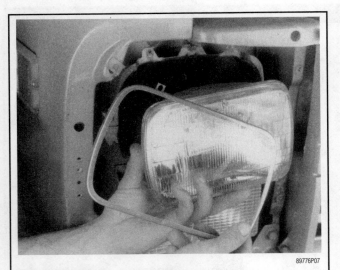

Hold the headlight and remove the retaining ring

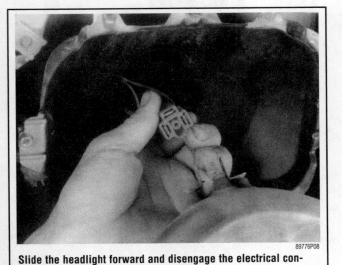

Slide the headlight forward and disengage the electrical connection

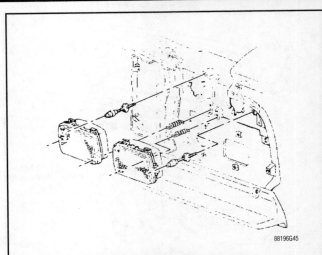

Fig. 47 Sealed headlamp mounting—model with a four headlamp assembly

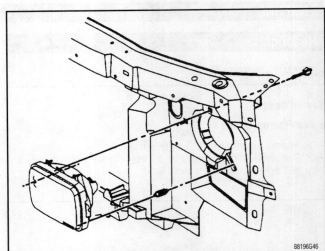

Fig. 48 Sealed headlamp mounting—model with a two headlamp assembly

Composite Type

▶ See Figure 49

BULB

1. Make sure the headlight switch is in the **OFF** position.
2. Reach behind the grille and disengage the electrical connector from the bulb.
3. Turn the bulb counterclockwise and disengage it from the headlamp.
4. Remove the bulb.

To install:

5. Insert the bulb and turn it clockwise to engage it in the headlamp.
6. Engage the electrical connection.

LENS

1. Remove the grille assembly.
2. Disconnect the negative battery cable.
3. Disengage the bulb socket's electrical connection.
4. Loosen the screws securing the lens housing to the frame.
5. Loosen the bolt securing the lens housing to the frame and remove the lens.
6. Installation is the reverse of removal.

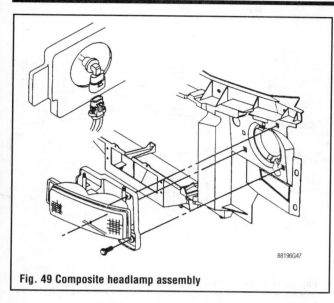

Fig. 49 Composite headlamp assembly

Loosen the headlight lens housing-to-frame bolt

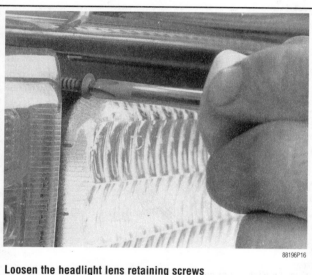

Loosen the headlight lens retaining screws

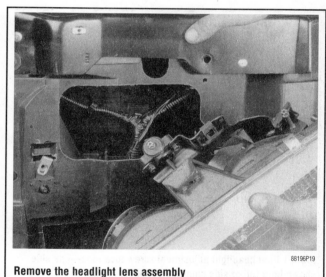

Remove the headlight lens assembly

AIMING THE HEADLIGHTS

▶ See Figures 50, 51, 52, 53 and 54

The headlights must be properly aimed to provide the best, safest road illumination. The lights should be checked for proper aim and adjusted as necessary. Certain state and local authorities have requirements for headlight aiming; these should be checked before adjustment is made.

✳✳ CAUTION

About once a year, when the headlights are replaced or any time front end work is performed on your vehicle, the headlight should be accurately aimed by a reputable repair shop using the proper equipment. Headlights not properly aimed can make it virtually impossible to see and may blind other drivers on the road, possibly causing an accident. Note that the following procedure is a temporary fix, until you can take your vehicle to a repair shop for a proper adjustment.

Disengage the bulb's electrical connection

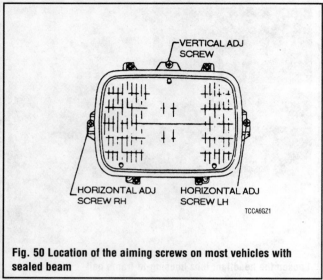

Fig. 50 Location of the aiming screws on most vehicles with sealed beam

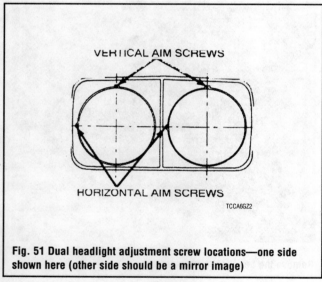

Fig. 51 Dual headlight adjustment screw locations—one side shown here (other side should be a mirror image)

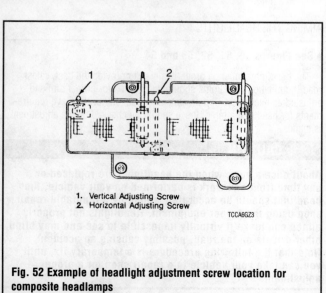

1. Vertical Adjusting Screw
2. Horizontal Adjusting Screw

Fig. 52 Example of headlight adjustment screw location for composite headlamps

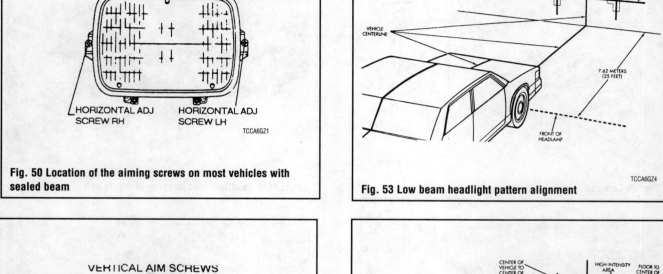

Fig. 53 Low beam headlight pattern alignment

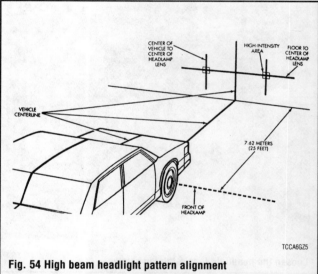

Fig. 54 High beam headlight pattern alignment

Headlight adjustment may be temporarily made using a wall, as described below, or on the rear of another vehicle. When adjusted, the lights should not glare in oncoming car or truck windshields, nor should they illuminate the passenger compartment of vehicles driving in front of you. These adjustments are rough and should always be fine-tuned by a repair shop which is equipped with headlight aiming tools. Improper adjustments may be both dangerous and illegal.

For most of the vehicles covered by this manual, horizontal and vertical aiming of each sealed beam unit is provided by two adjusting screws which move the retaining ring and adjusting plate against the tension of a coil spring. There is no adjustment for focus; this is done during headlight manufacturing.

➡**Because the composite headlight assembly is bolted into position, no adjustment should be necessary or possible. Some applications, however, may be bolted to an adjuster plate or may be retained by adjusting screws. If so, follow this procedure when adjusting the lights, BUT always have the adjustment checked by a reputable shop.**

Before removing the headlight bulb or disturbing the headlamp in any way, note the current settings in order to ease headlight adjustment upon reassembly. If the high or low beam setting of the old lamp still works, this can be done using the wall of a garage or a building:

1. Park the vehicle on a level surface, with the fuel tank about ½ full and with the vehicle empty of all extra cargo (unless normally carried). The vehicle should be facing a wall which is no less than 6 feet (1.8m) high and 12 feet (3.7m) wide. The front of the vehicle should be about 25 feet (7.6m) from the wall.

2. If aiming is to be performed outdoors, it is advisable to wait until dusk in order to properly see the headlight beams on the wall. If done in a garage, darken the area around the wall as much as possible by closing shades or hanging cloth over the windows.

3. Turn the headlights **ON** and mark the wall at the center of each light's low beam, then switch on the "brights" and mark the center of each light's high beam. A short length of masking tape which is visible from the front of the vehicle may be used. Although marking all four positions is advisable, marking one position from each light should be sufficient.

4. If neither beam on one side is working, and if another like-sized vehicle is available, park the second one in the exact spot where the vehicle was and mark the beams using the same-side light. Then switch the vehicles so the one to be aimed is back in the original spot. It must be parked no closer to or farther away from the wall than the second vehicle.

5. Perform any necessary repairs, but make sure the vehicle is not moved, or is returned to the exact spot from which the lights were marked. Turn the headlights **ON** and adjust the beams to match the marks on the wall.

6. Have the headlight adjustment checked as soon as possible by a reputable repair shop.

Signal and Marker Lights

REMOVAL & INSTALLATION

Front Turn Signal and Parking Lights

1987–95 MODELS

◆ See Figure 55

1. Disconnect the negative battery cable.
2. Remove the four bezel retaining screws.
3. Remove the bezel.
4. Remove the parking lamp retainers.
5. Remove the parking lamp.
6. Disengage the electrical connector from the parking lamp.
7. To remove a light bulb with retaining pins from its socket, grasp the

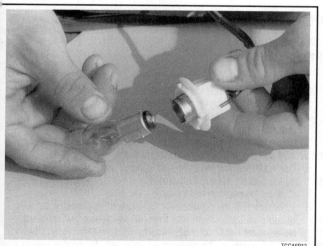

Depress and twist this type of bulb counterclockwise, then pull the bulb straight from its socket

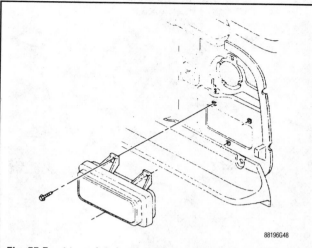

Fig. 55 Front turn signal and parking light mounting—1987–95 models

bulb, then gently depress and twist it ⅛ turn counterclockwise, and pull it from the socket.

8. To remove a light bulb with a flat base (and no retaining pins), simply grasp and pull it straight from its socket.

To install:

9. Before installing a light bulb into the socket, ensure that all electrical contact surfaces are free of corrosion or dirt.

➡**Before installing the light bulb, note the positions of the two retaining pins on the bulb. They will likely be at different heights on the bulb, to ensure that the bulb is installed correctly. If, when installing the bulb, it does not turn easily, do not force it. Remove the bulb and rotate it 180 degrees from its former position, then reinsert it into the bulb socket.**

10. Insert the light bulb into the socket and, while depressing the bulb, twist it ⅛ turn clockwise until the two pins on the light bulb are properly engaged in the socket.

11. To install a light bulb with a flat base (and no retaining pins), simply grasp the bulb and push it straight into its socket.

12. If applicable, install the socket and bulb assembly into the rear of the lens housing; otherwise, install the lens over the bulb.

13. Engage the electrical connection to the lamp.
14. Connect the negative battery cable.
15. To ensure that the replacement bulb functions properly, activate the applicable switch to illuminate the bulb which was just replaced. If the replacement light bulb does not illuminate, either it too is faulty or there is a problem in the bulb circuit or switch. Correct if necessary.
16. Install the bezel and tighten the screws.

1996–97 MODELS

◆ See Figures 56 and 57

1. Disconnect the negative battery cable.
2. Loosen the lens-to-grille retaining screws.
3. Remove the lens assembly and disengage the socket from the lens.
4. To remove a light bulb with retaining pins from its socket, grasp the bulb, then gently depress and twist it ⅛ turn counterclockwise, and pull it from the socket.
5. To remove a cylindrical light bulb with a flat base (and no retaining pins), simply grasp and pull it straight from its socket.

To install:

6. Before installing a light bulb into the socket, ensure that all electrical contact surfaces are free of corrosion or dirt.

Loosen the lens retaining screws and remove the lens

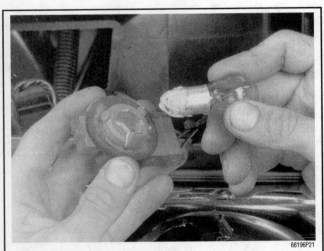

Depress and twist the bulb ⅛ turn counterclockwise to remove it from the socket

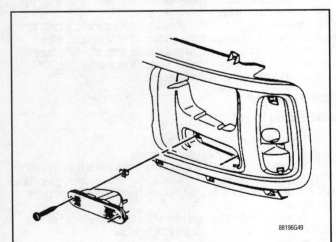

Fig. 56 Front turn signal and parking light mounting—1996–97 base models

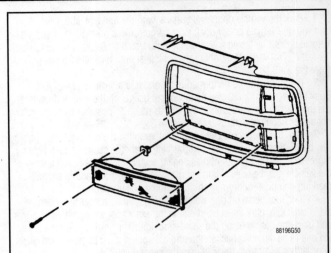

Fig. 57 Front turn signal and parking light mounting—1996–97 optional models

➡Before installing the light bulb, note the positions of the two retaining pins on the bulb. They will likely be at different heights on the bulb, to ensure that the bulb is installed correctly. If, when installing the bulb, it does not turn easily, do not force it. Remove the bulb and rotate it 180 degrees from its former position, then reinsert it into the bulb socket.

7. Insert the light bulb into the socket and, while depressing the bulb, twist it ⅛ turn clockwise until the two pins on the light bulb are properly engaged in the socket.

8. To install a light bulb with a flat base (and no retaining pins), simply grasp the bulb and push it straight into its socket.

9. Connect the negative battery cable.

10. To ensure that the replacement bulb functions properly, activate the applicable switch to illuminate the bulb which was just replaced. If the replacement light bulb does not illuminate, either it too is faulty or there is a problem in the bulb circuit or switch. Correct if necessary.

11. Engage the socket to the lamp housing by lining up the projections on the socket with the cutout in the lamp housing, then twisting the socket clockwise.

12. Install the lamp housing and tighten the screws.

Front Side Marker Lights

1987–95 MODELS
▶ See Figure 58

1. Disconnect the negative battery cable.
2. Unfasten the two side marker lamp retaining screws.
3. Remove the side marker lamp assembly.
4. Remove the light bulb from its socket.

To install:

5. Before installing the light bulb into the socket, ensure that all electrical contact surfaces are free of corrosion or dirt.

6. Line up the base of the light bulb with the socket, then insert the light bulb into the socket until it is fully seated.

7. Connect the negative battery cable.

8. To ensure that the replacement bulb functions properly, activate the applicable switch to illuminate the bulb which was just replaced. If the replacement light bulb does not illuminate, either it too is faulty or there is a problem in the bulb circuit or switch. Correct as necessary.

9. Install the lamp and tighten the screws.

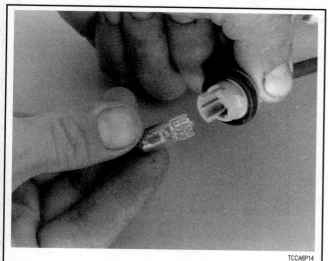

Simply pull this side marker light bulb straight from its socket

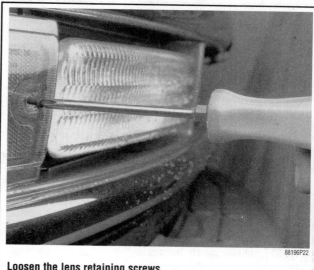

Loosen the lens retaining screws

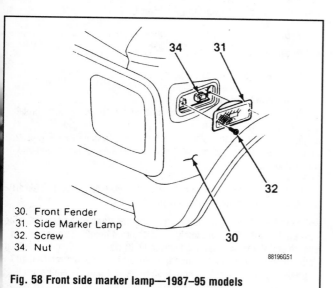

30. Front Fender
31. Side Marker Lamp
32. Screw
34. Nut

Fig. 58 Front side marker lamp—1987–95 models

Remove the lens from the grille, then twist the socket assembly and disengage it from the lens

1996–97 MODELS

◆ See Figures 59 and 60

1. Disconnect the negative battery cable.
2. Loosen the lens-to-grille retaining screws.
3. On base model vans, lift the side marker lamp up and out to disengage the tab.
4. On up-level vans, remove the side marker lens and/or the reflector from the grille.
5. Disengage the bulb socket from the lamp.

To install:

6. Before installing a light bulb into the socket, ensure that all electrical contact surfaces are free of corrosion or dirt.
7. To install a light bulb with a flat base (and no retaining pins), simply grasp the bulb and push it straight into its socket.
8. Connect the negative battery cable.
9. To ensure that the replacement bulb functions properly, activate the applicable switch to illuminate the bulb which was just replaced. If the replacement light bulb does not illuminate, either it too is faulty or there is a problem in the bulb circuit or switch. Correct if necessary.
10. Engage the socket to the lamp.

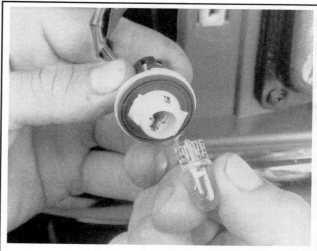

Grasp the bulb and pull it from the socket

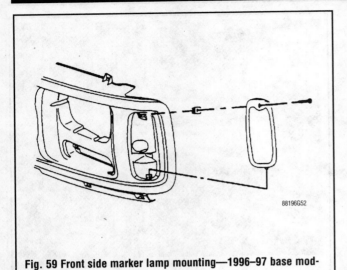

Fig. 59 Front side marker lamp mounting—1996–97 base models

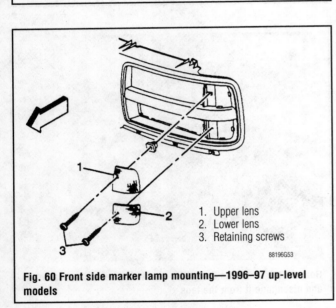

1. Upper lens
2. Lower lens
3. Retaining screws

Fig. 60 Front side marker lamp mounting—1996–97 up-level models

11. On up-level vans, install the side marker lens and/or the reflector to the grille.
12. On base model vans, engage the side marker lamp to the grille.
13. Tighten the lens retaining screws.

Rear Side Marker Lights

▶ See Figure 61

1. Disconnect the negative battery cable.
2. Remove the housing retaining screws.
3. Remove the housing.
4. Gently pull out the bulb socket.
5. Remove the bulb.
To install:
6. Insert the bulb into the socket.
7. Install the bulb socket.
8. Install the housing and tighten the screws.
9. Connect the negative battery cable and check for proper operation.

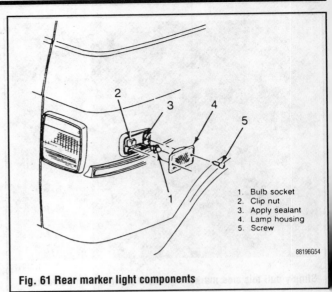

1. Bulb socket
2. Clip nut
3. Apply sealant
4. Lamp housing
5. Screw

Fig. 61 Rear marker light components

Rear Turn Signal, Brake and Parking Lights

1987–95 MODELS

▶ See Figure 62

1. Disconnect the negative battery cable.
2. Remove the lens housing retaining screws.
3. Remove the lamp housing.
4. Remove the bulb socket by squeezing the retention lock and rotating the socket counterclockwise.
5. To remove a light bulb with retaining pins from its socket, grasp the bulb, then gently depress and twist it 1/8 turn counterclockwise, and pull it from the socket.
To install:
6. Before installing a light bulb into the socket, ensure that all electrical contact surfaces are free of corrosion or dirt.

➡Before installing the light bulb, note the positions of the two retaining pins on the bulb. They will likely be at different heights on the bulb, to ensure that the bulb is installed correctly. If, when installing the bulb, it does not turn easily, do not force it. Remove the bulb and rotate it 180 degrees from its former position, then reinsert it into the bulb socket.

Loosen the lens retaining screws

Slide the lens assembly forward

89776P20

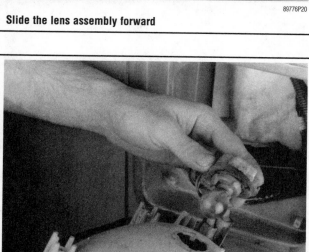

Disengage the bulb assembly from the lens

89776P21

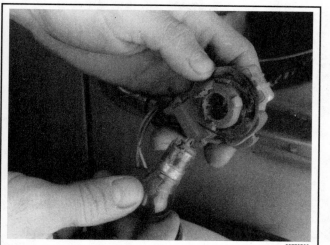

Depress the bulb and twist it about ⅛ turn counterclockwise, then remove it from the socket

89776P22

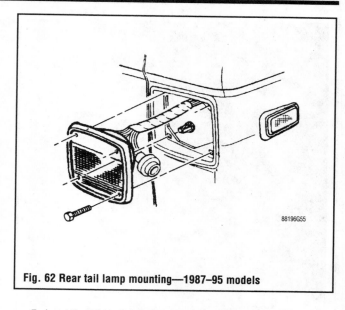

Fig. 62 Rear tail lamp mounting—1987-95 models

88196G55

7. Insert the light bulb into the socket and, while depressing the bulb, twist it ⅛ turn clockwise until the two pins on the light bulb are properly engaged in the socket.

8. Connect the negative battery cable.

9. To ensure that the replacement bulb functions properly, activate the applicable switch to illuminate the bulb which was just replaced. If the replacement light bulb does not illuminate, either it too is faulty or there is a problem in the bulb circuit or switch. Correct if necessary.

10. Install the socket into the housing and turn it clockwise until it is seated.

11. Install the lens and tighten the screws.

1996–97 MODELS

▶ See Figure 63 (p. 41)

1. Disconnect the negative battery cable.
2. Remove the upper quarter panel appliqué by loosening the retainers.
3. Loosen the lens retainers and remove the lens.
4. Disconnect the bulb socket(s) from the lens.
5. To remove a light bulb with retaining pins from its socket, grasp the bulb, then gently depress and twist it ⅛ turn counterclockwise, and pull it from the socket.

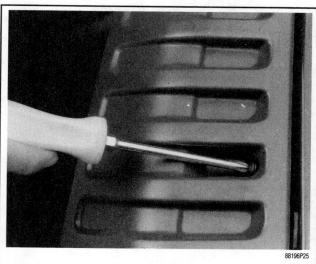

Loosen the quarter panel appliqué screws . . .

88196P25

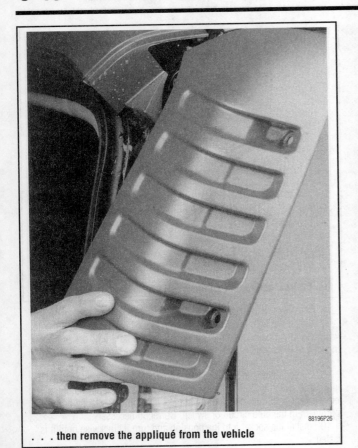

. . . then remove the appliqué from the vehicle

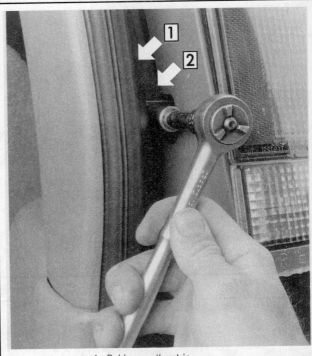

1. Rubber weatherstrip
2. Upper tail light lens retainer

Push the rubber weatherstrip aside to access the upper trim nut, then loosen the nut

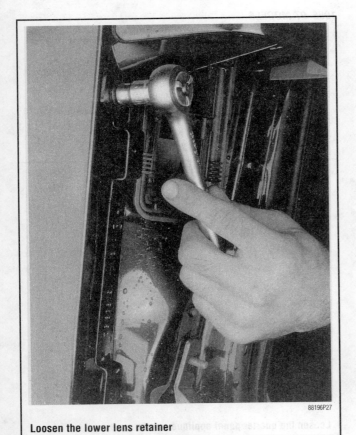

Loosen the lower lens retainer

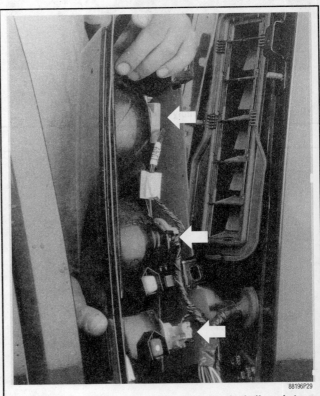

Pull the lens out far enough to gain access to the bulb socket assemblies (arrows)

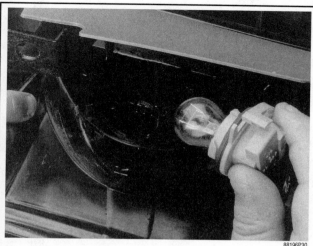

Twist the bulb socket assembly and disengage it from the lens assembly

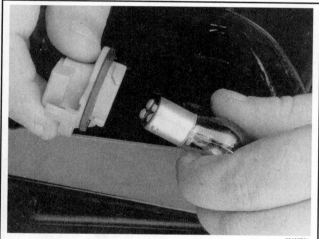

Depress the bulb and twist it about ⅛ turn counterclockwise, then remove it from the socket

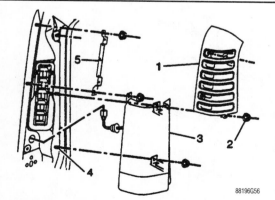

1. Upper quarter panel appliqué
2. Tail lamp assembly nut
3. Tail lamp lens
4. Tail lamp assembly stud
5. Upper quarter panel appliqué bracket

Fig. 63 Rear tail lamp assembly components—1996–97 models

To install:

6. Before installing a light bulb into the socket, ensure that all electrical contact surfaces are free of corrosion or dirt.

➡️**Before installing the light bulb, note the positions of the two retaining pins on the bulb. They will likely be at different heights on the bulb, to ensure that the bulb is installed correctly. If, when installing the bulb, it does not turn easily, do not force it. Remove the bulb and rotate it 180 degrees from its former position, then reinsert it into the bulb socket.**

7. Insert the light bulb into the socket and, while depressing the bulb, twist it ⅛ turn clockwise until the two pins on the light bulb are properly engaged in the socket.
8. Connect the negative battery cable.
9. To ensure that the replacement bulb functions properly, activate the applicable switch to illuminate the bulb which was just replaced. If the replacement light bulb does not illuminate, either it too is faulty or there is a problem in the bulb circuit or switch. Correct if necessary.
10. Engage the bulb socket(s) to the lens.
11. Install the lens and tighten the retainers. Tighten the retainers to 44 inch lbs. (5 Nm).
12. Install the appliqué and tighten the retainers.

High-Mount Brake Light

1987–95 MODELS

▶ See Figure 64

1. Disconnect the negative battery cable.
2. Loosen the screws and lift the lamp assembly to disengage the lens from the harness.

To install:

3. Engage the electrical connector to the harness.
4. Install the lamp assembly and tighten the screws to 17 inch lbs. (2 Nm).
5. Connect the negative battery cable and check for proper operation.

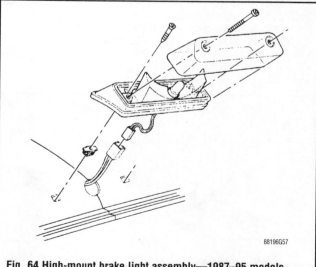

Fig. 64 High-mount brake light assembly—1987–95 models

1996–97 MODELS

▶ See Figure 65

1. Disconnect the negative battery cable.
2. Loosen the lens screws and remove the lens.
3. Remove the bulb from its socket.

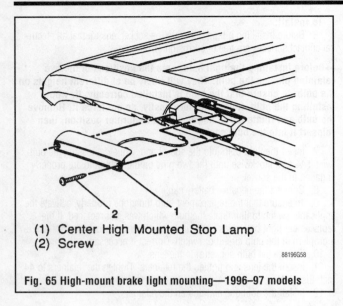

(1) Center High Mounted Stop Lamp
(2) Screw

Fig. 65 High-mount brake light mounting—1996–97 models

Grasp the dome lamp bulb and pull it from the socket

To install:

4. Before installing a light bulb into the socket, ensure that all electrical contact surfaces are free of corrosion or dirt.
5. Insert the bulb into its socket.
6. Connect the negative battery cable and check for proper operation.
7. Install the lens assembly and tighten the screws.

Dome Lamp

▶ See Figures 66 and 67

1. Gently pry the dome lamp lens to disengage the retaining tabs and remove it from the housing.
2. Pull the bulb from the socket.

To install:

3. Before installing a light bulb into the socket, ensure that all electrical contact surfaces are free of corrosion or dirt.
4. Install the bulb by pressing it into place.
5. Check for proper operation and correct if necessary.
6. Install the cover and engage the retaining tabs.

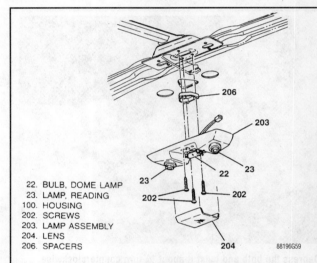

22. BULB, DOME LAMP
23. LAMP, READING
100. HOUSING
202. SCREWS
203. LAMP ASSEMBLY
204. LENS
206. SPACERS

Fig. 66 Dome lamp components—1987–95 models

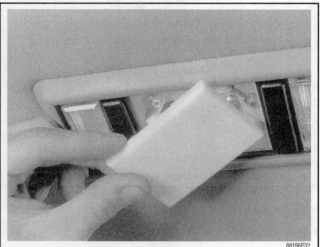

Gently pry the dome lamp lens to disengage the tabs from the housing

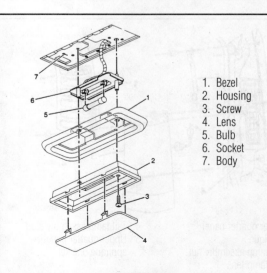

1. Bezel
2. Housing
3. Screw
4. Lens
5. Bulb
6. Socket
7. Body

Fig. 67 Dome lamp assembly—1996–97

License Plate Lamp

1987–95 MODELS

▶ **See Figure 68**

1. Loosen the lens retainers.
2. Remove the lens.
3. Remove the bulb.

To install:

4. Before installing a light bulb into the socket, ensure that all electrical contact surfaces are free of corrosion or dirt.
5. Insert the bulb.
6. Check for proper operation and correct if necessary.
7. Install the lens assembly and tighten the screws.

1996–97 MODELS

▶ **See Figure 69**

1. Loosen the retainers holding the lamp to the pocket.
2. Remove the lamp from the pocket.
3. Twist the electrical socket approximately 1/4 turn counterclockwise and remove it from the lamp.

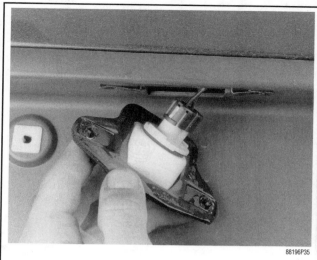

Remove the lamp from the pocket . . .

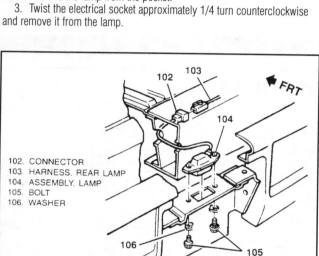

102. CONNECTOR
103. HARNESS, REAR LAMP
104. ASSEMBLY, LAMP
105. BOLT
106. WASHER

Fig. 68 License plate lamp components—1987–95 models

. . . then twist the bulb socket and disengage the socket from the lens

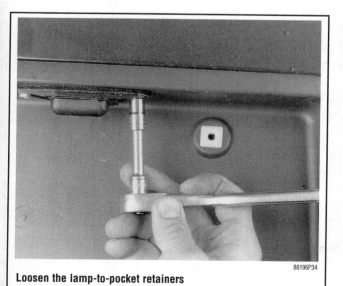

Loosen the lamp-to-pocket retainers

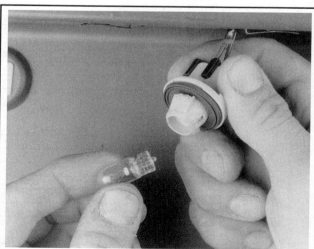

Grasp the bulb and pull it straight from the socket

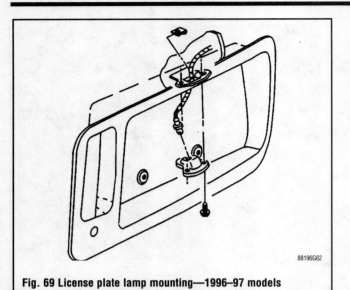

Fig. 69 License plate lamp mounting—1996–97 models

4. Pull the bulb straight out of the socket.

To install:

5. Before installing a light bulb into the socket, ensure that all electrical contact surfaces are free of corrosion or dirt.

6. Align the bulb's base with the socket and push the bulb straight in.

7. Check for proper operation and correct if necessary.

8. Insert the electrical socket into the lamp and twist it clockwise.

9. Install the lamp in the pocket and tighten the screws.

LIGHT BULB CHARTS

LAMP SPECIFICATIONS

P-TRUCK				G-TRUCK			
USED IN	QUAN.	TRADE #	POWER	USED IN	QUAN.	TRADE #	POWER
Dome Lamps: Cab	1	1004	15 CP	Dome lamps	2	211-2	12 CP
Oil Pressure indicator lamp[1]	1	168	3 CP	Oil pressure indicator lamp	1	161	1 CP
Generator indicator lamp[1]	1	168	3 CP	Generator indicator lamp	1	194	2 CP
Instrument cluster lamps[2]	5	168	3 CP	Instrument cluster lamps[11]	1	161	1 CP
Headlamp beam indicator lamp	1	168	3 CP	Headlamp beam indicator lamp	1	161	1 CP
Lamp assembly—tail & stop lamp	2	1157	3-32 CP	Park, directional signal lamps	2	1157	3-32 CP
License lamp[4]	1	67	4 CP	Tail, stop lamps	2	1157	3-32 CP
Directional signal (front park lamps)[6]	2	1157	3-32 CP	License lamp	1	67	4 CP
Head lamps	2	6014	50-60 W	Head lamps[12]	2	6014	50-60 W
Temperature indicator lamp	1	168	3 CP	Temperature indicator lamp	1	194	2 CP
Directional signal indicator lamp	2	168	3 CP	Directional signal indicator lamp	2	194	2 CP
Clearance and marker lamps	4	168	3 CP	Marker lamps	4	168	3 CP
Roof marker lamps[5]	5	194	2 CP	Brake warning indicator lamp	1	194	2 CP
Brake warning indicator lamp	1	168	3 CP	Back-up lamp	2	1156	32 CP
Transmission control (auto)	1	1445	0.7 CP	Radio dial lamp	1	1893	2 CP
Backing lamp (exc. motor home)	2	1156	32 CP	Heater or A/C illum. lamp	1	194	2 CP
Backing lamp (motor home)	2	1295	50 CP	Transmission control w/tilt wheel illum. lamp	1	1445	0.7 CP
Heater or A/C illum. lamp	1	161	1 CP	W/S wiper switch lamp	1	161	1 CP
Corner marker lamps (platform)	7	67	4 CP	Transmission control illum. lamp	1	73	.3 CP
Radio dial lamp — AM	1	216	1 CP	Choke heater indicator lamp	1	1893	2 CP
— AM/FM	1	216	1 CP	Seat belt warning lamp	1	194	2 CP
Courtesy lamp	1	1003	15 CP	Instrument cluster lamps[9]	5	194	2 CP
Windshield wiper switch lamp	1	161	1 CP	Instrument cluster lamps[10]	1	168	3 CP
Clock lamp	1	168	3 CP				
Rear identification[7] lamp	10	1895	2 CP				
Underhood lamp	1	93	15 CP				
Seat belt warning lamp	1	168	3 CP				
Cargo/dome lamp	2	211-2	12 CP				
Choke heater indicator lamp	1	168	3 CP				

[2]3 lamps used on instrument cluster on P models or RV w/o gages.
[3]Double filament sealed beam 60W high beam, 50W low beam.
[4]2 lamps used with step bumper and P models.
[5]4 required on P models.
[8]'P' truck only.
[9]'G' model w/o gages; 1 lamp with gages.
[10]'G' model w/o gages; 3 lamps with gages.
[11]'G' model with gages only.
[12]Double filament sealed beam 60W high beam, 50W low beam.

88196C01

Fig. 70 Light bulb specifications chart—1987–90 G and P models

SPECIFICATIONS
REPLACEMENT LAMPS

Lamp Usage	Quantity	Trade No.	Power Rating at 12.8V, Watts
Headlamps—Quad System			
High Beam Lamp	1	H4701	65
Low Beam Lamp	1	H4703	55
Headlamps—Dual System			
Combination Lamp	2	H6054*	35/65*
			Candle Power
Exterior Lamps			
Backup Lamps	2	1156	32
CHMSL			NOT SERVICED
License Lamp	1	67	4
Marker Lamps	4	194	2
Park & Turn Signal Lamp Bulbs—Dual Headlamp System	4	3157NA	32-3*
Park Lamp Bulbs—Quad Headlamp System	2	3157NA	32-3*
Tail, Stop Lamps	2	2057	2-32*
Turn Signal Lamp Bulbs—Quad Headlamp System	2	194NA	2
Underhood Lamp	1	232	9.9
Interior Lamps			
Dome Lamps	2	211-2	12
Reading Lamp	2/4	906	6
Stepwell Lamp	2	212-2	6
Transmission Indicator Dial with Tilt Wheel	1	1445	0.7
Transmission Indicator Dial w/o Tilt Wheel	1	73	0.3
Instrument Cluster Lamps			
Air Bag Indicator Lamp	1	PC74	.7
Antilock Brake Indicator Lamp	1	PC74	.7
Brake System Warning Indicator Lamp	1	PC74	.7
Brake Warning Indicator Lamp	1	PC74	.7
Daytime Running Lights Indicator Lamp	1	PC118	.7
Glow Plugs Lamp	1	194	2.0
Headlamp Beam Indicator Lamp	1	PC74	.7
Heater or A/C Control Lamp	1	194	2.0
Instrument Cluster Illumination Lamps	2	194	2.0
Instrument Cluster Illumination Lamps	3	168	—
Low Coolant Lamp (Diesel)	1	PC74	.7
Malfunction Indicator (Service Engine Soon) Lamp	1	PC74	.7
Seat Belt Warning Lamp	1	PC160	.9
Servive Throttle Soon Lamp (Diesel)	1	194	2.0
Sunshade Vanity Mirror Lamp	4	7065	1.0
Turn Signal Indicator Lamp	2	PC74	.7
Water in Fuel Lamp (Diesel)	1	194	2.0

*Double filament bulb

88196C02

Fig. 71 Light bulb specifications chart—1991-95 G models

SPECIFICATIONS
LAMP AND BULB REPLACEMENT—P MODEL COMMERCIAL

Lamp Usage	Quantity	Trade No.	Power Rating at 12V, Watts
Headlamp (2 Headlamp System)	2	6014	50/60W
			Candle Power
Park & Turn Signal Lamp[4]	2	2057	32-2
Tail & Stop Lamp[4]	2	1157	32-3
Tail & Stop Lamp[5]	2	2057	32-2
Front Side Marker Lamp	2	194	2
Rear Side Marker Lamp	2	194	2
License Lamp[1]	2	67	4
Backup Lamp[1]	N/A	N/A	N/A
Instrument Cluster Illumination Lamp	6	PC194	2
Directional Signal Indicator Lamp	2	PC194	2
Headlamp High Beam Indicator Lamp	1	PC74	.7
Service Brake Warning Indicator Lamp	1	PC74	.7
Park Brake Warning Indicator Lamp	1	PC74	.7
Transmission Control Illumination Lamp	1	73	.3
Low Coolant Indicator Lamp[2]	1	PC74	.7
Glow Plugs Indicator Lamp[2]	1	PC74	.7
Water In Fuel Indicator Lamp[2]	1	PC74	.7
Malfunction Indicator Lamp	1	PC74	.7
Trans. Indicator Lamp[2]	1	PC74	.7
Fasten Safety Belts Indicator Lamp[3]	1	PC74	.7
Door Ajar Indicator Lamp[3]	1	PC74	.7
Daytime Running Lights Indicator Lamp[6]	1	PC118	.7

[1] Refer to Body Manufacturer
[2] Diesel Engines Only
[3] Supplied by Body Manufacturer. May vary.
[4] Union City Body Co.
[5] Except Union City Body Co.
[6] Canada Only
N/A Not Available

88196C03

Fig. 72 Light bulb specifications chart—1991-95 P models (commercial)

SPECIFICATIONS

LAMP AND BULB REPLACEMENT—P MODEL MOTORHOME

Lamp Usage		Quantity	Trade No.	Power Rating at 12V, Watts
Headlamp	(2 Headlamp System)	2	6052	50/60W
	(4 Headlamp System)	2	4651	50W
		2	4652	60/40W
				Candle Power
Park & Turn Signal Lamp		2	2057	32-2
Tail & Stop Lamp[1]		N/A	N/A	N/A
License Lamp		N/A	N/A	N/A
Marker Lamp[1]		N/.A	N/A	N/A
Backup Lamp[1]		N/A	N/A	N/A
Instrument Cluster Illumination Lamp		6	PC194	2
Directional Signal Indicator Lamp		2	PC194	2
Headlamp High Beam Indicator Lamp		1	PC74	.7
Service Brake Warning Indicator Lamp		1	PC74	.7
Park Brake Warning Indicator Lamp		1	PC74	.7
Transmission Control Illumination Lamp		1	73	.3
Low Coolant Indicator Lamp[2]		1	PC74	.7
Glow Plugs Indicator Lamp[2]		1	PC74	.7
Water In Fuel Indicator Lamp[2]		1	PC74	.7
Malfunction Indicator Lamp		1	PC74	.7
Trans. Indicator Lamp[2]		1	PC74	.7
Fasten Safety Belts Indicator Lamp[3]		1	PC74	.7
Door Ajar Indicator Lamp[3]		1	PC74	.7
Daytime Running Lights Indicator Lamp[4]		1	PC118	.7

[1] Refer to Body Manufacturer
[2] Diesel Engines Only
[3] Supplied by Body Manufacturer. May vary.
[4] Canada Only
N/A Not Available

88196C04

Fig. 73 Light bulb specifications chart—1991–95 P models (motorhome)

SPECIFICATIONS

Replacement Bulbs

Location	Trade Number
Back Up Lamp	1141
Center High Mounted Stop Lamp (CHMSL)	L912
Dome Lamp	L211-2
Front Park/Turn Signal Lamp—Base	2057NA
Front Park/Turn Signal Lamp—Optional	2057NA
Front Side Marker Lamp—Base	L194
Front Side Marker Lamp—Optional	L194
Headlamp (Low Beam)—Optional	9005
Headlamp (High Beam)—Optional	9006
Headlamp—Base	H5054
License Plate Lamp	L194
Reading Lamp	L562
Stepwell	L212-2
Taillamp	2057
Underhood Lamp	L561

88196C05

Fig. 74 Light bulb specifications chart—1996–97 models

TRAILER WIRING

Wiring the vehicle for towing is fairly easy. There are a number of good wiring kits available and these should be used, rather than trying to design your own.

All trailers will need brake lights and turn signals as well as tail lights and side marker lights. Most areas require extra marker lights for overwide trailers. Also, most areas have recently required back-up lights for trailers, and most trailer manufacturers have been building trailers with back-up lights for several years.

Additionally, some Class I, most Class II and just about all Class III trailers will have electric brakes. Add to this number an accessories wire, to operate trailer internal equipment or to charge the trailer's battery, and you can have as many as seven wires in the harness.

Determine the equipment on your trailer and buy the wiring kit necessary. The kit will contain all the wires needed, plus a plug adapter set which includes the female plug, mounted on the bumper or hitch, and the male plug, wired into, or plugged into the trailer harness.

When installing the kit, follow the manufacturer's instructions. The color coding of the wires is usually standard throughout the industry. One point to note: some domestic vehicles, and most imported vehicles, have separate turn signals. On most domestic vehicles, the brake lights and rear turn signals operate with the same bulb. For those vehicles without separate turn signals, you can purchase an isolation unit so that the brake lights won't blink whenever the turn signals are operated, or, you can go to your local electronics supply house and buy four diodes to wire in series with the brake and turn signal bulbs. Diodes will isolate the brake and turn signals. The choice is yours. The isolation units are simple and quick to install, but far more expensive than the diodes. The diodes, however, require more work to install properly, since they require the cutting of each bulb's wire and soldering in place of the diode.

One final point: the best kits are those with a spring loaded cover on the vehicle mounted socket. This cover prevents dirt and moisture from corroding the terminals. Never let the vehicle socket hang loosely; always mount it securely to the bumper or hitch.

CIRCUIT PROTECTION

Fuses

The fuses are located on a fuse block, they provide increased circuit protection and reliability. The fuse block is located under the left side of the instrument panel and steering column. The fuse block should be visible from underneath the steering column, near the pedal bracket. If the block is not visible, check for a removable compartment door or trim panel which may be used on later models to hide the block. On 1996–97 models, there is also a fuse/relay panel mounted underhood.

If a fuse blows, the cause should be investigated and corrected before the installation of a new fuse. This, however, is easier to say than to do. Because each fuse protects a limited number of components, your job is narrowed down somewhat. Begin your investigation by looking for obvious fraying, loose connections, breaks in insulation, etc. Use the techniques outlined at the beginning of this section. Electrical problems are almost always a real headache to solve, but if you are patient and persistent, and approach the problem logically (that is, don't start replacing electrical components randomly), you will eventually find the solution.

Each fuse block uses miniature fuses (normally plug-in blade terminal-type for these vehicles) which are designed for increased circuit protection and greater reliability. The compact plug-in or blade terminal design allows for fingertip removal and replacement.

Although most fuses are interchangeable in size, the amperage values are not. Should you install a fuse with too high a value, damaging current could be allowed to destroy the component you were attempting to protect by using a fuse in the first place. The plug-in type fuses have a volt number molded on them and are color coded for easy identification. Be sure to only replace a fuse with the proper amperage rated substitute.

A blown fuse can easily be checked by visual inspection or by continuity checking.

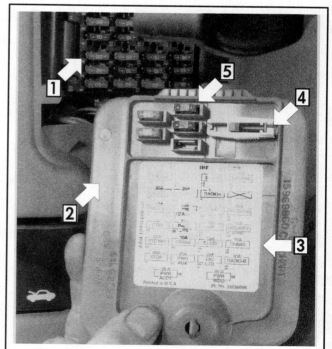

1. Fuse panel
2. Fuse panel cover
3. Fuse location diagram
4. Fuse puller
5. Spare fuses

88196P39

Some fuse panel covers contain a fuse puller, spare fuses and a diagram of the fuse locations

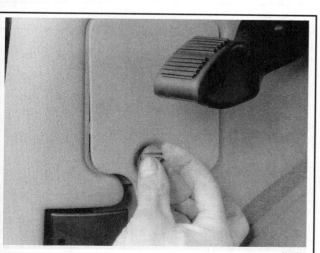

88196P38

If the fuse panel has a concealed cover, unscrew or unclip the retainer and remove the cover

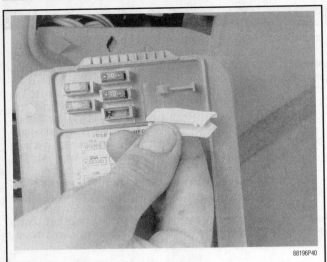

Remove the fuse puller from the panel cover . . .

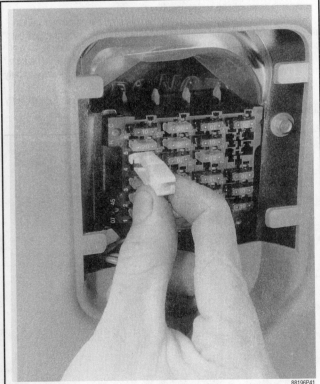

. . . then grasp the fuse to be removed with the puller and disengage it from the fuse panel

REPLACEMENT

1. Locate the fuse for the circuit in question.

➡**When replacing the fuse, DO NOT use one with a higher amperage rating.**

2. Check the fuse by pulling it from the fuse block and observing the element. If it is broken, install a replacement fuse the same amperage rating. If the fuse blows again, check the circuit for a short to ground or faulty device in the circuit protected by the fuse.

3. Continuity can also be checked with the fuse installed in the fuse block with the use of a test light connected across the 2 test points on the end of the fuse. If the test light lights, replace the fuse. Check the circuit for a short to ground or faulty device in the circuit protected by the fuse.

Fusible Links

In addition to fuses, the wiring harness incorporates fusible links (in the battery feed circuits) to protect the wiring. Fusible links are 4 in. (102mm) sections of copper wire, 4 gauges smaller than the circuit(s) they are protecting, designed to melt under electrical overload. There are 4 different gauge sizes used. The fusible links are color coded so that they may be installed in their original positions.

REPLACEMENT

▶ **See Figures 75 and 76**

Fusible links are usually located in the following circuits. Refer to the wiring diagrams for specific fusible link information.
- ECM circuit
- Air conditioning blower circuit

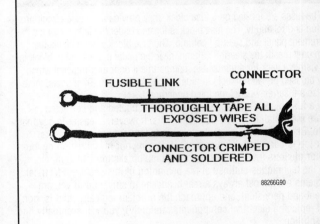

Fig. 75 New fusible links are spliced and soldered to the wire

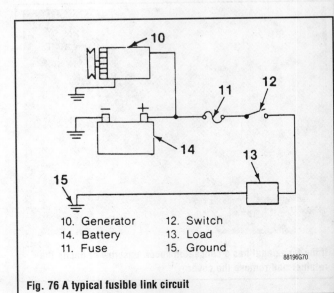

10. Generator 12. Switch
14. Battery   13. Load
11. Fuse   15. Ground

Fig. 76 A typical fusible link circuit

- Fuel pump circuit
- Ignition switch circuit
- Alternator circuit

Circuit Breakers

One device used to protect electrical components from burning out due to excessive current is a circuit breaker. Circuit breakers open and close the plow path for the electricity rapidly in order to protect the circuit if the current is excessive. A circuit breaker is used on components which are more likely to draw excessive current such as a breaker often found in the light switch that protects the headlight circuit. Circuit breakers may be found in various locations on the vehicle on/in the protected component, on a firewall bracket, the fuse block or in the fuse relay center in the engine compartment.

RESETTING

Locate the circuit breaker on the fuse block, then push the circuit breaker in until it locks. If the circuit breaker kicks itself Off again, locate and correct the problem in the electrical circuit. The windshield wiper motor has a self setting circuit breaker built into the motor assembly. This breaker is non-serviceable and requires replacement of the wiper motor unit if defective.

Flashers

The turn signal flasher is mounted to the fuse block.
The flasher unit is replaced by simply pulling it from the fuse block and pressing in a new flasher unit.

WIRING DIAGRAMS

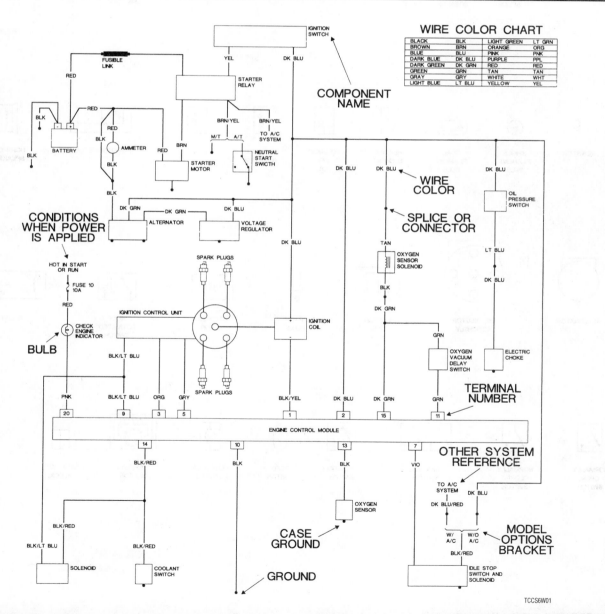

Fig. 77 Sample diagram—how to read and interpret wiring

WIRING DIAGRAM SYMBOLS

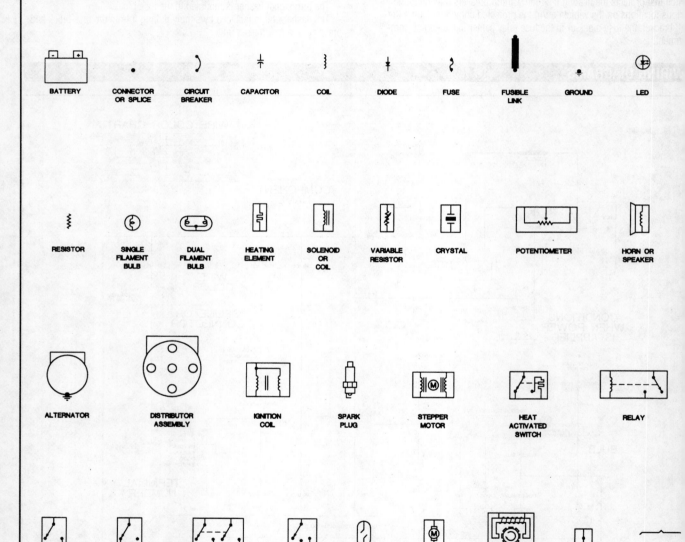

Fig. 78 Common wiring diagram symbols

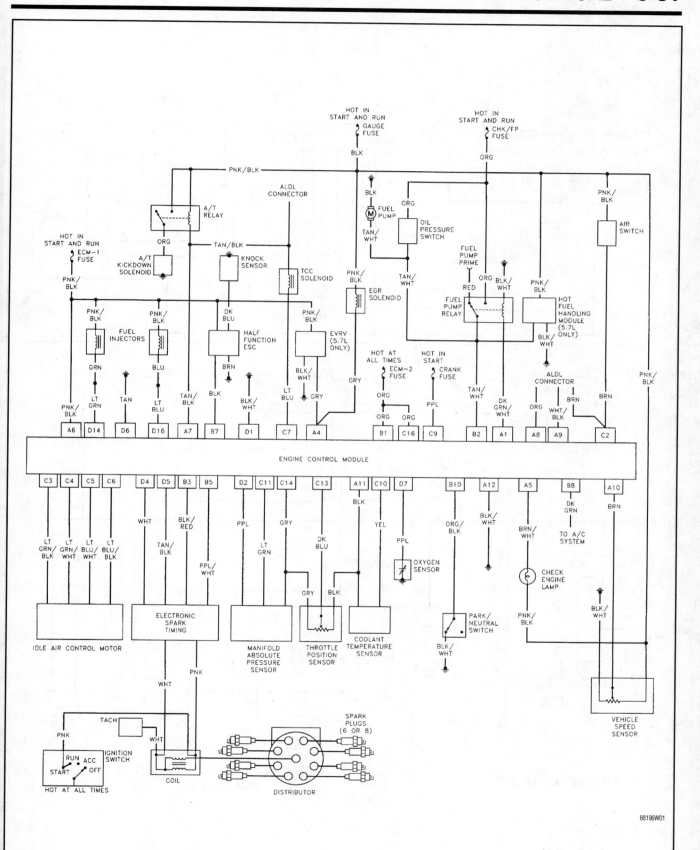

Fig. 79 Engine wiring—1987 G-series gasoline engine

88196W01

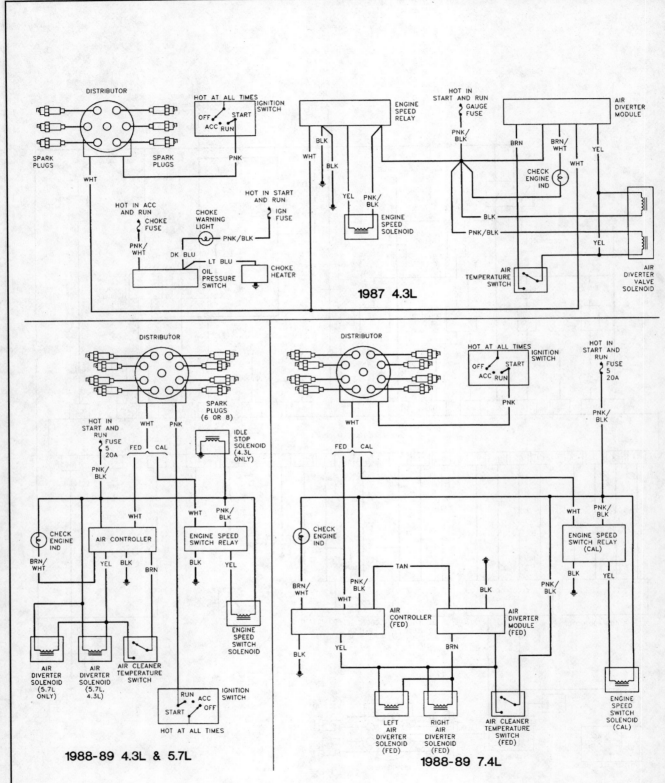

Fig. 80 Engine wiring—1987–89 P-series gasoline engine (carbureted)

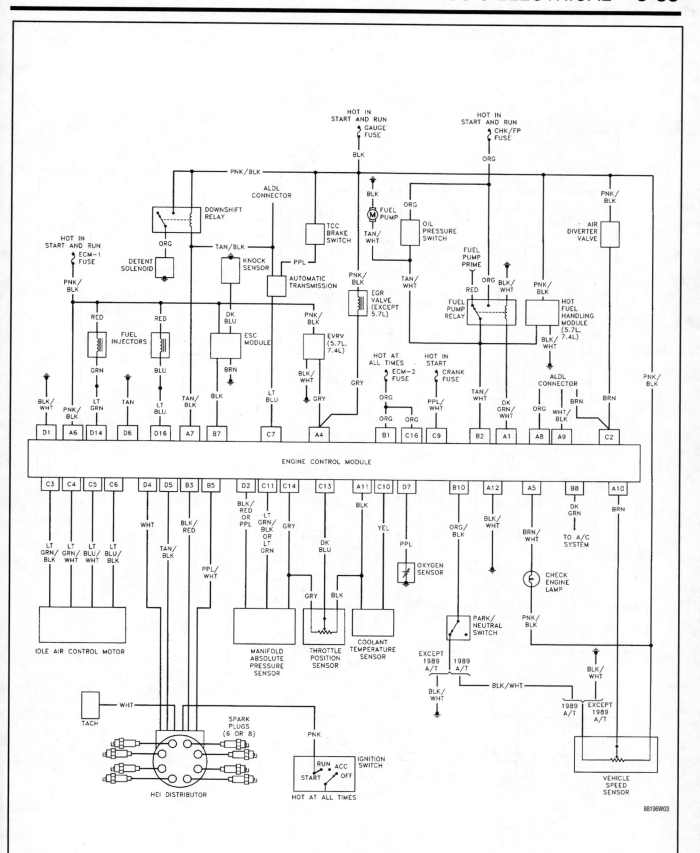

Fig. 81 Engine wiring—1988–89 G-series gasoline engine

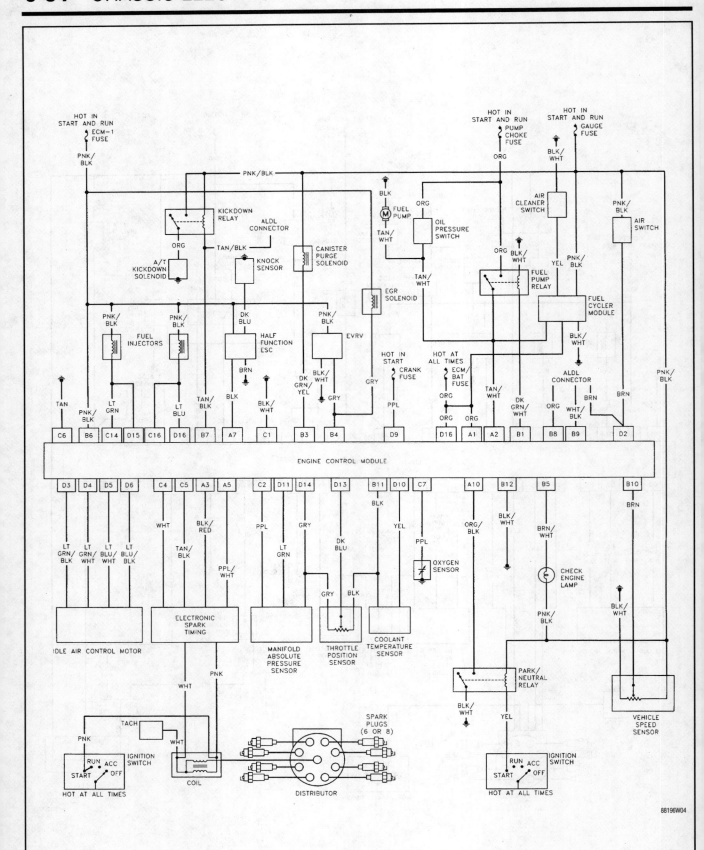

Fig. 82 Engine wiring—1987 5.7L P-series gasoline engine (fuel injected)

88196W04

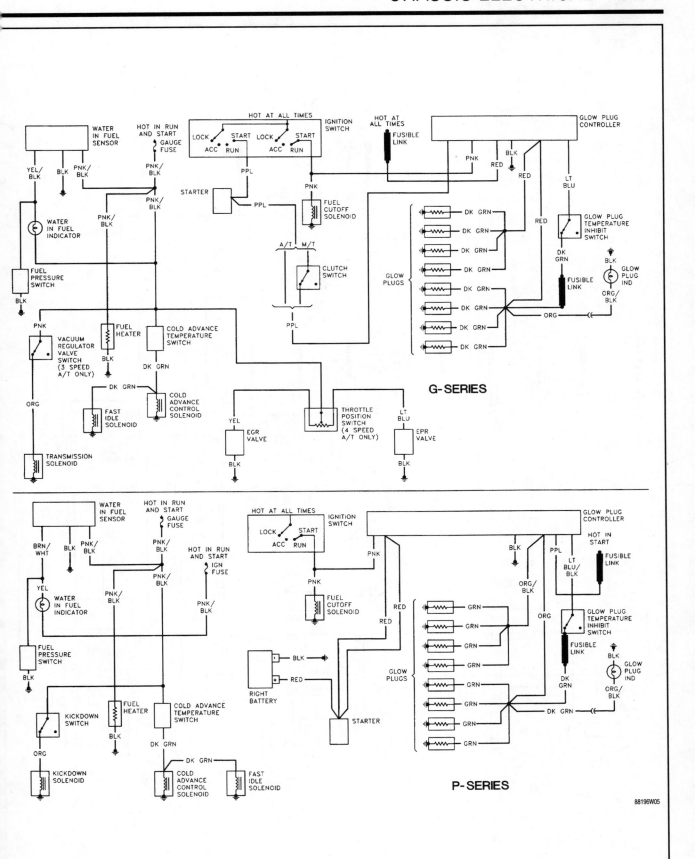

Fig. 83 Engine wiring—1987 diesel engines

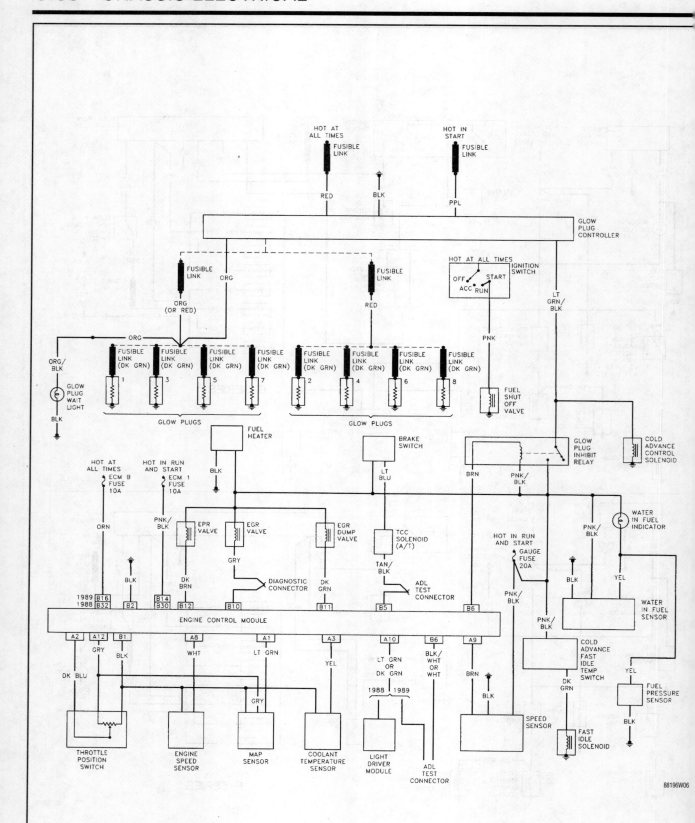

Fig. 84 Engine wiring—1988-89 diesel engine G-van

88196W06

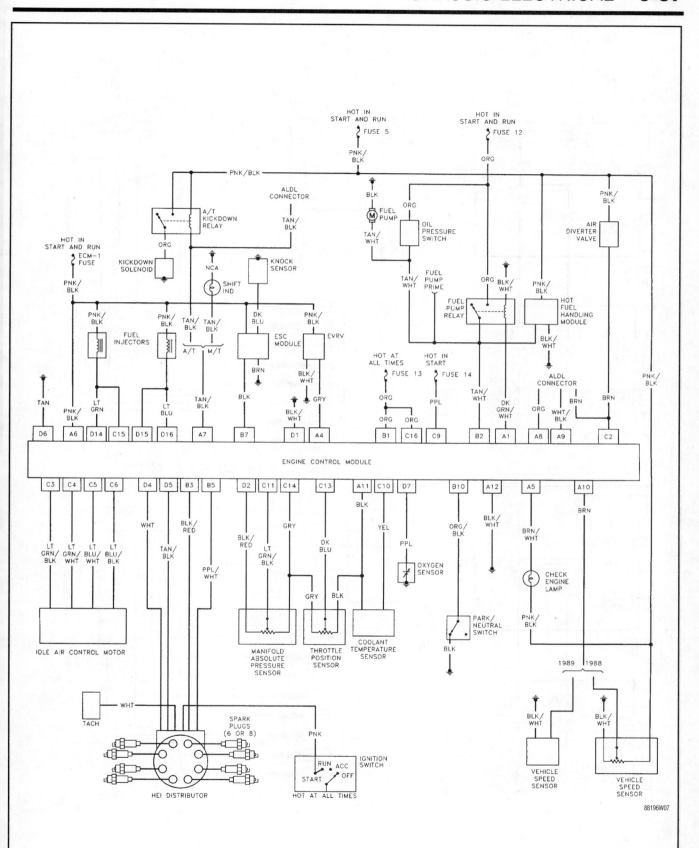

Fig. 85 Engine wiring—1988–89 P-series gasoline engines with EFI

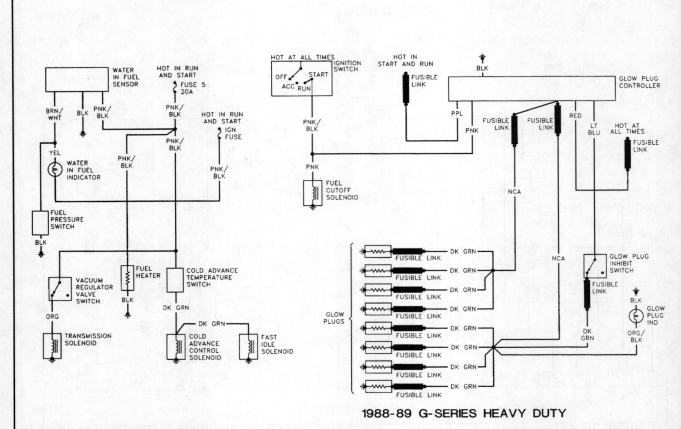

1988-89 G-SERIES HEAVY DUTY

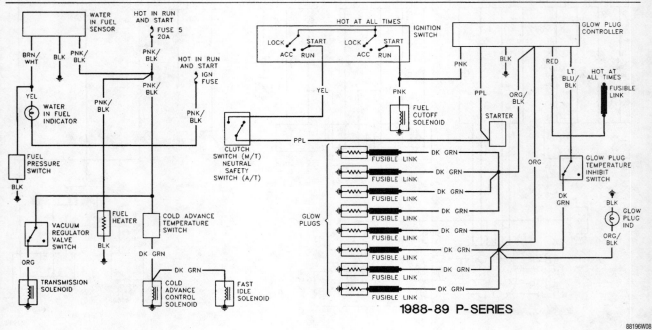

1988-89 P-SERIES

Fig. 86 Engine wiring—1988–89 diesel engines

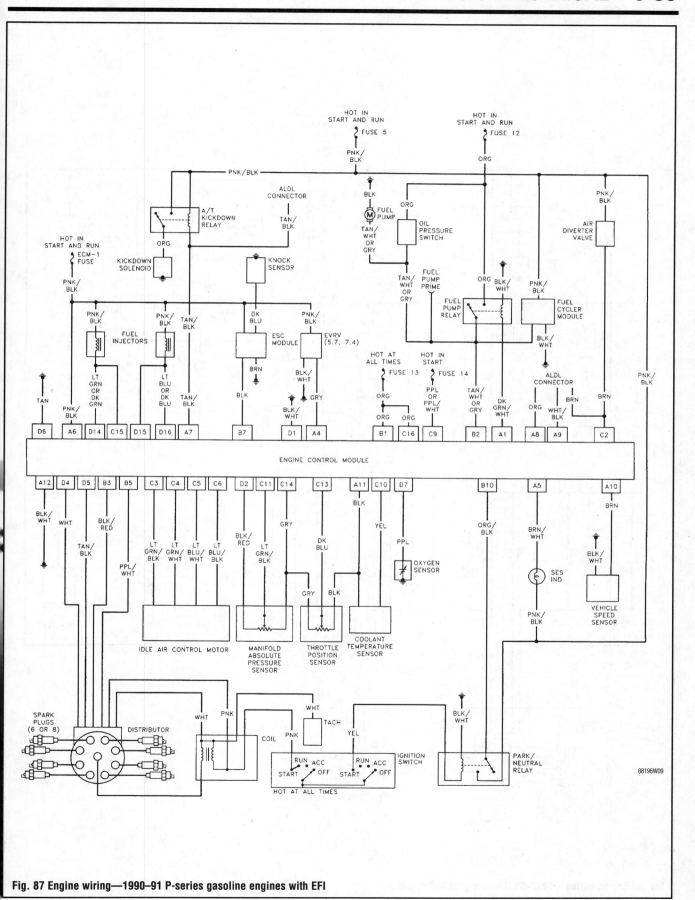

Fig. 87 Engine wiring—1990–91 P-series gasoline engines with EFI

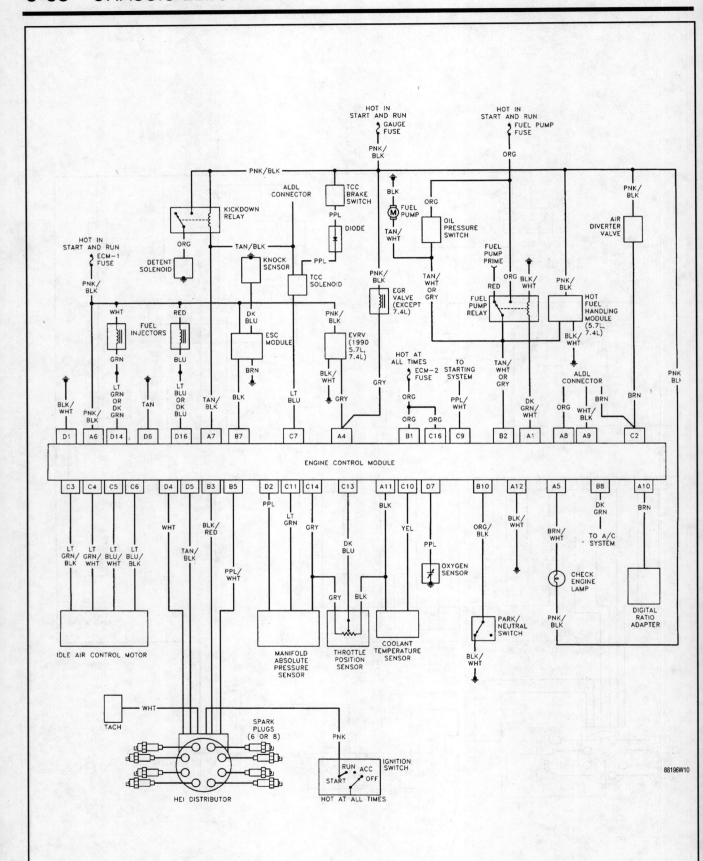

Fig. 88 Engine wiring—1990-91 G-series gasoline engines

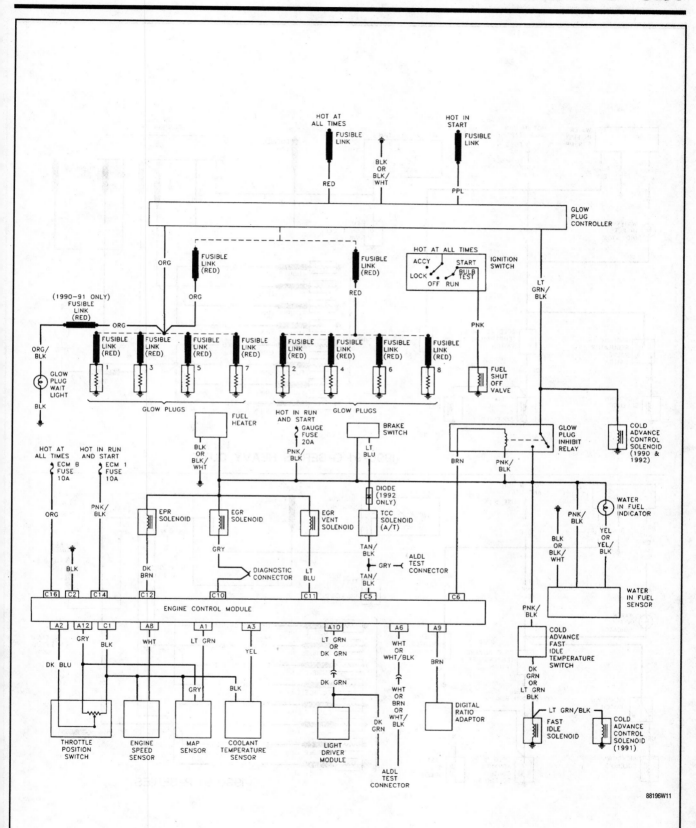

Fig. 89 Engine wiring—1990–91 G-series and 1992 G-series diesel engines with 4L60E transmission

88196W11

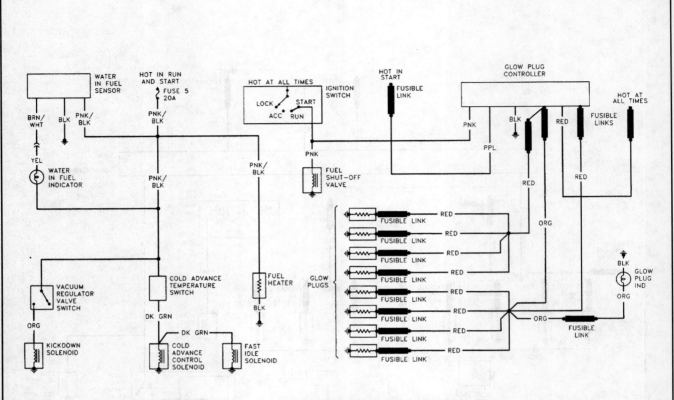

1990-91 G-SERIES HEAVY DUTY

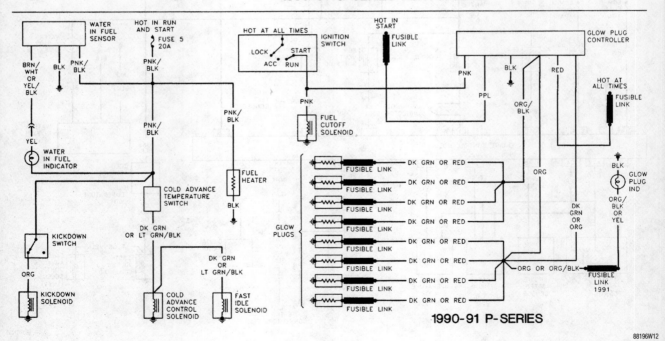

1990-91 P-SERIES

88196W12

Fig. 90 Engine wiring—1990-91 G and P-series diesel engines

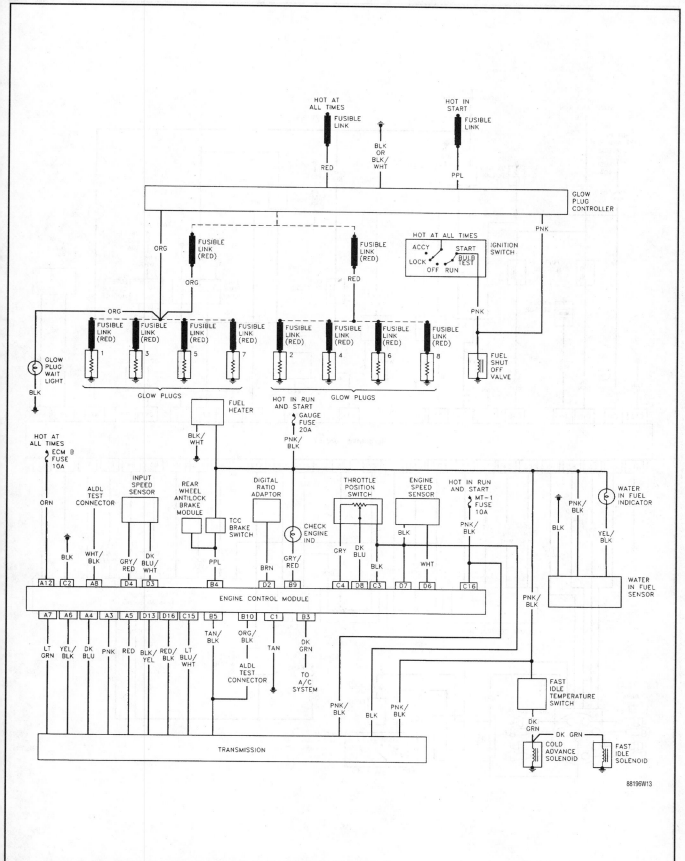

Fig. 91 Engine wiring—1992 G-series diesel engines with 4L80E transmission

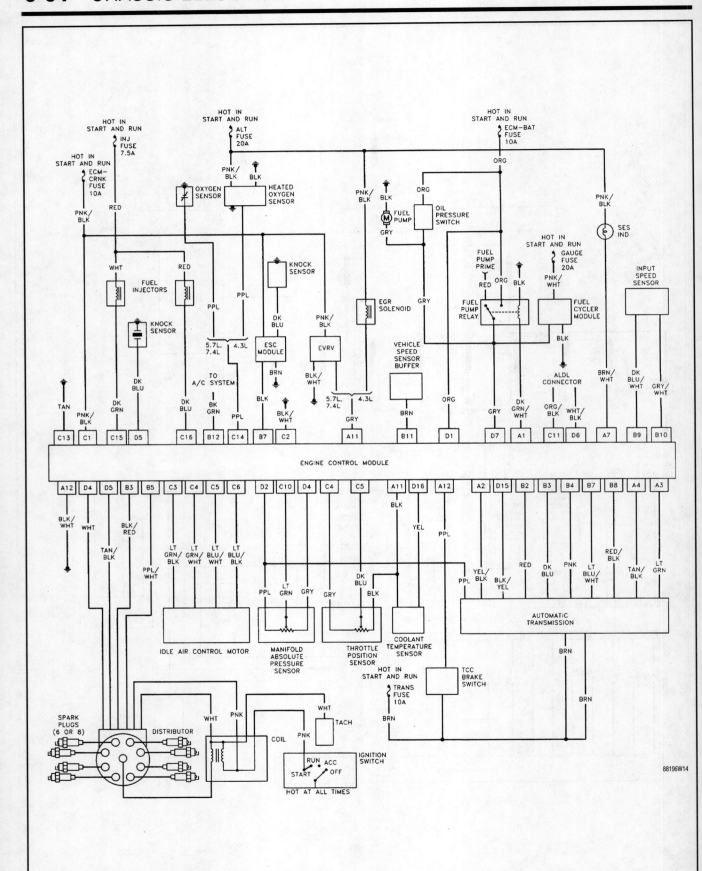

Fig. 92 Engine wiring—1992 P-series models with automatic transmission

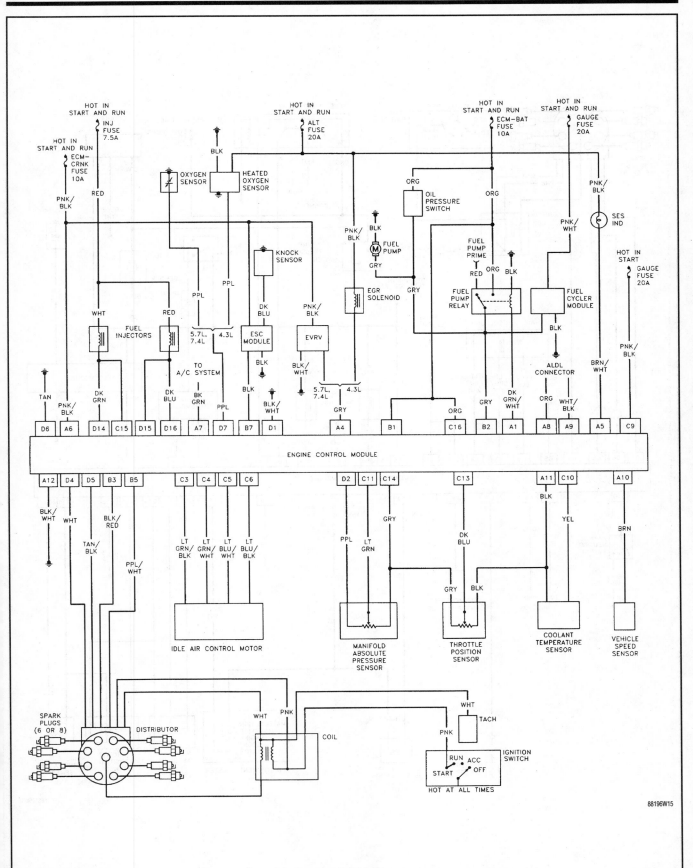

Fig. 93 Engine wiring—1992–93 P-series gasoline engines without 4L80E transmission

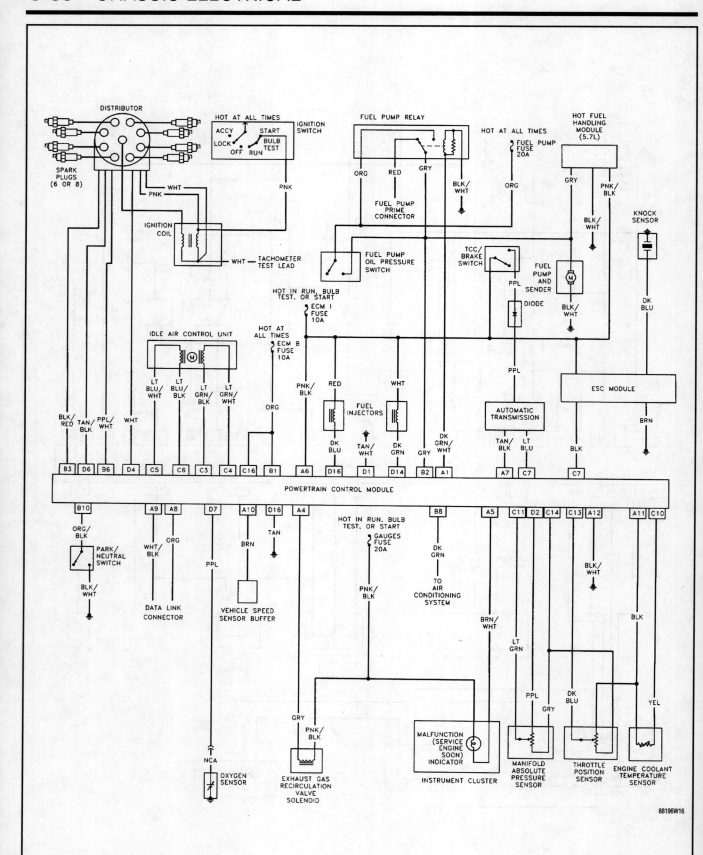

Fig. 94 Engine wiring—1992 G-series gasoline engines with 4L60E transmission

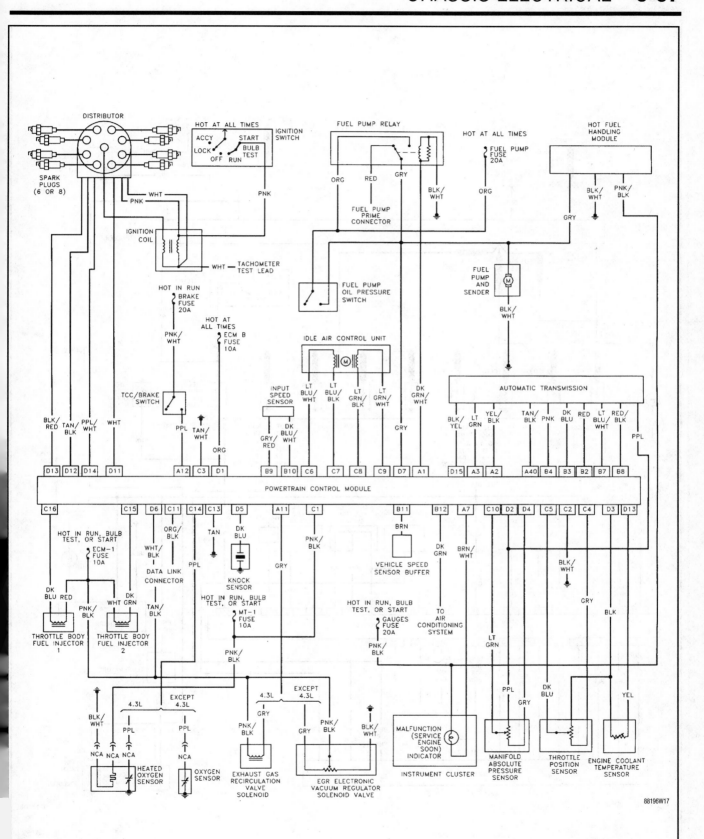

Fig. 95 Engine wiring—1992 G-series gasoline engines with 4L80E transmission

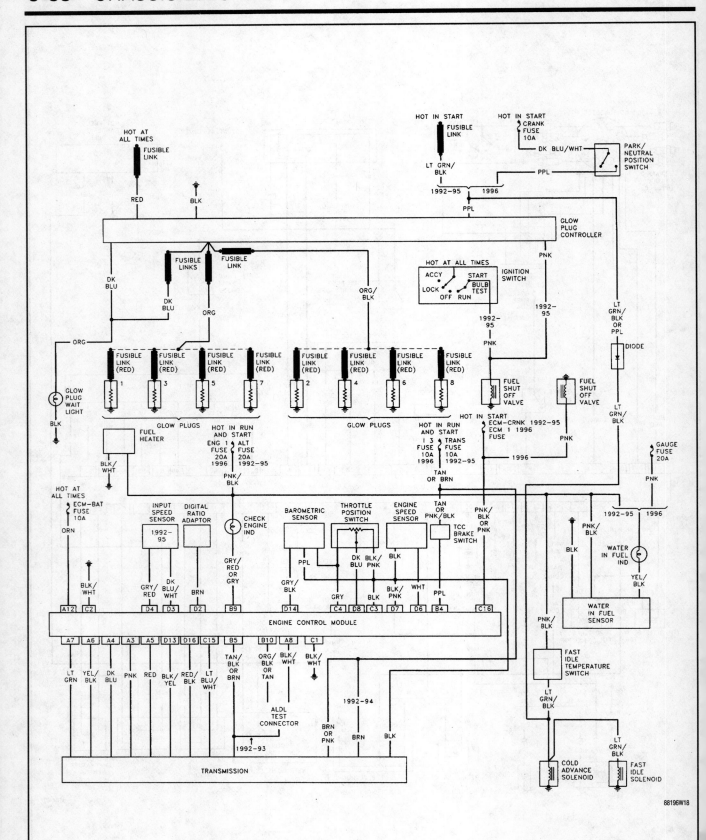

Fig. 96 Engine wiring—1992–96 P-series standard and heavy duty models with diesel engines and automatic transmissions

88196W18

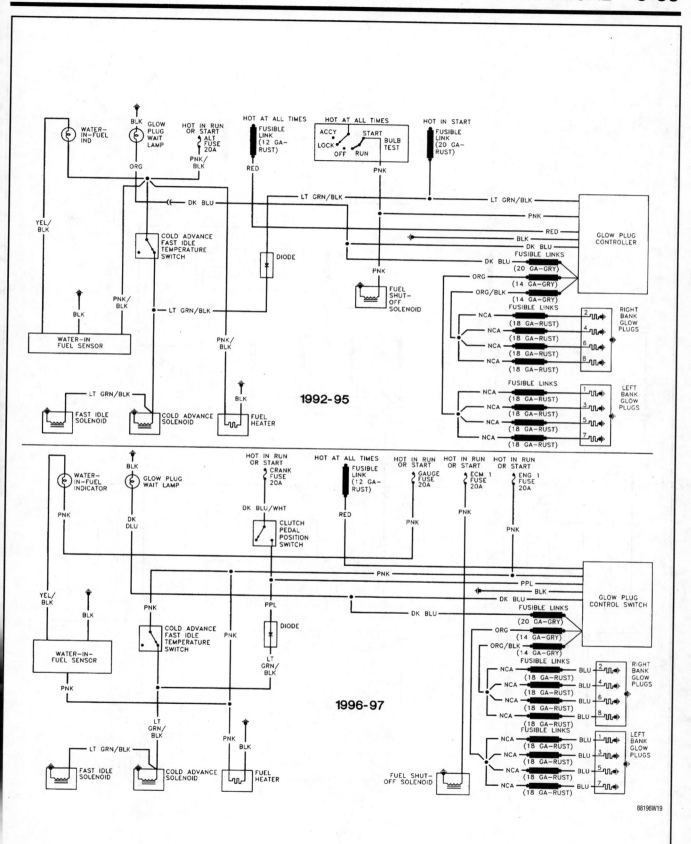

Fig. 97 Engine wiring—1992–97 P-series models with manual transmission

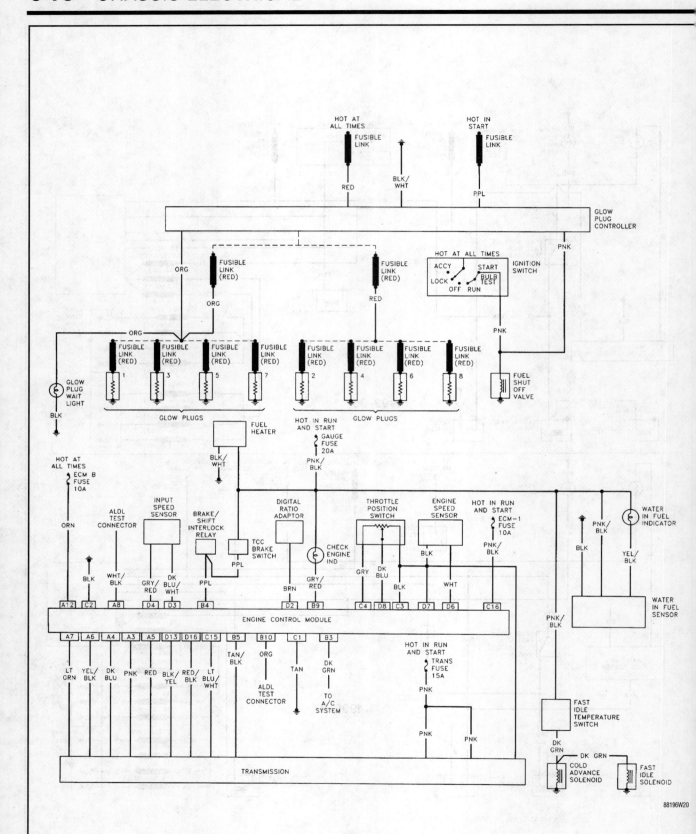

Fig. 98 Engine wiring—1993 G-series diesel engines with 4L80E transmission

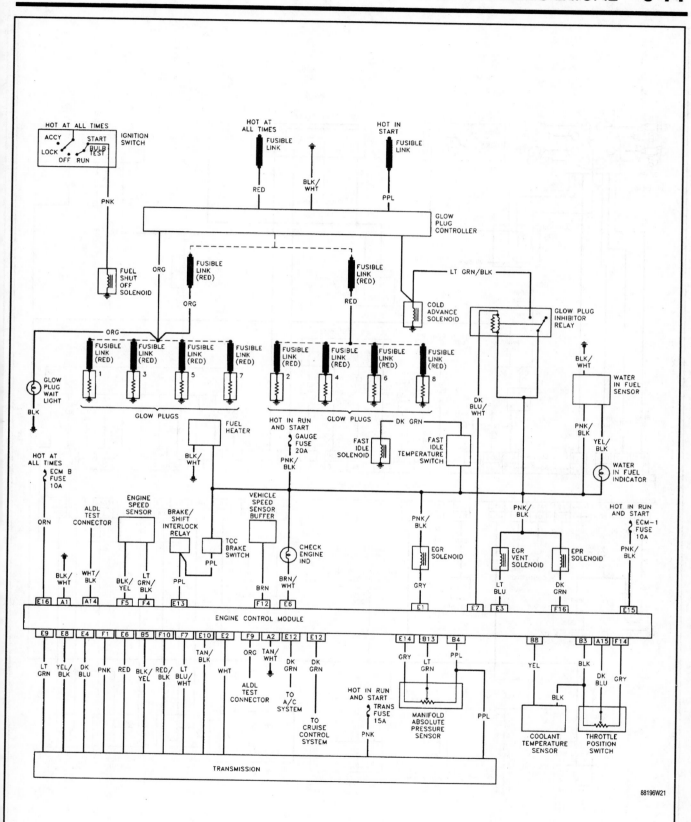

Fig. 99 Engine wiring—1993 G-series diesel engines with 4L60E transmission

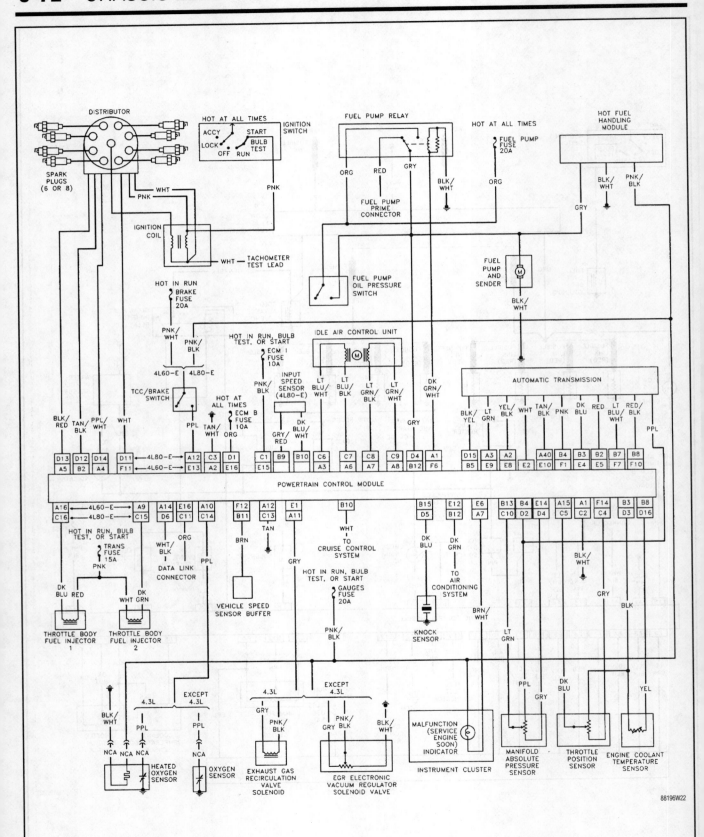

Fig. 100 Engine wiring—1993 G-series gasoline engines

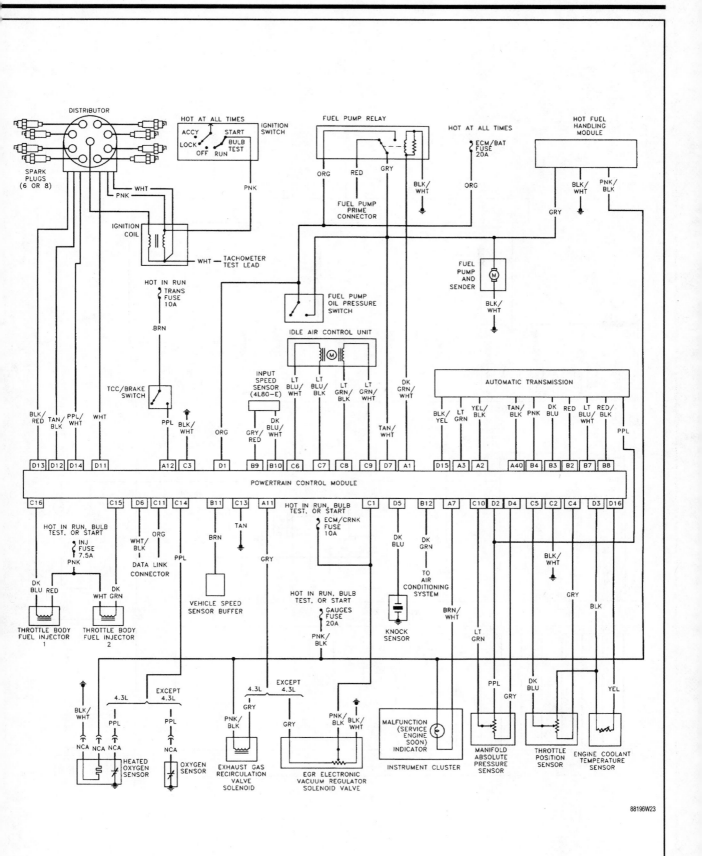

Fig. 101 Engine wiring—1993 P-series gasoline engines with 4L80E transmission

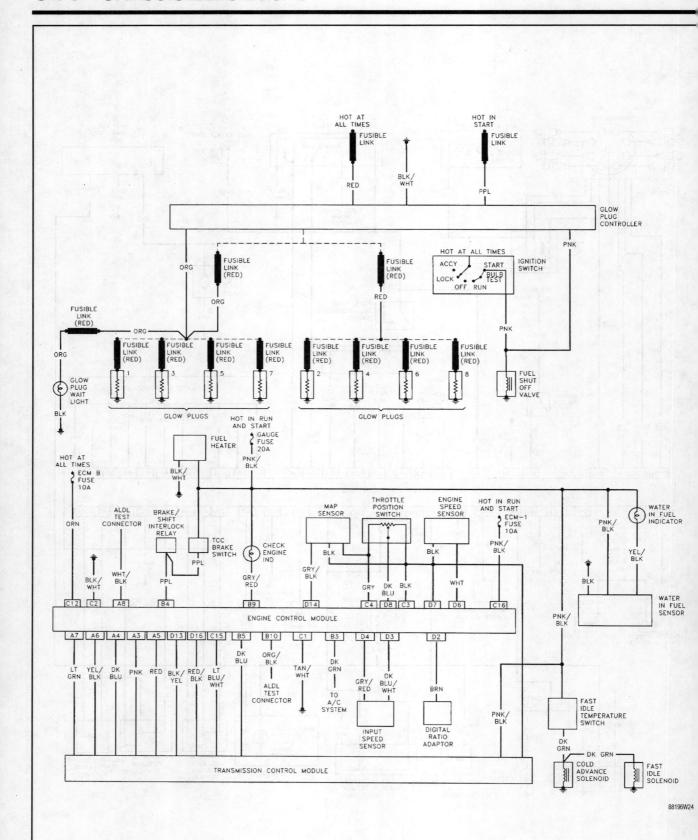

Fig. 102 Engine wiring—1994 G-series diesel engines with 4L80E transmission

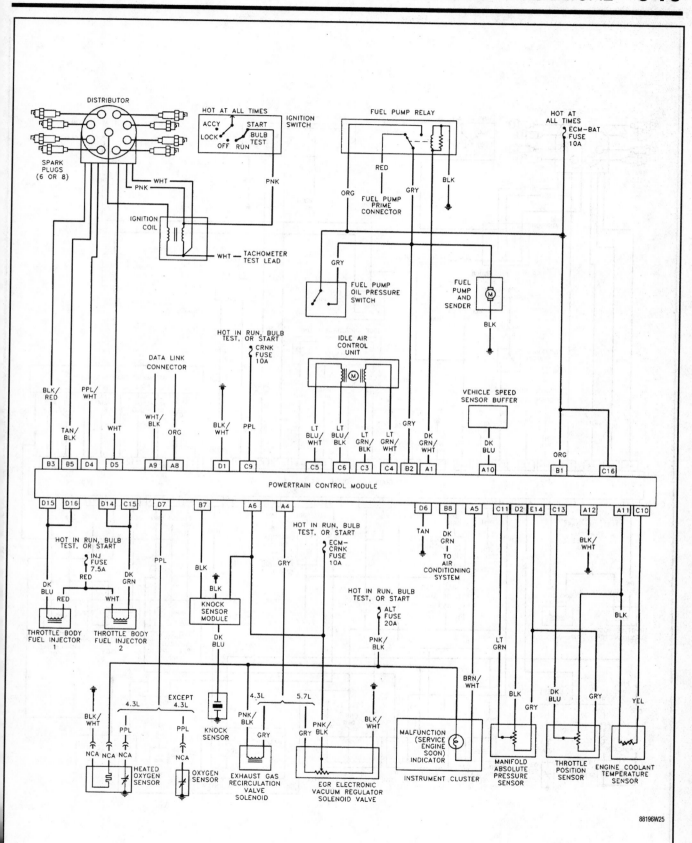

Fig. 103 Engine wiring—1994 P-series gasoline engines with manual transmission

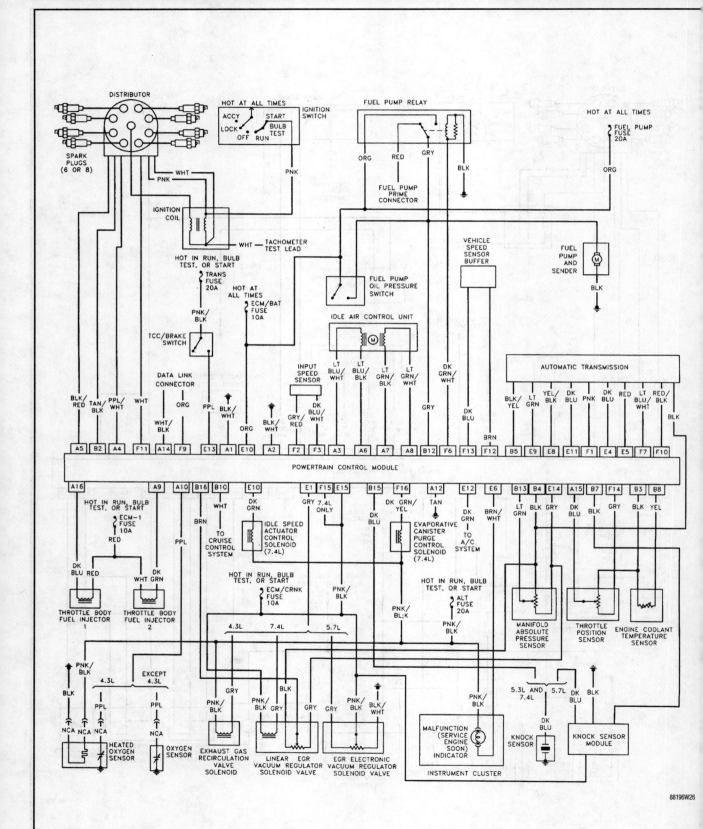

Fig. 104 Engine wiring—1994-95 P-series gasoline engines with automatic transmission

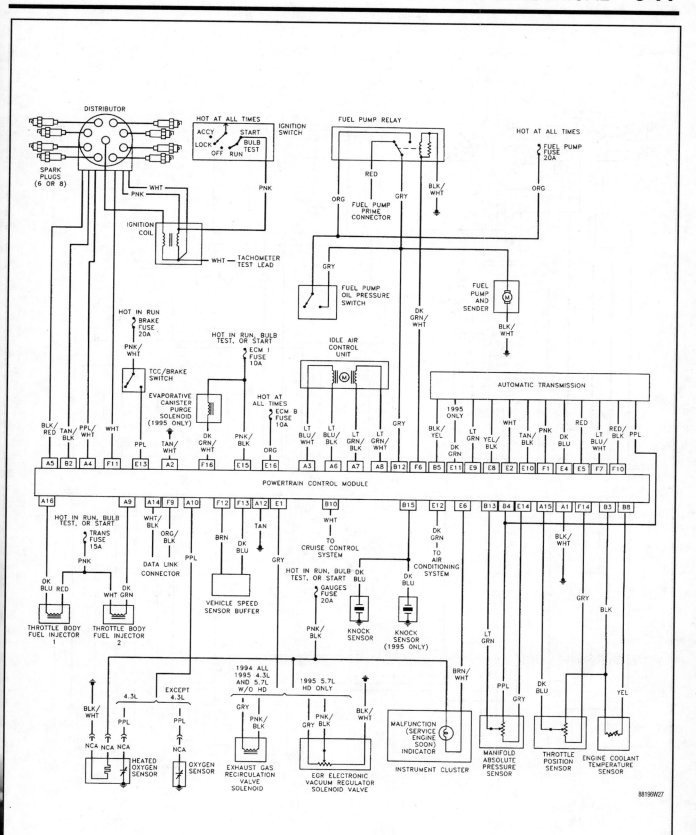

Fig. 105 Engine wiring—1994–95 G-series gasoline engines with 4L60E transmission

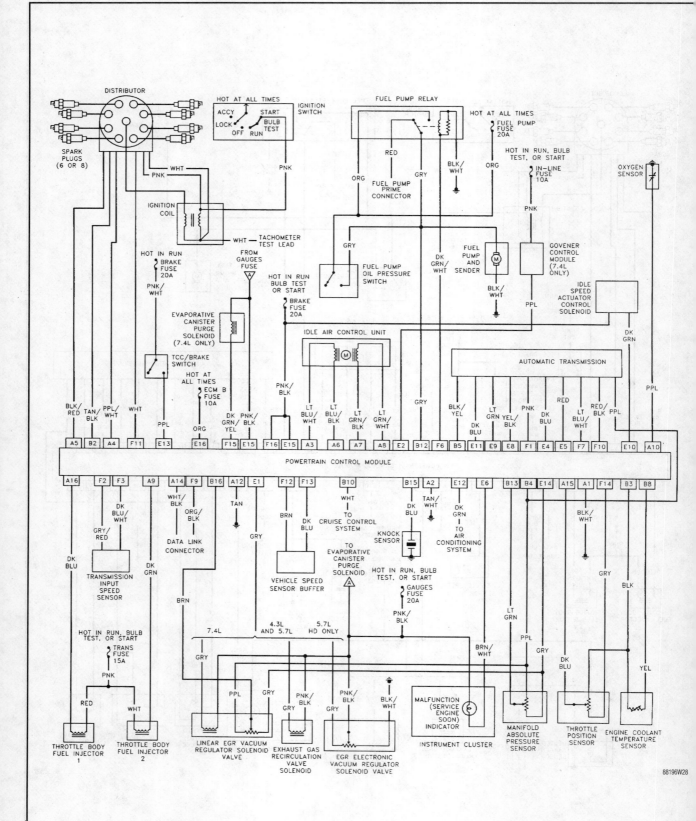

Fig. 106 Engine wiring—1994–95 G-series gasoline engines with 4L80E transmission

88196W28

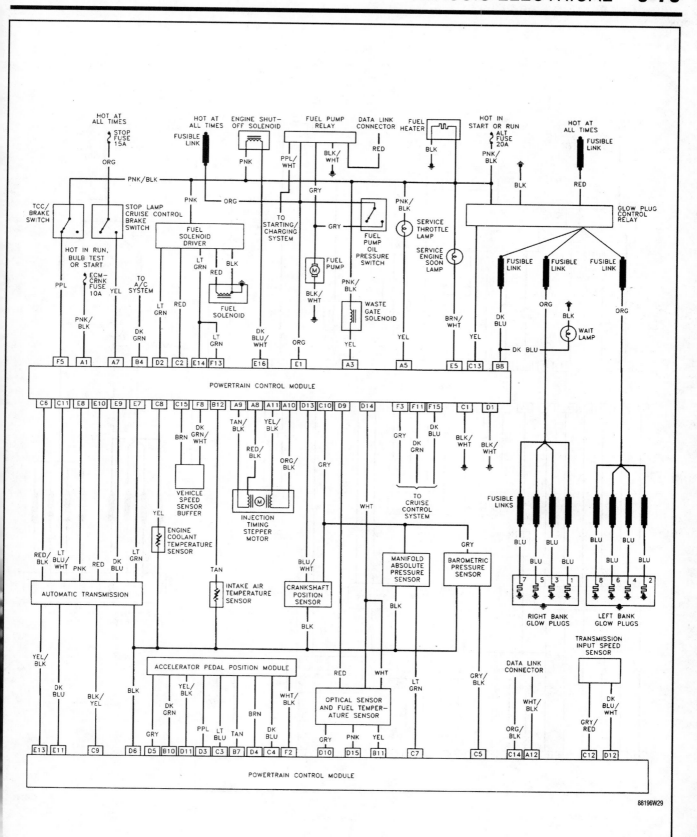

Fig. 107 Engine wiring—1994–95 P-series turbo diesel engines

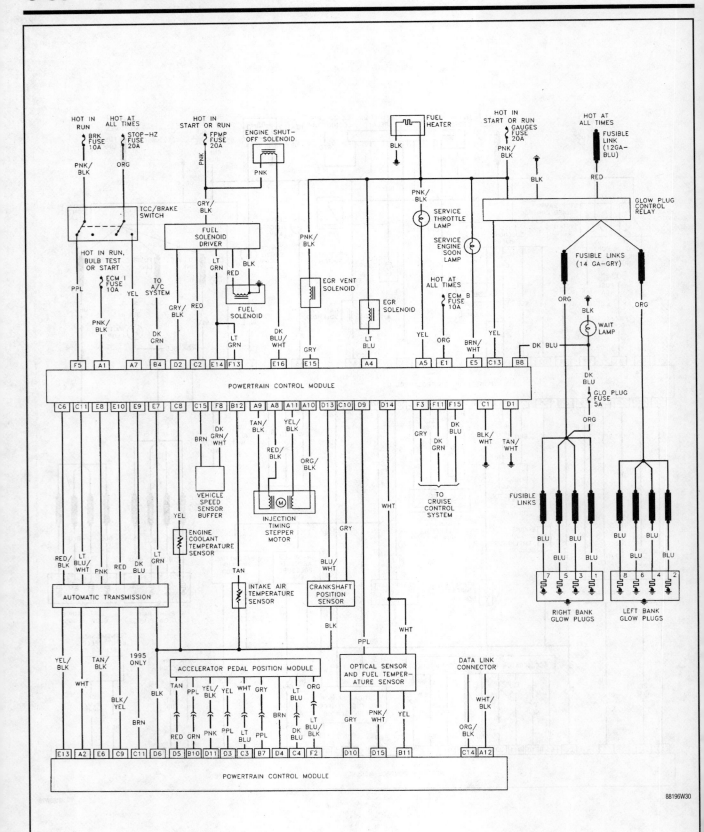

Fig. 108 Engine wiring—1994–95 G-series diesel engines with 4L60E transmission

88196W30

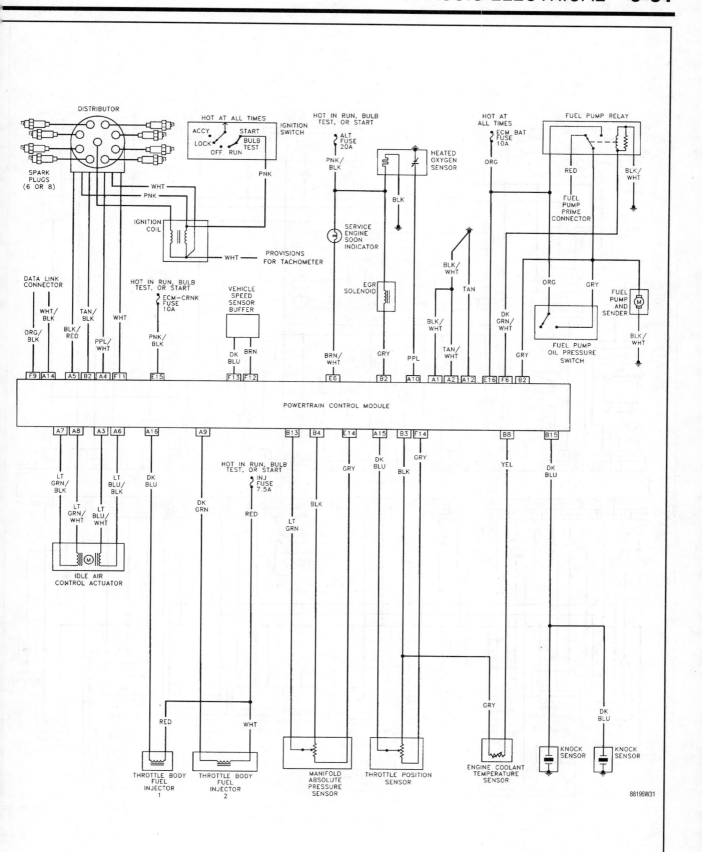

Fig. 109 Engine wiring—1995 P-series gasoline engines with manual transmission

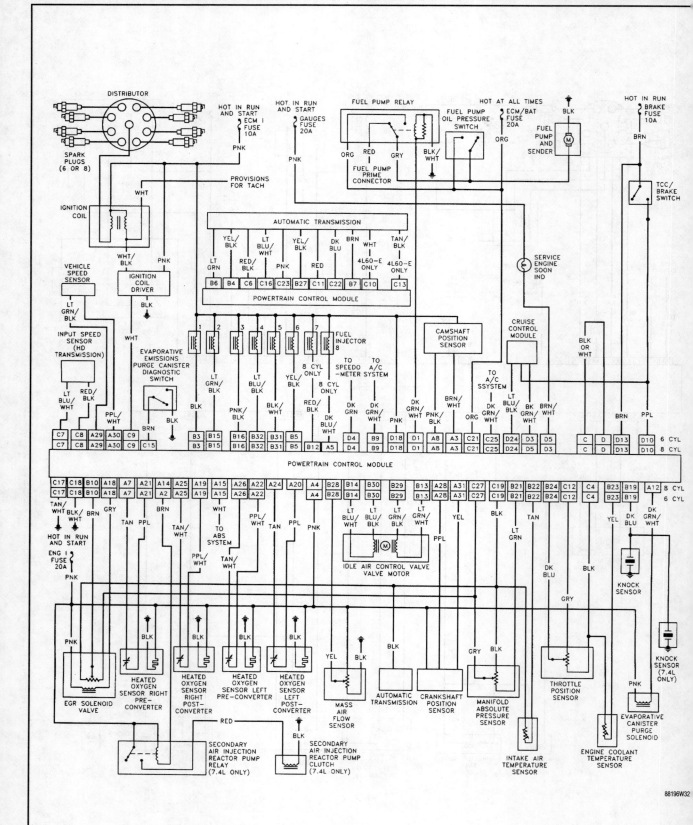

Fig. 110 Engine wiring—1996–97 G-series gasoline engines

88196W32

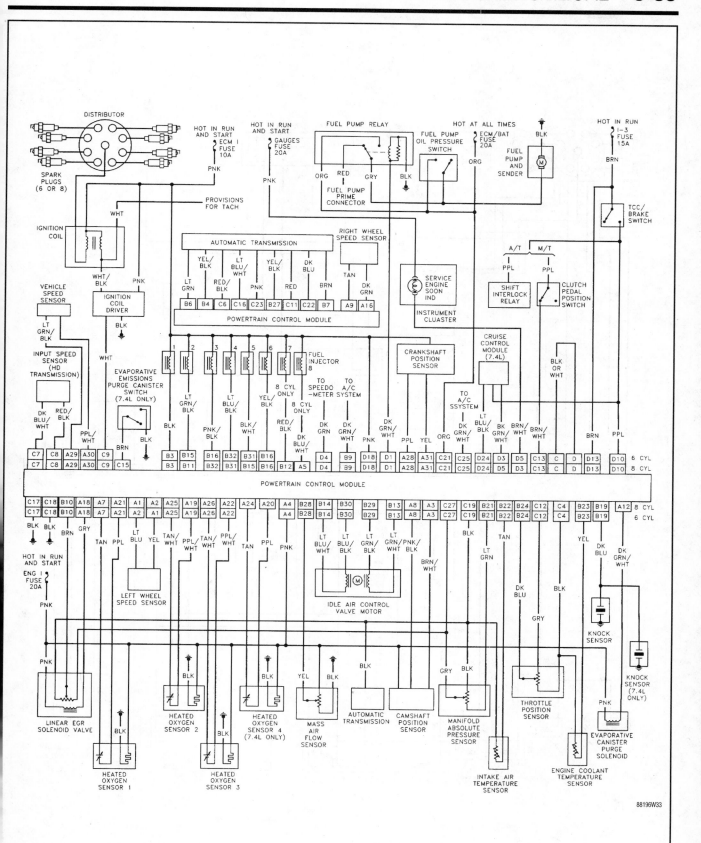

Fig. 111 Engine wiring—1996–97 P-series gasoline engines without TBI

88196W33

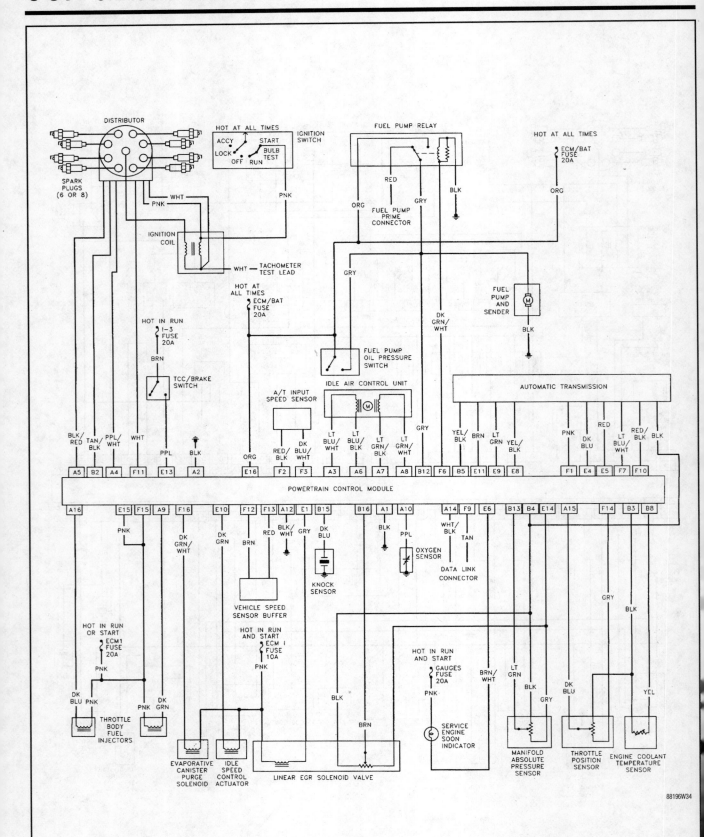

Fig. 112 Engine wiring—1996–97 7.4L P-series gasoline engines with TBI

88196W34

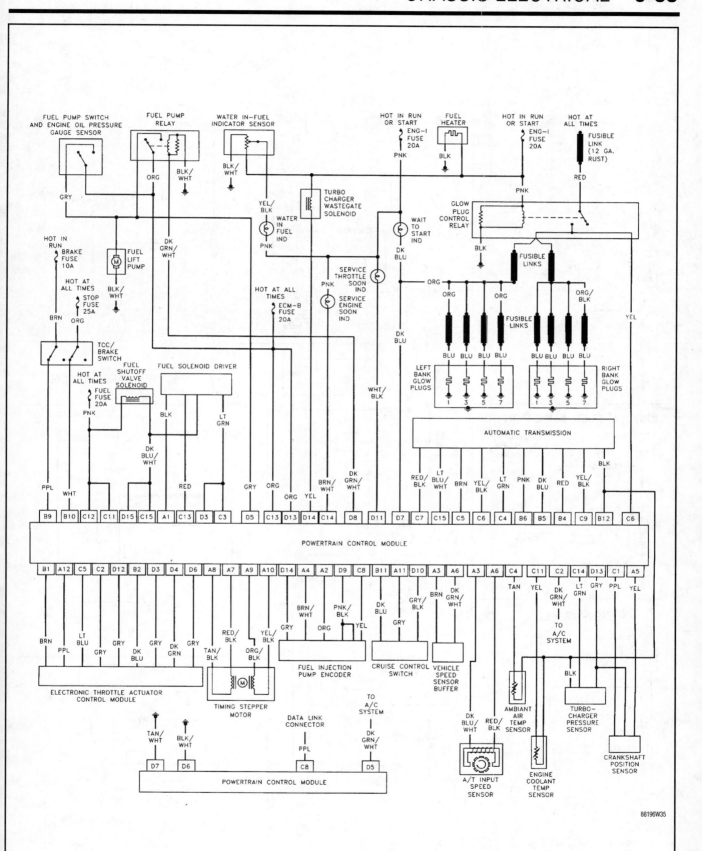

Fig. 113 Engine wiring—1996-97 G-series turbo diesel engines

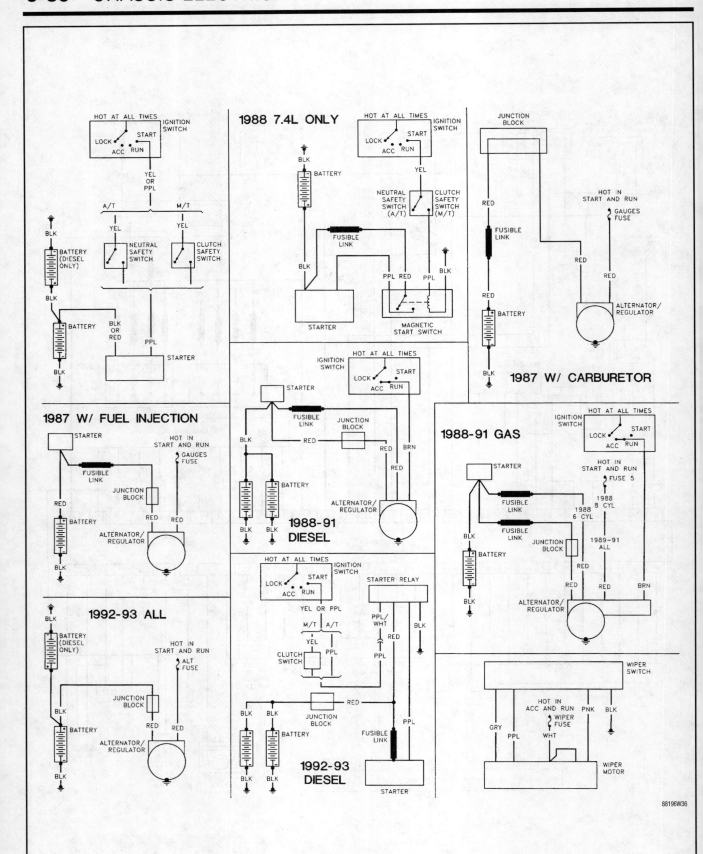

Fig. 114 Chassis wiring—1987–93 P-series

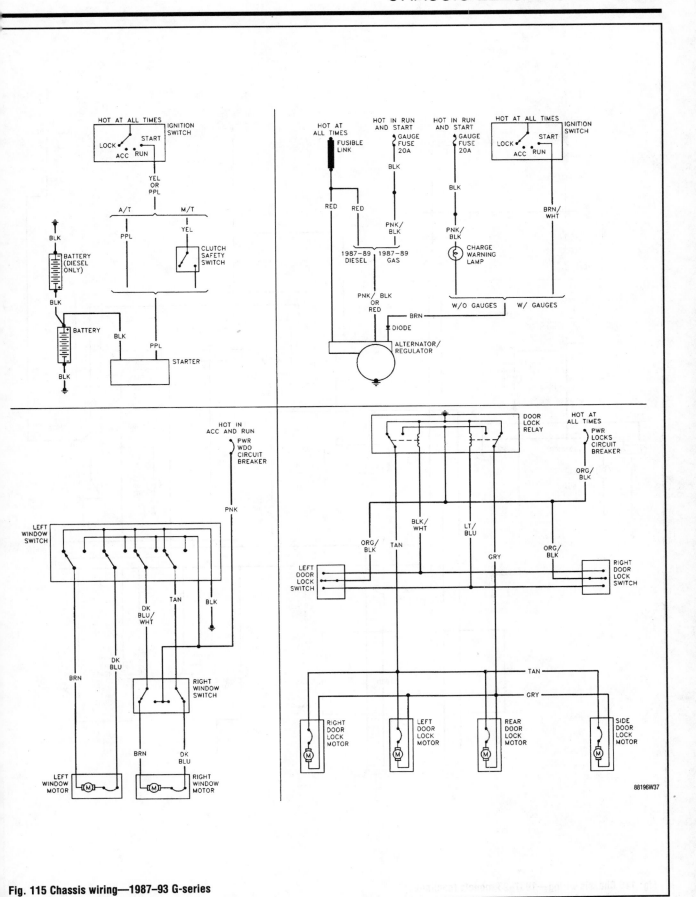

Fig. 115 Chassis wiring—1987–93 G-series

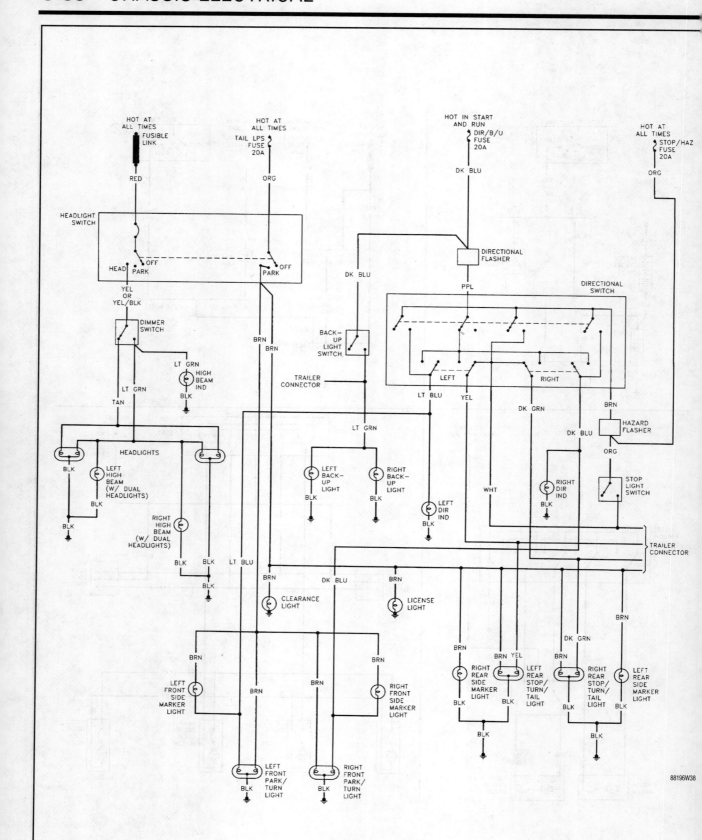

Fig. 116 Chassis wiring—1987-93 models (continued)

88196W38

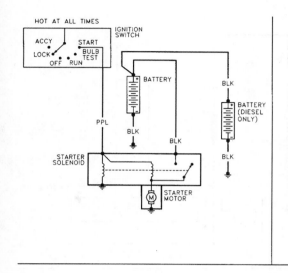

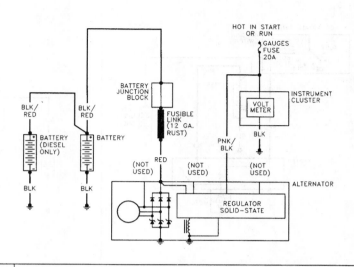

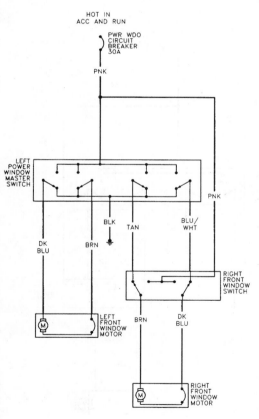

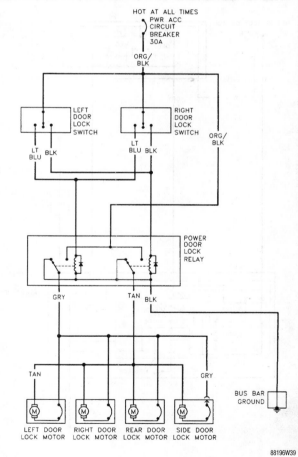

Fig. 117 Chassis wiring—1994–95 G-series

88196W39

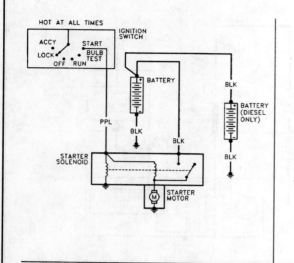

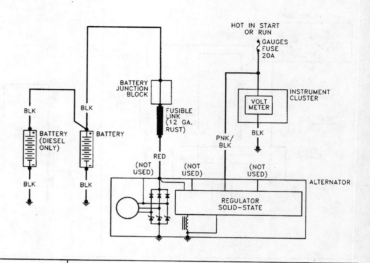

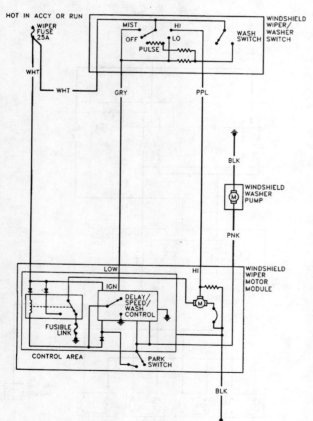

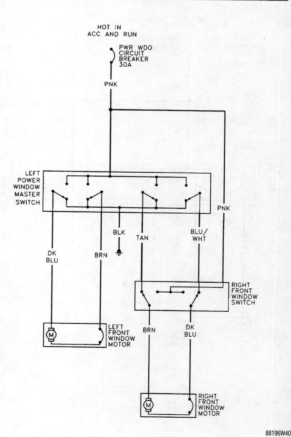

Fig. 118 Chassis wiring—1994-95 P-series

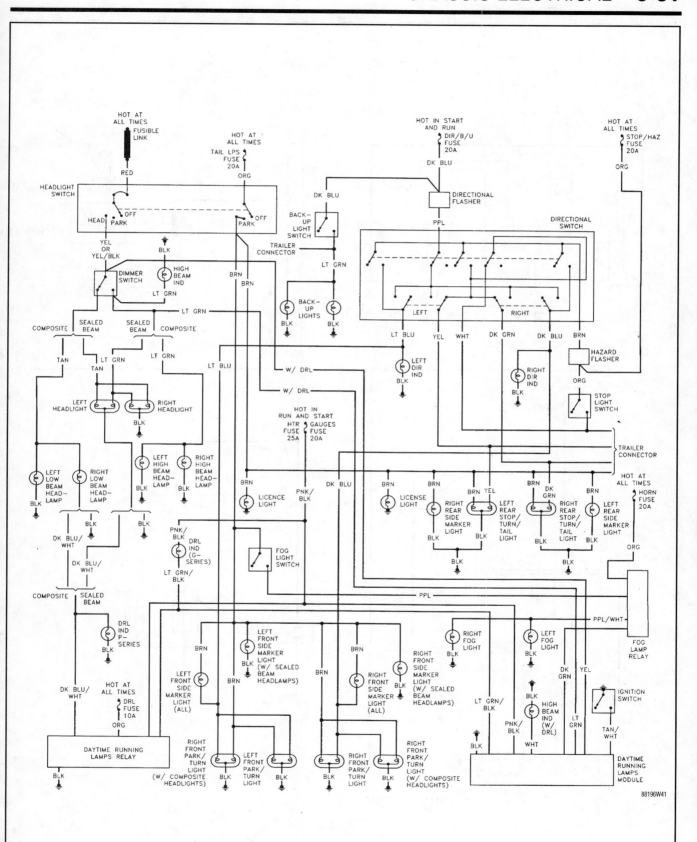

Fig. 119 Chassis wiring—1994-95 G-series and 1994-97 P-series (continued)

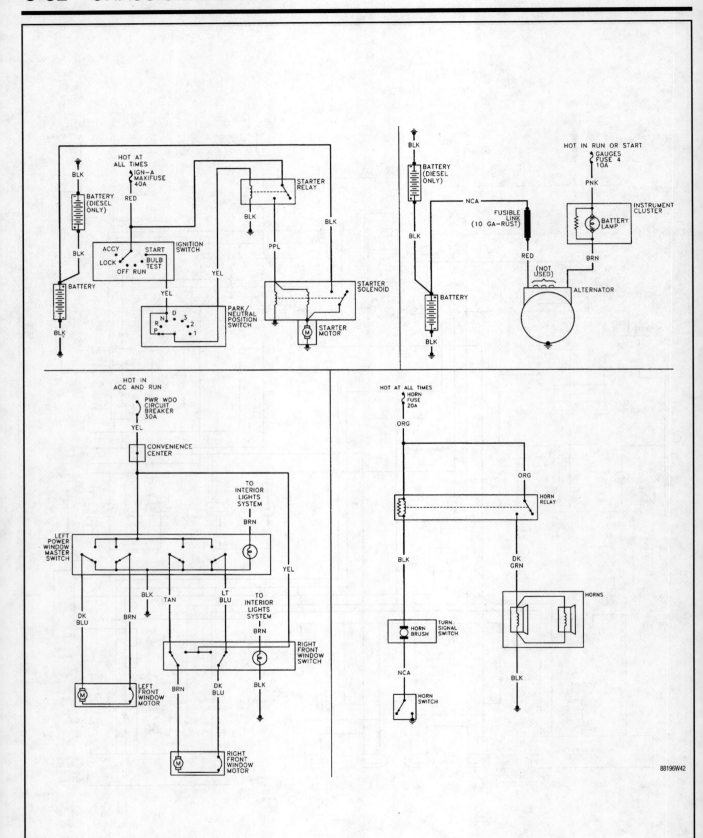

Fig. 120 Chassis wiring—1996–97 G-series

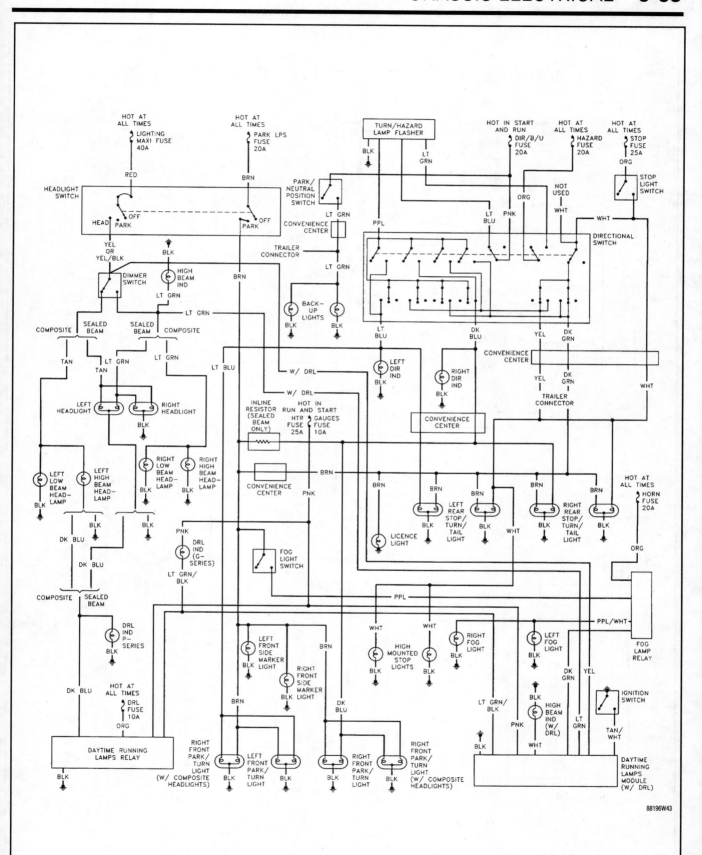

Fig. 121 Chassis wiring—1996-97 G-series (continued)

88196W43

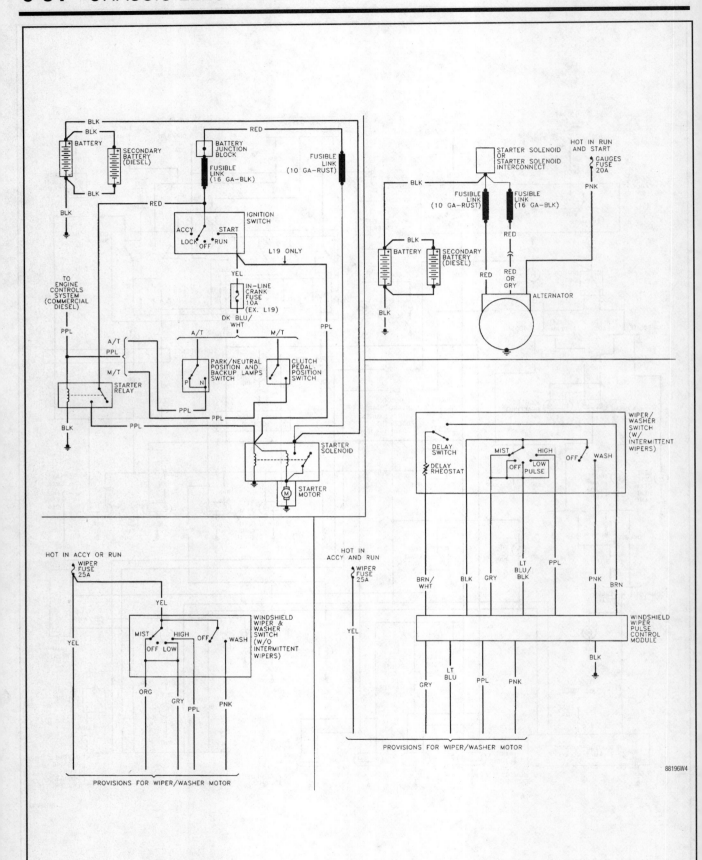

Fig. 122 Chassis wiring—1996–97 P-series

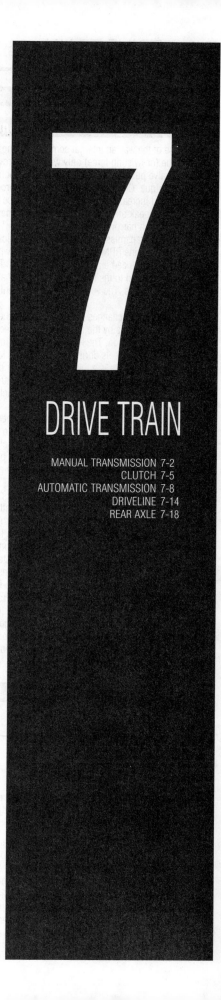

7
DRIVE TRAIN

MANUAL TRANSMISSION

Understanding the Manual Transmission

Because of the way an internal combustion engine breathes, it can produce torque (or twisting force) only within a narrow speed range. Most overhead valve pushrod engines must turn at about 2500 rpm to produce their peak torque. Often by 4500 rpm, they are producing so little torque that continued increases in engine speed produce no power increases.

The torque peak on overhead camshaft engines is, generally, much higher, but much narrower.

The manual transmission and clutch are employed to vary the relationship between engine RPM and the speed of the wheels so that adequate power can be produced under all circumstances. The clutch allows engine torque to be applied to the transmission input shaft gradually, due to mechanical slippage. The vehicle can, consequently, be started smoothly from a full stop.

The transmission changes the ratio between the rotating speeds of the engine and the wheels by the use of gears. 4-speed or 5-speed transmissions are most common. The lower gears allow full engine power to be applied to the rear wheels during acceleration at low speeds.

The clutch driveplate is a thin disc, the center of which is splined to the transmission input shaft. Both sides of the disc are covered with a layer of material which is similar to brake lining and which is capable of allowing slippage without roughness or excessive noise.

The clutch cover is bolted to the engine flywheel and incorporates a diaphragm spring which provides the pressure to engage the clutch. The cover also houses the pressure plate. When the clutch pedal is released, the driven disc is sandwiched between the pressure plate and the smooth surface of the flywheel, thus forcing the disc to turn at the same speed as the engine crankshaft.

The transmission contains a mainshaft which passes all the way through the transmission, from the clutch to the driveshaft. This shaft is separated at one point, so that front and rear portions can turn at different speeds.

Power is transmitted by a countershaft in the lower gears and reverse. The gears of the countershaft mesh with gears on the mainshaft, allowing power to be carried from one to the other. Countershaft gears are often integral with that shaft, while several of the mainshaft gears can either rotate independently of the shaft or be locked to it. Shifting from one gear to the next causes one of the gears to be freed from rotating with the shaft and locks another to it. Gears are locked and unlocked by internal dog clutches which slide between the center of the gear and the shaft. The forward gears usually employ synchronizers; friction members which smoothly bring gear and shaft to the same speed before the toothed dog clutches are engaged.

Shift Linkage

ADJUSTMENT

3-Speed Column Shift

▶ **See Figure 1**

➡ **The gearshift linkage should be adjusted each time it is disturbed or removed. The 1st/reverse rod must be adjusted before the 2nd/3rd rod.**

1. Loosen the shift rod-to-transmission lever bolt.
2. Move the 1st/reverse transmission lever to the front detent, or, the 2nd/3rd transmission lever to the front detent, then back 1 detent.
3. Put the 1st/reverse column lever into reverse and lock the column, or, put the 2nd/3rd column lever into Neutral.
4. Using a ¼ in. (6mm) drill bit as a gauge pin, place the bit through the holes in the column levers and the relay lever. All should align.
5. Hold the shift rod down tightly in the swivel and tighten the bolt. Remove the gauge pin.

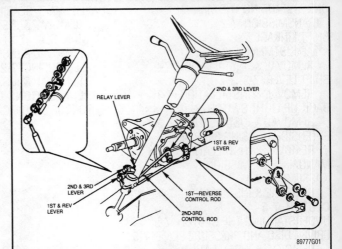

Fig. 1 Exploded view of the 3-speed column shift linkage—Muncie 3-speed transmission

Floor Mounted Shift

▶ **See Figure 2**

1. Loosen the nuts on either side of the swivel. Refer to the illustration of the floor shift linkage for component location.
2. Move the shift control lever to neutral and move the control levers to the front detent and then back one. This will place the transmission in neutral.
3. Place a 0.249–0.250 in. (6–7mm) gauge pin through the control levers and hold the shift rod levers forward tightly and tighten the nuts.
4. Remove the gauge pin and lubricate the levers.

REMOVAL & INSTALLATION

3-Speed Column Shift

1. Raise and support the front end on jackstands.
2. Remove the rod-to-column clips.
3. Disconnect the linkage at the column levers.
4. Disconnect the linkage at the transmission levers by removing the swivel bolts.

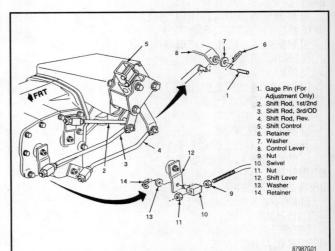

1. Gage Pin (For Adjustment Only)
2. Shift Rod, 1st/2nd
3. Shift Rod, 3rd/OD
4. Shift Rod, Rev.
5. Shift Control
6. Retainer
7. Washer
8. Control Lever
9. Nut
10. Swivel
11. Nut
12. Shift Lever
13. Washer
14. Retainer

Fig. 2 Exploded view of the shift lever and components—89mm 4-speed overdrive transmission

5. Unbolt the rods at the cross lever.
6. Remove the cross lever and linkage rods.
7. Installation is the reverse of removal. Lightly grease all moving parts.

Floor Mounted Shift

1. Remove the cotter pin and the washer.
2. Disconnect the shift rod from the control lever and remove the retainer and washer.
3. Disconnect the shift rod from the shift lever and remove the nuts and swivel.

To install:

4. Install but do not tighten the nuts and swivel.
5. Connect the shift rod to the shift lever.
6. Install the washer and new retainer.
7. Connect the shift rod to the control lever and install the washer and new retainer.
8. Adjust the shift linkage as outlined in this section.

Shift Lever

REMOVAL & INSTALLATION

117mm 4-Speed

▶ **See Figure 3**

1. On 4WD models, remove the transfer case lever boot.
2. Remove the transmission lever boot retaining ring.
3. Remove the boot retaining screws.
4. Remove the boot.
5. Push downward on the cap at the bottom of the lever and turn it counterclockwise. Pull the lever from the transmission.
6. Installation is the reverse of removal.

NVG 4500

▶ **See Figure 4**

1. Remove the shift boot retaining ring.
2. Remove the boot retaining screws and lift off the boot.
3. Loosen the jam nut and unscrew the lever.

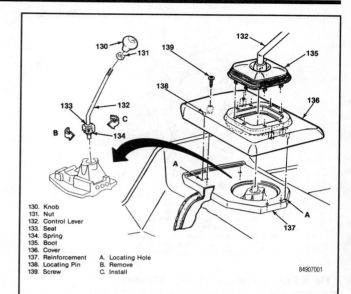

130. Knob
131. Nut
132. Control Lever
133. Seat
134. Spring
135. Boot
136. Cover
137. Reinforcement
138. Locating Pin
139. Screw

A. Locating Hole
B. Remove
C. Install

84907001

Fig. 3 Shift lever and components—117mm transmission

Back-up Light Switch

REMOVAL & INSTALLATION

▶ **See Figure 5**

1. Disconnect the negative battery cable.
2. Raise the vehicle and support it safely.
3. Unplug the electrical connector at the switch.
4. Unscrew the switch from the transmission case.
5. Installation is the reverse of removal.

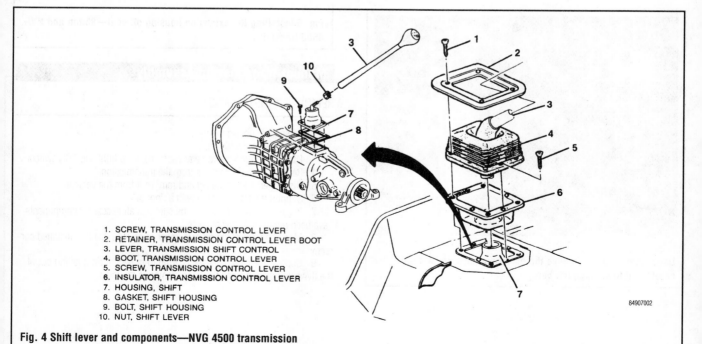

1. SCREW, TRANSMISSION CONTROL LEVER
2. RETAINER, TRANSMISSION CONTROL LEVER BOOT
3. LEVER, TRANSMISSION SHIFT CONTROL
4. BOOT, TRANSMISSION CONTROL LEVER
5. SCREW, TRANSMISSION CONTROL LEVER
6. INSULATOR, TRANSMISSION CONTROL LEVER
7. HOUSING, SHIFT
8. GASKET, SHIFT HOUSING
9. BOLT, SHIFT HOUSING
10. NUT, SHIFT LEVER

84907002

Fig. 4 Shift lever and components—NVG 4500 transmission

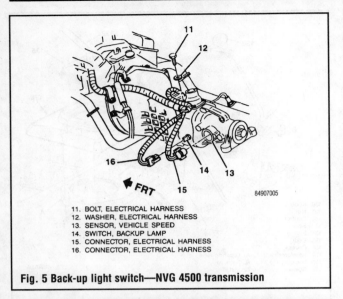

11. BOLT, ELECTRICAL HARNESS
12. WASHER, ELECTRICAL HARNESS
13. SENSOR, VEHICLE SPEED
14. SWITCH, BACKUP LAMP
15. CONNECTOR, ELECTRICAL HARNESS
16. CONNECTOR, ELECTRICAL HARNESS

Fig. 5 Back-up light switch—NVG 4500 transmission

Extension Housing Rear Seal

REMOVAL & INSTALLATION

▶ **See Figure 6**

1. Raise and support the van end on jackstands.
2. Drain the transmission oil.
3. Matchmark and disconnect the driveshaft.
4. Remove the parking brake, if necessary and the yoke.
5. Deform the seal with a punch and pull it from the housing.

To install:

6. Install the seal using a seal installation tool.
7. Install the yoke and the parking brake, if removed.
8. Install the driveshaft and refill the transmission with the proper quality and quantity of oil.
9. Lower the vehicle and check for leaks.

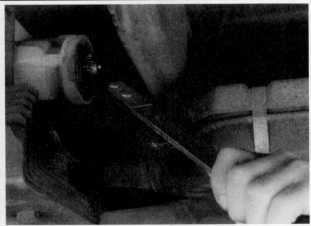

Use a seal puller to remove the extension housing seal (be careful not to damage the bore)

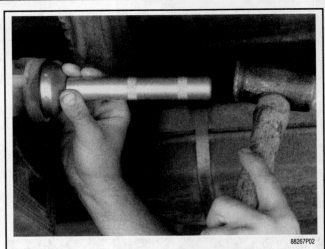

Use a driver to install the replacement seal—automatic transmission shown, manual similar

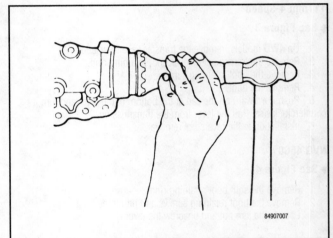

Fig. 6 Installing the extension housing oil seal—85mm and NVG 4500 transmissions

Manual Transmission Assembly

REMOVAL & INSTALLATION

1. Raise and support the van.
2. Drain the transmission.
3. Disconnect the speedometer cable, back-up light and TCS switch.
4. Remove the shift controls from the transmission.
5. Disconnect the driveshaft and remove it from the vehicle.
6. Support the transmission with a floor jack.
7. Inspect the transmission to be sure that all necessary components have been removed or disconnected.
8. Mark the front of the crossmember to be sure that it is installed correctly.
9. Support the clutch release bearing to prevent it from falling out of the flywheel housing when the transmission is removed.

10. Remove the flywheel housing under pan and transmission mounting bolts.

11. Move the transmission slowly away from the engine, keeping the mainshaft in alignment with the clutch disc hub. Be sure that the transmission is supported.

12. Remove the transmission from under the vehicle.

To install:

13. Installation is the reverse of removal. Please note the following important steps:

a. Inspect the transmission to be sure that all necessary components have been installed or connected.

b. Lightly coat the mainshaft with high temperature grease. Do not use much grease since, under normal operation, the grease will be thrown onto the clutch, causing it to fail.

c. Shift the transmission into high gear prior to installation on the 117mm 4-speed.

d. On the Muncie transmission, tighten the crossmember bolts to 50 ft. lbs. (67 Nm).

e. Tighten the transmission-to-clutch housing bolts to 75 ft. lbs. (100 Nm).

CLUTCH

Understanding the Clutch

The purpose of the clutch is to disconnect and connect engine power at the transmission. A vehicle at rest requires a lot of engine torque to get all that weight moving. An internal combustion engine does not develop a high starting torque (unlike steam engines) so it must be allowed to operate without any load until it builds up enough torque to move the vehicle. To a point, torque increases with engine rpm. The clutch allows the engine to build up torque by physically disconnecting the engine from the transmission, relieving the engine of any load or resistance.

The transfer of engine power to the transmission (the load) must be smooth and gradual; if it weren't, drive line components would wear out or break quickly. This gradual power transfer is made possible by gradually releasing the clutch pedal. The clutch disc and pressure plate are the connecting link between the engine and transmission. When the clutch pedal is released, the disc and plate contact each other (the clutch is engaged) physically joining the engine and transmission. When the pedal is pushed in, the disc and plate separate (the clutch is disengaged) disconnecting the engine from the transmission.

Most clutch assemblies consists of the flywheel, the clutch disc, the clutch pressure plate, the throw out bearing and fork, the actuating linkage and the pedal. The flywheel and clutch pressure plate (driving members) are connected to the engine crankshaft and rotate with it. The clutch disc is located between the flywheel and pressure plate, and is splined to the transmission shaft. A driving member is one that is attached to the engine and transfers engine power to a driven member (clutch disc) on the transmission shaft. A driving member (pressure plate) rotates (drives) a driven member (clutch disc) on contact and, in so doing, turns the transmission shaft.

There is a circular diaphragm spring within the pressure plate cover (transmission side). In a relaxed state (when the clutch pedal is fully released) this spring is convex; that is, it is dished outward toward the transmission. Pushing in the clutch pedal actuates the attached linkage. Connected to the other end of this is the throw out fork, which hold the throw out bearing. When the clutch pedal is depressed, the clutch linkage pushes the fork and bearing forward to contact the diaphragm spring of the pressure plate. The outer edges of the spring are secured to the pressure plate and are pivoted on rings so that when the center of the spring is compressed by the throw out bearing, the outer edges bow outward and, by so doing, pull the pressure plate in the same direction − away from the clutch disc. This action separates the disc from the plate, disengaging the clutch and allowing the transmission to be shifted into another gear. A coil type clutch return spring attached to the clutch pedal arm permits full release of the pedal. Releasing the pedal pulls the throw out bearing away from the diaphragm spring resulting in a reversal of spring position. As bearing pressure is gradually released from the spring center, the outer edges of the spring bow outward, pushing the pressure plate into closer contact with the clutch disc. As the disc and plate move closer together, friction between the two increases and slippage is reduced until, when full spring pressure is applied (by fully releasing the pedal) the speed of the disc and plate are the same. This stops all slipping, creating a direct connection between the plate and disc which results in the transfer of power from the engine to the transmission. The clutch disc is now rotating with the pressure plate at engine speed and, because it is splined to the transmission shaft, the shaft now turns at the same engine speed.

The clutch is operating properly if:
- It will stall the engine when released with the vehicle held stationary
- The shift lever can be moved freely between 1st and reverse gears when the vehicle is stationary and the clutch disengaged

Driven Disc and Pressure Plate

REMOVAL & INSTALLATION

▶ **See Figures 7 thru 15 (p. 6–7)**

✳✳ CAUTION

The clutch driven disc may contain asbestos, which has been determined to be a cancer causing agent. Never clean clutch surfaces with compressed air! Avoid inhaling any dust from any clutch surface! When cleaning clutch surfaces, use a commercially available brake cleaning fluid.

➡**Before removing the bell housing, the engine must be supported. This can be done by placing a hydraulic jack, with a board on top, under the oil pan.**

1. Remove the transmission.
2. Remove the actuator assembly.
3. Remove the bell housing cover.
4. Remove the bell housing from the engine.
5. Remove the throwout spring and fork.
6. Remove the ballstud from the bellhousing.
7. Install a pilot tool (an old input shaft makes a good pilot tool) to hold the clutch while you are removing it.

➡**Before removing the clutch from the flywheel, mark the flywheel, clutch cover and one pressure plate lug, so that these parts may be assembled in their same relative positions. They were balanced as an assembly.**

8. Loosen the clutch attaching bolts one turn at a time to prevent distortion of the clutch cover until the tension is released.
9. Remove the clutch pilot tool and the clutch from the vehicle.
10. Check the pressure plate and flywheel for signs of wear, scoring, overheating, etc. If the clutch plate, flywheel, or pressure plate is oil-soaked, inspect the engine rear main seal and the transmission input shaft seal, and correct leakage as required. Replace any damaged parts.

To install:

11. Install a new pilot bearing. Lubricate with a few drops of machine oil.
12. Install the pressure plate in the cover assembly, aligning the notch in the pressure plate with the notch in the cover flange. Install pressure plate retracting springs, lockwashers and drive strap-to-pressure plate bolts. Tighten to 11 ft. lbs. (15 Nm). The clutch is now ready to be installed.

➡**The manufacturer recommends that new pressure plate bolts and washers be used.**

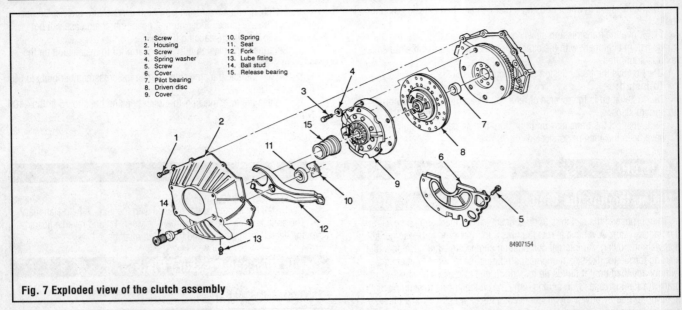

1. Screw
2. Housing
3. Screw
4. Spring washer
5. Screw
6. Cover
7. Pilot bearing
8. Driven disc
9. Cover
10. Spring
11. Seat
12. Fork
13. Lube fitting
14. Ball stud
15. Release bearing

84907154

Fig. 7 Exploded view of the clutch assembly

TCCS7116

Fig. 8 Removing the clutch and pressure plate bolts

TCCS7118

Fig. 10 Removing the clutch and pressure plate

TCCS7117

Fig. 9 Removing the clutch and pressure plate assembly

TCCS7124

Fig. 11 Be sure that the flywheel surface is clean, before installing the clutch

Fig. 12 Install a clutch alignment arbor, to align the clutch assembly during installation

Fig. 13 Apply a thread locking agent to clutch assembly bolts

Fig. 14 Be sure to use a torque wrench to tighten the bolts

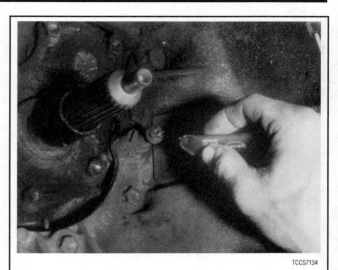

Fig. 15 Grease the clutch release fork ball

13. Turn the flywheel until the **X** mark is at the bottom.

14. Install the clutch disc, pressure plate and cover, using an old input shaft as an aligning tool.

15. Turn the clutch until the **X** mark or painted white letter on the clutch cover aligns with the **X** mark on the flywheel.

16. Install the attaching bolts and tighten them a little at a time in a crossing pattern until the spring pressure is taken up. Tighten to 22 ft. lbs. (30 Nm) on 4.3L, 5.0L and 5.7L engines; 32 ft. lbs. (43 Nm) on 6.2L and 6.5L engines; and 24 ft. lbs. (33 Nm) on 7.4L engines.

17. Remove the aligning tool.

18. Coat the rounded end of the ballstud with high temperature wheel bearing grease.

19. Install the ballstud in the bellhousing. Pack the ballstud from the lubrication fitting. Coat the rounded end of the ballstud with grease.

20. Pack the inside recess and the outside groove of the release bearing with high temperature wheel bearing grease and install the release bearing and fork.

21. Install the release bearing seat and spring.

22. Install the clutch housing. Tighten the bolts to 29 ft. lbs. (39 Nm).

23. Install the cover.

24. Install the actuator assembly.

25. Install the transmission.

26. Bleed the hydraulic system.

Clutch Master Cylinder, Reservoir and Actuator

REMOVAL & INSTALLATION

▶ **See Figures 16 and 17**

1. Disconnect the negative battery cable.

2. Disconnect the pushrod from the clutch pedal.

3. Disconnect the reservoir hose.

4. Disconnect the secondary cylinder hydraulic line to the master cylinder.

5. Remove the master cylinder retaining nuts.

6. Remove the nut and washer from the mounting clip.

7. Disconnect the master cylinder from the coupling using tool J-36221 or its equivalent by depressing the white plastic sleeve with the tool to separate the connection.

8. Remove the master cylinder.

9. Remove the retaining nuts and remove the reservoir from the firewall.

10. Unfasten the actuator-to-cylinder retainers and remove the actuator assembly

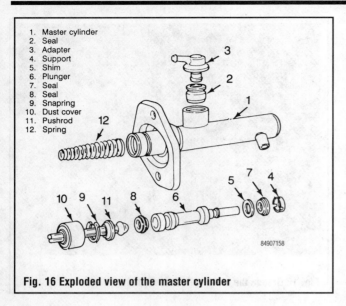

1. Master cylinder
2. Seal
3. Adapter
4. Support
5. Shim
6. Plunger
7. Seal
8. Seal
9. Snapring
10. Dust cover
11. Pushrod
12. Spring

84907158

Fig. 16 Exploded view of the master cylinder

To install:

11. Install the actuator assembly and tighten the retainers to 13 ft. lbs. (17 Nm).

※※ WARNING

Do not remove the plastic pushrod retainer from the actuator cylinder. The straps will break on the first clutch pedal application

12. Engage the master cylinder to the coupling.

➡**If a hard coupling effort is experienced, make sure the clutch pedal and master cylinder pushrods are fully retracted. Also make the actuator pushrod may be pressing against the clutch fork. If this is the case, loosen the actuator mounting nuts and complete the coupling procedure, then retighten the retainers.**

13. Install the washer and nut, then tighten the clip nut to 18 ft. lbs. (25 Nm).
14. Install the master cylinder and tighten the nuts to 13 ft. lbs. (17 Nm).
15. Engage the pushrod to the clutch pedal.

➡**Press the pedal down several times to break the plastic retaining straps on the actuator pushrod. Do not remove the plastic button on the end of the pushrod**

16. Connect the negative battery cable.
17. Bleed the clutch system.

HYDRAULIC SYSTEM BLEEDING

1. Disconnect the master cylinder pushrod from the clutch pedal and remove the actuator cylinder from the clutch master cylinder.
2. Remove the reservoir cap and slowly depress the actuator cylinder pushrod until it reaches the bottom of the bore.

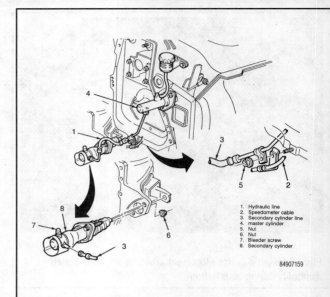

1. Hydraulic line
2. Speedometer cable
3. Secondary cylinder line
4. master cylinder
5. Nut
6. Nut
7. Bleeder screw
8. Secondary cylinder

84907159

Fig. 17 Clutch hydraulic system

3. Hold the actuator pushrod at the bottom of the bore and fill the reservoir with brake fluid. If necessary release actuator pushrod.
4. Hold the actuator assembly vertically so that the pushrod end faces the ground and the assembly is lower than the master cylinder.
5. Depress the actuator assembly pushrod slowly with short strokes of 5–10mm and watch the reservoir for air bubbles. Repeat this procedure until all the air is expelled.
6. Install the actuator assembly and if necessary, replenish the reservoir with brake fluid.
7. Install the reservoir cap and connect the master cylinder pushrod to the clutch pedal.

Adjustments

CLUTCH PEDAL FREE-PLAY

This adjustment is for the amount of clutch pedal free travel before the throwout bearing contacts the clutch release fingers. It is required periodically to compensate for clutch lining wear. Incorrect adjustment will cause gear grinding and clutch slippage or wear.

1. Disconnect the clutch fork return spring at the fork on the clutch housing.
2. Loosen the outer locknut on the adjusting rod.
3. Move the clutch fork back until clutch spring pressure is felt.
4. Hold the clutch pedal against its bumper and turn the inner adjusting nut until it is 0.28 in. (7mm) from the cross lever.
5. Tighten the locknut against the cross lever.
6. Install the return spring.
7. Check the free travel at the pedal and readjust as necessary. It should be 1⅜ in. (34mm).

AUTOMATIC TRANSMISSION

Understanding Automatic Transmissions

The automatic transmission allows engine torque and power to be transmitted to the rear wheels within a narrow range of engine operating speeds. It will allow the engine to turn fast enough to produce plenty of power and torque at very low speeds, while keeping it at a sensible rpm at high vehicle speeds (and it does this job without driver assistance). The transmission uses a light fluid as the medium for the transmission of power. This fluid also works in the operation of various hydraulic control circuits and as a lubricant. Because the transmission fluid performs all of these functions, trouble within the unit can easily travel from one part to another. For this reason, and because of the complexity and unusual operating principles of the transmission, a very sound understanding of the basic principles of operation will simplify troubleshooting.

TORQUE CONVERTER

♦ See Figure 18

The torque converter replaces the conventional clutch. It has three functions:
- It allows the engine to idle with the vehicle at a standstill, even with the transmission in gear.
- It allows the transmission to shift from range-to-range smoothly, without requiring that the driver close the throttle during the shift.
- It multiplies engine torque to an increasing extent as vehicle speed drops and throttle opening is increased. This has the effect of making the transmission more responsive and reduces the amount of shifting required.

The torque converter is a metal case which is shaped like a sphere that has been flattened on opposite sides. It is bolted to the rear end of the engine's crankshaft. Generally, the entire metal case rotates at engine speed and serves as the engine's flywheel.

The case contains three sets of blades. One set is attached directly to the case. This set forms the torus or pump. Another set is directly connected to the output shaft, and forms the turbine. The third set is mounted on a hub which, in turn, is mounted on a stationary shaft through a one-way clutch. This third set is known as the stator.

A pump, which is driven by the converter hub at engine speed, keeps the torque converter full of transmission fluid at all times. Fluid flows continuously through the unit to provide cooling.

Under low speed acceleration, the torque converter functions as follows:

The torus is turning faster than the turbine. It picks up fluid at the center of the converter and, through centrifugal force, slings it outward. Since the outer edge of the converter moves faster than the portions at the center, the fluid picks up speed.

The fluid then enters the outer edge of the turbine blades. It then travels back toward the center of the converter case along the turbine blades. In impinging upon the turbine blades, the fluid loses the energy picked up in the torus.

If the fluid was now returned directly into the torus, both halves of the converter would have to turn at approximately the same speed at all times, and torque input and output would both be the same.

In flowing through the torus and turbine, the fluid picks up two types of flow, or flow in two separate directions. It flows through the turbine blades, and it spins with the engine. The stator, whose blades are stationary when the vehicle is being accelerated at low speeds, converts one type of flow into another. Instead of allowing the fluid to flow straight back into the torus, the stator's curved blades turn the fluid almost 90∫ toward the direction of rotation of the engine. Thus the fluid does not flow as fast toward the torus, but is already spinning when the torus picks it up. This has the effect of allowing the torus to turn much

faster than the turbine. This difference in speed may be compared to the difference in speed between the smaller and larger gears in any gear train. The result is that engine power output is higher, and engine torque is multiplied.

As the speed of the turbine increases, the fluid spins faster and faster in the direction of engine rotation. As a result, the ability of the stator to redirect the fluid flow is reduced. Under cruising conditions, the stator is eventually forced to rotate on its one-way clutch in the direction of engine rotation. Under these conditions, the torque converter begins to behave almost like a solid shaft, with the torus and turbine speeds being almost equal.

PLANETARY GEARBOX

♦ See Figures 19, 20 and 21

The ability of the torque converter to multiply engine torque is limited. Also, the unit tends to be more efficient when the turbine is rotating at relatively high speeds. Therefore, a planetary gearbox is used to carry the power output of the turbine to the driveshaft.

Planetary gears function very similarly to conventional transmission gears. However, their construction is different in that three elements

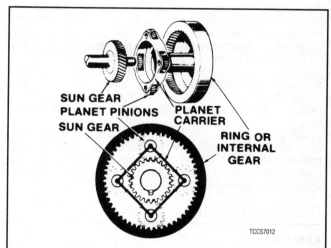

Fig. 19 Planetary gears work in a similar fashion to manual transmission gears, but are composed of three parts

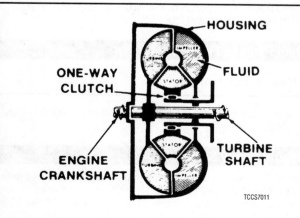

Fig. 18 The torque converter housing is rotated by the engine's crankshaft, and turns the impeller—The impeller then spins the turbine, which gives motion to the turbine shaft, driving the gears

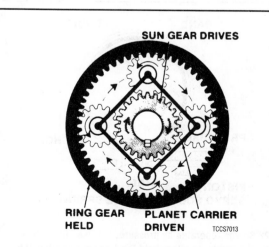

Fig. 20 Planetary gears in the maximum reduction (low) range. The ring gear is held and a lower gear ratio is obtained

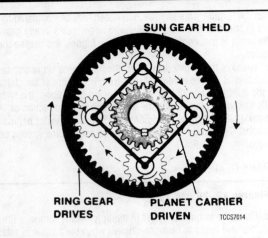

Fig. 21 Planetary gears in the minimum reduction (drive) range. The ring gear is allowed to revolve, providing a higher gear ratio

make up one gear system, and, in that all three elements are different from one another. The three elements are: an outer gear that is shaped like a hoop, with teeth cut into the inner surface; a sun gear, mounted on a shaft and located at the very center of the outer gear; and a set of three planet gears, held by pins in a ring-like planet carrier, meshing with both the sun gear and the outer gear. Either the outer gear or the sun gear may be held stationary, providing more than one possible torque multiplication factor for each set of gears. Also, if all three gears are forced to rotate at the same speed, the gearset forms, in effect, a solid shaft.

Most automatics use the planetary gears to provide various reductions ratios. Bands and clutches are used to hold various portions of the gearsets to the transmission case or to the shaft on which they are mounted. Shifting is accomplished, then, by changing the portion of each planetary gearset which is held to the transmission case or to the shaft.

SERVOS & ACCUMULATORS

▶ **See Figure 22**

The servos are hydraulic pistons and cylinders. They resemble the hydraulic actuators used on many other machines, such as bulldozers.

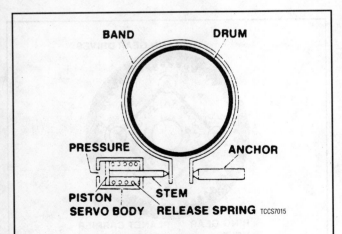

Fig. 22 Servos, operated by pressure, are used to apply or release the bands, to either hold the ring gear or allow it to rotate

Hydraulic fluid enters the cylinder, under pressure, and forces the piston to move to engage the band or clutches.

The accumulators are used to cushion the engagement of the servos. The transmission fluid must pass through the accumulator on the way to the servo. The accumulator housing contains a thin piston which is sprung away from the discharge passage of the accumulator. When fluid passes through the accumulator on the way to the servo, it must move the piston against spring pressure, and this action smooths out the action of the servo.

HYDRAULIC CONTROL SYSTEM

The hydraulic pressure used to operate the servos comes from the main transmission oil pump. This fluid is channeled to the various servos through the shift valves. There is generally a manual shift valve which is operated by the transmission selector lever and an automatic shift valve for each automatic upshift the transmission provides.

➡ **Many new transmissions are electronically controlled. On these models, electrical solenoids are used to better control the hydraulic fluid. Usually, the solenoids are regulated by an electronic control module.**

There are two pressures which affect the operation of these valves. One is the governor pressure which is effected by vehicle speed. The other is the modulator pressure which is effected by intake manifold vacuum or throttle position. Governor pressure rises with an increase in vehicle speed, and modulator pressure rises as the throttle is opened wider. By responding to these two pressures, the shift valves cause the upshift points to be delayed with increased throttle opening to make the best use of the engine's power output.

Most transmissions also make use of an auxiliary circuit for downshifting. This circuit may be actuated by the throttle linkage the vacuum line which actuates the modulator, by a cable or by a solenoid. It applies pressure to a special downshift surface on the shift valve or valves.

The transmission modulator also governs the line pressure, used to actuate the servos. In this way, the clutches and bands will be actuated with a force matching the torque output of the engine.

General Information

A number of transmission are available depending on selected drivetrain combinations and GVW packages. They are the Turbo Hydra-Matic 400 3-speed, the Turbo Hydra-Matic 700R4 4-speed overdrive, the 4L60E and 4L80E electronically controlled transmissions.

In 1990 the designations were changed, while the transmissions remained essentially the same. The THM 400 3-speed became the 3L80; the THM 700R4 became the 4L60.

Fluid Pan and Filter

REMOVAL & INSTALLATION

This procedure is covered in Section 1 of this manual under the Fluids and Lubricants heading.

Neutral Safety Switch

On 1987–95 vehicles covered by this manual, the Neutral Safety Switch is a part of the back-up light switch and is mounted to the steering column. For replacement or adjustment, please refer to the back-up light switch procedure.

On 1996–97 models, the neutral safety switch was relocated to the side of the transmission assembly. This change corresponds to the change made that year from shift linkage to a shift cable.

REPLACEMENT & ADJUSTMENT

▶ **See Figures 23 and 24**

➡Any removal of the switch will require that the switch is adjusted before installation. Switch adjustment should only be accomplished using J-41364-A or an equivalent switch adjustment and alignment tool. If the tool is not available, you may be able to successfully adjust the switch using a hit and miss method, moving the switch slightly each time and rechecking to verify that the switch works properly (the vehicle starts ONLY when the transmission is in Park or Neutral). But, this could take some time and be quite frustrating, so an attempt to buy or borrow the adjustment tool first may be well worth it.

1. Firmly apply the parking brake and block the rear wheels.
2. Disconnect the negative battery cable for safety.
3. Shift the transmission into Neutral.
4. Raise and support the front of the vehicle safely using jackstands.
5. Before attempting to remove or adjust the switch, make sure that the transmission is in the mechanical Neutral position. You can verify this at the control lever on the transmission assembly by rotating it clockwise until

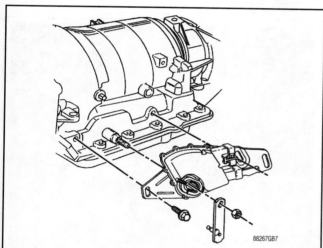

Fig. 23 Exploded view of the transmission mounted neutral safety switch—1996–97 models only

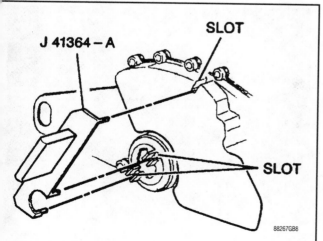

Fig. 24 Use the adjustment tool to greatly ease your job during neutral safety switch adjustment or installation

it reaches the FULL STOP position, then rotating it back counterclockwise 2 detents.

6. Disconnect the shift cable end from the transmission shift control lever by pulling the cable end from the lever ball stud.
7. Remove the nut securing the control lever to the manual shaft.
8. Disengage the wiring connectors from the neutral safety/back-up light switch.
9. Remove the 2 bolts which secure the switch to the transmission assembly.
10. Slide the switch from the manual shaft. If there is difficulty removing the switch, file the outer edge of the manual shaft lightly to remove any burrs from the shaft.

To adjust:

11. Position J-41364-A, or an equivalent adjustment tool, onto the neutral safety switch, making sure that the 2 slots on the switch (located where the manual shaft is inserted) are aligned with the 2 lower tabs on the tool. Then, rotate the tool until the tool's upper locator pin is aligned with the slot on the top of the switch.

➡**During installation, leave the adjustment tool mounted to the switch until the switch is secured and the position cannot change.**

To install:

12. Check the outer edge of the manual shaft to make sure there are no burrs which could prevent switch installation. If necessary, file the edge lightly to remove any remaining burrs.
13. Align the switch hub flats with the flats on the manual shaft.
14. Slide the switch onto the transmission manual shaft until the switch mounting bracket contacts the mounting bosses on the transmission.
15. Secure the switch to the transmission using the 2 retaining bolts. Tighten the bolts to 21 ft. lbs. (28 Nm).
16. Remove the switch adjustment tool from the switch assembly.
17. Engage the wiring harness connectors to the switch.
18. Install the transmission control lever to the manual shaft, then secure using the retaining nut. Tighten the nut to 21 ft. lbs. (28 Nm).
19. Connect the negative battery cable, then verify proper switch operation. The engine MUST start ONLY with the transmission in Park or Neutral. If further adjustment is required, loosen the switch retaining bolts and rotate the switch slightly, then tighten the bolts and check for proper operation.
20. Remove the jackstands and carefully lower the vehicle.

Vacuum Modulator

REMOVAL & INSTALLATION

THM 400

1. Raise and support the front end on jackstands.
2. Disconnect the vacuum line at the modulator.
3. Remove the screw and retaining clamp.
4. Remove the modulator. Be careful! Some fluid may run out.
5. Installation is the reverse of removal. Don't kink the vacuum line. Replace any lost fluid.

Back-up Light Switch

REMOVAL & INSTALLATION

Automatic Transmission

▶ **See Figure 25**

Vehicles up to and including 1995 model year have the back-up light switch mounted on the steering column. On the 1996 model year vehicles, the back-up light switch is part of the neutral safety switch mounted on the side of the transmission. Refer to the procedure for replacement of the neutral safety switch is this section.

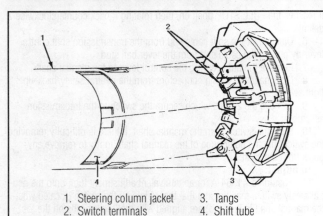

1. Steering column jacket
2. Switch terminals
3. Tangs
4. Shift tube

88266G45

Fig. 25 The back-up light switch also contains the neutral safety switch on automatic transmission equipped vehicles—1987–95 models

1. Disconnect the negative battery cable from the battery.
2. From the steering column, disconnect the electrical harness connector from the back-up light switch.
3. Using a small prybar, expand the back-up switch-to-steering column retainers and remove the switch from the steering column.

To install:

4. Place the gear selector in **NEUTRAL** and align the actuator on the switch with the hole in the shift tube. Align the mounting tangs with the mounting holes and press down to lock in place.
5. Connect the electrical harness connector to the back-up light switch.
6. Connect the negative battery cable to the battery.
7. Move the gear selector through all the positions including **PARK** and **LOW**. This should ratchet the switch and self adjust it.
8. Place the gear shift lever in the **REVERSE** position and check that the back-up lights turn on.

Extension Housing Seal

REMOVAL & INSTALLATION

1. Disconnect the negative battery cable for safety.
2. Block the front wheels.
3. Raise and support the rear of the vehicle safely using jackstands. Raise the rear of the vehicle sufficiently to keep all of the fluid in the transmission, away from the rear extension housing. If this cannot be done, the transmission pan will have to be removed in order to drain the fluid.
4. Matchmark and remove the driveshaft as outlined in this section.
5. Using a suitable prybar or better yet, a seal removal tool (these are usually inexpensive and make the job much easier), pry the rear seal out of the extension housing.

❊❊ WARNING

The use of an improper tool to pry the seal from the housing could allow the bore to be damaged, preventing the seal's replacement from fully "sealing" the transmission. Fluid leaks could result.

To install:

6. Coat the outside of the seal with a suitable non-hardening sealer.
7. Install the new seal with a suitable driver or seal installer.
8. Align and install the driveshaft.

9. Remove the jackstands and carefully lower the vehicle.
10. Connect the negative battery cable.

Automatic Transmission Assembly

REMOVAL & INSTALLATION

1. Disconnect the battery cable.
2. Remove the air cleaner.
3. Raise the vehicle and support it with jackstands.
4. Disconnect the shift linkage.
5. Tag and disengage all electrical connections, vacuum hoses and cables which will interfere with the transmission removal.
6. Drain the transmission.
7. Remove the driveshaft, after matchmarking its flange.
8. Disconnect the fluid cooler lines at the transmission.
9. Support the transmission and unbolt the rear mount from the cross member.
10. Remove the crossmember.
11. Remove the converter cover, matchmark the flywheel and converter, and remove the converter bolts.

88267P03

Remove the driveshaft for access to the rear transmission (extension housing) seal

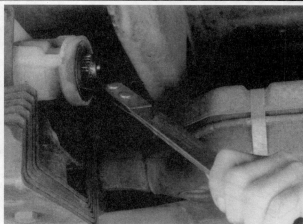

88267P01

Use a seal puller to remove the extension housing seal (BE CAREFUL not to damage the bore)

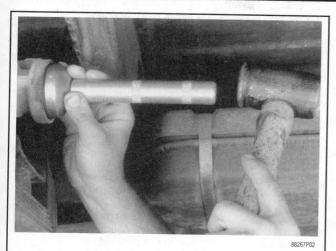

Use a suitable driver to install the replacement seal into the housing

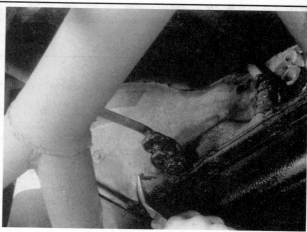

Pull out the cotter pin (if applicable), then disconnect the shift linkage from the transmission

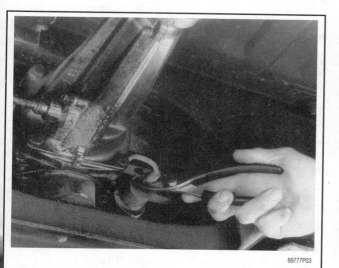

Disconnect the vacuum modulator hose . . .

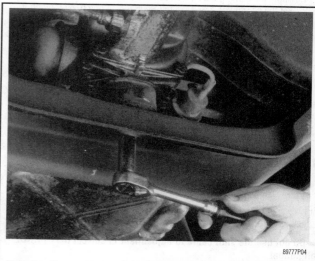

Unfasten the rear transmission mount from the crossmember

12. Support the engine and lower the transmission slightly for access to the upper transmission to engine bolts.

13. Remove the transmission-to-engine bolts and pull the transmission back. Remove the filler tube. Rig up a strap or keep the front of the transmission up so the converter doesn't fall out.

To install:

14. Installation is the reverse of removal. Please note the following important steps.

15. Check all seals and fittings for leaks.

16. Tighten the converter bolts to 50 ft. lbs. (65 Nm) on 700-R4 and 400 models and 46 ft. lbs. (63 Nm) on 4L60-E and 4L80-E models.

17. Tighten the transmission-to-engine bolts to 35 ft. lbs. (47 Nm) on 700-R4 and 400 models and 23 ft. lbs. (32 Nm) on 4L60-E and 4L80-E models.

18. Engage all lines, hoses and fittings that were disconnected during removal.

19. Fill the transmission with the correct amount and quality transmission fluid.

. . . and the speedometer cable from the transmission (if equipped)

Adjustments

SHIFT LINKAGE

1. Raise and support the front end on jackstands.
2. Loosen the shift lever bolt or nut at the transmission lever so that the lever is free to move on the rod.
3. Set the column shift lever to the Neutral gate notch, by rotating it until the shift lever drops into the Neutral gate. Do not use the indicator pointer as a reference to position the shift lever, as this will not be accurate.
4. Set the transmission lever in the neutral position by moving it clockwise to the Park detent, then counterclockwise 2 detents to Neutral.
5. Hold the rod tightly in the swivel and tighten the nut or bolt to 17 ft. lbs. (23 Nm).
6. Move the column shifter to Park and check that the engine starts. Check the adjustment by moving the selector to each gear position.

SHIFT CABLE

1993–95 P Models With 4L60-E and 4L80-E Transmissions

1. Apply the parking brake, then remove the pin and clevis pin.
2. Set the column shift lever to the Neutral gate notch, by rotating it until the shift lever drops into the Neutral gate. Do not use the indicator pointer as a reference to position the shift lever, as this will not be accurate.
3. Put the transmission in the Neutral by moving the shift lever to the forward position, then back to the back to the second detent.
4. Turn the clevis until it can be placed on the transmission stud and install the clevis pin and pin.
5. Check the adjustment as follows:
   a. The column selector must go into all the positions.
   b. The vehicle must start in Neutral and Park only.
6. Align the indicator if necessary and release the parking brake

1993–95 P/G Models With 4L60-E and 4L80-E Transmissions

1. Check the vehicle will only start in Park or Neutral.
2. Place the transmission in Neutral and check the position of the "PRNDL" indicator (needle). If it is not between the uprights of the "N" adjust as follows:

➡**Do not use the shift cable to adjustment to correct the "PRNDL" alignment**

   a. On models with a standard steering column, adjust column indicator by loosening the pointer retaining screw and adjust as necessary, then tighten the screw.
   b. On models with a tilt steering column, adjust the indicator by depressing the spring clip pointer attachment and adjust accordingly.
3. Check the position of the indicator in each of the drive positions. If the indicator does not cover a portion of the letter, the indicator must be readjusted.

1996–97 4L60-E and 4L80-E Transmissions

1. Place the transmission in park and apply the parking brake.
2. Raise and support the vehicle on jackstands.
3. On the shift cable end slide the black retaining clip forward just enough to allow the white lock button to be out.

➡**Do not push the white lock button completely out.**

4. Push the white lock button out just far enough to free the metal core adjust body inside the core.
5. Inspect the core adjust body for dirt or debris that may restrict its travel.
6. If there are any restrictions found the shift cable end should be washed with soap and water. If after cleaning the cable the travel of the core adjust body is still restricted the shift cable assembly must be replaced.
7. Lower the vehicle, turn the ignition switch **ON** and move the transmission lever from park to 1 ten times.
8. Place the shift lever in park and turn the ignition switch **OFF**. Raise and support the vehicle on jackstands.
9. Make sure the transmission is in mechanical park by rotating the control lever clockwise until it stops.
10. Push the white lock button in to secure the core adjuster body adjuster and slide the black retainer clip rearward until it covers the white lock button and locks in place over the shift cable end.
11. Lower the vehicle and turn the ignition switch **ON**.
12. Move the shifter through the gear ranges and ensure that the light comes on under the shift column letter when the shifter is positioned under that letter.
13. Ensure that the engine starts only when the transmission is placed in park or neutral. Adjust the park/neutral switch if necessary. Refer to the park/neutral switch adjustment procedure in this section.
14. Turn the ignition switch to the **LOCK** position and ensure that the key can be removed in the park position only.
15. Release the parking brake, start the engine and check for proper transmission shift operation.

THROTTLE VALVE CABLE

➡**This procedure applies to the THM 700R4 transmission.**

The adjustment is made at the engine end of the cable with the engine off, by rotating the throttle lever by hand. DO NOT use the accelerator pedal to rotate the throttle lever.
1. Remove the air cleaner.
2. Depress and hold down the metal adjusting tab at the end of the cable.
3. Move the slider until it stops against the fitting.
4. Release the adjusting tab.
5. Rotate the throttle lever to the full extent of it travel.
6. The slider must move towards the lever when the lever is at full travel. Make sure that the cable moves freely.

➡**The cable may appear to function properly with the engine cold. Recheck it with the engine hot.**

7. Road test the van.

DOWNSHIFT ADJUSTMENT

Turbo Hydra-Matic 400

When installing a new downshift switch, press the plunger as far forward as possible. The switch will adjust itself the first time the accelerator is floorboarded.

DRIVELINE

Tubular driveshafts are used on all models incorporating needle bearing U-joints. An internally splined sleeve at the forward end compensates for variation in distance between the rear axle and the transmission.

Long wheelbase models use a 2-piece driveshaft with a center support bearing. The front section is supported at the rear end by a rubber cushioned ball bearing mounted in a bracket attached to the frame crossmember. The ball bearing is permanently sealed and lubricated.

Driveshaft and U-Joints

REMOVAL & INSTALLATION

1. Raise the vehicle and support it on jackstands. There is less chance of lubricant leakage from the rear of the transmission if the rear is raised.

Unfasten the driveshaft retaining bolts

87987P05

Remove the driveshaft retaining straps

87987P06

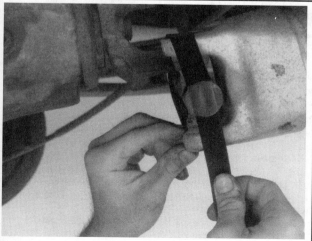

Tape the bearings into place to avoid losing them

87987P07

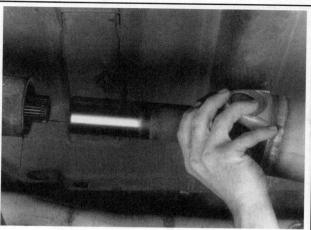

Lower the rear end of the shaft, then pull it back out of the transmission

87987P08

2. Matchmark the driveshaft and rear pinion flange and if equipped both halves of the 2-piece driveshaft.

3. Remove the U-bolts or straps at the rear axle. Tape the bearing cups to the trunnions.

4. On models with a 2-piece driveshaft, remove the bolts attaching the bearing support to the frame crossmember.

5. Slide the driveshaft forward and lower it. Slide the driveshaft toward the rear of the vehicle and disengage the splined sleeve from the output shaft of the transmission.

6. Remove the driveshaft from under the van.

To install:

7. Installation is the reverse of removal. Use the matchmarks made previously to help facilitate alignment. For models with 2-piece driveshaft, install the front half into the transmission and install the support to the crossmember. Rotate the shaft so that the front U-joint trunnions so that all are vertical. Rotate the rear shaft 4 splines to the left of the vehicle and connect the front and rear shaft. Some 2-piece driveshafts can only be assembled one way, in which case these instructions can be ignored. Attach the rear U-joint to the axle. On automatic transmission models, lubricate the internal yoke splines at the transmission end of the shaft with lithium base grease. The grease should seep out through the vent hole.

➡A thump in the rear driveshaft sometimes occurs when releasing the brakes after braking to a stop, especially on a downgrade. This is most common with automatic transmission. It is often caused by the driveshaft splines binding and can be cured by removing the driveshaft, inspecting the splines for rough spots or sharp edges, and carefully lubricating.

OVERHAUL

There are two types of U-joints used in these vans. The first is held together by wire snaprings in the yokes. The second type is held together with injection molded plastic retainer rings. This type cannot be reassembled with the same parts, once disassembled. However, repair kits are available.

Snapring Type

◗ See Figures 26, 27, 28 and 29

1. Remove the driveshaft from the van.

2. Remove the lockrings from the yoke and remove the lubrication fitting.

3. Support the yoke in a bench vise. Never clamp the driveshaft tube.

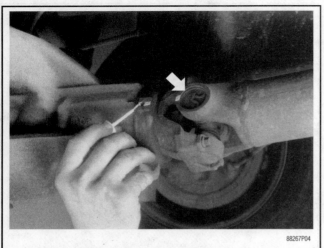

An external snapring type U-joint is easily identified by the visible snapring in the yoke bore

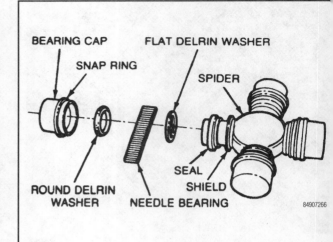

Fig. 28 Exploded view of the internal snapring U-joint

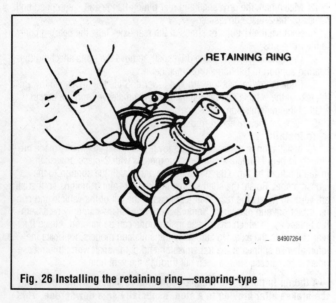

Fig. 26 Installing the retaining ring—snapring-type

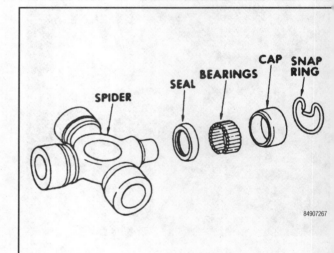

Fig. 29 Exploded view of the external snapring U-joint

4. Use a soft drift pin and hammer to drive against one trunnion bearing to drive the opposite bearing from the yoke.

➡ **The bearing cap cannot be driven completely out.**

5. Grasp the cap and work it out.

6. Support the other side of the yoke and drive the other bearing cap from the yoke and remove as in Steps 4 and 5.

7. Remove the trunnion from the driveshaft yoke.

8. If equipped with a sliding sleeve, remove the trunnions bearings from the sleeve yoke in the same manner as above. Remove the seal retainer from the end of the sleeve and pull the seal and washer from the retainer.

To remove the bearing support:

9. Remove the dust shield, or, if equipped with a flange, remove the cotter pin and nut and pull the flange and deflector assembly from the shaft

10. Remove the support bracket from the rubber cushion and pull the cushion away from the bearing.

11. Pull the bearing assembly from the shaft. If equipped, remove the grease retainers and slingers from the bearing.

Assemble the bearing support as follows:

12. Install the inner deflector on the driveshaft and punch the deflector on 2 opposite sides to be sure that it is tight.

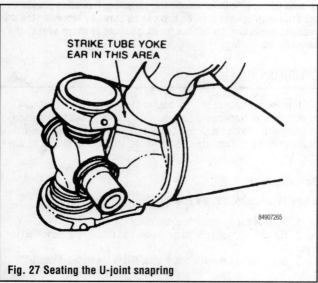

Fig. 27 Seating the U-joint snapring

13. Pack the retainers with special high melting grease. Insert a slinger (if used) inside one retainer and press this retainer over the bearing outer race.

14. Start the bearing and slinger on the shaft journal. Support the driveshaft and press the bearing and inner slinger against the shoulder of the shaft with a suitable pipe.

15. Install the second slinger on the shaft and press the second retainer on the shaft.

16. Install the dust shield over the shaft (small diameter first) and press it into position against the outer slinger or, if equipped with a flange, install the flange and deflector. Align the centerline of the flange yoke with the centerline of the driveshaft yoke and start the flange straight on the splines of the shaft with the end of the flange against the slinger.

17. Force the rubber cushion onto the bearing and coat the outside diameter of the cushion with clean brake fluid.

18. Force the bracket onto the cushion.

Assemble the trunnion bearings:

19. Repack the bearings with grease and replace the trunnion dust seals after any operation that requires disassembly of the U-joint. But be sure that the lubricant reservoir at the end of the trunnion is full of lubricant. Fill the reservoirs with lubricant from the bottom.

20. Install the trunnion into the driveshaft yoke and press the bearings into the yoke over the trunnion hubs as far as it will go.

21. Install the lockrings.

22. Hold the trunnion in one hand and tap the yoke slightly to seat the bearings against the lockrings.

23. On the rear driveshafts, install the sleeve yoke over the trunnion hubs and install the bearings in the same manner as above.

Molded Retainer Type

See Figures 30, 31, 32 and 33

1. Remove the driveshaft.

2. Support the driveshaft in a horizontal position. Place the U-joint so that the lower ear of the shaft yoke is supported by a 1⅛ in. socket. Press the lower bearing cup out of the yoke ear. This will shear the plastic retaining the lower bearing cup.

►**Never clamp the driveshaft tubing in a vise.**

3. If the bearing cup is not completely removed, lift the cross, insert a spacer and press the cup completely out.

4. Rotate the driveshaft, shear the opposite plastic retainer, and press the other bearing cup out in the same manner.

5. Remove the cross from the yoke. Production U-joints cannot be

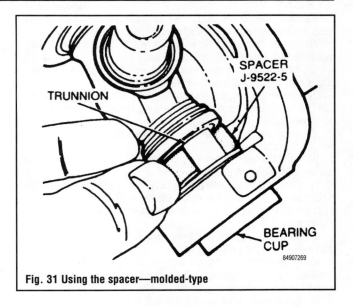

Fig. 31 Using the spacer—molded-type

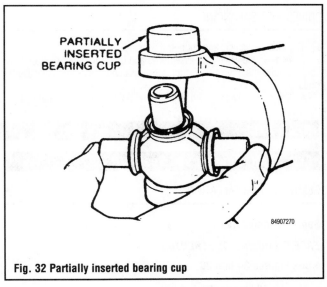

Fig. 32 Partially inserted bearing cup

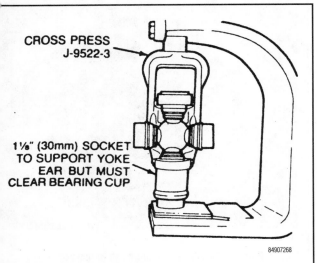

Fig. 30 Pressing out the U-joint

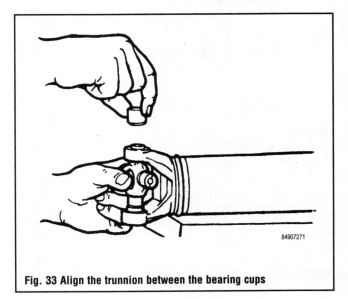

Fig. 33 Align the trunnion between the bearing cups

reassembled. There are no bearing retainer grooves in the cups. Discard all parts that we removed and substitute those in the overhaul kit.

6. Remove the sheared plastic bearing retainer. Drive a small pin or punch through the injection holes to aid in removal.

7. If the front U-joint is serviced, remove the bearing cups from the slip yoke in the manner previously described.

8. Be sure that the seals are installed on the service bearing cups to hold the needle bearings in place for handling. Grease the bearings if they aren't pregreased.

9. Install one bearing cup partway into one side of the yoke and turn this ear to the bottom.

10. Insert the opposite bearing cup partway. Be sure that both trunnions are started straight into the bearing cups.

11. Press against opposite bearing cups, working the cross constantly to be sure that it is free in the cups. If binding occurs, check the needle rollers to be sure that one needle has not become lodged under an end of the trunnion.

12. As soon as one bearing retainer groove is exposed, stop pressing and install the bearing retainer snapring.

13. Continue to press until the opposite bearing retainer can be installed. If difficulty installing the snaprings is encountered, tap the yoke with a hammer to spring the yoke ears slightly.

14. Assemble the other half of the U-joint in the same manner.

DRIVESHAFT BALANCING

1. Raise the vehicle and support it with jackstands.
2. Remove the wheel, tire assemblies and brake drums or rotors.
3. Inspact the driveshaft for dirt, loose retainers, dame and defective U-joints.
4. Clean the driveshaft and U-joints and tighten any loose retainers.

REAR AXLE

Axle Shaft, Bearing and Seal

REMOVAL & INSTALLATION

Semi-Floating Axles

EXCEPT LOCKING DIFFERENTIAL

▶ **See Figures 34 thru 39**

1. Support the axle on jackstands.
2. Remove the wheels and brake drums.
3. Clean off the differential cover area, loosen the cover to drain the lubricant, and remove the cover.
4. Turn the differential until you can reach the differential pinion shaft lockscrew. Remove the lockscrew and the pinion shaft.
5. Push in on the axle end. Remove the C-lock from the inner (button) end of the shaft.
6. Remove the shaft, being careful of the oil seal.
7. You can pry the oil seal out of the housing by placing the inner end of the axle shaft behind the steel case of the seal, then prying it out carefully.
8. A puller or a slide hammer is required to remove the bearing from the housing.

To install:

9. Pack the new or reused bearing with wheel bearing grease and lubricate the cavity between the seal lips with the same grease.
10. The bearing has to be driven into the housing. Don't use a drift, you might cock the bearing in its bore. Use a seal installation tool or its equivalent. Drive only on the outer bearing race. In a similar manner, drive the seal in flush with the end of the tube.
11. Slide the shaft into place, turning it slowly until the splines are engaged with the differential. Be careful of the oil seal.

5. Run the vehicle in gear at the same speed that the problem occurs.
6. If the problem does repeats, shut off the engine and remove the dri veshaft as outlined in this section.
7. Rotate the driveshaft 180 degrees from its original position.
8. Install the driveshaft and repeat Step 5. If the problem occurs again repeat Step 6.
9. Keep performing Steps 5 and 6 until a position is reached that give the best balance.
10. Install the rotors or drums and the wheel and tire assemblies.
11. Lower the vehicle and check for proper operation.

Center Bearing

REMOVAL & INSTALLATION

➡**The use of a suitable press is required for this procedure**

1. Raise the vehicle and support it with jackstands.
2. Remove the driveshaft as outlined in this section.
3. Disconnect the front driveshaft from the rear driveshaft by pulling rearward on the rear to disengage the slip yoke.
4. Remove the center bearing as follows:
   a. Press off the center bearing slinger retaining ring from the drive-shaft.
   b. Press the driveshaft down and off the center bearing.

To install:

5. Assemble the bearing a follows:
   a. Press the center bearing onto the shaft.
   b. Press the center bearing slinger retaining ring onto the driveshaft.
6. Install the driveshaft.
7. Lower the vehicle and check for proper operation.

12. Install the C-lock on the inner axle end. Pull the shaft out so that the C-lock seats in the counterbore of the differential side gear.

13. Position the differential pinion shaft through the case and the pinio gears, aligning the lockscrew hole. Install the lockscrew.

14. Install the cover with a new gasket and tighten the bolts evenly in a criss-cross pattern.

15. Fill the axle with lubricant as specified in Section 1.

16. Replace the brake drums and wheels.

87987P14

Fig. 34 Remove the differential pinion shaft lockscrew

Fig. 35 Remove the pinion shaft

Fig. 36 Remove the C-lock from the inner (button) end of the shaft

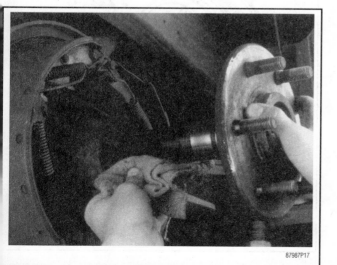

Fig. 37 Remove the axle shaft from the vehicle

Fig. 38 Use a puller to remove the oil seal

Fig. 39 Install the oil seal using a seal installer

LOCKING DIFFERENTIAL

◗ See Figures 40 and 41

This axle uses a thrust block on the differential pinion shaft.

1. Support the axle on jackstands.
2. Remove the wheels and brake drums.
3. Clean off the differential cover area, loosen the cover to drain the lubricant, and remove the cover.
4. Rotate the differential case so that you can remove the lockscrew and support the pinion shaft so it can't fall into the housing. Remove the differential pinion shaft lockscrew.
5. Carefully pull the pinion shaft partway out and rotate the differential case until the shaft touches the housing at the top.
6. Use a screwdriver to position the C-lock with its open end directly inward. You can't push in the axle shaft till you do this.
7. Push the axle shaft in and remove the C-lock.
8. Remove the shaft, being careful of the oil seal.
9. You can pry the oil seal out of the housing by placing the inner end of the axle shaft behind the steel case of the seal, then prying it out carefully.
10. A puller or a slide hammer is required to remove the bearing from the housing.

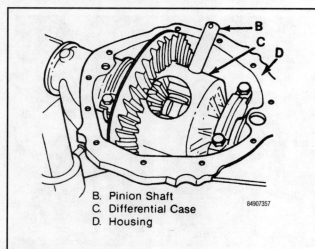

B. Pinion Shaft
C. Differential Case
D. Housing

84907357

Fig. 40 Positioning the case for the best clearance—semi-floating axle with locking differential

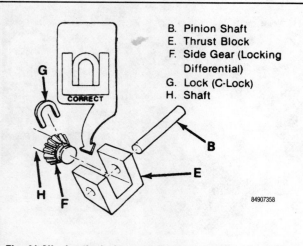

B. Pinion Shaft
E. Thrust Block
F. Side Gear (Locking Differential)
G. Lock (C-Lock)
H. Shaft

CORRECT

84907358

Fig. 41 Aligning the lock—semi-floating axle w/locking differential

To install:

11. Pack the new or reused bearing with wheel bearing grease and lubricate the cavity between the seal lips with the same grease.

12. The bearing has to be driven into the housing. Don't use a drift, you might cock the bearing in its bore. Use a piece of pipe or a large socket instead. Drive only on the outer bearing race. In a similar manner, drive the seal in flush with the end of the tube.

13. Slide the shaft into place, turning it slowly until the splines are engaged with the differential. Be careful of the oil seal.

14. Keep the pinion shaft partway out of the differential case while installing the C-lock on the axle shaft. Put the C-lock on the axle shaft and carefully pull out on the axle shaft until the C-lock is clear of the thrust block.

15. Position the differential pinion shaft through the case and the pinion gears, aligning the lockscrew hole. Install the lockscrew.

16. Install the cover with a new gasket and tighten the bolts evenly in a criss-cross pattern.

17. Fill the axle with lubricant as specified in Section 1.

18. Replace the brake drums and wheels.

Full-Floating Axles

▶ **See Figures 42, 43, 44 and 45**

The procedures are the same for locking and non-locking axles.

The best way to remove the bearings from the wheel hub is with an arbor press. Use of a press reduces the chances of damaging the bearing races,

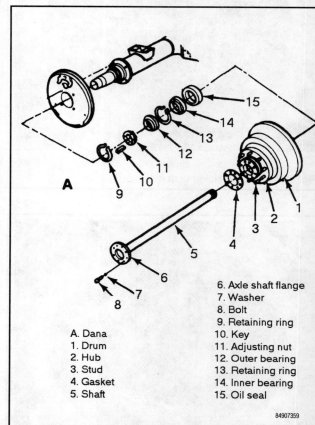

A. Dana
1. Drum
2. Hub
3. Stud
4. Gasket
5. Shaft

6. Axle shaft flange
7. Washer
8. Bolt
9. Retaining ring
10. Key
11. Adjusting nut
12. Outer bearing
13. Retaining ring
14. Inner bearing
15. Oil seal

84907359

Fig. 42 Exploded view of the axle, hub and drum assembly—full-floating axle, 9¾ and 10½ in.

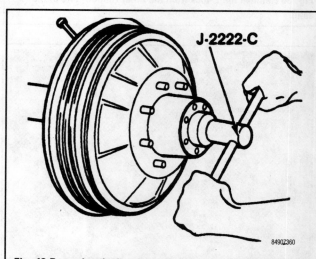

J-2222-C

84907360

Fig. 43 Removing the bearing adjusting nut—full-floating axle, 9¾ and 10½ in.

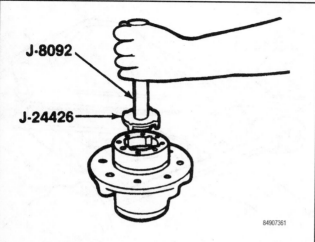

Fig. 44 Removing the bearing outer cup—full-floating axle, 9¾ and 10½ in.

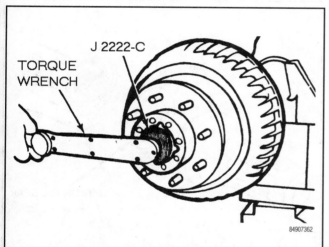

Fig. 45 Tightening the adjusting nut—full-floating axle, 9¾ and 10½ in.

cocking the bearing in its bore, or scoring the hub walls. A local machine shop is probably equipped with the tools to remove and install bearings and seals. However, if one is not available, the hammer and drift method outlined can be used.

1. Support the axles on jackstands.
2. Remove the wheels.
3. Remove the bolts and lock washers that attach the axle shaft flange to the hub.
4. Rap on the flange with a soft faced hammer to loosen the shaft. Grip the rib on the end of the flange with a pair of locking pliers and twist to start shaft removal. Remove the shaft from the axle tube.
5. The hub and drum assembly must be removed to remove the bearings and oil seals. You will need a large socket to remove and later adjust the bearing adjustment nut. There are also special tools available.
6. Disengage the tang of the locknut retainer from the slot or slat of the locknut, then remove the locknut from the housing tube.
7. Disengage the tang of the retainer from the slot or flat of the adjusting nut and remove the retainer from the housing tube.
8. Remove the adjusting nut from the housing tube.
9. Remove the thrust washer from the housing tube.
10. Pull the hub and drum straight off the axle housing.
11. Remove the oil seal and discard.

12. Use a hammer and a long drift to knock the inner bearing, cup, and oil seal from the hub assembly.
13. Remove the outer bearing snapring with a pair of pliers. It may be necessary to tap the bearing outer race away from the retaining ring slightly by tapping on the ring to remove the ring.
14. Drive the outer bearing from the hub with a hammer and drift.
To install:
15. Place the outer bearing into the hub. The larger outside diameter of the bearing should face the outer end of the hub. Drive the bearing into the hub using a washer that will cover both the inner and outer races of the bearing. Place a socket on top of this washer, then drive the bearing into place with a series of light taps. If available, an arbor press should be used for this job.
16. Drive the bearing past the snapring groove, and install the snapring. Then, turning the hub assembly over, drive the bearing back against the snapring. Protect the bearing by placing a washer on top of it. You can use the thrust washer that fits between the bearing and the adjusting nut for the job.
17. Place the inner bearing into the hub. The thick edge should be toward the shoulder in the hub. Press the bearing into the hub until it seats against the shoulder, using a washer and socket as outlined earlier. Make certain that the bearing is not cocked and that it is fully seated on the shoulder.
18. Pack the cavity between the oil seal lips with wheel bearing grease, and position it in the hub bore. Carefully press it into place on top of the inner bearing.
19. Pack the wheel bearings with grease, and lightly coat the inside diameter of the hub bearing contact surface and the outside diameter of the axle housing tube.
20. Make sure that the inner bearing, oil seal, axle housing oil deflector, and outer bearing are properly positioned. Install the hub and drum assembly on the axle housing, being careful so as not to damage the oil seal or dislocate other internal components.
21. Install the thrust washer so that the tang on the inside diameter of the washer is in the keyway on the axle housing.
22. Install the adjusting nut. Tighten to 50 ft. lbs. (68 Nm) while rotating the hub. Back off the nut and retighten to 35 ft. lbs. (47 Nm), then back off ¼ turn.
23. Install the tanged retainer against the inner adjusting nut. Align the adjusting nut so that the short tang of the retainer will engage the nearest slot on the adjusting nut.
24. Install the outer locknut and tighten to 65 ft. lbs. (88 Nm). Bend the long tang of the retainer into the slot of the outer nut. This method of adjustment should provide 0.001–0.010 in. (0.0254–0.254mm) end-play.
25. Place a new gasket over the axle shaft and position the axle shaft in the housing so that the shaft splines enter the differential side gear. Position the gasket so that the holes are in alignment, and install the flange-to-hub attaching bolts. Tighten to 115 ft. lbs. (156 Nm).

➡**To prevent lubricant from leaking through the flange holes, apply a non-hardening sealer to the bolt threads. Use the sealer sparingly.**

26. Replace the wheels.

Pinion Seal

REMOVAL & INSTALLATION

Semi-Floating Axles

▶ **See Figures 46, 47, 48, 49 and 50**

1. Raise and support the truck on jackstands. It would help to have the front end slightly higher than the rear to avoid fluid loss.
2. Matchmark and remove the driveshaft.
3. Release the parking brake.
4. Remove the rear wheels. Rotate the rear wheels by hand to make sure that there is absolutely no brake drag. If there is brake drag, remove the drums.
5. Using a torque wrench on the pinion nut, record the force needed to rotate the pinion.

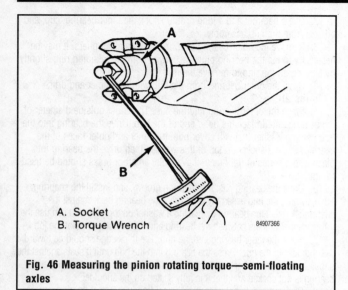

Fig. 46 Measuring the pinion rotating torque—semi-floating axles

A. Socket
B. Torque Wrench

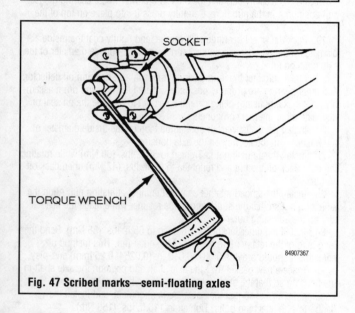

SOCKET

TORQUE WRENCH

Fig. 47 Scribed marks—semi-floating axles

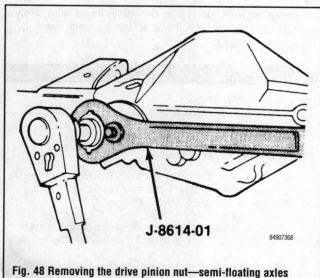

J-8614-01

Fig. 48 Removing the drive pinion nut—semi-floating axles

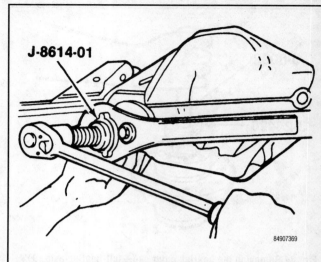

J-8614-01

Fig. 49 Removing the drive pinion flange—semi-floating axles

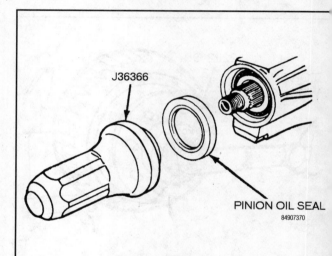

J36366

PINION OIL SEAL

Fig. 50 Installing the pinion seal—semi-floating axles

6. Matchmark the pinion shaft, nut and flange. Count the number of exposed threads on the pinion shaft.

7. Install a holding tool on the pinion. A very large adjustable wrench will do, or, if one is not available, put the drums back on and set the parking brake as tightly as possible.

8. Remove the pinion nut.

9. Slide the flange off of the pinion. A puller may be necessary.

10. Centerpunch the oil seal to distort it and pry it out of the bore. Be careful to avoid scratching the bore.

To install:

11. Pack the cavity between the lips of the seal with lithium-based chassis lube.

12. Position the seal in the bore and carefully drive it into place. A seal installer is VERY helpful in doing this.

13. Pack the cavity between the end of the pinion splines and the pinion flange with Permatex No.2® sealer, or equivalent non-hardening sealer.

14. Place the flange on the pinion and push it on as far as it will go.

15. Install the pinion washer and nut on the shaft and force the pinion into place by turning the nut.

❋❋ **WARNING**

Never hammer the flange into place!

16. Tighten the nut until the exact number of threads previously noted appear and the matchmarks align.

17. Measure the rotating torque of the pinion under the same circumstances as before. Compare the two readings. As necessary, tighten the pinion nut in VERY small increments until the torque necessary to rotate the pinion is 3 inch lbs. higher than the originally recorded torque.

18. Install the driveshaft.

Full Floating Axles

1. Raise and support the truck on jackstands. It would help to have the front end slightly higher than the rear to avoid fluid loss.

2. Matchmark and remove the driveshaft.

3. Matchmark the pinion shaft, nut and flange. Count the number of exposed threads on the pinion shaft.

4. Install a holding tool on the pinion. A very large adjustable wrench will do, or, if one is not available, set the parking brake as tightly as possible.

5. Remove the pinion nut.

6. Slide the flange off of the pinion. A puller may be necessary.

7. Centerpunch the oil seal to distort it and pry it out of the bore. Be careful to avoid scratching the bore.

To install:

8. Pack the cavity between the lips of the seal with lithium-based chassis lube.

9. Position the seal in the bore and carefully drive it into place. A seal installer is VERY helpful in doing this.

10. Place the flange on the pinion and push it on as far as it will go.

11. Install the pinion washer and nut on the shaft and force the pinion into place by turning the nut.

❋❋ **WARNING**

Never hammer the flange into place!

12. Tighten the nut until the exact number of threads previously noted appear and the matchmarks align.

13. Install the driveshaft.

Axle Housing

REMOVAL & INSTALLATION

1. Raise and support the rear end on jackstands.

2. For the 9¾ in. ring gear and the 10½ in. ring gear axles, place jackstands under the frame side rails for support.

3. Drain the lubricant from the axle housing and remove the driveshaft.

4. Remove the wheel, the brake drum or hub and the drum assembly.

5. Disconnect the parking brake cable from the lever and at the brake flange plate.

6. Disconnect the hydraulic brake lines from the connectors.

7. Disconnect the shock absorbers from the axle brackets.

8. Remove the vent hose from the axle vent fitting (if used).

9. Disconnect the height sensing and brake proportional valve linkage (if used).

10. Support the stabilizer shaft assembly with a hydraulic jack and remove (if used).

11. Remove the nuts and washers from the U-bolts.

12. Remove the U-bolts, spring plates and spacers from the axle assembly.

13. Lower the jack and remove the axle assembly.

To install:

14. Raise the axle assembly into position.

15. Install the U-bolts, spring plates and spacers.

16. Install the nuts and washers on the U-bolts.

17. Install the stabilizer shaft.

18. Connect the height sensing and brake proportional valve linkage.

19. Install the vent hose at the axle vent fitting.

20. Connect the shock absorbers at the axle brackets.

21. Connect the hydraulic brake lines.

22. Connect the parking brake cable.

23. Install the wheels.

24. Install the driveshaft.

25. Fill the axle housing.

TORQUE SPECIFICATIONS

System	Component		Ft. Lbs.	Nm
Manual Transmission				
	Crossmember bolts		50	67
	Bell transmission-to-clutch housing bolts		75	100
Clutch				
	Strap-to-pressure plate bolts		11	15
	Clutch cover bolts			
		4.3L, 5.0L and 5.7L engines	22	30
		6.2L and 6.5L engines	32	43
		7.4L engines	24	33
	Clutch housing bolts		29	39
	Actuator retainers		13	17
	Clip nut		18	25
	Clutch master cylinder nuts		13	17
Automatic Transmission				
	Neutral Safety switch bolts		21	28
	control lever nut		21	28
	Converter bolts			
		700-R4 and 400 models	50	65
		4L60-E and 4L80-E models	46	63
	Transmission-to-engine bolts			
		700-R4 and 400 models	35	47
		4L60-E and 4L80-E models	23	32
	Shift linkage rod nut or bolt		17	23
Full Floating Axle				
	Outer locknut		65	88
	Flange-to-hub bolts		115	156

88197C01

8

SUSPENSION AND STEERING

WHEELS

Wheels

REMOVAL & INSTALLATION

▶ **See Figure 1**

1. Park the vehicle on a level surface.
2. Remove the jack, tire iron and, if necessary, the spare tire from their storage compartments.
3. Check the owner's manual or refer to Section 1 of this manual for the jacking points on your vehicle. Then, place the jack in the proper position.
4. If equipped with lug nut trim caps, remove them by either unscrewing or pulling them off the lug nuts, as appropriate. Consult the owner's manual, if necessary.
5. If equipped with a wheel cover or hub cap, insert the tapered end of the tire iron in the groove and pry off the cover.
6. Apply the parking brake and block the diagonally opposite wheel with a wheel chock or two.

➡**Wheel chocks may be purchased at your local auto parts store, or a block of wood cut into wedges may be used. If possible, keep one or two of the chocks in your tire storage compartment, in case any of the tires has to be removed on the side of the road.**

7. If equipped with an automatic transmission, place the selector lever in **P** or Park; with a manual transmission, place the shifter in Reverse.
8. With the tires still on the ground, use the tire iron/wrench to break the lug nuts loose.

➡**If a nut is stuck, never use heat to loosen it or damage to the wheel and bearings may occur. If the nuts are seized, one or two heavy hammer blows directly on the end of the bolt usually loosens the rust. Be careful, as continued pounding will likely damage the brake drum or rotor.**

9. Using the jack, raise the vehicle until the tire is clear of the ground. Support the vehicle safely using jackstands.
10. Remove the lug nuts, then remove the tire and wheel assembly.

. . then remove the tire from the van

To install:

11. Make sure the wheel and hub mating surfaces, as well as the wheel lug studs, are clean and free of all foreign material. Always remove rust from the wheel mounting surface and the brake rotor or drum. Failure to do so may cause the lug nuts to loosen in service.
12. Install the tire and wheel assembly and hand-tighten the lug nuts.
13. Using the tire wrench, tighten all the lug nuts, in a crisscross pattern, until they are snug.
14. Raise the vehicle and withdraw the jackstand, then lower the vehicle.

Loosen the wheel lug nuts . . .

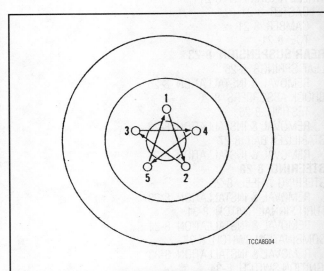

Fig. 1 Typical wheel lug tightening sequence

15. Using a torque wrench, tighten the lug nuts in a crisscross pattern to 100 ft. lbs. (140 Nm) on 15, 20/25 models. On 30/35 single wheel models tighten the nuts to 120 ft. lbs. (160 Nm) and 140 ft. lbs. (190 Nm) on 30/35 models with the dual wheels. Check your owner's manual or refer to Section 1 of this manual for the proper tightening sequence.

✳✳ WARNING

Do not overtighten the lug nuts, as this may cause the wheel studs to stretch or the brake disc (rotor) to warp.

16. If so equipped, install the wheel cover or hub cap. Make sure the valve stem protrudes through the proper opening before tapping the wheel cover into position.
17. If equipped, install the lug nut trim caps by pushing them or screwing them on, as applicable.
18. Remove the jack from under the vehicle, and place the jack and tire iron/wrench in their storage compartments. Remove the wheel chock(s).
19. If you have removed a flat or damaged tire, place it in the storage compartment of the vehicle and take it to your local repair station to have it fixed or replaced as soon as possible.

INSPECTION

Inspect the tires for lacerations, puncture marks, nails and other sharp objects. Repair or replace as necessary. Also check the tires for treadwear and air pressure as outlined in Section 1 of this manual.
Check the wheel assemblies for dents, cracks, rust and metal fatigue. Repair or replace as necessary.

Wheel Lug Studs

REMOVAL & INSTALLATION

With Disc Brakes

♦ See Figures 2, 3 and 4

1. Raise and support the appropriate end of the vehicle safely using jackstands, then remove the wheel.
2. Remove the brake pads and caliper. Support the caliper aside

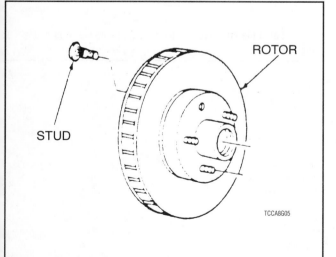

Fig. 2 View of the rotor and stud assembly

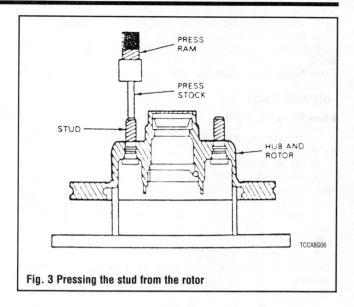

Fig. 3 Pressing the stud from the rotor

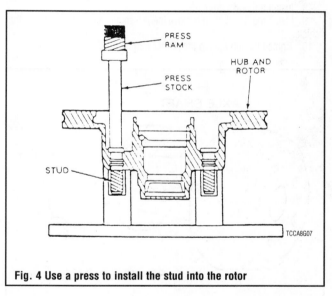

Fig. 4 Use a press to install the stud into the rotor

using wire or a coat hanger. For details, please refer to Section 9 of this manual.
3. Remove the outer wheel bearing and lift off the rotor. For details on wheel bearing removal, installation and adjustment, please refer to Section 1 of this manual.
4. Properly support the rotor using press bars, then drive the stud out using an arbor press.

➡ **If a press is not available, CAREFULLY drive the old stud out using a blunt drift. MAKE SURE the rotor is properly and evenly supported or it may be damaged.**

To install:
5. Clean the stud hole with a wire brush and start the new stud with a hammer and drift pin. Do not use any lubricant or thread sealer.
6. Finish installing the stud with the press.

➡ **If a press is not available, start the lug stud through the bore in the hub, then position about 4 flat washers over the stud and thread the lug nut. Hold the hub/rotor while tightening the lug nut, and the stud should be drawn into position. MAKE SURE THE STUD IS FULLY SEATED, then remove the lug nut and washers.**

7. Install the rotor and adjust the wheel bearings.

8. Install the brake caliper and pads.

9. Install the wheel, then remove the jackstands and carefully lower the vehicle.

10. Tighten the lug nuts to the proper torque.

With Drum Brakes

▶ See Figures 5, 6 and 7

1. Raise the vehicle and safely support it with jackstands, then remove the wheel.

2. Remove the brake drum.

3. If necessary to provide clearance, remove the brake shoes, as outlined in Section 9 of this manual.

4. Using a large C-clamp and socket, press the stud from the axle flange.

5. Coat the serrated part of the stud with liquid soap and place it into the hole.

To install:

6. Position about 4 flat washers over the stud and thread the lug nut. Hold the flange while tightening the lug nut, and the stud should be drawn into position. MAKE SURE THE STUD IS FULLY SEATED, then remove the lug nut and washers.

7. If applicable, install the brake shoes.

8. Install the brake drum.

9. Install the wheel, then remove the jackstands and carefully lower the vehicle.

10. Tighten the lug nuts to the proper torque.

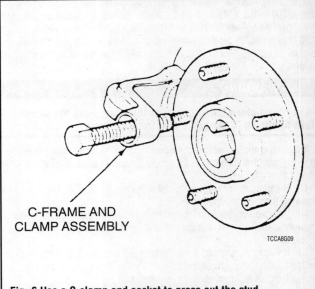

C-FRAME AND CLAMP ASSEMBLY

TCCA8G09

Fig. 6 Use a C-clamp and socket to press out the stud

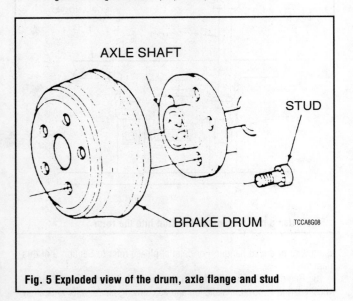

AXLE SHAFT

STUD

BRAKE DRUM

TCCA8G08

Fig. 5 Exploded view of the drum, axle flange and stud

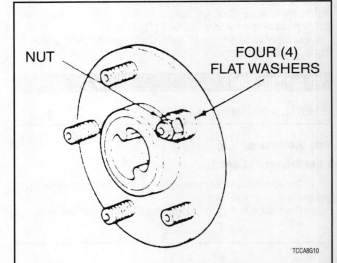

NUT

FOUR (4) FLAT WASHERS

TCCA8G10

Fig. 7 Force the stud onto the axle flange using washers and a lug nut

FRONT SUSPENSION

INDEPENDENT FRONT SUSPENSION AND STEERING COMPONENTS

1. Lower control arm
2. Shock absorber lower mounting
3. Upper ball joint
4. Tie rod end
5. Lower ball joint
6. Stabilizer bar
7. Stabilizer link
8. Tie rod adjuster sleeve
9. Center link
10. Idler arm
11. Pitman arm
12. Drag link

Vans are equipped with either an independent coil spring front suspension or an I-beam suspension.

> ❊❊❊ **CAUTION**
>
> **All suspension and steering fasteners are important attaching parts in that they could affect the performance of vital components and systems, and/or could result in major repair expense. They must be replaced with one of the same part number or with an equivalent part if replacement becomes necessary. Do not use a replacement part of lesser quality or substitute design. Torque values must be used as specified during reassembly to assure proper retention of these parts. Observe all nut and bolt torque**

Coil Springs

> ❊❊❊ **CAUTION**
>
> **Coil springs are under considerable tension. Be very careful when removing and installing them; they can exert enough force to cause serious injury. Always use spring compressors or a safety chain when removing a coil spring or releasing spring tension!**

REMOVAL & INSTALLATION

▶ **See Figure 8**

1. Raise and support the van under the frame rails. The control arms should hang freely.
2. Remove the wheel.
3. Disconnect the shock absorber at the lower end and move it aside.
4. Disconnect the stabilizer bar from the lower control arm.
5. Support the lower control arm and install a spring compressor on the spring, or chain the spring to the control arm as a safety precaution.

➡**On vans with an air cylinder inside the spring, remove the valve core from the cylinder and expel the air by compressing the cylinder with a prybar. With the cylinder compressed, replace the valve core so that the cylinder will stay in the compressed position. Push the cylinder as far as possible towards the top of the spring.**

6. Raise the jack to remove the tension from the lower control arm cross-shaft and remove the two U-bolts securing the cross-shaft to the crossmember.

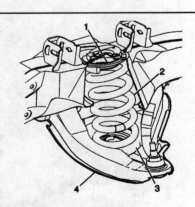

(1) Insulator, Upper Coil Spring
(2) Spring, Coil
(3) Insulator, Lower Coil Spring
(4) Arm, Lower Control   88198G01

Fig. 8 Typical installation of the coil spring—1997 model shown, others similar

> ❊❊❊ **CAUTION**
>
> **The cross-shaft and lower control arm keeps the coil spring compressed. Use care when you lower the assembly.**

7. Slowly release the jack and lower the control arm until the spring can be removed. Be sure that all compression is relieved from the spring.
8. If the spring was chained, remove the chain and spring. If you used spring compressors, remove the spring and slowly release the compressors.
9. Remove the air cylinder, if so equipped.
To install:
10. Install the air cylinder so that the protector plate is towards the upper control arm. The Schraeder valve should protrude through the hole in the lower control arm.
11. Install the chain and spring. If you used spring compressors, install the spring and compressors.
12. Slowly raise the jack and lower the control arm. Line up the indexing hole in the shaft with the crossmember attaching studs.
13. Install the two U-bolts securing the cross-shaft to the crossmember. Tighten the nuts to 65 ft. lbs. (88 Nm) for 10/1500 and 20/2500 series; 85 ft. lbs. (115 Nm) for 30/3500 series.
14. Remove the jack.
15. Connect the stabilizer bar to the lower control arm. Tighten the nuts to 24 ft. lbs. (32 Nm) on 1987–95 models and on 1996–97 models tighten the bolts to 36 ft. lbs. (35 Nm).
16. Connect the shock absorber at the lower end and tighten the bolt.
17. If equipped with air cylinders, inflate the cylinder to 60 psi.
18. Install the wheel.
19. Lower the van. Once the weight of the van is on the wheels, reduce the air cylinder pressure to 50 psi.
20. Have the alignment checked.

Leaf Springs

REMOVAL & INSTALLATION

▶ **See Figures 9 and 10 (p. 7–8)**

A special heavy duty front suspension is available on some P and P/G models which utilize a solid I-beam axle which incorporates the use of leaf springs instead of coil springs.

1. Raise the van and support the axle with safety stands. Remove the tire.
2. Disconnect the lower shock absorber mount at the axle.
3. Disconnect the stabilizer bar link from the bar. Remove the nut, washer and insulator and pull the link from the axle—don't lose the other insulator and retainer.
4. Remove the nuts and washers and lift out the U-bolts and spacer. Disconnect the spring from the axle.
5. Disconnect and separate the spring from the rear shackle and the front hanger. Remove the spring.
To install:
6. Position the spring so it lines up with the shackle and the hanger. The double wrap end should face forward.
7. Insert the hanger and shackle bolts and tighten to 92 ft. lbs. (125 Nm).
8. Position the spring spacer so that the aligning pin contacts the edge of the spring and tighten the U-bolt nuts, diagonally to 18 ft. lbs. (25 Nm). Retighten the nuts to 80 ft. lbs. (109 Nm).
9. Attach the retainer and insulator and then insert the stabilizer link into the proper hole in the axle. Tighten the nut until the distance between each retainer is 38mm (1½ in.).
10. Attach the link to the bar and tighten the nut to 50 ft. lbs. (68 Nm).
11. Install the shock to the axle and tighten the lower mounting nut to 37 ft. lbs. (50 Nm).
12. Install the wheel, lower the van and check the alignment.

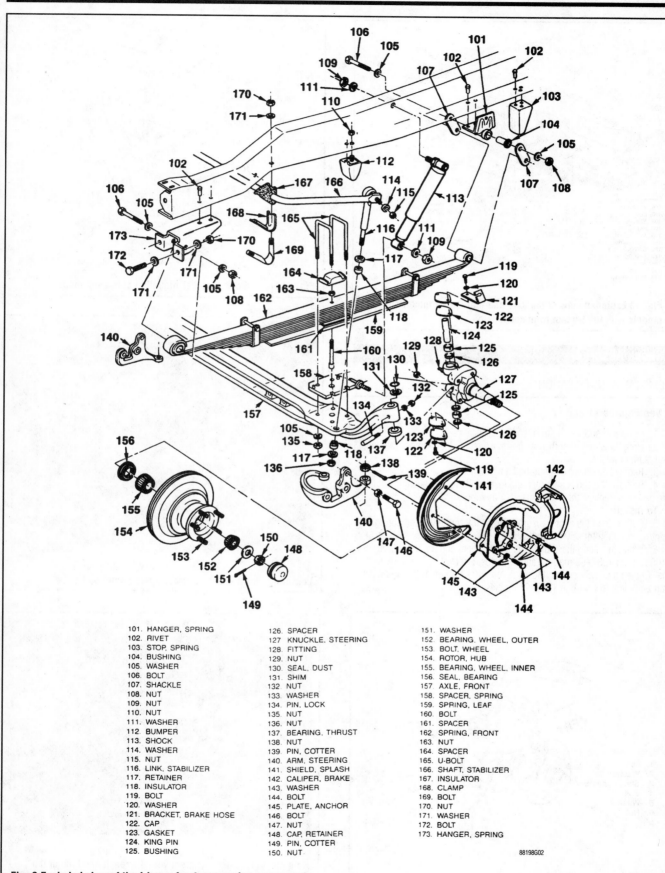

101. HANGER, SPRING	126. SPACER	151. WASHER
102. RIVET	127. KNUCKLE, STEERING	152. BEARING, WHEEL, OUTER
103. STOP, SPRING	128. FITTING	153. BOLT, WHEEL
104. BUSHING	129. NUT	154. ROTOR, HUB
105. WASHER	130. SEAL, DUST	155. BEARING, WHEEL, INNER
106. BOLT	131. SHIM	156. SEAL, BEARING
107. SHACKLE	132. NUT	157. AXLE, FRONT
108. NUT	133. WASHER	158. SPACER, SPRING
109. NUT	134. PIN, LOCK	159. SPRING, LEAF
110. NUT	135. NUT	160. BOLT
111. WASHER	136. NUT	161. SPACER
112. BUMPER	137. BEARING, THRUST	162. SPRING, FRONT
113. SHOCK	138. NUT	163. NUT
114. WASHER	139. PIN, COTTER	164. SPACER
115. NUT	140. ARM, STEERING	165. U-BOLT
116. LINK, STABILIZER	141. SHIELD, SPLASH	166. SHAFT, STABILIZER
117. RETAINER	142. CALIPER, BRAKE	167. INSULATOR
118. INSULATOR	143. WASHER	168. CLAMP
119. BOLT	144. BOLT	169. BOLT
120. WASHER	145. PLATE, ANCHOR	170. NUT
121. BRACKET, BRAKE HOSE	146. BOLT	171. WASHER
122. CAP	147. NUT	172. BOLT
123. GASKET	148. CAP, RETAINER	173. HANGER, SPRING
124. KING PIN	149. PIN, COTTER	
125. BUSHING	150. NUT	

88198G02

Fig. 9 Exploded view of the I-beam front suspension components

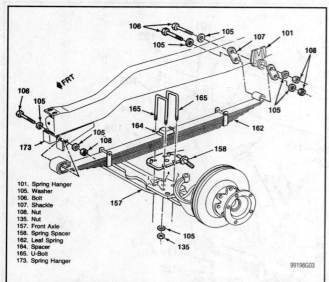

101. Spring Hanger
105. Washer
106. Bolt
107. Shackle
108. Nut
135. Nut
157. Front Axle
158. Spring Spacer
162. Leaf Spring
164. Spacer
165. U-Bolt
173. Spring Hanger

Fig. 10 Exploded view of the axle and leaf spring mounting—P models with the I-beam front suspension

Shock Absorbers

REMOVAL & INSTALLATION

▶ **See Figures 11 and 12**

1. Raise and support the front end on jackstands.
2. Hold the shock absorber stem with a wrench, then remove the upper end nut and washer.
3. Remove the lower end nut, bolt and washer.
4. Remove the shock absorber and inspect the rubber bushings. If these are defective, replace the shock absorber assembly.

To install:

5. Fully extend the shock absorber, insert it through the coil spring and control arm, then loosely install the retainers.
6. When installing the shock, tighten the upper end nut to 80 ft. lbs. (108 Nm) on 1987–95 models; and 12 ft. lbs. (16 Nm) on 1996–97 models. Tighten the lower end bolt to 74 ft. lbs. (101 Nm) on 1987–95 models; and 24 ft. lbs. (33 Nm) on 1996–97 models.

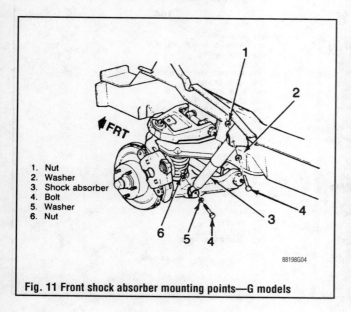

1. Nut
2. Washer
3. Shock absorber
4. Bolt
5. Washer
6. Nut

Fig. 11 Front shock absorber mounting points—G models

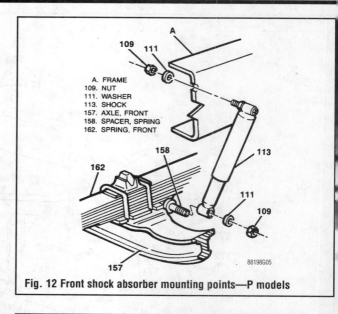

A. FRAME
109. NUT
111. WASHER
113. SHOCK
157. AXLE, FRONT
158. SPACER, SPRING
162. SPRING, FRONT

Fig. 12 Front shock absorber mounting points—P models

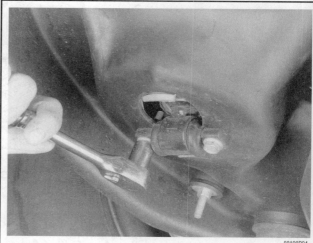

Loosen the front shock absorber lower mounting bolts

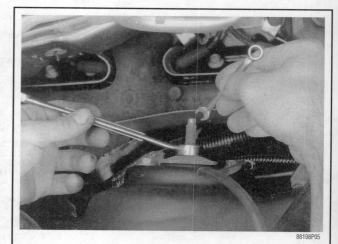

Hold the shock absorber stem with a wrench and loosen the upper nut

TESTING

The purpose of the shock absorber is simply to limit the motion of the spring during compression and rebound cycles. If the vehicle is not equipped with these motion dampers, the up and down motion would multiply until the vehicle was alternately trying to leap off the ground and to pound itself into the pavement.

Countrary to popular rumor, the shocks do not affect the ride height of the vehicle. This is controlled by other suspension components such as springs and tires. Worn shock absorbers can affect handling; if the front of the vehicle is rising or falling excessively, the "footprint" of the tires changes on the pavement and steering is affected.

The simplest test of the shock absorber is simply push down on one corner of the unladen vehicle and release it. Observe the motion of the body as it is released. In most cases, it will come up beyond it original rest position, dip back below it and settle quickly to rest. This shows that the damper is controlling the spring action. Any tendency to excessive pitch (up-and-down) motion or failure to return to rest within 2–3 cycles is a sign of poor function within the shock absorber. Oil-filled shocks may have a light film of oil around the seal, resulting from normal breathing and air exchange. This should NOT be taken as a sign of failure, but any sign of thick or running oil definitely indicates failure. Gas filled shocks may also show some film at the shaft; if the gas has leaked out, the shock will have almost no resistance to motion.

While each shock absorber can be replaced individually, it is recommended that they be changed as a pair (both front or both rear) to maintain equal response on both sides of the vehicle. Chances are quite good that if one has failed, its mate is weak also.

When fluid is seeping out of the shock absorber, it's time to replace it

Upper Ball Joint

INSPECTION

▶ **See Figures 13 and 14**

Excessive ball joint wear will usually show up as wear on the inside of the front tires. Don't jump to conclusions; front end misalignment can give the same symptom. The lower ball joint gets the most wear due to the distribution of suspension load. The wear limits given are the manufacturer's recommendation; they may not agree with your state's inspection law.

➡**Before performing this inspection, make sure the wheel bearings are adjusted correctly and that the control arm bushings are in good condition.**

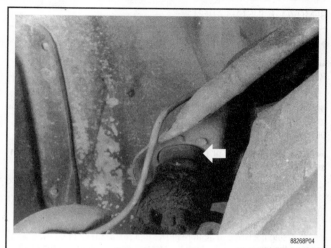

Fig. 13 To check the ball joint, first wipe the grease and road crud off of it for a visual inspection

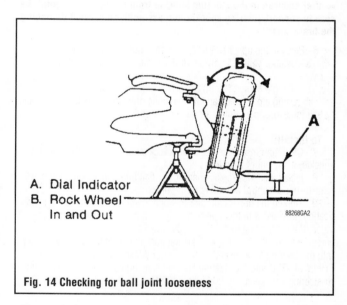

A. Dial Indicator
B. Rock Wheel In and Out

Fig. 14 Checking for ball joint looseness

1. Raise and support the front of the vehicle by placing jackstands under each lower control arm as close as possible to each lower ball joint.

➡**Before performing the upper ball joint inspection, be sure the vehicle is stable and the lower control arm bumpers are not contacting the frame.**

2. Wipe the ball joints clean and check the seals for cuts or tears. If a seal is damaged the ball joint MUST be replaced.

3. Position a dial indicator so it contacts the wheel rim.

4. To measure the horizontal deflection, perform the following procedures:

a. Grasp the tire (top and bottom), then pull outward on the top and push inward on the bottom; record the reading on the dial indicator.

b. Grasp the tire (top and bottom), then pull outward on the bottom and push inward on the top; record the reading on the dial indicator.

c. If the difference in the dial indicator reading is more than 0.08 in. (2mm), or if the ball joint can be twisted in its socket (with finger pressure) once it is disconnected from the knuckle, it must be replaced.

REMOVAL & INSTALLATION

▶ **See Figures 15, 16, 17 and 18**

➡**The following procedure requires the use of the GM Ball Joint Remover tool No. J-23742 or equivalent.**

1. Raise and support the front of the vehicle by placing jackstands under the lower control arms, between the spring seat and the lower ball joint. If jackstands are placed anywhere else, a floor jack MUST be used between the spring seat and the lower ball joint.

➡**Allow the jackstand or jack to remain under the lower control arm seat, to retain the spring and the lower control arm position.**

2. Remove the tire and wheel assembly.
3. From the upper ball joint, remove the cotter pin, loosen the nut 2 turns but do not remove.
4. Remove the brake caliper assembly.
5. Using the GM Ball Joint Remover tool No. J-23742 or equivalent, separate the upper ball joint from the steering knuckle. unfasten the bolt and pull the steering knuckle free of the ball joint after removal and wire it to the body.

➡**After separating the steering knuckle from the upper ball joint, be sure to support steering knuckle/hub assembly to prevent damaging the brake hose.**

6. Remove the upper ball joint from the upper control arm:
   a. Using a ⅛ in. (3mm) bit, drill a ¼ in. (6mm) deep hole into each rivet.
   b. Using a ½ in. (13mm) bit, drill off the rivet heads.
   c. Using a pin punch and the hammer, drive the rivets from the upper ball joint-to-upper control arm assembly and remove the upper ball joint.

To install:

7. Clean and inspect the steering knuckle hole. Replace the steering knuckle, if any out of roundness is noted.
8. Install a service replacement upper ball joint, positioning the ball joint-to-upper control arm bolts facing upward.
9. Tighten the upper ball joint-to-upper control arm bolts to the specification provided with the replacement joint. If no specification was provided, tighten the bolt to 18 ft. lbs. (25 Nm).
10. Remove the steering knuckle support, then seat the upper ball joint into the steering knuckle and install the nut. Make sure the ball joint is FULLY SEATED into the steering knuckle, then tighten the upper ball joint-to-steering knuckle nut to 90 ft. lbs. (122 Nm) on P and P/G models, 50 ft.

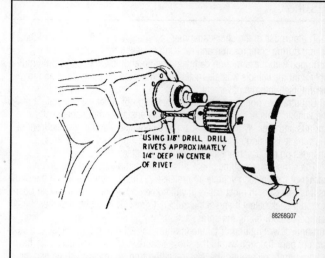

Fig. 16 Drill pilot holes in the upper ball joint rivets . . .

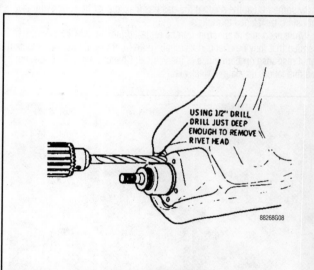

Fig. 17 . . . then drill off the rivet heads

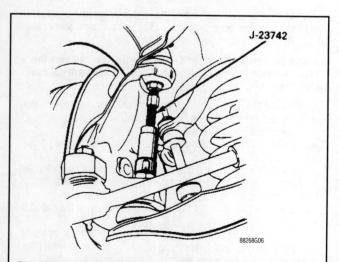

Fig. 15 Use a separator tool to free the upper ball joint from the steering knuckle

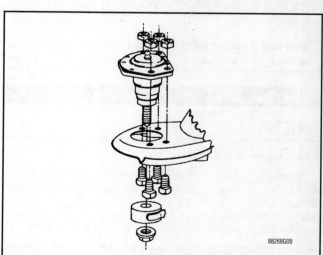

Fig. 18 When installing a service replacement upper ball joint, be sure the bolts are positioned on the bottom (nuts on top)

lbs. (68 Nm) for 1987–95 G model vehicles, or to 74 ft. lbs. (100 Nm) on 1996–97 vehicles.

11. Install a new cotter pin to the lower ball joint stud.

➡**When installing the cotter pin through the upper ball joint-to-steering knuckle nut, if the hole is not clear, always tighten the castle nut additionally to expose the cotter pin hole. NEVER loosen the nut for alignment.**

12. Install the brake caliper.
13. Install the grease fitting, then lubricate the upper ball joint using a grease gun.
14. Install the tire and wheel assembly.
15. Inspect and/or adjust the wheel bearing and the front end alignment.
16. Remove the jackstands and carefully lower the vehicle.

Lower Ball Joint

INSPECTION

▶ **See Figure 19**

1. Support the weight of the control arm at the wheel hub.
2. Wipe the ball joints clean and check the seals for cuts or tears. If a seal is damaged the ball joint MUST be replaced.
3. Measure the distance between the tip of the ball joint stud and the grease fitting below the ball joint.
4. Move the support to the control arm and allow the hub to hang free. Measure the distance again. If the variation between the two measurements exceeds $3/32$ in. (2.4mm) the ball joint should be replaced.

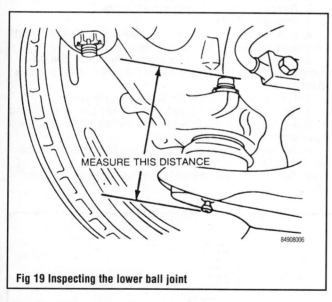

Fig 19 Inspecting the lower ball joint

REMOVAL & INSTALLATION

▶ **See Figures 20, 21 and 22**

1. Raise and support the front end on jackstands.
2. Support the lower control arm with a floor jack.
3. Remove the wheel.
4. Remove the lower stud cotter pin and loosen, but do not remove, the stud nut.
5. Loosen the ball joint with a forcing-type ball joint tool. It may be necessary to remove the brake caliper and wire it to the frame to gain enough clearance.
6. When the stud is loose, remove the tool and ball stud nut.
7. Install a spring compressor on the coil spring for safety.

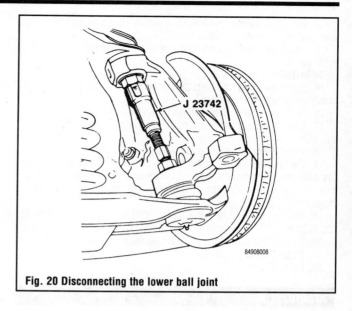

Fig. 20 Disconnecting the lower ball joint

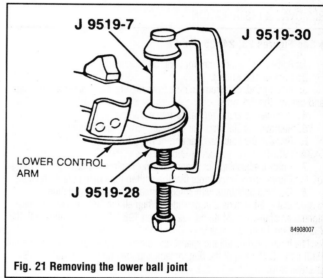

Fig. 21 Removing the lower ball joint

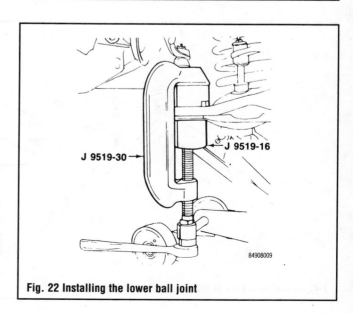

Fig. 22 Installing the lower ball joint

8. Pull the brake disc and knuckle assembly up and off the ball stud and support the upper arm with a block of wood.

9. Remove the ball joint from the control arm with a ball joint fork or other suitable tool.

To install:

10. Start the new ball joint into the control arm. Position the bleed vent in the rubber boot facing inward.

11. Turn the screw until the ball joint is seated in the control arm.

12. Lower the upper arm and match the steering knuckle to the lower ball stud.

13. Install the brake caliper, if removed.

14. On 1987–95 models, install the ball stud nut and tighten it to 90 ft. lbs. (122 Nm), plus the additional torque necessary to align the cotter pin hole. Do not exceed 130 ft. lbs. (176 Nm) or back the nut off to align the holes with the pin.

15. On 1996–97 models, install the ball stud nut and tighten it to 94 ft. lbs. (128 Nm).

16. Install a new lube fitting and lubricate the new joint.

17. Install the tire and wheel.

18. Lower the van.

Stabilizer Bar

REMOVAL & INSTALLATION

▶ See Figures 23, 24, 25 and 26

1. Raise and support the front end on jackstands.
2. Remove the wheels.
3. If equipped, unfasten the nuts from the link bolt spacer assemblies and remove the link bolts.
4. Remove the stabilizer bar-to-frame clamps.
5. Remove the stabilizer bar-to-lower control arm clamps.
6. Remove the stabilizer bar and bushings.

To install:

7. Check the bushings for wear or splitting. Replace any damaged bushings.
8. During installation, note that the split in the bushing faces forward.
9. Coat the bushings with silicone grease prior to installation.
10. Install all fasteners finger-tight. When all the fasteners are in place, tighten all of them to 24 ft. lbs. (32 Nm) on 1987–95 models and 26 ft. lbs. (35 Nm) on 1996–97 models.
11. If removed install the spacer and link bolt assemblies. Install the nut until it meets the end of the bolt threads and then tighten the nuts to 13 ft. lbs. (18 Nm).

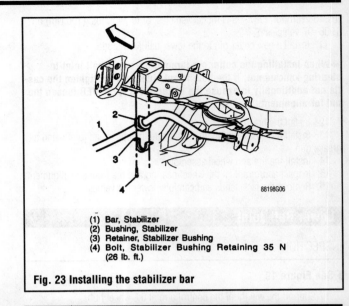

(1) Bar, Stabilizer
(2) Bushing, Stabilizer
(3) Retainer, Stabilizer Bushing
(4) Bolt, Stabilizer Bushing Retaining 35 N (26 lb. ft.)

Fig. 23 Installing the stabilizer bar

Upper Control Arm

REMOVAL & INSTALLATION

▶ See Figures 27 and 28 (p. 13–14)

1. Raise and support the van on jackstands.
2. Support the lower control arm with a floor jack.
3. Remove the wheel and tire.
4. If necessary, remove the caliper assembly or the brake hose bracket. Do not allow the caliper to hang by the brake hose.
5. Remove the cotter pin from the upper control arm ball stud and loosen the stud nut until the bottom surface of the nut is slightly below the end of the stud.
6. Install a spring compressor on the coil spring for safety.
7. Loosen the upper control arm ball stud in the steering knuckle using a ball joint stud removal tool. Remove the nut from the ball stud and raise the upper arm to clear the steering knuckle.
8. Remove the nuts securing the control arm shaft studs to the crossmember bracket and remove the control arm.
9. Tape the shims and spacers together and tag for proper reassembly.

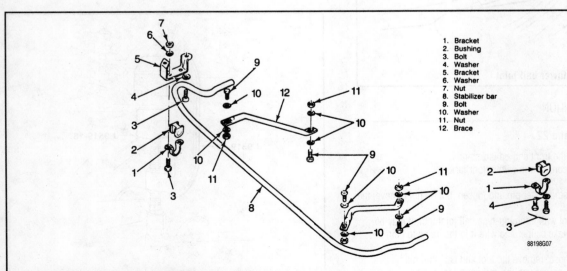

1. Bracket
2. Bushing
3. Bolt
4. Washer
5. Bracket
6. Washer
7. Nut
8. Stabilizer bar
9. Bolt
10. Washer
11. Nut
12. Brace

Fig. 24 Exploded view of the stabilizer bar mounting

Fig. 25 Loosen the stabilizer bar link nut, while using a wrench to hold the bolt from turning . . .

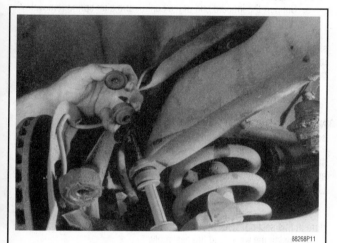

Fig. 26 . . . then remove the bolt, gathering each of the link components and keeping them in order

To install:

10. Place the control arm in position and install the nuts. Before tightening the nuts, insert the caster and camber shims in the same order as when removed.

11. Install the nuts securing the control arm shaft studs to the crossmember bracket. Tighten the nuts to 70 ft. lbs. (95 Nm) for 10/1500 and 20/2500 series; 105 ft. lbs. (142 Nm) for 30/3500 series on 1987–95 models and 140 ft. lbs. (190 Nm) on 1996–97 models.

12. Install the ball stud nut. Tighten the nut to 90 ft. lbs. (122 Nm) for 10/1500 series 130 ft. lbs. (176 Nm) for 30/3500 series 1987–95 models and on 1996–97 models, install the ball stud nut and tighten it to 94 ft. lbs. (128 Nm) on the lower nut and 74 ft. lbs. (100 Nm) on the upper nut.

13. Install the cotter pin. Never back off the nut to install the cotter pin. Always advance it.

14. Install the brake caliper.

15. Remove the spring compressor.

16. Install the wheel and tire.

17. Have the front end alignment checked, and as necessary adjusted.

CONTROL ARM BUSHING REPLACEMENT

10/1500 Series

➡**The following special tools, or their equivalents, are necessary for this procedure: J–24435–1, J–24435–3, J–24435–4, J–24435–5 and J–24435–7.**

1. Remove the upper control arm as explained earlier in this section.

2. Remove the pivot shaft nuts and washers.

3. Assemble tool J–24435–1. J–24435–3, and J–24435–7 on the control arm. Tighten the tool until the front bushing is forced out.

4. Remove the pivot shaft.

5. Use the forcing procedure to remove the rear bushing.

To install:

6. Position the new front bushing in the arm and assemble tools J–24435–4, J–24435–5 and J–24435–7. Force the bushing into place until it is fully seated.

7. Install the pivot shaft.

8. Repeat the forcing procedure to install the rear bushing.

9. Install the lower control arm.

10. Install the nuts and washers. Tighten the nuts to 115 ft. lbs. (156 Nm).

11. Install the control arm.

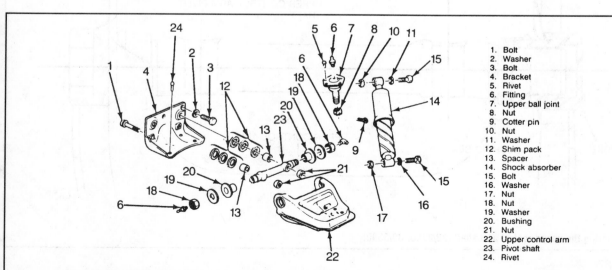

1. Bolt
2. Washer
3. Bolt
4. Bracket
5. Rivet
6. Fitting
7. Upper ball joint
8. Nut
9. Cotter pin
10. Nut
11. Washer
12. Shim pack
13. Spacer
14. Shock absorber
15. Bolt
16. Washer
17. Nut
18. Nut
19. Washer
20. Bushing
21. Nut
22. Upper control arm
23. Pivot shaft
24. Rivet

Fig. 27 Exploded view of the upper control arm—1987–95 models

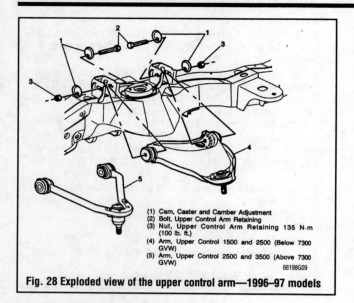

(1) Cam, Caster and Camber Adjustment
(2) Bolt, Upper Control Arm Retaining
(3) Nut, Upper Control Arm Retaining 135 N.m (100 lb. ft.)
(4) Arm, Upper Control 1500 and 2500 (Below 7300 GVW)
(5) Arm, Upper Control 2500 and 3500 (Above 7300 GVW)

88198G09

Fig. 28 Exploded view of the upper control arm—1996–97 models

20/2500 and 30/3500 Series

▶ **See Figure 29**

1. Raise and support the front end on jackstands.
2. Take up the weight of the suspension with a floor jack positioned under the lower control arm as near to the ball joint as possible.
3. Loosen, but do not remove, the pivot shaft-to-frame nuts.
4. Tape together and matchmark each shim pack's position for exact installation.
5. Install a chain over the control arm, inboard of the stabilizer bar and outboard of the shock absorber to hold the control arm close to the crossmember.
6. Remove the pivot shaft nuts, bolts and spacers.
7. Remove the grease fittings and unscrew the bushings from the control arm.
8. Remove the pivot shaft. Discard the seals.

To install:

9. Install new seals on the pivot shaft.
10. Slide the shaft into the arm.

11. Start the bushings into the arm and center the shaft in the bushings. Hand tighten the bushings to make sure the shaft doesn't bind.
12. Tighten the bushings to 190 ft. lbs. (257 Nm).
13. Check the pivot shaft for free rotation.
14. Install the grease fittings and lubricate the bushings.
15. Position the control arm on the frame and install the shim packs, spacers, nuts and bolts. Tighten the nuts to 105 ft. lbs. (142 Nm).
16. Remove the chain and install the wheel.
17. Have the alignment checked.

Lower Control Arm

REMOVAL & INSTALLATION

▶ **See Figures 30 and 31**

1. Raise and support the van on jackstands.
2. Remove the wheel and tire assembly.
3. Remove the caliper assembly. Do not allow the caliper to hang by the brake hose.
4. Remove the spring assembly. Refer to the spring removal and installation procedure.
5. Support the inboard end of the control arm after spring removal.
6. Remove the cotter pin from the lower ball stud and loosen the nut.
7. Loosen the lower ball stud in the steering knuckle using a ball joint stud removal tool. When the stud is loose, remove the nut from the stud. It may be necessary to remove the brake caliper and wire it to the frame to gain clearance.
8. Remove the lower control arm.

To install:

9. Install the lower control arm. Tighten the U-bolts to 65 ft. lbs. (88 Nm) on 10/1500 and 20/2500 series; 85 ft. lbs. (115 Nm) on 30/3500 series on 1987–95 models and 115 ft. lbs. (155 Nm) on 1996–97 models.
10. Install the ball stud nut. Tighten the nut to 90 ft. lbs. (122 Nm) for 10/1500 series 130 ft. lbs. (176 Nm) for 30/3500 series 1987–95 models and on 1996–97 models, install the ball stud nut and tighten it to 94 ft. lbs. (128 Nm) on the lower nut and 74 ft. lbs. (100 Nm) on the upper nut.
11. Install the brake caliper.
12. Install the spring. Refer to the spring removal and installation procedure in this section.
13. Install the wheel and tire assembly.

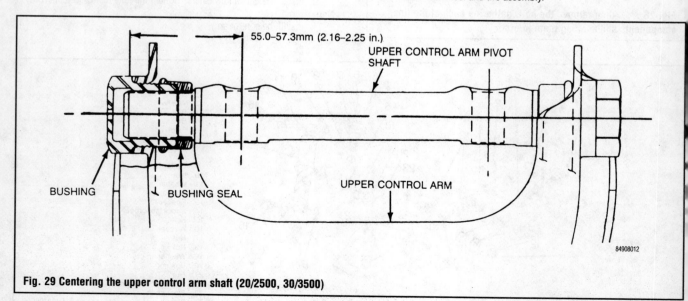

55.0–57.3mm (2.16–2.25 in.)

UPPER CONTROL ARM PIVOT SHAFT

BUSHING

BUSHING SEAL

UPPER CONTROL ARM

84908012

Fig. 29 Centering the upper control arm shaft (20/2500, 30/3500)

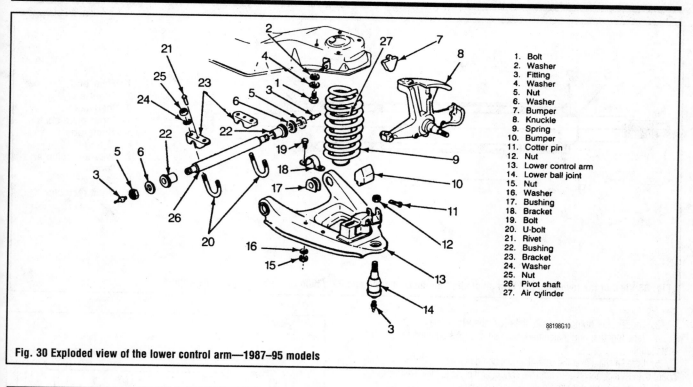

Fig. 30 Exploded view of the lower control arm—1987–95 models

1. Bolt
2. Washer
3. Fitting
4. Washer
5. Nut
6. Washer
7. Bumper
8. Knuckle
9. Spring
10. Bumper
11. Cotter pin
12. Nut
13. Lower control arm
14. Lower ball joint
15. Nut
16. Washer
17. Bushing
18. Bracket
19. Bolt
20. U-bolt
21. Rivet
22. Bushing
23. Bracket
24. Washer
25. Nut
26. Pivot shaft
27. Air cylinder

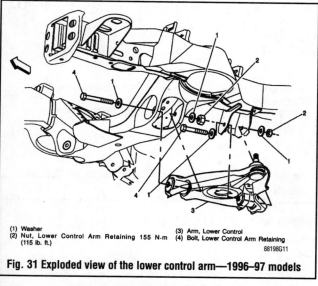

(1) Washer
(2) Nut, Lower Control Arm Retaining 155 N·m (115 lb. ft.)
(3) Arm, Lower Control
(4) Bolt, Lower Control Arm Retaining

Fig. 31 Exploded view of the lower control arm—1996–97 models

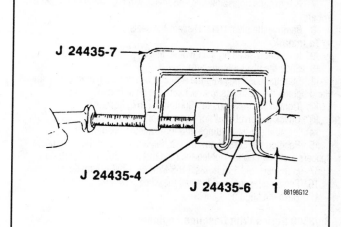

Fig. 32 Removing or installing the lower control arm bushings— G/101500 and G20/2500 models

CONTROL ARM BUSHING REPLACEMENT

10/1500 Series With Gasoline Engines

◆ See Figures 32 and 33

➡The following tools, or their equivalents, are necessary for this procedure: J-24435-1, J-24435-3, J-24435-4, J-24435-5 and J-24435-7.

1. Remove the upper control arm as explained earlier in this section.
2. Remove the pivot shaft nuts and washers.
3. Assemble tool J-24435-1, J-24435-3, and J-24435-7 on the control arm. Tighten the tool until the front bushing is forced out.
4. Remove the pivot shaft.
5. Use the forcing procedure to remove the rear bushing.

To install:

6. Position the new front bushing in the arm and assemble tools J-24435-4, J-24435-5 and J-24435-7. Force the bushing into place until it is fully seated.
7. Install the pivot shaft.
8. Install the nuts and washers. Tighten the nuts to 115 ft. lbs. (156 Nm).
9. Repeat the forcing procedure to install the rear bushing.
10. Stake the bushings in at least 2 places.
11. Install the lower control arm.

20/2500 Series With Gasoline Engines

1. Raise and support the front end on jackstands.
2. Take up the weight of the suspension with a floor jack positioned under the lower control arm as near to the ball joint as possible.

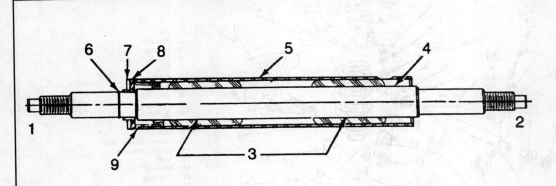

1. Rear end
2. Front end
3. Insulators
4. Inner pivot shaft
5. Shaft tube
6. O-ring
7. Washer, collar and flange
8. Bumper
9. Shaft restrictor

88198G13

Fig. 33 View of the lower control arm pivot shaft on the G10/1500 and G20/2500 models with gasoline engines

3. Loosen, but do not remove, the pivot shaft-to-frame nuts.
4. Tape together and matchmark each shim pack's position for exact installation.
5. Install a chain over the control arm, inboard of the stabilizer bar and outboard of the shock absorber to hold the control arm close to the crossmember.
6. Remove the pivot shaft nuts, bolts and spacers.
7. Remove the grease fittings and unscrew the bushings from the control arm.
8. Remove the pivot shaft. Discard the seals.

To install:
9. Install new seals on the pivot shaft.
10. Slide the shaft into the arm.
11. Start the bushings into the arm and center the shaft in the bushings. Hand tighten the bushings to make sure the shaft doesn't bind.
12. Tighten the bushings to 190 ft. lbs. (257 Nm).
13. Check the pivot shaft for free rotation.
14. Install the grease fittings and lubricate the bushings.
15. Position the control arm on the frame and install the shim packs, spacers, nuts and bolts. Tighten the nuts to 105 ft. lbs. (142 Nm) on 1987–95 models and 115 ft. lbs. (155 Nm) on 1996–97 models.
16. Remove the chain and install the wheel.
17. Have the alignment checked.

30/3500 Series With Gasoline Engines

▶ **See Figure 34**

1. Remove the lower control arm.
2. Remove the grease fittings and unscrew the bushings.
3. Slide out the pivot shaft.
4. Discard the old seals.

To install:
5. Install new seals on the pivot shaft.
6. Slide the shaft into the arm.
7. Start the bushings into the arm and center the shaft in the bushings. Hand tighten the bushings to make sure the shaft doesn't bind.
8. Tighten the bushings to 280 ft. lbs. (380 Nm).
9. Check the pivot shaft for free rotation.
10. Install the grease fittings and lubricate the bushings.
11. Install the lower arm.

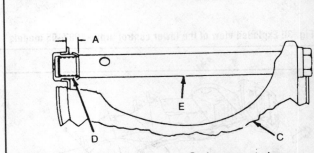

A. 29.96 – 31.9mm to properly center the pivot shaft
B. Bushing seal
C. Lower control arm
D. Bushing
E. Pivot shaft

88198G14

Fig. 34 Centering the lower control arm shaft on the G30/3500 models

20/2500 Series With Diesel Engines

▶ **See Figures 35 and 36**

1. Remove the lower control arm as explained earlier in this Section.
2. Assemble tools J-24435-7, J-24435-3, and J-24435-1 on the control arm. Tighten the tool until the front bushing is forced out.
3. Remove the pivot shaft.
4. Repeat the forcing procedure for the other bushing.

To install:
5. Position the new front bushing in the arm and assemble tools J-24435-4, J-24435-5 and J-24435-7. Force the bushing into place until it is fully seated.
6. Install the pivot shaft.
7. Repeat the forcing procedure to install the rear bushing.
8. Install the lower control arm.

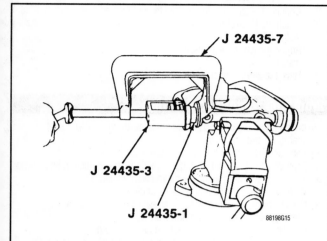

Fig. 35 Removing the lower control arm bushing—G20/2500 models with diesel engines

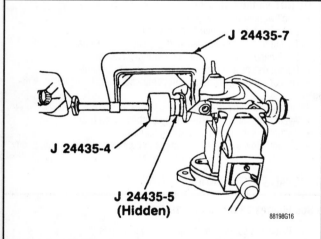

Fig. 36 Installing the lower control arm bushing—G20/2500 models with diesel engines

Steering Knuckle

REMOVAL & INSTALLATION

Independent Front Suspension

▶ See Figures 37 and 38

1. Raise and support the front end on jackstands.
2. Remove the wheels.
3. Dismount the caliper and suspend it out of the way without disconnecting the brake lines.
4. Remove the hub/rotor assembly.
5. Unbolt the splash shield and discard the old gasket.
6. Using a ball joint separator, disconnect the tie rod end from the knuckle. The procedure is explained later in this Section.
7. Position a floor jack under the lower control arm, near the spring seat. Raise the jack until it **just** takes up the weight of the suspension, compressing the spring. Safety-chain the coil spring to the lower arm.
8. Remove the upper and lower ball joint nut.
9. Using tool J-23742, or equivalent, break loose the upper ball joint from the knuckle.
10. Raise the upper control arm just enough to disconnect the ball joint.
11. Using the aforementioned-mentioned tool, break loose the lower ball joint.
12. Lift the knuckle off of the lower ball joint.
13. Inspect and clean the ball stud bores in the knuckle. Make sure that there are no cracks or burrs. If the knuckle is damaged in any way, replace it.
14. Check the spindle for wear, heat discoloration or damage. If at all damaged, replace it.

To install:

15. Maneuver the knuckle onto both ball joints.
16. Install both nuts. On 10/1500 series and 20/2500 series, tighten the upper nut to 50 ft. lbs. (68 Nm) and the lower nut to 90 ft. lbs. (122 Nm). On 30/3500 series, tighten both nuts to 90 ft. lbs. (122 Nm). On 1996–97 models, install the ball stud nut and tighten it to 94 ft. lbs. (128 Nm) on the lower nut and 74 ft. lbs. (100 Nm) on the upper nut.
17. Install the cotter pins. Always advance the nut to align the cotter pin hole. NEVER back it off! On the upper nut which was originally tightened to 50 ft. lbs. (68 Nm), don't exceed 90 ft. lbs. (122 Nm) when aligning the hole. On nuts tightened originally to 90 ft. lbs. (122 Nm), don't exceed 130 ft. lbs. (176 Nm) to align the hole.
18. Remove the floor jack.

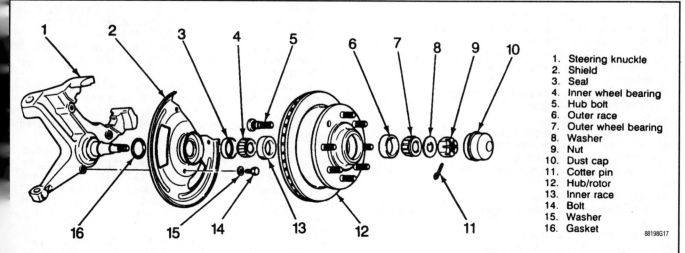

1. Steering knuckle
2. Shield
3. Seal
4. Inner wheel bearing
5. Hub bolt
6. Outer race
7. Outer wheel bearing
8. Washer
9. Nut
10. Dust cap
11. Cotter pin
12. Hub/rotor
13. Inner race
14. Bolt
15. Washer
16. Gasket

Fig. 37 Exploded view of the steering knuckle assembly—1987–95 models with an independent front suspension

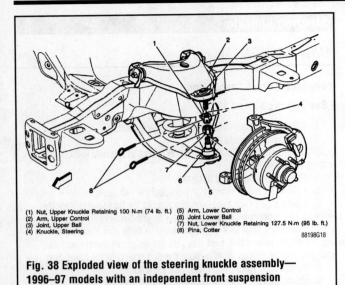

(1) Nut, Upper Knuckle Retaining 100 N·m (74 lb. ft.) (5) Arm, Lower Control
(2) Arm, Upper Control (6) Joint Lower Ball
(3) Joint, Upper Ball (7) Nut, Lower Knuckle Retaining 127.5 N·m (95 lb. ft.)
(4) Knuckle, Steering (8) Pins, Cotter

88198G18

Fig. 38 Exploded view of the steering knuckle assembly— 1996–97 models with an independent front suspension

19. Install a new gasket and the splash shield. Tighten the bolts to 19 ft. lbs. (26 Nm).
20. Connect the tie rod end.
21. Install the hub/rotor assembly.
22. Install the caliper.
23. Adjust the wheel bearings.
24. Install the wheels.
25. Have the alignment checked.

I-Beam Front Suspension

1. Raise and support the front end on jackstands.
2. Remove the wheels.
3. Dismount the caliper and suspend it out of the way without disconnecting the brake lines.
4. Remove the hub/rotor assembly.
5. Unfasten the bolts retaining the anchor plate, splash shield and the steering arm.
6. Pull the anchor plate and splash off the knuckle and let the hang by the tie rods.
7. Unfasten the anchor plate-to-splash shield retainers and separate both components.
8. Disengage the steering arm from the tie rods.
9. Remove the brake hose bracket retainers and the bracket and the gaskets.
10. Remove the steering knuckle caps.
11. Unfasten the lock pin retainers and remove the lock pin.
12. Remove the king pin from the steering knuckle by driving it out with a hammer and drift. The spacers and bushings will be driven out also.
13. Remove the steering knuckle, dust seal, shim, and thrust bearing.

To install:

14. Install new bushings in the bores, then ream them to 1.1804–1.1820 in. (29.982–30.022mm).
15. Install the steering knuckle.
16. Prelube and install thrust bearing, then install shim and dust seal.
17. Prelube the king pin, then install the king pin, lock pin and insert the spacers in the reverse order of removal.
18. Install the washer and nut, then tighten the nut to 29 ft. lbs. (40 Nm).
19. Install the gaskets and caps.
20. Install the brake hose bracket, washers and tighten the bolts to 5 ft. lbs. (7 Nm).
21. Install the bolts and washers and engage the splash shield to the anchor plate and install the bolts, washers and nuts to attach the anchor plate and steering arm to the steering knuckle. Tighten the bolts to 12 ft. lbs. (16 Nm) and the nuts to 230 ft. lbs. (312 Nm).

22. Connect the steering arm to the steering linkage.
23. Install the hub/rotor assembly.
24. Install the caliper.
25. Adjust the wheel bearings.
26. Install the wheels.
27. Have the alignment checked.

Front Hub, Rotor and Bearings

Before handling the bearings, there are a few things that you should remember to do and not to do.
Remember to DO the following:
• Remove all outside dirt from the housing before exposing the bearing.
• Treat a used bearing as gently as you would a new one.
• Work with clean tools in clean surroundings.
• Use clean, dry canvas gloves, or at least clean, dry hands.
• Clean solvents and flushing fluids are a must.
• Use clean paper when laying out the bearings to dry.
• Protect disassembled bearings from rust and dirt. Cover them up.
• Use clean rags to wipe bearings.
• Keep the bearings in oil-proof paper when they are to be stored or are not in use.
• Clean the inside of the housing before replacing the bearing.
Do NOT do the following:
• Don't work in dirty surroundings.
• Don't use dirty, chipped or damaged tools.
• Try not to work on wooden work benches or use wooden mallets.
• Don't handle bearings with dirty or moist hands.
• Do not use gasoline for cleaning; use a safe solvent.
• Do not spin-dry bearings with compressed air. They will be damaged.
• Do not spin dirty bearings.
• Avoid using cotton waste or dirty cloths to wipe bearings.
• Try not to scratch or nick bearing surfaces.
• Do not allow the bearing to come in contact with dirt or rust at any time.

REMOVAL & INSTALLATION

▶ **See Figures 39 thru 54 (p. 19–21)**

1. Raise and support the front end on jackstands.
2. Remove the wheel.
3. Dismount the caliper and wire it out of the way.
4. Pry out the grease cap, remove the cotter pin, spindle nut, and washer.
5. Remove the hub/rotor assembly. Do not drop the wheel bearings.
6. Remove the outer roller bearing assembly from the hub. The inner bearing assembly will remain in the hub/rotor assembly and may be removed after prying out the inner seal. Discard the seal.
7. Using a hammer and drift, remove the bearing races from the hub/rotor assembly. They are driven out from the inside out.

To install:

8. Clean all parts in a non-flammable solvent and let them air dry. Never spin-dry a bearing with compressed air! Check for excessive wear and damage.
9. When installing new races, make sure that they are not cocked and that they are fully seated against the hub/rotor assembly shoulder.
10. Pack both wheel bearings using high melting point wheel bearing grease for disc brakes. Ordinary grease will melt and ooze out ruining the pads. Bearings should be packed using a cone-type wheel bearing greaser tool. If one is not available they may be packed by hand. Place a healthy glob of grease in the palm of one hand and force the edge of the bearing into it so that the grease fills the bearing. Do this until the whole bearing is packed.
11. Place the inner bearing in the hub/rotor assembly and install a new inner seal, making sure that the seal flange faces the bearing race.
12. Carefully install the wheel hub/rotor assembly over the spindle.

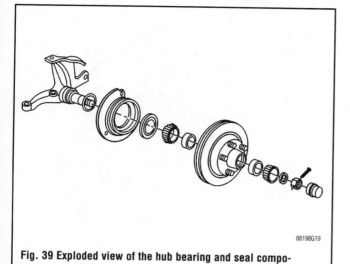

Fig. 39 Exploded view of the hub bearing and seal components—1996–97

Fig. 42 If difficulty is encountered, gently tap on the pliers with a hammer to help free the cotter pin

Fig. 40 Pry the dust cap from the hub taking care not to distort or damage its flange

Fig. 43 Loosen and remove the castellated nut from the spindle

Fig. 41 Once the bent ends are cut, grasp the cotter pin and pull or pry it free of the spindle

Fig. 44 Remove the washer from the spindle

TCCS8029

Fig. 45 With the nut and washer out of the way, the outer bearings may be removed from the hub

TCCS8032

Fig. 48 With the seal removed, the inner bearing may be withdrawn from the hub

TCCS8030

Fig. 46 Pull the hub and inner bearing assembly from the spindle

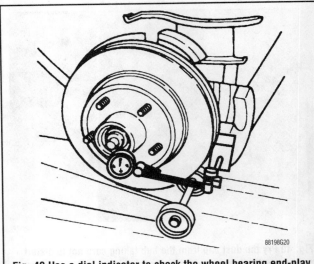

88198G20

Fig. 49 Use a dial indicator to check the wheel bearing end-play

TCCS8031

Fig. 47 Use a small prytool to remove the old inner bearing seal

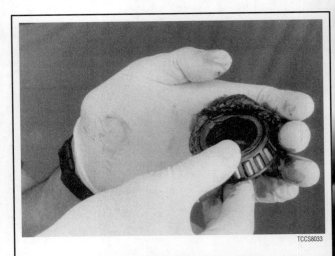

TCCS8033

Fig. 50 Thoroughly pack the bearing with fresh, high temperature wheel-bearing grease before installation

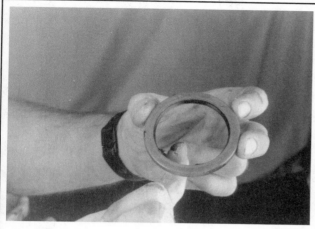

Fig. 51 Apply a thin coat of fresh grease to the new inner bearing seal lip

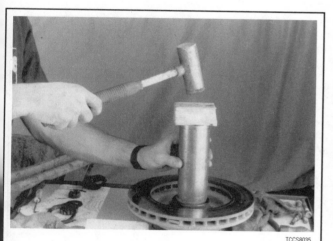

Fig. 52 Use a suitably sized driver to install the inner bearing seal to the hub

Fig. 53 With new or freshly packed bearings, tighten the nut to 12 ft. lbs. while gently spinning the wheel, then adjust the bearings

Fig. 54 After the bearings are adjusted, install the dust cap by gently tapping on the flange—DO NOT damage the cap by hammering on the center

13. Using your hands, firmly press the outer bearing into the hub. Install the spindle washer and nut.

14. Spin the wheel hub by hand and tighten the nut until it is just snug—12 ft. lbs. (16 Nm). Back off the nut until it is loose, then tighten it finger tight. Loosen the nut until either hole in the spindle lines up with a slot in the nut and insert a new cotter pin. There should be 0.001–0.005 in. (0.025–0.127mm) end-play. This can be measured with a dial indicator, if you wish.

15. Replace the dust cap, wheel and tire.

Wheel Alignment

If the tires are worn unevenly, if the vehicle is not stable on the highway or if the handling seems uneven in spirited driving, the wheel alignment should be checked. If an alignment problem is suspected, first check for improper tire inflation and other possible causes. These can be worn suspension or steering components, accident damage or even unmatched tires. If any worn or damaged components are found, they must be replaced before the wheels can be properly aligned. Wheel alignment requires very expensive equipment and involves minute adjustments which must be accurate; it should only be performed by a trained technician. Take your vehicle to a properly equipped shop.

Following is a description of the alignment angles which are adjustable on most vehicles and how they affect vehicle handling. Although these angles can apply to both the front and rear wheels, usually only the front suspension is adjustable.

CASTER

▶ **See Figure 55**

Looking at a vehicle from the side, caster angle describes the steering axis rather than a wheel angle. On vehicles equipped with an independent front suspension, the steering knuckle is attached to a control arm or strut at the top and a control arm at the bottom. On vehicles equipped with an I-beam (solid) front axle, the steering knuckle is attached to the axle yoke through ball joints or king pins. The wheel pivots around the line between these points to steer the vehicle. When the upper point is tilted back, this is described as positive caster. Having a positive caster tends to make the wheels self-centering, increasing directional stability. Excessive positive caster makes the wheels hard to steer, while an uneven caster will cause a pull to one side. Overloading the vehicle or sagging rear springs will affect caster, as will raising the rear of the vehicle. If the rear of the vehicle is lower than normal, the caster becomes more positive.

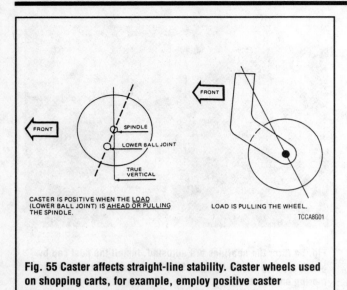

Fig. 55 Caster affects straight-line stability. Caster wheels used on shopping carts, for example, employ positive caster

CAMBER

▶ **See Figure 56**

Looking from the front of the vehicle, camber is the inward or outward tilt of the top of wheels. When the tops of the wheels are tilted in, this is negative camber; if they are tilted out, it is positive. In a turn, a slight amount of negative camber helps maximize contact of the tire with the road. However, too much negative camber compromises straight-line stability, increases bump steer and torque steer.

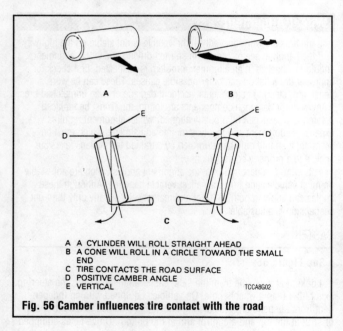

A A CYLINDER WILL ROLL STRAIGHT AHEAD
B A CONE WILL ROLL IN A CIRCLE TOWARD THE SMALL END
C TIRE CONTACTS THE ROAD SURFACE
D POSITIVE CAMBER ANGLE
E VERTICAL

Fig. 56 Camber influences tire contact with the road

TOE

▶ **See Figures 57, 58 and 59**

Looking down at the wheels from above the vehicle, toe angle is the distance between the front of the wheels, relative to the distance between the back of the wheels. If the wheels are closer at the front, they are said to be toed-in or to have negative toe. A small amount of negative toe enhances directional stability and provides a smoother ride on the highway.

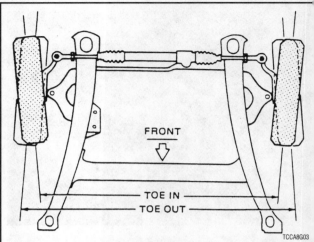

Fig. 57 With toe-in, the distance between the wheels is closer at the front than at the rear

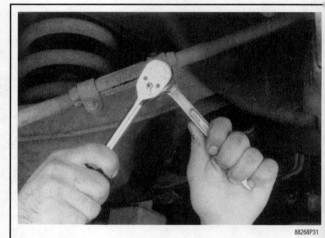

Fig. 58 To adjust toe, first loosen the tie rod adjuster clamp bolts . . .

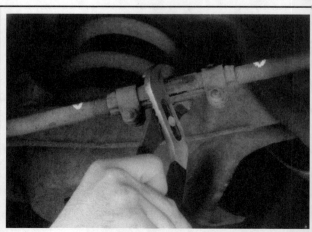

Fig. 59 . . . then turn the adjuster tube as necessary to achieve the required toe-in specification

REAR SUSPENSION

TYPICAL REAR SUSPENSION COMPONENTS

1. Leaf spring
2. U-bolts and nuts
3. Axle tube
4. Shock absorber lower mounting

88198P06

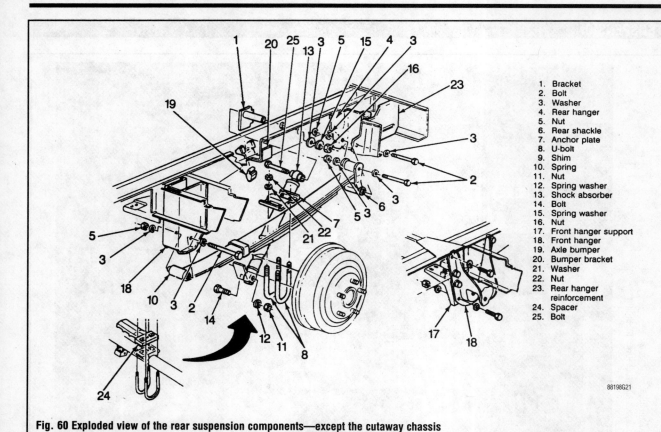

1. Bracket
2. Bolt
3. Washer
4. Rear hanger
5. Nut
6. Rear shackle
7. Anchor plate
8. U-bolt
9. Shim
10. Spring
11. Nut
12. Spring washer
13. Shock absorber
14. Bolt
15. Spring washer
16. Nut
17. Front hanger support
18. Front hanger
19. Axle bumper
20. Bumper bracket
21. Washer
22. Nut
23. Rear hanger reinforcement
24. Spacer
25. Bolt

88198G21

Fig. 60 Exploded view of the rear suspension components—except the cutaway chassis

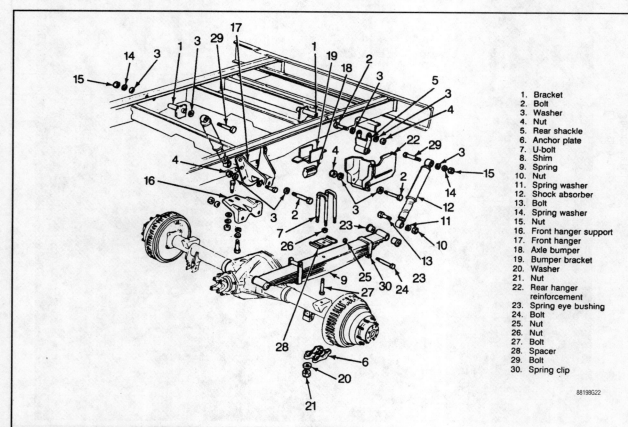

1. Bracket
2. Bolt
3. Washer
4. Nut
5. Rear shackle
6. Anchor plate
7. U-bolt
8. Shim
9. Spring
10. Nut
11. Spring washer
12. Shock absorber
13. Bolt
14. Spring washer
15. Nut
16. Front hanger support
17. Front hanger
18. Axle bumper
19. Bumper bracket
20. Washer
21. Nut
22. Rear hanger reinforcement
23. Spring eye bushing
24. Bolt
25. Nut
26. Nut
27. Bolt
28. Spacer
29. Bolt
30. Spring clip

88198G22

Fig. 61 Exploded view of the rear suspension components—30/3500 cutaway chassis

These vans have leaf spring rear suspension. Staggered rear shock absorbers are used to control axle hop on acceleration and braking. Heavy duty shock absorbers and springs have been available on most models.

❊❊ CAUTION

All suspension and steering fasteners are important attaching parts in that they could affect the performance of vital components and systems, and/or could result in major repair expense. They must be replaced with one of the same part number or with an equivalent part if replacement becomes necessary. Do not use a replacement part of lesser quality or substitute design. Torque values must be used as specified during reassembly to assure proper retention of these parts. Observe all nut and bolt torque specifications.

Leaf Springs

REMOVAL & INSTALLATION

▶ **See Figures 62, 63 and 64**

1. Raise the vehicle and support it so that there is no tension on the leaf spring assembly.
2. Remove the stabilizer bar.
3. Loosen the spring-to-shackle retaining bolts. (Do not remove these bolts).
4. Remove the bolts which attach the shackle to the spring hanger.
5. Remove the nut and bolt which attach the spring to the front hanger.
6. Remove the U-bolt nuts.
7. Remove the stabilizer bar anchor plate, spacers, and shims. Take note of their positions.

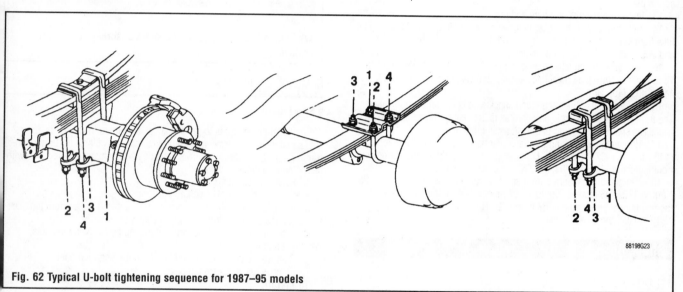

Fig. 62 Typical U-bolt tightening sequence for 1987–95 models

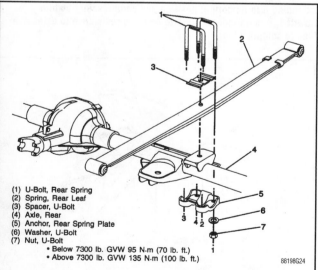

(1) U-Bolt, Rear Spring
(2) Spring, Rear Leaf
(3) Spacer, U-Bolt
(4) Axle, Rear
(5) Anchor, Rear Spring Plate
(6) Washer, U-Bolt
(7) Nut, U-Bolt
• Below 7300 lb. GVW 95 N·m (70 lb. ft.)
• Above 7300 lb. GVW 135 N·m (100 lb. ft.)

Fig. 63 Rear spring-to-axle bolt tightening sequence for 1996–97 models

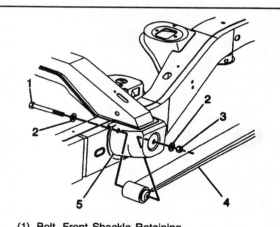

(1) Bolt, Front Shackle Retaining
(2) Washer, Front Shackle
(3) Nut, Front Shackle 110 N·m + 200° (80 lb. ft.)
(4) Spring, Leaf
(5) Frame

Fig. 64 Rear axle and spring-to-frame mounting—1996–97 models

8. If so equipped, remove the auxiliary spring.
9. Pull the spring from the vehicle.
10. Inspect the spring and replace any damaged components.

➡**If the spring bushings are defective, use the following procedures for Removal & Installation. ¾ ton and 1 ton vans use bushings that are staked in place. The stakes must first be straightened. When a new bushing is installed stake it in 3 equally spaced locations. Using a press or vise, remove the bushing and install the new one.**

To install:

11. Place the spring assembly onto the axle housing. Position the front and rear of the spring at the hangers. Raise the axle with a floor jack as necessary to make the alignments. Install the front and rear hanger bolts loosely.
12. Install the spacers, shims, auxiliary spring and anchor plate or spring plate.
13. Install the U-bolts, washers and nuts.
14. Tighten the nuts, in a diagonal sequence, to 18 ft. lbs. (24 Nm), then final tighten the retainers to 192 ft. lbs. (260 Nm) on 1987–95 P models and 205 ft. lbs. (155 Nm) on G models.
15. On 1996–97 models vehicles below 7300 GVW tighten the nuts to 70 ft. lbs. (95 Nm) and on vehicles above 7300 GVW tighten the nuts to 115 ft. lbs. (150 Nm).
16. Make sure that the hanger and shackle bolts are properly installed. The front hanger bolt head is outboard as is the rear spring-to-shackle bolt head. The shackle-to-hanger bolt head faces inboard.
17. Tighten the leaf spring front and rear hanger bolts to 107 ft. lbs. (145 Nm) on 1987–95 models. On 1996–97 models tighten the spring-to-front hanger nut to 80 ft. lbs. (110 Nm) + a 200 degree turn.
18. Tighten the leaf spring front and rear hanger nuts to 92 ft. lbs. (125 Nm) on 1987–95 models. On 1996–97 models tighten the rear shackle to the rear hanger and spring to 67 ft. lbs. (90 Nm).
19. Install the stabilizer bar.

Shock Absorbers

TESTING

The purpose of the shock absorber is simply to limit the motion of the spring during compression and rebound cycles. If the vehicle is not equipped with these motion dampers, the up and down motion would multiply until the vehicle was alternately trying to leap off the ground and to pound itself into the pavement.

Countrary to popular rumor, the shocks do not affect the ride height of the vehicle. This is controlled by other suspension components such as springs and tires. Worn shock absorbers can affect handling; if the front of the vehicle is rising or falling excessively, the "footprint" of the tires changes on the pavement and steering is affected.

The simplest test of the shock absorber is simply push down on one corner of the unladen vehicle and release it. Observe the motion of the body as it is released. In most cases, it will come up beyond it original rest position, dip back below it and settle quickly to rest. This shows that the damper is controlling the spring action. Any tendency to excessive pitch (up-and-down) motion or failure to return to rest within 2-3 cycles is a sign of poor function within the shock absorber. Oil-filled shocks may have a light film of oil around the seal, resulting from normal breathing and air exchange. This should NOT be taken as a sign of failure, but any sign of thick or running oil definitely indicates failure. Gas filled shocks may also show some film at the shaft; if the gas has leaked out, the shock will have almost no resistance to motion.

While each shock absorber can be replaced individually, it is recommended that they be changed as a pair (both front or both rear) to maintain equal response on both sides of the vehicle. Chances are quite good that if one has failed, its mate is weak also.

TCCA8P73

When fluid is seeping out of the shock absorber, it's time to replace it

REMOVAL & INSTALLATION

▶ **See Figure 65**

The usual procedure is to replace shock absorbers in axle pairs, to provide equal damping. Heavy duty replacements are available for firmer control. Air adjustable shock absorbers can be used to maintain a level rid with heavy loads or when towing.

1. Raise and support the van.
2. Support the rear axle with a floor jack.
3. If the van is equipped with air lift shocks, bleed the air from the lines and disconnect the line from the shock absorber.
4. Disconnect the shock absorber at the top by removing the nuts, washer and bolt.
5. Remove the nut, washer, and bolt from the bottom mount.
6. Remove the shock from the van.

To install:

➡**Before installation, purge the new shock of air by repeatedly extending it in its normal position and compressing it while inverted. It is normal for there to be more resistance to extension than to compression.**

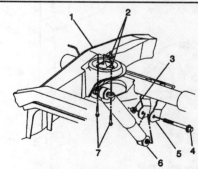

(1) Frame
(2) Nut, Upper Shock Absorber
(3) Nut, Lower Shock Absorber 80 N·m (60 lb. ft.)
(4) Bolt, Lower Shock Absorber
(5) Axle, Rear
(6) Absorber, Shock
(7) Bolt, Upper Shock Absorber 25 N·m (20 lb. ft.)

88198G26

Fig. 65 Typical shock absorber mounting—1996–97 model shown other models similar

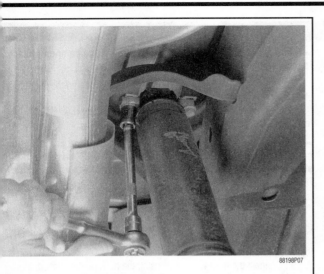

Loosen the rear shock absorber upper mounting bolts . . .

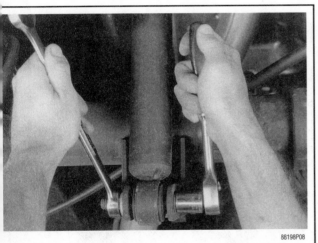

. . . then loosen the lower mounting bolts and remove the shock absorber

7. If the van is equipped with air lift shock absorbers, inflate them to 10–15 psi minimum air pressure.

8. Install the shock absorber in the vehicle.

9. Tighten the shock absorber mounting nuts as follows:

- 1987–92 P models: 114 ft. lbs. (155 Nm)
- 1987–95 G models: 75 ft. lbs. (102 Nm)
- 1993–94 P models shock absorber-to-frame nut: 40 ft. lbs. (55 Nm)
- 1993–94 P models shock absorber-to-axle nut: 125 ft. lbs. (170 Nm)
- 1996–97 G models upper shock absorber bolts: 20 ft. lbs. (25 Nm)
- 1996–97 G models lower shock absorber nut and bolt: 60 ft. lbs. (80 Nm)

Stabilizer Bar

REMOVAL & INSTALLATION

▶ See Figure 66

1. Raise and support the rear end on jackstands.
2. Remove the stabilizer bar bolts, washers and brackets. Take note of their respective positions for installation.
3. Remove the clamps securing the stabilizer bar to the anchor arms.
4. Remove the bar.
5. Remove the insulators from the bar.

To install:

6. Install the insulators.
7. Install the bar onto the anchor plates.
8. Install the brackets and tighten the nuts to 33 ft. lbs. (45 Nm).
9. Engage the bar to the frame, route the parking brake cable over the stabilizer bar, install the brackets and tighten the nuts to 30 ft. lbs. (40 Nm).
10. Lower the vehicle.

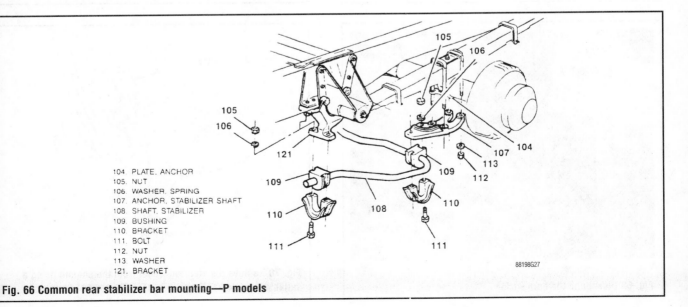

104. PLATE, ANCHOR
105. NUT
106. WASHER, SPRING
107. ANCHOR, STABILIZER SHAFT
108. SHAFT, STABILIZER
109. BUSHING
110. BRACKET
111. BOLT
112. NUT
113. WASHER
121. BRACKET

Fig. 66 Common rear stabilizer bar mounting—P models

STEERING

Steering Wheel

REMOVAL & INSTALLATION

Vehicles Without Air Bag

♦ See Figures 67 thru 74

➡The following procedure requires the use of the GM Steering Wheel Puller tool No. J-1859-03 or equivalent.

1. Disconnect the negative battery cable.
2. Rotate the steering wheel so it is in the horizontal position.
3. If equipped with a horn cap, pry the cap from the center of the steering wheel. If equipped with a steering wheel shroud, remove the screw(s) from the rear of the steering wheel and remove the shroud.

➡If the horn cap or shroud is equipped with an electrical connector, disengage it.

4. Remove the steering wheel-to-steering shaft retainer (snapring) and nut.

➡Since the steering column is designed to collapse upon impact, is recommended NEVER to hammer on it.

5. Matchmark the relationship of the steering wheel to the steering shaft in order to assure proper alignment upon installation.
6. Using the GM Steering Wheel Puller tool No. J-1859-03 or equivalent, press the steering wheel from the steering column.

➡Before installing the steering wheel, be sure the combination control switch is in the Neutral position. DO NOT misalign the steering wheel more than 1 in. (25mm) from the vertical centerline.

To install:

7. Install the steering wheel by aligning the matchmarks and carefully pushing it onto the steering shaft splines.
8. Install the steering wheel-to-steering shaft nut and tighten to 30 ft. lbs. (41 Nm).
9. Connect the horn wire, then install the horn pad or shroud, as applicable.
10. Connect the negative battery cable and check operation.

Fig. 67 Remove the horn button cap

Fig. 69 Remove the snapring from the steering shaft

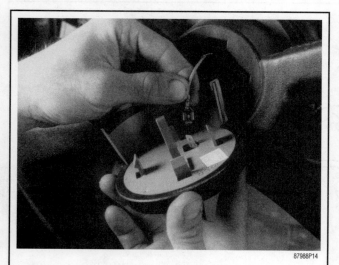

Fig. 68 Disengage the horn wiring

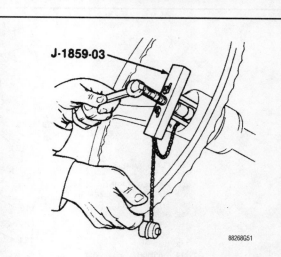

Fig. 70 Remove the steering wheel from the column using a suitable threaded puller

Fig. 71 Remove the nut and washer from the steering shaft

Fig. 72 Use a puller to remove the steering wheel

Fig. 73 Remove the steering wheel

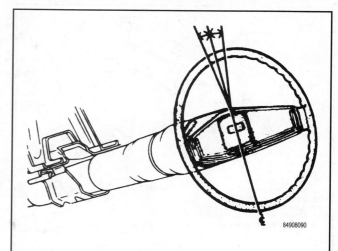

Fig. 74 Steering wheel alignment. Dimension A is 1 in. to either side of the centerline

Vehicles With Air Bag

EXCEPT 1996–97 MODELS

▶ See Figure 75

1. Properly disable the SIR (air bag) system, then disconnect the negative battery cable. For details on disabling the air bag system, please refer to Section 6 of this manual.

2. Remove the SIR inflator module from the steering wheel as follows:

   a. Remove the screws from the back of the steering wheel.

   b. Carefully lift the module away from the wheel, then push down and twist the horn contact lead to the right in order to remove it from the cam tower.

   c. Remove the Connector Position Assurance (CPA) retainer, then disengage the SIR wiring connector from the inflator module.

   d. Carefully remove the inflator module and position it aside in a safe place. MAKE SURE THE MODULE IS FACING UPWARD to leave space for air bag inflation should the unlikely event of an accidental deployment occur.

✳✳ CAUTION

ALWAYS be very cautious when handling a live (undeployed) SIR module. Always leave room for air bag expansion should a deployment occur. This means it should always be placed face up, without ANYTHING on top of it. You should also carry it facing away from you for the same reason.

3. Loosen and remove the steering wheel retaining nut.

4. If applicable, disengage the horn lead assembly.

5. Matchmark the relationship of the wheel to the steering shaft. This is necessary to assure proper alignment upon installation.

6. Remove the wheel from the shaft using a suitable threaded steering wheel puller such as J-1859-03 or equivalent.

To install:

7. Make sure the turn signal lever is in the neutral (no signal) position before attempting to install the steering wheel.

8. Slide the wheel onto the shaft splines while aligning the matchmarks made earlier. DO NOT misalign the wheel more than 1 in. (25mm) from the horizontal centerline.

9. If applicable, engage the horn lead assembly.

10. Install the steering wheel retaining nut and tighten to 30 ft. lbs. (40 Nm).

11. Install the SIR inflator module

   a. Position the module at the steering wheel, then engage the SIR connector and install the CPA retainer.

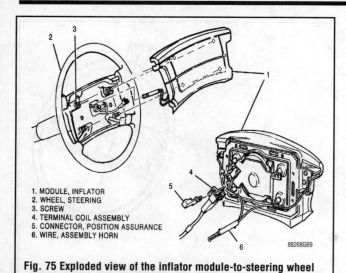

1. MODULE, INFLATOR
2. WHEEL, STEERING
3. SCREW
4. TERMINAL COIL ASSEMBLY
5. CONNECTOR, POSITION ASSURANCE
6. WIRE, ASSEMBLY HORN

88268GB9

Fig. 75 Exploded view of the inflator module-to-steering wheel mounting—except 1996–97 models

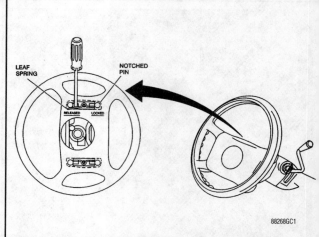

LEAF SPRING   NOTCHED PIN

RELEASED   LOCKED

88268GC1

Fig. 76 The inflator module is secured to the steering wheel using leaf springs and notched pins—1996–97 models

b. Position the SIR wires into the channel in the lower right portion of the steering wheel.

c. Route the horn contact lead through the wheel and into the cam tower. Press the lead into the tower and twist to the right (to the locked position).

d. Install the module to the steering wheel (starting with the top) while making sure NONE of the wires are pinched.

e. Install the retaining screws through the back of the module assembly and tighten to 27 inch lbs. (3 Nm).

12. Make sure the ignition is **OFF**, then connect the negative battery cable.

13. Properly enable the SIR system.

1996–97 MODELS

▶ **See Figures 76 and 77**

1. Properly disable the SIR (air bag) system, then disconnect the negative battery cable. For details on disabling the air bag system, please refer to Section 6 of this manual.

2. Remove the SIR inflator module from the steering wheel:

a. Turn the steering wheel 90 degrees to access the rear shroud hole for the inflator module.

b. Carefully insert a screwdriver and push the leaf spring to release the pin.

c. Turn the wheel 180 degrees to access the remaining rear shroud holes.

d. Again, insert the screwdriver and push the leaf spring to release the pin.

e. Tilt the module rearward from the top in order to access the wiring.

f. Disconnect the lead wire from the clip on the inflator module and from the clip on the steering wheel.

g. Remove the Connector Position Assurance (CPA) retainer from the module connector, then disengage the wiring.

h. Carefully remove the inflator module and position it aside in a safe place. MAKE SURE THE MODULE IS FACING UPWARD to leave space for air bag inflation should the unlikely event of an accidental deployment occur.

❈❈❈ CAUTION

ALWAYS be very cautious when handling a live (undeployed) SIR module. Always leave room for air bag expansion should a deployment occur. This means it should always be placed face up, without ANYTHING on top of it. You should also carry it facing away from you for the same reason.

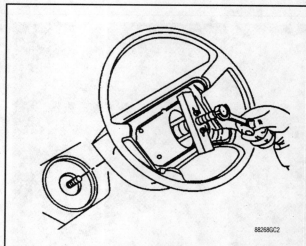

88268GC2

Fig. 77 Once the air bag is removed, steering wheel removal is much the same as it is for non-air bag models

3. Loosen and remove the steering wheel retaining nut.

4. If applicable, remove the horn plunger contact.

5. Matchmark the relationship of the wheel to the steering shaft. This is necessary to assure proper alignment upon installation.

6. Remove the wheel from the shaft using a suitable threaded steering wheel puller such as J-1859-A or equivalent.

To install:

7. Slide the wheel onto the shaft splines while aligning the matchmarks made earlier. DO NOT misalign the wheel more than 1 in. (25mm) from the horizontal centerline.

8. If applicable, install the horn plunger contact.

9. Install the steering wheel retaining nut and tighten to 30 ft. lbs. (40 Nm).

10. Install the SIR inflator module

a. Position the module at the steering wheel, then engage the SIR connector and install the CPA retainer.

b. Secure the SIR lead wire to the clips on the steering wheel and the module.

c. Install the module to the steering wheel by pressing it firmly into the wheel until all 4 notched pins are engaged in the leaf springs. DO NOT pinch the wires during this.

11. Make sure the ignition is **OFF**, then connect the negative battery cable.

12. Properly enable the SIR system.

Turn Signal Switch

✳✳ CAUTION

When servicing any components on the steering column, should any fasteners require replacement, be sure to use only nuts and bolts of the same size and grade as the original fasteners. Using screws that are too long could prevent the column from collapsing during a collision.

REMOVAL & INSTALLATION

Vehicles Without Air Bag

▶ **See Figures 78, 79 and 80**

➡The following procedure requires the use of the GM Lock Plate Compressor tool No. J-23653 or equivalent.

1. Disconnect the negative battery cable.
2. Refer to the Steering Wheel removal and installation procedures earlier in this section and remove the steering wheel.
3. If necessary, remove the steering column-to-lower instrument panel cover. Disengage the electrical harness connector from the steering column jacket (under the dash).
4. Using a small prytool, insert into the slots between the steering shaft lock plate cover and the steering column housing, then pry upward to remove the cover from the lock plate.
5. Using the GM Lock Plate Compressor tool No. J-23653 or equivalent, screw the center shaft onto the steering shaft (as far as it will go), then screw the center post nut clockwise until the lock plate is compressed.
6. Using a small prybar, carefully pry the snapring from the steering shaft slot.

➡If the steering column is being disassembled on a bench, the steering shaft will slide out of the mast jacket when the snapring is removed.

7. Remove the GM Lock Plate Compressor tool No. J-23653 or equivalent, and the lock plate.
8. Remove the multi-function lever-to-switch screw and the lever.
9. To remove the hazard warning switch, press the knob inward and unscrew it.
10. Remove the turn signal switch assembly-to-steering column screws.

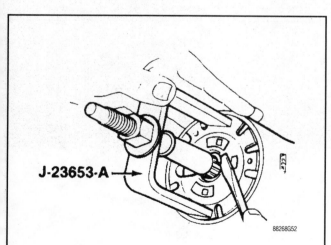

Fig. 78 Compress the steering shaft locking plate using this special tool for access to the snapring

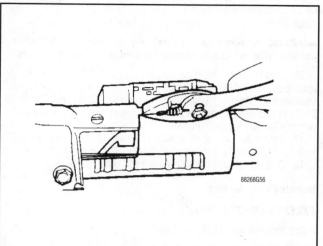

Fig. 79 Removing the turn signal wiring harness protective cover from the column

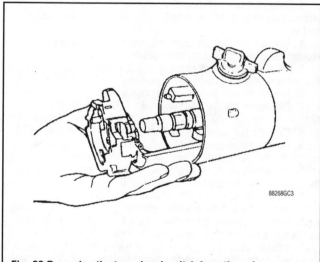

Fig. 80 Removing the turn signal switch from the column

11. Lift the turn signal switch assembly from the steering column, then slide the electrical connector through the column housing and the protector.

➡If the steering column is the tilting type, position the steering housing into the Low position.

12. To remove the harness cover, pull it toward the lower end of the column; be careful not to damage the wires.
13. To remove the wire protector, grab the protector's tab with a pair of pliers, then pull the protector downward, out of the steering column.

➡When assembling the steering column, use only fasteners of the correct length; overlength fasteners could prevent a portion of the assembly from compressing under impact.

To install:

14. Install the turn signal switch electrical connector:
   a. On the non-tilt columns, be sure the electrical connector is on the protector, then feed it and the cover down through the housing and under the mounting bracket.
   b. On the tilt columns, feed the electrical connector down through the housing and under the mounting bracket, then install the cover onto the housing.
15. Install the electrical connector to the clip on the jacket, the turn sig-

nal switch-to-steering column mounting screws, the lower instrument trim panel, the turn signal lever/screws and the hazard warning knob.

➡**With the multi-function lever installed, place it into the Neutral position. With the hazard warning knob installed, pull it outward.**

16. Onto the upper end of the steering shaft, install the washer, the upper bearing preload spring, the canceling cam, the lock plate and a new retaining ring (snapring). Using the GM Lock Plate Compressor tool No. J-23653 or equivalent, compress the lock plate and slide the new retaining ring into the steering shaft groove.

17. Tighten the multi-function switch-to-steering column screws to 35 inch lbs. (4 Nm) and the steering wheel nut to 30 ft. lbs. (41 Nm).

18. Connect the negative battery cable and check operation.

Vehicles With Air Bag

EXCEPT 1996–97 MODELS

♦ **See Figures 81, 82, 83 and 84**

1. Properly disable the SIR (air bag) system, then disconnect the negative battery cable. For details on disabling the air bag system, please refer to Section 6 of this manual.

2. Matchmark and remove the steering wheel.

3. Remove the SIR coil assembly retaining ring, then remove the coil assembly and allow it to hang freely from the wiring. Remove the wave washer.

4. Push downward on the shaft lock assembly until the snapring is exposed using the shaft lock compressor tool.

5. Remove the shaft lock retaining snapring, then carefully release the tool and remove the shaft lock from the column.

6. Remove the turn signal canceling cam assembly.

7. S0>Remove the upper bearing spring, inner race seat and inner race.

8. Move the turn signal lever upward to the "Right Turn" position.

9. Remove the access cap and disengage the multi-function lever harness connector, then grasp the lever and pull it from the column.

10. Loosen and remove the hazard knob retaining screw, then remove the screw, button, spring and knob.

11. Remove the screw and the switch actuator arm.

12. Remove the turn signal switch retaining screws, then pull the switch forward and allow it to hang from the wires. If the switch is only being removed for access to other components, this may be sufficient.

13. If the switch is to be replaced, cut the wires near the top of the switch and discard the switch. Before cutting the wires, verify that the wire color codes are the same. Secure the connector of the new switch to the old wires, and pull the new harness down through the steering column while removing the old switch.

14. If the original switch is to be reused, attach a piece of wire or string around the connector and pull the harness up through the column, while pulling the string up through the column and leaving the string or wire in position to help with reinstallation later.

15. After freeing the switch wiring protector from its mounting, pull the turn signal switch straight up and remove the switch, switch harness, and the connector from the column.

➡**On some vehicles access to the connector may be difficult. If necessary, remove the column support bracket assembly and properly support the column, and/or remove the wiring protectors.**

To install:

16. Install the switch and wiring harness to the vehicle. If the switch was completely removed, use the length of mechanic's wire or string to pull the switch harness through the column, then engage the connector.

➡**If the column support bracket or wiring protectors were removed, install them before proceeding.**

17. Position the switch in the column and secure using the retaining screws.

18. Install the switch actuator arm and retaining screw.

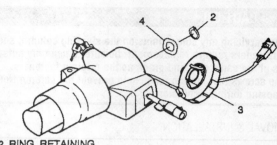

2 RING, RETAINING
3 COIL ASM, SIR
4 WASHER, WAVE

88268GC4

Fig. 81 Exploded view of the SIR coil mounting in the upper steering column

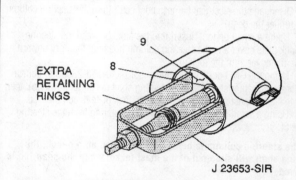

EXTRA RETAINING RINGS

J 23653-SIR

8 RING, RETAINING
9 LOCK, SHAFT

88268GC5

Fig. 82 Use a shaft lock compressor tool to expose the shaft lock snapring (retaining ring)

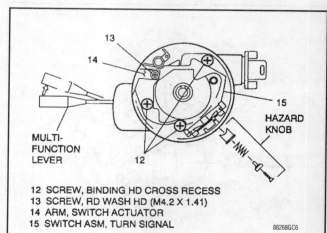

MULTI-FUNCTION LEVER

HAZARD KNOB

12 SCREW, BINDING HD CROSS RECESS
13 SCREW, RD WASH HD (M4.2 X 1.41)
14 ARM, SWITCH ACTUATOR
15 SWITCH ASM, TURN SIGNAL

88268GC6

Fig. 83 View of the turn signal switch and related component mounting in the upper steering column

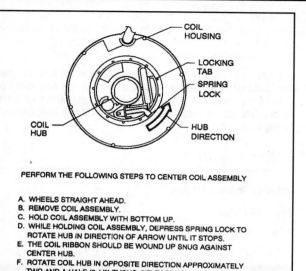

PERFORM THE FOLLOWING STEPS TO CENTER COIL ASSEMBLY

A. WHEELS STRAIGHT AHEAD.
B. REMOVE COIL ASSEMBLY.
C. HOLD COIL ASSEMBLY WITH BOTTOM UP.
D. WHILE HOLDING COIL ASSEMBLY, DEPRESS SPRING LOCK TO
   ROTATE HUB IN DIRECTION OF ARROW UNTIL IT STOPS.
E. THE COIL RIBBON SHOULD BE WOUND UP SNUG AGAINST
   CENTER HUB.
F. ROTATE COIL HUB IN OPPOSITE DIRECTION APPROXIMATELY
   TWO AND A HALF (2-1/2) TURNS. RELEASE SPRING LOCK
   BETWEEN LOCKING TABS.
                                            88268GC7

Fig. 84 Centering the SIR coil assembly

19. Install the hazard knob assembly, then install the multi-function lever.
20. Install the inner race, upper bearing race seat and upper bearing spring.
21. Lubricate the turn signal canceling cam using a suitable synthetic grease (usually included in the service kit), then install the cam assembly.
22. Position the shaft lock and a new snapring, then use the lock compressor to hold the lock down while seating the new snapring. Make sure the ring is firmly seated in the groove, then carefully release the tool.

→The coil assembly will become uncentered if the steering column is separated from the steering gear and allowed to rotate or if the centering spring is pushed down, letting the hub rotate while the coils assembly is removed from the steering column.

23. Make sure the coil is centered, then install the wave washer, followed by the coil and the retaining ring. The coil ring must be firmly seated in the shaft groove.
24. Align and install the steering wheel.
25. Make sure the ignition is **OFF**, then connect the negative battery cable.
26. Properly enable the SIR system.

1996–97 MODELS

Instead of the long time used steering column found on most older GM vehicles the 1996–97 vans are equipped with a new column that uses a multi-function combination switch mounted at the head of the column (below the steering wheel) and an upper/lower shroud assembly. The combination switch performs such functions as the wiper switch and the turn signal switch along with any other duties of the multi-function lever.

→When servicing any components on the steering column, should any fasteners require replacement, be sure to use only nuts and bolts of the same size and grade as the original fasteners. Using screws that are too long could prevent the column from collapsing during a collision.

Combination Switch

REMOVAL & INSTALLATION

♦ See Figures 85 and 86

→Removal of the SIR coil is not necessary during this procedure. Avoid removing the coil and make sure the steering column, if disconnected from the gear, is not allowed to rotate excessively. This is to prevent uncentering and damaging the coil. Should the coil become uncentered, it must be removed, centered and repositioned on the steering column.

1. Properly disable the SIR (air bag) system, then disconnect the negative battery cable. For details on disabling the air bag system, please refer to Section 6 of this manual.
2. Matchmark and remove the steering wheel from the column. For details, please refer to the procedure earlier in this section.
3. Either lower the steering column from the instrument panel for access or unbolt and remove the column. If the column is removed, prevent it from rotating so the SIR coil does not become uncentered.
4. If applicable, remove the tilt lever by pulling outward.
5. Remove the 2 Torx screws or pan head tapping screws (as applicable) from the lower column shroud, then tilt the shroud down and slide it back to disengage the locking tabs. Remove the lower shroud.
6. Remove the 2 Torx head screws from the upper shroud.
7. Lift the upper shroud for access to the lock cylinder hole. Hold the key in the **START** position and use a ¹⁄₁₆ in. Allen wrench to push on the lock cylinder retaining pin.
8. Release the key to the **RUN** position and pull the steering column lock cylinder set from the lock module assembly. Remove the upper shroud.
9. If necessary, remove the shift lever clevis, then remove the lever.
10. Remove the wiring harness straps (noting the positioning for installation purposes), then disengage the steering column bulkhead connector from the vehicle wiring harness.
11. Disengage the gray and black connectors for the multi-function combination switch from the column bulkhead connector.
12. Remove the 2 Torx switch retaining screws, then remove the switch from the steering column.

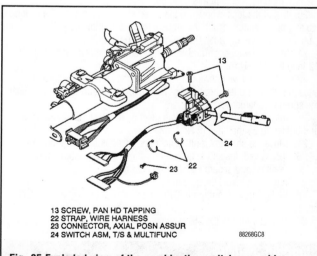

13 SCREW, PAN HD TAPPING
22 STRAP, WIRE HARNESS
23 CONNECTOR, AXIAL POSN ASSUR
24 SWITCH ASM, T/S & MULTIFUNC   88268GC8

Fig. 85 Exploded view of the combination switch assembly mounting—1996–97 vehicles only

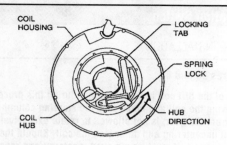

COIL HOUSING
LOCKING TAB
SPRING LOCK
HUB DIRECTION
COIL HUB

PERFORM THE FOLLOWING STEPS TO CENTER COIL ASSEMBLY

A. WHEELS STRAIGHT AHEAD.
B. REMOVE COIL ASSEMBLY.
C. HOLD COIL ASSEMBLY WITH BOTTOM UP.
D. WHILE HOLDING COIL ASSEMBLY, DEPRESS SPRING LOCK TO ROTATE HUB IN DIRECTION OF ARROW UNTIL IT STOPS.
E. THE COIL RIBBON SHOULD BE WOUND UP SNUG AGAINST CENTER HUB.
F. ROTATE COIL HUB IN OPPOSITE DIRECTION APPROXIMATELY TWO AND A HALF (2-1/2) TURNS. RELEASE SPRING LOCK BETWEEN LOCKING TABS.

88268GC9

Fig. 86 The SIR coil MUST be centered if it is allowed to uncenter (unwind) during steering column service

To install:

13. Position the multi-function switch assembly, then use a suitable small bladed tool to compress the electrical contact while moving the switch into position. Make sure the electrical contact rests on the canceling cam assembly.

14. Install the switch retaining screws and tighten to 53 inch lbs. (6.0 Nm).

15. Engage the gray and black multi-function switch connectors to the column bulkhead connector.

16. Install the wiring harness straps as noted during removal.

17. If removed, install the shift lever and secure the clevis.

18. Position the shift lever and multi-function lever seals to ease installation of the upper and lower shrouds.

19. Install the upper shroud and lock cylinder. With the key installed to the lock cylinder and turned to the **RUN** position, make sure the sector in the lock module is also in this position.

20. Install the lock cylinder to the upper shroud, then align the locking tab and positioning tab with the slots in the lock module assembly. With the tabs aligned, carefully push the cylinder into position.

21. Install the upper shroud Torx head retaining screws and tighten to 12 inch lbs. (1.4 Nm).

22. Install the lower shroud, making sure the slots on the shroud engage with the upper shroud tabs. Tilt the lower shroud upward and snap the shrouds together.

23. Install the 2 lower shroud pan head or Torx head retaining screws and tighten to 53 inch lbs. (6 Nm).

24. Move the shift and multi-function lever seals into position.

25. If removed, install the tilt lever by aligning and pushing inward.

26. Position and secure the steering column.

27. Align and install the steering wheel.

28. Make sure the ignition is **OFF**, then connect the negative battery cable.

29. Properly enable the SIR system.

Ignition Switch

For anti-theft reasons, on all models covered by this manual, the ignition switch is located where access is difficult. On all except 1996 vehicles, the switch is located inside the channel section of the brake pedal support and is completely inaccessible without first lowering the steering column. The switch is actuated by a rod and rack assembly. A gear on the end of the lock cylinder engages the toothed upper end of the actuator rod.

For 1996–97 models, the redesigned steering column relocated the ignition switch up the column, under the upper shroud and attached to the lock cylinder housing assembly. Although access is arguably easier here than in the channel of earlier columns, it still requires some effort.

➡ When servicing any components on the steering column, should any fasteners require replacement, be sure to use only nuts and bolts of the same size and grade as the original fasteners. Using screws that are too long could prevent the column from collapsing during a collision.

REMOVAL & INSTALLATION

Vehicles Without Air Bag

1987–93 MODELS

▶ See Figure 87

The switch is on the steering column, behind the instrument panel.

> ✳✳ **CAUTION**
>
> Extreme care is necessary to prevent damage to the collapsible column.

1. Lower and support the steering column as follows:
   a. Disconnect the battery ground.
   b. Disconnect the transmission control linkage at the column.
   c. Matchmark the intermediate shaft upper yoke and the steering shaft.
   d. Remove the upper yoke pinch bolt.
   e. Remove the column-to-instrument panel bolts and nuts and carefully lower the column to the seat.

2. Make sure the switch is in the Lock position. If the lock cylinder is out, pull the switch rod up to the stop, then go down 1 detent.

3. Remove the two screws and the switch.

To install:

4. Before installation, make sure the switch is in the Lock position.

5. Install the switch using the original screws.

> ✳✳ **CAUTION**
>
> Use of screws that are too long could prevent the column from collapsing on impact.

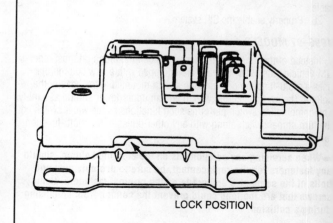

LOCK POSITION

84908096

Fig. 87 Ignition switch used on 1987–93 models

6. Replace the column as follows:

7. Loosely install the column-to-instrument panel bolts.

8. Guide the steering shaft into the yoke, aligning the matchmarks.

9. Install the pinch bolt, making sure it passes through the undercut in the shaft. Tighten the bolt to 35 ft. lbs. (47 Nm). Make sure that the angle of the yoke does not exceed 39° or be less than 34°.

10. Tighten the column bolts to 22 ft. lbs. (29 Nm).

11. Connect all wiring harness connectors.

12. Connect the transmission linkage.

13. Connect the battery ground cable.

1994–95 MODELS

▶ See Figure 88

1. Remove the lower column trim panel, then remove the steering column-to-instrument panel fasteners and carefully lower the column for access to the switch.

2. If equipped, remove the dimmer switch as follows:

    a. Disconnect the negative battery cable, then remove the Torx screw.

    b. Remove the hexagon nut and the ground ring terminal from the stud.

    c. Disconnect the dimmer switch assembly from dimmer switch rod.

3. Unfasten the 2 dimmer switch screws.

4. Disconnect the ignition switch from the choke and actuator assembly

5. Disengage any electrical connects from the switch and remove the switch.

To install:

6. Before installing the ignition switch, place it in the **Locked** position, then make sure the lock cylinder and actuating rod are in the **Locked** position (1st detent from the top).

7. Engage any electrical connections to the switch.

8. Install the choke and actuator rod into the ignition switch and assemble the switch onto the steering column. Tighten the ignition switch-to-steering column screws to 35 inch lbs. (4 Nm).

➡**When installing the ignition switch, use only the specified screws since overlength screws could impair the collapsibility of the column.**

9. Install the dimmer switch as follows:

    a. Connect the dimmer switch rod to the switch.

    b. Install the ground ring terminal and tighten the hexagon nut.

    c. Install the Torx screw and tighten it to 35 inch lbs. (4 Nm).

10. Raise the column into position and secure, then install any necessary trim plates.

11. Connect the negative battery cable and check for proper operation.

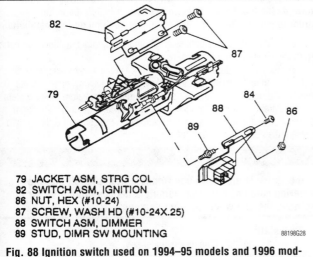

79 JACKET ASM, STRG COL
82 SWITCH ASM, IGNITION
86 NUT, HEX (#10-24)
87 SCREW, WASH HD (#10-24X.25)
88 SWITCH ASM, DIMMER
89 STUD, DIMR SW MOUNTING

88198G28

Fig. 88 Ignition switch used on 1994–95 models and 1996 models without an air bag

Vehicles With Air Bag

EXCEPT 1996–97 MODELS

1. Properly disable the SIR (air bag) system, then disconnect the negative battery cable. For details on disabling the air bag system, please refer to Section 6 of this manual.

2. Remove the lower column trim panel, then remove the steering column-to-instrument panel fasteners and carefully lower the column for access to the switch.

3. On some vehicles, the dimmer switch must be removed in order to remove the ignition switch. If necessary, remove the dimmer switch.

4. Place the ignition switch in the **OFF-LOCK** position.

➡**If the lock cylinder was removed, the switch slider should be moved to the extreme left position, then 1 detent to the right.**

5. Remove the ignition switch-to-steering column retainers and disengage the switch wiring, then remove the assembly.

To install:

6. Before installing the ignition switch, place it in the **OFF-LOCK** position, then make sure the lock cylinder and actuating rod are in the **Locked** position (1st detent from the top or 1st detent to the right of far left detent travel).

➡**Most replacement switches are pinned in the OFF-LOCK position for installation purposes. If so, the pins must be removed after installation or damage may occur. You can make your own pin by insert a ³⁄₃₂ in. drill bit into the adjustment hole provided in the switch in order to limit switch travel. Just remember to remove the bit before attempting to place the switch in service.**

7. Install the activating rod into the ignition switch and assemble the switch onto the steering column. Once the switch is properly positioned, tighten the ignition switch-to-steering column retainers to 35 inch lbs. (4.0 Nm).

➡**When installing the ignition switch, use only the specified screws since over length screws could impair the collapsibility of the column.**

8. If removed, install the dimmer switch.

9. Raise the column into position and secure, then install any necessary trim plates.

10. Make sure the ignition is **OFF**, then connect the negative battery cable.

11. Properly enable the SIR system.

1996–97 MODELS

▶ See Figures 89 and 90

1. Properly disable the SIR (air bag) system, then disconnect the negative battery cable. For details on disabling the air bag system, please refer to Section 6 of this manual.

2. Either lower the steering column from the instrument panel for access or unbolt and remove the column. If the column is removed, prevent it from rotating so the SIR coil does not become uncentered.

3. Remove the combination switch from the steering column.

4. If equipped, remove the alarm switch from the lock module assembly by gently prying the retaining clip on the alarm switch using a small blade prytool. Then, rotate the alarm switch ¼ turn and remove

5. S0>Remove the 2 ignition switch self-tapping retaining screws.

6. Disengage the connector, then remove the wiring harness from the slot in the steering column. Remove the ignition and key alarm switch.

To install:

7. Position the switch to the column. Route the wire harness through the slot in the column housing assembly. Secure the harness using a wire strap through the hole located in the bottom of the housing assembly.

8. Install the switch retaining screws and tighten to 12 inch lbs. (1.4 Nm) in order to secure the switch.

9. If applicable, install the alarm switch to the lock module assembly by aligning the switch (with the retaining clip) parallel to the lock cylinder, then rotating the switch ¼ turn until locked in place.

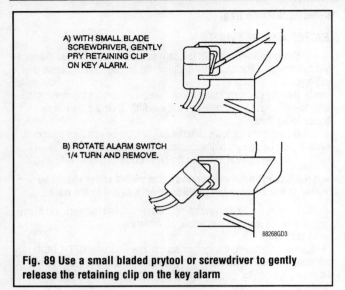

Fig. 89 Use a small bladed prytool or screwdriver to gently release the retaining clip on the key alarm

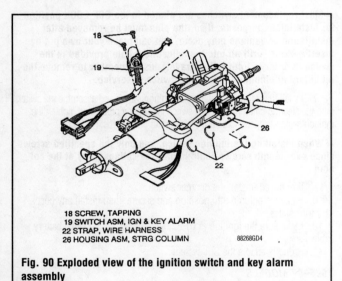

18 SCREW, TAPPING
19 SWITCH ASM, IGN & KEY ALARM
22 STRAP, WIRE HARNESS
26 HOUSING ASM, STRG COLUMN

Fig. 90 Exploded view of the ignition switch and key alarm assembly

10. Install the combination switch to the steering column.
11. Position and secure the steering column.
12. Make sure the ignition is **OFF**, then connect the negative battery cable.
13. Properly enable the SIR system.

Ignition Lock Cylinder

REMOVAL & INSTALLATION

Vehicles Without Air Bag

◆ See Figure 91

1. Remove the steering wheel.
2. Remove the turn signal switch. It is not necessary to completely remove the switch from the column. Pull the switch rearward far enough to slip it over the end of the shaft, but do not pull the harness out of the column.
3. Turn the lock to **RUN**.
4. Remove the lock retaining screw and remove the lock cylinder.

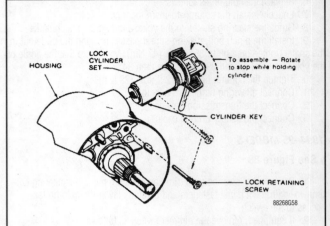

Fig. 91 Exploded view of the lock cylinder mounting—early model shown (late model, except 1996–97, similar)

→If the retaining screw is dropped on removal, it may fall into the column, requiring complete disassembly of the column to retrieve the screw.

5. Rotate the key to the stop while holding onto the cylinder.
6. Push the lock all the way in.
7. Install the screw. Tighten the screw to 40 inch lbs. (4.5 Nm) for regular columns, 22 inch lbs. for adjustable columns.
8. Install the turn signal switch and the steering wheel.

Vehicles With Air Bag

EXCEPT 1996–97 MODELS

1. Properly disable the SIR (air bag) system, then disconnect the negative battery cable. For details on disabling the air bag system, please refer to Section 6 of this manual.
2. Matchmark and remove the steering wheel.
3. Remove the SIR coil assembly retaining ring, then remove the coil assembly and allow it to hang freely from the wiring. Remove the wave washer.

→On some SIR equipped vehicles, it may be necessary to completely remove the coil and wiring from the steering column before removing the lock cylinder assembly. If so, attach a length of mechanic's wire to the coil connector at the base of the column, then carefully pull the harness and wire through the steering column towards the top. Leave the wire in position inside the column in order to pull the harness back down into position during installation.

4. Remove the turn signal switch from the column and allow it to hang from the wires (leaving them connected).
5. Remove the buzzer switch assembly. On some vehicles it may be necessary to temporarily remove the key from the lock cylinder in order to remove the buzzer. If so, the key should be reinserted before the next step.
6. Carefully remove the lock cylinder screw and the lock cylinder. If possible, use a magnetic tipped screwdriver on the screw in order to help prevent the possibility of dropping it.

❊❊ WARNING

If the screw is dropped upon removal, it could fall into the steering column, requiring complete disassembly in order to retrieve the screw and prevent damage.

To install:
7. Align and install the lock cylinder set.
8. Push the lock cylinder all the way in, then carefully install the retain-

ing screw. Tighten the screw to 22 inch lbs. (2.5 Nm) on tilt columns or to 40 inch lbs. (4.5 Nm) on standard non-tilt columns.

9. If necessary, install the buzzer switch assembly.
10. Reposition and secure the turn signal switch assembly

➡**The coil assembly will become uncentered if the steering column is separated from the steering gear and allowed to rotate or if the centering spring is pushed down, letting the hub rotate while the coils assembly is removed from the steering column.**

11. Make sure the coil is centered, then install the wave washer, followed by the coil and the retaining ring. The coil ring must be firmly seated in the shaft groove.
12. Align and install the steering wheel.
13. Make sure the ignition is **OFF**, then connect the negative battery cable.
14. Properly enable the SIR system.

1996–97 MODELS

▶ See Figures 92, 93 and 94

※※ **CAUTION**

When performing service around the SIR system components or wiring, the SIR system MUST be disabled. Failure to do so could result in possible air bag deployment, personal injury or unneeded SIR system repairs.

When carrying a live inflator module, make sure that the bag and trim cover are pointed away from you. Never carry the inflator module by the wires or connector on the underside of the module. In case of accidental deployment, the bag will then deploy with minimal chance of injury.

When placing a live inflator module on a bench or other surface, always face the bag and trim cover up, away from the surface.

1. Disconnect the negative battery cable and disable the SIR system. Refer to the procedure in Section 6.
2. Remove the upper and lower shroud, air bag module and the steering column.
3. Remove the retaining ring, SIR coil assembly, wave washer.
4. Remove the shaft lock retaining ring using tool J 23653-SIR or its equivalent to push down the shaft lock shield assembly. Discard the ring.
5. Remove the shaft lock shield and turn signal cancel cam assembly.
6. Remove the park lock cable assembly from the lock module assembly.
7. Remove the key alarm switch, if equipped by gently prying the alarm switch retaining clip with a small screwdriver. Rotate the alarm switch ¼ in. turn and remove.
8. Remove the two tapping screws and the ignition key and alarm assembly. Let the switch hang freely.

※※ **CAUTION**

The lock assembly is under slight spring tension. Hold the lock bolt in place while removing the lock module assembly.

9. Remove the three pan head tapping screws and the lock module assembly.
10. Remove the backing plate from the module.

➡**Mark the two sector gears at the OFF-LOCK position to ensure proper reassembly.**

11. Remove the sector gears.
12. Remove the positioning tab on the end of the lock cylinder using an ⅛ in. burring tool. Remove all burrs from the lock module and cylinder assembly.
13. Push on the locking tab of the lock cylinder from inside the lock module assembly and remove the lock cylinder.

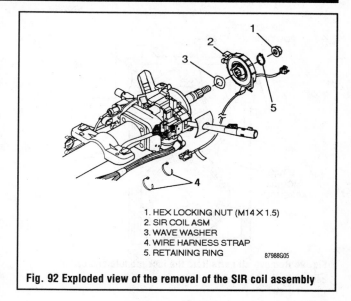

1. HEX LOCKING NUT (M14 × 1.5)
2. SIR COIL ASM
3. WAVE WASHER
4. WIRE HARNESS STRAP
5. RETAINING RING   87988G05

Fig. 92 Exploded view of the removal of the SIR coil assembly

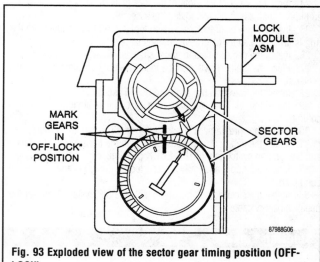

LOCK MODULE ASM

MARK GEARS IN "OFF-LOCK" POSITION

SECTOR GEARS

87988G06

Fig. 93 Exploded view of the sector gear timing position (OFF-LOCK)

To install:

14. Align the marks on the sector gears and install the gears and the backing plate to the lock module assembly.
15. Install the lock cylinder set and ensure that the lock module assembly is in the **OFF-LOCK** position.
16. Install the key in the lock cylinder and ensure that it is in the **OFF-LOCK** position.
17. Line up the locking tab with the slots in the lock module assembly and push the cylinder into position.
18. Rotate the lock cylinder to the **ACC** position. The alignment arrows on the sector gears should be pointing towards each other.
19. Rotate the lock cylinder to the **LOCK** position. Push the lock bolt in until it is flush and align the lock module assembly with the head assembly and install the lock module assembly.
20. Install the three pan head screws and tighten to 53 inch lbs. (6 Nm).
21. Install the ignition and key alarm switch assembly and the fasteners. Tighten the fasteners to 12 inch lbs. (1.4 Nm).
22. Install the key alarm switch. Make sure the retaining clip is parallel to the lock cylinder. Rotate the alarm switch ¼ in. turn until locked in place.
23. Lubricate the lower brass surface of the turn signal cancel cam assembly with synthetic grease and install the assembly.

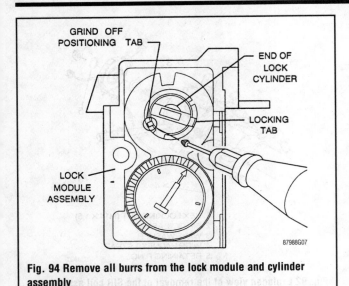

Fig. 94 Remove all burrs from the lock module and cylinder assembly

24. Align the inner block tooth of the lock plate to block tooth of race and upper shaft assembly and install the assembly.

25. Install a new shaft lock ring using tool J 23653-SIR and ensure the ring is firmly seated in the groove on the shaft.

26. Install the center race and upper shaft assembly.

27. Place the ignition switch to the lock assembly and ensure the coil is centered.

28. Install the wave washer and the SIR coil assembly.

29. Install the retaining ring and route the coil wire along the steering column.

30. Install the wire harness straps to the steering column harness.

31. Install the park lock cable assembly with the transmission in Park and the ignition switch in the **OFF-LOCK** position.

32. Install the upper and lower covers, lock cylinder set and tilt lever (if equipped).

33. Install the steering column and enable the SIR system. Connect the negative battery cable.

Steering Linkage

REMOVAL & INSTALLATION

Pitman Arm

▶ **See Figure 95**

1. Raise and support the front end on jackstands.
2. Remove the relay rod or connecting rod nut and cotter pin.
3. Disconnect the relay rod or connecting rod from the Pitman arm using a puller. Do not hammer on the Pitman arm. Damage could result to the steering gear.
4. Remove the Pitman arm nut and washer.
5. Remove the Pitman arm with a puller.

To install:

6. On commercial models, install the Pitman arm on the Pitman shaft and tighten the washer and nut to 184 ft. lbs. (250 Nm) on 1987–95 models

7. Engage the relay or connecting rod to the Pitman arm and make sure the seal is on the stud. Tighten to 40 ft. lbs. (54 Nm).

8. On motor home and I-beam front axle models, install the Pitman arm on the Pitman shaft and tighten the washer and nut to 125 ft. lbs. (170 Nm) on 1987

9. Install the idler arm ball stud in the relay rod, making certain the seal is positioned properly. Tighten a steering linkage installation tool to 35 ft. lbs.

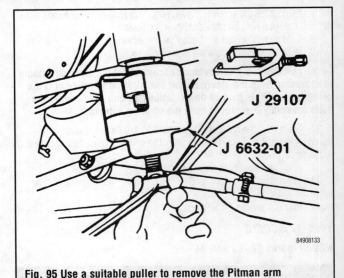

Fig. 95 Use a suitable puller to remove the Pitman arm

(47 Nm) to seat the tapers, remove the tool and tighten the nut to 66 ft. lbs. (90 Nm) on 1987–95 models and 35 ft. lbs. (47 Nm) on 1996–97 models. Always advance the nut to align the cotter pin hole. NEVER back it off!

10. Lower the vehicle to the floor.

Idler Arm

▶ **See Figures 96, 97, 98 and 99**

1. Raise and support the front end on jackstands.
2. Remove the nut from ball stud at the relay rod.
3. Using a screw-type ball joint tool, separate the ball stud from the relay rod.
4. Remove the idler arm to frame bolts and remove the idler arm assembly.

To install:

5. Position the idler arm on the frame and install the mounting bolts. Tighten the bolts to 30–35 ft. lbs. (40–47 Nm) on 1987–95 models and 74 ft. lbs. (100 Nm) +40 degrees on 1996–97 models.

6. Make sure that the threads on the ball stud and in the ball stud nut are clean and smooth. If threads are not clean and smooth, ball stud may turn in the socket when attempting to tighten nut. Check condition of ball stud seal; replace if necessary.

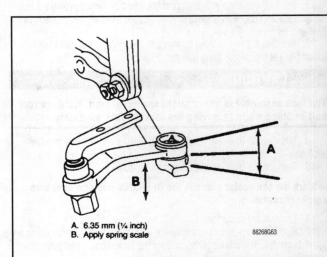

A. 6.35 mm (¼ inch)
B. Apply spring scale

Fig. 96 Idler arm inspection should be conducted using a spring scale

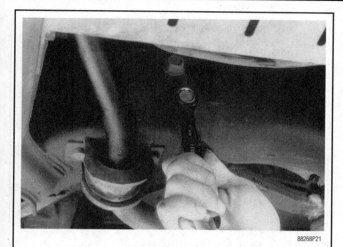

Fig. 97 Loosen and remove the idler arm-to-frame mounting bolts . . .

Fig. 98 . . . then separate the idler arm ball stud from the relay rod . . .

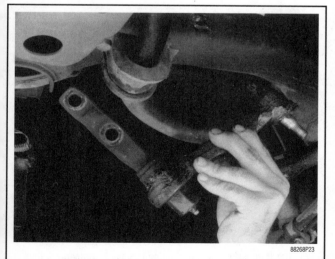

Fig. 99 . . . and remove the idler arm from the vehicle

7. Install the idler arm ball stud in the relay rod, making certain the seal is positioned properly. Tighten a steering linkage installation tool to 35 ft. lbs. (47 Nm) to seat the tapers, remove the tool and tighten the nut to 66 ft. lbs. (90 Nm) on 1987–95 models and 35 ft. lbs. (47 Nm) on 1996–97 models. Always advance the nut to align the cotter pin hole. NEVER back it off!

8. Lower the vehicle to the floor.

Tie Rod Ends

INDEPENDENT FRONT SUSPENSION

♦ See Figures 100 thru 108 (p. 39–41)

1. Loosen the tie rod adjuster sleeve clamp nuts.
2. If equipped, disconnect the steering shock absorber from the tie rod assembly.

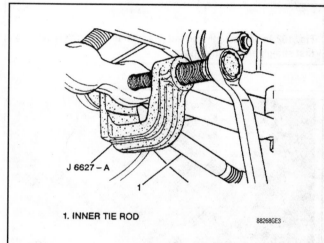

Fig. 100 Inner tie rod and relay rod connections require the use of a press-type linkage/wheel stud remover

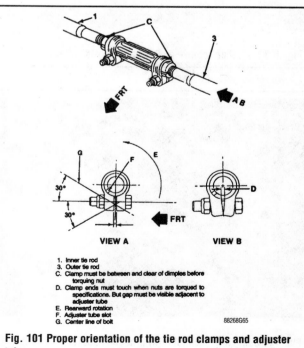

1. Inner tie rod
3. Outer tie rod
C. Clamp must be between and clear of dimples before torquing nut
D. Clamp ends must touch when nuts are torqued to specifications. But gap must be visible adjacent to adjuster tube
E. Rearward rotation
F. Adjuster tube slot
G. Center line of bolt

Fig. 101 Proper orientation of the tie rod clamps and adjuster tube

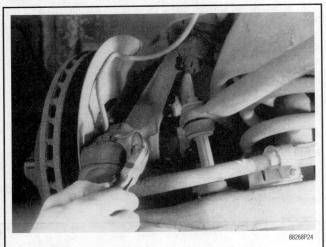

Fig. 102 To separate the tie rod end from the steering knuckle, first straighten the cotter pin . . .

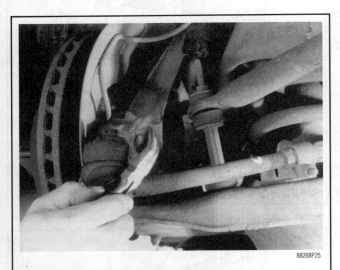

Fig. 103 . . . then remove and discard the old cotter pin

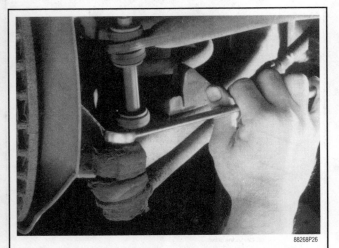

Fig. 104 Using a wrench (shown) or a deep socket, loosen the tie rod stud retaining nut

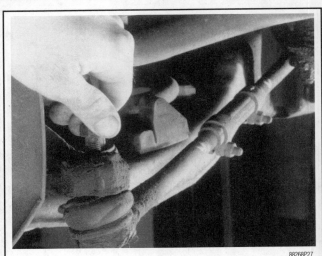

Fig. 105 Unthread the nut from the stud . . .

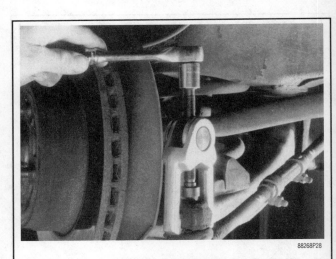

Fig. 106 . . . then use a universal steering linkage puller to free the stud from the knuckle

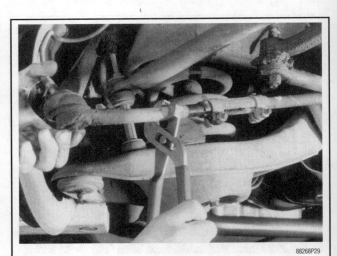

Fig. 107 If only the rod end is being removed, matchmark the threads (to preserve toe adjustment) . . .

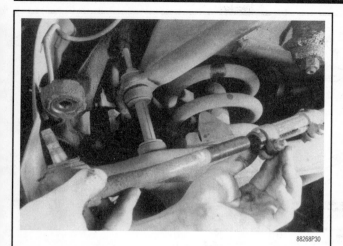

Fig. 108 . . . then loosen the adjuster clamp bolt and unthread the end from the adjuster tube

3. Remove the tie rod end stud cotter pin and nut.
4. Use a screw-type tie rod removal tool to loosen the outer stud.
5. Remove the inner stud in the same way.
6. Unscrew the tie rod end from the threaded sleeve. The threads may be left or right-hand threads. Count the number of turns required to remove it.

To install:

7. Grease the threads and turn the new tie rod end in as many turns as were needed to remove it. This will give approximately correct toe-in.
8. Tighten the inner tie rod ball stud in the relay rod, making certain the seal is positioned properly. Tighten a steering linkage installation tool to 35 ft. lbs. (47 Nm) to seat the tapers, remove the tool and tighten the nut to 66 ft. lbs. (90 Nm) on 1987–95 models and 35 ft. lbs. (47 Nm) on 1996–97 models. Always advance the nut to align the cotter pin hole. NEVER back it off!
9. Adjust the toe-in.
10. Before tightening the clamp nuts:
   a. Each clamp must be positioned between the locating dimples at each end of the adjuster.
   b. The inner and outer tie rods must rotate for their travel. The position of the tie rods must be maintained while the clamps are tightened.
   c. The split in the sleeve must be position at a point just above the clamp nut.

d. The clamps must be positioned with the nut facing forward and within 45 degrees of horizontal (60° on 1992–95 models).
11. Tighten the adjuster clamp bolts to 14 ft. lbs. (19 Nm) on 1987–95 models and 18 ft. lbs. (25 Nm) on 1996–97 models.

I-BEAM (SOLID) FRONT AXLE

▶ See Figure 109

1. Loosen the tie rod adjuster sleeve clamp nuts.
2. If equipped, disconnect the steering shock absorber from the tie rod assembly.
3. Remove the tie rod end stud cotter pin and nut.
4. Use a screw-type tie rod removal tool to loosen the outer stud from the steering knuckle.
5. Unscrew the tie rod end from the threaded sleeve. The threads may be left or right hand threads. Count the number of turns required to remove it.

To install:

6. Grease the threads and turn the new tie rod end in as many turns as were needed to remove it. This will give approximately correct toe-in.
7. Engage the outer tie rod ball stud to the steering knuckle, tighten the nut to 162 ft. lbs. (220 Nm) and install the a new cotter pin.
8. If equipped install the steering shock absorber, tighten the shock absorber nut to 46 ft. lbs.(62 Nm) and install a new cotter pin.
9. Adjust the toe-in.
10. Tighten the adjuster clamp bolts to 14 ft. lbs. (19 Nm).

Manual Steering Gear

REMOVAL & INSTALLATION

▶ See Figure 110

1. Set the front wheels in straight ahead position by driving vehicle a short distance on a flat surface.
2. Matchmark the relationship of the universal yoke to the wormshaft.
3. Remove the universal yoke pinch bolt.
4. Mark the relationship of the Pitman arm to the Pitman shaft.
5. Remove the Pitman shaft nut and then remove the Pitman arm from the Pitman shaft, using puller J-6632.
6. Remove the steering gear to frame bolts and remove the gear assembly.

To install:

7. Place the steering gear in position, guiding the steering gear shaft into the universal yoke.

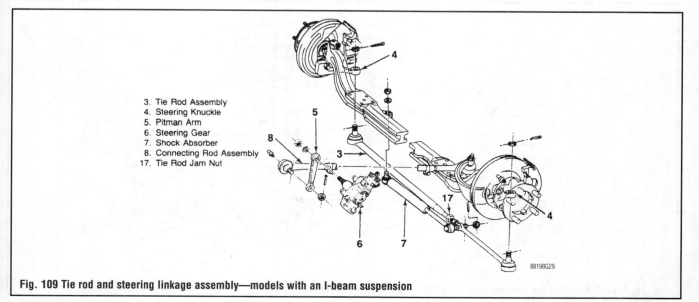

3. Tie Rod Assembly
4. Steering Knuckle
5. Pitman Arm
6. Steering Gear
7. Shock Absorber
8. Connecting Rod Assembly
17. Tie Rod Jam Nut

Fig. 109 Tie rod and steering linkage assembly—models with an I-beam suspension

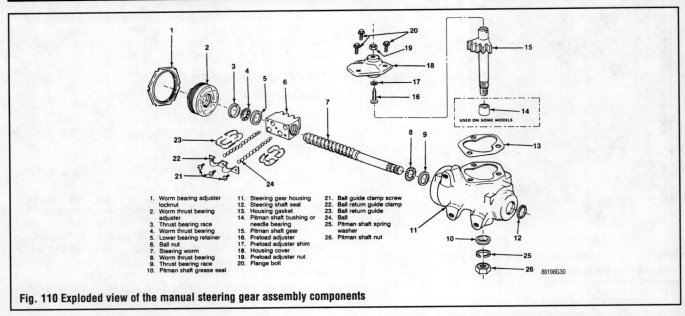

1. Worm bearing adjuster locknut
2. Worm thrust bearing adjuster
3. Thrust bearing race
4. Worm thrust bearing
5. Lower bearing retainer
6. Ball nut
7. Steering worm
8. Worm thrust bearing
9. Thrust bearing race
10. Pitman shaft grease seal
11. Steering gear housing
12. Steering shaft seal
13. Housing gasket
14. Pitman shaft bushing or needle bearing
15. Pitman shaft gear
16. Preload adjuster
17. Preload adjuster shim
18. Housing cover
19. Preload adjuster nut
20. Flange bolt
21. Ball guide clamp screw
22. Ball return guide clamp
23. Ball return guide
24. Ball
25. Pitman shaft spring washer
26. Pitman shaft nut

88198G30

Fig. 110 Exploded view of the manual steering gear assembly components

8. Install the steering gear to frame bolts and tighten to 75 ft. lbs. (101 Nm).

9. Install the yoke pinch bolt. Tighten the pinch bolt to 45 ft. lbs. (61 Nm).

10. Install the Pitman arm onto the Pitman shaft, lining up the marks made at removal. Install the Pitman shaft nut torque to 185 ft. lbs. (250 Nm).

Power Steering Gear

REMOVAL & INSTALLATION

1987–94 Models

▶ **See Figures 111, 112 and 113**

1. Raise and support the front end on jackstands.
2. Set the front wheels in the straight ahead position.
3. Disconnect the battery ground cable.
4. Place a drain pan under the gear and disconnect the fluid lines. Cap the openings.

5. Remove the flexible coupling pinch bolt (708 models) or the cardan joint clip bolt and nut (710 models).

6. On 710, remove the cardan joint from the steering gear stub shaft.

7. Mark the relationship of the Pitman arm to the Pitman shaft.

8. Remove the Pitman shaft nut and then remove the Pitman arm from the Pitman shaft, using a puller.

9. Remove the steering gear to frame bolts and remove the gear assembly.

To install:

10. Place the steering gear in position, guiding the wormshaft into flexible coupling. Align the flat in the coupling with the flat on the wormshaft.

11. Install the steering gear to frame bolts and tighten to 66 ft. lbs. (89 Nm) on the 708 models and 175 ft. lbs. (277 Nm) on the 710 models.

12. On 708 models, install the coupling pinch bolt. Tighten the pinch bolt to 75 ft. lbs. (102 Nm).

13. On 710 models, install the cardan joint to the steering gear and tighten the bolt to 35 ft. lbs. (48 Nm).

14. Install the Pitman arm.

15. Connect the fluid lines and refill the reservoir. Bleed the system.

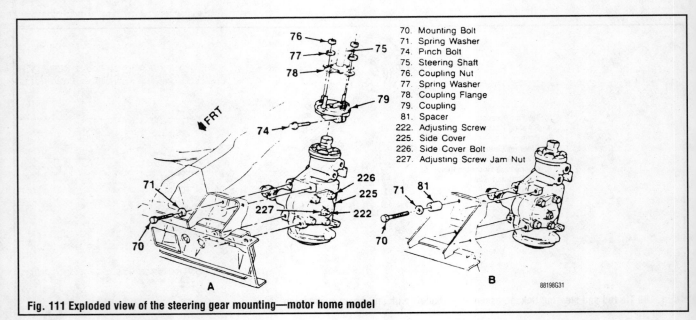

70. Mounting Bolt
71. Spring Washer
74. Pinch Bolt
75. Steering Shaft
76. Coupling Nut
77. Spring Washer
78. Coupling Flange
79. Coupling
81. Spacer
222. Adjusting Screw
225. Side Cover
226. Side Cover Bolt
227. Adjusting Screw Jam Nut

88198G31

Fig. 111 Exploded view of the steering gear mounting—motor home model

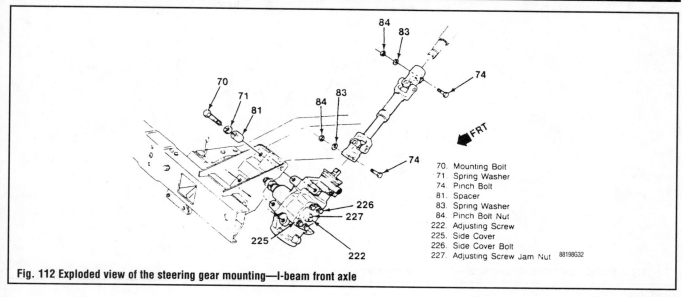

70. Mounting Bolt
71. Spring Washer
74. Pinch Bolt
81. Spacer
83. Spring Washer
84. Pinch Bolt Nut
222. Adjusting Screw
225. Side Cover
226. Side Cover Bolt
227. Adjusting Screw Jam Nut

88198G32

Fig. 112 Exploded view of the steering gear mounting—I-beam front axle

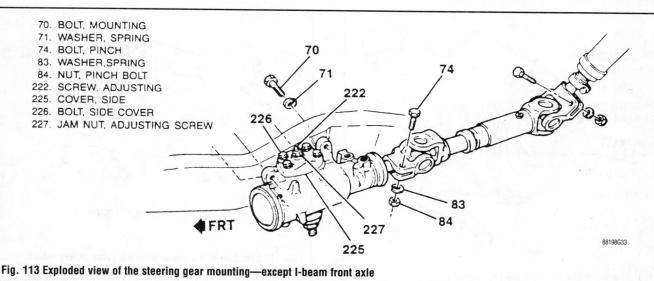

70. BOLT, MOUNTING
71. WASHER, SPRING
74. BOLT, PINCH
83. WASHER, SPRING
84. NUT, PINCH BOLT
222. SCREW, ADJUSTING
225. COVER, SIDE
226. BOLT, SIDE COVER
227. JAM NUT, ADJUSTING SCREW

88198G33

Fig. 113 Exploded view of the steering gear mounting—except I-beam front axle

1995–97 Models

▶ **See Figure 114**

1. Raise and support the front end on jackstands.
2. Set the front wheels in the straight ahead position.
3. Disconnect the battery ground cable.
4. Place a drain pan under the gear and disconnect the fluid lines. Cap the openings.
5. Remove the intermediate shaft pinch bolt.
6. Matchmark the relationship of the cardan yoke to the stub shaft.
7. Remove the Pitman shaft nut and then remove the Pitman arm from the Pitman shaft, using a puller.
8. Remove the steering gear to frame bolts and remove the gear assembly.

To install:

9. Place the steering gear in position, guiding the wormshaft into flexible coupling. Align the flat in the coupling with the flat on the wormshaft.
10. Install the steering gear to frame bolts and tighten to 98 ft. lbs. (135 Nm).
11. Install the intermediate shaft pinch bolt. Tighten the pinch bolt to 46 ft. lbs. (62 Nm).

12. Install the Pitman arm onto the Pitman shaft.
13. Connect the fluid lines and refill the reservoir. Bleed the system.

Power Steering Pump

REMOVAL & INSTALLATION

▶ **See Figures 115, 116, 117, 118 and 119 (p. 44–46)**

1. Disconnect the hoses at the pump. When the hoses are disconnected, secure the ends in a raised position to prevent leakage. Cap the ends of the hoses to prevent the entrance of dirt.
2. Cap the pump fittings.
3. Loosen the bracket-to-pump mounting nuts.
4. Remove the pump drive belt.
5. Remove the pulley with a puller such as J 25034-B, except for the 7.4L engine (on which the power steering pump pulley can be replaced after removal).
6. Remove the bracket-to-pump bolts and remove the pump from the van.

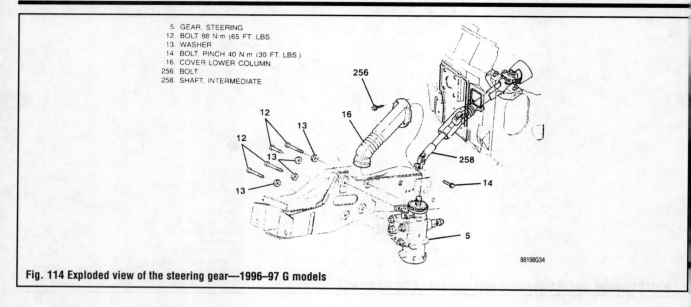

5. GEAR, STEERING
12. BOLT 88 N·m (65 FT. LBS.)
13. WASHER
14. BOLT PINCH 40 N·m (30 FT. LBS.)
16. COVER LOWER COLUMN
256. BOLT
258. SHAFT, INTERMEDIATE

88198G34

Fig. 114 Exploded view of the steering gear—1996–97 G models

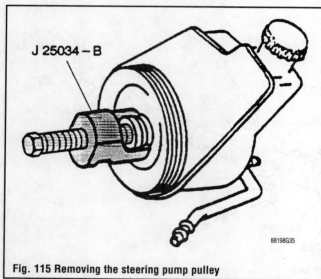

J 25034 – B

88198G35

Fig. 115 Removing the steering pump pulley

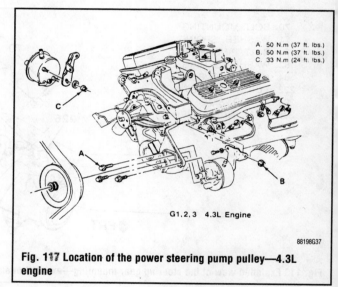

A. 50 N·m (37 ft. lbs.)
B. 50 N·m (37 ft. lbs.)
C. 33 N·m (24 ft. lbs.)

G1,2,3 4.3L Engine

88198G37

Fig. 117 Location of the power steering pump pulley—4.3L engine

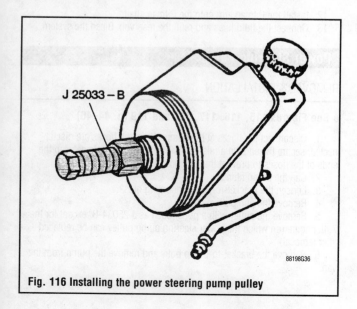

J 25033 – B

88198G36

Fig. 116 Installing the power steering pump pulley

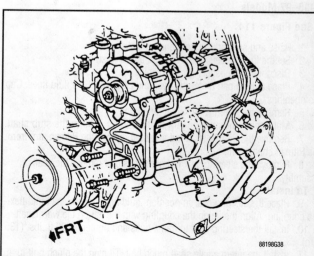

FRT

88198G38

Fig. 118 Location of the power steering pump pulley—5.7L engine

To install:

➡On 7.4L engines, install the pulley on the new pump with a forcing screw and washer tool (such as J 25033-B) before installing the pump.

7. Install the pump, then install the pulley on the new pump with a forcing screw and washer tool, then tighten all bolts and nuts securely.

8. Fill the reservoir and bleed the pump by turning the pulley counterclockwise (as viewed from the front) until bubbles stop forming.

9. Install the drive belt.

10. Bleed the system as outlined below.

BLEEDING

1987–95 Models

1. Fill the reservoir to the proper level and let the fluid remain undisturbed for at least 2 minutes.

2. Start the engine and run it for only about 2 seconds.

3. Add fluid as necessary.

4. Repeat Steps 1–3 until the level remains constant.

5. Raise the front of the vehicle so that the front wheels are off the ground. Set the parking brake and block both rear wheels front and rear. Manual transmissions should be in Neutral; automatic transmissions should be in Park.

6. Start the engine and run it at approximately 1500 rpm.

7. Turn the wheels (off the ground) to the right and left, lightly contacting the stops.

8. Add fluid as necessary.

9. Lower the vehicle and turn the wheels right and left on the ground.

10. Check the level and refill as necessary.

11. If the fluid is extremely foamy, let the van stand for a few minutes with the engine off and repeat the procedure. Check the belt tension and check for a bent or loose pulley. The pulley should not wobble with the engine running.

12. Check that no hoses are contacting any parts of the van, particularly sheet metal.

13. Check the oil level and refill as necessary. This step and the next are very important. When filling, follow Steps 1–10.

14. Check for air in the fluid. Aerated fluid appears milky. If air is present, repeat the above operation. If it is obvious that the pump will not respond to bleeding after several attempts, a pressure test may be required.

The procedures for maintaining, adjusting, and repairing the power steering systems and components discussed in this section are to be done only after determining that the steering linkages and front suspension systems are correctly aligned and in good condition. All worn or damaged parts should be replaced before attempting to service the power steering system. After correcting any condition that could affect the power steering, do the preliminary tests of the steering system components.

1996–97 Models

1. Turn the ignition **OFF**.

2. Raise the front of the vehicle so that the front wheels are off the ground.

3. Turn the steering wheel to its **full** left position.

4. Fill the reservoir to the **Full Cold** level and leave the cap off.

5. With the ignition still in the **OFF** position, turn the wheel lock-to-lock at least 20 times (on models with long return lines perform this procedure 40 times).

6. Ensure that the fluid level remains at the **Full Cold** level and that there is no spilled fluid or air bubbles that could indicate a loose connection or leaking O-ring seal.

7. Turn the ignition **ON** and with the engine idling, check the fluid level. If the level is correct install the cap.

8. Return the wheels to the center position and lower the vehicle.

9. With engine still running, turn the wheel from side-to-side. If there is a smooth, noiseless and leak free operation the procedure is complete.

10. If there is a problem, check that the fluid is free of bubbles and that the O-rings and clamps are in good condition. If not replace the worn or damaged part(s) and repeat the bleeding procedure.

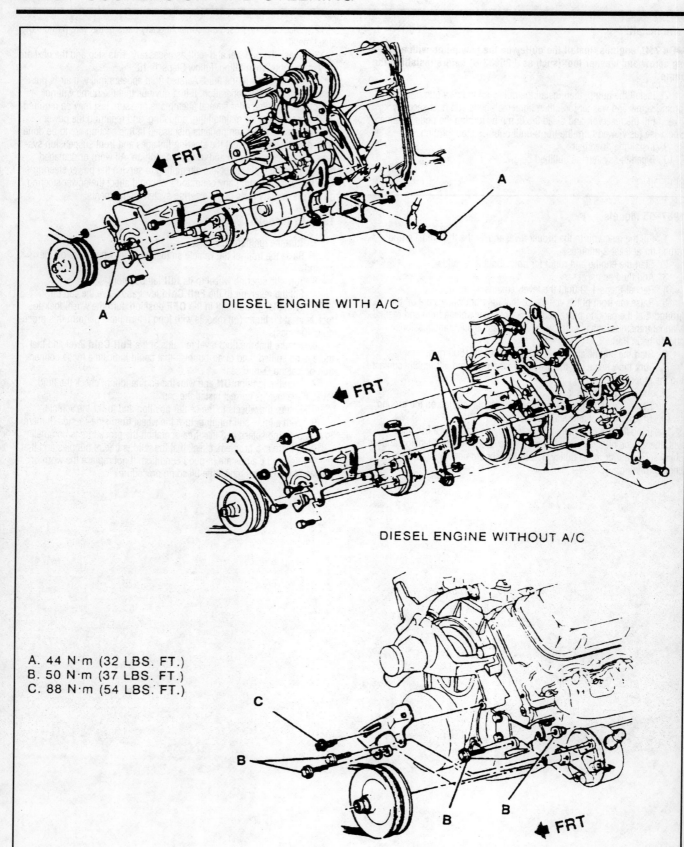

← FRT

DIESEL ENGINE WITH A/C

A

← FRT

A

A

DIESEL ENGINE WITHOUT A/C

A. 44 N·m (32 LBS. FT.)
B. 50 N·m (37 LBS. FT.)
C. 88 N·m (54 LBS. FT.)

C

B

B

B

← FRT

88198G39

7.4 ENGINE

Fig. 119 Location of the power steering pump pulley—6.5L diesel and 7.4L gasoline engines

TORQUE SPECIFICATIONS

System	Component			Ft. Lbs.	Nm
Front Suspension					
	Coil Spring				
	U-bolt nuts				
		10/1500 and 20/2500 series		65	88
		30/3500 series		85	115
	Shock Absorber				
		1987–95 models	Upper	80	108
			Lower	74	101
		1996–97 models	Upper	12	16
			Lower	24	33
	Upper Ball Joint				
	Nuts			18	25
	Stud nut				
		P/PG models		90	122
		1987–95 G models		50	68
		1996–97 models		74	100
	Lower Ball Joint				
	Stud nut				
		1987–95 models		90	122
		1996–97 models		94	128
	Leaf Spring				
	Shackle bolts			92	125
		U-bolt nuts	First pass	18	25
			Second pass	80	109
		Front eye bolt		92	125
	Stabilizer Bar				
	Bar-to-lower control arm				
		1987–95 models		24	33
		1996–97 models		26	35
	Upper Control Arm				
	Ball stud				
		1987–95 models			
		10/1500 and 20/2500		90	122
		30/3500		130	176
		1996–97 models		94	128
	Lower Control Arm				
	Ball stud				
		1987–95 models			
		10/1500 and 20/2500		90	122
		30/3500		130	176
		1996–97 models		94	128
Rear Suspension					
	Leaf Spring				
	U-bolt nuts				
		1987–95 models			
			P models	192	260
			G models	155	210
		1996–97 models			
			Below 7300 GVW	70	95
			Above 7300 GVW	115	150

TORQUE SPECIFICATIONS

System	Component			Ft. Lbs.	Nm
	Shock Absorber				
		P models			
		1987–92 models		114	155
		1993–94 models			
			Shock-to-frame nut	40	55
			Shock-to-axle nut	125	170
		G models			
		1987–95 models		75	102
		1996–97 models			
			Upper	20	25
			Lower	60	80
	Stabilizer Shaft				
		Shaft bracket-to-hanger nut		30	40
		Shaft bracket-to-frame nut		40	55
		Shaft-to-anchor nut		33	45
		Shaft-to-frame bolt		30	40
Steering					
	Steering Wheel Nut			30	40
	Pitman Arm-to-Shaft				
		Commercial		184	250
		Motor home and I-beam		125	170
	Idler Arm				
		Arm-to-frame			
		1987–95 models		30-35	40-47
		1996–97 models		74 + 100 degrees	100 +100 degrees
	Tie Rod End				
		Except I-beam			
		Stud nut			
		1987–95 models		66	89
		1996–97 models		35	47
		Clamp bolts			
		1987–95 models		14	19
		1996–97 models		18	25
		I-Beam			
		Stud nut		162	220
		Clamp bolts		14	19
	Manual Steering Gear				
		Gear-to-frame bolts		75	101
		Yoke pinch bolt		45	61
	Power Steering Gear				
		Gear-to-frame bolts			
		1987-95 models		66	89
		1996-97 models		98	133
		Coupling pinch bolt (model 708)		75	102
		Cardan joint bolt (model 710)		35	48

88198C02

9

BRAKES

BRAKE OPERATING SYSTEM

Basic Operating Principles

Hydraulic systems are used to actuate the brakes of all modern automobiles. The system transports the power required to force the frictional surfaces of the braking system together from the pedal to the individual brake units at each wheel. A hydraulic system is used for two reasons.

First, fluid under pressure can be carried to all parts of an automobile by small pipes and flexible hoses without taking up a significant amount of room or posing routing problems.

Second, a great mechanical advantage can be given to the brake pedal end of the system, and the foot pressure required to actuate the brakes can be reduced by making the surface area of the master cylinder pistons smaller than that of any of the pistons in the wheel cylinders or calipers.

The master cylinder consists of a fluid reservoir along with a double cylinder and piston assembly. Double type master cylinders are designed to separate the front and rear braking systems hydraulically in case of a leak. The master cylinder coverts mechanical motion from the pedal into hydraulic pressure within the lines. This pressure is translated back into mechanical motion at the wheels by either the wheel cylinder (drum brakes) or the caliper (disc brakes).

Steel lines carry the brake fluid to a point on the vehicle's frame near each of the vehicle's wheels. The fluid is then carried to the calipers and wheel cylinders by flexible tubes in order to allow for suspension and steering movements.

In drum brake systems, each wheel cylinder contains two pistons, one at either end, which push outward in opposite directions and force the brake shoe into contact with the drum.

In disc brake systems, the cylinders are part of the calipers. At least one cylinder in each caliper is used to force the brake pads against the disc.

All pistons employ some type of seal, usually made of rubber, to minimize fluid leakage. A rubber dust boot seals the outer end of the cylinder against dust and dirt. The boot fits around the outer end of the piston on disc brake calipers, and around the brake actuating rod on wheel cylinders.

The hydraulic system operates as follows: When at rest, the entire system, from the piston(s) in the master cylinder to those in the wheel cylinders or calipers, is full of brake fluid. Upon application of the brake pedal, fluid trapped in front of the master cylinder piston(s) is forced through the lines to the wheel cylinders. Here, it forces the pistons outward, in the case of drum brakes, and inward toward the disc, in the case of disc brakes. The motion of the pistons is opposed by return springs mounted outside the cylinders in drum brakes, and by spring seals, in disc brakes.

Upon release of the brake pedal, a spring located inside the master cylinder immediately returns the master cylinder pistons to the normal position. The pistons contain check valves and the master cylinder has compensating ports drilled in it. These are uncovered as the pistons reach their normal position. The piston check valves allow fluid to flow toward the wheel cylinders or calipers as the pistons withdraw. Then, as the return springs force the brake pads or shoes into the released position, the excess fluid reservoir through the compensating ports. It is during the time the pedal is in the released position that any fluid that has leaked out of the system will be replaced through the compensating ports.

Dual circuit master cylinders employ two pistons, located one behind the other, in the same cylinder. The primary piston is actuated directly by mechanical linkage from the brake pedal through the power booster. The secondary piston is actuated by fluid trapped between the two pistons. If a leak develops in front of the secondary piston, it moves forward until it bottoms against the front of the master cylinder, and the fluid trapped between the pistons will operate the rear brakes. If the rear brakes develop a leak, the primary piston will move forward until direct contact with the secondary piston takes place, and it will force the secondary piston to actuate the front brakes. In either case, the brake pedal moves farther when the brakes are applied, and less braking power is available.

All dual circuit systems use a switch to warn the driver when only half of the brake system is operational. This switch is usually located in a valve body which is mounted on the firewall or the frame below the master cylinder. A hydraulic piston receives pressure from both circuits, each circuit's pressure being applied to one end of the piston. When the pressures are in balance, the piston remains stationary. When one circuit has a leak, however, the greater pressure in that circuit during application of the brakes will push the piston to one side, closing the switch and activating the brake warning light.

In disc brake systems, this valve body also contains a metering valve and, in some cases, a proportioning valve. The metering valve keeps pressure from traveling to the disc brakes on the front wheels until the brake shoes on the rear wheels have contacted the drums, ensuring that the front brakes will never be used alone. The proportioning valve controls the pressure to the rear brakes to lessen the chance of rear wheel lock-up during very hard braking.

Warning lights may be tested by depressing the brake pedal and holding it while opening one of the wheel cylinder bleeder screws. If this does not cause the light to go on, substitute a new lamp, make continuity checks, and, finally, replace the switch as necessary.

The hydraulic system may be checked for leaks by applying pressure to the pedal gradually and steadily. If the pedal sinks very slowly to the floor, the system has a leak. This is not to be confused with a springy or spongy feel due to the compression of air within the lines. If the system leaks, there will be a gradual change in the position of the pedal with a constant pressure.

Check for leaks along all lines and at wheel cylinders. If no external leaks are apparent, the problem is inside the master cylinder.

DISC BRAKES

Instead of the traditional expanding brakes that press outward against a circular drum, disc brake systems utilize a disc (rotor) with brake pads positioned on either side of it. An easily-seen analogy is the hand brake arrangement on a bicycle. The pads squeeze onto the rim of the bike wheel, slowing its motion. Automobile disc brakes use the identical principle but apply the braking effort to a separate disc instead of the wheel.

The disc (rotor) is a casting, usually equipped with cooling fins between the two braking surfaces. This enables air to circulate between the braking surfaces making them less sensitive to heat buildup and more resistant to fade. Dirt and water do not drastically affect braking action since contaminants are thrown off by the centrifugal action of the rotor or scraped off the by the pads. Also, the equal clamping action of the two brake pads tends to ensure uniform, straight line stops. Disc brakes are inherently self-adjusting. There are three general types of disc brake:

- A fixed caliper
- A floating caliper
- A sliding caliper

The fixed caliper design uses two pistons mounted on either side of the rotor (in each side of the caliper). The caliper is mounted rigidly and does not move.

The sliding and floating designs are quite similar. In fact, these two types are often lumped together. In both designs, the pad on the inside of the rotor is moved into contact with the rotor by hydraulic force. The caliper, which is not held in a fixed position, moves slightly, bringing the outside pad into contact with the rotor. There are various methods of attaching floating calipers. Some pivot at the bottom or top, and some slide on mounting bolts. In any event, the end result is the same.

DRUM BRAKES

Drum brakes employ two brake shoes mounted on a stationary backing plate. These shoes are positioned inside a circular drum which rotates with the wheel assembly. The shoes are held in place by springs. This allows them to slide toward the drums (when they are applied) while keeping the linings and drums in alignment. The shoes are actuated by a wheel cylinder which is mounted at the top of the backing plate. When the brakes are applied, hydraulic pressure forces the wheel cylinder's actuating links outward. Since these links bear directly against the top of the brake shoes, the tops of the shoes are then forced against the inner side of the drum. This action forces the bottoms of the two shoes to contact the brake drum by rotating the entire assembly slightly (known as servo action). When pressure within the wheel cylinder is relaxed, return springs pull the shoes back away from the drum.

Most modern drum brakes are designed to self-adjust themselves during application when the vehicle is moving in reverse. This motion causes both shoes to rotate very slightly with the drum, rocking an adjusting lever, thereby causing rotation of the adjusting screw. Some drum brake systems are designed to self-adjust during application whenever the brakes are applied. This on-board adjustment system reduces the need for maintenance adjustments and keeps both the brake function and pedal feel satisfactory.

POWER BOOSTERS

Virtually all modern vehicles use a vacuum assisted power brake system to multiply the braking force and reduce pedal effort. Since vacuum is always available when the engine is operating, the system is simple and efficient. A vacuum diaphragm is located on the front of the master cylinder and assists the driver in applying the brakes, reducing both the effort and travel he must put into moving the brake pedal.

The vacuum diaphragm housing is normally connected to the intake manifold by a vacuum hose. A check valve is placed at the point where the hose enters the diaphragm housing, so that during periods of low manifold vacuum brakes assist will not be lost.

Depressing the brake pedal closes off the vacuum source and allows atmospheric pressure to enter on one side of the diaphragm. This causes the master cylinder pistons to move and apply the brakes. When the brake pedal is released, vacuum is applied to both sides of the diaphragm and springs return the diaphragm and master cylinder pistons to the released position.

If the vacuum supply fails, the brake pedal rod will contact the end of the master cylinder actuator rod and the system will apply the brakes without any power assistance. The driver will notice that much higher pedal effort is needed to stop the car and that the pedal feels harder than usual.

Vacuum Leak Test

1. Operate the engine at idle without touching the brake pedal for at least one minute.
2. Turn off the engine and wait one minute.
3. Test for the presence of assist vacuum by depressing the brake pedal and releasing it several times. If vacuum is present in the system, light application will produce less and less pedal travel. If there is no vacuum, air is leaking into the system.

System Operation Test

1. With the engine **OFF**, pump the brake pedal until the supply vacuum is entirely gone.
2. Put light, steady pressure on the brake pedal.
3. Start the engine and let it idle. If the system is operating correctly, the brake pedal should fall toward the floor if the constant pressure is maintained.

Power brake systems may be tested for hydraulic leaks just as ordinary systems are tested.

Brake Adjustments

DRUM BRAKES

▶ See Figures 1 and 2

These brakes are equipped with self-adjusters and no manual adjustment is necessary, except when brake linings are replaced.

➡**The following procedure requires the use of GM brake adjustment tool J-4735 or its equivalent.**

1. Raise and support the rear of the vehicle on jackstands.
2. Using a punch and a hammer, at the rear of the backing plate, knock out the lanced metal area near the star wheel assembly.

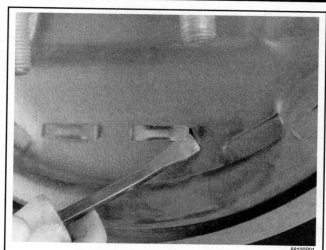
Fig. 1 Remove the metal tab from the backing plate. DO NOT allow it to fall into the drum

Fig. 2 Use a brake adjusting spoon to turn the starwheel. A screwdriver just won't work that well

➡**When knocking out the lanced metal area from the backing plate, the wheels must be removed and all of the metal pieces discarded.**

3. Using the GM Brake Adjustment tool No. J-4735 or equivalent, insert it into the slot and engage the lowest possible tooth on the star wheel. Move the end of the brake tool downward to move the star wheel upward and expand the adjusting screw. Repeat this operation until the brakes lock the wheel.
4. Insert a small screwdriver or piece of firm wire (coat hanger wire) into the adjusting slot and push the automatic adjuster lever out and free of the star wheel on the adjusting screw.
5. While holding the adjusting lever out of the way, engage the topmost tooth possible on the star wheel (with the brake tool). Move the end of the adjusting tool upward to move the adjusting screw star wheel downward and contact the adjusting screw. Back off the adjusting screw star wheel until the wheel spins freely with a minimum of drag. Keep track of the number of turns the star wheel is backed off.
6. Repeat this operation for the other side. When backing off the brakes on the other side, the adjusting lever must be backed off the same number of turns to prevent side-to-side brake pull.

➡ **Backing off the star wheel 12 notches (clicks) is usually enough to eliminate brake drag.**

7. Repeat this operation on the other side of the rear brake system.

8. After the brakes are adjusted, install a rubber hole cover into the backing plate slot. To complete the brake adjustment operation, make several stops while backing the vehicle to equalize the wheels.

9. Road test the vehicle.

DISC BRAKES

These brakes are inherently self-adjusting and no adjustment is ever necessary or possible.

Master Cylinder

REMOVAL & INSTALLATION

▶ **See Figure 3**

✳ WARNING

Clean any master cylinder parts in alcohol or brake fluid. Never use mineral based cleaning solvents such as gasoline, kerosene, carbon tetrachloride, acetone, or paint thinner as these will destroy rubber parts. Do not allow brake fluid to spill on the vehicle's finish, it will remove the paint. Flush the area with water.

1. Using a clean cloth, wipe the master cylinder and its lines to remove excess dirt and then place cloths under the unit to absorb spilled fluid.

2. Remove the hydraulic lines from the master cylinder and plug the outlets to prevent the entrance of foreign material. On vans with ABS, disconnect the lines at the isolation/dump valve.

3. Remove the master cylinder attaching bolts or, on vans with ABS, the attaching bolts from the isolation/dump valve, and remove the master cylinder from the brake booster, or, on vans with manual brakes, the firewall.

✳ WARNING

On vans with ABS, never let brake fluid or your skin touch the ECU electrical connections! Also, never let the isolation/dump valve hang by its wiring!

To install:

4. Position the master cylinder or, on vans with ABS the master cylinder and isolation/dump valve, on the booster or firewall. Tighten the nuts to 20 ft. lbs. (27 Nm) on 1987–93 models and 27 ft. lbs. (36 Nm) on 1994–97 models.

5. Connect the brake lines and tighten them to 13 ft. lbs. (17 Nm). Fill the master cylinder reservoirs to the proper levels.

6. Bleed the brakes master cylinder, then the complete system.

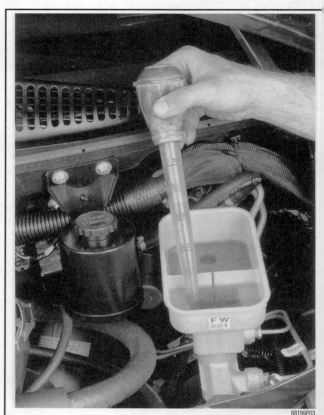

Use a suction device to remove about a third of the brake fluid from the master cylinder

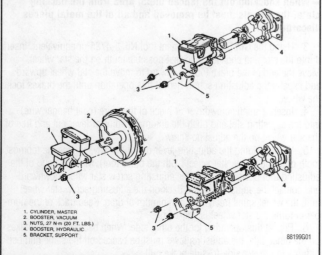

1. CYLINDER, MASTER
2. BOOSTER, VACUUM
3. NUTS, 27 N·m (20 FT. LBS.)
4. BOOSTER, HYDRAULIC
5. BRACKET, SUPPORT

88199G01

Fig. 3 Typical master cylinder mountings

Place a rag under the line wrench to help minimize spillage when disconnecting the brake lines

Loosen the master cylinder mounting nuts and remove the master cylinder

Vacuum Booster

REMOVAL & INSTALLATION

▶ **See Figure 4**

1. Unbolt the master cylinder from the booster and pull it off the studs, CAREFULLY! It is not necessary to disconnect the brake lines.
2. Disconnect the vacuum hose from the check valve.
3. Disconnect the booster pushrod at the brake pedal.
4. If necessary, unfasten the power brake booster nuts from the brake pedal bracket.

5. Remove the booster mounting nuts, located on the inside of the firewall.
6. Lift off the booster.
To install:
7. To install the booster with a new gasket.
8. Tighten the booster mounting nuts to 22 ft. lbs. (30 Nm) on 1987–95 models or 27 ft. lbs. (36 Nm) on 1996–97 models.
9. Install the master cylinder and bleed the system.

Hydro-Boost

Some models are equipped with the Bendix Hydro-Boost system. This power brake booster obtains hydraulic pressure from the power steering pump, rather than vacuum pressure from the intake manifold, as in most gasoline engine brake booster systems.

SYSTEM CHECKS

1. A defective Hydro-Boost cannot cause any of the following conditions:
   a. Noisy brakes
   b. Fading pedal
   c. Pulling brakes
If any of these occur, check elsewhere in the brake system.
2. Check the fluid level in the master cylinder. It should be within ¼ in. (6mm) of the top. If is isn't, add only DOT-3 or DOT-4 brake fluid until the correct level is reached.
3. Check the fluid level in the power steering pump. The engine should be at normal running temperature and stopped. The level should register on the pump dipstick. Add power steering fluid to bring the reservoir level up to the correct level. Low fluid level will result in both poor steering and stopping ability.

✷✷ CAUTION

The brake hydraulic system uses brake fluid only, while the power steering and Hydro-Boost systems use power steering fluid only. Don't mix the two!

4. Check the power steering pump belt tension, and inspect all the power steering/Hydro-Boost hoses for kinks or leaks.
5. Check and adjust the engine idle speed, as necessary.
6. Check the power steering pump fluid for bubbles. If air bubbles are present in the fluid, bleed the system:

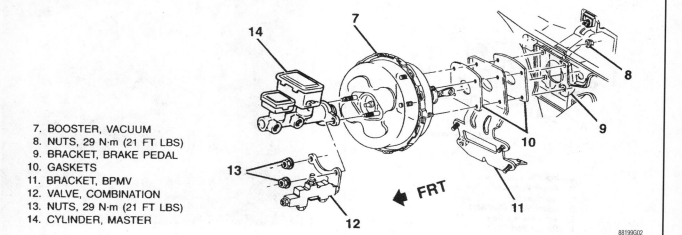

7. BOOSTER, VACUUM
8. NUTS, 29 N·m (21 FT LBS)
9. BRACKET, BRAKE PEDAL
10. GASKETS
11. BRACKET, BPMV
12. VALVE, COMBINATION
13. NUTS, 29 N·m (21 FT LBS)
14. CYLINDER, MASTER

Fig. 4 Vacuum booster mounting

a. Fill the power steering pump reservoir to specifications with the engine at normal operating temperature.

b. With the engine running, rotate the steering wheel through its normal travel 3 or 4 times, without holding the wheel against the stops.

c. Check the fluid level again.

REMOVAL & INSTALLATION

▶ **See Figures 5 thru 14**

✳✳ CAUTION

Power steering fluid and brake fluid cannot be mixed. If brake seals contact the steering fluid or steering seals contact the brake fluid, damage will result!

1. Apply the parking brake.
2. Turn the engine off and pump the brake pedal 4 or 5 times to deplete the accumulator inside the unit.
3. Remove the two nuts from the master cylinder, and remove the cylinder keeping the brake lines attached. Secure the master cylinder out of the way.
4. Remove the hydraulic lines from the booster.

5. Loosen the retainers and separate the booster unit from the firewall.
6. Disconnect the pushrod from the brake pedal and remove the unit

To install:

7. Engage the pushrod to the brake pedal and install the unit.
8. Tighten the booster mounting nuts to 22 ft. lbs. (30 Nm) on 1987–95 models and 27 ft. lbs. (36 Nm) on 1996–97 models.
9. Install the master cylinder.
10. Bleed the Hydro-Boost system.

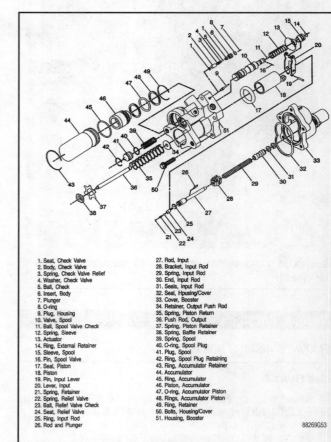

1. Seat, Check Valve	27. Rod, Input
2. Body, Check Valve	28. Bracket, Input Rod
3. Spring, Check Valve Relief	29. Spring, Input Rod
4. Washer, Check Valve	30. End, Input Rod
5. Ball, Check	31. Seals, Input Rod
6. Insert, Body	32. Seal, Hpusing/Cover
7. Plunger	33. Cover, Booster
8. O-ring	34. Retainer, Output Push Rod
9. Plug, Housing	35. Spring, Piston Return
10. Valve, Spool	36. Push Rod, Output
11. Ball, Spool Valve Check	37. Spring, Piston Retainer
12. Spring, Sleeve	38. Spring, Baffle Retainer
13. Actuator	39. Spring, Spool
14. Ring, External Retainer	40. O-ring, Spool Plug
15. Sleeve, Spool	41. Plug, Spool
16. Pin, Spool Valve	42. Ring, Spool Plug Retaining
17. Seal, Piston	43. Ring, Accumulator Retainer
18. Piston	44. Accumulator
19. Pin, Input Lever	45. Ring, Accumulator
20. Lever, Input	46. Piston, Accumulator
21. Spring, Retainer	47. O-ring, Accumulator Piston
22. Spring, Relief Valve	48. Rings, Accumulator Piston
23. Ball, Relief Valve Check	49. Ring, Retainer
24. Seat, Relief Valve	50. Bolts, Housing/Cover
25. Ring, Input Rod	51. Housing, Booster
26. Rod and Plunger	

88269G53

Fig. 7 Exploded view of the Hydro-Boost unit

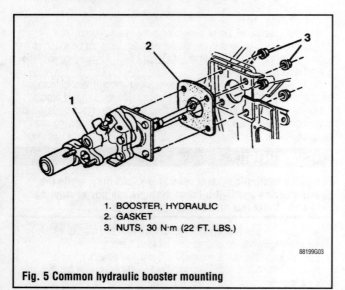

1. BOOSTER, HYDRAULIC
2. GASKET
3. NUTS, 30 N·m (22 FT. LBS.)

88199G03

Fig. 5 Common hydraulic booster mounting

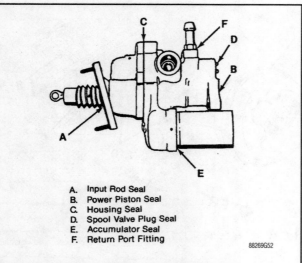

A. Input Rod Seal
B. Power Piston Seal
C. Housing Seal
D. Spool Valve Plug Seal
E. Accumulator Seal
F. Return Port Fitting

88269G52

Fig. 6 Potential leakage points on the Hydro-Boost unit

988269P11

Fig. 8 Use a rag to catch the fluid when disconnecting the pressure hoses

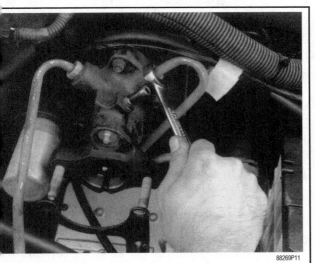

Fig. 9 Always use a flare wrench on the fittings

Fig. 12 Disconnect the pushrod from the pedal

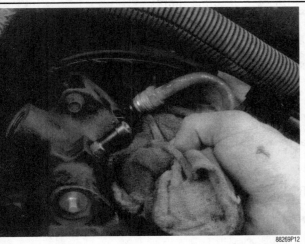

Fig. 10 Note the O-ring on the end of the fitting. Use a new one when reconnecting

Fig. 13 Withdraw the booster assembly by pulling straight out

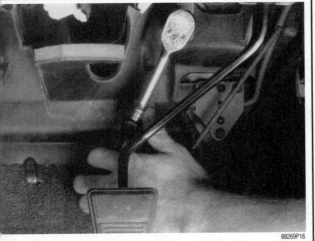

Fig. 11 Loosen and remove the booster mounting nuts from inside the vehicle

Fig. 14 Once the booster is out far enough to clear the pushrod, it can be removed from the vehicle

BLEEDING

The system should be bled whenever the booster is removed and installed.

1. Fill the power steering pump until the fluid level is at the base of the pump reservoir neck. Disconnect the battery lead from the distributor.

➡**Remove the electrical lead to the fuel solenoid terminal on the injection pump before cranking the engine.**

2. Jack up the front of the vehicle, turn the wheels all the way to the left, and crank the engine for a few seconds.

3. Check steering pump fluid level. If necessary, add fluid to the "ADD" mark on the dipstick.

4. Lower the car, connect the battery lead, and start the engine. Check fluid level and add fluid to the "ADD" mark, as necessary. With the engine running, turn the wheels from side to side to bleed air from the system. Make sure that the fluid level stays above the internal pump casting.

5. The Hydro-Boost system should now be fully bled. If the fluid is foaming after bleeding, stop the engine, let the system set for one hour, then repeat the second part of Step 4.

The preceding procedures should be effective in removing the excess air from the system, however sometimes air may still remain trapped. When this happens the booster may make a gulping noise when the brake is applied. Lightly pumping the brake pedal with the engine running should cause this noise to disappear. After the noise stops, check the pump fluid level and add as necessary.

Combination Valve

This valve is used on all models with disc brakes. The valve itself is a combination of:

1. The metering valve, which will not allow the front disc brakes to engage until the rear brakes contact the drum.

2. The failure warning switch, which notifies the driver if one of the systems has a leak.

3. The proportioner which limits rear brake pressure and delays rear wheel skid.

REMOVAL & INSTALLATION

1987–95 Models

▶ **See Figure 15**

1. Disconnect the hydraulic lines and plug to prevent dirt from entering the system.

2. Disconnect the warning switch harness.

3. Remove the retaining bolts and remove the valve. Tighten the bo 18 ft. lbs. (25 Nm).

4. Install the valve and bleed the brake system.

1996–97 Models

1. Raise the vehicle and support it with jackstands.

2. Remove the shield retainers and shield from the vehicle.

3. Disconnect the brake lines at the valve. Plug or cap the lines an ports.

4. Unplug the electrical connector.

5. Unfasten the Allen bolts connecting the valve to the Brake Press Modulator Valve (BPMV).

6. Remove the valve, then transfer the tubes to the new valve.

To install:

7. Install the tubes until they are firmly seated.

8. Install the valve. Tighten the bolts in two steps, first tighten the bolts to 6 ft. lbs. (8 Nm) and then to 12 ft. lbs. (16 Nm).

9. Connect the brake lines and engage the electrical connector.

10. Install the shield and tighten the retainers to 8 ft. lbs. (12 Nm).

11. Bleed the system.

Brake Hoses and Lines

Metal lines and rubber brake hoses should be checked frequently fo leaks and external damage. Metal lines are particularly prone to crushin and kinking under the vehicle. Any such deformation can restrict the pr flow of fluid and therefore impair braking at the wheels. Rubber hoses should be checked for cracking or scraping; such damage can create a weak spot in the hose and it could fail under pressure.

Any time the lines are removed or disconnected, extreme cleanliness must be observed. Clean all joints and connections before disassembly (use a stiff bristle brush and clean brake fluid); be sure to plug the lines and ports as soon as they are opened. New lines and hoses should be flushed clean with brake fluid before installation to remove any contami tion.

REMOVAL & INSTALLATION

▶ **See Figures 16, 17, 18 and 19**

1. Disconnect the negative battery cable.

2. Raise and safely support the vehicle on jackstands.

3. Remove any wheel and tire assemblies necessary for access to t particular line you are removing.

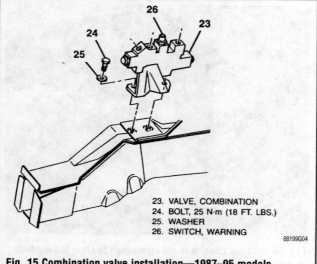

23. VALVE, COMBINATION
24. BOLT, 25 N·m (18 FT. LBS.)
25. WASHER
26. SWITCH, WARNING

88199G04

Fig. 15 Combination valve installation—1987–95 models

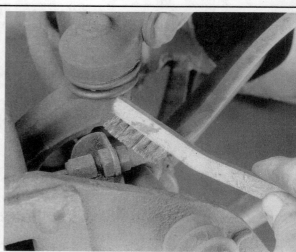

TCCA9

Fig. 16 Use a brush to clean the fittings of any debris

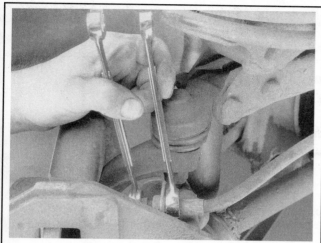

Fig. 17 Use two wrenches to loosen the fitting. If available, use flare nut type wrenches

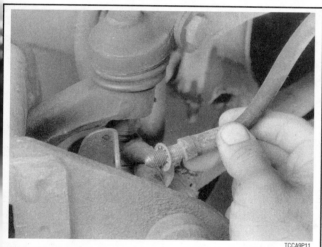

Fig. 18 Any gaskets/crush washers should be replaced with new ones during installation

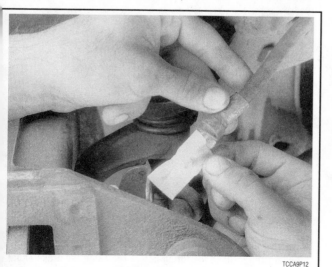

Fig. 19 Tape or plug the line to prevent contamination

4. Thoroughly clean the surrounding area at the joints to be disconnected.

5. Place a suitable catch pan under the joint to be disconnected.

6. Using two wrenches (one to hold the joint and one to turn the fitting), disconnect the hose or line to be replaced.

7. Disconnect the other end of the line or hose, moving the drain pan if necessary. Always use a back-up wrench to avoid damaging the fitting.

8. Disconnect any retaining clips or brackets holding the line and remove the line from the vehicle.

➡️If the brake system is to remain open for more time than it takes to swap lines, tape or plug each remaining clip and port to keep contaminants out and fluid in.

To install:

9. Install the new line or hose, starting with the end farthest from the master cylinder. Connect the other end, then confirm that both fittings are correctly threaded and turn smoothly using finger pressure. Make sure the new line will not rub against any other part. Brake lines must be at least 1/2 in. (13mm) from the steering column and other moving parts. Any protective shielding or insulators must be reinstalled in the original location.

✳️ WARNING

Make sure the hose is NOT kinked or touching any part of the frame or suspension after installation. These conditions may cause the hose to fail prematurely.

10. Using two wrenches as before, tighten each fitting.
11. Install any retaining clips or brackets on the lines.
12. If removed, install the wheel and tire assemblies, then carefully lower the vehicle to the ground.
13. Refill the brake master cylinder reservoir with clean, fresh brake fluid, meeting DOT 3 specifications. Properly bleed the brake system.
14. Connect the negative battery cable.

BRAKE LINE FLARING

▶ See Figures 20 and 21

Use only brake line tubing approved for automotive use; never use copper tubing. Whenever possible, try to work with brake lines that are already cut to the length needed. These lines are available at most auto parts stores and have machine made flares, the quality of which is hard to duplicate with most of the available inexpensive flaring kits.

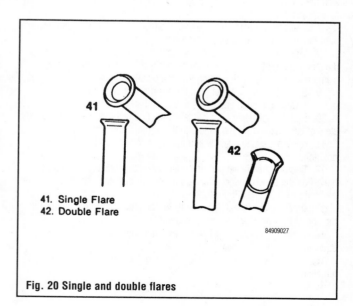

41. Single Flare
42. Double Flare

Fig. 20 Single and double flares

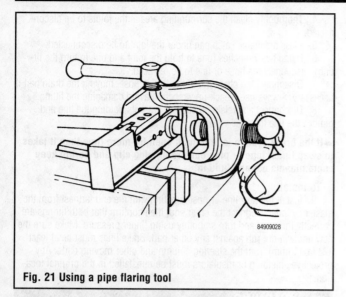

Fig. 21 Using a pipe flaring tool

When the brakes are applied, there is a great amount of pressure developed in the hydraulic system. An improperly formed flare can leak with resultant loss of stopping power. If you have never formed a double-flare, take time to familiarize yourself with the flaring kit; practice forming double-flares on scrap tubing until you are satisfied with the results.

The following procedure applies to the SA9193BR flaring kit, but should be similar to commercially available brake-line flaring kits. If these instructions differ in any way from those in your kit, follow the instructions in the kit.

1. Determine the length necessary for the replacement or repair and allow an additional 1/8 in. (3.2mm) for each flare. Select a piece of tubing, then cut the brake line to the necessary length using an appropriate saw. Do not use a tubing cutter.

2. Square the end of the tube with a file and chamfer the edges. Remove burrs from the inside and outside diameters of the cut line using a deburring tool.

3. Install the required fittings onto the line.

4. Install SA9193BR, or an equivalent flaring tool, into a vice and install the handle into the operating cam.

5. Loosen the die clamp screw and rotate the locking plate to expose the die carrier opening.

6. Select the required die set (4.75mm DIN) and install in the carrier with the full side of either half facing clamp screw and counter bore of both halves facing punch turret.

7. Insert the prepared line through the rear of the die and push forward until the line end is flush with the die face.

8. Make sure the rear of both halves of the die rest against the hexagon die stops, then rotate the locking plate to the fully closed position and clamp the die firmly by tightening the clamp screw.

9. Rotate the punch turret until the appropriate size (4.75mm DIN) points towards the open end of the line to be flared.

10. Pull the operating handle against the line resistance in order to create the flare, then return the handle to the original position.

11. release the clamp screw and rotate the locking plate to the open position.

12. Remove the die set and line, then separate by gently tapping both halves on the bench. Inspect the flare for proper size and shape. Dimension A should be 0.272–0.286 in. (6.92–7.28mm).

13. If necessary, repeat Steps 2–12 for the other end of the line or for the end of the line which is being repaired.

14. Bend the replacement line or section using SA91108NE, or an equivalent line bending tool.

15. If repairing the original line, join the old and new sections using a female union and tighten.

EXCEPT HYDRO-BOOST OR ABS

Manual Bleeding

◆ **See Figures 22 and 23**

The brake system must be bled when any brake line is disconnected or there is air in the system.

➡**Never bleed a wheel cylinder when a drum is removed.**

1. Clean the master cylinder of excess dirt and remove the cylinder cover and the diaphragm.

2. Fill the master cylinder to the proper level. Check the fluid level periodically during the bleeding process and replenish it as necessary. Do not allow the master cylinder to run dry, or you will have to start over.

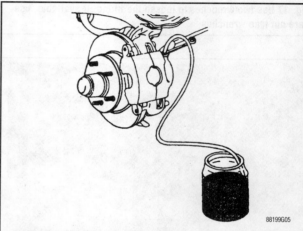

Fig. 22 Attach a length of vinyl hose to the bleeder screw of the brake to be bled. Insert the other end of the hose into a clear jar half full of clean brake fluid

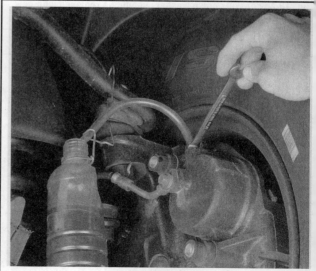

Have your assistant hold the brake pedal down, then open the bleeder fitting. Close the fitting before releasing the brake pedal

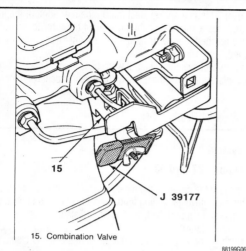

Fig. 23 Use a tool such as J 39177 to depress and hold the combination valve stem

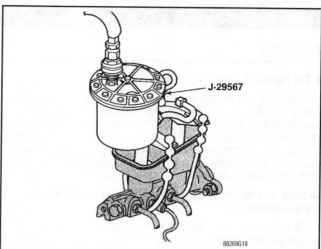

Fig. 24 The GM Pressure Bleeder adapter, J-29567 or equivalent, is needed when using this bleeding technique

3. Before opening any of the bleeder screws, you may want to give each one a shot of penetrating solvent. This reduces the possibility of breakage when they are unscrewed.

4. Attach a length of vinyl hose to the bleeder screw of the brake to be bled. Insert the other end of the hose into a clear jar half full of clean brake fluid, so that the end of the hose is beneath the level of fluid. The correct sequence for bleeding is to work from the brake farthest from the master cylinder to the one closest; right rear, left rear, right front, left front.

5. The combination valve must be held open during the bleeding process. A clip, tape, or other similar tool (or an assistant) can be used to hold in the metering pin.

6. Depress and release the brake pedal three or four times to exhaust any residual vacuum.

7. Have an assistant push down on the brake pedal and hold it down. Open the bleeder valve slightly. As the pedal reaches the end of its travel, close the bleeder screw and release the brake pedal. Repeat this process until no air bubbles are visible in the expelled fluid.

➡**Make sure your assistant presses the brake pedal to the floor slowly. Pressing too fast will cause air bubbles to form in the fluid.**

8. Repeat this procedure at each of the brakes. Remember to check the master cylinder level occasionally. Use only fresh fluid to refill the master cylinder, not the stuff bled from the system.

9. When the bleeding process is complete, refill the master cylinder, install its cover and diaphragm, and discard the fluid bled from the brake system.

Pressure Bleeding

▶ **See Figure 24**

➡**The following procedure requires the use of the GM Brake Bleeder Adapter tool No. J-29567 or equivalent, and the GM Combination Valve Depressor tool No. J-35856 or equivalent.**

1. Using the GM Brake Bleeder Adapter tool No. J-29567 or equivalent, fill the pressure tank to at least ⅓ full of brake fluid. Using compressed air, charge the pressure tank to 20–25 psi. (138–172 kPa), then install it onto the master cylinder.

2. Using the GM Combination Valve Depressor tool No. J-35856 or equivalent, install it onto the combination valve to hold the valve open during the bleeding operation.

3. Bleed each wheel cylinder or caliper in the following sequence: right rear, left rear, right front and left front.

4. Connect a hose from the bleeder tank to the adapter at the master cylinder, then open the tank valve.

5. Attach a clear vinyl hose to the brake bleeder screw, then immerse the opposite end into a container partially filled with clean brake fluid.

6. Open the bleeder screw ¾ turn and allow the fluid to flow until no air bubbles are seen in the fluid, then close the bleeder screw.

7. Repeat the bleeding process to each wheel.

8. Inspect the brake pedal for sponginess and if necessary, repeat the entire bleeding procedure.

9. Remove the depressor tool from the combination valve and the bleeder adapter from the master cylinder.

10. Refill the master cylinder to the proper level with brake fluid.

WITH ABS

Refer to the ABS system bleeding procedure outlined later in this section.

FRONT DISC BRAKES

On 1987–95 models, two different caliper designs are used. A Delco disc brake system is used on all models except G-30 and 3500 motor home chassis. The motor home chassis use the Bendix disc brake system. The difference will be noted in the following procedures.

On 1996–97 models three different Delco caliper designs are used. The 3400 series calipers with 75mm bore are used on models with 6100, 7100 and 7300 lb. Gross Vehicle Weight (GVW) ratings. The calipers with 80mm bore are used on models with 8600 and 9500 lb. GVW ratings, and the calipers with an 86mm bore are used on vehicles with dual rear wheels or with a 10,000 lb. and higher GVW.

✳✳ CAUTION

Brake pads may contain asbestos, which has been determined to be a cancer causing agent. Never clean the brake surfaces with compressed air! Avoid inhaling any dust from any brake surface! When cleaning brake surfaces, use a commercially available brake cleaning fluid.

Brake Pads

INSPECTION

♦ **See Figures 25 and 26**

Support the vans on jackstands and remove the wheels. Look in at the ends of the caliper to check the lining thickness of the outer pad. Look through the inspection hole in the top of the caliper to check the thickness of the inner pad. On 1987–95 models the minimum acceptable pad thickness is 1/32 in. (0.8mm) from the rivet heads on original equipment riveted linings and 1/2 in. (13mm) lining thickness on bonded linings. On 1996–97 models the minimum acceptable pad thickness is 0.030 in. (0.76mm).

➡**These manufacturer's specifications may not agree with your state inspection law.**

All original equipment pads are the riveted type; unless you want to remove the pads to measure the actual thickness from the rivet heads, you will have to make the limit for visual inspection 1/16 in. (1.6mm) or more. The same applies if you don't know what kind of lining you have. Original equipment pads and GM replacement pads have an integral

wear sensor. This is a spring steel tab on the rear edge of the inner pad which produces a squeal by rubbing against the rotor to warn that the pads have reached their wear limit. They do not squeal when the brakes are applied.

The squeal will eventually stop if worn pads aren't replaced. Should this happen, replace the pads immediately to prevent expensive rotor (disc) damage.

REMOVAL & INSTALLATION

Delco System

♦ **See Figures 27 thru 33**

1. Remove the cover on the master cylinder and siphon out 2/3 of the fluid. This step prevents spilling fluid when the piston is pushed back.
2. Raise and support the front end on jackstands.
3. Remove the wheels.
4. Push the brake piston back into its bore using a C-clamp to pull the caliper outward.
5. Remove the two bolts which hold the caliper and then lift the caliper off the disc.

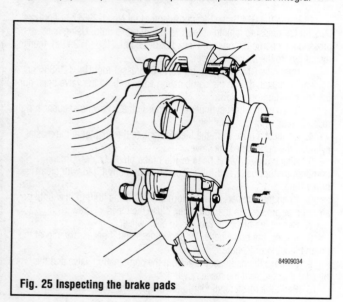

Fig. 25 Inspecting the brake pads

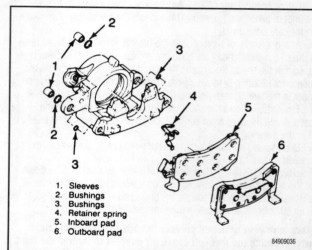

1. Sleeves
2. Bushings
3. Bushings
4. Retainer spring
5. Inboard pad
6. Outboard pad

Fig. 27 Delco brake pad and caliper assembly—1987–95 models

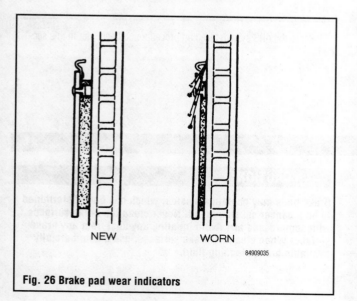

NEW   WORN

Fig. 26 Brake pad wear indicators

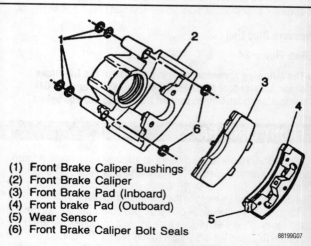

(1) Front Brake Caliper Bushings
(2) Front Brake Caliper
(3) Front Brake Pad (Inboard)
(4) Front brake Pad (Outboard)
(5) Wear Sensor
(6) Front Brake Caliper Bolt Seals

Fig. 28 Delco brake pad and caliper assembly—1996–97 models with a GVW rating of 6100 to 9500 lbs.

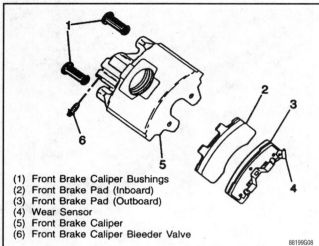

(1) Front Brake Caliper Bushings
(2) Front Brake Pad (Inboard)
(3) Front Brake Pad (Outboard)
(4) Wear Sensor
(5) Front Brake Caliper
(6) Front Brake Caliper Bleeder Valve

Fig. 29 Delco brake pad and caliper assembly—1996–97 models with a minimum GVW rating of 10,000 lbs.

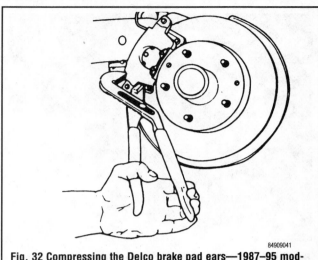

Fig. 32 Compressing the Delco brake pad ears—1987–95 models

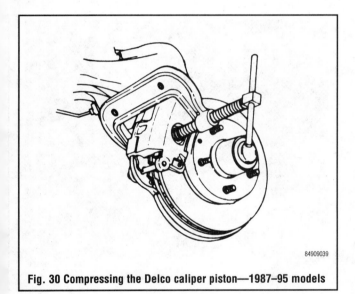

Fig. 30 Compressing the Delco caliper piston—1987–95 models

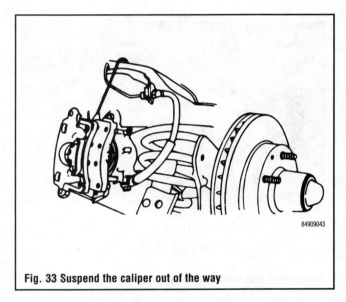

Fig. 33 Suspend the caliper out of the way

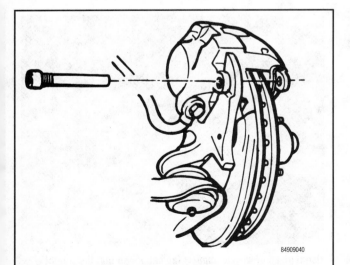

Fig. 31 Removing the Delco caliper bolts—1987–95 models

✳✳ WARNING

Do not let the caliper assembly hang by the brake hose.

6. Remove the inboard and outboard shoe. Use a small prybar to disengage the buttons on the outboard shoe from the holes in the caliper housing.

➡**If the pads are to be reinstalled, mark them inside and outside.**

7. Remove the pad support spring from the piston.
To install:
8. Position the support spring and the inner pad into the center cavity of the piston, snap the retaining spring into the piston. The outboard pad has ears which are bent over to keep the pad in position while the inboard pad has ears on the top end which fit over the caliper retaining bolts. A spring which is inside the brake piston hold the bottom edge of the inboard pad.

9. Push down on the inner pad until it lays flat against the caliper. It is important to push the piston all the way into the caliper if new linings are installed or the caliper will not fit over the rotor.

Remove the wheel to gain access to the caliper and pad assembly

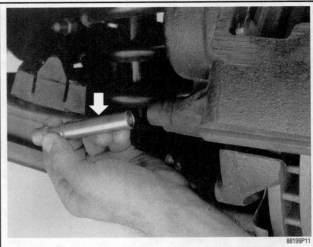

. . . then remove the mounting bolts and, if applicable, the sleeves

Typical front disc brake assembly

Grasp the caliper assembly and pull it off the rotor

Loosen the caliper mounting bolts . . .

Use a piece of wire to support the caliper so that the weight does not pull on the brake line

Remove the outboard brake pad . . .

88199P14

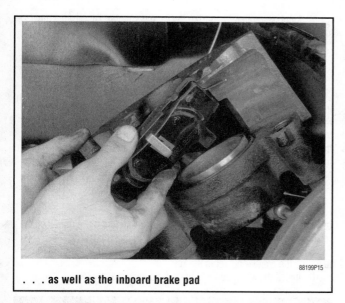

. . . as well as the inboard brake pad

88199P15

10. Position the outboard pad with the ears of the pad over the caliper ears and the tab at the bottom engaged in the caliper cutout.

11. With the two pads in position, place the caliper over the brake disc and align the holes in the caliper with those of the mounting bracket.

❋❋ WARNING

Make certain that the brake hose is not twisted or kinked.

12. Install the mounting bracket bolts through the sleeves in the inboard caliper ears and through the mounting bracket, making sure that the ends of the bolts pass under the retaining ears on the inboard pad.

➥**For best results, always use new bushings, bolt sleeves and bolt boot.**

13. Tighten the mounting bolts to 38 ft. lbs. (51 Nm). Pump the brake pedal to seat the pad against the rotor. Don't do this unless both calipers are in place. Use a pair of channel lock pliers to bend over the upper ears of the outer pad so it isn't loose.

➥**After tightening the mounting bolts, there must be clearance between the caliper and knuckle at both the upper and lower edge. The clearance must be 0.010–0.024 in. (0.26–0.60mm). If not, loosen the bolts and reposition the caliper.**

14. Install the wheel and lower the vans.

15. Add fluid to the master cylinder reservoirs so that they are ¼ in. (6mm) from the top.

16. Test the brake pedal by pumping it to obtain a hard pedal. Check the fluid level again and add fluid as necessary. Do not move the vehicle until a hard pedal is obtained.

Bendix System

◆ See Figures 34 thru 39

1. Remove approximately ⅓ of the brake fluid from the master cylinder. Discard the used brake fluid.

2. Jack up your vehicle and support it with jackstands.

3. Push the piston back into its bore. This can be done by suing a C-clamp.

4. Remove the bolt at the caliper support key. Use a brass drift pin to remove the key and spring.

5. Rotate the caliper up and forward from the bottom and lift it off the caliper support.

6. Tie the caliper out of the way with a piece of wire. Be careful not to damage the brake line.

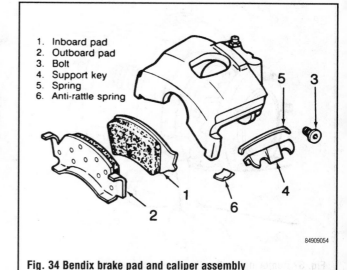

1. Inboard pad
2. Outboard pad
3. Bolt
4. Support key
5. Spring
6. Anti-rattle spring

84909054

Fig. 34 Bendix brake pad and caliper assembly

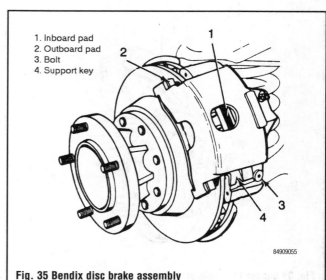

1. Inboard pad
2. Outboard pad
3. Bolt
4. Support key

84909055

Fig. 35 Bendix disc brake assembly

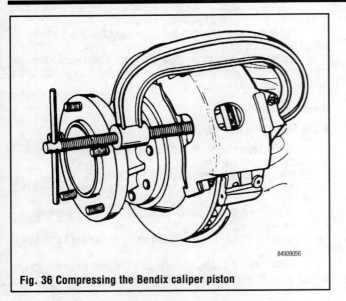
Fig. 36 Compressing the Bendix caliper piston

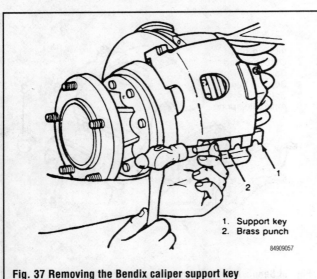

1. Support key
2. Brass punch

Fig. 37 Removing the Bendix caliper support key

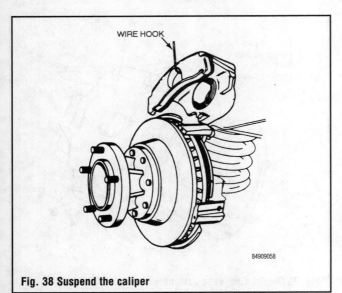

WIRE HOOK

Fig. 38 Suspend the caliper

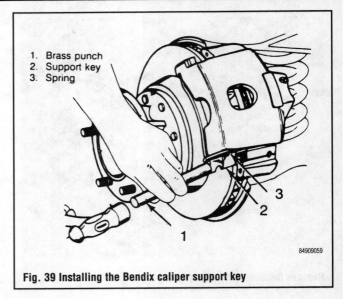

1. Brass punch
2. Support key
3. Spring

Fig. 39 Installing the Bendix caliper support key

7. Remove the inner pad from the caliper support. Discard the inner shoe clip.

8. Remove the outer pad from the caliper.

To install:

9. Lubricate the caliper support and support spring, with silicone.

10. Install a NEW inboard shoe clip on the shoe.

11. Install the lower end of the inboard shoe into the groove provided in the support. Slide the upper end of the shoe into position. Be sure the clip remains in position.

12. Position the outboard shoe in the caliper with the ears at the top of the shoe over the caliper ears and the tab at the bottom of the shoe engaged in the caliper cutout. If assembly is difficult, a C-clamp may be used. Be careful not to mar the lining.

13. Position the caliper over the brake disc, top edge first. Rotate the caliper downward onto the support.

14. Place the spring over the caliper support key, install the assembly between the support and lower caliper groove. Tap into place until the key retaining screw can be installed.

15. Install the screw and tighten to 15 ft. lbs. (20 Nm). The boss must fit fully into the circular cutout in the key.

16. Install the wheel and add brake fluid as necessary.

Brake Caliper

REMOVAL & INSTALLATION

Delco System

1. Remove the cover on the master cylinder and siphon enough fluid out of the reservoirs to bring the level to ⅓ full. This step prevents spilling fluid when the piston is pushed back.

2. Raise and support the vehicle. Remove the front wheels and tires.

3. Push the brake piston back into its bore using a C-clamp to pull the caliper outward.

4. Remove the two bolts which hold the caliper and then lift the caliper off the disc.

✳✳ WARNING

Do not let the caliper assembly hang by the brake hose.

5. Remove the inboard and outboard shoe.

➡If the pads are to be reinstalled, mark them inside and outside.

6. Remove the pad support spring from the piston.

7. Remove the two sleeves from the inside ears of the caliper and the 4 rubber bushings from the grooves in the caliper ears.

8. Remove the hose from the steel brake line and tape the fittings to prevent foreign material from entering the line or the hoses.

9. Remove the retainer from the hose fitting.

10. Remove the hose from the frame bracket and pull off the caliper with the hose attached.

11. Check the inside of the caliper for fluid leakage; if so, the caliper should be overhauled.

✳ WARNING

Do not use compressed air to clean the inside of the caliper, as this may unseat the dust boot.

To install:

12. Connect the brake line to begin installation. Lubricate the sleeves, rubber bushings, bushing grooves, and the end of the mounting bolts using silicone lubricant.

13. Install new bushing in the caliper ears along with new sleeves. The sleeve should be replaced so that the end toward the shoe is flush with the machined surface of the ear.

14. Position the support spring and the inner pad into the center cavity of the piston, snap the retaining spring into the piston. The outboard pad has ears which are bent over to keep the pad in position while the inboard pad has ears on the top end which fit over the caliper retaining bolts. A spring which is inside the brake piston hold the bottom edge of the inboard pad.

15. Push down on the inner pad until it lays flat against the caliper. It is important to push the piston all the way into the caliper if new linings are installed or the caliper will not fit over the rotor.

16. Position the outboard pad with the ears of the pad over the caliper ears and the tab at the bottom engaged in the caliper cutout.

17. With the two pads in position, place the caliper over the brake disc and align the holes in the caliper with those of the mounting bracket.

✳ WARNING

Make certain that the brake hose is not twisted or kinked.

18. Fill the cavity between the bolt bushings with silicone grease. Install the mounting bracket bolts through the sleeves in the inboard caliper ears and through the mounting bracket, making sure that the ends of the bolts pass under the retaining ears on the inboard pad.

➡ **For best results, always use new bushings, sleeves and bolt boots.**

19. Tighten the mounting bolts to 38 ft. lbs. (51 Nm). Pump the brake pedal to seat the pad against the rotor. Don't do this unless both calipers are in place. Use a pair of channel lock pliers to bend over the upper ears of the outer pad so it isn't loose.

➡ **After tightening the mounting bolts, there must be clearance between the caliper and knuckle at both the upper and lower edge. The clearance must be 0.010–0.024 in. (0.26–0.60mm). If not, loosen the bolts and reposition the caliper.**

20. Install the front wheel and lower the van.

21. Add fluid to the master cylinder reservoirs so that they are ¼ in. (6mm) from the top.

22. Test the brake pedal by pumping it to obtain a hard pedal. Check the fluid level again and add fluid as necessary. Do not move the vehicle until a hard pedal is obtained.

Bendix System

1. Remove approximately ⅓ of the brake fluid from the master cylinder. Discard the used brake fluid.

2. Raise and support the front end on jackstands.

3. Push the piston back into its bore. This can be done by suing a C-clamp.

4. Remove the bolt at the caliper support key. Use a brass drift pin to remove the key and spring.

5. Rotate the caliper up and forward from the bottom and lift it off the caliper support.

6. Unscrew the brake line at the caliper. Plug the opening. Discard the copper washer. Be careful not to damage the brake line.

7. Remove the outer shoe from the caliper.

To install:

8. Using a new copper washer, connect the brake line at the caliper. Tighten the connector to 32 ft. lbs. (43 Nm)

9. Lubricate the caliper support and support spring with silicone.

10. Position the outboard shoe in the caliper with the ears at the top of the shoe over the caliper ears and the tab at the bottom of the shoe engaged in the caliper cutout. If assembly is difficult, a C-clamp may be used. Be careful not to mar the lining.

11. Position the caliper over the brake disc, top edge first. Rotate the caliper downward onto the support.

12. Place the spring over the caliper support key, install the assembly between the support and lower caliper groove. Tap into place until the key retaining screw can be installed.

13. Install the screw and tighten to 15 ft. lbs. (20 Nm). The boss must fit fully into the circular cutout in the key.

14. Install the wheel and add brake fluid as necessary.

OVERHAUL

◆ **See Figures 40 thru 52 (p. 17–20)**

The following procedure applies to both the Delco and Bendix types of calipers.

✳ WARNING

Use only denatured alcohol to clean metal parts and brake fluid to clean rubber parts. Never use any mineral based cleaning solvents such as gasoline or kerosene, as these solvents will deteriorate rubber parts.

1. Remove the caliper, clean it and place it on a clean and level work surface.

2. Remove the brake hose from the caliper and discard the copper gasket. Check the brake hose for cracks or deterioration. Replace the hose as necessary.

3. Drain the brake fluid from the caliper.

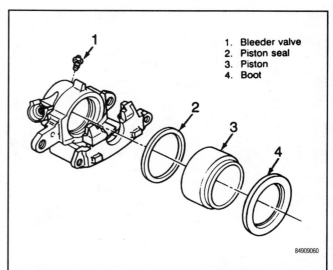

1. Bleeder valve
2. Piston seal
3. Piston
4. Boot

84909060

Fig. 40 Exploded view of the Delco caliper—1987–95 models

Fig. 41 Force the piston out with compressed air—Delco

Fig. 43 Prying out the piston boot—Delco

Fig. 42 Remove the piston from the caliper

Fig. 44 Remove the piston seal from the caliper

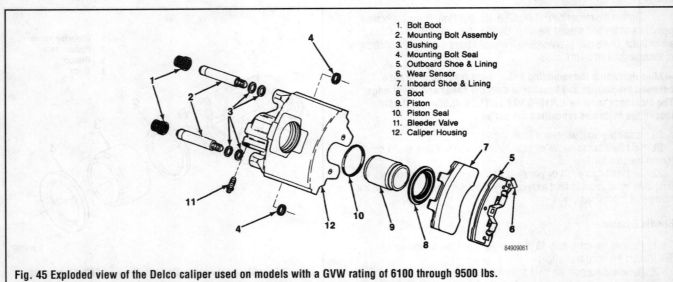

1. Bolt Boot
2. Mounting Bolt Assembly
3. Bushing
4. Mounting Bolt Seal
5. Outboard Shoe & Lining
6. Wear Sensor
7. Inboard Shoe & Lining
8. Boot
9. Piston
10. Piston Seal
11. Bleeder Valve
12. Caliper Housing

Fig. 45 Exploded view of the Delco caliper used on models with a GVW rating of 6100 through 9500 lbs.

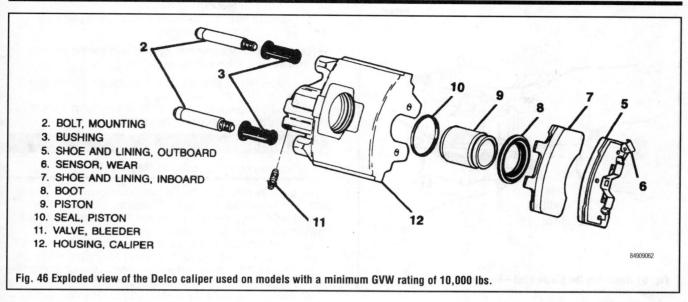

2. BOLT, MOUNTING
3. BUSHING
5. SHOE AND LINING, OUTBOARD
6. SENSOR, WEAR
7. SHOE AND LINING, INBOARD
8. BOOT
9. PISTON
10. SEAL, PISTON
11. VALVE, BLEEDER
12. HOUSING, CALIPER

Fig. 46 Exploded view of the Delco caliper used on models with a minimum GVW rating of 10,000 lbs.

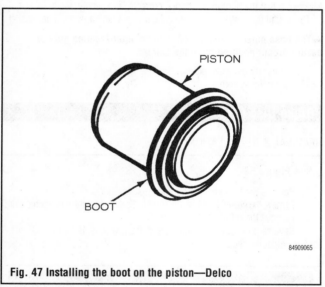

Fig. 47 Installing the boot on the piston—Delco

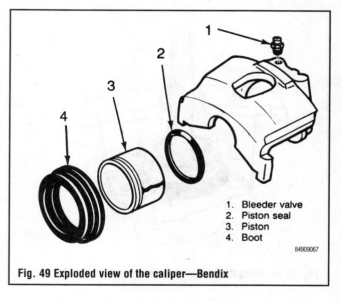

1. Bleeder valve
2. Piston seal
3. Piston
4. Boot

Fig. 49 Exploded view of the caliper—Bendix

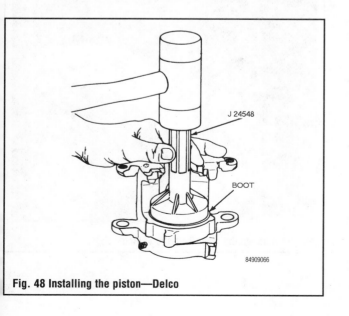

Fig. 48 Installing the piston—Delco

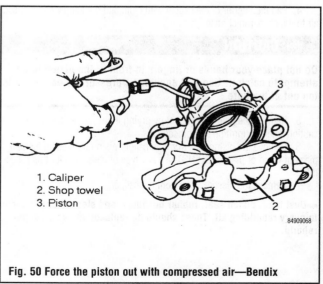

1. Caliper
2. Shop towel
3. Piston

Fig. 50 Force the piston out with compressed air—Bendix

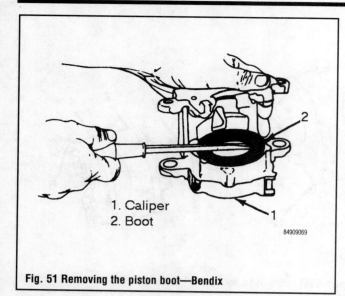

1. Caliper
2. Boot

84909069

Fig. 51 Removing the piston boot—Bendix

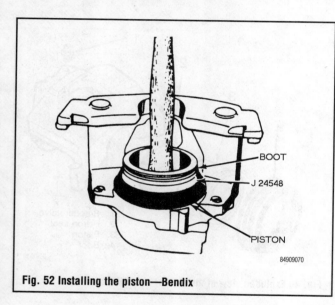

BOOT

J 24548

PISTON

84909070

Fig. 52 Installing the piston—Bendix

4. Pad the interior of the caliper with cloth and then apply compressed air to the caliper inlet hose.

✳✳ CAUTION

Do not place your hands or fingers in front of the piston in an attempt to catch it! Use just enough air pressure to ease the piston out of the bore.

5. Remove the piston dust boot by prying it out with a screwdriver. Use caution when performing this procedure.
6. Remove the piston seal from the caliper piston bore using a small piece of wood or plastic. DO NOT use any type of metal tool for this procedure.
7. Remove the bleeder valve from the caliper.

➡**Dust boot, piston seal, rubber bushings, and sleeves are included in every rebuilding kit. These should be replaced at every caliper rebuild.**

8. Clean all parts in the recommended solvent and dry them completely using compressed air if possible.

➡**The use of shop air hoses may inject oil film into the assembly; use caution when using such hoses.**

9. Examine the mounting bolts for rust or corrosion. Replace them as necessary.
10. Examine the piston for scoring, nicks, or worn plating. If any of these conditions are present, replace them as necessary.

✳✳ WARNING

Do not use any type of abrasive on the piston!

11. Check the piston bore. Small defects can be removed with crocus cloth. If the bore cannot be cleaned in this manner, replace the caliper.
12. Lubricate the piston bore and the new piston seal with brake fluid. Place the seal in the caliper bore groove.
13. Lubricate the piston in the same manner and position the new boot into the groove in the piston so that the fold faces the open end of the piston.
14. Place the piston into the caliper bore using caution not to unseat the seal. Force the piston to the bottom of the bore.
15. Place the dust boot in the caliper counterbore and seat the boot. Make sure that the boot in positioned correctly and evenly.
16. Install the brake hose in the caliper inlet using a new copper gasket.

➡**The hose must be positioned in the caliper locating gate to assure proper positioning of the caliper.**

17. Replace the bleeder screw.
18. Bleed the system.

Brake Disc (Rotor)

REMOVAL & INSTALLATION

▶ **See Figure 53**

1. Remove the brake caliper as previously outlined.
2. Remove the outer wheel bearing. Refer to Section 1 for the proper procedure.
3. Remove the rotor from the spindle.
4. Reverse procedure to install. Adjust the bearings. Refer to Section 1 for the proper procedure.

87989P15

Fig. 53 Remove the rotor from the vehicle

SPECTION

1. Raise and support the front of the van with jackstands, then remove wheel assemblies.
2. To check the disc run-out, perform the following procedures:
    a. Using a dial indicator, secure and position it so that the button contacts the disc about 1 in. (25 mm) from the outer edge.
    b. Rotate the disc. The lateral run-out should not exceed 0.004 in. (0.10mm) on 1987–95 models. On 1996–97 models the run-out should not exceed 0.003 in. (0.08mm) or 0.010 in. (0.25mm) on 3500 models.

If the reading is excessive, recondition or replace the rotor.
3. To check the thickness variation, perform the following procedures:
    a. Using a micrometer, check the thickness at four (4) locations around the disc, at the same distance from the edge.
    b. The thickness should not vary by more than 0.0005 in. (0.013mm). If the reading is excessive, recondition or replace the rotor.
4. The surface finish must be relatively smooth to avoid pulling and erratic performance, also, to extend the lining life. Light rotor scoring of up to 0.06 in. (1.5mm) in depth, can be tolerated. if the scoring depths are excessive, recondition or replace the rotor.

REAR DRUM BRAKES

Brake Drums

REMOVAL & INSTALLATION

With Semi-Floating Axle

1. Raise and support the rear end on jackstands.
2. Remove the wheel.

3. On some models it may be necessary to bend back the locking tangs with pliers.
4. Pulling the drum from the brake assembly. If the brake drums have been scored from worn linings, the brake adjuster must be backed off so that the brake shoes will retract from the drum. The adjuster can be backed off by inserting a brake adjusting tool through the access hole provided. In some cases the access hole is provided in the brake drum. A metal cover plate is over the hole. This may be removed by using a hammer and chisel.
5. To install, reverse the removal procedure.

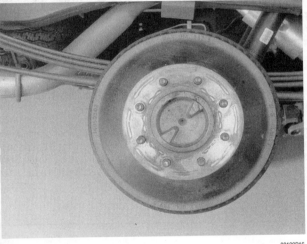

Typical rear brake drum

88199P16

A penetrating lubricant may also be required to make drum removal easier

88199P18

In some cases, it may be necessary to bend back the locking tabs with pliers

88199P17

Remove the brake drum from the axle

88199P19

With Full Floating Axle

To remove the drums from full floating rear axles, use the Axle Shaft removal and installation procedure in Section 7. Full floating rear axles can readily be identified by the bearing housing protruding through the center of the wheel.

➡**Make sure all metal particles are removed from the brake drum before reassembly.**

INSPECTION

When the drum is removed, it should be inspected for cracks, scores, or other imperfections. These must be corrected before the drum is replaced.

❊❊ WARNING

If the drum is found to be cracked, replace it. Do not attempt to service a cracked drum.

Minor drum score marks can be removed with fine emery cloth. Heavy score marks must be removed by turning the drum. This is removing metal from the entire inner surface of the drum on a lathe in order to level the surface. Automotive machine shops and some large parts stores are equipped to perform this operation.

If the drum is not scored, it should be polished with fine emery cloth before replacement. If the drum is resurfaced, it should not be enlarged more than 0.060 in. (1.524mm).

➡ **Your state inspection law may disagree with this specification.**

It is advisable, while the drums are off, to check them for out-of-round. An inside micrometer is necessary for an exact measurement, therefore unless this tool is available, the drums should be taken to a machine shop to be checked. Any drum which is more than 0.006 in. (0.1524mm) out-of-round will result in an inaccurate brake adjustment and other problems, and should be refinished or replaced.

➡**Make all measurements at right angles to each other and at the open and closed edges of the drum machined surface.**

Brake Shoes

INSPECTION

Remove the drum and inspect the lining thickness on both brake shoe A front brake lining should be replaced if it is less than ⅛ in. (3mm) thic at the lowest point on the brake shoe. The wear limit for rear brake lining is 0.030 in. (0.76mm).

➡**Brake shoes should always be replaced in axle sets. The wear specifications given may disagree with your state inspection rules**

REMOVAL & INSTALLATION

With Full Floating Axle

♦ **See Figures 54 and 55 (p. 22–24)**

1. Raise and securely support the vehicle using jackstands.
2. Loosen the parking brake equalizer enough to remove all tension c the brake cable.
3. Remove the brake drums.

❊❊ WARNING

The brake pedal must not be depressed while the drums are removed!

4. Using a brake tool, remove the shoe return springs. You can do th with ordinary tools, but it isn't easy.
5. Remove the self-adjuster actuator spring.
6. Remove the link from the secondary shoe by pulling it from the anchor pin.
7. Remove the hold-down pins. These are the brackets which run though the backing plate. They can be removed with a pair of pliers. Reach around the rear of the backing plate and hold the back of the pin. Turn the top of the pin retainer 45° with the pliers. This will align the elongated tan with the slot in the retainer. Be careful, as the pin is spring loaded and ma fly off when released. Use the same procedure for the other pin assembly.
8. Remove the adjuster actuator assembly.

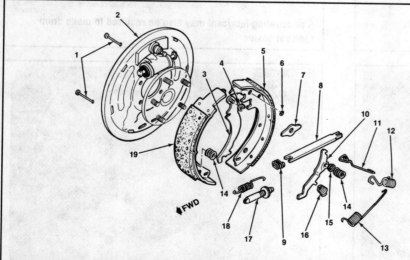

1. Hold-down pins
2. Backing plate
3. Parking brake lever
4. Washer
5. Secondary shoe
6. Retaining ring
7. Shoe guide
8. Parking brake strut
9. Strut spring
10. Actuator lever
11. Actuator link
12. Return spring
13. Return spring
14. Hold-down spring
15. Lever pivot
16. Lever return spring
17. Adjusting screw
18. Adjusting screw spring
19. Primary show

Fig. 54 Exploded view of the duo-servo drum brake—1987–92 models

84909087

DRUM BRAKE COMPONENTS

1. Return springs
2. Shoe guide
3. Brake shoes
4. Hold-down assembly pin
5. Hold-down spring
6. Hold-down assembly plate
7. Actuator link
8. Parking brake strut
9. Parking brake actuator lever
10. Adjusting screw spring
11. Adjusting screw

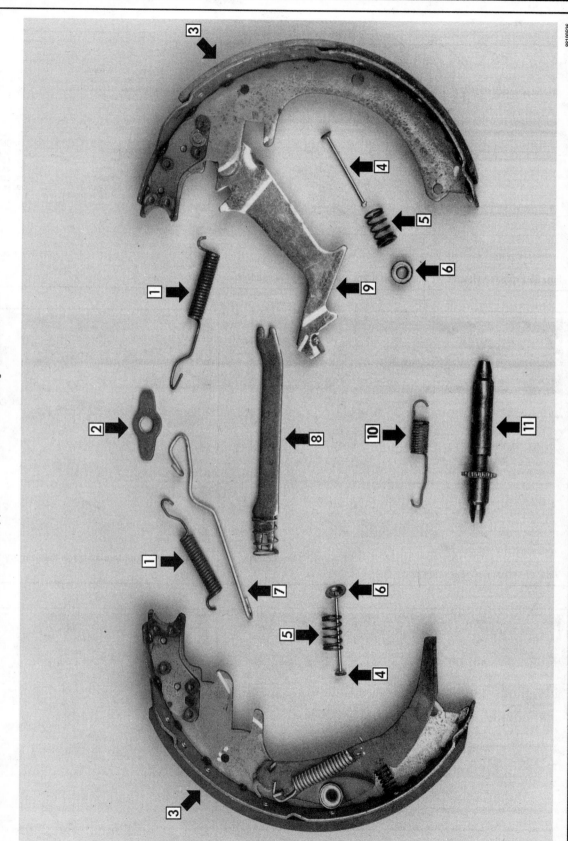

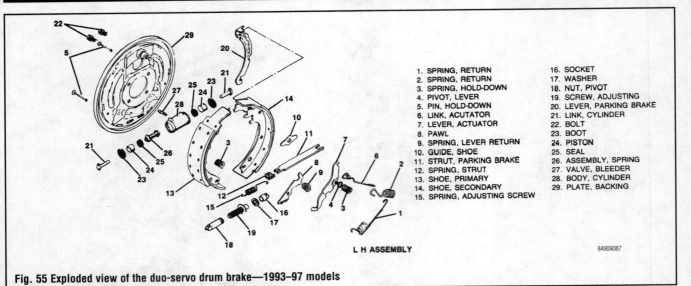

1. SPRING, RETURN
2. SPRING, RETURN
3. SPRING, HOLD-DOWN
4. PIVOT, LEVER
5. PIN, HOLD-DOWN
6. LINK, ACUTATOR
7. LEVER, ACTUATOR
8. PAWL
9. SPRING, LEVER RETURN
10. GUIDE, SHOE
11. STRUT, PARKING BRAKE
12. SPRING, STRUT
13. SHOE, PRIMARY
14. SHOE, SECONDARY
15. SPRING, ADJUSTING SCREW
16. SOCKET
17. WASHER
18. NUT, PIVOT
19. SCREW, ADJUSTING
20. LEVER, PARKING BRAKE
21. LINK, CYLINDER
22. BOLT
23. BOOT
24. PISTON
25. SEAL
26. ASSEMBLY, SPRING
27. VALVE, BLEEDER
28. BODY, CYLINDER
29. PLATE, BACKING

L H ASSEMBLY

84909087

Fig. 55 Exploded view of the duo-servo drum brake—1993–97 models

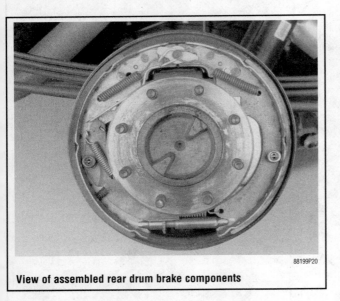

88199P20

View of assembled rear drum brake components

88199P22

Use the brake tool to disengage the primary shoe return spring . . .

88199P21

Use an evaporative spray brake cleaner to remove brake dust from the components

88199P23

. . . then unhook and remove the spring from the shoe

A pair of brake pliers is helpful when separating the secondary return spring from the actuator link

Remove the actuator link

Unhook and remove the spring from the secondary shoe

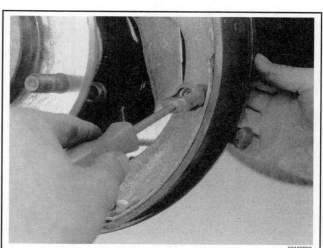

Use the brake tool to compress the hold-down spring and twist the plate to free the pin

Remove the shoe guide from the stud at the top of the backing plate

Once the pin and the slot on top of the plate are aligned, separate the hold-down spring and pin

Remove the parking brake strut and spring

Remove the parking brake lever from the secondary shoe using a pair of pliers

Remove the starwheel adjuster screw assembly . . .

Remove the secondary shoe from the backing plate

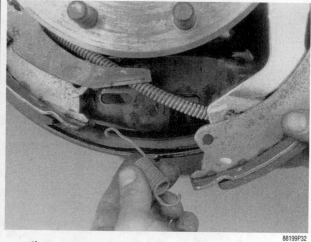

. . . then remove the starwheel adjuster screw spring and primary brake shoe

➡Since the actuator, pivot, and override spring are considered an assembly it is not recommended that they be disassembled.

9. Remove the shoes from the backing plate. Make sure that you have a secure grip on the assembly as the bottom spring will still exert pressure on the shoes. Slowly let the tops of the shoes come together and the tension will decrease and the adjuster and spring may be removed.

➡If the linings are to be reused, mark them for identification.

10. Remove the parking brake lever from the secondary shoe. Using a pair of pliers, pull back on the spring which surrounds the cable. At the same time, remove the cable from the notch in the shoe bracket. Make sure that the spring does not snap back or injury may result.

To install:

11. Use a brake cleaning fluid to remove dirt from the brake drum. Check the drums for scoring and cracks. Have the drums checked for out-of-round and service the drums as necessary.

12. Check the wheel cylinders by carefully pulling the lower edges of the wheel cylinder boots away from the cylinders. If there is excessive leakage, the inside of the cylinder will be moist with fluid. If there is any leakage at all, a cylinder overhaul is in order. DO NOT delay, as a brake failure could result.

→**A small amount of fluid will be present to act as a lubricant for the wheel cylinder pistons.**

13. Check the flange plate, which is located around the axle, for leakage of differential lubricant. This condition cannot be overlooked as the lubricant will be absorbed into the brake linings and brake failure will result. Replace the seals as necessary.

→**If new linings are being installed, check them against the old units for length and type.**

14. Check the new linings for imperfections.

⁜ WARNING

It is important to keep your hands free of dirt and grease when handling the brake shoes. Foreign matter will be absorbed into the linings and result in unpredictable braking.

15. Lightly lubricate the parking brake and cable and the end of the parking brake lever where it enters the shoe. Use high temperature, waterproof, grease or special brake lube.

16. Install the parking brake lever into the secondary shoe with the attaching bolt, spring washer, lockwasher, and nut. It is important that the lever move freely before the shoe is attached. Move the assembly and check for proper action.

17. Lubricate the adjusting screw and make sure that it works freely. Sometimes the adjusting screw will not move due to lack of lubricant or dirt contamination and the brakes will not adjust. In this case, the adjuster should be disassembled, thoroughly cleaned, and lubricated before installation.

18. Connect the brake shoe spring to the bottom portion of both shoes. Make certain that the brake linings are installed in the correct manner, the primary and secondary shoe in the correct position. If you are not sure remove the other brake drum and check it.

19. Install the adjusting mechanism below the spring and separate the top of the shoes.

20. Make the following checks before installation:
   a. Be certain that the right hand thread adjusting screw is on the left hand side of the vehicle and the left hand screw is on the right hand side of the vehicle.
   b. Make sure that the star adjuster is aligned with the adjusting hole.
   c. The adjuster should be installed with the starwheel nearest the secondary shoe and the tension spring away from the adjusting mechanism;
   d. If the original linings are being reused, put them back in their original locations.

21. Install the parking brake cable.

22. Position the primary shoe (the shoe with the short lining) first. Secure it with the hold-down pin and with its spring by pushing the pin through the back of the backing plate and, while holding it with one hand, install the spring and the retainer using a pair of needlenose pliers. Install the adjuster actuator assembly.

23. Install the parking brake strut and the strut spring by pulling back the spring with pliers and engaging the end of the cable onto the brake strut and then releasing the spring.

24. Place the small metal guide plate over the anchor pin and position the self-adjuster wire cable eye.

⁜ WARNING

The wire should not be positioned with the conventional brake installation tool or damage will result. It should be positioned on the actuator assembly first and then placed over the anchor pin stud by hand with the adjuster assembly in full downward position.

25. Install the actuator return spring. DO NOT pry the actuator lever to install the return spring. Position it using the end of a screwdriver or another suitable tool.

Using the proper tool, install the brake shoe return springs

→**If the return springs are bent or in any way distorted, they should be replaced.**

26. Using the brake installation tool, place the brake return springs in position. Install the primary spring first over the anchor pin and then place the spring from the secondary show over the wire link end.

27. Pull the brake shoes away from the backing plate and apply a thin coat of high temperature, waterproof, grease or special brake lube in the brake shoe contact points.

⁜ WARNING

Only a small amount of lubricant is necessary. Be sure to keep it away from the brake linings.

28. Once the complete assembly has been installed, check the operation of the self-adjusting mechanism by moving the actuating lever by hand.

29. Adjust the brakes.
   a. Turn the star adjuster until the drum slides over the brakes shoes with only a slight drag. Remove the drum:
   b. Turn the adjuster back 1¼ turns.
   c. Install the drum and wheel and lower the vehicle.

⁜ WARNING

Avoid overtightening the lug nuts to prevent damage to the brake drum. Alloy wheels can also be cracked by overtightening. Use of a torque wrench is highly recommended.

   d. If the adjusting hole in the drum has been punched out, make certain that the insert has been removed from the inside of the drum. Install a rubber hole cover to keep dirt out of the brake assembly. Also, be sure that the drums are installed in the same position as they were when removed, with the locating tang in line with the locating hole in the axle shaft flange.
   e. Make the final adjustment by backing the vehicle and pumping the brakes until the self-adjusting mechanisms adjust to the proper level and the brake pedal reaches satisfactory height.

30. Adjust the parking brake. Refer to the procedure in this section.

With Semi-Floating Axle

◗ See Figures 56, 57 and 58 (p. 28–29)

1. Jack up and securely support the vehicle using jackstands.
2. Loosen the parking brake equalizer enough to remove all tension on the brake cable.

3. Remove the brake drums. If difficulty is till encountered, remove the access hole plug in the backing plate and insert a metal rod to push the parking brake lever off its stop.

➡ **The brake pedal must not be depressed while the drums are removed!**

4. Raise the lever arm of the actuator until the upper end is clear of the slot in the adjuster screw. Slide the actuator off the adjuster pin.

5. Disconnect the actuator from the brake shoe.

6. Remove the hold-down pins. These are the brackets which run though the backing plate. They can be removed with a pair of pliers. Reach around the rear of the backing plate and hold the back of the pin. Turn the top of the pin retainer 45° with the pliers. This will align the elongated tang with the slot in the retainer. Be careful, as the pin is spring loaded and may fly off when released. Use the same procedure for the other pin assembly.

7. Pull the lower ends of the shoes apart and lift the lower return spring over the anchor plate. Remove the spring from the shoes.

8. Lift the shoes and upper return spring along with the adjusting screw, from the backing plate. Some spreading of the shoes is necessary to clear the wheel cylinder and axle flange. Remove the upper spring.

9. Remove the retaining ring, pin, spring washer and parking brake lever.

➡ **If the linings are to be reused, mark them for identification.**

To install:

10. Use a brake cleaning fluid to remove dirt from the brake drum. Check the drums for scoring and cracks. Have the drums checked for out-of-round and service the drums as necessary.

11. Check the wheel cylinders by carefully pulling the lower edges of the wheel cylinder boots away from the cylinders. If there is excessive leakage, the inside of the cylinder will be moist with fluid. If there is any leakage at all, a cylinder overhaul is in order. DO NOT delay, as a brake failure could result.

➡ **A small amount of fluid will be present to act as a lubricant for the wheel cylinder pistons.**

12. Check the flange plate, which is located around the axle, for leakage of differential lubricant. This condition cannot be overlooked as the lubricant will be absorbed into the brake linings and brake failure will result. Replace the seals as necessary.

➡ **If new linings are being installed, check them against the old units for length and type.**

13. Check the new linings for imperfections.

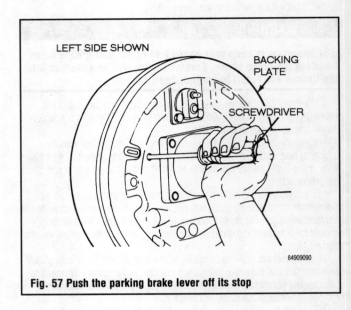

Fig. 57 Push the parking brake lever off its stop

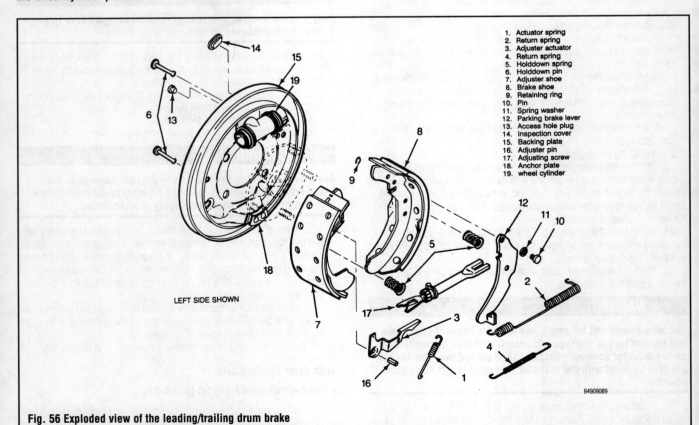

1. Actuator spring
2. Return spring
3. Adjuster actuator
4. Return spring
5. Holddown spring
6. Holddown pin
7. Adjuster shoe
8. Brake shoe
9. Retaining ring
10. Pin
11. Spring washer
12. Parking brake lever
13. Access hole plug
14. Inspection cover
15. Backing plate
16. Adjuster pin
17. Adjusting screw
18. Anchor plate
19. wheel cylinder

Fig. 56 Exploded view of the leading/trailing drum brake

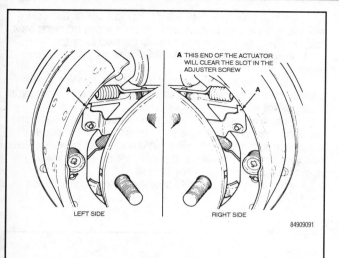

Fig. 58 Removing the adjuster actuator

✷✷ **WARNING**

It is important to keep your hands free of dirt and grease when handling the brake shoes. Foreign matter will be absorbed into the linings and result in unpredictable braking.

14. Install the parking brake lever assembly The concave side of the washer should be against the shoe.

15. Install the adjuster pin in the shoe so that the pin projects 0.268–0.276 in. (6.8–7.0mm) from the side of the shoe where the actuator is installed.

16. Apply an approved brake lubricant grease to the threads of the adjuster screw, socket and socket face.

17. Make certain that the brake linings are positioned correctly and connect the upper spring. If you are not sure of which shoe goes where, remove the other brake drum and check it. Don't over-stretch the spring; you'll ruin it. The spring can't be stretched, safely, more than 8.04 in. (204mm).

18. Install the adjusting mechanism between the shoes. Make the following checks before installation:

   a. Be certain that the adjusting screw assembly engages the adjuster shoe and parking brake lever.

   b. Make sure that the spring clip is positioned towards the backing plate.

   c. The linings are in the correct positions. The shoe with the parking brake lever is the rear shoe.

19. Coat the shoe mounting pads on the backing plate with a thin coat of lithium grease.

20. Position the assembly on the backing plate, engaging the upper shoe ends with the wheel cylinder pushrods.

21. Hook the lower return spring into the shoe ends and spread the shoes, guiding the lower spring over the anchor plate. Don't over-stretch the spring; you'll ruin it. The spring can't be stretched, safely, more than 4¼ in. (108mm).

22. Install the hold-down spring assemblies.

23. Place the adjuster actuator over the end of the adjusting pin so its top leg engages the notch in the adjuster screw.

24. Install the actuator spring. Make sure that the free end of the actuator engage the notch of the adjuster nut. Don't over-stretch the spring. Its maximum stretch is 3¼ in. (83mm).

25. Connect the parking brake cable to the lever. Adjust the parking brake:

   a. Measure the brake drum inside diameter.

   b. Turn the adjuster nut until the brake shoe maximum diameter is 0.01–0.02 in. (0.25–50mm) less than the brake drum diameter.

   c. Make sure that the stops on the parking brake levers are against the edge of the brake shoe web. If the cable is holding the stops off the edge, loosen the adjustment.

   d. Tighten the cable at the adjuster nut until the lever stops begin to

move off the shoe webs.

   e. Loosen the adjustment nut until the lever stops are **just** touching the shoe webs. There should be no more than 0.5mm clearance between the stops and the webs.

26. Install the drums and wheels.

27. Pump the brake pedal 30–35 times with normal force. Pause about 1 second between each stroke.

28. Depress the parking brake pedal 6 clicks. The wheels should be locked.

29. Release the parking brake. The wheels should rotate freely.

Wheel Cylinders

REMOVAL & INSTALLATION

▶ **See Figure 59**

1. Raise and support the vehicle using jackstands.
2. Remove the wheel and tire.
3. Back off the brake adjustment if necessary and remove the drum.
4. Disconnect and plug the brake line.
5. Remove the brake shoes as described above.

Typical wheel cylinder assembly

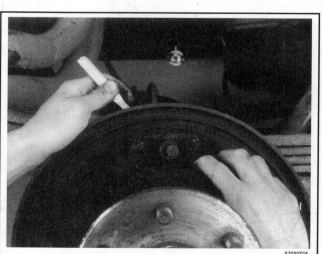

Remove the bolts securing the wheel cylinder to the backing plate

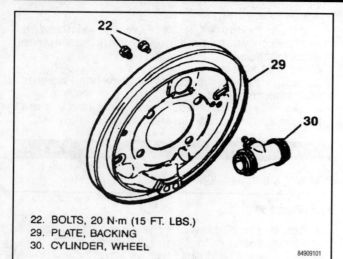

22. BOLTS, 20 N·m (15 FT. LBS.)
29. PLATE, BACKING
30. CYLINDER, WHEEL

84909101

Fig. 59 Wheel cylinder replacement

6. Remove the bolts securing the wheel cylinder to the backing plate.

7. Install the wheel cylinder. Tighten the mounting bolts to 15 ft. lbs. (20 Nm). Tighten the brake pipes to 13 ft. lbs. (17 Nm). Bleed the system.

OVERHAUL

◆ **See Figures 60 thru 69 (p. 30–32)**

Wheel cylinder overhaul kits may be available, but often at little or no savings over a reconditioned wheel cylinder. It often makes sense with these components to substitute a new or reconditioned part instead of attempting an overhaul.

If no replacement is available, or you would prefer to overhaul your wheel cylinders, the following procedure may be used. When rebuilding and installing wheel cylinders, avoid getting any contaminants into the system. Always use clean, new, high quality brake fluid. If dirty or improper fluid has been used, it will be necessary to drain the entire system, flush the system with proper brake fluid, replace all rubber components, then refill and bleed the system.

1. Remove the wheel cylinder from the vehicle and place on a clean workbench.

2. First remove and discard the old rubber boots, then withdraw the pistons. Piston cylinders are equipped with seals and a spring assembly, located behind the pistons in the cylinder bore.

3. Remove the remaining inner components, seals and spring assembly. Compressed air may be useful in removing these components. If no compressed air is available, be VERY careful not to score the wheel cylinder bore when removing parts from it. Discard all components for which replacements were supplied in the rebuild kit.

4. Wash the cylinder and metal parts in denatured alcohol or clean brake fluid.

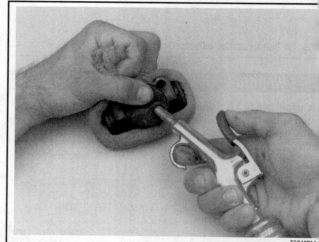

TCCA9P14

Fig. 61 Compressed air can be used to remove the pistons and seals

TCCA9P13

Fig. 60 Remove the outer boots from the wheel cylinder

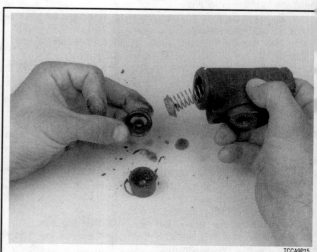

TCCA9P15

Fig. 62 Remove the pistons, cup seals and spring from the cylinder

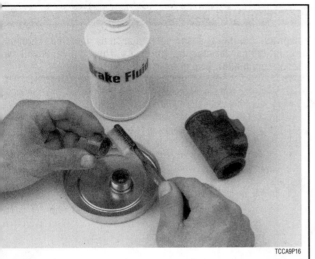

Fig. 63 Use brake fluid and a soft brush to clean the pistons . . .

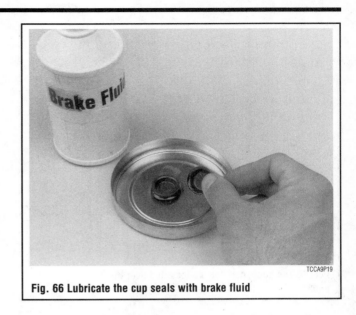

Fig. 66 Lubricate the cup seals with brake fluid

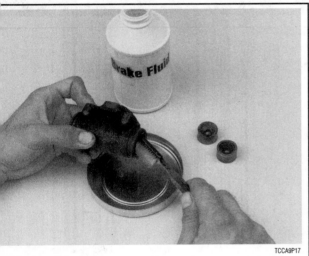

Fig. 64 . . . and the bore of the wheel cylinder

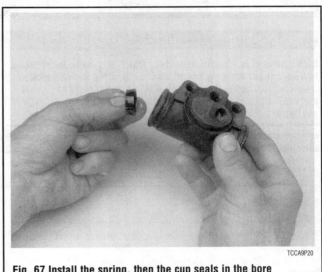

Fig. 67 Install the spring, then the cup seals in the bore

Fig. 65 Once cleaned and inspected, the wheel cylinder is ready for assembly

Fig. 68 Lightly lubricate the pistons, then install them

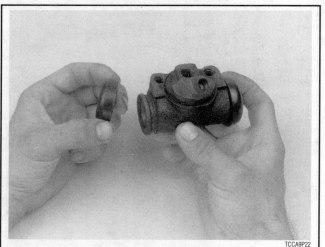

TCCA9P22

Fig. 69 The boots can now be installed over the wheel cylinder ends

⁂ WARNING

Never use a mineral-based solvent such as gasoline, kerosen or paint thinner for cleaning purposes. These solvents will sw rubber components and quickly deteriorate them.

5. Allow the parts to air dry or use compressed air. Do not use rags cleaning, since lint will remain in the cylinder bore.
6. Inspect the piston and replace it if it shows scratches.
7. Lubricate the cylinder bore and seals using clean brake fluid.
8. Position the spring assembly.
9. Install the inner seals, then the pistons.
10. Insert the new boots into the counterbores by hand. Do not lubric the boots.
11. Install the wheel cylinder.

REAR DISC BRAKES

⁂ CAUTION

Brake pads may contain asbestos, which has been determined to be a cancer causing agent. Never clean the brake surfaces with compressed air! Avoid inhaling any dust from any brake surface! When cleaning brake surfaces, use a commercially available brake cleaning fluid.

Brake Pads

INSPECTION

▶ **See Figures 70 and 71**

Support the vans on jackstands and remove the wheels. Look in at the ends of the caliper to check the lining thickness of the outer pad. Look through the inspection hole in the top of the caliper to check the thickness of the inner pad. Minimum acceptable pad thickness is 1/32 in. (0.8mm) from the rivet heads on original equipment riveted linings and 1/2 in. (13mm) lining thickness on bonded linings.

NEW   WORN
84909073

Fig. 71 Brake pad wear indicator

➡ **The manufacturer's specifications may not agree with your state inspection law.**

All original equipment pads are the riveted type; unless you want to remove the pads to measure the actual thickness from the rivet heads, you will have to make the limit for visual inspection 1/16 in. (1.6mm) or more. The same applies if you don't know what kind of lining you have Original equipment pads and GM replacement pads have an integral wear sensor. This is a spring steel tab on the rear edge of the inner pad which produces a squeal by rubbing against the rotor to warn that the pads have reached their wear limit. They do not squeal when the brake are applied.

The squeal will eventually stop if worn pads aren't replaced. Should thi happen, replace the pads immediately to prevent expensive rotor (disc) damage.

REMOVAL & INSTALLATION

▶ **See Figures 72 thru 78 (p. 33–34)**

1. Remove approximately 1/3 of the brake fluid from the master cylinder. Discard the used brake fluid.

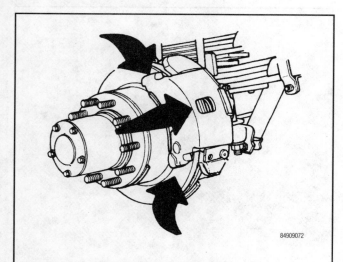

84909072

Fig. 70 Brake pad inspection points

2. Jack up your vehicle and support it with jackstands.

3. Push the piston back into its bore. This can be done by suing a C-clamp.

4. Remove the bolt at the caliper support key. Use a brass drift pin to remove the key and spring.

5. Rotate the caliper up and forward from the bottom and lift it off the caliper support.

6. Tie the caliper out of the way with a piece of wire. Be careful not to damage the brake line.

7. Remove the inner shoe from the caliper support. Discard the inner shoe clip.

8. Remove the outer shoe from the caliper.

To install:

9. Lubricate the caliper support and support spring, with silicone.

10. Install a NEW inboard shoe clip on the shoe.

11. Install the lower end of the inboard shoe into the groove provided in the support. Slide the upper end of the shoe into position. Be sure the clip remains in position.

12. Position the outboard shoe in the caliper with the ears at the top of the shoe over the caliper ears and the tab at the bottom of the shoe engaged in the caliper cutout. If assembly is difficult, a C-clamp may be used. Be careful not to mark the lining.

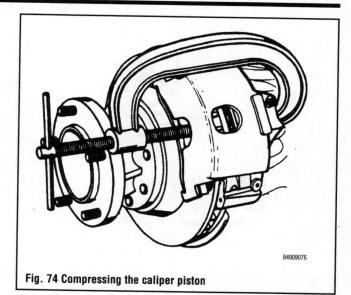

84909076

Fig. 74 Compressing the caliper piston

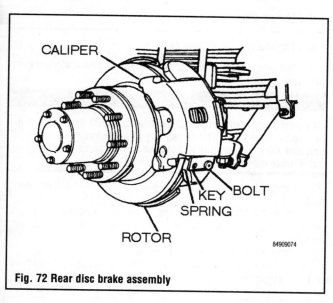

84909074

Fig. 72 Rear disc brake assembly

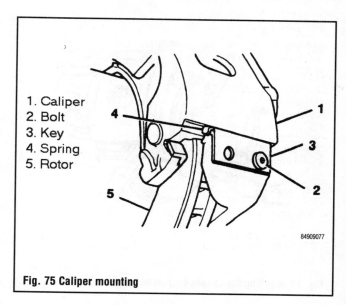

1. Caliper
2. Bolt
3. Key
4. Spring
5. Rotor

84909077

Fig. 75 Caliper mounting

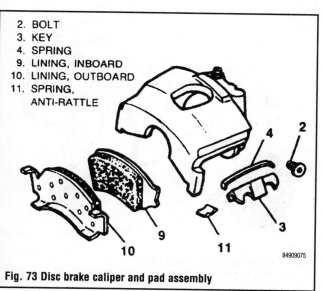

2. BOLT
3. KEY
4. SPRING
9. LINING, INBOARD
10. LINING, OUTBOARD
11. SPRING, ANTI-RATTLE

84909075

Fig. 73 Disc brake caliper and pad assembly

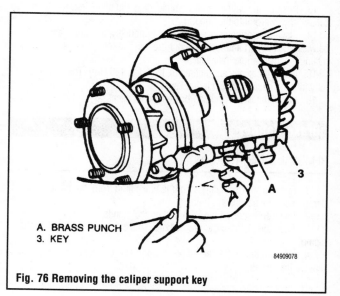

A. BRASS PUNCH
3. KEY

84909078

Fig. 76 Removing the caliper support key

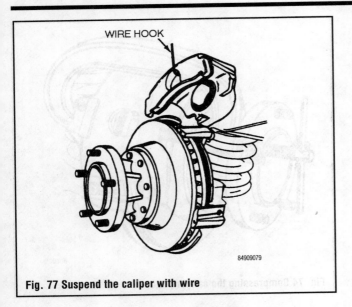

WIRE HOOK

84909079

Fig. 77 Suspend the caliper with wire

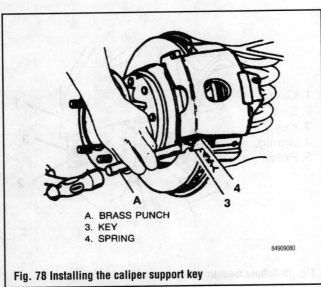

A. BRASS PUNCH
3. KEY
4. SPRING

84909080

Fig. 78 Installing the caliper support key

13. Position the caliper over the brake disc, top edge first. Rotate the caliper downward onto the support.

14. Place the spring over the caliper support key, install the assembly between the support and lower caliper groove. Tap into place until the key retaining screw can be installed.

15. Install the screw and tighten to 15 ft. lbs. (20 Nm). The boss must fit fully into the circular cutout in the key.

16. Install the wheel and add brake fluid as necessary.

Brake Caliper

REMOVAL & INSTALLATION

1. Remove approximately ⅓ of the brake fluid from the master cylinder. Discard the used brake fluid.

2. Raise and support the front end on jackstands.

3. Push the piston back into its bore. This can be done by suing a C-clamp.

4. Remove the bolt at the caliper support key. Use a brass drift pin to remove the key and spring.

5. Rotate the caliper up and forward from the bottom and lift it off the caliper support.

6. Unscrew the brake line at the caliper. Plug the opening. Discard the copper washer. Be careful not to damage the brake line.

7. Remove the outer shoe from the caliper.

To install:

8. Using a new copper washer, connect the brake line at the caliper. Tighten the connector to 33 ft. lbs. (45 Nm)

9. Lubricate the caliper support and support spring with silicone.

10. Position the outboard shoe in the caliper with the ears at the top of the shoe over the caliper ears and the tab at the bottom of the shoe engaged in the caliper cutout. If assembly is difficult, a C-clamp may be used. Be careful not to mar the lining.

11. Position the caliper over the brake disc, top edge first. Rotate the caliper downward onto the support.

12. Place the spring over the caliper support key, install the assembly between the support and lower caliper groove. Tap into place until the key retaining screw can be installed.

13. Install the screw and tighten to 15 ft. lbs. (20 Nm). The boss must fit fully into the circular cutout in the key.

14. Install the wheel and add brake fluid as necessary.

OVERHAUL

◆ **See Figures 79, 80, 81 and 82**

The following procedure applies to both the Delco and Bendix types of calipers.

⁑ WARNING

Use only denatured alcohol to clean metal parts and brake fluid to clean rubber parts. Never use any mineral based cleaning solvents such as gasoline or kerosene as these solvents will deteriorate rubber parts.

1. Remove the caliper, clean it and place it on a clean and level work surface.

2. Remove the brake hose from the caliper and discard the copper gasket. Check the brake hose for cracks or deterioration. Replace the hose as necessary.

3. Drain the brake fluid from the caliper.

4. Pad the interior of the caliper with cloth and then apply compressed air to the caliper inlet hose.

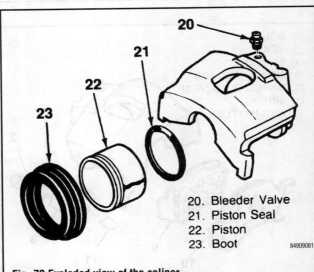

20. Bleeder Valve
21. Piston Seal
22. Piston
23. Boot

84909081

Fig. 79 Exploded view of the caliper

✳✳ CAUTION

Do not place your hands or fingers in front of the piston in an attempt to catch it! Use just enough air pressure to ease the piston out of the bore.

5. Remove the piston dust boot by prying it out with a screwdriver. Use caution when performing this procedure.

6. Remove the piston seal from the caliper piston bore using a small piece of wood or plastic. DO NOT use any type of metal tool for this procedure.

7. Remove the bleeder valve from the caliper.

➡**Dust boot, piston seal, rubber bushings, and sleeves are included in every rebuilding kit. These should be replaced at every caliper rebuild.**

8. Clean all parts in the recommended solvent and dry them completely using compressed air if possible.

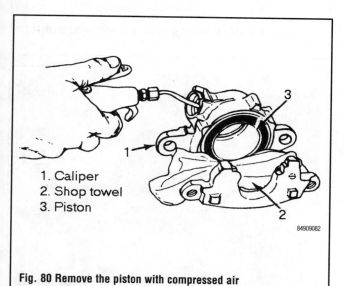

1. Caliper
2. Shop towel
3. Piston

84909082

Fig. 80 Remove the piston with compressed air

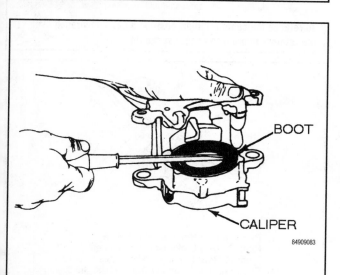

84909083

Fig. 81 Pry out the piston boot

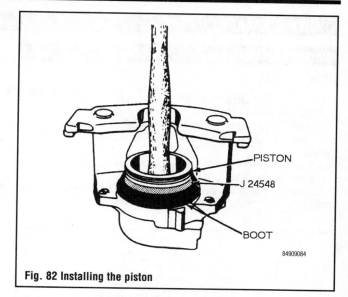

84909084

Fig. 82 Installing the piston

➡**The use of shop air hoses may inject oil film into the assembly; use caution when using such hoses.**

9. Examine the mounting bolts for rust or corrosion. Replace them as necessary.

10. Examine the piston for scoring, nicks, or worn plating. If any of these conditions are present, replace them as necessary.

✳✳ WARNING

Do not use any type of abrasive on the piston!

11. Check the piston bore. Small defects can be removed with crocus cloth. If the bore cannot be cleaned in this manner, replace the caliper.

12. Lubricate the piston bore and the new piston seal with brake fluid. Place the seal in the caliper bore groove.

13. Lubricate the piston in the same manner and position the new boot into the groove in the piston so that the fold faces the open end of the piston.

14. Place the piston into the caliper bore using caution not to unseat the seal. Force the piston to the bottom of the bore.

15. Place the dust boot in the caliper counterbore and seat the boot. Make sure that the boot in positioned correctly and evenly.

16. Install the brake hose in the caliper inlet using a new copper gasket.

➡**The hose must be positioned in the caliper locating gate to assure proper positioning of the caliper.**

17. Replace the bleeder screw.
18. Bleed the system.

Brake Disc (Rotor)

REMOVAL & INSTALLATION

1. Remove the brake caliper as previously outlined.
2. Remove the outer wheel bearing. (Refer to Section 1 for the proper procedure).
3. Remove the rotor from the spindle.
4. Reverse the procedure to install. Adjust the wheel bearings as described in Section 1.

PARKING BRAKE

Parking Brake Lever Pin-Up Procedure

▶ See Figure 83

This procedure is required on 1996–97 models only.
1. Remove the left kick panel.
2. Place the parking brake lever in the full upward position.
3. Raise the vehicle and support it with jackstands with a helper in the vehicle.
4. Pull the front of the cable strand rearward until the parking brake lever drum reaches its full reset position.
5. Insert a scribe or nail into the lever to hold the tension to its full reset position.

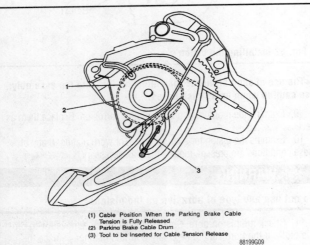

(1) Cable Position When the Parking Brake Cable Tension is Fully Released
(2) Parking Brake Cable Drum
(3) Tool to be Inserted for Cable Tension Release

88199G09

Fig. 83 Insert a scribe or nail into the lever to hold the tension at its full reset position—1996–97 models

Cables

REMOVAL & INSTALLATION

Front Cable

▶ See Figure 84

1. Raise the vehicle and support it with jackstands.
2. On 1996–97 models, perform the brake lever pin-up procedure, as described earlier in this section.
3. Remove adjusting nut from equalizer.
4. Remove retainer clip from rear portion of front cable at frame and from lever arm.
5. Disconnect the front brake cable from the parking brake pedal. Remove the front brake cable. On some models, it may assist installation of a new cable if a heavy cord is tied to the other end of the old cable before removal, to help route it properly.
6. Install the cable by reversing the removal procedure.
7. Adjust parking brake.

Rear Cable

▶ See Figure 85

1. Raise the vehicle and support it with jackstands.
2. On 1996–97 models, perform the brake lever pin-up procedure, as described earlier in this section.

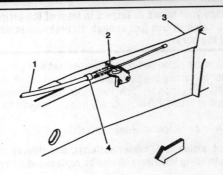

(1) Front Parking Brake Cable
(2) Front Parking Brake Cable Bracket
(3) Frame
(4) Front Parking Brake Cable Grommet

88199G10

Fig. 84 Front parking brake cable mounting—1996–97 models shown

88199P38

To release the cable retainer, position a box end wrench over the retainer in order to compress the fingers

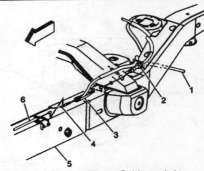

(1) Rear Parking Brake Cable to Axle
(2) Rear Parking Brake Cable Grommet
(3) Front to Rear Parking Brake Cable Equalizer
(4) Front and Rear Parking Brake Cable Installation
(5) Frame
(6) Front Parking Brake Cable

88199G11

Fig. 85 Rear parking brake cable mounting—1996–97 models shown

3. Remove rear wheel and brake drum.
4. Loosen adjusting nut at equalizer.
5. Disengage rear cable at connector.
6. Bend the retainer fingers.
7. Disengage the cable at the brake shoe operating lever.
8. Install the new cable by reversing the removal procedure.
9. Adjust the parking brake.

ADJUSTMENT

1987–95 Models

Before attempting parking brake adjustment, make sure that the rear brakes are fully adjusted by making several stops in reverse.
1. Raise and support the rear axle. Release the parking brake.
2. Apply the pedal 4 clicks.
3. Adjust the cable equalizer nut under the vans until a moderate drag can be felt when the rear wheels are turned forward.
4. Release the parking brake and check that there is no drag when the wheels are turned forward.

➡**If the parking brake cable is replaced, prestretch it by applying the parking brake hard about three times before attempting adjustment.**

1996–97 Models

▶ **See Figure 86**

1. Place the parking brake lever in the full up position.
2. Refer to the accompanying illustration and adjust the threads on the equalizer as follows:
• Passenger/Cargo to 0.511 in. (13mm)

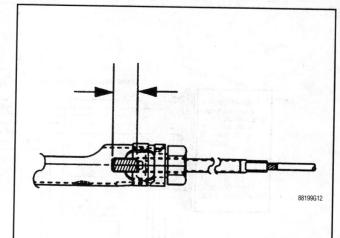

Fig. 86 Measure the threads on the equalizer between the points indicated by the arrows—1996–97 models

• Cutaway/Upfitters to 1.062 in. (27mm)
3. Lower the vehicle and check the parking brake will hold the vehicle by applying the lever.
4. If further adjustment is necessary, raise the vehicle and adjust the equalizer nut in 0.196 in. (5mm) increments until a moderate drag is reached on the rear wheels.
5. Back off the adjuster nut until the drag is no longer there, lower the vehicle and check the parking brake will hold the vehicle by applying the lever.

ANTI-LOCK BRAKE SYSTEMS

General Information

▶ **See Figures 87 thru 100 (p. 37–43)**

There are two basic types of anti-lock systems available for this vehicle; a Rear Wheel Anti-Lock (RWAL) brake system and 4 Wheel Anti-Lock (4WAL) brake system.

The RWAL system components consist of the Vehicle Speed Sensor (VSS), the Electronic Control Unit (ECU), the isolation/dump valve and the Vehicle Speed Sensor Buffer (also known as the Digital Ratio Adapter). The ECU also receives signals from various brake switches.

The 4WAL system components consist of the Electro-Hydraulic Control Unit (ECHU) valve (also known as the Brake Pressure Modulator Valve or BPMV), the wheel speed sensors, Vehicle Speed Sensor (VSS) on 3 sensor systems and the VSS Buffer.

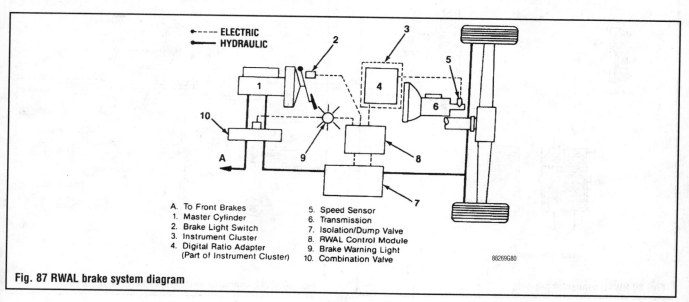

Fig. 87 RWAL brake system diagram

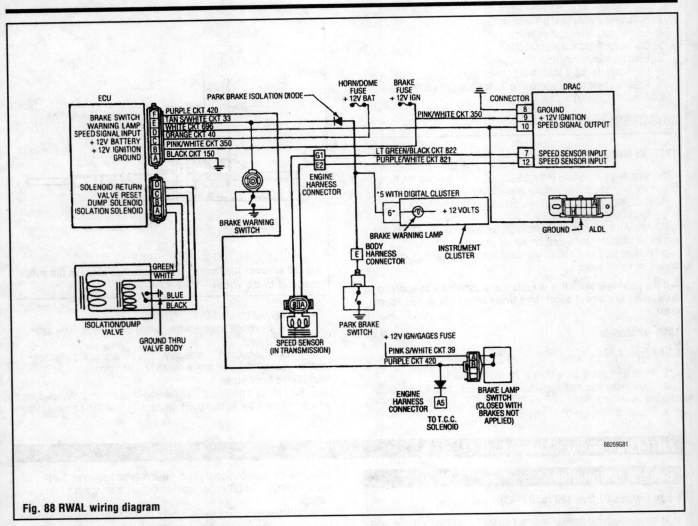

Fig. 88 RWAL wiring diagram

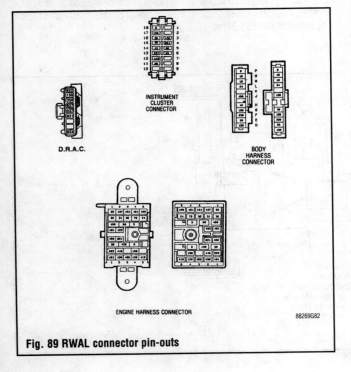

Fig. 89 RWAL connector pin-outs

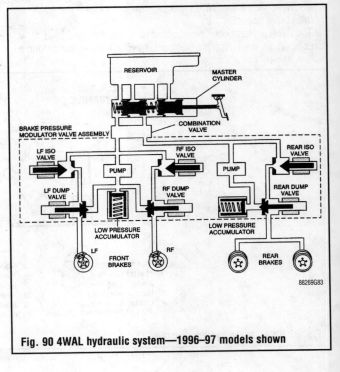

Fig. 90 4WAL hydraulic system—1996–97 models shown

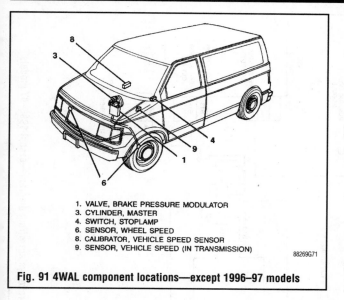

Fig. 91 4WAL component locations—except 1996–97 models

1. VALVE, BRAKE PRESSURE MODULATOR
3. CYLINDER, MASTER
4. SWITCH, STOPLAMP
6. SENSOR, WHEEL SPEED
8. CALIBRATOR, VEHICLE SPEED SENSOR
9. SENSOR, VEHICLE SPEED (IN TRANSMISSION)

88269G71

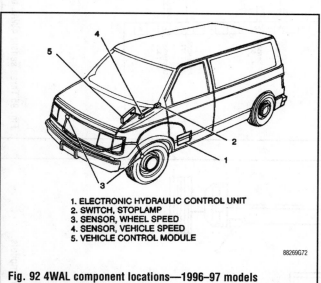

1. ELECTRONIC HYDRAULIC CONTROL UNIT
2. SWITCH, STOPLAMP
3. SENSOR, WHEEL SPEED
4. SENSOR, VEHICLE SPEED
5. VEHICLE CONTROL MODULE

88269G72

Fig. 92 4WAL component locations—1996–97 models

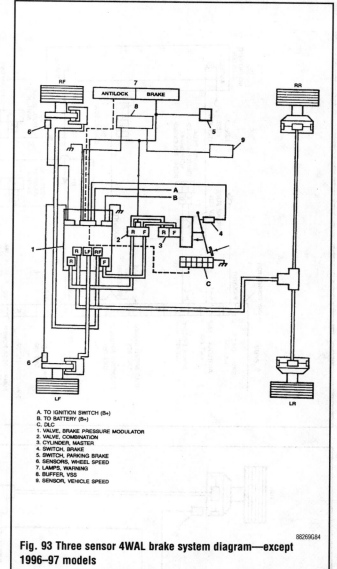

A. TO IGNITION SWITCH (B+)
B. TO BATTERY (B+)
C. DLC
1. VALVE, BRAKE PRESSURE MODULATOR
2. VALVE, COMBINATION
3. CYLINDER, MASTER
4. SWITCH, BRAKE
5. SWITCH, PARKING BRAKE
6. SENSORS, WHEEL SPEED
7. LAMPS, WARNING
8. BUFFER, VSS
9. SENSOR, VEHICLE SPEED

88269G84

Fig. 93 Three sensor 4WAL brake system diagram—except 1996–97 models

EHCU Valve/BPMV (4WAL)

REMOVAL & INSTALLATION

Except 1996–97 Models

▶ See Figures 101 and 102 (p. 43)

The EHCU valve is not serviceable. Replace the valve only when defective.

1. Disconnect the negative battery cable.
2. Raise the vehicle and support it with jackstands.
3. Tag and disengage the electrical connections from the EHCU/BPMV.
4. Disconnect the brake pipes from the EHCU/BPMV.
5. Unfasten the retaining bolts and remove the EHCU/BPMV from its mounting bracket.
6. Remove the EHCU/BPMV from the vehicle.

To install:

7. Install the EHCU/BPMV onto the bracket. Tighten the mounting bolt to 84 inch lbs. (9 Nm).

8. Install the EHCU/BPMV and tighten the retainers to 55 ft. lbs. (75 Nm).
9. Connect the electrical connectors and hydraulic lines. Torque the line fittings to 16 ft. lbs. (25 Nm).
10. Bleed the system and the EHCU/BPMV.
11. Connect the negative battery cable, pump the brakes before road test and road test

1996–97 Models

▶ See Figures 103 and 104 (p. 44)

1. Disconnect the negative battery cable.
2. Raise and safely support the vehicle.
3. Remove the EHCU shield retainers and shield.
4. Unplug the electrical connectors from the unit.
5. Using a flare wrench, disconnect the hydraulic lines from the unit.
6. Unfasten the bolts and remove the BPMV and bracket.
7. Remove the bolts that hold the unit to the bracket.
8. If necessary, unfasten the EBCM-to-BPMV retaining bolts and separate the units.
9. Unfasten the Allen bolts, then remove the combination valve.
10. Remove the transfer tubes.

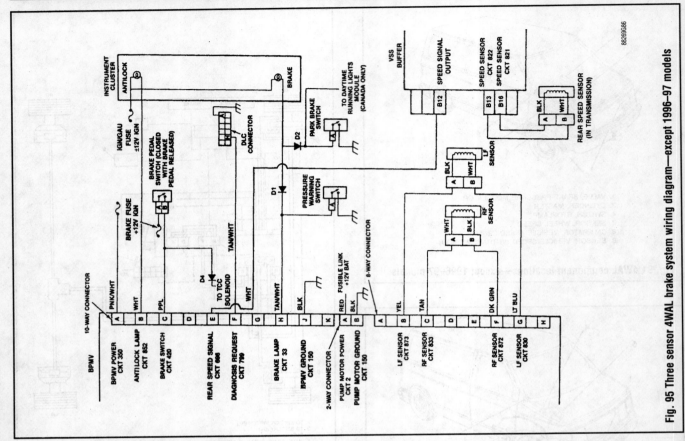

Fig. 95 Three sensor 4WAL brake system wiring diagram—except 1996–97 models

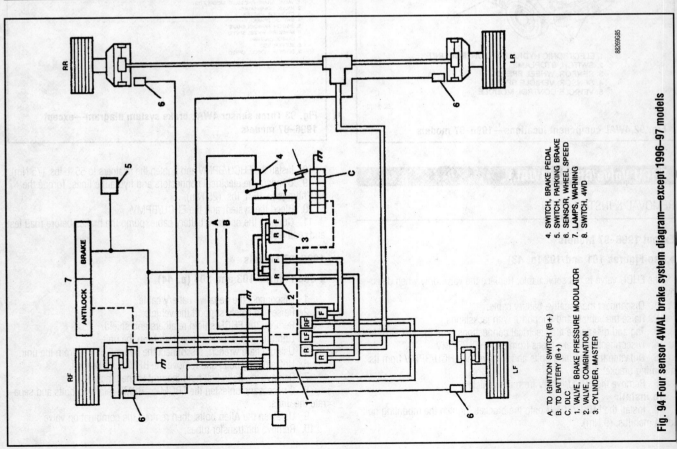

Fig. 94 Four sensor 4WAL brake system diagram—except 1996–97 models

A. TO IGNITION SWITCH (B+)
B. TO BATTERY (B+)
C. DLC
1. VALVE, BRAKE PRESSURE MODULATOR
2. VALVE, COMBINATION
3. CYLINDER, MASTER
4. SWITCH, BRAKE PEDAL
5. SWITCH, PARKING BRAKE
6. SENSOR, WHEEL SPEED
7. LAMPS, WARNING
8. SWITCH, 4WD

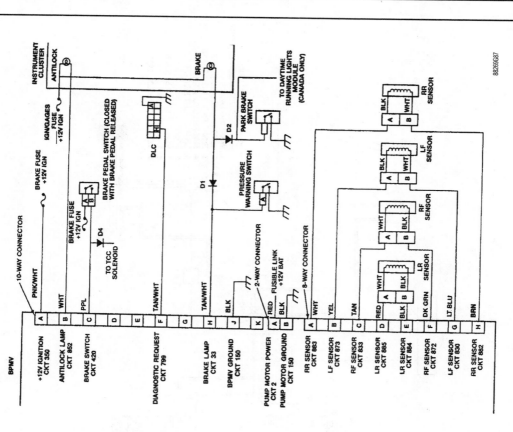

8826 9G88

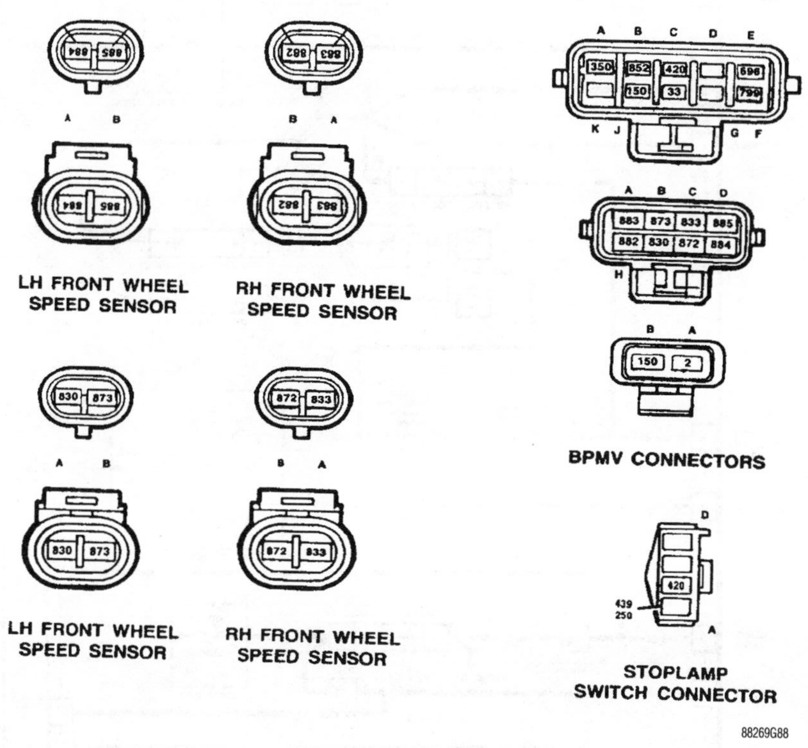

Fig. 97 4WAL connector pin-outs—except 1996–97 models

BPMV CONNECTORS

STOPLAMP SWITCH CONNECTOR

RH FRONT WHEEL SPEED SENSOR

LH FRONT WHEEL SPEED SENSOR

RH FRONT WHEEL SPEED SENSOR

LH FRONT WHEEL SPEED SENSOR

8826 9G87

Fig. 96 Four sensor 4WAL brake system wiring diagram—except 1996–97 models

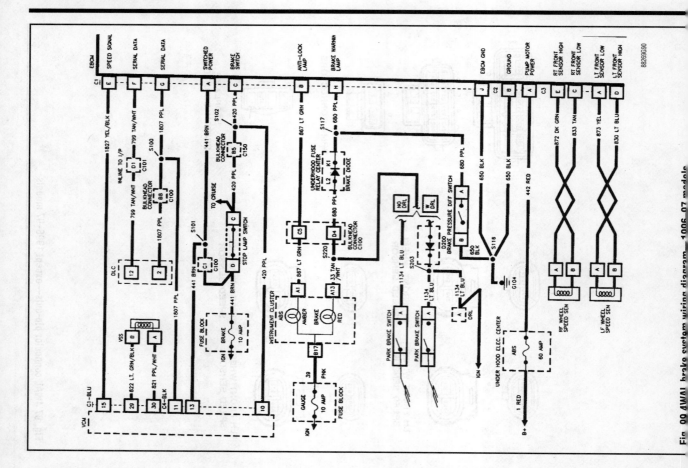

Fig. 99 4WAL brake system wiring diagram—1996-97 models

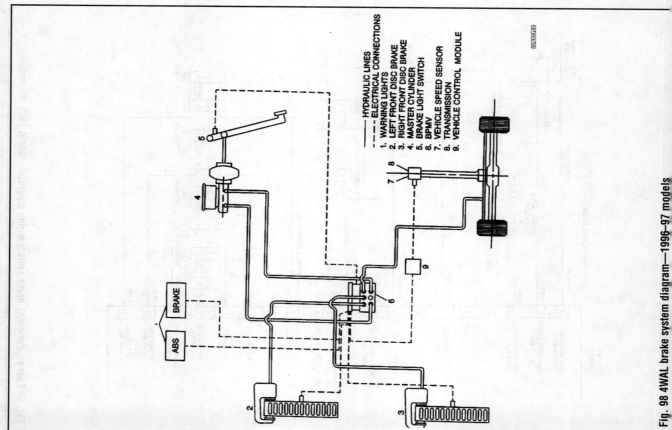

Fig. 98 4WAL brake system diagram—1996-97 models

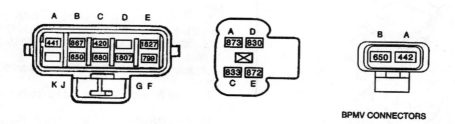

TERMINAL	CIRCUIT NO.	COLOR	CIRCUIT DESCRIPTION
A	441	BRN	SWITCHED IGNITION POWER
B	867	LT GRN	ABS WARNING LAMP CONTROL
C	420	PPL	BRAKE SWITCH INPUT
D	PLUGGED		NOT USED
E	1827	YEL/BLK	VEHICLE SPEED SIGNAL INPUT
F	799	TAN/WHT	SERIAL DATA LINE
G	1807	PPL	SERIAL DATA LINE
H	680	PPL	BRAKE WARNING LAMP CONTROL
J	650	BLK	EBCM GROUND
K	PLUGGED		NOT USED

EBCM 10-WAY CONNECTOR

TERMINAL	CIRCUIT NO.	COLOR	CIRCUIT DESCRIPTION
A	873	YEL	LT FRONT SENSOR LOW
B	PLUGGED		NOT USED
C	833	TAN	RT FRONT SENSOR LOW
D	830	LT BLU	LT FRONT SENSOR HIGH
E	872	DRK GRN	RT FRONT SENSOR HIGH

EBCM 5-WAY CONNECTOR

TERMINAL	CIRCUIT NO.	COLOR	CIRCUIT DESCRIPTION
A	442	RED	PUMP MOTOR POWER
B	650	BLK	GROUND

EBCM 2-WAY CONNECTOR

88269G91

Fig. 100 4WAL brake system connector pin-outs—1996–97 models

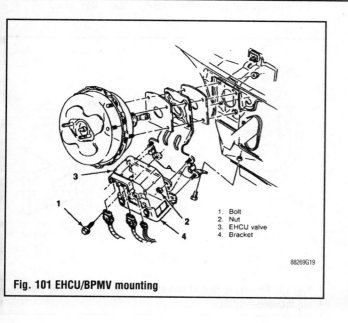

1. Bolt
2. Nut
3. EHCU valve
4. Bracket

88269G19

Fig. 101 EHCU/BPMV mounting

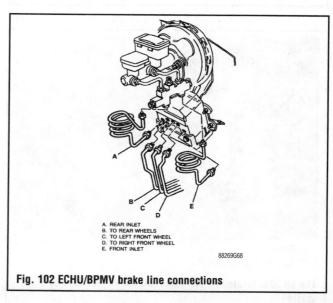

A. REAR INLET
B. TO REAR WHEELS
C. TO LEFT FRONT WHEEL
D. TO RIGHT FRONT WHEEL
E. FRONT INLET

88269G68

Fig. 102 ECHU/BPMV brake line connections

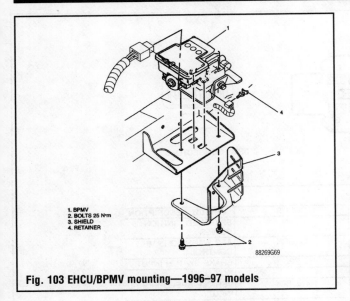

1. BPMV
2. BOLTS 25 N•m
3. SHIELD
4. RETAINER

88269G69

Fig. 103 EHCU/BPMV mounting—1996–97 models

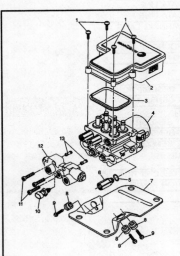

1. Bolt/screw 5 N•m
2. Module, electronic brake control
3. Gasket
4. Valve, brake pressure modulator
5. Seal, ruuber O ring
6. Tube adapters
7. Bracket
8. Grommet
9. Bolt/screw 9 N•m
10. Switch, brake pressure differential
11. Bolt/screw 16 N•m
12. Valve, combination
13. Transfer tubes

88269G70

Fig. 104 EHCU/BPMV exploded view—1996–97 models

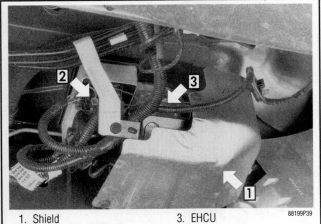

1. Shield
2. Electrical connection
3. EHCU

88199P39

The EHCU is located on the frame rail and is protected by a shield

To install:

11. Install the transfer tubes into the combination valve until fully seated.

12. Engage the combination valve to the BPMV and tighten the Allen bolts in two steps to 6 ft. lbs. (8 Nm) and then to 12 ft. lbs. (16 Nm).

13. Install a new gasket and engage the EBCM to the BPMV and tighten the retainers to 39 in. lbs. (5 Nm).

14. Install the unit onto the bracket and tighten the bolts to 7 ft. lbs. (9 Nm).

15. Install the unit and bracket and tighten the bolts to 9 ft. lbs. (12 Nm).

16. Connect the hydraulic lines. Torque the fittings to 22 ft. lbs. (30 Nm).

17. Engage the electrical connections and replace the EHCU shield and tighten the retainers to 8 ft. lbs. (12 Nm).

18. Connect the negative battery cable.

19. Bleed the hydraulic system.

20. Lower the vehicle.

Electronic Control Unit (RWAL)

REMOVAL & INSTALLATION

▶ **See Figure 105**

The ECU is not serviceable. Replace the unit only when defective.

➡ **Do not touch the electrical connections and pins or allow them to come in contact with brake fluid as this may damage the ECU.**

1. Disconnect the negative battery cable and ECU connectors.

2. Remove the ECU by prying the tab at the rear of the ECU and pulling it toward the front of the vehicle.

To install:

3. Install the ECU by sliding the unit into the bracket until the tab locks into the hole.

4. Connect the electrical connectors and negative battery cable.

Isolation/Dump Valve

TESTING

1. Disconnect the negative battery cable.

2. Disconnect the isolation/dump valve harness from the ECU.

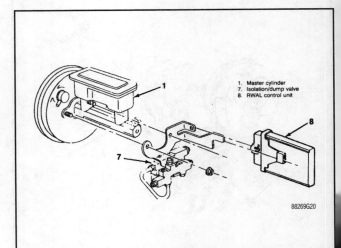

1. Master cylinder
7. Isolation/dump valve
8. RWAL control unit

88269G20

Fig. 105 Electronic control unit and isolation/dump valve mounting location—RWAL

3. Check the dump valve coil resistance between terminals B and D. If the resistance is greater than 3.0 ohms, replace the assembly. The resistance should be between 1.0 and 3.0 ohms.

4. Check the isolation valve coil resistance between terminals A and D. The resistance should be between 3.0 and 6.0 ohms. Replace the assembly if the resistance is above 6.0 ohms.

5. Check the resistance of the anti-lock valve switch between terminals C and D and then check it between C and the assembly body. If the resistance is less than 50,000 ohms in either test, replace the assembly.

REMOVAL & INSTALLATION

The isolation/dump valve is not serviceable. Replace the unit only when defective.
1. Disconnect the negative battery cable.
2. Disconnect the brake line fittings using a flare nut wrench.
3. Disconnect the bottom electrical connector from the ECU. Do not allow the isolation/dump valve to hang by the pigtail.
4. Remove the valve from the vehicle.
To install:
5. Install the valve and torque the bolts to 21 ft. lbs. (29 Nm).
6. Connect the electrical connectors and reconnect the brake lines using a flare nut wrench. Torque the fittings to 18 ft. lbs. (24 Nm).
7. Connect the negative battery cable and bleed the system.

Front Wheel Speed Sensor

TESTING

♦ See Figures 106 and 107

1. Disconnect the negative battery cable.
2. Raise the vehicle and support with jackstands. Remove the wheel and tire assembly.
3. Disconnect the front wheel speed sensor.
4. Measure the resistance of the sensor and compare to the chart.
5. Replace the sensor if the resistance does not meet specification.

REMOVAL & INSTALLATION

There are two basic styles of front wheel sensor, integral and non-integral. The integral sensor is mounted in the hub bearing assembly, while the non-integral is mounted on the backing plate.

WHEEL SPEED SENSOR TEMPERATURE VS. SENSOR RESISTANCE (APPROXIMATE)		
TEMP. (°C)	TEMP. (°F)	RESISTANCE (OHMS)
-40 TO 4	-40 TO 40	920 TO 1387
5 TO 43	41 TO 110	1125 TO 1620
44 TO 93	111 TO 200	1305 TO 1900
94 TO 150	201 TO 302	1530 TO 2200

88269G76

Fig. 106 Front wheel speed sensor resistance chart—Non-integral sensors

WHEEL SPEED SENSOR TEMPERATURE VS. SENSOR RESISTANCE (APPROXIMATE)		
TEMP. (°C)	TEMP. (°F)	RESISTANCE (OHMS)
-40 TO 4	-40 TO 40	1900 TO 2950
5 TO 43	41 TO 110	2420 TO 3450
44 TO 93	111 TO 200	2810 TO 4100
94 TO 150	201 TO 302	3320 TO 4760

88269G77

Fig. 107 Front wheel speed sensor resistance chart—integral sensors

Integral Sensors

♦ See Figures 108, 109, 110, 111 and 112

1. Disconnect the negative battery cable.
2. Raise the vehicle and support with jackstands. Remove the wheel and tire assembly.

❊❊ CAUTION

Brake pads may contain asbestos, which has been determined to be a cancer causing agent. Never clean the brake surfaces with compressed air! Avoid inhaling any dust from any brake surface! When cleaning brake surfaces, use a commercially available brake cleaning fluid.

3. Remove the brake caliper and rotor.
4. Remove the sensor wire clips from the frame and the control arm.
5. Disconnect the sensor electrical connector.
6. Remove the sensor from the bearing assembly.
To install:
7. Install a new O-ring on the sensor. Do not contaminate the lubricant in the sealed bearing.

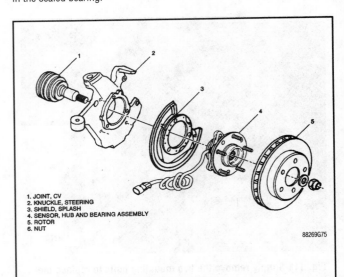

1. JOINT, CV
2. KNUCKLE, STEERING
3. SHIELD, SPLASH
4. SENSOR, HUB AND BEARING ASSEMBLY
5. ROTOR
6. NUT

88269G75

Fig. 108 Integral front wheel speed sensor

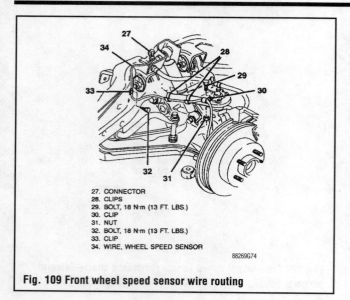

27. CONNECTOR
28. CLIPS
29. BOLT, 18 N·m (13 FT. LBS.)
30. CLIP
31. NUT
32. BOLT, 18 N·m (13 FT. LBS.)
33. CLIP
34. WIRE, WHEEL SPEED SENSOR

Fig. 109 Front wheel speed sensor wire routing

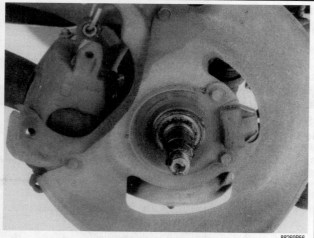

Fig. 110 The front wheel speed sensor is accessible after removing the hub and rotor

Fig. 111 Simply remove the two mounting bolts to replace the sensor

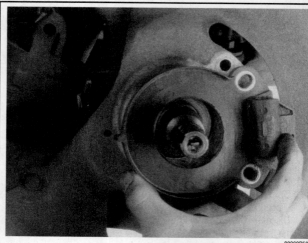

Fig. 112 Pull the sensor off the backing plate and route the wires through the opening

8. Install the sensor into the bearing assembly and torque the bolts to 13 ft. lbs. (18 Nm).
9. Connect the sensor wire.
10. Install the sensor wire in the clips..
11. Install the rotor and caliper.
12. Install the front wheel and torque the lug nuts.
13. Connect the negative battery cable and check operation.

Non-Integral Sensors

▶ See Figure 113

1. Disconnect the negative battery cable.
2. Raise the vehicle and support with jackstands. Remove the wheel and tire assembly.

✳✳ CAUTION

Brake pads may contain asbestos, which has been determined to be a cancer causing agent. Never clean the brake surfaces with compressed air! Avoid inhaling any dust from any brake surface! When cleaning brake surfaces, use a commercially available brake cleaning fluid.

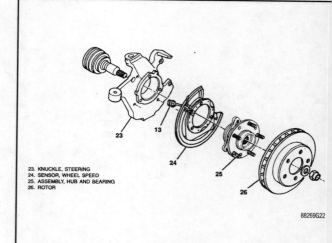

23. KNUCKLE, STEERING
24. SENSOR, WHEEL SPEED
25. ASSEMBLY, HUB AND BEARING
26. ROTOR

Fig. 113 Non-integral front wheel speed sensor

3. Remove the brake caliper and rotor.
4. Remove the hub and bearing assembly.
5. Disconnect the sensor electrical connector.
6. Remove the splash shield with the sensor from the steering knuckle.

To install:

7. Install the splash shield with the sensor onto the steering knuckle and torque the bolts to 11 ft. lbs. (15 Nm).
8. Connect the sensor wire.
9. Install the hub and bearing assembly.
10. Install the rotor and caliper.
11. Install the front wheel and torque the lug nuts to 100 ft. lbs. (136 Nm).
12. Connect the negative battery cable and check operation.

Rear Wheel Speed Sensors

On early model vehicles, the rear wheel speed sensors are held by 2 bolts at each rear wheel. The brake drum and primary brake shoe must be removed for access.

Late models vehicles receive the rear wheel speed signal from the Vehicle Speed Sensor (VSS) buffer. The VSS is located at the left rear of the transmission. The buffer, a unit for interpreting the electrical signal from the sensor, is located behind the instrument cluster. The buffer, formerly known as the Digital Ratio Adapter Controller (DRAC), is matched to the final drive and tire size of each vehicle. If the final drive or tire size is changed, the buffer unit must be replaced to maintain accurate speedometer/odometer readings and proper ABS function.

TESTING

▶ See Figure 114

1. Disconnect the negative battery cable.
2. Raise the vehicle and support with jackstands. Remove the wheel and tire assembly.
3. Disconnect the rear wheel speed sensor.
4. Measure the resistance of the sensor and compare to the chart.
5. Replace the sensor if the resistance does not meet specification.

REMOVAL & INSTALLATION

Early Model Vehicles

▶ See Figure 115

1. Elevate and safely support the vehicle.
2. Remove the wheel.
3. Remove the brake drum.

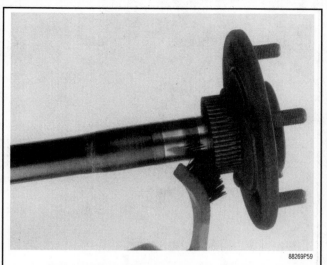
Fig. 115 The tone ring splines need to be clean to work properly

4. Remove the primary brake shoe.
5. Disconnect the sensor wiring at the connector.
6. Remove the sensor wire from the rear axle clips.
7. Remove the retainer(s) holding the sensor.
8. Remove the sensor by tracking the wire through the hole in the backing plate.

To install:

9. Route the wire through the hole in the backing plate and fit the sensor into position.
10. Install the retainer(s); tighten them to 26 ft. lbs. (35 Nm).
11. Secure the sensor wire within the rear axle clips.
12. Connect the sensor wiring to the harness connector.
13. Install the primary brake shoe.
14. Install the brake drum.
15. Install the wheel. Lower the vehicle to the ground.

Late Model Vehicles

WITH 4L60E TRANSMISSION

▶ See Figures 116, 117, 118, 119 and 120

➡Speed sensor removal/installation tool J-38417 or its equivalent is required for this procedure.

WHEEL SPEED SENSOR TEMPERATURE VS. SENSOR RESISTANCE (APPROXIMATE)		
TEMP. (°C)	TEMP. (°F)	RESISTANCE (OHMS)
-40 TO 4	-40 TO 40	920 TO 1387
5 TO 43	41 TO 110	1125 TO 1620
44 TO 93	111 TO 200	1305 TO 1900
94 TO 150	201 TO 302	1530 TO 2200

88269G76

Fig. 114 Rear wheel speed sensor resistance chart

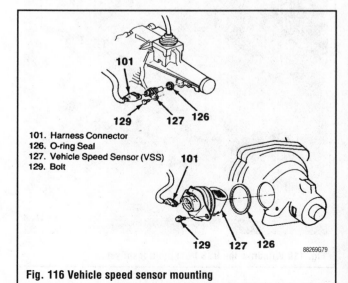

101. Harness Connector
126. O-ring Seal
127. Vehicle Speed Sensor (VSS)
129. Bolt

Fig. 116 Vehicle speed sensor mounting

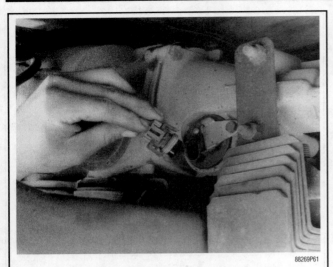

Fig. 117 Unplug the weatherpak connector from the VSS

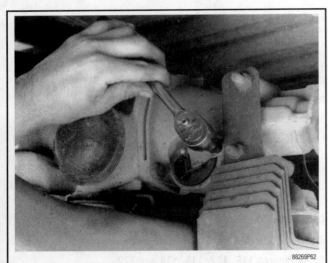

Fig. 118 The VSS is held by the one bolt and clamp

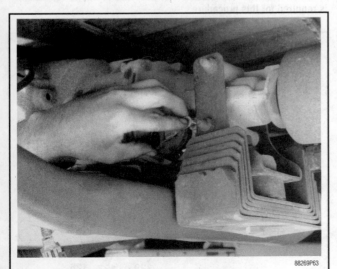

Fig. 119 Withdraw the VSS from the transmission

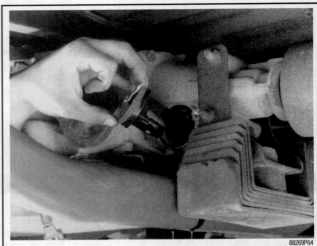

Fig. 120 Fluid will come out of the VSS opening so be ready to catch the spillage

1. Elevate and safely support the vehicle. The speed sensor is located on the left side of the transmission.
2. Disconnect the sensor wiring connector.
3. Remove the retaining bolt holding the sensor.
4. Using the removal tool, remove the sensor from the transmission case. Have a pan available to catch fluid spillage.

To install:

5. Coat the O-ring on the sensor with a thin coat of transmission fluid.
6. Using the installation tool, install the sensor into the case. Tighten the mounting bolt to 8 ft. lbs. (11 Nm).
7. Connect the sensor to the wiring harness.
8. Lower the vehicle to the ground. Check the transmission fluid level and fill to the correct level if necessary.

WITH W4L80E TRANSMISSION

1. Elevate and safely support the vehicle. Both speed sensors are located on the left side of the transmission.
2. Disconnect the sensor wiring connector(s).
3. Remove the retaining bolt holding the sensor.
4. Remove the sensor from the transmission case. Have a pan available to catch fluid spillage.

To install:

5. Coat the O-ring on the sensor with a thin coat of transmission fluid.
6. Install the sensor(s) into the case. Tighten the mounting bolt to 5 ft. lbs. (7 Nm).
7. Connect the sensor to the wiring harness.
8. Lower the vehicle to the ground. Check the transmission fluid level and fill to the correct level if necessary.

WITH MANUAL TRANSMISSION

1. Elevate and safely support the vehicle. The speed sensor is located on the left side of the transmission.
2. Disconnect the sensor wiring connector.
3. Remove the retaining bolt holding the sensor.
4. Remove the sensor from the transmission case. Have a pan available to catch fluid spillage.

To install:

5. Coat the O-ring on the sensor with a thin coat of transmission fluid.
6. Install the sensor into the case. Tighten the mounting bolt to 5 ft. lbs. (7 Nm).
7. Connect the sensor to the wiring harness.
8. Lower the vehicle to the ground. Check the transmission fluid level and fill to the correct level if necessary.

Vehicle Speed Sensor

The vehicle speed sensor is mounted in the transmission tail housing.

TESTING

▶ See Figure 121

1. Disconnect the negative battery cable.
2. Raise the vehicle and support with jackstands.
3. Disconnect the vehicle speed sensor wiring.
4. Measure the resistance of the sensor and compare to the chart.
5. Replace the sensor if the resistance does not meet specification.

WHEEL SPEED SENSOR TEMPERATURE
VS. SENSOR RESISTANCE (APPROXIMATE)

TEMP. (°C)	TEMP. (°F)	RESISTANCE (OHMS)
-40 TO 4	-40 TO 40	920 TO 1387
5 TO 43	41 TO 110	1125 TO 1620
44 TO 93	111 TO 200	1305 TO 1900
94 TO 150	201 TO 302	1530 TO 2200

88269G76

Fig. 121 Vehicle speed sensor resistance chart

REMOVAL & INSTALLATION

Refer to the Rear Wheel Speed Sensor procedure in this section.

Self-Diagnostics

READING TROUBLE CODES

▶ See Figure 122

Rear Wheel Anti-Lock Brakes

The trouble codes are read by jumping terminal **A** and terminal **H** of the ALDL (assembly line diagnostic link) with a jumper wire. Observe the flashing of the brake warning light. The terminals must be jumped for about 20 seconds before the code will begin to flash.

Count the number of short flashes starting from the long flash. Include the long flash as a count. Sometimes the first count sequence will be short, however, following counts will be accurate.

If there is more than one failure, only the first recognized code will be retained and flashed.

- Code 1—ECU malfunction
- Code 2—Open isolation valve or faulty ECU
- Code 3—Open dump valve or faulty ECU
- Code 4—Grounded anti-lock valve switch
- Code 5—Excessive dump valve activity during stop
- Code 6—Erratic speed system
- Code 7—Shorted isolation valve or faulty ECU

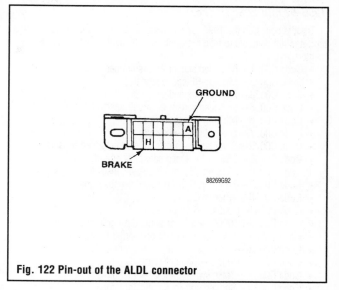

Fig. 122 Pin-out of the ALDL connector

- Code 8—Shorted dump valve or faulty ECU
- Code 9—Open speed signal circuit
- Code 10—Brake lamp switch circuit
- Code 11—Faulty ECU
- Code 12—Faulty ECU
- Code 13—Faulty ECU
- Code 14—Faulty ECU
- Code 15—Faulty ECU

4-Wheel Anti-Lock Brakes

EXCEPT 1996–97 MODELS

The trouble codes are read by jumping terminal **A** and terminal **H** of the ALDL (assembly line diagnostic link) with a jumper wire. Observe the flashing of the ANTI-LOCK warning light. The terminals must be jumped for about 20 seconds before the code will begin to flash.

Count the number of short flashes starting from the long flash. Include the long flash as a count. Sometimes the first count sequence will be short, however, following counts will be accurate.

If there is more than one failure, only the first recognized code will be retained and flashed.

- Code 21—RF speed sensor or circuit open
- Code 22—Missing RF speed signal
- Code 23—Erratic RF speed sensor
- Code 25—LF speed sensor or circuit open
- Code 26—Missing LF speed signal
- Code 27—Erratic LF speed sensor
- Code 29—Simultaneous drop out of front speed sensors
- Code 31—RR speed sensor or circuit open
- Code 32—Missing RR speed signal
- Code 33—Erratic RR speed signal
- Code 35—VSS or LR speed sensor or circuit open
- Code 36—Missing VSS or LR speed sensor or circuit open
- Code 37—Erratic VSS or LR speed sensor signal
- Code 38—Wheel speed error
- Code 41–54—Control valves
- Code 61–63—Reset switches
- Code 65–66—Open or shorted pump motor relay
- Code 67—Open motor circuit or shorted BPMV output
- Code 68—Locked motor or shorted motor circuit
- Code 71–74—Memory errors
- Code 81—Brake switch circuit shorted or open
- Code 86—Shorted anti-lock indicator lamp
- Code 88—Shorted brake warning lamp

1996–97 MODELS

Trouble codes on the 1996–97 vehicles can only be read using a scan tool. It is not possible to read the trouble codes by the flashing light method.

- Code C0021—RF speed sensor or circuit open
- Code C0022—Missing RF speed signal
- Code C0023—Erratic RF speed sensor
- Code C0025—LF speed sensor or circuit open
- Code C0026—Missing LF speed signal
- Code C0027—Erratic LF speed sensor
- Code C0029—Simultaneous drop out of front speed sensors
- Code C0035—VSS or LR speed sensor or circuit open
- Code C0036—Missing VSS or LR speed sensor or circuit open
- Code C0037—Erratic VSS or LR speed sensor signal
- Code C0038—Wheel speed error
- Code C0041– C0054—Control valves
- Code C0065– C0066—Open or shorted pump motor relay
- Code C0067—Open motor circuit or shorted BPMV output
- Code C0068—Locked motor or shorted motor circuit
- Code C0071– C0074—Memory errors
- Code C0081—Brake switch circuit shorted or open
- Code C0086—Shorted anti-lock indicator lamp
- Code C0088—Shorted brake warning lamp

CLEARING TROUBLE CODES

On 1987–95 vehicles the trouble codes may be cleared using a Tech I scan tool or by performing the following procedures. On 1996–97 vehicles, the trouble codes can only be cleared by the appropriate scan tool.

1. Turn the ignition switch to the **RUN** position.
2. Use a jumper wire to ground the ALDL terminal **A** to **H** for 2 seconds.
3. Remove the jumper wire for 2 seconds.
4. Repeat the grounding and ungrounding 2 more times.
5. Check that the memory is cleared by making a diagnostic request.
6. Turn the ignition switch **OFF**.

Bleeding The ABS System

The brake system must be bled when any brake line is disconnected or there is air in the system.

➡**Never bleed a wheel cylinder when a drum is removed.**

1. Clean the master cylinder of excess dirt and remove the cylinder cover and the diaphragm.
2. Fill the master cylinder to the proper level. Check the fluid level periodically during the bleeding process, and replenish it as necessary. Do not allow the master cylinder to run dry, or you will have to start over.
3. Before opening any of the bleeder screws, you may want to give each one a shot of penetrating solvent. This reduces the possibility of breakage when they are unscrewed.
4. Attach a length of vinyl hose to the bleeder screw of the brake to be bled. Insert the other end of the hose into a clear jar half full of clean brake fluid, so that the end of the hose is beneath the level of fluid. The correct sequence for bleeding is to work from the brake farthest from the master cylinder to the one closest; right rear, left rear, right front, left front.
5. The combination valve must be held open during the bleeding process. A clip, tape, or other similar tool (or an assistant) will hold the metering pin in.
6. Depress and release the brake pedal three or four times to exhaust any residual vacuum.
7. Have an assistant push down on the brake pedal and hold it down. Open the bleeder valve slightly. As the pedal reaches the end of its travel, close the bleeder screw and release the brake pedal. Repeat this process until no air bubbles are visible in the expelled fluid.

➡**Make sure your assistant presses the brake pedal to the floor slowly. Pressing too fast will cause air bubbles to form in the fluid.**

8. Repeat this procedure at each of the brakes. Remember to check the master cylinder level occasionally. Use only fresh fluid to refill the master cylinder, not the stuff bled from the system.
9. When the bleeding process is complete, refill the master cylinder, install its cover and diaphragm, and discard the fluid bled from the brake system.
10. If the BPMV has been replaced, perform 4 function tests with the TECH 1 scan tool. The brake pedal **must** be firmly applied.
11. On models with rear wheel ABS:
   a. Refill the jar with clean brake fluid and attach the bleed hose to the bleed valve on the Isolation/Dump valve.
   b. Have your assistant slowly depress the brake pedal and hold it. Loosen the bleed valve and expel the air. Tighten the valve and slowly release the pedal.
   c. Wait 15 seconds and repeat this procedure. Repeat bleeding the Isolation/Dump valve until all the air is expelled.
12. On models with 4 wheel ABS, repeat Steps 1–9.

BRAKE SPECIFICATIONS

Year	Brake Disc Original Thickness	Brake Disc Maximum Refinish	Maximum Run-out	Brake Drum Diameter Original Inside Diameter	Brake Drum Diameter Max. Wear Limit	Minimum Lining Thickness Front	Minimum Lining Thickness Rear
1987	1.280 in.	1.230 in.	0.004	11.00	11.06	0.030	0.142
	1.540 in.	1.480 in.	0.004	13.00	13.06	0.030	0.142
1988	1.280 in.	1.230 in.	0.004	11.00	11.06	0.030	0.142
	1.540 in.	1.480 in.	0.004	13.00	13.06	0.030	0.142
1989	1.280 in.	1.230 in.	0.004	11.00	11.06	0.030	0.142
	1.540 in.	1.480 in.	0.004	13.00	13.06	0.030	0.142
1990	1.280 in.	1.230 in.	0.004	11.00	11.06	0.030	0.142
	1.540 in.	1.480 in.	0.004	13.00	13.06	0.030	0.142
1991	1.280 in.	1.230 in.	0.004	11.00	11.06	0.030	0.142
	1.540 in.	1.480 in.	0.004	13.00	13.06	0.030	0.142
1992	1.280 in.	1.230 in.	0.004	11.00	11.06	0.030	0.142
	1.540 in.	1.480 in.	0.004	13.00	13.06	0.030	0.142
1993	1.280 in.	1.230 in.	0.004	11.00	11.06	0.030	0.142
	1.540 in.	1.480 in.	0.004	13.00	13.06	0.030	0.142
1994	1.280 in.	1.230 in.	0.004	11.00	11.06	0.030	0.142
	1.540 in.	1.480 in.	0.004	13.00	13.06	0.030	0.142
1995	1.280 in.	1.230 in.	0.004	11.00	11.06	0.030	0.142
	1.540 in.	1.480 in.	0.004	13.00	13.06	0.030	0.142
1996	1.250 in. ①	1.230 in.	0.004	11.15	13.00 ①	0.030	0.142
	1.260 in. ②	1.230 in.	0.004	21.00	13.06 ②	0.030	0.142
	1.500 in. ③	1.480 in.	0.004	21.00	13.06 ③	0.030	0.142
1997	1.250 in. ①	1.230 in.	0.004	11.15	13.00 ①	0.030	0.142
	1.260 in. ②	1.230 in.	0.004	21.00	13.06 ②	0.030	0.142
	1.500 in. ③	1.480 in.	0.004	21.00	13.06 ③	0.030	0.142

① 1500 series
② 2500 series
③ 3500 series

88199C01

Troubleshooting the Brake System

Problem	Cause	Solution
Low brake pedal (excessive pedal travel required for braking action.)	· Excessive clearance between rear linings and drums caused by inoperative automatic adjusters	· Make 10 to 15 alternate forward and reverse brake stops to adjust brakes. If brake pedal does not come up, repair or replace adjuster parts as necessary.
	· Worn rear brakelining	· Inspect and replace lining if worn beyond minimum thickness specification
	· Bent, distorted brakeshoes, front or rear	· Replace brakeshoes in axle sets
	· Air in hydraulic system	· Remove air from system. Refer to Brake Bleeding.
Low brake pedal (pedal may go to floor with steady pressure applied.)	· Fluid leak in hydraulic system	· Fill master cylinder to fill line; have helper apply brakes and check calipers, wheel cylinders, differential valve tubes, hoses and fittings for leaks. Repair or replace as necessary.
	· Air in hydraulic system	· Remove air from system. Refer to Brake Bleeding.
	· Incorrect or non-recommended brake fluid (fluid evaporates at below normal temp).	· Flush hydraulic system with clean brake fluid. Refill with correct-type fluid.
	· Master cylinder piston seals worn, or master cylinder bore is scored, worn or corroded	· Repair or replace master cylinder
Low brake pedal (pedal goes to floor on first application—o.k. on subsequent applications.)	· Disc brake pads sticking on abutment surfaces of anchor plate. Caused by a build-up of dirt, rust, or corrosion on abutment surfaces	· Clean abutment surfaces
Fading brake pedal (pedal height decreases with steady pressure applied.)	· Fluid leak in hydraulic system	· Fill master cylinder reservoirs to fill mark, have helper apply brakes, check calipers, wheel cylinders, differential valve, tubes, hoses, and fittings for fluid leaks. Repair or replace parts as necessary.
	· Master cylinder piston seals worn, or master cylinder bore is scored, worn or corroded	· Repair or replace master cylinder
Decreasing brake pedal travel (pedal travel required for braking action decreases and may be accompanied by a hard pedal.)	· Caliper or wheel cylinder pistons sticking or seized	· Repair or replace the calipers, or wheel cylinders
	· Master cylinder compensator ports blocked (preventing fluid return to reservoirs) or pistons sticking or seized in master cylinder bore	· Repair or replace the master cylinder
	· Power brake unit binding internally	· Test unit according to the following procedure: (a) Shift transmission into neutral and start engine (b) Increase engine speed to 1500 rpm, close throttle and fully depress brake pedal (c) Slow release brake pedal and stop engine (d) Have helper remove vacuum check valve and hose from power unit. Observe for backward movement of brake pedal. (e) If the pedal moves backward, the power unit has an internal bind—replace power unit

TCCA9C01

Troubleshooting the Brake System (cont.)

Problem	Cause	Solution
Spongy brake pedal (pedal has abnormally soft, springy, spongy feel when depressed.)	• Air in hydraulic system	• Remove air from system. Refer to Brake Bleeding.
	• Brakeshoes bent or distorted	• Replace brakeshoes
	• Brakelining not yet seated with drums and rotors	• Burnish brakes
	• Rear drum brakes not properly adjusted	• Adjust brakes
Hard brake pedal (excessive pedal pressure required to stop vehicle. May be accompanied by brake fade.)	• Loose or leaking power brake unit vacuum hose	• Tighten connections or replace leaking hose
	• Incorrect or poor quality brakelining	• Replace with lining in axle sets
	• Bent, broken, distorted brakeshoes	• Replace brakeshoes
	• Calipers binding or dragging on mounting pins. Rear brakeshoes dragging on support plate.	• Replace mounting pins and bushings. Clean rust or burrs from rear brake support plate ledges and lubricate ledges with molydisulfide grease. **NOTE:** If ledges are deeply grooved or scored, do not attempt to sand or grind them smooth—replace support plate.
	• Caliper, wheel cylinder, or master cylinder pistons sticking or seized	• Repair or replace parts as necessary
	• Power brake unit vacuum check valve malfunction	• Test valve according to the following procedure: (a) Start engine, increase engine speed to 1500 rpm, close throttle and immediately stop engine (b) Wait at least 90 seconds then depress brake pedal (c) If brakes are not vacuum assisted for 2 or more applications, check valve is faulty
	• Power brake unit has internal bind	• Test unit according to the following procedure: (a) With engine stopped, apply brakes several times to exhaust all vacuum in system (b) Shift transmission into neutral, depress brake pedal and start engine (c) If pedal height decreases with foot pressure and less pressure is required to hold pedal in applied position, power unit vacuum system is operating normally. Test power unit. If power unit exhibits a bind condition, replace the power unit.
	• Master cylinder compensator ports (at bottom of reservoirs) blocked by dirt, scale, rust, or have small burrs (blocked ports prevent fluid return to reservoirs).	• Repair or replace master cylinder **CAUTION:** Do not attempt to clean blocked ports with wire, pencils, or similar implements. Use compressed air only.
	• Brake hoses, tubes, fittings clogged or restricted	• Use compressed air to check or unclog parts. Replace any damaged parts.
	• Brake fluid contaminated with improper fluids (motor oil, transmission fluid, causing rubber components to swell and stick in bores	• Replace all rubber components, combination valve and hoses. Flush entire brake system with DOT 3 brake fluid or equivalent.
	• Low engine vacuum	• Adjust or repair engine

Troubleshooting the Brake System (cont.)

Problem	Cause	Solution
Grabbing brakes (severe reaction to brake pedal pressure.)	• Brakelining(s) contaminated by grease or brake fluid	• Determine and correct cause of contamination and replace brakeshoes in axle sets
	• Parking brake cables incorrectly adjusted or seized	• Adjust cables. Replace seized cables.
	• Incorrect brakelining or lining loose on brakeshoes	• Replace brakeshoes in axle sets
	• Caliper anchor plate bolts loose	• Tighten bolts
	• Rear brakeshoes binding on support plate ledges	• Clean and lubricate ledges. Replace support plate(s) if ledges are deeply grooved. Do not attempt to smooth ledges by grinding.
	• Incorrect or missing power brake reaction disc	• Install correct disc
	• Rear brake support plates loose	• Tighten mounting bolts
Dragging brakes (slow or incomplete release of brakes)	• Brake pedal binding at pivot	• Loosen and lubricate
	• Power brake unit has internal bind	• Inspect for internal bind. Replace unit if internal bind exists.
	• Parking brake cables incorrrectly adjusted or seized	• Adjust cables. Replace seized cables.
	• Rear brakeshoe return springs weak or broken	• Replace return springs. Replace brakeshoe if necessary in axle sets.
	• Automatic adjusters malfunctioning	• Repair or replace adjuster parts as required
	• Caliper, wheel cylinder or master cylinder pistons sticking or seized	• Repair or replace parts as necessary
	• Master cylinder compensating ports blocked (fluid does not return to reservoirs).	• Use compressed air to clear ports. Do not use wire, pencils, or similar objects to open blocked ports.
Vehicle moves to one side when brakes are applied	• Incorrect front tire pressure	• Inflate to recommended cold (reduced load) inflation pressure
	• Worn or damaged wheel bearings	• Replace worn or damaged bearings
	• Brakelining on one side contaminated	• Determine and correct cause of contamination and replace brakelining in axle sets
	• Brakeshoes on one side bent, distorted, or lining loose on shoe	• Replace brakeshoes in axle sets
	• Support plate bent or loose on one side	• Tighten or replace support plate
	• Brakelining not yet seated with drums or rotors	• Burnish brakelining
	• Caliper anchor plate loose on one side	• Tighten anchor plate bolts
	• Caliper piston sticking or seized	• Repair or replace caliper
	• Brakelinings water soaked	• Drive vehicle with brakes lightly applied to dry linings
	• Loose suspension component attaching or mounting bolts	• Tighten suspension bolts. Replace worn suspension components.
	• Brake combination valve failure	• Replace combination valve
Chatter or shudder when brakes are applied (pedal pulsation and roughness may also occur.)	• Brakeshoes distorted, bent, contaminated, or worn	• Replace brakeshoes in axle sets
	• Caliper anchor plate or support plate loose	• Tighten mounting bolts
	• Excessive thickness variation of rotor(s)	• Refinish or replace rotors in axle sets

TCCA9C03

10

BODY & TRIM

EXTERIOR

Front Doors

REMOVAL & INSTALLATION

1987–95 Models

▶ **See Figure 1**

1. Remove the door trim panel and disconnect the electrical wiring harness from the door (if equipped).
2. Remove the kick panel (if equipped).
3. Remove the hinge bolt cover plate. Mark the position of the hinges on the door and the door pillar.
4. Support the door and remove the door frame to hinge bolts.
5. Remove the door from the vehicle.
6. Remove the hinge to door bolts and remove the hinges from the door.

To install:

7. Install the door and line up the hinge with the marks made during removal.
8. Install the hinge-to-frame bolts and tighten them to 25 ft. lbs. (33 Nm).
9. Install the hinge bolt cover plate.
10. Install the kick panel and engage the electrical wiring harness (if equipped).
11. Install the door trim panel.

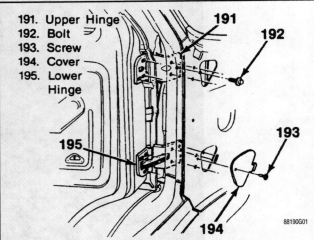

191. Upper Hinge
192. Bolt
193. Screw
194. Cover
195. Lower Hinge

Fig. 1 Exploded view of the door hinge components—1987–95 models

1996–97 Models

▶ **See Figure 2**

1. Disconnect the negative battery cable.
2. Remove the hinge pillar trim, then tag and disengage the wiring connectors for the door in the pillar.
3. Remove the rubber conduit by pushing it out from the door pillar and disengage the wiring harness from the pillar.
4. Remove the check link from the pillar.
5. Mark the position of the hinges on the door and the door pillar.
6. Remove the lower hinge pin retainer.
7. Use a soft faced mallet and a pair of locking pliers to grasp the pin and drive it from the hinge.

➡ **Install a bolt through the lower hinge temporally to hold the door in place until the top hinge is disconnected.**

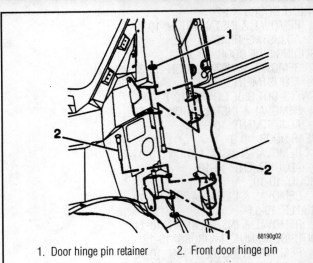

1. Door hinge pin retainer   2. Front door hinge pin

Fig. 2 Installing the door hinge pin—1996–97 models

8. Remove the upper hinge pin retainer and the upper hinge pin in the same manner as the lower pin.
9. Remove the bolt inserted to temporarily hold the bottom hinge, then remove the door.

To install:

10. Install the door and line up the hinge with the marks made during removal.
11. Install the bolt through the lower hinge temporally to hold the door in place until the top hinge is secured.
12. Install the upper hinge pin with the pointed end up and a new pin retainer.
13. Remove the bolt inserted to temporarily hold the bottom hinge.
14. Install the lower pin with the pointed end down and a new pin retainer.
15. Install the check link, wiring harness and rubber conduit to the pillar.
16. Engage the door electrical connections.
17. Lubricate the hinge pins with clean engine oil.
18. Install the hinge pillar trim and connect the negative battery cable.

ADJUSTMENT

1987–95 Models

▶ **See Figure 3**

There is no adjustment for the 1996–97 models.

➡ **Special tool J-29843-9 door striker wrench, or its equivalent is required to perform this procedure.**

1. Remove the lock striker protector screw.
2. Remove the lock striker protector.
3. Remove the spring.
4. Remove the door striker using Tool J-29843-9 or its equivalent.
5. Remove the spacer.
6. Remove the kick panel (if equipped).
7. Remove the hinge bolt cover screw.
8. Remove the hinge bolt cover.
9. Loosen the door hinge bolts as needed to adjust the door. Adjust the door up or down, forward or rearward, and in or out at the door hinges.
10. Adjust the door to obtain a gap of 0.16–0.20 in. (4–4.61mm) between the front door and the roof panel. door striker wrench
   The gap between the rocker panel and the front door at its base should be 0.23–0.25 in. (5.84mm–6.61mm).
11. Adjust the door to obtain a gap of 0.16 –0.20 in. (4–4.61mm) between the doors rear edge and the rear door pillar.

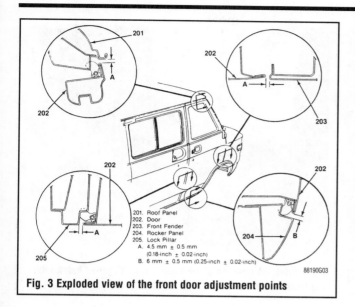

Fig. 3 Exploded view of the front door adjustment points

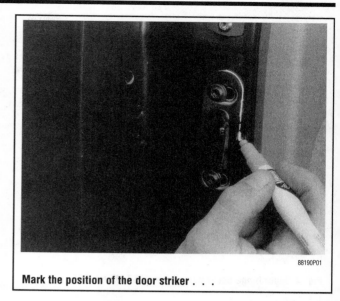

Mark the position of the door striker . . .

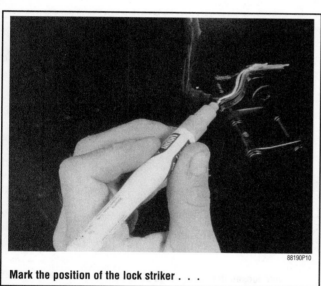

Mark the position of the lock striker . . .

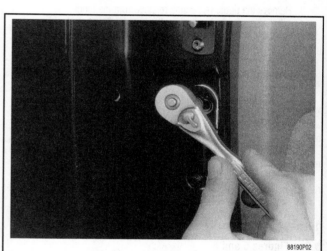

. . . then loosen the retainers and adjust the striker to the desired position

The gap between the door's front edge and the rear edge of the fender should be 0.16–0.20 in. (4–4.61mm).

To install:

12. Tighten the door hinge bolts that were loosened.
13. Install the hinge-to-frame bolts and tighten them to 25 ft. lbs. (33 Nm).
14. Install the hinge bolt cover plate.
15. Install the kick panel and engage the electrical wiring harness (if equipped).
16. Install the spacer to the door striker using tool J-29843-9 door striker wrench or its equivalent . Tighten the retainers to 45 ft. lbs. (62 Nm).
17. Install the spring, lock striker protector and pin.

Sliding Side Door

REMOVAL & INSTALLATION

1987–95 Models

▶ See Figure 4

1. Remove the upper track cover and the hinge cover.
2. Open the door completely. Mark the position of the roller assembly on the door and remove the upper front roller assembly.

. . . and loosen the retainers, then adjust the door to its desired position before tightening the retainers

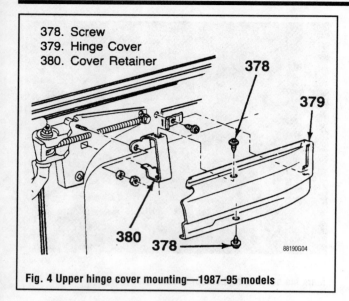

378. Screw
379. Hinge Cover
380. Cover Retainer

Fig. 4 Upper hinge cover mounting—1987–95 models

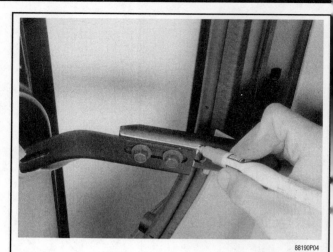

Matchmark the position of the hinge; this will prove helpful during installation . . .

3. Remove the upper rear hinge retainer from the hinge.
4. Lift the upper rear hinge off of the track and remove the hinge.
5. Pivot the door away from the vehicle to disengage the rollers and lower the front roller from the track.
6. Disengage the wiring harness (if equipped).
7. Remove the door from the vehicle.

To install:
8. Engage the wiring harness (if equipped).
9. Insert the lower front roller in the track.
10. Pivot the door away from the vehicle to engage the rollers to the track, then pivot the door towards the vehicle.
11. Insest the upper rear hinge to the upper rear track and lift the hinge roller onto the track.
12. Install the upper rear hinge retainer to the hinge and the upper front roller assembly to the door. Align the roller assembly to the mark made earlier
13. Install the upper rear track cover and the hinge cover.

1996–97 Models

▶ **See Figures 5 and 6**

1. Open and support the door, then remove the interior quarter trim panel.
2. Unfasten the center track bumper nut and washer, then remove the bumper.

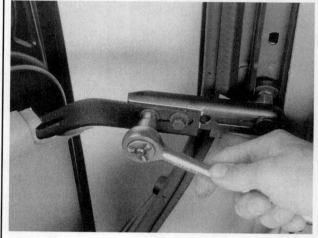

. . . then loosen the upper hinge bolts

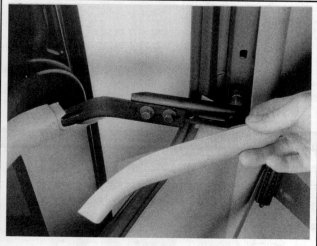

Remove the sliding side door upper roller high trim piece

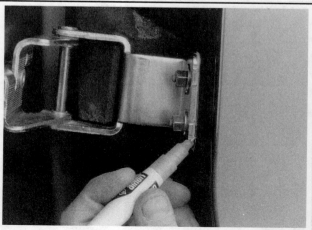

To ease installation, matchmark the position of the center track hinge

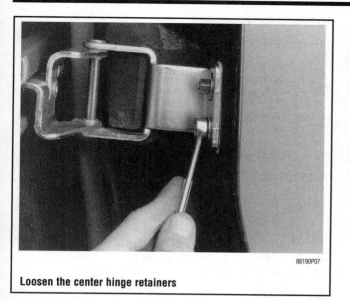

Loosen the center hinge retainers

88190P07

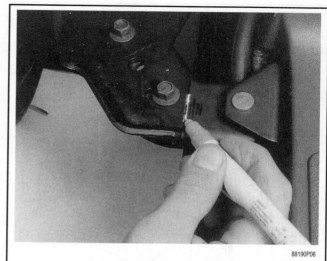

Matchmark the hinge position on the lower hinge . . .

88190P08

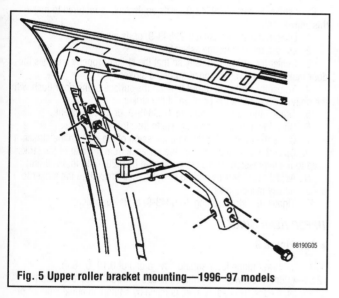

Fig. 5 Upper roller bracket mounting—1996–97 models

88190G05

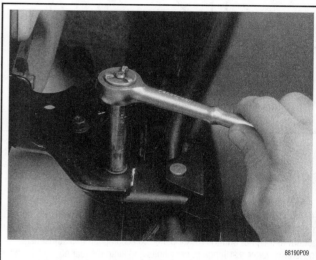

. . . then remove the hinge retainers

88190P09

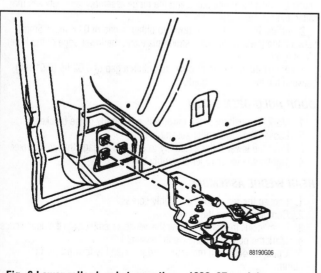

Fig. 6 Lower roller bracket mounting—1996–97 models

88190G06

3. Loosen the center track cap nut and plate, then remove the cap.

4. Remopve the upper and lower roller bolts.

5. With the aid of an assistant, slide the door out the rear of the center track.

To install:

6. With the aid of an assistant, slide the door in the rear of the center track.

7. Install the upper and lower roller bolts, then tighten them to 18 ft. lbs. (25 Nm).

8. Install the cap, center track cap nut and plate.

9. Install the bumper, center track bumper nut and washer.

10. Install the interior quarter trim panel.

ADJUSTMENTS

1987–95 Models

UP-AND-DOWN

▶ See Figure 7

➡Door striker wrench J-29843-9, or its equivalent, is required to perform this procedure.

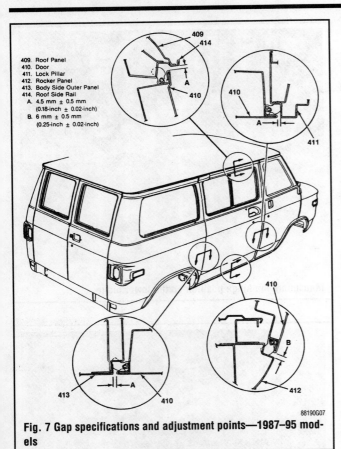

409. Roof Panel
410. Door
411. Lock Pillar
412. Rocker Panel
413. Body Side Outer Panel
414. Roof Side Rail
A. 4.5 mm ± 0.5 mm
   (0.18-inch ± 0.02-inch)
B. 6 mm ± 0.5 mm
   (0.25-inch ± 0.02-inch)

88190G07

Fig. 7 Gap specifications and adjustment points—1987–95 models

1. Remove the upper rear hinge cover.
2. Remove the front lock striker.
3. Remove the rear lock striker using tool J-29843-9, or its equivalent.
4. Remove the rear door wedge assembly.
5. Adjust the rear edge of the door to obtain a gap of 0.16–20 in. (4–4.61mm) between the top of the door and the roof side rail. This adjustment should provide a gap of 0.23–0.25 in. (5.84mm–6.61mm) between the bottom of the door and the rocker panel. To accomplish this adjustment, loosen the upper rear hinge to door bolts and align the rear edge of the door up and down. Next, tighten the upper rear hinge to door bolts.

Adjust the front edge of the door by loosening the upper front roller bracket to door bolts and the lower hinge to door bolts. Align the door to obtain the same gap as in step 5, then tighten the lower hinge to door bolts.

Adjust the upper front roller bracket up and down so that the roller is centered in the track. The roller must not touch the top or bottom of the track. Tighten the upper front roller bracket to door bolts.

Install the door wedge assembly and the front and rear lock strikers.
6. Install the upper hinge cover.

IN-AND-OUT

1. Remove the front lock striker.
2. Loosen the nut retaining the upper front roller to the upper roller bracket.
3. Loosen the lower front roller assembly to roller assembly bracket bolts.
4. Loosen the rear door lock striker.
5. Adjust the door in or out until the surface of the door is flush with the surface of the body.
6. Tighten the rear door lock striker.
7. Tighten the lower front roller assembly to roller assembly bracket bolts.
8. Tighten the nut retaining the upper front roller to the upper roller bracket.
9. Install the front lock striker.

FORWARD-AND-REARWARD

1. Mark the position of the front and rear latch strikers on the body pillars.
2. Remove the front and rear lock strikers.
3. Remove the upper front track cover.
4. Loosen the upper rear hinge striker.
5. Adjust the door forward or rearward to obtain a gap of 0.16–20 in. (4–4.61mm) between the left and right door edge and the door pillars
Tighten the upper rear hinge striker.
Install the upper front track cover.
Install the front and rear lock strikers at the position previously marked.

FRONT STRIKER

1. Loosen the front latch striker bolts.
2. Slide the door toward the striker.
3. The guide on the door must fit snugly into the rubber lined opening in the striker assembly.
4. Check that the latch fully engages the striker. Add or delete shims behind the striker to accomplish this adjustment.
5. Tighten the striker bolts.

REAR STRIKER

Door striker wrench J-29843-9, or its equivalent, is required to make this adjustment.
1. Loosen the striker using J-29843-9, or its equivalent.
2. Loosen the rear wedge assembly.
3. Center the striker vertically so that the striker properly engages the door lock. Mark the vertical position of the striker.
4. Adjust the striker in or out to align the surface of the door flush with the body surface. Mark the position of the striker.
5. Tighten the striker using tool J-29843-9, or its equivalent.
6. Open the door and apply grease to the striker.
7. Close the door and make an impression of the lock on the striker.
8. Open the door and measure the distance from the rear of the striker head to the impression. The distance should be 0.20–0.30 in. (5–8mm).
9. Adjust the striker by adding or deleting shims. Align the striker to the previously made marks.
10. Tighten the striker using J-29843-9, or its equivalent.

UPPER REAR HINGE

▶ See Figure 8

1. The lower hinge lever should have a gap of 0.10–0.16 in. (2.54–4.06mm) between the outer edge of the lower hinge lever and the striker latch edge. This adjustment is made by adding an equal amount of shims between the guide block and the hinge assembly, and between the roller and the hinge assembly.
2. Adjust the striker up or down to obtain a gap of 0.06 in. (1.5mm) between the lower edge of the striker plate and the lower edge of the lower hinge lever.
3. Adjust the guide up or down to obtain a gap of 0.02 in. (0.51mm) between the track and the guide.

DOOR HOLD-OPEN CATCH

1. Mark the position of the lower roller assembly to the bracket.
2. Loosen the lower roller assembly bolts.
3. Pivot the lower roller assembly to properly engage the latch striker.
4. Tighten the lower roller assembly bolts.

REAR WEDGE ASSEMBLY

1. Loosen the rear wedge assembly screws.
2. Completely close the door.
3. From inside the vehicle, center the wedge assembly onto the door wedge.
4. Mark the position of the wedge assembly.
5. Open the door, and move the wedge assembly forward ³⁄₁₆ in. (4.76mm).
6. Tighten the rear wedge assembly screws.

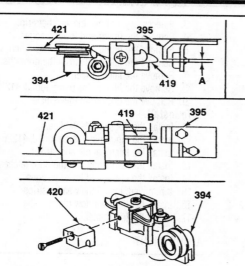
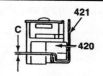

A. 2.5 mm to 4 mm (0.10-inch to 0.16-inch)
B. 1.5 mm (0.06-inch)
C. 0.5 mm (0.02-inch)
394. Hinge Assembly
395. Striker
419. Lower Hinge Lever
420. Guide Block
421. Track

88190G08

Fig. 8 Adjustment points and gap specifications on the upper rear hinge—1987–97 models

1996–97 Models

UP-AND-DOWN

1. Remove the upper and lower trim.
2. Loosen the bolts retaining the upper and lower front roller to the door and the nuts retaining the lower front roller to the door.
3. Adjust the door up and down until the desired position is achieved.
4. Tighten the nuts retaining the rear roller to the door to 18 ft. lbs. (25 Nm).
5. Tighten the bolts retaining the upper and lower front roller to the door to 18 ft. lbs. (25 Nm).
6. Install the upper and lower trim.

IN-AND-OUT

1. Remove the upper and lower trim.
2. Loosen the bolts retaining the upper and lower front roller to the bracket.
3. Loosen the nuts retaining the rear roller to the bracket.
4. Adjust the door in and out until the desired position is achieved.
5. Tighten the nuts retaining the rear roller to the bracket to 18 ft. lbs. (25 Nm).
6. Tighten the bolts retaining the upper and lower front roller to the bracket to 18 ft. lbs. (25 Nm).
7. Install the upper and lower trim.

Swing-Out Side Doors

REMOVAL & INSTALLATION

1987–95 Models

▶ **See Figure 9**

1. Open the door, remove the door trim panel and disconnect the electrical wiring harness (if equipped). Then mark the position of the door on the hinges using a wax pencil.
2. Remove the hinge hole plugs on the body side pillar.
3. Remove the strap pin from the bracket, then remove the snapring from the pin, and pull the pin.
4. Support the door safely, and remove the hinge to body pillar bolts.
5. Remove the door from the vehicle.
To install:
6. Install the door and door hinge-to-pillar bolts (finger-tight only).
7. Align the hinges with the marks made during removal. Tighten the bolts to 30 ft. lbs. (43 Nm).

1. POWER LOCK MOTOR
2. POWER LOCK MOTOR CONNECTOR
3. POWER LOCK HARNESS CONNECTOR

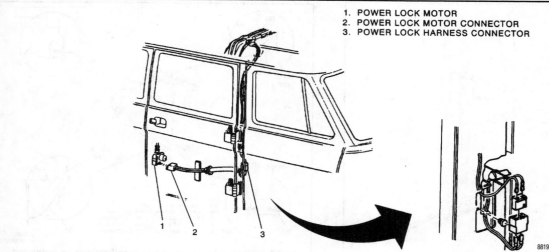
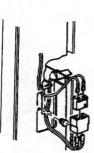

88190G09

Fig. 9 Side door wiring harness components—1987–97 models

8. Install the strap pin in the bracket and then the snap-ring to the pin.

9. Install the hinge hole caps.

10. Engage the electrical connections (if equipped).

11. Install door trim panel.

1996–97 Models

SIDE FRONT DOOR

▶ See Figure 10

Tool J-41226-50 hinge pin kit or its equivalent is required for this procedure.

1. Remove the door trim panel and the swing out window.

2. Remove the inside and outside handles.

3. If necessary, remove the weatherstrip.

4. Remove the upper and lower wedges.

5. Remove the lock rod retainers by rotating it 90 degrees and pulling it out.

6. Remove the door latch, then tag and disengage the electrical connections.

7. Remove the door check strap by unfastening the bolts retaining.

8. Remove the check strap seal using a 3M® release agent or its equivalent, then clean all the old adhesive residue.

9. Remove the hinge pins using tool J-41226-50, or its equivalent.

10. Remove the door from the vehicle.

To install:

11. Install the door on the vehicle.

12. Install the hinge pins using tool J-41226-50 or its equivalent.

13. Install the check strap seal and the check strap. Hook the strap in the door and pull to engage it, then tighten the bolts to 89 inch lbs. (10 Nm).

14. Engage all electrical connections and install the door latch.

15. Install the lock rod retainers by inserting them into the door and rotating them 90 degrees.

16. Install the upper and lower wedges.

17. Install the weatherstrips.

18. Install the inside and outside door handles.

19. Install the door glass and the trim panel.

SIDE REAR DOOR

Tool J-41226-50 hinge pin kit or its equivalent is required for this procedure.

1. Remove the door trim panel and the swing out window.

2. Remove the door glass.

3. If necessary, remove the weatherstrip.

4. Remove the upper and lower wedges.

5. Remove the upper and lower door latches.

6. Remove the latch rods from the door, then remove the latch handle.

7. Remove the latch striker.

8. Remove the hinge pins using tool J-41226-50, or its equivalent.

9. Remove the door from the vehicle.

To install:

10. Install the door on the vehicle.

11. Install the hinge pins using tool J-41226-50 or its equivalent.

12. Install the latch handle and striker.

13. Install the latch rods and the door latches.

14. Install the upper and lower wedges.

15. If removed, install the weatherstrips.

16. Install the door window glass.

17. Install the trim panel.

ADJUSTMENT

1987–95 Models

▶ See Figure 11

Door striker wrench J-29843-9, or its equivalent, is required to make this adjustment.

1. Remove the door lock striker from the rear intermediate door using J-29843-9, or its equivalent.

2. Remove the upper and lower rear intermediate door strikers.

3. Loosen the hinge bolts as necessary to adjust the doors.

4. Each of the two doors must first be adjusted in the door opening before adjusting the door to door clearance.

5. Adjust the door up and down, forward and rearward, and in and out, at the door hinges.

6. Adjust the door height so that there is a gap of 0.16–20 in. (4–4.5mm) between the door and the roof panel.

Adjust the gap between the door and the rocker panel to 0.23–24 in. (5.59mm–6.61mm).

7. Adjust the gap between the doors and the body at the hinge pillars to 0.16–15.98 in. (3.59–4.61mm).

8. Adjust the gap between the front and rear intermediate doors to 0.23–24 in. (5.59mm–6.61mm).

9. Tighten the hinge bolts that were loosened.

10. Install the upper and lower rear intermediate door strikers to the body.

11. Install the door lock striker to the rear intermediate door using J-29843-9, or its equivalent.

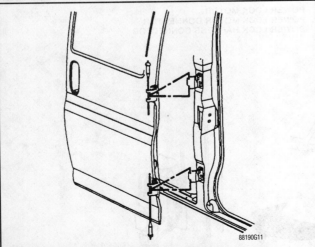

Fig. 10 The hinge pins must be removed when removing the side doors—1996–97 models

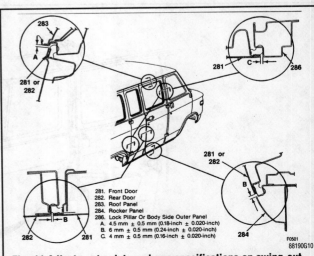

281. Front Door
282. Rear Door
283. Roof Panel
284. Rocker Panel
286. Lock Pillar Or Body Side Outer Panel
A. 4.5 mm ± 0.5 mm (0.18-inch ± 0.020-inch)
B. 6 mm ± 0.5 mm (0.24-inch ± 0.020-inch)
C. 4 mm ± 0.5 mm (0.16-inch ± 0.020-inch)

Fig. 11 Adjustment points and gap specifications on swing-out side door—1987–95 models

12. Adjust the upper and lower intermediate door striker to door clearance so that there is 0.172 in. (4.37mm) between the striker and the door latch when the door is in the secondary latch position. (The door is latched but not fully closed.) An $^{11}/_{64}$ in. diameter drill bit may be used to gauge this clearance.

13. Adjust the front intermediate striker on the rear door so that the front door lock properly engages the rear door, and so that the front door is flush with the rear door.

Rear Door

REMOVAL & INSTALLATION

1987–95 Models

▶ **See Figure 12**

1. Open the door, remove the door trim panel and disconnect the electrical wiring harness (if equipped). Then mark the position of the door on the hinges using a wax pencil.
2. Remove the hinge hole plugs on the body side pillar.
3. Remove the strap pin from the bracket, then remove the snapring from the pin, and pull the pin.
4. Support the door safely, and remove the hinge to body pillar bolts.
5. Remove the door from the vehicle.

To install:

6. Install the door on the vehicle.
7. Align the hinges to the marks made during removal, then install the bolts.
8. Install the door pin, snap-ring and strap pin.
9. Engage the electrical connections and install the trim panel.

1996–97 Models

LEFT SIDE

▶ **See Figure 13**

1. Remove the trim panel.
2. Remove the door extension as follows:
    a. Unfasten the extension retaining bolts.
    b. Close the door partially and pull the extension rearward from the door.
3. Remove the door latches and latch handle.
4. Tag and disengage the electrical connections from the door.
5. Remove the door glass.
6. Remove the weatherstrips.

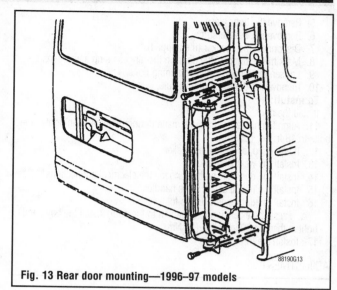

Fig. 13 Rear door mounting—1996–97 models

7. Disconnect the speaker (if equipped).
8. Mark the position of the door on the hinges using a wax pencil.
9. Loosen the hinge-to-body retaining bolts.
10. Remove the door from the vehicle.

To install:

11. Position the door. Align the hinges with marks made during removal, then tighten the bolts to 18 ft. lbs. (25 Nm).
12. If equipped, connect the speaker.
13. Install the weatherstrips.
14. Instaal the door glass, then engage the electrical connections.
15. Install the latch handle and latches.
16. Install the door extension as follows:
    a. Press the extension to engage it to the door, install the bolts and tighten them to 89 inch lbs. (10 Nm).
17. Install the trim panel.

RIGHT SIDE

1. Remove the trim panel.
2. Remove the door extension as follows:
    a. Unfasten the extension retaining bolts.
    b. Close the door partially and pull the extension rearward from the door.
3. Remove the inside and outside door handle.
4. Tag and disengage the electrical connections from the door.

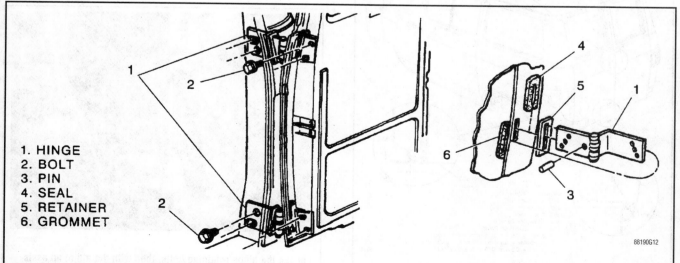

1. HINGE
2. BOLT
3. PIN
4. SEAL
5. RETAINER
6. GROMMET

Fig. 12 Rear door mounting—1987–95 models

5. Remove the door glass.
6. Remove the weatherstrips.
7. Disconnect the speaker (if equipped).
8. Mark the position of the door on the hinges using a wax pencil.
9. Loosen the hinge-to-body retaining bolts.
10. Remove the door from the vehicle.

To install:
Install the door.
11. Align the hinges with marks made during removal, then tighten the bolts to 18 ft. lbs. (25 Nm).
12. If equipped, connect the speaker.
13. Install the weatherstrips.
14. Install the door glass, then engage the electrical connections.
15. Install the inside and outside handles.
16. Install the door extension as follows:
  a. Press the extension to engage it to the door, install the bolts and tighten them to 89 inch lbs. (10 Nm).
17. Install the trim panel.

ADJUSTMENT

1987–95 Models

▶ **See Figure 14**

There is no adjustment for the 1996–97 models.

➡**Each of the two doors must first be adjusted in the door opening before adjusting the door-to-door clearance.**

1. Adjust the door height so that there is a gap of 0.23–0.27 in. (5.84mm–6.86mm) between the roof panel and the rear door panel.
Adjust the gap between the bottom of the door panel (not the bottom of the outer panel) and the platform panel should be 0.23–0.27 in.

(5.84mm–6.86mm). This measurement should be taken on each door individually from the side of the door. The door should be in its normal closed position. The outer rear door panel is 0.58–62 in. (14.75–15.75mm) away from the rear platform panel when normally closed.
Adjust the rear door outer panel to the body side outer panel gap to 0.14–18 in. (3.59–4.61mm).
2. The door to door clearance between the left and right outer door panels should be 0.23–0.27 in. (5.84mm–6.86mm).

Hood

REMOVAL & INSTALLATION

1987–95 Models

▶ **See Figure 15**

1. Open the hood.
2. Mark the area around the hinges to make installation easier.
3. Support the hood and remove the hinge to hood frame bolts.
4. With the aid of and assistant, remove the hood from the van.

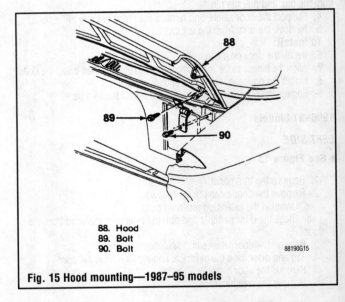

88. Hood
89. Bolt
90. Bolt

88190G15

Fig. 15 Hood mounting—1987–95 models

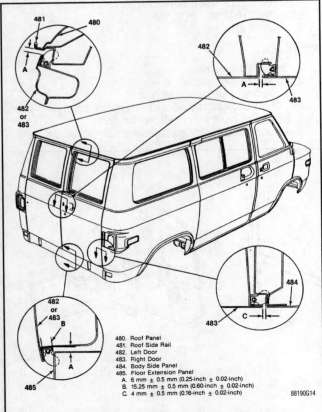

480. Roof Panel
481. Roof Side Rail
482. Left Door
483. Right Door
484. Body Side Panel
485. Floor Extension Panel
  A. 6 mm ± 0.5 mm (0.25-inch ± 0.02-inch)
  B. 15.25 mm ± 0.5 mm (0.60-inch ± 0.02-inch)
  C. 4 mm ± 0.5 mm (0.16-inch ± 0.02-inch)

88190G14

Fig. 14 Adjustment and gap specifications—1987–95 models

88190P12

Loosen the hinge retaining bolts, then with the aid of an assistant, remove the hood

To install:

5. With aid of an assistant, install the hood and align the hinges with the marks made during removal.

6. Install the hood-to-hinge bolts and tighten them to 13 ft. lbs. (17 Nm).

7. Adjust the hood bumpers until a gap of ¾ in. (19mm) is achieved between the hood and the top of the radiator grille.

1996–97 Models

▶ **See Figures 16 and 17**

1. Remove the wiper arms, then open and support the hood.
2. Disconnect the underhood lamp and harness.
3. Unfasten the air inlet grille panel screws and remove the grille.
4. Mark the area around the hinges to make installation easier.
5. With the help of an assistant, remove the hood.

To install:

6. With aid of an assistant, install the hood on the vehicle.
7. Align the hinges with the marks made during removal.
8. Install the hood bolts an d tighten them to 18 ft. lbs. (25 Nm),
9. Connect the underhood lamp and harness.
10. Install the air inlet grille panel and tighten the screws.
11. Install the wiper arms.

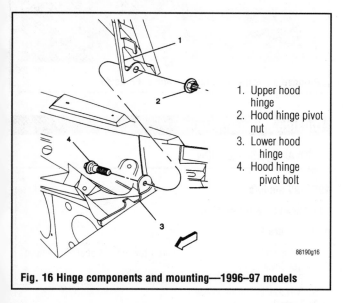

1. Upper hood hinge
2. Hood hinge pivot nut
3. Lower hood hinge
4. Hood hinge pivot bolt

88190g16

Fig. 16 Hinge components and mounting—1996–97 models

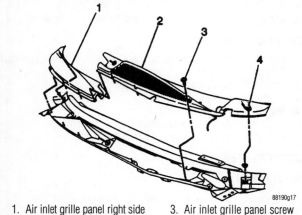

1. Air inlet grille panel right side
2. Air inlet grille panel left side
3. Air inlet grille panel screw
4. Air inlet grille panel retainer

88190g17

Fig. 17 The wiper arms and air inlet grille must be removed to facilitate hood removal—1996–97 models

Grille

REMOVAL & INSTALLATION

1987–95 Models

▶ **See Figure 18**

1. Raise and support the hood.
2. Disconnect the negative battery cable.
3. Remove the headlamp bezels.
4. Remove the sheet metal cross panel-to-grille retainers.
5. Remove the grille-to-lower front end panel retainers.
6. Lift the grille from the van.

To install:

7. Install the grille on the vehicle.

8. Install the grille-to-lower front end panel retainers and tighten them to 12 inch lbs. (1.4 Nm).

9. Install the sheet metal cross panel-to-grille retainers and tighten them to 12 inch lbs. (1.4 Nm).

10. Install the headlamp bezels, connect the negative battery cable and close the hood.

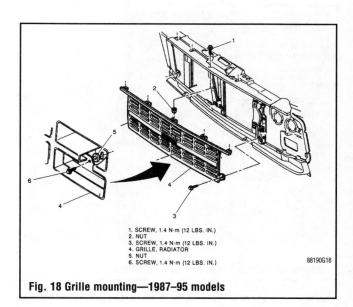

1. SCREW, 1.4 N·m (12 LBS. IN.)
2. NUT
3. SCREW, 1.4 N·m (12 LBS. IN.)
4. GRILLE, RADIATOR
5. NUT
6. SCREW, 1.4 N·m (12 LBS. IN.)

88190G18

Fig. 18 Grille mounting—1987–95 models

1996–97 Models

▶ **See Figure 19**

1. Raise and support the hood.
2. Disconnect the negative battery cable.
3. Disconnect the side marker lamp.
4. Loosen the grille-to-radiator support retainers.

5. Loosen the retainers at the top of the grille from the radiator support.

6. Lift the grille to disengage the locating pins on the bottom of the grille-to-radiator support

7. Remove the grille from the van.

To install:

8. Install the grille and align the locking pins and lower them into position, then push to engage them.

9. Tighten all the grille retainers to 18 inch lbs. (2 Nm).

10. Connect the side marker lamp and the negative battery cable.

11. Close the hood.

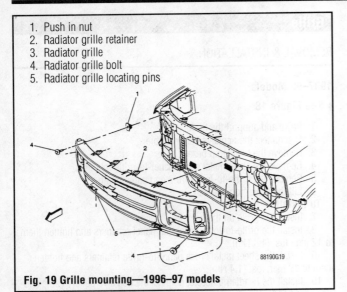

1. Push in nut
2. Radiator grille retainer
3. Radiator grille
4. Radiator grille bolt
5. Radiator grille locating pins

88190G19

Fig. 19 Grille mounting—1996–97 models

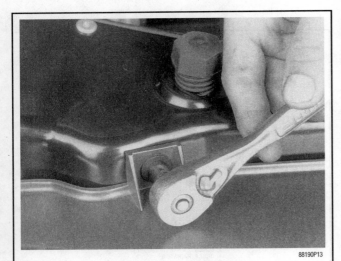

88190P13

Remove the grille's upper and lower retainers

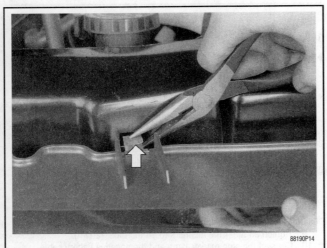

88190P14

It may be necessary to use a pair of pliers to slightly AND GENTLY depress the clips in order to disengage them

88190P15

Remove the grille from the van and set it aside

Outside Manual Mirrors

REMOVAL & INSTALLATION

1987–95 Models

BELOW EYE LEVEL MIRROR

♦ See Figure 20

1. Lift the mirror cover, pivot the mirror towards the door and remove the mirror cover screw.
2. Remove the mirror-to-door retainers.
3. Remove the mirror and seal.
To install:
4. Position the mirror and seal.
5. Install the mirror-to-door retainers and the mirror cover screw.

WEST COAST MIRRORS

1. Remove the mirror bracket-to-door bracket nuts, bolts and bushings.
2. Remove the mirror bracket from the door.
3. Remove the door bracket nuts and bolts.
4. Remove the brackets from the door.
To install:
5. Install the door bracket, then fasten the nuts and bolts
6. Install the mirror bracket, nuts, bolts and bushings.

CAMPER MODELS

♦ See Figure 21

1. Loosen the set screw, then remove the bolt and washers.
2. Remove the mirror head.
3. Loosen the arm bolts and remove the bolts.
4. Loosen the brace bolts and the brace.
To install:
5. Install the brace and the bolts finger tighten only.

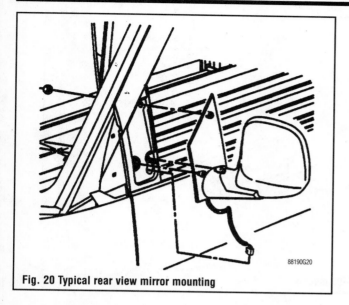

Fig. 20 Typical rear view mirror mounting

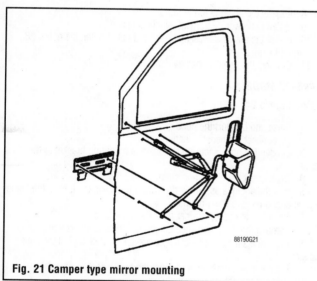

Fig. 21 Camper type mirror mounting

6. Install the arm and the bolts, then tighten the brace and arm bolts to 32 inch lbs. (4 Nm).

7. Install the mirror head, washer and bolt, then tighten the bolt to 27 ft. lbs. (37 Nm).

8. Install the set screw and tighten it to 15 inch lbs. (2 Nm).

COMMERCIAL MODELS

▶ See Figure 22

1. Loosen the mirror arm bolts, then remove the mirror arm from the van.
2. Loosen the mirror-to-clamp retaining fasteners and remove the mirrors.
3. Loosen both bracket retainers and remove the bracket.
4. Remove the insulator and bolt.
To install:
5. Install the insulator and fingertighten the bolt.
6. Install the lower bracket and tighten nuts to 41 inch lbs. (5 Nm) and the bolts to 18 inch lbs. (2 Nm).
7. Install the mirror arm and retainers, then position the arm 90 degrees to the door panel and tighten the upper and lower bracket pivot arm nuts to 106 inch lbs. (12 Nm).
8. Install the mirrors and tighten the clamp retainers to 41 inch lbs. (5 Nm).

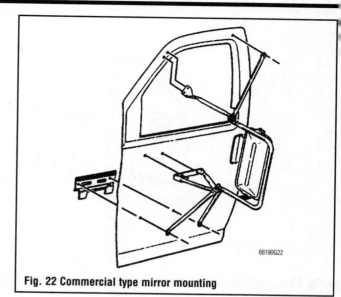

Fig. 22 Commercial type mirror mounting

Outside Power Mirrors

REMOVAL & INSTALLATION

1987–95 Models

1. Unfasten the mirror cover screw and slide the cover out of the way.
2. Remove the bracket and gasket.
3. Disengage the electrical connection and remove the mirror.
To install:
4. Engage the electrical connection and install the mirror assembly.
5. Install the mirror bracket and gasket, then install the nut and washer onto the studs and tighten the nut to 33 inch lbs. (4 Nm).
6. Install the mirror cover and tighten the screw to 17 inch lbs. (2 Nm).
7. Remove the door garnish molding.
8. Unfasten the mirror-to-door retainers and remove the mirror.
To install:
9. Install the mirror and tighten the retainers to 89 inch lbs. (10 Nm).
10. Install the garnish molding.

1996–97 Models

1. Install the front door trim panel and disengage the electrical connection from the mirror.
2. Unfasten the mirror retaining nuts, then remove the mirror and harness.
To install:
3. Install the mirror and harness, then tighten the retaining nuts to 89 inch lbs. (10 Nm).
4. Engage the electrical connection to the mirror harness.
5. Install the trim panel.

Antenna

REMOVAL & INSTALLATION

Fixed Mast Antenna

1987–95 MODELS

▶ See Figure 23

1. Disconnect the battery ground cable.
2. Unplug the antenna lead from the back of the radio.

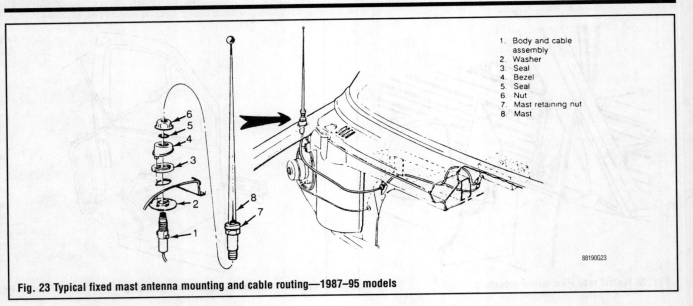

Fig. 23 Typical fixed mast antenna mounting and cable routing—1987–95 models

1. Body and cable assembly
2. Washer
3. Seal
4. Bezel
5. Seal
6. Nut
7. Mast retaining nut
8. Mast

88190G23

3. Remove the mast retaining nut and lift the mast from the base.
4. Remove the antenna base nut and remove the bezel and seal.
5. Pull the antenna base and cable assembly out of the fender. At this point the cable can be unscrewed from the base. If the cable is being removed, carefully remove it from any under-dash clamps and thread it slowly through the firewall and out.

To install:

6. Install the cable (if removed).
Install the antenna base and cable assembly.
7. Install the seal, bezel and nut.
8. Install the mast and retaining nut.
9. Connect the antenna lead to the radio.
10. Connect the negative battery cable.

1996–97 MODELS

1. Remove the right side knee bolster from inside the vehicle.
2. Disconnect the antenna cable connector located behind the knee bolster panel.
3. Push the cable grommet through the cowl panel.
4. Raise and support the hood, then loosen the bolts securing the antenna mounting bracket to the inner fender.
5. Pull the antenna assembly downward to disengage it from the fender grommet and remove the grommet.
6. Remove the antenna assembly.

To install:

7. Engage the antenna cable and grommet to the fender.
8. Push the antenna assembly up to engage the grommet.
9. Install the bolts the secure the mounting bracket to the fender and tighten the bolts to 97 inch lbs. (11 Nm).
10. From inside the van, pull the cable grommet through the cowl panel and engage the connector behind the knee bolster panel.
11. Install the knee bolster panel.

Power Antenna

1987–95 MODELS

1. Disconnect the negative battery cable.
2. Remove the antenna nut and bezel.
3. Remove the lower instrument panel extension.
4. Disconnect the antenna from the radio.
5. Disengage the electrical connections, as necessary.
6. Loosen the antenna bracket screw and remove the antenna.

To install:

7. Install the antenna and tighten the bracket retaining screw to 71 inch lbs. (8 Nm).

8. Engage the antenna to the radio.
9. Install the lower instrument panel extension.
10. Install the antenna bezel and retaining nut. Tighten the nut to 38 inch lbs. (4 Nm).
11. Connect the negative battery cable.

1996–97 MODELS

▶ See Figure 24

1. Raise and support the hood.
2. Disconnect the negative battery cable.
3. Loosen the bolts securing the antenna mounting bracket to the inner fender.
4. Disconnect the grounding strap.
5. Pull the antenna assembly downward to disengage it from the fender grommet and remove the grommet.
6. Renmove the cable retainer from the inner fender.
7. Remove the right side knee bolster from inside the vehicle.
8. Disconnect the antenna cable connector located behind the knee bolster panel.
9. Push the cable grommet through the cowl panel.
10. Remove the antenna assembly.

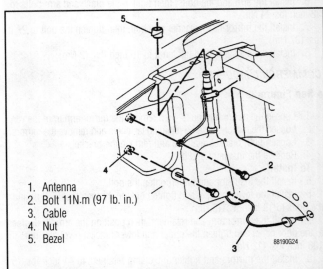

1. Antenna
2. Bolt 11N.m (97 lb. in.)
3. Cable
4. Nut
5. Bezel

88190G24

Fig. 24 Power antenna mounting—1996–97 models

To install:

11. Engage the antenna cable and grommet to the fender.
12. Engage the cable retainer to the inner fender.
13. Push the antenna assembly up to engage the grommet.
14. Install the bolts the secure the mounting bracket to the fender and tighten the bolts to 97 inch lbs. (11 Nm).
15. From inside the van, pull the cable grommet through the cowl panel and engage the connector behind the knee bolster panel.
16. Install the knee bolster panel.

Fender

REMOVAL & INSTALLATION

▶ **See Figure 25**

1. Disconnect the negative battery cable.
2. Remove the headlight bezel, bumper and cowl vent grille.
3. Raise and support the hood.
4. Remove the hood-to-fender nut and bolt.
5. If equipped, unbolt the splash shields.
6. Remove the front wheelhouse extension and fender-to-body bolts.
7. With an assistant, remove the fender from the vehicle. Be careful not to damage the painted surfaces.

To install:

8. Install the fender-to-body bolts and tighten to 18 ft. lbs. (25 Nm). If equipped, install the splash shield.
9. Install the front wheelhouse extension and hood-to-fender nuts and bolts.
10. Install the cowl vent grille, bumper and headlight bezel.
11. Connect the negative battery cable and align the fender.

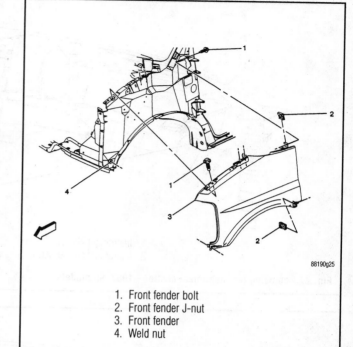

1. Front fender bolt
2. Front fender J-nut
3. Front fender
4. Weld nut

Fig. 25 Exploded view of a typical fender mounting

INTERIOR

Instrument Panel and Pad

REMOVAL & INSTALLATION

1987–95 Models

▶ **See Figures 26, 27 and 28**

1. Disconnect the negative battery cable.
2. If equipped, disable the SIR system.

3. Loosen the instrument panel lower extension screws and remove the lower extension.
4. Disengage the cigarette lighter and lamp electrical connections.
5. Loosen the steering column opening filler screws.
6. Remove the knee bolster.
7. Loosen the lower instrument panel screws (4).
8. Loosen the lower radio bracket screw, then use a prytool to remove the radio bezel.
9. Remove the radio screws (2) and disengage the antenna from the radio.
10. Disengage all the radio electrical connections.

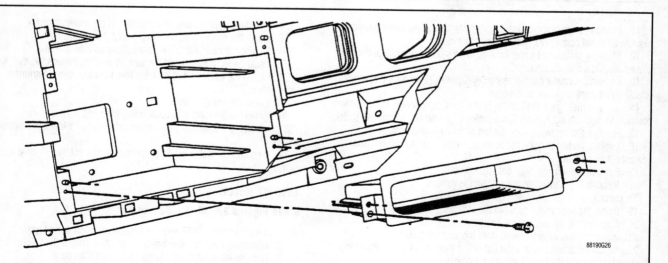

Fig. 26 Instrument panel lower mounting—1987–95 models

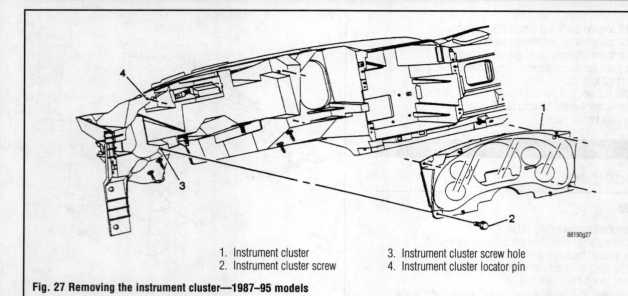

1. Instrument cluster
2. Instrument cluster screw
3. Instrument cluster screw hole
4. Instrument cluster locator pin

Fig. 27 Removing the instrument cluster—1987–95 models

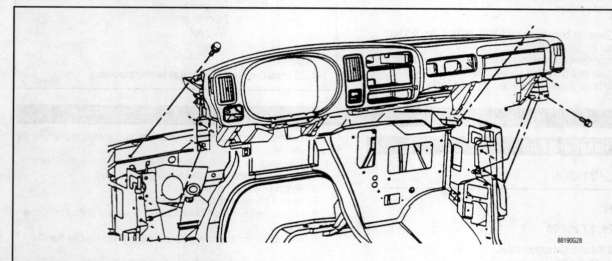

Fig. 28 Installing the instrument panel carrier—1987–95 models

11. Loosen the instrument cluster trim plate screws (6) and the lower instrument panel screws (2). Remove the cluster.

12. Slide the instrument panel forward, then tag and disengage the two cluster electrical connections.

13. Loosen the heater control assembly screws (3). Leave the assembly attached and position towards the cowl.

14. Tag and disengage the headlamp electrical connection. Pull out the rosebud to cigarette lighter harness connector located on instrument panel.

15. Remove the screws across the top of the instrument panel (8).

16. Loosen the two nuts on the lower side the steering column and lower column to seat.

17. Remove the left and right defogger ducts.

18. Remove the instrument panel from the vehicle.

To install:

19. Install the instrument panel in the vehicle.

20. Connect the left and right defogger ducts.

21. Install the two nuts removed from the steering column.

22. Install the screws across the top of the instrument panel. Press in the rosebud to cigarette lighter electrical harness.

23. Engage the headlamp and instrument panel cluster electrical connections.

24. Install the cluster assembly and tighten the lower screws.

25. Install the cluster trim plate and fasten the screws.

26. Engage the radio electrical connections and the antenna.

27. Install the radio screws and the bezel by pushing the tabs into their slots.

28. Fasten the lower radio bracket screw, then the lower instrument panel screws.

29. Install the knee bolster.

30. Install the steering column opening filler and screws.

31. Install the instrument panel lower extension and lower and upper screws.

32. If equipped, enable the SIR system and connect the negative battery cables.

1996–97 Models

▶ **See Figures 29, 30, 31, 32 and 33**

1. Turn the engine **OFF** and put the transmission in first gear.

2. Disconnect the negative battery cable and disable the SIR system.

3. Remove the instrument cluster lower trim filler panel.

4. Remove the instrument cluster trim panel and lower instrument panel center trim.

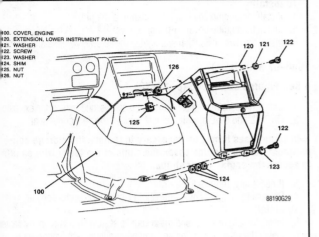

00. COVER, ENGINE
20. EXTENSION, LOWER INSTRUMENT PANEL
21. WASHER
22. SCREW
23. WASHER
24. SHIM
25. NUT
26. NUT

Fig. 29 Removing the instrument lower extension—1996–97 models

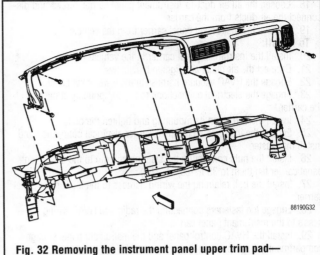

Fig. 32 Removing the instrument panel upper trim pad—1996–97 models

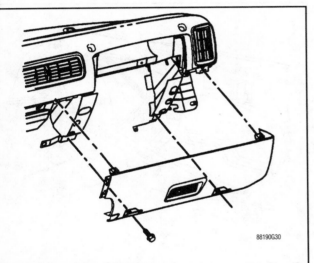

Fig. 30 Remove the passenger knee bolster . . .

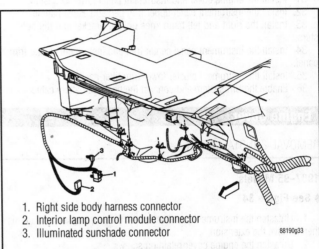

1. Right side body harness connector
2. Interior lamp control module connector
3. Illuminated sunshade connector

Fig. 33 Engage the instrument panel harness (right side) electrical connections—1987–95 models

5. Remove the left and right knee bolsters and their brackets.
6. Remove the instrument panel assist handle and upper trim panel.
7. Remove the instrument panel lower extension and the engine cover.
8. Remove the radio or CD player and brackets, if equipped.
9. If equipped, remove the instrument panel storage compartments.
10. Remove the heating and A/C (HVAC) control panel.
11. Disengage the fasteners retaining the radio and heating and A/C wiring to the instrument panel carrier.
12. Unfasten the bolts retaining the steering column wiring harness and steering column to the instrument panel carrier.
13. Remove the instrument cluster and disengage the wiring harness from the instrument panel carrier.
14. Unfasten the bolts retaining the instrument panel carrier.
15. Slide the carrier forwards and downwards to gain access any other components.
16. Tag and disengage all electrical connections.

➥**Do not disconnect any HVAC vacuum harness retainers from the air ducts**

17. Disengage the HVAC vacuum connector at the lower right of the carrier.

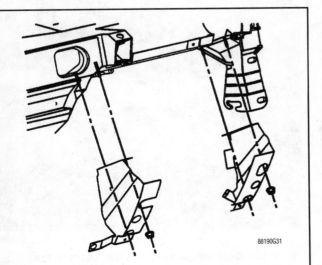

Fig. 31 . . . then remove the inner and outer brackets

18. Loosen the all air duct-to-instrument panel carrier screws and disconnect the air ducts from the carrier.

19. Remove the instrument panel carrier from the vehicle.

To install:

20. Install the instrument panel carrier in the vehicle.

21. Connect the air ducts and tighten the screws.

22. Engage the HVAC vacuum harness at the lower cowl panel.

23. Engage the electrical connections to the components at the rear of the carrier.

24. Install the carrier on its mounting and tighten the bolts.

25. Engage the instrument cluster-to-carrier electrical connection and install the cluster.

26. Install the nuts connecting the steering column to the instrument panel carrier ten them to 35 ft. lbs. (47 Nm).

27. Install the bolt retaining the wiring harness to the instrument panel carrier.

28. Engage the fasteners connecting the radio and HVAC wiring harness's to the instrument panel carrier.

29. Install the HVAC control panel and the instrument panel storage compartments, if equipped.

30. If equipped, install the radio and CD player brackets and components.

31. Install the engine cover and instrument panel lower extension.

32. Install the instrument panel upper trim pad and assist handle.

33. Install the right and left hand knee bolster bracket and the bolsters.

34. Install the instrument panel center trim and instrument cluster trim panel.

35. Install the instrument cluster lower trim filler panel.

36. Enable the SIR system and connect the negative battery cable.

Engine Cover

REMOVAL & INSTALLATION

1987–95 Models

▶ **See Figure 34**

1. Unfasten the instrument panel extension screws, washers and shims, then remove the extension.

2. Unfasten the engine cover retaining screws.

3. Remove the clamp from the pin and the engine cover from the vehicle.

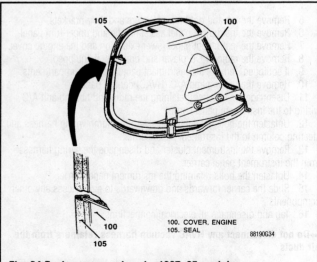

Fig. 34 Engine cover and seal—1987–95 models

To install:

4. Install the engine cover and the clamp to the pin.

5. Install the engine cover-to-panel screws.

6. Install the lower extension and tighten the screws, washers and shims.

1996–97 Models

▶ **See Figures 35 thru 45 (p. 18–20)**

1. Unfasten the instrument panel extension screws, and remove the extension.

2. On 7.4L and 6.5L diesel engines, remove the passenger seat.

➡ **In some cases it may be necessary to remove the storage compartment from the engine cover and some of the lower trim panels to access the engine cover straps.**

3. If necessary, remove the air duct.

4. Release the engine cover straps and remove the engine cover.

To install:

5. Install the engine cover and make sure its sealing strip is properly seated.

6. Install the retaining straps and any components removed to gain access to the straps.

7. If removed, install the passenger seat.

8. Install the instrument panel lower extension and tighten the screws.

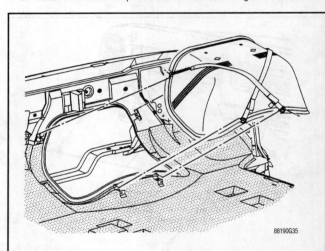

Fig. 35 Engine cover mounting—1996–97 models

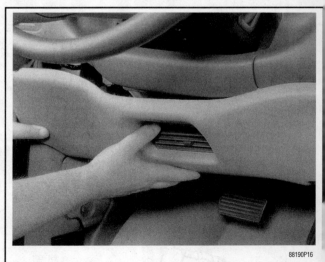

Fig. 36 Unbolt and remove the driver's side lower trim panel . . .

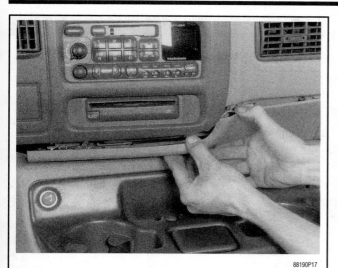

Fig. 37 . . . then unsnap and remove the center trim panel

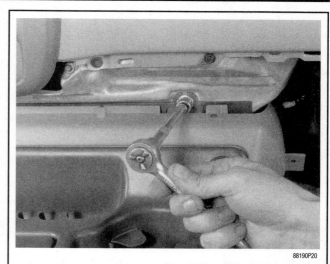

Fig. 40 Loosen the storage compartment retaining bolts

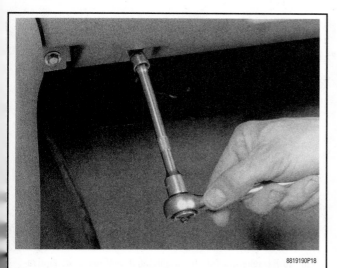

Fig. 38 Loosen the passenger side lower trim panel retainers . . .

Fig. 41 Slide the storage compartment forward . . .

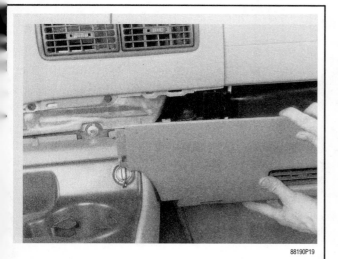

Fig. 39 . . . then remove the trim panel

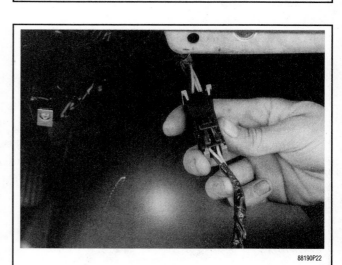

Fig. 42 . . . and disengage any electrical connections, then move the storage compartment aside

Fig. 43 If applicable, remove the air duct from the front of the engine cover

Fig. 44 Detach the engine cover straps . . .

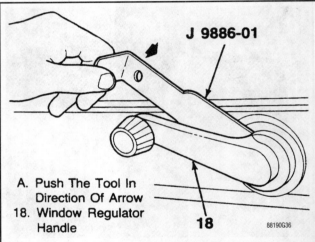

Fig. 45 . . . and remove the engine cover from the van

Door Panels

REMOVAL & INSTALLATION

Front Door

1987–95 MODELS

♦ See Figures 46 and 47

➡ Door handle clip remover Tool J-9886-01, or its equivalent, is required to perform the following procedure.

1. Remove the window regulator handle using tool J-9886-01 or its equivalent.
2. Remove the window regulator handle bezel.
3. Remove the door lock assembly handle using J-9886-01 or its equivalent.
4. Remove the control assembly handle bezel.
5. Remove the assist handle (if equipped).
6. Remove the armrest (if equipped).
7. if equipped, remove the door trim outer panel screws and pull the panel away from the retainer.

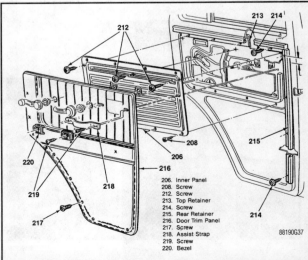

A. Push The Tool In Direction Of Arrow
18. Window Regulator Handle

Fig. 46 Remove the door handle using J-9886-01 or its equivalent—1987–95 models

206. Inner Panel
208. Screw
212. Screw
213. Top Retainer
214. Screw
215. Rear Retainer
216. Door Trim Panel
217. Screw
218. Assist Strap
219. Screw
220. Bezel

Fig. 47 Front door side trim panel mounting—1987–95 models

8. Remove the door trim inner panel screws and remove the trim inner panel.

To install:

9. Install the trim panel and fasten the screws.
10. If equipped, install the door trim outer panel, engage the retainers by pushing them into the door and then fasten the screws.
11. If equipped, install the arm rest.
12. If equipped, install the assist handle.
13. Install the control assembly handle bezel and the door lock assembly.
14. Install the window regulator bezel and handle.

1996–97 MODELS

♦ See Figures 48 thru 54

➡**Door handle clip remover Tool J-9886-01, or its equivalent, is required to perform the following procedure.**

1. Remove the window regulator handle using tool J-9886-01 or its equivalent.
2. Remove the window regulator handle bezel.
3. Remove the front door garnish and trim plate.
4. Unfasten the screws from the armrest.

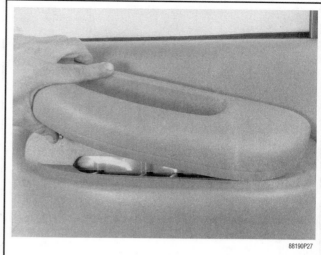

fig. 50 . . . then remove the armrest from the door

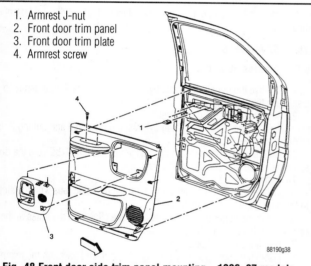

1. Armrest J-nut
2. Front door trim panel
3. Front door trim plate
4. Armrest screw

Fig. 48 Front door side trim panel mounting—1996–97 models

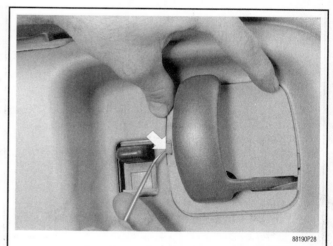

fig. 51 Use a small pick or prytool to disengage the inside handle trim piece

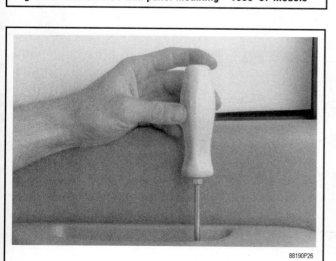

Fig. 49 Use a screwdriver to loosen the armrest retaining screws . . .

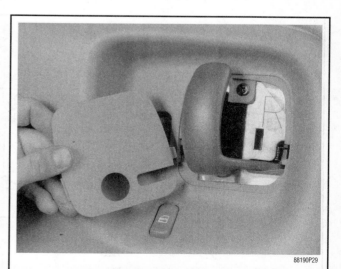

Fig. 52 Remove the inside handle trim piece from the door

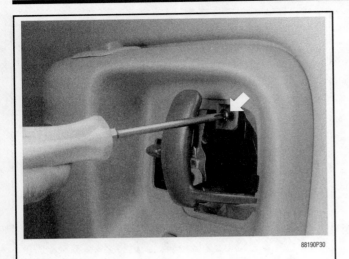

Fig. 53 Loosen the door trim panel retaining screws

Fig. 54 Use a prytool to carefully unsnap the retaining clips, then remove the panel

5. Lift up on the trim panel to release the retaining tabs on the lower portion of the trim panel.

6. Remove the trim panel from the vehicle.

To install:

7. Install the trim panel and align the retaining tabs with holes in the door and push down to lock it in place.

8. Fasten the screws in the armrest and install the door garnish.

9. Install the trim plate.

10. Install the window regulator handle bezel and regulator handle.

Sliding Door

1987–95 MODELS

♦ See Figure 55

1. Unfasten the inside door handle screw and remove the handle.

2. Remove the inside door handle cover.

3. Remove the lock knob by pulling it from the door.

4. Unfasten the assist strap screws and remove the strap.

5. Unfasten the trim panels screws and remove the trim panel from the van.

To install:

6. Install the trim panel on the door and tighten the screws.

7. Install the assist strap and tighten the screw.

8. Install the lock knob.

9. Install the inside door handle cover, inside door handle and fasten the screw.

1996–97 MODELS

♦ See Figures 56 and 57

1. Remove the upper trim panel by grasping it and pulling it gently to disengage the retaining clips.

2. Remove the inside door bezel.

3. Remove the upper trim panel by grasping the panel and pulling it up to disengage the retaining clips.

4. Lift the lower trim panel to disengage the retaining tabs from the door and remove the trim panel from the van.

To install:

5. Install the lower trim panel and align the retaining tabs with the slots in the door and lower it into place.

6. Install the upper trim panel and align the clips with the holes in the retainers on the door and push.

7. Install the inside handle bezel.

8. Install the upper panel by sliding it in place and pressing the retaining clips into place.

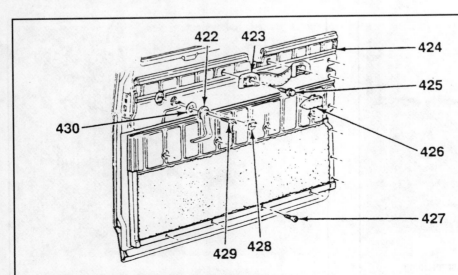

422. Inside Handle
423. Assist Strap
424. Door Trim Panel
425. Screw
426. Cover
427. Screw
428. Lock Knob
429. Screw
430. Cover

Fig. 55 Sliding side door trim panel components—1987–95 models

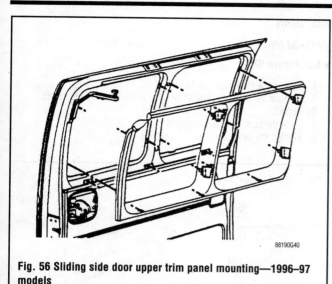

Fig. 56 Sliding side door upper trim panel mounting—1996–97 models

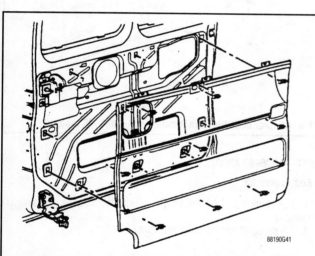

Fig. 57 Remove the lower trim panel by grasping it and pulling to disengage the retaining clips—1996–97 sliding door models

Swing-Out Side Doors

FRONT—1987–95 MODELS

▶ See Figure 58

1. Remove the door strap by prying the lock knob off the lock rod, with the knob in the unlocked position.
2. Unfasten the door handle bezel screws, then remove the bezel and lock knob.
3. Loosen the trim panel retaining screws, pull the panel from the retainers and remove the panel.
4. Loosen the retainer screws and remove the retainer.
5. Loosen the garnish screws and remove the garnish.

To install:

6. Install the garnish and tighten the screws.
7. Install the retainer and tighten the screws.
8. Install the trim panel and push edge of the panel into the retainers, then tighten the panel screws.
9. Install the handle bezel and lock knob, place the lock knob onto the lockrod and tighten the screws.
10. Install the door strap and tighten the screws to 17 inch lbs. (2 Nm).

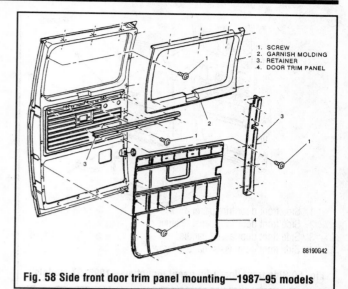

Fig. 58 Side front door trim panel mounting—1987–95 models

REAR—1987–95 MODELS

▶ See Figure 59

1. Loosen the trim panel retaining screws and pull the panel from the retainers.
2. Loosen the side garnish molding screws and remove the garnish molding.
3. Loosen the retainer screws and remove the retainer.
4. Loosen the upper garnish screws and remove the upper garnish.

To install:

5. Install the upper garnish and tighten the screws.
6. Install the retainer and tighten the screws.
7. Install the side garnish and tighten the screws.
8. Install the trim panel and push edge of the panel into the retainers, then tighten the panel screws.

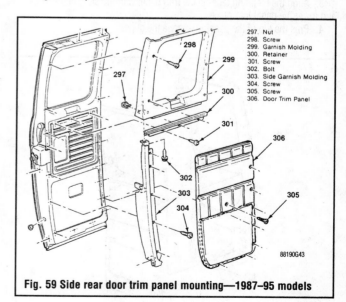

Fig. 59 Side rear door trim panel mounting—1987–95 models

FRONT—1996–97 MODELS

▶ See Figure 60

1. Loosen the assist handle screws, then remove the assist handle.
2. Remove the inside handle and the trim plate.

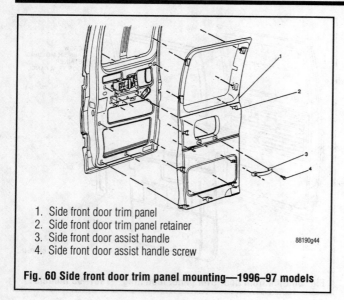

1. Side front door trim panel
2. Side front door trim panel retainer
3. Side front door assist handle
4. Side front door assist handle screw

88190g44

Fig. 60 Side front door trim panel mounting—1996–97 models

3. Pull on the top of the trim panel to unsnap the retaining clips.
4. Lift the panel up to disengage it from the door.

To install:

5. Align the retaining tabs on the trim panel with the slots on the door and lower the panel into place.
6. Pres the top of the panel to engage the clips.
7. Install the trim plate and handle bezel.
8. Install the assist handle and tighten the screws.

REAR—1996–97 MODELS

▶ **See Figure 61**

1. Pull on the top of the trim panel to unsnap the retaining clips.
2. Lift the panel up to disengage it from the door.

To install:

3. Align the retaining tabs on the trim panel with the slots on the door and lower the panel into place.
4. Pres the top of the panel to engage the clips.

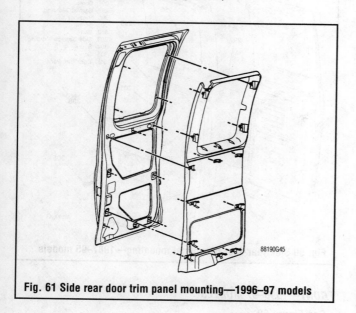

88190G45

Fig. 61 Side rear door trim panel mounting—1996–97 models

Rear Doors

1987–95 MODELS

▶ **See Figure 62**

1. Loosen the trim panel screws.
2. Remove the trim panel by sliding the panel out of the retainers.

To install:

3. Slide the panel into the retainers.
4. Tighten the trim panel retaining screws.

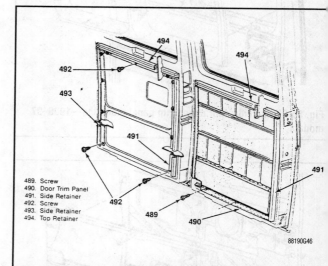

489. Screw
490. Door Trim Panel
491. Side Retainer
492. Screw
493. Side Retainer
494. Top Retainer

88190G46

Fig. 62 Rear door trim panel mounting—1987–95 models

LEFT—1996–97 MODELS

▶ **See Figure 63**

1. Pull on the top of the trim panel to unsnap the retaining clips around the window.
2. Lift the panel up to disengage it from the door.

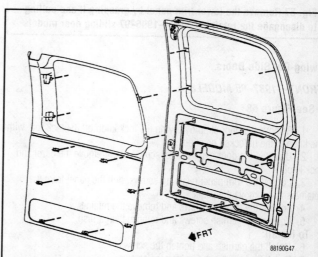

88190G47

Fig. 63 Left side rear door trim panel mounting—1996–97 models

To install:

3. Align the retaining tabs on the trim panel with the slots on the door and lower the panel into place.

4. Press the top of the panel to engage the clips.

RIGHT—1996–97 MODELS

▶ **See Figure 64**

1. Unfasten the door handle bezel screws.
2. Unfasten the trim plate screws, then remove the trim plate.
3. Pull on the top of the trim panel to unsnap the retaining clips.
4. Lift the panel up to disengage it from the door.

To install:

5. Align the retaining tabs on the trim panel with the slots on the door and lower the panel into place.
6. Pres the top of the panel to engage the clips.
7. Install the trim plate and tighten the screws.
8. Install the handle bezel.

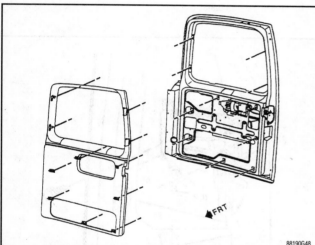

Fig. 64 Right side rear door trim panel mounting—1996–97 models

88190G48

Door Locks

REMOVAL & INSTALLATION

Front Doors

1987–95 MODELS

▶ **See Figure 65**

1. Raise the window completely.
2. Remove the trim panel and lock knob.
3. Remove the inside door handle.
4. If equipped, remove the remote control assembly.
5. Remove the rear glass run channel.
6. Unfasten the lock screws.
7. Remove the lock by lowering it in the door far enough to provide clearance for the inside lock rod.

To install:

8. Install the lock and align the lock rod with the hole in the top of the panel.
9. Tighten the lock retaining screws to 25 ft. lbs. (33 Nm).
10. Install the remote control assembly, if equipped.
11. Install rear glass run channel
12. Install the lock knob and trim panel.

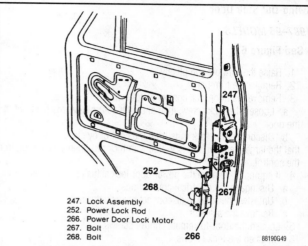

247. Lock Assembly
252. Power Lock Rod
266. Power Door Lock Motor
267. Bolt
268. Bolt

Fig. 65 Exploded view of the front door lock assembly—1987–95 models

88190G49

1996–97 MODELS

▶ **See Figure 66**

1. Raise the window completely.
2. Remove the trim panel and water deflector.
3. Remove the rear run channel.
4. Discoconnect the lock rods from the lock.
5. Disengage the electrical connections.
6. Disconnect the lock rod guide from the lock.
7. Unfasten the lock screws.
8. Remove the lock by lowering it in the door far enough to provide clearance for the inside lock rod.

To install:

9. Install the lock and tighten the lock retaining screws to 89 inch lbs. (10 Nm).
10. Connect the lock rod guide.
11. Engage the electrical connections and the lock rods to the lock.
12. Install the rear run channel.
13. Install the water deflector and trim panel.

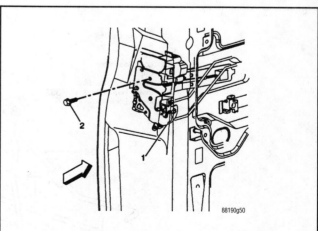

1. Front door lock   2. Door lock bolt

Fig. 66 Exploded view of the front door lock assembly—1996–97 models

88190g50

Swing-Out Side Door

1987–95 MODELS

▶ **See Figure 67**

1. Raise the window completely.
2. Remove the trim panel.
3. Remove the door lock control as follows:
   a. Loosen the lock screw, then slide the control towards the front of the door.
   b. Disconnect the lock rods from the control by sliding the clip so that the large diameter slot is in line with lock rod, then pull the rod from the control.
4. If equipped, remove the power door lock actuator as follows:
   a. Disengage the electrical connections.
   b. Unfasten the screws, disconnect the actuator rod.
   c. Remove the actuator.
5. Loosen the door-to-remote control screws.
6. Unfasten the lock screws.
7. Remove the lock and remote control with the rods.

To install:

8. Install the lock and remote control with the rods.
9. Tighten the lock retaining screws to 25 ft. lbs. (33 Nm).
10. Install the door-to-remote control screws and tighten them to 97 inch lbs. (11 Nm).
11. If equipped, install the power door lock actuator as follows:
    a. Install the actuator and connect the lock rod.
    b. Install the actuator screws and engage the electrical connection.
    c. Install the door lock control as follows:
    d. Engage the rod lock to the control, then the control to the door and tighten the screws.
12. Install the trim panel.

1996–97 MODELS

▶ **See Figure 68**

1. Remove the trim panel.
2. Disconnect the lock rods from the lock.
3. Disengage the electrical connections.
4. Loosen the lock-to-door screws and remove the lock.

To install:

5. Install the lock on the door and tighten the screws to 89 inch lbs. (10 Nm).
6. Engage the electrical connections an lock rods to the lock.
7. Install the trim panel.

Sliding Side Door

FRONT—1987–95 MODELS

▶ **See Figure 69**

1. Remove the trim panel, then the lock access panel by loosening the screws and pulling it up to disengage the clips.
2. Remove the outside door handle.
3. Loosen the lock-to-door screws and disconnect the lock rods from lock.
4. Disconnect the lower latch rod from the lock.
5. Disconnect the lock cylinder rod clips and remove the lock assembly.

To install:

6. Engage the lock assembly to the door and the rod clips to the lock.
7. Connect the lower latch rod and the rear door lock rods.
8. Install the lock-to-door screws and the outside handle.
9. Install the lock trim panel and screws.
10. Install the trim panel.

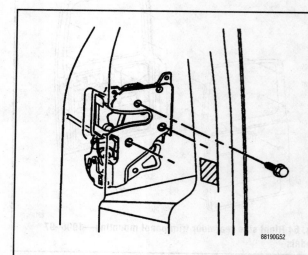

Fig. 68 Swing-out door lock mounting—1996–97 models

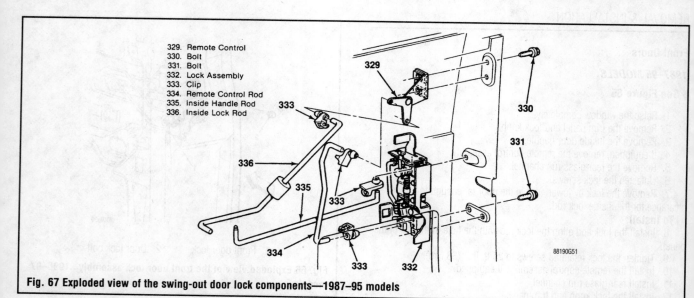

329. Remote Control
330. Bolt
331. Bolt
332. Lock Assembly
333. Clip
334. Remote Control Rod
335. Inside Handle Rod
336. Inside Lock Rod

Fig. 67 Exploded view of the swing-out door lock components—1987–95 models

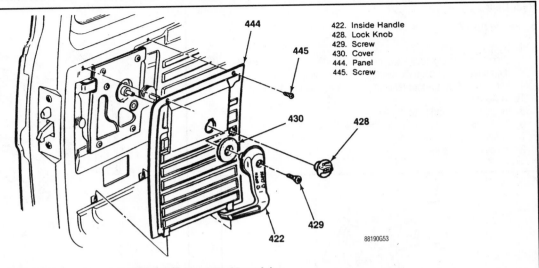

422. Inside Handle
428. Lock Knob
429. Screw
430. Cover
444. Panel
445. Screw

Fig. 69 Remove the door lock panel to gain access to the front lock—1987–95 models

REAR—1987–95 MODELS

See Figure 70

1. Disconnect the lock rods from the lock.
2. Loosen the lock-to-door screws and remove the lock from the door.

To install:

3. Install the lock and tighten the screws.
4. Engage the lock rods to the lock.

1996–97 MODELS

See Figure 71

1. Remove the trim panel.
2. Disconnect the lock rods from lock.
3. Loosen the lock retaining bolts and remove the lock.

To install:

4. Install the lock and tighten the bolts to 18 ft. lbs. (25 Nm).
5. Engage the lock rods to the lock.

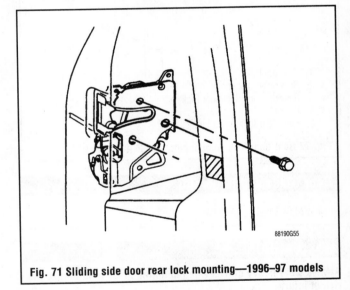

Fig. 71 Sliding side door rear lock mounting—1996–97 models

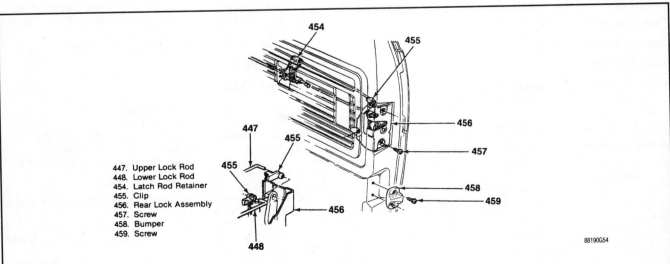

447. Upper Lock Rod
448. Lower Lock Rod
454. Latch Rod Retainer
455. Clip
456. Rear Lock Assembly
457. Screw
458. Bumper
459. Screw

Fig. 70 Sliding side door rear lock mounting—1987–95 models

Rear Door

▶ **See Figure 72**

1. Remove the trim panel.
2. Disconnet the lock rods from the lock.
3. If equipped, disengage the electrical connections.
4. Loosen the lock-to-door retaining screws and remove the lock.

To install:

5. Install the lock and tighten the screws.
6. If equipped, engage the electrical connections.
7. Connect the lock rods.
8. Inside the trim panel.

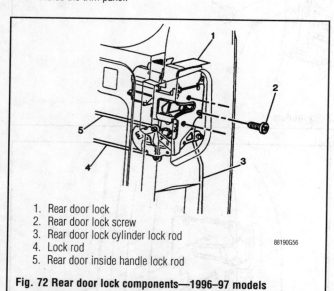

1. Rear door lock
2. Rear door lock screw
3. Rear door lock cylinder lock rod
4. Lock rod
5. Rear door inside handle lock rod

88190G56

Fig. 72 Rear door lock components—1996–97 models

Door Glass and Regulator

REMOVAL & INSTALLATION

✳✳ CAUTION

Always wear heavy gloves when handling glass to minimize the risk of injury.

Door Glass and Regulator

1987–95 MODELS

▶ **See Figure 73**

Remove the door glass as follows:

1. Lower the glass to the bottom of the door and remove the door trim panel.
2. Remove the door vent/window channel run assembly.

➡**Mask or cover any sharp edges that could scratch the glass.**

3. Slide the glass forward until the front roller is in line with the notch in the sash channel.
4. Disengage the roller from the channel.
5. Push the window forward, then tilt it up until the rear roller is disengaged.
6. Place the window in a level position, and raise it straight up and out of the door.

Remove the regulator as follows:

7. Raise the window and tape the glass in the full up position using cloth body tape.

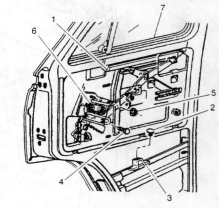

1. SASH CHANNEL
2. BUMPER
3. STOP
4. BOLT
5. NUT
6. REGULATOR
7. OUTER WINDOW WEATHERSTRIP

88190G57

Fig. 73 Window and regulator components—1987–95 models

8. Remove the door trim panel and the door panel to regulator bolts.
9. Slide the regulator rearward to disengage the rear roller from the sash channel. Then disengage the lower roller from the regulator rail.
10. Disengage the forward roller from the sash channel at the notch in the sash channel.
11. Collapse the regulator and remove it through the access hole in the door.

To install:

Install the regulator as follows.

12. Lubricate the regulator and the sash channel and regulator rails with Lubriplate® or its equivalent.
13. Collapse the regulator and insert it through the access hole.
14. Engage the forward roller to the sash channel at the notch.
15. Slide the regulator rearward to engage the rear roller to the sash channel and also connect the lower roller to the to the regulator rail.
16. Slide the regulator into position and install the regulator drive.
17. Install the door panel to regulator bolts and tighten them to 84 inch lbs. (9 Nm).
18. Install the trim panel and remove the tape from the window.

Install the glass as follows:

19. Lower the window into the door, push it forward, tilt it up and slide the rear roller into the sash channel.
20. Slide the window back until the front roller is in line with the notch in the sash channel, then engage the roller to the channel.
21. Slide the window rearward into the run channel.
22. Remove the masking tape and install the trim panel.

1996–97 MODELS

▶ **See Figures 74 and 75**

1. Remove the front and rear door garnish.
2. Remove the trim panel and water deflector.
3. Lower window, then remove the inner and outer sealing strip.
4. Loosen the front run channel bolt and remove the channel.
5. Raise the window half way to gain access to the nuts retaining the window to the sash and loosen the nuts.
6. Remove the window.
7. Loosen the rear run channel retaining bolts and remove the channel.
8. Remove the inside door handle.
9. Remove the lock rods from the door regulator.
10. Tag and disengage any electrical connections that will hamper regulator (module) removal.
11. Drill out the rivets retaining the regulator assembly (module to the door.
12. Remove the regulator (module) from the door.

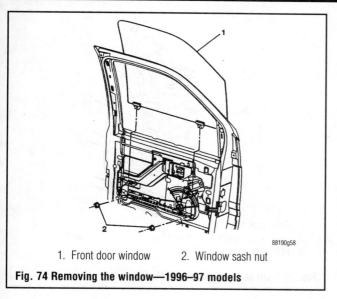

1. Front door window   2. Window sash nut

Fig. 74 Removing the window—1996–97 models

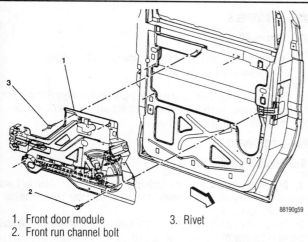

1. Front door module   3. Rivet
2. Front run channel bolt

Fig. 75 Removing the regulator (module assembly)—1996–97 models

To install:

13. Install the regulator and rivet it to the door.
14. Engage all the electrical connections.
15. Connect the lock rods to the regulator.
16. Install the door handle.
17. Install the rear run channel. Tighten the run channel bolt to 97 inch lbs. (11 Nm).
18. Install the window and the nuts, then tighten the nuts to 97 inch lbs. (11 Nm).
19. Lower the front window and install the front run channel. Tighten the bolt to 97 inch lbs. (11 Nm).
20. Install the inner and outer sealing strips
21. Install the water deflector and the front and rear door garnish.
22. Install the trim panel.

Electric Window Motor

REMOVAL & INSTALLATION

▶ **See Figure 76**

1. Disconnect the negative battery cable.
2. Remove the trim panel and water deflector.
3. Remove the window regulator for clearance (if necessary).
4. Disengage the wiring connector to the window motor.
5. Remove the motor to door frame retainers.
6. Remove the window motor.

To install:

7. Install the motor and tighten the retainers.
8. Engage the electrical connection.
9. If removed, install the regulator.
10. Install the water deflector and trim panel.
11. Connect the negative battery cable.

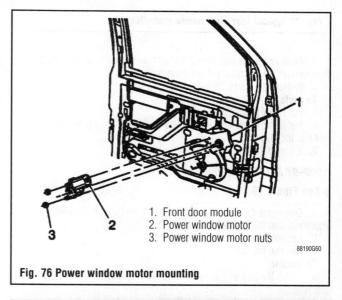

1. Front door module
2. Power window motor
3. Power window motor nuts

Fig. 76 Power window motor mounting

Inside Rear View Mirror

▶ **See Figure 77**

1. Loosen the setscrew and remove the mirror from the base.
2. Installation is the reverse of removal.

Seats

REMOVAL & INSTALLATION

Front

1987–95 MODELS

▶ **See Figure 78**

1. Disconnect the seat belt.
2. Raise the van and support it with jackstands.

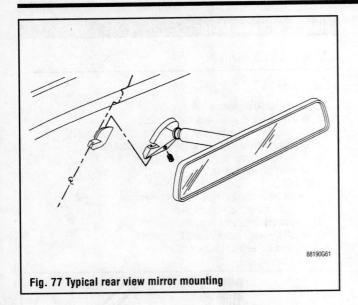

Fig. 77 Typical rear view mirror mounting

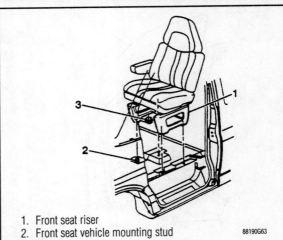

1. Front seat riser
2. Front seat vehicle mounting stud
3. Front seat retaining nut

Fig. 79 Front seat mounting—1996–97 models

3. From under the van, loosen the seat riser-to-floor panel retainers, then remove the washers and reinforcements.

4. Remove the seat.

To install:

5. Install the seat.

6. Install the reinforcements, washer and retainers. Tighten the retainers to 47 ft. lbs. (65 Nm).

7. Connect the seat belt.

1996–97 MODELS

◆ See Figure 79

1. Disengage the electrical connections from the seat adjuster (if equipped) and the seat belt buckle.

2. Loosen the seat-to-vehicle retainers.

3. Remove the seat.

To install:

4. Install the seat and its retainers and tighten the retainers to 63 ft. lbs. (85 Nm).

5. Engage the electrical connections.

Center and Rear

1987–95 MODELS

◆ See Figure 80

1. Unlatch the seat, and pull it towards the rear of the vehicle.

2. Remove the seat from the vehicle.

To install:

3. Place the seat in the vehicle and install the hooked retainers onto the pins.

4. Latch the seat into position, then push the seat backwards and forwards to ensure that it is seated properly.

1996–97 MODELS

◆ See Figures 81 and 82

1. Disconnect the quick release latch plates for the lap or shoulder belts by pressing a drift punch or equivalent tool into the release hole of the belt buckle while pulling on the belt.

2. Remove the locking pin from its retaining clip and insert it in the hole provided in the rear of the seat riser.

3. Lift the seat up and off the rails and out of the vehicle.

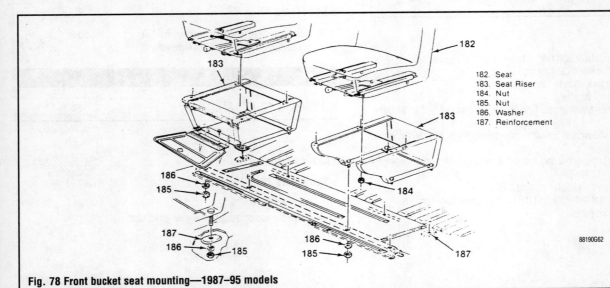

182. Seat
183. Seat Riser
184. Nut
185. Nut
186. Washer
187. Reinforcement

Fig. 78 Front bucket seat mounting—1987–95 models

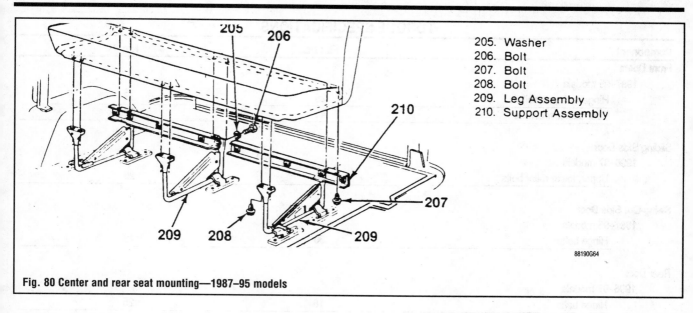

205. Washer
206. Bolt
207. Bolt
208. Bolt
209. Leg Assembly
210. Support Assembly

Fig. 80 Center and rear seat mounting—1987–95 models

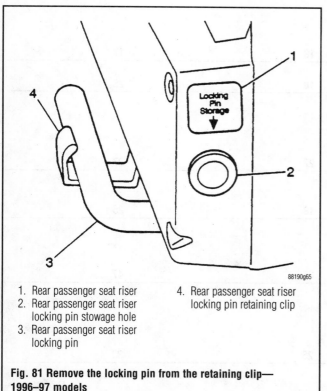

1. Rear passenger seat riser
2. Rear passenger seat riser locking pin stowage hole
3. Rear passenger seat riser locking pin
4. Rear passenger seat riser locking pin retaining clip

Fig. 81 Remove the locking pin from the retaining clip—1996–97 models

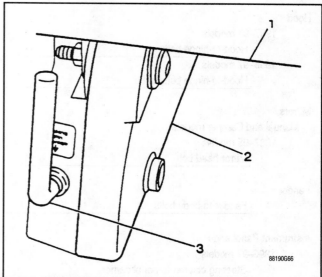

1. Rear passenger seat
2. Rear passenger seat riser
3. Rear passenger seat riser locking pin stowed position

Fig. 82 Insert the pin before removing the center and rear seats—1996–97 models

To install:
4. Install the seat in the vehicle and align the attaching points on the rails.
5. Push the seat forward to lock the front of the seat risers onto the pins on the inside of the floor rail.
6. Remove the locking pin and store the pin in its retaining clip.
7. Connect the quick release latch plate for the lap or shoulder belt by inserting the latch plate into the seat belt buckle and pushing to engage the latch plate with the belt buckle.

Power Seat Motor

REMOVAL & INSTALLATION

1. Raise the seat to the full height position to gain access to the motor.
2. Disengage the electrical connection.
3. Remove the seat from the vehicle.
4. Loosen the motor retainers and remove the motor.
To install:
5. Install the motor and tighten the retainers.
6. Install the seat in the vehicle.
7. Engage the electrical connection.
8. Check the seat for proper operation.

TORQUE SPECIFICATIONS

Component	Ft. Lbs.	Nm
Front Doors		
1987–95 models		
Hinge-to-frame bolts	25	33
Door striker retainers	45	62
Sliding Side Door		
1996–97 models		
Upper, lower roller bolts	18	25
Swing-Out Side Door		
1987–95 models		
Hinge bolts	30	43
Rear Door		
1996–97 models		
Hinge bolts	18	25
Hood		
1987–95 models		
Hood-to-hinge bolts	13	17
1996–97 models		
Hood-to-hinge bolts bolts	18	25
Mirrors		
Manual and Camper models		
1987–95 models		
Mirror head bolt	27	37
Fender		
Fender-to-body bolts	18	25
Instrument Panel and Pad		
1996–97 models		
Steering column-to-panel carrier	35	47
Door Locks		
Front Door		
1987–95 models		
Lock retaining screws	25	33
Swing-Out Side Door		
1987–95 models		
Lock retaining screws	25	33
Seats		
Front		
1987–95 models		
Seat riser-to-floor retainers.	47	65
1996–97 models		
Seat retainers	63	85

88190C01

GLOSSARY

AIR/FUEL RATIO: The ratio of air-to-gasoline by weight in the fuel mixture drawn into the engine.

AIR INJECTION: One method of reducing harmful exhaust emissions by injecting air into each of the exhaust ports of an engine. The fresh air entering the hot exhaust manifold causes any remaining fuel to be burned before it can exit the tailpipe.

ALTERNATOR: A device used for converting mechanical energy into electrical energy.

AMMETER: An instrument, calibrated in amperes, used to measure the flow of an electrical current in a circuit. Ammeters are always connected in series with the circuit being tested.

AMPERE: The rate of flow of electrical current present when one volt of electrical pressure is applied against one ohm of electrical resistance.

ANALOG COMPUTER: Any microprocessor that uses similar (analogous) electrical signals to make its calculations.

ARMATURE: A laminated, soft iron core wrapped by a wire that converts electrical energy to mechanical energy as in a motor or relay. When rotated in a magnetic field, it changes mechanical energy into electrical energy as in a generator.

ATMOSPHERIC PRESSURE: The pressure on the Earth's surface caused by the weight of the air in the atmosphere. At sea level, this pressure is 14.7 psi at 32°F (101 kPa at 0°C).

ATOMIZATION: The breaking down of a liquid into a fine mist that can be suspended in air.

AXIAL PLAY: Movement parallel to a shaft or bearing bore.

BACKFIRE: The sudden combustion of gases in the intake or exhaust system that results in a loud explosion.

BACKLASH: The clearance or play between two parts, such as meshed gears.

BACKPRESSURE: Restrictions in the exhaust system that slow the exit of exhaust gases from the combustion chamber.

BAKELITE: A heat resistant, plastic insulator material commonly used in printed circuit boards and transistorized components.

BALL BEARING: A bearing made up of hardened inner and outer races between which hardened steel balls roll.

BALLAST RESISTOR: A resistor in the primary ignition circuit that lowers voltage after the engine is started to reduce wear on ignition components.

BEARING: A friction reducing, supportive device usually located between a stationary part and a moving part.

BIMETAL TEMPERATURE SENSOR: Any sensor or switch made of two dissimilar types of metal that bend when heated or cooled due to the different expansion rates of the alloys. These types of sensors usually function as an on/off switch.

BLOWBY: Combustion gases, composed of water vapor and unburned fuel, that leak past the piston rings into the crankcase during normal engine operation. These gases are removed by the PCV system to prevent the buildup of harmful acids in the crankcase.

BRAKE PAD: A brake shoe and lining assembly used with disc brakes.

BRAKE SHOE: The backing for the brake lining. The term is, however, usually applied to the assembly of the brake backing and lining.

BUSHING: A liner, usually removable, for a bearing; an anti-friction liner used in place of a bearing.

CALIPER: A hydraulically activated device in a disc brake system, which is mounted straddling the brake rotor (disc). The caliper contains at least one piston and two brake pads. Hydraulic pressure on the piston(s) forces the pads against the rotor.

CAMSHAFT: A shaft in the engine on which are the lobes (cams) which operate the valves. The camshaft is driven by the crankshaft, via a belt, chain or gears, at one half the crankshaft speed.

CAPACITOR: A device which stores an electrical charge.

CARBON MONOXIDE (CO): A colorless, odorless gas given off as a normal byproduct of combustion. It is poisonous and extremely dangerous in confined areas, building up slowly to toxic levels without warning if adequate ventilation is not available.

CARBURETOR: A device, usually mounted on the intake manifold of an engine, which mixes the air and fuel in the proper proportion to allow even combustion.

CATALYTIC CONVERTER: A device installed in the exhaust system, like a muffler, that converts harmful byproducts of combustion into carbon dioxide and water vapor by means of a heat-producing chemical reaction.

CENTRIFUGAL ADVANCE: A mechanical method of advancing the spark timing by using flyweights in the distributor that react to centrifugal force generated by the distributor shaft rotation.

CHECK VALVE: Any one-way valve installed to permit the flow of air, fuel or vacuum in one direction only.

CHOKE: A device, usually a moveable valve, placed in the intake path of a carburetor to restrict the flow of air.

CIRCUIT: Any unbroken path through which an electrical current can flow. Also used to describe fuel flow in some instances.

CIRCUIT BREAKER: A switch which protects an electrical circuit from overload by opening the circuit when the current flow exceeds a predetermined level. Some circuit breakers must be reset manually, while most reset automatically.

COIL (IGNITION): A transformer in the ignition circuit which steps up the voltage provided to the spark plugs.

COMBINATION MANIFOLD: An assembly which includes both the intake and exhaust manifolds in one casting.

COMBINATION VALVE: A device used in some fuel systems that routes fuel vapors to a charcoal storage canister instead of venting them into the atmosphere. The valve relieves fuel tank pressure and allows fresh air into the tank as the fuel level drops to prevent a vapor lock situation.

COMPRESSION RATIO: The comparison of the total volume of the cylinder and combustion chamber with the piston at BDC and the piston at TDC.

CONDENSER: 1. An electrical device which acts to store an electrical charge, preventing voltage surges. 2. A radiator-like device in the air conditioning system in which refrigerant gas condenses into a liquid, giving off heat.

CONDUCTOR: Any material through which an electrical current can be transmitted easily.

CONTINUITY: Continuous or complete circuit. Can be checked with an ohmmeter.

COUNTERSHAFT: An intermediate shaft which is rotated by a mainshaft and transmits, in turn, that rotation to a working part.

CRANKCASE: The lower part of an engine in which the crankshaft and related parts operate.

CRANKSHAFT: The main driving shaft of an engine which receives reciprocating motion from the pistons and converts it to rotary motion.

CYLINDER: In an engine, the round hole in the engine block in which the piston(s) ride.

CYLINDER BLOCK: The main structural member of an engine in which is found the cylinders, crankshaft and other principal parts.

CYLINDER HEAD: The detachable portion of the engine, usually fastened to the top of the cylinder block and containing all or most of the combustion chambers. On overhead valve engines, it contains the valves and their operating parts. On overhead cam engines, it contains the camshaft as well.

DEAD CENTER: The extreme top or bottom of the piston stroke.

DETONATION: An unwanted explosion of the air/fuel mixture in the combustion chamber caused by excess heat and compression, advanced timing, or an overly lean mixture. Also referred to as "ping".

DIAPHRAGM: A thin, flexible wall separating two cavities, such as in a vacuum advance unit.

DIESELING: A condition in which hot spots in the combustion chamber cause the engine to run on after the key is turned off.

DIFFERENTIAL: A geared assembly which allows the transmission of motion between drive axles, giving one axle the ability to turn faster than the other.

DIODE: An electrical device that will allow current to flow in one direction only.

DISC BRAKE: A hydraulic braking assembly consisting of a brake disc, or rotor, mounted on an axle, and a caliper assembly containing, usually two brake pads which are activated by hydraulic pressure. The pads are forced against the sides of the disc, creating friction which slows the vehicle.

DISTRIBUTOR: A mechanically driven device on an engine which is responsible for electrically firing the spark plug at a predetermined point of the piston stroke.

DOWEL PIN: A pin, inserted in mating holes in two different parts allowing those parts to maintain a fixed relationship.

DRUM BRAKE: A braking system which consists of two brake shoes and one or two wheel cylinders, mounted on a fixed backing plate, and a brake drum, mounted on an axle, which revolves around the assembly.

DWELL: The rate, measured in degrees of shaft rotation, at which an electrical circuit cycles on and off.

ELECTRONIC CONTROL UNIT (ECU): Ignition module, module, amplifier or igniter. See Module for definition.

ELECTRONIC IGNITION: A system in which the timing and firing of the spark plugs is controlled by an electronic control unit, usually called a module. These systems have no points or condenser.

END-PLAY: The measured amount of axial movement in a shaft.

ENGINE: A device that converts heat into mechanical energy.

EXHAUST MANIFOLD: A set of cast passages or pipes which conduct exhaust gases from the engine.

FEELER GAUGE: A blade, usually metal, or precisely predetermined thickness, used to measure the clearance between two parts.

FIRING ORDER: The order in which combustion occurs in the cylinders of an engine. Also the order in which spark is distributed to the plugs by the distributor.

FLOODING: The presence of too much fuel in the intake manifold and combustion chamber which prevents the air/fuel mixture from firing, thereby causing a no-start situation.

FLYWHEEL: A disc shaped part bolted to the rear end of the crankshaft. Around the outer perimeter is affixed the ring gear. The starter drive engages the ring gear, turning the flywheel, which rotates the crankshaft, imparting the initial starting motion to the engine.

FOOT POUND (ft. lbs. or sometimes, ft.lb.): The amount of energy or work needed to raise an item weighing one pound, a distance of one foot.

FUSE: A protective device in a circuit which prevents circuit overload by breaking the circuit when a specific amperage is present. The device is constructed around a strip or wire of a lower amperage rating than the circuit it is designed to protect. When an amperage higher than that stamped on the fuse is present in the circuit, the strip or wire melts, opening the circuit.

GEAR RATIO: The ratio between the number of teeth on meshing gears.

GENERATOR: A device which converts mechanical energy into electrical energy.

HEAT RANGE: The measure of a spark plug's ability to dissipate heat from its firing end. The higher the heat range, the hotter the plug fires.

HUB: The center part of a wheel or gear.

HYDROCARBON (HC): Any chemical compound made up of hydrogen and carbon. A major pollutant formed by the engine as a byproduct of combustion.

HYDROMETER: An instrument used to measure the specific gravity of a solution.

INCH POUND (inch lbs.; sometimes in.lb. or in. lbs.): One twelfth of a foot pound.

INDUCTION: A means of transferring electrical energy in the form of a magnetic field. Principle used in the ignition coil to increase voltage.

INJECTOR: A device which receives metered fuel under relatively low pressure and is activated to inject the fuel into the engine under relatively high pressure at a predetermined time.

INPUT SHAFT: The shaft to which torque is applied, usually carrying the driving gear or gears.

INTAKE MANIFOLD: A casting of passages or pipes used to conduct air or a fuel/air mixture to the cylinders.

JOURNAL: The bearing surface within which a shaft operates.

KEY: A small block usually fitted in a notch between a shaft and a hub to prevent slippage of the two parts.

MANIFOLD: A casting of passages or set of pipes which connect the cylinders to an inlet or outlet source.

MANIFOLD VACUUM: Low pressure in an engine intake manifold formed just below the throttle plates. Manifold vacuum is highest at idle and drops under acceleration.

MASTER CYLINDER: The primary fluid pressurizing device in a hydraulic system. In automotive use, it is found in brake and hydraulic clutch systems and is pedal activated, either directly or, in a power brake system, through the power booster.

MODULE: Electronic control unit, amplifier or igniter of solid state or integrated design which controls the current flow in the ignition primary circuit based on input from the pick-up coil. When the module opens the primary circuit, high secondary voltage is induced in the coil.

NEEDLE BEARING: A bearing which consists of a number (usually a large number) of long, thin rollers.

OHM: (Ω) The unit used to measure the resistance of conductor-to-electrical flow. One ohm is the amount of resistance that limits current flow to one ampere in a circuit with one volt of pressure.

OHMMETER: An instrument used for measuring the resistance, in ohms, in an electrical circuit.

OUTPUT SHAFT: The shaft which transmits torque from a device, such as a transmission.

OVERDRIVE: A gear assembly which produces more shaft revolutions than that transmitted to it.

OVERHEAD CAMSHAFT (OHC): An engine configuration in which the camshaft is mounted on top of the cylinder head and operates the valve either directly or by means of rocker arms.

OVERHEAD VALVE (OHV): An engine configuration in which all of the valves are located in the cylinder head and the camshaft is located in the cylinder block. The camshaft operates the valves via lifters and pushrods.

OXIDES OF NITROGEN (NOx): Chemical compounds of nitrogen produced as a byproduct of combustion. They combine with hydrocarbons to produce smog.

OXYGEN SENSOR: Use with the feedback system to sense the presence of oxygen in the exhaust gas and signal the computer which can reference the voltage signal to an air/fuel ratio.

PINION: The smaller of two meshing gears.

PISTON RING: An open-ended ring with fits into a groove on the outer diameter of the piston. Its chief function is to form a seal between the piston and cylinder wall. Most automotive pistons have three rings: two for compression sealing; one for oil sealing.

PRELOAD: A predetermined load placed on a bearing during assembly or by adjustment.

PRIMARY CIRCUIT: the low voltage side of the ignition system which consists of the ignition switch, ballast resistor or resistance wire, bypass, coil, electronic control unit and pick-up coil as well as the connecting wires and harnesses.

PRESS FIT: The mating of two parts under pressure, due to the inner diameter of one being smaller than the outer diameter of the other, or vice versa; an interference fit.

RACE: The surface on the inner or outer ring of a bearing on which the balls, needles or rollers move.

REGULATOR: A device which maintains the amperage and/or voltage levels of a circuit at predetermined values.

RELAY: A switch which automatically opens and/or closes a circuit.

RESISTANCE: The opposition to the flow of current through a circuit or electrical device, and is measured in ohms. Resistance is equal to the voltage divided by the amperage.

RESISTOR: A device, usually made of wire, which offers a preset amount of resistance in an electrical circuit.

RING GEAR: The name given to a ring-shaped gear attached to a differential case, or affixed to a flywheel or as part of a planetary gear set.

ROLLER BEARING: A bearing made up of hardened inner and outer races between which hardened steel rollers move.

ROTOR: 1. The disc-shaped part of a disc brake assembly, upon which the brake pads bear; also called, brake disc. 2. The device mounted atop the distributor shaft, which passes current to the distributor cap tower contacts.

SECONDARY CIRCUIT: The high voltage side of the ignition system, usually above 20,000 volts. The secondary includes the ignition coil, coil wire, distributor cap and rotor, spark plug wires and spark plugs.

SENDING UNIT: A mechanical, electrical, hydraulic or electro-magnetic device which transmits information to a gauge.

SENSOR: Any device designed to measure engine operating conditions or ambient pressures and temperatures. Usually electronic in nature and designed to send a voltage signal to an on-board computer, some sensors may operate as a simple on/off switch or they may provide a variable voltage signal (like a potentiometer) as conditions or measured parameters change.

SHIM: Spacers of precise, predetermined thickness used between parts to establish a proper working relationship.

SLAVE CYLINDER: In automotive use, a device in the hydraulic clutch system which is activated by hydraulic force, disengaging the clutch.

SOLENOID: A coil used to produce a magnetic field, the effect of which is to produce work.

SPARK PLUG: A device screwed into the combustion chamber of a spark ignition engine. The basic construction is a conductive core inside of a ceramic insulator, mounted in an outer conductive base. An electrical charge from the spark plug wire travels along the conductive core and jumps a preset air gap to a grounding point or points at the end of the conductive base. The resultant spark ignites the fuel/air mixture in the combustion chamber.

SPLINES: Ridges machined or cast onto the outer diameter of a shaft or inner diameter of a bore to enable parts to mate without rotation.

TACHOMETER: A device used to measure the rotary speed of an engine, shaft, gear, etc., usually in rotations per minute.

THERMOSTAT: A valve, located in the cooling system of an engine, which is closed when cold and opens gradually in response to engine heating, controlling the temperature of the coolant and rate of coolant flow.

TOP DEAD CENTER (TDC): The point at which the piston reaches the top of its travel on the compression stroke.

TORQUE: The twisting force applied to an object.

TORQUE CONVERTER: A turbine used to transmit power from a driving member to a driven member via hydraulic action, providing changes in drive ratio and torque. In automotive use, it links the driveplate at the rear of the engine to the automatic transmission.

TRANSDUCER: A device used to change a force into an electrical signal.

TRANSISTOR: A semi-conductor component which can be actuated by a small voltage to perform an electrical switching function.

TUNE-UP: A regular maintenance function, usually associated with the replacement and adjustment of parts and components in the electrical and fuel systems of a vehicle for the purpose of attaining optimum performance.

TURBOCHARGER: An exhaust driven pump which compresses intake air and forces it into the combustion chambers at higher than atmospheric pressures. The increased air pressure allows more fuel to be burned and results in increased horsepower being produced.

VACUUM ADVANCE: A device which advances the ignition timing in response to increased engine vacuum.

VACUUM GAUGE: An instrument used to measure the presence of vacuum in a chamber.

VALVE: A device which control the pressure, direction of flow or rate of flow of a liquid or gas.

VALVE CLEARANCE: The measured gap between the end of the valve stem and the rocker arm, cam lobe or follower that activates the valve.

VISCOSITY: The rating of a liquid's internal resistance to flow.

VOLTMETER: An instrument used for measuring electrical force in units called volts. Voltmeters are always connected parallel with the circuit being tested.

WHEEL CYLINDER: Found in the automotive drum brake assembly, it is a device, actuated by hydraulic pressure, which, through internal pistons, pushes the brake shoes outward against the drums.

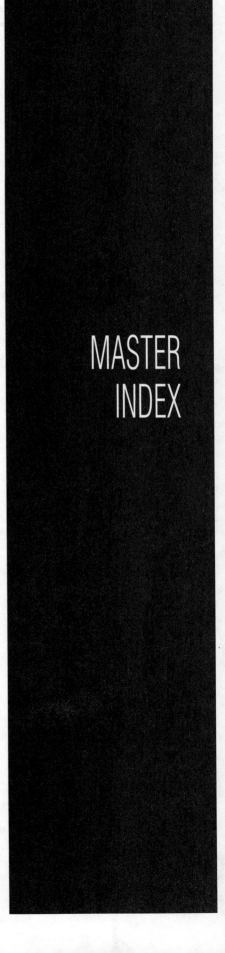

MASTER
INDEX

3 1221 05672 0746